# The Complete Everyday Cookbook

Compiled and tested
by Better Cooking Library

Publishers · WESTPORT CORP · New York

Rhubard Pie
p. 329
Good.

# Contents

# BARBECUE

Today, every one in the country seems to be cooking outdoors. Some families have built-in barbecue units in the yard, complete with picnic table and outdoor lights. With the multitude of outdoor grills on the market, it is comparatively simple to cook in the back yard, at the beach, near a lake or a stream, or even on the tail gate of a station wagon parked along a country road.

This book will tell you how to cook and what to cook on your outdoor barbecue. Of course you all know how to cook steak. And chicken can be broiled in many different ways. But how many times have you cooked fish over glowing coals. Or have you ever wrapped different combinations of foods in aluminum foil and let them cook over hot charcoal. Next time you might try barbecuing turkey or duckling.

Be sure to look at the pages on vegetables and "go-alongs." While the dinner is cooking, it is nice to have something to nibble on. And don't forget, a steak will not make a whole meal, and we have several suggestions for goodies you may not have cooked before.

So, during the summer months under a sunny sky, or under a starlit sky, at the beach or even cooking in your indoor fireplace while winter winds are howling outside; why not discover the delights of cooking over glowing coals.

## Barbecue Sauces

**Liquid dressings of condiments and herbs accentuate natural flavors of foods and add zest to barbecue cooking— outside or indoors.**

### Barbecue Sauce No. 1

**2 tablespoons salad oil**
**1 medium onion, chopped**
**2 teaspoons salt**
**½ teaspoon monosodium glutamate**
**½ teaspoon pepper**
**1 cup tomato juice**
**1 teaspoon vinegar**
**1½ teaspoons flour**
**2 tablespoons catsup**
**1 tablespoon sugar**
**1 tablespoon Worcestershire**
**½ teaspoon dry mustard dissolved in 1 tablespoon warm water**

In a large saucepan, saute chopped onions in salad oil. When onions are tender, add remaining ingredients and mix well. Heat thoroughly and serve over grilled halibut steaks. Makes 1½ cups of sauce, or enough for four servings.

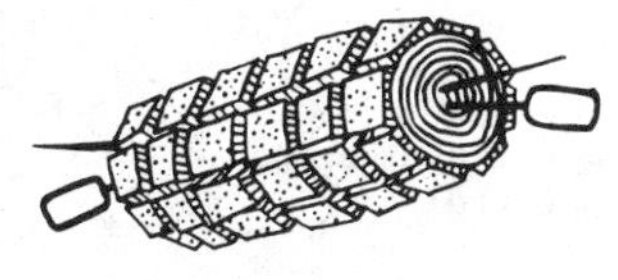

### Tabasco Steak Marinade

**½ cup salad oil**
**½ cup red wine**
**1 teaspoon dry mustard**
**⅛ teaspoon marjoram**
**⅛ teaspoon thyme**
**¼ cup lime juice**
**½ teaspoon Tabasco**
**½ teaspoon salt**

Combine all ingredients and blend well. Pour over steak and let stand at least 5 hours, turning once. Makes enough marinade for 1 4-pound steak.

### West Indies Barbecue Sauce

**¼ cup unsulphured molasses**
**1 tablespoon prepared mustard**
**1 tablespoon vinegar**
**1 tablespoon Worcestershire sauce**
**1 can (8-ounces) tomato sauce**
**2 tablespoons finely chopped onion**
**¼ teaspoon Tabasco**

Combine all ingredients in saucepan. Bring to a boil; boil 1 minute. Use to brush chicken during broiling or grilling. Makes 1⅓ cups sauce.

American Molasses

McIlhenney's Tabasco

# Tabasco Roquefort Steak Spread

½ teaspoon Tabasco
2 tablespoons butter
1 package 3-ounces)
Roquefort cheese

Cream together all ingredients until blended. Spread over broiled steak. Makes enough for 2 4-pound steaks.

# Garlic Spread for Hamburgers

1 slick (½ cup) butter or margarine
1 teaspoon dry mustard
1 teaspoon salt
1 teaspoon paprika
½ teaspoon garlic salt
½ tablespoon sugar
1 tablespoon lemon juice
1 tablespoon vinegar
1 tablespoon Worcestershire sauce

Combine all ingredients and blend thoroughly. Use on buns with hamburgers, hot dogs or steak. Makes about ½ cup spread.

# Special Hamburger Toppings

1. Combine 1 cup sour cream, 2 tablespoons chopped green-onion tops, 1 teaspoon dried herbs. Blend well.
2. Combine ¾ cup mayonnaise, ½ cup prepared mustard and two tablespoons horse-radish. Goes with dill pickle slices.
3. Peel and dice 1 cucumber, add ½ teaspoon salt, 1 tablespoon sugar, 2 tablespoons wine vinegar and 2 tablespoons chopped fresh mint. Let stand awhile before using.
4. Combine 2 cups sliced green onion with a few caraway seeds and 2 tablespoons vinegar. Season to taste.
5. Combine ½ cup chili sauce, ¼ cup steak sauce, 2 tablespoons prepared mustard, 1½ teaspoons dry mustard, 1½ teaspoons prepared horse-radish, few drops lemon juice. Blend well and let stand for several hours before using.

# Tomato Spread

1 can (6 ounces) tomato paste
2 tablespoons prepared mustard
2 tablespoons lemon juice
½ teaspoon Tabasco
2 teaspoons Worcestershire sauce
2 teaspoons horse-radish
¼ teaspoon salt

Combine all ingredients and blend well. Use for steak or hamburgers. Makes 1 cup.

# Tabasco Butter

½ cup butter
2 tablespoons lemon juice
½ teaspoon Tabasco

Melt butter; stir in lemon juice and Tabasco. Wonderful on steak or hot corn on the cob. Makes sauce for 2 steaks or 1 dozen ears of corn.

# Ripe Olive Sauce

2 tablespoons butter or margarine
¼ teaspoon salt
⅛ teaspoon pepper
2 tablespoons flour
1 cup water
1 cup ripe olives, slivered

Melt butter. Stir in flour and seasonings. Cook butter and flour together until lightly browned. Stir in water, bring to boiling and cook stirring constantly for about 2 minutes. Stir in olives.

# Sparerib Special

¼ cup salad oil
⅓ cup vinegar
½ cup canned fruit juice
½ cup catsup
¼ cup minced onion
¼ cup Worcestershire sauce
1 teaspoon Tabasco sauce
2 teaspoons salt
1 teaspoon chili powder
½ teaspoon cayenne pepper
¼ teaspoon oregano

Combine all ingredients in a saucepan, bring to a boil and simmer 10 minutes. Brush sauce generously over spareribs, before and during cooking time. Wonderful also with poultry and seafood.

# Mock Catsup for Hamburgers

¼ cup mayonnaise
2 tablespoons prepared mustard
2 tablespoons tomato paste
½ teaspoon sugar
¼ teaspoon monosodium glutamate
Dash pepper

Blend mayonnaise and mustard together. Add remaining ingredients and blend well. Perfect for hamburgers. Makes ⅓ cup.

# Mustard Butter

¼ cup butter
2 tablespoons prepared mustard
¼ teaspoon Tabasco

Cream butter; gradually stir in mustard and Tabasco. Spread over steak or hamburgers when done. Enough butter for 2 steaks or 8 hamburgers.

# Lemon-Cucumber Sauce

½ lemon
1 small onion
1 cucumber
1 cup mayonnaise
Dash of cayenne
½ teaspoon salt
¼ teaspoon dry mustard
¼ teaspoon Worcestershire sauce
Pinch of thyme

Put lemon, onion and cucumber through coarse blade of food chopper. Combine with remaining ingredients. Chill before serving. Good with shrimp. Makes 1 pint.

# Wine Marinade for Lamb

1 cup Sauterne or other white dinner wine
2 tablespoons wine vinegar
2 teaspoons dried tarragon
½ teaspoon garlic salt
¼ teaspoon powdered thyme
¼ teaspoon powdered rosemary
Dash Cayenne pepper

Combine all ingredients, crumbling herbs very fine, if they are not powdered. To use, pour over lamb chops and let stand about 2 hours in refrigerator. Drain thoroughly, and broil over very hot coals, basting occasionally with marinade. Makes enough marinade for 6 to 8 large chops.

Wine Institute

# Perfect Barbecue Sauce

½ cup beer
2 tablespoons vinegar
2 tablespoons Worcestershire sauce
2 tablespoons lemon juice
1 cup chili sauce

Combine all ingredients in a small saucepan. Bring to a boil and keep warm on edge of barbecue grill. Use to baste frankfurters, hamburgers or other meats during grilling.

# Steak Sauce Angostura

½ cup butter or margarine
¼ cup finely chopped onion
½ teaspoon Angostura aromatic bitters

Melt butter, add onion and Angostura bitters. Broil steak on both sides according to directions. Spread butter mixture on top side during last 5 minutes of cooking.

# Tomato Mustard Sauce

2 tablespoons butter
¼ cup minced celery
2 tablespoons minced onion
2 tablespoons flour
2 tablespoons prepared mustard
1 teaspoon salt
⅛ teaspoon pepper
1¾ cups (No. 2 can) canned tomatoes, strained

Melt butter. Add celery and onion and cook until tender. Stir in flour and mix until smooth. Add mustard, salt and pepper. Gradually add tomatoes and cook over low heat until mixture boils and is thickened. Fine for hamburgers and frankfurters. Makes 1½ cups sauce.

# Barbecue Sauce for Suckling Pig

2 pounds butter or margarine
2½ quarts water
1½ tablespoons dry mustard
¼ cup sugar
3 tablespoons salt
3 tablespoons chili powder
½ teaspoon cayenne
2 tablespoons Worcestershire sauce
1 cup vinegar
2 teaspoons Tabasco
3 tablespoons pepper
4 tablespoons paprika
1 onion, chopped fine
2 cloves garlic, minced

Combine all ingredients in a large saucepan and simmer for at least 30 minutes before using.

# Barbecue Sauce for Turkey

¼ cup diced green pepper
1 small onion, minced
1 clove garlic, crushed
2 tablespoons oil
1 cup catsup
½ cup chili sauce
¼ cup water
1 teaspoon prepared mustard
½ teaspoon grated horse-radish
¼ cup lemon juice
2 tablespoons wine vinegar
¼ cup sugar
2 teaspoons Worcestershire sauce
¼ teaspoon paprika
½ teaspoon salt
¼ teaspoon black pepper
Dash chili powder

Sauté green pepper, onion and garlic in oil until lightly browned. Add remaining ingredients. Simmer over low heat for ¾ to 1 hour, stirring occasionally. Makes 1½ pints sauce.

# Bleu Cheese Basting Sauce

1 cup salad oil
1 cup lemon juice
½ cup finely crumbled bleu cheese
2 tablespoons Worcestershire sauce
1 teaspoon salt
¼ teaspoon pepper

Combine all ingredients and blend thoroughly. Let stand in refrigerator several hours before using to allow flavors to blend. This sauce is especially good with turkey or chicken. Makes about 1 pint sauce.

# All-Purpose Barbecue Sauce

½ cup butter or margarine
1 clove garlic, minced
1 onion, minced
Dash of Tabasco
½ cup ketchup
¾ teaspoon prepared mustard
1 tablespoon prepared horse-radish
1 tablespoon Worcestershire sauce
2 tablespoons vinegar
2 teaspoons sugar
1 teaspoon chili powder
1 teaspoon salt
½ teaspoon marjoram
½ teaspoon thyme
¼ teaspoon pepper
3 cups water

Combine all ingredients in a saucepan and simmer 35 minutes. This sauce may be used to marinate meat in before cooking or to brush meat with while cooking. Makes about 1 quart sauce.

American Molasses

# 1-2-3 Barbecue Sauce

1 cup unsulphured molasses
1 cup prepared mustard
1 cup vinegar

Combine molasses and mustard, mix thoroughly. Stir in vinegar. Makes 3 cups. One cup of sauce is sufficient to barbecue 8 broiler-fryer chicken halves, or 2 dozen hamburgers or frankfurters.

# Parsley Sauce

2 tablespoons butter or margarine
2 tablespoons flour
½ teaspoon salt
Dash of pepper
1 cup milk
¼ cup finely chopped parsley

Melt butter over low heat; add flour, salt and pepper, stir until well blended and bubbly. Remove from heat. Gradually stir in milk and return to heat. Cook, stirring constantly, until thick and smooth. Add parsley. Makes 1 cup.

# Deviled Sauce

1 tablespoon butter or margarine
½ teaspoon onion powder
⅛ teaspoon cayenne
2 teaspoons Worcestershire sauce
1 tablespoon ketchup
2 tablespoons prepared mustard

Melt butter. Stir in remaining ingredients. Simmer over low heat until well blended. This is especially good with broiled chicken livers. Makes ¼ cup sauce.

# Tabasco Barbecue Sauce

2 teaspoons Tabasco
2 tablespoons molasses
¼ cup prepared mustard
2 tablespoons vinegar or lemon juice
2 tablespoons Worcestershire sauce

Add Tabasco to molasses and mustard; blend well. Stir in vinegar and Worcestershire sauce. Use to brush chicken, spareribs, frankfurters during baking, broiling or grilling. Makes ⅔ cup.

# Tomato Barbecue Sauce

½ cup corn oil
¼ to ½ cup vinegar
¼ cup light corn syrup
¼ cup catsup
¼ cup chilli sauce
1 tablespoon lemon juice
1 tablespoon Worcestershire sauce
1 teaspoon monosodium glutamate
1 teaspoon dry mustard
1 small onion, finely chopped
1 small clove garlic

Combine all ingredients in a heavy saucepan. Bring to a boil, then simmer about ½ hour to blend flavors. Keep hot for basting and mix well before using each time. Serve extra mixture as sauce. Makes 1½ cups sauce.

Best Foods, Inc.

## Apple Curry Sauce

2 large green apples
2 large onions
4 sprigs parsley
1 slice garlic
3 tablespoons butter or margarine
2 teaspoons curry powder
½ teaspoon salt
Dash of nutmeg
Dash of cayenne
1½ cups milk
2 tablespoons flour

Put apples, onions, parsley, garlic through fine blade of food chopper. Sauté in fat until golden brown. Add seasonings. Blend in flour, stir in milk and cook, stirring constantly until thick. Excellent with shrimp. Makes 1 pint.

## Calypso Barbecue Sauce

¼ cup salad oil
1 medium onion, minced
¼ cup vinegar
1 cup tomato sauce
1 cup water
1 teaspoon salt
⅛ teaspoon red pepper
2 teaspoons Angostura aromatic bitters

Heat salad oil. Add onion and cook over low heat until yellow but not brown. Add vinegar, tomato sauce, water and salt. Add Angostura bitters. Brush chicken halves with mixture before cooking and again several times during cooking. Let remainder of sauce cook over low heat until slightly thick, and serve with chicken.

## Barbecue Sauce No. 2

2 tablespoons butter or margarine
1 medium onion, chopped
1 clove garlic, chopped
½ cup chopped celery
¼ cup chopped green pepper
1 No. 2 can tomatoes
1 6-ounce can tomato paste
1 bay leaf
3 tablespoons brown sugar
2 teaspoons dry mustard
⅓ cup vinegar
½ teaspoon cloves
½ teaspoon allspice
2 slices lemon
1½ teaspoons salt
2 teaspoons Tabasco

Melt butter; add onion and garlic and cook until tender but not brown. Add remaining ingredients and simmer 30 minutes. Let stand until cool. Strain if desired before using. Serve cool.

## Herb Barbecue Sauce

½ cup sherry wine
¼ cup salad oil
1 medium-sized onion, grated
1½ teaspoons Worcestershire sauce
1 tablespoon dry mustard
1½ teaspoons mixed fresh herbs
1½ teaspoons garlic salt
¼ teaspoon salt
½ teaspoon freshly ground pepper

Combine all ingredients in a jar and shake well. Makes about 1 cup sauce.

## Beer Barbecue Sauce

½ cup molasses or brown sugar
¼ cup prepared mustard
½ cup chili sauce
1 teaspoon Worcestershire sauce
½ cup finely minced onion
½ teaspoon salt
¼ teaspoon pepper
½ cup beer

Combine all ingredients in a saucepan; bring to a boil. Simmer 5 minutes. Use generously to baste hamburgers while broiling. To make basting easy over hot coals, supply the outdoor chef with a big mug with barbecue sauce and a long-handled brush.

## Creamy Mustard Frankfurter Topping

1 cup sour cream
2 tablespoons prepared mustard
1 tablespoon minced onion
1 teaspoon salt
Dash pepper
1 teaspoon Worcestershire sauce
1 tablespoon lemon juice
4 drops Tabasco

Combine all ingredients and stir until blended. Use to spread on frankfurters or hamburgers on rolls. Makes 1 cup topping.

## Molasses Barbecue Sauce

¼ cup molasses
1 tablespoon prepared mustard
1 tablespoon vinegar
1 8-ounce can tomato sauce
¼ cup chopped onion
¼ teaspoon Tabasco

Combine all ingredients in a saucepan. Bring to a boil and boil 1 minute. Makes ⅔ cup sauce.

## Herb Barbecue Sauce for Lamb

1 small onion, chopped
3 cloves garlic, chopped
1 teaspoon dried rosemary
12 fresh mint leaves
¼ cup vinegar
½ cup water

Chop onion and garlic very fine. Add rosemary and mint leaves which have been crushed. Add vinegar and water and let mixture stand overnight. When ready to barbecue steaks or chops, brush them thoroughly with the sauce. As the meat cooks, baste occasionally. Pass a tureen of the same sauce when serving the lamb.

## Special Steak Barbecue Sauce

⅔ cup butter or margarine
⅔ cup water
2 teaspoons A-1 sauce
1½ tablespoons lemon juice
¼ teaspoon Tabasco
2 teaspoons sugar
1 teaspoon salt
Few grains cayenne
2 teaspoons flour

Melt butter, add the water and other liquids. Combine dry ingredients and stir well into the liquid. Cook for 2 or 3 minutes, or until mixture thickens slightly.

# Cocktail Sauce

**2 tablespoons prepared horseradish**
**¾ cup ketchup**
**Dash of Tabasco**
**3 tablespoons chili sauce**
**2 tablespoons lemon juice**
**Salt to taste**

Mix together all ingredients. Sauce for 4 cocktails.

# Pickle Relish Barbecue Sauce

**2 medium onions chopped**
**1 green pepper, chopped**
**⅔ cup sweet pickle relish**
**⅔ cup vinegar**
**2 cups chili sauce**
**¼ cup firmly packed brown sugar**
**1 tablespoon prepared mustard**
**½ teaspoon Tabasco**

Combine all ingredients in a saucepan. Bring to boiling point, lower heat and simmer 20 minutes. Good with frankfurters. Makes 3 cups.

# Tabasco-Garlic Sauce

**2 tablespoons butter or margarine**
**1 medium onion, chopped**
**1 minced clove garlic**
**½ cup ketchup**
**¼ cup vinegar**
**1 tablespoon brown sugar**
**1 teaspoon salt**
**1 teaspoon Tabasco**
**½ teaspoon dry mustard**
**¼ cup water**

Combine all ingredients in a saucepan; bring to a boil. Use to brush frankfurters or hamburgers during broiling. Makes 1¼ cups sauce.

# Maitre D'Hotel Butter

**½ cup butter**
**1 teaspoon chopped parsley**
**½ teaspoon salt**
**Juice of ½ lemon**

Mix together all ingredients, stirring until creamy.

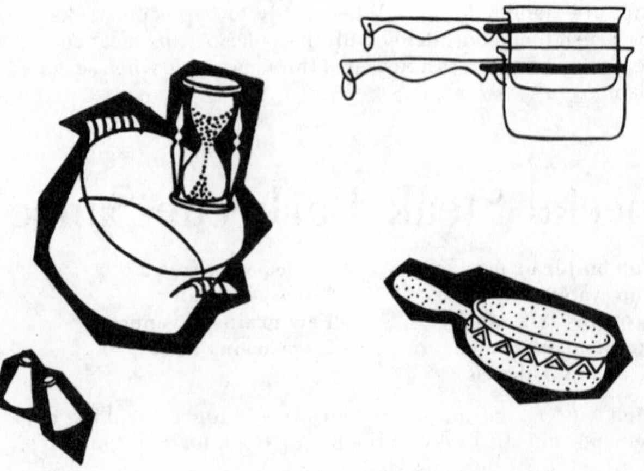

# White Wine Sauce

**2 tablespoons butter or margarine**
**2 tablespoons flour**
**1 cup water**
**2 bouillon cubes**
**2 cloves**
**1 bay leaf**
**½ cup white wine**
**¼ cup diced celery**
**1 tablespoon minced parsley**
**Salt and pepper**

**Melt butter, blend in flour, add water and bouillon cubes. Cook, stirring, until smooth. Add cloves and bay leaf, simmer about 10 minutes. Strain. Add wine, celery, parsley and seasonings to taste. Serve hot with baked or broiled fish. Makes about 1¼ cups sauce.**

# Steak Marinade

**½ cup salad oil**
**¼ cup lime juice**
**½ cup red wine**
**1 teaspoon dry mustard**
**¼ teaspoon thyme**
**1 bay leaf**
**½ teaspoon salt**
**⅛ teaspoon pepper**
**1 medium onion, minced**

**Combine all ingredients and blend well. Place steak in a shallow pan. Pour mixture over top of steak. Let stand in refrigerator about 5 hours or over night. Turn once during soaking period. Makes enough for 1 4-pound steak.**

# Roquefort Butter

**1 package (3-ounces) Roquefort cheese**
**2 tablespoons butter**
**¼ teaspoon Tabasco**

Cream butter; crumble cheese in butter and blend well. Stir in Tabasco. Spread over broiled steak or hamburgers. Makes enough for 2 steaks or 8 hamburgers.

# Cranberry Chutney Sauce

Combine 1 pound whole cranberry sauce with ½ cup raisins, ½ unpeeled cored apple, chopped, ½ cup finely chopped celery and 1 teaspoon ginger. Store in refrigerator for several hours before serving.

# Poultry

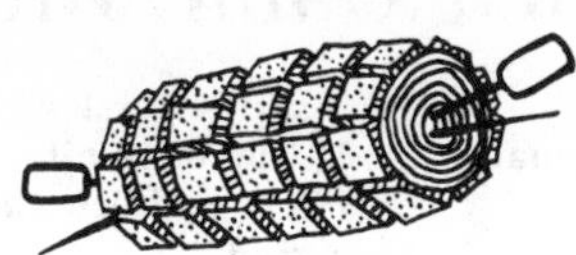

## Savory Chicken Dinner

**1 teaspoon salt**
**¼ teaspoon pepper**
**½ cup flour**
**1 4-pound chicken, cut in serving pieces**
**½ cup fat**
**1 clove garlic, quartered**
**1 cup uncooked rice**
**1 cup sliced onions**
**3 tomatoes, quartered**
**¼ cup diced green pepper**
**½ cup chili sauce**
**3 cups stock**
**1 pound green beans, halved lengthwise**
**1 cup uncooked peas**

Combine salt, pepper, and flour in a paper bag. Add chicken and shake well to coat the chicken with seasoned flour. Brown chicken in hot fat in a heavy Dutch oven. Add garlic and rice and cook a few minutes, stirring occasionally. Add remaining ingredients, except beans and peas. Cover tightly, and simmer over low coals about 30 minutes. Add beans and peas and cook until vegetables are tender. Makes 6 servings.

## Broiled Chicken Livers

Allow 2 or 3 chicken livers for each serving with 1 slice of bacon and about 3 mushroom caps. Cut livers in half and bacon into 1-inch squares. On each skewer string alternate pieces of mushroom caps, chicken livers and bacon. Sprinkle with salt and pepper and brush with melted butter or margarine. Place on grid over coals and cook slowly. Turn occasionally and serve immediately when well browned.

## Roast Turkey

Select a turkey weighing from 14 to 16 pounds. Truss the legs and the wings tightly to the body and fasten the neck skin to the back with a skewer. Insert spit through backbone about 1 inch above the tail and come out through extreme front end of breast bone. Fasten holding forks securely and balance well before cooking. Roast over moderate coals, basting if desired with a mixture of melted butter and white wine. Test for doneness by pulling the leg; it moves easily at the joint if it is done. A 14- to 16-pound turkey will take about 3 hours unstuffed, about 1 hour longer if stuffed.

## Maple Barbecue Broiler

**4 broiler halves**
**½ cup butter or margarine, melted**
**1 clove garlic, minced**
**3 tablespoons wine vinegar**
**1 tablespoon maple syrup**
**1 teaspoon salt**
**¼ teaspoon dry mustard**
**¼ teaspoon marjoram**
**Dash of pepper**

Place broiler halves on rack, skin side up, 4 to 5 inches from glowing coals. Combine remaining ingredients and blend well. Broil chicken halves 20 minutes, turn and brush with the maple mixture. Broil 20 minutes, turn skin side up and continue cooking 15 to 20 minutes longer, brushing with sauce frequently. Test for doneness by cutting into thickest part of thigh. Makes 4 servings.

## Barbecued Chicken No. 1

**½ cup corn oil**
**½ cup lemon juice**
**¼ cup water**
**2 teaspoons salt**
**¼ teaspoon pepper**
**1 tablespoon sugar**
**1 teaspoon paprika**
**1 tablespoon minced onion**
**3 broiler-fryer chickens, split**

Combine all ingredients, except chicken. Place chicken, skin side up, on grill 6 to 12 inches from hot coals. Brush chicken with barbecue mixture. Cook slowly until tender, turning and basting occasionally. Allow 1 to 1¼ hours total cooking time. To test for doneness, leg should twist easily out of thigh joint and pieces should be fork tender.

Broiler Council

## Chicken Sauté Au Vin

**2 3½-pound chickens**
**¼ cup flour**
**1 teaspoon salt**
**¼ teaspoon pepper**
**¼ cup butter or margarine**
**¼ cup salad oil**
**1 large onion, thinly sliced**
**¼ cup chopped parsley**
**Pinch of marjoram**
**1 8-ounce can mushrooms**
**2 cups red wine**

Have frying chickens cut in pieces for serving. Combine flour salt and pepper in a paper bag. Add a few pieces of chicken at a time and shake thoroughly so that each piece of chicken is lightly covered with seasoned flour. Heat butter and salad oil in a heavy Dutch oven. Add chicken and sauté until golden brown. Add onion, parsley, marjoram, mushrooms and wine. Cover tightly and simmer 45 minutes to 1 hour or until chicken is tender. Makes 8 servings.

# Chicken Oriental

2 large onions
2 seedless oranges
2 3-pound chickens, cut in frying pieces
Flour
¼ cup salad oil
½ cup brown rice
½ pound almonds, blanched and chopped
3 cups milk
3 tablespoons chopped pimiento
⅛ teaspoon pepper
¼ teaspoon dried thyme
2 teaspoons salt

Put the onions and oranges through the coarse blade of food chopper. Dredge the chicken in flour. Heat the salad oil in a very large cast iron skillet. (Use 2 small ones if you do not own a very large one.) Brown chicken quickly on all sides and remove from skillet. Add rice and almonds and cook until golden brown. Spread rice out on bottom of skillet. Add onions and orange. Arrange chicken on top of rice. Add remaining ingredients. Cover tightly and cook on outdoor grill about 1 hour. Makes 8 servings.

# Chicken Breasts Hawaiian

**2 chicken breasts**
**1 egg, slightly beaten**
**Finely sieved bread crumbs**
**1 teaspoon salt**
**Fat for frying**
**1 cup pineapple juice**
**2 tablespoons lemon juice**
**1 tablespoon cornstarch**
**¼ teaspoon curry powder**
**1 tablespoon sugar**
**4 slices toast**
**Slivered almonds**

Split breasts in half. Remove bones, keeping meat in one piece. Dip in egg. Roll in bread crumbs. Season with salt. Pan fry in ¼-inch of hot fat in a very heavy skillet until brown. Drain all fat from pan. Combine juices, cornstarch, curry powder and sugar. Pour over chicken. Cover tightly and simmer over low heat about 20 minutes, or until tender. Serve on hot toast topped with sauce and slivered almonds. Makes 4 servings.

# Broiler Turkey Barbecued Over Charcoal

**3- to 4-pound ready-to-cook broiler turkey, quartered**
**1⅓ cups Herb Barbecue Sauce**

If turkeys are quick frozen, thaw as label directs and quarter; break hip, knee and wing joints; remove wing tips and flatten pieces. Brush with sauce. Grease broiler rack thoroughly and place turkey quarters on rack, skin side down. Grill over glowing (not flaming) coals for 1½ hours or until done; turn and brush with barbecue sauce every 15 minutes. Test by cutting into thickest part of meat on drumstick. It should cut easily with no blood showing at bone. Serve extra sauce with turkey. Serves 4.

# Barbecued Game Birds

2 plump game birds, (partridge, grouse, quail, etc.)
1 clove garlic
Salt
2 small onions, quartered
2 celery tops
2 sprigs parsley
¼ cup olive oil
1 lemon, juice and grated rind
Dash Tabasco sauce
1 teaspoon onion juice
¼ teaspoon thyme

Clean birds thoroughly and rinse in cold water; pat dry. Rub inside and out with garlic and salt. Insert an onion, celery top and parsley sprig into each cavity. Shake oil, lemon juice and rind, Tabasco sauce, onion juice and thyme in a wide-mouth jar. Place birds on a rack in a covered roasting pan; roast in moderately hot oven 375°F. until done to your liking, basting with sauce every 10 minutes, or grill over faintly glowing coals on your outdoor grill turning and basting frequently until thoroughly done and tender. Serves 2 to 4.

# Barbecued Broilers

¼ cup prepared mustard
¼ cup molasses
¼ cup lime or lemon juice
2 tablespoons salad oil
2 tablespoons Worcestershire sauce
1 teaspoon Tabasco
½ teaspoon monosodium glutamate
½ teaspoon salt
Monosodium glutamate
4 broilers, halved

Combine mustard and molasses. Stir well. Add juice, salad oil, Worcestershire sauce, Tabasco, ½ teaspoon monosodium glutamate and salt. Blend well. Sprinkle additional monosodium glutamate over broiler halves. Brush with barbecue sauce. Arrange chicken, cut side down on greased grill over glowing coals. Grill slowly about 35 minutes, or until tender, turning with tongs and basting often with remaining sauce. Makes 8 servings.

# Grilled Chicken in Foil

2 packages frozen, precut chicken
6 large pieces aluminum foil
½ cup soft butter or margarine
Salt
Pepper
2 medium onions, chopped
2 tablespoons chopped parsley
½ pound mushrooms, chopped

Allow frozen chicken to defrost just enough to separate. Portion chicken pieces out into servings on the squares of aluminum foil. Spread with butter. Sprinkle with salt and pepper. Combine remaining ingredients and divide over pieces of chicken. Bring up sides of foil. Fold down onto chicken in tight double fold. Fold ends up in tight double folds. Place foil packages directly on hot coals over an outdoor fire. Grill 30 minutes, turning once during cooking time. Serve in opened packages. Makes 6 servings.

# Lemon Barbecued Chicken

2 broiling chickens
½ cup butter or margarine
1 clove garlic
1½ teaspoons salt
¼ cup salad oil
½ cup lemon juice
2 tablespoons minced onion
½ teaspoon pepper
½ teaspoon dried thyme

Split chicken in half. Rinse in cold water and dry Melt butter in a heavy skillet or pan. Brown chicken on both sides. Mash garlic clove, and add remaining ingredients. Pour over the chicken. Cover tightly. Cook over low heat about 40 minutes or until chicken is tender. Pour remaining sauce in pan over chicken when served. Makes 4 servings.

# Chicken Marinara

3 broiler-fryer chickens, halved or quartered
1 can (8-ounces) tomato sauce
1 tablespoon vinegar
1 tablespoon Worcestershire sauce
1 teaspoon salt
¼ teaspoon Tabasco
2 tablespoons salad oil
⅓ cup finely chopped onion

Place chicken halves or quarters, skin side up, on grate set 3 to 6 inches from hot coals. Combine remaining ingredients. Brush chicken with sauce. Cook until tender, turning and brushing occasionally. Allow from 45 minutes to 1¼ hours cooking time, depending on weight of chicken and distance from heat. To test for doneness, leg should twist easily out of thigh joint and pieces should be fork tender. Makes 6 servings.

National Broiler Council

## Chicken Chasseur

2½-pound frying chicken
¼ cup flour
2 teaspoons salt
¼ teaspoon pepper
¼ teaspoon thyme
3 tablespoons butter or margarine
4 green onions, chopped
¼ pound mushrooms, sliced thick
2 tablespoons lemon juice
1 teaspoon sugar
1 teaspoon salt
⅓ cup dry white wine
2 medium tomatoes, diced
2 tablespoons chopped parsley

Cut chicken into serving pieces. Combine flour, salt, pepper and thyme in a paper bag. Add the pieces of chicken and shake well to coat chicken with flour. Melt the butter in a heavy skillet. Brown the pieces of chicken on all sides. Add onions and mushrooms and cook about 5 minutes. Combine lemon juice, sugar, salt and wine and pour over chicken. Cover and simmer 5 minutes over low coals. Add tomatoes. Cook slowly, covered tightly, over low coals about 30 minutes or until chicken is tender. Sprinkle with parsley before serving. Makes 4 servings.

## Spit-Roasted Beltville Turkeys

4- to 5-pound ready-to-cook turkey
Salt
1 large onion
1 celery top
2 sprigs parsley
1 cup Barbecue Sauce

Rinse turkey and pat dry. Rub neck and abdominal cavities with salt. Stuff with onion, celery top and parsley. Fold neck skin over and skewer to back; sew openings; tie drumsticks securely. Fasten bird on spit securely. Roast about 6 inches from the glowing coals, turning (if spit is not automatic) and basting with sauce every 10 minutes for about 2½ hours or until the drumstick thigh joint breaks or moves easily. Beltville turkeys may be spit-roasted indoors in an oven equipped with a spit attachment or in an electric rotissiere. Serves 6 to 8.

## California Chicken

2 broilers, cut in serving pieces
Salt and pepper
¼ cup oil
1 clove garlic, minced
½ cup chopped onion
¼ cup chopped green pepper
4 to 6 small white onions
6 carrots, cut in quarters
2 cups dry sherry
1 bay leaf
¼ teaspoon rosemary

Wipe chicken pieces with a damp cloth and season with salt and pepper. Brown chicken in hot oil in a heavy skillet. Remove chicken. Add garlic, onion, green pepper, whole onion and carrots to skillet and brown lightly. Add sherry, bay leaf, rosemary and chicken. Cover tightly and cook over low coals about 45 minutes or until chicken is tender. Makes 4 to 6 servings.

## Tim's Wonderful Barbecued Chicken

2 3-pound ready-to-cook whole fryers
¼ teaspoon poultry seasoning
2 small onions, peeled
6 sprigs parsley
4 stalks celery
1 large clove garlic
1 teaspoon salt
Dash Tabasco sauce
½ cup bacon drippings

Start charcoal fire in grill which has a spit attachment about 30 minutes before cooking begins. Rinse and dry chickens. Dust cavities with poultry seasoning and place an onion, 3 sprigs parsley and 2 stalks celery in each. Mash garlic to a paste with salt and mix with Tabasco sauce and bacon drippings. When fire dies down and you have a nice bed of rosy coals secure birds on spit. Brush generously with sauce. Cook 8 inches from the coals for about 1¼ hours or until meat is done to the bone. Turn spit (if not automatic) every 10 minutes, basting with the sauce. *The chickens may be split or cut in pieces.* Brush with sauce and place skin side up on grill over the coals; turn occasionally brushing with sauce until thoroughly done, about 45 minutes to 1 hour. Serves 6.

# Charcoal Rotisseried Turkey Roll

Leave turkey roll in original wrapper and thaw in refrigerator from 1 to 2 days, or under running, cold water. Remove the wrapper and leave string in place while cooking.

Rinse turkey with cold water; drain and pat dry. If roll is not preseasoned, rub lightly with salt and pepper.

Insert spit rod through center of turkey roll. Insert skewers firmly in place in roll and screw tightly. Test the balance. Roll must balance on spit so it will rotate smoothly throughout the cooking period. Place spit in rotisserie. Brush roast with melted butter or margarine.

Arrange hot charcoal briquets at back of fire box. Attach spit with turkey roll carefully balanced and start rotisserie motor as manufacturer directs. No further basting is necessary. Barbecue sauce may be brushed over the last 30 to 45 minutes of cooking, if desired.

To test doneness, insert a meat thermometer in center of roll, being careful not to touch spit. Thermometer should register 170° to 175°F.

For best results in slicing, allow roast to stand 20 to 30 minutes to absorb the juices. Remove string; use a sharp knife or meat slicer and slice thinly across the roast.

**TIMETABLE**

| Purchased Ready-To-Cook Weight | Interior Temperature | Guide to Total Cooking Time |
|---|---|---|
| 3 to 5 lbs. | 170° to 175°F | 1¾ to 2¼ hours |
| 5 to 7 lbs. | 170° to 175°F | 2 to 3 hours |
| 7 to 9 lbs. | 170° to 175°F | 2¾ to 3½ hours |

Poultry and Egg National Board

# Barbecued Chicken No. 2

Cut a 2 to 2½-pound ready-to-cook broiler-fryer in halves or quarters. Break hip, knee and wing joints to keep bird flat during grilling. When coals are hot place chicken on greased grids, cut side down. Broil slowly, turning frequently with tongs, and brush often with barbecue sauce. Cook until chicken is tender and lightly browned, about 30 to 40 minutes.

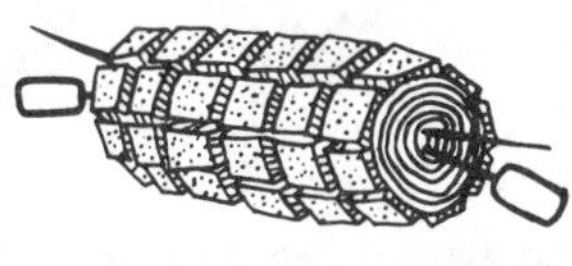

# Chicken Firecrackers

**2 cups diced cooked chicken**
**1½ cups diced celery**
**¼ cup slivered almonds, toasted**
**1 tablespoon diced onion**
**1 tablespoon lemon juice**
**1 teaspoon salt**
**⅛ teaspoon pepper**
**½ cup mayonnaise**
**¼ pound grated Cheddar cheese**
**8 French rolls**

Combine chicken, celery, almonds, onion, lemon juice, salt, pepper, mayonnaise, cheese; blend well. Scoop out center of each French roll; fill with chicken mixture. Wrap each roll in aluminum foil, twisting ends to resemble firecrackers. Place on grill of portable barbecue; heat about 20 minutes, turning several times. Makes 8 firecrackers.

Photo Courtesy Alcoa Wrap

McIlhenney's Tabasco

# "Cook Your Own" Barbecue

¾ pound boneless sirloin of beef, cut into thin slices
¾ pound chicken breasts, cut into thin slices
1 to 2 dozen cherry tomatoes *or* 12 tomato wedges
1 onion, thinly sliced and separated into rings
1 green pepper, thinly sliced into rings
1 cup soy sauce
½ teaspoon Tabasco

Arrange beef, chicken, tomatoes, onion and pepper rings attractively on serving plate or tray. Combine soy sauce and Tabasco; divide into 6 dishes. Let each guest dip bite-size portions of meat and vegetables into Soy-Tabasco mixture, then cook to desired doneness over the coals. Makes 6 servings.

# Curry Broiled Duckling

Allow 1 large sized duckling for each 4 persons; have them quartered. Brush both sides with a mixture of ¼ cup honey; ¼ cup lemon juice and 1 tablespoon curry powder. Use any leftover mixture for basting while cooking. Broil from 45 minutes to 1 hour on grill over low fire, turning a few times. During last few minutes of cooking regulate the grill or firebox so that coals are hotter and the skin of the duck will crisp.

# Rotisseried Duckling

Truss and center duckling on spit. Secure with food skewers. Cook duckling about 1 hour on high heat, or until duckling is tender and flesh is no longer pink at leg joints. About 10 minutes before duckling is done, brush all over with a mixture of honey, Kitchen Bouquet and ginger.

If you cook the duckling on a spit over your outdoor barbecue you will need a drip pan to catch the fat. Fashion one the correct shape for your grill from heavy aluminum freezer foil. Place in front of coals, directly under the turning spit.

Carve duck in the traditional manner and serve on toasted buns. Or simply cut the duckling in quarters with heavy kitchen or poultry shears.

# Charcoal Grilled Turkey Quarters

1 fryer-roaster turkey, 4 to 6 pounds, quartered
Melted butter or margarine for basting
Salt and pepper, as desired

To make a compact piece of meat for uniform cooking, fold wing tip back under wing. When wood charcoal briquets are all covered with fine white ash, place turkey quarters well brushed with melted butter or margarine on grill, skin side up. If desired, sprinkle turkey with salt and pepper. Turn quarters about every 15 minutes, basting as necessary. Cook slowly, keeping the turkey as far from the coals as possible, approximately 8 to 10 inches, to insure slow even cooking. Allow 2 to 2½ hours total cooking time for a 5 pound bird. Turkey is well-done when drumstick twists out of thigh joint readily and meaty portions are fork-tender. Serve with choice of favorite barbecue sauces. Makes 4 servings.

Poultry and Egg National Board

# Burgers and Franks

## Hot Chili Franks

Split frankfurter buns, partially fill with canned chili con carne or baked beans. Wrap each filled bun in a double thick square of foil, using tight double folds. Place bun packages on cooler side of grill. Heat buns for 10 minutes, turning frequently. Cook frankfurters over hot coals until heated through. To serve, open bun packages and place a broiled frankfurter in each.

Alcoa Wrap

## Frank and Bacon Twirls

**8 frankfurters**
**8 ounces Cheddar cheese**
**1 tablespoon prepared mustard**
**2 teaspoons grated onion**
**⅛ teaspoon Worcestershire sauce**
**8 slices bacon**
**8 frankfurter rolls**

Slice the frankfurters in half lengthwise. In a small bowl, mash the cheese with a fork, then blend in mustard, onion and Worcestershire sauce. Spread generously between frankfurter halves. Roll 1 strip of bacon around each of the frankfurters. Grill over hot coals, turning often until bacon is browned to taste. Serve in toasted frankfurter rolls. Makes 6 servings.

## Coney Island Beefwich

**1 pound ground beef**
**1½ cups chopped onions**
**1 cup chopped celery**
**1 teaspoon salt**
**⅛ teaspoon pepper**
**1 can condensed tomato soup**
**1½ tablespoons chili powder**
**¼ cup water**

Brown meat in a small amount of hot fat in a heavy skillet. Add onions and celery and cook until tender. Add remaining ingredients, using enough chili powder to suit taste. Simmer about 30 minutes. Serve over split, toasted buns. Makes 4 to 6 servings.

## Quick Frank Meal

**3 medium tomatoes, peeled**
**1 large onion, peeled**
**1 green pepper**
**1 pound frankfurters**
**1 cup grated cheese**
**½ teaspoon salt**
**1 teaspoon paprika**

Slice tomatoes into a heavy skillet. Top with thin slices of onion and strips of green pepper. Slice frankfurters in half, first lengthwise and then crosswise and place on vegetables. Cover and cook very slowly about 15 minutes. Sprinkle cheese, salt and paprika over the frankfurters. Cover tightly. Remove from hot grill and let stand long enough for cheese to melt. Makes 4 servings.

The Roguefort Association

## Grilled Roquefort Kabob Sandwiches

**1 pound ground beef round**
**1 tablespoon chopped parsley**
**½ cup crumbled Roquefort cheese**
**½ teaspoon garlic salt**
**⅛ teaspoon pepper**
**1 medium-sized green pepper, cut in quarters**
**1 medium-sized firm tomato, cut in quarters**
**4 whole cooked small white onions**
**¼ cup melted butter or margarine**
**4 indivdual loaves French bread**

Combine beef, parsley, cheese, garlic salt and pepper; mix well and shape into 16 balls. Arrange beef balls, green pepper wedges, tomato wedges and onions on skewers. Brush with some of butter or margarine. Broil 3-4 inches from source of heat or cook on outdoor grill 5 minutes on each side, or until beef balls are desired degree of doneness. Brush often during cooking period with remaining butter or margarine. Arrange meat balls and vegetables on bread to make sandwiches. Makes 4 servings.

National Live Stock & Meat Board

# Party Hamburgers

1 pound ground beef
3 tablespoons catsup
2 teaspoons prepared mustard
1½ teaspoons horse-radish
1 small onion, finely chopped
1 teaspoon salt
½ cup soft bread crumbs
¼ cup top milk
1½ teaspoons Worcestershire sauce

Combine all ingredients. Shape into 4 large or 8 small patties. Place on grill and cook about 6 minutes on each side for large patties, or 4 minutes for smaller patties. Or until browned on the outside and done to your liking on the inside. Makes 4 or 8 servings.

# Hamburger Chop Suey

3 large stalks celery
1 medium onion
3 tablespoons shortening
1 pound ground beef
1 beef bouillon cube
⅓ cup boiling water
2½ tablespoons cornstarch
1¾ teaspoons salt
½ teaspoon brown sugar
⅛ teaspoon pepper
2 tablespoons soy sauce
2 tablespoons cold water
1 can bean sprouts

Cut celery into thin slices and chop onion quite fine. Melt shortening in a heavy cast iron skillet and cook onions and ground beef over hot coals until meat is cooked through. Stir constantly so meat does not brown. Add celery slices and bouillon cube which has been dissolved in boiling water. Cover tightly and cook 5 minutes longer. Combine cornstarch, salt, brown sugar, pepper, soy sauce and cold water into a smooth paste, add to meat mixture and stir in thoroughly. Cook until thickened. Mix in well-drained bean sprouts and heat thoroughly. Makes 4 to 6 servings.

# Hamburgers on Skewers

1½ pounds ground beef
1 medium onion, chopped fine
2 slices bread, crumbled
1 egg
1 teaspoon Worcestershire sauce
1 teaspoon salt
6 small tomatoes
2 green peppers

Combine all ingredients except tomatoes and green peppers. Mix well and form into 18 small balls. Cut tomatoes in half. Remove stems from green peppers and cut each pepper into 6 large pieces. Arrange pepper slices, hamburger balls and tomato halves on 6 skewers. Broil over hot coals about 6 minutes on each side. Makes 6 servings.

Reynolds Metals Company

# Hamburger Balls

1 pound ground chuck
1 egg, beaten
½ cup bread crumbs
2 teaspoons grated onion
1 teaspoon horse-radish
1 teaspoon prepared mustard
2 teaspoons salt
¼ teaspoon pepper
1 round loaf pumpernickle bread

Combine all ingredients, except bread and shape into tiny balls. Form a pan of heavy duty aluminum foil. Place on grill over hot coals. Add 2 tablespoons butter or margarine and heat until hot. Add meat balls and brown quickly on all sides. Cut a slice from the top of the bread and hollow out loaf, leaving just the crust. Spread with softened butter. Place on one side of grill and as meat balls are browned and cook, place them in bread basket. Serve while piping hot.

# Chiliburgundies

**1 pound ground beef**
**3 tablespoons fat**
**2 cans (15 ounces) chili con carne with beans**
**⅔ cup red table wine**
**2 hamburger buns, halved and toasted**

Shape ground beef into 4 flat cakes of the same diameter as the hamburger buns. Brown well on both sides in fat in a heavy skillet. Heat chili con carne to boiling; stir in wine. Pour chili over cooked hamburgers, cover and simmer about 5 minutes. Place a bun half on a plate, top with a hamburger pattie and cover with chili mixture. Serve with additional toasted bun halves. Makes 4 servings.

# Burger Sûpreme

**1½ pounds ground chuck**
**1 teaspoon salt**
**⅛ teaspoon pepper**
**1 medium onion, sliced**
**1 medium tomato, sliced**
**¼ teaspoon Worcestershire sauce**
**Butter**
**4 hamburger buns**

Season meat with salt and pepper and blend lightly. Form into 8 thin patties. Place 1 slice of onion and tomato on each of 4 patties. Sprinkle with Worcestershire sauce. Cover with remaining patties, press edges of meat together to make a seal. Grill until brown on both sides. Butter split and toasted hamburger buns. Place patties between bun halves. Makes 4 servings.

# Double Decker Burgers

**1 pound ground beef**
**1 egg**
**1 teaspoon salt**
**Dash of pepper**
**¼ cup catsup**
**½ cup chopped onion**
**10 slices bacon**
**Frankfurter buns**

Combine meat, egg, salt, pepper and catsup and mix well. Form into 10 thin oblong patties, the shape of hot dog buns. Put 2 meat patties together with chopped onion between. Press edges together. Wrap each hamburger with 2 bacon slices and fasten ends with toothpicks. Broil patties on grill 3 to 5 inches from hot coals until bacon is cooked. Slip between hot dog buns and eat. Makes 5 servings.

# Franks in a Skillet

**3 tablespoons butter or margarine**
**8 medium onions, sliced**
**4 green peppers, sliced**
**1 pound frankfurters**
**½ teaspoon salt**
**⅛ teaspoon pepper**

Heat butter in a heavy skillet. Add remaining ingredients, cover tightly and simmer about 30 minutes, or until tender. Makes 4 servings.

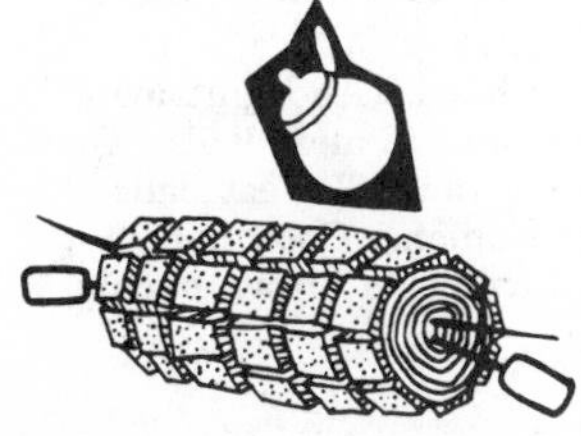

# Outdoor Barbecued Frankfurters

**½ cup chopped onion**
**2 tablespoons butter or margarine**
**3 tablespoons vinegar**
**3 tablespoons brown sugar**
**1 cup chili sauce**
**2 cups canned apple sauce**
**1 teaspoon salt**
**1 pound frankfurters**

Saute onion in butter until light brown. Add vinegar, brown sugar, chili sauce, apple sauce and salt. Add frankfurters and simmer over hot coals about 20 minutes. Serve in split, toasted frankfurter rolls, with spoonfuls of sauce. Makes 8 servings.

McIlhenney's Tabasco

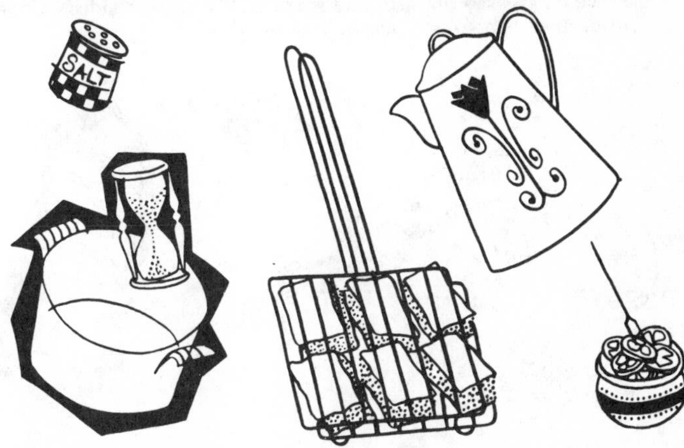

United Fresh Fruit and Vegetable Association

# Hamburger Kabob

**1½ pounds ground chuck**
**¼ teaspoon garlic salt**
**½ teaspoon onion salt**
**½ teaspoon celery salt**
**¼ teaspoon pepper**
**12 canned mushroom buttons**
**12 1-inch pieces green pepper**
**12 1-inch pieces tomato**
**12 1-inch pieces Bermuda onion**
**3 tablespoons salad oil**

Combine meat with salts and pepper. Form into 1½-inch balls. Thread on skewer, alternating with chunks of vegetables. Brush with oil and broil over hot coals, turning occasionally until well browned and of the desired doneness. Makes 6 servings.

# State Lake Hamburgers

**1 pound ground beef**
**¼ cup sour cream**
**1 teaspoon Worcestershire sauce**
**1 teaspoon monosodium glutamate**
**¼ cup chili sauce**

Combine all ingredients thoroughly. Shape into 4 patties. Place on greased hot grill and sear quickly on both sides. Cook to desired doneness. Makes 4 servings.

# Hamburgers DeLuxe

**1 pound ground beef**
**½ teaspoon salt**
**⅛ teaspoon pepper**
**¼ pound blue cheese**
**1 tablespoon Worcestershire sauce**
**2 tablespoons mayonnaise**
**½ teaspoon dry mustard**

Combine ground beef, salt and pepper and shape into 8 thin patties. With a fork crumble the cheese and combine with the remaining ingredients. Combine ¼ of the mixture between two patties and press edges together securely. Broil over hot coals on hand grill, or place on grill over hot coals. Brown first side, turn and brown second side. Makes 4 servings.

# Potato Burgers

**½ pound ground chuck**
**1 cup grated raw potatoes**
**3 tablespoons minced onions**
**⅛ teaspoon pepper**
**1 teaspoon salt**
**3 tablespoons butter or margarine**
**½ teaspoon dry mustard**
**2 tablespoons chopped parsley**

Mix together chuck, potato, onion, pepper and salt. Shape into 8 patties. Melt butter in a heavy skillet over hot coals. Fry patties until crisp and brown on both sides. Remove from skillet. Add mustard and parsley to drippings in pan, heat thoroughly and serve over burgers. Makes 4 servings.

# Savory Hamburger and Sauce Angostura

**2 pounds ground beef**
**2 teaspoons salt**
**½ teaspoon pepper**
**2 teaspoons angostura bitters**
**1 tablespoon lemon juice**
**1 can tomato sauce**
**¼ cup water**
**1 tablespoon minced onion**
**2 tablespoons minced green pepper**
**2 tablespoons minced celery**

Combine meat, salt, pepper, bitters and lemon juice. Blend thoroughly and form into four thick patties. Let stand while preparing sauce. Combine tomato sauce with the remaining ingredients in a small bowl. Brush cakes on both sides with this mixture. Place on rack and broil some distance from the hot coals, about 5 minutes on each side for rare. Broil longer for well done. Serve with remaining sauce. Makes 4 large servings.

# Heavenly Burger Bobs

**1 pound ground beef**
**¾ teaspoon monosodium glutamate**
**¾ teaspoon salt**
**¼ teaspoon pepper**
**1 large green pepper, cut in pieces**
**4 small white onions, halved**

Break up meat with fork in mixing bowl. Add glutamate, salt and pepper and toss gently. Shape into 12 meat balls. On green wooden sticks or metal skewers arrange 3 meat balls, 2 pieces of green pepper and 2 halves of onion. Cook over hot coals until meat is desired doneness, turning to brown evenly. Makes 4 servings.

# Just Right Burgers

½ teaspoon Tabasco
½ cup tomato juice
1 pound ground beef
1 teaspoon salt

Combine all ingredients and blend with a fork. Shape into 4 patties. Place in a folding wire grill and grill over hot coals 4 to 5 minutes on each side, or to desired doneness. Brush with favorite barbecue sauce during cooking if desired. Serve on toasted rolls. Makes 4 servings.

# Hamburger Cheese Scoops

5 slices bacon
2 pounds ground beef
2 tablespoons onion, chopped
1 can (10½ ounces) condensed tomato soup
1 cup cubed process American cheese
½ to 1 teaspoon caraway seed
Buns or rolls

Cut bacon into small pieces and pan-fry in a skillet until crisp. Remove bacon and pour off bacon fat. Brown ground beef and onion in skillet. Add bacon, tomato soup, cheese and caraway seed. Stir and cook for 10 minutes or until cheese is thoroughly melted. Scoop onto split buns or hard rolls. Makes 8 servings.

# Party Meat Logs

1 egg
½ cup tomato juice
2 cups fresh bread cubes
1 teaspoon seasoning salt
½ teapoon celery salt
1 pound ground beef
8 slices processed American cheese
8 buttered frankfurter rolls

Combine egg, tomato juice, bread cubes, seasoning salt and celery salt. Combine with ground beef and mix thoroughly. Chill mixture. Divide meat mixture into 8 portions. Form each portion into a log, about 4 inches long. Broil over hot coals until done. Place a slice of cheese on each frankfurter bun, place meat log on cheese slice. Serve immediately. Makes 8 servings.

R. T. French & Co.

# Dillburgers

1½ pounds ground beef
¼ teaspoon garlic salt
½ teaspoon onion salt
½ teaspoon celery salt
¼ teaspoon pepper
2 dill pickles
6 slices bacon

Combine ground beef with salts and pepper. Cut dill pickles into thirds, lengthwise. Shape meat mixture around each piece of pickle, so that it is entirely covered. Wrap a bacon slice around each bundle of meat. Place on grill over hot coals and cook until bacon is crispy and meat done. Serve between hot dog buns. Makes 6 servings.

# Cheddared Franks

With a sharp knife split frankfurters lengthwise almost all the way through. Stuff the slit in the frankfurters with very sharp cheddar cheese. Fasten a strip of bacon at one end of the frankfurter with a toothpick, wind bacon around frankfurter and fasten at other end with toothpick. Grill over hot coals until bacon is of desired doneness. Serve between toasted rolls with assorted relishes.

# Hot Dogs on a Skewer

**1 pound frankfurters, cut in 1-inch pieces**
**4 dill pickles, cut in chunks**
**1 can (1 pound) boiled potatoes, drained**
**French dressing**
**Prepared mustard**
**Garlic salt**

Place frankfurters, pickles and potatoes in a bowl. Cover with French dressing and let stand about 1 hour. Drain, saving French dressing. Place frankfurters, pickles and potatoes alternately on skewers. Broil on grill over hot coals until lightly browned, turning several times and brushing with French dressing. Serve with mustard seasoned with a little garlic salt. Makes 4 servings.

# Franks in Blankets

**1¼ cups prepared biscuit mix**
**⅓ cup milk**
**8 frankfurters**
**8 gherkins**
**Prepared mustard**

Make rolled biscuit dough as directed on the package, reducing milk to ⅓ cup. On floured board, roll dough to ⅛-inch thickness. Cut into four 3½-inch squares. Split frankfurters and pickles lengthwise. Spread center of each frankfurter with mustard and insert 2 pickle halves. Place 1 filled frankfurter on each square of dough and roll it so that the center portion of frankfurter is encased. Cook slowly over hot coals until dough is browned on all sides. Makes 8 sandwiches.

# Fish

# Skewered Scallops

**1 pound sea scallops**
**16 small white onions**
**3 green peppers**
**¾ pound large mushrooms**
**2 tablespoons lemon juice**
**¼ cup melted butter**
**Freshly ground black pepper**
**Garlic powder**
**Paprika**

Rinse scallops and pat dry. Peel onions and cut peppers into 1¼-inch pieces. Remove stems from mushrooms. Cook onions in boiling salted water about 8 minutes. Add pepper pieces and cook 2 minutes longer. Drain. Arrange scallops, onions, pepper and mushrooms on 8-inch skewers. Combine lemon juice and butter. Brush filled skewers with lemon butter, sprinkle with pepper and garlic powder. Sprinkle scallops with paprika. Broil 2 inches from source of heat, about 5 minutes, turning once. Makes 8 servings.

National Fisheries Institute

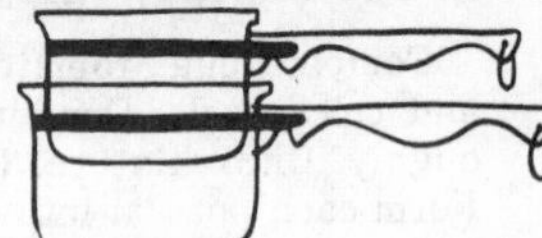

# Pan-Sautéed Scallops

**1½ pounds scallops**
**1 cup dry bread crumbs**
**¼ cup butter or margarine**
**¼ teaspoon salt**
**⅛ teaspoon pepper**
**Pinch of paprika**
**4 slices grilled toast**
**3 tablespoons dry white wine**

Roll scallops in bread crumbs. Melt butter in a heavy skillet. Add scallops and cook 5 minutes over very hot coals, turning constantly. Add salt, pepper and paprika. Remove scallops and arrange on grilled toast. Add wine to pan, swish it around once and pour mixture over scallops. Makes 4 to 6 servings.

# Crispy Fried Trout

**6 small trout**
**1 cup milk**
**½ teaspoon celery salt**
**½ teaspoon onion salt**
**½ teaspoon garlic salt**
**¼ teaspoon black pepper**
**⅔ cup white corn meal**
**12 slices bacon**
**⅓ cup butter or margarine**
**1 lemon**

Clean and split trout. Remove heads and tails. Dip in milk. Combine seasonings and sprinkle over fish. Dip in corn meal. Fry bacon until crisp. Reserve bacon in a warm place. Add butter to bacon fat. Heat. Fry fish gently in hot fat until crisp and brown. Serve garnished with bacon and lemon. Makes 6 servings.

# Broiled Lobster

To kill the lobster, insert a sharp knife between the body and tail shells; this severs the spinal cord. Place lobster on back and make a deep cut lengthwise from head to end of tail. Open and remove stomach, dark vein and liver. Crack large claws. Brush meat with melted butter or margarine and place cut side down on rack over hot coals. Cook about 5 minutes. Turn cut side up. Brush with melted butter and season with salt and pepper. Broil 10 to 15 minutes or until meat is tender. Time, of course, depends on size of lobster and distance from heat.

National Fisheries Institute

# Broiled or Grilled Smelt

Have smelt drawn (leaving heads and tails intact) or use frozen smelt. Sprinkle with salt and pepper and squeeze the juice of a lemon over all. Place under broiler or on grill so that smelt are 4 inches from the source of heat. Cook 4 minutes on each side. Serve with cold sliced cucumbers and a generous amount of watercress.

# Seafood Kabobs

**⅓ cup salad oil**
**3 tablespoons lemon juice**
**1 clove garlic, halved**
**½ teaspoon salt**
**2 tablespoons chili sauce**
**1 tablespoon soy sauce**
**1 pound large shrimp, fresh or frozen**
**½ pound sea scallops**
**2 rock lobster tails**

Combine oil with lemon juice, garlic, salt, chili and soy sauces; let stand. Shell and devein shrimp. Halve scallops. Cut away undershells of rock lobster tails with kitchen scissors; then carefully insert fingers between shell and raw rock lobster tail meat and work out meat from shell. Cut each lobster tail into 3 sections. Arrange seafoods on skewers, alternating varieties. Place skewers in shallow dish and pour marinade over them; let stand ½ to 3 hours. Remove skewers from marinade and broil until done about 5 minutes on each side. Makes 6 servings.

# Broiled Soft-Shell Crabs

Dust crabs very lightly with flour. Place crabs on grid that is about 6 inches from the hot coals. Broil small and medium-sized crabs 4 minutes on the first side and 4 minutes on the second side. Large crabs should be broiled about 5 minutes on each side. Do not baste during cooking period. When done, remove crabs, dot with butter and serve immediately. Two large or 3 small soft-shell crabs make 1 serving.

# Broiled Oysters

**36 shell oysters**
**½ teaspoon salt**
**⅛ teaspoon pepper**
**½ cup bread crumbs**
**2 tablespoons butter or margarine**

Shuck and drain oysters; place in deep half of the shells. Sprinkle with salt, pepper and buttered bread crumbs. Place on grill and cook over very hot coals until edges of oysters curl Makes 6 servings.

# Broiled Whole Fish

Any type of small whole fish can be barbecued. Clean and dress fish and place on the barbecue grill. Sprinkle with garlic salt and pepper. Place a square of butter on each fish. Cook about 10 minutes over glowing coals. To cook small fish properly, place grill about 3 inches from the hot coals. At the same time the fish is being grilled, grill large onion slices with a slice of tomato atop each.

# Broiled Haddock with Clam Sauce

**1½ pound haddock fillets**
**¼ teaspoon salt**
**⅛ teaspoon pepper**
**2 tablespoons oil**
**1 can condensed clam chowder**
**¼ cup tomato juice**
**⅛ teaspoon thyme**
**1 tablespoon minced parsley**

Preheat broiling compartment. Brush fillets with seasoned oil. Place on broiling pan or broil-and-serve platter 2 inches from heat. Broil about 6 minutes or until fish flakes easily with a fork. Meanwhile combine remaining ingredients in a 1-quart saucepan and simmer until hot. Serve fillets on a hot platter with clam sauce. Makes 6 servings.

# Fresh Vegetables and Shrimp en Brochette

**1 cup oil**
**½ cup white wine**
**1 teaspoon salt**
**¼ teaspoon pepper**
**2 teaspoons chopped parsley**
**2 medium tomatoes, quartered**
**2 medium green peppers, cut in cubes**
**2 medium onions, quartered**
**12 whole fresh mushrooms**
**20 to 24 peeled, cleaned uncooked shrimp**

Combine oil, wine, salt, pepper and parsley. Add vegetables and shrimp. Let stand for several hours. String shrimps on skewers alternately with vegetables. Broil over hot coals until nicely browned, turning and basting with marinade occasionally. Makes 4 servings.

# Manhattan Clam Chowder

**¼ pound salt pork, diced**
**1 large onion, diced**
**1 green pepper, diced**
**1 cup diced raw carrots**
**1 cup diced raw potatoes**
**1 cup diced celery**
**1 No. 2½ can tomatoes**
**3 cups water**
**2 teaspoons salt**
**¼ teaspoon pepper**
**2 dozen large clams, cleaned and chopped**
**Or 2 cups minced clams**
**½ cup fine cracker crumbs**

Cook pork in a heavy kettle until lightly brown; add onion and cook until golden brown. Add remaining vegetables, water and seasonings; cover and simmer 1 hour. Add clams and cook 5 minutes. Add cracker crumbs. Makes 6 to 8 servings.

# Frogs' Legs

**24 medium frogs' legs**
**Flour**
**Oil**
**2 tablespoons butter**
**1 cup finely chopped mushrooms**
**¼ cup finely chopped shallots**
**¼ cup finely chopped parsley**
**Salt and pepper**
**¼ cup dry white wine**

Have frogs' legs cleaned and skinned. Roll them in seasoned flour and fry in hot oil until golden brown in your outdoor skillet. In another skillet melt butter, add mushrooms, shallots and parsley. Sauté until just done and season with salt and pepper. Place frogs' legs on a very hot serving platter, cover with mushroom mixture and pour wine over the top. Makes 4 to 6 servings.

# Fisherman's Stew

**6 ounces salt pork**
**6 medium onions**
**4½ cups boiling water**
**5 medium potatoes**
**6 fish, 1½ pounds each**
**1½ cups cold water**
**½ cup nonfat dry milk**
**Salt to taste**
**Black pepper**
**Garlic powder to taste**
**Ground thyme to taste**
**¼ cup butter or margarine**

Slice salt pork in ⅛-inch slices and fry in a heavy Dutch oven until crisp. Remove pieces of salt pork from fat. Peel onion, slice and sauté in hot salt pork fat until limp. Add boiling water. Slice peeled potatoes ¼ inch thick and add to water. Cover and cook until potatoes are tender. Cook fish in boiling water until flesh is flaky, about 3 to 4 minutes. Remove from water. Slip off skin, lift out bones and break into chunks. Add to potato mixture along with salt pork. Mix cold water with dry milk and stir into stew. Add salt, pepper, garlic powder and thyme to taste. Stir in butter. Heat thoroughly and serve. Makes 8 to 9 servings.

# Barbecue Grilled Fish

**4 fish steaks, cut ¾-inch thick**
**2 tablespoons lemon juice**
**½ cup salad oil**
**1 teaspoon savory salt**

Place fish steaks in a shallow pan. Combine lemon juice, oil and savory salt. Pour over fish. Let stand in the refrigerator 2 hours. Arrange fish in a folding wire broiler. Brush well with marinade. Grill close to fire 3 minutes, or until fish is golden. Brush with marinade, turn and grill until fish is tender and browned. Makes 4 servings.

# Roast Fish

**1 3- to 4-pound fish**
**¼ cup butter**
**2 cloves garlic**
**2 tablespoons lemon juice**
**Salt and pepper**

Have the head and tail removed from the fish. Ask the fish dealer to remove the backbone, but do not cut the fish in half. Place butter and garlic in a saucepan and let butter melt slowly. Add lemon juice and let mixture stand a few minutes. Sprinkle inside of fish with salt and pepper and brush with butter mixture. Place fish in fold grill of rotisserie. Brush outside of fish with butter mixture. Place in preheated rotisserie. Cook until fish is just fork tender, from 15 to 25 minutes or according to directions of the rotisserie manufacturer. Brush fish once or twice with butter mixture during cooking period. Cook whole mushroom caps in bottom tray of rotisserie and hash browned potatoes in a skillet on the top at the same time that the fish is cooking.

## Down East Fish Chowder

**1½ pounds fresh or canned cod, haddock or other large fish**
**1 cup diced potatoes**
**1 cup diced carrots**
**1 quart water**
**1 small can shrimp, cut up**
**½ cup lobster meat**
**¼ pound salt pork, diced**
**1 onion, chopped**
**1 pint milk**
**Salt and pepper**

Cut fish in small pieces, removing bone and skin. Cook with potatoes and carrots in water for 15 minutes. Add shrimp and lobster. Fry the pork crisp in a heavy skillet. Add onions and cook until tender. Combine with milk, fish, and vegetables. Season to taste. Simmer gently for 10 minutes, stirring often. Makes 6 servings.

## Baked Stuffed Bass

**1 3- to 4-pound bass**
**1½ cups bread cubes**
**½ teaspoon salt**
**⅛ teaspoon pepper**
**¼ teaspoon thyme**
**½ onion, minced**
**½ cup butter or margarine, melted**
**2 tablespoons lemon juice**
**1 No. 2 can white onions**
**1 3-oz. can mushrooms**
**Salt and pepper**
**Chopped parsley**

Have fish cleaned with head and tail removed. Rub inside with salt. Combine bread cubes, salt, pepper, thyme, onion and ¼ cup of the butter. Place mixture in body cavity. Bind fish in about 3 places with string. Tear off a large piece of heavy duty foil and fold double to make a double thick wrap for the fish. Place fish on foil. Pour over it the remaining melted butter and lemon juice. Add onions and mushrooms. Sprinkle with salt, pepper and chopped parsley. Bring the foil up and over the fish and seal edges together tightly with a double fold. Place package of fish on grate over medium hot coals. Grill rather slowly allowing 15 to 20 minutes for each pound. Turn two or three times during cooking period. When cooked, place foil on a large serving tray, open foil and serve. Makes 6 to 8 servings.

## Shrimp, Scallops and Green Olives

**1 pound shrimp**
**½ pound scallops**
**1 can (No. 2½) pineapple chunks**
**1 can large stuffed green olives**
**¼ cup butter or margarine**
**Juice of ½ lemon**
**Salt and pepper**

Remove shells from shrimp. Cut down back of shrimp and remove sand vein. Cut scallops in pieces, two pieces if scallops are small, four pieces if they are large. Drain pineapple and olives. Place two shrimps together and thread on skewers alternately with scallops, pineapple and olives. Melt butter and add lemon juice and seasonings. Brush on shrimps and scallops. Place skewers over hot coals (the holder shown here is very handy for holding any kind of kabobs). Broil about 5 minutes, turning occasionally and brushing with melted butter. Makes 4 hearty servings.

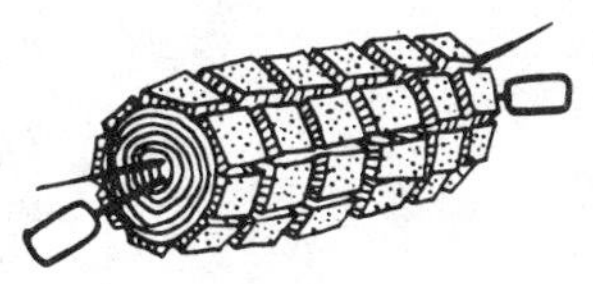

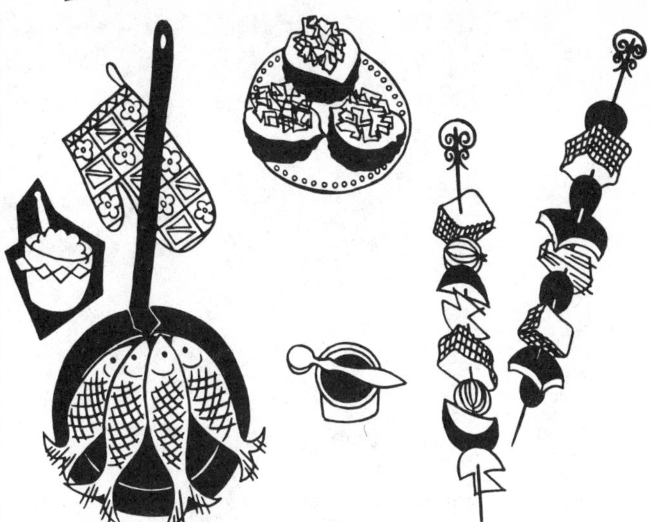

## Grilled Halibut Steaks with Barbecue Sauce

**1 pound halibut steaks fresh, or frozen**
**Juice of 1 lemon**
**½ cup salad oil**
**¼ teaspoon salt**
**⅛ teaspoon pepper**
**½ teaspoon dry mustard**

If halibut is frozen let thaw on refrigerator shelf or at room temperature. Arrange steaks in refrigerator dish. Combine remaining ingredients and pour over steaks. Cover dish and let marinate about 4 hours. Place on well-greased grill over low glowing coals. Grill 10 minutes, turn and grill 10 minutes more, or until fish is completely white and flakes easily when tested with a fork. Baste frequently with marinade during grilling. Makes 4 servings.

Halibut Association of North America

Shrimp Association of the Americas

# Grilled Marinated Shrimp

Split through the shell of 2 pounds of jumbo shrimp with a sharp knife. Remove the black vein but leave the shell intact. Place shrimp in a bowl or jar, with the following ingredients:

**3 cloves garlic, finely chopped**
**1 medium onion, finely chopped**
**¼ cup chopped parsley (optional)**
**1 teaspoon dried basil (optional)**
**1 teaspoon dry mustard**
**1 teaspoon salt**
**½ cup olive or peanut oil**
**Juice of 1 lemon**

Let the shrimp marinate in this mixture for several hours. Place shrimp on a grill over hot charcoal. Grill about 5 minutes.

# Broiled Salmon Steaks

Sprinkle salmon steaks with lemon juice, salt and pepper. Put on preheated broiling pan. Place pan 2 inches from source of heat. Broil 3 minutes. Turn carefully and broil 5 minutes.

# Brother Girard's Skewered Scallops

**¾ pound deep-sea scallops (12 scallops)**
**½ cup honey**
**¼ cup mustard**
**1 tablespoon lemon juice**
**2 teaspoons curry powder**
**½ teaspoon salt**
**Dash of pepper**
**8 tomatoes or tomato wedges**
**2 small green peppers, seeded and cut in quarters**

Wash and drain scallops. Mix honey, mustard, lemon juice, curry powder, salt and pepper in a bowl. Add scallops and stir to coat on all sides. Cover and let stand in refrigerator for several hours. When ready to cook, arrange on skewers alternately with tomatoes and pepper wedges. Grill over wood charcoal briquettes about 5 minutes, turning to brown both sides. Brush with sauce during cooking. Makes 4 servings.

Paper Cup and Plate Industries

American Institute of Baking

# Grilled Perch in a Bun

**6 pan-dressed perch or other fish fillets, frozen**
**⅓ cup creamy French dressing**
**1½ tablespoons lemon juice**
**¼ teaspoon pepper**
**6 frankfurter buns**

Thaw fish. Clean, wash, and dry each fish fillet. Combine French dressing, lemon juice, and pepper. Brush each fish fillet with the sauce. Grill over hot coals for about ten minutes; turn and brush with sauce. Grill for five minutes longer, or until the fish flakes easily when tested with a fork. Serve each fillet on a frankfurter bun, with or without tartar sauce.

# Outdoor Crab Newburg

**1 can condensed cream of mushroom soup**
**¼ cup milk**
**1 cup cooked or canned crab meat, flaked**
**2 tablespoons sherry**

Heat mushroom soup and milk in a heavy saucepan. Stir in crab meat. Heat to the boiling point. Remove from heat and stir in sherry. Serve at once over toast, crisp crackers or toasted noodles. Makes 4 servings.

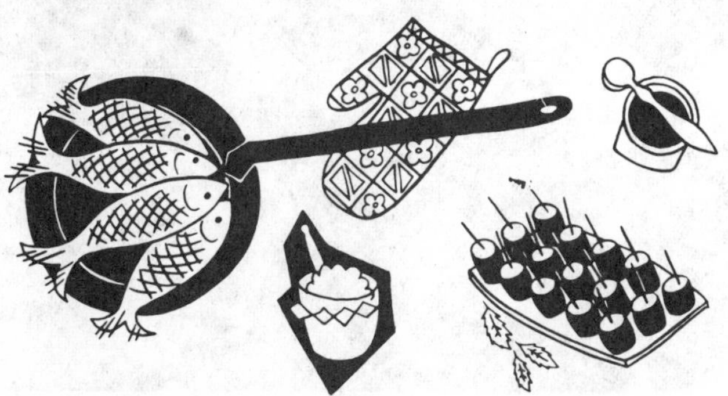

# Sweet-Sour Barbecued Fish

**½ cup lemon juice**
**½ teaspoon salt**
**¼ cup salad oil**
**½ teaspoon pepper**
**2 tablespoons grated onion**
**1 teaspoon dry mustard**
**2 tablespoons brown sugar**
**1 pound fish steaks**

Mix ingredients, stirring until sugar is completely dissolved. Place fish in heat-proof broiler platter and pour sauce over the top. Preheat broiling compartment and place steaks about 2 inches from heat. Broil about 3 minutes, turn and broil about 5 minutes or until fish flakes easily with a fork. Baste frequently during cooking time. Makes 3 to 4 servings.

# Grilled Oysters

**1 pint frying oysters**
**5 tablespoons oysters liquor**
**1 tablespoon lemon juice**
**2 tablespoons grated onion**
**1 tablespoon minced celery**
**1 teaspoon salt**
**¼ teaspoon pepper**
**1 tablespoon butter, softened**

Drain oysters and save liquor. Divide oysters and place on 5 squares of aluminum foil. Combine oyster liquor with remaining ingredients. Blend well and pour over oysters. Bring up sides of foil; fold down over oysters in tight double fold; fold ends up in tight double folds. Place each packet in another square of aluminum foil and wrap again in double folds. Place packages directly on hot coals; grill 10 to 12 minutes, turning once. Serve in opened packages. Makes 5 servings.

# Oysters Pepper Pan

**1 medium onion, minced**
**½ cup finely-diced green pepper**
**2 tablespoons butter or margarine**
**1 tablespoon chopped parsley**
**1 cup ketchup**
**1 pint oysters, drained**
**Grilled toast**

Cook onion and green pepper in butter in a heavy skillet until golden brown. Add the parsley and ketchup and bring to a boil. Add oysters and simmer about 4 minutes or until oysters are plump. Serve at once on toast. Makes 4 servings.

# Steamed Clams

Allow 15 to 25 clams for each person. Scrub clams thoroughly in plenty of clean water. Place clams in a large kettle with about ½ inch of water. Cover tightly and steam 6 to 10 minutes or until clams are just open. Do not overcook. Serve clams on plates with melted butter or margarine, seasoned with a few drops of lemon juice. Clam broth should be strained and served piping hot along with the clams.

American Institute of Baking

# Grilled Salmon-Slaw Sandwiches

2 tablespoons salad oil
⅓ cup lemon juice
8 small salmon steaks
8 sandwich buns
2⅔ cups Hot Cabbage Slaw recipe below)

Combine salad oil and lemon juice and brush both sides of salmon steaks. Wrap each steak in heavy aluminum foil, double folding the edges for tight seal. Place the wrapped steaks over the hot (not blazing) coals of the grill. Cook for 5 minutes on each side. Unwrap steaks and remove center bone by pushing it out with finger tip. Remove skin using paring knife or tweezers. Place a steak and ⅓ cup hot slaw between halves of heated bun. Serve immediately. Makes 8 sandwiches.

### Hot Cabbage Slaw

1 tablespoon sugar
3 tablespoons vinegar
¼ cup water
1 teaspoon salt
½ teaspoon caraway or poppy seeds
1 egg, beaten slightly
1 quart chopped, shredded cabbage

Combine sugar, vinegar, salt and seeds in a small saucepan. Add beaten egg and cook until thickened, stirring constantly. Pour over cabbage and toss together lightly. Makes 2⅔ cups Hot Cabbage Slaw.

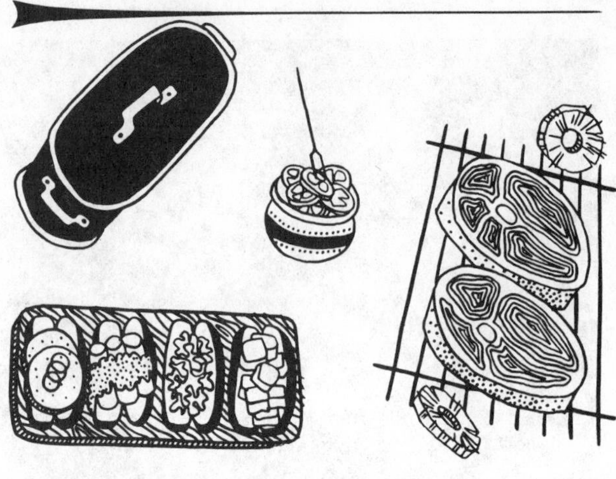

# Open-Grill Fish

2 pounds fish fillets or steaks
Salt
Paprika
⅓ cup melted butter
¼ teaspoon Tabasco

Cut fillets into serving-size pieces or leave whole. Sprinkle fish with salt and paprika. Place whole fillets or serving pieces on individual pieces of aluminum foil; bring up sides of foil. Combine butter and Tabasco; pour over fish. Secure foil tightly. Place on grill 4 inches from heat. Grill 8-10 minutes, or until easily flaked with a fork. Serve with lemon or lime wedges. *For pan-fried fish:* Dip fillets, steaks, or small whole fish into milk, evaporated milk or 1 egg beaten with two tablespoons water. Sprinkle with salt; roll in flour or fine dry bread crumbs. Place in hot (not smoking) fat in skillet. Cook quickly about 2-3 minutes on each side or until moist and easily flaked. Makes 4 servings.

McIlhenney's Tabasco

# Meat

## Barbecue Pot Roast

4 pounds blade-bone pot roast, 1½ inches thick
Salt and pepper
Barbeque Sauce (recipe below)
2 stalks celery, cut in diagonal slices
2 carrots, cut in diagonal slices
1 small onion, thinly sliced
½ green pepper, thinly sliced

Brown meat slowly for 20-30 minutes over low coals; season with salt, pepper. Tear off a 2½ foot length of 18-inch heavy-duty aluminum foil. Place ½ barbecue sauce in center of foil; place meat on top of sauce; pad sharp bones with pieces of foil. Cover top of meat with celery, carrot slices, remaining sauce; top with onion, pepper slices. Bring up torn edges of foil in tight double folds; fold ends up using tight double folds. Place package on grill over low coals for 1½ to 2 hours, or until tender; turn once during cooking time. Makes 6 servings.

### Barbecue Sauce

2 tablespoons butter
1 onion, chopped fine
½ cup chopped celery
¾ cup water
1 cup catsup
2 tablespoons vinegar
2 tablespoons lemon juice
2 tablespoons Worcestershire sauce
2 tablespoons brown sugar
1 teaspoon dry mustard
1 teaspoon salt
¼ teaspoon pepper

Melt butter; add onion, celery; cook until tender. Add water, catsup, vinegar, lemon juice, Worcestershire Sauce, brown sugar, dry mustard, salt, pepper. Simmer 15 minutes.

Alcoa Wrap

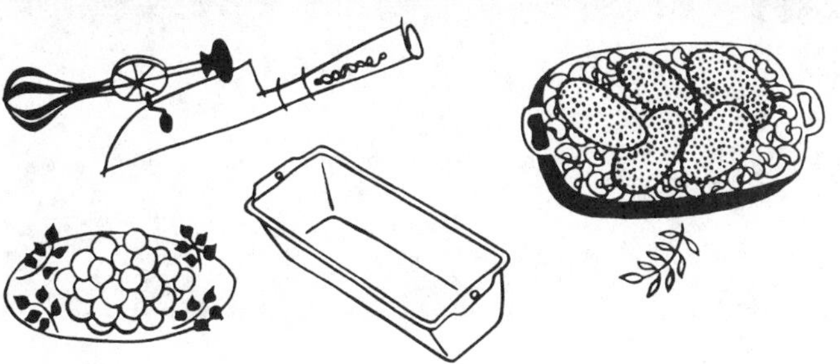

## Barbecued Pork Chops

8 ½-inch thick loin pork chops
Barbeque sauce
1 medium onion, sliced thin
1 small green pepper, cut in rings

Brown pork chops on both sides over hot coals. Pour 1 tablespoon of your favorite barbecue sauce in center of eight squares of foil; place chops on top; place 2 slices onion, 1 tablespoon barbecue sauce, 2 rings green pepper on top of each chop. Bring torn edges of foil together in tight double folds on top of chops; fold ends up using tight double folds. Place packages on grill over medium coals for 45-50 minutes, turning frequently. Makes 8 servings.

## Barbecued Short Ribs

1 cup tomato juice
1 teaspoon salt
½ teaspoon pepper
2 cloves minced garlic
1½ teaspoons dry mustard
½ teaspoon Worcestershire sauce
1 teaspoon brown sugar
½ cup red wine
3 pounds short ribs

Combine all ingredients except ribs and mix well. Add the ribs and let stand in the refrigerator overnight. Remove ribs, and drain well. Place ribs on a hot grill and cook over hot coals for about 30 minutes. Turn and baste frequently with the marinating sauce. Makes about 6 servings.

Pan American Coffee Bureau

# Barbecued London Broil

1 flank steak
¼ cup butter or margarine
½ cup strong coffee
Few drops bitters
2 tablespoons light molasses
½ teaspoon salt

Combine butter, coffee, bitters and molasses. Stir over low heat until butter melts. (This may be made in the kitchen and reheated over outdoor fire). Score steak, criss-cross fashion, on both sides and brush both sides with sauce. Grill, about 2 inches above glowing charcoal, basting often with sauce, for about minutes. Sprinkle with half the salt. Turn; grill 3 minutes longer, basting often. Sprinkle with remaining salt. Cut on the diagonal in very thin slices. Pour any remaining sauce over steak slices. Makes 4 generous servings.

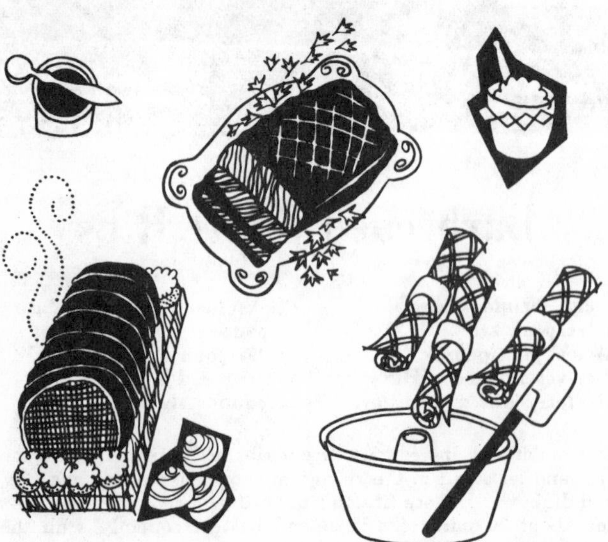

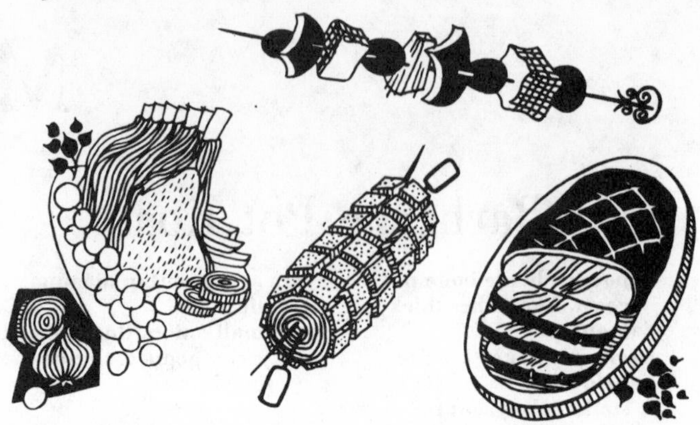

# Chicken Livers and Bacon en Brochette

Soak bamboo skewers in water, and string each with 4 or 5 halves of chicken livers that have been wrapped in bacon. Broil, or let the guests broil, over charcoal until the bacon is crisp. Each guest gets skewer and eats the tidbit from it.

# Barbecue Steak Sandwiches

½ cup sliced onion
½ cup butter or margarine
½ teaspoon salt
2 tablespoons Worcestershire sauce
2 tablespoons lemon juice
2 tablespoons sugar
½ teaspoon oregano
⅔ cup ketchup
1 cup canned apple sauce
6 cube steaks
6 hamburger rolls

Saute onion in butter until light brown. Stir in salt, Worcestershire sauce, lemon juice, sugar, oregano, ketchup and apple sauce. Mix thoroughly. Pour sauce over steaks and let stand 15 minutes. Lift out steaks and arrange on grill 2-inches from hot coals. Broil quickly on one side, about 3 minutes; baste with barbecue sauce and turn to cook other side. Spread hamburger rolls with soft butter or margarine. Toast on grill. Place steaks on rolls and top with some of remaining barbecue sauce. Makes 6 servings.

Processed Apples Institute, Inc.

Wish-Bone

# Spareribs with Ginger Barbecue Sauce

1 bottle (8-ounces) Italian dressing
¾ cup brown sugar, firmly packed
¾ cup catsup
1 cup water
1½ teaspoons celery salt
1½ teaspoons ginger
4 pounds spareribs

Combine all ingredients except spareribs, in a small saucepan. Simmer about 10 minutes, stirring occasionally. Place spareribs on a grill and cook for about 1 hour and 10 minutes turning and basting about every 15 minutes with the sauce. Makes about 4 servings.

# Ham on a Spit

Choose a fully cooked boneless ham roll for a quick outdoor meal. Leave the roll whole and skewer through the whole piece. Place on spit over hot coals and cook until well browned on the outside, about 45 minutes to 1 hour. While cooking brush with a sauce made from ¾ cup brown sugar, 3 tablespoons vinegar, ¼ cup pineapple juice, ½ cup apricot nectar, ¼ teaspoon powdered garlic and ¼ teaspoon powdered cloves.

A variation on this that is easy to make and looks very fancy: Cut the ham into slices, about 1-inch thick. Alternate slices with slices of canned pineapple. Place on skewer and fasten tightly with holding forks on both ends so that the whole assembly is smooth and looks to be in one piece. Brush during cooking with pineapple juice or the above mixture.

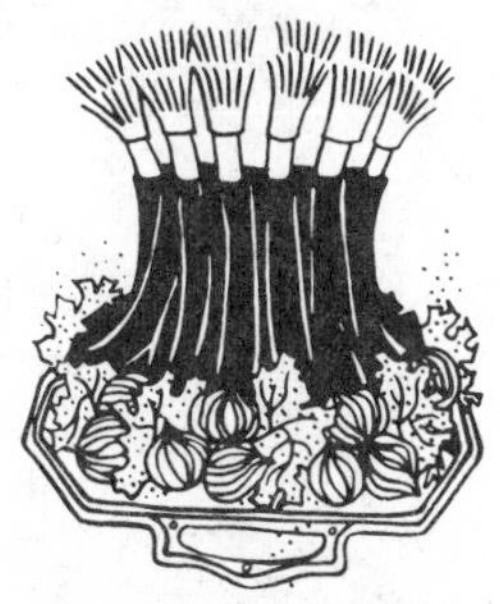

# Beef Bundles

**1 pound beef round, cut in ¾-inch cubes**
**2 medium onions, peeled and quartered**
**2 large potatoes, peeled and quartered**
**2 large tomatoes, halved**
**2 ears fresh corn, broken in halves**
**Aluminum foil**
**Seasoned salt**
**Pepper**

Divide meat and vegetables into four equal portions and place each portion on a 12-inch sheet of aluminum foil. Season to taste. Bring edges of foil together and seal with double folds. Place on grill over hot coal and cook 1 hour, turning occasionally. Serve right in foil packets. Makes 4 servings.

# Hawaiian Sweetbread Brochettes

**1 pound sweetbreads**
**2 tablespoons salad oil**
**2 tablespoons lemon juice**
**1 teaspoon salt**
**½ cup fine bread crumbs**
**4 slices bacon**
**8 pineapple chunks**

Place sweetbreads in boiling salted water. Simmer 25 minutes. Drain and cool. Remove thin membrane covering and divide into pieces about 1½ inches in diameter. Combine oil and lemon juice. Dip sweetbreads into this mixture then into bread crumbs to which salt has been added. Cut bacon into 2-inch pieces. Place on skewers, alternating the bacon between the pineapple and sweetbreads. Broil over hot coals about 10 minutes, turning to brown evenly. Makes 4 servings.

Pan American Coffee Bureau

# Rumaki

Cut bacon silces in 1½-inch pieces. Cut chiken livers in fourths. Drain canned, broiled, whole mushroom crowns. Drain canned water chestnuts. On short metal skewers alternate bacon, chicken liver pieces, mushrooms and water chestnuts. Grill over hot coals until chicken livers are done, turning often and basting with the following mixture. Combine ¼ cup butter or margarine, ½ cup strong coffee, 2 drops Angostura bitters and 2 tablespoons brown sugar. Heat until mixture is combined and use to brush Rumaki.

# California Barbecued Spareribs

**4 to 5 pounds spareribs in two pieces**
**Salt**
**Freshly ground pepper**
**California barbec ue sauce recipe (below)**

Salt & pepper spareribs and brown on grill over moderate fire, turning them once or twice. Prepare pan from double thickness of heavy aluminum foil to fit spareribs, by turning up edges of the foil 1½ inches all around. Mitre corners so it will be secure. As soon as spareribs have browned, transfer them to the foil pan and spoon over about 1 cupful of California barbecue sauce. Place the pan on the center of the grill and continue cooking for about 1½ hours longer. Baste with the sauce occasionally. To serve, transfer foil pan with the spareribs to platter. Ribs separate easily when cut with sharp knife. Makes 6 to 8 servings.

### California Barbecue Sauce

**½ cup honey**
**⅔ cup soy sauce**
**⅔ cup catsup**
**1 teaspoon dry mustard**
**1 teaspoon paprika**
**1 cup wine vinegar**
**½ teaspoon Tabasco sauce**
**1 clove garlic, finely mashed**
**1 teaspoon salt**
**1 cup fresh or reconstituted frozen orange juice**

Combine all the ingredients thoroughly

Reynolds Wrap

# Zesty Lamb Riblets

**3 pounds lamb riblets**
**1 teaspoon salt**
**¼ cup salad oil**
**¼ cup vinegar**
**½ cup chili sauce**
**1 tablespoon sugar**
**1 tablespoon Worcestershire sauce**
**1 teaspoon chili powder**
**½ teaspoon garlic salt**

Have lamb riblets cut into 2-rib portions. Combine remaining ingredients and pour over lamb pieces in a bowl. Keep in refrigerator 2 to 4 hours, turning occasionally. Remove ribs from sauce and grill over hot coals 30 to 40 minutes. Daub with remaining sauce and turn frequently during cooking period. Makes 4 to 6 servings.

# Lamb Steak with Tarragon

Use lamb steaks cut from either the leg or the shoulder. Rub with garlic and salt. Cover steak with 1 cup of white wine and 1½ teaspoons dry tarragon and let stand about 2 hours, turning frequently. Drain well. Melt 6 tablespoons of butter in a skillet; add the wine and tarragon and heat and serve. Grill steak over medium hot coals, brushing from time to time with the wine-tarragon mixture. A 1-inch thick steak will take 4 to 6 minutes for each side to cook medium-rare.

# Pork Steaks

**4 pork shoulder steaks**
**2 tablespoons fat**
**1 onion, sliced**
**2 tablespoons lemon juice**
**½ teaspoon dry mustard**
**1 teaspoon Worcestershire sauce**
**3 whole cloves**
**1 teaspoon salt**
**¾ cup hot water**
**Paprika**

Brown chops in hot fat in a heavy skillet. Pour off drippings. Cover with sliced onion. Combine lemon juice, mustard, sauce, cloves, salt and water. Pour over chops. Sprinkle with paprika. Cover tightly. Simmer about 1 hour. Makes 4 servings.

# Spicy Barbecued Ribs

**6 pounds spareribs**
**3 teaspoons salt**
**½ teaspoon pepper**
**2 onions, quartered**
**3 cans (8-ounces) tomato sauce**
**⅓ cup dark brown sugar**
**3 tablespoons chopped onion**
**Juice of 2 lemons**
**1 teaspoon prepared mustard**
**⅓ cup oil**
**2 tablespoons Angostura aromatic bitters**

Cut spareribs into generous serving pieces and salt and pepper them. Place with onion in large kettle, add water to cover, bring to boiling, reduce heat, simmer until just tender, about 1 hour. Drain. Meanwhile, combine rest of ingredients and simmer for 15 minutes. Pour over meat in a shallow pan and let stand in refrigerator for at least two hours. When ready to cook, drain, marinade and reserve. Brush spareribs with the sauce and grill slowly over hot coals, basting several times during roasting. Or place brushed ribs in uncovered baking pan and roast in hot oven (400° F.) for 45 minutes, or until browned and glazed, basting frequently with sauce. Makes 6 servings.

# Charcoal Grilled Chuck Steak

½ cup chopped onion
½ cup lemon juice
¼ cup salad oil
½ teaspoon salt
½ teaspoon celery salt
½ teaspoon pepper
½ teaspoon thyme
½ teaspoon oregano
½ teaspoon rosemary
1 clove garlic, minced
2 to 2½ pound chuck steak, ½ to ¾-inch thick

Combine all ingredients except steak. Pour over steak in a shallow pan. Let stand at room temperature about 4 hours, turning steak several times. Remove from liquid and place on grill over hot coals. Cook steak to desired doneness, turning once. Baste with remaining mixture during cooking time. Makes 4 servings.

# Shish Kabob

2 pounds lamb, neck or shank
½ cup olive oil
1 cup red wine
3 tablespoons wine vinegar
1 teaspoon salt
1 bay leaf, crushed
Parsley, chopped
2 cloves garlic, crushed
Dash of thyme
Dash of oregano
2 tomatoes, quartered
4 small onions
4 mushrooms

Cut meat into 2-inch pieces. Make a marinade of oil, wine, vinegar and seasonings. Soak lamb in marinade for several hours or overnight. Arrange lamb on skewers alternately with vegetables. Broil over hot coals, turning frequently until meat is done. Makes 4 servings.

# Minced Beef Cubes with Noodles

4 tablespoons butter or margarine
1 clove garlic, minced
3 tablespoons flour
3 pounds beef chunk, cut in 1-inch cubes
½ pound mushrooms, sliced
1 cup sliced onions
2 bouillon cubes
2½ cups hot water
3 tomatoes, peeled and chopped
1 tablespoon salt
⅛ teaspoon pepper
⅛ teaspoon thyme
⅛ teaspoon oregano
1 pound noodles, cooked

Melt butter in a large skillet. Add garlic. Sprinkle flour over meat cubes. Add to fat and cook over moderate heat until browned. Add mushrooms and onion; continue cooking until the onion is soft. Dissolve bouillon cubes in water, add to meat with tomatoes and seasonings. Cover and cook over low heat until meat is tender, about 1 hour. Add noodles just before serving. Makes 8 servings.

# Sukiyaki

2 medium onions
½ pound fresh mushrooms
1 bunch scallions
6 stalks celery
½ pound fresh spinach
1 can (8-ounce) bamboo shoots
1 pound round steak
3 tablespoons olive oil
½ cup beef consommé
¼ cup soy sauce
1 tablespoon sugar

Cut onions and mushrooms into thin slices, scallions into lengthwise halves and celery into 1-inch lengths. Chop spinach coarsely. Cut meat cross-grain into paper-thin slices. Heat olive oil in skillet. Add meat and sauté until browned. Add vegetables, cover and sauté 5 minutes, stirring frequently. Pour in combined beef consommé, soy sauce and sugar. Mix well. Cook uncovered over low coals, 15 minutes, or until vegetables are tender. Makes 6 servings.

# Cube Steaks, Horse-Radish Sauce

¼ cup mayonnaise
⅛ cup heavy cream or evaporated milk
2 tablespoons horse-radish
¾ teaspoon salt
⅛ teaspoon pepper
4 cube steaks
4 toasted buns

In a small bowl, blend mayonnaise with cream until smooth. Stir in horse-radish, ¼ teaspoon salt and a dash of pepper. Broil cube steaks very quickly over hot coals and season with remaining salt and pepper. Serve on toasted buns with blended horse-radish sauce. Makes 4 servings.

# Barbecued Baby Spareribs

4 pounds young pork spareribs
1 onion, peeled
4 whole cloves
2 peppercorns
2 teaspoons salt
1 can (16-ounce) beer

Ask meatman to cut spareribs into finger-size pieces. Place spareribs in a large kettle. Add remaining ingredients. Bring to a boil. Simmer, covered, 30 minutes. Remove ribs from brew and dip each rib into Oriental Barbecue Sauce. Place ribs on grill over hot coals. Grill, turning once until crisp and brown, 5 to 10 minutes. Makes 8 to 10 appetizer servings.

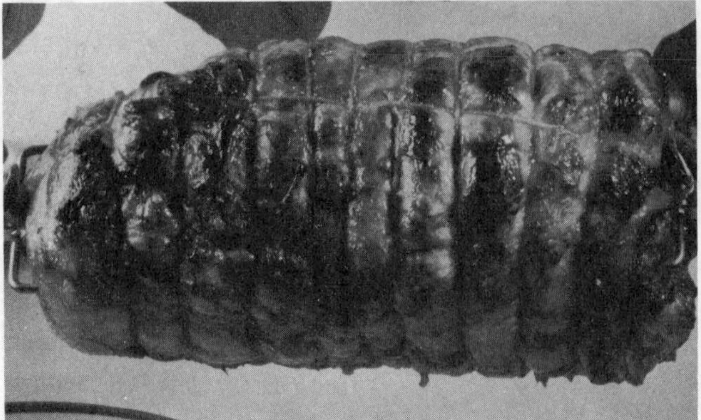

American Sheep Producers Council

# Barbecued Lamb Shoulder Roast

**1 5-pound boned shoulder of lamb, rolled and tied**
**1 teaspoon whole cloves**
**¼ cup salad oil**
**2 tablespoons dill pickle liquid**
**⅓ cup firmly-packed brown sugar**
**¼ cup finely chopped dill pickles**
**1 teaspoon salt**
**½ teaspoon allspice**

Stud lamb with cloves. Arrange lamb on spit. Cook in rotisserie or on outdoor grill about 2 to 2½ hours, or until meat thermometer registers 175-180° F. (depending upon desired degree of doneness). Combine remaining ingredients; stir and heat to boiling point. Baste lamb frequently with sauce while cooking. Makes 8 servings.

# Kalypso Kabobs

**1 pound diced lamb shoulder**
**1 can (1-pound 13-ounces) peach halves**
**4 medium bananas, cut in 1-inch slices**
**1 package (8-ounces) pitted dates**
**24 red marschino cherries (about ½ cup)**
**2 tablespoons butter or margarine, melted**
**1 tablespoon lemon juice**
**1 teaspoon cinnamon**
**¼ teaspoon cloves**

Arrange lamb on skewers. Drain peaches, reserving syrup. Coat banana slices with syrup. Arrange peach half, 3 dates, 3 banana slices and 3 cherries on each of 8 skewers. Combine melted butter or margarine, lemon juice, cinnamon and cloves for basting sauce. Broil lamb 3 to 4 inches from source of heat or cook on oudoor grill 5 to 7 minutes; turn. Add fruit skewers; brush with basting sauce; cook 5 to 7 minutes longer turning fruit skewers one; and brush with sauce frequently. Makes 4 servings.

Underwood Deviled Ham

# Deviled Ham Dogs

**1 can (4½-ounces) deviled ham**
**½ cup grated Cheddar cheese**
**¼ cup chopped, stuffed olives**
**2 tablespoons chopped onion**
**2 tablespoons mayonnaise**
**6 frankfurter or hamburg rolls**

Combine deviled ham, cheese, olives, onions and mayonnaise. Split rolls and fill with ham mixture; then wrap each roll securely in foil and heat over an open grille. Makes 6 rolls.

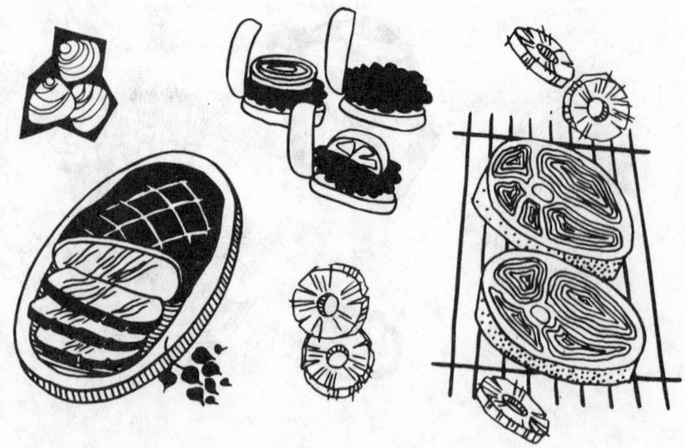

# Cantonese Kabobs

½ cup soy sauce
½ cup maraschino cherry juice
½ cup dry Sherry wine or ¼ cup lemon juice
¼ cup preserved ginger root syrup or ¼ cup honey plus ½ teaspoon powdered ginger
2 cloves garlic, crushed
¼ cup salad oil
3½ pounds lamb riblets
1 cup whole red maraschino cherries (about 40 cherries)
¾ cup preserved kumquats
1 can (1 pound) lychee nuts, drained or 1 can (13½-ounces) pineapple chunks, drained
¼ to ½ cup preserved ginger root, optional
1 can (11-ounces) mandarin orange segments, drained, or 2 oranges cut in wedges

Combine soy sauce, cherry juice, sherry, ginger root syrup, garlic and oil. Pour over lamb riblets and marinate 3 to 4 hours. Drain riblets and place on skewers. Broil 8 to 9 inches from source of heat, or cook on outdoor grill, 15 minutes on each side. Baste with marinade, if desired. Meanwhile, alternate cherries, kumquats, lychee nuts, ginger root and mandarin oranges on skewers. Cook with lamb last 5 minutes turning once. Makes 6 servings.

# Prem-Egglets

1 can (12-ounces) ham loaf
4 eggs
1 tablespoon butter

Cut the loaf into four ½ inch thick slices. Cut a square hole in the middle of each slice. Melt the butter in a skillet. Brown the small pieces of loaf, from the center of slices, on both sides. Push them to one side in the skillet. Brown each large slice of loaf on one side. Turn. Break one egg into the hole in each slice. Cover and cook until egg is cooked to desired doneness. Serve immediately with the small pieces. Makes 4 servings.

Swift & Co.

# Barbecued Rib Chops

**1 package (⅝-ounce) Italian salad dressing mix**
**1 can (6-ounces) tomato paste**
**8 lamb rib chops, ¾-inch thick**

Combine salad dressing mix and tomato paste; spread in thin layer over top side of chops. Broil 3 to 4 inches from source of heat, or cook on outdoor grill, 5-7 minutes. Turn, brush second side with sauce, cook 5 minutes longer, or until desired degree of doneness. Makes 8 servings.

# Liver and Bacon Brochettes

Cut calf, veal or lamb liver in 1-inch cubes. Fold strips of bacon in quarters. On a metal skewer start with chunks of tomato, alternate cubes of liver and the folded bacon and end with a tomato chunk. Brush with melted fat. Place on rack, about 5 inches from the hot coals. Cook, turning occasionally, until liver is browned and bacon crisp, about 15 minutes. Season with salt and pepper before serving.

# Ham Piquant

**¼ cup peanut butter**
**¼ cup orange marmalade**
**2 tablespoons soy sauce**
**1½ pounds center cut ham sliced**

Mix peanut butter, orange marmalade and soy sauce. Spread both sides of ham slice with peanut butter mixture. Grill over charcoal about 10 minutes. Turn to brown both sides. Makes 4 servings.

Peanut Growers of Alabama and Georgia

American Institute of Baking

# Chuck Wagon Steak Sandwich

**½ cup soy sauce**
**¼ cup water**
**2 tablespoons instant onion flakes**
**2 cloves garlic, crushed**
**2 tablespoons sugar**
**6 medium-sized cube steaks**
**½ cup butter or margarine**
**⅓ cup flour**
**1 teaspoon salt**
**¼ teaspoon pepper**
**2 teaspoons ground ginger**
**3 cups milk**
**½ pound sliced fresh mushrooms**
**1 loaf (1 pound) Vienna bread**
**1 tablespoon corn oil**
**2 medium-sized tomatoes, each cut into 6 slices**

Combine soy sauce, water, onion flakes, crushed garlic and sugar. Marinate cube steaks in soy mixture for at least one hour. To make sauce: melt ⅓ cup butter in a 1 quart saucepan. Combine flour, salt, pepper, and ginger; stir into butter. Gradually add milk, stirring constantly. Allow to cool two minutes after thickening. Saute sliced mushrooms in remaining butter and add them to sauce. Keep sauce hot. Cut Vienna bread into 12 slices. Butter slices, if desired, and toast in a hot oven (400° F.) for about fifteen minutes or wrap in foil and heat over grill. Cook marinated steaks on oiled griddle or grill over hot coals. To serve: Place one slice of toasted bread on plate. Top with steak, 2 tomato slices, another bread slice and about ½ cup hot ginger-mushroom sauce.

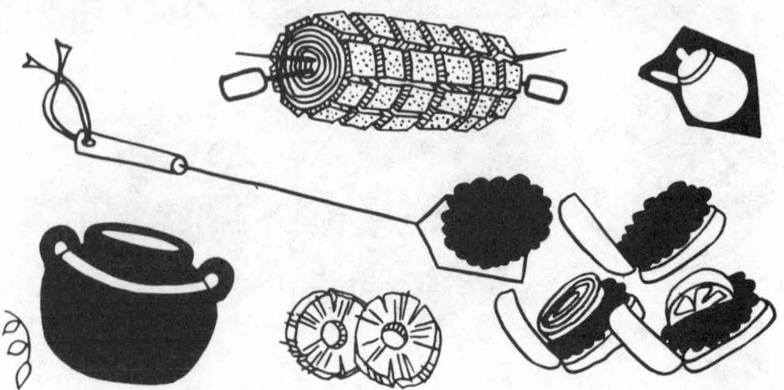

# Western Hash

2 tablespoons butter or margarine
¼ cup finely chopped onion
¼ cup chopped green pepper
1 pound ground beef
1 teaspoon salt, divided
1 teaspoon chili powder
¼ cup chopped ripe olives, optional
¼ cup molasses
¼ cup prepared mustard
2 tablespoons Worcestershire sauce
1 can (1 pound) tomatoes
1 cup raw rice

Melt butter in large skillet; add onion and green pepper and cook until onion is tender, but not brown. Add ground beef, ½ teaspoon of the salt and chili powder. Brown beef, breaking up into pieces with a fork. While beef is browning, combine molasses and prepared mustard. Stir in the Worcestershire sauce. Add to beef mixture with tomatoes and remaining ½ teaspoon salt. Gradually add rice. Cover; reduce heat and simmer 25 to 30 minutes, or until the rice is tender. Makes 6 servings.

American Molasses

# Marinated Shish Kabob

1½ teaspoons mixed pickling spices
½ teaspoon poultry seasoning
¼ teaspoon salt
1 cup beef bouillon
1½ teaspoons grated lemon rind
1½ teaspoons lemon juice
1 slice onion
1½ pounds lean leg of lamb
1 large onion, sliced
1 large green pepper, sliced
1 fresh tomato, sliced

Combine pickling spices, poultry seasoning, salt, beef bouillon, lemon rind, lemon juice and onion slice. Heat but do not boil. Cut lamb in 2-inch cubes. Pour marinade over lamb in a small bowl. Cool. Place in refrigerator for 24 hours turning several times. When ready to cook, alternate lamb pieces on skewers with slices of onion, green pepper and tomato. Cook over hot coals 25 to 30 minutes, turning to cook uniformly. Serve hot on frankfurter rolls if desired. Makes 4 servings.

Peanut Growers of Alabama and Georgia

# Spicy Pork Kabob

2 pounds lean, boneless pork
¼ cup smooth peanut butter
1½ teaspoons ground coriander
1½ teaspoons salt
½ teaspoon red pepper
1 teaspoon ground cumin
½ teaspoon freshly ground black pepper
4 medium sized onions, minced
1 clove garlic, minced
1½ tablespoons lemon juice
3 tablespoons soy sauce
1 tablespoon brown sugar

Cut pork into 1½-inch cubes. Mix peanut butter with remaining ingredients in a medium sized bowl. Add pork cubes. Stir until cubes are coated with ingredients on all sides. Cover and let stand in refrigerator for several hours.

When ready to cook put cubes on skewers. Broil in broiler or over charcoal coals 20-25 minutes, turning to brown both sides. Makes 6 servings.

# Wine Barbecued Spareribs

3 pounds spareribs, cut into 4-rib portions
1 cup white table wine
1½ teaspoons lemon juice
2 teaspoons sugar
1½ teaspoons salt
6 drops Angostura bitters
¼ cup chili sauce

Simmer spareribs in boiling salted water until almost tender, about 1 hour. Drain thoroughly. Cover with wine and let stand about 4 hours. Drain thoroughly and reserve wine. Combine wine with remaining ingredients and mix well. Place spareribs on barbecue rack. Baste with wine sauce. Broil spareribs, turning frequently and basting frequently, for about 25 minutes, or until meat is brown and tender. Serve at once. Makes 4 to 6 servings.

# Rotisserie Roast Beef

**1 4- to 5-pound rolled sirloin roast, 4 inches in diameter**
**2 cloves garlic**
**Salt**
**Pepper**

With the point of a sharp knife make several deep stabs in fat of rolled sirloin roast. Cut garlic cloves in thin slices and place one slice in each gash. Place roast on skewer spit and fasten in prongs on each end. Be sure that the skewer is centered in the roast and that the roast does not touch the rotisserie on either end. Place in rotisserie. Remove small drip tray and substitute a pan that is at least as wide as the roast beef and about 2 inches deep. Cook roast beef according to directions of rotisserie manufacturer. It will take about 1 to 1¼ hours for a piece of rare roast beef, although we suggest that you insert a meat thermometer in roast to judge the cooking time accurately. Remove the large drip tray ½ hour before the roast is finished cooking. Replace with regular drip pan. Make up a batter for Yorkshire pudding and pour into hot pan with the drippings from the roast beef. Cook until almost done in a hot oven (425° F.). Remove from oven when puffy and set, slide under roast beef in rotisserie and let the top brown during the last 10 minutes of cooking period.

# Chuck Steak Sandwiches

**½ cup chopped onion**
**½ cup lemon juice**
**¼ cup salad oil**
**½ teaspoon salt**
**½ teaspoon celery salt**
**½ teaspoon pepper**
**½ teaspoon thyme**
**½ teaspoon oregano**
**½ teaspoon rosemary**
**2 cloves garlic, minced**
**2 to 2½ pounds chuck steak, cut ½ inch thick**

Combine all ingredients except steak. Place steak in a shallow pan. Cover with mixture and let stand several hours, turning several times. Place on grill over hot coals and cook to desired degree of doneness. Baste with sauce during cooking time. Slice in very thin slices and place between cut halves of French bread. Makes about 6 servings.

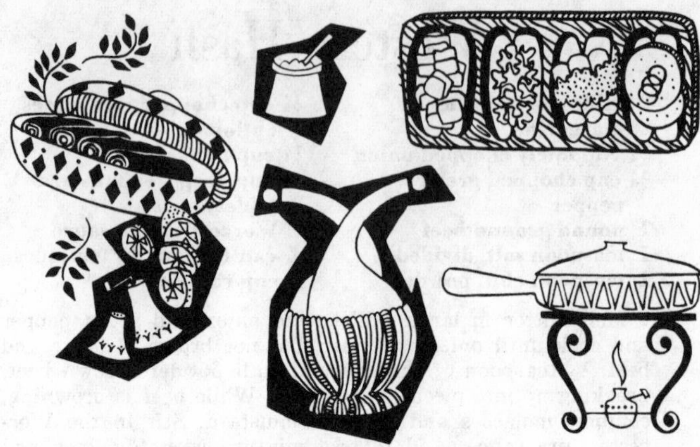

# Italian Steak

**1½ pounds round steak, cut ¾-inch thick**
**2 tablespoons fat**
**1 4-ounce can mushrooms, drained**
**½ cup sliced onion**
**2 tablespoons chopped green pepper**
**⅓ cup chili sauce**
**¼ cup water**
**1 teaspoon salt**
**⅛ teaspoon pepper**
**⅛ teaspoon garlic salt**
**½ teaspoon Worcestershire sauce**
**¼ cup sliced olives**

Brown steak on both sides in a heavy skillet in the fat. Remove steak. Add mushrooms, onions and green pepper to fat and cook 5 minutes. Blend in remaining ingredients. Add steak and cover tightly. Simmer about 1 hour, or until steak is tender. Makes 6 servings.

# Broiled Steak

Have a large enough fire to start with to have a good bed of coals, but don't start cooking until the flames die down and there is only a bed of glowing coals. Usually the grill is from 3 to 6 inches from the coals, depending on the thickness of the steaks and the degree of doneness—the thicker the steaks or the more well done you want them, the farther they should be placed from the coals. The steaks should be far enough from the coals so that flames caused by dripping fat will not touch the meat.

Choose top-quality steaks at least 1 inch thick. Tender steaks, porterhouse, T-bone, sirloin and club are the best choices for broiling. Trim off excess fat, leaving only a thin edge of fat. Score the fat to prevent curling during cooking. Broil one side until well browned. Turn with tongs, never a fork because piercing the meat releases the juices, and season. Broil second side to the desired degree of doneness or until well browned. Season and serve.

It is not possible to give an exact time for broiling steaks—variations in heat from coals, thickness of steak, distance from coals and many factors must be taken into consideration. Therefore it will be necessary to experiment a few times with your particular equipment to have steaks done to your preference. Roughly, for a 1-inch steak it takes about 20 minutes for medium rare, and about 40 minutes to cook a 2-inch steak medium rare.

To barbecue steaks, sear them quickly on both sides. Then turn frequently, and baste each time with barbecue sauce until cooked to the desired doneness.

You will find when you serve steaks, it is best to keep the rest of your meal fairly simple. Serve warmed potato chips or potato salad. Choose vegetables that can be munched in the hand. Add toasted rolls, French bread or garlic bread, mixed green salad and a choice of desserts. It is wise to provide plenty of good hot coffee for the finishing touch.

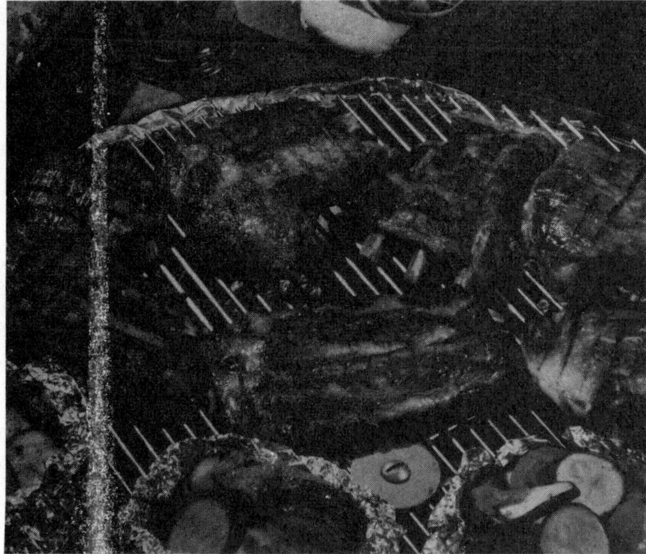

## Sweet-Sour Spareribs

3 to 4 pounds spareribs
2 tablespoons flour
2 cups meat stock
4 tablespoons vinegar
2 tablespoons brown sugar
1 bay leaf
⅛ teaspoon thyme
Salt and pepper to taste

Cut spareribs into serving pieces. Brown slowly in a heavy skillet. Remove spareribs and pour off all but 2 tablespoons of the drippings. Stir flour into drippings, add meat stock and cook until thickened. Add spareribs and remaining ingredients. Cover tightly and simmer 45 minutes. Makes 4 to 6 servings.

## Campfire Beef Stew

1 medium onion, chopped
2 tablespoons fat
1 tablespoon flour
1 cup Burgundy wine
2 cans (1 pound) beef stew
1 cup cooked peas
½ teaspoon Worcestershire sauce

Cook onion in fat over glowing coals until lightly browned. Blend in flour. Add wine and cook, stirring, until mixture boils and thickens. Add beef stew, peas and Worcestershire sauce. Heat thoroughly before serving. Makes 4 servings.

## Barbecue Pork Sandwiches

1 fresh pork butt (4 to 5 pounds)
Barbecue sauce
Butter
12 soft buns

Have butt boned and tied; balance on spit of outdoor rotisserie grill following manufacturer's directions. Cook about 4 inches above glowing coals for 3 to 4 hours or until temperature reaches 185° if meat thermometer is used. Baste with barbecue sauce occasionally during cooking. Cut into medium thin slices and serve on buttered, toasted buns. Add additional hot barbecue sauce if desired. Makes 12 to 15 servings.

### Barbecue Sauce

2 tablespoons salad oil
1 medium onion, chopped
2 teaspoons salt
½ teaspoon monosodium glutamate
½ teaspoon pepper
1 cup tomato juice
1 teaspoon vinegar
1½ teaspoons flour
2 tablespoons catsup
1 tablespoon sugar
1 tablespoon Worcestershire
½ teaspoon dry mustard dissolved in 1 tablespoon warm water

In a large saucepan, saute chopped onions in salad oil. When onions are tender, add remaining ingredients and mix well. Heat thoroughly and serve over grilled halibut steaks. Makes 1½ cups of sauce, or enough for four servings.

Campbell Soup Company

## Shish Kabob in Foil

2 pounds round steak, cut in 1½-inch cubes
½ pound cocktail frankfurters
½ pound mushrooms
3 tomatoes, sliced
¼ teaspoon Tabasco
½ cup ketchup
1 tablespoon vinegar
2 tablespoons brown sugar
1 teaspoon dry mustard
1 teaspoon salt
1 medium onion, finely chopped
2 tablespoons butter or margarine

Place alternate pieces of steak, frankfurters, mushrooms and tomatoes on 6 skewers. Place the filled skewers on a large square of foil. Combine remaining ingredients in a saucepan, bring to a boil and simmer 5 minutes. Brush kabob with barbecue sauce. Wrap foil around the meat, double-folding edges together and pinching ends tight to the skewers. Place on a grate over a hot fire and cook, turning frequently. It will take 15 to 30 minutes, depending on the intensity of the heat. Serve with remaining sauce. Makes 6 servings.

## Steak Sandwiches

Count on at least ½ pound of steak per person. Let the steaks stand at room temperature for at least ½ hour. Rub both sides with salt and pepper; spread with a thin layer of mustard. Grill over hot coals until desired doneness. Remove from heat and top with butter. Butter a split loaf of French bread. Place steaks on half the buttered bread. Top other half with onion and tomato slices. Put together to form a sandwich. Slice the French bread diagonally to make individual servings.

## The Whole Meal

String meat cubes, potatoes, mushrooms, tomatoes, onions or whatever kind of vegetables you choose on separate skewers. Then start grilling the foods that need the longest cooking first, and adding the others as you go along. Presto, everything comes out done at the same time, without some foods being overdone and some being underdone. Proceed as you do with Kabobs by brushing with melted butter or barbecue sauce as the foods are cooking.

## Tenderloin on a Spit

Purchase a whole tenderloin from your butcher and leave it in one piece. Remove excess fat from tenderloin. Lower grade tenderloin is leaner and needs little trimming. Fold slender tips back and hold in place. Pierce meat lengthwise with rod of the spit. Brush meat with melted butter or margarine, spicy French dressing or barbecue sauce. Place meat 5 to 6 inches from glowing coals. Turn spit so that meat browns uniformly. Brush occasionally with sauce during cooking time. This meat should be deeply browned on the outside and rare inside. About 1 hour is needed to cook to this degree, but if in doubt it is wise to use a meat thermometer. Cut meat in slices crosswise to serve.

## Barbecued Quickie-Q for Two

**1 package frozen ready-quick sandwich steaks**
**½ cup margarine or butter**
**1 teaspoon dry mustard**
**1 teaspoon salt**
**1 teaspoon paprika**
**½ teaspoon garlic salt**
**½ tablespoon sugar**
**1 tablespoon lemon juice**
**1 tablespoon vinegar**
**1 tablespoon Worcestershire sauce**
**2 tomatoes, sliced**
**1 large sweet onion, sliced**
**Long loaf rye bread**

Remove sandwich steaks from cardboard dividers. Allow to thaw just enough to bend. Combine margarine, mustard, salt, paprika, garlic salt, sugar, lemon juice, vinegar and Worcestershire sauce and blend until smooth. Spread each steak generously with this mixture. Fold steaks twice, into quarters, with spread inside and thread three steaks onto each of two long metal skewers, alternately with chunks of the dill pickle. Do not crowd. Broil over hot coals 10 to 15 minutes. Split loaf of rye bread in two, lengthwise and crosswise. Spread bottom halves with remaining butter-mustard mixture. Cover with sliced tomatoes and sliced onion. Push one skewer of barbecued beef and pickle onto the sliced onion on each bottom half. Cover with top portion of rye bread. Makes 2 servings.

## Pot Roast of Beef

**3 pounds chuck or round of beef**
**1 tablespoon fat**
**1 cup water**
**1 cup red wine**
**1½ teaspoons salt**
**4 peppercorns**
**6 medium potatoes**
**6 medium carrots**
**6 to 8 small onions**
**½ pound whole mushrooms, cleaned**

Brown beef on all sides in hot fat in a heavy Dutch oven. Add water, wine, salt and peppercorns. Cover tightly and move to slow coals and simmer about 2 hours. Add remaining ingredients and simmer about 45 minutes, or until vegetables are tender. Makes 6 servings.

# Smoke Barbecued Leg of Lamb with Mint Barbecue Sauce

**6 to 9 pound leg of lamb**
**1 clove garlic, minced**
**1 onion, minced**
**2 tablespoons olive oil**
**Grated rind of 2 lemons**
**½ cup lemon juice**
**3-inch sprig of fresh mint OR 2 tablespoons mint jelly**
**1 teaspoon prepared "herbs for salad" or 3 teaspoons combined minced fresh herbs (thyme, tarragon, rosemary, marjoram)**
**3 tablespoons brown sugar (reduce to 2 tablespoons if mint jelly is used)**
**2 teaspoons salt**
**1 teaspoon freshly ground black pepper**

Prepare lamb for roasting as usual. Form a pan of double-thick heavy duty aluminum wrap to fit lamb, turning up edges of foil 1 inch all around and mitering corners so it is firm. Prepare a barbecue sauce from the remaining ingredients as follows: Saute the garlic and onion 2 minutes in the olive oil. Add the remaining ingredients and simmer for 3 minutes. Brush the lamb on all sides with this sauce and let stand at room temperature for an hour or longer, brushing twice more. Have fire ready in smoke cooker (it takes about 25 minutes to kindle charcoal briquets.) Transfer lamb with pan to rack over the fire, close the hood, adjust vents half open and cook for 2½ to 3 hours. A meat thermometer inserted in the thickest part of the roast not touching the bone, should register (175°F.) when the meat is done. Baste several times during the roasting. Throw damp hickory chips or green twigs of wild cherry, apple or other savory wood on the fire about 1 hour before roasting is finished. When done, transfer meat to a warm carving board. Add any left-over barbecue sauce to drippings in the pan with boiling water, if necessary. Stir and cook to dissolve browned drippings and serve with the lamb.

# Breakfast Eggs and Sausages in Individual Pans

**Brown-and-serve sausages**
**Butter or margarine**
**Eggs**
**Salt and pepper**

Make double thick squares of aluminum foil 5 x 7 inches. Turn up edges ¾ inch all around and mitre corners to hold firm. Brown sausages quickly right on the grill over direct heat. Place little pans on grill and add a dab of butter or margarine to each. Place the sausages in pans and break in the eggs. Let eggs cook until firm. Sprinkle with seasonings. If the day is breezy, cover tops of pans with squares of foil so eggs will cook on top. Transfer pans with broad spatula to paper plates for serving.

# Hot Garlic Bread

Crush a clove of garlic with a very little salt in a small bowl, using the back of a spoon. Add softened butter and chopped parsley. Spread between slices of French or any "specialty" bread. Wrap in foil, leaving a small opening at top. Heat about 15 minutes on the grill.

# Breakfast Apples

Core large baking apples and peel skin from upper part. Place on squares of aluminum foil. Fill centers with orange marmalade, top with chopped walnuts and sprinkle with lemon juice to keep cut surface from discoloring. Wrap up in foil, twisting at top to close. Store in refrigerator until ready to cook. Place on the grill over medium heat and cook about 45 minutes. Test for doneness by piercing with fork through foil. To serve, turn back the foil attractively to form a foil dish.

# Poppy Seed Bread

Buy a homestyle loaf unsliced bread and cut in thick slices down to, but not through, the bottom crust. Stand on a large sheet of aluminum foil. Mix softened butter with poppy seeds, or sugar and cinnamon, if preferred. Bring the foil up over the bread and wrap, but leave opening at top for steam to escape. Heat for about 20 minutes on the grill over medium heat. Tip over on both sides for part of time for even heating. Serve from foil.

Campbell Soup Company

## Marinated Barbecued Lamb Chops

6 shoulder lamb chops, about ½-inch thick
½ cup salad oil
¼ cup vinegar
½ teaspoon salt
½ teaspoon oregano
Dash pepper
Dash garlic powder

Arrange chops in a shallow dish. Combine remaining ingredients in a jar with cover, shake well and pour over chops. After 15 minutes, turn chops and marinate another 15 minutes. Cook chops over hot glowing coals, about 20 minutes; brushing with marinade as chops are turned. Make 6 servings.

## London Broil

You'll need 2 Prime- or Choice-grade flank steaks for 6, unless they are very large ones. Remove the thin membrane, but do not score. Broil over a hot charcoal fire for 3 minutes on each side, a minute longer if you don't like very rare meat. (London Broil should always be rare, however, as it is tough otherwise.) Using a razor-sharp knife, slice very thin slices at a diagonal, across the grain. Each slice should be at least 2½ inches wide.

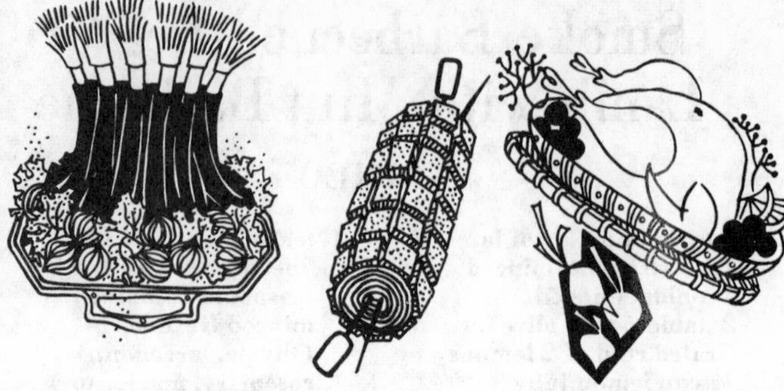

## Skewered Beef

½ cup salad oil
¼ cup tarragon vinegar
3 tablespoons lemon juice
2 tablespoons mustard
2 tablespoons soy sauce
½ teaspoon salt
1 teaspoon garlic salt
¼ teaspoon pepper
1 bay leaf
1 medium onion, sliced
2 pounds top round or sirloin steak
2 green peppers
⅓ pound whole mushrooms
4 tomatoes
1 jar (1-pound) whole onions

Combine salad oil, vinegar, lemon juice, mustard, soya sauce, salt, garlic salt, pepper, bay leaf and sliced onions. Let stand for a while for flavors to blend. Cut steak into 1-inch cubes, cover with sauce and let stand about 4 hours. Cut green peppers into cubes. Prepare mushrooms, drain onions and cut tomatoes into slices. Spear the meat on long skewers alternating with green pepper pieces, mushrooms and onions. Cook over hot coals, turning frequently and basting with marinade. Sprinkle with salt and pepper and serve with tomato slices, either cold or broiled. Makes about 4 servings.

## Spicy Fruit Kabobs

1½ pounds ground lamb
¼ cup water
Salt and pepper to taste
¼ teaspoon garlic powder
3 tablespoons vinegar
2 tablespoons brown sugar
¼ teaspoon ginger
¼ teaspoon cloves
⅓ cub salad oil
6 fresh or canned apricots pitted
2 pears, cored and cut in wedges

Combine lamb, 2 tablespoons water, salt and pepper to taste and garlic powder; mix well. Shape into 12 2-inch balls. Arrange lamb balls on skewers. Combine vinegar, sugar, ginger, cloves, oil and remaining 2 tablespoons water; stir well. Brush lamb with spice mixture. Broil lamb 3-4 inches from source of heat or cook on outdoor grill 5-7 minutes. Turn lamb. Arrange apricots and pears on skewers. Brush with spice mixture. Cook lamb and fruit 5-7 minutes, or until desired degree of doneness. Brush lamb and fruit frequently with spice mixture during cooking period. Makes 6 servings.

# Vegetables and Salads

## Baked Beans with Deviled Ham and Onions

**1 can plumped, chopped prunes (about 16)**
**6 plumped prune halves—for garnish**
**3 tablespoons chopped onion**
**1½ tablespoons butter or margarine**
**2 cans (1-pound) pork and beans in tomato sauce**
**1 can (2¼ ounce) deviled ham**
**¼ teaspoon dry mustard**
**½ cup tomato sauce**
**¼ cup brown sugar**
**¼ cup onion slices**

**Saute cut-up prunes and onions in butter or margarine in skillet over low heat until onions become transparent, about 5 minutes. Pour beans into medium-sized bowl. Add sauteed prunes and onions, deviled ham, mustard, tomato sauce and brown sugar. Stir well. Pour into 1½ quart buttered casserole. Place onion rings on top of beans. Arrange prune halves, cut side down, on top. Bake in hot oven (400°F.), 40 to 45 minutes, until hot and bubbly. Makes 5 to 6 servings.**

California Prune Advisory Board

Corn Products Company

## Old Fashioned Potato Salad

**6 cooked potatoes, cubed**
**¼ cup thinly sliced radishes**
**½ cup diced celery**
**¼ cup minced onion**
**4 hard-cooked eggs, diced**
**1 cup mayonnaise**

**Combine all ingredients and mix lightly. Chill well. Mound in a serving bowl on lettuce cups and garnish with hard-cooked eggs and tomato wedges. Makes 6 servings.**

## Baked Cheese-Stuffed Potatoes

**6 medium-sized potatoes (baking)**
**6 strips process cheese**

**Remove a lenghtwise piece from the center of each potato, using an apple corer to hollow out potatoes from each end. Insert a cheese strip into hollow section of each potato. Plug up ends with outer ½ inch chunk of potato removed with corer. Partially insert prongs of a fork into each potato. Wrap each potato tightly with heavy duty foil. Place on grill over hot coals, turn frequently during an hour of baking. Makes 6 servings.**

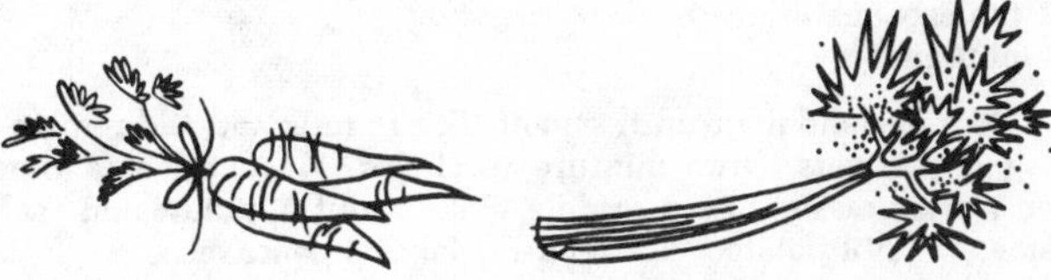

# Wagon Wheel Skillet

2 tablespoons butter or margarine
2 cloves garlic, crushed
2 teaspoons chopped chives
¼ teaspoon freshly ground black pepper
½ cup chicken stock
4 packages (10-ounces) frozen brussels sprouts
2 packages (10-ounces) frozen whole kernel corn
6 tomatoes, cut in wedges

Melt butter in a large skillet. Add garlic, chives and pepper; cook slowly about 5 minutes. Stir in chicken stock. Starting at outer edge of skillet, arrange rings of vegetables as follows; brussels sprouts, corn, tomatoes and again brussels sprouts. Cover and cook over low heat 25 minutes, or until brussels sprouts are tender.

# Potatoes Chantilly

4 medium potatoes
3 tablespoons butter or margarine
½ cup heavy cream
Salt and pepper
Chopped parsley
½ cup grated sharp cheese

Peel and cut potatoes into thin strips as for French fries. Place in center of a large piece of aluminum foil. Dot with butter, add cream, seasonings, parsley and cheese. Bring up foil over potatoes and seal all edges together to make a tight package. Place on grate over moderate fire and cook, turning two or three times for 30 to 40 minutes. Open package and allow people to help themselves. Makes 4 servings.

# Potato Pancakes O'Brien

1 egg, slightly beaten
3 tablespoons flour
¼ cup milk
2 tablespoons minced onion
2 tablespoons minced green pepper
2 tablespoons minced pimiento
¼ teaspoon monosodium glutamate
Salt and pepper to taste
2 cups, firmly packed, grated raw potatoes

Mix egg and flour until smooth. Stir in milk and add remaining ingredients. Drop mixture in circles, ¼ cupful at a time on a hot greased heavy griddle. Bake about 5 minutes on each side, or until potatoes are tender. Makes 8 pancakes.

# Buttered Vegetables in Foil

Use either one or two packages of frozen mixed vegetables, depending on the size of the party. Thaw just enough so that vegetables can be broken into chunks. Place vegetables on large squares of aluminum foil. Add plenty of butter and salt and pepper. Bring edges of foil together and seal with a double fold to form a neat package. Place the vegetables on top of the grill or right on the hot coals for about 10 minutes.

# Cabbage Salad Tokay

4 cups finely shredded cabbage
1 cup seeded Tokay grape halves
1 cup thick sour cream
3 tablespoons lemon juice
½ teaspoon salt
3 tablespoons sugar

Combine cabbage and grapes. Blend together remaining ingredients. Toss cabbage and grapes with sour cream mixture. Garnish with seeded grapes. Makes 6 servings.

# Coal-Grilled Vegetables

Potatoes: Wash potatoes, pierce skins with a fork and wrap each in a separate piece of aluminum foil, using only one layer. Bake on the grill or place in embers until potatoes are tender when tested with a pointed knife. Turn occasionally during cooking time to bake uniformly.

Carrots: Wash young baby garden carrots. Leave whole and unpeeled. Wrap in one piece of aluminum foil, 2 carrots to a package. Bake on the grill or in the embers 25 to 30 minutes or until tender when tested with a pointed knife, turning to cook uniformly. Serve hot with butter, salt and pepper.

Fresh Snap Beans: Wash and remove ends from snap beans. Place each serving on a square of aluminum foil. Sprinkle with salt, pepper and top with ½ pat of butter or margarine. Wrap tightly. Bake over barbecue grill 20 to 30 minutes or until tender, turning to cook uniformly.

Baked Onion Slices: Peel large Bermuda onions and slice ½ inch thick. Place each slice on a square of aluminum foil. Sprinkle with salt and pepper and top with ½ teaspoon of butter or margarine. Wrap securely. Bake on grill 20 minutes or until tender.

# Zucchini Parmesan

4 cups thinly sliced zucchini
1 small onion, sliced
1 tablespoon water
2 tablespoons butter or margarine
1 teaspoon salt
Dash of pepper
3 tablespoons grated Parmesan cheese

Put all ingredients except cheese in a heavy skillet. Cover and cook 1 minute. Uncover and continue to cook, turning with wide spatula until vegetables are barely tender, about 5 minutes. Sprinkle with cheese, toss lightly and serve. Makes 8 servings.

# Tossed Green Salad

Select a large bowl of wood, glass or pottery. Rub inside of bowl with cut clove of garlic. Fill with a variety of crisp, well-drained salad greens, broken into bite-sized pieces. Add some finely chopped chives, onion rings, carrot curls, sliced cucumbers, radishes and quartered tomatoes. Pour a small amount of French dressing over greens; toss lightly with a spoon and fork until all greens glisten. Taste and add more seasonings if necessary. Serve salad immediately.

# Brussels Sprouts en Brochette

**2 packages (10 ounces each) frozen brussels sprouts, thawed**
**1 can (1 pound) whole onions, drained**
**2 large tomatoes, cut in wedges**
**½ cup French dressing**

Arrange vegetables on 6 skewers, Brush kabobs well with French dressing. Broil or grill 3 to 5 inches from heat 5 minutes per side, basting frequently with dressing. Makes 6 servings.

Brussel Sprouts Marketing Program

# Grilled Corn

Strip husks down, remove the corn silks and fold husks back over the corn. Dip ears in water. Place on grill over hot coals and cook 20 minutes, or until corn is tender, turning often to cook evenly. Serve with melted butter flavored with onion salt or garlic salt. Allow 2 ears for each person.

# Braised Fresh Vegetables

Melt 3 tablespoons butter or margarine in a heavy skillet over hot coals. Add 2 cups each sliced fresh carrots, snap beans, broken into 1-inch pieces, sliced summer or zucchini squash, 1 cup sliced onion and ½ teaspoon salt. Cover and cook until just crisply-tender, 15 to 20 minutes, depending on heat of coals and distance from heat, stirring occasionally. Sprinkle with ground black pepper and serve piping hot. Makes 6 servings.

# Tomato-Corn-Onion Barbecue

Parboil small whole onions and fresh corn on the cob until almost done. Break ears of corn into halves or thirds. String onion, corn and small whole tomatoes on heavy skewers. Brush liberally with garlic butter. Place on grill over hot coals and continue cooking until onions are lightly browned. Turn and baste occasionally with additional garlic butter.

# Broiled Small Whole Onions

**Small unpeeled onions**
**Melted butter or margarine**
**Garlic or celery salt to taste**
**Black pepper**
**Salt**

Place onions on a grill over hot coals and cook until tender, about 30 minutes, turning frequently. When done, peel and dip in melted butter and sprinkle with garlic salt, black pepper and salt to taste.

## Green Pepper Cole Slaw

**4 cups shredded cabbage**
**1 cup chopped green pepper**
**½ cup grated carrots**
**1 teaspoon salt**
**⅛ teaspoon white pepper**
**2 tablespoons sugar**
**½ cup mayonnaise**
**1 tablespoon tarragon vinegar**
**1 teaspoon celery seed**
**Salad greens**
**Green pepper rings**

Combine cabbage, green pepper and carrot with seasonings. Mix together mayonnaise, vinegar and celery seed and add to cabbage mixture tossing lightly. Place in a bowl lined with salad greens and garnish with green pepper rings. Makes 6 servings.

## Potato Casserole

Cut potatoes in strips as for French fries. Arrange them in a buttered casserole in layers, sprinkling each layer with grated natural sharp cheddar cheese, salt, pepper and minced thyme, minced chives, a very little dill and parseley. (Prepared "herbs for salad" may be substituted.) Pour over half and half milk and cream to fill the casserole about ⅔ full. Top with a final layer of grated cheese. Cover casserole with aluminum foil and place on the grill 1 hour before the meat is finished. Remove the foil cover during the last 30 minutes of the cooking.

## Foil-Roasted Corn

Remove husks from corn and place each ear on a piece of aluminum foil. Brush with softened butter, salt and pepper. Wrap completely, twisting ends of foil. Place on grill 20 minutes before lamb is finished. Turn back foil; eat right from the foil.

## Corn Bundle

Use a sharp knife and cut kernels from ears not too close to the cob. Use the back of the knife and run it down the cob to remove milk. Place raw corn on a large square of heavy duty foil. Add slices of tomato, chopped onion and chopped green pepper. Dot with butter and season to taste. Fold foil over corn to make a tight package. Place on grate over medium hot coals and cook 25 minutes, turning once or twice. Serve from package.

## Zucchini Packet

Slice zucchini, cut peeled tomatoes in quarters and slice onions very thin. Combine sufficient for the number to be served on a large square of heavy duty foil. Season with salt, pepper and basil. Dot with butter. Bring foil over vegetables and seal to make a tight package. Place on grill over medium fire and cook about 30 minutes, turning once. Serve right from package.

## Hot Weather Salad

1 cucumber
1 pound boiled ham
1 pound American cheese
3 hard-cooked eggs
1 bunch scallions
Salad greens
¾ cup mayonnaise
¼ cup catsup

Score cucumber with a fork and slice in thin slices. Cut ham and cheese in finger strips. Slice eggs. Arrange ham, cheese, eggs, cucumber and scallions on crisp salad greens. Combine mayonnaise and catsup and serve on the side with the salad. Makes 6 servings.

## Carrots and Celery Basket

Scrape carrots and cut in strips. Cut celery in small pieces. Combine sufficient for all to be served on a large square of heavy duty foil. Add butter and seasonings. Sprinkle with a little chopped mint. Fold and seal package. Place on grill over medium fire and cook 35 to 40 minutes, turning once. Serve right from package.

## Baked Beans and Corn Casserole

2 1-pound cans baked beans with pork
1 No. 2 can whole kernel corn, drained
1½ cups grated American cheese
1 6-ounce can tomato paste
½ cup red wine
1 tablespoon minced onion
Salt and pepper to taste

Mix beans, drained corn, 1 cup of the cheese, tomato paste, wine, onion, salt and pepper. Turn into a heavy skillet or a Dutch oven; top with remaining cheese. Cover and bake in a slow oven about 1 hour; or place Dutch oven on grill, not directly over hottest part, and simmer gently while cooking meat. Makes 6 to 8 servings.

## Baked Butternut Squash

Select squash weighing from ½ to ¾ pound. Wash and split in half, lengthwise. Remove seeds. Stick a whole clove in each end of each half, and sprinkle with salt and pepper. Put 1½ teaspoons butter or margarine and 2 teaspoons brown sugar in one half of each squash. Cover with the other half. Wrap each whole squash in aluminum foil, folding and lapping edges over tightly. Bake over hot coals 2 hours, turning occasionally, or until soft to the touch.

# Go-Alongs

# *(for outdoor eating)*

## Creative Barbecue Canapés

*Marinated Crabmeat:* Combine 2 tablespoons mayonnaise, 1 tablespoon chili sauce and 1 teaspoon lemon juice. Blend well. Fold in 1 can (7¾-ounces) crabmeat, drained and flaked. Chill. Makes 1 cup.

*Barbecuer's Special:* Combine 1 pint dairy sour cream, ½ teaspoon salt, ⅛ teaspoon black pepper, 1 teaspoon lemon juice, 1 tablespoon finely chopped celery, 1½ tablespoons finely chopped chutney and 1 hard-cooked egg, finely chopped. Blend well and chill.

*Fruit Trio:* Peel and cut an avocado into ½-inch cubes. Sprinkle with lemon juice. Combine with sections from 1 grapefruit and 1 cup of canned pineapple chunks.

*Julienne Beets:* Drain 1 can (8-ounces) julienne beets and combine with ¼ cup dairy sour cream. Chill thoroughly.

*Dilled Cucumbers:* Blend together 1 tablespoon dill vinegar with 2 tablespoons olive oil. Beat until slightly thickened. Pour over 1 scored and sliced cucumber. Chill thoroughly.

National Biscuit Company

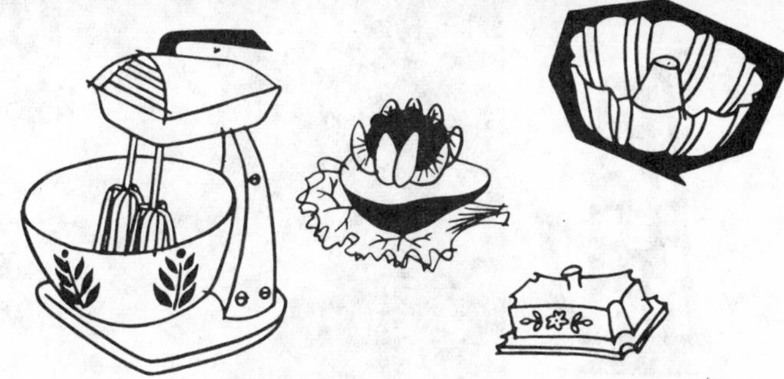

American Institute of Baking

# Grilled Bacon and Egg Sandwiches

8 slices enriched bread
1⅓ tablespoons soft butter or margarine
4 hard-cooked eggs, sliced
Salt and pepper to taste
4 slices bacon, cut in half crosswise

Spread each bread slice with ½ teaspoon butter. Arrange sliced eggs on half the bread slices. Sprinkle with salt and pepper. Top with remaining bread slices, butter side down. Place sandwiches in a long-handled, hinged wire broiler or toaster and top with 2 half slices of bacon, side by side. Brown both sides of sandwiches over hot coals, leaving the side with bacon until last, Serve hot. Makes 4 Grilled Bacon and Egg Sandwiches.

American Institute of Baking

# Chili and Cabbage Buns

1 can (15½ ounces) chili con carne
1 cup coarsely shredded or chopped cabbage
1 tablespoon lemon juice
½ teaspoon sugar
¼ teaspoon salt
6 sliced sandwich buns

Heat chili con carne and drain off any excess liquid. Combine cabbage, lemon juice, suger and salt. Place about 2½ tablespoons of chili in each bun and top with 2 tablespoons of cabbage mixture. Makes 6 Chili and Cabbage Buns.

# Brown 'n' serve Club Sandwiches

6 Brown 'n' Serve club or French rolls
2 tablespoons prepared mustard
3 tablespoons soft butter or margarine
3 slices boiled ham
12 thin lengthwise slices pickle
3 slices Swiss cheese
6 large or 12 small thin slices tomato

Slice each roll horizontally into 3 layers. Spread mustard on the bottom layers and butter on the other layers. Place ½ slice ham and 2 slices pickle on the mustard layer. Place ½ slice Swiss cheese and 1 or 2 slices tomato on the other layer. Top ham layers with cheese layers and cover with bun tops. Use toothpicks to hold sandwiches together, if necessary. Wrap each roll in heavy foil. Heat on outdoor grill over hot coals for 15 minutes, turning them over every 5 minutes. Makes 6 Brown 'n' Serve Club Sandwiches.

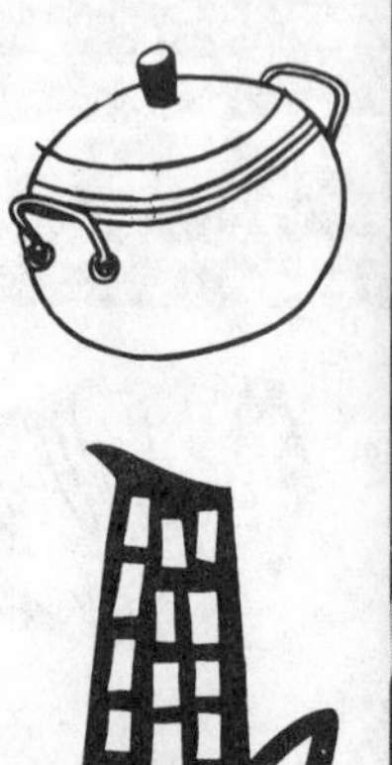

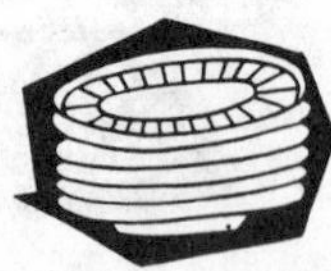

Sealtest Consumer Service

# Chocolate Waffles à la Mode

**3 tablespoons butter**
**1½ squares unsweetened chocolate**
**1¾ cups sifted flour**
**4 teaspoons baking powder**
**⅓ cup sugar**
**½ teaspoon salt**
**2 eggs, well beaten**
**1¼ cup chocolate milk**
**1 quart chocolate ice cream**
**Chopped nuts**

Melt butter and chocolate together over hot water. Sift flour, baking powder, sugar and salt into a mixing bowl. Add beaten eggs and chocolate milk; beat until smooth. Add melted butter and chocolate to batter and blend. Bake waffle batter in waffle iron. Serve waffles topped with ice cream and chopped nuts. Makes 8 servings.

# Outdoor Sundae

Cut ripe cantaloupes in halves and scoop out seeds. Top with your favorite ice cream or sherbet. Combine 1 cup maple syrup and ½ cup salted pecans. Warm thoroughly and serve over ice cream.

U. S. Brewers Association

# Camp-Out Chili with Corn Pancakes

**2 cans (1 pound) chili con carne**
**1 cup beer, divided**
**1 egg**
**1 cup corn muffin mix**

Combine chili con carne with ½ cup beer in a heavy pot. Simmer while making pancakes, adding additional beer if chili becomes too thick. Combine remaining beer and egg. Stir in muffin mix and stir until almost smooth. Bake on a hot, lightly greased griddle until golden. Place 2 or 3 pancakes on each plate and top with chili. Makes 5 to 6 servings.

# Avocado Chip-Dip

2 medium, ripe avocados, peeled and pitted
½ cup sour cream
2 tablespoons lemon juice
1 teaspoon grated onion
1 teaspoon salt
4 slices bacon, cooked and crumbled

Mash avocados well with a fork, or force through sieve. Add sour cream, lemon juice, onion and salt. Chill. Just before serving, stir in crumbled bacon, reserving a few bits for garnish. Serve with potato chips. Makes 1½ cups dip.

Campbell Soup Company

American Institute of Baking

# Mocha Ice Cream Soda

¼ cup instant coffee
2 tablespoons sugar
2 cups chilled milk
½ teaspoon almond extract
1 quart chocolate ice cream
3 bottles (6-ounces) sparkling water

Mix instant coffee and sugar together. Add a little milk to dissolve, then add remaining milk and almond extract. Place a small scoop of ice cream in each of 6 tall glasses. Divide milk mixture among the 6 glasses. Fill glasses almost to top with soda and stir gently to blend liquids. Top each glass with a large scoop of ice cream. Makes 6 servings.

National Dairy Council

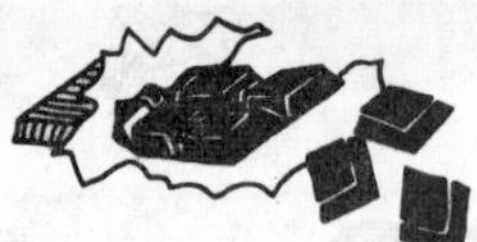

# Grilled Cheese and Peanut Butter Sandwiches

12 slices enriched bread
¾ cup peanut butter
6 slices American cheese
2 tablespoons soft butter or margarine

Spread the peanut butter on 6 slices of bread. Top with a cheese slice and another bread slice. Spread soft butter over outside of sandwiches, using ½ teaspoon for each side. Wrap tightly in heavy duty foil and place on grill over hot coals. Turn frequently until sandwiches are toasted, or about five minutes. Makes 6 sandwiches.

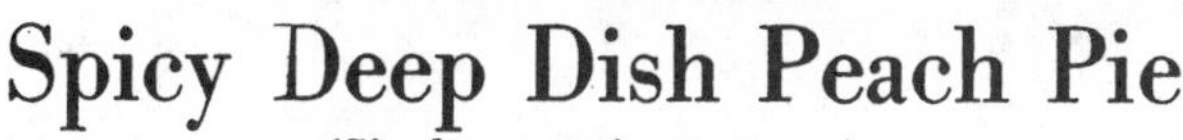

# Spicy Deep Dish Peach Pie

**(Single crust pie, top crust)**

**The Pastry:** Make up half the recipe for pie crust adding ¼ teaspoon each nutmeg, cinnamon and allspice to the flour.

**The Filling:**

**1 can (1 lb. 13 oz.) cling peach slices, or 4 cups fresh or frozen peach slices**
**½ cup sugar (¾ cup for fresh peaches)**
**¼ teaspoon nutmeg**
**2 tablespoons cornstarch**
**¼ teaspoon salt**
**1 teaspoon grated orange rind**
**1 tablespoon lemon juice**
**2 tablespoons butter or margarine**

Heat oven to very hot (425° F.). Grease an 8-inch round baking dish. Arrange peaches and syrup in the dish. Blend together sugar, nutmeg, cornstarch, salt and orange rind. Sprinkle over peaches. Sprinkle lemon juice over. Dot with bits of butter or margarine. Roll out the pastry ½ inch larger than the baking dish. Cut slits to let the steam escape and place over the peaches. Press the overhanging pastry firmly against the edge of the dish. Flute the edges. Bake 25 to 30 minutes.

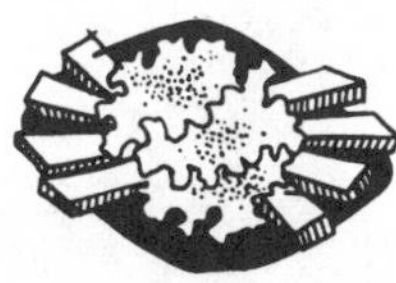

# Kraut Relish

**2 cups sauerkraut, drained and cut in short lengths**
**½ cup chopped green pepper**
**¼ cup canned pimientos, cut in strips**
**½ cup mayonnaise**
**1 tablespoon prepared horseradish**
**1 teaspoon Worcestershire sauce**
**½ teaspoon salt**
**⅛ teaspoon pepper**

Combine all ingredients; mix well. Chill. Serve with fried or barbecued chicken, if desired. Makes 4-6 servings.

# Beef Broth V-8 Cocktail

**1 can (10½ ounces) condensed beef broth**
**1 can (6 ounces) mixed vegetable juice**
**½ teaspoon Worcestershire sauce**
**Lemon wedges**
**Shaved ice**

Combine beef broth, vegetable juice and Worcestershire. Fill roomy glasses with shaved ice. Garnish each serving with a lemon wedge. Makes about 4 servings.

# Picnic Corn 'n' Seafood Chowder

**1 can (1 pound, 1 ounce) yellow cream style corn**
**1 can (10½ ounces) cream of potato soup**
**1 can (7½ ounces) minced or chopped clams**
**1 can (10 ounces) oysters**
**½ cup white dinner wine**
**1 pint milk**
**Salt and pepper**

Combine all ingredients in a large kettle. Heat slowly, stirring now and then to simmering. Chowder can be thinned with a little additional wine or milk. It can also be enriched with cooked vegetables such as canned mixed vegetables, carrots, green beans and peas. Makes 4 or 5 servings.

# NOTES

# BUDGET

Cooking on a budget aways seems to scare people. They think in terms of watered down soup and left overs. But this doesn't have to happen, as you will discover, if you look through this book. First; remember that any budget is a plan for spending. Sometimes it means spending your money wisely, sometimes it means spending your time wisely. You can spend your money on convenience foods and use your time for other things. Or you can spend lots of time cooking, when it is available, and save your money for other things. Either way you wish to budget, and here is a selection of recipes designed to suit your specific needs.

You will discover how to economically make your own soups, and how to combine canned soups when time is important; how to economize with casserole dishes, or how to cook "quick" meals in the broiler, many with a new flavor twist that give a gourmet's touch.

When it comes to desserts, we present more of the same. On one hand, you can start from scratch, or with a couple of quick tricks you can fancy up a "store-bought" cake so tasty, so different, that you will claim it as your very own.

## Soups

**Cold or hot, plain or fancy, soups can be a low cost, nutritious addition to your meals.**

### Chicken Gumbo Soup

Chicken gumbo soup, whether from a can or homemade, is a meal in itself. Serve it thick and hot with corn bread for a true creole treat. To make a real budget soup, use 8 chicken backs instead of the whole chicken.

**¼-pound cured bacon or jowl**
**4-pound stewing chicken**
**Seasoned flour**
**1 medium onion, chopped**
**3 cups cut okra, fresh, canned or frozen**
**2 cups canned tomatoes**
**1 tablespoon salt**
**7 cups hot water**
**1 bay leaf**
**2 small red pepper pods**
**½ clove garlic**
**1 tablespoon dry parsley**
**½ teaspoon thyme**
**½ teaspoon pepper**
**½ teaspoon brown sugar**
**1 cup uncooked rice**

Dice bacon or jowl and fry in a deep kettle until crisp. Remove. Cut chicken into serving pieces. Dredge with seasoned flour and brown well in bacon fat. Add remaining ingredients except rice. Simmer gently for three to four hours, adding water as needed. About 1 hour before serving add the rice. Stir occasionally.

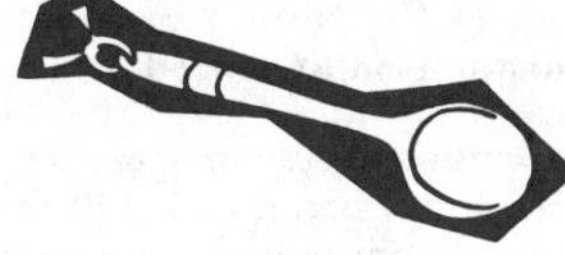

### Vichyssoise

**4 leeks, white part only**
**1 medium onion**
**½ stick (2 ounces) butter or margarine**
**5 medium potatoes, sliced finely**
**4 cups chicken consomme**
**Salt to taste**
**2 cups milk**
**2 cups cream**

Chop the leeks and onion finely and brown very lightly in butter. Add potatoes, consommé and salt and cook, covered, for 35 minutes. Put through a sieve and return to heat. Add the milk and heat but do not boil for five minutes. Cool. Add the cream and chill thoroughly before serving. Top with finely chopped chives. Makes 8 servings.

### Creamy Shrimp Gumbo

**1 can (10½ ounces) condensed cream of chicken soup**
**1½ soup cans water or milk**
**1 can (10½ ounces) condensed chicken gumbo soup**
**½ cup chopped cooked shrimp**

Blend cream of chicken soup with water; add chicken gumbo soup and shrimp. Heat, stirring occasionally. Makes 4 servings.

Campbell Soup Company

# Jellied Tomato Juice Consommé

**2 cups tomato juice**
**2 cans (10½ oz.) consomme**
**2 tablespoons chopped celery**
**½ bay leaf**
**2 thin slices onion**
**4 whole cloves**
**¼ cup lemon juice**
**1 tablespoon Worcestershire**
**1 package lemon gelatin**

Combine the tomato juice, consommé, celery, bay leaf, onion and cloves. Simmer for 10 minutes. Strain and measure 8 cups, adding boiling water if necessary. Pour the hot liquid, lemon juice and Worcestershire into the gelatin and stir until dissolved. Chill until firm. Beat lightly with a fork and serve in chilled cups. Garnish with a thin slice of lemon or with a spoonful of salted whipped cream. Makes 6 to 8 servings.

# Cream of Vegetable Soup

This is an excellent way to use leftover vegetables. The basic technique used in making this soup can be used to make any cream soup. In place of the vegetables in this recipe substitute 1 cup of any cooked and diced or puréed vegetable, and one teaspoon of grated onion.

**1 potato, diced**
**1 carrot, diced**
**½ cup diced celery**
**2 slices onion**
**1 cup water**
**1 cup canned peas**
**3 cups milk and vegetable liquid**
**3 tablespoons butter or margarine**
**3 tablespoons flour**
**1 teaspoon salt**
**Dash of pepper**

Place potato, carrot, celery and onion with water in a saucepan. Cover tightly and cook until vegetables are tender. Drain vegetables, reserving liquid. Drain peas, preserving liquid. Combine vegetable liquid with milk to make three cups. Melt butter in a saucepan. Add flour, salt and pepper and blend together. Remove from heat and add liquid gradually, stirring. Return to heat, bring to a boil and cook 1 minute, stirring constantly. Add vegetables and serve with minced parsley or a dash of paprika. Makes 4 generous servings.

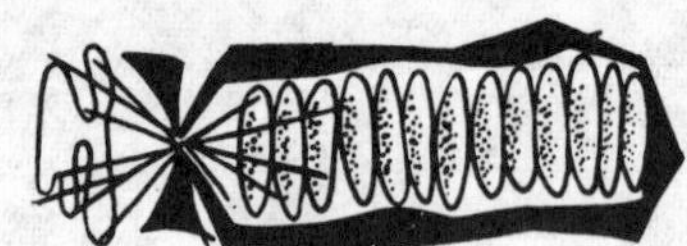

# Country Style Chicken Soup

**1 small stewing chicken or 6 backs and necks**
**8 cups water**
**1 cup chopped celery**
**1 cup sliced carrots**
**2 medium onions, sliced**
**1 small bay leaf or ½ teaspoon dill seeds**
**1 large potato, diced**
**2 teaspoons salt**
**¼ teaspoon pepper**

Simmer chicken in water 1 to 1½ hours. Add celery, carrots, onions and bay leaf or dill. Simmer thirty minutes. Remove meat from the frame of the chicken. Allow meat and vegetables to stand in broth overnight. Skim off excess fat, add potato and salt and pepper. Simmer thirty minutes longer. Makes 6 servings. You could use leftover chicken to make this soup and omit leaving it stand overnight.

Best Foods

# Golden Onion Soup

**3 cups water**
**1 envelope golden onion soup mix**

**Bring water to boil in saucepan. Stir in soup mix. Reduce heat; partially cover and boil gently 10 minutes. Makes 3 to 4 servings.**
**Note: Soup may be sprinkled with ¼ cup grated Parmesan cheese just before serving, if desired.**

### French Onion Soup

**Prepare Golden Onion Soup. Put 1 slice toasted French bread into each individual soup bowl; sprinkle with grated Parmesan or Swiss cheese. Pour hot soup over bread. Serve immediately, with additional grated cheese. Makes 3 to 4 servings.**

### Curried Onion Soup

**Prepare Golden Onion Soup. Add dash curry powder. Makes 3 to 4 servings.**

### Cream of Onion Soup

**Prepare Golden Onion Soup, reducing water to 1 cup, and stirring occasionally while simmering 10 minutes. Stir in 2 cups milk. Heat. Sprinkle with ¼ cup grated Parmesan cheese, if desired. Makes 3 to 4 servings.**

### Tomato-Onion Soup

**Follow recipe for Golden Onion Soup, substituting 1 cup tomato juice for 1 cup of the water. Makes 3 to 4 servings.**

# Icy Beet Borscht

**2 cans (10½ oz.) consomme**
**1 can (1 lb.) beets**
**1 medium onion, sliced**
**2 tablespoons lemon juice**
**2 teaspoons sugar**
**Sour cream**

Combine consommé, beets and onion. Cook 10 minutes. Add lemon juice, sugar, and chill thoroughly. Serve with a spoonful of sour cream in each bowl or cup. Makes 6 servings.

# Purée Mongole

1 can (10½ oz.) green pea soup
1 can (10½ oz.) tomato soup
Dash of curry powder
1 cup milk
1 cup water

Blend all ingredients. Heat but do not boil. Serve with a dab of lightly salted whipped cream. Makes 4 generous servings.

# Gloucester Fish Chowder

1 pound haddock fillets
½ cup flour
½ teaspoon salt
½ cup cubed salt pork
1 small onion, minced
1⅓ cups water
A few celery leaves
1 large potato, diced
1½ cups hot milk
1 tablespoon butter or margarine

Cut fish fillets into cubes. Combine flour and salt and dredge fish with it. Fry salt pork until brown in a deep kettle. Remove pork from kettle and brown onion in fat. Add fish, water, celery leaves and potato. Cover and simmer until vegetables are tender. Add milk, butter or margarine, and additional seasonings if necessary. Heat and serve with crackers. Makes 4 to 6 servings.

# Split Pea Soup

1 cup dried split peas
7 cups cold water
A ham bone or small shank end of ham
1 medium onion, sliced
1½ slices lemon
2 carrots, sliced
3 celery stalks with tops on, sliced
Salt and pepper to taste

Soak peas in 2 cups of the water for 4 hours or overnight. Remove a little of the ham fat and sauté onion in it until golden. Combine onion, peas, ham, lemon, carrots, celery, salt and pepper and remaining 5 cups water. Cover, bring to a boil, and simmer for 3 hours until the peas are tender and the soup, thick. If you like a smooth soup, rub through a coarse sieve. Skim off any surface fat. Serve with crisp croutons. Makes 4 servings.

# Tomato Bouillon

3 cups boiling water
3 beef bouillon cubes
2½ cups tomato juice
Salt and pepper to taste
Thin slices of lemon
1 tablespoon chopped parsley

Pour boiling water over bouillon cubes and stir until dissolved. Add tomato juice and heat. Season to taste. Serve in cups with a lemon slice and sprinkling of parsley on top.

Campbell Soup Company

# Mushroom-Shrimp Chowder

2 cans (10½ ounces each) condensed cream of mushroom soup
1 cup small shrimp, cooked or canned
1 soup can of milk
1 soup can water
1 to 2 tablespoons sherry, if desired
Butter

Combine 1 can of soup and shrimp in electric blender. Blend until smooth. Pour into saucepan; stir in remaining soup, milk, water and sherry. Heat, stirring now and then. Place a pat of butter on top of each serving. Makes 4 to 6 servings.

# Busy Day Luncheon Soup

1 pound ground beef
2¼ cups tomato juice
1½ cups diced potato
1 cup diced carrot
1 cup diced celery
½ cup diced onion
¼ cup uncooked rice
2 teaspoons salt
¼ teaspoon pepper
5 cups water

Crumble ground beef and place with remaining ingredients in a large kettle. Cover and simmer one hour. Serve with toast. Makes 8 servings.

# Washington Chowder

2 medium potatoes
1 medium onion
1½ cups boiling salted water
1 cup canned tomatoes
1 cup canned cream style corn
Dash of pepper
2 cups milk

Pare and thinly slice potatoes and onion. Cook in boiling salted water until tender. Add tomatoes, corn and pepper. Heat milk until just below boiling, and add vegetables just before serving. Makes 4 servings. Serve with crackers or top with freshly buttered popped corn.

# Beef and Bean Soup

1 tablespoon oil
1 large onion, chopped (1 cup)
1 can (10½ ounces) beef broth
1 package (10 ounces) frozen lima beans
1 can (14 ounces) red kidney beans
2 cans (1½ pounds) beef stew
2 tablespoons chili powder
½ teaspoon thyme
1 teaspoon salt

Heat oil in large aluminum Dutch oven. Add chopped onion and saute over low heat until tender. Add beef broth and lima beans. Cover and cook 10 minutes. Add remaining ingredients and bring to a boil. Makes 2¼ quarts or 8 one-cup servings.

Paper Cup & Plate Industries

Wine Institute

# Cream of Tomato Mushroom Soup

1 envelope of mushroom soup mix
1½ cups water
1 cup tomato juice
1 teaspoon minced onion
1 cup milk

Empty soup mix into saucepan. Gradually stir in water, tomato juice and onion. Bring to boil, stirring occasionally. Reduce; partially cover and simmer 5 minutes. Add milk; heat. Makes 4 servings.

### Tomato Mushroom Soup

Follow recipe for Cream of Tomato Mushroom Soup, adding 1 cup stewed tomatoes with milk. Makes 4 servings.

# Fruit Soup, Burgundy

1 (1-pound, 1-ounce) can pitted dark sweet cherries
½ teaspoon grated orange rind
¼ teaspoon ground cinnamon
⅛ teaspoon salt
2 tablespoons cornstarch
1 large orange
1 cup Sparkling Burgundy
Sour cream or whipped cream, for garnish

Combine undrained cherries, orange rind, cinnamon, salt and cornstarch in saucepan; stir gently to blend. Cook until mixture boils and thickens; remove from heat. Section orange. Squeeze all juice from membrane and add to cooling cherry base; chill slightly. Stir in chilled Sparkling Burgundy and orange sections (cut in half, if large). Spoon into sherbet glasses or small cups to serve. Top with a bit of sour cream or whipped cream, if desired. Makes 5 or 6 servings.

# Breads

**How to get the most out of this body building and energy food without waste.**

BREAD, the body building and energy food, is probably the food you buy most often. It may very well also be the one you waste the most.

To keep bread fresh as long as possible, leave it in the wrapper in which it came from the store and place it in a tightly covered container like a tin box. Bread, like bananas, should not be kept in the refrigerator. It will become stale more quickly there than in a bread box.

The best way to keep bread fresh for any length of time is to freeze it. Bread frozen while it is very fresh will have the same freshness thawed, as it did when it went into the freezer. There is no need to re-wrap or overwrap the bread, the moisture-proof wrapper in which it came from the store is very satisfactory. Just tuck the bread into the freezer in a spot where it will not be crushed.

To use the frozen bread, pop the slices in the toaster while still frozen, allowing a little more time to toast. Making sandwiches with frozen slices of bread is actually easier since it will not tear if the butter or spread is a little hard. The sandwich will thaw in two to three hours even when wrapped and packed in a lunch box.

Bread that has become too old to use as fresh bread can be made into crumbs, melba toast, croutons, or can be used in stuffings or bread puddings.

*Economy tip:* Whole grain, enriched or restored breads and cereals are usually priced at no more than refined products. They have a wealth of minerals and vitamins which refined grains have lost in processing.

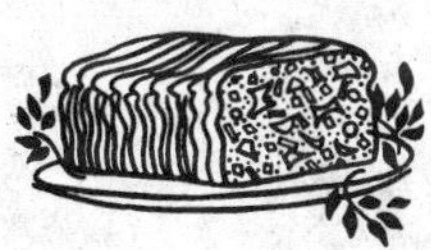

## Toast Cups

Trim the crusts from slices of bread. Brush one side with melted butter or margarine. Press each slice into a muffin cup. Bake in a very hot oven (450° F.) for 10 to 15 minutes or until crisp and brown. Fill with creamed foods.

## Peanut Butter Garlic Bread

**¼ cup smooth or crunchy peanut butter**
**½ cup softened butter or margarine**
**1 garlic bud, crushed**
**⅛ teaspoon salt**
**1 loaf French bread**

Mix peanut butter with butter, garlic and salt. Slice French bread in 1-inch slices, not quite through bottom of loaf. Spread peanut butter mixture between slices. Wrap in aluminum foil and bake in hot oven (400°F.) 10-15 minutes. Serve hot.

American Institute of Baking

## Bread Patty Shells

Use three slices of bread for each patty shell. Cut each slice into rounds with a large cookie cutter. Cut the center from two-thirds of the rounds with a small cookie cutter. You now have one round and two circles for each patty shell. Brush the top sides of the rounds and both sides of the circles with milk, and put two circles on top of each round. Brush top, sides and centers of the patty shells with melted butter and place on a greased baking sheet. Bake in a hot oven (400° F.) for 20 minutes or until shells are crisp and browned. Serve filled with creamed foods. Use the leftover bread and trimmings for crumbs or stuffings.

## Strawberry Coffee Buns

Form refrigerator dough into round buns. Combine ½ cup soft, fine bread crumbs, ¼ cup brown sugar and ¼ teaspoon cinnamon. Beat 1 egg white slightly. Dip each bun in egg white then in crumb mixture. Place on a greased baking sheet and let rise. When risen, make a deep indentation in the center of each bun with the thumb. Place 1 teaspoon strawberry preserves in each indentation. Bake in a moderate oven (375° F.) for about 25 minutes or until rolls are brown and preserves are bubbly.

## Waffled Bread

Trim the crusts from slices of bread. Dip in a mixture of 2 eggs, ½ cup milk, ⅛ teaspoon salt and 2 tablespoons melted butter. Place in the center of a heated waffle baker. Bake until brown and crisp. Serve with butter or margarine, and syrup.

## Bread Baskets

Trim the crusts from a large loaf of unsliced bread. Cut the bread into blocks 2x3x2 inches. With a sharp knife, cut centers from the blocks, leaving a cavity. Brush the baskets with melted butter. Place on a cookie sheet and toast under the broiler until a light golden brown. Serve with creamed foods. Makes 6 baskets.

# Crisp Cheese Baskets

Follow the directions for bread baskets. After brushing the baskets with melted butter, place some finely grated cheese on a piece of waxed paper and roll the baskets in the cheese until top and sides are well coated. Place on a cookie sheet and toast in a hot oven (400° F.) for 5 minutes or until the edges are slightly brown. Makes 6 baskets.

American Institute of Baking

# Orange Toast

**2 eggs, beaten**
**¼ cup milk**
**1 tablespoon sugar**
**1 tablespoon grated orange rind**
**¼ cup orange juice**
**Dash salt**
**6 slices bread**
**Butter or margarine**

Combine beaten eggs, milk, sugar, orange rind, juice, and salt. Mix well. Dip bread slices in egg mixture, lightly coating both sides. Heat butter or margarine in a skillet and brown bread on both sides in it. Serve at once with honey, syrup or applesauce, or place fresh or frozen strawberries or peaches between two layers of toast, sprinkle with confectioners' sugar and serve as a dessert.

# Refrigerator Rolls

**2 cakes compressed yeast**
**¼ cup lukewarm water**
**1 cup milk**
**1½ teaspoons salt**
**¼ cup sugar**
**½ cup shortening**
**5 cups sifted flour (about)**
**3 eggs, beaten**

Crumble the yeast into the lukewarm water and stir it. Heat, but do not boil the milk. Add the salt, sugar and shortening. Allow to cool until lukewarm. Add 2 cups of the flour and beat well. Add yeast and beaten eggs and blend thoroughly. Add remaining flour to make a soft dough. Turn out on a lightly floured board and knead until satiny. Place the dough in a lightly greased bowl, cover and let rise in a warm place (80 to 85° F.) away from drafts, until doubled in bulk. Punch down with fingers or fist and form into a smooth ball. Grease the surface of the ball lightly, then cover and put into the refrigerator. Punch it down occasionally. About 2 hours before baking, cut off the amount needed and return the remaining dough to the refrigerator. Shape into rolls and place on a greased baking sheet. Brush tops with melted butter or margarine. Let rise until light, about 1½ to 2 hours. Heat oven to moderately hot (400° F.) Bake 15 to 20 minutes. Makes about 3 dozen rolls. Here are 2 variations of Refrigerator Rolls:

# Old-fashioned Buns

Form refrigerator dough into balls ⅓ the size desired after baking. Grease a round pan well and place buns close together in it. Let rise and bake.

# Parkerhouse Rolls

Roll refrigerator dough ¼ inch thick. Cut out with a biscuit cutter. Brush each round with melted butter. Make a crease across each round and fold over so that top half slightly overlaps. Press edges together at the crease. Place close together on the pan. Let rise and bake.

American Institute of Baking

# French Toast

**2 eggs, beaten**
**½ teaspoon salt**
**1 tablespoon sugar**
**1 cup milk**
**12 slices bread**
**Butter or margarine**

Combine beaten eggs, salt, sugar and milk. Dip bread slices into the mixture. Fry in a small amount of butter or margarine until golden brown. Or heat oven to very hot (500° F.). Place slices of dipped bread on a well greased cookie sheet and place in the oven for ten minutes on each side or until brown. Serve with honey butter or maple flavored syrup.

# Baking Powder Biscuits

| | Family Size (20 biscuits) | Make-Your-Own Mix In Quantity |
|---|---|---|
| **Sift together:** | | |
| **Flour, sifted before measuring** | **2 cups** | **9 cups** |
| **Baking powder** | **2½ teaspoons** | **¼ cup (4 tablespoons)** |
| **Salt** | **1 teaspoon** | **1 tablespoon** |
| **Cut shortening in to resemble "meal"** | **⅓ cup** | **2 cups** |
| **Add milk just before mixing and baking** | **¾ cup** | **¾ cup milk to each three cups mix** |

• General directions: Heat oven to very hot (450° F.). Stir milk into desired quantity dry ingredients; form dough into a ball and knead lightly 6 times. Roll dough or pat it out with floured hand, ¼ inch thick for thin, crusty biscuits or ½ inch thick for softer biscuits. Cut close together with a floured biscuit cutter or for speed, cut in squares with a knife. Fit left-over pieces together but do not re-knead. Place 1 inch apart for crusty sides, or close together for soft sides. Bake in middle of oven for 10 to 12 minutes, until golden brown.

**Bacon Biscuits:** Cook 4 strips bacon until very crisp. Crumble and add to flour and shortening mixture in basic recipe.

**Cheese Biscuits:** Add ½ cup grated sharp American cheese to the flour and shortening mixture.

**Curry Biscuits:** Add ½ teaspoon curry powder to the dry ingredients in the basic recipe.

• Hints for better biscuits... Quantity mix may be stored in a canister on pantry shelf if fat not needing refrigeration is used... When ready to prepare biscuits for baking, stir in almost all of the milk. If dough does not seem pliable, add the rest. Use only enough to make a soft, puffy dough, easy to roll out. Too much milk makes the biscuits sticky; too little makes them dry... Too much handling makes biscuits tough, so don't overdo the kneading... A heavy or shiny pan helps prevent over-browning on the bottom.

# Dumplings

Follow the directions for Baking Powder Biscuits but increase the milk to 1 cup. Drop by spoonfuls onto the meat or chicken in the soup or stew, not into the liquid. Cover the kettle and cook 10 minutes. Uncover and cook another 10 minutes.

**Herb Dumplings:** Add ¼ teaspoon each sage and thyme and 1½ teaspoons caraway seeds to the dry ingredients.

**Parsley-Chive Dumplings:** Add 1½ tablespoons each, minced parsley and chives to the dry ingredients.

# Drop Biscuits

Follow the recipe for Baking Powder Biscuits but increase the milk to 1 cup. Drop from a spoon onto a greased baking pan and bake as in the basic recipe.

Pimiento Drop Biscuits: Coarsely chop enough pimiento to make ⅓ cup. Add to the dry ingredients with the milk. Drop and bake.

Blushing Biscuits. Use tomato juice in place of the milk. Drop and bake.

# Vari-Waffles

**3 eggs, separated**
**3¼ cups milk**
**½ cup melted butter or margarine**
**4½ cups variety baking mix**
**2 packages frozen chicken a la king, prepared as directed**
**1 cup pecans, chopped**
**Maple blended syrup**

Beat egg whites until stiff. Mix yolks, milk and cooled butter and stir into baking mix. Gently fold in beaten egg whites. Divide batter into two parts.

Bake one part of batter plain in waffle baker; divide waffles in quarters and top with approximately ½ cup prepared chicken a la king per serving

To make pecan waffles, add chopped pecans to other part of batter, bake in waffle baker and serve with syrup.

Makes enough waffles to serve 8 generously.

### Orange Waffles

Fold 1 tablespoon grated orange rind into ½ recipe of waffle batter. Bake and serve with vanilla ice cream and chocolate sauce.

### Date Waffles

Fold ½ cup chopped, pitted dates to ½ recipe of waffle batter. Bake and serve with lemon sauce.

### Blueberry Waffles

Fold 1 cup frozen blueberries into ½ recipe of waffle batter. Bake and serve with hard sauce.

Paper Cup and Plate Industries

# Creole Upside Down Cornbread

**1 package frozen creole succotash**
**1 package cornbread mix**
**1 tablespoon chopped chives**

Defrost frozen creole succotash by boiling 6 minutes and spread on the bottom of a buttered 8-inch square baking dish. Mix cornbread as directed on the package and add chives. Pour over succotash and bake over medium heat on grill or hibachi for about 30 minutes. Serves 6.

# Muffins

*Muffin Tip*: If muffins get done a little ahead of the rest of the meal, loosen them, tip them slightly in the pans, and keep them in the warm oven.

**2 cups flour, sifted before measuring**
**3 teaspoons baking powder**
**½ teaspoon salt**
**4 tablespoons sugar**
**4 tablespoons butter or shortening, melted**
**1 cup milk**
**1 egg, well beaten**

Heat oven to hot (400° F.). Grease muffin tins. Combine flour, baking powder, salt and sugar. Combine butter, milk and egg. Add liquid ingredients all at once to dry ingredients and mix just until the flour is moistened. The batter will look lumpy but do not mix it any more. Fill muffin cups ⅔ full of batter. Bake 20 to 25 minutes or until golden brown. Makes 12 muffins.

**Surprise Muffins:** Follow the recipe for Muffins. Fill the greased muffin cups half full of batter. Drop a scant teaspoonful of jelly on the center of the batter. Add more batter to fill cup two-thirds full. Bake as directed.

**Blueberry Muffins:** Add 1 cup fresh or well-drained canned or frozen blueberries to the batter. Bake as directed.

**Pineapple Nut Muffins:** Add ½ cup well-drained crushed pineapple and ½ cup chopped nuts to the batter. Bake as directed.

**Cranberry Muffins:** Increase the sugar to 8 tablespoons and add ¾ cup chopped cranberries and 2 tablespoons grated orange rind to the dry ingredients. Bake as directed.

# Banana Coffee Cake

Add 1 egg and 2 extra tablespoons sugar to the basic biscuit recipe. Use 1 cup mashed fully ripe banana in place of the milk. Follow directions for Orange Coffee Cake omitting the orange rind from the topping.

# Orange Coffee Cake

Heat oven to hot (400° F.). Grease an 8-inch layer cake pan. Add 1 egg and 2 extra tablespoons sugar to the basic biscuit recipe. Use ¾ cup orange juice in place of the milk. Stir together only until dry ingredients are dampened. The batter will be lumpy. Spread batter in layer cake pan. Sprinkle with the following topping: mix together ¼ cup chopped nuts, ½ cup brown sugar, ½ teaspoon cinnamon, 2 tablespoons soft butter and 1 tablespoon grated orange rind. Bake for 25 minutes or until browned.

# Lucky Corn Clovers

**2 packages compressed or dry yeast**
**¼ cup lukewarm water**
**1 teaspoon sugar**
**½ cup shortening**
**2 teaspoons salt**
**¼ cup sugar**
**1 cup scalded milk**
**2 eggs, beaten**
**1 cup corn meal**
**3½ cups sifted all-purpose flour**

Crumble or sprinkle yeast in lukewarm water in small bowl. Add 1 teaspoon sugar and mix well. Let stand until yeast is thoroughly dissolved (5 to 15 minutes) . . . Put shortening, salt and ¼ cup sugar in large bowl; add milk, and stir until shortening is melted, then cool to lukewarm. Add dissolved yeast and eggs and mix well. Add corn meal, then add flour gradually, beating thoroughly after each addition. Turn out on lightly floured board and knead to a smooth dough. Place in greased bowl and brush dough with melted shortening. Cover and let rise in warm place until double in bulk (about 1½ hours). Rub hands thoroughly with the shortening, take a small portion of dough and squeeze between thumb and forefinger into small balls. Place 4 balls in each cup of grease-coated muffin pans. Let rise in warm place until double in bulk (about 20 minutes). Bake in hot oven (425°F) for 12 to 15 minutes. Makes 2½ dozen rolls.

Lever Brothers Co.

# Banana Tea Loaf

**1¾ cups flour, sifted before measuring**
**3 teaspoons baking powder**
**½ teaspoon salt**
**⅓ cup shortening**
**⅔ cup sugar**
**2 eggs, well-beaten**
**1 cup mashed ripe bananas**

Heat oven to moderate (350° F.). Grease an 8x4x2-inch loaf pan. Combine and sift together flour, baking powder and salt. Beat shortening until creamy in a bowl. Add sugar gradually and continue beating until light and fluffy. Add eggs and beat well. Add flour mixture alternately with bananas, a small amount at a time, mixing after each addition only enough to moisten the dry ingredients. Pour into pan and bake about 1 hour and 10 minutes.

**Banana Raisin Loaf:** Add 1 cup seedless raisins to egg mixture.

**Banana Nut Loaf:** Add ½ cup coarsely chopped nuts to egg mixture.

**Apricot or Prune Banana Loaf:** Add 1 cup finely cut soaked and drained dried prunes or apricots to egg mixture.

# Popovers

**2 eggs**
**1 cup milk**
**½ teaspoon salt**
**1 cup flour, sifted before measuring**

Heat oven to hot (425° F.). *Generously* butter deep muffin cups or oven glass cups. Beat eggs, milk, flour and salt with a rotary egg beater until smooth. Pour batter into cups and fill half full. Bake for 35 to 40 minutes until puffed and brown. Serve immediately with butter or slit and fill with creamed foods. Makes 6 to 8 popovers.

# Swedish Cherry Ring

**1 recipe biscuit dough**
**Melted butter**
**¼ cup sugar**
**1 teaspoon cinnamon**
**¼ cup chopped nuts**
**Cherry preserves**

Heat oven to very hot (450° F.). Grease a cookie sheet. Roll dough into a rectangle ¼ inch thick. Spread with melted butter, and sprinkle with sugar, cinnamon and nuts. Roll dough jelly roll fashion and shape into a ring on a greased cookie sheet. Press ends together. With a scissors, snip from the outer edge almost to the center at 1 inch intervals. Turn each cut slice on its side so that cut surface is up. Place 1 teaspoon cherry preserves in the center of each slice. Bake about 15 minutes.

# Speedy-Quick Waffles

**2 cups pancake mix**
**2 tablespoons sugar**
**2 eggs, separated**
**1½ cups milk**
**¼ cup melted shortening or butter**

Heat waffle iron. Place pancake mix and sugar in a mixing bowl. Beat egg yolks. Combine milk, melted shortening or butter and egg yolks. Add liquid ingredients to dry ingredients and stir until smooth. Beat egg whites, fold in. Pour batter on iron and bake until steaming stops. Makes 6 waffles.

**Cheese and Bacon Waffles:** Add ½ cup grated American cheese to the batter. Sprinkle crisply cooked crumbled bacon over the batter in the waffle iron.

**Nut Waffles:** Sprinkle 2 tablespoons coarsely chopped nuts over the batter as soon as it has been poured onto the iron.

**Berry Waffles:** Sprinkle 2 tablespoons fresh or well drained canned or frozen berries over the batter as soon as it has been poured onto the iron.

# Sour Milk Griddle Cakes

**2 cups flour, sifted before measuring**
**1½ teaspoons baking soda**
**½ teaspoon salt**
**1 tablespoon sugar**
**1 egg**
**2 cups sour milk or buttermilk (see page 10 for how to sour milk)**
**1½ tablespoons melted butter or shortening**

Mix and sift flour, baking soda, salt and sugar. Combine egg and milk and add. Beat until free from lumps and add shortening. Heat a heavy ungreased griddle well. Pour batter from the tip of a large spoon or from a pitcher to form round cakes of the desired size. If you like thick pancakes, add 2 tablespoons extra flour to the batter. If you like thin cakes, add 2 tablespoons more milk. When pancakes are puffed and full of bubbles, turn and brown other side. Turn only once. Makes 2 dozen medium sized pancakes. Serve with butter and maple flavored syrup, crisply browned bacon or sausages.

**Company Griddlecakes:** Place chilled cottage cheese between two piping hot pancakes and top with warmed cherry preserves.

**Apple Spice Pancakes:** Add ¼ teaspoon each, cinnamon and nutmeg to the dry ingredients and use 1 cup applesauce for 1 cup of the sour milk.

*Pancake Pointers:*

1. If the batter has to stand for half an hour to an hour, add a little extra baking soda.

2. For Sweet Milk Pancakes, use sweet milk in place of the sour milk and use baking powder instead of baking soda.

3. To keep pancakes hot if you are making a great many, place them between the folds of a warm towel in a warm oven.

U. S. Brewers' Association

# Date and Nut Bread

2½ cups sifted all-purpose flour
4 teaspoons baking powder
1 teaspoon salt
1 cup sugar
⅓ cup shortening
1 cup beer or ale
1 egg
½ cup chopped nuts
1 cup finely cut dates

Sift together flour, baking powder, salt and sugar. Cut in shortening with two knives or pastry blender until mixture resembles coarse meal. Form a "well" in center of dry ingredients; add beer and egg; mix just until all flour mixture is dampened. Stir in nuts and dates. Turn into a well-greased 9x5x3-inch loaf pan. Spread mixture to sides of pan, leaving center slightly hollowed. Bake in a moderate oven (350°F.) 1 hour. Cool thoroughly before slicing. Makes 1 loaf.

# Date Oatmeal Muffins

¾ cup sifted all-purpose flour
2 teaspoons baking powder
¾ teaspoon salt
⅓ cup sugar
1 cup rolled oats
¼ cup shortening
2 eggs
½ cup beer or ale
½ cup finely cut dates

Sift together flour, baking powder, salt and sugar. Stir in rolled oats; cut in shortening. Beat together eggs and beer. Stir into dry ingredients only until blended. Stir in dates. Spoon into 12 greased 2½-inch muffin pans. Bake in a moderately hot oven (400°F.) 20 to 25 minutes. Makes 12 muffins.

# Pasta, Beans and Rice

**Choose one of these luscious concoctions that are easy on the palate, and the budget as well.**

THE term "macaroni" really includes macaroni, spaghetti and egg noodles in all the varied shapes and sizes in which these products can be found. The most familiar of these are: *macaroni,* a tube in long lengths or short elbows; *spaghetti,* a solid rod in varying degrees of thickness; *egg noodles,* ribbon-like pieces in varying widths. Among the other shapes are corrugated elbows, coiled or bunched rods, alphabets, shells, bows, stars and seeds. High quality macaroni products are made from semolina, the purified middlings of durum wheat, the hardest wheat known to man. Egg noodles are also made of semolina but they have egg yolk added to the dough.

Macaroni and spaghetti approximately double in volume when cooked. Egg noodles do not increase in volume.

Macaroni, rice and beans combine well with meat, cheese, eggs or fish to provide low cost, highly nutritious meals.

# Day-Before-Payday-Casserole

2 cans (6½ or 7 ounces each) tuna in vegetable oil
1 can condensed tomato soup
1 can (1 pound) cut green beans
Water
1 teaspoon salt
½ teaspoon thyme
1 teaspoon Worcestershire sauce
1 cup raw rice

Turn tuna with oil and soup into saucepan. Drain liquid from green beans into soup can; fill to top with water. Add to saucepan with remaining ingredients. Place over moderate heat and bring to a boil. Turn into 2-quart casserole; cover and bake in a moderate oven (375°) for 30 minutes. Remove. Arrange green beans in band around casserole; cover and return to oven 15 minutes longer. Makes 6 servings.

Tuna Research Foundation

The Borden Company

# Spaghetti and Meat Balls

*The spaghetti:* To make 8 servings, bring three quarts water and one tablespoon salt to a boil in a large kettle or saucepan. Lower eight ounces of spaghetti into the saucepan, holding it and pressing down as you ease it into the water gradually so that it doesn't break. Cook, uncovered, stirring occasionally, twelve to fifteen minutes or until tender but still chewy. Drain and rinse with warm water. Place on a warmed platter and serve with sauce and meat balls.

*The sauce:*

**¼ cup chopped onion**
**1 clove garlic**
**2 tablespoons olive oil**
**1 can (1 lb. 13 oz.) tomatoes, strained**
**1 can (10½ oz.) tomato puree**
**1 can (6 oz.) Italian tomato paste**
**1 bay leaf**
**¼ teaspoon oregano**
**¼ teaspoon basil**
**1 teaspoon sugar**
**Salt and pepper to taste**

Cook onion and garlic in olive oil until golden. Add tomatoes and tomato puree and cook 30 minutes. Add remaining ingredients. Cover and cook very slowly about 1 hour, stirring occasionally.

*The meat balls:* The secret of really tender meat balls is not to mix and handle them too much. Combine 1 pound ground beef with 1 egg, 1 cup dry bread crumbs, ¼ cup grated Parmesan cheese, 2 tablespoons minced parsley and 1 clove of garlic, minced. Mix well and form into 16 balls. Brown on all sides in hot olive oil. Add to the sauce and cook together for 30 minutes longer.

**Ranch House Spaghetti:** Combine 2 cans (1¾-cup size) spaghetti in tomato sauce with cheese, 1 cup cubed leftover meat, 1 can or 2 cups cooked green beans. Heat thoroughly and serve. Makes 6 servings.

# Camper's Kettle

**1 can (1 lb.) luncheon meat**
**1 tablespoon fat**
**1½ cups chopped onion**
**¼ cup chopped celery**
**2 cups canned tomatoes**
**1 cup cooked dried beans**
**1½ teaspoons salt**
**2 teaspoons sugar**
**¼ pound uncooked spaghetti**

Cube luncheon meat and brown in fat in a large skillet. Push to one side and add onions and celery. Brown lightly. Add tomatoes, beans and seasonings. Add uncooked spaghetti. Cook slowly for 45 minutes to 1 hour, stirring occasionally. Makes 6 servings.

# Macaroni Angostura

**1 pound elbow macaroni**
**¼ pound butter**
**½ cup sweet red onions, chopped**
**½ cup green pepper, chopped**
**2 teaspoons salt**
**1 teaspoon pepper**
**1 tablespoon Angostura aromatic bitters**
**1 cup creamed Ricotta cheese, or cottage cheese**
**1 cup grated Parmesan and Romano cheese, mixed**

**Cook elbow macaroni according to package directions. Saute onions and green pepper in some of the butter until onions are transparent, but not brown. Melt rest of butter; add salt, pepper and Angostura aromatic bitters. Drain macaroni and mix hot macaroni with onions, green pepper and seasoned butter. Add Ricotta or cottage cheese and mix thoroughly. Fold in grated cheese, mixing well. Place over very low flame until hot, stirring constantly. Serve immediately with additional grated cheese. Yield: 6 servings.**

Angostura Bitters

# Franks and Beans

(See picture opposite.)

8 frankfurters
2 large cans of baked beans

Brown the franks evenly under the broiler, turning frequently. Meanwhile heat the beans and pour into a shallow dish. Add the browned franks and serve.

# Beef Stew with Vegetables

(See picture opposite.)

2 lbs. stewing beef cut into 2-in. squares
6 small onions
½ lb. sliced carrots
1 stick of celery
2 small parsnips
4 potatoes

Brown the meat in a little fat, then slice and add 2 of the onions and brown. Add enough water to cover, salt and pepper to taste and add 4 grains of all spice. Simmer at low heat until meat is tender, approximately 1½ to 2 hours, stirring occasionally. About an hour before serving add the vegetables and if necessary a little water. The sauce may be thickened by adding one teaspoon of corn starch mixed in a little cold water about 5 minutes before serving.

# Chicken Tetrazzini

An elegant way to use leftover chicken:

**8 ounces spaghetti**
**3 tablespoons butter or margarine**
**½ cup sliced mushrooms**
**3 tablespoons flour**
**1 cup chicken bouillon**
**½ cup milk**
**½ cup cream**
**Dash each celery salt, salt, pepper**
**1 cup diced cooked chicken**
**¼ cup dry bread crumbs**
**¼ cup grated Parmesan cheese**

Cook spaghetti according to directions on package. Melt butter in a saucepan. Sauté mushrooms in it until lightly browned. Blend in flour then gradually add bouillon and milk. Cook, stirring, until smooth. Add cream and seasonings to taste. Combine spaghetti, sauce and chicken. Place in a buttered baking dish. Combine bread crumbs and cheese. Sprinkle over the top. Bake in a very hot oven (450° F.) for 20 minutes. Or place drained spaghetti on a heated platter, add chicken to sauce, pour over spaghetti on platter and sprinkle with crumb-cheese mixture. Makes 6 servings.

# Lumberjack Mac

**8 ounces macaroni, unbroken**
**2 cups medium sharp American cheese, grated**
**2 tablespoons Worcestershire**
**¼ cup chili sauce**
**¾ cup melted butter or margarine**

Cook macaroni according to directions on package. Spread it on a heated platter. Sprinkle with the cheese, Worcestershire and chili sauce. Pour melted butter or margarine over. Mix and toss with two forks until sauce is creamy. Makes 6 servings.

# Lamb Stew

(See picture opposite.)

2 lbs. stewing lamb
½ lb. carrots
6 small potatoes
2 cloves of garlic
½ lb. peas
2 onions

Slice the onions and crush the garlic. Cut meat into cubes and brown in a little fat. Add the onion and garlic and brown these also, being careful not to let them burn. Add water to cover, salt and pepper to taste, and simmer on a low flame until tender. About ¾ of an hour before the end of cooking time, add the potatoes, sliced carrots and peas, and add a little more water if necessary.

# Baked Macaroni Supreme

**8 ounces macaroni, broken in pieces**
**½ cup chopped green pepper**
**¼ cup chopped onion**
**3 tablespoons butter or margarine**
**½ cup sliced stuffed olives**
**½ cup sliced mushrooms**
**1½ cups cubed ham or leftover meat**
**1 cup sharp cheddar cheese**
**1 can tomato soup**
**3 strips bacon**

Cook macaroni according to directions on package. Sauté green pepper and onion in butter or margarine about 5 minutes, until soft. Combine remaining ingredients, except bacon, with macaroni, green pepper and onion. Place in a greased casserole. Top with bacon strips. Bake in a hot oven (400° F.) for 20 minutes or until macaroni casserole is bubbly and bacon is done. Makes 6 servings.

R. T. French Co.

# Macaroni Salad Loaf

**1 envelope white sauce mix**
**1 envelope unflavored gelatin**
**4 teaspoons sugar**
**2 teaspoons seasoning salt**
**1½ cups milk**
**¼ cup salad oil**
**¼ cup cider vinegar**
**2 tablespoons mustard**
**2 teaspoons minced green onion**
**2 cups elbow macaroni, uncooked**
**¼ pound Muenster or Cheddar cheese**
**½ pound thinly sliced boiled ham**
**4 hard-cooked eggs, diced**
**½ cup diced celery**
**½ cup diced radishes**

Empty white sauce mix into saucepan. Add gelatin, sugar, and seasoning salt. Add milk. Bring to a boil, stirring constantly. Remove from heat. Add salad oil, vinegar, mustard, and green onion. Meanwhile, cook macaroni; drain well. Add the cooked salad dressing. While mixture cools, prepare meat-cheese rolls. Cut cheese into 6 sticks about 3-inches long and ½-inch thick. Wrap a slice of ham around each stick. Arrange in 2 rows in bottom of large (8-cup) loaf pan. (If a round pan is used—arrange rolls in a circle like the spokes of a wheel.) Dice any cheese or ham that's left. Add to macaroni along with eggs, celery, and radishes. Spoon macaroni mixture into pan, to fill space between rolls. Fill pan. Chill several hours. Turn out on platter. Garnish with thin slices of fresh cucumber. Makes 8 servings.

*Cheese Sputnik, p. 417*

*Filled Avocados, p. 389*

# Quick Noodle Casserole

**1 can beef bouillon**
**½ soup can water**
**1 package (8-ounce) noodles**
**1 cup grated American cheese**
**1 can (3-ounce) sliced mushrooms and broth**
**Salt**
**Pepper**

Bring bouillon and water to boil in a 1-quart aluminum saucepan. Add noodles and cook 8 to 10 minutes or until bouillon is absorbed. Mix in cheese and mushrooms and stir over low heat until cheese is melted. Season with salt and pepper. Makes 4 servings.

# Baked Fish-Rolls with Filling

(See picture opposite.)

**1¼-1½ lbs. fillet of sole or cod**
**Salt, pepper**
**Lemon**
**3 tablespoons butter or margarine**
**Chopped parsley, chives and dill (equal portions)**
**Fine, dry, bread crumbs**
**½-¾ cup of cream**

Choose small fillets and prepare 2 for each person. Wash and dry fish, drip with lemon juice, salt and pepper. Work the chopped greens into the butter and lay a piece on each fillet before rolling up and placing in an ovenproof dish. Sprinkle dried bread crumbs over. Put butter on top of fillets and place in an oven 450-500 degrees. After 10 mins. add the cream and leave in oven 5-10 minutes more.

# White Cabbage Salad

(See picture opposite.)

**1 cup finely chopped cabbage**
**1 small can of pimento**
**Juice of 1 or 2 oranges**

Mix pimento and cabbage. Pour orange juice over mixture. Serve with fish dish.

## RICE

RICE is not just rice. There are two different types from which you can choose and several different forms in which it is processed. The two major types of rice are long-grain and short-grain. The long-grain is a little more expensive and cooks up into fluffy, separate grains. It is excellent as a vegetable or in a rice ring. Short-grain rice is a good buy and makes a nice creamy pudding or casserole.

*Milled white rice* is the product with which most of us are familiar. It has had the hull, bran and germ removed. It keeps well but is not a good source of vitamins. *Brown rice* has had only the hull removed. It has a pleasant nut-like flavor and is rich in vitamins and minerals. It does not keep as well as white rice and is a little less readily digestible. *Converted rice* is regular white rice that has been treated so that the B vitamins and the minerals normally dissolved during processing, remain in the interior of the rice granule. *Fortified rice,* available in some areas, has been treated so that the vitamins and minerals are locked in and cannot escape during the polishing process. *Precooked white rice* has been partially cooked before packing and produces fluffy grains in a very short time. *Wild rice* is not a true rice but the seed of a grass that grows wild in shallow lakes and marshy lands. It has a distinctive flavor that many people enjoy greatly, but it is very expensive.

# Old-fashioned Spanish Rice

**2 slices bacon, cut in small pieces**
**½ cup chopped onion**
**½ cup chopped green pepper**
**4 cups tomato juice**
**⅔ cup washed uncooked rice**
**1 teaspoon salt**
**⅛ teaspoon pepper**

Sauté bacon, onion and green pepper together until bacon is crisp. Place in top of a double boiler and add remaining ingredients. Cook over boiling water for 1 hour, stirring occasionally. Makes 8 servings.

# Sunshine Rice Casserole

**2 cups cooked rice**
**2½ cups finely grated carrots**
**1¼ cups grated American cheese**
**2 well-beaten eggs**
**¼ cup milk**
**1 tablespoon grated onion or ¼ teaspoon onion powder**
**1 tablespoon melted butter or margarine**
**1 teaspoon salt**
**⅛ teaspoon pepper**

Combine all ingredients. Toss well but lightly together. Place in a buttered 1½ quart casserole. Cover and bake in a slow oven (325° F.) for 45 minutes. Makes 6 servings.

# Green Rice Casserole

**2 tablespoons dehydrated onion flakes**
**2 tablespoons dehydrated parsley flakes**
**2 tablespoons dehydrated sweet pepper flakes**
**½ cup packaged pre-cooked rice**
**1 egg, beaten**
**⅓ cup salad oil**
**1 cup milk**
**1 teaspoon salt**
**1½ cups grated Parmesan and Romano cheese**
**½ cup buttered bread crumbs**

Rehydrate onion flakes, parsley flakes and pepper flakes as directed on package. Meanwhile cook rice according to directions on package. Lightly butter a 1-quart casserole. In large-sized mixing bowl, combine rice, egg, oil, milk and salt. Stir in rehydrated onion, parsley and green pepper. Stir in 1 cup of the cheese. Pour into casserole. Mix remaining cheese with bread crumbs; sprinkle on top of casserole. Bake in a moderate oven (350°F.) until sauce is thickened and top is golden brown, 35 to 40 minutes. Makes 5 to 6 servings.

The Borden Co.

# Oriental Chicken Pilaff

A most unusual way of serving leftover chicken:

**½ cup butter or margarine**
**2 cups cooked chicken cut into 1½ inch strips**
**¼ cup diced onion**
**2 teaspoons salt**
**⅛ teaspoon pepper**
**½ teaspoon oregano**
**1 cup uncooked white rice**
**2½ cups chicken bouillon**
**½ cup canned tomatoes, drained**
**½ cup chopped walnuts**

Melt the butter in a large saucepan. Add the chicken and onion and cook until the chicken is lightly browned. Add salt, pepper and oregano. Add the rice, and cook, stirring occasionally, for 5 minutes. Slowly add the chicken bouillon, then the tomatoes and walnuts. Bring to a boil. Cover and simmer 20 minutes or until rice is tender. Do not stir while cooking. Makes 8 servings.

## BEANS

DRIED beans are hearty and filling, high in food value and low in cost. As a general rule in using them, soak them several hours or overnight and then cook them in the same water in which they were soaked.

| | Dry Measure | Water to Soak | Added Water to Cook | Cooked Measure |
|---|---|---|---|---|
| Lentils | 1 cup | 2¼ cups | 1½ cups | 2½ cups |
| Navy Beans | ½ cup | ¾ cup | 3 cups | 1⅜ cups |
| *Pinto Beans | ½ cup | ¾ cup | 1½ cups | 1⅓ cups |
| Peas | ½ cup | ¾ cup | 4 cups | 1½ cups |
| *Kidney Beans | ½ cup | ¾ cup | 2 cups | 1½ cups |
| *Lima Beans | ½ cup | ¾ cup | 2½ cups | 1¼ cups |

***These beans come in 1 pound cans, cooked and slightly salted. They are a time and fuel saver for the busy homemaker since they require no soaking or long cooking.**

# Creole Pork and Beans

**3 slices bacon**
**½ cup chopped onion**
**½ cup diced green pepper**
**½ cup chopped celery**
**¼ cup dry bread crumbs**
**Salt**
**1 can (1 lb.) pork and beans**
**1 cup canned tomatoes**
**1 teaspoon sugar**

Sauté bacon until crisp. Remove from pan and break into small pieces. Drain off all but 3 tablespoons of the bacon fat. Place onion, green pepper and celery in bacon drippings and cook 3 minutes. Remove from heat. Add bread crumbs, salt and bacon. Place a layer of pork and beans in a casserole. Add a layer of vegetable and bacon mixture, then another layer of pork and beans. Top with tomatoes and sprinkle with sugar. Bake in a hot oven (425° F.) for 30 minutes. Makes 4 servings.

# Savory Baked Lima Beans

These beans are even better rewarmed for a second meal:

**1 pound (2½ cups) dried lima beans**
**½ teaspoon baking soda**
**4 ounces salt pork or 5 strips bacon**
**1 teaspoon dry mustard**
**1½ teaspoons salt**
**3 tablespoons brown sugar or molasses**
**¼ teaspoon paprika**
**1 cup bean liquid or water**
**1 cup catsup**
**1 medium onion, peeled but whole**

Pick over beans and wash them. Cover with 1½ quarts water and soak overnight. Add baking soda and meat to the beans the next day and cook ½ hour. Drain off liquid, saving 2 cups. Add seasonings to beans and turn into a baking dish that has a cover. Bury the onion in the center of the beans. Add one cup of the liquid. Cover and bake in a moderate oven (350° F.) for 2½ to 3 hours or until the beans are soft. Add the remaining cup of liquid gradually over the baking period as beans need it. Uncover last half hour of baking to brown the top. Makes 8 to 10 servings.

The Borden Co.

# Baked Lima Beans and Cheese

**1 package (12 ounces) frozen lima beans, cooked**
**4 hard-cooked eggs, sliced**
**1 cup (8-ounce can) tomato sauce**
**1 package (6 ounces) American cheese slices**

Place half the lima beans in bottom of an 8-inch square baking dish. Arrange half the egg slices on top of lima beans. Pour half the tomato sauce on top of egg slices. Place half the cheese slices on top. Repeat procedure, ending with cheese slices. Bake in a moderate oven (350°F.) until cheese is melted, 20 to 25 minutes. Serve at once. Makes 4 to 6 servings.

# Saturday Night Special

Brown 1 pound ground beef lightly in a skillet without any added fat, stirring frequently. Add 1 can (1 lb.) pork and beans, 1 can (1 lb.) tomatoes, and 1 teaspoon salt. Grease a baking dish. Pour half the mixture in. Cover with slices of onion. Add remaining meat-bean mixture. Top with strips of bacon and sprinkle with ¼ cup brown sugar. Bake in a moderate oven (350° F.) for 1 hour. Makes 8 servings.

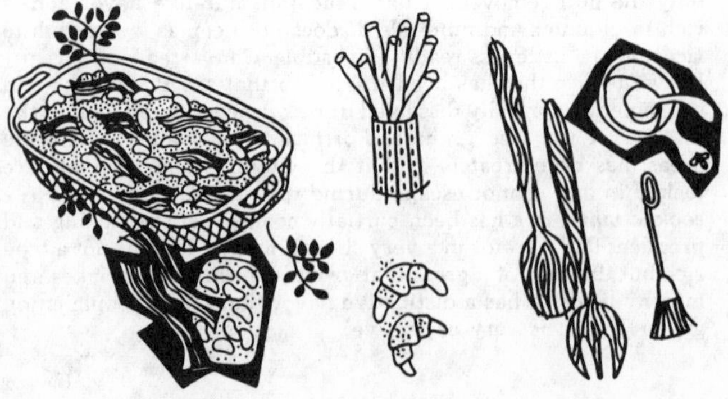

Campbell Soup Company

# Variations for Canned Pork and Beans

1. Place pork and beans in casserole. Top with thin slices of onion and a few strips of bacon before heating.

2. Sauté finely chopped green pepper and onion in a small amount of bacon drippings. Add to pork and beans and heat thoroughly.

3. Combine pork and beans with sliced frankfurters and minced onion before heating.

4. Combine pork and beans with browned ground beef, minced onion and molasses before heating.

5. Add chili sauce and browned seasoned pork sausage patties to pork and beans before heating.

# Texas Bean Pie

**1 pound ground beef**
**2 tablespoons fat**
**½ cup chopped onion**
**1 clove garlic, minced**
**¼ cup green pepper**
**1 teaspoon salt**
**1 tablespoon chili powder**
**1 teaspoon Worcestershire**
**2 cans (10½ oz.) tomato pureé**
**1 can (1 lb.) kidney beans**
**⅓ cup corn meal**
**1 cup cubed cheese**

Brown beef in hot fat. Add onion, garlic, green pepper, seasonings, tomato purée and kidney beans. Bring to a boil. Stir in the corn meal. The mixture will become very thick. Pour into a 2 quart casserole. Top with cheese. Bake in a moderate oven (350° F.) 10 to 15 minutes or until cheese melts and browns slightly. Makes 6 to 8 servings.

# Mexican Bean Pot

**1 pound dried kidney beans**
**3 cups water**
**2 cups California Burgundy or other red dinner wine**
**1 tablespoon plain or seasoned salt**
**3 tablespoons butter or bacon drippings**
**1 clove garlic**
**1 stick cinnamon**
**⅛ teaspoon powdered cloves**
**2 teaspoons dry mustard**
**2 teaspoons chili powder**
**2 tablespoons wine vinegar**
**½ cup spicy syrup from sweet pickles or spiced fruit**
**½ cup strong coffee**
**1 can (14½-ounce) stewed tomatoes**
**6 thick onion slices**

Measure beans, water and wine into a large saucepan. Bring slowly to a boil. Boil 2 minutes. Turn off heat, cover and let stand 1 hour. Then add salt, butter, garlic, cinnamon, cloves, mustard, and chili powder. Simmer, covered, until beans begin to get tender, about 1 hour and 20 minutes. Add remaining ingredients and cook uncovered until beans are completely tender, about 30 to 40 minutes longer. If thicker liquid is desired, mash about ½ cup of the beans and stir into the remaining bean mixture. To serve, spoon hot beans onto hot tortillas (or, squares of corn bread). Sprinkle with chopped green onion and grated sharp Cheddar cheese; top with sliced avocado.

# Ginger Peachy Baked Beans

**½ cup dark corn syrup**
**1 tablespoon finely chopped onion**
**1 teaspoon ginger**
**2 (1-pound) cans baked beans**
**1 (1-pound 13-ounce) can peaches, drained**
**Orange marmalade**

Combine corn syrup, onion and ginger. Spoon baked beans into 2-quart casserole. Stir in syrup mixture. Top with drained peaches inside up. Place a spoonful of orange marmalade in each indentation. Bake in a hot oven (400°F.) basting frequently, until peaches are well glazed and beans are hot, 1 to 1½ hours. Makes 6 servings.

Best Foods

# Eggs and Cheese

**From plain cooked eggs to elegant cheese soufflés and puffy omelets, these foods make excellent meals!**

EGGS and cheese cost less pound for pound than meat and supply the same kind of high-quality protein. Information on the carton gives size and quality. Here is what it means:

### Consider Size and Weight in Relation To Price When You Buy Eggs

| U.S. Size | Weight Per Dozen |
|---|---|
| Jumbo | 30 oz. |
| Extra Large | 27 oz. |
| Large | 24 oz. |
| Medium | 21 oz. |
| Small | 18 oz. |
| Peewee | 15 oz. |

### Consider Quality in Relation To Use When You Buy Eggs

A reliable guide to quality in eggs in government grading:

**U.S. Grade AA**—Egg covers small area, white is thick, yolk stands firm and high. Since there are a limited number of this grade, some may be included in the carton with grade A eggs.

**U.S. Grade A**—Egg covers moderate area, white is reasonably thick, yolk is firm and high. Found in almost all markets.

**U.S. Grade B**—Egg covers wide area, has only small amount of thick white, yolk is somewhat flattened and enlarged. Found in some markets.

### Know Your Eggs

- The shell color does not affect the flavor, food value or cooking performance. There is no advantage to paying more for eggs because they are brown or white.
- Buy eggs that have been under refrigeration and store them in your refrigerator in their cardboard carton, or small end down in an egg container.
- Don't wash eggs. The protective coating on the shell helps preserve them. If soiled, wipe with a cloth.
- Store leftover yolks under water in a covered jar in the refrigerator for 2 or 3 days; store leftover whites in a tightly covered jar in the refrigerator. These may be held a week to 10 days. Yolks separate from the whites more easily when they are cold.
- For highest volume, let egg whites stand at room temperature for a while before beating.

## Baked Eggs and Spinach

Sauté 2 tablespoons chopped onion in 3 tablespoons butter or margarine. Add 1 pound washed spinach, 1 teaspoon salt and a dash of pepper. Cover and cook about 5 minutes. Chop the spinach. Butter or grease 4 individual casseroles. Place spinach in them. Break an egg into each. Sprinkle with salt and pepper. Cover with foil and bake as above.

## Baked Eggs With Cheese Sauce

**2 tablespoons butter or margarine**
**2 tablespoons flour**
**¼ teaspoon salt**
**½ teaspoon prepared mustard**
**1 cup milk**
**¼ pound process American cheese, grated**
**¼ teaspoon Tabasco**
**8 eggs**

**Melt butter; blend in flour and seasonings. Add milk and cook stirring constantly until mixture thickens and comes to a boil. Remove from heat; add grated cheese, stirring occasionally until cheese is melted. Pour 2 tablespoons of sauce into each of 4 individual buttered baking dishes. Break 2 eggs into each dish and top with remaining sauce. Bake in a moderate oven (350°F.) until eggs are set, about 12 minutes. Makes 4 servings.**

McIlhenney's Tabasco

Poultry & Egg Natl. Board

# Puffy Omelet

Separate eggs. To the yolks add 1 tablespoon water or milk and a dash of salt and pepper for each egg used. Beat the whites until stiff. Beat the yolks until thick and lemon-colored. Carefully fold the yolks into the beaten whites. Put 1½ teaspoons butter or fat for each egg in a skillet and heat until sizzling. Pour eggs into skillet. Turn heat to low, and cook slowly about 10 minutes or until lightly browned on bottom. Heat oven to moderate (350° F.) and when bottom is browned, place skillet in oven. Bake about 10 to 15 minutes or until lightly browned on top. Make a deep crease in the center of the omelet, fold in half and roll out onto a warm platter. Serve with cheese sauce, tomato or Spanish sauce, creamed chicken, ham or asparagus. You can also add to the egg yolks 1 cup salmon or tuna combined with 1 tablespoon each minced parsley and onion, or 1 cup finely diced leftover meat or chicken.

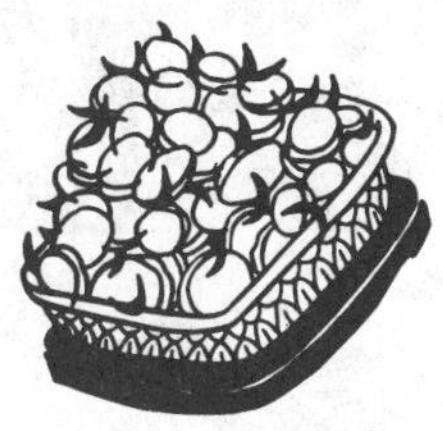

Poultry and Egg National Board

# French Omelet

In a bowl, place 1 tablespoon water or milk and a dash of salt and pepper for each egg used. Mix with a fork. Heat 1 teaspoon butter or fat for each egg in a skillet until sizzling. Pour egg mixture into sizzling fat and reduce heat at once. Cook slowly and as the mixture at the edges thickens, draw these portions with a fork or spatula toward center so that uncooked portion flows to the bottom. Shake the skillet to keep omelet sliding free. When eggs are set and bottom is slightly brown, sprinkle with meat, cheese or herbs, about ½ teaspoon per egg. Loosen edge, fold in half or roll onto hot platter.

# Fillings For French Omelets

- A combination of herbs—chives, parsley, basil, thyme, marjoram. This is called an omelet aux fines herbes.
- Finely minced and browned onion and chopped chicken liver.
- Finely minced and sautéed eggplant, garlic and tomato.
- Sautéed sliced or minced mushrooms.
- Crisp bits of bacon and grated cheese.
- Any tart jelly.

# Baked (Shirred) Eggs

Heat oven to slow (325° F.). Grease or butter individual shallow baking dishes. Break an egg into each dish. Dot with bits of butter and sprinkle with salt and pepper. Add 1 tablespoon milk or cream and bake 15 to 20 minutes or until set.

# Creamed Ham and Eggs

**1 can (3 or 4 ounces) mushrooms**
**Milk**
**¼ teaspoon Tabasco**
**⅓ cup butter or margarine**
**6 tablespoons flour**
**½ teaspoon salt**
**1 teaspoon dry mustard**
**4 hard cooked eggs, quartered**
**2½ cups diced cooked ham**

**Drain mushrooms; add enough milk to mushroom liquid to make 3 cups. Stir in Tabasco; reserve. Melt butter; add flour, salt and dry mustard; stir to a smooth paste. Gradually add milk and cook, stirring constantly, until mixture thickens and comes to a boil. Add drained mushrooms, hard cooked eggs and ham; heat to serving temperature. Turn into serving dish; garnish with toasted buttered bread crumbs, if desired. Makes 4 to 6 servings.**

**McIlhenney's Tabasco**

# Swiss Pie

*(See picture between pgs. 288-289.)*

**Pastry**
**2 cups of flour**
**1 cup margarine**
**½ teaspoon salt**
**5 teaspoons iced water**

**Filling**
**1 lb. lean ham cut into 9 slices**
**¾ to 1 lb. swiss cheese**
**1 large onion**

Mix flour and salt, crumble in margarine, and add water a little at a time to make a dough. Put aside to cool for 2 hours. Later roll out to a square and trim the edges. Lay 3 slices of ham on the pastry square, leaving the corner triangles free. Cover ham with slices of cheese and then the onion. Repeat the layers and then finish again with ham. Fold the corners in to the middle and nip together. Make a small decoration of pastry to place in the middle and then brush with egg. Bake in an oven at 450-500 degrees for 20-25 minutes until the pie is golden brown. Makes 6-8 servings.

Serve with a fresh salad of lettuce, cucumber and tomatoes sprinkled with lemon juice.

# Individual Cheese Pudding

**2 hard-cooked eggs**
**2 cups cottage cheese**
**3 egg yolks**
**1 cup sugar**
**¼ cup melted butter or margarine**
**3 tablespoons flour**
**½ cup raisins**
**½ teaspoon vanilla**
**3 egg whites**

Heat oven to slow (325° F.). Force hard-cooked eggs and cheese through sieve, mix thoroughly. Cream egg yolks, sugar and melted butter or margarine together. Add to cheese mixture and beat well. Fold in flour, raisins and vanilla. Beat egg whites until stiff and fold into cheese mixture. Pour into 8 greased custard cups. Bake about 45 minutes, or until knife comes out clean when inserted in center of each pudding. Cool thoroughly and turn from custard cups into dessert dishes.

# Poached Eggs

Place about 2 inches of water in a shallow pan. Bring to a boil, then reduce to a simmer. Break each egg into a saucer, and slip one at a time into the water. Cover the pan, and cook with the water barely simmering for 3 to 5 minutes. Lift eggs from the water one at a time with a slotted spoon. Drain, season with salt and pepper. Serve on hot buttered toast or English muffins. Milk or broth may be used instead of water. Pour the hot milk or broth over the eggs and toast.

# Cooked-in-the-Shell Eggs

### Hints To Help You

- Have eggs at room temperature to prevent cracking during cooking.
- Choose a large enough pan so that eggs are in single layer.
- Cover eggs completely with water, cold or boiling.
- Cook at temperatures below boiling, timing accurately with a clock.

*Cold Water Start:* Cover eggs in pan with at least one inch cold water. Bring rapidly to a boil. Remove pan from heat. Cover, and let stand off heat 2 to 4 minutes for soft-cooked eggs, 23 to 25 minutes for hard cooked eggs. Cool eggs in cold water for several seconds to prevent further cooking and to make handling easier.

*Boiling Water Start:* Bring water to boil in a saucepan. With a spoon, carefully lower eggs into water to prevent cracking the shell. Reduce heat to merest simmer. Cook 3 to 5 minutes for soft; 18 to 20 minutes for hard. Cool eggs to stop cooking, for easier handling.

# Cheese Soufflé

**½ pound Processed American cheese**
**4 tablespoons butter or margarine**
**4 tablespoons flour**
**1½ cups milk**
**1 teaspoon salt**
**Dash of cayenne pepper**
**6 eggs, separated**

Heat oven to slow (325° F.). Slice or break the cheese into small pieces. Melt the butter or margarine in a saucepan. Add the flour and combine. Add the milk, and cook, stirring constantly, until the mixture thickens. Add the salt and cayenne, then the cheese and stir until cheese melts. Remove from heat. Beat the egg yolks and add. Slightly cool the mixture. Beat the egg whites until stiff, then pour the cheese mixture slowly onto the beaten egg whites, cutting and folding until thoroughly blended. Pour the mixture into an ungreased 2 quart casserole. Run the tip of a teaspoon around the mixture, 1 inch from the edge, making a slight indentation all around. This forms the top hat effect. Bake for 1 to 1¼ hours. Makes 8 servings.

**Carrot Cheese Puff:** Add one cup grated raw carrot to the cheese mixture before folding into the whites.

**Tomato-Cheese Soufflé:** Follow the Cheese Soufflé recipe using tomato juice in place of the milk.

**Individual Cheese Soufflés:** Pour the cheese mixture into individual custard cups. Bake only 25 to 30 minutes.

**Mushroom-Cheese Soufflé:** When the soufflé is all mixed, carefully fold in 1 cup finely chopped sautéed mushrooms.

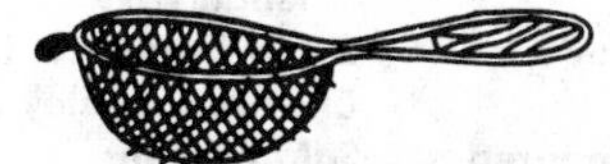

# Deviled Eggs

Hard-cook 6 eggs. Cut in halves and slip yolks into a bowl. Mash. Add ½ teaspoon salt, ⅛ teaspoon pepper, ½ teaspoon dry mustard and enough salad dressing or cream to moisten (about 3 tablespoons). Refill whites with seasoned yolks, heaping yolks up lightly.

# Special Deviled Eggs

Add to the egg yolks 2 tablespoons of any of the following: minced chives, parsley, pimiento, celery, crisp bacon, mashed sardines, salmon, shrimp or lobster.

# Cottage Cheese Stuffed Eggs

With the 6 yolks, combine ½ cup cottage cheese, 1 teaspoon each chopped chives and parsley. Add ½ teaspoon salt, ⅛ teaspoon pepper, 1 tablespoon salad dressing, ½ teaspoon vinegar.

Courtesy of Minute Tapioca

# Whole Strawberry Omelet

**2 tablespoons quick-cooking tapioca**
**¾ teaspoon salt**
**⅛ teaspoon pepper**
**¾ cup milk**
**1 tablespoon butter**
**4 eggs, separated**
**Sugar**
**1 package (1 pound) frozen whole strawberries, thawed**

Combine tapioca, salt, pepper, and milk in saucepan. Cook and stir over medium heat until mixture comes to a boil. Stir in butter. Remove from heat and allow to cool slightly.

Meanwhile, beat egg whites until they will form stiff shiny peaks. Beat egg yolks until thick and lemon colored. Gradually blend tapioca mixture into egg yolks. Fold tapioca mixture into the egg whites.

Pour into a hot, buttered, 10-inch skillet. Cook over low heat 3 minutes. Then bake in a moderate oven (350°F.) for 15 minutes. Omelet is sufficiently cooked when a knife inserted comes out clean. Sprinkle with sugar. Cut across center at right angles to handle of pan, being careful not to cut all the way through. Carefully fold from handle to opposite side and serve on hot platter. Again, sprinkle with sugar. Serve with berries. Makes 4 servings.

# Individual Lemon Soufflés

**6 eggs, separated**
**1 cup sugar**
**1½ teaspoons grated lemon rind**
**2 tablespoons lemon juice**

Heat oven to 325° F. (slow). Beat egg yolks until foamy. Slowly beat in ½ cup sugar, then lemon rind and juice. Add remaining sugar to egg whites. Beat until stiff, but not dry. Fold half the beaten whites thoroughly into yolk mixture. Fold in remaining whites using 8 slow strokes. Turn into 6 lightly buttered and sugared individual molds, filling them three-quarters full. Bake uncovered in 325° F. oven for 35 minutes. Serve at once. Makes 6 servings.

# Cottage Cheese-Corn Rolls

**2 cartons (8-ounce) creamed cottage cheese**
**1 egg, slightly beaten**
**1 cup fine dry bread crumbs**
**2 tablespoons finely chopped onion**
**1 can (12 ounce) niblet corn with peppers and pimiento, drained**
**¾ teaspoon salt**
**¼ teaspoon black pepper**
**½ teaspoon Worcestershire sauce**
**3 tablespoons butter**

**Combine all ingredients except ¼ cup of the bread crumbs and the butter. Divide mixture into 8 equal portions. Shape each portion as a cylinder or log and roll in crumbs until all surfaces are coated. Refrigerate at least ½ hour. Heat butter in frying pan until bubbling; place rolls in frying pan and fry, turning as needed, until golden brown. Serve with sour cream or tomato sauce. Makes 8 servings.**

The Borden Co.

# Fried Eggs, Sunny-Side-Up

Heat a thin layer of butter or bacon fat in a skillet until just hot enough to sizzle a drop of water. Break eggs into a saucer and slip into the hot skillet. Reduce heat immediately to low. Cook, 3 to 4 minutes, spooning the fat over the eggs. Sprinkle with salt and pepper and serve. To make Fried Eggs Over, when whites are set, turn the eggs and cook to the desired doneness.

# Baked Egg-Cheese Sandwiches

Trim the crusts from 8 slices of bread. Spread 4 slices with butter, then with mustard. Place in a flat baking dish. Slice 4 hard-cooked eggs, and arrange on bread. Top each with a slice of cheese and a second slice of bread, making 4 sandwiches in the dish. Beat 4 eggs; combine with 2 cups milk and ½ teaspoon salt. Pour evenly over sandwiches. Sprinkle with paprika and bake in a slow oven (325° F.) for 45 minutes or until an inserted knife comes out clean. Makes 4 servings.

## Eggs in Aspic

**1 envelope unflavored gelatin**
**2 cups well-seasoned chicken broth**
**1 teaspoon instant minced onion**
**½ teaspoon Ac'cent**
**4 hard-cooked eggs, halved lengthwise**
**2 pimientos, cut in strips**
**Chopped parsley and chives**
**Salad greens**
**Mayonnaise**

Soften gelatin in ½ cup of the chicken broth. Dissolve over hot water or low heat. Add to remaining broth with onion and Ac'cent. Pour half into a 10 x 6 x 2-inch pan. Chill until firm. Chill remaining half until thickened. Arrange eggs, cut side down, on firm mixture. Make a cross of pimiento on each. Sprinkle with herbs. Spoon remaining thickened mixture over eggs. Chill until firm. Cut in squares, and serve on greens on individual plates, with mayonnaise. Makes 4 servings.

## Layered Tomato-and-Cottage-Cheese Salad

**2 cups cottage cheese**
**½ cup mayonnaise**
**1 green onion, chopped**
**6 stuffed olives, chopped**
**Salt and pepper**
**6 large tomatoes**
**Lettuce**

Mix cottage cheese, mayonnaise, green onion, and olives. Season with salt and pepper. Cut a thin slice from stem ends of tomatoes; remove cores; cut each tomato into three slices. Put slices together with cheese mixture to make 6 servings. Serve on lettuce, Romaine, escarole, or other salad greens, and top with remaining cheese mixture. Makes 6 servings.

## Cheese Fondue

**3 tablespoons butter or margarine**
**5 slices bread cut in cubes or strips**
**1 cup (¼ pound) Processed American cheese, shredded**
**1 large egg, beaten**
**1 cup milk**
**½ teaspoon salt**
**⅛ teaspoon dry mustard**
**Dash of pepper**

Heat oven to moderate (350° F.). Melt the butter or margarine in a skillet. Add bread, and toss until lightly browned. Grease a 1 quart casserole. Alternate layers of bread then cheese in the casserole. Combine egg, milk and seasonings. Pour over bread and cheese. Set casserole in a pan containing 1 inch of water. Bake for 40 minutes. Makes 4 servings.

# Poultry and Fish

**Hints and helps on how to make the best use of these high-protein, low-waste foods.**

CHICKEN now comes Ready-To-Cook. It is drawn and cleaned and ready to pop in the oven. It may be fresh or frozen. It may also be whole, halved, quartered or disjointed. Many are cut up and tray packed in transparent wrap.

**How Much To Buy:** Figure on ¾ to 1 pound per person.

### What Kind Of Chicken To Buy

**For Frying or Broiling.** Buy broiler-fryers weighing from 1½ to 4 pounds. Use chickens 2½ pounds or under for broiling and have them split in half. Use chickens from 1½ to 4 pounds for frying. Have the smaller ones cut in quarters and the larger ones disjointed.

**For Roasting.** Buy a plump chicken weighing around 3 to 4 pounds, or a capon weighing more than 5 pounds.

**For Stewing or Fricasseeing.** Buy a stewing chicken or a fat hen weighing from 3½ to 6 pounds.

*To Store Uncooked Chicken:* Keep frozen chicken frozen until ready to use. Allow sufficient time for defrosting before cooking, 1 to 3 days in the refrigerator or 2 to 4 hours at room temperature. Cook promptly after defrosting.

Refrigerate tray-packed chickens as they come from the store. Wrap other fresh chicken loosely in foil or waxed paper and refrigerate. Use cut-up chickens within 1 or 2 days. Whole chickens may be kept slightly longer.

*To Store Cooked Chicken:* Refrigerate leftover chicken and gravy in well-covered containers as soon as possible after the meal. Remove stuffing if there is any, and refrigerate it separately in a well-covered container.

**Timetable For Roasting**

| Ready-To-Cook Weight | Oven Temperature | Time, Stuffed Bird |
|---|---|---|
| 1½ to 2½ lbs. | 325°F. | 1¼ to 2 hours |
| 2½ to 3½ lbs. | 325°F. | 2 to 3 hours |
| 3½ to 4¾ lbs. | 325°F. | 3 to 3½ hours |
| 4¾ to 6 lbs. | 325°F. | 3½ to 4 hours |

## Roast Chicken

Allow 1¼ cups stuffing per pound of ready-to-cook bird, 1 cup per pound of dressed bird. Combine the stuffing ingredients just before stuffing the bird. Stuff just before roasting. Rub cavity of bird with ½ to 1 teaspoon salt. Stuff body and wishbone cavities lightly. Close by placing skewers across the body opening and lacing shut with cord. Tie the drumsticks to the tail and fasten neck skin to the back with a skewer. Twist wing tips to lay under the back. Place bird on a rack in a shallow open pan. Brush the skin with an unsalted fat. Cover the top of the chicken with a fat-moistened thin cloth or a loose cap of aluminum foil, but do not wrap the bird in foil or cloth. Roast according to the timetable. If cloth dries during cooking, moisten with fat from bottom of pan. When bird is two-thirds done, cut the string between drumstick and tail. The bird is done when the drumstick meat feels very soft when pressed with the fingers and the drumstick-thigh bone, when grasped at the end of the leg, moves easily. Serve with cranberry sauce, parsley potatoes, mixed vegetables, lemon ice.

*Tip:* In cooking all kinds of poultry remember these don'ts—don't add any water, don't cover, don't sear at high temperatures, don't pierce the skin, don't overcook.

## Crusty Fried Chicken

Use young chickens which have been halved, quartered or disjointed into 11 or 12 pieces, each with its own section of skin. For each pound of chicken blend together ¼ cup flour, 1 teaspoon salt, 1 teaspoon paprika, ⅛ teaspoon pepper, ¼ teaspoon celery salt. Place in a paper bag. Add chicken and shake bag with 2 or 3 pieces at a time until all are evenly coated. Reserve leftover flour for gravy. Heat ½ inch of fat (part butter or margarine) in a deep, heavy skillet. Place meaty pieces in skillet, skin-side-down. Slip less meaty pieces in as chicken browns. When brown, cover tightly and cook slowly 20 to 40 minutes depending on the size and thickness of the pieces of chicken. Uncover the last 5 to 10 minutes to crisp the skin. Remove to a warm platter and make gravy.

**To Oven Fry Chicken.** Place ¼ cup butter or margarine in a shallow baking pan. Heat until bubbly. Place floured chicken in pan and cook until brown on one side then the other in a hot oven, 400° F. It takes 30 to 40 minutes.

**To Barbecue Chicken.** Either fry or oven-fry the chicken and when brown, pour over a sauce made of lemon juice, Worcestershire sauce, thyme, catsup, sugar and Tabasco, using ½ cup per pound of chicken.

Broiler Council

# Chicken Stoup

**1 broiler-fryer chicken, cut in serving pieces**
**¼ cup (½ stick) butter or margarine**
**2 cups sliced celery**
**1 large onion, chopped**
**1 green pepper, cut in strips and halved**
**2 cups water**
**3 medium potatoes, quartered**
**2 teaspoons salt**
**½ teaspoon paprika**
**¼ teaspoon black pepper**
**¼ teaspoon thyme**
**1 tablespoon Worcestershire sauce**
**1 can (1 pound) tomatoes**
**1 can (1 pound) whole kernel corn**

Melt butter in 5 or 6-quart kettle over medium heat; add chicken and brown on both sides. Remove chicken; add celery, onion, and green pepper to kettle and cook 5 minutes, stirring often. Add water, potatoes, salt, paprika, black pepper, thyme, Worcestershire sauce, and chicken; simmer 30 minutes. Add tomatoes and corn; simmer 10 to 15 minutes, until chicken is tender. Serve with corn sticks. (Serve in soup plates and eat with knife, fork and spoon.) Makes 4 to 6 servings.

# Deep-Dish Chicken Pies

**4-pound ready-to-cook fowl**
**1 tablespoon salt**
**1 stalk celery and leaves, chopped**
**1 small onion, sliced**
**6 tablespoons flour**
**½ cup cream**
**¼ pound ham, chopped**
**1½ cups cooked peas**
**½ cup diced, cooked celery**
**1 tablespoon minced parsley**
**6 or 8 small cooked onions**
**2 cups all-purpose flour**
**⅓ cup corn meal**
**1 teaspoon salt**
**⅔ cup softened lard**
**¼ cup water**

Place fowl in water to barely cover. Add salt, celery and onion. Cover and simmer for 2½ to 3 hours or until chicken is tender. Remove chicken; strain and measure 3 cups broth. Add flour stirred smooth in cream; simmer for 6 minutes. Remove chicken meat from bones in large pieces. Combine with ham, peas, celery and parsley. Place an onion and an equal division of chicken mixture in each of 6 or 8 individual casseroles. Pour broth over. Prepare crust by mixing flour, corn meal and salt; cut in lard. Sprinkle with water mixing with a fork until dough is moist enough to hold together though not sticky. Roll on a lightly floured board to ⅛ inch thickness and cut in circles 1 inch larger than top of casseroles. Place rounds on pies and crimp edges. Prick tops and bake in a hot oven 425°F. for 25 minutes or until golden brown on top. Makes 6 or 8 pies.

# Chicken Curry Buffet

**5-pound stewing chicken, cut in pieces**
**⅓ cup butter or margarine (part chicken fat may be used)**
**¼ cup minced onion**
**2 tablespoons curry powder**
**½ cup flour, scant**
**1½ cups milk**
**2 cups chicken broth**
**¼ teaspoon sugar**
**Salt**
**2 tablespoons sherry**

Steam chicken in kettle or pressure cooker until tender. Melt butter, and sauté onion until limp and golden. Blend in curry powder and flour. Gradually add milk and strained chicken broth; cook, stirring constantly, until mixture is thickened and smooth. Transfer to a double boiler. Add sugar and salt to taste. Remove cooked chicken meat from bones, cut in fairly good-sized pieces and add to sauce. Cover and cook over gently boiling water for 30 minutes. Just before serving, add sherry. Serve with rice and any or all of the following condiments—chutney (a "must,") shredded coconut, diced banana, sieved hard-cooked egg, crumbled crisp bacon, chopped salted peanuts. Serves 6 to 8.

# Jambolette

**3½-pound dressed fryer, cut in pieces**
**Salt**
**Pepper**
**Flour**
**3 tablespoons butter or margarine**
**3 tablespoons olive or salad oil**
**1 cup raw rice**
**2 green peppers, sliced thin**
**½ cup finely chopped celery**
**½ cup finely chopped onion**
**1 clove garlic, minced**
**1 bay leaf**
**¼ teaspoon thyme**
**Dash Tabasco**
**3-oz. can sliced mushrooms and juice**
**½ cup white wine**
**2 10½-oz. cans condensed tomato soup**
**1 cup water**

**Dust chicken with salt, pepper and flour. Sauté in hot butter and oil until nicely browned all over. Remove chicken pieces and sauté rice, green peppers, celery, onion and garlic for 15 minutes. Add chicken and remaining ingredients. Cover and cook for 25 minutes or until rice is tender. Stir occasionally and add water if needed. Serves 4 to 5.**

# Popovers with Creamed Chicken

**1 cup flour**
**½ teaspoon salt**
**2 eggs**
**1 cup milk**
**3 tablespoons butter or margarine**
**2 tablespoons flour**
**¾ cup chicken broth**
**1 cup cooked or canned chicken, cubed**
**⅓ cup canned drained mushrooms, chopped**
**½ teaspoon salt or seasoned salt**
**Dash nutmeg**
**1 egg**
**¼ cup cream**
**1 tablespoon sherry**

**Sift 1 cup flour; measure and sift again with salt. Beat eggs with rotary beater until thick and lemon colored; gradually add milk and 1 tablespoon melted butter. Stir in salted flour. Beat until mixture is smooth. Fill buttered custard cups a little less than half full. Bake in oven preheated to 425°F. about 40 minutes. Meanwhile, melt remaining 2 tablespoons butter and blend in 2 tablespoons flour; slowly add broth. Cook and stir until thickened. Add chicken, mushrooms, seasoned salt and nutmeg; heat through. Beat egg, cream and sherry together, then into chicken mixture. Split sides of hot popovers and fill with creamed chicken. Serves 6.**

# Crispy Broiled Chicken

Place chickens split in half lengthwise on the broiling pan. Rub the entire surface with lemon juice. Coat liberally with melted butter or margarine. Combine 1 teaspoon salt, 1 teaspoon sugar, ¼ teaspoon paprika and ⅛ teaspoon pepper for each half. Sprinkle over chicken. Place skin side down in the broiler pan (not rack) and place 6 to 9 inches from heat. Broil slowly for 40 to 60 minutes, turning and brushing with melted butter or margarine two or three times to insure even browning. Serve the pan drippings over the chicken. Serve with baked potatoes, asparagus with hollandaise sauce, combination salad, jelly roll.

# Hot Chicken Sandwich

**2 cups canned apple sauce**
**1 teaspoon prepared horseradish**
**1 tablespoon prepared mustard**
**1 tablespoon cornstarch**
**2 tablespoons cold water**
**1 cup chicken bouillon**
**8 slices bread, toasted**
**Sliced cold chicken**

Combine apple sauce, horseradish and mustard. Blend cornstarch and water until smooth. Combine chicken soup, 1 cup of the apple sauce mixture and cornstarch; cook until slightly thickened. Spread 4 slices toast with remaining 1 cup of seasoned apple sauce. Top with chicken slices and remaining toast. Serve with the hot apple sauce gravy. Makes 4 servings.

Processed Apples Institute, Inc.

# Chicken Cacciatore

Use a 2½ pound to 3½ pound chicken disjointed. Brown the chicken in ½ cup fat, preferably olive oil. Add 1 medium onion, thinly sliced and 1 clove garlic, finely minced and cook until onion is golden. Add 1 can (1 lb. 13 oz.) tomatoes, 1½ teaspoons salt, ¼ teaspoon pepper, ½ teaspoon oregano and cover. Simmer 40 to 50 minutes until chicken is tender and sauce thickened. Add ½ cup white wine the last 15 minutes of cooking. Makes 4 to 5 servings. Serve with still-chewy spaghetti, leaf spinach, lettuce and green pepper salad, fresh fruit.

# Chicken Veronique

**2 broiler-fryer chickens, cut serving pieces**
**2 teaspoons Ac'cent**
**Salt**
**Paprika**
**½ cup butter or margarine, divided**
**1 onion, finely chopped**
**1 clove garlic, minced**
**¼ pound mushrooms, sliced**
**4 tablespoons flour**
**1 teaspoon sugar**
**2 cups bouillon**
**2 tablespoons lemon juice**
**1 cup white grapes, removed from stem**
**8 large mushroom caps, sauteed**

**Sprinkle chickens with Ac'cent, salt and paprika. Melt ¼ cup of the butter in a large skillet; add chicken and brown well; remove chicken. Add remaining ¼ cup butter, onion and garlic; cook over low heat 5 minutes. Add mushrooms, cook over medium heat 2 minutes. Blend in flour and sugar. Add bouillon and lemon juice; bring to a boil, stirring. Add chicken, cover and simmer 30 minutes or until tender. Add grapes last 5 minutes of cooking time. Arrange chicken on platter and pour over sauce. Garnish with sauteed mushroom caps. Makes 6 servings.**

**Broiler Council**

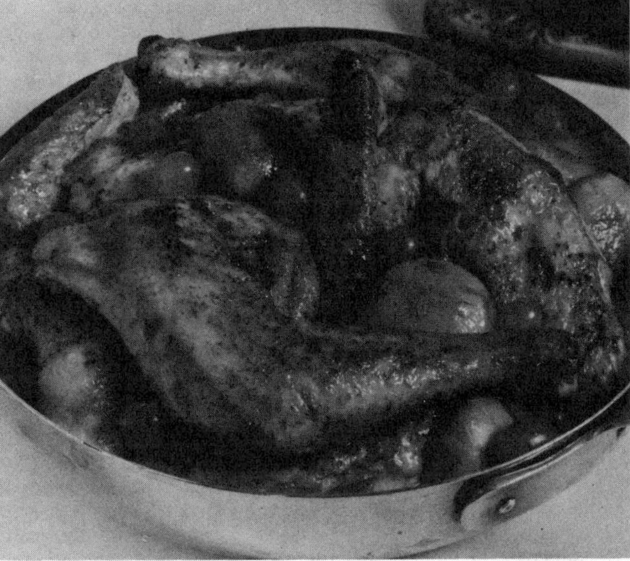

# Chicken and Macaroni Shell Hash

**½ pound macaroni shells**
**2 cups hot scalded milk**
**1 No. 2 can mixed vegetables**
**1 cup diced cooked or canned chicken**
**8-oz. can mushroom sauce**
**½ cup grated Parmesan cheese**
**1 teaspoon salt or seasoned salt**

Combine raw macaroni and hot milk in a buttered 2-quart casserole. Cover and let stand for 5 minutes. Add liquid from vegetables, chicken, mushroom sauce, cheese and salt to taste. Cover and bake 10 minutes in a hot oven 450°F. Stir in vegetables. Reduce heat to 375°F. and continue to bake, covered, for 20 minutes. Serves 4.

*Tip:* Serve leftover chicken in salads, pies, sandwiches.

## FISH

Buy fresh fish that has been stored and displayed on crushed ice, and buy it just before using. Frozen fish have the flavor and texture of fresh fish. Cook from the frozen state or thaw them just before using and never attempt to refreeze after thawing. Buy 1 pound per serving of whole fish, ½ pound per serving of dressed fish, ⅓ pound per serving of fillets, steaks and sticks. Buy lobster alive in amounts to provide the size servings you want.

### General Rule For How To Cook Fish

Cook fat fish like mackerel, pompano, salmon, ocean perch, herring, tuna, shad, whitefish and catfish by broiling or baking. Cook the lean fish like bass, haddock, pike, carp, halibut, cod, perch, flounder and whiting by frying, boiling, steaming. When broiling or baking brush with melted butter or margarine. The most important point to remember in cooking fish is not to overcook it.

# Broiled Frozen Fillets

Thaw just enough to separate the fillets, then season with salt and pepper. Brush with melted butter or margarine, or salad oil. Place on a greased pre-heated broiler rack, and place 2 or 3 inches from the source of heat. Broil until brown on one side, about 8 to 10 minutes. Baste with melted fat, turn and baste other side. Broil 8 to 10 minutes and serve promptly. To broil steaks, like salmon steak, sprinkle with lemon juice, salt and pepper, and place on a greased rack in a pre-heated broiler. Place 2 inches from the source of heat and broil 8 minutes on each side, turning fish carefully so as not to break it.

# Tuna Hominy Bake

**1 can (1 lb. 13 oz.) hominy**
**1 can (7 oz.) tuna**
**2 tablespoons oil from the can of tuna**
**1½ tablespoons flour**
**½ teaspoon salt**
**1½ cups tomato juice**
**1 tablespoon minced onion or ½ teaspoon onion powder**
**½ cup coarsely chopped ripe olives**

Drain the hominy. Drain the tuna saving the oil. Place 2 tablespoons of the oil in a saucepan. Blend in flour and salt. Gradually stir in tomato juice. Cook, stirring constantly, until thickened. Add onion and ripe olives. Place ⅔ of the hominy in a greased baking dish. Cover with pieces of tuna. Add remainder of hominy. Pour sauce over the hominy and bake in a moderately hot oven (375° F.) for 30 minutes. Makes 4 to 6 servings. Serve with carrot and raisin salad, broiled grapefruit.

# Baked Stuffed Fish

**6 pounds dressed fish (head, tail, fins, entrails removed)**
**Salt**
**¾ cup butter or margarine**
**6 cups toasted bread crumbs or day-old bread crumbs**
**4 tablespoons lemon juice**
**3 tablespoons chopped onion**
**2 tablespoons capers**
**2 tablespoons parsley flakes**
**¾ teaspoon each, salt, celery seed, thyme, marjoram**
**½ teaspoon pepper**

Heat oven to moderate (350° F.). Wash the whole fish. Pat dry with paper towels. Sprinkle inside and out with salt. Melt butter or margarine and toss lightly together with remaining ingredients. Stuff fish loosely and close with skewers and string, or a needle. Place fish on a shallow greased baking dish. Brush with melted fat. Bake for 1 to 1½ hours, basting occasionally with melted fat. Serve with scalloped tomatoes, succotash, lemon meringue pie.

# Sweet and Pungent Shrimp

**1 pound shrimp, fresh or frozen**
**1 flat can sliced pineapple**
**½ cup brown sugar**
**½ cup vinegar**
**2 tablespoons soy sauce**
**¼ cup water**
**3 tablespoons cornstarch**
**1 green pepper, cut in strips**
**1 tomato, cut into wedges**

Clean and cook shrimp. Drain syrup from pineapple into a saucepan. Cut pineapple slices in half and reserve. Add brown sugar, vinegar, soy sauce and 1 cup water to pineapple syrup. Bring to boil. Combine cornstarch and ¼ cup water. Add to sugar mixture. Cook stirring constantly until thickened. Add green pepper, pineapple, and tomato wedges. Cook 2 minutes. Add shrimp and cook to heat shrimp through. Serve immediately. Makes 4 servings.

Shrimp Association of the Americas

# Ginger Crisp Fillets

Thaw the fillets just enough to separate. Combine 1 cup very finely crushed corn flakes, ½ teaspoon salt and ½ teaspoon powdered ginger. Beat 2 eggs with a dash of salt and pepper. Dip fillets in crumbs, then egg, then crumbs again. Brown in hot fat in a skillet. Serve the fillets with minted peas, either French fried or mashed potatoes, cucumber and tomato salad, peach shortcake.

# Fish Stick Kabobs

Heat the broiler. Cut the fish sticks in thirds. On 6 inch skewers, alternate fish sticks and 2 or more of the following: bacon squares, mushroom crowns, pineapple chunks, dill pickle pieces, onion slices, tomato chunks, green pepper squares. Combine melted butter, minced onion, lemon juice, Worcestershire, dried savory or thyme. Brush over fish and vegetables. Sprinkle with salt and pepper. Broil 2 to 3 inches from the source of heat, turning until fish sticks are heated and vegetables lightly cooked.

# Quick Sardines Creole

**1 small onion, sliced**
**½ green pepper, diced**
**1 tablespoon sardine oil**
**⅛ teaspoon chili powder**
**1 teaspoon salt**
**⅛ teaspoon pepper**
**1 can (3¼ oz.) sardines**
**1 can (10½ oz.) condensed tomato soup, undiluted**
**¾ cup quick cooking rice**

Place onion, green pepper and oil in a saucepan. Heat until onion is golden. Add chili powder, salt, pepper, sardines and soup. Simmer over very low heat. Prepare rice according to the package directions. Place ring of rice around the edge of a round platter. Fill center with sardine mixture. Makes 2 servings. Serve with crisply cooked cabbage, carrot sticks and radishes, orange Bavarian cream.

# Pan-Fried Smelts

**2 pounds smelts**
**1 teaspoon salt**
**¼ teaspoon pepper**
**½ cup flour**
**1 egg, lightly beaten**
**1 tablespoon water**
**Bread crumbs**
**¼ cup fat**

Wipe smelts with damp cloth. Sprinkle with flour which has been seasoned with salt and pepper. Dip in combined egg and water, then roll in bread crumbs. Brown in hot fat in a shallow frying pan. Makes 4 to 6 servings.

# Paella Mediterraneo

**1 3-pound chicken, cut up**
**4½ cups water**
**2 teaspoons salt**
**4 tablespoons salad oil**
**1 cup sliced celery**
**½ cup chopped onion**
**½ pound cooked ham**
**1 small can mushroom crowns**
**½ teaspoon saffron (optional)**
**¼ teaspoon Tabasco**
**1 pound peeled, cooked shrimp**
**1 can (1 pound) green peas**
**1½ pounds mussels or clams in shells or 1 can (8 ounces) minced clams**
**4 cups packaged precooked rice**

Cover chicken giblets, neck and back with water. Simmer 1 hour. Measure 4 cups broth. Sprinkle remaining chicken with half the salt. Brown lightly in oil. Add celery, onions. Cook about 5 minutes. Cube ham and add. Drain liquid from mushrooms. Add liquid to broth with remaining salt, saffron and Tabasco. Add to chicken mixture with mushrooms, shrimp. peas and mussels. Bring to boil. Sprinkle in rice. Toss until rice is dampened. Simmer uncovered 5 minutes. Makes 8 servings.

Pan-American Coffee Bureau

Western Growers Association

# Fish and Vegetables on a Stick

1 pound fillet of sole, fresh or frozen
½ cup teriyaki marinade*
4 mushroom caps
2 large bell peppers, cut in squares
16 cherry tomatoes
2 large zucchini, parboiled for 4 minutes, cut in chunks

With scissors cut sole into long strips. Marinate for 30 minutes in the teriyaki marinade. Then thread on bamboo skewers alternating with mushroom caps and bell pepper squares. On other skewers alternate zucchini and tomatoes and bell pepper squares to make an interesting design. Broil sole kebabs for 5 to 7 minutes, 4 inches from flame, turning once. Broil tomato kebabs 3 to 4 minutes, 4 inches from the flame, turning once.

### *Teriyaki Marinade

½ cup soy sauce
1 tablespoon cooking oil
1 tablespoon sugar
½ teaspoon ginger

Combine all ingredients and blend well.

# Deviled Tuna

1 tablespoon chopped onion
1 can (4-ounce) sliced mushroom, drained
¼ cup butter or margarine
¼ cup flour
½ teaspoon salt
½ teaspoon dry mustard
¼ teaspoon paprika
⅛ teaspoon ground black pepper
Dash cayene pepper
1½ cups milk
½ teaspoon Worcestershire sauce
1 teaspoon lemon juice
2 hard-cooked eggs, sliced
1 (7 ounce) can tuna, drained
Round buttery crackers

Saute onion and mushrooms in butter or margarine. Stir in next 6 ingredients. Add milk, Worcestershire sauce and lemon juice. Cook stirring constantly until sauce thickens. Add sliced eggs and tuna. Heat, serve over crackers. Makes 4 to 6 servings.

# Fish Cutlets

1 pound fish, cooked and flaked
1 egg, slightly beaten
½ cup milk
½ teaspoon salt
2 tablespoons pickle relish
1 cup fine bread crumbs, divided
¼ cup fat

Blend together fish, egg, milk, salt, relish and ¾ cup of the bread crumbs. Shape into patties or cutlets, dredge in remaining crumbs. Fry in hot fat until brown. Serve with tomato sauce. Makes 6 to 8 cutlets.

# Tuna-Cheese Bake

¼ cup salad oil
2 cups (8 ounce) uncooked macaroni shells
½ cup chopped onion
½ cup chopped green pepper
1 tablespoon flour
2½ cups milk
1 cup chopped or shredded sharp process cheese
1 can flaked tuna, drained
Pimiento-stuffed green olives

Heat oil in skillet. Stir in macaroni shells, onion and pepper. Sprinkle with flour. Cook and stir over low heat until macaroni yellows, about 10 minutes. Stir in milk, cheese and tuna. Turn mixture into a greased casserole and sprinkle with crumbs, if desired. Bake in a hot oven (400°F.) about 35 minutes, or until macaroni shells are very tender. Garnish with sliced, pimiento-stuffed green olives. Makes 6 servings.

# Seafood Medley

½ pound scallops
1 teaspoon salt
1 cup water
½ pint oysters
1 cup shrimp
3 tablespoons butter or margarine
1 cup sliced mushrooms
3 tablespoons flour
½ cup light cream
2 tablespoons sherry
2 teaspoons lemon juice
3 cups rice cereal
2 tablespoons butter or margarine
½ cup grated cheese
Dash of paprika
1½ tablespoons finely chopped onion

Cut scallops into small cubes; add ½ teaspoon salt and the water. Bring to boiling point and simmer for 5 minutes. Drain, reserving stock. Drain oysters reserving liquor. Combine scallop stock, oyster liquor and shrimp stock, if any, to make 1 cup liquid. If more liquid is needed to make this amount, add milk. Heat butter; add mushrooms and onion; cook over low heat about 5 minutes until soft but not browned. Blend in flour and slowly add sea food liquid. Cook over low heat, stirring constantly, until thickened. Add cream, sherry, lemon juice, remaining salt, scallops, oysters and shrimp. Place in greased scallop shells or ramekins. Sprinkle with finely crushed rice cereal which has been mixed with melted butter and grated cheese. Sprinkle with paprika. Bake in a moderate oven (375°F.) about 25 minutes or until browned. Makes 6 servings.

# Codfish and Potato Casserole

1 package (12 ounces) frozen potato patties
¼ pound salted codfish, freshened*
2 tablespoons finely chopped onion
1 cup light cream
1 tablespoon butter

*To freshen salted codfish, place under cold running water about 5 minutes; then cover with cold water and let stand overnight. Drain and flake.

Place the potato patties in a greased 1½-quart casserole. Add the codfish; then add the onion. Pour on cream; dot with butter. Cover and bake in a moderate oven (350°F.) for 1 hour, or until potatoes are tender, stirring with a fork to break up potato patties after 15 and 45 minutes of baking. Garnish with slices of canned cranberry sauce cut in shape of fish, if desired. Makes 3 or 4 servings.

Courtesy of Birds Eye Potato Patties

# Tuna in Cheese Biscuit Baskets

2 tablespoons butter or margarine
2 tablespoons flour
1 cup milk
2 7-ounce cans tuna, drained and flaked
2 hard-cooked eggs, diced
3 tablespoons diced pimiento
3 cups biscuit mix
½ cup grated cheese, firmly packed
¾ cup milk

Melt butter over low heat. Stir in flour. Add milk and cook over low heat, stirring constantly until thickened. Add tuna, eggs, and pimiento. Keep warm. Measure biscuit mix into a bowl and stir in cheese. Add milk and stir only enough to moisten biscuit mix. Turn out on floured board and knead gently. Pat out to a rectangle 8 inches wide and ½ inch thick. Cut into 8 squares. Press each square down into cups of large greased muffin pan, covering sides and bottom. Spoon in creamed tuna mixture. Bake in a hot oven (425°F.) 20 to 25 minutes. Makes 6 to 8 servings.

# Bouillabaisse

1 medium carrot, sliced
2 medium onions, sliced
1 clove garlic
4 tablespoons butter or margarine
3 pounds fish, cooked and flaked (cod, whiting, haddock halibut, etc.)
1 cup tomatoes
1 bay leaf
2 cups fish stock or water
1 dozen oysters, clams or scallops
1 cup shrimp or crab
2 teaspoons salt
½ teaspoon pepper
2 tablespoons lemon juice
¼ cup cooking sherry

Cook carrot, onion, and garlic together in butter until golden brown, remove garlic. Add fish, tomatoes, bay leaf and stock. Cook over simmer heat 15 minutes. Add remaining ingredients except sherry. Continue cooking 5 minutes. Add sherry and serve immediately. Makes 6 to 8 servings.

# Spiced Salmon

1 can (1 lb.) red salmon
1 cup vinegar
1 teaspoon whole cloves
½ teaspoon allspice berries
8 whole peppercorns
¼ teaspoon salt

Remove skin and bones from salmon. Combine all the other ingredients in a saucepan and bring to a boil. Pour over fish. Cover and let stand 2 hours. Drain, chill and serve as a salad or on lettuce as an appetizer.

# Mardi Gras Jambalaya

6 cups water
1 teaspoon salt
1 bay leaf
1 stalk celery with leaves
2 pounds shrimp
1 1½-inch thick slice cooked ham (about ¾ pound)
4 tablespoons butter
¼ cup finely chopped onion
1 garlic clove, minced
1½ cups raw white rice
1 can (1 pound) tomatoes
¾ cup bouillon or water
1 teaspoon salt
½ teaspoon Tabasco
1 can (1 pound) okra

*Day Before:* Combine water, salt, bay leaf and celery in a deep saucepan. Bring to a boil. Add shrimp; return to boil, then reduce heat and simmer 5 minutes. Drain shrimp and cool quickly. Shell and clean. Cut ham into ½-inch cubes.

*To Serve:* Melt butter; add onion and garlic and cook until tender, but not brown. Stir in rice and toss lightly to coat with butter. Add tomatoes, bouillon, salt and Tabasco. Quickly bring mixture to boiling; reduce heat and cover. Cook, stirring occasionally, about 20 minutes. Add shrimp, ham and okra. Continue to cook, uncovered, until heated thoroughly, about 10 minutes. Makes 6 to 8 servings.

McIlhenney's Tabasco

# Seafood à la King

2 tablespoons chopped green pepper
2 tablespoons butter or margarine
2 tablespoons flour
½ teaspoon dry mustard
½ teaspoon salt
1 cup tomato juice
1 egg, slightly beaten
¾ cup milk
¾ cup grated cheese
1 cup flaked seafood
Toast squares

Cook green pepper in butter until soft; blend in flour and seasonings. Add combined tomato juice, egg and milk; cook over low heat, stirring constantly, only until thick. Remove from heat, add cheese and stir until melted. Add seafood; heat. Serve immediately on toast squares. Makes 4 servings.

# Broiled Mackerel with Onion Slices

**4 1-pound mackerel**
**3 onions, sliced**
**2 tablespoons butter**

Have mackerel cleaned but not split. Rub inside of fish with salt. Make several slits on each side of the fish. Slip a slice of onion and a dot of butter in each slit on the top side, pushing the slice of onion well into the slit. Place fish in preheated broiling compartment, about 6 inches from source of heat. Broil for 3 minutes, turn and insert onion slices and dots of butter. Broil 6 minutes or until fish flakes easily when tested with a fork. Makes 4 servings.

# Meats

**Here's how to buy various cuts of meat and use them as ingredients of savory dishes.**

### How Much To Buy

- A pound of meat with connective tissue and bone (shank, brisket, short ribs, spareribs, breast of veal and lamb) will give 1 to 2 servings.
- A pound of meat with a medium amount of bone (steaks, chops, shoulder and loin roast of beef, veal, pork, lamb, and smoked ham) will give 2 servings.
- A pound of meat with very little bone (center cut roasts and steaks from the beef round, leg of lamb, veal and pork) will give 2 to 3 servings.
- A pound of meat with no bone (ground meat, boneless stew meat, boneless roasts, liver, variety meats) will give 3 to 4 servings.

### How To Store

**Fresh Meats.** Remove peach colored butcher paper. Cover loosely with waxed paper. Place in the coldest part of the refrigerator and use within 2 to 3 days. Pre-packaged meats may be left in their original wrappings and placed in the coldest part of the refrigerator. Use within 3 days. To freeze, overwrap the transparent covering with a moisture-vaporproof freezer paper.

**Ground Meat.** Unwrap, cover loosely with waxed paper. Store as above but use within 24 hours, or wrap tightly and freeze.

**Variety Meats.** Liver, heart and kidney are treated just like ground meat.

**Cooked Meats.** Cool, cover tightly, and refrigerate. Do not cut, grind or slice until ready to use.

**Frozen Meats.** Store in the freezing unit in the unopened cartons. Keep frozen until ready to use. Use promptly after thawing. Do not refreeze.

### How To Cook Frozen Meats

Use the meats that have been longest in the freezer first. Most frozen meats may be cooked without thawing, or thaw in the unopened package. Figure thawing time from the size, shape, kind, cut and wrapping. A large roast will thaw in 24 to 72 hours in the refrigerator or in 5 to 12 hours at room temperature. Follow the same time and temperature directions for cooking thawed meats as for fresh. If you do not thaw, allow 15 to 20 minutes more cooking time per pound.

### Meat Cookery

Steady, low temperatures are money-savers because they cause less shrinkage and produce juicier, more flavorful roasts. The two principle methods used in meat cookery are dry heat, used for the more tender cuts, and moist heat, used for the less tender cuts.

### Oven Roasting (Dry Heat)

**Cuts to use.**

Beef: rib, sirloin
Pork: loin, shoulder, fresh or cured ham
Veal: rump, loin, shoulder
Lamb: leg, shoulder, ribs

**Method.**

1. Season with salt and pepper.
2. Place in open roasting pan, fat side up.
3. Insert meat thermometer into the thickest part of the meat.
4. Do not cover, do not add water, do not baste.
5. Roast in a slow oven (see temperature chart).
6. Roast to desired degree of doneness (see chart on time).

*Tip.* A meat thermometer takes the guesswork out of roasting. Insert the thermometer in the thickest part of the meat—not touching the bone and not resting in the fat.

### Broiling and Pan-Broiling (Dry Heat)

**Cuts to use.**

Beef: tenderloin, sirloin, porterhouse, T-bone, club, rib steaks and ground beef
Pork: Cured ham and bacon
Lamb: rib, loin, shoulder chops, ground lamb patties
Veal: loin chops

**Method—Broiling.**

1. Heat broiler for about 5 minutes.
2. Cut edges of fat about 2 inches apart to prevent curling.
3. Place meat 3 to 5 inches from source of heat. If steaks are used, they should be 1 to 2 inches thick. Thinner steaks should be pan-broiled.
4. Broil to desired brownness. Season. Turn once and broil other side to desired doneness. Season.

**Method—Pan-Broiling.**

1. Rub a heavy skillet lightly with fat trimmed from meat.
2. Heat pan until very hot. Add meat and brown well on both sides.
3. Reduce heat and turn meat occasionally.
4. Pour off fat as it accumulates so that meat will broil and not fry.

| | *1½ in. thick* | *2 in. thick* |
|---|---|---|
| To broil steaks rare | 9 min. | 16 min. |
| To broil steaks medium | 10 min. | 18 min. |
| To broil steaks well done | 12 min. | 20 min. |

### Braising and Pan-Roasting (Moist Heat)

**Cuts to use.**

Beef: chuck, short ribs, flank, round, rump, sirloin tip
Pork: chops, shoulder steaks, cutlets, fresh ham steaks
Lamb: neck slices, riblets, shanks, boneless stew meat
Veal: cutlets, steaks, chops, boneless stew meat

**Method.**

1. Brown meat in a small amount of fat in a heavy kettle. Season to taste.
2. Add a small amount of liquid—water, milk, stock or vegetable juice.
3. Cover and simmer until tender on top burners or in a slow oven (300° F.) about 40 minutes per pound.

### Stewing (Moist Heat)

**Cuts to use.**

Same as for braising.

**Method.**

1. Cut the meat in small pieces.
2. Add enough water to cover the meat. Season.
3. Cover and simmer until almost tender.
4. Add cut-up carrots, onions and potatoes the last 20 to 30 minutes.

### TIME AND TEMPERATURE CHART

| *Meat* | *Oven Temperature* | *Time Min. per lb.* | *Thermometer Temperature When Done* |
|---|---|---|---|
| **BEEF** | | | |
| Standing Rib Roast (over 5½ lbs.) | 300°F | 21—rare<br>26—medium<br>28—well done | 140°F<br>160°F<br>170°F |
| Standing Rib Roast (under 5½ lbs.) | 325°F | 25—rare<br>30—medium<br>35—well done | 140°F<br>160°F<br>170°F |
| Boneless Rib Roast | 300°F | 30—rare<br>35—medium<br>38—well done | 140°F<br>160°F<br>170°F |
| **HAM** | | | |
| Whole Ham (12 lbs. or larger) | 325°F | 10 | 150°F |
| (less than 12 lbs.) | 325°F | 12 | 150°F |
| Half Ham | 325°F | 20 | 150°F |
| Smoked Picnic | 325°F | 19 | 150°F |
| **PORK** | | | |
| Loin, shoulder or fresh ham | 350°F | 30 to 35 | 185°F |
| Fresh Picnic | 350°F | 35 to 40 | 185°F |
| **LAMB** | | | |
| Leg—5 to 6 lbs. | 325°F | 35 to 40 | 180°F |
| Shoulder—2½ to 3½ lbs. | 325°F | 35 to 40 | 180°F |
| Shoulder—rolled and boned | 325°F | 40 to 45 | 180°F |
| **VEAL** | | | |
| Shoulder—boned, rolled, stuffed | 300°F | 40 to 45 | 170°F |
| Rump, shoulder, breast, arm, blade | 300°F | 25 | 170°F |
| Loin | 300°F | 30 to 35 | 170°F |

### Types of Hams Available

**Uncooked** (cook-before-eating hams). These are the most generally available. They come whole, in halves or sliced. They require cooking before eating.

**Cooked** (ready-to-eat hams). These are completely cooked and may be sliced and served cold just as they come from the store without any additional cooking. They can also be served hot, but it is uneconomical to do so, since you can just as well buy the slightly less expensive uncooked ham for this purpose.

**Skinless and Shankless Hams.** These come cooked and uncooked and are very popular. They come whole, in halves or slices. There are actually more servings per pound since there is more edible meat and less waste.

**Canned Hams.** These are fully cooked and ready to serve hot or cold. They are boneless, skinless and defatted. Some are available already scored, glazed and decorated.

*Tip.* Leftover pork chops or pork loin can be slivered and made into chop suey or chow mein.

## VEAL

Veal is always cooked at low temperature until well done. It comes from a very young animal and is low in fat making it less suitable for broiling and pan-broiling than some of the other meats.

## VARIETY MEATS

Liver, heart, **kidney** and sweetbreads are highly nutritious and are excellent buys because there is no bone in them and practically no fat.

Best Foods

# Creamy Minced Veal

**3 tablespoons margarine**
**1 pound veal, cut into ¼-inch strips**
**1 envelope chunk chicken noodle soup mix**
**2 tablespoons corn starch**
**1½ cups water**
**2 tablespoons margarine**
**1 cup heavy cream**

Melt 3 tablespoons margarine in skillet. Add veal; saute until lightly browned. Combine soup mix and corn starch in saucepan. Gradually blend in water, then add 2 tablespoons margarine. Bring to boil, stirring constantly. Reduce heat; cover and simmer 5 minutes. Add veal and cream. Heat, but do not boil. Serve on rice or toast. Makes 3 to 4 servings.

*To prepare with cooked meat:* Substitute 2 cups diced cooked meat for sauteed veal, omitting 3 tablespoons margarine.

# Roast Pork Loin

**4 pound pork loin**
**1 teaspoon salt**
**¼ teaspoon pepper**
**½ teaspoon sage**

Sprinkle pork loin with seasonings and proceed according to the directions for oven roasting for the indicated length of time. Makes 6 servings. Serve with savory apples, made by placing cored thick apple slices in a shallow pan and topping with a mixture of 2 tablespoons lemon juice, 4 tablespoons brown sugar, 4 tablespoons catsup, 2 tablespoons melted butter or margarine and 2 tablespoons prepared horse-radish. Bake with the roast for the last 30 minutes, adding a bit of water if needed; baked sweet potatoes, buttered green beans, broiled grapefruit.

*Tip.* When buying a pork loin roast, have the backbone sawed from the ribs so that carving will be easier.

# Brazilian Beefsteak

**2 pounds beef round steak, sliced ¾-inch thick**
**¼ cup flour**
**1 teaspoon salt**
**⅛ teaspoon fresh ground pepper**
**4 tablespoons cooking oil**
**¾ cup chopped onion**
**1½ cups solid pack tomatoes**
**1 cup chicken or beef stock**
**½ cup peanut butter**

Cut steak into 6 servings. Mix flour with salt and pepper and coat meat with flour.

Heat oil in large skillet and brown meat on both sides. Remove meat and saute onion until tender, but not browned. Return meat to skillet. Add tomatoes and stock. Cover and cook over low heat 15 minutes. Stir in peanut butter and continue cooking 15 minutes or until meat is tender. Serve with rice. Makes 6 servings.

Peanut Growers of Alabama and Georgia

# Porcupine Meat Balls

**1½ pounds ground beef**
**1 teaspoon salt**
**½ teaspoon pepper**
**½ cup uncooked rice**
**1 small onion, finely minced**
**2 tablespoons fat, heated**
**1 can (10½ oz.) tomato purée**
**1 cup water**
**2 tablespoons diced green pepper**
**1 teaspoon sugar**

Combine ground beef, salt, pepper, rice and onion. Form into balls. Brown in a skillet in the hot fat. Add tomato purée, water, green pepper and sugar. Stir well. Cover and simmer slowly for 40 minutes or until rice is tender. Makes 6 to 8 servings.

# Pork Chops with Rosy Pineapple Rings

**6 pork chops, 1 inch thick**
**salt and pepper for sprinkling**
**½ cup hot water, tomato juice or bouillon**
**1 can (1 lb. 4 oz.) pineapple slices**
**½ cup red cinnamon candies**

Trim a little fat from the edges of the chops and heat in a heavy skillet. Remove the pieces of fat. Sprinkle the chops with salt and pepper and brown well in the hot fat. Add liquid, cover and cook over low heat for 45 minutes to 1 hour. Drain the syrup from the pineapple. Place in a saucepan with cinnamon candies. Heat slowly until candies have dissolved. Add pineapple slices and bring to a boil. Reduce heat, simmer 5 minutes. Chill and serve with pork chops. Serve with buttered rice, Brussels sprouts, crisp celery, prune and apricot pie.

The Aluminum Association

# Tasty Franks

**2 tablespoons bacon drippings**
**1 cup chopped onions**
**½ cup chopped green peppers**
**1½ cups all purpose barbecue sauce**
**2 tablespoons prepared mustard**
**1½ teaspoons Worcestershire sauce**
**8-10 frankfurters**

Sauté onion and green pepper in bacon drippings in a 10-inch aluminum skillet. Add barbecue sauce and seasonings, mixing well. Cover and simmer 10 minutes.

When ready to serve, heat sauce, add frankfurters, cover and simmer 10 minutes. Serve on buns.

# Veal Paprika

**1½-pound veal steak, about ½ inch thick**
**salt and pepper**
**4 tablespoons flour**
**1 tablespoon paprika**
**2 tablespoons each, fat and butter or margarine**
**1 medium onion, finely chopped**
**1 tablespoon lemon juice**
**¾ cup sour or sweet cream or undiluted evaporated milk**

Cut the veal in 4 or 5 portions. Sprinkle with salt and pepper and then with flour and paprika. Pound lightly with a knife. Heat the fat and butter in a heavy skillet, and sauté meat until lightly browned. Add onion and brown lightly. Sprinkle lemon juice over and stir to combine with pan juices. Add cream. Cover and cook *very* slowly for about 30 to 40 minutes, or until tender, adding a few tablespoons of water from time to time to prevent sticking. Serve with buttered poppy seed noodles, Bavarian red cabbage, grapefruit and romaine salad, fruit tarts.

# New England Boiled Dinner

**3 pounds corned beef**
**6 medium whole turnips**
**6 medium whole onions**
**4 potatoes, quartered**
**6 medium whole, carrots**
**1 head cabbage, cut in wedges**
**⅛ teaspoon pepper**

Modern corned beef is packaged with brine and spices included. To prepare, place meat and brine in a kettle. Cover with cold water and bring to a boil. Cover tightly and simmer 3 hours or until tender and most of the water has evaporated. One hour before serving time, add the turnips and onions. When these have cooked 15 minutes, add the potatoes, carrots and cabbage. Sprinkle with pepper. Cover and cook 45 minutes longer. Makes 6 servings. Serve with horse-radish sauce made by combining ½ cup salad dressing, ¼ cup whipped cream, ½ teaspoon salt and 2 tablespoons prepared horse-radish; radishes and ripe olives, fruit compote.

*Tip.* Leftover corned beef combines deliciously with potatoes, beets and onions to make a Red Flannel Hash meal.

# Golden Nugget Pie

2 teaspoons Ac'cent
2 pounds ground beef
1 cup evaporated milk
2 cups soft bread crumbs
2 eggs
2 teaspoons salt
2 teaspoons dry mustard
½ teaspoon pepper
½ teaspoon thyme
½ cup minced onion
4 ounces process American cheese, cut in cubes
1 envelope instant mashed potatoes

Sprinkle Ac'cent over beef in mixing bowl. Add remaining ingredients except instant potatoes. Mix with fork until blended. Turn into a 10-inch pie plate or shallow baking dish. Bake in a moderate oven (350°F.) 50 minutes. Remove from oven. Increase heat to hot (450°F.). While meat is baking, prepare potatoes according to package directions. Put through pastry tube in lattice design on top of meat. Dot with butter. Return to oven and bake 10 minutes longer. Makes 8 servings.

Ac'cent International

# Savory Liver

1 pound liver (veal, beef, pork or lamb)
French dressing
Flour seasoned with salt and pepper
2 tablespoons fat
1 green pepper, sliced
1 medium onion, sliced
1 teaspoon Worcestershire sauce
½ cup water

Cut the liver into small pieces. Marinate for several hours in the French dressing, then sprinkle with seasoned flour and brown in hot fat. Remove from pan and add green pepper and onion to fat, adding a little more fat if needed. Brown lightly. Add Worcestershire sauce, water, and stir until combined and thickened slightly. Season to taste then add liver just long enough to heat through. Makes 4 servings. Serve with brown rice, leaf spinach, tomato and cucumber salad, caramel custard.

Courtesy of Birds Eye Italian Green Beans

# Frankalaya

1 package (9 ounces) frozen Italian green beans
1½ tablespoons butter or margarine
¼ cup chopped onion
1 tablespoon chopped green pepper
2 tablespoons all-purpose flour
⅛ teaspoon salt
Dash of pepper
1 cup milk
1 pound frankfurter, cut into thirds
¾ cup grated sharp Cheddar cheese

Cook beans as directed on package. Drain if necessary. Meanwhile, melt butter in saucepan. Add onion and green pepper; sauté until tender—about 5 minutes. Blend in flour, salt, and pepper. Gradually stir in milk. Cook and stir over medium heat until sauce is thickened.

Place half of the beans in a 1-quart casserole. Add the frankfurters, cream sauce, and remaining beans. Sprinkle with cheese. Bake in a moderate oven (350°F.) for 20 minutes, or until mixture is bubbling hot and cheese is melted. Makes 4 servings.

# Savory Stew

**2 pounds boneless beef, cubed**
**seasoned flour (¼ cup flour, 2 teaspoons salt, ½ teaspoon pepper)**
**fat for browning**
**1 clove garlic**
**1 medium onion, sliced**
**water or bouillon**
**1 cup each diced potatoes, sliced carrots, celery**
**½ cup green peas**

Dredge the meat with the seasoned flour and in a heavy kettle, brown the meat in a little hot fat. Add the garlic and onion and brown. Add the water or bouillon to cover the meat. Cover and simmer for 2 hours. Add vegetables and cook 30 minutes longer. Season to taste and thicken the gravy if necessary. Makes 6 servings. Serve with crisp rolls, cucumber and tomato salad, peach custard.

*Tip.* Leftover stew combined with canned vegetables and topped with a pastry crust makes a tasty meat pie meal.

R. T. French Co.

# Potatoes-Franks Au Gratin

**1 package potatoes au gratin**
**3½ cups cold water**
**2 tablespoons butter or margarine**
**1½ cups diagonally-sliced celery**
**2 teaspoons mustard**
**1 pound frankfurters**
**salt and black pepper to taste**

Empty potatoes from package into a skillet with a tight fitting lid. Reserve envelope of cheese mix. Add water and butter. Bring to a boil. Reduce heat; cover; cook at a slow boil for 20 minutes. Meanwhile cut celery into slices about ¼-inch thick. Cut each frankfurter into four portions. When the 20 minutes are up, sprinkle the cheese mix over potatoes. Add mustard. Stir gently to blend. Add celery and frankfurters. Bring to a boil; reduce heat; cover; cook 10 minutes, stirring once or twice. Makes 6 servings.

# Braised Lamb Shanks with Vegetables

**4 lamb shanks**
**1 cut clove garlic**
**¼ cup flour**
**2 teaspoons salt**
**¼ teaspoon pepper**
**3 tablespoons salad oil**
**1 onion, sliced**
**½ cup catsup**
**12 ounces (bottle or can) beer or ale**
**8 pared carrots, quartered**
**8 small whole white onions, peeled**
**4 potatoes, peeled, cut into chunks**

Trim any extra fat from lamb shanks; rub well with cut garlic clove. Roll shanks in mixture of flour, salt and pepper to coat. Heat oil in Dutch oven or heavy kettle; add shanks and brown well on all sides, about 15 to 20 minutes. Add sliced onion, catsup and beer. Cover and simmer 1½ hours or until lamb is almost tender. Add vegetables and cook about 30 minutes longer until meat and vegetables are done. Makes 4 servings.

Brewers Association

Wine Institute

# California Jambalaya

1½ cups chopped onion (2 medium onions)
¾ cup chopped green pepper (1 medium pepper)
1 clove garlic, minced or crushed
1 bay leaf
1 teaspoon salt
2 tablespoons cooking oil
2 tablespoons butter or margarine
1½ cups raw regular brown rice
1 can (1 pound) stewed tomatoes
2 cans (14-ounce) chicken broth
¾ cup Rhine Wine, Sauterne, or other white dinner wine
1 to 2 cups diced cooked ham
1 to 2 cups diced cooked turkey or chicken

Combine all ingredients except ½ cup of the Rhine Wine, ham and turkey in a large pan or skillet. Bring to a boil, stirring; lower heat, cover and simmer about 45 minutes stirring occasionally. Remove cover, stir in ham and turkey; cook uncovered about 10 to 15 minutes longer or until rice is tender. Remove from heat and stir in remaining Rhine Wine. Garnish with chopped parsley or shredded Parmesan cheese, if desired. Makes 8 to 10 servings.

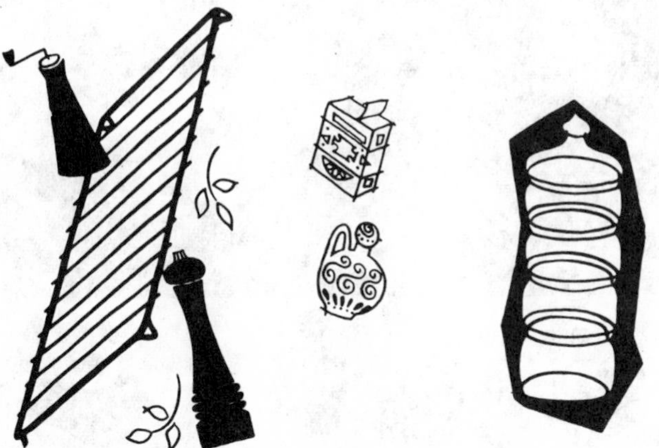

American Institute of Baking

# Hamburger Rolls with Sweet Pickle Stuffing

¼ cup butter or margarine
⅓ cup chopped onion
1 quart soft ½-inch bread cubes
½ cup piccalilli or chopped sweet pickles
½ teaspoon salt
⅛ teaspoon pepper
⅛ teaspoon sage or marjoram
¼ cup milk or water
1 pound hamburger
⅛ teaspoon pepper
1 teaspoon salt

Melt butter in a skillet; add onion and saute until tender. Pour over soft bread cubes, piccalilli, salt, pepper and sage. Add milk and mix well. Season meat with salt and pepper. Spread meat on lightly floured wax paper. Coat rolling pin with flour and roll meat into a rectangular sheet. Spread stuffing evenly on the meat, then roll up as a jelly roll by lifting waxed paper and gently rolling meat away from it. Bake in a loaf pan in a moderate oven (350°F.) for 50 minutes. Makes 6 servings.

# Beef Stew Bourbonnais

1½ pounds beef chuck, cut into 1-inch cubes
1 tablespoon shortening
1 clove garlic, minced
1 medium onion, chopped
½ teaspoon salt
⅛ teaspoon pepper
1 can (10¾ ounces) condensed tomato soup, undiluted
¾ cup red wine
¼ cup water
¼ teaspoon basil leaves, crushed
¼ teaspoon powdered thyme
½ cup tomato ketchup
3 medium carrots, cut in ½-inch diagonal pieces
1½ cups 1-inch diagonally cut celery
4 medium potatoes, pared and quartered
1 cup cooked cut green beans (optional)

Lightly brown beef in shortening. Add garlic and onion; sauté until onion is transparent. Sprinkle with salt and pepper. Stir in soup, wine and water. Cover; simmer 30 minutes. Stir in herbs and ketchup. Add carrots, celery and potatoes; cover; simmer 1½ hours or until meat and vegetables are tender. Add green beans during last few minutes of cooking to heat. Add more water if necessary. Makes 6 servings (approximately 8 cups).

H. J. Heinz Co.

# Stuffed Grilled Frankfurters with Ready-to-use Cheese Sauce

To stuff 1 pound (9) frankfurters, combine 1¼ cups (about 3 slices) fine bread crumbs, 1 tablespoon grated onion, ⅛ teaspoon black pepper, dash of rubbed sage, 1½ tablespoons melted butter and 2 tablespoons milk. Cut a deep lengthwise slit in frankfurters, brush cut surfaces with your favorite prepared mustard. Fill frankfurters with bread stuffing. Sauté 9 slices of bacon until half done. Wrap each frankfurter in a slice of bacon and fasten bacon ends with toothpicks. Broil until bacon is crisp, about 4 to 5 minutes. Meanwhile heat contents of an 8-ounce glass of ready-to-use cheese sauce in top of double boiler over hot water. Spiced peach halves topped with currant jelly are good eating with these frankfurters.

The Borden Company

American Institute of Baking

## Swedish Meat Balls

1 tablespoon shortening
⅓ cup chopped onion
1 pound ground beef
½ pound ground pork
1½ cups dry bread crumbs
2 eggs, beaten
1 tablespoon salt
1 tablespoon sugar
¼ teaspoon pepper
¼ teaspoon nutmeg
¾ cup water or milk
¼ cup melted shortening
3 beef bouillon cubes
3 cups water
5 tablespoons flour
1½ tablespoons lemon juice
3 bay leaves

Melt shortening in a skillet, add onion and sauté until tender. Combine sautéed onion, meats, dry bread crumbs, beaten eggs, salt, sugar, pepper, nutmeg and water or milk. Shape into 1½-inch balls, then brown in melted fat in a hot skillet. Remove meat balls from fat. Dissolve beef bouillon cubes in water. Blend flour into remaining fat in skillet, add bouillon water and lemon juice, stirring until thick. Add bay leaves and browned meat balls. Cook slowly for 1 hour. Makes 8 servings.

# Vegetables and Salads

**How-to make mouth-watering treats from healthful, nutritious, "must eat" vegetables.**

FROM the standpoint of nutrition as well as flavor, the best buys are vegetables at their peak—fresh, firm and free from blemishes. Occasionally, when soup is to be made, if slightly imperfect or withered vegetables are offered at a low price, they might prove satisfactory, but even here, the tastier the vegetables, the better the soup. In figuring how much of a vegetable to buy, keep in mind not only the number of people to be served, but also the number of times you can serve the vegetable while it is still at the peak of freshness.

### TO STORE VEGETABLES

Keep green leafy vegetables slightly moist in a ventilated container at refrigerator temperature (40° to 50°).

Keep tomatoes without cover at about 50°.

Asparagus is best used soon after purchase. To keep a short time stand it in about an inch of water in the refrigerator.

Shell, or husk corn, peas or lima beans just before cooking, and do not keep them even a few hours longer than necessary as they lose their delicate flavor and sugar content.

Store root vegetables like potatoes, parnsips, turnips in a dry, well-ventilated spot, at a temperature of about 60° F.

Store the strong-flavored vegetables like onions, cabbage, cauliflower, under the same conditions as the root vegetables, but not with them.

### TO BOIL VEGETABLES

**Fresh Vegetables:** Use only a small amount of boiling, salted water; cook, covered, for as short a time as possible; serve them immediately when done. Following these three simple rules will produce vegetables that will retain their color, their shape and texture and their food value. More specific cooking information is given for each vegetable in the recipes that follow, but since the age of the vegetable and the size of the pieces will affect the cooking time, only an approximate time can be given.

Overcooked green vegetables turn brown due to chemical changes in the green coloring matter. This is most likely to happen when the vegetables are cooked whole or in very large pieces since the outside may be done several minutes before the inside is tender. Bear this in mind when grooming vegetables for the pot and shred your cabbage, split the cores of Brussels sprouts and the stalks of broccoli. Cauliflower will have more flávor and better color if split into flowerets before cooking. Yellow vegetables can be cooked whole since their flavor and color are not affected by ordinary cooking.

**Frozen Vegetables:** Packaged frozen vegetables need no previous preparation and each package will have directions on it.

**Canned Vegetables:** Drain and boil down the liquid in the can to ½ its original volume, except in the case of tomatoes, asparagus and corn. Add vegetables, cover and heat slowly for 5 minutes. Season and serve.

# Scalloped Potatoes

6 medium potatoes
2 tablespoons flour
1 teaspoon salt
Dash of pepper
2 tablespoons grated onion
½ cup diced green pepper
2 tablespoons butter or margarine
2 cups milk (about), heated

Heat oven to moderate (350° F.). Wash, pare and thinly slice the potatoes. Butter a baking dish well. Place half the potatoes in baking dish. Sprinkle with half the flour, salt, pepper, onion, green pepper and butter or margarine. Add remainder of potatoes and sprinkle with remaining half of above-mentioned ingredients. Pour milk over potatoes. Cover and bake about 30 minutes. Remove cover and bake another 15 to 20 minutes or until a browned crust is formed on top.

The Borden Co.

# Ginger Glazed Carrots

6 medium to large carrots
3 tablespoons butter or margarine
3 tablespoons brown sugar
½ teaspoon ginger

Scrub, scrape and cut carrots into thin strips. Cook in boiling, salted water until tender. Drain. Heat oven to moderate (350° F). Place carrots in a shallow pan and dot with bits of butter. Sprinkle with brown sugar and ginger. Bake 10 to 15 minutes.

# Bavarian Red Cabbage

1⅓ pound head red cabbage
3 tablespoons butter or bacon drippings
1 large onion, minced
1 large tart apple, peeled and sliced
1 cup hot water
⅓ cup vinegar
2 tablespoons brown sugar
5 whole cloves
1 teaspoon salt

Shred the cabbage. Melt butter in pan in which cabbage is to be cooked. Add onion and cook slowly until soft and yellow. Add cabbage, apple, water, vinegar, sugar, cloves and salt. Toss together. Cover and cook just until cabbage is wilted. Uncover and cook 20 minutes, stirring occasionally.

Peanut Growers of Alabama & Georgia

# Southern Peanut Loaf

## (Meatless Meat Loaf)

1¼ cups crunchy peanut butter
1½ cups cooked baby lima beans
¼ cup onion, finely chopped
½ teaspoon basil
1 teaspoon salt
¼ teaspoon pepper
1¼ cups soft bread crumbs
1½ cups grated American cheese
1½ cups milk
2 tablespoons chopped parsley
4 eggs, well beaten
1½ cups well seasoned tomato sauce

Combine all ingredients except tomato sauce, mixing well. Spoon into a greased 9x5x3-inch loaf pan. Bake in a moderate oven (350°F.) 40 to 45 minutes. Serve hot with tomato sauce. If desired, garnish with green pepper strips and radish slices. Makes 8 servings.

# Herb Baked Tomatoes

3 large tomatoes
6 teaspoons butter or margarine
½ teaspoon salt
⅛ teaspoon pepper
¼ teaspoon each, basil, thyme, oregano, sugar
¼ cup potato chip crumbs

Heat oven to slow (300° F). Cut core from tomatoes and slice them in half. Place tomato halves in a shallow pan, cut side up. Place a teaspoon of butter on each half. Combine remaining ingredients and sprinkle over the tomatoes. Bake for 30 minutes.

# Scalloped Corn and Pepper

1 small onion, chopped
½ green pepper, diced
3 tablespoons butter or margarine
1 can (1 pound) whole kernel corn
¼ cup rich milk or light cream
¼ teaspoon salt
⅛ teaspoon pepper
2 cups crushed potato chips

Sauté onion and green pepper in the butter over low heat until tender but not brown. Add corn and liquid, milk, salt and pepper. Butter a casserole well. Heat oven to moderately hot (375° F). Place a layer of corn mixture in casserole and add a layer of potato chips. Repeat until casserole is full, ending with potato chips. Bake about 25 minutes or until top is crisp and brown. Makes 6 servings.

American Institute of Baking

# Carrot Timbales

2 tablespoons shortening
2 tablespoons flour
¼ teaspoon salt
½ cup milk
5 large carrots, cut in pieces
2 tablespoons butter or margarine
2 cups soft ¼ bread cubes
3 eggs, beaten
1 tablespoon chopped onion
⅛ teaspoon nutmeg
1½ teaspoons salt

Melt shortening in a saucepan. Blend in flour and salt. Add milk and cook until thick, stirring constantly. Cook carrots in small amount of water until tender. Drain off remaining liquid. Add butter to carrots and mash. Combine mashed carrots with soft bread cubes, beaten eggs, onion, parsley, nutmeg, salt and white sauce. Place mixture into 6 well-greased custard cups. Set custard cups in a pan of hot water and bake in a moderate oven (350°F.) for 35 minutes. Unmold and serve with cream pea sauce. Makes 6 servings.

# Cheese-Potato-Tomato Casserole

1 package (4⅛-ounce or 2 cups) instant whipped potatoes
1 egg, well beaten
¾ teaspoon salt
Pinch instant minced onions
½ pound cheese spread shredded (2 cups)
6 to 8 tomato slices
2 tablespoons butter, melted
¼ cup dry bread crumbs
Grated Parmesan and Romano cheese

Prepare whipped potatoes according to package directions; cool slightly. Stir in egg, salt, and minced onions. Spoon into buttered 9x12-inch rectangular baking dish. Make 6 to 8 shallow depressions in potato mixture and fill each with equal amounts of shredded cheese; top each with tomato slice. Mix together butter and bread crumbs. Sprinkle buttered crumbs and grated cheese on top mixture. Bake in a moderate oven (350°F.) for 30 minutes. Makes 6 to 8 servings.

# Speedy Tomato Aspic

2¼ cups tomato juice
1 bay leaf
6 whole cloves
2 slices onion
Several pieces celery, and leaves
1 package lemon gelatin dessert
1 teaspoon Worcestershire sauce

Simmer tomato juice, bay leaf, cloves, onion and celery for 10 minutes. Strain. Dissolve gelatin in the hot tomato juice. Add Worcestershire, pour into a lightly oiled mold and chill until firm. You can add minced celery and green pepper to the aspic when partially congealed. Makes 6 servings.

# Herbed Green Beans

1 pound fresh green beans
¼ cup minced onion
½ clove garlic, minced
¼ cup minced celery
4 tablespoons butter
¼ teaspoon rosemary
¼ teaspoon basil
¾ teaspoon salt

Wash beans, cut off ends and slice into 1-inch pieces. Soak in cold water for 15 minutes. Sauté onion, garlic and celery in butter in 1½-quart pan until tender but not browned. Add drained beans. Cover and cook over low heat 15-20 minutes. Add seasonings. Makes 4 servings.

The Aluminum Association

# Zucchini Casserole

1 package (6 ounce) Cheddar cheese slices
¼ cup (4 tablespoons) butter, melted
3 cups rye bread cubes
4 cups thinly sliced zucchini
2 tablespoons onion flakes
3 tomatoes, sliced
2 tablespoons sweet pepper flakes
½ teaspoon salt
Dash of black pepper

Cut extra long slices of cheese into three equal portions (this makes 12 slices). Pour melted butter over rye bread cubes; mix thoroughly. Grease a 1½-quart casserole. Alternately place layers of zucchini, onion, tomato, pepper, cheese and bread cubes in casserole. Sprinkle with salt and pepper. Repeat process twice ending with bread cubes. Cover and bake in a moderate oven (350° F.) for about 1 hour or until vegetables are tender. Serve hot. Makes 6 servings.

The Borden Company

Western Growers Association

# Celery Coronado

3 medium size hearts of celery
¼ cup butter or margarine
1 cup of chicken bouillon
½ cup California, dry Sauterne
1 small jar pimientos
Sliced almonds

Wash celery stalks and split them lengthwise from top to bottom. Sauté in butter, until golden green color in an electric skillet or large frying pan on medium heat. Turn halves over carefully. Add bouillon and wine. Cover and cook slowly until the celery is crisp-tender. Remove celery to hot platter and keep warm in oven. Reduce the sauce until it has a glazed appearance and pour over the celery. Garnish with sautéed almonds and ribbons of pimiento. Makes 4 to 6 servings.

# Chicken Salad

2 cups cold cooked chicken, cut in large pieces
1 cup sliced celery
The juice of 1 small lemon
Salt and pepper to taste
½ cup mayonnaise or salad dressing
2 chopped hard-cooked eggs

Combine chicken, celery, lemon juice, salt and pepper and mayonnaise. Toss lightly together. Fold in hard-cooked eggs. Serve in a lettuce cup garnished with parsley, pimiento or capers. Makes 4 to 5 servings. For a delicious variation add 1 cup well-drained pineapple cubes or seedless grapes.

*Economy Tip:* You can use leftover veal for half the chicken.

# Vegetable Whiz Casserole

2 large bermuda onions, sliced (about 1½ cups)
3 cups sliced carrots
1 jar (1-pound) pasteurized process cheese spread
36 round buttery crackers, finely rolled (about 1⅔ cups crumbs)
¼ teaspoon ground black pepper
½ teaspoon thyme leaves
1 jar (4-ounce) pimientos, chopped

Cook onions and carrots until tender. Drain. Heat cheese spread over boiling water. Combine cracker crumbs with pepper and thyme. Layer vegetables, melted cheese and crumb mixture in a greased shallow 2-quart baking dish. Sprinkle with chopped pimientos. Bake, covered, 15 minutes in a moderate oven (350°F.) then 15 minutes uncovered. Makes 6 to 8 servings.

# Baked Avocados with Tuna Salad

3 ripe avocados
1 tablespoon lemon juice
2 cups (2, 7-ounce cans) tuna
1 cup finely cut celery
2 teaspoons butter, melted
¼ teaspoon salt
⅛ teaspoon pepper
½ cup mayonnaise
1½ cups corn flakes

Cut each avocado in half lengthwise; remove seed. Brush with lemon juice. Combine tuna, celery, salt, pepper and mayonnaise. Fill avocado shells with mixture. Crush corn flakes slightly and mix with melted butter. Sprinkle over tuna salad. Place shells in lightly greased baking pan. Bake in slow oven (325°F.) about 15 minutes or until heated through. Serve at once. Makes 6 servings.

**SALADS**

GENERAL HINTS ON HOW TO PREPARE SALADS

- All ingredients for the salad should be clean, fresh and thoroughly chilled.
- All juicy fruits should be drained, all greens patted dry.
- Vegetables and fruits should be cut into pieces large enough to hold their shape when mixed in a salad.
- For a tossed salad, the ingredients should be combined with the dressing just before serving. For potato, meat and fish salads, you may want to marinate one or more of the ingredients for a few hours before serving.
- Plates or platters for salads should be large enough so that the salads don't brim over the edge.
- Pile tossed salads lightly into bowls or plates. Fix arranged salads neatly and artistically, but not so that they have a handled look.

WAYS WITH SALAD GREENS

Wash salad greens carefully in cold water. Drain thoroughly and store in the hydrator of the refrigerator or wrap in a slightly dampened cloth and store in any cold place.

Have parsley on hand for days by washing it and storing slightly wet in a tightly covered jar in the refrigerator. Water cress, on the other hand should be kept cold, but not separated. Clean it just before serving.

# Fruit Salads

Using lettuce as a background, arrange the different kinds of fruit in rows or in circles or in any other eye catching way. Or place the different fruits in individual lettuce cups. Pass the dressing. A bowl of cottage cheese with a sprinkling of paprika on top is an attractive addition to any fruit salad.

Tip: To keep fruit from discoloring, slice with a stainless steel knife at the last possible minute. Sprinkle with lemon or pineapple juice (which will add to the flavor as well as prevent discoloration) or combine as soon as cut with some cut-up citrus fruits. Store in a cool place.

Western Growers Association

# Waldorf Salad

Figure on ½ apple per person and dice apple with the skin on. Combine with half as much diced celery as you have apple and toss with salad dressing. Just before serving add coarsely chopped walnuts or pecans. Top with a maraschino cherry or a nut half. Delicious variations of Waldorf salad can be made by combining the apple with other fruits like seeded grape halves, pears or avocado.

# Ruby Beet Salad Mold

**1 can (1 pound) diced beets**
**1 envelope unflavored gelatine**
**¼ cup cold beet juice**
**½ cup hot beet juice**
**¼ cup sugar**
**½ teaspoon salt**
**⅓ cup vinegar or lemon juice**
**2½ tablespoons prepared horse-radish**
**2 tablespoons chopped onion**
**½ cup finely diced celery**
**¼ cup finely diced green pepper**

Drain the beets reserving the liquid. Place the gelatine in the cold beet juice to soften. Heat ½ cup of the beet juice and dissolve the gelatine in it. Add beets, sugar, salt, vinegar or lemon juice, horse-radish, onion, celery and green pepper. Pour into a lightly oiled mold. Chill until firm. Unmold and serve on greens. Makes 6 to 8 servings.

# Olive Tuna Salad

**1 can (7 oz.) tuna fish**
**1 bottle (2 oz.) stuffed olives, drained and sliced**
**1 cup diced celery**
**1 hard-cooked egg, diced**
**¾ cup salad dressing**

Drain tuna and place in a bowl. Add olives, celery, egg and dressing. Toss lightly together. Chill and serve on lettuce leaves. Makes 4 servings.

# Jellied Cranberry Salad

**1 pound fresh cranberries**
**2 large apples, cored but not peeled**
**1 large orange, washed, but with skin on**
**2 cups sugar**
**½ cup nuts**
**½ cup seedless white grapes**
**1 package lemon gelatin dessert**
**½ cup boiling water**

Put cranberries, apples and orange through the food grinder using the coarse attachment. Add sugar and stir until it is dissolved. Add nuts and grapes. Dissolve gelatin in boiling water. Add to 3 cups of the cranberry mixture and chill until firm in a lightly oiled 1 quart ring mold. Serve remaining cranberry mixture as a relish. It may be stored in the refrigerator for several weeks.

# Curried Shrimp Salad

**1 pound raw shrimp**
**1 tablespoon lemon juice**
**2 cups diced celery**
**3 tablespoons chopped pimiento**
**3 hard-cooked eggs, coarsely chopped**
**⅔ cup curried dressing (see below)**

Cook the shrimp and if necessary, peel and devein them. Chill, then either leave whole or cut in pieces and sprinkle with lemon juice. Let stand 10 to 15 minutes. Add celery, pimiento, and eggs. Just before serving, add curried dressing and toss together. Makes 6 servings.

# California Carrot Casserole

**18-20 medium carrots (2½ pounds) peeled,**
**Salt and pepper to taste**
**2 teaspoons candied ginger, chopped fine**
**4 tablespoons butter or margarine, divided**
**2 tablespoons evaporated milk**
**½ cup chopped walnuts**

Simmer carrots, covered, in small amount of boiling salted water until tender. Drain and mash well; season with salt and pepper, ginger and 2 tablespoons butter. Beat well, adding milk. Pile in buttered 1-quart casserole. Sprinkle with nuts and dot with 2 tablespoons butter. Bake in a moderate oven (350°F.) for 30 minutes. Makes 6 servings.

Western Growers Association

# Sour Cream Potato Salad

**4 cups cooked, diced potatoes**
**⅓ cup diced cucumber**
**2 teaspoons finely minced onion**
**1 teaspoon celery seed**
**1¼ teaspoons salt**
**¼ teaspoon pepper**
**5 hard-cooked eggs**
**½ cup thick sour cream**
**½ cup salad dressing**
**1½ teaspoons vinegar**
**1 teaspoon prepared mustard**

Lightly toss together potatoes, cucumber, onion, celery seed, salt and pepper. Chop the whites of the eggs and add. Put the yolks through a sieve and combine with sour cream, salad dressing, vinegar and mustard. Add sour cream mixture to potatoes. Toss together. Chill. Serve on crisp greens. Makes 6 servings.

SALAD DRESSINGS

# Zesty French Dressing

**1 cup salad oil**
**¼ cup vinegar**
**1½ teaspoons salt**
**⅛ teaspoon pepper**
**¼ teaspoon paprika**
**Dash of celery salt**
**¾ teaspoon sugar**
**2 tablespoons catsup**
**1 tablespoon lemon juice**
**1½ teaspoons Worcestershire sauce**
**2 cloves garlic, cut in two**

Combine all ingredients in a bottle or a jar. Cover tightly, shake well and chill several hours. Remove garlic and shake well before each use. Makes 1⅓ cups.

Chiffonade Dressing: To ¾ cup of French Dressing recipe add 2 tablespoons chopped hard-cooked egg, 1 tablespoon chopped green pepper, 2 tablespoons chopped beets, 1 teaspoon minced parsley and ¼ teaspoon onion juice.

Roquefort Dressing: To ¾ cup of French Dressing recipe add ⅓ cup crumbled Roquefort or Blue cheese.

Lorenzo Dressing: To ¾ cup of French Dressing recipe add ¼ cup chili sauce and ¼ cup chopped water cress.

MAYONNAISE AND SALAD DRESSINGS

**Pink Fruit Salad Dressing:** Blend together ½ cup whipped cream and ½ cup cold cranberry sauce. Add ⅔ cup mayonnaise or salad dressing. Beat well until combined.

**Curried Dressing:** Combine 1 cup mayonnaise or salad dressing, ½ teaspoon curry powder and a dash of Tabasco. Mix well.

# Desserts and Fruit

**From Apples to Zabaglione — —**

**desserts to count your pennies by — —**

# Apple Mince Tarts

**Pastry for a 2-crust 9-inch pie**
**1 jar (28 oz.) moist mincemeat**
**3 apples, cored, peeled and coarsely chopped**
**¼ cup brown sugar**
**½ teaspoon salt**
**¼ cup brandy**
**1 tablespoon butter or margarine**

Heat oven to hot (425° F.). Roll the pastry and cut into rounds. Fit into fluted tart pans or muffin pans. Combine mincemeat, apples, sugar, salt and brandy. Fill tart shells. Dot with bits of the butter and bake about 20 minutes.

**Toppings For Mince Tarts:**

- Whipped cream with grated orange rind folded in.
- Cream cheese creamed with milk with chopped nuts added.
- Meringue made with egg whites and sugar. Place this on top of the cooled tart and bake in a 350° F. oven for 15 minutes.

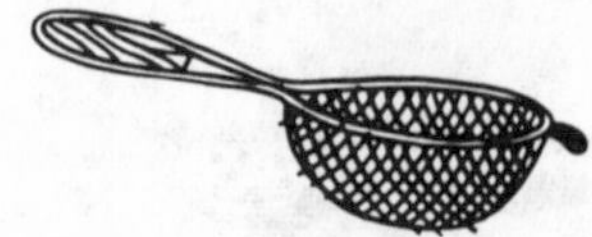

# Apple Dumplings

**Pastry for a 2-crust 9-inch pie**
**1 cup sugar**
**¼ teaspoon cinnamon**
**¼ teaspoon nutmeg**
**2 cups pineapple juice**
**3 tablespoons butter or margarine**
**½ cup broken pecans or walnuts**
**6 medium, tart apples**
**½ cup sugar**
**1 teaspoon cinnamon**
**1 tablespoon butter or margarine**

Heat oven to hot (425° F.). Roll out the pastry and cut into 6 squares of about 7 inches each. Combine sugar, cinnamon, nutmeg, pineapple juice and butter or margarine. Cook for 5 minutes. Remove from heat and add nuts. Peel and core the apples. Combine sugar and cinnamon. Place one apple on each square of dough. Sprinkle with sugar and cinnamon and fill the cavity with it. Dot with bits of the butter. Bring opposite points of the pastry up over the apple. Overlap, then moisten and press together. Lift carefully into an oblong baking dish and pour the hot syrup around (not over) the dumplings. Bake 40 to 45 minutes. Serve with the syrup and cream.

R. T. French Co.

# Jellied Tropicana

**1 package orange gelatin dessert**
**1 cup blended orange-grapefruit juice, heated**
**1 can (1 lb. 4 oz.) crushed pineapple**
**½ cup shredded coconut**
**½ cup chopped nuts**

Dissolve orange gelatin in hot juice. Drain the pineapple, reserving the juice. Add to orange mixture 1 cup of the juice drained from the pineapple. Pour one-half this mixture into a lightly oiled mold. Chill until partly congealed, then fold in coconut and nuts. Chill remaining gelatin mixture until thick and syrupy and beat with a rotary egg beater until frothy. Fold in crushed pineapple and pour over stiffened gelatin in the mold. Chill until firm. Garnish with pineapple and cut marshmallows.

# Party Baked Apples

**½ cup corn syrup**
**½ cup water**
**¼ teaspoon cinnamon**
**1 teaspoon grated lemon rind**
**1 tablespoon butter or margarine**
**2 tablespoons sugar**
**4 baking apples**
**1 egg white**
**2 tablespoons sugar**
**Blanched, slivered almonds, about 14**

Heat oven to moderate (350° F.). Combine syrup, water, cinnamon, lemon rind, butter or margarine, and the first 2 tablespoons sugar in a saucepan. Bring to a boil. Remove from heat. Core apples and peel the upper half. Place in a shallow baking dish. Pour syrup mixture over and bake about 1 hour, basting frequently. Remove from oven. Beat the egg white until foamy; add the remaining 2 tablespoons sugar gradually.

Top each apple with meringue. Stick almonds in meringue and return to the oven for 15 minutes.

**Banana-Berry Apples.** Combine ½ cup chopped cranberries, ½ cup chopped banana, ½ cup sugar and ½ teaspoon cinnamon. Cut off stem and blossom end from 6 large tart apples, and core them. Remove part of the pulp and add to the cranberry mixture. Place apples in a baking dish and fill centers with chopped fruit mixture. Chop 2 tablespoons nuts and sprinkle over the tops of the apples. Bake in a moderate oven (350° F.) 30 to 40 minutes. Serve with cream.

# Chocolate Velvet

**2½ squares (2½ oz.) unsweetened chocolate**
**½ cup milk**
**⅔ cup sugar**
**5 eggs, separated**
**1 cup butter or margarine**
**1 cup confectioners' sugar (xxxx)**
**1 cup (about 14) graham crackers rolled to fine crumbs**

Melt chocolate and cool. Combine milk, sugar and beaten egg yolks, in the top of a double boiler. Cook over boiling water, stirring constantly until thickened. Cool. Cream together the butter or margarine, confectioners' sugar and the cooled chocolate. Blend into the cold egg yolk mixture. Beat egg whites until stiff. Fold chocolate mixture into the egg whites. Blend well. Sprinkle half the crumbs over the bottom of an 8-inch-square pan. Pour chocolate mixture into pan and top with remaining crumbs. Chill overnight. Cut into squares to serve. Makes about 12 servings.

*Tip.* You can also put this mixture into a chocolate or graham cracker crumb crust, and serve as a pie.

# Orange Pineapple Fluff

**Butter cookies**
**1 package orange gelatin dessert**
**⅔ cup well-drained crushed pineapple**
**1 cup (½ pint) heavy cream, whipped**

Line bottoms and sides of dessert dishes with cookies. Prepare the package of orange gelatin dessert according to directions on package. Chill until thick and syrupy, then whip with a rotary egg beater until frothy. Fold in the crushed pineapple and then the whipped cream. Pile lightly on top of cookies in dessert dishes. Chill thoroughly. Makes 6 servings.

# Danish Apple Bake

1 quart applesauce
2 cups toasted bread crumbs
3 egg yolks, beaten
⅓ cup melted butter or margarine
½ teaspoon cinnamon
¼ cup sugar
3 egg whites
6 tablespoons sugar
½ teaspoon vanilla extract

Combine applesauce, toasted bread crumbs, beaten egg yolks, butter, cinnamon and sugar. Bake in a greased 2-quart casserole in a moderate oven (325°F.) for forty-five minutes. Remove from oven. Beat egg whites until stiff. Add sugar gradually, continuing to beat until mixture stands in peaks. Add vanilla extract. Top apple bake with meringue and return to oven for fifteen minutes, or until brown. Makes 8 servings.

American Institute of Baking

# Pineapple Mallow

1 recipe chocolate crumb crust
½ pound marshmallows
⅓ cup evaporated milk
3 tablespoons lemon juice plus pineapple juice to make ½ cup
1 teaspoon grated lemon rind
¾ cup well-drained, crushed pineapple
⅔ cup evaporated milk, chilled icy cold

Prepare 1 recipe crumb crust using chocolate wafers but do not pack in pie plate. Place marshmallows and the ⅓ cup evaporated milk in top of a double boiler. Heat over boiling water until marshmallows are melted. Remove from heat. As mixture cools, add lemon and pineapple juices, lemon rind and crushed pineapple. When cool and thickened, whip the evaporated milk until very stiff. Add the cooled marshmallow mixture and mix quickly but well. Put two-thirds of the chocolate crumbs in the bottom of a 9-inch square pan. Pour mallow mixture over. Top with remaining crumbs. Chill 1½ hours or until set. Cut in squares to serve. Makes 6 to 8 servings.

Processed Apples Institute

# Apple Crisp

1 can (1 lb. 4 oz.) sliced apples
1 tablespoon lemon juice
¾ cup flour
¾ cup brown sugar
¼ teaspoon salt
¾ teaspoon cinnamon
6 tablespoons butter or margarine

Heat oven to moderate (375° F.). Place apples in an oblong baking dish reserving a few for garnishing. Sprinkle with lemon juice. Combine flour, sugar, salt, cinnamon and butter or margarine. With a pastry blender or the fingers, work together until coarse crumbs are formed. Sprinkle over apples. Garnish with reserved apple slices. Bake 30 minutes or until crumbs are lightly browned. Serve hot or cold, with cream. Makes 6 servings.

# Banana Polka Dot

⅓ cup seedless raisins
1 cup water
1 teaspoon butter or margarine
Dash of salt
1 tablespoon lemon juice
⅓ cup sugar
1 tablespoon cornstarch mixed to a paste with 2 tablespoons orange juice
3 large underripe bananas

Heat oven to hot (400° F.). In a saucepan, combine raisins, water, butter or margarine, salt, lemon juice, sugar and cornstarch. Cook over low heat, stirring constantly until mixture begins to bubble and thicken. Remove from heat. Peel bananas and cut in half crosswise. Place in a shallow baking pan and pour sauce over. Bake 10 minutes, basting several times. Makes 6 servings.

# Wacky Apple Cake

2 tablespoons butter
1 cup sugar
1 egg, beaten
2 cups flour
2 teaspoons baking powder
1 teaspoon salt
¼ teaspoon nutmeg
½ teaspoon cinnamon
¾ cup milk
2 peeled, thinly sliced apples
2 tablespoons melted butter
2 tablespoons sugar
½ cup table cream

Cream butter and sugar, add egg and beat well. Sift and measure flour, add baking powder, salt and spices, sifting two more times. Add to creamed mixture alternately with the milk. Pour into a greased 8x8-inch cake pan. Place apple slices in rows until the batter is completely covered. Pour melted butter over all, sprinkle with sugar and place in moderate oven (375°F.). Bake ½ hour and then pour cream over cake and return to the oven to continue baking for another ½ hour or until cake tests done with a toothpick.

The Apple Pantry

# Mock Apple Pie

Pastry for 2 crust 9-inch pie
1 stack pack of round buttery crackers (about 36)
2 cups water
2 cups sugar
2 teaspoons cream of tartar
2 tablespoons lemon juice
grated rind of one lemon
Butter or margarine
Ground cinamon

Roll out bottom crust of pastry and fit into 9-inch pie plate. Break crackers coarsely into pastry-lined plate. Combine water, sugar and cream of tartar in saucepan; boil gently for 15 minutes. Add lemon juice and rind; cool. Pour syrup over crackers. Dot generously with butter or margarine and sprinkle with cinnamon. Cover with top crust. Trim and flute edges together. Cut slits in top crust to let steam escape. Bake in a hot oven (425°F.) 30 to 35 minutes, until crust is crisp and golden. Serve warm. Makes 6 to 8 servings.

National Biscuit Company

# Golden Cheese Sponge

4 eggs, separated
½ cup sugar
3 tablespoons flour
2 tablespoons lemon juice
1 tablespoon lemon rind
¼ teaspoon salt
1 cup sour cream
1 cup cottage cheese
¼ cup melted butter
Fresh strawberries
Sweetened whipped cream

Beat egg yolks until thick and lemon colored. Add sugar gradually, beating well. Add flour, lemon juice, rind, salt, sour cream, cottage cheese and butter; beat until almost smooth. Pour mixture into a 1½-quart casserole; bake in a slow oven (300°F.) for 1 hour or until set. Serve cool or well chilled topped with fresh strawberries and whipped cream. Makes 4 to 6 servings.

# Old-Fashioned Noodle Pudding

**5 tablespoons butter**
**2½ cups peeled cooking apples cut in ½-inch slices**
**7 tablespoons sugar**
**⅓ cup packed dark brown sugar**
**1¾ teaspoons ground cinnamon, divided**
**2 tablespoons finely chopped walnuts**
**2½ cups drained, cooked broad noodles**
**½ cup sour cream**
**1¼ cups creamed cottage cheese, sieved**
**½ teaspoon salt**
**2 eggs well beaten**

Melt 3 tablespoons butter in heavy skillet. Add sliced apples; sprinkle with 3 tablespoons sugar. Stir until apples are completely coated with butter. Cover; cook over low heat about 8 minutes.

Mix brown sugar, ¼ teaspoon cinnamon and nuts well. Spread mixture evenly over bottom of well-greased 8x8x2-inch pan. Add 2 tablespoons butter to noodles and toss until well-coated. Add sour cream, cottage cheese, salt, eggs, cooked apples and their liquid and 2 tablespoons sugar which has been mixed with 1 teaspoon cinnamon; blend well. Put noodle mixture over brown sugar layer in pan. Bake in moderate oven (325°F.) for 50 minutes, or until done. Immediately sprinkle a mixture of 2 tablespoons sugar and ½ teaspoon cinnamon over top and serve at once. Makes 7 servings.

Sealtest Kitchens

# Zabaglione

This simple but elegant dish can be served as a dessert or as a sauce over ice cream or stewed fruits.

**6 egg yolks**
**6 tablespoons sugar**
**Dash of salt**
**½ cup sherry, marsala or madeira**

Combine the egg yolks, sugar and salt in the top part of a double boiler, not over water. Beat with a rotary egg beater or a whisk until thick and lemon colored. Gradually beat in the wine. Place over hot water (not boiling) and beat with the rotary egg beater or whisk until thick and fluffy, about 5 minutes. Remove from heat and serve immediately in individual dessert dishes. Makes 4 servings.

Wine Institute

# French Cherry Dessert

**2 cups corn flakes or**
**½ cup packaged corn flake crumbs**
**3 tablespoons confectioners' sugar**
**½ cup sifted flour**
**½ cup butter or margarine**
**¼ cup sifted flour**
**½ teaspoon baking powder**
**¼ teaspoon salt**
**2 eggs, well-beaten**
**½ cup maraschino cherries halved and drained**
**1 cup sugar**
**1 teaspoon vanilla flavoring**
**½ cup chopped nutmeats**
**½ cup flaked coconut**

If using corn flakes, crush into fine crumbs. Combine confectioners' sugar, flour and corn flake crumbs in mixing bowl. Cut in butter until mixture resembles coarse corn meal. Press into bottom of 8x8-inch baking pan. Bake in moderate oven (350°F.) about 25 minutes or until lightly browned.

Sift together flour, baking powder and salt. Blend eggs, sugar and vanilla. Stir in sifted dry ingredients. Fold in nutmeats, coconut and cherries. Spread over baked crust. Bake in slow oven (325°F.) about 45 minutes or until done. Cool. To serve, cut into squares and top with whipped cream or ice cream, if desired. Makes 9 servings.

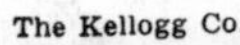

The Kellogg Co.

# Cakes

**Here are reliable, tested recipes plus suggestions for enhancing quick mixes and ready-cooked products.**

A GOOD cake starts with a good recipe. Those included here are reliable and tested. Read and follow them carefully. They are based on exact, standard measurements, and all measurements are level.

### Pick The Proper Pan Size

Picking the proper size pan can make all the difference in the success of your cake. Too big a pan will make the layers flat and shrunken looking; too small a pan will cause spillover and an overhanging edge with even the most accurate measurements. Try to find the exact size pan called for in the recipe. You can check your cake pan sizes by measuring the diameter and the depth with a ruler. It is a good idea to mark the sizes on the underside with nail polish or paint. You can then check your pan size very quickly by turning it over.

### Pick The Proper Kind Of Pan

Shiny pans of medium to lightweight metal make the best cake baking pans. They heat rapidly, yet reflect the heat so that the cakes brown delicately. Dark or dull pans absorb more heat and give a deeper brown and a heavier crust. If using glass baking dishes, reduce the temperature 25° F.

### Prepare The Pans

Before you start your measuring or mixing, there are two things that come first in baking. One is to start your oven heating, the other is to prepare your pans. For greasing, use oil or very soft shortening. Dip a pastry brush or piece of crumpled paper in the shortening, and grease the bottom and sides of the pans thoroughly. Sprinkle a little flour into the greased pan and shake the pan to coat it evenly. Overturn the pan to remove any excess. If oblong cake pans are being used, cut pieces of heavy waxed paper or brown paper to fit the bottoms, leaving little ears for easier removal. Fit the paper into the pan and grease the bottom and sides thoroughly. You can save wear and tear on your hands in cleaning the muffin pans, by baking cupcakes in little crinkled paper cups.

This is the good old way of mixing cakes. While it may be traditional, it is by no means old-fashioned, and many people still prefer the open texture and chewiness of cakes made by this method.

All ingredients should be at room temperature (75° to 80° F.), although in the summer time, the *milk and eggs* may be used right out of the refrigerator. The *shortening* may be butter, margarine, hydrogenated vegetable shortening or all-purpose shortening. Cane and beet *sugar* are equally good. A double-acting *baking powder* will give the most reliable results, and either cake flour or all-purpose *flour* should be used according to what the recipe calls for.

### Chiffon Cakes

These are cakes made with a liquid shortening. They have a delightfully different texture, lighter than solid shortening cakes, not quite as light as sponge. They serve equally well the purposes of both.

### Three Quick and Easy Frostings

**No-Cook Chocolate Frosting.** Combine 2 squares (2 oz.) chocolate, melted with ¼ cup undiluted evaporated milk, ⅛ teaspoon salt, 1 teaspoon melted butter or margarine, ½ teaspoon vanilla. Add enough confectioners' sugar (xxxx) to make into spreading consistency. Makes enough to frost the tops of two 9-inch layers or the tops and sides of two 8-inch layers.

**Strawberry Speed Frosting.** Place 1 unbeaten egg white and ½ cup strawberry preserves, and ¼ teaspoon salt in the top of a double boiler. Beat with a rotary egg beater or an electric beater until foamy. Then place over rapidly boiling water and beat constantly for 3 minutes or until frosting stands in peaks. Remove, cool, then spread on cake. Makes enough frosting for one large angel cake or the top and sides of two 9-inch layers.

**Wonder Frosting.** Combine two (3 oz.) packages cream cheese with 4 tablespoons milk and blend. Add 4 cups confectioners' sugar (xxxx) 1 cup at a time, blending after each addition. Melt 4 squares (4 oz.) unsweetened chocolate and add with a dash of salt, and beat until smooth. Add a teaspoon more milk if necessary to bring to spreading consistency. Makes enough for tops and sides of two 9-inch layers. This frosting, if tightly covered can be kept in the refrigerator several days before using.

### What You Can Do With A Cake Mix!

**White Upside Down Cake.** Heat oven to moderate (375° F.). Drain and reserve the juice from 1 can (1 pound 4 oz.) crushed pineapple. Combine ⅔ cup of the juice with ⅓ cup melted butter, ⅔ cup firmly packed brown sugar. Divide this mixture into two 8x1½- or 9x1½-inch round layer pans. Cover with drained pineapple. Prepare 1 package white cake mix according to the manufacturer's directions. Pour batter over fruit in pans. Bake 25 to 35 minutes. Invert on a wire rack for 5 minutes. Remove pans and cool. Place one layer on top of the other to serve.

**White Nut Cake.** Fold 1 cup finely chopped nuts into the batter.

**Polka Dot White Cake.** Shave 2 squares (2 oz.) sweet or semi-sweet chocolate and fold into the batter.

**Gingerbread-Orange Ring.** Prepare gingerbread mix according to the manufacturer's directions but bake it in a greased ring mold. Combine 1 cup cream, whipped with 2 tablespoons of sugar and 1 tablespoon grated orange rind. Place in the center of the ring of gingerbread and top with orange slices or sections.

**Ginger Coffee Cake.** Combine ½ cup firmly packed brown sugar with 2 tablespoons flour, and 2 teaspoons cinnamon. Blend in 2 tablespoons melted butter or margarine and ½ cup chopped nuts. Prepare gingerbread mix as directed and pour into pans. Top with the sugar-nut mixture and bake.

**Maple Nut Yellow Cake.** To the liquid called for in the yellow cake, add 1½ teaspoons maple flavoring. To the batter, add ½ cup finely chopped nuts.

**Frozen Orange Yellow Cake.** Use 1 cup diluted frozen orange juice (do not use fresh) in place of 1 cup liquid called for in the instructions.

**Spice Cake Party Layers.** Bake 1 package spice cake mix according to the manufacturer's directions. Cool. Whip 1 pint cream until stiff. Blend in ¼ cup sugar and 2 teaspoons grated lemon rind. Using a thread and gentle sawing motion or a sharp, thin knife, cut each layer in two. Spread whipped cream between the layers and over the top and sides. Sprinkle with chopped pecans. Chill until serving time.

**Orange Spice Cake.** Add the grated rind of two oranges to the Spice Cake batter and frost with an orange-flavored butter icing.

**Quick Prune Spice Cake.** Cook 1 pound prunes until just tender. Drain, cool and cut in small pieces. Be sure the pieces are small or they will sink to the bottom of the cake. Add the cut prunes (it will make about 1½ cups) and ⅓ cup finely chopped nuts to the batter.

**Almond Angel Cake.** Replace the vanilla flavoring with 1 teaspoon almond flavoring in making the angel food mix. Bake, cool, then cover sides and top with almond-flavored whipped cream and garnish with chopped toasted almonds.

**Angel Petit Fours.** This is an excellent way to use leftover angel food cake. Cut the cake into 2 inch squares. Spread top and sides with cocoa-flavored sweetened whipped cream. Roll in shredded coconut.

**Orange Date Devil's Food Cake.** Prepare and bake the devil's food mix according to the manufacturer's directions. Cool. Chop 1 cup pitted dates and simmer in 1 cup water 10 minutes. Drain and cool. Add ⅛ teaspoon salt, ¼ teaspoon grated orange rind, 2 teaspoons orange juice and 2 tablespoons dark corn syrup. Mix well and spread between the layers. Frost with an orange-flavored butter frosting.

**Pep-O-Nut Devil's Food Cake.** Add 2 drops oil of peppermint and ⅔ cup chopped nuts to the batter.

**Creole Devil Cake.** Add 1 teaspoon cinnamon, ½ teaspoon nutmeg and ¼ teaspoon cloves to the dry ingredients of the mix. Bake, cool and frost with a butter frosting to which chopped nuts and raisins have been added.

# Pound Cake Pudding

**1 (4½-ounce) package butterscotch pudding**
**1 (14-ounce) loaf pound cake**

Prepare butterscotch pudding according to direction on package. Cut pound cake in half lengthwise. With a 2-inch cookie cutter, cut each lengthwise strip into 3 circles. Arrange cake circles in dessert dishes. Pour butterscotch pudding over each circle. Makes 6 servings.

American Institute of Baking

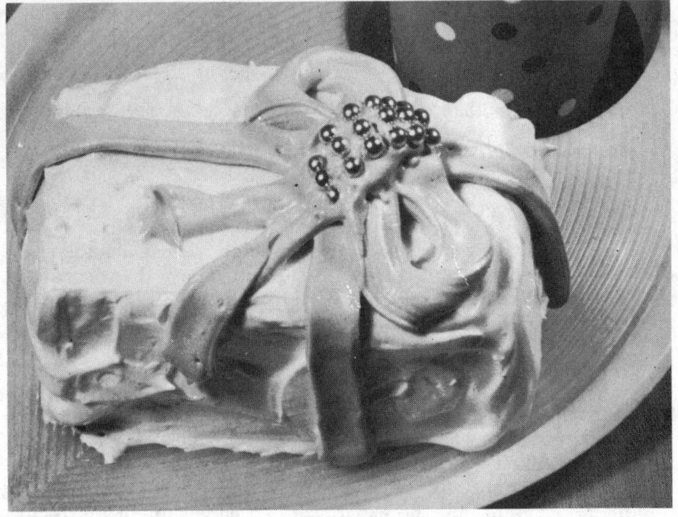

National Biscuit Company

# Surprise Packages

**1 package (14-ounce) gingerbread mix**
**1 cup water**
**1½ cups milk**
**1 package vanilla pudding and pie filling mix**
**1½ tablespoons grated orange rind**
**2 egg whites**
**Few drops red food coloring**
**1½ cups sugar**
**⅓ cup orange juice**
**2 tablespoons water**
**1 tablespoon light corn syrup**
**½ teaspoon salt**
**1 teaspoon grated orange rind**

Prepare gingerbread mix according to package directions. Pour into a greased and floured 9-inch square pan. Bake in a moderate oven (350°F.) 40 to 45 minutes or until center springs back when touched lightly with fingertips. Cool. Add milk to pudding mix. Cook over low heat until thick. Stir in orange rind. Cool. Slice cake in 3 layers. Spread 2 layers with cooled filling. Stack. Cut into 10 bars.

For frosting, combine egg whites with next 5 ingredients in top of double boiler. Beat one minute. Place over boiling water and beat until mixture forms peaks. Remove from boiling water. Add orange rind. Continue heating until thick enough to spread. Reserve ¾ cup frosting. Frost each bar. Add food coloring to reserved frosting and using a pastry tube or spatula decorate each with ribbon bows. Decorate bows with silver dragees. Makes 10 bars.

# Chocolate Fudge Cake

4 squares (4 oz.) unsweetened chocolate
½ cup hot water
½ cup sugar
2 cups cake flour, sifted before measuring
1 teaspoon baking soda
1 teaspoon salt
½ cup shortening
1¼ cups sugar
3 eggs, unbeaten
Milk—¾ cup with shortening, ⅔ cup with butter or margarine
1 teaspoon vanilla

Heat oven to moderate (350° F.). Read the recipe through. Assemble all the ingredients. Prepare two 9x1½-inch round layer pans. Heat chocolate and water in the top part of a double boiler over hot water. Cook and stir until chocolate is melted and mixture thickens. Add the ½ cup sugar. Cook and stir 2 minutes longer. Cool to lukewarm. Combine flour, baking soda and salt. Sift together 3 times. Cream the shortening, adding the 1¼ cups sugar gradually. Cream together until light and fluffy. Add eggs, one at a time, beating thoroughly after each. Then add flour, alternately with the milk, starting with the flour and ending with the flour, beating after each addition just enough to blend smoothly. Be careful not to overbeat or the volume will be reduced. Add vanilla, then the chocolate mixture, and blend. If there were nuts or raisins in the recipe they would be added now. Pour batter equally into layer pans and bake about 30 minutes or until cake has pulled away from the sides and springs back when lightly touched.

# Rich Golden Cake

2¼ cups cake flour, sifted before measuring
1½ cups sugar
3 teaspoons baking powder
1 teaspoon salt
⅔ cup soft shortening
1 cup milk
1½ teaspoons vanilla
3 eggs

Heat oven to moderate (350° F.). Read the recipe through. Assemble all ingredients. Prepare two 9x1½-inch round layer pans or one 13x9-inch oblong pan. Combine and sift together, flour, sugar, baking powder and salt into a mixing bowl. Add soft shortening, then about two-thirds of the milk. Beat with mixer at medium speed for 2 minutes, scraping the bowl constantly, or beat vigorously with a spoon 150 strokes per minute for 2 minutes. If you stop to rest, count only the actual beating time or strokes. Add remaining milk, vanilla and unbeaten eggs. Beat 2 minutes more, scraping bowl frequently. This batter will be thinner than the conventional cake batter. Pour batter into prepared pans, dividing it evenly between them. Place in the oven so that layers are staggered in opposite corners, slightly apart and away from the oven walls. The top of the cake should be about midway in the oven. Bake about 30 to 35 minutes or until cake tests done. The oblong pan will take 40 to 45 minutes. Cool 5 to 10 minutes only, then fill with a lemon pudding filling, and frost with a white frosting and grated coconut.

# Citrus Frosting

¾ cup sugar
1½ tablespoons flour
¼ teaspoon salt
2 teaspoons grated orange peel
⅓ cup orange juice
2½ tablespoons fresh lemon juice
1 egg, slightly beaten
1 tablespoon butter or margarine
1 cup whipping cream

Mix sugar, flour and salt in top of double boiler. Add grated orange peel, orange and lemon juice and egg, mixing well. Cook over hot water until thickened, stirring frequently. Add butter and cool. Whip cream until stiff and fold into cooked orange mixture. Use as filling and frosting for 3 layers of cooled carrot cake. Garnish with flowers, made by cutting thin carrot rings into petal pattern and using strips of orange peel for the flower stems.

Western Growers Association

# Springtime Carrot Cake

1½ cups salad oil
2 cups sugar
3½ teablespoons hot water
5 egg yolks
2½ cups sifted cake flour
2½ teaspoons cinnamon
1½ teaspoons nutmeg
1½ teaspoons baking soda
½ teaspoon salt
1½ cups grated raw carrots (3 large)
1 cup finely chopped nutmeats
5 egg whites

Combine salad oil, sugar, hot water and egg yolks; beat on low speed of electric mixer until well blended, but do not overbeat. Sift together flour, cinnamon, nutmeg, soda and salt. Add egg yolk mixture alternately with carrots and nutmeats to dry ingredients, blending well after each addition. Beat egg whites until they stand in stiff peaks but are not dry; fold carefully into cake batter. Pour batter into 3 well-greased 8 or 9-inch round cake pans and bake in warm oven (300°F.) for 50 to 60 minutes, or until done.

# Sherry Gold Cake

**2¼ cups sifted cake flour**
**1 cup sugar**
**2 teaspoons baking powder**
**1 teaspoon salt**
**¼ cup soft butter or margarine**
**¼ cup soft shortening**
**1 teaspoon vanilla**
**¼ teaspoon almond extract**
**5 egg yolks**
**½ cup milk**
**¼ cup Sherry wine**
**Sherry Butter Icing**

Sift flour, sugar, baking powder and salt into a mixing bowl. Add butter, shortening, flavoring, yolks and milk. Beat 2 minutes at medium speed on mixer, or vigorously by hand (300 strokes). Scrape sides and bottom of bowl frequently. Add wine and beat 2 minutes more. Turn into a paper-lined, greased loaf pan about 9x5x2½ inches. Bake in a moderate oven (350°F.) 55 to 60 minutes. When cool spread top of cake with Sherry Butter Icing. Makes 1 loaf.

# Sherry Butter Icing

**2 tablespoons butter or margarine**
**1½ cups sifted powdered sugar**
**1 tablespoon Sherry wine**
**Cream**

Heat butter until bubbly and lightly browned. Remove from heat and add sugar and wine. Stir vigorously until blended. Add a few drops of cream until of thick spreading consistency.

Wine Institute

American Institute of Baking

# Fruit Cake a la Mode

**1 quart vanilla ice cream**
**9 slices bakers' fruit cake**
**1⅛ cups Sherry Butter Sauce**

Place a large scoop of ice cream on each fruit cake slice. Serve 2 tablespoons Sherry Butter Sauce over each serving. Makes 9 servings.

### Sherry Butter Sauce

**¼ cup melted butter**
**1 cup sugar**
**2 tablespoons water**
**1 tablespoon lemon juice**
**1 tablespoon grated lemon rind**
**Dash nutmeg**
**¼ cup Sherry wine**

Combine butter, sugar and water in a saucepan. Cook until thick and blended, stirring constantly. Add lemon juice and rind, nutmeg and wine. Makes 1⅛ cups Sherry Butter Sauce.

# Strawberry Angel Food Cake

**1 (9-ounce) baker's angel food cake**
**½ cup heavy cream, whipped**
**1 cup fresh whole strawberries**
**1 cup fresh strawberries, crushed**

Cut baker's angel food cake in half, horizontally. Place whipped cream between cake halves. Fill center of cake with whole strawberries and spread crushed strawberries over sides of cake. Serve immediately. Makes 6 servings.

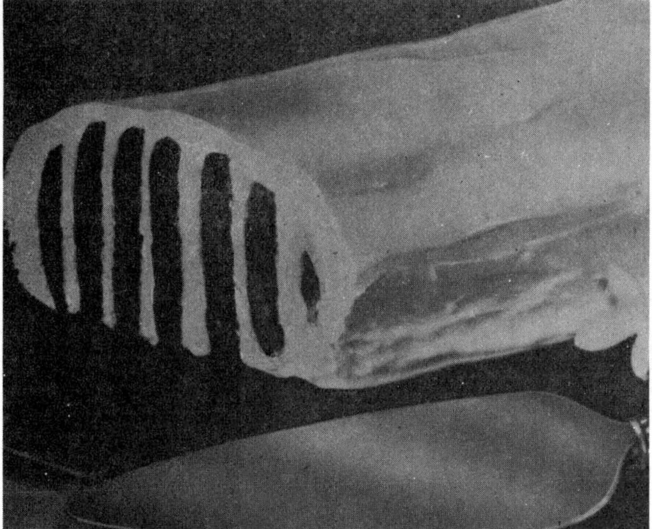

# Famous Chocolate Refrigerator Cake

**1½ cups heavy cream**
**¼ cup confectioners' sugar**
**½ teaspoon vanilla extract**
**20 chocolate wafers**

Whip cream with sugar and vanilla, until stiff. Spread about 1 tablespoon of cream on each wafer. Put together in stacks of 4 or 5. Chill 15 minutes. Stand stacks on edge of plate to make one long roll. Frost outside of roll with remaining cream. Refrigerate three hours. Cut roll diagonally at a 45° angle. Makes 6 to 8 servings. Cake may be frozen after chilling, if desired.

American Institute of Baking

# Individual Baked Alaskas

**4 egg whites**
**¼ teaspoon vanilla extract**
**¼ cup sifted confectioners' sugar**
**1 pint ice cream**
**6 individual sponge cake shells**

Beat egg whites until stiff, but not dry. Add vanilla extract. Add confectioners' sugar gradually. Continue beating until meringue stands in peaks. Divide ice cream into 6 portions and place a portion in the center of each sponge cake shell. Cover cake and ice cream closely with meringue. Place on a cookie sheet and brown quickly in a hot oven (450°F.) for about 5 minutes. Serve immediately. Makes 6 Baked Alaskas.

NOTE: The Alaskas may be made oven-ready in advance. Keep frozen for 2 weeks in freezer or 2 days in refrigerator freezing compartment.

# Chocolate Lovelight Cake

**2 eggs, separated**
**1½ cups sugar**
**1¾ cups cake flour, sifted before measuring**
**¾ teaspoon baking soda**
**¾ teaspoon salt**
**⅓ cup salad oil**
**1 cup buttermilk or sour milk**
**2 squares (2 ounces) unsweetened chocolate, melted**

Heat oven to moderate (350° F.). Read the recipe through. Assemble all ingredients. Prepare two 9x1½-inch round layer pans. Beat egg whites until frothy. Gradually beat in ½ cup of the sugar. Continue beating until very stiff and glossy. Combine remaining sugar, flour, baking soda, and salt, and sift into another bowl. Add salad oil and half the buttermilk. Beat 1 minute, medium speed on a mixer or 150 vigorous strokes by hand, scraping the sides and bottom of the bowl constantly. Add remaining buttermilk, egg yolks and chocolate. Beat 1 minute more, scraping bowl constantly. Fold in beaten egg whites. Pour, dividing equally, into prepared pans. Bake 30 to 35 minutes. Cool and frost with cocoa-flavored sweetened whipped cream.

# Fudge Frosting

**2 cups sugar**
**¾ cup light cream**
**2 squares (2 oz.) unsweetened chocolate**
**2 tablespoons light corn syrup**
**⅛ teaspoon salt**
**2 tablespoons butter or margarine**
**1 teaspoon vanilla**

Combine in a heavy saucepan, the sugar, cream, chocolate, corn syrup and salt. Cook over low heat and stir until dissolved. Continue cooking until a little of the syrup dropped in a cup of cold water forms a very soft ball (230° to 234° F.), but do not stir while cooking. Remove from heat. Add the butter, and allow to cool to lukewarm. Add the vanilla, then beat until the mixture begins to thicken and lose its gloss. Add a little more cream, a teaspoon at a time until of spreading consistency. Makes enough for two 8- or 9-inch layers. To prevent hardening while spreading, place the bowl of frosting over hot water.

# Orange Butter Frosting

**¼ cup butter or margarine**
**2 cups confectioners' sugar (xxxx)**
**2 teaspoons grated orange rind**
**dash of salt**
**about 3 tablespoons cream, or 2 tablespoons orange juice and 1 egg yolk**

Cream butter or margarine until soft. Gradually stir in 1 cup of the sugar, creaming well. Add orange rind and salt. Add remaining cup of sugar alternately with cream or juice and egg yolk, beating after each addition until smooth. Add only enough cream to make proper spreading consistency. Makes enough for top and sides of two 8-inch layers or tops of two 9-inch layers.

# Seven Minute Fluff

**2 egg whites**
**¾ cup sugar**
**⅓ cup light corn syrup**
**2 tablespoons water**
**¼ teaspoon cream of tartar**
**¼ teaspoon salt**
**1 teaspoon vanilla**

Combine egg whites, sugar, light corn syrup, water, cream of tartar and salt in the top of a double boiler over rapidly boiling water. Cook, beating constantly with a rotary egg beater, until mixture stands in peaks. Remove from heat. Add vanilla and continue beating until thick enough to spread. Frost cooled cake and decorate. Makes enough to frost two 8- or 9-inch layers. Overcooking will give this type of frosting a sugary texture. Undercooking will leave it too soft and runny. The ideal time is about 7 minutes.

# NOTES

# Buffet

Just the word "buffet" connotates a party. It inspires the vision of a table, spread with a colorful cloth and decorated with candles and flowers. But most of all a picture of food, spread out in colorful casseroles and serving dishes for the enjoyment of invited guests.

This book is not going to tell you how to set your table or how many guests to have. It is simply chock full of casserole dishes for you to try, cook, sample and serve. We do not profess that they are all "fancy." Some of them are downright homey, using left over meat, plus bits of this and that, for the times when you want to put your feet up and relax. Many of them are fancy and start with fresh lobster tails, whole chickens and other goodies, that take more time, money and effort on your part.

We have also added a special section on chafing dish recipes. Many of you may have had a chafing dish for years, but never have found the courage to use it. Many of you may have received chafing dishes for wedding presents and are eager to try them. If you don't want to cook in your chafing dish, they make perfect serving dishes on a buffet table and for this we have included a few dishes that can be cooked on top of the stove and then transferred to the chafing dish for gracious service.

# How to Prepare a Casserole

**Saute rice in remaining pan juices until it is golden brown. Keep stirring the rice constantly. Now combine seasonings. Grease inside of a 3-quart casserole and arrange food in layers. Seasonings—salt, chili powder, pepper and the dry mustard—should be sprinkled on each layer.**

## Southwestern Range Supper

**2½ pounds 1-inch diced boneless chuck or round steak**
**¼ cup salad or olive oil**
**1 cup chopped onions**
**1 clove garlic, minced**
**2 cups raw rice**
**1 tablespoon salt**
**2 teaspoons chili powder (about)**
**¼ teaspoon pepper**
**½ teaspoon dry mustard**
**2 No. 2 cans tomatoes (5 cups)**
**No. 2 can kidney beans (2½ cups)**
**½ cup diced green pepper**
**1 cup stale beer**

Heat oven to 350° F. (moderate). Brown meat in a skillet in salad oil. Add onions and garlic. Cook until onions are soft. Remove from pan. Sauté rice in remaining pan juices until golden brown, stirring constantly. Combine seasonings. In a 3-quart greased casserole arrange 2 alternate layers each of rice, meat-onion combination and tomatoes, sprinkling each layer with seasonings. Top with kidney beans and a layer of tomatoes. Sprinkle with green pepper. Add beer. Cover and bake for 3 hours or until all rice is thoroughly cooked. Add hot water (if necessary) throughout cooking. Makes 8 servings.

**Layers should be alternate: rice in one, then meat and onions, then tomatoes. Top with kidney beans.**

After sprinkling top with green pepper, add beer, cover and bake for 3 hours: it's a delicious dish!

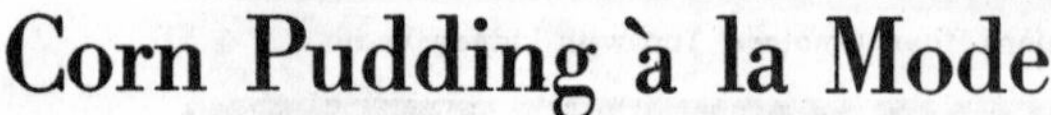

# Corn Pudding à la Mode

- 2 tablespoons butter or margarine
- 1 small onion, chopped
- ¼ cup thinly sliced celery
- 1 sweet red pepper, chopped
- No. 303 can cream-style corn (2 cups)
- 1 small green pepper, sliced
- 1 cup cooked lima beans
- ½ teaspoon salt
- ¼ teaspoon pepper
- ¼ teaspoon dry mustard
- 2 eggs, slightly beaten
- 2 3½-ounce cans Vienna sausages
- 2 ripe tomatoes, sliced

Heat oven to 350° F. (moderate). Melt butter in a saucepan and sauté onion and celery until tender. Combine with red pepper, corn, green pepper, lima beans, seasonings and eggs. Slice contents of 1 can Vienna sausages and add to corn mixture. Arrange tomato slices on bottom of a 1½-quart greased baking dish. Pour over corn mixture. Bake uncovered in 350° F. oven for 45 minutes. Arrange remaining sausage sliced in two lengthwise over top and continue to bake 15 minutes. Garnish with parsley sprigs. Makes 6 servings.

Arrange tomato slices on bottom of 1½-quart greased baking dish. Slice Vienna sausages.

Combine sauté of onion-celery with red, green peppers, corn, lima beans, seasonings and eggs.

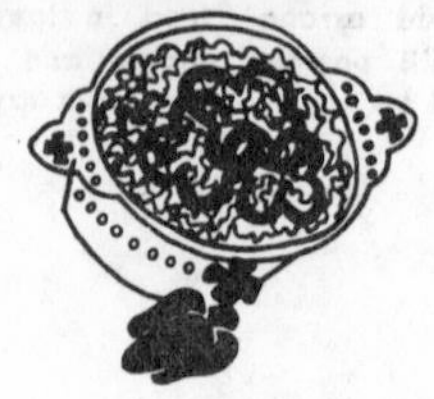

Add Vienna sausages to this corn mixture. Pour the whole over tomato slices in the baking dish.

Bake uncovered in oven for 45 minutes. Garnish with parsley sprigs: economical and delicious.

# Fish Fillets with Sauce Sûpreme

6 flounder fillets, about ½ pound each
⅓ cup salad oil
Salt
White pepper
¼ cup lemon juice
½ pound mushrooms, sliced
1 medium onion, sliced
2 tablespoons chopped parsley
2 teaspoons cornstarch
1¾ cups milk
2 egg yolks
1½ pounds fresh or frozen asparagus, cooked

Heat oven to 425° F. (hot). Brush fillets with oil. Sprinkle lightly with salt, pepper and 1 tablespoon lemon juice. Allow to stand for 15 minutes. Sauté mushrooms and onion in 2 tablespoons oil in a skillet until tender. Combine with parsley. Spread over fillets. Roll and tie fillets at each end with string. Place on greased baking dish and bake uncovered in 425° F. oven for 25 minutes. Meanwhile combine cornstarch, 1 teaspoon salt and a dash of white pepper in a saucepan. Mix with 2 tablespoons milk until smooth. Pour in remaining milk and stir over low heat until mixture thickens and boils. Boil for 1 minute, stirring constantly. Remove from heat. Mix in egg yolks, then remaining lemon juice and salad oil, beating until smooth. Arrange asparagus around fish. Cover fish and asparagus with sauce. Place under broiler, 3 inches from heat until browned. Serves 6.

Combine tender mushrooms and onion with parsley. Spread over fillets. Roll and tie with string.

Add a tbsp. lemon juice and allow to stand in dish 15 minutes. Sauté mushrooms and onion in oil.

While fillets are baking, mix cornstarch, salt and white pepper in pan. Mix with milk smoothly.

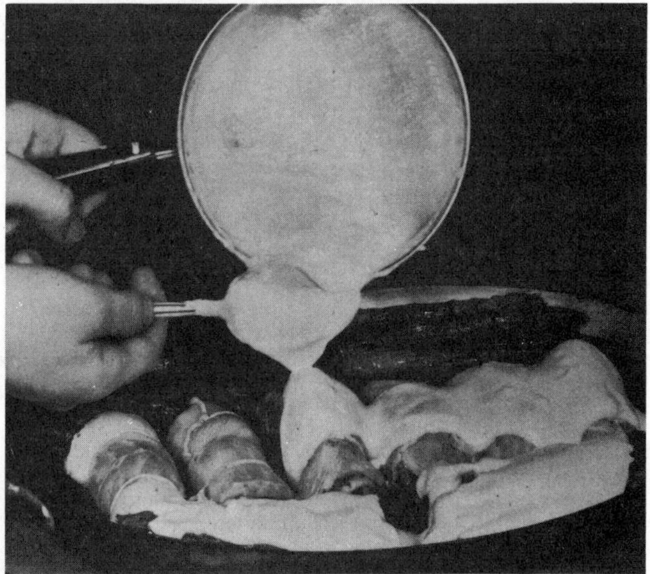

Place fillets on greased baking dish in oven, uncovered and bake 25 minutes, more or less. Boil sauce, add egg yolks, lemon juice, salad oil to it: a tasty combination with the fillets!

# Chicken and Turkey

## Wonderful New Chicken Pudding

- 2 cups finely diced, cooked chicken
- 1 cup cooked whole kernel corn
- 1 cup cooked peas
- 2 tablespoons grated onion
- 2 tablespoons finely minced parsley
- 1 cup cracker crumbs
- 1 teaspoon salt
- ¼ teaspoon pepper
- ⅛ teaspoon MSG
- 3 eggs, well beaten
- ¾ cup sour cream

Heat oven to 350° F. (moderate). Combine all of the ingredients in the order given and blend well. Pour into a 2½-quart greased casserole. Bake uncovered in 350° F. oven for 45 minutes or until set. Makes 6 servings.

## Chicken Dandy

- 3 cups diced cooked chicken
- 2 cups cooked rice
- 1 cup fresh bread crumbs
- ¼ cup chopped green pepper
- ¼ cup chopped sweet red pepper
- 1 teaspoon salt
- ½ teaspoon curry powder
- ⅛ teaspoon pepper
- ¼ cup finely chopped peanuts
- 3 cups chicken broth or milk
- 4 eggs, well beaten

Heat oven to 350° F. (moderate). Combine all of the ingredients in the order given. Blend well. Pour into a greased rectangular baking dish about 2 inches deep. Bake in 350° F. oven for 1 hour or until set. To serve cut in squares or oblongs. Makes 6 to 8 servings.

Best Foods

## Savory Baked Stuffed Chicken Breasts

- 4 boned chicken breasts
- 1½ cups cooked rice
- 1 medium onion, chopped
- 2 tablespoons chopped parsley
- 2½ teaspoons salt, divided
- Pepper
- ¾ cup corn oil, divided
- ¼ cup flour
- ½ teaspoon paprika
- ¾ cup lemon juice
- ¼ cup water
- 3 tablespoons sugar
- 1½ teaspoons Tabasco

Wash chicken breasts and dry thoroughly; place skin side down. Combine rice, onion, parsley, ½ teaspoon salt, dash of pepper and ¼ cup of the corn oil. Blend well. Spoon into hollows of chicken breasts. Lap sides together and fasten with wooden toothpicks. Dust each breast lightly with a mixture of flour and paprika. Place chicken pieces skin side up in a shallow baking pan, lined with aluminum foil. Bake in a very hot oven (450° F.) about 25 minutes. Reduce heat to 325° F. Combine remaining corn oil, lemon juice, water, remaining salt, sugar and Tabasco sauce. Heat to boiling. Baste chicken with sauce. Bake about 25 more minutes or until tender; baste frequently to use all of the sauce. Makes 4 servings.

# Turkey Tetrazzini

¼ cup butter, divided
½ pound mushrooms, sliced
2 tablespoons flour
1 teaspoon salt
1½ cups milk
1 bouillon cube
¼ teaspoon Tabasco
2 cups diced cooked turkey
2 tablespoons diced pimiento
2 cups fine noodles, cooked
¼ cup grated Parmesan cheese
1 cup soft buttered bread crumbs

Melt 3 tablespoons of the butter in a saucepan. Add sliced mushrooms and cook 5 minutes. Blend in flour and salt. Gradually stir in milk; add bouillon cube. Cook over medium heat, stirring constantly, until mixture thickens and comes to a boil. Remove from heat; stir in Tabasco. Place turkey, pimiento and noodles in a shallow baking dish. Pour mushroom sauce over all. Sprinkle with cheese and dot with remaining butter. Sprinkle buttered bread crumbs around edge. Bake in a moderate oven (375° F.) 20 minutes or until browned. Makes 4 servings.

McIlhenney's Tabasco

# Turkey Mandarin

2 tablespoons finely chopped green onion
1½ cups diced celery
2 tablespoons salad oil
2 cups 1-inch diced, cooked turkey
¼ cup coarsely chopped toasted almonds
Grated rind of ½ lemon (yellow only)
1 tablespoon lemon juice
⅔ cup mayonnaise
Salt
Pepper
1 cup crushed potato chips
½ cup grated Cheddar cheese

Heat oven to 375° F. (moderate). Sauté onion and celery in oil until tender. Combine with turkey, almonds, lemon rind and juice in a mixing bowl. Add mayonnaise and toss lightly to blend ingredients. If necessary, add additional salt and pepper. Sprinkle 4 12-ounce greased casseroles or a 2-quart greased casserole with fine potato chips. Divide mixture into casseroles. Sprinkle cheese over top and scatter remaining potato chips around edges. Bake uncovered in a 375° F. oven for 25 minutes, or until cheese begins to bubble. Makes 4 servings. Double recipe for 8 servings.

# Chicken and Macaroni au Gratin

4 tablespoons butter
2 tablespoons flour
3-ounce package cream cheese
1 teaspoon salt
Dash cayenne
¼ teaspoon garlic salt
Dash nutmeg
1 cup milk
1 cup chicken bouillon
2 tablespoons chopped pimiento
1 cup sautéed mushrooms
2½ cups 1-inch diced, cooked chicken
2 cups cooked macaroni
½ cup grated Swiss cheese

Heat oven to 350° F. (moderate). Melt butter over low heat and blend in flour, cream cheese and seasonings. Gradually add milk and bouillon, stirring constantly until slightly thickened. Combine with pimiento, mushrooms, chicken and macaroni. Turn into a 2-quart greased casserole, top with cheese and bake uncovered in 350° F. oven for 25 minutes, or until lightly browned on top. Makes 8 servings.

# Baked Turkey Hash

1½ cups diced turkey
1 medium onion, diced
1 medium potato, diced
1 pimiento, diced
2 medium carrots
1 teaspoon salt
2 teaspoons minced parsley
¼ teaspoon poultry seasoning
½ cup seasoned thin gravy

Cube turkey, onion, potato and pimiento. Combine with coarsely grated carrots, salt, parsley and poultry seasoning. Mix lightly to distribute seasoning evenly throughout mixture. Blend in gravy and stir until all ingredients are moistened. Spoon into a greased 1-quart casserole. Cover and bake in a moderate oven 350°F. for 45 minutes. Remove cover and continue to bake uncovered for 15 minutes. Serve with reheated extra gravy.

# Turkey Divan

¼ cup butter or margarine
¼ cup flour
¼ teaspoon salt
2 cups chicken stock
¼ teaspoon Tabasco
¼ cup grated Parmesan cheese
½ cup heavy cream
4 ounces rigatoni, cooked
1 package (10-ounces) frozen broccoli, thawed
1½ cups diced cooked turkey

Melt butter, stir in flour and salt. Gradually add chicken stock and cook, stirring constantly, until mixture thickens and comes to a boil. Remove from heat; stir in Tabasco, cheese and cream. Put hot cooked rigatoni in a greased 2-quart casserole. Top with broccoli and turkey; pour sauce over all. Bake in a moderate oven (350° F.) 40 minutes, or until broccoli is tender. Sprinkle with additional grated cheese. Makes 4 servings.

# Turkey-Green Bean Puff

10½-ounce can condensed cream of chicken soup
⅓ cup milk
2 tablespoons melted butter or margarine
½ teaspoon onion salt
Dash cayenne
1 cup cooked turkey or chicken, cut in small thick slices
2 cups 1-inch piece cooked green beans
½ cup chopped peanuts
4 eggs, separated
¼ cup grated Swiss cheese

Heat oven to 375° F. (moderate). Combine soup, milk, butter and seasonings in a 1½-quart greased casserole. Stir in chicken, beans and peanuts. Bake uncovered in 375° F. oven for 10 minutes. Meanwhile, beat egg yolks until foamy and add cheese. Fold into stiffly beaten egg whites. Pile fluffy egg topping on casserole ingredients. Continue baking uncovered for 30 minutes. Serve at once. Makes 6 servings.

# Duckling California-Style

6-pound duckling
Salt
Pepper
¼ cup salad oil
1 clove garlic
1 cup seedless raisins
1 cup crushed pineapple and juice
2 cups apricot juice
1 cup water
½ cup Sauterne
1 teaspoon cornstarch

Heat oven to 350° F. (moderate). Cut duckling in serving-size pieces. Season with salt and pepper and sauté in oil united with garlic. Drain. Place browned duck in a large casserole. Add remaining ingredients. Bake covered in 350° F. oven for 1¼ to 1½ hours or until tender. Stir the mixture occasionally to prevent sticking. Makes 6 servings.

Thicken the sauce with cornstarch mixed with a little water. if desired.

# Deviled Duck

2 4-pound ducklings
Salt
Pepper
¼ cup shortening
¼ cup flour
2 cups consommé or water
½ cup catsup
1 teaspoon dry mustard
1 teaspoon salt
⅛ teaspoon Tabasco sauce
1 tablespoon A-1 sauce

Heat oven to 350° F. (moderate). Cut duckling in serving-size pieces. Season with salt and pepper and sauté in shortening until browned on all sides. Sprinkle with flour. Place in a large casserole. Combine remaining ingredients and pour over. Cover and bake in 350° F. oven for 1 to 1¼ hours or until tender. Stir occasionally to distribute gravy. Makes 6 to 8 servings.

R. T. French

# Savory Chicken Pie

4 tablespoons butter or margarine
4 tablespoons flour
1 teaspoon salt
1 cup chicken broth
1 cup milk
1 tablespoon mustard
¼ teaspoon rosemary, crushed
2 cups diced cooked chicken
1 can (8 ounces) tiny whole boiled onions
1 cup cooked peas
1 can (3 ounces) mushrooms, drained
1 envelope instant mashed potato granules
Melted butter

Melt butter in saucepan; blend in flour and salt. Add chicken broth and milk; cook over low heat until smooth and thickened, stirring constantly. Blend in mustard and crushed rosemary. Add diced chicken, drained onions, peas and mushrooms. Pour mixture into a 1½ quart casserole; bake in a moderate oven (350° F.) about 30 minutes. Meanwhile prepare mashed potato as directed on envelope. Remove casserole from oven, pipe mashed potatoes around edge. Brush potatoes with melted butter and then paprika, continue baking about 15 minutes or until lightly browned. Makes 6 servings.

# Cornwall Duck Pastry

2 cups sifted all-purpose flour
1 teaspoon salt
⅓ cup corn meal
⅔ cup shortening
4 to 5 tablespoons cold water
2 cups diced cooked duck
1 cup diced cooked carrots
6 medium onions, cooked
2 tablespoons chopped parsley
10½-ounce can cream of celery soup
1 cup light cream
½ teaspoon salt

Mix sifted flour, salt and corn meal. Cut in shortening with 2 knives or pastry blender until mixture resembles coarse meal. Add water, mixing with a fork, until dough will hold together but is not sticky. Roll ⅛-inch thick and cut in 6 circles. Heat oven to 425° F. (hot). Combine remaining ingredients and divide evenly into 6 individual greased baking dishes. Top with pastry. Press to rim of dish with fork. Make several slits in the top. Bake in 425° F. oven 25 to 50 minutes or until browned and sauce bubbles through the slits. Makes 6 servings.

# Super Chicken Casserole

2 ounces medium noodles
1 medium onion, chopped
1 tablespoon butter or margarine
1 can (10½ ounces) condensed cream of chicken soup
½ cup milk
1 can (5 ounces) boned chicken or turkey
½ cup drained cooked lima beans
½ cup shredded Cheddar cheese

Cook noodles in lighly salted water; drain. Meanwhile, cook onion in butter until golden brown; combine with soup, milk, chicken, beans, and cooked noodles. Pour into a 1-quart casserole; top with cheese. Bake in a moderate oven (375° F.) about 25 minutes or until hot and bubbling. Makes 4 servings.

**Note:** 1 cup diced cooked chicken or turkey may be used in place of boned chicken or turkey, if desired.

# Giblet Pie

1½ cups thinly sliced potatoes
1 cup thinly sliced onions
1 cup chopped cooked spinach, drained
1½ cups chopped cooked turkey or chicken giblets
1 cup sauteed sliced mushrooms
1 cup chopped cooked turkey or chicken
1 teaspoon salt
⅛ teaspoon pepper
⅛ teaspoon nutmeg
⅛ teaspoon thyme
1 cup giblet broth
2 tablespoons melted butter or margarine
½ cup sour cream
½ recipe standard pastry

Heat oven to 350° F. (moderate). Layer bottom of a 2-quart greased casserole with potato slices, then onion slices, spinach, giblets, mushrooms and turkey, sprinkling layers with mixed seasonings. Repeat layers, ending with potatoes. Cover with broth blended with butter and cream. Top with pastry. Pinch to edge of casserole and make several slits in top. Bake uncovered in 350° F. oven for 1¼ hours or until brown. Makes 6 servings.

# Lancaster Roast Duckling

6-pound duckling
Salt
Pepper
Powdered garlic
2 tart green apples
6 cups sauerkraut
1 teaspoon caraway seeds
1 cup water
3 tablespoons brown sugar
1 teaspoon salt
¼ teaspoon pepper

Heat oven to 350° F. (moderate). Wipe duckling, prick to allow fat to drain and season cavity with salt, pepper and a dash of garlic. Bake uncovered in a large baking dish in 350° F. oven for 45 minutes, turning occasionally to brown evenly. Pour off fat. Core, pare and slice apples. Combine the remaining ingredients and arrange over the duckling. Cover and bake 2 hours longer, stirring occasionally, until the duckling is tender. Makes 6 servings.

Campbell Soup Company

# Chicken Fricarole

5- to 6-pound stewing chicken, disjointed
1 stalk celery, cut in pieces
2 tablespoons chopped parsley
1 small onion, sliced
1 bay leaf
6 peppercorns
2 teaspoons salt
½ cup chopped onions
2 tablespoons chicken fat or butter
1 pound (two 8-ounce packages) medium-wide noodles
2 cups cooked, 1-inch asparagus pieces
1 cup diced cooked ham
½ cup sliced stuffed olives
10½-ounce can condensed cream of chicken soup
1 cup grated American cheese

Heat oven to 350° F. (moderate). Place chicken in a large casserole with celery, parsley, sliced onion, bay leaf, peppercorns and salt. Add water to barely cover. Cover and cook in 350° F. oven for 2 hours. Pour off and reserve broth, removing peppercorns and bay leaf. Meanwhile sauté chopped onions in fat until tender and cook noodles according to package directions (do not overcook). Scatter onions, noodles, asparagus pieces, ham and olives over chicken. Combine soup with chicken broth and ½ cup cheese. Pour over all. Sprinkle with remaining cheese. Return to oven and continue to cook uncovered, stirring several times, for 45 minutes or until bubbling hot and delicately browned. Makes 8 servings.

# Cream Chicken Casserole

2 fryers (3 to 3½ pounds), ready to cook
¾ cup flour
1½ tablespoons paprika
2 teaspoons salt
¼ teaspoon pepper
¼ teaspoon thyme
1 teaspoon dill seed
¾ cup shortening
1 cup chopped onion
1 tablespoon chopped pimiento
1 cup light cream or evaporated milk
1 cup bouillon (or 1 cube dissolved in 1 cup hot water)
¼ cup fresh lemon juice

Have fryers cut in serving-size pieces. Put flour, paprika, salt, pepper, thyme and dill seeds in a paper bag and shake a few pieces of chicken in at a time until they are well coated with the flour mixture. Brown chicken on both sides in hot shortening. Remove and brown chopped onions lightly. Add pimiento and stir in the remainder of the seasoned flour from the chicken pieces. Stir in cream or evaporated milk, blending well. Add the bouillon and fresh lemon juice. Place chicken in a casserole dish and pour sauce over. Cover and bake in moderate oven (325° F.), 50 to 60 minutes. Makes 10 servings.

Sunkist Growers

# Tangy Chicken

2 broiler-fryer chickens, cut in serving pieces
2½ cups water
2 bay leaves
1 onion, stuck with cloves
2 stalks celery
2 teaspoons salt
¼ teaspoon each pepper and thyme
3 tablespoons flour
1 lemon, sliced
Parsley

Put chicken in deep kettle with tight-fitting lid. Add water, bay leaves, onion, celery, salt, pepper and thyme; cover. Bring to a boil; reduce heat and simmer 40 to 50 minutes. Remove from heat. Strain broth and measure 2½ cups. Combine flour with ½ cup of the cooled stock; beat until smooth. Add lemon slices to remaining stock. Gradually add flour mixture to stock, stirring constantly and cook until thickened. Add chicken; heat. Garnish with parsley. Makes 8 servings.

Broiler Council

# Capon and Savory Dressing en Casserole

5- to 6-pound capon, cut in pieces (or two 3-pound fryers)
½ cup flour
½ teaspoon salt
¼ teaspoon pepper
½ cup shortening
¼ cup chopped onion
½ cup chopped celery and leaves
5 cups dry bread cubes
¾ teaspoon salt
¼ teaspoon pepper
⅛ teaspoon garlic salt
¼ teaspoon sage
¼ teaspoon thyme
½ cup sliced stuffed olives
½ cup melted butter or margarine
2 cups chicken broth

Heat oven to 350° F. (moderate). Toss capon pieces in a clean paper bag with flour, salt and pepper. Fry in hot shortening until evenly browned. Arrange around sides of a large casserole. Sauté onion and celery in remaining shortening until tender. Combine with bread cubes, seasonings, olives, butter and ½ cup chicken broth. Place stuffing in center of casserole. Pour remaining broth over capon, cover and bake in 350° F. oven for 1½ hours, or until capon is tender. Remove cover and continue to bake for 15 minutes to lightly brown dressing. Gravy may be made from drippings in skillet. Makes 8 to 10 servings.

# Chicken Baked with Fresh Tomatoes

**2 2½-pound frying chickens**
**⅓ cup flour**
**½ teaspoon paprika**
**3 teaspoons salt**
**⅓ cup bacon drippings**
**1 clove garlic**
**¾ cup chopped onion**
**¾ cup chopped green peppers**
**4 medium tomatoes**
**2 cups beer**
**¼ cup tomato paste**
**½ teaspoon thyme**

Heat oven to 350° F. (moderate). Coat chickens with flour seasoned with paprika and 1 teaspoon salt. Brown in drippings with garlic. Transfer chickens to a large greased casserole. Discard garlic. Sauté onions and green peppers until tender. Sprinkle over chickens. Peel and quarter tomatoes and arrange over chickens. Blend beer, tomato paste, 2 teaspoons salt and thyme. Pour over all. Bake covered in 350° F. oven for 1¼ hours. Makes 6 to 8 servings.

Campbell Soup Company

# Chicken with Pineapple and Almonds

**½ cup canned pineapple cubes**
**2 tablespoons butter or margarine**
**1½ tablespoons cornstarch**
**1 teaspoon salt**
**Dash cayenne**
**Dash cinnamon**
**Dash ground cloves**
**½ cup pineapple juice**
**2 tablespoons minced chutney**
**2 cups chicken stock**
**2 cups 1-inch diced, cooked chicken**
**½ cup sliced celery**
**½ cup slivered blanched almonds**

Heat oven to 350° F. (moderate). Sauté pineapple cubes in butter for 5 minutes. Mix cornstarch and seasonings. Combine with pineapple juice, chutney and stock. Add to pineapple cubes and stir over low heat until thickened. Place chicken, celery and ¼ cup almonds in a 1½-quart greased casserole. Pour sauce over and mix well. Sprinkle with remaining almonds and bake uncovered in 350° F. oven for 25 minutes. Makes 4 servings. Double recipe for 8 servings.

# Chicken Potatopies

**6 tablespoons butter or margarine**
**8 tablespoons flour**
**1 quart seasoned chicken stock**
**1 cup light cream or top milk**
**3 cups 2-inch diced, cooked chicken**
**½ cup diced ham**
**6-ounce can sliced mushrooms, drained**
**1 cup finely diced celery**
**12-ounce package frozen peas, thawed**
**3 cups seasoned mashed potatoes**
**Melted butter**

Heat oven to 400° F. (hot). Heat butter, blend in flour and gradually add chicken stock. Simmer until slightly thickened. Add cream, chicken, ham, mushrooms, celery and thawed peas. Simmer for 15 minutes. Pour into eight 12-ounce greased casseroles. Pile mashed potatoes in crowns around edges of casseroles. Brush with butter. Bake uncovered in 400° F. oven for 25 minutes or until golden brown. Makes 8 servings.

# Cracker-Crust Chicken Pie

**2 tablespoons butter or margarine**
**3 tablespoons flour**
**1 cup milk**
**1 teaspoon salt**
**Dash cayenne**
**1 teaspoon curry powder**
**3 cups coarsely chopped cooked chicken**
**2 cups light cream**
**1 tablespoon finely chopped parsley**
**2 cups coarse cracker crumbs**
**½ pound sliced mushrooms, sautéed**
**1 pimiento (optional)**

Heat oven to 400° F. (hot). Melt butter, blend in flour. Gradually add milk and stir over low heat until thickened. Add seasonings. Cook chicken in cream over low heat for 5 minutes. Mix with cream-curry sauce and parsley. Spoon into a 2½-quart greased baking dish. Bake uncovered in 400° F. oven for 10 minutes. Remove. Arrange cracker crumbs around edge of casserole. Make a series of neat circles of overlapping mushroom slices in the center. Cut pimiento into shape of a chicken. Place in center of mushrooms. Return to oven for 5 minutes. Makes 6 servings.

# Hot Buffet Salad

**2 tablespoons butter or margarine**
**2 tablespoons flour**
**1½ cups milk**
**½ cup pickle relish**
**¼ cup mayonnaise**
**2 tablespoons lemon juice**
**1 teaspoon salt**
**⅛ teaspoon pepper**
**2 cups cooked elbow macaroni**
**2 cups 1-inch diced, cooked chicken**
**1 large tart apple, chopped**
**3 stalks celery, chopped**
**2 pimientos, chopped**
**½ cup finely chopped pecans**

Heat oven to 350° F. (moderate). Melt butter over low heat. Blend in flour, then milk, stirring constantly until smooth and thick. Combine all remaining ingredients except pecans. Turn into a 2-quart greased casserole. Sprinkle with pecans. Bake uncovered in 350° F. oven for 30 minutes. Makes 4 to 6 servings.

# Baked Chicken

**2 broiler-fryers, cut in pieces**
**½ cup melted butter or margarine**
**¼ cup lemon juice**
**1 tablespoon dried tarragon**
**Dash pepper**

**Arrange chicken in shallow baking dish. Combine remaining ingredients; mix well. Brush chicken thoroughly with butter mixture. Bake in moderate oven (350°F.) one hour, or until tender, basting occasionally. Makes 6 servings.**

California Prune Advisory Board

# Prune Dressing with Casserole Baked Chicken

**2 large onions (or 2 cups sliced)**
**¼ lb. butter**
**2 teaspoons poultry seasoning**
**1 teaspoon salt**
**Few grains pepper**
**8 cups bread cubes**
**2 cups chopped uncooked prunes**
**½ cup boiling water**
**1 chicken, split**
**Whole plumped prunes for garnish**

Sauté sliced onions in butter until golden brown. Add poultry seasoning, salt and pepper. Combine bread cubes and prunes. Add onion mixture and water; mix well. Place in bottom of casserole, set split chicken or chicken pieces on top, brush with melted butter; cover. Bake about 1½ hours in moderate oven (350° F.), or until chicken is tender, uncovering the last ½ hour to brown chicken. Just before serving, heat whole plumped prunes for garnish on casserole.

**Note:** If desired, 2 packages of prepared stuffing can be used. Simply follow directions on package and add chopped prunes.

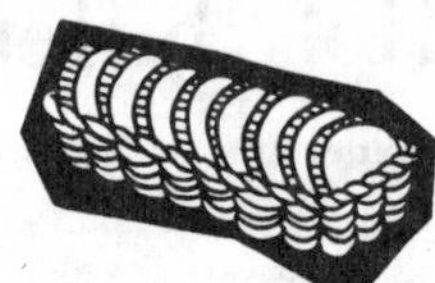

# Chicken and Stuffing Casserole

**⅓ cup chopped onion**
**¼ cup melted butter or margarine**
**5 cups soft bread cubes**
**½ teaspoon salt**
**Dash of pepper**
**¼ teaspoon sage**
**2½ tablespoons cornstarch**
**½ cup milk**
**2 cups chicken broth**
**1 cup drained cooked peas**
**2 cups diced cooked chicken or turkey**

Add onion to melted butter and simmer until onion is tender, about 15 minutes. Combine soft bread cubes, salt, pepper and sage. Add onion mixture and mix well. Combine cornstarch with milk in a 2-quart saucepan and blend well. Add chicken broth. Bring to a boil over medium heat, stirring constantly. Add peas and chicken to sauce. Place half of the stuffing mixture in a greased 8-inch square baking dish. Pour half of chicken mixture over stuffing. Repeat. Bake in a moderate oven (350° F.) 30 minutes. Makes 6 servings.

# Chicken and Ham Royale

**3 chicken breasts, (about 1 pound each) split**
**2 cups hot water**
**1 slice of onion**
**2 celery tops**
**1 teaspoon salt**
**8 ounces medium noodles**
**6 tablespoons melted butter**
**1 envelope a la king sauce mix**
**1¾ cup chicken broth**
**½ cup light cream**
**1 egg yolk**
**6 thin slices boiled ham**
**2 tablespoons toasted slivered almonds**

Place chicken breasts in water with onion, celery tops, and salt. Cover; cook over low heat about 30 minutes, or until tender. Let chicken cool in broth. Remove breast meat in one piece, discarding skin and bones. (Refrigerate, if made ahead). Strain broth and reserve. Cook noodles according to package directions; drain. Add 2 tablespoons of the butter to the noodles and keep hot. To make sauce, empty sauce mix into small saucepan. Add chicken broth; bring to a boil over moderate heat, stirring constantly. Blend together light cream and egg yolk. Add to hot sauce gradually. Bring again to boiling point, stirring constantly; remove from heat. Meanwhile lightly brown chicken pieces in remaining 4 tablespoons butter. Turn hot noodles into a large platter. Place slices of ham over top. Top each piece of ham with a piece of chicken. Spoon sauce over meat and noodles. Sprinkle with almonds. Noodles and meat can be assembled in a casserole, covered and kept hot in a warm oven (300°F.). Spoon sauce over when ready to serve. Makes 6 servings.

R. T. French Co.

# Seafood

## Artichoke Lobster Newburg

1 package (9 ounces) frozen artichoke hearts
1 bay leaf (optional)
1 can (5-ounces) lobster, cut in bite-size pieces
1 can (10½ ounces) condensed cream of mushroom soup
2 tablespoons Sherry wine
2 teaspoons chopped onion
½ teaspoon salt
⅛ teaspoon garlic salt
⅛ teaspoon pepper
½ cup grated Cheddar cheese
Wild rice, noodles or toast points

Cook artichokes as directed on package, adding bay leaf before simmering. Drain; remove bay leaf. Then arrange artichokes and lobster in 1-quart casserole. Combine soup, Sherry, onion, salt, garlic salt, and pepper; mix well. Pour over artichokes and lobster in casserole. Top with cheese. Bake in hot oven (400° F.) for about 15 minutes. Serve with wild rice. Makes 4 servings.

Birds Eye Artichoke Hearts

## Shrimp Olivia

¾ cup corn meal
3 cups boiling water
2 teaspoons salt
1 medium onion, chopped
1 small green pepper, chopped
2 tablespoons olive or salad oil
2 large ripe tomatoes, peeled and diced
Dash Tabasco sauce
½ teaspoon Worcestershire sauce
1½ cups cooked cleaned shrimp
1 cup chopped ripe olives
¾ cup grated American cheese

Heat oven to 350° F. (moderate). Gradually pour corn meal into boiling salted water. Cook and stir over low heat until thickened. Sauté onion and green pepper in oil until tender. Add tomatoes and seasoning sauces and simmer for 10 minutes. Place layer of cooked corn meal in a 2-quart greased casserole then a layer of shrimp, olives, tomato mixture and cheese. Repeat the layers. Make ribbons of ripe olives and shrimp on top of casserole. Bake uncovered in 350° F. oven for 30 minutes. Makes 6 servings.

## Salem-Town Lobster Bake

2 7-ounce cans lobster meat (about 2 cups)
1½ cups thin cream
¾ cup soft bread crumbs
2 eggs, slightly beaten
1 tablespoon chopped parsley
1 teaspoon grated onion
1½ teaspoons dry mustard
½ teaspoon salt
⅛ teaspoon pepper
⅛ teaspoon Worcestershire sauce
1 cup buttered toast cubes

Heat oven to 375° F. (moderate). Remove membrane from lobster and flake with a fork. Heat cream until small bubbles appear around edges of pan. Stir in bread crumbs and lobster. Slowly add eggs, blending well. Cook and stir until thickened. Add parsley, onion and seasonings. Pour into a 1½-quart greased casserole. Top with toast cubes. Bake in 375° F. oven for 15 minutes or until bubbling. Makes 6 to 8 servings.

## Sea Food Scallop

1 pint shucked scallops
½ pint shucked oysters
7-ounce can tuna
¼ cup white wine
2 tablespoons chopped green onion
2 tablespoons chopped green pepper
2 tablespoons butter or margarine
2 eggs, well beaten
2 tablespoons chopped pimiento
½ cup chili sauce
2 cups boiled rice
1 teaspoon salt
⅛ teaspoon pepper

Drain scallops and oysters. Reserve liquor. Drain and flake tuna. Mix with scallops and oysters. Pour over wine and let stand 25 minutes. Heat oven to 350° F. (moderate). Sauté onion and green pepper in butter until tender. Beat reserved sea food liquor and eggs until foamy. Add all the remaining ingredients and mix lightly with a fork until well blended. Pour into a 2-quart greased casserole and bake uncovered in 350° F. oven for 25 to 30 minutes or until just set. Makes 6 servings.

## Ocean Swell

7-ounce can crab meat
7-ounce can bonita
2 hard-cooked eggs, diced
⅓ cup pickle relish
2 tablespoons lemon juice
3 eggs, separated
½ cup milk
½ teaspoon salt
½ teaspoon celery salt
Dash cayenne

Heat oven to 350° F. (moderate). Remove membrane from crab meat; drain bonita and break into flakes. Mix seafood with eggs, relish and lemon juice. Beat egg yolks until thick and lemon-colored. Blend in milk and seasonings. Add fish mixture and mix well. Beat egg whites until stiff but not dry. Fold into egg-fish mixture. Pour into a 1½-quart greased casserole. Bake in 350° F. oven for 45 to 50 minutes or until set. Makes 6 servings.

# Rock Lobster Party Casserole

**6 (4-ounce) South African rock lobster tails**
**4 tablespoons butter**
**4 tablespoons flour**
**2 cups tomato juice**
**1 can (3-ounces) sliced mushrooms**
**1 small green pepper, finely chopped**
**1 teaspoon scraped onion**
**1 tablespoon catsup**
**½ teaspoon salt**
**1 teaspoon paprika**

Drop frozen South African rock lobster tails into boiling salted water. When water reboils, cook for 2 minutes. Drain immediately and drench with cold water. (Rock lobster should not be thoroughly done—it finishes cooking in the sauce.) Remove meat carefully from shells and dice it. Melt butter in saucepan over low heat. Gradually blend in flour. Add tomato juice gradually and cook slowly until thickened. Drain mushrooms and sauté them along with green pepper in small amount of butter. Add to sauce mixture along with remaining ingredients. Stir in South African rock lobster meat. Heat thoroughly and keep warm on buffet table. Serve over fluffy rice. Makes 6 servings.

South African Lobster Association

# Down-East Clam Pie

**2 dozen clams, shucked**
**¼ pound salt pork, diced**
**1 medium onion, sliced**
**2 medium carrots, diced**
**4 medium potatoes, diced**
**Clam liquor**
**1 bay leaf**
**¼ teaspoon celery salt**
**Dash Tabasco sauce**
**4 peppercorns**
**1 tablespoon cornstarch**
**2 tablespoons cold water**
**1 cup cooked peas**
**½ recipe standard pastry**

Drain clams and reserve liquor. Clean and chop clams. Set aside. Sauté salt pork until lightly browned. Add onion, carrots and potatoes. Cook, stirring occasionally, until lightly browned. Gradually stir in 3 cups clam liquor or clam liquor and water. Add seasonings. Simmer 10 minutes. Add clams and simmer 10 minutes longer. Blend cornstarch with the cold water and slowly add to clam mixture. Cook and stir until thickened. Add peas. Heat oven to 425° F. (hot). Pour mixture into a 2-quart greased casserole. Roll pastry to fit top. Trim edges and press with tines of a fork. Make several slits for steam to escape. Bake in 425° F. oven for 20 minutes or until top is browned and sauce bubbles through slits. Makes 6 servings.

# Hot Crab Meat Salad

**1 pound fresh crab meat or two 7-ounce cans**
**1 tablespoon lemon juice**
**4 tablespoons butter**
**4 tablespoons flour**
**2 cups milk**
**½ teaspoon salt**
**¼ teaspoon pepper**
**1 tablespoon chopped chives**
**3 hard-cooked eggs, chopped**
**1 cup sour cream**
**¼ cup sliced stuffed olives**
**1 bunch water cress**

Heat oven to 375° F. (moderate). Remove shell particles from crab meat. Sprinkle with lemon juice. Melt butter in a saucepan. Stir in flour until smooth. Add milk gradually, stirring until thickened and smooth. Combine with seasonings, chives, crab meat and chopped eggs. Pour into a shallow greased baking dish and bake in a 375° F. oven for 20 minutes. Remove and spread warm sour cream over surface. Top with olive slices. Continue to bake for 5 minutes or until cream is thoroughly heated. Serve hot on beds of water cress garnished with olive slices. Makes 6 servings.

# Sea Food Soufflé

**1 cup finely chopped, cooked or canned crab meat, shrimps or flaked fish**
**2 tablespoons lemon juice**
**Dash cayenne**
**½ teaspoon salt**
**2 tablespoons minced chives or parsley**
**4 tablespoons butter**
**4 tablespoons flour**
**1 cup milk**
**4 eggs, separated**

Heat oven to 350° F. (moderate). Combine your choice of seafood with lemon juice, cayenne, salt and chives. Melt butter in a saucepan and blend in flour. Add milk and stir over low heat until slightly thickened. Add seasoned seafood. Beat egg yolks well and stir gradually into mixture. Beat egg whites until stiff but not dry. Fold about half into the mixture, blending thoroughly. Fold in remaining egg whites, using 8 slow strokes. Turn into a 1½-quart greased casserole with straight sides. Place in a pan of hot water and bake in 350° F. oven for 1 hour. Serve with Mushroom-Cheese Sauce. Makes 4 servings.

**MUSHROOM-CHEESE SAUCE**

**10½-ounce can condensed cream of mushroom soup**
**1 tablespoon butter or margarine**
**Dash cayenne**
**¼ cup grated American cheese**

Mix ingredients. Stir over low heat until heated through and well blended. Makes about 1⅔ cups.

# Clam-Tamale Pie

½ cup finely chopped green pepper
½ cup finely chopped onion
¼ cup butter or margarine
2 or 3 teaspoons chili powder
1 can (8-ounces) chopped clams
1 can (1 pound-1 ounce) cream style corn
1 can (1 pound) stewed tomatoes
1 cup Sauterne, Chablis or other white dinner wine
1 cup uncooked yellow corn meal
Salt
½ cup pitted ripe olives

Cook green pepper and onion in butter until soft but not browned. Stir in chili powder (using amount most suited to your taste); cook a few minutes longer. Add undrained clams, corn, tomatoes and wine. Slowly stir in cornmeal. Taste and add salt, if needed; add olives. Turn mixture into casserole. Bake in a moderate oven (350° F.) for 30 minutes. Makes 6 servings.

Wine Institute

# Crab Chicken Ramekins

¾ cup uncooked rice
1 envelope Swiss recipe chunk chicken noodle soup mix
1 tablespoon margarine
1 teaspoon salt
2 cups water
1 can (7½-ounces) crabmeat, flaked
1 tomato, sliced
Finely shredded Cheddar cheese

Combine rice, soup mix, margarine and salt in 3-quart saucepan. Add water. Bring to boil, stirring occasionally. Cover, reduce heat and simmer until rice is tender and liquid is absorbed, about 15 minutes. Stir in crabmeat. Heat. Spoon into individual ramekins. Top each with tomato slice and shredded cheese. Broil until cheese melts and browns slightly. Makes 2 to 3 servings.

Best Foods

# Zippy Tuna Puff

3 7½-ounce cans tuna
1 teaspoon celery salt
¾ cup milk
3 cups grated Cheddar cheese (¾ pound)
½ teaspoon salt
1 teaspoon horse-radish
⅛ teaspoon pepper
Dash cayenne
3 cups soft ½-inch bread cubes

Heat oven to 375° F. (moderate). Drain tuna and break in flakes with a fork. Place in a 2-quart greased casserole. Sprinkle with celery salt. Heat milk over low heat. Add cheese and seasonings. Stir until cheese melts (Do not overcook). Add bread cubes and pour over tuna. Bake uncovered in 375° F. oven for 25 to 30 minutes or until lightly browned and set. Serve at once. Makes 6 servings.

# Tuna Pin Wheel

2 7-ounce cans tuna
2 16- or 17-ounce cans macaroni and cheese
2 tablespoons chopped parsley
2 tablespoons grated onion
3 firm tomatoes
Salt
Pepper
1 cup grated Cheddar cheese

Heat oven to 350° F. (moderate). Drain tuna, break in pieces and mix with macaroni, parsley and onion. Pour into a 2-quart greased casserole. Cut tomatoes in slices and arrange on macaroni. Sprinkle with salt, pepper and cheese. Bake uncovered in 350° F. oven for 25 minutes or until cheese melts and is lightly browned. Makes 6 to 8 servings.

# Deviled Oyster Scallop

1 quart unshucked oysters
¾ cup oyster liquor
½ cup catsup
1 tablespoon horse-radish
Dash Tabasco sauce
1 cup finely crushed potato chips
¼ cup shortening
10½-ounce can condensed cream of mushroom soup
½ cup coarsely crushed potato chips

Heat oven to 350° F. (moderate). Drain oysters, reserving ¾ cup of liquor. Mix catsup, horse-radish and Tabasco sauce. Dip oysters in seasoned catsup. Roll in a cup of fine crumbs. Sauté in hot shortening until lightly browned. Drain on absorbent paper. Mix soup and reserved oyster liquor and remaining catsup mixture. Arrange layers of oysters and soup with a top layer of soup in a 2-quart greased casserole. Sprinkle with the ½ cup of coarse crumbs. Bake uncovered in 350° F. oven for 20 minutes or until heated through. Makes 6 servings.

# Oysters à la Maddux

1 quart shucked oysters
¼ cup butter or margarine
3 tablespoons flour
1 teaspoon salt
¼ teaspoon pepper
¼ teaspoon curry powder
2 tablespoons lemon juice
½ cup mayonnaise
1 cup undiluted evaporated milk
2 tablespoons prepared mustard
2 tablespoons minced chives or parsley
1½ cups buttered bread cubes

Heat oven to 400° F. (hot). Clean and drain oysters. Melt butter in a saucepan. Sauté oysters over low heat until they are plump and edges curl slightly. Sprinkle with combined flour and seasonings, then lemon juice. Beat mayonnaise, milk, mustard and chives until blended. Fold oysters into sauce. Turn into a 2-quart greased baking dish. Top with buttered bread cubes. Bake in 400° F. oven for 15 minutes. Makes 6 servings.

# French-Toasted Salmon Doublettes

1 cup finely chopped celery
¼ cup chopped green pepper
2 tablespoons minced onion
1-pound can salmon
½ teaspoon salt
⅛ teaspoon pepper
1 teaspoon lemon juice
½ cup mayonnaise
16 slices bread
2 eggs, slightly beaten
1 cup milk
¼ cup butter

**Preparation:** Chop vegetables; drain and flake salmon. Combine with chopped vegetables, seasonings, lemon juice and mayonnaise.

**Performance:** Make eight double sandwiches of bread and filling and dip in mixture of egg and milk. Heat butter in blazer pan and brown sandwiches until golden brown on both sides. Serve at once. Makes 8 sandwiches.

# Stuffed Smelts

2 dozens smelts
2 tablespoons lemon juice
2 dozen anchovy fillets
¼ cup melted butter or margarine
½ cup white wine
Salt
Pepper
2 tablespoons fine dry bread crumbs

Heat oven to 375° F. (moderate). Split smelts lengthwise and remove bones. Brush each fish with lemon juice. Place an anchovy fillet on each smelt and roll. Secure with toothpicks. Place on shallow greased baking pan. Drizzle with butter and wine. Sprinkle with salt, pepper and bread crumbs. Bake uncovered in 375° F. oven for 25 to 30 minutes or until smelts are tender. Makes 6 servings.

# Tuna-Mushroom Strata

1 cup sliced mushrooms
¼ cup butter or margarine
3 cups buttered day-old bread cubes
7-ounce can tuna, drained
2½ cups milk, scalded
3 eggs, slightly beaten
1 teaspoon salt
⅛ teaspoon pepper
⅛ teaspoon oregano

Heat oven to 325° F. (slow). Sauté mushrooms in butter until tender and lightly browned. Place 1 cup bread cubes on bottom of a 2-quart greased casserole. Top with layer of tuna and mushrooms. Repeat layers, having the top layer mushrooms. Slowly mix milk, eggs and seasonings. Pour into casserole. Set dish in pan of hot water and bake uncovered in 325° F. oven for 60 minutes or until set. Makes 6 servings.

# Columbia Salmon Supreme

2-pound piece fresh salmon, boned
Salt
Pepper
1 teaspoon dill or dill seasoning
2 tablespoons French dressing
1 tablespoon lemon juice
1 cup sour cream
Paprika for garnish

Heat oven to 375° F. (moderate). Wipe boned salmon with a damp cloth. Sprinkle both sides with salt, pepper and dill. Place on shallow greased baking dish. Mix French dressing and lemon juice and drizzle over the fish. Spread sour cream over fish. Sprinkle top with paprika. Bake uncovered in 375° F. oven for 60 minutes or until fish flakes easily when tested with a fork and sauce is lightly browned. Makes 6 servings.

# Perch Oceania

2 12-ounce packages frozen perch fillets
6 medium potatoes
2 medium onions, finely chopped
1 small green pepper, finely chopped
1½ cups tomato juice
½ cup chili sauce
¼ cup salad oil
1 teaspoon
⅛ teaspoo

Thaw perch fillets according to package skin and cut in 2-inch pieces. Pare and th. Crisp in cold water. Heat oven to 375° F. (m maining ingredients. Place alternate layers o: tatoes and tomato mixture in 2½-quart grease and bake 40 minutes. Remove cover and con 30 minutes or until potatoes are tender. Make

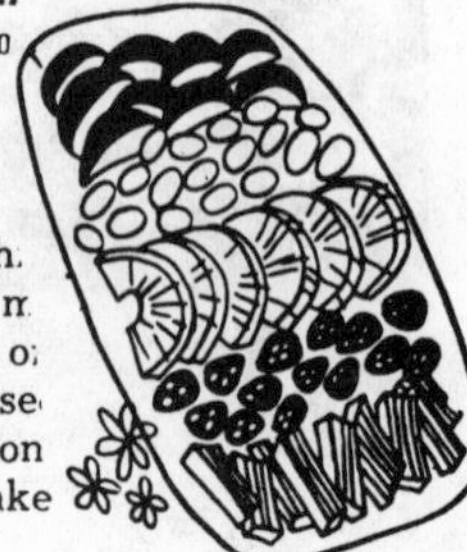

## Scallops Baked in Batter

**1 quart scallops**
**½ cup fine cracker crumbs**
**1 teaspoon salt**
**½ teaspoon paprika**
**¼ cup salad oil**
**2 eggs, slightly beaten**
**1 cup flour**
**½ teaspoon salt**
**2 cups milk**
**1 tablespoon finely chopped parsley**

Wipe scallops and roll in cracker crumbs seasoned with salt and paprika. Sauté in oil until evenly browned. Heat oven to 425° F. (hot). Mix remaining ingredients and beat until smooth. Place scallops in an irregular pattern in a shallow baking dish. Pour over batter. Bake uncovered in 425° F. oven for 30 to 35 minutes or until puffed and brown. Makes 6 servings.

## Spicy Baked Mackerel Fillets

**3 pounds mackerel fillets**
**1 teaspoon dried tarragon**
**1 teaspoon salt**
**¼ teaspoon pepper**
**½ cup diced onion**
**¼ cup lemon juice**
**¼ cup melted butter or margarine**
**½ cup catsup**

Heat oven to 425° F. (moderate). Wipe fillets and place on greased shallow baking dish. Mix tarragon, salt and pepper. Sprinkle over fillets. Mix remaining ingredients and pour evenly over the fish. Bake in 425° F. oven for 25 to 30 minutes or until fish flakes easily when tested with a fork. Makes 6 servings.

## Baked Clams and Eggplant

**¼ cup butter or margarine**
**½ cup chopped onion**
**1 large eggplant, peeled and diced**
**1 pint shucked clams**
**2 cups coarse bread crumbs**
**½ teaspoon salt**
**¼ teaspoon pepper**
**½ teaspoon celery salt**
**½ cup clam liquor**
**2 slices bacon, chopped**

Heat oven to 350° F. (moderate). Melt butter in a saucepan and sauté onion and eggplant until tender. Clean and mince clams. Place alternate layers of bread crumbs, clams and onion-eggplant mixture in a 2-quart greased casserole, ending with bread crumbs; sprinkle each layer with a mixture of seasonings. Pour clam liquor over. Top with bacon bits. Bake uncovered in a 350° F. oven for 45 minutes. Makes 6 servings.

## Shrimp and Swiss Cheese Fonduette

**2 5-ounce cans shrimps**
**2 cups grated Swiss cheese**
**8-ounce can undiluted evaporated milk**
**1 cup stale beer**
**¼ teaspoon salt**
**1 teaspoon Worcestershire sauce**
**2 cups cooked rice**
**½ cup finely chopped celery**
**2 cups toasted bread cubes**
**¼ cup melted butter or margarine**

Heat oven to 350° F. (moderate). Drain and de-vein shrimps. Combine cheese, milk and beer in saucepan. Stir over low heat until cheese melts and mixture is smooth. Add seasonings. Fold in shrimp, rice and celery. Turn into a 2-quart greased baking dish. Toss bread cubes in melted butter and arrange in a border on top. Bake uncovered in 350° F. oven for 30 minutes. Makes 6 servings.

## French Baked Fish Steaks

**4 bay leaves**
**1 large onion, thinly sliced**
**2 fish steaks, about 1½ pounds each (halibut, haddock or cod)**
**3 or 4 tablespoons salad oil**
**½ teaspoon salt**
**¼ teaspoon pepper**
**¼ teaspoon savory**
**⅓ cup slivered blanched almonds**
**2 green onions, chopped**
**1 tablespoon lemon juice**
**1 teaspoon grated lemon rind**
**2 tablespoons finely chopped parsley**
**2 tablespoons white wine**
**1 chicken bouillon cube**
**⅓ cup boiling water**

Heat oven to 350° F. (moderate). Place bay leaves in bottom of a large shallow baking dish. Cover with onion slices. Brush steaks with 2 tablespoons oil and lightly sprinkle with salt, pepper and savory. Brown almonds in remaining 2 tablespoons salad oil. Add green onions, lemon juice, lemon rind, parsley, wine, and bouillon cube dissolved in boiling water. Stir until blended and heated through. Pour over fish. Bake uncovered in 350° F. oven for 30 minutes. Makes 6 servings.

## Fish Fillets with Parslied Biscuit-Rolls

**1 pound fish fillets**
**3 hard-cooked eggs, chopped**
**1 tablespoon grated onion**
**1½ cups cubed potatoes**
**½ teaspoon salt**
**⅛ teaspoon white pepper**
**½ teaspoon curry powder**
**2 tablespoons flour**
**10½-ounce can condensed lobster bisque**
**¾ cup thin cream**
**2 tablespoons butter or margarine**
**2 cups biscuit mix (1 package)**
**½ cup finely chopped parsley**

Heat oven to 375° F. (moderate). Cut fillets in 1-inch pieces. Combine with eggs, onion and potatoes. Place in a 2-quart greased casserole. Mix seasonings and flour in a saucepan. Gradually add bisque and cream stirring over low heat until thickened and smooth. Pour over fish mixture in casserole. Dot with butter. Prepare biscuit mix, according to package directions. Roll dough to a thin sheet. Brush with melted butter or margarine. Sprinkle with parsley. Roll like a jelly roll. Slice in ¾ inch coils and arrange 6 or 8 on top of casserole. Bake uncovered in 375° F. oven for about 20 minutes or until biscuit-rolls are well browned. Bake extra biscuit-rolls at the same time on a lightly greased pan. Makes 6 servings.

## Salmon au Gratin on Lemon Toast

**1½ cups canned salmon (12 ounces)**
**1 tablespoon minced parsley**
**1 teaspoon minced fresh dill**
**1 tablespoon minced onion**
**½ cup minced celery**
**2 hard-cooked eggs, coarsely chopped**
**5 tablespoons butter or margarine**
**2 tablespoons flour**
**2 cups buttermilk**
**1 cup fine dry bread crumbs**
**½ teaspoon salt**
**⅛ teaspoon pepper**
**6 slices lightly browned toast**
**1 teaspoon lemon juice**
**½ teaspoon lemon rind**
**Lemon and paprika for garnish**

Heat oven to 350° F. (moderate). Skin and flake salmon. Do not drain. Combine with parsley, dill, onion, celery and eggs. Melt 2 tablespoons butter in a saucepan and blend in flour. Gradually add buttermilk and bread crumbs, stirring until thickened. Season with salt and pepper. Fold salmon mixture into sauce and turn into a 1½-quart greased baking dish. Bake uncovered in 350° F. oven for 50 minutes. Meanwhile butter toast with a mixture of 3 tablespoons butter, lemon juice and rind. Place in hot oven for 3 to 5 minutes so butter will saturate toast. Serve salmon on lemon toast garnished with lemon wedges dipped in paprika. Makes 6 servings.

## Creamy Fish Hash

**1 pound fillets of flounder**
**¼ cup dry white wine**
**⅛ teaspoon thyme**
**1 teaspoon chopped fresh dill**
**2 tablespoons grated onion**
**4 tablespoons flour**
**1 cup rich milk**
**4 tablespoons butter or margarine**
**1 cup fish broth, made from fish bones and trimmings**
**1 teaspoon salt**
**Dash cayenne**
**1 cup grated Swiss cheese**
**1 clove garlic**
**2 cups grated potatoes**

Heat oven to 350° F. (moderate). Cut fish in 1-inch pieces and sprinkle with wine, thyme, dill and grated onion. Melt butter in a saucepan. Blend in flour, then milk and fish broth. Stir over low heat until thickened and smooth. Season with salt and cayenne. Add ¾ cup cheese to sauce and stir till melted. Rub a 2-quart casserole with cut clove of garlic, and grease it. Alternate two layers each of fish mixture, potatoes and sauce. Sprinkle with remaining cheese. Bake uncovered in 350° F. oven for 45 minutes, or until top is delicately browned. Makes 6 servings.

# Lamb and Veal

## Veal Kidneys in Claret

**6 veal kidneys**
**3 tablespoons butter**
**1 clove garlic**
**2 medium onions, thinly sliced**
**1 pound mushrooms, cleaned and sliced**
**3 tablespoons flour**
**1 cup finely cut celery**
**¼ teaspoon rosemary**
**1 cup claret**
**1 cup stock**
**Salt**
**Pepper**
**Toast**

Split and clean kidneys, removing skin and tissue. Soak in cold water for ½ hour. Heat oven to 350° F. (moderate). Cut kidneys in ½-inch slices and sauté in butter with cut clove of garlic for 5 minutes. Remove kidneys, discard garlic and sauté onions and mushrooms until tender. Sprinkle with flour and blend well. Combine with kidneys in a 2½-quart greased casserole. Add celery, rosemary, claret and stock. Cover tightly and bake in 350° F. oven for 20 minutes. Remove cover, season to taste with salt and pepper and continue to bake for 10 minutes or until tender. Serve on buttered toast. Makes 6 to 8 servings.

# Oven Kebabs

2 pounds 1½-inch diced tender lean lamb (or beef)
½ cup wine vinegar
¼ cup olive or salad oil
1 clove garlic, minced
1 teaspoon mixed salad herbs
¼ pound large mushrooms
1 onion
4 small firm tomatoes
2 green peppers
Salt
Pepper
8-ounce can tomato sauce

Place lamb cubes in well blended marinade of vinegar, oil, garlic and herbs. Store in refrigerator for 10 hours, turning occasionally. Heat oven to 400° F. (hot). Cut mushrooms in thick slices. Slice onion, tomatoes and peppers in pieces about 1½ inches square. Loosely string alternate pieces of pepper, onion, meat, mushroom and tomato on long skewers repeating twice Brush with marinade and sprinkle with salt and pepper. Place in a large baking dish and cover with tomato sauce and remaining marinade. Bake uncovered in 400° F. oven for 1 hour, turning and basting every 15 minutes. Serve piping hot on skewers. Makes 6 to 8 servings.

# Lamb and Eggplant Dardanella

1 large eggplant, diced
1 large onion, sliced
⅓ cup olive or salad oil
1½ pounds ground lamb
1 teaspoon salt
¼ teaspoon pepper
¼ teaspoon rosemary
4 medium tomatoes, sliced
3 tablespoons chopped parsley
¼ cup grated American cheese

Heat oven to 350° F. (moderate). Sauté eggplant and onion in hot oil until tender. Remove from pan and drain on absorbent paper. Mix lamb with salt, pepper and rosemary and form into 6 patties. Brown in same pan as vegetables, adding more oil if necessary. Alternate layers of eggplant and onion with tomato slices and lamb patties in a 3-quart greased casserole ending with tomato slices; sprinkle each layer with parsley. Scatter cheese over top. Bake uncovered in 350° F. oven for 45 minutes. Makes 6 servings.

American Lamb Council

# Lamb Casserole

2 tablespoons salad oil
2 pounds cubed lamb shoulder (about 1½ inch cubes)
½ cup all-purpose flour
2½ teaspoons salt
¼ teaspoon pepper
½ teaspoon rosemary
3 cups beef bouillon
1½ cups chopped celery
1½ cups diced potatoes
1 cup thinly sliced carrots
½ cup chopped green peppers
1 cup sliced onions

Heat oil. Add lamb and cook over low heat until browned on all sides. Drain on absorbent paper. Combine flour, salt, pepper and rosemary. Gradually add bouillon and cook over low heat, stirring constantly, until thickened. Combine lamb, bouillon mixture, celery, potatoes, carrots, green pepper and onions; mix well. Turn into 2½-quart casserole. Cover and bake in moderate oven (350° F.) 1½ hours, or until lamb and vegetables are tender. Makes 8 servings.

*To Freeze:* Cool quickly (set uncovered casserole in iced or very cold water). Cover with moisture-proof material and seal with freezetape. To heat, uncover and bake in moderate oven (375° F.), 30-45 minutes, stirring occasionally, or until thoroughly heated.

# Lamb Pie with Sweet Potato Topping

2 cups 1-inch diced, cooked lamb
1 cup rich lamb gravy
1 cup bouillon
12 small cooked white onions
2 cups peas
1 cup diced celery
¼ teaspoon thyme
¼ teaspoon ground allspice
Salt
Pepper
2 cups mashed sweet potatoes
½ cup buttermilk
¼ teaspoon baking powder
1 tablespoon brown sugar

Heat oven to 400° F. (hot). Combine lamb, gravy, bouillon, onions, peas, celery, thyme and allspice. Season to taste with salt and pepper. Turn into a 2½-quart greased casserole, or 6 individual greased casseroles. Bake uncovered in 400° F. oven for 15 minutes. Beat potatoes, buttermilk, baking powder, ½ teaspoon salt and brown sugar. Arrange on top of casserole or casseroles as the case may be. Return to the oven and continue to bake for 15 to 20 minutes or until topping is heated through and lightly browned. Makes 6 servings.

# Lamb Hash Gratiné

1 medium onion, chopped
2 tablespoons butter or margarine
3 cups finely chopped cooked lamb
6 medium potatoes, cooked and diced
1 green pepper, finely chopped
¼ cup chili sauce
1 teaspoon Worcestershire sauce
1 teaspoon salt
¼ teaspoon pepper
⅓ cup grated American cheese
⅓ cup coarse bread crumbs

Heat oven to 400° F. (hot). Sauté onion in butter until tender. Combine with lamb, potatoes, green pepper, chili and Worcestershire sauces, salt and pepper. Mix well and spread in a shallow baking dish to a depth of about 1½ inches. Toss cheese and bread crumbs and sprinkle over the top. Bake uncovered in 400° F. oven for 30 minutes or until cooked through and browned. Makes 6 servings.

# Cranberry Lamb Shanks

**6 lamb shanks**
**Salt**
**Pepper**
**Flour**
**3 tablespoons fat**
**3 cups whole cranberry sauce**
**1 cup orange juice**
**¼ teaspoon powdered cloves**
**2 tablespoons sugar**

Heat oven to 350° F. (moderate). Wipe lamb shanks and sprinkle with salt, pepper and flour. Brown in hot fat. Transfer to a large casserole and pour over combined cranberry sauce, orange juice, cloves and sugar. Cover and bake for 2¼ hours or until meat is tender. Makes 6 servings.

# Party Veal Chops

**8 loin veal chops**
**¼ cup flour**
**½ teaspoon salt**
**¼ teaspoon paprika**
**¼ teaspoon pepper**
**¼ cup olive or salad oil**
**1½ cups light stock or consommé**
**½ cup white wine**
**2 large firm tomatoes**
**½ cup buttered bread crumbs**
**⅓ cup shredded cheese**
**⅓ cup sliced stuffed olives**

Heat oven to 325° F. (moderate). Dredge chops in flour seasoned with salt, paprika and pepper. Brown chops in hot oil in a large skillet. Transfer to a large shallow baking dish. Pour in stock and wine. Bake uncovered in 325° F. oven for 30 minutes, basting and turning occasionally. Cut tomatoes in 8 thick slices; place one on each chop. Return to oven and bake for 7 or 8 minutes. Top tomatoes with buttered bread crumbs, shredded cheese and olive slices. Increase heat to 400° F. (hot). Return to oven until cheese is melted and bubbling. Makes 8 servings.

# Stuffed Veal Chops with Herbed Spaghetti

**⅓ pound sliced cooked ham**
**2 slices processed cheese, cut in half**
**6 veal chops, cut with pockets**
**Salt and pepper**
**4 tablespoons olive or salad oil**
**3 cups cooked spaghetti**
**1 cup bouillon**
**¼ cup butter or margarine**
**¼ teaspoon oregano**
**1 tablespoon chopped chives**
**1 tablespoon minced parsley**

Heat oven to 350° F. (moderate). Divide ham and cheese in 4 portions and stuff into veal chops. Fasten openings with toothpicks. Sprinkle chops with salt and pepper. Brown on both sides in hot oil. Arrange spaghetti in a large open baking dish with chops on top. Combine bouillon, butter and herbs. Pour over all. Bake covered in 350° F. oven for 35 minutes. Remove cover and continue to bake for 10 minutes or until chops are tender, adding hot water as needed. Makes 6 servings.

# Country Lamb Stew

**2 pounds lean, boneless lamb shoulder, cubed**
**¼ cup flour**
**2 teaspoons salt**
**½ teaspoon celery salt**
**3 tablespoons shortening**
**4 cups hot water**
**Dash Tabasco**
**6 peppercorns**
**2 tablespoons fresh minced dill or 2 teaspoons dill seasoning**
**12 small white onions**
**6 small carrots**
**1 small summer squash, cut in 2-inch pieces**
**2 green tomatoes, quartered**
**1 cup cooked peas**

Heat oven to 350° F. (moderate). Dredge lamb with flour seasoned with salt and celery salt. Brown in hot shortening. Place in a 4-quart casserole and cover with water. Add Tabasco sauce, peppercorns and 1 tablespoon minced dill. Cover and bake in 350° F. oven for 1¼ hours. Add onions, carrots, squash and tomatoes. Replace cover and cook for 45 minutes. Add peas and remaining dill and cook uncovered for 10 minutes. Makes 6 servings.

# Veal Stew with Sweet Potatoes

**1 pound veal, cut thin**
**2 tablespoons flour**
**2 tablespoons salad oil**
**1 clove garlic, minced**
**10-ounce can condensed tomato soup**
**1 bouillon cube**
**½ cup hot water**
**1 teaspoon salt**
**½ teaspoon paprika**
**2 bay leaves**
**4 tomatoes, peeled and quartered**
**2 medium onions, sliced**
**12-ounce package frozen mixed vegetables, partly thawed**
**2 cups mashed, seasoned sweet potatoes**
**2 tablespoons melted butter or margarine**
**⅓ cup milk**
**1 seasoned dried mint**

Heat oven to 350° F. (moderate). Cut veal in 1-inch strips. Dredge in flour. Brown in hot oil with garlic. Combine with soup, bouillon cube dissolved in hot water, and seasonings. Turn into a 2½-quart casserole. Add tomatoes, onions and mixed vegetables. Bake covered in 350° F. oven for 45 minutes. Meanwhile whip sweet potatoes, butter, milk and mint until fluffy. When veal is tender, spoon in mounds over casserole. Bake uncovered 15 minutes or until potatoes are heated through. Makes 6 servings.

# Lamb Chops in Sour Cream

**6 large loin lamb chops**
**¼ cup fat**
**1 clove garlic**
**3 bay leaves**
**¼ cup water**
**1 cup sour cream**
**2 tablespoons A-1 sauce**
**½ teaspoon salt**
**¼ teaspoon pepper**
**¼ teaspoon marjoram**
**2 tablespoons minced water cress**

Heat oven to 350° F. (moderate). Trim chops and brown in hot fat with garlic, in a skillet. Discard garlic. Place bay leaves in bottom of a shallow greased baking dish with lamb chops over them. Bring water to a boil in skillet and loosen brown particles. Add sour cream, A-1 sauce and seasonings. Pour over meat and bake uncovered for 40 minutes or until chops are tender. Garnish with water cress. Makes 6 servings.

# Cream-Crowned Veal Continental

¼ cup butter
6 tablespoons onion flakes
1½ cups cooked rice
1 tablespoon salt
½ teaspoon black pepper
4 drops Tabasco sauce
2 cups sour cream
1½ pounds ground, cooked veal
1 egg, slightly beaten
Parsley or watercress, if desired

In large skillet over low heat melt butter. Rehydrate onions according to directions on package. Sauté onions until tender and lightly browned. Add rice; saute until golden brown. Remove from heat. Stir in seasonings. Combine rice mixture, ½ cup of the sour cream and veal. Press about ¾ cup mixture lightly into each of six individual casseroles. Bake in a moderate oven (350° F.) for 20 minutes. Combine remaining sour cream and egg. Spoon sour cream mixture evenly over veal or around edges. Return casseroles to oven; bake until sour cream is set, about 5 minutes. If desired, garnish with parsley or watercress. Makes 6 servings.

The Borden Company

# Pork and Ham

## Baked Ham and Cottage Cheese

½ cup milk
1½ cups soft bread crumbs
1 cup (8 ounces) cottage cheese
1 egg
1 pound ground ham
Apple rings (raw *or* pan-fried)
Parsley, if desired

Combine milk, bread crumbs, cottage cheese and egg; blend well. Mix in ham. Turn into 10 x 6 x 2-inch baking dish. Bake in moderate oven (375° F.) until top is lightly browned, 45 to 50 minutes. Serve with raw or pan-fried apple rings. Garnish with parsley. Makes 4 to 6 servings.

*Variation:* Omit apple rings and parsley; before baking arrange 4 pineapple slices on top and sprinkle with 2 tablespoons of brown sugar.

The Borden Company

# Flemish Pork Stew

**3 pounds lean pork, cut in bite-size pieces**
**Salt**
**Pepper**
**2 tablespoons rendered pork fat or drippings**
**3 medium onions**
**1 clove garlic**
**2 green peppers**
**3 stalks celery**
**1 bunch small carrots**
**3 tablespoons minced parsley**
**1 bay leaf**
**¼ teaspoon thyme**
**¼ teaspoon ground allspice**
**8 medium potatoes**
**1½ tablespoons cornstarch**
**½ teaspoon nutmeg**

Heat oven to 350° F. (moderate). Sprinkle pork pieces with salt and pepper; brown in hot fat. Chop onions, garlic, green peppers and celery; add to meat and cook until lightly browned. Place in a large casserole; add water to cover. Cook covered in 350° F. oven for 25 minutes. Meanwhile, scrape carrots, leaving them whole; add to stew with parsley, bay leaf, thyme, allspice, and salt and pepper to taste. Return to oven and cook, covered for 20 minutes. Pare and quarter potatoes and add to casserole. Continue to cook until potatoes and pork are tender. Skim off fat and thicken with cornstarch mixed to a paste with ¼ cup cold water. Sprinkle with nutmeg. Makes 8 servings.

# Pork Chops Baked in Applesauce

**8 large loin pork chops**
**1 clove garlic**
**Salt**
**Pepper**
**1 teaspoon fat**
**2 cooking apples, cored and cut in ½-inch slices**
**2 medium onions, sliced**
**3 tablespoons flour**
**2 cups boiling water**
**1 tablespoon lemon juice**
**2 cups applesauce**
**¼ teaspoon allspice**
**¼ teaspoon cinnamon**

Heat oven to 350° F. (moderate). Rub chops with garlic; sprinkle with salt and pepper. Lightly brush a large skillet with fat and quickly brown chops. Line a 3-quart greased casserole with a layer of apple and onion slices. Arrange pork chops over onions. Blend flour with pan juices in the skillet and add water. Cook and stir until slightly thickened. Add lemon juice, applesauce and spices. Pour over chops. Cover and bake in 350° F. oven for 1 hour. Remove cover and continue to bake for 30 minutes. Makes 8 servings.

# Baked Pork Tenderloin with Mixed Beans

**6 tenderloin cutlets or slices, about 1 inch thick**
**2 tablespoons fat**
**½ cup chopped onion**
**1 clove garlic**
**1 green pepper, chopped**
**1 teaspoon salt**
**1 teaspoon chili powder**
**¼ teaspoon pepper**
**No. 3 can kidney beans (4 cups)**
**12-ounce package frozen lima beans, thawed**
**1 tablespoon lemon juice**
**⅓ cup tomato catsup**

Heat oven to 350° F. (moderate). Fry cutlets in hot fat until well browned. Remove cutlets and sauté onion and garlic until tender. Discard garlic. Combine onion, green pepper, seasonings and kidney beans; place in a 3-quart shallow greased casserole. Cover with lima beans. Sprinkle with lemon juice and catsup. Arrange cutlets over limas. Cover and bake in 350° F. oven for 35 minutes. Remove cover and continue to bake 10 minutes. Makes 6 servings.

# Pancake Enchiladas

**½ pound sausage meat**
**1 clove garlic, minced**
**1 cup finely chopped onion**
**¾ pound chopped beef**
**1 teaspoon salt**
**½ teaspoon chili powder**
**1 teaspoon Kitchen Bouquet**
**1½ cups chopped cooked spinach**
**3-ounce can sliced mushrooms, drained and chopped**
**1¼ cups milk**
**3 eggs**
**½ teaspoon salt**
**⅔ cup all-purpose flour**
**⅓ cup corn meal**
**8-ounce can tomato sauce**
**¼ cup chili sauce**

Heat oven to 350° F. (moderate). Cook sausage meat in a skillet over medium heat until browned. Add garlic, onion and beef and continue to cook, stirring frequently for 10 minutes. Mix in salt, chili powder, Kitchen Bouquet, spinach and mushrooms. Beat milk, eggs, salt, flour and corn meal until smooth. Spoon onto a greased griddle, making 12 thin, 6-inch pancakes. Brown on one side. Place ⅓ cup filling on uncooked side of each cake and roll up. Arrange in a large shallow baking dish. Heat tomato and chili sauces. Pour around pancakes. Bake uncovered in 350° F. oven for 25 minutes. Makes 6 servings.

# Ham-Vegetables Au Gratin

**1 package potatoes au gratin**
**1½ cups boiling water**
**1¼ cups milk**
**2 tablespoons butter or margarine**
**1 tablespoon instant minced onion**
**1 tablespoon mustard**
**1 package (10-ounces) frozen succotash, thawed**
**2 cups diced cooked ham**
**2 tablespoons diced green pepper**
**3 green pepper rings**

Empty potatoes into a 2-quart casserole. Sprinkle packet of cheese sauce mixture over potatoes. Add boiling water, milk, butter, onion, mustard. Stir gently. Add thawed succotash, ham and diced green pepper. Cover and bake in a hot oven (400° F.) 50 minutes. To lightly brown top, uncover last 10 minutes of baking. Garnish top with pepper rings. Makes 4 to 6 servings.

R. T. French Co.

# Frankfurters Monterey

8-ounce package noodles
1 medium onion, chopped
1 green pepper, chopped
3 tablespoons salad oil
1 tablespoon Worcestershire sauce
2 tablespoons brown sugar
½ teaspoon salt
⅛ teaspoon pepper
1 lemon
1 pound frankfurters

Heat oven to 375° F. (moderate). Cook noodles according to package directions. Drain. Sauté onion and pepper in oil until tender. Add Worcestershire sauce, brown sugar, seasonings, juice of lemon and a thin strip of lemon rind. Simmer for 15 minutes, stirring occasionally. Remove lemon rind. Arrange frankfurters over noodles in a large greased baking dish and pour sauce over. Bake uncovered in 375° F. oven for 30 minutes. Makes 6 servings.

Corn Products Company

# Pepperoni Pizza

½ package hot roll mix
2 tablespoons olive or salad oil
¼ pound bland white cheese, shredded (1 cup)
1 small onion
1 clove garlic
1 large ripe tomato, peeled and diced
3 tablespoons tomato paste
½ teaspoon salt
⅛ teaspoon oregano
⅛ teaspoon pepper
¼ teaspoon sugar
6-ounce can sliced mushrooms
½ cup sliced pepperoni or other Italian sausage
2 tablespoons chopped parsley
¼ cup grated Parmesan cheese

Prepare dough according to package instructions. Divide in half and make a thick bottom crust on two 9- or 10-inch pie pans. Brush with 1 tablespoon oil. Cover with half of shredded cheese. Heat oven to 450° F. (very hot). Sauté onion and garlic in 1 tablespoon hot oil until tender. Discard garlic. Add tomato, tomato paste and seasonings. Cook for 10 minutes over low heat. Pour into pie crusts. Top with remaining shredded cheese, mushrooms and sausage. Sprinkle with parsley and Parmesan cheese. Bake uncovered in 450° F. oven for 18 minutes. Makes 8 servings.

# Pizza a la Reine

(See picture between pgs. 288-289.)

2¼ cups self-raising flour
1 cup butter
1 cup margarine
½ teaspoon salt
Water for mixing

Sift flour and salt, work in butter and margarine and add water a little at a time until a light, pliable dough is formed. Roll out lightly and cut to the size of a deep, heatproof, baking dish. Trim and flute the edges.

The fillings for the pizza are placed in three different sections and it is important that these must not be too moist or the pie will be too wet to bake.

No. 1 - Fried mushrooms, seasoned with a few drops of garlic, basil, salt and pepper.

No. 2 - Lay strips of ham on a bed of shredded Parmesan cheese. Make Bechamel sauce and add Parmesan cheese to taste (stiff consistency), use 1 cup. Decorate with fried tomatoes and green olives.

No. 3 - Place slices of Mozzarella and Gruyere cheese in the last section. Make sauce Mornay (thick white sauce seasoned with cayenne pepper and cut-up sharp cheese). Decorate with tomatoes, red pimentos (Spanish peppers in cans) and black olives. Rolled sardines can also be used if liked.

The Pizza must be placed in a very hot oven, after which bake at moderate heat from 15-20 minutes. Serve warm with a salad.

# Bechamel Sauce

(See picture between pgs. 288-289.)

1½ cups chicken stock
1 slice onion
1 slice carrot
Bay leaf
Sprig of parsley
6 peppercorns
¼ cup butter
¼ cup flour
1 cup scalded milk
½ teaspoon salt
⅛ teaspoon pepper

Cook stock 20 minutes with onion, carrot, bay leaf, parsley, and peppercorns. Strain. Melt butter. Add flour and gradually add hot stock and milk. Season with salt and pepper.

# Ham Tetrazzini

¼ cup finely chopped onion
½ cup butter
½ pound mushrooms, sliced
⅓ cup flour
2 cups milk
2 cups light cream
3 tablespoons Sherry
¼ teaspoon salt
Dash garlic salt
Dash pepper
¾ cup shredded Parmesan cheese
1 package (7-ounces) spaghetti, cooked
2 cups small, cooked ham pieces

Sauté onion in butter until transparent; add mushrooms and cook until tender. Blend in flour. Stir in milk and cream: continue stirring until mixture is smooth and thickened. Add sherry, salts and pepper. Mix together ½ cup cheese and spaghetti in bottom of a 2-quart shallow baking dish. Cover with alternate layers of sauce and ham, ending with sauce. Sprinkle remaining cheese over top. Bake in a moderate oven (375° F.) about 20 to 25 minutes, or until bubbly around edges and brown on top. Makes 6 to 8 servings.

# Marinated Pork Chops

1 envelope Swiss recipe cream of mushroom soup mix
2 cups water
2 tablespoons vinegar
2 teaspoons sugar
4 pork chops, about 1-inch thick
2 tablespoons corn oil (approximately)

Empty soup mix into saucepan. Gradually stir in water. Bring mixture to boil, stirring constantly. Reduce heat; partially cover and simmer 5 minutes. Remove from heat; cool Stir in vinegar and sugar. Arrange chops in marinade; cover. Let marinate in refrigerator 2 to 3 hours, turning once and spooning sauce over chops.

Heat corn oil in skillet over low heat. Remove chops from marinade, reserving marinade, and cook in corn oil, turning once, until lightly browned on both sides. Drain if necessary, then arrange in shallow baking dish. Spoon marinade over chops. Cover. Bake in moderate oven (350° F.) basting once, until meat is tender, 45 to 60 minutes. Makes 4 servings.

Best Foods

# Buffet Brunch

1 pound link sausages
1 tablespoon butter or margarine
½ cup fine bread crumbs
1 tablespoon minced parsley or chives
¼ teaspoon paprika
½ teaspoon salt
½ cup rich cream
6 eggs

Cut sausages apart and prick lightly. Place in a heat-proof baking dish on upper shelf of cold oven. Set oven heat to 325° F. and bake sausages for 25 minutes or until nicely browned. Pour off fat and turn sausages several times. While sausages are cooking, butter 6 flat shirring or baking dishes. Dust with bread crumbs mixed with parsley, paprika and salt. Spoon 2 teaspoons cream and carefully break an egg into each dish. Spoon 2 teaspoons cream over each egg. Arrange dishes on a cookie sheet and bake on lower shelf of 325° F. oven for 15 to 20 minutes or until firm. Arrange sausages over eggs. Makes 6 servings.

# Spareribs in Red Wine

4 pounds spareribs
1 teaspoon salt
¼ teaspoon pepper
¼ teaspoon garlic powder
½ cup chopped onion
½ lemon, sliced thin
1½ cups red wine
2 tablespoons Worcestershire sauce
4 medium-size tomatoes, peeled and diced

Heat oven to 450° F. (very hot). Wipe spareribs and sprinkle with salt, pepper and garlic powder. Place in a large baking dish. Cover with onion and lemon slices. Bake uncovered in 450° F. oven for 20 minutes. Pour off excess fat. Heat wine with Worcestershire sauce. Reduce oven heat to 350° F. (moderate). Sprinkle tomatoes over spareribs and pour heated wine over. Continue to bake uncovered at 350° F. for 1 hour, basting occasionally. Makes 6 servings.

# Yamboree

1½ pounds cooked ham
No. 2½ can drained sweet potatoes (about 3 cups)
⅓ cup brown sugar, firmly packed
½ cup pineapple juice
½ cup pineapple bits
1 medium onion
2 tablespoons ham or bacon drippings

**Preparation:** Cut ham in 2-inch lengths. Slice sweet potatoes ¼ inch thick. Combine sugar, pineapple juice and bits. Chop onion.

**Performance:** Heat drippings in blazer pan. Sauté onion until tender. Stir in pineapple mixture. Arrange ham slices in center and sweet potatoes around edge of blazer pan. Baste with sauce. Cover and simmer over low flame for 15 minutes, basting twice. Makes 6 servings.

# Ohio Ham Birds

2 cups cooked rice
1 tablespoon grated onion
⅛ teaspoon powdered cloves
½ cup minced celery
½ teaspoon salt
¼ teaspoon pepper
12 thin slices cooked ham
1 cup apple sauce
1 red apple
Melted butter or margarine
Dash cinnamon

Heat oven to 400° F. (hot). Combine rice, onion, cloves, celery, salt and pepper. Spread ham slices with stuffing nearly to the edge. Roll tightly and tie or fasten with small skewers. Place in a low flat casserole. Distribute apple sauce evenly around birds. Core but do not pare apple and cut in ½-inch slices. Arrange over birds. Brush with butter and sprinkle with cinnamon. Bake uncovered in 400° F. oven 30 minutes or until apples are browned. Makes 6 servings.

# Canadian Bacon-Pineapple Ruffles

No. 2 can sweet potatoes (2 cups)
⅔ cup brown sugar
⅛ teaspoon cinnamon
¼ teaspoon salt
½ pound Canadian bacon, thinly sliced
No. 2 can pineapple slices
¼ cup pineapple juice
2 tablespoons butter or margarine
Parsley for garnish

Heat oven to 325° F. (slow). Slice sweet potatoes in half lengthwise and arrange in two rows in a 2-quart greased baking dish. Sprinkle with brown sugar, cinnamon and salt. Arrange alternate slices of bacon and pineapple over potatoes. Pour pineapple juice over all. Dot with butter and bake uncovered in 325° F. oven for 45 minutes or until bacon is browned at edges. Garnish with parsley before serving. Makes 6 servings.

Ralston Purina

# Jackcake and Creamed Ham

**1¾ cups sifted enriched flour**
**¼ cup sugar**
**3 teaspoons baking powder**
**½ teaspoon salt**
**½ teaspoon soda**
**2¼ cups bite-sized toasted corn cereal crushed to 1 cup**
**1 egg**
**¾ cup sour milk**
**1 tablespoon light molasses**
**¼ cup salad oil or melted shortening**

Butter an 8-inch square baking pan. Sift together flour, sugar, baking powder, salt and soda. Stir in cereal crumbs. Beat together egg, milk and molasses. Mix in oil. Add to dry ingredients. Stir only until blended. Pour into buttered pan. Bake 20 minutes or until browned, in a hot oven (400° F.).

### Creamed Ham

**¼ cup butter or margarine**
**¼ cup flour**
**2 cups milk**
**1¼ cups shredded sharp Cheddar cheese**
**¾ teaspoon Worcestershire sauce**
**2½ cups diced cooked ham**

Melt butter. Add flour. Blend. Stir in milk gradually. Heat and stir until boiling and thickened. Add cheese and Worcestershire sauce. Stir until cheese is melted. Add ham. Heat thoroughly. Serve over Jackcake. Makes 6 to 8 servings.

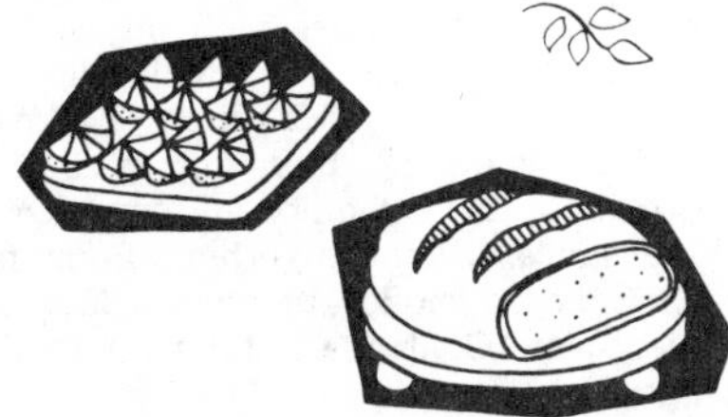

# Baked Mince Sausage Casserole

**1 package condensed mince meat**
**1 cup water**
**1 pound pork sausage meat**
**4 cups cooked, ½-inch thick sweet potato slices**
**½ teaspoon vinegar**
**3 tablespoons butter**
**2 cups sliced apples**
**¼ cup brown sugar, firmly packed**

Break mince meat into small pieces into small saucepan. Add water. Place over low heat and stir until lumps are broken. Increase heat and boil briskly for 5 minutes, stirring often. Slowly heat sausage in heavy frying pan until well browned, breaking the meat into small pieces with a fork as it cooks. Remove from heat; pour off fat and drain sausage meat on absorbent paper. Combine the cooked sausage and mince meat. Put half the potatoes on bottom of greased 2-quart casserole. Sprinkle with half the vinegar and dot with half the butter. Cover with mince meat-sausage mixture. Add apples, arranging in a layer; sprinkle with brown sugar. Arrange remaining potatoes in a layer over top; sprinkle with vinegar and dot with butter. Cover casserole and bake in a moderate oven (350° F.) for 30 minutes. Uncover and continue baking until apples are tender and potatoes are lightly browned, about 25 minutes. Makes 6 servings.

The Borden Company

# Country Cousin Supper

**4 cups sauerkraut**
**1 medium onion, sliced**
**½ teaspoon caraway seed**
**¼ teaspoon pepper**
**1½ pounds frankfurters**
**2 bay leaves**
**½ cup grated American cheese**
**2 cups seasoned mashed potatoes**
**1 tablespoon melted butter or margarine**

Heat oven to 350° F. (moderate). Combine partially drained sauerkraut, onion, caraway seed and pepper. Cut frankfurters in ¼-inch discs. Place bay leaves in bottom of a 2-quart greased casserole. Cover with layers of seasoned sauerkraut and frankfurters, ending with sauerkraut. Sprinkle with cheese. Bake covered in 350° F. oven for 20 minutes. Remove cover. Trim top of casserole with a decorative border of potatoes. Brush with melted butter. Increase heat to 425° F. (hot). Bake uncovered until potato border is lightly browned. Makes 6 servings.

# Ham Parisienne

2 12-ounce packages frozen broccoli
Salt
Paprika
6 ¼-inch slices boiled ham
10½-ounce can condensed cream of mushroom soup
4-ounce can sliced mushrooms and juice
2 tablespoons sherry
¼ cup grated Parmesan cheese

Heat oven to 425° F. (hot). Cook broccoli according to package directions, and arrange in a 2-quart greased rectangular baking dish. Season with a light sprinkling of salt and paprika. Top with ham slices in a neat row or pattern. Blend soup, 2 tablespoons mushroom juice and sherry. Pour sauce over ham. Sprinkle with cheese. Bake uncovered in 425° F. oven for 15 minutes or until heated through and delicately browned. Makes 6 servings.

Campbell Soup Company

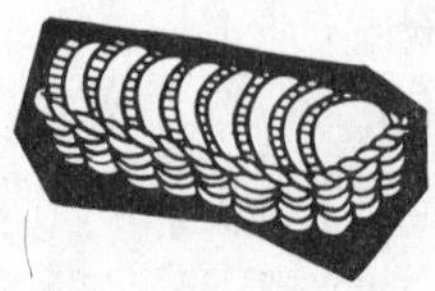

# Pork Paprika

2 medium onions, chopped
1 sweet red pepper, chopped
1 stalk celery, chopped
3 tablespoons pork drippings
4 cups thinly sliced potatoes
2 tablespoons flour
1 teaspoon salt
3 cups 1-inch diced, cooked pork
1 teaspoon paprika
10½-ounce can condensed cream of celery soup
1 cup buttermilk

Heat oven to 350° F. (moderate). Sauté onions, red pepper and celery in drippings until tender. Combine with potato slices. Sprinkle with flour and salt and arrange in a large baking dish. Sprinkle pork with paprika until lightly coated. Place over vegetables. Combine soup and buttermilk. Pour over pork. Sprinkle with paprika. Bake in 350° F. oven for 50 minutes or until browned on top and potatoes are tender. Makes 6 servings.

R. T. French Co.

# Country Pork Chops

6 loin or rib pork chops, 1-inch thick
½ cup finely diced carrot (1 small)
½ cup finely diced celery
¾ cup water
¼ cup catsup
2 tablespoons instant minced onion
2 tablespoons prepared mustard
2 teaspoons Worcestershire sauce

Lightly grease bottom of large skillet with a little fat trimmed from chops. Season chops on both sides with salt and pepper. Brown chops well on both sides, over medium heat; about 15 minutes. Meanwhile, sprinkle chopped carrots and celery in bottom of 2-quart shallow casserole. Arrange browned chops on top. Pour excess fat from skillet. Combine water, catsup, instant onion, prepared mustard, and Worcestershire sauce. Blend together. Pour mixture over chops. Cover. Bake in moderate oven (350° F.) for 50 minutes. Remove cover. Continue baking 15 to 20 minutes. Makes 6 servings.

# Spaghetti Fegato

**2 tablespoons olive or salad oil**
**½ pound pork sausage**
**1 cup chopped onion**
**1 clove garlic, minced**
**½ pound ground beef liver**
**No. 2½ can Italian-style tomatoes (3½ cups)**
**6-ounce can tomato paste**
**1 cup rich beef stock**
**2 tablespoons chopped parsley**
**½ bay leaf**
**¼ teaspoon dried basil**
**¼ teaspoon dried thyme**
**1 tablespoon salt**
**½ teaspoon pepper**
**1 cup chopped ripe olives**
**½ pound spaghetti**

Heat oven to 350° F. (moderate). Heat oil in a saucepan and brown sausage meat. Add onion, garlic and liver. Cook for 10 minutes. Combine with tomatoes, tomato paste, stock, parsley and seasonings and simmer 1 hour. Add olives cut in large pieces. Cook spaghetti in boiling salted water, according to package directions, until tender. Drain. Spoon meat sauce over and mix lightly with a fork. Turn into a shallow 2½-quart greased casserole. Bake uncovered in 350° F. oven for 30 minutes. Makes 6 servings.

# Reveler's Reward

**36 salted soda crackers, finely crushed**
**⅓ cup melted butter or margarine**
**¾ pound pork sausage meat**
**2 medium onions, finely chopped**
**1 cup cooked rice**
**3 eggs, slightly beaten**
**1½ cups milk**
**2 tablespoons chopped green pepper**
**½ pound Cheddar cheese, grated (2 cups)**
**Pimiento for garnish**

Thoroughly blend cracker crumbs and butter. Press one-third against bottom of a 2-quart baking dish and chill. Heat oven to 350° F. (moderate). Cook sausage meat and onions in a skillet until no pink shows in the meat. Mix with rice and arrange over crust. Add eggs to milk. Stir in green peppers and cheese. Pour over sausage mixture. Make a crust of remaining buttered crumbs leaving a circle in center uncovered. Bake uncovered in 350° F. oven for 45 minutes. Garnish with pimiento strips to form quarter hour divisions and hands of clock. Makes 8 servings.

# Beef

## Baked Stuffed Lasagne

**¼ cup salad or olive oil**
**½ pound ground beef**
**⅓ cup chopped onion**
**¼ cup diced celery**
**1 clove garlic, minced**
**Dash Tabasco sauce**
**8-ounce can tomato sauce**
**½ cup water**
**1¼ teaspoons salt**
**⅛ teaspoon pepper**
**½ teaspoon oregano**
**¼ cup chopped parsley**
**3 cups cooked wide noodles**
**8-ounce package cottage cheese**
**1 cup grated Parmesan cheese**

Heat oven to 350° F. (moderate). Heat oil in a saucepan and cook beef until nicely browned. Remove from pan. Add onion, celery and garlic; cook until tender, but do not brown. Add Tabasco sauce, tomato sauce, water, seasonings and parsley. Simmer for 10 minutes. Pour ½ cup sauce into bottom of a 2-quart greased casserole; add layers of cooked noodles, cottage cheese, grated cheese, meat and repeat layers until all ingredients are used, ending with a generous layer of grated cheese. Bake uncovered in 350° F. oven for 30 minutes. Makes 6 servings.

McIlhenney's Tabasco

## Cauliflower Beef Casserole

**1 medium head of cauliflower**
**1½ pounds ground beef**
**1 small onion, chopped**
**½ teaspoon salt**
**¼ teaspoon Tabasco**
**1 tablespoon flour**
**1 cup milk**
**1 tablespoon oil**
**¼ teaspoon Tabasco**
**½ pound Cheddar cheese, grated**
**1 cup seasoned bread cubes**

Separate cauliflower buds. Cook in salted water until partially tender. Sauté beef with onion, salt and ¼ teaspoon Tabasco. Meanwhile combine flour, milk, oil and Tabasco in a small saucepan. Stir over low heat until thickened. Add cheese; heat until melted. Put meat into a 2-quart casserole; cover with a layer of bread cubes. Add cauliflower and pour cheese sauce over all. Bake in a moderate oven (375° F.) 30 minutes, or until casserole is heated through and sauce is bubbly. Makes 6 servings.

# Mexican Chili Con Carne

**1 pound chuck**
**1 large onion, chopped**
**2 cloves garlic, minced**
**3 tablespoons bacon drippings**
**1½ teaspoons salt**
**2 tablespoons chili powder**
**1 teaspoon oregano**
**¼ teaspoon cummin**
**1 bay leaf, crushed**
**No. 2 can tomatoes (2½ cups)**
**No. 2 can red kidney beans (2½ cups)**

Have beef coarsely ground or chop it fine. Heat oven to 325° F. (slow). Brown meat, onion and garlic in drippings. Sprinkle with seasonings. Combine with tomatoes and turn into a 2-quart greased casserole. Cover and bake in 325° F. oven for 1½ hours. Remove from oven. Stir in heated beans. Replace cover and continue baking for 20 minutes. (The cooking may be done on the top of the stove. Place casserole on an asbestos pad to protect it from direct heat. Cook over low heat for 2 hours. Add beans and heat through.) Makes 6 servings.

American Spice Trade Association

Sunkist Growers

# Filled Cabbage Rolls

**1 medium head cabbage**
**¼ cup minced onion**
**½ pound ground round steak**
**½ cup coarse cracker crumbs**
**3 tablespoons chopped raisins**
**¼ teaspoon salt**
**¼ teaspoon celery salt**
**Pinch each of oregano, allspice and pepper**
**2 cans (8-ounce) tomato sauce**
**3 tablespoons fresh lemon juice**
**1 lemon, sliced**

Remove 6 outer leaves from cabbage. Trim off thick part from each one. Cover with boiling water and allow to stand for a few minutes to wilt. Drain and cool. Combine onion, beef, crumbs, raisins and seasonings with enough tomato sauce to moisten. Divide filling into six portions; place mound of meat mixture in cup part of each cabbage leaf; loosely fold over sides of each leaf; roll up. Shred some of remaining cabbage and put on bottom of 1½-quart casserole. Arrange filled rolls, with seam side down, over shredded cabbage. Combine remaining tomato sauce with lemon juice and pour over rolls. Tuck lemon slices in between each roll. Bake in a moderate oven (350° F.) 30 to 40 minutes. Makes 6 servings.

# Frizzled Beef and Potato Scallop

6-ounce jar dried beef
4 tablespoons shortening
3 tablespoons flour
3 cups milk
¼ teaspoon pepper
½ teaspoon dill seasoning salt
6 medium potatoes, sliced
1 cup thin onion slices
½ cup chopped celery
1 cup shredded American cheese

Heat oven to 325° F. (slow). Shred beef and soak in boiling water for 5 minutes. Drain and pat dry with absorbent paper. Sauté in shortening until lightly browned. Remove beef from pan. Blend flour into remaining drippings. Add milk gradually, stirring over low heat until thickened and smooth. Add seasonings. Arrange potatoes, beef, onions, celery and cheese in alternate layers in a 3-quart greased casserole ending with cheese. Pour sauce over. Bake uncovered in a 325° F. oven for 1 hour or until potatoes are tender and cheese is browned. Makes 6 to 8 servings.

# Snow-Capped Pie

2 tablespoons butter or margarine
1 medium onion, chopped
1 pound ground beef
½ teaspoon celery salt
½ teaspoon salt
⅛ teaspoon pepper
1 teaspoon A-1 sauce
2 cups cooked sliced carrots
¼ cup carrot liquid
2½ cups well seasoned mashed potatoes
Melted butter or margarine
Parsley for garnish

Heat oven to 400° F. (hot). Melt butter in skillet. Sauté onion and beef until lightly brown. Add celery salt, salt, pepper and A-1 sauce. Place carrots and liquid in a 2-quart greased casserole. Put browned beef mixture on top of carrots. Top with mashed potatoes. For a decorative finish, put some of mashed potatoes in a pastry tube or a cake decorator and make a fluted or scalloped edging around top. Brush with butter. Bake uncovered in 400° F. oven for 15 to 20 minutes or until potatoes are lightly browned and food is thoroughly heated. Garnish with parsley. Makes 6 servings.

# Chipped Beef and Green Beans in Cheese Sauce

8-ounce jar dried beef
3 tablespoons butter or margarine
2 cups cooked green beans, cut in slivers or French style
12 small cooked or canned white onions, cut in quarters
¼ teaspoon pepper
1 teaspoon curry powder
2 tablespoons flour
1 cup grated Parmesan cheese
1 can condensed cream of mushroom soup
1 cup milk

Heat oven to 350° F. (moderate). Shred beef and soak in boiling water for 5 minutes. Drain and pat dry with absorbent paper. Sauté in butter until lightly browned. Place beans in a large greased baking dish, cover with onions and frizzled beef, sprinkling each layer lightly with a mixture of seasonings, flour and cheese. Combine soup and milk and mix until smooth. Pour over all. Bake uncovered in 350° F. oven for 40 minutes until bubbling and browned on top. Makes 6 servings.

# Apple Kraut Special

1 can (No. 2) sauerkraut
1 can (12-ounces) frankfurters
2 cups canned apple sauce
1 cup sour cream
½ cup finely chopped onion
1½ cups sifted all-purpose flour
2 teaspoons baking powder
¼ teaspoon salt
2 tablespoons caraway seeds
6 tablespoons shortening
½ cup milk

Combine sauerkraut, frankfurters cut in 1" pieces, apple sauce, sour cream and onions. Mix well. Put into shallow baking dish, 9" x 9" x 2". Sift together flour, baking powder and salt; add caraway seeds. Cut in shortening with 2 knives or pastry blender. Add enough milk to hold ingredients together. Pat out dough on floured board to 1" thickness. Cut with round cutter. Place biscuits on sauerkraut mixture. Bake in hot oven (400° F.) 45 minutes. Makes 4-6 servings.

Processed Apples Institute, Inc.

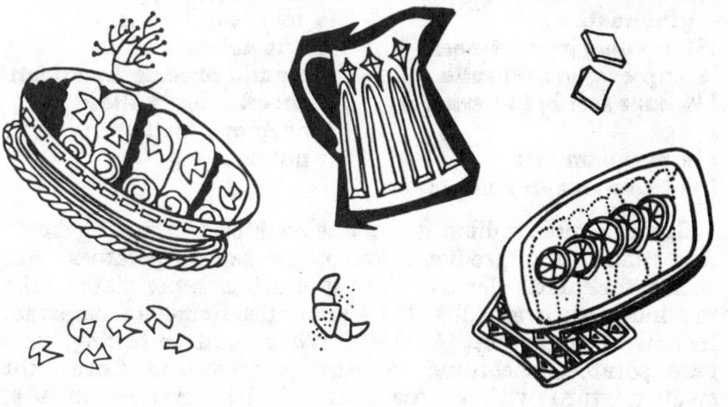

# Oxtail Ragout

2 oxtails, disjointed
¼ cup flour
1 teaspoon salt
¼ teaspoon pepper
2 medium onions, sliced
2 garlic cloves, minced
4 tablespoons bacon drippings
3 cups beef stock or canned consommé
2 large tomatoes, diced
1 bay leaf
2 sprigs parsley
3 medium potatoes
4 carrots
4 stalks celery
2 green peppers
1 cup red wine

Heat oven to 350° F. (moderate). Cover oxtail joints with cold water. Bring to a boil and simmer 10 minutes. Drain and pat dry with absorbent paper. Dredge with flour seasoned with salt and pepper. Brown with onion and garlic in drippings. Combine with stock, tomatoes, bay leaf, parsley and flour left from dredging. Turn into a 5-quart casserole. Cover tightly and bake in 350° F. oven for 3 hours. Meanwhile dice potatoes, carrots, celery and green peppers. Remove casserole from oven and skim off fat. Add vegetables and wine. Replace cover and continue to cook for 45 minutes or until vegetables are tender. Remove bay leaf. Add seasonings to taste. Makes 8 to 10 servings.

Ac'cent International

# Meat 'N' Tater

1½ teaspoons monosodium glutamate
1½ pounds ground beef
¾ cup evaporated milk
1½ cups soft bread crumbs
1 egg
1½ teaspoon salt
1½ teaspoons dry mustard
¼ teaspoon pepper
¼ teaspoon thyme
½ cup minced onion
¼ pound process American cheese, thinly sliced
1 envelope instant mashed potatoes

Sprinkle monosodium glutamate over beef in mixing bowl. Add remaining ingredients except cheese and potatoes. Mix with a fork until blended. Turn into a 9-inch pie plate. Bake in a moderate oven (350° F.) 40 minutes. Remove from oven. Increase heat to hot (450° F.). While meat is baking, prepare potatoes according to package directions. Cover hot meat mixture with cheese slices. Swirl potatoes on top. Return to hot oven and bake 10 minutes. Makes 6 servings.

# Beef Ragout with Catsup

1 pound round steak, (½ inch thick)
1 medium onion, chopped
2 tablespoons shortening
2 cups water
2 bouillon cubes
1 green pepper, chopped
½ cup catsup
1 teaspoon salt
⅛ teaspoon pepper
½ cup washed raw rice
Parsley for garnish

Heat oven to 325° F. (slow). Cut meat into ½-inch cubes Brown meat and onion in shortening, then stir in remaining ingredients. Turn into a 2-quart greased casserole. Cover and bake in 325° F. oven for 1 hour. Garnish with parsley sprigs. Makes 6 servings.

# Happy-Go-Lucky Supper

4 medium carrots
1 medium onion
1 large green pepper
2 10½-ounce cans condensed cream of celery soup
2 cups bouillon
2 cups cooked rice
12-ounce can corned beef, cubed
⅛ teaspoon pepper
⅛ teaspoon thyme

Heat oven to 350° F. (moderate). Cut vegetables in thin slivers. Combine soup and bouillon. Stir until smooth. Add vegetables, rice, meat and seasonings. Turn into a 3-quart greased casserole. Cover and bake in 350° F. oven for 45 minutes. Remove cover and continue to bake for 15 minutes. Cover and reserve in a warm oven until ready to use. Waiting won't hurt this dish. Makes 6 servings.

# Nina's Steak and Mushroom Casserole

4 cube steaks
4 tablespoons bacon drippings
2 medium onions, sliced
1 pound mushrooms, sliced
1 can condensed cream of mushroom soup
⅔ cup buttermilk
2 tablespoons minced parsley
1 teaspoon salt
¼ teaspoon pepper
¼ teaspoon dry mustard
4 medium potatoes, sliced

Heat oven to 350° F. (moderate). Brown steaks in drippings. Remove steaks from pan and sauté onion and mushroom slices until tender. Drain steak, onions and mushrooms on absorbent paper. Combine soup, buttermilk, parsley and seasonings. Place alternate layers of potatoes, onion and mushroom slices and steaks in a 2½-quart greased casserole. Pour a little soup mixture on each layer. Bake uncovered in 350° F. oven for 1 hour. Makes 4 servings.

# Liver Bordelaise

4 slices bacon, chopped
2½ pounds beef liver
No. 2 can small white onions and liquid
1 carrot, grated
1 teaspoon salt
¼ teaspoon pepper
Dash ground allspice
2 cups red wine
1 teaspoon cornstarch
2 tablespoons chopped parsley

Heat oven to 325° F. (slow). Fry bacon bits until crisp; set aside. Cut liver in 2-inch strips and brown in bacon fat, adding drained onions when partially browned. Transfer to a 3-quart casserole; sprinkle with carrot and seasonings and pour in wine and onion liquid. Cover and cook in 325° F. oven for 1¼ hours or until tender. Thicken liquid with cornstarch, mixed to a paste with ¼ cup water, if desired. Sprinkle with bacon bits and parsley. Makes 6 to 8 servings.

United Fresh Fruit and Vegetable Association

# Brown Beef Stew

**3 pounds lean chuck**
**¼ cup flour**
**½ teaspoon salt**
**⅛ teaspoon pepper**
**3 tablespoons beef drippings**
**1 teaspoon sugar**
**2 medium onions, chopped**
**1 clove garlic, minced**
**2 cups bouillon**
**¼ teaspoon thyme**
**2 whole cloves**
**½ teaspoon chili powder**
**3 tomatoes, quartered**
**6 small carrots, quartered**
**1 green pepper, cut in slices**
**3 stalks celery, cut in pieces**
**10-ounce can small potatoes, drained**

Heat oven to 325° F. (slow). Cut meat into 1½-inch cubes. Dredge with flour seasoned with salt and pepper. Sear in hot beef drippings. Sprinkle with sugar and continue to brown until well darkened. Remove meat to a large casserole. Sauté onions and garlic in the same fat until tender. Add to meat with bouillon and seasonings. Cover tightly and cook in 325° F. oven for 1½ hours. Add tomatoes, carrots, green pepper and celery. Cook covered for 40 minutes. Add potatoes and cook 10 minutes longer, just enough to heat them through. Makes 6 to 8 servings.

# Corned Beef and Succotash Dinner

**12-ounce package frozen lima beans**
**12-ounce package frozen corn kernels**
**12-ounce can corned beef, cubed**
**2 tablespoons minced onion**
**2 tablespoons butter or margarine**
**2 tablespoons flour**
**Dash Tabasco sauce**
**2 cups undiluted evaporated milk**
**½ cup fine bread crumbs**
**1 cup shredded Cheddar cheese**

Heat oven to 350° F. (moderate). Cook beans and corn according to package directions. Add corned beef cubes and turn into a 2-quart greased casserole. Sauté onion in butter until tender. Blend in flour and Tabasco sauce. Gradually add milk stirring constantly until slightly thickened. Mix lightly with vegetables and meat in casserole. Combine crumbs and cheese and sprinkle over top. Bake uncovered in 350° F. oven until bubbly, about 20 minutes. Makes 6 servings.

# Layered Casserole

**2 pounds ground beef**
**2 tablespoons shortening**
**1 clove garlic**
**1 tablespoon oil**
**4 cups sliced potatoes**
**12-ounce package frozen green beans, thawed**
**12-ounce can small white onions**
**1½ teaspoons salt**
**¼ teaspoon pepper**
**¼ teaspoon thyme**
**1 tablespoon cornstarch**
**8-ounce can tomato sauce**
**⅔ cup bouillon**
**¼ cup grated Cheddar cheese**
**¼ cup bread crumbs**
**3 tablespoons melted butter**

Heat oven to 350° F. (moderate). Sauté beef in shortening until browned and crumbling. Rub a 3-quart casserole with cut clove garlic and oil. Arrange in it a layer each of half the potatoes, meat, beans, and all the onions. Finish with layers of remaining beans, meat and finally potatoes, sprinkling salt, pepper and thyme on each layer. Mix cornstarch to a thin paste with a little tomato sauce. Mix with remaining tomato sauce and bouillon. Pour over potatoes. Top with a mixture of grated cheese and bread crumbs. Drizzle butter over all. Bake uncovered in 350° F. oven for 1¼ hours. Makes 6 to 8 servings.

The Best Foods, Inc.

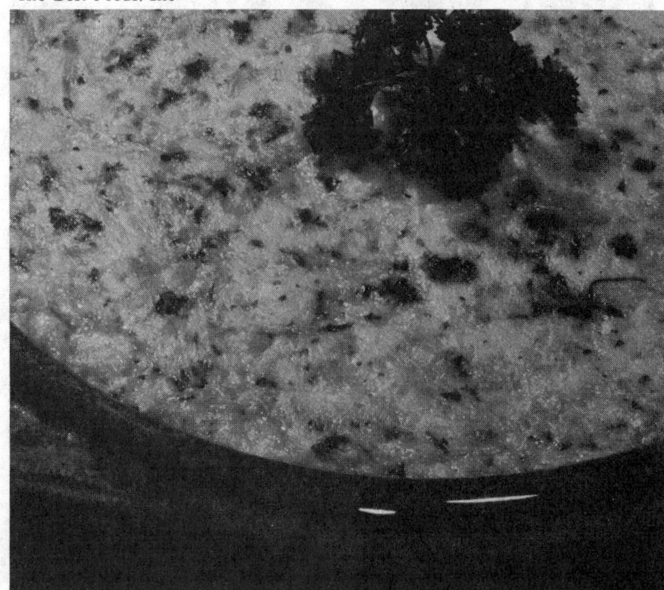

# Cheese, Eggs, Vegetables and Pasta

## Cheese and Onion Pie

**1½ sticks packaged pie crust mix**
**1 quart sliced onion rings**
**3 eggs, slightly beaten**
**½ cup light cream**
**1 teaspoon monosodium glutamate**
**½ teaspoon salt**
**1½ cups shredded sharp Cheddar cheese**

**Prepare pie crust according to package directions. Line a deep 8-inch pan with the pastry and form a high fluted edge. Do not prick shell. Parboil onions for 5 minutes in a small amount of water. Drain well. Combine eggs, cream, monosodium glutamate and salt. Place a layer of onions in pie shell, then a layer of cheese. Repeat. Pour custard mixture over filling. Bake in a hot oven (425° F.) 15 minutes. Reduce heat to 350° F. and bake about 20 minutes more, or until a knife inserted into center of pie comes out clean. Let stand for a few minutes before cutting. Makes 6 servings.**

**Ac'cent International**

## Swedish Oven Omelet

**½ pound sharp cheese**
**½ cup undiluted evaporated milk**
**2 teaspoons minced chives**
**¾ teaspoon salt**
**¼ teaspoon paprika**
**6 egg yolks, lightly beaten**
**6 egg whites, beaten stiff**

Heat oven to 325° F. (slow). Cut cheese in slivers and melt in top of a double boiler. Add milk gradually, stirring until smooth. Add chives and seasonings. Remove from heat. Slowly add cheese sauce to egg yolks. Fold into stiffly beaten egg whites. Pour into well greased 9-inch metal skillet, or shallow ovenproof casserole. Bake uncovered in 325° F. oven for 25 to 30 minutes. Cut into pie-shaped wedges and serve immediately. Makes 6 servings.

## Tecumseh Pudding-Pie

**3 eggs**
**2 cups undiluted evaporated milk**
**2 cups fresh or frozen whole kernel corn**
**½ cup sliced stuffed olives**
**½ cup minced water cress**
**1 tablespoon grated onion**
**½ teaspoon sugar**
**½ teaspoon salt**
**Dash Tabasco sauce**
**½ standard recipe pastry**

Heat oven to 425° F. (hot). Beat eggs until foamy. Add milk and beat for 3 minutes. Mix in corn, olives, water cress, onion and seasonings. Stir over low heat until slightly thickened. Fit pastry into a low 1½-quart casserole. Pour in corn mixture and bake uncovered in 425° F. oven for 10 minutes. Reduce heat to 325° F. and continue to bake 45 to 50 minutes, or until mixture is just set. Cool slightly. Serve in wedges. Makes 6 servings.

## Polenta with Tomato Sauce

**¾ cup corn meal**
**2 cups milk**
**1 egg, slightly beaten**
**1 cup grated Parmesan cheese**
**1½ teaspoons salt**
**⅛ teaspoon pepper**
**½ cup salad oil**
**2 cloves garlic**
**½ cup chopped onions**
**6-ounce can tomato paste**
**No. 2 can tomatoes (2½ cups)**
**1 teaspoon salt**
**¼ teaspoon pepper**

Heat oven to 400° F. (hot). Place corn meal in saucepan; gradually add milk. Stir over low heat until mixture thickens and comes to a boil. Simmer 3 minutes and remove from heat. Beat in egg. Add ½ cup cheese, salt, pepper and ¼ cup salad oil. Spread about 1½ inches deep in pan and cool. Cut in 3-inch rounds and arrange in shallow baking dish. Heat remaining oil in a saucepan; add garlic and onions and cook 3 minutes. Discard garlic. Add remaining ingredients and mix well. Pour around corn-meal rounds. Sprinkle with remaining cheese. Bake uncovered in 400° F. oven for 30 minutes. Makes 6 servings.

## Celery en Casserole

**1 large bunch celery**
**Boiling water**
**3 bouillon cubes**
**4 slices bacon**
**1 small onion, chopped**
**¾ cup grated Swiss cheese**
**¼ cup melted butter or margarine**

Wash, remove leaves from celery and cut in pieces. Cook in boiling water to cover with bouillon cubes until tender. While celery cooks, fry bacon until crisp. Break in crumbles. Sauté onion in bacon fat until tender. Heat oven to 400° F. (hot). Drain celery and arrange in a 2-quart greased casserole. Scatter over onion and bacon crumbles. Sprinkle with grated cheese. Drizzle butter over cheese. Bake in 400° F. oven for 10 minutes or until cheese melts. Makes 6 servings.

## Hominy-Cheese Delight

**2 cups cooked large hominy**
**1 cup grated Swiss cheese**
**3 eggs, slightly beaten**
**1 teaspoon salt**
**1 teaspoon Worcestershire sauce**
**1 tablespoon chopped chives**
**1 tablespoon chopped pimento**
**1¼ cups light cream, scalded**

Heat oven to 350° F. (moderate). Combine all ingredients in order given. Pour into 6 buttered individual baking dishes. Place in a pan of hot water. Bake uncovered in 350° F. oven for 30 minutes or until set. Makes 6 servings.

## Spinach Desireé

**1½ cups chopped cooked spinach, drained**
**½ teaspoon salt**
**¼ teaspoon pepper**
**⅛ teaspoon nutmeg**
**1 teaspoon grated onion**
**1 egg, slightly beaten**
**⅔ cup undiluted evaporated milk**
**1 tablespoon butter or margarine**
**1 hard-cooked egg, chopped**
**2 firm tomatoes**
**1 tablespoon grated cheese**
**1 tablespoon fine bread crumbs**

Heat oven to 350° F. (moderate). Combine spinach, seasonings, onion, egg, milk, butter and hard-cooked egg. Mix well and pour into 6 greased custard cups. Set in a pan of hot water. Bake uncovered in 350° F. oven for 40 minutes or until firm. Cut tomatoes in 6 slices. Place on a baking sheet. Mix cheese with bread crumbs and sprinkle over tomato slices. Broil until lightly browned. Place a spinach mound on each tomato slice. Makes 6 servings.

## Macaroni Caprice

**4 cups cooked macaroni**
**2 cups cooked green beans, cut in 1-inch pieces**
**1 cup chopped cooked ham**
**10½-ounce can condensed cream of celery soup**
**1 tablespoon A-1 sauce**
**⅛ teaspoon pepper**
**¾ cup milk**
**1 cup grated American cheese**
**½ cup buttered whole wheat crumbs**

Heat oven to 375° F. (moderate). Place 2 cups macaroni in a 2½-quart greased casserole. Cover with a layer of green beans, a layer of ham, and remaining macaroni. Beat soup, seasonings, milk and cheese until smooth. Pour over macaroni. Top with well-buttered crumbs. Bake uncovered in 375° F. oven for 30 minutes or until bubbling hot and slightly browned. Makes 4 to 6 servings.

## Savory Potatoes Under Cheese

**1 cup bread crumbs**
**1 teaspoon salt**
**⅛ teaspoon pepper**
**¼ teaspoon dry mustard**
**¼ teaspoon dill seasoning**
**3 tablespoons melted butter or margarine**
**8 medium potatoes, thinly sliced**
**6 green onions, chopped**
**2 cups milk**
**8 slices processed American cheese**

Heat oven to 350° F. (moderate). Mix bread crumbs with salt, pepper, mustard, dill seasoning and butter. Place a layer of potatoes in a 2-quart greased baking dish. Sprinkle with seasoned crumbs and onions. Repeat several times. Pour milk over potatoes and lay slices of cheese on top. Bake uncovered in 350° oven for 1 hour or until potatoes are tender. Makes 6 servings.

## Bacon and Egg Soufflés

**6 strips bacon**
**8 eggs, separated**
**1 cup light cream**
**½ teaspoon salt**
**¼ teaspoon celery salt**

Heat oven to 350° F. (moderate). Fry bacon until crisp, drain on absorbent paper and crumble to bits. Beat egg yolks until thick and lemon-colored. Add cream, seasonings, and bacon bits. Blend well. Beat egg whites until stiff but not dry. Fold into bacon-mixture. Pour into 6 individual greased baking dishes. Place in a pan of hot water and bake uncovered in 350° F. oven for 25 to 30 minutes or until puffed. Makes 6 servings.

## Italian Risotto

**½ cup butter**
**½ cup chopped onion**
**1 clove garlic, minced**
**2 cups raw rice**
**Pinch saffron**
**3 cups veal or other light stock**
**6-ounce can sliced mushrooms**
**½ cup grated Parmesan cheese**
**Salt**

Heat oven to 350° F. (moderate). Heat butter in a saucepan until it bubbles. Add onion and garlic. Gradually add rice, stirring constantly with a wooden spoon. Cook and stir over low heat until onion is tender and rice is yellow. Stir in saffron, then stock, a little at a time. Add mushrooms and juice, cheese and salt to taste. Turn into a 3-quart casserole. Cover tightly and cook in 350° F. oven for 30 minutes or until rice is tender. Makes 8 servings.

## Spring-Time Egg Casserole

**½ cup sliced mushrooms**
**2 tablespoons butter**
**8 hard-cooked eggs, sliced**
**1 cup cooked cut asparagus**
**10½-ounce can condensed cream of chicken or celery soup**
**1 teaspoon salt**
**8 cooked asparagus tips**
**1 tablespoon melted butter or margarine**

Heat oven to 350° F. (moderate). Sauté the mushrooms in butter until lightly browned. Blend with eggs, cut asparagus, soup and salt. Pour into a 1½-quart greased casserole. Arrange asparagus tips on top. Brush with melted butter. Bake uncovered in 350° F. oven for 25 minutes or until bubbling. Makes 6 servings.

# Ham-Flavored Cheese Pudding

**6 slices boiled ham, shredded**
**2 cups grated Swiss cheese**
**2 cups heavy cream**
**3 eggs, well beaten**
**1 teaspoon salt**
**Nutmeg for garnish**

Heat oven to 350° F. (moderate). Distribute the ham evenly over the bottom of 1½-quart greased casserole. Mix all ingredients except nutmeg. Pour over ham. Sprinkle top lightly with nutmeg. Bake uncovered in 350° F. oven for 40 minutes or until set. Makes 6 servings.

# Eggs Diable

**8 hard-cooked eggs**
**4 tablespoons finely chopped canned mushrooms**
**1 tablespoon chopped chives**
**4 anchovy fillets, minced**
**2 tablespoons cream**
**Dash Tabasco sauce**
**10½-ounce can condensed tomato soup**
**½ cup milk**
**¼ cup grated Cheddar cheese**

Heat oven to 375° F. (moderate). Cut eggs in half lengthwise. Scoop out yolks and mix with mushrooms, chives, anchovy fillets, cream and Tabasco sauce. Stuff into egg whites. Place on shallow greased baking dish. Mix soup and milk. Pour over eggs. Top with cheese. Bake uncovered in 375° F. oven for 25 minutes or until cheese melts and sauce bubbles. Makes 6 servings.

# Macaroni with Salami and Olives

**½ pound processed cheese, shredded (2 cups)**
**1 cup undiluted evaporated milk**
**½ cup sliced stuffed olives**
**½ pound salami sausage, diced**
**½ teaspoon salt**
**⅛ teaspoon pepper**
**1 teaspoon prepared mustard**
**4 cups cooked elbow macaroni**
**1 cup buttered soft bread crumbs**

Heat oven to 375° F. (moderate). Melt cheese in top of a double boiler. Gradually add milk, stirring constantly until the sauce is smooth. Add olives, salami, seasonings and macaroni. Pour into 6 individual greased casseroles or a 2-quart greased casserole. Sprinkle with buttered crumbs and bake uncovered in a 375° F. oven for 20 minutes or until crumbs are lightly browned. Makes 6 servings.

# Neopolitan Dinner

**1 cup lentils**
**3 slices bacon, chopped**
**½ cup chopped onion**
**1 clove garlic, minced**
**green or red sweet pepper, chopped**
**¼ cup chopped celery**
**½ pound Italian sausage or salami, sliced**
**1 teaspoon salt**
**¼ teaspoon pepper**
**4 cups cooked elbow macaroni**
**1 cup tomato sauce**
**¼ cup grated Parmesan cheese**

Wash and pick over lentils. Soak in cold water overnight. Fry bacon, onion and garlic until soft, in a saucepan. Add drained lentils, 2½ cups lentil water, green pepper, celery, sausage, salt and pepper. Cover and cook over moderate flame for 15 minutes or until beans are tender. Heat oven to 350° F. (moderate). Combine with macaroni and tomato sauce. Turn into a 3-quart greased casserole. Sprinkle with cheese and bake uncovered in 350° F. oven for 30 minutes. Makes 8 servings.

# Macaroni-Clam Shell Casserole

**3 cups macaroni shells**
**7-ounce can minced clams**
**1 cup diced cooked ham**
**1 green pepper, chopped**
**¼ cup butter or margarine**
**1 teaspoon seasoned salt**
**¼ teaspoon pepper**
**½ teaspoon paprika**
**1 cup grated American cheese**
**1 clove garlic**
**8-ounce can tomato sauce**
**1 cup soft bread crumbs**

Heat oven to 400° F. (hot). Cook macaroni shells according to package directions. Drain. Pour off liquid from clams and set aside. Lightly toss macaroni, clams, ham, green pepper, 2 tablespoons butter, seasonings, and ½ cup cheese. Rub a 2½-quart casserole with a cut clove of garlic and grease it. Turn macaroni into casserole; pour in combined clam liquid and tomato sauce. Toss bread crumbs with remaining butter and scatter over all. Top with remaining cheese and bake uncovered in 400° F. oven for 30 minutes or until crumbs are golden brown. Makes 8 servings.

# Green Rice with Lamb Kidneys

**2 cups raw long grain rice**
**12 lamb kidneys, sliced**
**1 cup minced water cress**
**8 green onions, chopped**
**¼ teaspoon pepper**
**1 teaspoon celery salt**
**5 cups consommé or stock**

Heat oven to 350° F. (moderate). Place washed rice in a large casserole. Mix in kidneys, water cress, onions and seasonings. Pour in consommé, cover tightly and cook in 350° F. oven for 1 hour. Reduce heat to 300° F. (slow). Remove cover from casserole and cook until all liquid is absorbed but rice is still moist. Makes 8 servings.

# Mexican Bean Chowder

**1 cup dried lima beans**
**1½ cups minced onions**
**1 cup diced celery**
**4 tablespoons butter or margarine**
**1 cup raw rice**
**1 cup mashed potatoes**
**No. 303 can cream-style corn (2 cups)**
**2 teaspoons salt**
**¼ teaspoon pepper**
**6-ounce can sliced mushrooms**

Soak beans overnight. Cook in boiling salted water for 1 hour. Drain. Heat oven to 350° F. (moderate). Sauté onions and celery in butter until soft. Place all ingredients except mushrooms in a large casserole. Add 3 quarts boiling water. Cover and cook in 350° F. oven for 1½ hours. Taste for seasoning. Float sliced mushrooms on surface. Serve from casserole. Makes 8 to 10 servings.

# Tomato-Zucchini Surprise

**4 medium zucchini**
**¼ cup salad oil**
**1 clove garlic**
**4 large firm tomatoes, peeled and sliced**
**¼ teaspoon oregano**
**Salt**
**Pepper**
**4 tablespoons grated Parmesan cheese**
**¼ pound processed Swiss cheese slices, cut in strips**

Heat oven to 375° F. (moderate). Wash and cut zucchini in slices. Sauté with garlic in oil until lightly browned. Discard garlic. Arrange alternate layers of zucchini and tomatoes in a 2-quart greased casserole, sprinkling each layer with oregano, salt, pepper and grated cheese. Cover top layer with cheese strips. Bake uncovered in 375° F. oven for 30 minutes or until cheese is melted and browned. Makes 6 servings.

# Vegetable Carnival

**½ cup cooked peas**
**½ cup cooked sliced carrots**
**½ cup cooked snapbeans or green beans**
**½ cup cooked sliced celery**
**1 small onion, grated**
**⅓ cup tomato catsup**
**10½-ounce can condensed cream of mushroom soup**
**½ teaspoon salt**
**⅛ teaspoon pepper**
**½ cup coarse bread crumbs**
**3 slices bacon**

Heat oven to 375° F. (moderate). Arrange peas, carrots, beans and celery in layers in a 1½-quart greased casserole. Combine onion, catsup, soup and seasonings. Pour over vegetables. Top with crumbs and bacon slices. Bake in 375° F. oven for 30 minutes or until bubbling, and crumbs and bacon are browned and crisp. Makes 6 servings.

# Stuffed Beets

**6 large whole beets**
**6 tablespoons grated sharp cheese**
**2 tablespoons fine dry bread crumbs**
**2 tablespoons sour cream**
**1 tablespoon pickle relish**
**1 teaspoon salt**
**⅛ teaspoon pepper**
**⅛ teaspoon MSG**
**¼ cup butter**
**¼ cup white wine**

Cook whole beets until tender. Cool, remove skins and carefully scoop out centers leaving a shell. Heat oven to 350° F. (moderate). Mix beet pulp, cheese, bread crumbs, cream, pickle relish and seasonings. Stuff into beets. Place on a shallow greased baking dish. Brush with butter. Bake uncovered in 350° F. oven for 15 to 20 minutes, basting occasionally with butter mixed with wine. Makes 6 servings.

# Broccoli-Lima Bean Casserole

**3 tablespoons butter or margarine**
**¾ teaspoon curry powder**
**4 cups bite-size shredded rice biscuits**
**1 package (10 ounces) frozen broccoli, cooked**
**1 package (10 ounces) frozen lima beans cooked**
**1 can (10½ ounces) condensed cream of celery soup**
**1 can (10½ ounces) condensed cream of mushroom soup**

Melt butter in a skillet. Stir in curry powder and shredded rice biscuits. Stir over low heat for 5 minutes to coat and crisp cereal. Set aside. Cut broccoli in small pieces. Mix with lima beans and soups. Stir in 1 cup of the crisped rice biscuits. Place in a baking dish. Top with remaining cereal, crumbled. Bake in a moderate oven (350° F.) 30 minutes, or until brown and bubbly. Makes 6 servings.

Ralston Purina

# Stuffed Potato Boats

**6 large potatoes**
**1 pound sausage meat**
**1 cup soft bread crumbs**
**1 tablespoon chopped parsley**
**1 tablespoon chopped onion**
**1 teaspoon salt**
**¼ teaspoon poultry seasoning**
**2 tablespoons melted butter or margarine**
**1 teaspoon paprika**

Heat oven to 375° F. (moderate). Boil potatoes with skins on for 15 minutes. Drain, pare and carefully scoop out a deep hole for stuffing. Sauté the sausage meat until brown and crumbly. Add crumbs, parsley, onion, salt, and poultry seasoning. Mix well and stuff into the potatoes. Place in a shallow greased casserole. Brush with butter mixed with paprika. Bake in 375° F. oven for 25 to 30 minutes, basting with more butter if necessary, until tender. Makes 6 servings.

# Green Noodles for Friday

**½ pound mushrooms, sliced**
**4 tablespoons butter or margarine**
**2 cups crab meat (2 6½-ounce cans)**
**6 cups cooked green noodles**
**2 pimientos, diced**
**1 teaspoon salt**
**¼ teaspoon pepper**
**1 clove garlic**
**1 tablespoon salad oil**
**3 eggs**
**1 cup milk**
**¼ cup fine bread crumbs**
**¼ cup grated Swiss cheese**

Heat oven to 350° F. (moderate). Sauté mushrooms in 2 tablespoons butter until soft. Flake crab meat removing tendons and mix with mushrooms, noodles, pimientos, salt and pepper. Place in a 3-quart casserole rubbed with cut clove of garlic and oil. Beat eggs and milk together and pour over. Melt remaining butter and toss with bread crumbs and cheese. Sprinkle over top of casserole. Bake uncovered in 350° F. oven for 30 minutes or until delicately browned. Makes 6 to 8 servings.

# Wagon Wheel Casserole

**1 cup (4 ounces) uncooked macaroni in shape of wheels or in any other form desired**
**Boiling salted water**
**1½ cups grated Cheddar cheese**
**½ cup Rhine wine, Sauterne or Chablis**
**2 tablespoons butter or margarine**
**¼ cup finely chopped onion**
**1½ tablespoons flour**
**1 cup rich milk**
**⅛ teaspoon salt**
**⅛ teaspoon curry powder**
**Dash pepper**
**¼ cup sliced green stuffed olives**
**1 large fresh tomato**
**¼ cup buttered bread crumbs**

Cook macaroni in boiling salted water until barely tender; drain well. Melt cheese in wine over very low heat. Blend in butter, onion and flour. Slowly stir in milk. Cook, stirring constantly, until mixture thickens. Add salt, curry powder and pepper, add drained macaroni and olives. Simmer gently about 10 minutes. Turn into heat-proof serving dish or casserole. Slice tomato and arrange over macaroni; sprinkle with buttered crumbs. Place under broiler 4 or 5 minutes until crumbs turn golden brown. Makes 4 servings.

**Wine Institute**

**Swiss Fondue is only one of many basic chafing dish preparations that are both delicious and enticing.**

# How to Cook in a Chafing Dish

WHILE the chafing dish has a long and honorable ancestry dating back many hundreds of years, today's version is a light, portable unit—skillfully planned to blend utility with gracious design. Because of this adroit use of craftsmanship, the chafing dish plays an important role in today's scheme of living. It can be carried easily into the living room, rumpus room or terrace. It doubles in brass, fitting easily into elegant after-theater suppers, or helping serve impromptu snacks on the porch. Wherever it goes, it is most decorative.

The most popular and useful type of chafing dish on the market today is made of copper, and the blazer pan, with a two-quart capacity, is block tin or silver-lined.

The heating unit may require either alcohol or Sterno. Note the illustration on the opposite page which shows you the various component parts.

Your chafing dish has two main functions: one is to cook and the other, to keep food warm. In cooking many dishes such as veal scallopine, it is essential to brown the meat in the blazer pan directly over the heat, not using the water pan. The water pan acts as an insulating factor between the flame and blazer pan and is used much as a double boiler. For instance, use it when making newburg dishes or creamed potatoes, and for keeping hot hors d'oeuvre warm. Among the recipes in this book we will designate for you when and when not to use the water pan.

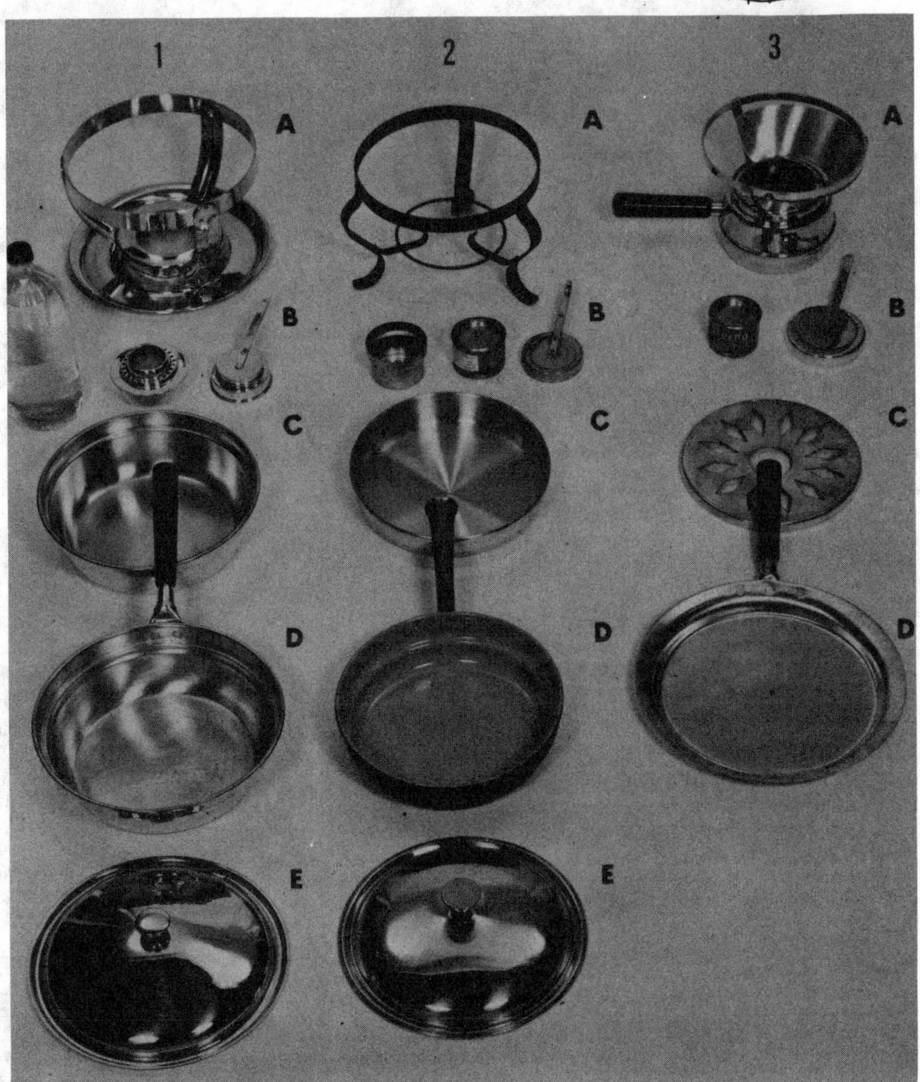


**Above are shown 3 different kinds of chafing dishes: 1. is the alcohol burner type with built-in tray and is claimed to develop more intense heat than others by its manufacturer; it may easily be converted to Sterno type by changing fuel; 2. is the actual Sterno chafing dish, which is economical and exceptionally portable; 3. is the Rechaud burner kind of dish, a traditional favorite of the French hotel and restaurant head waiter. This type is generally used for dishes involving flaming brandy, such as crêpes suzette and peach flambeau. It may also be used for such directly-over-the-flame cooking as is required by veal scallopini. The lettering above refers to parts of the various chafing dishes: under 1. is A.—brass stand with built-in copper tray; B.—bottle of fuel, denatured alcohol; C.—water pan; D.—blazer pan; E.—cover for blazer pan. Under 2. is A.—stand; B.—receptacle for Sterno can, which fits into bottom of stand (shown also are a can of Sterno and the flame adjuster); C.—water pan; D.—blazer pan, and E.—blazer pan cover. Under 3. is A.—the stand; B.—a can of Sterno and flame adjuster; C.—pan-rest, which sits atop the stand; D.—the blazer pan, which is shallower and wider than the one used in other illustrated chafing dishes.**

First step in the creation of a tasty fondue is grating of the cheese. Then add 2 tablespoonfuls of flour and toss until both are well mixed.

# Swiss Fondue

2 cups coarsely grated Swiss cheese
2 tablespoons flour
1 clove garlic
1 cup dry white wine
Salt
1 teaspoon dry mustard
1 teaspoon Worcestershire sauce
Dash nutmeg
Toast points

**Preparation:** Grate cheese and toss with flour.

**Performance:** Rub blazer pan with cut clove of garlic and place over hot water. Pour in wine and heat to simmering (never let it boil). Stir in half cup cheese at a time with a silver fork, allowing cheese to completely melt each time before adding more. Stir until mixture bubbles slightly. Add salt to taste and seasonings. Serve on toast points or let each guest dunk toast points in fondue with a fork. Makes 6 servings.

After tossing, rub blazer pan with cut clove of garlic.

The above photo shows blazer pan set over hot water, as wine is poured in to simmer, not boil.

As wine simmers, stir in half cup of cheese at a time with silver fork, allowing it to melt.

When all of cheese-flour mix has been added, is melted, stir with fork until it bubbles slightly.

Finally, add salt and seasonings to taste. Serve on toast points or allow guests to dunk the toast.

A tasty and unusually simple dish to make with holiday leftovers is this combination of vegetables and fowl. It will be a hit with guests.

# Turkey à la Mayfair

**2 cups cooked or canned peas**
**3 cups 1-inch diced, cooked turkey**
**3 stalks celery, thinly diced**
**2 green onions, diced**
**1 pimiento, diced**
**½ cup sliced stuffed olives**
**2 tablespoons cornstarch**
**¼ teaspoon thyme**
**½ teaspoon salt**
**⅛ teaspoon white pepper**
**1 cup undiluted evaporated milk**
**1 cup turkey broth**
**Pastry shells**
**Parsley for garnish**

**Preparation:** Cook peas if fresh peas are used. Dice turkey, celery, green onions and pimiento. Slice olives. Combine cornstarch, thyme, salt and pepper. Combine milk and broth. Combine celery and onion.

**Performance:** Blend seasoned cornstarch with ¼ cup milk-broth to a smooth paste. Place in blazer pan with remaining milk and broth. Heat over boiling water and stir until smooth. Add celery and onion. Cover and simmer for 15 minutes, stirring occasionally. Add peas, turkey, pimiento, olives. Simmer until heated through and bubbling hot. Serve in pastry shells garnished with parsley. Makes 8 to 10 servings.

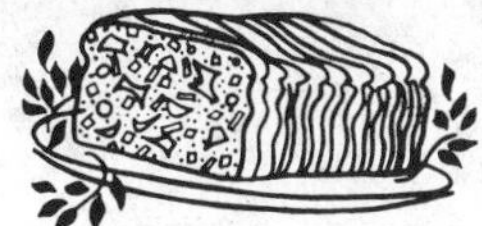

First, cook peas, if fresh ones are used. Then dice turkey, green onions, pimiento. Slice olives. Combine all this with cornstarch, thyme, salt and pepper. Add milk, broth, celery and onion. Blend seasoned cornstarch with ¼ cup milk-broth to smooth paste and then place all in a blazer pan. Heat over boiling water and stir until smooth. Add celery, onion. Cover and simmer for ¼ hour. Now add peas, turkey, pimiento, olives. Simmer until bubbling hot. Serve in fancy pastry shells.

# Chafing Dish Recipes

## Lobster Tails Harlequin

**6 frozen rock lobster tails (3 packages, 8 ounces each)**
**¼ cup butter or margarine**
**¼ cup chopped green pepper**
**¼ cup flour**
**1 teaspoon salt**
**¼ teaspoon pepper**
**¼ teaspoon nutmeg**
**1 can (14½ ounces) chicken broth**
**½ cup milk**
**½ cup heavy cream**
**¼ cup Sherry**
**½ cup diced cooked ham (if desired)**
**1 can (3 ounces) ripe olives, pitted sliced**
**4 cups hot cooked rice**
**3 tablespoons butter or margarine**
**2 tablespoons grated Parmesan cheese**

Following package directions, cook rock lobster tails in boiling salted water until tender. With kitchen scissors, cut around thin transparent undershell. Remove the meat and dice or flake. Save the cleaned shells. Melt the ¼ cup of butter in chafing dish. Add green pepper and cook until tender. Stir in flour, salt, pepper and nutmeg and stir to blend. Gradually stir in chicken broth, then milk and cream and continue to cook, stirring constantly, until smooth and thickened. Add Sherry, ham, olives and flaked lobster meat. Stir to blend. Keep warm over hot water. Toss rice with three tablespoons butter; then pile into cleaned lobster shells. (Fan out end of tail for a prettier appearance.) Top rice with Parmesan. Keep warm in slow oven (250° F.) until serving time; then, if desired, run under broiler long enough to toast cheese. Serve chafing dish of lobster sauce surrounded by rice in shells. Makes 6 servings.

National Fisheries Institute

# One-Bite Meat Balls (hors d'oeuvre)

1 pound ground beef
1 cup grated raw potatoes
2 tablespoons minced onion
1 tablespoon minced parsley
½ teaspoon salt
½ teaspoon celery salt
¼ teaspoon pepper
2 tablespoons cream
¼ cup flour
3 tablespoons grated Parmesan cheese
3 tablespoons shortening or bacon drippings

**Preparation:** Mix meat, potatoes, onion, parsley, seasonings and cream until blended. Roll into balls the size of marbles. Coat with flour mixed with cheese. Set in refrigerator until chafing time.

**Performance:** Heat shortening in blazer pan. Brown balls, doing only as many as fit in bottom of pan at one time. Serve on toothpicks with a selection of mustard, relish and catsup nearby. Makes about 28 balls.

# Ham Chafing Discs (hors d'oeuvre)

3-ounce jar deviled ham
1 cup processed sharp cheese
¼ cup grated onion
2 tablespoons pickle relish
1 teaspoon Worcestershire sauce
2 to 3 tablespoons mayonnaise
1 small loaf white bread, unsliced fresh
¼ cup butter or margarine
Chopped parsley for garnish

**Preparation:** Combine ham, cheese, onion, relish and Worcestershire sauce. Mash to a paste, using enough mayonnaise to moisten. Slice loaf of bread lengthwise, remove crusts and spread each slice with paste. Roll and hold in place with toothpicks. Wrap in wax paper or foil and store in refrigerator until chafing time. Slice in discs ½ inch thick.

**Performance:** Heat 2 tablespoons butter in blazer pan. Fry discs in small batches until delicately browned on both sides adding butter as needed. Garnish with chopped parsley. Makes about 24 to 30 discs.

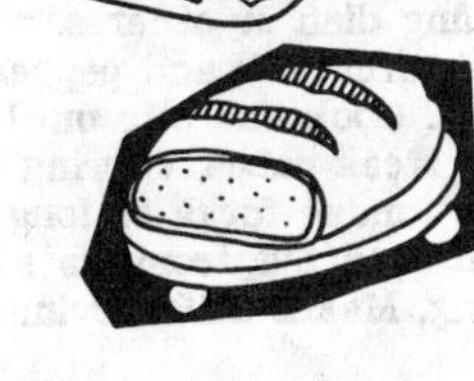
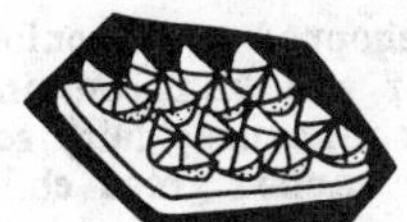

# Clam Bisque

1 medium onion, minced
2 tablespoons finely shredded water cress
1 quart shucked clams
Evaporated milk
2 tablespoons butter
½ teaspoon salt
⅛ teaspoon garlic salt
Dash Tabasco sauce

**Preparation:** Mince onion, shred water cress. Drain and chop clams very fine. Combine clam liquid with milk to make 3 cups.

**Performance:** Heat butter in blazer pan and sauté onion until soft but not brown. Add liquid, clams and seasonings. Cook, stirring occasionally with a wooden spoon, for 10 minutes. Do not allow to boil. Serve from chafing dish into bowls. Sprinkle with water cress. Makes 6 servings.

# Scallops Delmonico

2 pounds scallops
½ cup white wine
1 small onion
1 tablespoon minced parsley
4 egg yolks
1 cup cream
1 tablespoon lemon juice
2 tablespoons butter or margarine
1 tablespoon cornstarch
3-ounce can sliced mushrooms
1 teaspoon salt
Dash Tabasco sauce

**Preparation:** Place scallops and wine in a saucepan. Barely cover with boiling water and simmer for 3 minutes. Drain, reserving the liquid. Cut scallops in uniform bite-size pieces. Chop onion and parsley. Beat egg yolks with cream. Squeeze lemon juice.

**Performance:** Heat butter in blazer pan and sauté onion until tender. Add corn starch blended to a smooth paste with a little of the scallop liquid. Gradually stir in 1 cup of scallop liquid. Add parsley, mushrooms, seasonings and scallops. Heat to simmering. Place over hot water and pour in egg-cream mixture. Cook and stir gently until mixture thickens. Just before serving blend in lemon juice. Serve in pastry shells. Makes 6 to 8 servings.

# Oyster-Milk Toast

1 quart shucked oysters
1 quart scalded rich milk
3 tablespoons butter or margarine
1 teaspoon celery salt
¼ teaspoon white pepper
¼ teaspoon Worcestershire sauce
Buttered whole wheat toast points
Paprika for garnish

**Preparation:** Clean oysters and strain liquid. Heat milk just before chafing time, being careful not to scorch it.

**Performance:** Heat oysters and liquid, butter and seasonings in blazer pan over hot water. Cook until oysters begin to curl at the edges. Add hot milk and cook for 1 minute. Serve over toast points in individual soup bowls and garnish with paprika. Makes 6 servings.

# Seafood Mushroom Newburg

1 package (11½ ounces) frozen lobster Newburg
1 can (6½ ounces) crabmeat, flaked
1 can (3 ounces) sliced broiled-in-butter mushrooms
½ can (⅔ cup) condensed cream of mushroom soup
1 cup frozen peas
1 tablespoon lemon juice
Freshly ground black pepper
Hot cooked rice

Defrost lobster Newburg for about 1 hour. Place Newburg in blazer pan of chafing dish over hot water. Heat until hot and well blended. Add crabmeat, mushrooms with liquid, mushroom soup and peas. Heat over hot water, stirring several times, about 15 minutes, until thoroughly heated. Just before serving, stir in lemon juice and pepper. Serve over hot cooked rice. Makes 4 to 6 servings.

Paper Cup and Plate Industries

Wine Institute

# Party Steak Pot

2 pounds tender beef steak (cut about 1-inch thick)
¼ cup butter
1½ teaspoons plain or seasoned salt
⅜ cup white dinner wine
¼ cup catsup
2 teaspoons cornstarch
¼ teaspoon dried dill
Freshly ground black pepper
Assorted Go-Alongs

Trim all excess fat from meat. Cut steak into bite-size cubes, about ½-inch thick (should be about 48 cubes). Brown steak quickly in heated butter, turning and sprinkling meat with salt during browning. Do not crowd skillet so meat will brown nicely. This quick-browning will cook tender steak to rare or medium-rare doneness. Remove steak cubes to heated chafing dish or other serving container. Blend wine, catsup, cornstarch, dill and pepper to taste; stir into rich pan drippings. Cook and stir until mixture boils and thickens. Pour over steak cubes, stirring to combine meat and sauce. Serve with fondue forks or long cocktail picks for spearing meat. Meat is lifted from its sauce and dipped into desired Go-Along. Makes 8-10 servings.

### Go-Alongs

Finely chopped green onion or parsley; toasted sesame seeds; half and half container of prepared mustard and catsup or chili sauce; dairy sour cream mixed with chopped chutney or canned green chili.

The Borden Company

# Cheese and Lobster

**6 tablespoons butter**
**½ pound mushrooms, sliced**
**2 tablespoons flour**
**½ teaspoon paprika**
**2 cups light cream**
**½ pound American cheese, finely diced**
**4 cups cooked lobster meat, cut in pieces**
**½ cup Sherry**

**Melt butter in a blazer pan of chafing dish over direct flame. Add mushrooms; cook until tender, about 3 minutes. Blend in flour and paprika. Add cream and cheese. Place blazer pan over hot water. Cook, stirring, until cheese is melted and mixture thickens slightly. Add lobster and Sherry. Cover and heat thoroughly. Serve over crispy waffles. Makes 8 servings.**

# Shrimp Elegante´

**½ pound mushrooms**
**⅔ cup bouillon**
**½ teaspoon salt**
**¼ teaspoon pepper**
**1 bay leaf**
**3 tablespoons salad oil**
**3½ cups canned or frozen shrimp (1½ pounds)**
**1 tablespoon tomato paste**
**1 strip lemon peel**
**1½ cups sour cream**

**Preparation:** Wipe mushrooms with a damp cloth and slice. Combine bouillon and seasonings.

**Performance:** Heat oil in blazer pan and sauté mushrooms Add shrimp, tomato paste, seasoned bouillon and lemon peel. Cover and simmer gently over hot water for 15 minutes. Stir in sour cream and heat through. Do not bring to a boil. Remove bay leaf before serving. Makes 6 servings.

# Meat Balls in Sour Cream Sauce

**1 egg, slightly beaten**
**1 cup milk**
**1 teaspoon salt**
**¼ teaspoon pepper**
**1 cup fine dry bread crumbs**
**1 teaspoon grated onion**
**1½ pounds ground lean beef**
**2 tablespoons bacon drippings**
**1 medium onion, chopped**
**2 tablespoons flour**
**2 8-ounce cans tomato sauce**
**1 cup sour cream**
**1 cup coarsely chopped ripe olives**

**Preparation:** Beat egg with milk, salt, pepper, crumbs and grated onion. Allow to stand for a few minutes. Add ground beef, mix lightly with a fork and shape into 2-inch balls. Cover with wax paper or foil and store in refrigerator until chafing time.

**Performance:** Heat drippings in blazer pan. Fry meat balls until uniformly browned. This may have to be done in two or three batches, depending on the size of your pan. Remove from pan. Sauté onion in pan juices for 5 minutes. Stir in flour until blended. Add tomato sauce, and meat balls. Place over hot water. Cover and simmer 30 minutes. Add sour cream and mix gently with a wooden spoon until meat balls are coated with cream. Scatter olives over all. Heat through and serve. Makes 6 to 8 servings.

# Penny's Million Dollar Mushrooms (hors d'oeuvre)

**1 pound large mushrooms**
**½ pound chicken livers**
**½ cup butter or margarine**
**3 tablespoons tomato juice**
**2 hard-cooked eggs, chopped**
**2 anchovies, minced**
**2 tablespoons grated onion**
**1 teaspoon Worcestershire sauce**
**½ teaspoon salt**
**Dash Tabasco sauce**
**¼ cup chopped parsley**
**Juice 1 lemon**

**Preparation:** Wipe mushrooms with a damp cloth and remove stems. Sauté chicken livers in 2 tablespoons butter for 2 minutes. Sprinkle with tomato juice and mash to a paste. Combine with chopped eggs, anchovies, onion and seasonings. Stuff firmly into mushroom caps. Reserve in refrigerator until chafing time. Just before cooking roll in parsley flakes.

**Performance:** Heat 2 tablespoons butter in blazer pan. Sauté parslied mushrooms until browned all over and a little wrinkled. Sprinkle with lemon juice. Repeat until all mushrooms are cooked, adding butter as needed. Serve on toothpicks or toast rounds. Makes about 24 stuffed mushroom caps.

# Mushrooms Polonaise

1 pound medium mushrooms
2 tablespoons minced parsley
2 tablespoons minced chives
1 teaspoon Worcestershire sauce
3 tablespoons butter or margarine
1 clove garlic
½ teaspoon salt
¼ teaspoon pepper
1 cup sour cream
Toast

**Preparation:** Choose mushrooms as uniform as possible. Wipe them with a damp cloth; remove and chop stems. Mince parsley and chives; combine with chopped mushroom stems and Worcestershire sauce. Stuff mixture into mushroom caps.

**Performance:** Heat butter in blazer pan and sauté garlic clove and mushroom caps, stuffed side down, for 3 minutes. Turn carefully and continue to cook until tender. Discard garlic. Sprinkle with salt and pepper. Fold in sour cream and heat through. Serve at once on buttered toast. Makes 6 servings.

# Emerald Rice

1 cup raw rice
3 green onions
1 cup minced parsley
¼ pound American cheese
2 eggs
1 cup milk
1 teaspoon salt
¼ teaspoon pepper

**Preparation:** Cook rice according to package directions. Mince green onions and parsley as finely as possible. Grate cheese. Beat eggs until frothy. Scald milk, being careful not to scorch it.

**Performance:** Pour heated milk into blazer pan over hot water. Add rice, onions, parsley, seasonings and eggs. Cook and stir until mixture begins to thicken. Sprinkle with cheese and mix well. Cover and cook until set. This is delicious served with ham or veal. Makes 6 servings.

# Mixed Cheese Fondue

¼ pound Cheddar cheese
¼ pound pimiento cheese
¼ pound bleu cheese
2 eggs
3 tablespoons butter or margarine
1 cup undiluted evaporated milk
Dash Tabasco sauce

**Preparation:** Shred cheese, and beat eggs.

**Performance:** Melt butter in blazer pan over boiling water. Stir in cheeses, working to a smooth paste with a wooden spoon. Add milk and Tabasco sauce, stirring constantly until blended. Just before serving beat in eggs, one at a time. Serve over toasted English muffins. Makes 6 servings.

# Chinese Scrambled Seafood

½ pound scallops, cooked and chopped fine
½ pound shrimp, cooked and chopped fine
6 eggs
4 tablespoons cream
½ teaspoon salt
⅛ teaspoon pepper
Dash Tabasco sauce
1 tablespoon Worcestershire sauce
1 teaspoon finely chopped ginger
2 tablespoons butter or margarine

**Preparation:** Cook and chop scallops and shrimp. Beat eggs, cream and seasonings together.

**Performance:** Heat butter in blazer pan. Scramble egg mixture until it begins to set. Add chopped seafood. Continue to stir until moistly set. Serve with rice. Makes 6 servings.

# Asparagus Tips Monte Carlo (hors d'oeuvre)

12-ounce package frozen asparagus tips
⅓ cup grated American cheese
15 to 18 slices cooked tongue
3 tablespoons butter or margarine
1 lemon, cut in wedges

**Preparation:** Defrost asparagus tips, cook until almost tender. Drain and roll in grated cheese. Cut meat in even slices and roll around tips. Secure with toothpicks. Cover with wax paper and store in refrigerator until chafing time.

**Performance:** Heat butter in blazer pan. Sauté asparagus rolls, turning often until heated through and browned. Sprinkle with lemon juice. Keep hot over water pan. Have cocktail napkins handy. Makes about 15 to 18 hors d'oeuvre.

# Eggs Aurora

2 medium-size ripe tomatoes
1 small onion
6 medium mushroom caps
6 eggs
½ teaspoon salt
⅛ teaspoon pepper
Dash Tabasco sauce
2 tablespoons butter or margarine
1 tablespoon capers
Toast

**Preparation:** Peel and chop tomatoes and onion. Slice mushrooms. Beat eggs with seasonings until lemon-colored.

**Performance:** Melt butter in blazer pan and sauté onion and mushrooms until tender. Add tomatoes and cook for 10 minutes. Place blazer pan over hot water. Turn in eggs and capers. Stir slowly with a wooden spoon until eggs are moistly set. Serve at once on toast triangles. Makes 6 servings.

# Spaghetti with White Clam Sauce

1 pound spaghetti
2 cloves garlic
8-ounce can minced clams
¼ cup minced parsley
½ cup olive oil
½ teaspoon salt
¼ teaspoon pepper
Dash cayenne
½ cup grated Parmesan cheese

**Preparation:** Cook spaghetti according to package directions. Keep hot. Split garlic cloves. Drain clams. Mince parsley.

**Performance:** Heat oil in blazer pan and cook garlic until browned. Discard garlic. Add clams, parsley and seasonings. Heat through and pour over hot spaghetti. Sprinkle with cheese. Toss until well mixed. Serve at once with additional cheese. Makes 6 servings.

# Shrimp Chafing Discs (hors d'oeuvre)

½ pound shrimp, cleaned and cooked
3-ounce package cream cheese
2 teaspoons lemon juice
1 tablespoon minced chives
2 tablespoons prepared horse-radish
Dash cayenne
½ teaspoon celery salt
¼ teaspoon salt

**Preparation:** Put shrimps through meat grinder, using medium blade. Combine cream cheese, lemon juice, chives, horse-radish and seasonings, whipping until smooth. Beat in ground shrimp. Spread on bread sliced lengthwise and proceed as for Ham Chafing Discs .

# Fillets of Sole with Green Grapes

**½ pound seedless green grapes**
**Juice 1 lemon**
**3 pounds fillets of sole or flounder**
**1 teaspoon salt**
**½ teaspoon paprika**
**3 tablespoons butter or margarine**

**Preparation:** Place grapes in boiling water and simmer for 2 minutes. Drain. Squeeze lemon. Sprinkle fish fillets with salt and paprika.

**Performance:** Heat butter in blazer pan until bubbling. Sauté fillets until golden brown on both sides and tender. It will be necessary to do this in several batches so keep cooked fish warm on a hot platter. Return to blazer pan. Sprinkle with lemon juice and scatter grapes over. Cover and allow to heat through. Makes 6 servings.

# Curried Eggs with Peas

**6 eggs**
**1 teaspoon grated onion**
**½ teaspoon lemon juice**
**6 hamburger-type buns**
**4 tablespoons flour**
**¼ teaspoon mustard**
**1 teaspoon curry powder**
**½ teaspoon salt**
**4 tablespoons butter or margarine**
**¼ teaspoon Worcestershire sauce**
**2 cups milk**
**No. 303 can peas (2 cups)**

**Preparation:** Cook eggs in gently boiling water for 20 minutes. Crack shells and roll eggs between palms of hands. Slip off shells. Grate onion. Squeeze lemon juice. Combine flour, mustard, curry powder and salt. Split and toast buns.

**Performance:** Melt butter in blazer pan over boiling water. Blend in seasoned flour, grated onion and Worcestershire sauce. Gradually add milk, stirring until smooth and thickened. Add eggs and peas and continue to cook over boiling water until thoroughly heated. Stir in lemon juice. Serve over toasted buns. Makes 6 servings.

# Lima Bean Rabbit

**1½ cups large dry lima beans**
**⅓ cup dry white wine**
**2 small onions**
**3 medium tomatoes**
**2 pimientos**
**¾ pound Monterey Jack cheese (or any bland yellow cheese)**
**3 tablespoons butter or margarine**
**1 teaspoon celery salt**
**Dash cayenne**

**Preparation:** Soak and cook lima beans according to package directions. Drain and just before chafing time heat with wine. Chop onions. Peel and dice tomatoes and pimientos. Shred cheese.

**Performance:** Heat butter in blazer pan till bubbling. Sauté onions until tender. Add tomatoes, cover and cook slowly for 10 minutes. Place over hot water pan and gradually blend in cheese, stirring until melted. (Don't rush this part or the cheese will be tough and stringy.) Add pimientos, seasonings, lima beans and wine. Heat through. Keep hot over hot water. Makes 6 servings.

Poultry and Egg National Board

# Chafing Dish Scrambled Eggs

**9 eggs**
**9 tablespoons light cream**
**Pinch baking powder**
**1 teaspoon salt**
**¼ teaspoon pepper**
**¼ teaspoon paprika**
**Few drops Worcestershire sauce (optional)**
**3 tablespoons butter or margarine**

**Preparation:** Break eggs into a bowl and beat until frothy. Combine with cream, baking powder and seasonings.

**Performance:** Melt butter in blazer pan over hot water. Pour in seasoned eggs and cook slowly, stirring from bottom of pan with a wooden spoon, until a desired consistency. Makes 6 servings.

Vary this simple recipe by adding one of the following:

**¼ cup minced ham**
**1 tablespoon finely chopped parsley or chives**
**⅓ cup grated Swiss cheese**
**½ cup chopped cooked brains or chicken livers**
**¼ cup sliced sautéed mushrooms**
**4 anchovies, finely chopped**

# Fish Fillets Duglere

1 pound frozen fish fillets
2 tablespoons butter or margarine
1 medium onion, chopped
1 clove garlic, minced
1 can (No. 2) tomatoes
¼ cup white wine or lemon juice
1 tablespoon minced parsley
1 tablespoon flour
¼ teaspoon oregano
2 tablespoons heavy cream

Let fillets thaw on the bottom shelf of the refrigerator or at room temperature. Cut fillets in serving-size pieces. Melt 1 tablespoon butter or margarine in a skillet; add onion and garlic. Place fish on top: cover with tomatoes, wine or lemon juice and parsley. Bring to a boil; lower heat; cover skillet and cook 10 to 15 minutes. Remove fish to chafing dish to keep warm. Cream remaining butter with flour and stir into sauce. Add oregano. Cook, stirring occasionally, for about 5 minutes. Blend in heavy cream. Pour over fish in chafing dish. Garnish with additional parsley. Makes 4 servings.

National Fisheries Institute

# Canton Sub-Gum Soup

6 cups seasoned chicken broth
½ cup slivered cooked chicken
3 eggs
1 teaspoon soy sauce
No. 2 can Chinese mixed vegetables (2¼ cups)
Parsley for garnish

**Preparation:** Prepare chicken broth or use canned broth. Cut chicken meat in slivers. Beat eggs with soy sauce until frothy. Mince drained Chinese vegetables and parsley.

**Performance:** Heat broth in blazer pan with chicken and vegetables for 10 minutes. Slowly stir eggs into broth with a rotating motion to form small flowers. Serve at once garnished with parsley. Makes 8 servings.

# Apricots Jubilee

No. 2 can apricot halves
2 lemon slices
¼ teaspoon powdered cloves
⅓ cup brandy
1 quart banana ice cream
½ cup macaroon crumbs

**Preparation:** Drain apricots and bring juice to a boil. Simmer with lemon slices and cloves until reduced to half the original quantity. Heat brandy just before chafing time.

**Performance:** Heat apricot juice in blazer pan; add apricot halves and heat through. Ignite heated brandy and pour over. When flame dies, serve over ice cream with a sprinkling of macaroon crumbs. Makes 6 servings.

# Italian Nimbus

1 teaspoon grated orange rind
1 tablespoon orange juice
6 egg yolks
⅓ cup sugar
½ cup sweet sherry

**Preparation:** Grate orange rind and squeeze juice. Just before chafing time beat egg yolks and sugar together until light.

**Performance:** Place egg yolks in blazer pan. Cook over barely simmering water which does not touch blazer pan. Beat constantly with a wire whisk until smooth and thickened. If curdling starts remove from heat and beat smooth. Add orange rind, orange juice and sherry and continue to beat for 2 or 3 minutes. Serve hot in sherbet glasses. Makes 6 servings.

# Chicken à la King

¼ cup butter or margarine
1 cup sliced mushrooms
¼ cup flour
1 cup chicken stock
1½ cups half and half milk
½ cup diced pimiento
3 cups diced cooked chicken
2 egg yolks, slightly beaten
Salt and pepper to taste

Heat butter in blazer pan of chafing dish over direct heat. Add mushrooms and cook until tender, about 5 minutes. Stir in flour. Add stock and half and half milk. Place blazer pan over hot water. Cook, stirring occasionally, until thickened and smooth. Add pimiento and chicken. Heat thoroughly. Stir a little of the hot sauce into the egg yolks. Add slowly to remaining sauce, and stir, until smooth and hot. Serve over crispy waffles. Makes 6 servings.

# Chicken Liver Bisque

½ pound chicken livers
1 medium onion
2 tablespoons butter
3 tablespoons flour
¼ teaspoon rosemary
3 cups chicken broth
1 cup undiluted evaporated milk
½ teaspoon salt or more to taste
¼ cup sherry
Minced water cress for garnish

**Preparation:** Clean chicken livers, removing any greenish portions. Cut in small pieces. Mince onion and water cress.

**Performance:** Heat butter in blazer pan and sauté chicken livers and onion until soft. Sprinkle with flour and rosemary and stir until blended. Gradually add chicken broth and milk. Continue to stir until mixture begins to thicken. Place pan over boiling water and cook for 10 minutes. Add salt and sherry. Cook 2 minutes longer. Serve in individual bowls with a garnish of water cress. Makes 6 servings.

# Creamed Ham and Eggs

**6 tablespoons butter**
**6 tablespoons flour**
**½ teaspoon salt**
**3 tablespoons prepared mustard**
**3 cups milk**
**2 cups cooked ham, cubed**
**4 hard-cooked eggs, diced**

**Melt butter in blazer pan of chafing dish over direct flame. Stir in flour, salt and mustard. Remove from flame. Gradually stir in milk. Place blazer pan over hot water. Cook, stirring until mixture thickens. Blend in ham and eggs. Cook 5 minutes longer or until ham and eggs are thoroughly heated. Serve over crisp waffles. Makes 6 to 8 servings.**

National Fisheries Institute

# Crabmeat à la Dewey

**2 tablespoons butter or margarine**
**2 large mushrooms, finely chopped**
**1½ tablespoons flour**
**¼ teaspoon salt**
**Freshly ground black pepper**
**1 cup light cream**
**1 egg yolk**
**¼ cup Sherry**
**1 pound lump crabmeat, picked over**

Melt butter in blazer pan of chafing dish. Cook mushrooms until tender. Add flour and seasonings and blend thoroughly. Place blazer pan over hot water. Stir in cream, and cook, stirring until smooth and thickened. Beat together egg yolk and Sherry. Add a little of hot cream sauce to mixture. Return to chafing dish and cook, stirring, until smooth and heated through. Add crabmeat and cook just long enough to heat. Serve over crisp toast points. Makes 4 to 6 servings.

# Roast Beef Omelet

**2 cups diced cooked beef**
**2 slices bacon**
**1 small onion**
**3 eggs**
**¼ teaspoon curry powder**
**¼ teaspoon salt**
**⅛ teaspoon pepper**

**Preparation:** Dice beef and bacon. Grate onion. Beat eggs to a froth. Combine seasonings.

**Performance:** Fry diced bacon in blazer pan until almost crisp. Add beef and onion and cook for 5 minutes, stirring with a wooden spoon. Add eggs and seasonings. Place over hot water and cook until eggs are set. Do not stir. Crease lightly through center with a spatula and fold. Serve at once. Makes 4 servings.

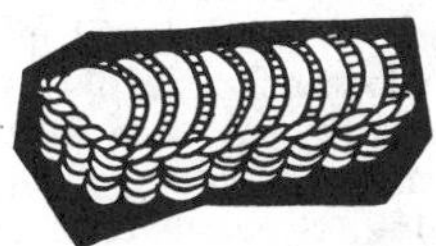

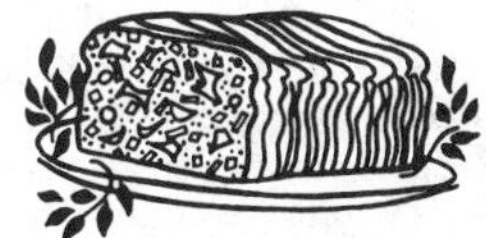

# Skillet Supper Italiano

**2 tablespoons butter or margarine**
**3 tablespoons chopped onion**
**1 cup sliced mushrooms**
**¾ pound ground chuck**
**1 teaspoon salt**
**⅛ teaspoon pepper**
**1 can (15½-ounces) Marinara sauce**
**1 beef bouillon cube**
**½ cup hot water**
**1½ cups medium, uncooked noodles**

Melt butter in a large aluminum skillet. Add onions and mushrooms and cook until tender. Add meat and cook until browned. Add salt, pepper, Marinara sauce. Dissolve bouillon cube in hot water and add to skillet mixture. Heat to a boil; reduce heat and simmer 5 minutes. Add noodles. Cover and cook over low heat for 8-10 minutes. Makes 6 servings.

The Aluminum Association

# Buffet Shrimp Pineapple

2 packages (8-ounces) peeled and deveined shrimp, raw
3 tablespoons butter
2 tablespoons cornstarch
¾ cup dry white table wine
1 can (9-ounces) pineapple tidbits with syrup
3 tablespoons lime juice
½ teaspoon cloves
½ teaspoon salt
½ teaspoon sugar

If shrimp are large, split lengthwise and crosswise. Melt butter in blazer pan of chafing dish over direct heat. Add shrimp and cook, stirring constantly, until pink and lightly tinged with brown. Remove shrimp from pan and place in a bowl. Combine cornstarch and table wine and stir until smooth. Pour into blazer pan of chafing dish. Add pineapple tidbits and syrup and cook, stirring constantly, until thickened and clear. Stir in lime juice, cloves, salt and sugar. Return shrimp to pan and stir to blend with pineapple. Place blazer pan over hot water for serving. Serve over toast, waffles or hot cooked rice. Makes 4 to 6 servings.

Shrimp Association of the Americas

# Chop Suey

2 cups chopped cooked meat (chicken, pork, veal or beef)
2 small onions
4 stalks celery
1¼ cups consommé
1 tablespoon soy sauce
½ teaspoon sugar
⅛ teaspoon pepper
No. 2 can Chinese mixed vegetables (2¼ cups)
¼ cup peanut or salad oil
1 tablespoon cornstarch

**Preparation:** Chop meat, onions and celery. Mix 1 cup consommé, soy sauce, sugar, and pepper. Drain vegetables.

**Performance:** Heat oil in blazer pan over hot fire. Brown meat quickly. Add onions and celery and cook for 5 minutes. Pour in seasoned consommé and heat through. Add vegetables and heat to boiling point. Stir in cornstarch combined with remaining ¼ cup consommé. Cook for 5 minutes. Keep hot over hot water. Serve Chinese-style with fried noodles, fluffy hot rice, slivered almonds and additional soy sauce. Makes 6 servings.

# Toddie's Heavenly Cheese Soup

1 small onion
2 stalks celery
½ small green pepper
½ pound Cheddar cheese
3 cups milk
10-ounce can consommé
3 tablespoons margarine or butter
3 tablespoons flour
1 tablespoon tomato paste
½ teaspoon salt
Dash cayenne
Water cress for garnish

**Preparation:** Mince vegetables and water cress. Grate cheese. Combine milk and consommé.

**Performance:** Heat margarine in blazer pan. Sauté vegetables until tender. Stir in flour until well blended. Slowly add milk-consommé mixture. Sprinkle in grated cheese, stirring until melted. Add tomato paste and seasonings. Cook over hot water until smooth. Garnish with water cress. Makes 6 servings.

The Best Foods, Inc.

# Chinese Fried Rice with Pork

5 cups cooked rice (about 1½ cups raw rice)
1½ cups, 1-inch diced, cooked pork
3 green onions, finely chopped
3 tablespoons salad oil
2 eggs, slightly beaten
2 tablespoons soy sauce

**Preparation:** Cook rice according to package directions. Dice pork and chop green onions.

**Performance:** Heat oil in blazer pan and sauté pork and about two-thirds of the onions until pork is lightly browned. Add rice and cook for 10 minutes. Beat eggs with soy sauce and pour over. Scramble all together until eggs are set. Sprinkle with remaining green onions. Makes 6 servings.

# Calfs' Liver in White Wine

**1½ pounds calfs' liver, thinly sliced**
**3 tablespoons flour**
**1 teaspoon salt**
**¼ teaspoon pepper**
**1 small onion**
**1 small green pepper**
**3 tablespoons minced parsley**
**¼ cup butter or margarine**
**⅓ cup dry white wine**

**Preparation:** Coat liver slices with combined flour and seasonings. Mince onion, green pepper and parsley.

**Performance:** Heat 2 tablespoons butter in blazer pan and brown liver slices on both sides over a lively flame. Transfer to a hot platter. Sauté onion and green pepper until tender. Add wine and simmer for 8 minutes. Add remaining butter. Return liver slices to pan to heat through. Sprinkle with parsley. Makes 6 servings.

Processed Apples Institute, Inc.

# Curried Rice and Apple Sauce

**1 cup sliced onions**
**⅓ cup butter or margarine**
**1½ cups cooked rice**
**2 cups apple sauce**
**1 teaspoon curry powder**
**Few grains of salt**

Cook onion in butter of blazer pan of chafing dish over direct flame. Stir and cook until tender and golden brown. Add rice and apple sauce. Mix curry powder with a little cold water; add with salt. Heat thoroughly. Serve as an accompaniment to lamb stew, lamb chops or chicken fricassee. Makes 4 to 6 servings.

# Sea Food Newburg au Gourmet

**1½ cups cooked shrimps**
**1½ cups cooked fillet of flounder**
**½ cup sliced ripe olives**
**3 tablespoons butter or margarine**
**2 tablespoons flour**
**½ teaspoon salt**
**⅛ teaspoon pepper**
**Dash Tabasco sauce**
**1½ cups light cream**
**6-ounce can mushroom caps**
**3 egg yolks, well beaten**
**⅓ cup sherry**
**Toast**

**Preparation:** Cook shrimps and fish; flake fish. Slice olives in large chunks.

**Performance:** Melt butter in blazer pan. Stir in flour and seasonings. Gradually add cream, stirring constantly. Add shrimps, fish, drained mushrooms and ripe olives. Stir in egg yolks and sherry. Cook, stirring gently, until mixture thickens. Serve on toast. Makes 6 servings.

# Hot Pickle Rolls (hors d'oeuvre)

**2 cups watermelon pickle chunks**
**6 ounces cream cheese, at room temperature**
**½ pound Canadian bacon, thinly sliced at a slant**
**¼ cup butter or margarine**
**Dash cayenne**

**Preparation:** Drain pickles and soften cream cheese. Spread cream cheese around pickle chunks and wrap them in bacon slices. Secure with toothpicks. Store in refrigerator until chafing time.

**Performance:** Melt butter in blazer pan of chafing dish. Add a dash of cayenne. Sauté pickle rolls until heated through. Place over hot water to keep warm. Let guests serve themselves from chafing dish, lifting rolls by securing toothpicks. Makes about 24 hors d'oeuvre.

# Apples and Sweet Potatoes Flambé

**6 medium-size sweet potatoes**
**1 large firm cooking apple**
**⅓ cup brown sugar**
**3 tablespoons butter or margarine**
**3 tablespoons applejack or rum**

**Preparation:** Just before chafing time cook sweet potatoes in boiling salted water for 30 minutes and peel. Cut in ½ inch slices. Core but do not pare apple and cut in ½ inch slices. Sprinkle with 2 tablespoons brown sugar. Heat applejack.

**Performance:** Melt butter in blazer pan and sauté potatoes until browned. Sprinkle with 4 tablespoons brown sugar. Turn slices to coat evenly with melted sugar and cook until glazed. Push to sides of blazer pan and fry apple rings until tender and brown on both sides. Arrange potatoes over apple rings. Ignite applejack and pour over. Allow flames to burn out before serving. Makes 6 servings.

# Fruited Sweet-Sour Pork

**2 tablespoons butter or margarine**
**1½ pounds pork, sliced in thin strips (2-2½ pound pork shoulder, boned)**
**1 can (13½-ounces) pineapple tidbits**
**½ cup bottled Russian Dressing**
**¾ cup water**
**2 tablespoons cornstarch**
**1½ tablespoons soy sauce**
**1 teaspoon vinegar**
**¼ teaspoon salt**
**1 medium-size green pepper, sliced thin**
**½ cup thinly sliced onions**
**2 cups hot cooked rice**

Preheat fry pan at 350 degrees; melt butter or margarine. Add pork and sauté about 2 to 3 minutes or until meat is browned. Drain pineapple, reserving about ¾ cup syrup. Combine pineapple syrup, Russian dressing, water, cornstarch, soy sauce, vinegar and salt; pour over meat and stir until thickened. Cover. Turn control dial down to 225° and simmer ½ hour, or until meat is fork tender. Add green pepper, onion, and pineapple tidbits. Cover and cook 5 minutes. Serve over hot cooked rice. Makes 4 servings.

Wish-Bone

# COOKIE

Cookies are for fun. Before the holidays, let the children help make up batches of rolled cookies. Let them frost and decorate them with love and imagination and give them to friends and relatives for holiday presents.

Cookies are to cheer one up. On a gloomy, rainy, winter day, bake a batch of cookies – the odor of cinnamon and spices wafting through the house, will lift the lagging spirits and make the day seem sunny.

Cookies are for hurry up. When time is short, but dessert for dinner is important. A batch of quick stir and drop cookies can be put together and baked, even while dinner is still cooking.

Cookies can be done ahead. Try a batch of refrigerator cookies, keep the dough in the refrigerator and have hot fresh from the oven cookies baked in minutes.

Or maybe just because you like cookies. Here are a whole range, kind and variety of cookies for you to bake and enjoy.

# Drop Cookies

**Spring these treats on your family—Coffee Pecan Delights, Jubilee Jumbles, Festive Butter Wafers.**

## Sherried Butter-Nut Drops

**1½ cups butter or margarine**
**1¾ cups sifted confectioners' sugar**
**¼ teaspoon salt**
**3⅓ cups sifted flour**
**½ cup sherry wine**
**1 cup finely-chopped pecans**

Cream together butter and sugar until light and fluffy. Add salt and continue mixing. Add flour alternately with sherry wine, beating well after each addition. Stir in nuts. Drop from teaspoon onto greased baking sheet. Bake in a moderate oven (350° F) 20 to 25 minutes. Makes about 100 drops.

## Coffee Pecan Delights

**4 teaspoons instant coffee**
**1 tablespoon hot water**
**2 egg whites**
**⅛ teaspoon salt**
**1 cup sugar**
**1 cup fine vanilla-cookie crumbs**
**1 cup chopped pecans**

Dissolve coffee in hot water; cool. Beat egg whites and salt until stiff. Add sugar and coffee, alternately, beating well after each addition. Fold in crumbs and nuts. Drop from a teaspoon onto greased baking sheets, about 2 inches apart. Bake in a slow oven (300°F) about 15 minutes, or until golden brown. Makes 3 dozen cookies.

## Baked Fudge Drops

**3 tablespoons cocoa**
**⅔ cup sweetened condensed milk**
**1½ cups shredded coconut**
**⅛ teaspoon salt**
**¼ teaspoon vanilla**

Combine cocoa, milk, coconut, salt and vanilla. Drop from a teaspoon onto a greased baking sheet. Bake in a moderate oven (350°F) 15 minutes. Makes 2 dozen drops.

After batter is thoroughly mixed, stir in finely-chopped pecans. Set out a greased baking sheet.

Drop from teaspoon onto greased baking sheet. Bake in a moderate oven (350° F) 20-25 minutes.

Remove baking sheet from oven and place hot cookies on a rack. Allow to cool before storing.

## Crunchies

1½ cups corn flakes, crushed
¾ cup sifted flour
¾ cup sugar
¾ cup shredded coconut
¼ teaspoon salt
½ cup butter
1 tablespoon light corn syrup
1 teaspoon soda
1 teaspoon vanilla

Combine cereal, flour, sugar, coconut and salt in a bowl. Set aside. Melt butter in a saucepan over medium heat. Add corn syrup and cook, stirring until mixture comes to a boil. Add soda and stir rapidly to blend. When foam settles, remove from heat at once, add vanilla and blend. Pour over dry ingredients and mix thoroughly. Mixture will be dry and crumbly. Shape into rounds by pressing mixture by tablespoonfuls against side of mixing bowl. Place carefully on ungreased baking sheet, placing cookies about 2 inches apart. Press with fork to flatten slightly. Bake in a moderately-hot oven (375°F) 7 to 8 minutes, or until lightly browned. Cool about 2 minutes, then remove carefully. Makes 2½ dozen cookies.

## Molasses Jumbles

½ cup shortening
½ cup sugar
1 egg
2½ cups sifted flour
1 teaspoon soda
½ teaspoon cinnamon
¼ teaspoon salt
⅛ teaspoon ginger
½ cup light molasses
½ cup sour milk
1 package (1 cup) semi-sweet chocolate morsels

Cream together shortening and sugar until light and fluffy. Beat in egg. Sift together flour, soda, cinnamon, salt and ginger. Add to creamed mixture alternately with blended molasses and milk. Beat well after each addition. Fold in chocolate morsels. Drop from a teaspoon onto a greased baking sheet. Bake in a moderately-hot oven (375° F) 15 minutes. Makes 6 dozen jumbles.

## Angostura Snaps

½ cup butter or margarine
¼ cup molasses
½ cup sugar
2 teaspoons Angostura bitters
1 cup sifted flour
1 teaspoon ground ginger
¼ teaspoon salt

Melt butter in a saucepan. Stir in molasses and sugar and stir until sugar dissolves. Remove mixture from heat and add bitters. Sift together flour, ginger and salt. Add to molasses mixture and beat until smooth. Drop from a teaspoon onto greased baking sheet. Bake in a very hot oven (450° F) about 14 minutes. Allow cookies to cool slightly before removing from baking sheet. Makes 2½ dozen cookies.

## Father's Molasses Cookies

½ cup butter or margarine
⅓ cup sugar
½ cup molasses
2 eggs, well beaten
2 tablespoons sour milk
2½ cups sifted flour
½ teaspoon salt
1 teaspoon soda
¾ teaspoon ginger
½ cup seedless raisins, chopped

Cream together butter and sugar until light and fluffy. Stir in molasses, eggs and milk. Beat well. Sift together flour, salt, soda and ginger. Stir into creamed mixture. Stir in raisins. Drop from a teaspoon onto greased baking sheet. Bake in a moderately-hot oven (375° F) 12 to 15 minutes. Makes about 3 dozen cookies.

## Frosted Ginger Cookies

⅓ cup margarine
½ cup brown sugar, firmly packed
1 egg, well beaten
¼ cup molasses
½ cup boiling water
1⅔ cups sifted flour
½ teaspoon soda
1½ teaspoons baking powder
½ teaspoon salt
1 teaspoon cinnamon
1 teaspoon cloves
1 teaspoon ginger
2 cups sifted confectioners' sugar
½ cup margarine, melted
1 teaspoon grated lemon rind
¼ cup lemon juice

Cream together margarine and sugar until fluffy. Add egg and blend well. Stir in molasses. Add boiling water, stirring to blend well. Sift together flour, soda, baking powder, salt and spices. Add to creamed mixture and beat until well blended. Chill about 2 hours. Drop from a teaspoon onto greased baking sheet. Bake in a hot oven (400°F) 10 to 12 minutes. Remove to rack and cool. Combine confectioners' sugar and melted margarine and blend well. Add lemon rind and lemon juice, blending to a smooth consistency. Cover tops of ginger cookies with this frosting. Makes about 2½ dozen cookies.

Corn Products Co.

# Chocolate Kisses

3 egg whites
1 cup sifted confectioners' sugar
⅓ cup salted cracker crumbs
1 package (1 cup) semi-sweet chocolate morsels
½ teaspoon vanilla

Beat egg whites until stiff but not dry. Gradually beat in sugar, and continue beating until stiff and satiny. Fold in cracker crumbs. Melt chocolate morsels over hot water. Cool and fold into egg whites with vanilla. Drop from a teaspoon onto greased baking sheets. Bake in a moderate oven (350° F) 12 to 15 minutes. Makes 4 dozen cookies.

# German Chocolate Cookies

2 eggs
1 cup dark brown sugar, firmly packed
1 cup sifted flour
1 teaspoon baking powder
½ teaspoon salt
¼ teaspoon cinnamon
2 tablespoons grated lemon rind
1⅓ cups blanched almonds, chopped
½ package (½ cup) semi-sweet chocolate morsels, chopped

Beat eggs. Add sugar and continue beating until thick. Sift together flour, baking powder, salt and cinnamon. Stir into beaten eggs. Add remaining ingredients and blend well. Drop from teaspoon onto greased baking sheet. Bake in a moderately-hot oven (375° F) 12 minutes. Makes 4 dozen cookies.

# Drop and Bake Cookies

1 cup seedless raisins
½ cup shredded coconut
¼ cup citron
¾ cup chopped walnuts
½ cup shortening
⅓ cup sugar
2 eggs, separated
⅔ cup sweetened condensed milk
1½ cups sifted flour
2 teaspoons baking powder
¼ teaspoon salt
1 teaspoon vanilla extract
1 tablespoon grated orange rind

Put raisins, coconut, citron and walnuts through food chopper, using medium blade. Cream shortening and sugar together until light and fluffy. Mix in egg yolks and milk. Sift together flour, baking powder and salt. Blend into creamed mixture and mix well. Stir in vanilla, orange rind and ground fruits. Blend well. Beat egg whites until stiff. Fold into cookie mixture. Drop from a teaspoon onto greased baking sheet. Bake in a hot oven (400° F) 12 to 15 minutes. Makes about 2½ dozen cookies.

Lever Bros. Co.

# Frosted Chocolate Nut Drops

½ cup shortening
1 cup brown sugar, firmly packed
1 egg
2 squares unsweetened chocolate, melted
1 teaspoon vanilla
1⅓ cups sifted cake flour
½ teaspoon salt
¼ teaspoon soda
½ cup buttermilk
1 cup walnuts, chopped

Cream together shortening and sugar until light and fluffy. Add egg, chocolate and vanilla and beat well. Sift together flour, salt and soda. Add to creamed mixture alternately with buttermilk. Mix well. Stir in nuts. Drop rounded tablespoons of dough onto greased baking sheet. Bake in a moderate oven (350°F) 12 to 15 minutes. Frost tops of cookies with chocolate frosting when cold. Makes about 3 dozen cookies.

### Chocolate Frosting

1 tablespoon shortening
1 tablespoon butter or margarine
2½ squares unsweetened chocolate, melted
¼ cup scalded milk
1¼ cups sifted confectioners' sugar
Dash of salt
½ teaspoon vanilla

Melt shortening, butter and chocolate over hot water. Pour hot milk over combined sugar and salt and stir until sugar is dissolved. Add vanilla; then add chocolate mixture and beat until thick enough to spread.

# Chocolate Banana Cookies

1 package (1 cup) semi-sweet chocolate morsels
⅔ cup shortening
1 cup sugar
2 eggs
2¼ cups sifted flour
2 teaspoons baking powder
½ teaspoon salt
¼ teaspoon soda
1 cup mashed bananas, (2, fully ripe)

Melt chocolate morsels over hot (not boiling) water. Cream together shortening and sugar until light and fluffy. Add eggs, one at a time, and beat well after each addition. Sift together flour, baking powder, salt and soda. Add to creamed mixture with cooled chocolate and the bananas. Blend thoroughly. Drop from a teaspoon onto a greased baking sheet. Bake in a hot oven (400° F) 12 minutes. Makes 7 dozen cookies.

# Florentines

3 eggs
1¼ cups sugar
3 tablespoons sifted flour
¼ teaspoon baking powder
1 package (1 cup) semi-sweet chocolate morsels, ground
⅓ cup chopped candied orange peel
1½ cups blanched almonds, finely chopped
¼ teaspoon vanilla
¼ teaspoon cinnamon
¼ teaspoon cloves
¼ teaspoon nutmeg
1 teaspoon grated lemon rind

Beat eggs until thick. Add sugar gradually and continue beating until very thick. Combine flour and baking powder and add to egg mixture. Add remaining ingredients and blend well. Drop from teaspoon onto a baking sheet lined with browned paper, 2 inches apart. Bake in a hot oven (400° F) 10 minutes. Cool on brown paper. Wet paper underneath cookies and peel them off. Makes 5 dozen.

# Almond Frosts

2 eggs
¾ cup sugar
1 teaspoon lemon juice
1 teaspoon vanilla
1½ cups finely-chopped, unblanched almonds
1 cup sifted flour
½ teaspoon salt
⅓ cup melted shortening
7 tablespoons confectioners' sugar
½ teaspoon vanilla
2½ teaspoons warm water

Beat eggs until thick and lemon-colored. Add sugar, 2 tablespoonfuls at a time, beating well after each addition. Blend in lemon juice, vanilla and almonds. Sift together flour and salt and add to egg mixture. Blend well. Stir in shortening. Drop from a teaspoon onto lightly-greased baking sheet, about 3 inches apart. Bake in a moderately-hot oven (375° F) about 12 minutes. Remove from baking sheet while warm. Combine confectioners' sugar, vanilla and water. Stir until smooth. Brush tops of cooled cookies with sugar mixture. Makes about 4½ dozen small cookies.

# Good Luck Roll-Ups

½ cup margarine
1 cup brown sugar, firmly packed
2 eggs, well beaten
1 teaspoon grated orange rind
4 tablespoons sifted cake flour
½ teaspoon salt
½ cup pecans, finely chopped

Cream together margarine and sugar until light and fluffy. Add eggs and orange rind and blend well. Add flour and salt and mix thoroughly. Fold in nuts. Drop from a teaspoon onto a greased baking sheet, leaving a 4-inch space between each spoonful of batter. Spread mixture as thin as possible with a spatula. Bake in a moderately-slow oven (325°F) 10 to 12 minutes. Remove from oven and let stand 1 minute. Loosen cookies from baking sheet with a broad spatula. Working quickly, roll warm cookies, one at a time, around the handle of a wooden spoon. Place on a rack and let cool. If cookies cool and cannot be rolled easily, return them to warm oven for a few minutes. Makes about 2 dozen cookies.

Lever Bros. Co.

# Almond Fruit Cookies

1 cup shortening
1½ cups sugar
3 eggs, beaten
¾ teaspoon maple flavoring
3 cups sifted flour
1 teaspoon salt
1 teaspoon soda
1 teaspoon nutmeg
1 cup quick-cooking oats
1 cup chopped, roasted blanched almonds
1½ cups cooked, chopped prunes

Cream together shortening and sugar until light and fluffy. Add eggs and maple flavoring and mix well. Sift together flour, salt, soda and nutmeg. Stir into creamed mixture. Add oats, almonds and prunes and combine thoroughly. Drop from a teaspoon onto ungreased baking sheets, about 2 inches apart. Bake in a hot oven (400° F) 12 to 15 minutes. Makes about 6 dozen cookies.

# Almond Snowdrifts

2 egg whites
1 cup sugar
¼ teaspoon salt
1 teaspoon vanilla
1½ cups finely-chopped, unblanched almonds
1 tablespoon flour

Beat egg whites until stiff but not dry. Beat in sugar, about 2 tablespoonfuls at a time, beating well after each addition. Fold in salt, vanilla, almonds and flour; blend well. Drop from a teaspoon onto a lightly-floured baking sheet, about 2 inches apart. Bake in a moderately-slow oven (325° F) 15 to 17 minutes. Remove from baking sheet while still warm. Makes about 3½ dozen cookies.

# Jubilee Jumbles

½ cup shortening
1 cup brown sugar, firmly packed
½ cup sugar
2 eggs
1 cup evaporated milk
1 teaspoon vanilla
2¾ cups sifted flour
½ teaspoon soda
1 teaspoon salt
1 cup chopped walnuts

Cream together shortening and sugars until light and fluffy. Add eggs and beat well. Stir in milk and vanilla. Sift together flour, soda and salt. Stir into creamed mixture. Add walnuts and blend thoroughly. Drop rounded tablespoonfuls of dough onto greased baking sheet, about 2 inches apart. Bake in a moderately-hot oven (375°F) 10 minutes, or until delicately browned. Remove from baking sheets and cool. Heat 2 tablespoons of butter until golden brown. Beat in 2 cups sifted confectioners' sugar and ¼ cup evaporated milk. Continue beating until smooth. Frost cookies with this mixture. Makes about 4 dozen cookies.

# Latin American Cookies

⅓ cup butter
¼ cup sugar
1½ cups sifted flour
½ teaspoon salt
1 teaspoon baking powder
½ teaspoon soda
1 teaspoon cinnamon
½ teaspoon nutmeg
¼ teaspoon ginger
⅓ cup light molasses
⅓ cup double-strength, cold coffee
1 package semi-sweet chocolate morsels

Cream together butter and sugar until light and fluffy. Sift together flour, salt, baking powder, soda, cinnamon, nutmeg and ginger. Add to creamed mixture alternately with combined molasses and coffee. Blend well after each addition. Fold in chocolate morsels. Drop from a teaspoon onto a greased baking sheet. Bake in a moderately-hot oven (375° F) 15 minutes. Makes 3 dozen cookies.

# Almond Roll Cookies

⅔ cup almonds, blanched
½ cup sugar
½ cup butter or margarine
1 tablespoon flour
2 tablespoons milk

Put almonds through coarse blade of food chopper; then through fine blade. Combine with remaining ingredients in a skillet. Heat slowly until butter melts. Drop by half teaspoonfuls, 3 inches apart, onto greased baking sheet. Bake in moderate oven (350° F) 8 minutes, or until cookies are lacey and lightly browned. Cool slightly. Remove from baking sheet with broad spatula and roll around the handle of a wooden spoon. If cookies become hard on sheet, return to oven for a few minutes to soften. Makes 30 cookies.

Lever Bros. Co.

# Coconut Orange Jumbos

¾ cup shortening
½ cup sugar
½ cup light corn syrup
2 eggs
2 cups chopped, shredded coconut
3 tablespoons grated orange rind
2½ cups sifted flour
¼ teaspoon salt
½ teaspoon soda
½ cup orange juice

Cream together shortening and sugar until light and fluffy. Add syrup and blend well. Add eggs, one at a time, beating well after each addition. Stir in coconut and orange rind. Sift together flour, salt and soda. Add to creamed mixture alternately with orange juice, mixing well after each addition. Drop from teaspoon onto lightly-greased baking sheet. Bake in a moderate oven (350° F) 15 minutes. Makes 5 dozen cookies.

# Almond Oat Wafers

¼ cup shortening
⅔ cup sugar
2 eggs, well beaten
½ cup quick-cooking oats
¾ cup finely-chopped, unblanched almonds
1 teaspoon lemon extract
¼ teaspoon salt
⅓ cup sifted flour

Cream together shortening and sugar until light and fluffy. Blend in eggs. Stir in oats, almonds, flavoring, salt and flour. Mix well. Drop from a teaspoon onto greased and floured baking sheets, about 3 inches apart. Bake in a moderate oven (350° F) 13 to 14 minutes. Remove from baking sheet while cookies are warm. Makes about 4½ dozen wafers.

# Grape-Nuts Raisin Cookies

**1 cup milk**
**¾ cup wheat and barley kernels**
**½ cup butter or margarine**
**¾ cup light brown sugar, firmly packed**
**1 egg**
**½ cup coarsely-cut raisins**
**2 cups sifted flour**
**1½ teaspoons double-acting baking powder**
**½ teaspoon salt**
**½ teaspoon mace**
**⅛ teaspoon cinnamon**
**⅛ teaspoon cloves**
**1 teaspoon vanilla**

Pour milk over cereal and let stand about 5 minutes. Cream butter and sugar together until light and fluffy. Add egg and beat thoroughly. Add raisins and mix well. Sift together flour, baking powder, salt, mace, cinnamon and cloves. Add flour, alternately with cereal mixture, beating well after each addition. Add vanilla. Drop from a teaspoon onto greased baking sheet. Bake in a moderate oven (350°F) 15 minutes. Makes 4 dozen cookies.

# Lacy Corn Flake Crisps

**¼ cup butter**
**¼ cup sugar**
**⅓ cup light molasses**
**1 package (1 cup) semi-sweet chocolate morsels**
**4 cups corn flakes**

Combine butter, sugar and molasses in a saucepan. Bring to a full rolling boil, stirring constantly. Remove from heat and add remaining ingredients and mix well. Drop by half-teaspoons onto an ungreased baking sheet. Bake in a moderate oven (350° F) 6 to 8 minutes. Makes 5 dozen cookies.

# Banana-Oatmeal Drops

**¾ cup shortening**
**1 cup sugar**
**1 egg**
**1 medium-sized banana, mashed**
**½ teaspoon lemon juice**
**1½ cups sifted flour**
**½ teaspoon soda**
**1 teaspoon salt**
**¾ teaspoon cinnamon**
**¼ teaspoon nutmeg**
**1½ cups quick-cooking oats**
**½ cup chopped walnuts**

Cream together shortening and sugar until light and fluffy. Beat in egg. Stir in banana and lemon juice. Sift together flour, soda, salt, cinnamon and nutmeg. Stir into creamed mixture. Mix in oats and walnuts. Drop from a teaspoon onto greased baking sheets, about 2 inches apart. Bake in a moderate oven (350°F) 12 to 15 minutes, or until edges turn golden. Makes about 4 dozen cookies.

Lever Bros. Co.

# Old Time Nutmeg Hermits

**1 cup butter or margarine**
**2 cups brown sugar, firmly packed**
**4 eggs**
**4 cups sifted flour**
**1 teaspoon soda**
**1½ teaspoons nutmeg**
**½ teaspoon salt**
**¼ cup milk**
**2 cups seedless raisins**
**1 cup chopped nuts**

Cream together butter and brown sugar until light and fluffy. Beat in eggs. Sift together flour, soda, nutmeg and salt. Add to creamed mixture alternately with milk, beating well after each addition. Stir in raisins and nuts. Drop from a teaspoon onto lightly-greased baking sheets. Bake in a moderately-hot oven (375°F) 12 to 15 minutes. Makes about 5 dozen cookies.

American Spice Trade Assn.

# Peanut Brittle Cookies

**¾ cup shortening**
**1½ cups sugar**
**¼ cup water**
**½ teaspoon vanilla**
**2 cups sifted flour**
**⅛ teaspoon soda**
**1 teaspoon salt**
**1 cup crushed peanut brittle**

Cream together shortening and sugar until light and fluffy. Stir in water and vanilla and blend well. Sift together flour, soda and salt. Add to creamed mixture and blend. Stir in peanut brittle. Drop from teaspoon onto well-greased baking sheet, about 2 inches apart. Bake in a moderately-hot oven (375° F) 10 minutes, or until lightly browned. Makes about 8½ dozen cookies.

## Soft Spiced Molasses Cookies

**1 cup shortening**
**2 cups sugar**
**1 cup molasses**
**2 eggs**
**5 cups sifted flour**
**2 teaspoons salt**
**1½ teaspoons soda**
**1 teaspoon ginger**
**1 teaspoon mace**
**2 teaspoons cinnamon**
**½ teaspoon cloves**
**½ cup sour milk**
**1½ cups seedless raisins**

Cream together shortening, sugar and molasses until light and fluffy. Beat in eggs. Sift together flour, salt, soda, ginger, mace, cinnamon and cloves. Add to creamed mixture alternately with sour milk. Beat well. Stir in raisins. Drop from teaspoon onto greased baking sheet Bake in a moderately-hot oven (375° F) 15 minutes. Makes 7 dozen cookies.

## Prune Molasses Cookies

**½ cup shortening**
**¾ cup sugar**
**⅓ cup molasses**
**2½ cups sifted flour**
**½ teaspoon soda**
**¾ teaspoon ginger**
**1 teaspoon salt**
**¼ cup water**
**¾ cup cooked, chopped prunes**

Cream together shortening, sugar and molasses until light and fluffy. Sift together flour, soda, ginger and salt. Stir into creamed mixture alternately with water, blending well after each addition. Stir in prunes. Drop from teaspoon onto greased baking sheets. Bake in a moderately-hot oven (375° F) 12 to 15 minutes. Makes about 40 cookies.

## Very Special Cookies

**1 cup butter or margarine**
**1 cup sugar**
**1 cup brown sugar, firmly packed**
**2 eggs, beaten**
**1 cup unsweetened applesauce**
**4 cups sifted flour**
**1 teaspoon salt**
**1 teaspoon soda**
**1 teaspoon nutmeg**
**1 teaspoon mace**
**2 teaspoons cinnamon**
**½ teaspoon cloves**
**¼ cup thinly cut preserved lemon peel**
**¼ cup thinly cut preserved orange peel**
**½ cup sliced candied cherries**
**1 cup chopped walnuts**
**1½ cups seedless raisins**

Cream together butter and sugars until light and fluffy. Stir in eggs and applesauce and beat well. Sift together flour, salt, soda and spices. Add to creamed mixture and blend thoroughly. Add lemon peel, orange peel, cherries, walnuts and raisins and mix well. Drop from a teaspoon onto an ungreased baking sheet, about 2 inches apart. Bake in a hot oven (400° F) about 15 minutes. Makes about 6 dozen cookies.

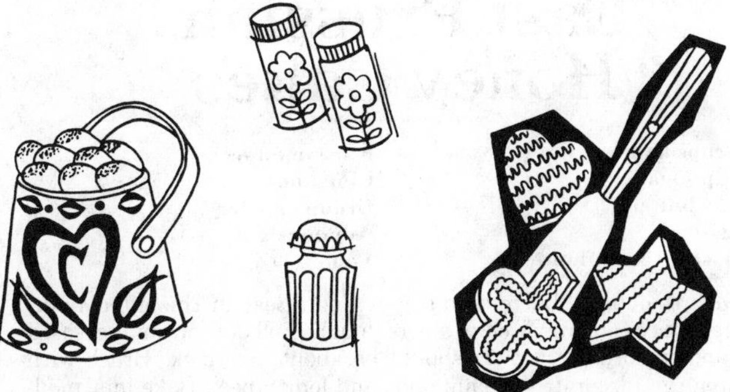

## Sherried Fig-Coconut Cookies

**1 cup dried figs**
**¾ cup shortening**
**1½ cups sugar**
**2 eggs, well beaten**
**1 cup shredded coconut**
**3 cups sifted flour**
**3 teaspoons baking powder**
**¾ teaspoon salt**
**½ cup sherry wine**

Cover figs with boiling water; let stand 10 minutes and drain. Snip off stems and cut figs into small pieces with scissors. Cream shortening. Gradually add sugar and cream until light and fluffy. Beat in eggs. Stir in coconut and figs. Sift together flour, baking powder and salt. Add dry ingredients alternately with sherry, mixing well after each addition. Drop from teaspoon, 2 to 3 inches apart, onto greased baking sheet. Bake in a hot oven (400° F) about 10 minutes. Makes about 7 dozen cookies.

## Mincemeat Cookies

**1 cup shortening**
**1¼ cups sugar**
**3 eggs, slightly beaten**
**1½ cups ready-to-use mincemeat**
**3¼ cups sifted flour**
**½ teaspoon salt**
**1 teaspoon soda**

Cream together shortening and sugar until light and fluffy. Add eggs and beat until smooth. Stir in mincemeat. Sift together flour, salt and soda. Add to shortening mixture and mix thoroughly. Drop from teaspoon onto greased baking sheet, about 2 inches apart. Bake in a moderately-hot oven (375° F) about 12 minutes, or until golden brown. Makes 6 dozen cookies.

## Israeli Honey Cookies

**½ cup shortening**
**½ cup honey**
**1 egg**
**1 teaspoon vanilla**
**1 cup sifted flour**
**1 teaspoon baking powder**
**¼ teaspoon salt**
**½ cup quick-cooking oats**
**½ cup chopped nuts**
**½ cup seedless raisins**
**1 package (1 cup) semi-sweet chocolate morsels, chopped**

Cream together shortening and honey until light and fluffy. Add egg and vanilla and beat well. Sift together flour, baking powder and salt and add to creamed mixture. Add remaining ingredients and blend well. Drop from teaspoon onto greased baking sheet. Flatten with tines of a fork. Bake in a moderately-hot oven (375° F) 10 minutes. Makes 4 dozen cookies.

# Shortcake Cookies

*(See picture opposite.)*

1 lb. flour
2 teaspoons baking powder
2 eggs
1 tablespoon rum
Vanilla, few drops
Grated rind of ½ lemon
½ lb. margarine

Mix all the ingredients to a stiff dough. Work with fingers until smooth and pliable. Leave for at least one hour in refrigerator to get cold and firm. Roll out thinly and cut into various shapes. Bake in a moderate oven for 10 to 12 minutes. Decorate with coarse sugar, currants, colored sugar, chocolate or lemon frosting, or sandwich together with jam.

# Filled Marzipan Cookies

*(See picture opposite.)*

½ lb. ground almonds
½ lb. powdered sugar
1 egg
Shortcake cookies
Pineapple, 1 in. pieces
Ginger
Walnut halves

Make a marzipan by mixing the almonds, sugar and egg to a stiff paste. Roll out ½" thick, cut into 1" strips and place around the cookies, leaving a space in the middle. Sprinkle the pineapple with ginger, and fill the center of the marzipan cookies. Cover with chocolate frosting and decorate with walnuts.

# Marzipan Cookies

*(See picture opposite.)*

½ lb. ground almonds
½ lb. powdered sugar
1 egg
3 egg whites
Lemon peel, grated
1 oz. almonds
Candied fruit

Mix the ground almonds with the powdered sugar and eggs to make a firm paste. Mix in the grated lemon peel to taste. Grease a baking sheet thoroughly. Roll out paste and cut small rounds. Decorate with almonds and fruit. Bake in a hot oven until slightly golden brown. When cold, cover bottoms and sides with chocolate frosting.

# Pineapple-Ade Cookies

¾ cup shortening
½ cup granulated sugar
½ cup brown sugar, firmly packed
2 eggs
1 tablespoon grated lemon rind
1 teaspoon vanilla
2 cups sifted flour
1 teaspoon baking powder
¼ teaspoon soda
½ teaspoon salt
7 tablespoons pineapple juice
¾ cup walnuts, chopped

Cream together shortening, sugar and brown sugar until light and fluffy. Add eggs, lemon rind and vanilla and beat well. Sift together flour, baking powder, soda and salt. Add to creamed mixture alternately with pineapple juice, beating well after each addition. Blend in walnuts. Drop rounded tablespoons of dough onto greased baking sheet. Bake in a moderately-hot oven (375°F) 10 to 15 minutes. Frost with Pineapple Icing when cool. Makes 4 dozen cookies.

## Pineapple Icing

1 tablespoon shortening
1 tablespoon butter
¼ teaspoon salt
½ teaspoon grated lemon rind
¼ cup hot pineapple juice
3 cups confectioners' sugar

Blend together shortening, butter, salt and lemon rind. Add pineapple juice alternately with confectioners' sugar, beating well after each addition.

# French Lace Cookies

½ cup light corn syrup
¼ cup butter
¼ cup shortening
⅔ cup brown sugar, firmly packed
1 cup sifted all-purpose flour
1 cup finely chopped nuts

Combine corn syrup, butter, shortening and brown sugar in a saucepan. Bring to a boil and then remove immediately from the heat. Blend in flour and nuts gradually. Drop by rounded teaspoonfuls onto a greased baking sheet about 3 inches apart. Bake in a slow oven (325°F.) 8 to 10 minutes. Cool 1 minute. Remove carefully from baking sheet with a spatula. If desired cookies may be rolled into cone shape while still warm. Makes about 5 dozen cookies.

# Molasses Snaps

¾ cup margarine
1 cup sugar
1 egg, well beaten
1 cup light molasses
½ cup hot water
4 cups sifted flour
¼ teaspoon ginger
1 teaspoon salt
1 teaspoon soda

Cream together margarine and sugar until light and fluffy. Add egg and beat well. Add molasses and hot water. Sift together flour, ginger, salt and soda. Stir into molasses mixture. Drop from teaspoon onto greased baking sheets. Bake in a moderate oven (350°F) 12 to 15 minutes. Makes 5 dozen cookies.

# Gay Peppernuts

*(See picture opposite.)*

1 lb. honey
¾ cup sugar
½ cup butter
⅔ cup chopped almonds
Vanilla, few drops
½ teaspoon mixed spice
2 lbs. self-rising flour

Melt the honey, butter and sugar. Add the spices, mix well and leave to cool. Add the flour and let dough stand for one hour. Roll out ¾" thick and bake in a greased tin in a moderate oven. When cool cut into various shapes.

1½ cups powdered sugar
3 tablespoons water
2 teaspoons cocoa

Mix the sugar and water. Flavor half with the cocoa. For decoration: almonds, walnuts, sugar-pearls.

# East Prussian Honey Cakes

*(See picture opposite.)*

1½ cups honey
¾ cup sugar
½ cup butter
3 eggs
1 lb. self-rising flour
Kardamon seeds
Cinnamon
Ground ginger
Almonds
Lemon peel

Melt the honey, butter and sugar. Cool. Beat in the sifted flour, 2 eggs, spices and mix well to a firm dough. Roll out, put in a greased tin and smooth the top. It should be about ½" thick. Brush with beaten egg, decorate with almonds and lemon peel. Bake in a moderate oven for about 30 minutes. Allow to cool slightly before cutting. However, be certain to remove from tin before cold.

*Columbian Torte*, p. 211

*Nut Pudding with Vanilla Sauce, p. 241*

# Konigsberger Marzipan

(See picture opposite.)

5 cups sweet almonds
3 teaspoons bitter almonds
2½ cups powdered sugar
6-8 tablespoons rose-water

Scald almonds and skin, rinse thoroughly, spread on cloth and dry over night. Mix almonds and sugar and pass twice through almond grinder. Add rose-water and knead dough until smooth. Sprinkle powdered sugar on baking pan. Roll dough knife-thin, cut into ¼ in. strips and different shapes. Brush edges with rose-water. Place ¼ in. strip around edge to form a rim and make a pattern on it. Cover inside with white paper, so that only the rim gets brown with help of a red glowing iron spade held over them. A skillfully handled toaster or grill will do the same job. Remove paper, fill forms with sugar icing or chocolate icing.

# Chocolate Icing

(See picture opposite.)

Sweet or semi-sweet chocolate bars

Melt in a double boiler. Cool to touch. If the chocolate seems stiff, beat in a little cream.

# Sugar Icing

(See picture opposite.)

2½ cups powdered sugar
Lemon juice to taste
2 tablespoons water
½ teaspoon vanilla

Combine above ingredients until smooth.

# Chocolate Drop Chews

**1 package (1 cup) semi-sweet chocolate morsels**
**⅔ cup condensed milk**
**1 cup chopped nuts**
**Pinch of salt**
**1 teaspoon vanilla**

Heat the chocolate morsels and condensed milk together over hot water. Beat until smooth with a rotary beater. Add remaining ingredients. Drop from teaspoon onto well-greased baking sheet. Bake in a moderate oven (350° F) 10 to 12 minutes. Makes 3 dozen chews.

# Oatmeal Macaroons

**½ cup shortening**
**1 cup sugar**
**1 tablespoon molasses**
**1 teaspoon vanilla**
**1 egg**
**1 cup sifted flour**
**1 teaspoon salt**
**1 teaspoon cinnamon**
**¾ teaspoon soda**
**1 cup quick-cooking oats**
**⅓ cup seedless raisins**
**⅓ cup chopped dates**

Cream together shortening and sugar until light and fluffy. Add molasses, vanilla and egg and beat well. Sift together flour, salt, cinnamon and soda. Add to creamed mixture and mix well. Stir in oats, raisins and dates. Drop from a teaspoon onto a greased baking sheet. Bake in a moderate oven (350°F) 10 to 15 minutes. Makes 4 dozen macaroons.

# Raisin Crunchies

**½ cup shortening**
**½ cup sugar**
**1 egg, beaten**
**1½ tablespoons grated orange rind**
**1 cup sifted flour**
**1 teaspoon baking powder**
**½ teaspoon salt**
**½ cup quick-cooking oats**
**½ cup shredded coconut**
**¾ cup seedless raisins**

Cream together shortening and sugar until light and fluffy. Blend in egg and orange rind. Sift together flour, baking powder and salt. Stir into creamed mixture. Blend in oats, coconut and raisins. Drop from a teaspoon onto greased baking sheet. Bake in a moderately-hot oven (375° F) 12 to 15 minutes. Makes 3½ dozen cookies.

# Dad's Oatmeal Cookies

**1 cup prunes**
**½ cup shortening**
**1 cup sugar**
**2 eggs, beaten**
**6 tablespoons milk**
**1½ cups sifted flour**
**3 teaspoons baking powder**
**½ teaspoon salt**
**1½ cups quick-cooking oats**
**1 teaspoon vanilla**
**½ cup chopped walnuts**

Cover prunes with water and boil for 20 minutes. Cool, drain and cut from pits into small pieces. Cream shortening and sugar together until light and fluffy. Stir in eggs and milk. Sift together flour, baking powder and salt. Combine with oats and stir into creamed mixture. Add vanilla, nuts and prunes and blend thoroughly. Drop from a teaspoon onto greased baking sheets. Bake in a hot oven (400° F) about 15 minutes. Makes 2½ dozen cookies.

# Double Chocolate Cookies

**1 cup plus 2 tablespoons sifted flour**
**½ teaspoon soda**
**½ teaspoon salt**
**½ cup sugar**
**¼ cup brown sugar, firmly packed**
**1 egg**
**½ cup butter or margarine**
**1 teaspoon vanilla**
**½ cup chopped nuts**
**1 package (1 cup) semi-sweet chocolate morsels**

Sift together flour, soda and salt. Add sugar, brown sugar, egg, butter and vanilla. Blend well. Melt ⅓ cup of the chocolate morsels over hot water. Cool and add to the flour mixture. Stir in nuts and remaining chocolate morsels. Drop from teaspoon onto ungreased baking sheet, about 2 inches apart. Bake in a moderately-hot oven (375° F) 10 to 12 minutes. Makes about 4 dozen cookies.

# Prune Maple Cookies

**1½ cups cooked prunes**
**1 cup shortening**
**1½ cups sugar**
**3 eggs, well beaten**
**½ teaspoon maple extract**
**3 cups sifted flour**
**1½ teaspoons salt**
**1 teaspoon baking powder**
**1 cup quick-cooking oats**
**1 cup chopped nuts**

Cut prunes from pits into small pieces. Cream shortening and sugar together until light and fluffy. Add eggs and maple extract and mix well. Sift together flour, salt and baking powder. Combine with oats and stir into creamed mixture. Add nuts and mix well. Drop from a teaspoon onto greased baking sheets, about 2 inches apart. Bake in a hot oven (400° F) 12 to 15 minutes. Makes about 5 dozen cookies.

# Cookie-Pops

¾ cup shortening
1 cup brown sugar, firmly packed
¼ cup molasses
½ teaspoon salt
1 egg, unbeaten
2 cups sifted flour
2 teaspoons soda
1 teaspoon ginger
1 teaspoon cinnamon
½ teaspoon cloves
21 drinking straws, cut in half

Cream together shortening and sugar until light and fluffy. Add molasses, salt and egg and beat well. Sift together flour, soda, ginger, cinnamon and cloves. Add to shortening mixture and blend well. Measure out level tablespoons of dough onto greased baking sheets. Insert half a drinking straw in each mound of dough, straws parallel with sheet. Sprinkle dough with sugar. Bake in a moderately-hot oven (375°F) 11 to 14 minutes. Cool about 2 minutes before removing cookies from baking sheets. Makes about 3½ dozen Cookie-Pops.

Lever Bros. Co.

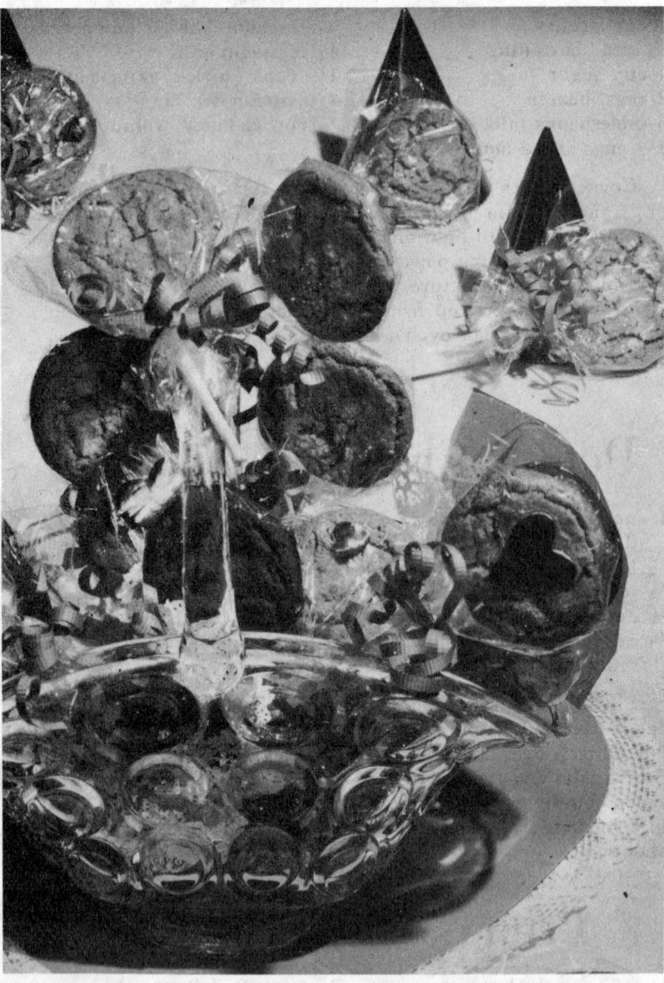

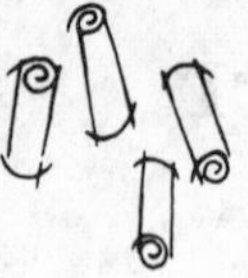

# Ginger Honeys

½ cup shortening
½ cup sugar
½ cup honey
1 egg
2 cups sifted flour
½ teaspoon salt
1 teaspoon ginger
1 teaspoon cinnamon
1 teaspoon soda
1 egg white, slightly beaten
¾ cup salted blanched peanuts, finely chopped

Cream together shortening, sugar and honey until light and fluffy. Add egg and beat well. Sift together flour, salt, ginger, cinnamon and soda. Add to shortening mixture and mix well. Drop level tablespoons of batter onto greased baking sheet. Flatten cookies with bottom of a glass. Brush with beaten egg white. Sprinkle with chopped peanuts. Bake in a moderate oven (350°F) 12 to 15 minutes. Makes about 3 dozen cookies.

Lever Bros. Co.

# Brazil Nut Scotchies

1 cup sugar
½ cup shortening
1 tablespoon molasses
1 teaspoon salt
1 teaspoon cinnamon
1 teaspoon vanilla
1 egg
1 cup sifted flour
¼ teaspoon soda
1 teaspoon baking powder
1 cup quick-cooking oats
1 cup chopped Brazil nuts
Sliced Brazil nuts

Cream together sugar and shortening until light and fluffy. Add molasses, salt, cinnamon, vanilla and egg and beat thoroughly. Sift together flour, soda and baking powder. Add to shortening mixture and mix well. Stir in oats and nuts. Drop from a level tablespoon onto greased baking sheets. Top with sliced nuts. Bake in a moderate oven (350°F) 10 to 12 minutes. Makes 3½ dozen cookies.

# Salted Peanut Cookies

½ cup shortening
1¼ cups brown sugar, firmly packed
1 egg
1½ cups sifted flour
½ teaspoon baking powder
¾ teaspoon soda
½ teaspoon salt
¼ cup milk
1½ cups grape nuts flakes
¾ cup chopped salted peanuts

Cream together shortening and sugar until light and fluffy. Add egg and beat well. Sift together flour, baking powder, soda and salt. Add flour mixture to creamed mixture alternately with milk, mixing well after each addition. Stir in cereal and peanuts. Drop from teaspoon onto greased baking sheets. Bake in a moderately-hot oven (375° F) 8 minutes, or until done. Makes about 4 dozen cookies.

# Quick Raisin Cookies

½ cup shortening
1¼ cups brown sugar, firmly packed
2 eggs
¼ cup milk
2 cups sifted flour
1 teaspoon salt
½ teaspoon baking powder
1 teaspoon cinnamon
½ teaspoon nutmeg
¼ teaspoon cloves
1 cup seedless raisins

Melt shortening in a large saucepan. Stir in sugar. Cool to lukewarm. Add eggs, one at a time, beating thoroughly after each addition. Stir in milk. Sift together flour, salt, baking powder, cinnamon, nutmeg and cloves. Blend into shortening mixture. Stir in raisins. Drop from tablespoon onto greased baking sheets. Bake in a moderate oven (350°F) about 15 to 20 minutes. Makes about 4 dozen cookies.

# Oatmeal Cookies

2 cups sifted flour
1 teaspoon baking powder
1 teaspoon salt
1 teaspoon cinnamon
½ teaspoon baking soda
3 cups pan-toasted old fashioned or quick oats or instant oatmeal
1 cup raisins
1¼ cups margarine
1¼ cups sugar
2 eggs, slightly beaten
¼ cup milk

Sift flour. baking powder, salt, cinnamon and baking soda together into bowl. Mix in oats or instant oatmeal and raisins. Cream margarine and sugar in mixing bowl. Add eggs; beat until fluffy. Stir in half the dry ingredients, then milk, then remaining dry ingredients. Drop batter by teaspoonsful, 2-inches apart, onto ungreased cooky sheet. Bake in hot oven (400°F.) until lightly browned, 10 to 12 minutes. Remove from cooky sheet immediately. Makes 6 dozen.

Best Foods

### Chocolate Chip Oatmeal Cookies

Follow recipe for Oatmeal Cookies, substituting 1 cup chocolate chips for raisins.

### Fruit Oatmeal Cookies

Follow recipe for Oatmeal Cookies, subsituting 1 cup chopped candied fruit for raisins.

### Mincemeat Oatmeal Cookies

Follow recipe for Oatmeal Cookies, substituting 1 cup ready-to-use or reconstituted mincemeat for raisins.

### Nutmeg Oatmeal Cookies

Follow recipe for Oatmeal Cookies, substituting ½ teaspoon nutmeg for 1 teaspoon cinnamon.

### Date Oatmeal Cookies

Follow recipe for Oatmeal Cookies, substituting 1 cup cut dates for raisins.

### Nut Oatmeal Cookies

Follow recipe for Oatmeal Cookies, substituting 1 cup chopped nuts for raisins.

### Citrus Oatmeal Cookies

Follow recipe for Oatmeal Cookies, substituting 1 teaspoon grated lemon or orange rind for cinnamon.

# Orange Oatmeal Cookies

½ cup shortening
½ cup sugar
1 egg
1 cup quick-cooking oats
1 cup sifted flour
½ teaspoon soda
¼ teaspoon salt
½ teaspoon cinnamon
5 tablespoons orange juice
¾ cup seedless raisins

Cream together shortening and sugar until light and fluffy. Add egg and beat well. Stir in oats. Sift together flour, soda, salt and cinnamon. Add to creamed ingredients, alternately with orange juice, beating well after each addition. Stir in raisins. Drop from teaspoon onto greased baking sheet. Bake in a moderate oven (350° F) 10 to 12 minutes. Makes about 4 dozen cookies.

American Spice Trade Assn.

# Spiced Black Pepper Cookies

2 cups sifted all-purpose flour
¼ teaspoon salt
1 teaspoon double-acting baking powder
½ cup shortening
1 teaspoon ground ginger
1 teaspoon ground cinnamon
½ teaspoon ground nutmeg
¼ teaspoon ground black pepper
1 cup sugar
⅓ cup molasses
1 large egg
1 tablespoon milk
Raisins, optional

Sift together flour, salt and baking powder and set aside. Mix together shortening and spices, into which gradually blend in sugar and molasses. Beat in egg and milk. Mix in dry ingredients. Drop a rounded teaspoon of dough one at a time onto lightly greased cooky sheets, or if desired, drop a heaping teaspoon dough onto lightly greased cooky sheets and top each with a raisin. Bake in a preheated moderate oven (350° F.) 15 minutes or until browned around the edges. Cool on wire racks. Store in a tightly closed container. Makes 3 dozen large cookies or 5 dozen 1-inch cookies.

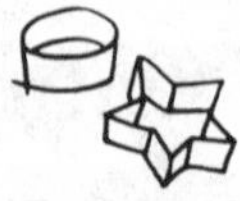
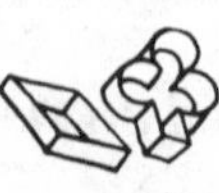

# Golden Raisin Lacies

1 egg
½ cup brown sugar, firmly packed
¼ teaspoon salt
¼ teaspoon nutmeg
¼ teaspoon vanilla
1 cup quick-cooking oats
½ cup golden raisins

Beat egg well. Add sugar gradually, beating thoroughly after each addition. Add salt, nutmeg, vanilla, oats and raisins and blend well. Drop from a teaspoon onto a greased baking sheet. Bake in a moderately-hot oven (375° F) 10 to 12 minutes. Remove from baking sheet at once. Makes about 2 dozen cookies.

# Chocolate Brazil Nut Cookies

½ cup butter or margarine
1 cup sugar
1 egg
1 teaspoon vanilla
2 squares candy-making chocolate, melted
¾ cup sifted flour
¼ teaspoon salt
½ cup chopped Brazil nuts

Cream together butter and sugar until light and fluffy. Add egg and beat well. Blend in vanilla and chocolate. Sift together flour and salt, add to butter mixture and mix well. Add Brazil nuts. Drop level tablespoons of batter onto a lightly-greased baking sheet, about 2 inches apart. Spread batter with a knife into flat rounds about 2 inches in diameter. Bake in a slow oven (325°F) about 15 minutes. Makes 3 dozen cookies.

Brazil Nut Assn.

# Ginger Orange Drops

½ cup shortening
½ cup sugar
1 egg
6 tablespoons fresh-frozen orange juice (undiluted)
2 cups sifted flour
⅛ teaspoon salt
¼ teaspoon baking soda
2 teaspoons baking powder
½ teaspoon ginger
½ cup seedless raisins

Cream shortening and sugar until light and fluffy. Blend in egg. Stir in orange juice, a tablespoonful at a time, and mix well. Sift together flour, salt, baking soda, baking powder and ginger. Add gradually to sugar mixture and blend well. Stir in raisins. Drop from teaspoon onto greased baking sheet. Bake in moderate oven (350° F) 10 to 15 minutes, or until golden brown. Cool. Makes about 5 dozen cookies.

# Oatmeal Fig Cookies

1 cup dried figs
¾ cup shortening
1 cup sugar
1 egg
2 tablespoons milk
1 teaspoon vanilla
1½ cups sifted flour
1 teaspoon salt
1 teaspoon baking powder
1 teaspoon cinnamon
2 cups quick-cooking oats

Cover figs with boiling water and let stand 10 minutes. Drain, clip stems and cut in small pieces. Cream together shortening and sugar until light and fluffy. Add egg, milk and vanilla and blend well. Sift together flour, salt, baking powder and cinnamon. Stir into creamed mixture. Add oats and figs and mix thoroughly. Drop from a teaspoon onto greased baking sheets. Bake in a moderate oven (350° F) 12 to 15 minutes. Makes about 4 dozen cookies.

# Nut Crumb Drops

1 package (1 cup) semi-sweet chocolate morsels
1⅓ cups condensed milk
1 teaspoon cinnamon
½ teaspoon salt
½ teaspoon vanilla
¾ cup chopped nuts
1 cup fine, dry bread crumbs

Combine chocolate morsels and condensed milk. Heat together over hot water. Beat until smooth with a rotary beater. Stir in remaining ingredients. Drop from teaspoon onto well-greased baking sheet. Bake in a moderately-hot oven (375° F) 12 minutes. Remove cookies from baking sheet as soon as they are done. Makes 4 dozen drops.

Pan American Coffee Bureau

# Chocolate Chip Coffee Kisses

2 egg whites
⅛ teaspoon cream of tartar
⅛ teaspoon salt
½ cup sugar
1 tablespoon instant coffee
1 package (1 cup) semi-sweet chocolate morsels
½ teaspoon vanilla

Combine egg whites, cream of tartar and salt in a mixing bowl; beat until foamy. Combine sugar and instant coffee. Add to egg whites, 2 tablespoonfuls at a time, beating after each addition. Continue beating until mixture will stand in stiff peaks. Fold in chocolate morsels and vanilla. Drop from teaspoon onto well-greased baking sheet. Bake in a slow oven (300° F) 25 minutes. Makes about 3 dozen kisses.

# Danish Cream Cones

⅓ cup butter or margarine
⅓ cup sugar
½ cup sifted all-purpose flour
4 egg whites
Strawberry jam
½ cup heavy cream

Melt butter. Stir in sugar and flour. Stir until smooth. Beat egg whites stiff. Fold in. Drop from measuring tablespoon onto hot, well-greased baking sheet, spacing well apart. Bake only 2 or 3 at a time. Spread each mound into paper-thin oblong about 4" x 5". Bake at 400° 5 minutes or until deep golden brown. Quickly remove and roll into cones while hot. Continue until batter is used. Fill bottom of cooled cones with strawberry jam. Whip cream. Fill large ends of cones with whipped cream forced through pastry tube. Store unused cones in a tightly-covered metal container to prevent softening. Makes 10 cones.

# Gail's Brown Sugar Cookies

½ cup shortening
1 cup brown sugar, firmly packed
1 egg
1 teaspoon vanilla
1½ cups sifted flour
½ teaspoon salt
2 teaspoons baking powder
2 tablespoons hot water
½ cup chopped dates
½ cup chopped pecans

Cream together shortening and sugar until light and fluffy. Add egg and vanilla and beat well. Sift together flour, salt and baking powder. Add half the flour to the creamed mixture and blend well. Stir in hot water. Add remaining flour and blend well. Add dates and pecans. Drop level tablespoons of the dough onto greased baking sheets. Press cookies lightly with the tines of a fork. Bake in a moderate oven (350° F) 10 to 15 minutes. Makes 3 dozen cookies.

# Angostura Pecan Crisps

1 cup butter or margarine
2 cups brown sugar, firmly packed
2 eggs
2 cups plus 3 tablespoons sifted cake flour
½ teaspoon salt
½ teaspoon soda
½ pound shelled pecans, finely ground
1 teaspoon Angostura bitters
Pecan halves

Cream together butter and sugar until light and fluffy. Add eggs and beat well. Sift together flour, salt and soda. Add to creamed mixture and blend well. Add ground nuts and bitters. Drop from a teaspoon onto ungreased baking sheets, about 2½ inches apart. Place a pecan half in center of each cookie. Bake in a hot oven (400° F) about 14 minutes. Cool slightly before removing from baking sheets. Makes about 3 dozen crisps.

# Lace Cookies

3 tablespoons sugar
2 tablespoons light molasses
3 tablespoons butter or margarine
4 teaspoons water
⅓ cup sifted flour
½ teaspoon baking powder
Dash of salt
½ teaspoon cinnamon
¼ cup finely-chopped pecans

Combine sugar, molasses, butter and water in a saucepan. Heat to boiling. Remove from heat and stir until butter is melted. Sift together flour, baking powder, salt and cinnamon. Add to molasses mixture and stir until well blended. Stir in pecans. Bake cookies one at a time. Put 1 tablespoon of the batter on a well-greased baking sheet and spread as thin as possible. Bake in a moderately-slow oven (325° F) 9 to 10 minutes. Remove from oven and allow to cool ½ minute. Remove cookie from sheet and curve over a greased glass. Makes about 1 dozen cookies.

# Applesauce Cookies

¾ cup shortening
1 cup sugar
1 egg
1¾ cups sifted flour
½ teaspoon baking powder
1 teaspoon soda
¼ teaspoon salt
1 teaspoon cinnamon
½ teaspoon cloves
½ teaspoon nutmeg
1 cup thick sweetened applesauce
½ cup seedless raisins
1 cup corn flakes, crushed

Cream together shortening and sugar until light and fluffy. Add egg and beat well. Sift together flour, baking powder, soda, salt and spices. Add to creamed mixture alternately with applesauce, mixing thoroughly. Add raisins and cereal and mix thoroughly. Drop from teaspoon onto greased baking sheet, about 2 inches apart. Bake in a moderately-hot oven (375° F) 10 minutes. Makes about 5½ dozen cookies.

Processed Apple Institute

# Corn Flake Meringoons

2 egg whites
1 cup sifted confectioners' sugar
¼ teaspoon salt
1 cup shredded coconut
2 cups corn flakes
1 package (1 cup) semi-sweet chocolate morsels
½ teaspoon vanilla

Beat egg whites until stiff but not dry. Gradually add sugar and salt and continue beating until stiff and satiny. Fold in coconut, corn flakes, chocolate morsels and vanilla. Drop from a teaspoon onto well-greased baking sheet. Bake in a moderate oven (350° F) 25 minutes. Makes 3 dozen cookies.

# Cinnamon Hermits

3½ cups all-purpose flour
4½ teaspoons double-acting baking powder
1½ teaspoons salt
2 cups light brown sugar
½ cup shortening
1½ teaspoons ground cinnamon
½ teaspoon ground cloves
3 large eggs
2 tablespoons milk
2 cups raisins

Sift the first three ingredients together and set aside to use later. Gradually add sugar to shortening and spices. Beat in eggs. Blend in milk and raisins. Gradually stir in sifted flour mixture. Drop from a teaspoon onto lightly greased cooky sheet. Bake in a preheated moderate oven (375° F.) 15 to 18 minutes. Makes 6 dozen cookies.

American Spice Trade Assn.

# Chocolate Oatmeal Chews

1 12-ounce jumbo package *or* 2 6-ounce packages (2 cups) semi-sweet chocolate morsels
½ cup shortening
½ teaspoon salt
3 eggs
¾ cup sugar
1 cup rolled oats
1 teaspoon vanilla

Melt semi-sweet chocolate morsels over hot (not boiling) water. Remove from water; stir in shortening and salt. Beat eggs until thick and lemon-colored. Gradually add sugar, beating until very thick. Stir in chocolate mixture, oats and vanilla. Drop by rounded teaspoonsful on greased cookie sheet. Bake in a moderate oven (375° F.) 6 to 8 minutes. Remove from sheet while warm. Makes 6 dozen.

# Quick and Easy

½ cup bacon drippings
¾ cup molasses
2 tablespoons sugar
2 cups sifted flour
¾ teaspoon salt
1 teaspoon soda
1 teaspoon cinnamon
¾ teaspoon ginger
¼ teaspoon cloves
1 egg

Blend together bacon drippings, molasses and sugar. Sift together flour, salt, soda and spices. Stir a small amount of flour mixture into molasses mixture. Beat in egg. Add remaining flour, blending until smooth. Drop from teaspoon onto greased baking sheet, about 2½ inches apart. Bake in a moderate oven (350° F) 15 minutes. Makes 3½ dozen cookies.

The Nestle Co.

## Brownie Candy Cookies

*½ cup (approximately) sweetened condensed milk
¼ cup sugar
¼ teaspoon salt
1 egg
1 6-ounce package (1 cup) semi-sweet chocolate morsels
2 tablespoons butter or margarine
¼ cup water
1 teaspoon vanilla
¼ cup sifted all-purpose flour
1 cup coarsely chopped nuts

Combine condensed milk, sugar and salt in saucepan; bring to a boil, stirring constantly. Beat egg slightly. Add a little of condensed milk mixture, stirring rapidly. Add egg mixture to remaining condensed milk mixture and cook, stirring over moderate heat, 1 minute. Remove from heat. Add semi-sweet chocolate morsels, butter, water and vanilla, stirring until smooth. Stir in flour and nuts. Drop by teaspoonful on an ungreased foil-lined cookie sheet. Bake in a moderate oven (350° F.) 12 to 15 minutes. Cool thoroughly and peel off foil. Makes 7 dozen.
*Remainder of 14 ounce can, after making Short Cut Fudge.

## Festive Butter Wafers

1 cup butter or margarine
1 cup sugar
2 eggs
2 cups sifted flour
½ teaspoon salt
1 teaspoon vanilla
⅔ cup chopped walnuts
⅔ cup seedless raisins
⅔ cup shredded coconut

Cream together butter and sugar until light and fluffy. Blend in eggs and beat well. Sift together flour and salt and stir into creamed mixture. Blend in vanilla, walnuts, raisins and coconut. Drop from teaspoon onto greased baking sheet. Bake in a moderate oven (350° F) 10 to 12 minutes. Makes 5 to 6 dozen cookies.

The Nestle Co.

## Chocolate Oatmeal Cartwheels

1 cup butter or margarine
2 cups firmly packed brown sugar
2 eggs
1 tablespoon water
1½ teaspoon grated orange rind
2 cups sifted all-purpose flour
2 teaspoons baking powder
¾ teaspoon baking soda
1 teaspoon salt
1½ cups rolled oats
1 6-ounce package (1 cup) semi-sweet chocolate morsels
½ cup chopped walnuts

Cream together butter and sugar. Beat in eggs, one at a time, with water and orange rind. Sift in flour, baking powder, soda and salt; mix until blended. Stir in oats, semi-sweet chocolate morsels and walnuts. Drop by rounded tablespoonsful on lightly greased cookie sheet. Bake in a moderate oven (375° F.) 10 to 12 minutes. Makes 4 dozen.

Baker's German's Sweet Chocolate

## Tandies

½ cup dark corn syrup
⅓ cup butter
1 package (4 ounces) sweet cooking chocolate
½ cup firmly packed light brown sugar
1 cup sifted flour
⅔ cup flaked coconut

Heat corn syrup to a boil. Blend in butter. Add chocolate and melt in the syrup over low heat stirring constantly until smooth. Remove from heat. Stir in sugar, flour, and coconut. Drop by teaspoonfuls onto a lightly greased baking sheet. Bake in a slow oven (300° F.) for 15 minutes. Cool 1 to 2 minutes, then remove carefully from baking sheet, using a thin knife or spatula. If wafers harden on pan, return to oven for a few minutes. Makes about 5 dozen wafers.

*Note:* If desired roll cookies over the handle of a wooden spoon, or form into cornucopias by shaping over a cornucopia made of aluminum foil. Cool on rack. Fill with sweetened whipped cream.

# Crunch Drops

1 cup shortening
1 cup brown sugar, firmly packed
1 cup sugar
2 eggs
1 teaspoon vanilla
2 cups sifted flour
1 teaspoon soda
½ teaspoon salt
2 cups quick-cooking oats
2 cups crisp rice cereal
1 cup shredded coconut

Cream together shortening and sugars until light and fluffy. Add eggs, one at a time, and beat well after each addition. Stir in vanilla. Sift together flour, soda and salt. Add to creamed mixture and mix well. Add oats, rice cereal and coconut and blend well. Drop from a teaspoon onto a greased baking sheet, about 2 inches apart. Bake in a moderate oven (350° F) 12 to 15 minutes. Makes 5 dozen drops.

# German's Chocolate Drop Cookies

1 package (4 ounces) sweet cooking chocolate
2 cups sifted flour
½ teaspoon baking soda
½ teaspoon salt
¾ cup butter or other shortening
¾ cup sugar
2 eggs, unbeaten
½ teaspoon vanilla
½ cup chopped black walnuts
Chocolate Glaze

Place chocolate in small bowl and set over hot water until melted; cool. Sift flour once, measure, add soda and salt, and sift again. Cream shortening, add sugar gradually, and cream together until light and fluffy. Add eggs and beat well. Add melted chocolate; blend. Then add flour and mix well. Add vanilla and nuts. Drop from teaspoon on greased baking sheet. Bake in a moderate oven (350° F.) for 10 to 12 minutes. Spread warm cookies with Chocolate Glaze. Makes about 4 dozen cookies.

### Chocolate Glaze

Melt 1 package (4 ounces) sweet cooking chocolate. Spread thinly over cookies.

Baker's German's Sweet Chocolate

# Almond Crispies

½ cup shortening
1 cup brown sugar, firmly packed
2 eggs, well beaten
½ cup sifted flour
1 teaspoon baking powder
¼ teaspoon salt
1 teaspoon cinnamon
¾ cup fine dry bread crumbs
⅔ cup ground, unblanched almonds
¼ cup chopped seedless raisins

Cream together shortening and sugar until light and fluffy. Blend in eggs. Sift together flour, baking powder, salt and cinnamon. Add to creamed mixture and blend well. Stir in crumbs, almonds and raisins. Drop from a teaspoon onto ungreased baking sheets, about 3 inches apart. Bake in a moderate oven (350° F) 12 to 15 minutes. Makes 4 dozen Almond Crispies.

# Almond Drops

1 egg
¼ teaspoon salt
⅛ teaspoon cream of tartar
⅔ cup sugar
2 tablespoons flour
2 teaspoons cold water
1 cup ground, unblanched almonds
1 teaspoon lemon extract

Combine egg, salt and cream of tartar and beat until thick and lemon-colored. Beat in sugar, a small amount at a time, and continue beating until sugar is dissolved. Blend in flour. Stir in water, almonds and flavoring. Drop in small mounds on greased and floured baking sheet. Bake in a moderately-hot oven (375° F) 12 to 13 minutes. Remove from baking sheet immediately. Makes 2½ dozen drops.

# Prune Drops

½ cup shortening
1 cup brown sugar, firmly packed
1 teaspoon vanilla
1 egg
1¼ cups sifted flour
1 teaspoon baking powder
½ teaspoon salt
½ teaspoon cinnamon
¼ cup liquid from prunes
1 cup cooked, chopped prunes

Cream together shortening and sugar until light and fluffy. Add vanilla and egg and beat well. Sift together flour, baking powder, salt and cinnamon. Add to creamed mixture alternately with prune liquid. Add prunes and blend well. Drop from a teaspoon onto greased baking sheet. Bake in a moderate oven (350° F) 12 to 15 minutes. Makes about 3½ dozen cookies.

# Holiday Fruit Cookies

1 cup shortening
2 cups brown sugar, firmly packed
2 eggs
½ cup sour milk
3½ cups sifted flour
1 teaspoon soda
1 teaspoon salt
1½ cups broken pecans
2 cups candied cherry halves
2 cups chopped dates

Cream together shortening and sugar until light and fluffy. Add eggs and milk and beat well. Sift together flour, soda and salt. Add to creamed mixture and blend well. Add remaining ingredients. Drop from a teaspoon onto lightly-greased baking sheets. Bake in a hot oven (400°F) 8 to 10 minutes. Makes about 7 dozen cookies.

# Coconut Flake Cookies

1⅓ cups sifted flour
2 teaspoons double-acting baking powder
½ teaspoon salt
¾ cup butter or other shortening
1¼ cups firmly packed brown sugar
2 eggs
2 teaspoons vanilla
2½ cups corn flakes
¾ cup flaked coconut

Measure sifted flour, add baking powder and salt, and sift together. Cream shortening, gradually add sugar and cream thoroughly. Add eggs, one at a time, beating well after each. Add vanilla. Then add flour, a small amount at a time, mixing well after each addition. Stir in cereal and coconut.

Drop from teaspoon onto ungreased baking sheet. Bake in a moderate oven (375°F) for 10 to 12 minutes, or until cookies are golden brown. Makes about 4½ dozen cookies.

Baker's Angel Flake Coconut

# Holland Snaps

1 package (1 cup) semi-sweet chocolate morsels
½ cup butter
¼ cup light corn syrup
⅓ cup sugar
1 cup sifted flour
⅛ teaspoon salt
½ teaspoon soda
1 teaspoon vanilla
1 egg, beaten

Combine chocolate morsels, butter, corn syrup and sugar and melt over hot (not boiling) water. Remove from heat and let stand 5 minutes. Sift together flour, salt and soda. Add to chocolate mixture and blend well. Add remaining ingredients and mix thoroughly. Drop by half teaspoons onto a greased baking sheet. Bake in a moderate oven (350° F) 10 minutes. Makes 6 dozen snaps.

# Strawberry Jam Cookies

⅔ cup butter or margarine
1 cup brown sugar, firmly packed
2 eggs
½ cup crushed pineapple, well drained
1 teaspoon vanilla
3 cups sifted flour
1 teaspoon soda
1 teaspoon baking powder
½ teaspoon salt
Strawberry jam

Cream together butter and sugar until light and fluffy. Add eggs, one at a time, and beat well. Stir in pineapple and vanilla. Sift together flour, soda, baking powder and salt. Drop from a teaspoon onto a well-greased baking sheet. Top each cookie with a bit of strawberry jam. Bake in a moderately-hot oven (375° F) 10 to 12 minutes, or until slightly browned. Makes 4 dozen cookies.

# Peanut Butter Drops

¾ cup shortening
1 cup brown sugar, firmly packed
½ cup peanut butter
2 eggs, beaten
¼ cup milk
2 cups sifted flour
¾ teaspoon salt
2 teaspoons baking powder
½ teaspoon cloves
¼ teaspoon mace
1 teaspoon cinnamon
¾ cup seedless raisins

Cream together shortening and sugar until light and fluffy. Stir in peanut butter and beat well. Add eggs and milk. Sift together flour, salt, baking powder, cloves, mace and cinnamon. Blend into creamed mixture. Stir in raisins. Drop from teaspoon onto greased baking sheet. Flatten each cookie with a fork. Bake in a moderately-hot oven (375° F) 10 to 12 minutes, or until golden brown. Makes 3½ dozen cookies.

National Dairy Council

# Butter Cookie Cones

3 eggs, beaten
1 cup sugar
½ teaspoon nutmeg
1 teaspoon lemon extract
¼ cup butter, melted
1 cup sifted all-purpose flour

Add sugar to eggs gradually; beat mixture until fluffy and a light yellow color. Add nutmeg and lemon extract; blend. Add melted butter and flour and mix well. Pour 1 teaspoonful of batter onto very well buttered 5-inch circle on cookie sheet. Bake in a moderate oven, (350° F.), until a light brown (12 to 15 minutes). Remove from oven. Loosen cookie from sheet with spatula or pancake turner and roll immediately onto the handle of a large wooden spoon. Remove cookie from spoon handle and place on wire rack to cool. For best results when rolling cookies bake no more than 2 at a time. If cookies harden before rolled return pan to oven to warm cookies. Makes about 36 cones.

## Sesame Seed Cookies

**¾ cup butter or margarine**
**2 cups sifted brown sugar (do not pack)**
**1 egg, beaten**
**1 teaspoon vanilla**
**½ cup sesame seed**
**1 cup sifted flour**
**¼ teaspoon salt**

Cream together butter and brown sugar until light and fluffy. Add egg, vanilla and sesame seed and beat well. Add flour and salt and blend well. Drop by half teaspoons onto greased baking sheet, about 3 inches apart. Bake in a moderate oven (350° F) 4 to 5 minutes. Cool cookies about 2 minutes before removing from baking sheet. If difficult to remove, reheat slightly. Makes about 100 cookies.

# Refrigerator Cookies

**One refrigerator makes possible 20 kinds of cookies, including Petticoat Tails, Orange Brans, Circle-Circles!**

## Basic Refrigerator Cookies

**1 cup shortening**
**1 cup sugar**
**2 eggs**
**1 teaspoon vanilla**
**3 cups sifted flour**
**3 teaspoons baking powder**
**1 teaspoon salt**

Cream shortening until soft. Add sugar slowly and cream together until light and fluffy. Add eggs and vanilla and beat until well blended. Sift together flour, baking powder and salt. Stir into creamed mixture; mix until well blended. Divide dough in half. Shape each half into a roll about 3 inches in diameter. Wrap in waxed paper. Chill several hours or overnight. Slice rolls into ⅛-inch slices. Place slices on a greased baking sheet. Bake in a moderately-hot oven (375° F) about 8 minutes. Remove from sheet immediately. Makes about 5 dozen cookies.

## Circle-Circle Cookies

**¾ cup butter or margarine**
**1 cup sugar**
**2 eggs**
**1 teaspoon vanilla**
**1 cup finely-crushed corn flakes**
**3 cups sifted flour**
**1½ teaspoons baking powder**
**¼ teaspoon salt**
**2 squares unsweetened chocolate, melted**
**2 tablespoons sugar**
**1 tablespoon milk**

Cream together butter and sugar until light and fluffy. Add eggs and vanilla and beat well. Add crushed corn flakes and blend. Sift together flour, baking powder and salt. Add to creamed mixture and blend thoroughly. Divide dough into two parts, making one part slightly larger. To the smaller part, add the melted chocolate, 2 tablespoons sugar and milk. Blend well. Divide the vanilla and chocolate dough into 4 parts each and shape into eight rolls, ¾ inch thick and about 13 inches long. Wrap each roll tightly in waxed paper and chill until firm enough to slice. Cut rolls in ⅛-inch slices. Use 2 vanilla and 2 chocolate circles for each cookie, placing them on an ungreased baking sheet so that edges of the 4 circles just touch. Bake in a hot oven (425° F) 7 to 8 minutes, or until done. Makes 12 dozen cookies.

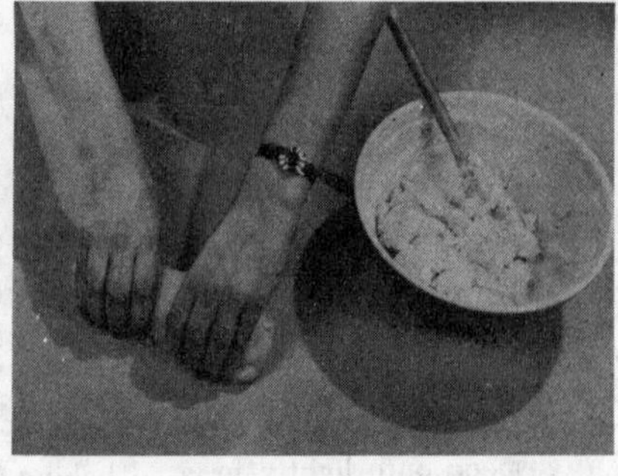

When dough for refrigerator cookies is well blended, halve into rolls 3 inches in diameter.

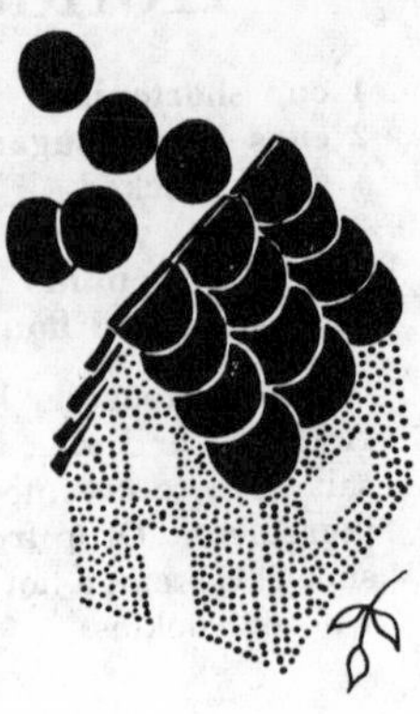

Wrap each 3-in. roll tightly in waxed paper. Place in refrigerator to chill several hours or overnight.

Remove rolls from refrigerator and cut in slices about ⅛ in. thick. Place on greased baking sheet.

Bake in moderately-hot oven (375° F) 8 minutes or until lightly browned around edges. Cool on racks.

## Prune Pinwheel Cookies

**¾ cup chopped, pitted, unsweetened, cooked prunes**
**¼ cup cooking liquid from prunes**
**¼ cup sugar**
**¼ teaspoon grated lemon rind**
**½ cup shortening**
**1 cup brown sugar, firmly packed**
**1 egg**
**1 teaspoon vanilla**
**1¾ cups sifted flour**
**1 teaspoon salt**
**½ teaspoon baking powder**

Combine prunes, cooking liquid and sugar. Cook over low heat, stirring frequently until thick. Remove from heat and add lemon rind. Cool thoroughly. Cream together shortening and sugar until light and fluffy. Blend in egg and vanilla. Sift together flour, salt and baking powder and blend into creamed mixture. Chill dough for a while. Turn out onto a sheet of waxed paper and pat into rectangular shape. Roll to a rectangle about 9 by 12 inches. Spread cooled prune filling over dough and roll as for a jelly roll. Pinch edge to seal. Roll in waxed paper and chill for several hours. Cut into ¼-inch slices with sharp knife. Place on greased baking sheet. Bake in a moderately-hot oven (375° F) 12 to 15 minutes. Makes about 3 dozen cookies.

Lever Bros. Co.

## Orange-Pecan Refrigerator Cookies

**1 cup shortening**
**½ cup brown sugar, firmly packed**
**½ cup sugar**
**1 egg, unbeaten**
**1 tablespoon grated orange rind**
**2 tablespoons orange juice**
**2¾ cups sifted flour**
**¼ teaspoon soda**
**1 teaspoon salt**
**½ cup finely-chopped pecans**

Cream together shortening and sugars until light and fluffy. Add egg, orange rind and orange juice and beat thoroughly. Sift together flour, soda and salt. Add to creamed mixture and blend. Add pecans and mix well. Shape into rolls, 2 inches in diameter. Wrap in waxed paper and chill in refrigerator several hours or overnight. Cut in ¼-inch slices. Place on greased baking sheet. Bake in a hot oven (400° F) 8 to 10 minutes. Makes 5 dozen cookies.

## Petticoat Tails

**1 cup soft butter**
**1 cup sifted confectioners' sugar**
**1 teaspoon vanilla**
**2½ cups sifted flour**
**¼ teaspoon salt**

Cream together butter and sugar until light and fluffy. Beat in vanilla. Stir in flour and salt and mix well. Mix thoroughly with the hands. Shape into a long, smooth roll about 2 inches in diameter. Wrap in waxed paper and chill several hours or overnight. With a sharp knife cut in thin, ⅛-inch slices. Place on ungreased baking sheet. Bake in a hot oven (400° F) 8 to 10 minutes or until lightly browned. Makes about 6 dozen 2-inch cookies.

## Nut Slices

**1 cup soft shortening (part butter)**
**½ cup sugar**
**½ cup firmly packed brown sugar**
**2 eggs**
**2¾ cups flour, sifted before measuring**
**½ teaspoon baking soda**
**1 teaspoon salt**
**2 to 3 teaspoons cinnamon**

Heat oven to hot (400° F.). Combine shortening, sugars and eggs. Mix thoroughly. Combine and sift together, flour, baking soda, salt and cinnamon. Stir into creamed mixture and mix thoroughly with the hands. Press and mold into a long, smooth roll as big around as you want the cookies to be. Wrap in waxed paper, twisting the ends. Place in the freezing compartment to chill quickly or in the refrigerator if you have time. Slice thinly with a thin, very sharp knife. Return any unused dough to the refrigerator. Place slices on an ungreased baking sheet a little apart and bake 6 to 8 minutes or until lightly browned. Makes about 6 dozen.

## Date Pinwheel Cookies

**¾ cup pitted, diced dates**
**6 tablespoons sugar**
**6 tablespoons water**
**2 teaspoons lemon juice**
**½ teaspoon grated lemon rind**
**¼ cup finely-chopped nuts**
**⅔ cup butter or margarine**
**1¼ cups brown sugar, firmly packed**
**1½ teaspoons grated orange rind**
**1 egg**
**1 tablespoon vinegar**
**2 cups sifted flour**
**¼ teaspoon baking soda**
**¼ teaspoon salt**

Combine dates, sugar and water in a heavy saucepan. Cook until thickened, about 5 minutes, stirring constantly. Remove from heat. Blend in lemon juice, lemon rind and nuts. Cool. Cream together butter and brown sugar until light and fluffy. Beat in orange rind, egg and vinegar. Sift together flour, soda and salt. Add to creamed mixture and blend well. Chill dough thoroughly. Roll dough into a 15 by 10-inch rectangle. Spread with date mixture. Starting from long side, roll as for a jelly roll. Chill about 1 hour. Slice into ¼-inch slices. Place on greased baking sheet. Bake in a moderately-hot oven (375° F) 12 to 15 minutes, or until lightly browned. Makes about 5 dozen cookies.

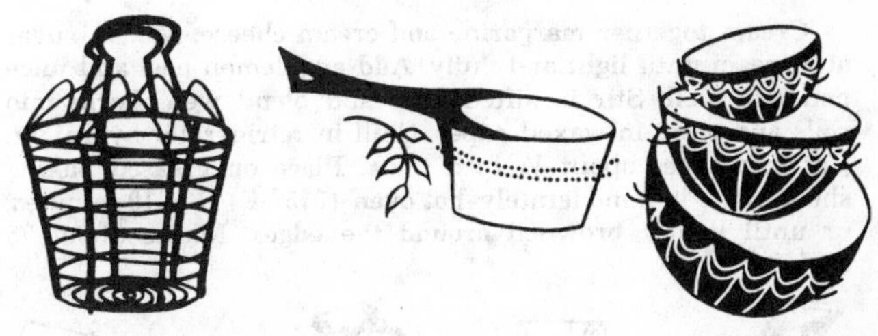

## Chocolate Nut Slices

¾ cup shortening
1¾ cups sugar
2 teaspoons vanilla
1 egg
squares unsweetened chocolate, melted
1 tablespoon vinegar
2 cups sifted flour
¼ teaspoon soda
½ teaspoon salt
¾ cup chopped pecans

Cream together shortening and sugar until light and fluffy. Beat in vanilla, egg and chocolate. Stir in vinegar. Sift together flour, soda and salt. Stir into creamed mixture. Add nuts and blend well. Shape into 2 rolls about 2 inches in diameter. Wrap in waxed paper. Chill several hours or overnight. Slice dough into ¼-inch slices. Place on greased baking sheet. Bake in a moderately-hot oven (375° F) about 10 minutes. Makes 7 dozen cookies.

## Honey Cookies

½ cup shortening
½ cup sugar
½ cup honey
1 egg
½ cup chopped nuts
2½ cups sifted flour
1 teaspoon baking powder
¼ teaspoon soda
¼ teaspoon salt

Cream together shortening, sugar and honey until light and fluffy. Stir in egg. Add nuts and mix well. Sift together flour, baking powder, soda and salt. Add to honey mixture and blend well. Divide dough in half. Shape each half into a long roll. Wrap in waxed paper and chill in refrigerator about 2 hours. Cut into slices about ⅛ inch thick. Place slices on ungreased baking sheet. Bake in a hot oven (400° F) 8 to 10 minutes. Makes about 4 dozen cookies.

## Spice Cookies

1 cup butter or margarine
¾ cup sugar
½ cup dark corn syrup
4 cups sifted flour
1 teaspoon cinnamon
¼ teaspoon mace
½ teaspoon cloves
½ teaspoon ginger
½ teaspoon cardamom
½ teaspoon salt
¼ teaspoon pepper
1 teaspoon soda
½ cup sour cream

Cream together butter and sugar until light and fluffy. Add syrup and beat well. Sift together flour, spices, salt, pepper and soda. Add to creamed mixture alternately with sour cream, mixing well after each addition. Divide dough in half. Shape into diamond-shaped strips. Wrap in waxed paper and chill in refrigerator several hours or overnight. Cut in thin slices about 1/16 inch, with a sharp knife. Place on greased baking sheet. Bake in a moderately-hot oven (375° F) 8 to 10 minutes. Makes 10 dozen cookies.

## Tender Tea Wafers

1 cup margarine
1 3-ounce package cream cheese
1 cup sugar
1 egg
Grated peel of 1 lemon
1 tablespoon lemon juice
3 cups sifted flour

Cream together margarine and cream cheese. Mix in sugar and cream until light and fluffy. Add egg, lemon peel and juice and mix well. Stir in sifted flour and blend well. Form into rolls and wrap in waxed paper. Chill in refrigerator overnight. Cut into slices about ¼ inch thick. Place on greased baking sheet. Bake in a moderately-hot oven (375° F) 8 to 10 minutes, or until lightly browned around the edges. Makes about 75 cookies.

## Pinwheels

½ package (½ cup) semi-sweet chocolate morsels
¼ cup butter
½ cup sugar
1 egg
3 tablespoons milk
1 teaspoon vanilla
2½ cups sifted cake flour
1 teaspoon salt
1 teaspoon baking powder
1 cup finely-ground nuts

Melt chocolate morsels over hot water. Cream together butter and sugar until light and fluffy. Add egg, milk and vanilla and beat well. Sift together flour, salt and baking powder. Add to creamed mixture with nuts and knead well. Divide dough in half. Roll out one half on a lightly-floured board to ⅛-inch thickness. Add melted chocolate to other half. Roll chocolate half out to ⅛-inch thickness. Place chocolate dough over white dough and press with a rolling pin. Roll up into rolls, 1 inch in diameter. Wrap in waxed paper. Chill until firm. Cut in slices, ⅛ inch thick. Place on ungreased baking sheet. Bake in a moderately-hot oven (375° F) 12 minutes. Makes 9 dozen cookies.

## Coconut Crisps

¾ cup butter or margarine
1 cup brown sugar, firmly packed
1 egg
2 tablespoons honey
½ teaspoon vanilla
2 cups sifted flour
1½ teaspoons baking powder
¼ teaspoon salt
1 cup coconut

Cream together butter and sugar until light and fluffy. Add egg, honey and vanilla and mix well. Sift together flour, baking powder and salt. Add to butter mixture and blend well. Add coconut and mix thoroughly. Shape into a roll about 2 inches in diameter and wrap in waxed paper. Chill in refrigerator overnight. Cut dough with a sharp knife into slices about ¼ inch thick. Place on ungreased baking sheet. Bake in a moderately-hot oven (375° F) 12 to 15 minutes. Makes 6 dozen cookies.

## Semi-Sweet Sour Cream Wafers

⅓ cup butter
⅓ cup shortening
2 cups brown sugar, firmly packed
1 tablespoon vanilla
1 egg
½ cup sour cream
3½ cups sifted flour
1 teaspoon baking soda
½ teaspoon salt
½ teaspoon nutmeg
1 package (1 cup) semi-sweet chocolate morsels, finely chopped

Cream together butter, shortening and sugar until light and fluffy. Add vanilla and egg and beat well. Stir in sour cream. Sift together flour, soda, salt and nutmeg. Add to creamed mixture and blend well. Stir in chocolate. Line a 10 by 5 by 3-inch loaf pan with waxed paper. Pack dough firmly into pan. Chill overnight. Slice loaf lengthwise into thirds; then cut each third into slices ⅛ inch thick. Place on ungreased baking sheet. Bake in a hot oven (400° F) 8 minutes. Makes 4 dozen cookies.

## Coconut Slices

2 cups sifted flour
¼ teaspoon salt
1 cup butter or margarine
1 cup sugar
2 cups shredded coconut
1 egg

Sift flour and salt into a mixing bowl. Cut in butter with a pastry blender or 2 knives until mixture has consistency of corn meal. Add sugar, coconut and egg. Mix well with hands until dough holds together. Shape dough into a roll, wrap in waxed paper and chill in refrigerator about 2 hours. Cut off slices with a sharp knife, about ⅛ inch thick. Place on ungreased baking sheet. Bake in a moderately-hot oven (375° F) 10 to 12 minutes. Makes about 7 dozen cookies.

# Oatmeal Crispies

½ cup margarine
½ cup white sugar
½ cup brown sugar, firmly packed
2 eggs
1 teaspoon vanilla
¾ cup sifted flour
½ teaspoon salt
½ teaspoon soda
1½ cups quick-cooking oats
¼ cup chopped walnuts

Cream together margarine and sugars until light and fluffy. Add eggs, one at a time, beating well after each addition. Add vanilla. Sift together flour, salt and soda. Stir in oats and walnuts. Add to creamed mixture and blend thoroughly. Form into 2 rolls. Wrap in waxed paper and chill in refrigerator several hours, or overnight. Slice in ⅛-inch-thick slices. Place on ungreased baking sheet. Bake in a moderate oven (350° F) 10 to 12 minutes. Makes 3 dozen cookies.

Lever Bros. Co.

# Good Luck Cookies

1 cup margarine
½ cup sugar
1 egg yolk
1 teaspoon grated lemon rind
2½ cups sifted flour

Cream together margarine and sugar until light and fluffy. Add egg yolk and lemon rind and mix well. Add flour and mix until well blended. Shape dough into long rolls about ½ inch thick. Wrap in waxed paper and chill about 30 minutes. Cut off thin slices of dough and place 4 slices together on a baking sheet to resemble a 4-leaf clover. Insert an additional small piece of dough to resemble a stem. Bake in a moderately-hot oven (375° F) about 8 minutes, or until lightly browned around the edges. Makes about 6 dozen cookies.

# Refrigerator Thins

½ cup butter or margarine
1 cup sugar
½ cup brown sugar, firmly packed
1 tablespoon lemon juice
3 cups sifted flour
½ teaspoon baking powder
½ teaspoon soda
1 tablespoon cinnamon
⅓ cup milk
1 cup ground pecans

Cream together butter and sugars until light and fluffy. Stir in lemon juice. Sift together flour, baking powder, soda and cinnamon. Add to creamed mixture alternately with the milk, stirring well after each addition. Stir in pecans. Divide dough in half. Pat into triangular strips. Wrap in waxed paper. Chill in refrigerator several hours or overnight. With a very sharp knife, cut into slices about $\frac{1}{16}$ inch thick. Place on greased baking sheet. Bake in a hot oven (400° F) 10 minutes. Makes 8 dozen cookies.

# Almond Refrigerator Cookies

½ cup shortening
½ cup sugar
½ cup brown sugar, firmly packed
1 egg
½ teaspoon vanilla
1¾ cups sifted flour
½ teaspoon salt
½ teaspoon soda
1 teaspoon cinnamon
¾ cup finely-chopped, toasted almonds

Cream together shortening and sugars until light and fluffy. Add egg and vanilla and beat well. Sift together flour, salt, soda and cinnamon. Blend into creamed mixture. Add almonds and mix thoroughly. Shape into two long rolls about 1½ inches in diameter. Wrap in waxed paper and chill overnight or for several hours. Cut into slices ⅛ inch thick. Place on an ungreased baking sheet. Bake in a moderate oven (350° F) 10 to 12 minutes. Makes about 6 dozen cookies.

# Chocolate Pinwheels

½ cup butter or margarine
⅔ cup sugar
1 egg
1 tablespoon milk
2 cups sifted flour
1 teaspoon double-acting baking powder
½ teaspoon salt
1 square unsweetened chocolate, melted

Cream together butter and sugar until light and fluffy. Add egg and milk and beat well. Sift together flour, baking powder and salt. Gradually add to creamed mixture and mix well. Divide dough into two parts. To one part, add the melted chocolate and blend well. Chill dough until firm enough to roll. Roll each half of dough on floured waxed paper into a rectangular sheet about ⅛ inch thick. Turn sheet of plain dough over chocolate sheet. Remove waxed paper. Roll as for a jelly roll. Chill until firm enough to slice. Cut in ⅛-inch-thick slices. Bake on ungreased baking sheet in moderately-hot oven (375° F) 10 minutes. Makes about 5 dozen pinwheels.

# Prune Icebox Cookies

1 cup shortening
1 cup brown sugar, firmly packed
½ cup sugar
2 eggs
1 tablespoon vinegar
1 teaspoon vanilla
1 cup chopped, cooked prunes
4 cups sifted flour
1 teaspoon soda
1½ teaspoons salt

Cream together shortening and sugars until light and fluffy. Add eggs, vinegar and vanilla and beat well. Add prunes. Sift together flour, soda and salt. Add to creamed mixture and blend thoroughly. (This is a stiff dough and it may be necessary to use the hands for a well-blended mixture.) Shape in 2 rolls about 2 inches in diameter. Wrap in waxed paper. Chill a few hours or overnight. Slice ⅛ inch thick. Place on greased baking sheet. Bake in a hot oven (400° F) about 10 minutes. Makes about 6 dozen cookies.

# Orange Bran Cookies

1¼ cups butter or margarine
2 cups brown sugar, firmly packed
2 eggs, well beaten
1 cup bran
Grated rind of 1 orange
3 cups sifted flour
2 teaspoons baking powder

Cream together butter and sugar until light and fluffy. Add eggs and beat. Add bran and grated orange rind. Sift together flour and baking powder. Add to orange mixture and blend thoroughly. Divide dough in half and shape into two rolls. Wrap in waxed paper and chill in refrigerator several hours or overnight. With a very sharp knife, cut into slices about $\frac{1}{16}$ inch thick. Place on greased baking sheet. Bake in a hot oven (400° F) 8 to 10 minutes. Makes 6 dozen cookies.

# Christmas Bells

½ cup shortening (part butter)
½ cup sugar
1 egg
1 teaspoon vanilla
1½ cups sifted flour
¼ teaspoon soda
½ teaspoon salt

Cream together shortening and sugar until light and fluffy. Add egg and vanilla and blend well. Sift together flour, soda and salt. Stir into creamed mixture. Take out two-thirds of the dough and color red or green with food coloring. Mold this dough into a 1½ by 10-inch roll; then squeeze top half together, leaving lower half flared and curving like a bell. Chill. Save ¼ cup of remaining dough for clappers. On waxed paper, roll out remaining dough into a 10 by 14-inch rectangle large enough to cover colored dough. Trim edges. Wrap around colored dough. Chill thoroughly. Slice dough in ⅛-inch slices. Place on ungreased baking sheet. Press tiny ball of dough at bottom of each bell for the clapper. Bake 8 to 10 minutes. Makes about 5 dozen bells.

# Molded Cookies

## Here are varied taste-treats that can be shaped attractively without bother of rolling the dough.

IN THESE COOKIES the dough as a rule is quite stiff. It is similar to the type used for rolled cookies, but using the methods shown in the following pictures, you can obtain almost the same shapes without the bother of rolling the dough on a floured board.

For perfect molded cookies, roll bits of dough, roughly walnut-sized, in the palm of your hand.

Flatten each bit of dough by pressing with the bottom of a glass that has been dipped in sugar.

Place on a baking sheet and press in criss-cross pattern with flour- or sugar-dipped fork tines.

Dip them in sugar and cinnamon, chopped nuts or almost any cookie decoration that appeals to you.

# Almond Patties

½ cup butter
¼ cup sugar
1 teaspoon vanilla
½ cup sifted flour
¼ teaspoon salt
1 cup finely-ground, blanched almonds
½ package (½ cup) semi-sweet chocolate morsels

Cream together butter, sugar and vanilla until light and fluffy. Sift together flour and salt and add to creamed mixture. Add almonds and chocolate and blend thoroughly. Shape into 1-inch balls. Place on ungreased baking sheet. Bake in a moderately-hot oven (375° F) 12 minutes. Makes 4 dozen patties.

# Gala Holiday Wreaths

½ cup margarine
¼ cup sifted brown sugar
1 egg, separated
1 cup sifted flour
1 cup finely-chopped nuts
Raspberry jam

Cream margarine and sugar together until light and fluffy. Add egg yolk and beat well. Add flour. Chill dough. Form into small balls. Dip in egg white and then roll in nuts. Place on a baking sheet. Press a hole in center of each cookie with the handle of a knife. Bake in a very slow oven (300° F). After 8 minutes of baking, press in center of cookies again and continue baking 10 minutes. Remove to rack and cool. Fill center with jam. Makes 2½ dozen cookies.

# Crisp Almond Cookies

1 cup butter or margarine
1 cup sugar
1 cup sour cream
⅛ teaspoon soda
2 egg yolks
1½ teaspoons grated lemon rind
1 teaspoon soda
½ teaspoon salt
3½ cups sifted flour
¾ cup finely-chopped, toasted almonds
2 tablespoons sugar

Combine butter, sugar, cream and ⅛ teaspoon soda in a heavy saucepan. Place over low heat. Stir until sugar is dissolved. Boil, stirring occasionally, until thickened, about 10 to 15 minutes. Cool. Beat in egg yolks, lemon rind, soda and salt. Add flour and blend well. Chill dough. Roll dough, about ½ teaspoonful at a time, in palms of hands to form small balls. Place 3 inches apart on an ungreased baking sheet. Press flat with bottom of a glass dipped in sugar. Combine almonds and sugar. Sprinkle on cookies. Bake in a moderately-slow oven (325° F) 10 to 12 minutes, or until edges are delicately browned. Makes 7 dozen cookies.

# Brazil Nut Swedish Cookies

½ cup butter or margarine
¼ cup sugar
½ teaspoon vanilla
1 egg yolk
1 cup sifted flour
¼ teaspoon salt
1 egg white, unbeaten
¾ cup finely-chopped Brazil nuts

Cream together butter and sugar until light and fluffy. Blend in vanilla and egg yolk and beat well. Sift together flour and salt. Add to creamed mixture and blend thoroughly. Shape into balls about ¾ inch in diameter. Dip into unbeaten egg white and roll lightly in Brazil nuts. Place on ungreased baking sheet. Bake in a moderately-hot oven (375° F) about 15 minutes, or until delicately browned. Remove from baking sheet immediately. Makes 3 dozen cookies.

# Swedish Oatmeal Cookies

⅔ cup butter or margarine
3 cups quick-cooking oats
½ cup sugar
1 egg, beaten
1 teaspoon almond extract

Place butter, oats and sugar in a bowl. Using hands, knead together into a solid mass. Add egg and almond extract and knead until a smooth dough is formed. Shape into balls the size of marbles. Place on greased baking sheet. Press tops of each ball down with tines of a fork. Bake in a slow oven (325° F) 10 to 15 minutes or until golden brown. Makes 2½ dozen cookies.

# Cherry-Oat Party Cookies

1 cup shortening
1 cup brown sugar, firmly packed
1 cup sugar
½ teaspoon salt
½ teaspoon vanilla
2 eggs
½ cup chopped walnuts
1¼ cups sifted flour
1 teaspoon soda
3 cups quick-cooking oats
18 candied cherries, quartered

Cream together shortening and sugars until light and fluffy. Add salt, vanilla and eggs and beat well. Stir in nuts. Sift together flour and soda, add to creamed mixture and blend well. Add oats and mix well. Shape into 1-inch balls with the hands. Roll in sugar and place on greased baking sheets, about 2 inches apart. Top each ball with a piece of candied cherry. Bake in a moderate oven (350° F) 12 to 15 minutes. Cool 2 minutes before removing from baking sheets. Makes 6 dozen cookies.

# French-Swiss Cookies

1 cup butter or margarine
1 cup sugar
1 egg yolk
2 cups sifted flour
2½ teaspoons cinnamon
1 egg white
Ground nuts

Cream together butter and sugar until light and fluffy. Beat in egg yolk. Add flour and cinnamon and blend thoroughly. Chill dough. Roll pieces of the dough into 1-inch balls. Place on ungreased baking sheet about 2 inches apart. Press out, paper-thin, with a floured spatula. Brush tops with egg white and sprinkle with nuts. Bake in a moderate oven (350° F) 10 to 12 minutes. Makes 6 dozen cookies.

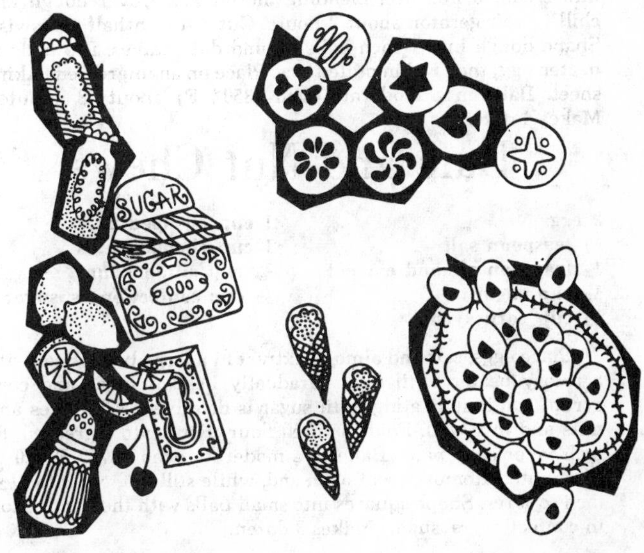

# Coconut Pompons

1 cup margarine
½ cup sugar
2 teaspoons vanilla
2 cups sifted flour
¼ teaspoon salt
½ pound pecan halves
Chopped, shredded coconut

Cream together margarine, sugar and vanilla until light and fluffy. Sift together flour and salt. Add to creamed mixture and blend thoroughly. Shape dough around pecan halves to form 1-inch balls. Roll in shredded coconut. Place on an ungreased baking sheet. Bake in a slow oven (325° F) about 20 minutes. Remove to wire rack and cool. Makes 6 dozen cookies.

Swift & Co.

# Porcupines

1 cup butter or margarine
½ cup sugar
1½ teaspoons vanilla
1 tablespoon vinegar
2½ cups sifted flour
½ teaspoon salt
¼ teaspoon baking soda
24 pitted dates
1 egg, slightly beaten
1½ cups puffed rice

Cream together butter and sugar until light and fluffy. Stir in vanilla and vinegar. Sift together flour, salt and soda. Stir into creamed mixture, blending thoroughly. Cover dough and chill in refrigerator about 2 hours. Cut dates in half crosswise. Shape dough into 1-inch balls around date halves. Dip balls in beaten egg; then roll in puffed rice. Place on an ungreased baking sheet. Bake in a moderate oven (350° F) about 18 minutes. Makes 4 dozen.

# Date and Nut Chews

2 eggs
¾ teaspoon salt
½ teaspoon almond extract
½ cup sugar
½ cup corn syrup
1 cup chopped dates
1 cup chopped nuts
¾ cup sifted flour
⅓ cup confectioners' sugar

Place eggs, salt and almond extract in a large bowl. Beat with a rotary beater until light. Gradually beat in sugar and corn syrup; continue beating until sugar is dissolved. Add dates and nuts and mix well. Fold in sifted flour. Pour into 2 greased, 8-inch layer cake pans. Bake in a moderate oven (375° F) 20 to 25 minutes. Remove from oven and, while still hot, cut into 1½-inch squares. Shape squares into small balls with the hands. Roll in confectioners' sugar. Makes 3 dozen.

# Pineapple Crunchies

1 No. 2 can crushed pineapple
¾ cup butter or margarine
1 cup brown sugar, firmly packed
1 teaspoon vanilla
1½ cups sifted flour
1 teaspoon soda
1¾ cups corn flakes
½ cup chopped walnuts

Drain pineapple, reserving syrup. Cream together butter and sugar until light and fluffy. Add vanilla and 1 tablespoon pineapple syrup. Sift together flour and soda. Stir into creamed mixture. Add corn flakes and blend well. With hands, press into balls about 1¼ inches in diameter. Place on a baking sheet and make an indentation in top of each with the thumb. Fill with crushed pineapple and sprinkle with chopped nuts. Bake in a moderate oven (350° F) 20 minutes. Makes about 2½ dozen cookies.

Lever Bros. Co.

# Cookie Delights

½ cup margarine
1 cup sugar
4 egg yolks
1 teaspoon vanilla
1½ cups sifted flour
1 teaspoon baking powder
¾ cup finely-chopped pecans
1½ teaspoons cinnamon

Cream together margarine and sugar until light and fluffy. Beat egg yolks until thick and lemon-colored. Add to first mixture with vanilla and mix thoroughly. Sift together flour and baking powder. Add to mixture and blend well. Chill dough. Shape into ¾-inch balls. Roll each ball in a mixture of pecans and cinnamon. Place on a greased baking sheet about 3 inches apart. Bake in a moderate oven (350° F) 10 to 12 minutes. Makes about 4 dozen cookies. For variety, roll the balls of dough in tiny multicolored candies or chocolate sprinkles instead of nuts.

# Almond Crescents

1 cup soft butter
⅓ cup sugar
1⅔ cups sifted flour
¼ teaspoon salt
⅔ cup ground, blanched almonds

Cream together butter and sugar until light and fluffy. Stir in flour and salt and mix well. Add almonds and blend. Chill dough thoroughly. Roll into long rolls about the size of pencils. Cut into 2½-inch lengths. Pull ends around to form crescents. Place on ungreased baking sheet. Bake in a moderately-slow oven (325° F) 14 to 16 minutes. Makes about 60 cookies.

# Gingersnap Cookies

**¾ cup shortening**
**¾ cup brown sugar, firmly packed**
**1 egg**
**¾ cup molasses**
**3 cups sifted flour**
**¼ teaspoon salt**
**2 teaspoons soda**
**½ teaspoon cloves**
**1 teaspoon cinnamon**
**1 teaspoon ginger**
**Sugar**

Cream together shortening and brown sugar until light and fluffy. Add egg and molasses and mix well. Sift together flour, salt and spices. Mix well. Chill thoroughly in refrigerator. Form into ½-inch balls. Roll in sugar. Place 2 inches apart on an ungreased baking sheet. Bake in a moderately-hot oven (375° F) 10 to 15 minutes. Makes 10 dozen cookies.

# Cherry Kislings

**1 cup butter**
**¼ cup sugar**
**2 cups sifted flour**
**¼ teaspoon salt**
**½ cup sliced maraschino cherries, well drained**
**½ cup chopped walnuts**
**Confectioners' sugar**

Cream together butter and sugar until light and fluffy. Add flour and salt and blend well. Add cherries and walnuts. Shape dough into small balls. Place on ungreased baking sheet and bake in a slow oven (300° F) 20 to 30 minutes. Remove from baking sheet and roll in confectioners' sugar. Cool and again roll in sugar. Makes 3 dozen cookies.

# Coconut Macaroons

**1¼ cups shortening**
**1 cup sugar**
**1 cup brown sugar, firmly packed**
**2 eggs, beaten**
**2¼ cups sifted flour**
**⅓ teaspoon baking soda**
**2 teaspoons baking powder**
**½ teaspoon salt**
**1 cup rolled oats**
**1 cup chopped walnuts**
**2 cups chopped coconut**

Cream shortening until fluffy. Add sugars gradually and cream until light and fluffy. Beat in eggs. Sift together flour, soda, baking powder and salt. Stir into creamed mixture. Add oats, walnuts and coconut and mix thoroughly. (This may be easier to mix with the hands.) Roll dough into balls about the size of walnuts. Place on ungreased baking sheet about 3 inches apart. Bake in a moderate oven (350° F) 12 to 15 minutes or until golden. Cool slightly on baking sheet and then remove cookies to wire rack. Makes about 8 dozen cookies.

# Pecan Crescents

**¼ cup butter**
**¾ cup shortening**
**1 teaspoon vanilla**
**2 cups sifted flour**
**¼ cup sugar**
**1 package (1 cup) semi-sweet chocolate morsels, coarsely chopped**
**2 cups chopped pecans**

Cream together butter, shortening and vanilla. Sift together flour and sugar and stir into creamed mixture. Add remaining ingredients and blend well. With the hands, shape dough into pencil-thick lengths about 1½ inches long. Shape into crescents. Place on ungreased baking sheet and bake in a moderate oven (350° F) 15 minutes. Makes 7 dozen cookies.

# Brazil Nut Snowballs

**¾ cup butter or margarine**
**½ cup sugar**
**1 egg**
**2 teaspoons vanilla**
**2 cups sifted flour**
**½ teaspoon salt**
**2 cups ground Brazil nuts**
**Confectioners' sugar**

Cream together butter and sugar until light and fluffy. Stir in egg and vanilla and beat well. Sift together flour and salt. Stir into creamed mixture. Add Brazil nuts and blend well. Shape into small balls about ⅔ inch in diameter. Place on baking sheet and bake in a moderate oven (350° F) 20 minutes. Cool slightly; then roll in confectioners' sugar. When thoroughly cool, roll in sugar again. Makes about 6 dozen.

Brazil Nut Assn.

Lever Bros. Co.

# Golden Nuggets

**1 cup margarine**
**½ cup sugar**
**1 egg yolk**
**1 teaspoon grated orange rind**
**2½ cups sifted flour**
**24 pitted dates**
**Walnuts**
**Confectioners' sugar**

Cream together margarine and sugar until light and fluffy. Add egg yolk and rind and mix until evenly blended. Add flour gradually, mixing thoroughly after each addition. Continue mixing until a smooth compact ball of dough is formed. Cut the dates in half crosswise. Insert a small piece of walnut in each half. Pinch off small pieces of dough, press date into each piece, and shape dough into a smooth ball covering the date. Place balls on a lightly greased baking sheet. Bake in a moderately-slow oven (325° F) 25 to 30 minutes. While cookies are still hot, roll in confectioners' sugar. Cool and cover with sugar again. Makes about 4 dozen cookies.

# Berliner Kranze

**1½ cups shortening (half butter)**
**1 cup sugar**
**Grated rind of 1 orange**
**2 eggs**
**4 cups sifted flour**
**1 egg white**
**2 tablespoons sugar**

Cream together shortening and sugar until very light and fluffy. Add orange rind and eggs and beat very well. Stir in sifted flour and blend until well mixed. Chill dough thoroughly. Break off small pieces of dough and form into pencil-length rolls about 7 by ¼ inches. Form a circle with each piece, bringing ends through in a single knot. Leave about ½ inch of end on each side. Beat egg white until stiff, gradually add sugar and continue beating until stiff and glossy. Place cookies on an ungreased baking sheet and brush tops with meringue mixture. Bake in a hot oven (400° F) 10 to 15 minutes. Makes 72 cookies.

# Black-Eyed Susans

**½ cup shortening**
**¾ cup granulated sugar**
**1 egg**
**¾ teaspoon vanilla**
**¾ cup sifted flour**
**½ teaspoon salt**
**1¼ cups quick-cooking oats**
**¾ cup chopped coconut**
**1 cup cooked, chopped prunes**
**¼ cup granulated sugar**

Cream shortening until light. Add sugar and mix until light and fluffy. Add egg and vanilla and beat well. Sift together flour and salt. Add oats and stir into creamed mixture. Blend well. Chill dough thoroughly. Shape dough into small balls and roll each ball in coconut. Place on a greased baking sheet and make a dent in the top of each with the handle of a knife. Bake in a slow oven (300° F) 25 to 30 minutes. Remove to wire rack to cool. Combine prunes and sugar. Cook over low heat, stirring constantly, until mixture is thick. Cool. Place a spoonful of prune mixture in hollow of each cookie. Makes about 3 dozen cookies

# Lemon Snowballs

**½ cup shortening**
**⅔ cup sugar**
**2 teaspoons grated lemon rind**
**1 egg**
**3 tablespoons lemon juice**
**1 tablespoon water**
**1¾ cups sifted flour**
**¼ teaspoon soda**
**¼ teaspoon cream of tartar**
**½ teaspoon salt**
**½ cup finely-chopped nuts**
**Confectioners' sugar**

Cream together shortening and sugar until light and fluffy. Add lemon rind and egg and beat well. Stir in lemon juice and water. Sift together flour, soda, cream of tartar and salt. Add to creamed ingredients and blend well. Stir in nuts. Chill dough. Flour hands and form dough into small balls. Place about 1 inch apart on ungreased baking sheet. Bake in a moderate oven (350° F) 10 to 15 minutes. Remove immediately from baking sheet and roll in confectioners' sugar. Makes 3 to 4 dozen cookies.

# Chinese Almond Cakes

**2½ cups sifted flour**
**¾ cup sugar**
**¼ teaspoon salt**
**1 teaspoon baking powder**
**¾ cup shortening**
**1 egg**
**2 tablespoons water**
**1 teaspoon almond extract**
**⅓ cup blanched almonds**

Sift together flour, sugar, salt and baking powder. Cut in shortening with a pastry blender or 2 knives until mixture resembles corn meal. Add egg, water and almond extract and stir until mixture comes away from sides of bowl. Knead with the hands until smooth. Chill dough 1 hour. Pinch off balls of dough the size of walnuts. Roll and flatten with hands to about ¼-inch thickness. Press an almond in the center of each cookie. Bake in a moderate oven (350° F) 20 to 25 minutes. Makes 2½ dozen cakes.

# Coconut Gumdrop Cookies

**½ cup butter or margarine**
**½ cup brown sugar, firmly packed**
**½ cup granulated sugar**
**1 egg**
**1 cup sifted flour**
**½ teaspoon double-acting baking powder**
**½ teaspoon soda**
**¼ teaspoon salt**
**1½ cups shredded coconut**
**½ cup finely-cut gumdrops**
**2 cups corn flakes**
**½ teaspoon vanilla**

Cream butter and sugars together until light and fluffy. Add egg and beat well. Sift together flour, baking powder, soda and salt. Add to creamed mixture and stir well. Add coconut, gumdrops, cereal and vanilla. Beat until well blended. Chill dough. Shape into small balls and place on an ungreased baking sheet. Press down with a fork. Bake in a moderate oven (350° F) 15 minutes, or until lightly browned. Makes 3 dozen cookies.

## Almond Secrets

1 cup margarine
½ cup sugar
1 egg yolk, unbeaten
½ teaspoon almond extract
2½ cups sifted flour
4 dozen almonds
Confectioners' sugar

Cream together margarine and sugar until light and fluffy. Add egg yolk and almond extract and beat well. Add flour gradually, mixing well after each addition. Chill dough. Spread almonds in a shallow pan and toast in a moderate oven (350° F) 15 to 20 minutes. Cool. Pinch off small pieces of dough, press a cooled almond into each and shape into smooth balls covering the almond. Place on lightly-greased baking sheet. Bake in a moderately-slow oven (325° F) 25 to 30 minutes, or until very lightly browned. While cookies are hot, roll in confectioners' sugar. Cool and coat with sugar again. Makes about 4 dozen.

## Soft Molasses Cookies

1 cup shortening
1½ cups molasses
¼ cup sugar
4 cups sifted flour
1½ teaspoons salt
2 teaspoons soda
2 teaspoons cinnamon
1½ teaspoons ginger
½ teaspoon cloves
1 egg

Melt shortening in a saucepan large enough for mixing dough. Stir in molasses and sugar and cool. Sift together flour, salt, soda, cinnamon, ginger and cloves. Mix a small amount of flour into shortening mixture. Beat in egg. Add remaining flour and blend until smooth. Chill dough about 2 hours. Shape into 1¼-inch balls. Place on baking sheets about 2 inches apart. Bake in a moderate oven (350° F) about 15 minutes. Remove to wire racks. While still warm, spread half the cookies with confectioners' sugar icing. Makes 4 dozen cookies.

Grandma's Unsulphured Molasses

## Russian Nut Balls

1 cup butter
½ cup sugar
1 teaspoon vanilla
2¼ cups sifted flour
¼ teaspoon salt
1 cup finely-chopped walnuts

Cream together butter and sugar until light and fluffy. Stir in vanilla. Add flour and salt and mix until a smooth dough is formed. Stir in nuts. Chill. Form into 1-inch balls. Place about 2 inches apart on baking sheet. Bake in a hot oven (400° F) 14 to 17 minutes until very delicately browned. While still warm, roll in confectioners' sugar. Cool and then roll in confectioners' sugar again. Makes about 5 dozen cookies.

## Gold Cookies

½ cup shortening
1½ cups sugar
4 egg yolks
2 tablespoons milk
1 teaspoon vanilla
1½ cups sifted flour
½ teaspoon baking powder
¼ teaspoon salt
¾ cup finely-chopped nuts
2 teaspoons cinnamon

Cream together shortening and sugar until light and fluffy. Add egg yolks, milk and vanilla and beat well. Sift together flour, baking powder and salt. Add to creamed mixture and blend thoroughly. Chill. Roll dough into balls the size of walnuts. Combine nuts and cinnamon. Roll balls in this mixture. Place 3 inches apart on an ungreased baking sheet. Bake in a hot oven (400° F) 12 to 15 minutes. Makes about 60 cookies.

## Walnut Festival Cookies

½ cup butter or margarine
¾ cup sugar
1 teaspoon grated orange rind
1 egg, beaten
3 tablespoons milk
2½ cups sifted flour
¼ teaspoon salt
½ teaspoon soda
½ cup chopped walnuts
½ cup seedless raisins

Cream together butter and sugar until light and fluffy. Blend in orange rind, egg and milk. Sift together flour, salt and soda. Stir into creamed mixture. Stir in walnuts and raisins. Roll into small balls between palms of hands and place on a greased cookie sheet. Flatten slightly with a fork dipped in milk. Bake in a hot oven (425° F) 7 to 9 minutes. Makes about 3 dozen cookies.

American Spice Trade Assn.

## Nutmeg Butterballs

1⅓ cups blanched almonds
1 cup butter or margarine
½ cup sugar
1 teaspoon vanilla
2 cups sifted flour
½ cup confectioners' sugar
2 teaspoons nutmeg

Put almonds through coarse blade of food chopper. Cream together butter and sugar until light and fluffy. Blend in almonds and vanilla. Add flour and mix well. Chill dough thoroughly. Shape dough into balls about the size of walnuts. Place on greased baking sheets. Bake in a slow oven (300° F) 15 to 20 minutes, or until lightly browned. Combine confectioners' sugar and nutmeg. Roll cookies in this mixture while hot. When cool, roll in sugar-nutmeg mixture again. Makes 6 dozen cookies.

# Mandel Kager

½ cup shortening
½ cup butter
½ cup sugar
1 egg
1⅔ cups sifted flour
½ teaspoon baking powder
1 teaspoon cinnamon
1 teaspoon ground cardamom
½ cup chopped, toasted almonds
1 egg yolk
1 tablespoon water

Cream together shortening, butter and sugar until light and fluffy. Beat in egg. Sift together flour, baking powder, cinnamon and cardamom. Add to creamed mixture and blend well. Stir in almonds. Chill. Shape into balls the size of hickory nuts; flatten slightly. Beat together egg yolk and water. Brush tops of cookies with this mixture. Bake in a moderately-hot oven (375° F) about 10 minutes. Makes about 3½ dozen cookies.

# Mexican Wedding Cakes

1 cup butter or margarine
⅓ cup sugar
1 teaspoon almond flavoring
2½ cups sifted flour
½ teaspoon salt
1 cup finely chopped Brazil nuts
Red and green food coloring

Work butter and sugar in a bowl until creamy. Stir in flavoring. Stir in flour, salt and nuts and mix thoroughly. Divide dough in half. Stir a few drops of red coloring into one half; green coloring into the other. Chill several hours. Form into 1-inch balls. Place on greased baking sheets. Cover the bottom of a glass with damp cheesecloth and use it to flatten each ball to ¼-inch thickness. Bake in a moderately low oven (325°F.) 12 to 15 minutes or until the cookies start to brown a little around the edges. Makes about 3 dozen.

# Cocoa Bourbon Balls

1 cup finely crushed vanilla wafers
1 cup sifted confectioners' sugar
Chopped pecans
Cocoa
2 tablespoons light corn syrup
¼ cup bourbon
Granulated sugar
Chocolate shot

Combine wafer crumbs, confectioners' sugar, 1 cup pecans and 2 tablespoons cocoa. Add corn syrup and bourbon and mix well. Shape in 1-inch balls. Roll some in granulated sugar, others in chopped pecans, cocoa or chocolate shot. Store in tight cans for a few days. Makes 3 dozen balls.

# Pfeffernuesse

4 cups sifted flour
1 teaspoon baking soda
½ teaspoon salt
1 tablespoon cinnamon
1 teaspoon cloves
1 teaspoon nutmeg
¼ teaspoon black pepper
1 tablespoon crushed cardamom seeds
1 teaspoon anise
¼ pound candied orange peel, ground fine
½ pound citron, ground fine
2 tablespoons butter
2½ cups confectioners' sugar
5 eggs, separated
1½ teaspoons grated lemon rind
¼ cup milk
1 cup confectioners' sugar

Sift together flour, soda, salt and spices. Stir in seeds and orange peel and citron. Mix together butter and sugar. Beat egg yolks well and add to butter mixture with lemon peel. Stir in flour-fruit mixture. Fold in stiffly beaten egg whites. Chill for about 1 hour. Shape with well floured hands into balls about the size of hickory nuts. Place on a greased baking sheet, cover with a towel and let stand overnight. Combine milk and 2½ cups confectioners' sugar. Brush cookies with this mixture. Bake in a moderate oven (350°F.) 15 to 20 minutes. Cool. Store in a tightly covered container to age. Roll in confectioners' sugar before serving. Makes about 7 dozen cookies.

# Frosties

1 package (1 cup) semi-sweet chocolate morsels
3 tablespoons light corn syrup
3 cups sifted confectioners' sugar
1 cup chopped nuts
⅓ cup orange juice
1¾ cups crumbled vanilla wafers
Confectioners' sugar

Melt chocolate morsels over hot water. Cool slightly and add remaining ingredients. Knead well. Form into 1-inch balls and roll in confectioners' sugar. Store in a covered container a few days to ripen. Makes 6 dozen Frosties.

# Peanut Butter Crisps

4 cups corn flakes *or* 1 cup corn flake crumbs
1 cup soft butter or margarine
½ cup peanut butter
½ cup granulated sugar
½ cup brown sugar, firmly packed
1 egg
1 teaspoon vanilla flavoring
1⅓ cups sifted flour
Spanish salted peanuts

If using corn flakes, crush into fine crumbs. Blend butter and peanut butter; blend in sugars. Add egg and vanilla; beat well. Stir in flour, mixing thoroughly. Shape dough into small balls; roll in corn flake crumbs. Place on greased baking sheets. Press one peanut into each ball. Bake in moderate oven (350° F.) about 15 minutes. Makes about 4 dozen cookies.

Peanut Growers of Alabama & Georgia

# Crisp Peanut Butter Cookies

1 cup margarine
1 cup creamy or chunk style peanut butter
1 cup sugar
1 cup firmly packed brown sugar
2 eggs, beaten
1 teaspoon vanilla
2½ cups sifted flour
1 teaspoon baking powder
1 teaspoon baking soda
1 teaspoon salt

Cream margarine, peanut butter, and sugars. Mix in eggs and vanilla. Sift flour, baking powder, baking soda and salt together over creamed mixture. Stir until well blended. Chill dough until it can be easily handled. Shape into 1-inch balls. Place about 2 inches apart on greased cooky sheet. Flatten with floured bottom of glass or with floured fork, making crosswise pattern on each if fork is used. Bake in moderate over (350°F.) until lightly browned, 12 to 15 minutes. Makes about 6 dozen.

Note: Fork may be dipped into fortified chocolate syrup before pressing cookies.

### Orange Peanut Butter Cookies

Follow recipe for Crisp Peanut Butter Cookies, adding 2 tablespoons grated orange rind with eggs and vanilla.

### Coconut Patties

Follow recipe for Crisp Peanut Butter Cookies, rolling 1-inch balls of dough in flaked coconut before placing on cooky sheet and flattening them with floured bottom of glass.

### Peanut Butter Sandwich Cookies

Prepare Crisp Peanut Butter Cookies. Make sandwiches with cookies, using peanut butter as filling.

### Jelly Thumb Print Cookies

Follow recipe for Crisp Peanut Butter Cookies, pressing small indentation into each 1-inch ball of dough with thumb after placing on cooky sheet instead of flattening. Remove from cooky sheet while still warm and press again with thumb. Cool. Fill each indentation with desired jelly or jam.

### Peanut Butter Spritz Cookies

Prepare dough as directed for Crisp Peanut Butter Cookies. Chill. Put through cooky press onto greased cooky sheet, making desired shaped. Bake. Makes about 8 dozen.

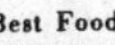

Best Foods

# Russian Tea Cakes

1 cup soft butter
½ cup sifted confectioners' sugar
1 teaspoon vanilla
2¼ cups sifted flour
¼ teaspoon salt
¾ cup finely chopped nuts
Confectioners' sugar

Cream together butter, sugar and vanilla until smooth. Sift together flour and salt and stir into butter mixture. Stir in nuts. Chill dough. Roll in 1-inch balls. Place about 2 inches apart on an ungreased baking sheet. Bake in a hot oven (400°F.) about 10 to 12 minutes, until set but not browned. While still warm roll in confectioners' sugar. Cool. Roll in sugar again before serving. Makes about 4 dozen tea cakes.

# Scandinavian Cookies

½ cup butter or margarine
½ cup brown sugar, firmly packed
1 egg, separated
1 cup sifted flour
Chopped nuts or sesame seed

Cream butter and sugar together until smooth. Add egg yolk and mix well. Stir in flour and mix until a stiff dough is formed. Shape dough into small balls, about the size of walnuts. Beat egg white slightly. Dip balls in beaten egg white and roll in chopped nuts or sesame seed. Place on a lightly greased baking sheet. Bake in a moderate oven (350°F.) 15 to 20 minutes. Makes 2 dozen cookies.

# Rolled Cookies

**There are mouth-watering wonders for every taste and occasion in this big, gem-bright collection.**

# Basic Rolled Cookie Dough

1 cup (2 sticks) margarine
1½ cups sugar
1 egg, unbeaten
1½ teaspoons vanilla
3½ cups sifted flour
1 teaspoon salt

Cream margarine in a bowl until light and fluffy. Add sugar gradually, creaming until thoroughly blended. Add egg and vanilla and beat thoroughly. Sift together flour and salt. Sift into creamed mixture. Mix well, first with a spoon, and then with hands to make a smooth dough. Chill dough thoroughly in refrigerator before using. This dough is for filled cookies.

For Basic Rolled Cookie Dough, first cream 1 cup (2 sticks) margarine with wooden spoon until light.

To the creamed margarine gradually add 1½ cups sugar; continue creaming until light and fluffy.

To the sugar-margarine mixture you next add 1 egg and 1 tsp. of vanilla and beat thoroughly.

Now sift flour out onto a square of waxed paper.

Measure 3½ cups of it and 1 tsp. salt into sifter.

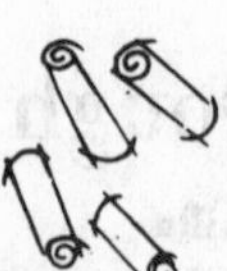

Sift flour and salt right into the creamed mixture. Stir with spoon as much as you possibly can.

With hands, continue blending into smooth
Chill the Basic Rolled Cookie Dough befo

# My Favorite Filled Cookies

Follow the recipe for Basic Rolled Cookie Dough. When dough is well chilled, roll, a small amount at a time, on a floured board to thickness of 1/8 inch. Cut dough into rounds with a 2½-inch cookie cutter. Cut a hole in the center of half the rounds with the tiniest cookie cutter you have or cut 3 tiny holes with a thimble. Place the plain rounds on a lightly-greased baking sheet. Place a spoonful of any of the fillings that follow on each, spreading the filling to within ½ inch of the edge. Cover with cut-out round. Seal edges by pressing with the tines of a fork. Bake in a moderately-hot oven (375°F) 12 to 15 minutes. Transfer cookies to wire racks to cool.

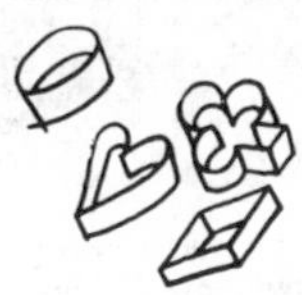

### Fruit Filling

Cut up enough dried fruits (raisins, dates, figs) to make 1½ cups. Place fruits in a saucepan with ½ cup sugar, ½ cup water and juice of ½ lemon. Cook over low heat, stirring occasionally, until thickened, about 5 to 10 minutes. Cool before using.

### Pineapple Filling

In a saucepan, combine ½ cup sugar, 1 tablespoon cornstarch, 1 tablespoon butter, 1½ cups drained crushed pineapple, a dash of salt and a pinch of nutmeg. Cook, stirring, until thick and clear. Cool before using.

### Date Filling

In a saucepan, mix 1 cup chopped pitted dates, ¼ cup brown sugar, ⅔ cup water, ½ cup chopped nuts, 1 tablespoon lemon juice. Bring to a boil over moderate heat, stirring constantly, and continue to boil until mixture is thick enough to spread. Cool before using.

**Place plain rounds on a lightly-greased baking sheet, top with selected filling and spread it to within ½ inch of edge. Top each with a holed round and carefully seal edges with the floured tines of a fork. Cook them in a moderately-hot oven (375° F) for 12 to 15 minutes and transfer to wire racks to cool.**

# Old-Fashioned Sugar Cookies

**3 cups sifted flour**
**1 teaspoon baking powder**
**¼ teaspoon salt**
**1¼ cups sugar**
**1 cup margarine**
**3 eggs, unbeaten**
**1 teaspoon vanilla**

Sift flour, baking powder, salt and sugar together into a mixing bowl. Cut in margarine with a pastry blender or 2 knives until mixture has consistency of corn meal. Add eggs and vanilla and mix until well blended. Chill dough in the refrigerator, at least one hour. On a well-floured board or baking sheet, roll out a small amount of the dough to a thickness of about 1/8 inch. Cut cookies with 4-inch floured cutter. If dough is rolled on a board, remove rounds to a baking sheet. If dough is rolled on a baking sheet, remove excess dough from around the cookies. Sprinkle cookies with sugar and bake in a moderately-hot oven (375°F) 12 to 15 minutes or until golden brown around the edges. Transfer cookies to a wire rack to cool. Makes about 3 dozen 4-inch cookies.

**For Old-Fashioned Sugar Cookies, sift flour onto waxed paper; measure 3 cups back into the sifter.**

To the 3 cups of flour in the sifter, you now add 1 tsp. of baking powder and ¼ tsp. of salt.

Cut it in with a pastry blender. Or, if no blender is available, 2 knives will serve the purpose.

Now add 1¼ cups of sugar to the mixture in the sifter and sift all into a large mixing bowl.

The dough should now possess the consistency of corn meal. Three eggs are added next, unbeaten.

Next comes margarine. Add 1 cup (2 sticks) to the sifted dry ingredients in the mixing bowl.

And, finally, with the addition of 1 tsp. of vanilla, your cookie dough is ready for blending.

Blend thoroughly and refrigerate for at least 1 hour before rolling. This is very soft dough.

Next, using a spatula, carefully remove excess flour and dough from around cookies, as shown.

To save handling, roll it directly onto a well-floured baking sheet. Roll a little at a time.

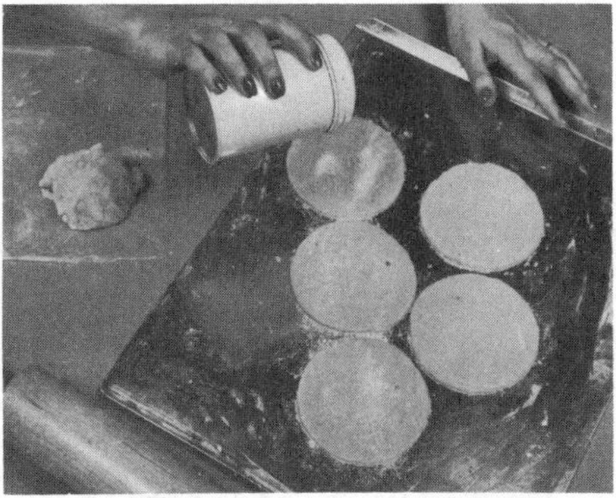

Sprinkle liberally with sugar or sugar-cinnamon mixture and bake in moderately-hot (375° F) oven.

From dough of ⅛-inch thickness, cut out your cookies with floured, 4-inch round cookie cutter.

Bake for 12 to 15 minutes, or until golden brown around edges. Transfer to a wire rack to cool.

# Pink Peppermint Cookies

½ cup shortening
¾ cup sugar
1 egg
¼ teaspoon essence of peppermint
12 drops red vegetable food coloring
1¼ cups sifted flour
½ cup instant non-fat dry milk
½ teaspoon baking powder
½ teaspoon salt
Chopped nuts

Cream together shortening and sugar until light and fluffy. Add egg, peppermint and food coloring and beat until well blended. Sift together flour, milk, baking powder and salt; add to creamed mixture and blend thoroughly. Chill dough about ½ hour. Roll out half the dough between two sheets of waxed paper to ⅛-inch thickness. Cut with a 2-inch cookie cutter. Place on ungreased baking sheet; top with chopped nuts. Bake in a moderate oven (350°F) 8 to 10 minutes or until edges are lightly browned. Makes about 4 dozen cookies.

# Chocolate Derbies

½ cup butter
2 tablespoons sugar
¼ cup brown sugar, firmly packed
1 egg yolk
1⅓ cups sifted flour
¼ teaspoon salt
¼ teaspoon soda
½ package (½ cup) semi-sweet chocolate morsels

Cream together butter, sugar and brown sugar until light and fluffy. Beat in egg yolk. Sift together flour, salt and soda. Blend into creamed mixture and mix well. Roll dough out thin between two sheets of waxed paper. Remove top sheet of paper. Cut into 1½-inch circles. Place circles on ungreased baking sheet. Top each circle with 5 to 6 chocolate morsels and cover with another circle. Seal edges together with a fork. Bake in a very hot oven (425° F) 10 minutes. Makes 3 dozen cookies.

# Cardamom Cookies

1 cup butter or margarine
1 cup sugar
2 teaspoons ground cardamom
2 teaspoons grated lemon rind
2 eggs
4 cups sifted flour

Cream together butter and sugar until light and fluffy; add cardamom and lemon rind. Add eggs, one at a time, and beat well after each addition. Add flour and blend thoroughly. Roll dough to ⅛ inch thick on a lightly-floured board. Cut into desired shapes. Bake in a moderately-hot oven (375°F) 10 minutes or until edges are lightly browned. Makes about 6 dozen cookies.

National Dairy Council

# Ginger Cookies

5 cups sifted flour
1 teaspoon soda
1 teaspoon salt
1 teaspoon cinnamon
1 teaspoon nutmeg
3 teaspoons ginger
⅔ cup butter
1 cup sugar
1 cup dark molasses
2 eggs, beaten

Sift together flour, soda, salt and spices. Cream butter; add sugar and beat until light and fluffy. Blend in molasses and eggs. Add dry ingredients; mix well. Chill dough in refrigerator several hours or overnight. Roll dough out on lightly floured board or pastry cloth to ⅛-inch thickness. Cut with floured cookie cutters. Place on buttered baking sheets. Bake in a moderate oven (375° F.) for 10 to 12 minutes. Cool on rack. Decorate with butter cream frosting and cookie decorations, if desired. Makes 4 dozen cookies.

# Sugar Cookies

5½ cups sifted flour
2 teaspoons baking powder
2 teaspoons salt
1½ cups butter (3 sticks)
2 cups sugar
4 eggs
2 tablespoons grated orange rind or 1 tablespoon vanilla

Sift together flour, baking powder and salt. Cream butter; add sugar and beat until light and fluffy. Blend in eggs and grated orange rind or vanilla. Add dry ingredients; mix well. Chill dough in refrigerator several hours or overnight. Roll dough out on lightly floured board or pastry cloth to ⅛-inch thickness. Cut with floured cookie cutters. Place on ungreased baking sheets. Sprinkle with sugar. Bake in a hot oven (400° F.) for 6 to 8 minutes or until done and delicately browned. Cool on rack. Decorate with butter cream frosting and cookie decorations, if desired. Makes 8 dozen cookies.

# Coconut-Wine Filled Cookies

**1 cup shredded coconut**
**1 cup seedless raisins**
**¾ cup port wine**
**1 tablespoon sugar**
**Dash of salt**
**½ cup shortening**
**¾ cup sugar**
**1 egg**
**½ teaspoon vanilla**
**2¼ cups sifted flour**
**¼ teaspoon double-acting baking powder**
**½ teaspoon soda**
**½ teaspoon salt**
**½ cup sour cream**

Combine coconut and raisins and put through food chopper. Add wine, 1 tablespoon sugar and dash of salt. Place over low heat and cook until mixture is thickened, stirring constantly; cool. Cream together shortening and sugar until light and fluffy; add egg and vanilla and beat thoroughly. Sift flour, baking powder, soda and salt. Add to creamed mixture, alternately with sour cream, beating well after each addition. Chill dough until firm enough to roll. Roll dough, a small amount at a time, to ¼ inch on a well-floured board. Cut with 2½-inch cutter. Place half of cookies on ungreased baking sheet; place a heaping teaspoon full of coconut mixture in center of each. Top with another cookie and press edges together with a fork. Bake in a moderately-hot oven (375°F) 12 to 15 minutes. Makes about 2½ dozen filled cookies.

# Pineapple Cookie Dessert

**1 No. 2 can sliced pineapple**
**½ cup shortening**
**¾ cup sugar**
**1 egg, well beaten**
**2 cups sifted flour**
**½ teaspoon baking powder**
**¼ teaspoon salt**
**¼ cup brown sugar**
**1 pint vanilla ice cream**

Drain pineapple, reserving 2 tablespoons of the syrup. Pat slices dry on paper toweling and let stand. Cream together shortening and sugar until light and fluffy; blend in egg and pineapple syrup. Sift together flour, baking powder and salt. Add to shortening mixture and mix thoroughly. Wrap dough in waxed paper and chill. Roll out ¼ inch thick on a lightly-floured board. Cut into rounds, using the washed, dried and floured pineapple can; place on baking sheet. Top ten of the rounds with pineapple slices. Sprinkle pineapple generously with brown sugar. Bake in a moderately-hot oven (375°F) 12 to 15 minutes or until lightly browned around edges. Top each pineapple-topped slice with a scoop of vanilla ice cream and serve for dessert. Makes 10 pineapple cookies and about 14 plain rounds.

# Bran Delights

**1½ teaspoons grated orange rind**
**½ cup butter**
**1 cup sugar**
**1 egg, well beaten**
**1 tablespoon milk**
**1 tablespoon orange juice**
**1¼ cups sifted flour**
**2 teaspoons baking powder**
**½ teaspoon salt**
**1¼ cups bran flakes**

Add orange rind to butter and cream well; add sugar gradually and cream until light and fluffy. Add egg, milk and orange juice and beat well. Sift together flour, baking powder and salt; add to creamed mixture and blend well. Stir in cereal; chill about 1 hour. Roll dough out, a small amount at a time, on a lightly-floured board, to about ⅛ inch thick. Cut with a 2½-inch cookie cutter. Bake on a greased baking sheet in a hot oven (425°F) 6 to 8 minutes. Makes about 3½ dozen cookies.

Best Foods

# Hamantashen

**4 eggs**
**1 cup corn oil margarine, melted**
**¾ cup sugar**
**Grated rind of 1 orange**
**5 cups sifted self rising cake flour**
**Lekvar or apple butter**

Beat eggs slightly, then beat in margarine, sugar and orange rind, continuing beating until mixture is fluffy and thick. Gently stir in flour. Chill until firm, about 1½ hours. Divide dough into quarters. Roll out each on floured board or cloth to ¼-inch thickness. Cut into 3-inch circles and place on greased cookie sheet. Spoon 1 tablespoon lekvar or apple butter into center of each. Form tricorns, bringing up edges of dough almost to center and making three seams. (Some filling should show in center.) Pinch seams together tightly. Bake in a moderate oven (350° F.) until golden brown, about 20 minutes. Makes about 3 dozen.

# Raisin Rounds

1 cup seedless raisins
⅓ cup honey
⅓ cup orange juice
1 teaspoon grated orange rind
1 tablespoon butter
½ cup shortening
1 cup sugar
2 eggs
1 teaspoon vanilla
2 cups sifted flour
2½ teaspoons baking powder
½ teaspoon salt

Combine raisins, honey, orange juice and rind in a saucepan. Cook over low heat, about 5 minutes, stirring constantly. Blend in butter; cool. Cream together shortening and sugar until light and fluffy. Beat in eggs and vanilla. Sift together flour, baking powder and salt. Stir into creamed mixture and blend thoroughly; chill. Roll out to ⅛-inch thickness on a lightly-floured board. Cut into 2-inch rounds. Place half of rounds on ungreased baking sheet. Spread with raisin mixture. Cut small holes in remaining circles. Place on top of filling and seal edges together with a fork. Bake in a hot oven (400°F) 10 to 12 minutes. Makes about 2 dozen cookies.

# Cinnamon Stars

½ pound blanched almonds
½ cup egg whites
2 cups sifted confectioners' sugar
½ teaspoon grated lemon rind
½ teaspoon cinnamon

Put almonds through coarse blade of food chopper first, then through fine blade. Beat egg whites until stiff but not dry. Gradually add sugar; continue beating until mixture is completely blended—about 5 minutes. Beat in lemon rind. Reserve ¾ cup of this mixture for topping. Blend together cinnamon and ground almonds and fold into remaining beaten egg whites. If batter is too soft for rolling, let it stand at room temperature until stiffened to proper consistency. Roll out, a small amount at a time, on a cloth-covered board which has been heavily dusted with confectioners' sugar, to ⅛ inch. Cut into star shapes. Place cookies on a well-greased and floured baking sheet. Top each star with ½ teaspoon of the reserved egg-white mixture. Bake in a moderate oven (350°F) 12 minutes. Makes about 4½ dozen cookies.

# Swiss Almond Bites

1 pound shelled almonds
4 squares unsweetened chocolate
2 cups and 2 tablespoons sugar
1 teaspoon cinnamon
¼ teaspoon cloves
¼ teaspoon salt
3 eggs

Put almonds through coarse blade of food chopper; put almonds and chocolate through fine blade. Mix thoroughly with remaining ingredients. Sprinkle a board with a mixture of half flour and half sugar. Pat out small amounts of the dough to ¼-inch thickness. Cut into any desired shape. Place on greased baking sheet and let stand in a cool place overnight. Bake in a slow oven (325°F) about 15 minutes. Cool slightly before removing from pan. Makes about 3 dozen cookies.

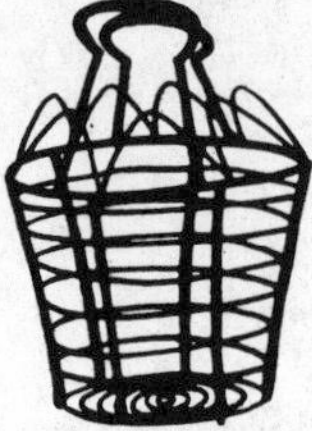

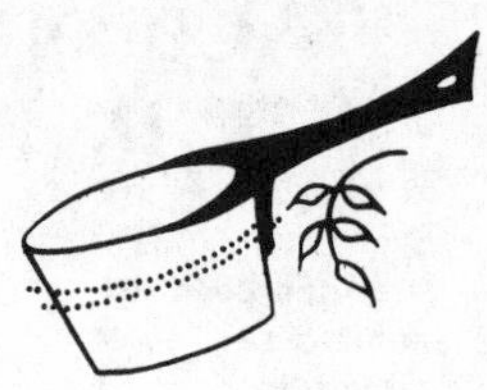

# Fancy Filled Cookies

1 cup butter or margarine, soft
1 cup sifted confectioners' 10X sugar
1 egg
1 teaspoon vanilla
½ teaspoon cinnamon
2½ cups sifted enriched flour
½ teaspoon baking powder
1 cup quick rolled oats, uncooked
2 tablespoons plum preserves
2 tablespoons apricot preserves

Beat together butter, sugar, egg, vanilla and cinnamon. Sift together flour and baking powder. Add to butter mixture. Beat well. Blend in oats. Chill. Roll out dough on lightly floured board or canvas to ⅛-inch thickness. Cut 48 cookies with well-floured 2½-inch round cutter. Place 24 unbaked cookies on ungreased cookie sheets. Cut circle (about ¾-inch in diameter) from center of remaining cookies. For each cookie, place about ½ teaspoon preserves in center of each plain cookie. Place cookies with cut-out center over filling; seal edges carefully. Bake in a moderate oven (375° F.) 12 to 15 minutes or until delicately browned around edges. Remove from cookie sheets immediately. Cool. Makes 2 dozen.

Pan American Coffee Bureau

# Moravian Cookies

1 cup molasses
½ cup shortening
⅓ cup brown sugar, firmly packed
1 teaspoon salt
¾ teaspoon soda
¾ teaspoon cinnamon
¾ teaspoon ginger
¾ teaspoon cloves
¼ teaspoon nutmeg
¼ teaspoon allspice
3¾ cups sifted flour

Heat molasses to boiling point and remove from heat. Add shortening and stir until well blended. Stir in sugar, salt, soda and spices; then stir in flour and blend thoroughly. Cover and store in refrigerator from 5 days to 2 weeks. (Dough does not hold together unless thoroughly chilled.) Roll out, a small amount at a time, on a lightly-floured board to $\frac{1}{16}$ inch. Cut in desired shape. Place on baking sheet. Bake in a moderately-hot oven (375°F) 5 to 6 minutes. Makes about 200 small cookies.

# Peek-A-Boo Dates

**2 cups sifted flour**
**2 teaspoons grated lemon rind**
**⅔ cup margarine**
**1¼ cups creamed cottage cheese**
**1 pound pitted dates**
**1 egg white**
**3 tablespoons sugar**

Combine flour and lemon rind. Cut in margarine with a pastry blender or 2 knives until mixture has consistency of corn meal. Add cottage cheese and mix lightly until concoction will stick together; chill. Roll out, a small amount at a time, on a lightly-floured board to about ¼ inch thick. Cut in 2½-inch squares. Place a date diagonally upon each square and roll up. Press corners firmly to seal. Brush lightly with egg white; sprinkle with sugar. Bake in a moderately-hot oven (375°F) 15 to 20 minutes. Makes about 3 dozen cookies.

Processed Apple Institute

# Apple Cheesettes

**2 cups sifted all-purpose flour**
**½ teaspoon salt**
**½ teaspoon baking powder**
**⅔ cup shortening**
**⅔ cup grated American cheddar cheese**
**3-4 tablespoons ice water**
**2½ cups sliced apples**
**1 tablespoon grated orange rind**
**3 dozen pecans or walnuts**
**Brown sugar**

Sift together flour, salt and baking powder; cut in shortening with 2 knives or pastry blender. Add cheese; mix well. Add enough water to hold ingredients together. Chill. Drain liquid from canned apples; add rind; mix well. Roll out pastry to ⅛-inch thickness; cut with 3-inch round cutter. Place apple slice on one-half of circle of pastry; add walnut or pecan, and sprinkle lightly with sugar. Moisten edges of pastry; fold over; press edges together. Flute with pastry wheel. Pierce with fork or make gash in center of each. Place on baking sheet; bake in hot oven (425°), for 10-15 minutes. Makes 3 dozen.

American Molasses Co.

# Ginger Sprites

**½ cup shortening**
**½ cup sugar**
**½ cup molasses**
**1 egg**
**2½ cups sifted flour**
**½ teaspoon soda**
**1 teaspoon baking powder**
**1 teaspoon ginger**
**1½ teaspoons cloves**
**1½ teaspoons cinnamon**
**⅛ teaspoon nutmeg**

Cream together shortening and sugar until light and fluffy; add molasses and egg and beat well. Sift together flour, soda, baking powder and spices; add to molasses mixture and blend thoroughly. Chill in refrigerator. Roll out on a lightly-floured board to about ¼-inch thickness. Cut with a 6-inch, "ginger-bread-man" cookie cutter. Place on a greased baking sheet. Bake in a moderate oven (350°F) 10 to 12 minutes. Makes about 1½ dozen Ginger Sprites.

# Maraschino Cherry Roll-Ups

**1 3-ounce package cream cheese**
**½ cup butter or margarine**
**1 cup sifted flour**
**Dash of salt**
**½ cup confectioners' sugar**
**4 dozen maraschino cherries, well drained**
**Confectioners' sugar**

Blend together cream cheese and butter. Add flour and salt and blend well; chill. Roll dough ⅛ inch thick on a lightly-floured board; sprinkle with confectioners' sugar. Cut into 1 by 3-inch rectangles. Place a cherry on each rectangle and roll up. Place on ungreased baking sheet and bake in a moderate oven (350°F) 15 to 17 minutes. Sprinkle with confectioners' sugar. Makes 4 dozen cookies.

# Brazil Nut Sugar Cookies

**1 cup butter or margarine**
**1 cup sugar**
**2 eggs, well beaten**
**1½ teaspoons vanilla**
**3 cups sifted flour**
**1 teaspoon baking powder**
**¼ teaspoon salt**
**Sliced Brazil nuts**

Cream together butter and sugar until light and fluffy; add eggs and vanilla and blend well. Sift together flour, baking powder and salt; add to creamed mixture and blend thoroughly. Chill about ½ hour. Roll dough out ⅛ inch thick on a lightly-floured board. Cut with star-shaped cookie cutters. Press Brazil nut slice in center of each cookie. Bake on an ungreased baking sheet in a moderate oven (350°F) about 12 minutes. Makes 3 dozen cookies.

# Brazil Nut Treasure Rounds

**⅔ cup finely-cut, pitted dates**
**¼ cup finely-chopped Brazil nuts**
**¼ cup brown sugar, firmly packed**
**2 tablespoons water**
**½ cup butter or margarine**
**¼ pound sharp cheddar cheese, grated**
**1 cup plus 2 tablespoons sifted flour**

Combine dates, Brazil nuts, sugar and water in a saucepan; cook over low heat, stirring constantly, until soft. Cool. Cream together butter and cheese, and blend in flour. Chill dough about 1 hour. Roll dough out ⅛ inch thick on a lightly-floured board. Cut into rounds with a 2-inch cutter. Top half the rounds with a teaspoon of the date filling. Cut center of remaining rounds with small star cookie cutter and place on top of the date filling. Press edges together with a fork. Bake in a moderate oven (350°F) 15 minutes. Makes 2 dozen cookies.

# Snappy Sugar Crisps

**½ cup margarine**
**¾ cup sugar**
**1 egg**
**1 teaspoon vanilla**
**1½ cups sifted flour**
**¼ teaspoon baking powder**
**½ teaspoon salt**

Melt margarine in a large saucepan; remove from heat. Add sugar, egg and vanilla and beat until light and fluffy. Sift together flour, baking powder and salt; add to first mixture and blend thoroughly. Chill dough in refrigerator about 30 minutes. Shape according to variations that follow. Bake in a moderate oven (350°F) 12 to 15 minutes. Makes about 40 cookies.

### Diamonds

Roll out half the dough about ⅛ inch thick on a greased, floured baking sheet. Mark with well-floured knife or pastry wheel in diamond shapes. Top each diamond with raisins and bake. When done, break cookies apart.

### Cinnamon Fans

Shape chilled dough into 1-inch balls. Place on greased and floured baking sheet about 3 inches apart. Using edge of a teaspoon, cut 5 gashes from outside almost to center of balls. Flatten each section with a well-floured spoon; sprinkle with cinnamon and sugar.

### Chocolate Cookies

Following the basic recipe, melt ½ cup semi-sweet chocolate pieces with the margarine. Roll half of chilled dough ⅛ inch thick on a greased and floured baking sheet. Draw a well-floured fork down and across dough to make waffle pattern; divide into squares with knife or a wheel. Bake, cool and break apart.

# Orange Cookies

**¼ cup margarine**
**1 cup sugar**
**Grated rind of ½ orange**
**4 egg yolks, beaten**
**2 tablespoons orange juice**
**2½ cups sifted flour**
**2 teaspoons baking powder**
**⅛ teaspoon salt**
**1 egg white, beaten**
**½ cup chopped almonds**
**¼ cup sugar**

Cream together margarine and sugar until light and fluffy. Add orange rind, egg yolks and orange juice and mix thoroughly. Sift together flour, baking powder and salt. Add to creamed mixture and mix thoroughly; chill. Roll dough out on a lightly-floured board to ⅛ inch thick; cut in desired shapes. Brush with beaten egg whites. Combine almonds and sugar and sprinkle over tops of cookies. Place on greased baking sheet and bake in a moderately-hot oven (375°F) 7 to 8 minutes. Makes about 50 cookies.

# Apricot Thimble-itas

**1 cup drained, cooked dried apricots**
**½ cup sugar**
**6 tablespoons apricot juice**
**⅛ teaspoon salt**
**1 tablespoon orange juice**
**⅔ cup shortening**
**1 cup brown sugar, firmly packed**
**1 teaspoon salt**
**1 teaspoon grated orange rind**
**1 egg**
**2¼ cups sifted flour**
**1 teaspoon baking powder**
**½ teaspoon soda**
**3 tablespoons milk**

Mash apricots to a smooth pulp. Add ½ cup sugar, apricot juice, salt and orange juice. Cook over low heat, stirring constantly for about 15 minutes and cool. Cream together shortening and brown sugar until light and fluffy. Add salt, orange rind and egg and beat well. Sift together flour, baking powder and soda. Add half of flour to creamed mixture and blend well. Add milk, then add remaining flour and blend well. Chill dough about 1 hour. Roll small portions of dough on a lightly-floured board to ⅛ inch thick. Cut out rounds with a 2½-inch cookie cutter. Place one rounded teaspoon of the apricot mixture on each of half the cookies. With a thimble, cut a hole in center of remaining rounds and place over top of apricot filling. Press cookies' edges together with tines of a fork and place on greased baking sheet. Bake in a moderately-hot oven (375°F) 8 to 10 minutes. Makes 2 dozen cookies.

Lever Bros. Co.

American Spice Trade Assn.

# Spiced Cinnamon Cookies

**2 cups sifted flour**
**1 cup brown sugar**
**½ teaspoon nutmeg**
**1 teaspoon cinnamon**
**1 teaspoon ginger**
**⅔ cup butter or margarine**
**1 egg, beaten**
**1 tablespoon cold water**

Combine flour, sugar and spices in a mixing bowl. Cut in butter with a pastry blender or 2 knives until mixture resembles corn meal. Mix egg and water and stir into flour mixture, blending thoroughly. Chill dough until stiff enough to roll. Roll out, a small amount at a time, to ⅛ inch thick, on a lightly-floured board. Shape as desired with cookie cutters. Bake in a hot oven (400°F) 6 to 7 minutes until edges are lightly browned. Cool. Makes 5 dozen cookies.

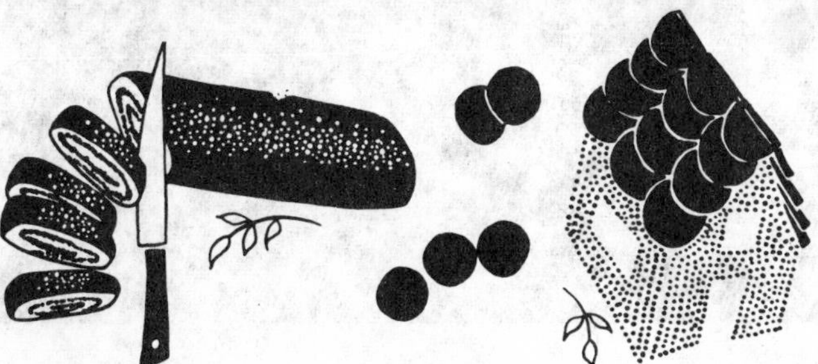

# Stone Jar Molasses Cookies

**1 cup molasses**
**½ cup shortening**
**1 teaspoon soda**
**2¼ cups sifted flour**
**1¾ teaspoons baking powder**
**1 teaspoon salt**
**1½ teaspoons ginger**

Heat molasses to boiling point; remove from heat, add shortening and soda, and stir until well blended. Sift together remaining ingredients and stir into molasses mixture. Blend thoroughly; chill. Roll dough out to $\frac{1}{16}$ inch on a lightly-floured board and cut with a 1½-inch cookie cutter. Bake in a moderate oven (350°F) 5 to 7 minutes. Makes about 8 dozen cookies.

# Anise Cookies

**1 cup butter or margarine**
**1 cup sugar**
**2 teaspoons whole anise seeds**
**2 teaspoons grated lemon rind**
**2 eggs**
**4 cups sifted flour**

Cream together butter and sugar until light and fluffy; add anise and lemon rind. Add eggs, one at a time, and beat well after each addition. Stir in flour and blend well. Roll dough to ⅛ inch thick on a lightly-floured board. Cut into desired shapes with cookie cutter. Bake in a moderately-hot oven (375°F) about 10 minutes, or until only edges have browned lightly. Makes about 6 dozen cookies.

# Chocolate Crown Cookies

**½ cup butter or margarine**
**½ cup sugar**
**1 egg**
**½ teaspoon vanilla**
**2 squares unsweetened chocolate, melted**
**2 cups sifted flour**
**1 teaspoon double-acting baking powder**
**½ teaspoon salt**
**1 tablespoon milk**
**¼ cup butter**
**2 cups sifted confectioners' sugar**
**1 tablespoon milk**
**¼ teaspoon peppermint extract**

Cream together butter and sugar until light and fluffy. Add egg and vanilla, mix thoroughly, then add chocolate and beat well. Sift together flour, baking powder and salt, and add to creamed mixture, blending well. Add milk and blend. Chill dough. Roll out ⅛ inch thick on a lightly-floured board. Cut out crown shapes, using a paper pattern and sharp knife or cut out rounds, using a 2-inch cookie cutter. Place on ungreased baking sheet. Bake in a moderate oven (350°F) 10 minutes. Cream ¼ cup of butter. Add confectioners' sugar, milk and peppermint extract and mix thoroughly. Put icing in a pastry tube or paper cone. Outline a crown on the round cookies, and decorate crown-shaped cookies as desired. Makes about 5 to 6 dozen cookies.

# Almond Teas

**1 cup butter or margarine**
**⅔ cup sugar**
**3 egg yolks**
**2½ cups sifted flour**
**½ teaspoon salt**
**½ cup ground blanched almonds**
**½ teaspoon vanilla**
**Blanched almond halves**

Cream together butter and sugar until light and fluffy; beat in egg yolks. Stir in flour, salt, almonds and vanilla. Work mixture with hands until smooth. Roll dough to ⅛-inch thickness on a lightly-floured board and cut into desired shapes. Top each with an almond half. Place on greased baking sheet and bake in a hot oven (400°F) about 8 to 10 minutes or until lightly browned. Makes about 5 dozen cookies.

## Coffee Wafers

**¾ cup shortening**
**½ cup sugar**
**1½ tablespoons vinegar and enough strong, cold coffee to make ¼ cup liquid**
**¼ cup molasses**
**2 cups sifted flour**
**½ teaspoon soda**
**¼ teaspoon salt**
**¼ teaspoon cloves**
**¼ teaspoon ginger**

Cream together shortening and sugar until light and fluffy. Combine vinegar, coffee and molasses. Sift together flour, soda, salt, cloves and ginger. Add to sugar mixture, alternately with molasses mixture, mixing thoroughly after each addition; chill well. Roll, a small amount at a time, on a lightly-floured board to ⅛ inch. Cut into desired shapes. Place on a greased baking sheet. Bake in a moderately-hot oven (375°F) 6 to 8 minutes. Makes about 5 dozen wafers.

## Sesame Seed Anise Cookies

**1 tablespoon anise seed**
**2 tablespoons boiling water**
**⅔ cup sugar**
**¾ cup butter or margarine**
**⅛ teaspoon soda**
**1 large egg**
**2 cups sifted all-purpose flour**
**1 large egg, lightly beaten**
**Toasted sesame seed**

Combine anise seed and boiling water and steep while mixing dough. Gradually blend sugar with butter or margarine and soda. Beat in egg. Drain anise seed and add. Stir in flour, a little at a time. Mix well. Chill dough overnight or until stiff enough to handle. Roll dough into ¼-inch balls. Place on ungreased cooky sheets 3 inches apart. Place a piece of waxed paper over cookies and flatten to 1/16-inch thickness with the bottom of a glass. Remove waxed paper. Brush tops with lightly beaten egg. Sprinkle each with toasted sesame seeds. Bake in a preheated hot oven (400° F.) 7 to 8 minutes or until lightly browned. Makes about 6 dozen.

### To Toast Sesame Seed

Sprinkle sesame seeds in a large shallow pan. Place in a preheated moderate oven (350° F.) 22 to 25 minutes or until golden brown.

## Lemon Filled Cookies

**½ cup sugar**
**2 tablespoons cornstarch**
**¼ teaspoon salt**
**½ cup orange juice**
**1 tablespoon grated lemon rind**
**¼ cup lemon juice**
**1 tablespoon margarine**
**¾ cup margarine**
**1 cup sugar**
**1 egg, well beaten**
**1½ teaspoons vanilla**
**2½ cups sifted flour**
**¾ teaspoon baking powder**
**¼ teaspoon salt**

Combine ½ cup sugar, cornstarch, salt, orange juice, lemon rind, lemon juice and 1 tablespoon margarine in a saucepan. Bring to a rolling boil and boil 1 minute, stirring constantly. Chill thoroughly before using. Cream together margarine and sugar until light and fluffy; add egg and vanilla and blend well. Sift together flour, baking powder and salt; add to creamed mixture and blend well. Chill dough. Roll out on a lightly-floured board ⅛ inch thick; cut with fluted cookie cutter. Place a spoonful of lemon filling on each of half the cookies. Cut 2 gashes in other rounds and place over filling. Gently lift points so filling will show. Press edges together with a fork. Place on a greased baking sheet and bake in a moderately-hot oven (375°F) 8 to 10 minutes. Makes about 40 filled cookies.

Corn Products Co.

# Bar Cookies

**Whether they're plain Brownies or Brazil Nut Triple Layer Bars, they satisfy big appetites!**

## Brownies

**⅓ cup butter or margarine**
**2 squares unsweetened chocolate**
**1 cup sugar**
**2 eggs, well beaten**
**⅔ cup sifted flour**
**½ teaspoon baking powder**
**¼ teaspoon salt**
**½ cup chopped walnuts**
**1 teaspoon vanilla**

Melt butter and chocolate together over hot water. Gradually add sugar to beaten eggs and beat thoroughly. Add chocolate mixture and blend well. Sift together flour, baking powder and salt and stir into chocolate mixture. Add nuts and vanilla and mix well. Spread mixture in a greased 8 by 8 by 2-inch pan. Bake in a moderate oven (350° F) 25 to 30 minutes. Cool in pan. Cut into squares for serving. Makes about 16 Brownies.

**For Brownies, first melt butter and chocolate over hot water, break two eggs into mixing bowl and beat.**

Gradually add 1 cup sugar to beaten eggs and beat mixture thoroughly after each addition of sugar.

Take butter and chocolate mixture from stove and add to batter in bowl. Stir until well-blended.

Sift together flour, baking powder and salt in proportions shown in recipe and stir into batter.

Add ½ cup chopped walnuts and 1 teaspoon vanilla to rest of batter in the bowl and blend together.

Turn mixture into a greased 8x8x2-inch pan and bake in a moderate oven (350° F) 25 to 30 minutes.

Cool baked loaf in pan and then cut into squares to serve. Recipe makes approximately 16 Brownies.

# Chocolate Squares

2 squares unsweetened chocolate
½ cup shortening
1 cup sugar
3 eggs
¾ cup sifted cake flour
1 teaspoon baking powder
1 cup chopped nuts
2 squares unsweetened chocolate
1 square sweet chocolate
3 tablespoons butter or margarine
1¾ cups sifted confectioners' sugar
5 tablespoons hot milk
½ teaspoon vanilla

Melt chocolate and shortening in a heat-resistant glass bowl in the oven. Cool slightly. Beat in sugar. Add eggs, one at a time, beating well after each addition. Sift together flour and baking powder. Add to chocolate mixture. Add nuts and blend well. Pour into a greased 2-quart, heat-resistant glass utility dish. Bake in a moderate oven (325° F) about 35 minutes. Melt unsweetened chocolate, sweet chocolate and butter together in a heat-resistant glass bowl in the oven. Combine sugar and hot milk. Pour into chocolate mixture. Add vanilla and beat until thick enough to spread. Spread over top of baked squares. Cut in squares or bars. Makes 15 to 24.

Best Foods

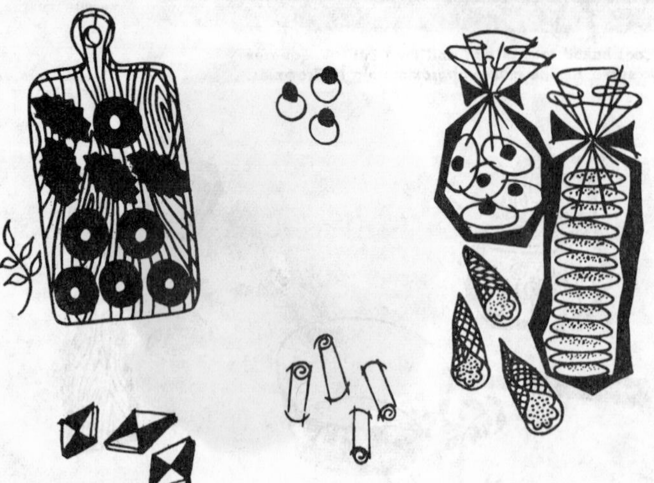

# Date Layers

1 pound pitted dates, cut up
½ cup sugar
¾ cup light corn syrup
¼ cup orange juice
2 teaspoons grated orange rind
¼ teaspoon salt
2½ cups sifted flour
1 teaspoon soda
1 teaspoon salt
1 cup shortening
1 cup brown sugar, firmly packed
½ cup water
2½ cups uncooked rolled oats

Combine dates, sugar, corn syrup, orange juice, orange rind and salt in a saucepan. Bring to a boil; cook slowly, stirring frequently until thick. Cool. Sift together flour, soda and salt into a large bowl. Add shortening and blend in well with a fork. Add brown sugar and water and work until smooth. Stir in oats. Knead with fingers if necessary to blend well. Spread half of dough over greased 15 by 11-inch baking pan. Roll remaining dough between 2 sheets of waxed paper into a rectangle the same size as the pan. Chill about 10 minutes. Spread date mixture over oatmeal layer in pan. Cover with chilled layer of oatmeal mixture. Bake in a moderate oven (350° F) 30 minutes. Cool in pan and cut into squares. Makes 70 to 80 bars.

# Chewy Cookie Bars

2 eggs
1 cup brown sugar, firmly packed
¼ cup melted shortening
¾ cup sifted flour
½ teaspoon baking powder
½ teaspoon salt
½ teaspoon cinnamon
½ teaspoon vanilla
1 cup seedless raisins
½ cup chopped walnuts

Beat eggs well. Beat in sugar and shortening. Sift together flour, baking powder, salt and cinnamon. Blend into egg mixture. Stir in vanilla, raisins and nuts. Turn into a greased 9-inch-square pan. Bake in a moderate oven (350° F) 30 minutes. Cool in pan and cut into bars. Makes 36 bars.

Best Foods

# Pineapple Brownies

½ cup shortening
2 squares unsweetened chocolate
1 cup sugar
2 eggs, well beaten
1 flat can crushed pineapple, well drained
½ teaspoon vanilla
1 cup sifted flour
½ teaspoon baking powder
¼ teaspoon soda
¼ teaspoon salt
½ cup chopped nuts

Melt shortening and chocolate in top of double boiler over hot water. Blend in sugar. Remove from heat and blend in eggs, pineapple and vanilla. Sift together flour, baking powder, soda and salt. Add to pineapple mixture and blend well. Stir in chopped nuts. Pour into well-greased, 8-inch-square pan. Bake in a moderate oven (350° F) 35 to 40 minutes. While still warm, cut into squares. Makes 16 brownies.

# Fruity Walnut Bars

⅓ cup shortening
1 cup sugar
2 eggs, beaten
¾ cup sifted flour
3 tablespoons cocoa
½ teaspoon salt
½ teaspoon baking powder
½ teaspoon vanilla
½ cup chopped walnuts
1 cup cooked prunes, pitted and chopped

Melt shortening. Blend in sugar and eggs and beat well. Sift together flour, cocoa, salt and baking powder. Stir into shortening mixture. Add vanilla, walnuts and prunes and mix well. Turn batter into a greased, 9-inch-square pan. Bake in a moderate oven (350° F) 25 to 30 minutes. Cool and cut into bars. Makes about 2 dozen bars.

# Raisin Cookie Strips

⅓ cup shortening
⅓ cup sugar
3 tablespoons honey
3 tablespoons peanut butter
1 egg
1 tablespoon milk
½ cup sifted flour
¼ teaspoon salt
¼ teaspoon mace
½ teaspoon cinnamon
¾ teaspoon baking powder
⅓ cup seedless raisins
⅔ cup quick-cooking oats
1 tablespoon honey
1 teaspoon melted butter

Cream together shortening and sugar until light and fluffy. Add honey and peanut butter and continue beating. Beat in egg and milk. Sift together flour, salt, mace, cinnamon and baking powder; stir into shortening mixture. Stir in raisins and oats. Spread in a greased, 8-inch-square pan. Combine honey and melted butter and pour evenly over top of dough. Bake in a moderately-hot oven (375° F) about 15 minutes. Cut into strips. Makes 32 strips.

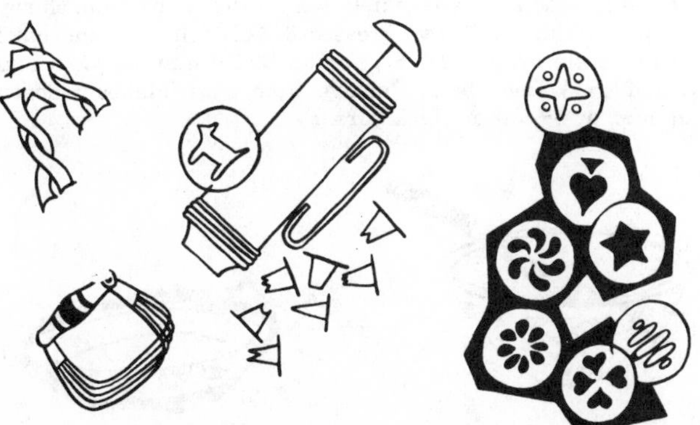

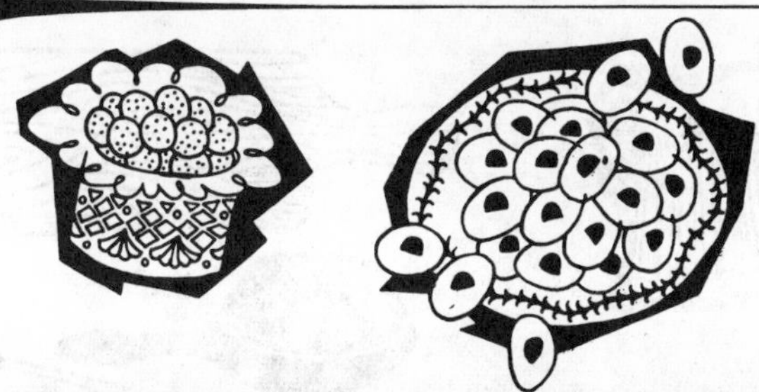

The Kellogg Co.

# Fruit-Filled Crumb Bars

6 cups corn flakes *or* 1½ cups packaged corn flake crumbs
2 cups sifted flour
1 cup brown sugar, firmly packed
½ teaspoon baking soda
1 teaspoon salt
1 cup soft butter or margarine

If using corn flakes, crush into fine crumbs. Sift together flour, soda and salt. Blend butter and sugar; add sifted dry ingredients together with corn flake crumbs, mix well. Press half of mixture into greased 13x9-inch baking pan. Spread evenly with desired filling; cover with remaining crumb mixture, pat down lightly. Bake in moderate oven (350° F.) about 35 minutes, or until lightly browned. Cool. Cut into bars about 2x2½ inches. Top with ice cream if desired. Makes about 18 bars, 2x2½ inches.

## Date-Apricot Filling

1 cup cut, pitted dates
½ cup sugar
2 tablespoons juice drained from apricots
2 cups mashed, drained, cooked dried apricots

Combine all ingredients in medium-sized saucepan and cook over low heat, stirring constantly until thickened, about 5 minutes. Cool.

## Prune-Orange Filling

3 cups cut, pitted cooked prunes
½ cup sugar
½ cup orange juice
2 tablespoons grated orange rind
2 tablespoons lemon juice

Prepare as Date-Apricot Filling.

## Chocolate Raisin Brownies

**2 squares unsweetened chocolate**
**¼ cup butter or margarine**
**1 cup sugar**
**⅛ teaspoon salt**
**1 teaspoon vanilla**
**2 eggs, well beaten**
**¾ cup sifted flour**
**¾ cup seedless raisins**

Combine chocolate and butter. Heat over hot water until melted. Remove from heat and stir in sugar, salt, vanilla and eggs. Beat well. Fold in flour and raisins. Pour into a shallow, greased, 8-inch-square pan. Bake in a moderate oven (350° F) 25 to 30 minutes. When cool, cut into strips and dust with confectioners' sugar if desired. Makes 32 strips.

## Bran-Molasses Brownies

**6 tablespoons butter or margarine**
**¼ cup molasses**
**2 eggs**
**¾ cup sugar**
**⅔ cup sifted flour**
**½ cup cocoa**
**½ cup bran**
**½ cup chopped dates**

Melt butter and stir in molasses. Beat eggs in a large mixing bowl Add sugar and beat until well blended. Stir in molasses mixture. Mix together flour, cocoa, bran and dates. Stir into molasses mixture until flour is just dampened. Turn into a greased, 8-inch-square pan. Bake in a moderate oven (350° F) 25 to 30 minutes. When cool, cut into 2-inch bars. Makes 16 bars.

## Florida Orange Nut Bars

**¼ cup shortening**
**1½ cups sugar**
**2 egg yolks**
**1 egg**
**⅔ cup orange juice**
**Grated rind 1 orange**
**2 cups sifted cake flour**
**2 teaspoons baking powder**
**¼ teaspoon salt**
**2 egg whites**
**⅔ cup pecan halves**

Cream shortening thoroughly. Add 1 cup sugar and cream until light and fluffy. And egg yolks and whole egg, one at a time, and beat well after each addition. Combine orange juice and rind. Sift together flour, baking powder and salt. Add alternately with orange juice to shortening mixture, mixing well after each addition. Spread in a well-greased, 15 by 9½-inch pan. Beat egg whites until stiff, gradually add remaining half cup of sugar and continue beating until the mixture is stiff and glossy. Spread on top of batter and top with pecan halves. Bake in a moderate oven (350° F) 25 minutes. Cut into 1 by 3-inch bars. When cool, remove from pan. Makes 45 bars.

Baker's Angel Flake Coconut

## Coconut Fig Bars

**1¼ cups sifted cake flour**
**1½ teaspoons double-acting baking powder**
**½ teaspoon salt**
**1 cup sugar**
**2 eggs, well beaten**
**1 tablespoon melted butter or other shortening**
**¾ cup finely cut dried figs**
**1 teaspoon grated lemon rind**
**1 cup flaked coconut**
**1 tablespoon hot water**

Sift flour once, measure, add baking powder and salt, and sift again. Add sugar gradually to eggs, beating thoroughly. Add shortening, then figs, lemon rind, and coconut. Mix thoroughly. Add flour alternately with water. For a thin, chewy bar, spread mixture in two greased 8x8x2-inch pans and bake in a moderate oven (325° F.) for about 35 minutes. Cool and cut in 2½x1¼-inch bars. Remove from pans. Makes 3 dozen thin bars, or 1½ dozen thick bars.

# Ginger Fruit Bars

1 egg, beaten
1 cup dark brown sugar, firmly packed
¼ cup butter or margarine, melted
2 tablespoons milk
1 cup sifted flour
½ teaspoon salt
⅛ teaspoon soda
½ teaspoon ginger
½ teaspoon cinnamon
1 cup mixed glazed fruit
½ cup chopped nuts

Combine egg, brown sugar and butter and mix well. Stir in milk. Sift together flour, salt, soda, ginger and cinnamon. Stir into egg mixture. Blend in fruit and nuts. Pour batter into a greased and floured 9-inch-square pan. Bake in a moderate oven (350° F) about 45 minutes. When cool, cut into bars. Makes about 32 bars.

# Gingercrisps

¾ cup shortening
¾ cup sugar
½ cup unsulphured molasses
1 egg
2¼ cups sifted all-purpose flour
1½ teaspoons baking soda
1 teaspoon cinnamon
½ teaspoon ginger
¼ teaspoon salt
⅛ teaspoon ground cloves

Cream together shortening and sugar until light and fluffy. Add molasses and egg; mix well. Sift in remaining ingredients; mix thoroughly. Place in freezer 1 hour or chill in refrigerator 2 hours. Form into approximately 1-inch balls; roll in granulated sugar. Bake on greased baking sheets in a moderate oven (375° F.) 10 to 12 minutes. Makes approximately 4 dozen cookies.

# Hermits

½ cup butter or margarine
½ cup sugar
½ cup unsulphured molasses
2 eggs
2 cups sifted all-purpose flour
½ teaspoon salt
¼ teaspoon baking soda
2 teaspoons baking powder
1 teaspoon cinnamon
½ teaspoon ground cloves
¼ teaspoon mace
¼ teaspoon nutmeg
⅛ teaspoon allspice
¾ cup raisins
½ cup chopped nuts

Cream together butter and sugar until light and fluffy. Add molasses and eggs; beat well. Sift together flour, salt, baking soda, baking powder and spices; stir in raisins and nuts. Add to molasses mixture; blend well. Spread evenly in greased 12x 8x2-inch baking pan. Bake in a moderate oven (350° F.) 30 minutes. If desired, spread with Confectioners' Sugar Icing while warm. Cool; cut into squares. Makes 2 dozen Hermits.

# Hazelnut Bars

2 egg whites
1 cup sugar
1 tablespoon flour
1 teaspoon vanilla
1½ cups coarsely-ground, unblanched hazelnuts

In the top of a double boiler beat the egg whites until stiff. Gradually beat in the sugar and continue beating until mixture stands in peaks. Fold in flour. Cook over boiling water about 3 minutes, stirring constantly. Remove from water and blend in vanilla and nuts. Spread dough in ungreased, paper-lined, 13 by 9-inch oblong pan. Bake in a moderate oven (350° F) 15 to 20 minutes or until top looks dull. While warm, cut into bars 1½ by 2 inches. Cool slightly. Turn bars out of pan, paper and all. Dampen paper with cold water. When paper is thoroughly wet, remove bars. Makes about 32 bars.

# Apple Spice Bars

¼ cup shortening
½ cup sugar
1 egg
½ cup molasses
2 cups sifted flour
1½ teaspoons baking powder
¼ teaspoon salt
¼ teaspoon soda
1 teaspoon cinnamon
1 teaspoon nutmeg
½ cup milk
1 cup chopped dates
1½ cups diced, raw apple

Cream together shortening and sugar until light and fluffy. Add egg and molasses and beat well. Sift together flour, baking powder, salt, soda, cinnamon and nutmeg. Add to creamed mixture alternately with milk. Add dates and diced apple. Pour into a greased, floured 10 by 12-inch pan. Bake in a moderate oven (350° F) 25 minutes. When cool, cut into 1 by 3-inch bars and roll in confectioners' sugar. Makes 2½ dozen bars.

# Molasses Chew-Chews

⅓ cup shortening
1 cup sugar
1 cup molasses
½ cup egg whites
1¾ cups sifted flour
¼ teaspoon soda
½ teaspoon salt
1½ cups shredded coconut

Cream shortening until light. Add sugar and molasses and beat until light and fluffy. Beat in egg whites. Sift together flour, soda and salt and stir into molasses mixture. Add coconut and mix until blended. Spread batter on a greased, waxed-paper-lined jelly roll pan, 15 x 10 x 1 inch. Bake in a moderate oven (350° F) 30 to 35 minutes. Turn out on a baking sheet, remove paper and turn right side up. When cool, cut into 1 x 2-inch bars. Makes 75 bars.

# Pineapple Scotch Bars

1½ cups crushed pineapple, lightly drained
3 tablespoons apricot jam
¼ cup sugar
1½ tablespoons cornstarch
1½ cups sifted flour
½ teaspoon soda
½ teaspoon salt
1½ cups quick-cooking oats
1 cup brown sugar, firmly packed
¾ cup shortening

Combine pineapple and jam in a saucepan. Blend together sugar and cornstarch and stir into pineapple mixture. Cook over low heat, stirring constantly, until mixture is thick and clear. Cool. Sift together flour, soda and salt into a bowl. Add the oats and brown sugar and mix. Cut in shortening until mixture has the consistency of corn meal. Pat half of this mixture into a 9-inch-square pan. Spread pineapple filling over top of crumb mixture. Press remaining crumb mixture over the top. Bake in a moderately-hot oven (375° F) 35 to 40 minutes. Cool and cut into bars. Makes 24 bars.

Pan American Coffee Bureau

# Peanut Butter Brownies

½ cup sifted flour
¼ teaspoon salt
½ cup crunchy-style peanut butter
¼ cup butter
1 teaspoon vanilla
1 cup firmly packed brown sugar
2 eggs, unbeaten
1 cup chopped peanuts

Mix and sift flour and salt. Cream peanut butter, butter and vanilla. Add sugar gradually, creaming until well-blended. Add eggs 1 at a time, beating well after each addition. Blend in flour. Stir in peanuts. Spoon into greased 8-inch square cake pan. Spread evenly. Bake in moderate oven (350° F.) 30 to 35 minutes or until center is firm. Cool in pan 5 minutes. Cut into squares. Remove from pan. Cool on cake rack.

# Congo Squares

⅔ cup shortening
2¼ cups brown sugar, firmly packed
3 eggs
2⅔ cups sifted flour
2½ teaspoons baking powder
½ teaspoon salt
1 cup chopped nuts
1 package (1 cup) semi-sweet chocolate morsels

Melt shortening in a large saucepan. Stir in brown sugar and cool slightly. Beat in eggs, one at a time. Sift together flour, baking powder and salt. Add to shortening mixture with remaining ingredients. Blend well. Pour into a greased, waxed-paper-lined pan, 15 by 10 by 1 inch. Bake in a moderate oven (350° F) 25 to 30 minutes. Makes 36 squares.

# Oatmeal Bars

⅓ cup shortening
⅔ cup brown sugar, firmly packed
1 egg
1 cup sifted flour
¼ teaspoon salt
¼ teaspoon soda
1¼ cups quick-cooking oats
½ cup milk
1 package (1 cup) semi-sweet chocolate morsels
¼ cup sugar
1 tablespoon orange juice
1 tablespoon grated orange rind

Cream together shortening and sugar until light and fluffy. Add egg and beat well. Sift together flour, salt and soda. Add to creamed mixture. Add oats, milk and chocolate morsels. Pour into a greased pan, 10 by 5 by 3 inches. Bake in a moderately-hot oven (375° F) 35 to 40 minutes. Combine sugar and orange juice and bring to a boil. Add orange rind. Pour over top of baked cookies. When cool, cut into bars. Makes 2 dozen bars.

# Neapolitans

Dark Dough:
1 cup shortening
1½ cups brown sugar, firmly packed
2 eggs
3 cups sifted flour
¼ teaspoon salt
1 teaspoon soda
½ teaspoon cinnamon
½ teaspoon cloves
1 cup coarsely-ground nuts
1 package (1 cup) semi-sweet chocolate morsels, ground

Light Dough:
½ cup shortening
¾ cup sugar
1 egg
1 teaspoon vanilla
½ teaspoon almond extract
2 tablespoons water
2 cups sifted flour
½ teaspoon salt
¼ teaspoon soda
¾ cup raisins, finely chopped
12 candied cherries, chopped

For dark dough, cream together shortening and sugar until light and fluffy. Add eggs and beat well. Sift together flour, salt, soda, cinnamon and cloves. Add to creamed mixture and blend well. Add nuts and ground chocolate and mix well. Line a loaf pan, 10 by 5 by 3 inches, with waxed paper. Pack half of the dark dough firmly into pan. For light dough, cream together shortening and sugar until light and fluffy. Add egg, vanilla, almond extract and water and beat thoroughly. Sift together flour, salt and soda and add to creamed mixture. Add remaining ingredients and blend well. Pack on top of dark dough in loaf pan. Add remaining dark dough and pack well. Refrigerate for 24 hours. Turn out; cut in thirds, lengthwise. Cut each third into slices, ¼ inch thick. Bake in a hot oven (400° F) 10 minutes. Makes 8 dozen Neapolitans.

# Jiffy California Walnut Bars

½ cup softened butter or margarine
3 tablespoons powdered sugar
1 cup sifted all-purpose flour
2 eggs
2 tablespoons all-purpose flour
1 teaspoon baking powder
¼ teaspoon salt
1 cup chopped walnuts
½ cup quick-cooking oats
½ cup flaked coconut
1 cup brown sugar, firmly packed
½ teaspoon vanilla

Cream butter or margarine until soft and fluffy; blend in sugar. Add flour a little at a time, mixing until smooth after each addition. Pat into a 9-inch square pan (not necessary to grease with all the butter in the shortbread). Bake in a moderate oven (375° F.) for 15 minutes. Beat eggs lightly in mixing bowl. Sift in flour, baking powder and salt. Stir in walnuts, oats, coconut, brown sugar and vanilla. Spoon over shortbread. Reduce heat to 325° and bake 25 to 30 minutes longer. Cut into 1x3-inch bars. Makes about two dozen bars.

Diamond Walnuts

California Prune Advisory Board

# Prune Chewies

½ cup butter
1 cup light brown sugar, firmly packed
1 cup flour
1 tablespoon cornstarch
¼ teaspoon salt
¼ cup prune juice
1½ cups chopped plumped prunes
1 cup chopped walnut meats
2 teaspoons grated lemon rind
2 tablespoons lemon juice
2 eggs
1 4-ounce can angel flake coconut
1 teaspoon vanilla extract

Cream together butter, ½ cup brown sugar and flour until crumbly. Pat out into greased 9″ x 9″ x 2″ pan, having mixture 1″ high around edge. Bake in moderate oven (350°F.), 20 minutes. Combine remaining ½ cup brown sugar, cornstarch, salt, prune juice, prunes, lemon rind and juice; cook until thickened. Add walnuts; spread out over baked mixture. Beat eggs; add coconut and vanilla extract. Spoon evenly over prune mixture. Bake at 350° F., 35 minutes. Cool. Cut in squares. Makes 16 squares.

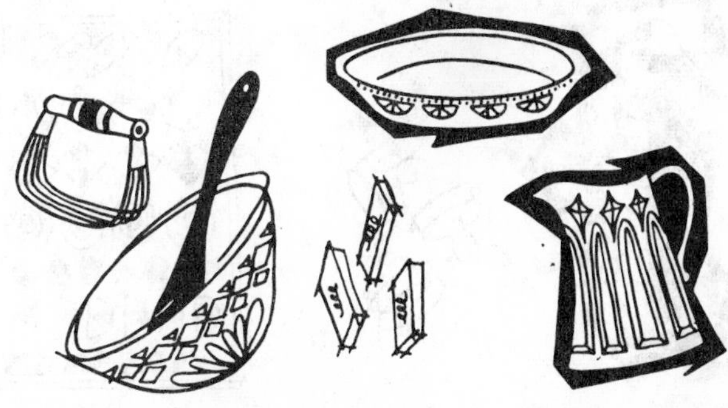

# Fruit Filled Bars

⅓ cup seedless raisins, chopped
½ cup chopped cooked prunes
⅓ cup chopped, cooked dried apricots
⅓ cup granulated sugar
1 tablespoon lemon juice
½ cup shortening
¼ cup evaporated milk
½ teaspoon vanilla
1¾ cups sifted flour
½ teaspoon salt
⅓ cup confectioners' sugar

Combine raisins, prunes, apricots, sugar and lemon juice in a saucepan. Cook over low heat until thick. Cool. Cream shortening thoroughly. Blend in milk and vanilla. Sift together flour, salt and sugar and blend into shortening and milk. Pat half the dough firmly into bottom of a greased, 8-inch-square pan. Spread filling over the dough. Place remaining dough between 2 squares of waxed paper. Roll out into an 8-inch square. Place on top of filling. Bake in a moderately-hot oven (375° F) about 30 to 35 minutes. Cut into squares while warm. Cool in pan. Makes about 18 bars.

# Graham Brownies

1 package (1 cup) semi-sweet chocolate morsels
2¼ cups graham cracker crumbs
1 can condensed milk
1 teaspoon cinnamon
¼ teaspoon salt
1 teaspoon vanilla
1 cup chopped nuts

Melt chocolate over hot water. Cool slightly and combine with remaining ingredients. Spread in an 8-inch-square pan lined with waxed paper. Bake in a moderately-hot oven (375° F) 25 minutes. Makes sixteen 2-inch squares.

# Jelly Meringue Bars

½ cup shortening
½ cup sifted confectioners' sugar
2 eggs
1 cup sifted flour
¾ cup jelly
2 egg whites
½ cup sugar
¼ teaspoon cinnamon
1 cup ground nuts

Cream together shortening and sugar until light and fluffy. Beat in eggs. Add flour and blend well. Press with hand into bottom of ungreased, 13 by 9-inch oblong pan. Bake in a moderate oven (350° F) 10 minutes. Remove from oven. Cool slightly and spread with jelly. Beat egg whites until stiff. Gradually add sugar and cinnamon and beat until glossy. Fold in nuts. Pile on top of jelly. Return to 350° F oven and continue baking 25 minutes or until topping is golden brown. Cool slightly and cut into bars. Makes about thirty 1 by 3-inch bars.

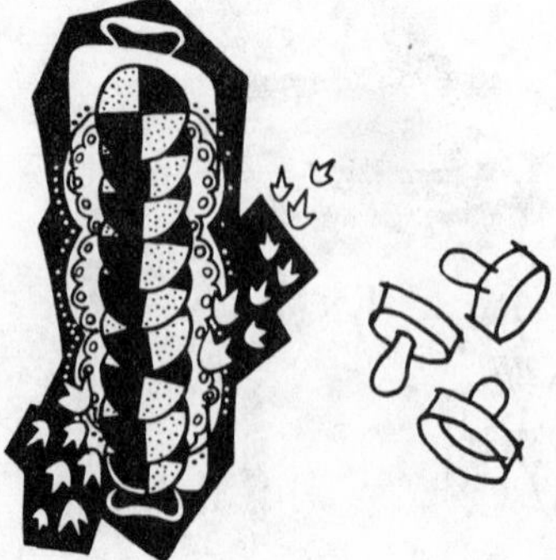

# Toffee Nut Bars

½ cup shortening
½ cup brown sugar, firmly packed
1 cup sifted flour
2 eggs
1 cup brown sugar, firmly packed
1 teaspoon vanilla
2 tablespoons flour
1 teaspoon baking powder
½ teaspoon salt
1 cup shredded coconut
1 cup chopped almonds

Cream together shortening and sugar until light and fluffy. Stir in 1 cup flour and blend well. Press with hand into bottom of an ungreased, 13 by 9-inch oblong pan. Bake in a moderate oven (350° F) 10 minutes. Beat eggs well. Beat in 1 cup brown sugar and vanilla. Mix together flour, baking powder and salt. Stir into egg mixture. Fold in coconut and almonds. Pile egg mixture over top of baked dough in pan. Return to 350° F oven and bake about 25 minutes. Cool slightly; then cut into bars. Makes about 2½ dozen 1 by 3-inch bars.

# Butterscotch Brownies

¼ cup butter or margarine
1 cup light brown sugar, firmly packed
1 egg
½ cup sifted flour
1 teaspoon baking powder
½ teaspoon salt
½ teaspoon vanilla
½ cup chopped walnuts

Melt butter in a saucepan over low heat. Remove from heat and stir in sugar. Mix until blended. Cool. Stir in egg. Sift together flour, baking powder and salt. Add to butter mixture and blend well. Stir in vanilla and nuts. Pour into a greased and floured, 8-inch-square pan. Bake in a moderate oven (350° F) 20 to 25 minutes. Cut into squares while warm. Makes about 16 brownies.

# Spicy Raisin Squares

1 egg
⅔ cup sugar
⅓ cup melted butter or margarine
1 cup sifted flour
½ teaspoon mace
½ teaspoon cinnamon
½ teaspoon nutmeg
½ teaspoon salt
¼ teaspoon soda
⅓ cup drained crushed pineapple
½ cup seedless raisins
¼ cup sugar
2 tablespoons light cream

Beat egg and sugar together. Stir in butter. Sift flour with spices, salt and soda and stir into egg mixture. Mix in pineapple and raisins. Turn into a greased baking pan about 11 by 7 by 1½ inches. Smooth top with a spatula. Combine ¼ cup sugar and cream. Pour over top of dough in pan. Bake in a hot oven (400° F) 20 to 25 minutes. Cut in squares and serve hot. Makes about 2 dozen squares.

Wine Institute

# Sherry Cashew Strips

1 cup dried golden figs
½ cup Sherry
½ cup soft butter or margarine
¾ cup brown sugar (packed)
1 egg, beaten
2 cups sifted all-purpose flour
1½ teaspoons baking powder
1 teaspoon salt
½ teaspoon ginger
⅓ cup milk
½ cup chopped cashews
Sherry Glaze

Clip stems from figs; cut figs into small pieces. Combine with Sherry and let stand ½ hour. Cream butter, brown sugar and egg until light and fluffy. Resift flour with baking powder, salt and ginger. Add to creamed mixture alternately with milk. Stir in figs and nuts. Turn into a greased and floured 13x9-inch baking pan, spreading batter evenly. Bake in a moderately hot oven (375° F.) until golden brown, about 20 to 25 minutes. Remove from oven and let cool in pan. When cold, spread with Sherry Glaze. Sprinkle with additional chopped cashews, if desired. Cut into strips about 1½ by 3 inches. Makes 2 dozen.

### Sherry Glaze

Beat 1 tablespoon soft butter, 1½ cups sifted powdered sugar and 2 tablespoons Sherry together until smooth.

# Viennese Waffles

**¾ cup unblanched almonds**
**2 cups sifted flour**
**½ teaspoon baking powder**
**½ cup sugar**
**½ cup butter or margarine**
**1 egg, beaten**
**⅔ cup jam**
**Confectioners' sugar**

Put almonds through coarse blade of food chopper; then through finest blade. Sift flour and baking powder together in a mixing bowl. Add almonds and sugar. Cut in the butter with a pastry blender or two knives until mixture has consistency of corn meal. Add egg and blend well. Cut dough in half and roll each half into a rectangle 8 by 10 inches, ¼ inch thick. Place on ungreased baking sheets. Bake in a moderate oven (350° F) 20 minutes or until edges brown very lightly. While still hot, loosen each layer carefully. Spread one layer with jam and put second layer on top. Cut into 2-inch squares with a sharp knife. Sprinkle lightly with confectioners' sugar. Makes 16 squares.

# Bran Fruit Squares

**3 cups 40% bran flakes**
**1½ cups chopped raisins**
**¾ cup chopped dried figs**
**¾ cup chopped dates**
**1 cup chopped walnuts**
**¾ cup sweetened condensed milk**
**1 tablespoon lemon juice**
**1 tablespoon honey**

Combine ingredients and mix until well blended. Press in a 9-inch-square pan and cut into squares. Place on a platter and let dry for several hours. Wrap in waxed paper. Makes about 3 dozen squares.

# Ginger Nut Bars

**2 eggs, beaten**
**1⅓ cups dark brown sugar, firmly packed**
**⅔ cup sifted flour**
**¾ teaspoon baking powder**
**¼ teaspoon salt**
**½ teaspoon ginger**
**3 tablespoons butter or margarine**
**¾ cup chopped nuts**
**⅓ cup confectioners' sugar**
**1 tablespoon milk**

Beat eggs and sugar in top of a double boiler until thoroughly mixed. Cook over hot water until thoroughly heated and of custard-like consistency. Sift together flour, baking powder, salt and ginger. Beat flour into egg-sugar mixture, 1 tablespoon at a time, with a rotary beater. Grease a 9-inch-square pan with part of the butter. Dot remaining butter over bottom of pan. Sprinkle with chopped nuts. Pour batter over top of nuts. Bake in a slow oven (300° F) 25 to 30 minutes. Mix together confectioners' sugar, and milk. Spread over top of cookies. Cool. Cut into squares. Makes 36 squares.

# Raisin Oat Squares

**⅓ cup shortening**
**⅔ cup brown sugar, firmly packed**
**2 tablespoons molasses**
**1 egg**
**½ cup sifted flour**
**¼ teaspoon salt**
**¼ teaspoon soda**
**¾ cup quick-cooking oats**
**1 cup seedless raisins**

Melt shortening in a medium-sized saucepan. Remove from heat and stir in sugar and molasses. Add egg and beat thoroughly. Sift together flour, salt and soda. Add flour mixture, oats and raisins to molasses mixture and mix well. Turn into a greased, 8-inch-square pan. Bake in a moderate oven (350° F) about 25 minutes. Cool and cut into squares. Makes about 16 squares.

# Sugar-Dusted Bars

3 eggs
1 cup sugar
1¼ cups sifted flour
1 teaspoon baking powder
½ teaspoon salt
¼ teaspoon cinnamon
¼ teaspoon allspice
2 teaspoons grated orange rind
1 cup seedless raisins
1 cup cooked dried apricots, chopped
1 cup cooked prunes, pitted and chopped
1 cup chopped walnuts
Confectioners' sugar

Beat eggs until very light. Gradually beat in sugar and beat until thick and light in color. Sift together flour, baking powder, salt, cinnamon and allspice; fold gradually into egg mixture. Fold in rind, raisins, apricots, prunes and walnuts. Pour into a greased, 9 by 14-inch pan. Bake in a slow oven (300° F) about 40 minutes. Cool. Cut into bars or squares. Roll in confectioners' sugar. Makes about 3 dozen bars.

# Almond Cookie Strips

2 tablespoons shortening
½ cup sugar
1 egg
1½ tablespoons orange marmalade
⅓ cup ground almonds
½ cup sifted flour
½ teaspoon baking powder
½ teaspoon salt
¼ cup brown sugar
1 tablespoon cream
½ teaspoon cinnamon

Cream together shortening and sugar until light and fluffy. Stir in egg, marmalade and almonds. Sift together flour, baking powder and salt. Blend into shortening mixture. Spread dough in a greased, 9-inch-square pan. Combine sugar, cream and cinnamon. Pour evenly over top of dough. Bake in a moderately-hot oven (375° F) about 20 minutes. Cool to lukewarm. Cut into strips. Makes 36 strips.

# Gumdrop Squares

2 eggs
1 cup sugar
1 teaspoon vanilla
1 cup sifted flour
½ teaspoon salt
½ cup chopped, toasted, blanched almonds
½ cup gumdrops, cut up

Beat eggs until foamy. Add sugar gradually and continue beating until smooth. Add vanilla. Sift together flour and salt. Stir into egg mixture and blend well. Add almonds and gumdrops. Spread in a well-greased and floured 9-inch-square pan. Sprinkle extra cut up gumdrops over top. Bake in a moderately-slow oven (325° F) 30 to 35 minutes. Cut into squares while warm. Cool and then remove from pan. Makes 16 squares.

# Banana Fudge Bars

⅓ cup melted margarine
3 tablespoons cocoa
1 cup sugar
2 eggs, beaten
1 teaspoon vanilla
1 tablespoon milk
½ cup sifted flour
¼ teaspoon salt
1 teaspoon baking powder
1 cup mashed, ripe bananas
1 cup chopped nuts

Combine margarine, cocoa and sugar. Mix eggs, vanilla and milk. Sift together flour, salt and baking powder. Add egg mixture and cocoa mixture to sifted dry ingredients. Stir in bananas and nuts and mix well. Pour into a greased, 8-inch-square baking pan. Bake in a moderate oven (350° F) about 50 minutes. While still warm, cut into bars. Makes about 12 bars.

# Crisp Wafers

⅓ cup butter
⅔ cup semi-sweet chocolate morsels
½ cup sugar
1 egg
½ cup sifted flour
⅛ teaspoon salt
1 teaspoon vanilla
⅓ cup chopped nuts
⅓ cup semi-sweet chocolate morsels

Combine butter and ⅔ cup chocolate morsels in top of double boiler. Melt over hot water. Remove from heat and stir until well blended. Stir in sugar. Add the egg and beat well. Stir in flour, salt and vanilla. Spread in a well-greased pan, 15 by 10 by 1 inch. Sprinkle nuts and remaining chocolate over top. Bake in a hot oven (400° F) 12 minutes. Cut into squares immediately. Makes 3 dozen wafers.

Processed Apple Institute

# Dream Squares

½ cup butter
1½ cups brown sugar
1 cup sifted all-purpose flour
2 eggs
1 teaspoon vanilla extract
¼ cup flour
¼ teaspoon salt
½ teaspoon baking powder
1 4-ounce can flaked coconut
2½ cups (1 can) sliced apples
1 cup chopped nut meats

Cream together butter, ½ cup brown sugar and 1 cup flour until crumbly. Pat out into greased 9"x9"x2" baking pan. Bake in moderate oven (350° F.), 20 minutes. Beat eggs, add vanilla extract and remaining 1 cup brown sugar with ¼ cup flour, salt and baking powder. Mix well. Add apples, coconut and nut meats. Pour over baked squares in pan. Return to moderate oven (350° F.), and bake 30 minutes. Cool 5 minutes. Cut in squares. Serve plain or topped with whipped cream or ice cream. Yields 16 servings.

# Almond Butterscotch Squares

**½ cup butter or margarine**
**1 cup brown sugar, firmly packed**
**1 egg**
**½ teaspoon vanilla**
**1 cup sifted flour**
**1 teaspoon baking powder**
**½ teaspoon salt**
**¼ cup chopped almonds**
**½ cup blanched almond halves**

Cream together butter and sugar until light and fluffy. Add egg and vanilla and beat well. Sift together flour, baking powder and salt and stir into butter mixture. Stir in chopped almonds. Spread mixture in a greased 8-inch-square pan and top with blanched almonds. Bake in a moderate oven (350° F) 30 to 35 minutes. Cool in pan. Cut into squares. Makes sixteen 2-inch bars.

# Molasses Date-Nut Bars

**1 egg, beaten**
**½ cup sugar**
**½ cup molasses**
**¼ cup shortening, melted**
**½ teaspoon vanilla**
**1 cup sifted flour**
**½ teaspoon salt**
**⅛ teaspoon soda**
**⅔ cup chopped nuts**
**1 7-ounce package pitted dates, cut fine**
**½ cup confectioners' sugar**
**3 teaspoons water**

Combine egg, sugar, molasses, shortening and vanilla. Sift together flour, salt and soda. Stir into shortening mixture with nuts and dates. Turn into a greased, lightly-floured 9-inch-square pan. Bake in a moderate oven (350° F) 40 minutes, or until done. Mix confectioners' sugar and water until smooth. Cover half the pan of cookies with frosting before cutting into bars. Makes 1½ dozen bars.

# Plantation Fruit Bars

**¼ cup shortening**
**½ cup sugar**
**1 egg**
**½ cup molasses**
**2 cups sifted flour**
**¼ teaspoon salt**
**¼ teaspoon soda**
**1½ teaspoons baking powder**
**½ cup milk**
**1 cup chopped nuts**
**1 cup chopped dates**

Cream together shortening and sugar until light and fluffy. Beat in egg and molasses. Sift together flour, salt, soda and baking powder. Stir into creamed mixture alternately with milk. Stir in dates and nuts. Spread in a greased, 8 by 12-inch baking pan. Bake in a moderate oven (350° F) 25 to 30 minutes. When cool, cut into bars, 1 by 2 inches. Makes 48 bars.

Brazil Nut Assn.

# Brazil Nut Triple Layer Bars

### Step 1:

**¼ cup butter or margarine**
**1 cup sifted flour**
**¼ teaspoon salt**

Cream butter. Add flour and salt and mix until thoroughly blended. Turn into a 7 by 11 by 1½-inch oblong pan. Spread evenly over the bottom of pan and press down with a spatula. Bake in a moderately-hot oven (375° F) 15 minutes.

### Step 2:

**2 eggs, well beaten**
**¾ cup brown sugar, firmly packed**
**1 cup finely-chopped Brazil nuts**
**½ cup shredded coconut**
**1 teaspoon vanilla**
**¼ teaspoon salt**
**2 tablespoons flour**

Combine eggs and sugar and blend well. Mix in nuts, coconut and vanilla. Add remaining ingredients and blend. Spread evenly over baked first layer. Bake in a moderately-hot oven (375° F) 15 minutes. Remove from oven and cool in pan.

### Step 3:

**2 tablespoons butter or margarine**
**1 tablespoon grated orange rind**
**1¼ cups confectioners' sugar**
**2 tablespoons orange juice**
**½ cup chopped Brazil nuts**

Cream butter and orange rind together. Add confectioners' sugar and orange juice; mix until smooth. Spread evenly over cookies in pan. Sprinkle with chopped nuts. Let stand 30 minutes. Cut into 1 by 2¼-inch bars. Makes 35 bars.

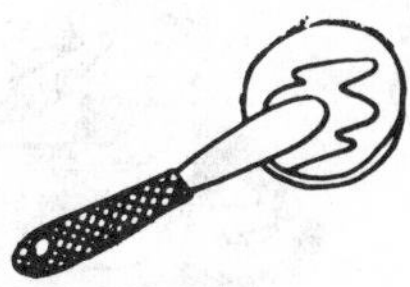

# Date Nut Squares

2 eggs
½ cup sugar
½ teaspoon vanilla
½ cup sifted flour
½ teaspoon baking powder
½ teaspoon salt
1 cup chopped walnuts
2 cups finely-cut-up dates
Confectioners' sugar

Beat eggs until foamy. Beat in sugar and vanilla and beat until well blended. Sift together flour, baking powder and salt. Stir into egg mixture. Add walnuts and dates and blend well. Spread in a well-greased, 8-inch-square pan. Bake in a moderately-slow oven (325° F) 25 to 30 minutes. Cut into squares while warm. Remove from pan and roll carefully in confectioners' sugar. Makes 16 squares.

# Cherry Date Nut Squares

2 eggs
½ cup sugar
½ teaspoon vanilla
½ cup sifted flour
½ teaspoon baking powder
½ teaspoon salt
1 cup chopped walnuts
1 cup chopped maraschino cherries
1 cup chopped pitted dates

Beat eggs until foamy. Beat in sugar and vanilla. Sift together flour, baking powder and salt. Add to egg mixture and blend well. Fold in nuts, cherries and dates. Spread in a well-greased, 8-inch-square pan. Bake in a moderately-slow oven (325° F) 35 to 40 minutes. Cool and cut into squares. Makes 16 squares.

# Prune Apricot Squares

¾ cup cooked prunes, pitted and chopped
½ cup cooked, chopped dried apricots
⅓ cup sugar
1 tablespoon flour
1 teaspoon grated lemon rind
1 tablespoon lemon juice
1 cup sifted flour
½ teaspoon salt
1 cup quick-cooking oats
¾ cup brown sugar, firmly packed
½ cup shortening

Combine prunes, apricots, sugar, flour, grated lemon rind and lemon juice in a saucepan. Cook over low heat, stirring occasionally until thick. Cool. Sift together flour and salt; add oats and brown sugar. Cut in shortening until mixture is crumbly. Pack half the dough in bottom of a greased, 8-inch-square pan. Spread cooled filling over it. Top with remaining crumbly mixture. Pat down lightly. Bake in a moderate oven (350° F) about 35 minutes. Cool. Cut into squares. Makes 16 squares.

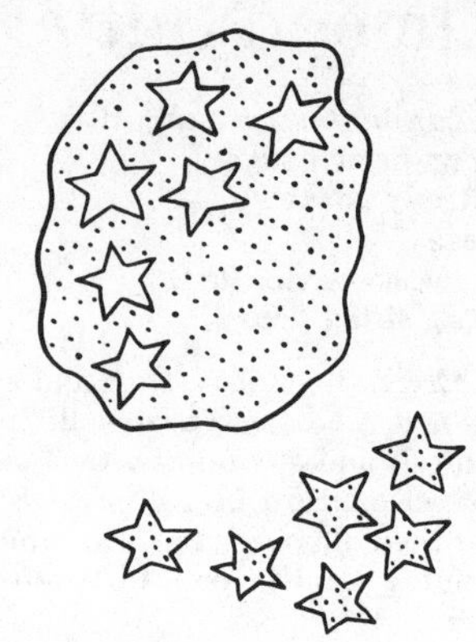

# Sandwich Squares

1 cup sifted flour
1 teaspoon soda
2 cups quick-cooking oats
1 cup brown sugar, firmly packed
¾ cup melted butter
1 package (7 ounces) dates, finely cut
1 tablespoon flour
1 cup water
1 package (1 cup) semi-sweet chocolate morsels
1 teaspoon vanilla

Sift together flour and soda. Add oats, brown sugar and melted butter and blend well. Spread half of this mixture in a greased, 12 by 8 by 2-inch pan. Combine dates, flour and water and chocolate morsels in a saucepan. Cook over low heat, stirring until thick, about 10 minutes. Stir in vanilla. Spread over mixture in pan. Sprinkle remaining oat mixture over chocolate layer. Press down. Bake in a moderately-hot oven (375° F) 20 minutes. Makes 24 squares.

# Chocolate Fruit Sticks

1 package (1 cup) semi-sweet chocolate morsels
2 tablespoons shortening
¾ cup sugar
4 eggs
½ cup light molasses
1½ cups sifted flour
1 teaspoon baking powder
1½ teaspoons cinnamon
½ teaspoon cloves
½ teaspoon salt
1 cup mixed, diced candied fruits
1 cup chopped nuts

Melt chocolate morsels over hot (not boiling) water. Cream together shortening and sugar. Add eggs one at a time and beat well after each addition. Stir in cooled chocolate and molasses. Sift together flour, baking powder, cinnamon, cloves and salt. Add to creamed mixture and blend well. Stir in remaining ingredients. Spread in a greased pan, 15 by 10 by 1 inch. Bake in a moderate oven (350° F) 25 to 30 minutes. Makes 6 dozen sticks.

# Scotchbread Dominoes

2¾ cups sifted flour
¾ cup sifted confectioners' sugar
1 cup butter
½ cup blanched almonds, finely chopped
½ teaspoon salt
1 teaspoon almond extract
1 package (1 cup) semi-sweet chocolate morsels

Sift together flour and sugar. Cut in butter until mixture has consistency of corn meal. Add almonds, salt and almond extract and blend well. Press mixture into a greased pan, 11 by 7 by 1½ inches. Pierce dough with a fork. Sprinkle chocolate morsels over top. Bake in a moderately-hot oven (375° F) 30 to 35 minutes. Makes 4 dozen bars.

# Walnut Apricot Bars

**⅔ cup dried apricots**
**¼ cup sugar**
**1⅓ cups sifted flour**
**½ cup butter or margarine**
**2 eggs**
**1 cup brown sugar, firmly packed**
**½ teaspoon baking powder**
**¼ teaspoon salt**
**½ teaspoon vanilla**
**½ cup chopped walnuts**
**Confectioners' sugar**

Rinse apricots; cover with water and boil 10 minutes. Drain, cool and chop. Sift together sugar and 1 cup of the flour. Cut in butter until mixture is crumbly. Pack into the bottom of a greased, 8-inch-square pan. Bake in a moderate oven (350° F) about 15 minutes, or until lightly browned. Beat eggs until light. Gradually beat in brown sugar and continue beating until thick. Sift remaining ⅓ cup flour with baking powder and salt. Stir into egg mixture. Fold in vanilla, nuts and apricots. Spread over baked layer. Bake in a 350° F oven about 30 minutes longer. Cool. Cut into bars and roll in confectioners' sugar. Makes about 3 dozen bars.

# Butterscotch Raisin Bars

**½ cup shortening**
**1 cup brown sugar, firmly packed**
**2 eggs, beaten**
**1 cup sifted flour**
**½ teaspoon salt**
**1 teaspoon baking powder**
**2 teaspoons grated orange rind**
**½ cup seedless raisins**

Cream together shortening and sugar until light and fluffy. Blend in eggs. Sift together flour, salt and baking powder. Blend into creamed mixture. Stir in rind and raisins. Spread in a greased, shallow pan about 7 by 10 by 1½ inches. Bake in a moderate oven (350° F) 30 to 35 minutes. Cool in pan before cutting. Makes about 36 bars.

# Raisin Coconut Bars

**⅓ cup shortening**
**1 cup brown sugar, firmly packed**
**1 egg**
**⅔ cup sifted flour**
**½ teaspoon baking powder**
**¼ teaspoon salt**
**½ teaspoon vanilla**
**¾ cup seedless raisins**
**⅓ cup shredded coconut**

Melt shortening and blend in sugar. Add egg and beat thoroughly. Sift together flour, baking powder and salt; stir into first mixture. Blend in vanilla and raisins and mix well. Spread in a greased, 8-inch-square pan. Sprinkle with coconut. Bake in a moderate oven(350° F) 30 minutes. Cool and cut into bars. Makes 2 dozen bars.

Ralston Purina Co.

# Mincemeat Bars

**7 tablespoons butter or margarine**
**½ cup brown sugar, firmly packed**
**¼ teaspoon rum extract**
**1¼ cups sifted enriched flour**
**¼ teaspoon salt**
**¼ teaspoon baking soda**
**½ cup instant or regular whole wheat cereal**
**1 cup drained prepared mincemeat**

Heat oven to moderate (350° F.). Butter an 8-inch square pan. Cream butter and sugar. Add extract. Sift together flour, salt and soda. Stir in cereal. Add to creamed mixture. Mix well to form crumbs. Pack ½ of crumb mixture in bottom of pan. Spread with mincemeat. Sprinkle remaining crumb mixture over top. Pat lightly. Bake 20 minutes or until lightly browned. Cut into 12 bars. Remove from pan. Heat bars before serving. Serve with hard sauce or ice cream. Makes 12 servings.

## NOTES

# DESSERT

Have you always dreamed of being able to bake a fabulous dessert such as Napoleons, Crêpes Suzettes or Creamy Cheese Cake? Here is the cook book to make all of your dreams and wishes a reality.

With easy to follow recipes and pictures, you will find luscious Chocolate Eclairs and Cream Puffs, a whole section on tortes and a chapter on fancy yeast breads, including breakfast Brioche and Croissants.

Pancakes for supper? Of course! When you discover the chapter on pancakes, you will find ways to roll them, stuff them, and stack them that will turn pancakes into a dessert fit for a king.

No matter if your tastes are plain or fancy; or if you are lazy or ambitious, you are sure to find a new and wonderful treat if you try any of the fancy desserts in this book.

# Cakes and Tortes

## Fresh Blueberry Cake

**2 cups fresh cultivated blueberries**
**2¼ cups flour**
**1 cup sugar**
**4 tablespoons butter**
**2 eggs**
**¾ cup milk**
**2 teaspoons baking powder**
**1 teaspoon vanilla**
**1 tablespoon butter**
**1 teaspoon cinnamon**

Wash fresh cultivated blueberries and spread on paper toweling. Sprinkle with a little sugar and let dry while making batter. In a bowl, cut butter into flour and sugar as if for a pie crust. When thoroughly mixed, take out ¾ cup of the crumb mixture and set aside. To remainder in bowl, add eggs, milk, baking powder and vanilla. Beat thoroughly until all sugar is assimilated and batter is not grainy. Pour batter into buttered 9-inch spring pan and work up around sides of pan to form a lining of dough. Place blueberries into hollow of batter. To the reserved ¾ cup of crumbs, add 1 tablespoon butter and cinnamon and work with fingers to make crumbly. Sprinkle crumbs over top of berries. Bake in a very hot oven at (450° F.) for 5 minutes. Reduce heat to (350° F.) and continue baking for 20 minutes more. Serve warm or cold. Makes 8 large servings.

The Blueberry Institute

## Petits Fours

**2¼ cups sifted cake flour**
**3 teaspoons double-acting baking powder**
**½ teaspoon salt**
**1¼ cups sugar**
**1¼ cups heavy cream**
**4 egg whites**
**1 teaspoon vanilla**

Sift together cake flour, baking powder, salt, and sugar. Whip cream until thick. Add sifted dry ingredients, egg whites and vanilla. Beat for 2 minutes in an electric mixer or 300 strokes by hand. Pour into a well-greased lightly floured 13x9x2-inch pan. Bake in a moderate oven (350°F.) 35 to 50 minutes. Cool 10 to 15 minutes; turn out on a cake rack. Cool thoroughly. Cut with fancy cutters or a sharp knife into small squares, diamonds or any desired shape. Frost with petit fours frosting. Decorate with ornamental frosting. Makes 2½ dozen petits fours.

### PETITS FOURS FROSTING

**2 cups sugar**
**1 cup water**
**⅛ teaspoon cream of tartar**
**1 to 2 cups sifted confectioners' sugar**

Combine sugar, water and cream of tartar. Cook over direct heat to a thin syrup or (226°F.) Stir only until sugar dissolves. Remove from heat and pour into the top of a double boiler and cool to lukewarm (110°F.) Add only enough confectioners' sugar so that the frosting is consistency to pour. Place a few cakes in rows on wire rack over cookie sheet, allowing space between cakes. Pour frosting over cakes, covering tops and sides, allowing frosting to drip onto cookie sheet. Scrape frosting from sheet, reheat over hot water and use for other cakes. Repeat process until all cakes are completely coated.

### ORNAMENTAL FROSTING

**2 tablespoons butter or margarine**
**2 cups sifted confectioners' sugar**
**3 tablespoons hot cream**
**½ teaspoon vanilla**

Cream butter. Blend in sugar, mixing well. Add hot cream a little at a time. Add vanilla. Blend until frosting is consistency to force through a decorating tube, adding a little more cream if needed. Place frosting in a decorating tube and decorate tops of cakes as desired. Let stand until frosting is well set.

# Party Cheese Cake

**6 3-ounce packages cream cheese**
**⅔ cup zwieback crumbs, lightly packed**
**1 teaspoon vanilla extract**
**½ cup egg whites (4 to 5 eggs)**
**1 cup sugar**
**Sweetened fresh or frozen or canned fruits**

Let cream cheese stand at room temperature until softened. Sprinkle bottom and side of a buttered 8-inch spring form pan with zwieback crumbs, pressing any extra crumbs evenly on bottom of pan. Put cream cheese into a mixing bowl. Add vanilla and cream until fluffy. Beat egg whites until foamy. Beat in sugar, ⅓ cup at a time, beating well after each addition. Then beat until whites are stiff enough to hold a peak but not dry. Fold gently into cheese. Turn into lined spring form pan. Bake in a moderate oven (350°F.) 25 minutes; center will be soft. Cool away from drafts. Then chill in refrigerator 3 to 4 hours. Remove side of spring form pan. Top with sweetened fruit before serving. Cut cake with angel food cutter or thin, sharp knife as the texture is light and moist. Makes 12 to 14 servings.

# California Cheese Cake

**1 cup ginger snap cookie crumbs, lightly packed**
**½ cup plus 1 tablespoon sugar**
**2 tablespoons butter, melted**
**4 3-ounce packages cream cheese**
**1½ teaspoons vanilla**
**2 eggs, well beaten**
**1 cup sour cream**
**2 tablespoons chopped nuts**

Combine cookie crumbs and 2 tablespoons of the sugar; blend in butter. Press mixture evenly on sides and bottom of 8-inch cake pan with a removable bottom. Let cream cheese stand at room temperature until softened; beat until fluffy. Bend in 6 tablespoons of the sugar gradually. Mix in 1 teaspoon of the vanilla. Beat in eggs. Turn into lined cake pan. Bake in a moderate oven (350°F.) about 30 minutes, or until firm in center. Remove from oven and let stand in pan, away from drafts, 5 minutes. Mix sour cream, 1 tablespoon of the sugar and ½ teaspoon of the vanilla. Spread on top of cake and sprinkle with nuts. Return to oven and bake until cream is set, about 5 minutes. Remove from oven and let cool in pan away from drafts. Remove side of pan. Chill in refrigerator about 4 hours before serving. Makes one 8-inch cake.

# Almond Cream Torte

**10 egg whites**
**1⅓ cups sugar**
**1 teaspoon vanilla**
**1⅓ cups finely ground blanched almonds**

Beat egg whites until stiff but not dry. Beat in sugar a little at a time. Add vanilla. Then fold in almonds. Pour into two 10-inch greased and floured layer cake pans. Bake in a slow oven (325°F.) for 50 minutes. Cool. Before serving spread the following filling between and on top of layers.

**10 egg yolks**
**10 tablespoons sugar**
**½ teaspoon salt**
**1 cup sweet butter**
**1 teaspoon vanilla**

Beat egg yolks, in the top of a double boiler over hot water, until creamy. Stir in sugar and salt. Remove from heat and cool. Cream butter until soft and stir into egg mixture with vanilla. Spread between and on top of torte layers. Makes 10 servings.

# Creamy Cheese Cake

**Crust:**

**6 cups cornflakes *or* 1½ cups packaged corn flake crumbs**
**⅓ cup soft butter or margarine**
**¼ cup sugar**

**Filling:**

**3 8-ounce packages cream cheese, softened**
**1⅓ cups (15-ounce can) sweetened condensed milk**
**4 eggs, separated**
**1 cup sour cream**
**1 tablespoon confectioners' sugar**
**1 teaspoon vanilla flavoring**
**1 teaspoon grated orange or lemon rind**
**½ teaspoon salt**

If using corn flakes, crush into fine crumbs. Combine corn flake crumbs, butter and sugar; mix well. Reserve ½ crumbs mixture for topping; press remainder evenly and firmly into bottom of 10-inch spring form pan.

Using electric mixer, combine cheese and milk. Increase speed while adding egg yolks, one at a time, beating well after each addition until mixture is very smooth. Decrease speed slightly and add sour cream, sugar, vanilla and orange rind. Beat egg whites with salt until stiff but not dry; fold into cheese mixture. Pour into crumb-lined pan; top with reserved crumbs mixture. Bake in slow oven (300°F.) about 1½ hours, or until knife inserted near center comes out clean. Cool in oven with door open. Do not remove from pan until completely cold. Garnish with sweetened sliced strawberries, if desired. Makes 1 10-inch cheese cake.

The Kellog Co.

# Fluffy Pecan Torte

**3 egg whites**
**1 cup sugar**
**1 teaspoon baking powder**
**Dash salt**
**1 teaspoon vanilla**
**1 cup chopped pecans**
**3 cups bite-size toasted corn cereal crushed to 1 cup**

Heat oven to moderate (350°F.). Butter generously an 8 or 9-inch pie plate. Beat egg whites until soft peaks form. Add sugar, baking powder and salt. Beat until sugar is dissolved and meringue is stiff. Stir in vanilla, pecans and cereal crumbs. Spread evenly on buttered pie plate. Bake 30 minutes or until lightly browned. Cool. Serve with ice cream or whipped cream and sprinkle with nuts. Makes 1 (8 or 9-inch) torte.

Ralston Purina

# Prize Cheese Cake

**¾ package zwieback**
**2 tablespoons butter or margarine**
**2 tablespoons sugar**
**¼ teaspoon ground cinnamon**
**1 pound cream cheese**
**2 tablespoons flour**
**½ cup sugar**
**¼ teaspoon salt**
**1 teaspoon vanilla**
**4 eggs, separated**
**1 cup light cream**
**Grated rind of 1 lemon**

Roll zwieback into fine crumbs; makes about 1½ cups. Soften butter. Blend into crumbs with sugar and cinnamon. Press three-fourths of the mixture on the bottom of a buttered 9-inch spring form baking pan. Blend together cream cheese, flour, sugar, salt and vanilla. Add egg yolks, one at a time, blending well after each yolk is added. Add cream and lemon rind; mix completely. Whip egg whites until stiff. Gently fold cheese mixture into egg whites. Pour on the crumb layer in the pan. Sprinkle remaining crumbs on the top. Bake in a moderately low oven (325°F.) 1 hour or until set in the center. Cool cake in the pan. Cut around edge of cake and carefully remove the rim of the pan. Serve from bottom round. Makes 8 to 10 servings.

# Chocolate Meringue Torte

**1 package (6-ounce) chocolate pieces**
**3 egg whites**
**1 cup sifted confectioners' sugar**
**10 soda crackers, coarsely crushed**
**½ teaspoon vanilla**
**1 pint vanilla ice cream**

Melt chocolate over hot water. Beat egg whites until stiff but not dry; gradually beat in sugar and continue beating until mixture stands in peaks. Fold in cracker crumbs, chocolate and vanilla. Cover a cookie sheet with heavy brown paper. Pour mixture on brown paper and form into two 8-inch circles. Bake in a moderate oven (350°F.) 12 minutes. Cool thoroughly. When cool, wet bottom of brown paper and peel paper off cakes. Just before serving spread ice cream between layers, top with a few scoops of ice cream. Makes 8 servings.

# Almond Torte

**6 eggs, separated**
**1 cup sugar**
**Grated rind of 1 lemon**
**Juice of 1 lemon**
**1 teaspoon cinnamon**
**1 cup ground almonds**
**¾ cup fine bread crumbs**
**¼ teaspoon salt**

Beat egg yolks until thick and light in color. Gradually beat in sugar and continue beating until light and fluffy. Add lemon rind, juice, cinnamon, almonds and bread crumbs. Blend well. Whip egg whites and salt until stiff. Fold carefully into yolk mixture. Pour into a greased 8-inch tube pan and bake in a moderate oven (350°F.) about 1 hour. Let cool in pan. Remove from pan and frost as desired. Makes one 8-inch torte.

# Genoise à la Ritz Pistache

**1 cup eggs, about 5**
**1 cup sugar**
**½ teaspoon salt**
**1 teaspoon vanilla**
**1¼ cups sifted flour**

Beat eggs until light and fluffy. Gradually add sugar, salt and vanilla and beat until thick and lemon-colored. Fold in flour, 2 tablespoons at a time. Pour batter into a 15x10-inch shallow pan which has been greased and lined with waxed paper. Bake in a moderate oven (350°F.) 18 to 20 minutes. Turn out immediately on a towel sprinkled with confectioners' sugar. Remove paper; trim edges of cake. Roll warm cake in towel, starting from 15-inch edge; cool on a rack.

**¾ cup sugar**
**2 tablespoons cornstarch**
**3 eggs**
**1½ cups milk**
**Green food coloring**
**½ cup soft butter or margarine**
**1 teaspoon vanilla**
**½ cup pistachio nuts, chopped**
**Whipped cream**

Combine sugar and cornstarch in a saucepan. Mix well. Add eggs and beat until light and fluffy. Stir in milk, and cook over low heat until thick, stirring constantly. Remove from heat. Add a few drops of food coloring to make a light delicate green color. Blend in butter and vanilla. Cool. Fold in nuts. Unroll cake and fill with pistachio nut mixture. Bring sides of cake together so they just meet. Place seam-side down on waxed paper; chill. Transfer to serving plate. Cover with whipped cream and additional whole pistachio nuts. Makes 1 cake roll.

National Banana Association

# Banana Spook Cake

**1 package (1 pound, 3 ounces) white cake mix**
**4 medium bananas, all-yellow yellow**
**1 cup sugar**
**1/4 cup lemon juice**
**1 cup heavy cream, whipped**
**1/4 cup butter or margarine**
**1/2 cup semi-sweet chocolate pieces (plus 8 pieces for decoration)**
**1 egg**
**2 medium bananas, all-yellow**
**Lemon juice**
**4 strips licorice**
**Marshmallow cat faces**

Prepare cake mix and bake in 2 layer pans according to package directions. Cool. Meanwhile, mash 4 bananas in saucepan; add sugar and 1/4 cup lemon juice. Cook, stirring constantly until mixture comes to a full boil. Chill; fold in whipped cream. Combine 1/2 cup semi-sweet chocolate pieces and butter in saucepan; cook over low heat, stirring constantly until smooth. Beat egg until frothy; gradually stir in chocolate mixture and beat until smooth. Chill until spreading consistency. Spread about 1/3 of banana cream between cake layers. Spread chocolate glaze over top of cake. Frost sides with remaining banana cream. Just before serving, halve 2 bananas and brush with lemon juice; insert chocolate pieces for eyes and licorice for mouths. Insert toothpicks in cut parts of bananas and secure spooks on top of cake. Secure marshmallow cat faces on toothpicks and insert around sides of cake.

# Peachy Cake Roll

**Cake:**
**1/4 teaspoon salt**
**3 eggs**
**3/4 cup sugar**
**1/2 teaspoon vanilla**
**3/4 cup pancake mix**

**Filling:**
**1 1/2 cups finely chopped peaches (fresh, frozen or canned, drained)**
**1 tablespoon lemon juice**
**1 teaspoon grated lemon rind**
**1 pint vanilla ice cream**

**Topping:**
**1 cup whipping cream**
**3 tablespoons confectioners' sugar**
**1/2 teaspoon vanilla**
**1/2 cup toasted flaked or shredded coconut**
**8 peach slices**

For cake, add salt to eggs; beat until thick and lemon colored. Add sugar to eggs, a little at a time, beating well after each addition. Add vanilla and pancake mix; stir until smooth. Spread evenly in greased waxed paper-lined pan. Bake in hot oven (400°F.) 8 to 10 minutes. While cake roll is baking, sprinkle a towel well with confectioners' sugar.

Immediately on taking cake from oven, loosen edges and turn out on towel. Peel waxed paper carefully from cake; trim off edges. Roll cake in towel. Let stand 20 minutes, then unroll. Combine peaches, lemon juice, rind and softened ice cream; spread over cake roll. Roll up quickly. Wrap cake roll in aluminum foil; place in freezer several hours. (May be made a day to two in advance.)

Just before serving, whip cream until stiff; fold in sugar and vanilla; frost top and sides of cake. Sprinkle with coconut. Garnish with peach slices. Makes 8 servings.

The Quaker Oats Company

## Pecan Cake

**½ pound shelled pecans**
**6 tablespoons flour**
**1 teaspoon cream of tartar**
**10 eggs, separated**
**1¼ cups sugar**
**1 teaspoon vanilla**

Put the pecans through the food grinder. Sift together flour and cream of tartar and mix with the ground nuts. Beat egg yolks until light and fluffy. Gradually beat in sugar and continue beating until yolks are thick and smooth. Stir in vanilla. Beat egg whites until very stiff. Fold flour-nut mixture into beaten egg yolks. Fold in beaten egg whites. Fit a piece of paper in the bottom of a 10-inch tube pan. Grease the paper. Pour batter into the pan. Bake in a moderately hot oven (375°F.) about 50 minutes. Invert cake and cool thoroughly. Remove from pan. Makes one cake.

## Italian Cheese Pie

**1 recipe pastry**
**1 pound Italian Ricotta cheese or small-curd cottage cheese**
**3 eggs, beaten**
**¼ cup sugar**
**½ cup chopped pistachio nuts**
**¼ teaspoon salt**
**1 tablespoon slivered citron**
**1 tablespoon chopped candied orange peel**

Line an 8-inch pie plate with ½ the pastry. Combine remaining ingredients and mix well. Pour into pastry shell. Roll out remaining dough and cut in strips. Arrange in lattice fashion on top of filling. Bake in a moderately hot oven (375°F.) 20 to 30 minutes, or until browned. Serve warm or cold.

## Applesauce Cake Roll

**3 eggs**
**1 cup sugar, divided**
**½ cup sweetened applesauce**
**1 cup sifted flour**
**½ teaspoon baking powder**
**½ teaspoon cinnamon**
**¼ teaspoon baking soda**
**¼ teaspoon salt**
**¼ teaspoon cloves**
**½ cup raisins**
**Confectioners' sugar**
**2 3-ounce packages cream cheese**
**4 tablespoons milk**
**1 tablespoon grated orange rind**

Beat eggs until very thick and lemon-colored. Gradually beat in ¾ cup of the sugar and beat well. Add applesauce. Sift together flour, baking powder, cinnamon, baking soda, salt and cloves. Fold gently into egg mixture. Add raisins. Line the bottom of a 10x15x1-inch pan with waxed paper. Grease bottom and sides of pan. Pour batter in pan. Bake in a moderately hot oven (375°F.) 20 to 25 minutes. Turn out on brown paper dusted with confectioners' sugar. Remove pan and paper from cake. Trim off any hard edges. Roll up like a jelly roll in the paper, set aside to cool. Blend together cream cheese, milk, orange rind and remaining sugar. Unroll cake. Spread cheese mixture on cake and reroll. Sprinkle top with confectioners' sugar. Makes 4 to 6 servings.

## Prune Torte

**½ cup butter**
**½ cup light brown sugar**
**1 cup sifted flour**
**½ cup chopped nuts**
**4 egg whites**
**Pinch of salt**
**½ tablespoon lemon juice**
**¼ cup plus 2 tablespoons sugar**
**½ cup cooked, pitted prunes, chopped**
**1 cup heavy cream**
**Garnish: 10 cooked pitted prunes**
**3 maraschino cherries**
**Chopped nuts**

Cream butter with brown sugar. Mix flour in thoroughly. Stir in nuts. Pat the dough into the bottom of a 9-inch cake pan that has been lined with heavy duty aluminum foil. Bake in a moderate oven (350° F.) for 20 minutes. Beat egg whites with salt and lemon juice until they are stiff. Slowly beat in sugar. Fold prunes into this mixture. Pour over mixture in cake pan. Bake in a slow oven (300° F.) for 1 hour. Whip cream. Sweeten as desired. Spread over cooled torte. Garnish with cooked prunes, nuts and maraschino cherries. Makes 10 servings.

## Columbian Torte

*(See picture between pgs. 160-161.)*

**2½ tablespoons cocoa**
**1 cup of milk**
**1 cup of sugar**
**1½ sticks of butter or margarine**
**2 eggs**
**2 cups of flour**
**1½ teaspoons baking powder**
**1 teaspoon vanilla**

Mix the cocoa, milk and ½ cup of sugar in a pan. Bring to a boil and let cool. Mix the butter (or margarine) with sugar until white and porous. Add vanilla; add eggs, one at a time. Add flour and baking powder, alternately with the cooled cocoa mixture. Pour into a greased form and bake in a moderate oven 350 degrees for 45-50 minutes. When cold, cut cake into 3 layers.

**1½ cups whipped cream**
**½-1¼ cups finely chopped nuts**
**2 tablespoons strong, cold coffee or 1 tablespoon instant coffee**
**1 can mandarin oranges**
**Rum**
**Grated chocolate**

Whip the cream and add coffee and chopped nuts. Mix mandarin juice and rum, pouring a little onto the cake layers before spreading cream between the layers. Spread the rest of the cream on top of the cake and decorate with mandarin slices and grated chocolate. Serves 12 to 16.

## Peach-Apricot Torte

**2 cups very fine zwieback crumbs**
**1 No. 2½ can cling peach halves**
**1 No. 2½ can apricot halves**
**1 cup sugar**
**3 eggs, slightly beaten**
**¾ cup sour cream**
**¼ teaspoon nutmeg**
**1½ teaspoons vanilla**
**½ teaspoon almond flavoring**

Pat ⅔ of the zwieback crumbs in the bottom of a well-greased 8-inch spring form pan. Drain the peaches and apricots thoroughly. Arrange the peaches, cut side up, on the crumbs. Fill in the spaces with apricot halves. Save a few apricots to garnish top of torte. Combine sugar, eggs, sour cream, nutmeg, vanilla and almond flavoring. Pour over fruit. Bake in a moderate oven (350°F.) 1 hour. Cool. Remove sides of pan. Garnish top of torte with apricot halves.

## Brazil Nut Torte

**½ cup sifted flour**
**2 teaspoons double-acting baking powder**
**2 cups fine graham cracker crumbs**
**½ cup butter or margarine**
**1 cup granulated sugar**
**3 egg yolks**
**¾ cup chopped Brazil nuts**
**1 teaspoon vanilla**
**1 cup milk**
**3 egg whites, stiffly beaten**
**1 package vanilla pudding or pie filling**
**1½ cups milk**
**½ cup heavy cream**

Sift together flour and baking powder; add cracker crumbs. Cream butter and sugar together until smooth. Beat in yolks singly, beating well after each addition. Add nuts and vanilla. Beat in flour mixture alternately with milk, beating well after each addition. Fold in stiffly beaten egg whites. Line bottoms of two 8-inch layer cake pans with waxed paper. Pour cake batter in tins. Bake in a moderately hot oven (375°F.) 30 minutes or until done. Cool in pans. Combine vanilla pudding with milk and cook over medium heat until mixture comes to a boil. Remove from heat and chill thoroughly. Beat pudding until smooth. Whip cream and fold into pudding. Remove cakes from pan. Split each cake layer in half crosswise, making four layers in all. Spread filling between layers and on top of cake. Refrigerate at least 1 hour before serving.

## Poppy Seed Torte

**¼ cup butter**
**½ cup sugar**
**6 eggs, separated**
**½ cup fine bread crumbs**
**¼ pound semi-sweet chocolate, melted**
**⅓ cup ground poppy seeds**
**Apricot jam**

Cream together the butter and sugar until light and fluffy. Beat egg yolks until thick and lemon-colored. Beat in the butter-sugar mixture. Add the crumbs and mix until well blended. Add chocolate and poppy seeds and mix thoroughly. Beat egg whites until stiff. Fold gently into poppy seed mixture. Pour mixture into two buttered 8-inch layer cake pans. Bake in a slow oven (325°F.) 30 minutes or until a light touch leaves no depression. Turn cake out of pans at once. When cool put layers together with apricot jam. Frost cake either with sweetened whipped cream or chocolate frosting.

## Fyrstekake

**1 cup butter**
**2 cups sifted flour**
**2 teaspoons double-action baking powder**
**½ cup sugar**
**1 egg, beaten**
**½ pound blanched almonds, cut fine**
**2 cups confectioners' sugar**
**1 egg white**
**3 tablespoons white wine**

Cut butter into the flour with a pastry blender or two knives. Add baking powder, sugar and beaten egg. Mix well. Divide dough in half. Roll out half on a lightly floured board into a rectangle 9x12 inches. Place in a greased 9x12-inch baking pan. Combine almonds, sugar, egg white and wine. Mix well and spread over bottom layer of cake. Roll out second part of dough. Cut in strips with a sharp knife and place over top of almond filling. Bake in a moderately hot oven (375°F.) 30 to 35 minutes, or until lightly browned. Makes 12 servings.

## Nut Torte

**½ package zwieback**
**1 teaspoon baking powder**
**1 cup chopped walnuts**
**4 eggs, separated**
**½ cup sugar**
**Dash of salt**
**1 cup heavy cream**

Roll zwieback into fine crumbs with a rolling pin. Mix with baking powder and nuts. Beat egg yolks until thick and lemon-colored; beat in sugar and salt and stir in crumb-nut mixture. Beat egg whites until stiff and fold into yolk mixture. Turn into two prepared 9-inch layer cake pans. Bake in a moderately hot oven (375°F.) about 10 minutes; cool. Remove from pans and put layers together with the cup of heavy cream which has been whipped and sweetened to taste. Makes one 9-inch torte.

## Meringue Nut Torte

**1½ cups finely crushed saltine crumbs**
**2 cups chopped pecans**
**2 teaspoons baking powder**
**6 egg whites**
**2 cups sugar**
**2 tablespoons almond extract**
**Sweetened whipped cream**

Be sure the saltine cracker crumbs are rolled really fine. Mix with pecans and baking powder. Beat the egg whites until stiff but not dry, add the sugar a tablespoonful at a time, beating well between each addition. Continue beating until mixture stands in stiff peaks. Beat in extract. Fold in cracker crumb mixture carefully. Grease and lightly coat with flour two 9-inch cake pans. Use the ones with removable slip bottoms if you have them. Divide mixture into cake pans. Bake in a slow oven (325°F.) about 40 minutes. Remove torte from pans and cool in a rack. Put the layers together with whipped cream. Makes 6 to 8 servings.

## Fruit Nut Torte

**1½ cups whole wheat flakes**
**¼ cup sifted flour**
**½ teaspoon baking powder**
**½ teaspoon salt**
**½ cup nuts, chopped**
**1 cup finely cut dried fruit, apricots or peaches**
**2 eggs, separated**
**1 cup brown sugar**

Crush wheat flakes into fine crumbs; combine with mixed and sifted dry ingredients. Add nuts and dried fruits. Beat egg yolks until thick and lemon-colored; beat in sugar. Stir into flour and nut mixture. Beat egg whites until stiff but not dry and fold into egg yolk mixture. Cover the bottom of an 8-inch square cake pan with waxed paper. Pour batter into pan. Bake in a slow oven (325°F.) 30 to 35 minutes. Cool. Cut into squares and serve with whipped cream if desired. Makes 16 squares.

## Grandmother's Nut Torte

**3 eggs, separated**
**6 tablespoons sugar, divided**
**6 tablespoons sifted flour**
**½ teaspoon baking powder**
**½ teaspoon salt**
**1 tablespoon dark corn syrup**
**6 tablespoons chopped nuts**
**1 cup heavy cream**

Beat the egg yolks until thick and lemon-colored. Beat in 3 tablespoons of the sugar. Beat egg whites until stiff but not dry. Gradually beat in remaining sugar. Sift flour, baking powder and salt together. Add to yolk mixture and stir until smooth. Add syrup, fold in egg whites and chopped nuts. Line the bottom of a 9-inch square cake pan with waxed paper. Pour batter into pan. Bake in a moderate oven (350°F.) 30 minutes. Cool. Whip cream and flavor to taste. Cover cake with cream before serving. Makes 6 servings.

# Lemon-Apple Cheese Cake

1 package lemon flavored gelatin
¾ cup boiling water
1 envelope unflavored gelatin
1 package (8 ounces) cream cheese
¾ cup sugar
2 cups canned apple sauce
1 teaspoon vanilla
1⅔ cups (1 tall can) evaporated milk
1 cup graham cracker or gingersnap crumbs
2 tablespoons brown sugar
¼ cup butter or margarine, melted
½ cup chopped walnuts

Thoroughly mix lemon gelatin and unflavored gelatin; add boiling water and stir until dissolved, then cool. Combine cream cheese and sugar, blend until smooth and creamy; blend in apple sauce, vanilla and cooled gelatin mixture. Chill until mixture is well thickened. At same time, in separate bowl, chill evaporated milk until icy.

Mix crumbs, brown sugar, melted butter or margarine and ¼ cup chopped nuts. Press crumb mixture firmly into the bottom and about an inch up on the sides of a greased 7 or 8-inch spring form pan.

Whip thickened apple-gelatin mixture while gradually adding chilled milk. When mixtures are blended, continue to whip on high speed until very light and fluffy and about doubled in volume. Turn into prepared pan and sprinkle top with remaining ¼ cup nuts. Chill until set, at least 5 hours, or overnight. Makes 12 servings. Variation: For a Florida Apple Cheese Cake, substitute lime flavored gelatin for the lemon.

Processed Apples Institute, Inc.

# Fig Torte

½ cup fine cookie crumbs
4 egg whites
½ cup sugar
1 teaspoon vanilla
¼ teaspoon salt
1 cup chopped nuts
1 cup chopped dried figs

Line the bottom of an 8-inch spring form pan with waxed paper. Press cookie crumbs on bottom and sides of pan. Beat egg whites until stiff but not dry; add sugar gradually and beat until mixture stands in peaks. Fold in remaining ingredients. Pour into spring form pan. Bake in a moderate oven (350°F.) about 50 minutes. Let cool in pan before removing.

# Deluxe Cheese Cake

1 cup sifted flour
¼ cup sugar
1 teaspoon grated lemon rind
¼ teaspoon vanilla
1 egg yolk
½ cup butter

Combine flour, sugar, lemon rind and vanilla. Make a well in the center and add egg yolk and butter; blend together. Wrap in waxed paper and chill in refrigerator 1 hour. Roll about ⅓ of the dough between floured pieces of waxed paper into a circle 9½ inches in diameter and ⅛ inch thick. Place on bottom of a spring form pan and trim to fit pan. Bake in a hot oven (400°F.) about 10 minutes, or until light, golden brown. Cool. Butter sides of pan and place over filled base. Roll remaining dough to a rectangle 4 inches wide and 15 inches long. Cut in half lengthwise. Line sides of pan with cookie strips.

2½ pounds cream cheese
1¾ cups sugar
3 tablespoons flour
¼ teaspoon salt
½ teaspoon grated orange rind
½ teaspoon grated lemon rind
¼ teaspoon vanilla
5 medium-sized eggs
2 egg yolks
¼ cup heavy cream

Let cream cheese stand at room temperature until softened; beat until fluffy. Combine sugar, flour, salt, fruit rinds and vanilla; blend into cream cheese gradually, keeping mixture smooth. Add eggs and egg yolks, one at a time, blending well after each addition. Gently stir in cream. Turn into lined pan. Bake in a very hot oven (500°F.) 12 to 15 minutes, or until cookie dough is light, golden brown. Reduce oven temperature to 200°F. and continue baking for 1 hour. Remove from oven and place away from drafts until well cooled. Remove side of pan.

1 quart strawberries
½ cup sugar
¼ cup water
4 teaspoons cornstarch
1 teaspoon butter
Red food coloring

Wash and hull strawberries. Crush enough berries to fill ½ cup; keep remaining berries whole. Put crushed berries, sugar, water and cornstarch in saucepan. Bring to a boil and boil 2 minutes. Stir in butter and a few drops of food coloring. Strain. Cool slightly. Arrange whole berries on top of cheese cake. Pour sauce over berries. Chill in refrigerator before serving. Makes 12 servings.

# Russian Paskha

**1 pound very dry cottage cheese**
**2 hard-cooked eggs**
**½ cup sugar**
**¼ cup sweet butter**
**2 tablespoons sour cream**
**1 vanilla bean**
**½ teaspoon salt**
**½ cup seedless raisins**
**½ teaspoon grated orange rind**

Put the cottage cheese through a very fine sieve. Then put the eggs through a sieve. Combine cheese and eggs and put through the fine sieve again. Cream together the sugar and butter. Add sour cream. Cut the vanilla bean very fine and add to butter mixture. Combine with cheese mixture. Add salt, raisins and orange rind. Press into a wooden paskha mold lined with a linen napkin. If you do not have a paskha mold, line a clean flower pot with waxed paper. Poke a hole through the wax paper where the hole is in the pot. Line the pot with a linen napkin. Press the paskha down in mold firmly. Place a saucer over the paskha and put a weight on the saucer so that the moisture is forced from the cheese. Chill in the refrigerator at least 12 hours before serving. Unmold and serve in small portions.

# Spitzer's Kirchentorte

**1 No. 2 can dark red cherries**
**½ cup brandy**
**2 cups sifted cake flour**
**2 teaspoons baking powder**
**½ teaspoon baking soda**
**½ teaspoon salt**
**½ cup butter**
**1 cup sugar**
**1 teaspoon vanilla**
**2 eggs**
**3 squares unsweetened chocolate, melted**
**1 cup milk**
**2 teaspoons instant coffee**
**1 pint heavy cream**
**Semi-sweet chocolate**

Combine cherries and brandy and let stand in refrigerator about 2 days. Stir occasionally so that all cherries can absorb brandy flavor. Sift together flour, baking powder, soda and salt. Cream butter until smooth; gradually add sugar, beating until very fluffy. Beat in vanilla and 1 tablespoon of the cherry-brandy juice. Beat in eggs, one at a time, beating well after each addition. Beat in chocolate. Combine milk and instant coffee. Add flour alternately with milk, beating until smooth after each addition. Turn into prepared 9-inch layer cake pans and bake in a moderate oven (350°F.) 30 minutes. Cool slightly, and turn cakes out of pans onto cooling racks. Whip cream until very stiff. Sweeten to taste and flavor with a little brandy. Drain cherries. Spread a thick layer of cream over one layer of cake and dot with well-drained cherries. Top with second layer. Cover top and sides with remaining whipped cream. Arrange remaining cherries on top of cake. Shave pieces of semi-sweet chocolate and place on sides of cake. Chill cake in the refrigerator for at least 12 hours before serving. Makes one 9-inch torte.

# Apricot Cheese Flan

**1 cup sifted flour**
**½ teaspoon salt**
**⅓ cup butter or margarine**
**1 egg yolk**
**2 tablespoons milk**
**1 No. 2 can apricot halves**
**2 eggs**
**1 cup cottage cheese**
**Dash of cinnamon**
**Juice of ½ lemon**
**Sour cream**

Sift together flour and salt. Cut in butter until the mixture is consistency of corn meal. Combine yolk and milk. Stir into flour mixture and mix just enough to stick together. Form into a ball and turn out on a lightly floured board. Roll out into a 10-inch circle and fit into a 9-inch layer pan. Drain apricot halves well and save juice. Spread apricots over bottom of pan. Beat eggs; beat in apricot juice and cheese. Add cinnamon and lemon juice. Pour over top of apricots. Bake in a hot oven (400°F.) about 30 minutes or until cheese custard is set. Remove from oven and let stand about 10 minutes. Spread top of flan with sour cream and sprinkle with additional cinnamon, if desired. Makes 6 servings.

# Linzer Torte

**½ cup sweet butter**
**¼ cup shortening**
**½ teaspoon brandy flavoring**
**1 teaspoon orange flavoring**
**1 cup sugar**
**2 eggs**
**1½ cups sifted flour**
**½ teaspoon baking powder**
**¼ teaspoon cinnamon**
**⅛ teaspoon cloves**
**1 tablespoon cocoa**
**1½ cups ground almonds**
**¾ cup fine white bread crumbs**
**Lingonberry jam**

Cream together butter, shortening, brandy flavoring and orange flavoring. Add sugar and beat until light and fluffy. Add eggs singly and beat well after each addition. Sift together flour, baking powder, cinnamon, cloves and cocoa. Stir into butter mixture and mix well. Fold in ground almonds and bread crumbs. Take out ¾ cup of this mixture. Pat remaining mixture about ½-inch thick on bottom and sides of a 9-inch cake pan. Cover with lingonberry jam. Roll out reserved ¾ cup of the dough on a lightly floured board about ⅛ inch thick. Cut into ½-inch strips. Arrange over filling cross-cross fashion. Cover the end of the lattice strips with another strip, circling the cake pan, press to seal. Bake in a moderate oven (350°F.) about 1 hour or until pastry edge is lightly browned and a little crisp. Remove from oven and put more jam between lattice top strips. Cool. When cold wrap in aluminum foil and store from 1 to 2 weeks to age before eating. Makes one torte.

United Fresh Fruit and Vegetable Association

# Fresh Raspberry Refrigerator Cake

**2 pints fresh raspberries**
**⅓ cup sugar**
**1 teaspoon vanilla**
**2 cups (1 pint) heavy cream**
**3 pkgs. (3 oz. each) lady fingers**

Rinse raspberries lightly and set aside to drain. Save out a few for a garnish. Add sugar and vanilla to cream and beat until it is stiff enough to stand in soft, stiff peaks. Fill an 8-inch spring form pan with alternating layers of lady fingers, raspberries and whipped cream, beginning with lady fingers and ending with cream. Chill overnight or 10 to 12 hours. Just before serving, remove sides from the spring form pan and place cake on a serving plate. Stand remaining lady fingers around the sides of mold. Garnish as desired with the raspberries saved for this purpose. Makes 10 servings.

# Peach Kuchen

**2 cups sifted flour**
**2 tablespoons sugar**
**¼ teaspoon baking powder**
**½ teaspoon salt**
**½ cup butter or margarine**
**12 peach halves, canned or fresh**
**1 cup light brown sugar**
**1 teaspoon cinnamon**
**2 egg yolks**
**1 cup heavy cream**

Mix and sift together flour, sugar, baking powder and salt. With a pastry blender or two knives cut in the butter to the consistency of corn meal. Sprinkle the mixture over the bottom and sides of a greased 9-inch cake pan. Place the peaches cut side up over the dough. Combine the brown sugar and cinnamon and sprinkle over the peach halves. Bake in a hot oven (400°F.) 15 minutes. Combine the egg yolks and cream. Pour over peaches and continue to bake 30 minutes or until browned. Cool. Serve with whipped cream, if desired. Makes 6 servings.

# Eight Layer Torte

**¾ cup sifted cake flour**
**¾ teaspoon double-acting baking powder**
**¼ teaspoon salt**
**4 eggs**
**¾ cup sugar**
**1 teaspoon vanilla**

Sift together flour, baking powder and salt. Beat eggs in a small bowl with an egg beater or at high speed of an electric mixer. Add sugar gradually and beat thoroughly until mixture becomes fluffy and thick and light-colored. Gradually fold in flour and vanilla. Pour batter into a 15x10x1-inch pan which has been lined on bottom with waxed paper. Bake in a hot oven (400°F.) 13 minutes. Turn cake out onto a cloth which has been lightly sprinkled with confectioners' sugar. Quickly remove paper and cut off crisp edges of cake. Let cool on cake rack.

**4½ squares unsweetened chocolate**
**½ cup butter**
**3 cups sifted confectioners' sugar**
**⅓ cup milk**
**2 egg whites**
**1 teaspoon vanilla**

Melt chocolate and butter together. Add sugar, milk, egg whites and vanilla. Mix well. Place in a bowl of ice and water and beat with a rotary beater until of spreading consistency. Cut cake into 4 equal parts and split each quarter horizontally through the middle, making 8 thin layers. Spread a thin layer of frosting (about ¼ cup) on a layer of cake. Place another layer of cake on top and repeat until all 8 layers of cake are used. Frost tops and sides of the torte with remaining frosting. Chill several hours before serving. Makes 12 servings.

# Mocha Torte

**2 cups shelled walnuts**
**1½ cups sifted confectioners' sugar**
**6 egg whites**

Put walnuts through the food chopper. Mix with confectioners' sugar. Beat egg whites until stiff. Fold walnut mixture into egg whites. Cover 2 baking sheets with brown paper. Draw two 8-inch circles on each sheet. Oil the circles. Smooth one-fourth of batter into each circle. Bake in a moderate oven (350°F.) 30 to 35 minutes. Cool and loosen carefully with a spatula.

**½ cup butter or margarine**
**1½ cups sifted confectioners' sugar**
**1 teaspoon vanilla**
**1 tablespoon instant coffee concentrate**
**4 egg yolks**

Beat butter until creamy. Gradually beat in sugar until soft and smooth. Add vanilla and coffee. Beat in egg yolks one at a time. Spread filling between each layer and over top of the torte. Makes one 8-inch torte.

# California Walnut Party Torte

6 eggs, separated
½ cup granulated sugar
1 tablespoon instant coffee dissolved in 3 tablespoons cold water
2 tablespoons graham cracker crumbs
2 tablespoons flour
1 cup ground walnuts
2 teaspoons baking powder
¼ teaspoon salt
½ teaspoon vanilla
2 tablespoons granulated sugar

Beat egg yolks until light and lemon colored; beat in the ½ cup sugar gradually, then beat for 5 minutes. Beat in coffee. Stir in ground walnuts, crumbs, flour, baking powder, salt and vanilla. Beat egg whites until stiff. Beat in the two tablespoons sugar and fold into yolk mixture. Turn into three 9-inch pans, greased and floured. Bake in slow oven, (300° F.) for 30 minutes, or until top springs back. Turn out and cool.

### Chocolate Filling

1 6-ounce package semi-sweet chocolate morsels (1 cup)
2 cups rich milk
2 teaspoons instant coffee
2 eggs
2 tablespoons cornstarch
2 tablespoons cold water
½ teaspoon vanilla
½ cup whipping cream

Melt chocolate morsels in milk, along with instant coffee, in top of double boiler. Beat eggs and mix in cornstarch dissolved in cold water; stir in part of the chocolate milk. Return to double boiler and cook until thickened. Stir in vanilla. Cool. Spread filling between layers and frost top with whipping cream, whipped and sweetened to taste. Makes 10 to 12 servings.

Diamond Walnuts

# Seven Layer Cake

6 eggs, separated
1¼ cups sugar
2 tablespoons lemon juice
¾ cup sifted flour
¼ cup cornstarch
½ teaspoon salt

Beat egg yolks until thick and lemon-colored. Add sugar gradually, beating constantly with a rotary beater; add 1 tablespoon lemon juice. Sift in dry ingredients alternately with remaining lemon juice, beating until smooth. Fold in stiffly beaten egg whites. Spread a few tablespoonfuls of the batter in each of two or three 8-inch round layer pans, lined on bottoms with waxed paper, then greased. Bake in a very hot oven (450°F.) about 5 minutes, or until lightly browned. Turn out on racks to cool. Remove paper. Repeat baking process until all the batter is used and 7 layers are baked.

### CHOCOLATE FROSTING

4 squares unsweetened chocolate
4 egg yolks
⅔ cup sugar
½ cup heavy cream
⅛ teaspoon salt
1¼ cups sweet butter

Melt chocolate in top part of double boiler over hot water. Beat egg yolks with sugar; add cream and salt. Pour slowly over chocolate, stirring constantly. Cook over hot water for 5 minutes, or until thickened, stirring constantly. Cream butter; add chocolate mixture, 1 tablespoonful at a time, beating until blended. Chill until of spreading consistency. Spread between layers and on top and sides of 7 layer cake.

# Linzer Torte II

1 egg
⅓ cup sugar
¼ cup sifted flour
¼ teaspoon salt
1½ cups milk
1 teaspoon vanilla
1 package thawed, frozen raspberries, undrained
2 tablespoons sugar
2 tablespoons cornstarch
1 tablespoon lemon juice

Beat egg until fluffy. Add sugar and beat until thick and lemon-colored. Blend in flour and salt. Add milk. Cook over low heat, stirring constantly, until mixture is thick and smooth. Add vanilla and cool. Combine raspberries, sugar, cornstarch and lemon juice. Bring to a boil and cook 5 to 10 minutes until mixture begins to thicken. Cool.

1½ cups sifted flour
¼ cup sugar
½ teaspoon double-acting baking powder
½ teaspoon salt
½ teaspoon cinnamon
½ cup firmly packed brown sugar
½ cup butter or margarine
1 egg
½ cup ground unblanched almonds

Sift together flour, sugar, baking powder, salt and cinnamon. Cut in brown sugar and butter. Add egg and almonds. Blend with a fork until well mixed. Take out ½ cup of this mixture and chill. Press remaining dough evenly into bottom and sides of an 8-inch pie pan (do not cover rim of pie pan). Fill with vanilla cream filling. Spread raspberry sauce over the top. Roll out remaining ½ cup of dough on a lightly floured board to ⅛-inch thickness. Cut into ½-inch strips with pastry wheel or knife. Arrange over filling, criss-cross fashion. Cover the end of the lattice strips with another strip, circling the pie but not covering rim of pie pan. Press to seal. Bake in a moderately hot oven (375°F.) 30 to 35 minutes.

R. T. French Co.

Pacific Kitchen

# Filbert Cream Crunch Cake

**1 cup chopped filberts**
**1 package angel food cake mix**
**1 package vanilla pudding mix**
**1/3 cup chopped maraschino cherries**
**1 cup whipping cream**
**3 tablespoons sugar**
**1 teaspoon vanilla**

Toast filberts 20 minutes in (275° F.) oven. Prepare angel food mix according to directions on package label. Cut cooled cake in three layers. Prepare pudding mix according to directions on package. Pile one-half of cooled pudding on bottom layer of cake. Sprinkle with 1/4 cup filberts and half the cherries. Repeat same procedure for second layer. Place third layer on top. Chill well. Swirl flavored and sweetened whipped cream on sides and top. Sprinkle sides with the remaining 1/2 cup chopped nuts. Let chill to set. Cut and serve. Makes 10 to 12 servings.

# Banana Cream Torte

**2 cups graham cracker crumbs, finely rolled**
**1/3 cup softened butter or margarine**
**2 tablespoons sugar**
**2 packages prepared vanilla pudding**
**2 bananas**
**3 egg whites**
**6 tablespoons sugar**

Combine cracker crumbs, butter and sugar. Press 2/3 of crumb mixture firmly against sides and bottom of well-buttered spring form pan. Prepare vanilla pudding according to directions on package. Cool. Pour into crumb lined pan. Slice bananas over top of pudding. Beat egg whites until stiff but not dry. Beat in sugar gradually, and continue beating until smooth and glossy. Spread meringue on top of bananas. Sprinkle remaining 1/3 crumb mixture on top of meringue. Bake in a moderate oven (350°F.) 20 minutes. Chill overnight before removing from pan. Makes 6 to 8 servings.

# Greek Nut Cake

**2 cups shelled pecans**
**1/4 cup ground zwieback**
**Grated rind of 1 medium orange**
**Grated rind of 1 large lemon**
**6 eggs**
**1/2 cup sugar**
**1/2 teaspoon vanilla**
**1 tablespoon whiskey**
**1 tablespoon water**
**1/2 teaspoon cinnamon**
**1/2 teaspoon cloves**
**1 1/2 teaspoons baking powder**
**3/4 cup honey**
**1/4 cup water**
**1 teaspoon lemon juice**

Put pecans and zwieback through the food chopper. Grate rind from orange and lemon. Separate eggs. Beat yolks until light in color. Add sugar gradually and continue beating until mixture is smooth and all the sugar is absorbed. Stir in the vanilla, whiskey, water, cinnamon, cloves, baking powder, pecans, zwieback and grated orange and lemon rind. Beat egg whites until they stand in points. Fold whites gently into yolk mixture. Pour into a greased 13x9x2-inch baking pan. Bake in a moderate oven (350°F.) about 30 minutes or until done. Cool in pan on a wire rack. Poke tiny holes in cake with a toothpick. Combine honey, water and lemon juice and cook until mixture is hot. Cool to lukewarm and pour over entire surface of cool cake in the pan. Let stand until syrup is absorbed. Cut in squares to serve.

# Danish Cinnamon Cake

**3/4 cup butter or margarine**
**3/4 cup sugar**
**1 egg**
**1 1/2 teaspoons cinnamon**
**1 1/2 cups sifted flour**
**1 1/2 cups heavy cream**

Cream butter until soft. Gradually add sugar and continue creaming until light. Add egg and beat well. Add cinnamon and flour and mix well. Spread about 1/3 of the batter on an ungreased baking sheet into a rectangle about 10x12 inches. Bake in a hot oven (400°F.) 7 to 8 minutes, or until lightly browned. Remove from oven and let stand a few minutes. Cut cake into 3 equal rectangles and transfer to cooling rack. Repeat process with the remaining batter. Whip cream until stiff. Flavor to taste. Spread a thin layer of cream between each piece of cake. Top with any remaining cream and serve immediately. Makes 6 to 8 servings.

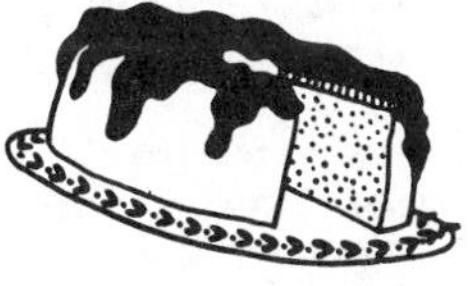

# Zuppa Inglaise

**8 eggs**
**1/2 cup sugar**
**2 tablespoons flour**
**1 quart milk**
**5 slices lemon rind**
**1 10-inch sponge cake**
**Port or sherry**

Beat eggs in the top of a double boiler. Slowly beat in sugar until mixture is thick. Add the flour and milk and blend well. Add lemon rind. Cook over hot water, stirring constantly, until mixture thickens. Allow to cool and remove lemon rind. Slice sponge cake into 3 or 4 layers. Dip a layer of the cake into the port or sherry and place on a large cake plate. Cover generously with the custard. Repeat with remaining layers. Pour remaining custard over top of cake and serve immediately. Makes 10 servings.

# Genoise

1 cup eggs, about 5
1 cup sugar
½ teaspoon salt
1 teaspoon vanilla
1¼ cups sifted flour

Beat the eggs with a rotary beater until light and fluffy. Gradually add sugar, salt and vanilla. Beat until thick and lemon-colored. Fold in flour, 2 tablespoonfuls at a time. Fold all in gently but thoroughly. Line two 8-inch cake pans with waxed paper on the bottoms. Grease well. Pour batter into cake pan. Bake in a moderate oven (350°F.) 25 to 30 minutes. Cool in pans. Remove from pans and split each layer in half to form 2 layers.

¾ cup sugar
2 tablespoons cornstarch
3 eggs
1½ cups milk
1 teaspoon vanilla
½ cup butter or margarine

Combine sugar and cornstarch in a saucepan. Mix well. Add eggs. Beat until light and fluffy. Stir in milk. Cook over medium heat, stirring constantly, until thick. Remove from heat and add vanilla. Cool. Cream butter. Add cooked sauce and blend well. Cool thoroughly. Spread between layers of cake. Spread on sides of cake. Cover top of cake with your favorite chocolate confectioners' sugar icing. Decorate sides of cake with toasted slivered almonds or grated chocolate.

# Eggnog Torte

11 egg yolks
2 cups sugar
2¼ cups sifted cake flour
2 teaspoons baking powder
⅛ teaspoon salt
1 cup milk, scalded
1½ teaspoons vanilla
½ cup melted butter or margarine
1 envelope unflavored gelatin
1 cup milk
2 eggs, separated
½ cup sugar
1 teaspoon vanilla
¼ teaspoon nutmeg
1 cup heavy cream, whipped

Beat egg yolks until very thick and lemon-colored. Add sugar slowly, beating well after each addition. Sift together flour, baking powder and salt. Add dry ingredients alternately with the milk and vanilla. Fold in melted butter and mix just enough to make a smooth batter. Line the bottom of two 9-inch cake pans with waxed paper. Pour batter into pans. Bake in a moderate oven (350°F.) 30 to 35 minutes. Cool in pans for 10 minutes. Turn out and cool thoroughly. Combine gelatin and milk. Beat egg yolks slightly with the sugar. Add to milk and cook over hot water in the top of a double boiler, stirring constantly, until mixture thickens slightly. Remove from heat. Add vanilla and nutmeg. Cool until slightly thickened. Beat egg whites until stiff. Fold in heavy cream. Fold in egg yolk mixture. Chill a few minutes longer, but do not let get stiff. Split each layer of cake into two layers. Fill between layers with custard mixture. Place in refrigerator until serving time. Just before serving frost entire cake with sweetened whipped cream.

# Cinnamon-Chocolate Sponge Roll

4 large eggs
¾ teaspoon double-acting baking powder
¼ teaspoon salt
¾ cup sugar
1 teaspoon vanilla
½ teaspoon ground cinnamon
¾ cup sifted cake flour
Cinnamon-Chocolate Frosting

Beat eggs with baking powder and salt in a bowl set over hot water (not in it) until foamy. Mix sugar with cinnamon and gradually beat into eggs. Continue beating until the mixture is very thick. Remove bowl from over the hot water and beat in vanilla. Fold in cake flour. Line a greased 15½ x 10½ x 1-inch jelly roll pan with waxed or brown paper. Grease paper. Pour batter into pan and spread it uniformly over the bottom. Bake in a preheated hot oven (400° F.) 12 to 13 minutes or until cake springs back when touched with fingers. Turn out upside down on a cloth dusted with confectioners' sugar. Quickly remove paper and trim off edges of cake. Roll up in cloth in jelly roll fashion. Cool. Unroll and spread with Cinnamon-Chocolate Frosting. Roll again. Frost outside of cake with same frosting or dust with confectioners' sugar.

### Cinnamon-Chocolate Frosting

12-ounce package semi-sweet chocolate pieces
¼ cup (½ stick) butter or margarine
sugar
⅔ cup sifted confectioners'
¾ teaspoon ground cinnamon
¼ cup evaporated milk or top milk
1 teaspoon vanilla
⅛ teaspoon salt

Melt chocolate and butter or margarine over hot water. Remove from heat. Stir in sugar, cinnamon, milk, vanilla and salt. Beat until smooth and of spreading consistency. Makes 12 servings.

American Spice Trade Association

# Brazilian Chocolate Chiffon Cake

2¼ cups sifted cake flour
1⅔ cups sugar
3 teaspoons baking powder
2 teaspoons powdered instant coffee
1 teaspoon salt
¼ teaspoon cinnamon
½ cup salad oil
6 eggs, separated
¾ cup water
2 teaspoons vanilla
3 squares unsweetened chocolate, melted
½ teaspoon cream of tartar

Mix and sift first six ingredients. Make a well and add in order, salad oil, egg yolks, water and vanilla. Beat with a spoon until smooth. Add melted chocolate and blend well. Add cream of tartar to egg whites. Beat until egg whites form very stiff peaks. Gently fold egg yolk and chocolate mixture into egg whites until well blended. Fold, do not stir. Turn batter into an ungreased 10-inch tube pan. Bake in a slow oven (325°F.) 70 to 75 minutes or until cake springs back when touched lightly with finger. Invert pan and let stand until cool. Loosen cake from sides of pan and remove.

# Chocolate Log

⅔ cup sifted cake flour
1¼ teaspoons baking powder
⅓ teaspoon salt
2½ squares unsweetened chocolate
5 eggs
1¼ cups sugar
1¼ teaspoons vanilla extract
⅓ teaspoon baking soda
4 tablespoons cold water
Confectioners' sugar

Line the bottom of a 16x11x1-inch pan with waxed paper. Grease bottom and sides of pan. Sift together flour, baking powder and salt. Melt chocolate over hot water. Beat eggs until very thick and light in color. Beat in sugar, 1 tablespoonful at a time. Sift flour mixture into beaten eggs and mix thoroughly. Combine chocolate, vanilla, baking soda and water. Add immediately to cake mixture and mix well. Pour into lined pan. Bake in a moderate oven (350°F.) 20 minutes. Remove cake from oven and dust lightly with confectioners' sugar. Turn upside down on a piece of brown paper. Remove pan and peel off waxed paper. Cut off crisp edges of cake with a knife. Roll cake up lengthwise and let stand while preparing the filling.

⅓ cup sugar
5 tablespoons flour
1 teaspoon grated orange rind
¼ teaspoon salt
1 cup milk
½ cup orange juice
1 egg

Mix sugar, flour, orange rind and salt in top part of double boiler. Add milk gradually and stir until mixture is smooth. Stir in orange juice. Cook over boiling water 10 minutes, stirring frequently. Beat egg slightly. Pour hot mixture over egg and mix well. Return mixture to double boiler and cook for 2 minutes, stirring constantly. Cool. Open chocolate roll and spread filling evenly over cake. Reroll in paper and let stand a while. Melt 2 squares unsweetened chocolate with 2 teaspoons butter over boiling water. Mix well. Place chocolate log on a plate. Swirl chocolate mixture over top while it is still hot. Makes 1 chocolate log.

# Chiffon Cheese Cake

1½ cups vanilla cookie crumbs, firmly packed
¼ cup butter, melted
3 8-ounce packages creamed cottage cheese, sieved
1 cup sugar, divided
⅓ cup flour
¼ teaspoon salt
2 tablespoons lemon juice
1 teaspoon vanilla
3 eggs, separated
1 cup heavy cream, whipped

Blend together cookie crumbs and butter. Press evenly on sides and bottom of a lightly greased 9-inch spring form pan. Combine cottage cheese, ¾ cup of the sugar, flour and salt. Stir in lemon juice and vanilla extract. Beat egg yolks until thick. Beat egg whites until stiff; gradually beat in ¼ cup of the sugar, beating until mixture forms stiff peaks. Fold egg yolks into cheese mixture; fold in whipped cream and then egg whites. Turn into lined pan. Bake in a very slow oven (300°F.) 1 hour. Turn off oven heat and let cake remain in oven one hour, with door closed. Place on a cake rack in pan and let cool. Remove side of pan. Chill in refrigerator. Makes 12 servings.

The Borden Company

# Chocolate Almond Delight

4 egg whites (at room temperature)
¼ teaspoon cream of tartar
1 cup sugar
1 teaspoon instant coffee
½ teaspoon vanilla extract
2 quarts chocolate ice cream
1 cup (½ pint) heavy cream, whipped
Chocolate sauce
Shelled blanched whole almonds

Beat egg whites until frothy; sprinkle with cream of tartar. Beat until stiff but not dry. Slowly beat in sugar (about a tablespoon at a time) adding the instant coffee with the last tablespoon of sugar. Beat until the mixture is very stiff. Fold in vanilla extract. Use a 10-inch pie plate to outline a circle on unglazed paper. Place paper on a baking sheet. Spread meringue about 1-inch deep over the circle. Evenly spoon remaining meringue around edge of circle to build up edge. Bake in slow oven (250° F.) until light brown and dry and crisp to the touch, about 1 hour. Cool away from drafts. When ready to serve fill shell with ice cream. Circle ice cream with whipped cream. Garnish with chocolate syrup and almonds. Makes 12 servings.

# Chocolate Cream Cheese Dessert

**2 packages (8 ounces each) cream cheese**
**1½ cups crushed vanilla wafers (approx. 38 wafers)**
**¼ cup melted butter**
**½ cup sugar**
**½ cup chocolate flavored mix**
**1 teaspoon vanilla extract**
**Dash salt**
**4 eggs, separated**
**1 cup (½-pint container) sour cream**
**⅓ cup sugar**
**½ cup heavy cream, optional**
**2 tablespoons sugar, optional**
**Shaved chocolate, optional**

Let cream cheese stand at room temperature until softened. In large size mixing bowl blend crushed wafers and melted butter. Evenly line well-buttered 9-inch spring form pan with crumb mixture. Refrigerate until chilled. In large size mixing bowl beat the cheese until fluffy. Combine the ½ cup sugar, chocolate-flavored mix, vanilla extract and salt; stir into slightly beaten egg yolks. Blend chocolate mixture until they hold a soft peak. Gradually whip in the ⅓ cup sugar; continue to whip until whites hold firm peaks. Gently fold into cheese mixture. Pour into crumb-lined pan. Bake in slow oven (250° F.) for 2 hours. (DO NOT OPEN OVEN DURING BAKING.) Remove from oven. Set away from drafts until well cooled. Remove sides of pan. To serve: Whip heavy cream with 2 tablespoons sugar and garnish cake with whipped cream and shaved chocolate. Makes a 9-inch cake *or* 10 to 12 servings.

**Note:** This dessert cuts best with moistened cake breaker or thin, sharp knife, as the texture is light and moist.

The Borden Company

# Cottage Cheese Cake

**1½ cups graham cracker crumbs, lightly packed**
**1¼ cups sugar, divided**
**¼ cup butter, melted**
**4 eggs**
**¼ cup flour**
**¼ teaspoon salt**
**2 tablespoons lemon juice**
**¼ teaspoon grated lemon rind**
**¾ cup heavy cream**
**3 8-ounce packages cottage cheese, sieved**

Combine cracker crumbs and ¼ cup of the sugar. Blend in butter. Press mixture evenly on sides and bottom of a greased 8-inch spring form pan. Beat eggs until thick; beat in remaining 1 cup sugar gradually; beat in flour and salt. Mix in lemon juice, rind, heavy cream and cottage cheese; beat until well blended. Turn into lined pan. Bake in a slow oven (325°F.) 1¼ hours. Turn off oven heat and let cake remain in oven 1 hour with the door closed. Place on cake rack in pan and let cool. Remove side of pan. Chill before serving. Makes 6 to 8 servings.

# Sherry-Cream Filled Angel Food Cake

**1 (10-ounce) package angel food cake mix**
**¾ teaspoon vanilla**
**¾ teaspoon almond extract**
**1 envelope plain gelatin**
**3 tablespoons cold water**
**⅔ cup sweet sherry wine**
**¼ cup sugar**
**Dash of salt**
**1 pint heavy cream, whipped**
**1 cup crushed peanut brittle**

Prepare angel food cake mix according to directions on package, adding vanilla and almond extracts to the batter. Bake in a 10-inch tube pan. Invert until thoroughly cool. Remove from pan and cut crosswise into 2 layers. Soften gelatin in cold water. Heat sherry to simmering; add gelatin, sugar and salt and stir until dissolved. Cool. Chill until mixture begins to thicken. Fold in whipped cream. Chill again just until thick enough to spread. Put cake layers together with some of the mixture between layers. Spread remaining mixture over top and sides of cake. Chill for several hours. Sprinkle peanut brittle over top of cake about 1 hour before serving. Makes 8 to 10 servings.

# Fried Cakes

## Mitzie's Doughnuts

**3½ cups sifted flour**
**4 teaspoons baking powder**
**1 teaspoon salt**
**2 egg yolks**
**½ cup sugar**
**2 tablespoons lemon juice**
**2 teaspoons grated orange rind (optional)**
**3 tablespoons corn oil or 3 tablespoons margarine, melted**
**½ cup milk**
**2 egg whites, stiffly beaten**
**Corn oil, for frying (about 1 quart)**

Sift flour, baking powder and salt together. Beat egg yolks in large mixing bowl until thick and lemon colored; gradually add sugar, beating constantly, alternately add lemon juice, orange rind and corn oil, a little at a time; then beat in 2 cups sifted dry ingredients alternately with milk, adding flour mixture in 3 additions. Fold in beaten egg whites, then remaining dry ingredients. Knead on floured board until smooth. Pat or roll out to ¼-inch thickness. Cut with floured doughnut cutter. Pour corn oil into sturdy, flat bottomed kettle or deep fryer, filling utensil ⅓ full. Heat over medium heat (375°F.) or until a 1-inch cube of bread turns brown in 40 seconds. Fry doughnuts and centers in hot oil, turning once, until golden brown on all sides, about 4 minutes. Drain on absorbent paper. If desired, roll in confectioners' sugar. Makes about 1½ dozen doughnuts and 1½ dozen centers.

*To prepare doughnut centers only:* Cut doughnut dough with 1-inch cooky cutter or center of doughnut cutter. Fry in hot oil as directed in basic recipe. Roll in confectioners' sugar and serve on toothpicks, if desired.

*Pressed doughnut variations:* Prepare dough according to above directions, reducing flour to 2⅔ cups, and baking powder to 3 teaspoons. *Do not knead.* Place dough in doughnut gun and follow manufacturer's directions for forming doughnuts. Heat oil and fry as directed above.

# Dried Pear Fritters

**8 dried pear halves**
**½ cup sifted flour**
**½ teaspoon baking powder**
**1 tablespoon sugar**
**⅛ teaspoon salt**
**⅛ teaspoon ginger**
**1 egg**
**¼ cup milk**
**½ tablespoon butter or margarine**
**2 tablespoons shortening**
**Lemon juice**

Wash pears, cut out any core or stem. Soak overnight and drain well. Sift flour, baking powder, sugar, salt and ginger. Beat egg, add milk and mix well. Add to flour mixture and stir until smooth. Add melted butter. Dip pears in batter to coat well. Brown on both sides in hot shortening in a frying pan. Drain on absorbent paper. Serve with a little lemon juice and a sprinkling of confectioners' sugar. Makes 4 servings.

# Scotch Cream Scones

**2 cups sifted flour**
**¾ teaspoon salt**
**1 teaspoon sugar**
**1 teaspoon baking powder**
**5 tablespoons butter**
**1 teaspoon soda**
**2 tablespoons water**
**1 cup sour cream**
**1 cup currants**

Sift together flour, salt, sugar and baking powder. Cut in butter with a pastry blender or two knives. Combine soda, water and sour cream and stir into flour mixture. Add currants. Turn out onto a lightly floured board. Divide dough into four parts. Pat each part into a round about ½ inch thick. Cut rounds in quarters. Cook slowly on a greased hot griddle about 20 minutes, turning frequently for even browning on both sides. Makes 16 scones.

# Cherry Crisps

**3 eggs**
**¼ cup sugar**
**1 cup sifted flour**
**⅓ cup milk**
**½ cup white wine**
**1 pound ripe red cherries**
**Deep fat**
**Confectioners' sugar**
**Cinnamon**

Beat eggs until light and frothy. Beat in sugar and flour until smooth. Add milk and wine and mix until well blended. Wash and dry cherries, retaining them in clusters as much as possible. Dip a cluster of cherries in batter and drop into deep hot fat (370°F.). When browned remove cherries and drain. Sprinkle with sugar and cinnamon and serve hot. Be careful to warn guests of the pits. Makes about 6 servings.

# Prune Fritters

**1 cup sifted all-purpose flour**
**1½ teaspoons baking powder**
**¼ teaspoon salt**
**3 tablespoons confectioners' sugar**
**⅓ cup milk**
**1 egg, beaten**
**1 cup chopped plumped prunes**
**2 tablespoons lemon juice**

Sift together flour, baking powder, salt and confectioners' sugar; gradually add milk beating until smooth. Add egg, prunes and lemon juice; mix well. Drop by teaspoons into deep hot fat heated to 375°F. Fry 3 to 5 minutes, or until delicate brown. Drain on absorbent paper. If desired, serve hot with lemon sauce or maple syrup or roll in a mixture of confectioners' sugar and cinnamon. Makes 24 fritters.

# Banana Fritters

**1 cup sifted flour**
**2 teaspoons baking powder**
**1¼ teaspoons salt**
**¼ cup sugar**
**1 egg, well beaten**
**⅓ cup milk**
**2 teaspoons melted shortening**
**3 firm yellow bananas**
**Flour**
**Deep fat for frying**

Sift together flour, baking powder, salt and sugar. Combine egg, milk and shortening. Add to dry ingredients and mix until batter is smooth. Cut bananas into 4 diagonal pieces. Roll in flour. Dip into batter, completely coating the banana pieces with the batter. Heat deep fat to a temperature of 375°F. Drop about 3 or 4 pieces of coated banana into the hot fat and cook about 6 minutes, or until well-browned. Turn fritters frequently to brown evenly. Drain on a rack. Serve piping hot for dessert with a hot fruit sauce or liberal servings of whipped cream spiced with cinnamon. Makes 12 fritters.

United Fruit Co.

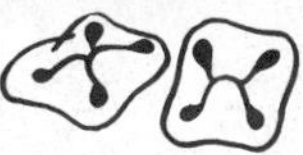

# Fried Fruit Pies

**½ pound dried prunes**
**½ pound dried apricots**
**¾ cup sugar**
**2 cups sifted flour**
**1 teaspoon salt**
**⅔ cup shortening**
**¼ cup ice water**
**Fat for frying**

Soak prunes and apricots if necessary. Simmer with just enough water to cover until tender. Cool. Pit prunes and return to pan with apricots. Stir in sugar and bring to a boil. Cool. If there is any juice left drain it off. Mix remaining pulp thoroughly. Sift together flour and salt. Cut in half the shortening with a pastry blender until the mixture resembles corn meal. Cut in remaining shortening to the size of peas. Sprinkle ice water over mixture, and toss with a fork just until dough sticks. Shape into a ball in waxed paper and chill in refrigerator about 1 hour. Divide dough into 8 parts. Roll each piece into a 5-inch circle. Place ⅛ of the filling on half of each circle, leaving ½-inch edge of pastry. Moisten the pastry edges. Fold the other half of the circle up over the filling. Seal edges. Drop into deep hot fat (375°F.). Fry until golden brown on both sides, about 5 minutes. Drain on absorbent paper. Sprinkle with sugar and serve warm. Makes 8 servings.

# Golden Coated Pears

1 can (1-pound, 14-ounces) pears
½ cup corn oil
1 cup flour
1 egg
1½ cups milk
Corn oil, for frying
Flour, for dusting

Place pears in strainer to drain. Reserve syrup for sauce. Stir corn oil into flour, mixing until smooth. Add egg to milk and add all at once to flour and oil mixture. Beat with rotary beater until smooth and the consistency of heavy cream. Heat corn oil in skillet or heavy kettle to 375°F. or until a 1-inch cube of bread browns in 30 to 40 seconds. For best results, oil should be at least 1-inch deep but should not fill the skillet more than ⅓ full. Dust pears lightly but evenly with flour. Then dip in batter to coat entire surface; lift out with fork and drain off excess batter. Lower into heated corn oil. Fry until pears are golden brown. Turn to brown both sides. Drain on absorbent paper. Serve hot with roast or warm as dessert with Cinnamon Sauce. Makes 6 servings, 2 pear halves each. Batter keeps well. Store leftover batter in refrigerator.

### Cinnamon Sauce

1½ cups syrup from pears
¼ cup red cinnamon candies
1½ tablespoons corn starch
¼ cup water

Combine syrup drained from canned pears and cinnamon candies in saucepan and set over low heat until candies are melted; stir occasionally. Increase heat to bring mixture to a boil. Combine corn starch and water; stir gradually into boiling syrup. Continue boiling, stirring constantly, until mixture is slightly thickened and clear. Serve warm or chilled. Makes about 1½ cups.

Best Foods

# Strawberry Fritters

1 pint large fresh strawberries
¾ cup apricot jam
½ cup finely chopped almonds
1 cup salted cracker crumbs
2 eggs
Fat for deep frying

Wash berries, hull and drain well. Force jam through a strainer into a bowl. Place almonds in another bowl and cracker crumbs in another bowl. Beat eggs slightly. Dip berries in jam and then roll in almonds. Dip berries in beaten egg and roll in cracker crumbs. Do all the berries and chill for several hours. Heat deep fat to a temperature of 365°F. or until a cube of bread turns golden brown in one minute. Cook fritters in deep fat a few at a time, until they are golden brown. Remove from fat and drain well. Serve plain or dipped in confectioners' sugar. Makes 4 servings.

# Wirre Gedanken

4 egg yolks
3 tablespoons confectioners' sugar
5 tablespoons white wine
2 cups sifted flour
⅛ teaspoon salt
Fat for cooking
Confectioners' sugar

Beat egg yolks until light. Beat in sugar and wine. Stir in flour and salt. Turn out on a lightly floured board and knead until smooth. Chill in the refrigerator about 1 hour. Roll dough out on a lightly floured board to about ⅛ inch thickness. Cut into 3-inch circles. Make four sharp incisions in each circle. Thread the handle of a wooden spoon in and out of each hole. Hold spoon in hot deep fat (365°F.) and when done on one side, slip off spoon, turn and brown on other side. Remove from fat and drain on absorbent paper. Sprinkle with confectioners' sugar. Makes 4 dozen.

# Cherry Fritters

1 8-ounce can pitted cherries
2 eggs
1 8-ounce package cottage cheese
½ cup fine bread crumbs
½ cup sifted flour
2 tablespoons sugar
½ teaspoon salt
Dash of nutmeg
¼ cup butter or margarine, melted
Deep fat for frying
Confectioners' sugar

Drain cherries. In a large bowl beat eggs until frothy. Add cheese, bread crumbs, flour, sugar, salt, nutmeg and melted butter. Mix until smooth. With floured hands, form dough into 1-inch balls, enclosing a cherry in center of each. Melt fat and heat to a temperature of 375°F. Drop fritters into hot fat and cook about 2 minutes, turning occasionally, until golden brown. Remove from fat and drain on absorbent paper. Sprinkle with confectioners' sugar and serve immediately. Makes 6 servings.

# Swiss Crullers

2 egg yolks, slightly beaten
1 egg white, stiffly beaten
2 tablespoons sugar
2 tablespoons cream
2 tablespoons melted butter or margarine
2 teaspoons fruit juice
1⅔ cups sifted enriched flour
Confectioners' sugar

Fold egg yolks into egg white. Add sugar and blend. Add cream, butter and fruit juice and mix well. Add flour and combine thoroughly. Chill overnight. Roll out on a lightly floured board about ¼ inch thick. Cut into diamond shapes. Make a slit in the middle of diamond and draw one end through the slit. Fry in deep hot fat (375°F.) until golden brown on both sides. Drain on absorbent paper and sprinkle with confectioners' sugar. Makes about 2 dozencrullers.

# Fastnachts

3 medium potatoes, peeled and quartered
2 cups salted water
¾ cup sugar
1 teaspoon salt
7 to 8 cups sifted flour
1 package or cake yeast, active dry or compressed
¼ cup lukewarm water
½ cup soft butter or margarine
2 eggs
½ teaspoon nutmeg

Boil potatoes in salted water until tender. Drain; reserve 1 cup of water and pour into a large mixing bowl. Stir in sugar, salt and 1 cup of the flour. Beat until smooth. Add yeast to lukewarm water (warm, not hot, for active dry yeast; lukewarm for compressed yeast). Stir until dissolved. Stir into batter. Cover bowl with a cloth and let stand in a warm place until bubbly, about 4 hours. Mash hot potatoes, measure 1 cup into a mixing bowl and beat in butter, eggs and nutmeg. Stir potato mixture into yeast batter and add remaining flour or enough to make a stiff dough. Turn out on a lightly floured board and knead until smooth and elastic. Place dough in a greased bowl, cover and let rise in a warm place until double in bulk. Punch dough down and store in refrigerator until ready to use. Divide dough in half. Roll each half out on a lightly floured board to about ⅓ inch thick. Cut with a doughnut cutter. Place doughnuts on a floured board, cover with a cloth and let rise in a warm place until double in bulk. Drop doughnuts singly in deep hot fat (365°F.). Fry about 4 at one time. When they rise to the surface, turn with a long-handled fork to brown both sides. Drain on absorbent paper and sprinkle with sugar, if desired. Makes about 4 dozen Fastnachts.

# St. Joseph's Cream Puffs

½ cup butter
1 cup water
1 cup sifted flour
¼ teaspoon salt
4 eggs
1 tablespoon sugar
½ teaspoon grated orange rind
½ teaspoon grated lemon rind

Bring butter and water to a boil in a saucepan. Add flour all at once and stir vigorously over low heat until mixture forms a ball. Remove from heat. Add salt. Add eggs one at a time and beat well after each addition until mixture is smooth. Add sugar and orange and lemon rinds. Drop mixture by spoonfuls into deep hot fat (350°F.). Fry until golden brown and puffed.

1 pound ricotta cheese
2 tablespoons chocolate chips
1 tablespoon chopped candied orange peel
2 tablespoons crème de cacao
2 tablespoons sugar

Cream ricotta until smooth. Add remaining ingredients and mix thoroughly. When cream puffs are cool, split and fill with this ricotta filling. Makes 15 puffs.

# Russian Sirniki

3 pounds dry cottage cheese
3 tablespoons sour cream
4 eggs, beaten
1 tablespoon sugar
¼ cup sifted flour
Sour cream
Jam

Combine cottage cheese, sour cream, eggs, sugar and flour and beat well. Drop by spoonfuls into a hot buttered skillet and fry cakes until golden brown on both sides. Serve piping hot with sour cream and jam. Makes about 3 dozen cakes.

# Apple Fritters

1 cup sifted all-purpose flour
1½ teaspoons baking powder
3 tablespoons confectioners' sugar
¼ teaspoon salt
2½ cups well-drained canned apple slices
1 egg
Mace Sauce

Sift together flour, baking powder, salt and sugar. Drain apples; add. Beat egg; add. Mix well. Drop individual apple slices into deep fat or salad oil heated to 375°F.; fry, turning to brown all sides. Drain on absorbent paper; sprinkle with confectioners' sugar. Serve hot with sauce. Makes 6 servings.

### Mace Sauce

1½ cups apple juice
⅓ cup sugar
4 teaspoons cornstarch
½ teaspoon mace
2 tablespoons butter
Few grains salt
1 teaspoon lemon juice

Combine sugar, cornstarch, salt and mace; gradually add apple juice, stirring until blended. Cook, stirring constantly, until thickened. Add lemon juice and butter, stirring until melted. Makes 6 servings.

Processed Apples Institute

# French Fried Cookies

2 egg yolks
3 tablespoons butter or margarine, melted
3 tablespoons sugar
Dash of salt
1 teaspoon vanilla
4 tablespoons port wine
2¼ cups sifted flour
Apricot preserves

Beat together egg yolks, butter, sugar and salt. Add vanilla and wine. Add flour and stir to make a stiff dough. Wrap in waxed paper and chill in refrigerator for 1 hour. Roll dough out on a lightly floured board about ½ inch thick. Cut dough in 3-inch circles. Wet edges of circles with water. Place a teaspoon of preserves on cookie, fold over, and press wet edges together with a fork. Prick on top. Fry in deep hot fat (375°F.) until golden brown. Drain and sprinkle with confectioners' sugar. Serve hot or cold. Makes about 2 dozen cookies.

# Glazed Doughnut Puffs

2 tablespoons butter or margarine
½ cup sugar
2 eggs, well beaten
2 cups sifted flour
2 teaspoons baking powder
½ teaspoon salt
¼ teaspoon nutmeg
½ teaspoon mace
½ cup milk
2 teaspoons light corn syrup
2 tablespoons rum
1½ cups sifted confectioners' sugar
3 tablespoons hot water

Cream butter and sugar together until light and fluffy. Add eggs and beat well. Sift dry ingredients together and add, alternately with milk, to the first mixture. Chill dough thoroughly. Drop by rounded tablespoonfuls in deep hot fat (375°F.). As doughnuts rise to the surface turn, and turn again to brown all sides thoroughly. Drain on absorbent paper. Combine corn syrup, rum, confectioners' sugar and hot water to make a thin glaze. Dip doughnuts in this mixture while still warm. Makes 2½ dozen doughnut puffs.

# French Apple Fritters

1 egg, separated
1 teaspoon water
1 tablespoon oil
⅛ teaspoon salt
⅔ cup sifted flour
2 medium-sized apples
Confectioners' sugar

Beat egg yolk well with water, oil and salt. Add flour and beat well until smooth. Let stand at room temperature for about 2 hours. Peel and core apples. Cut into ¼-inch wedges. Just before frying, beat egg white until stiff. Fold into batter mixture. Dip apple slices into batter. Fry in hot deep fat (375°F.) until golden brown. Drain. Sprinkle with sugar before serving. Makes 4 to 6 servings.

# Fried Spice Balls

2 cups prepared biscuit mix
2 tablespoons sugar
½ teaspoon nutmeg
1 egg
1 tablespoon salad oil
Milk
Fat for deep frying
½ cup sugar
1 teaspoon cinnamon

Combine biscuit mix, sugar and nutmeg. Break the egg into a measuring cup. Beat with a fork, add the salad oil and enough milk to make ½ cup liquid. Beat until blended. Pour all at once over biscuit mix, stirring until just damp enough to drop from spoon. Heat fat to 375°F. Drop dough by teaspoonfuls into hot fat and fry about 2 minutes, turning to brown both sides. Drain on absorbent paper. Roll in sugar and cinnamon mixture. Makes 1½ dozen balls.

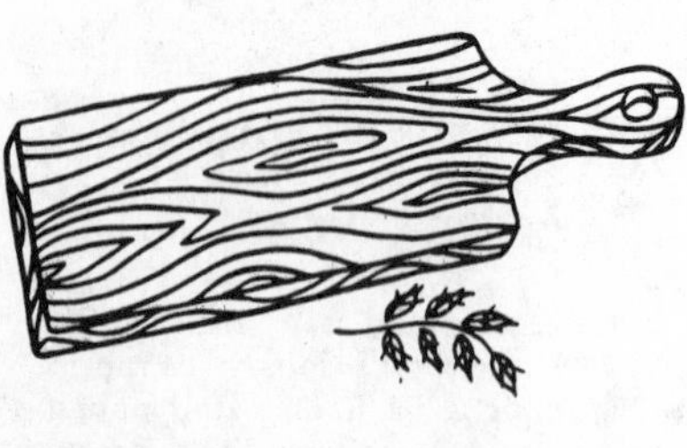

# Shrove Tuesday Cakes

2 cups sifted flour
¼ cup corn starch
2 tablespoons milk
2 tablespoons light cream
1 tablespoon margarine, melted
1 teaspoon kirsch (optional)
¼ teaspoon salt
3 eggs
1 quart corn oil (for frying)
Confectioners' sugar

Sift flour and corn starch together. Combine milk, cream, margarine, kirsch, salt and eggs; beat well with rotary beater. Stir in flour mixture, mixing until dough forms. Knead on floured board or cloth until dough is smooth and elastic, about 5 minutes. Cover; let rest in warm place 30 minutes. Divide into 16 equal parts. Roll out two parts to 3-inch circles on floured board, keeping other portions of dough covered. Sprinkle one circle generously with flour; place second circle on top. Roll out to thin circle, then carefully separate two pieces, over back of hand, if necessary. Stretch, if needed, to form 7-inch circles. Dust off excess flour and place circles between two layers of clean cloth. Continue rolling until all 16 pieces of dough are thin, 7-inch circles; keep covered. Then heat corn oil in deep skillet or large heavy saucepan to 375°F. (Oil must be at least 1-inch deep, but should not fill utensil more than ⅓ full). Drop two circles into hot oil, one at a time, and fry turning once, until light brown on both sides (about 2 minutes). Remove both cakes together; do not separate. Place in low oven to keep warm, if desired. Continue frying until all cakes have been cooked. Dust with confectioners' sugar before serving. Makes 8 cakes.

**Note:** If dough is rolled slightly larger than pan used for frying, edges of cakes will curl up and be more attractive.

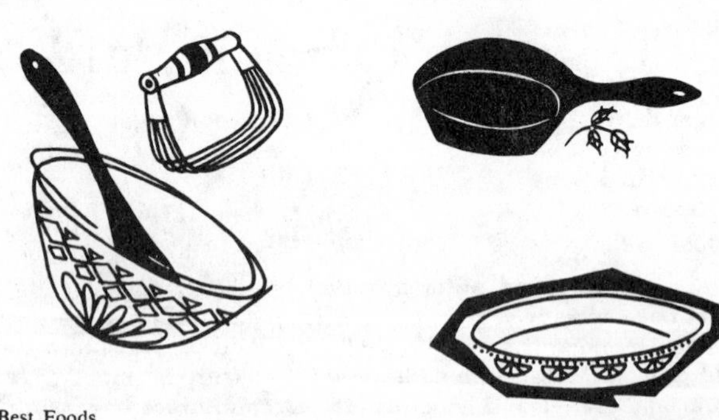

Best Foods

# Fried Cake

1 medium-sized stale spongecake
¼ cup milk
¼ cup heavy cream
1 tablespoon sugar
⅛ teaspoon vanilla
1 egg yolk
Pinch of salt
½ cup warm water
½ cup flour
2 egg whites, stiffly beaten
2 tablespoons butter, melted

Cut spongecake in slices ⅓ inch thick. Cut into round or square shapes with a cookie cutter. Combine milk, cream, sugar and vanilla. Dip pieces of cake in this mixture and allow to drain on absorbent paper. Combine egg yolk, salt and water and beat well. Stir in flour. Fold in egg whites and butter. Dip cake pieces in this batter and fry in deep hot fat (365°F.) until lightly browned on both sides. Serve piping hot, sprinkled with sugar if desired.

# Swiss Twists

1 cup light cream
2 eggs, well beaten
¼ teaspoon salt
2 cups sifted flour
½ cup butter
Sugar

Combine cream, eggs and salt and mix well. Add flour to make a soft dough. Turn onto a lightly floured board, dot with butter and work into the dough. Butter should be firm but not hard. Place dough in refrigerator several hours. Roll out on a lightly floured board about ⅛ inch thick. Cut into diamond or oblong shapes. Slash each cookie through the center with ½-inch gash. Fry in deep hot fat (375°F.) until browned. Drain on absorbent paper. Roll in granulated sugar while hot. Makes about 3 dozen twists.

# Banana Doughnuts

5 cups sifted flour
4 teaspoons baking powder
1 teaspoon soda
2 teaspoons salt
1 teaspoon nutmeg
¼ cup shortening
1 cup sugar
3 eggs, well beaten
¾ cup mashed bananas (about 2 bananas)
½ cup sour milk or buttermilk
1½ teaspoons vanilla
Fat for deep frying

Sift together flour, baking powder, soda, salt and nutmeg. Beat shortening until creamy. Add sugar gradually and continue beating until light and fluffy. Add eggs and beat well. Add combined bananas, milk and vanilla to creamed mixture and blend. Add flour mixture and mix until smooth. Turn a small amount of dough onto a lightly floured board. Knead very lightly. Roll dough out to ⅜-inch thickness. Cut with a floured 2½-inch doughnut cutter. Heat fat to 375°F. or until a 1-inch cube of bread will turn golden brown in about 40 seconds. Slip doughnuts, a couple at a time into the hot fat. Fry about 3 minutes, or until golden brown. Drain on absorbent paper. Makes 3½ dozen.

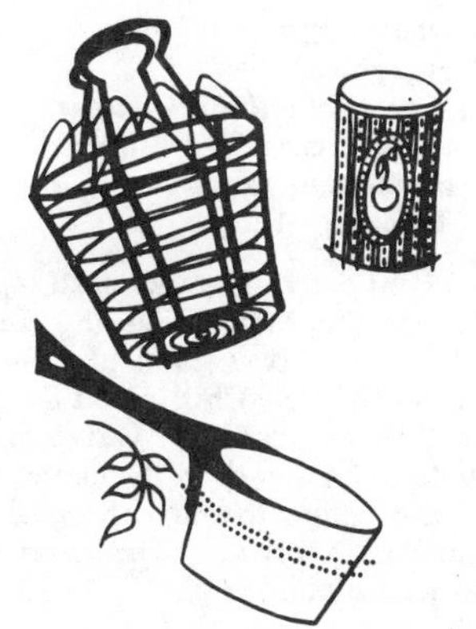

Best Foods

# Fruit Fritters

1 cup sifted flour
1 teaspoon baking powder
½ teaspoon salt
1 tablespoon sugar
2 egg yolks
¼ cup milk
1 tablespoon corn oil
1½ cup blueberries or chopped fruit
2 egg whites, stiffly beaten
Corn oil, for frying
Light, dark or mapley corn syrup

Sift together flour, baking powder, salt and sugar. Combine egg yolks, milk and corn oil. Add to dry ingredients; mix until well blended. Add fruit. Fold in stiffly beaten egg whites. For shallow frying, pour corn oil into skillet to a 1-inch depth. For deep frying, fill kettle ⅓ full. Heat oil to 375°F. Drop fritters by tablespoonfuls into hot oil and fry 3 to 4 minutes turning to brown evenly. Fry only a few fritters at a time. Drain on absorbent paper. Makes 4 to 6 servings. If desired, fritters may be pan fried. Heat about ½ cup corn oil in a skillet. Fry fritters to a golden brown on one side. Turn to brown on other side. Serve warm with corn syrup flavor of your choice.

# Apple Ring Fritters

**4 medium-sized tart apples**
**1 tablespoon lemon juice**
**1 teaspoon sugar**
**1 cup sifted flour**
**1½ teaspoons baking powder**
**¼ cup sugar**
**1½ teaspoons salt**
**1 egg, beaten**
**⅓ cup milk**
**1 tablespoon melted shortening**

Pare and core apples. Cut in ½-inch slices crosswise. Sprinkle slices with lemon juice and sugar and let stand. Sift together flour, baking powder, sugar and salt into a mixing bowl. Add combined egg, milk and shortening and beat until smooth. Dip apple rings in batter. Fry a few at a time in deep hot fat (375°F.) about 4 minutes, or until golden brown. Drain on absorbent paper. Serve piping hot with the following sauce.

**1 cup brown sugar**
**1 tablespoon cornstarch**
**¼ teaspoon cinnamon**
**⅛ teaspoon nutmeg**
**Dash of salt**
**1 cup apple juice**
**1 tablespoon butter or margarine**

Mix first five ingredients in a saucepan. Add apple juice and butter. Bring to a boil and boil 3 minutes. Keep hot to serve with apple rings. Makes about 12 fritters.

# Sockerstruvor (Rosettes)

**2 eggs**
**2 teaspoons sugar**
**1 cup milk**
**¼ teaspoon salt**
**1 teaspoon almond flavoring**
**1 cup sifted flour**
**Fat for deep frying**
**Confectioners' sugar**

Beat eggs until very light. Beat in sugar, milk, salt and flavoring. Finally beat in flour and continue beating until a smooth batter is formed. Heat fat to 365°F. or until a one-inch cube of bread browns in one minute. Heat Rosette Iron in hot fat. Dip hot iron in batter so that the batter comes just short of the top of the iron. Lower batter covered iron into hot fat and fry until delicately browned. If the rosette falls off the iron, fish it off with a fork when it is delicately browned. Drain on absorbent paper. Serve hot or cold sprinkled with confectioners' sugar. Makes about 35 rosettes.

You'll need a rosette iron in order to prepare Sockerstruvor.

Roll dough out as thin as possible, then cut dough into strips 2 inches long by 1 inch wide.

Fry in deep hot fat (365°F.) until light brown and drain on absorbent paper for the final step.

# Swedish Fattig Man

**2 whole eggs**
**2 egg yolks**
**¼ cup confectioners' sugar**
**2 teaspoons melted butter**
**1 tablespoon brandy flavoring**
**1 tablespoon grated lemon rind**
**1¾ cups sifted flour**
**Fat for frying**

Beat eggs and yolks until light and fluffy. Add sugar, butter, brandy and lemon rind and continue beating. Add flour gradually and mix well. Turn out on a lightly floured board and knead lightly. Chill. Roll dough out on a lightly floured board as thin as possible. Cut into strips 2 inches long by 1 inch wide. Cut a gash in the center of each strip and pull one corner of the dough through the gash. Fry in deep hot fat (365°F.) until light brown. Drain on absorbent paper. Makes about 50 Fattig Man.

Wrap cannoli around aluminum tubes or sticks; fill each shell, then sprinkle with confectioners' sugar.

Be sure to leave puffs in hot fat long enough to puff up just like cream puffs baked in oven, then drain.

# Fried Ribbon Cookies

**4 eggs**
**4 tablespoons sugar**
**¾ teaspoon salt**
**4 tablespoons butter, melted**
**2¾ cups sifted flour**
**2 teaspoons anise extract**
**2 teaspoons water**
**Confectioners' sugar**

Beat eggs until thick and lemon-colored. Gradually add sugar and salt and beat until dissolved. Stir in butter. Add half the flour and blend well. Stir in anise extract and water. Add remaining flour to make a stiff dough. Chill 15 minutes. Divide the dough into 5 or 6 parts. Roll one part at a time out on a lightly floured board until dough is nearly transparent. With a pastry wheel cut dough into strips 1 inch wide and 6 inches long. Roll strips very loosely over first two fingers. Slip ribbon of cookie onto tines of a large meat fork. Place cookie in hot deep fat (365°F.). As soon as the dough rises to the surface it will begin to unroll. As soon as it unrolls, twist it back into a roll again with the meat fork. Hold dough loosely against side of pan for a minute or two until the dough sets. Brown lightly on both sides. Drain on absorbent paper and sprinkle with confectioners' sugar. Makes about 120 cookies.

# Italian Cannoli

**3 cups sifted flour**
**½ teaspoon cinnamon**
**¼ teaspoon salt**
**1 tablespoon sugar**
**1 tablespoon butter**
**1 egg, beaten**
**2 tablespoons water**
**4 tablespoons white wine**
**Fat for frying**
**¼ cup chopped pistachio nuts**
**Confectioners' sugar**

Sift together flour, cinnamon, salt and sugar. Cut in butter. Add egg, water and wine and stir until stiff dough is formed. Turn out on a lightly floured board and knead until soft and smooth. Divide dough in half and chill for 30 minutes. Roll each half out to ⅛ inch thickness. Cut into 4-inch squares. Wrap each piece around aluminum tubes or wooden sticks about ¾ inch thick and 6 inches long. (If you have no aluminum tubes, 6-inch lengths of a thin broomstick work very well). Press edges together to seal, but do not press dough firmly against tube. Drop into hot deep fat (365°F.) and cook until dark brown. Remove cannoli carefully from sticks and cool.

**1¼ pounds pot cheese**
**5 tablespoons sugar**
**½ cup milk**
**1 tablespoon almond extract**
**1 tablespoon chopped candied fruit**
**1 tablespoon grated orange rind**

Combine cheese, sugar, milk and almond extract. Rub through a fine sieve. Add fruit and rind and blend well. Fill each cannoli shell. Dip ends in chopped nuts and sprinkle whole cannoli with confectioners' sugar. Makes about 20 cannoli.

# Miniature Puffs

**½ cup butter**
**1 cup boiling water**
**1 cup sifted flour**
**½ teaspoon salt**
**4 eggs**
**½ teaspoon vanilla**
**Fat for frying**

Melt butter in a saucepan; add boiling water. Add flour and salt all at once. Cook over medium heat, stirring constantly, until mixture leaves sides of pan and is smooth and compact, about 2 minutes. Remove from heat and cool about 1 minute. Beat in eggs, one at a time, beating vigorously after each addition until mixture is smooth and glossy. Add vanilla. Drop by teaspoonfuls into deep hot fat (365°F.). Fry for 4 to 6 minutes, or until golden brown. Be sure to leave them in the hot fat long enough to puff up just like cream puffs baked in the oven. Drain on absorbent paper. Sprinkle with confectioners' sugar and serve hot or cold. These may also be split open and filled as desired. Makes about 4 dozen miniature puffs.

# Koesisters

**2 tablespoons warm water**
**1 package or cake yeast, active dry or compressed**
**3 cups sifted enriched flour**
**1 cup brown sugar, firmly packed**
**½ cup butter or margarine**
**2 teaspoons cinnamon**
**1 teaspoon allspice**
**½ teaspoon salt**
**4 eggs, beaten**

Measure water into a large mixing bowl (warm, not hot water for active dry yeast; lukewarm for compressed yeast). Sprinkle or crumble in yeast. Stir until dissolved. Mix flour and sugar. Cut in butter or margarine. Add cinnamon, allspice and salt and mix thoroughly. Add eggs and yeast and beat well. Turn out on a lightly floured board and knead until smooth and satiny, adding more flour if necessary. Place in a lightly greased bowl. Cover. Let rise in a warm place, free from draft, until light, about 2 hours. Knead lightly again. Roll out on a lightly floured board about ¼ inch thick. Cut in 1½-inch squares. Place on a lightly greased baking sheet and let rise in a warm place, free from draft, overnight. Fry in deep hot fat (375°F.) until brown on both sides. Drain on absorbent paper. When cool dip in following syrup. Drain on a cooling rack. Serve when dry. Makes about 4 dozen.

Syrup:

**1¼ cups sugar**
**¼ teaspoon cinnamon**
**1 cup water**

Combine ingredients in a saucepan. Bring to a boil and boil about 5 minutes. Cool before using.

# French Market Doughnuts

**½ cup warm water**
**2 tablespoons corn oil**
**⅓ cup sugar**
**½ teaspoon salt**
**½ cup evaporated milk**
**¼ cup warm, not hot, water**
**1 package active dry yeast or 1 cake compressed yeast**
**4 cups sifted flour, about**
**2 eggs, beaten**
**Corn oil, for frying**

In a large mixing bowl combine warm water, corn oil, sugar, salt and evaporated milk. Sprinkle dry yeast into ¼ cup warm (not hot) water. (Crumble compressed yeast into lukewarm water.) Stir until dissolved. Add corn oil mixture. Stir in flour and eggs alternately, beating hard and briskly. If necessary add more flour to make a soft dough. Turn out on a lightly floured board, and knead dough lightly for about 5 minutes or until smooth and elastic. Place dough into an oiled bowl; brush lightly with corn oil; cover with a cloth and let stand for about ½ hour. The dough will not be doubled. Divide dough in half. Keep unused portion of dough covered. On a lightly floured board roll ½ dough at a time into a rectangle about ½-inch thick. Cut into small rectangles or triangles, about 1½ inches. Stretch with fingers until double in size and thin. Pieces should be slightly thinner in center. Fill a sturdy, flat-bottomed saucepan ⅓ full with corn oil. (Use 1-quart corn oil in a 3-quart pan.) Heat to 375°F. Add doughnuts slowly when correct temperature is reached. Fry only one layer at a time. Turn to cook and brown all sides evenly, about 2 to 4 minutes. Drain on absorbent paper. Dust with confectioners' sugar; serve hot if possible. Makes 4 dozen.

Best Foods

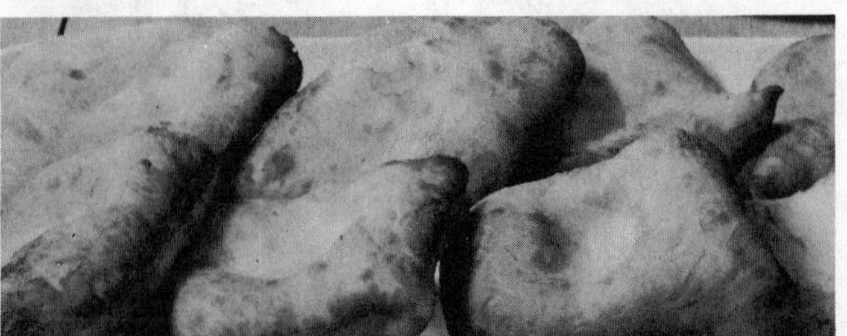

# Dessert Pancakes

## Fudge Nut Pancakes

**1½ squares (1½ ounces) unsweetened chocolate**
**3 tablespoons butter or margarine**
**1 cup sifted enriched flour**
**¾ cup sugar**
**2 teaspoons baking powder**
**½ teaspoon salt**
**½ teaspoon soda**
**⅔ cup bite-size shredded wheat biscuits crushed to ⅓ cup**
**½ cup chopped nuts**
**1 egg**
**1½ cups sour milk**
**1 teaspoon vanilla**

Melt chocolate and butter together over low heat. Cool slightly. Sift together flour, sugar, baking powder, salt and soda. Stir in cereal crumbs and nuts. Beat egg and cooled chocolate mixture. Beat in milk and vanilla. Add to dry ingredients. Stir just until blended. Pour from the tip of a large spoon onto hot griddle (about 1½ tablespoons of batter for a 2-inch pancake). Turn pancakes when puffed and bubbly. Brown on other side. To keep pancakes warm, place between folds of a towel and keep in a very slow oven (200° F.) until ready to serve. Serve with ice cream and chocolate sauce. Makes about 32—2-inch pancakes.

**Note:** These can be frozen, thawed and reheated between folds of a towel in a slow oven (300° F.) 15-20 minutes.

Ralston Purina

# Blintzes

**¾ cup sifted cake flour**
**¼ teaspoon soda**
**½ teaspoon salt**
**2 tablespoons sugar**
**3 eggs**
**2 tablespoons melted butter**
**1½ cups buttermilk**
**Cheese Filling, recipe below**
**Sour Cream**
**Cherry preserves**

Sift together flour, soda, salt and sugar. In a mixing bowl, beat eggs, butter and buttermilk. Add the dry mixture and beat until very smooth. Lightly grease a hot 7" skillet. Pour in 3 tablespoons of the batter at a time, tipping the pan quickly to spread batter over bottom. Fry each pancake slowly until lightly browned on one side only. Remove from skillet and stack pancakes brown side up on flat plate until cool. Place 1½ tablespoons of the Cheese Filling in center of each pancake on the browned side. Fold over the 4 edges to the middle and fry both sides in greased skillet until golden brown. Serve hot with sour cream and cherry preserves. Makes 20 Blintzes.

### Cheese Filling

**2½ cups creamed cottage cheese**
**3 tablespoons confectioners' sugar**
**3 egg yolks**
**¼ teaspoon salt**
**¾ teaspoon vanilla**
**¾ teaspoon ground cinnamon**

Combine ingredients thoroughly. Makes 2½ cups of filling.

### Crêpes

To make crêpes, follow recipe for Blintzes but brown crêpes on both sides turning only once. Serve with your favorite crêpe sauce. 20 Crêpes.

# Ice Cream Pancakes

**1 cup milk**
**2 eggs, beaten**
**½ cup pancake mix**
**1 pint vanilla ice cream**

Add milk to beaten eggs and blend well. Sprinkle pancake mix over surface of milk mixture; beat with a rotary beater until smooth and free from lumps. Pour about 2 tablespoons of the batter into a lightly greased 6-inch hot skillet. Cook over medium heat, until bubbles form over entire surface. Turn and cook other side. Remove from skillet to flat oven dish. Keep pancakes in warm oven while cooking remaining batter. Fill each pancake with spoonfuls of ice cream. Roll or fold edges of pancake around ice cream. Serve immediately. Makes 12 pancakes.

# German Pancakes

**3 eggs**
**¾ cup sifted flour**
**⅛ teaspoon salt**
**1 teaspoon sugar**
**1 cup milk**
**Butter or margarine**
**Cinnamon**
**1 lemon**
**Huckleberries, cooked and sweetened**

Beat eggs lightly. Beat in flour, salt, sugar and milk. Beat until batter is smooth and light. Melt enough butter in a large skillet to cover bottom and sides. The skillet should be at least 12 to 18 inches across. When hot pour in 4 to 6 tablespoons of the batter. Turn pan to make batter spread all over bottom. Cook until small bubbles are formed. Turn and brown other side. Slip onto a large hot platter. Sprinkle generously with sugar and cinnamon. Squeeze lemon juice over top of pancake. Cover with huckleberries. Roll quickly like a jelly roll. Sprinkle with sugar and cinnamon. Cut in half to serve 2 people. This recipe will make 2 or 3 pancakes, enough to serve about 6 people generously.

# Peach Crêpes

**¾ cup sifted enriched flour**
**¼ cup sugar**
**Pinch salt**
**⅔ cup bite-size shredded wheat biscuits crushed to ⅓ cup**
**3 eggs**
**1½ cups milk**
**1 tablespoon melted butter or margarine**
**1 egg white**
**3 medium peaches, finely diced (about 2 cups)**
**¼ cup sugar**
**¼ teaspoon ginger**
**3 tablespoons brown sugar**
**3 tablespoons melted butter**

### Crêpes

Sift together flour, sugar and salt. Stir in cereal crumbs. Beat eggs, milk and butter. Stir into dry ingredients. Stir until smooth. Let batter stand 2 hours. Heat lightly buttered 5—6-inch skillet. Stir batter. Spoon 2 tablespoons batter into skillet. Rotate pan to spread batter evenly. Cook over high heat ½ minute on each side or until slightly brown. Stack to keep warm. Fill with Peach Filling.

### Peach Filling

Heat oven to hot (400° F.). Butter baking dish. Beat egg white until soft peaks form. Fold in peaches, sugar and ginger. Fill crêpes with 1 heaping tablespoon. Fold or roll. Place in baking dish. Combine brown sugar and butter. Spoon over crêpes. Bake 10 minutes, or until brown sugar glazes crêpes. Makes 18 crêpes.

Ralston Purina

# Ginger Peach Pancakes

**½ cup flour**
**1 tablespoon sugar**
**⅛ teaspoon salt**
**2 eggs, well beaten**
**⅔ cup milk**
**1 tablespoon butter, melted**
**¼ teaspoon grated lemon rind**

Sift flour, sugar and salt. Combine eggs, milk, butter and lemon rind. Stir into flour mixture and mix until smooth. Heat a small 6-inch skillet over medium heat. Grease lightly with butter. Pour about 2 tablespoons of the batter into skillet, quickly tilt skillet to spread in a thin layer. Bake until set and browned; turn and brown on other side. Grease skillet again if necessary. As each pancake is baked, place on a shallow pan and roll. Cover with a clean towel.

**1 No. 2½ can sliced peaches**
**1½ tablespoons finely chopped crystallized ginger**
**2 teaspoons grated lemon rind**
**¼ cup sugar**
**1½ tablespoons cornstarch**
**Pinch of salt**
**1 tablespoon butter or margarine**

Drain syrup from peaches. Chop peaches into small pieces, stir in 1 tablespoon ginger and lemon rind. Let stand about 1 hour. Measure peach syrup and add enough water to make 1¾ cups liquid. Combine sugar, cornstarch, remaining ginger and salt in a small saucepan. Slowly stir in peach syrup. Cook over medium heat, stirring constantly, until sauce thickens and boils. Stir in butter. Place a tablespoon of the peach mixture in the center of each pancake and roll up. Place close together in a shallow pan. Pop under the broiler and let stand until pancakes are heated and slightly glazed. Serve immediately with hot peach syrup. Makes about 12 pancakes.

# Blini

**1 package dry or compressed yeast**
**¼ cup lukewarm water**
**¾ cup lukewarm milk**
**2 cups buckwheat pancake mix**
**½ teaspoon baking soda**
**2 cups buttermilk**
**4 eggs, separated**
**3 tablespoons melted butter**
**¼ teaspoon salt**
**Cottage cheese**
**Salmon caviar**

In a mixing bowl, dissolve yeast in water. Add milk and ¾ cup of the pancake mix. Mix until smooth. Cover with a towel and set aside in a warm place to rise for 2 hours. Add soda to buttermilk. Beat egg yolks well. Add melted butter, buttermilk and remaining pancake mix; mix well. Add to the raised mixture; mix well. Add salt to egg whites. Beat until stiff, but not dry, and fold into the batter.

For each pancake, drop 2 tablespoons batter onto well-greased griddle. Cook until browned on both sides, turning only once. Serve Blini warm, topped with cottage cheese and salmon caviar. About 44 four-inch pancakes or 10 to 12 servings.

Sealtest Consumer Service

# Chocolate Pancakes

**¼ cup butter**
**¼ cup sugar**
**⅔ cup sifted flour**
**2 cups milk**
**½ teaspoon vanilla**
**8 eggs, separated**
**2 ounces semi-sweet chocolate**

Melt the butter in a saucepan over low heat. Stir in sugar and flour. Gradually blend in milk and cook, stirring constantly, until mixture is smooth and thick. Remove from heat and cool slightly. Add vanilla. Beat egg yolks slightly and add to cooked mixture. Beat egg whites until stiff. Fold cooked mixture in. Butter a 6-inch skillet lightly. Pour a small amount of batter into skillet, tip so that it covers bottom. Cook until lightly browned on both sides. These pancakes will be light and should be handled carefully. Place pancake in a baking dish. Sprinkle with grated sweet chocolate. Top with second pancake and sprinkle with chocolate. Make piles of 3 or 4 pancakes and continue until all batter is used.

**3 egg whites**
**½ teaspoon vanilla**
**6 tablespoons sugar**

Beat egg whites until stiff. Gradually beat in sugar until whites stand in very high peaks. Fold in vanilla. Pile egg white mixture on stacked pancakes. Bake in a slow oven (325°F.) about 10 minutes, or until whites are lightly browned. To serve, cut pancake stacks pie fashion.

# Dessert Pancakes

**2 eggs, slightly beaten**
**1 cup sifted flour**
**1¼ cups milk**
**½ teaspoon salt**
**2 cups applesauce**
**2 tablespoons sugar**
**1 tablespoon grated lemon rind**
**1 tablespoon lemon juice**
**Confectioners' sugar**

Combine eggs, flour, milk and salt and beat until smooth with a rotary beater. Drop by spoonfuls on a hot, lightly greased griddle; spread thinly and cook over low heat until golden brown on both sides. Combine applesauce, sugar, lemon rind and juice. Spread over each pancake and roll as for jelly roll. Sprinkle with confectioners' sugar and serve piping hot. Makes 4 to 6 servings.

# Apricot Pancakes

**3 eggs**
**1 teaspoon salt**
**1½ teaspoons sugar**
**1 cup sifted flour**
**2 cups milk**
**3 tablespoons melted butter**
**2 cans apricot nectar**
**Grated rind of 1 orange**
**Juice of 1 lemon**
**2 tablespoons butter**
**Apricot preserves**
**¼ cup Cointreau**

Beat eggs until light. Add salt and sugar and continue beating. Add flour, milk and butter and beat until smooth. Lightly butter a small 6-inch hot skillet. Put a small amount of batter in skillet and tilt quickly so that the entire bottom of pan is covered thinly with the batter. Cook over medium heat until delicately browned, turn and brown other side. Transfer pancakes to a platter. Continue until all batter is used. Combine nectar, orange rind, lemon juice and butter and cook about 5 minutes. Spread pancakes with apricot preserves and roll up. Place in a single layer in a large pan. Combine sauce and Cointreau and stir well. Pour about ¼ of the sauce over pancakes. Place in a hot oven (400°F.) and heat about 5 minutes or until piping hot. Serve with remaining hot apricot sauce. Makes about 6 to 7 servings.

# Cottage Cheese Pancakes

**½ cup sifted flour**
**½ teaspoon salt**
**1 tablespoon sugar**
**2 eggs, well beaten**
**⅔ cup milk**
**1 tablespoon butter, melted**
**1 teaspoon grated orange rind, divided**
**1 cup cottage cheese**
**1 tablespoon sugar**
**¼ teaspoon cinnamon**
**1 cup maple-blended syrup**
**¾ cup canned crushed pineapple, drained**

Sift together flour, salt and sugar. Combine eggs, milk, butter and ½ teaspoon of the orange rind. Add to flour mixture and mix until smooth. Butter lightly a 4-inch skillet. Pour a spoonful of batter in the hot skillet, tilt to make pancake cover entire bottom of pan. Cook until browned, turn and brown other side. Remove pancakes to a warm platter. Combine cottage cheese, sugar, cinnamon and remaining orange rind. Place a scant tablespoon of this mixture in center of each pancake. Roll up. Keep in a warm oven until all pancakes are ready. Heat maple-blended syrup to boiling. Add pineapple. Pour over pancakes. Serve each person 3 pancakes. Makes 6 servings.

# Coffee Apple Pancake

**1 pound tart apples**
**⅓ cup melted butter**
**⅓ cup sugar**
**⅛ teaspoon nutmeg**
**¼ teaspoon cinnamon**
**2 large eggs**
**¼ cup strong coffee**
**¼ cup milk**
**½ cup sifted all-purpose flour**
**¼ teaspoon salt**
**5 tablespoons melted butter**
**¼ cup sugar**

Pare and core apples. Cut in thin slices. Cook in ⅓ cup butter 5 minutes. Combine ⅓ cup sugar, nutmeg and cinnamon. Add to apples, cover and cook over low heat 10 minutes longer, or until apples are crisply tender. Remove from heat. Cool to lukewarm. Combine eggs, coffee, milk, flour and salt. Beat with rotary beater or electric mixer 2 to 3 minutes (batter will be very thin). Heat 1 tablespoon of remaining butter in 10-inch frying pan and tilt to coat sides. When hot, pour batter into pan. Bake in oven at 450°F. for 15 minutes. When batter puffs up in center (about 3 minutes) puncture with fork, repeating as necessary. Lower heat to 350° F. Bake 10 minutes longer or until golden brown and crisp. (Batter will creep up on sides of pan forming shell.) Remove from oven. Pour half the remaining butter over surface. Sprinkle with half the remaining sugar. Spread apple mixture over half the surface. Fold as for an omelet. Remove to hot platter. Pour remaining butter on top. Sprinkle with remaining sugar. Makes 4 servings as a dessert, 2 as a main dish.

Pan American Coffee Bureau

# Danish Pancakes

**1½ cups sifted flour**
**2 tablespoons sugar**
**1 teaspoon salt**
**½ teaspoon cardamom**
**4 eggs, well beaten**
**1⅔ cups milk, at room temperature**
**½ cup butter, melted**
**½ lemon**
**½ orange**
**1 apple**
**2 cups raw cranberries**
**1½ cups maple-blended syrup**

Sift together flour, sugar, salt and cardamom. Combine eggs, milk and butter. Add to flour mixture gradually, beating until smooth. Bake on a hot, ungreased griddle, spreading quickly to make a very thin 6-inch pancake. Use about 3 tablespoons of the batter for each pancake. When pancakes are done, remove from the griddle, fold in half and then in half again to form a triangular shaped pancake. Arrange on a wire cake rack and place in a slow oven (300°F.) to keep hot until ready to serve. Remove seeds from lemon and orange. Core, peel and quarter apple. Put lemon, orange, apple and cranberries through medium grinder of the food chopper. Add maple-blended syrup and mix well. Chill in refrigerator several hours to blend flavors. Place 3 or 4 pancakes on a plate and serve with the sauce. Makes about 6 to 8 servings.

# Hawaiian Pancake Roll-ups

**2 cups sifted flour**
**¼ cup sugar**
**1 teaspoon baking powder**
**1 teaspoon salt**
**¼ cup shortening**
**1 teaspoon grated lemon rind**
**4 eggs, well beaten**
**2 cups milk**
**1 cup brown sugar, firmly packed**
**1 tablespoon cornstarch**
**1 cup unsweetened pineapple juice**
**1 tablespoon butter**
**1 tablespoon lemon juice**
**1 can crushed pineapple**

Sift together flour, sugar, baking powder and salt into a mixing bowl. Cut in shortening. Add lemon rind. Combine beaten eggs and milk and add to dry ingredients, mixing until smooth. Combine brown sugar and cornstarch in a saucepan. Add pineapple juice, and butter and boil about 3 minutes. Add lemon juice and keep syrup hot. For each pancake, pour about ⅓ cup of the batter onto a hot greased griddle and spread out batter as thin as possible. Turn when bubbles appear on the surface and edges of pancake are dry, and brown the other side. Spread top of pancake with crushed pineapple and roll up quickly. Serve immediately with the hot sauce. Makes 16 pancakes.

# Swedish Pancakes with Strawberry Sauce

**1 cup sifted flour**
**1/8 teaspoon salt**
**2 teaspoons baking powder**
**1 tablespoon sugar**
**1 egg, beaten**
**1 cup milk**
**1/4 cup salad oil**
**1 package (1 pound) frozen whole strawberries, thawed, but not drained**
**1/2 cup currant jelly**

### Swedish Pancakes

Sift together flour, salt, baking powder and sugar. Blend in egg and milk. Heat small amount of oil in skillet, tilting to coat bottom of skillet. Drop batter by tablespoonsful into skillet. Cook until lightly browned on both sides. Repeat, using remaining batter and oil; keep pancakes hot. Makes 4 to 6 servings.

### Strawberry Sauce

Combine strawberries and jelly. Stir over low heat 10 minutes.

California Strawberry Advisory Board

# Pear Pancake Pleaser

**1 (1 lb.) can pear halves**
**2 cups pancake mix**
**3 cups cottage cheese**
**1/2 cup chopped filberts**

Drain pear halves, reserving syrup. Prepare pancake mix according to directions on package label. Make four 8-inch pancakes. Stack pancakes, filling with cottage cheese mixed with nuts. Arrange pear quarters, fan shape, on top of stack. Cut in wedges and serve with spicy marmalade sauce. Makes 6 servings.

### Marmalade Sauce

**3/4 cup pear syrup**
**1 cup orange marmalade**
**1 tablespoon cornstarch**
**1/4 teaspoon mace**

Combine above ingredients. Cook until thickened. Serve over pancake stack.

Bartlett Pears

# how to make crêpes suzette

## Crêpes:

**4 eggs**
**2 cups milk**
**1 teaspoon vanilla**
**1 tablespoon sugar**
**½ teaspoon salt**
**1½ cups all-purpose flour**
**Butter or margarine**
**1 tablespoon brandy or Curacao**
**½ cup sugar**
**1 tablespoon orange rind**

**Preparation:** Beat eggs until frothy. Combine with milk, vanilla, and also the sugar and salt. Gradually beat into flour. Add 3 tablespoons melted butter and brandy. Beat smooth. The batter should be quite thin (this is the secret of good crêpes). Heat 1 tablespoon butter in a heavy 5- or 6-inch skillet. Pour in just enough batter to cover the bottom. Remember, you want a very thin pancake. Cook until bubbles appear and the underside is browned. Turn or flip and lightly brown the other side. Continue to make crêpes, one or several at a time, depending on how many little skillets you have and your dexterity. Heat a teaspoon of butter to sizzling for each crêpe. Cream ⅓ cup butter and ½ cup sugar with orange rind until smooth. Spread a little on the brownest side of each crêpe and fold it into a 4 layered triangle. Refrigerate until 1 hour before chafing time. Crêpes may be made several days in advance. Makes about 24 crêpes.

## Suzette Sauce:

**1 orange, grated rind and juice**
**⅓ cup hot brandy and/or Curaçao**
**2 tablespoons butter**
**2 tablespoons confectioner's sugar**

**Preparation:** Grate and juice orange. Just before chafing time heat brandy.

**Performance:** Melt butter in blazer pan of chafing dish. Add sugar, orange rind and juice. Cook until slightly thickened. Arrange crêpes in pan and spoon the hot sauce over them. When thoroughly heated, ignite hot brandy and pour over crêpes. Gently spoon syrup over crêpes as long as the flame lasts. Makes 8 servings.

**Crêpes Suzette are the traditional delicacy of the chafing dish crowd.**

**After beating eggs until frothy combine with milk, vanilla, also required sugar and salt.**

**Gradually beat into flour, add 3 tbsp. melted butter, brandy. Batter must be exceptionally thin.**

**Spoon a mixture of ⅓ cup butter, ½ cup sugar, orange rind on each crêpe and fold in triangles.**

**After cooking crêpes and folding in triangles, arrange them in blazer pan filled with sauce.**

**Final step: thoroughly heat crêpes in hot sauce: then ignite hot brandy and pour over the crêpes.**

# Parfaits, Puddings, Soufflés

## Baked Alaska

**6 cake shells**
**6 scoops ice cream, firmly frozen or,**
**6 dixie cups, firmly frozen**
**5 egg whites**
**6 tablespoons granulated sugar**

Arrange cake shells on a cookie sheet, leaving about 1½ inches between each dessert shell. Beat egg whites until they stand in peaks. To test, lift the beater and see if the meringue actually does form peaks that don't flatten out. Gradually add sugar, a tablespoon at a time, beating after each addition, until the meringue becomes stiff and looks glossy. Place one scoop of ice cream on the top of each cake shell. Generously ice each dessert using all the meringue. Brown the alaskas immediately in a very hot oven (450°F.) for about five minutes or until brown. Serve immediately.

Ward Foods Inc.

California Strawberry Advisory Board

## French Pancakes with Brandied Strawberries

**1 package (1 pound) frozen whole strawberries, thawed, but not drained**
**2 tablespoons brandy**
**1 cup sifted flour**
**½ teaspoon baking soda**
**¼ teaspoon salt**
**2 tablespoons sugar**
**1 egg, beaten**
**1 cup milk**
**2 tablespoons vinegar**
**⅓ cup melted butter or margarine**
**Combine: 1 package (8 ounces) cream cheese, softened**
**2 tablespoons lemon juice**
**¼ cup sugar**
**¼ teaspoon almond extract**

Combine strawberries with brandy. Let stand 30 minutes to mellow. Sift together flour, baking soda, salt and 2 tablespoons sugar. Blend egg, milk and vinegar; beat into flour mixture until smooth. Pour 1 teaspoon butter into 5½ inch skillet. Add enough batter to cover bottom of pan and brown on both sides. Repeat, using remaining batter. Spread cream cheese mixture on pancakes and roll up. Brush pancake rolls with remaining melted butter. Cover and heat to serving temperature. Serve with brandied strawberries. Makes 6 servings.

## Chocolate Ice Cream Roll

**¾ cup sifted cake flour**
**¼ teaspoon salt**
**⅓ cup cocoa**
**1 tablespoon lemon juice**
**5 eggs, separated**
**1 cup sugar**
**1 quart vanilla ice cream**

Sift flour, salt and cocoa together 2 times. Add lemon juice to egg yolks and beat until thick and lemon-colored. Whip egg whites until soft peaks form. Add sugar gradually and continue beating until stiff peaks are formed. Fold in egg yolks. Then fold in sifted dry ingredients. Pour into a 10½x5x1-inch pan lined with waxed paper. Bake in a moderate oven (350°F.) 15 to 18 minutes. Sift additional cocoa on a clean dish towel. As soon as cake is baked, loosen sides from the pan and turn out on towel. Remove waxed paper and trim off crusts. Roll up tightly in the towel and cool. Unroll carefully and spread with softened ice cream. Reroll tightly. Place in freezer or freezing compartment of refrigerator until serving time. Makes 6 servings.

# Biscuit Tortoni

2 cups heavy cream
⅓ cup confectioners' sugar
2 egg whites
½ cup crushed macaroons
¾ cup minced, blanched and toasted almonds
1½ teaspoons sherry

Beat cream until thick but not too stiff. Beat in sugar. Beat egg whites until stiff and fold into cream. Fold in macaroons, almonds and sherry. Pour into small paper cups. Sprinkle tops with macaroon crumbs. Place in freezing trays of automatic refrigerator and freeze until firm. Makes about 12 cups.

# Chocolate Soufflé

2 squares unsweetened chocolate
2 cups milk
½ cup sugar
⅓ cup flour
½ teaspoon salt
2 tablespoons butter or margarine
1 teaspoon vanilla
4 egg yolks, beaten until thick and lemon-colored
4 egg whites, stiffly beaten
Whipped cream, sweetened

Melt chocolate in milk in top part of double boiler over boiling water. Beat with rotary beater until well blended. Mix sugar, flour and salt; add small amount of chocolate mixture, stirring until smooth. Return to double boiler containing rest of chocolate mixture, and cook until thickened, stirring constantly. Continue cooking for 5 minutes, stirring occasionally. Add butter and vanilla; cool slightly. Add egg yolks, mix well. Fold into egg whites. Pour into buttered 1½-quart casserole. Put in pan of hot water and bake in a moderate oven (350°F.) 1 hour and 15 minutes, or until firm. Serve at once with whipped cream. Makes 8 servings.

# Walnut Soufflé

4 eggs, separated
10 tablespoons confectioners' sugar
½ teaspoon vanilla
¾ cup ground walnuts
⅛ teaspoon salt

Beat egg yolks until light; gradually add sugar and beat until creamy. Mix in vanilla and walnuts. Beat egg whites and salt together until mixture stands in stiff peaks. Fold into yolk mixture. Pour into a greased 2-quart baking dish. Set in a pan of hot water. Bake in a slow oven (325°F.) 45 to 55 minutes or until firm. Serve at once with brandy flavored whipped cream if desired. Makes 6 servings.

# Oeufs à la Neige

1½ cups milk
1½ cups heavy cream
4 tablespoons sugar
1 1-inch piece vanilla bean
2 egg whites
4 egg yolks
3 tablespoons cognac
Nutmeg

In a large saucepan combine milk, cream, 2 tablespoons of the sugar and the vanilla bean. Heat until tiny bubbles form. Meanwhile beat egg whites until they hold soft peaks. Gradually beat in remaining sugar, and continue beating until whites hold in stiff peaks. Drop by spoonfuls into hot milk; cook 3 minutes, turning 2 or 3 times during cooking time. Drain on absorbent paper. In the top of a double boiler beat the egg yolks until light. Strain hot milk mixture. Cool slightly and stir into egg yolks. Cook over boiling water, stirring occasionally, until custard thickens. Remove from heat. Cool. Add cognac. Pour custard into serving dishes. Chill. Just before serving place an egg white mound on each custard and sprinkle with nutmeg. Makes 6 servings.

# Orange Soufflé

4 eggs
2 tablespoons grated orange rind
1½ tablespoons sugar
3 tablespoons butter
3 tablespoons flour
1 cup orange juice

Separate the eggs into 2 large bowls. Combine the rind and sugar with the egg yolks. In the top of a double boiler blend the butter and the flour. Stir in orange juice. Cook over boiling water, stirring occasionally, until mixture thickens. Gradually stir into the egg yolk mixture; let cool until lukewarm. Meanwhile beat the egg whites until they stand in soft peaks. Gently fold egg whites into the cooled orange mixture. Spoon into a 1½-quart casserole and bake in a moderately hot oven (375°F.) 50 minutes or until top is golden brown. Serve immediately. Makes 6 servings.

# Semi-Sweet Chocolate Casserole Pudding

1 6-ounce package (1 cup) semi-sweet chocolate morsels, divided
¼ cup sugar
½ teaspoon salt
1 teaspoon grated lemon rind
1½ cups crumbled doughnuts (approximately 3)
2 cups milk
Nutmeg (optional)
1 cup heavy cream
2 tablespoons sugar
½ teaspoon vanilla

Melt 1 cup less 1 tablespoon semi-sweet chocolate morsels over hot (not boiling) water. Remove from water. Add sugar, salt, lemon rind, doughnuts and milk. Beat thoroughly with rotary beater. Pour into 1 quart greased casserole. Sprinkle lightly with nutmeg (optional). Bake moderate oven (350°F.) for 45 minutes. Cool. Combine cream, sugar, and vanilla. Beat till stiff. Drop by tablespoonfuls on top of cooled pudding. Sprinkle reserved tablespoon morsels over cream. Chill several hours or overnight. Makes 6 to 8 servings.

Nestle Co.

Baker's Angel Flake Coconut

# Jellied Coconut Ring

**1 regular size package (3 ounce) black cherry flavor gelatin**
**1¼ cups boiling water**
**¾ cup milk**
**½ cup sugar**
**Dash of salt**
**½ cup whipping cream**
**½ cup flaked coconut**
**2 cups Bing cherries (pitted fresh or drained canned)**

Dissolve gelatin in boiling water. Allow to cool to lukewarm. Scald milk. Add sugar and salt and stir until dissolved. Cool to lukewarm. Then add milk to gelatin *very gradually,* stirring constantly. Chill until slightly thickened. Beat gelatin mixture until fluffy and thick. Whip cream. Then fold whipped cream and coconut into the gelatin mixture. Pour into a 1½-quart ring mold and chill until firm. Unmold and fill center of ring with Bing cherries. Makes 6 to 8 servings.

# Baked Crême Brulée

**2 cups heavy cream**
**4 egg yolks, well beaten**
**2 tablespoons white sugar**
**1 teaspoon vanilla**
**½ cup brown sugar**

Heat oven to 325° F. (slow). Scald cream in double boiler. Pour in a slow stream into egg yolks, mixing well. Add white sugar and vanilla. Pour into a buttered baking dish to a depth of 2 inches. Place in a pan of hot water and bake uncovered in 325° F. oven until set, about 45 minutes. Chill for 4 hours. Cover with a layer of brown sugar. Broil until sugar carmelizes or until just melted. Serve at once. Makes 6 servings.

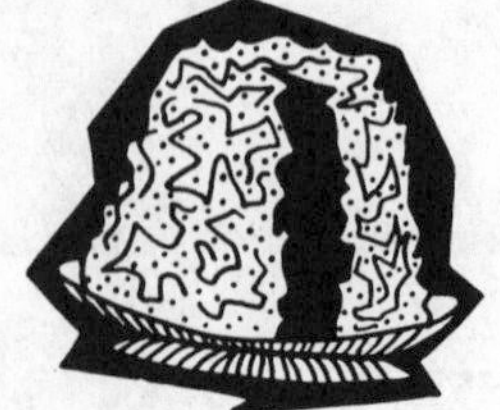

# Quick Apricot Soufflé

**3 eggs, separated**
**2 tablespoons sugar**
**1 tablespoon flour**
**½ cup apricot puree**
**1 tablespoon butter**
**2 tablespoons dry bread crumbs**
**Whipped cream**

Beat egg yolks until thick. Add sugar and continue beating until very thick and light in color. Beat in flour. Fold in apricot purée. Beat egg whites until stiff and fold into egg yolk mixture. Butter the top of a 2-quart double boiler and coat it with bread crumbs. Pour in egg mixture. Cover tightly and cook over gently boiling water about 35 minutes. Do not remove cover during cooking period. Serve immediately with whipped cream. Makes about 3 servings.

# Chocolate Baskets

**⅔ cup butter**
**1 cup sifted flour**
**10 eggs, separated**
**1 cup sugar**
**1⅓ cups ground nuts**
**⅔ cup chocolate bits**

Cut butter into the flour. Blend in the egg yolks and mix until a smooth dough is formed. Separate the dough into 12 portions and chill for several hours. Shape each piece into a ball and roll out on a floured board into a very thin circle. Fit into small buttered pie tins or shallow large custard cups. Beat egg whites until stiff. Beat in sugar until mixture stands in stiff peaks. Fold in nuts and chocolate bits. Fill the lined tins with this mixture. Bake in a moderate oven (350°F.) about 20 minutes, or until golden brown. Makes about 12 baskets.

# Almond-Strawberry Puffette

**1 cup milk**
**2 tablespoons flour**
**2 tablespoons butter**
**⅛ teaspoon salt**
**½ teaspoon almond extract**
**¼ teaspoon vanilla extract**
**3 tablespoons finely crushed almonds**
**3 tablespoons sugar**
**4 eggs, separated**
**2 cups sweetened whipped cream (about ¾ cup)**
**½ cup sweetened crushed strawberries**

Heat oven to 350° F. (moderate). Scald milk in top of double boiler. Cream flour and butter and gradually blend in hot milk. Cook in top of double boiler over hot water, stirring, for 10 minutes. Add salt, extracts, almonds, sugar and well beaten egg yolks. Fold in stiffly beaten egg whites. Turn into a 1½-quart buttered casserole with straight sides and place in a pan of hot water. Bake uncovered in 350° F. oven for 50 minutes or until puffed and firm. Serve at once with whipped cream mixed with strawberries. Makes 6 servings.

# Soufflé Rothschild

¼ cup glace mixed fruit, finely chopped
1 jar (8 ounces) red glace cherries, or red maraschino cherries, drained and finely chopped (about 20 maraschino cherries or 30 glace cherries)
¼ cup kirsch
Sugar
3 tablespoons sifted all-purpose flour
¾ cup milk
⅓ cup sugar
4 egg yolks
2 tablespoons butter
5 egg whites
⅛ teaspoon salt
1 tablespoon sugar
2 teaspoons vanilla

Combine glace mixed fruit, ¼ cup finely chopped glace or maraschino cherries (well drained) and kirsch; mix well and allow to stand 30 minutes, stirring occasionally to moisten fruit. Tear off a length of wax paper long enough to go around and slightly overlap a 7-inch diameter soufflé dish or 1½ quart straight-sided casserole. Fold paper in half lengthwise and butter it well on one side. Wrap it around the dish, butter side inside, so that it stands above the rim about 4 inches; secure with string. Butter the inside of the dish and sprinkle sugar over the entire inner surface. In enamel or glass saucepan, combine flour with a small amount of the milk to give a smooth paste. Gradually add remaining milk and ⅓ cup sugar; stir until well blended. Cook over medium heat, stirring constantly, until mixture thickens and comes to a boil. Boil, stirring, 30 seconds. Remove from heat and beat 2 minutes. Add egg yolks, 1 at a time, beating well after each addition. Beat in 1 tablespoon butter and dot top of sauce with remaining 1 tablespoon butter. Beat egg whites and salt together until soft peaks form. Sprinkle 1 tablespoon sugar over whites and beat until stiff, but not dry. Drain mixed fruits, reserving liquid. Add liquid with vanilla to sauce and beat well. Fold ¼ of beaten egg whites thoroughly into sauce. Fold in remaining egg whites. Pour a third of soufflé mixture into prepared dish and sprinkle with drained glace fruit. Cover with maining soufflé mixture. Bake in moderate oven (375°F.) 30 to 35 minutes or until soufflé is nicely browned and puffed. Garnish with remaining ¼ cup red glace or maraschino cherries. Serve immediately. Makes 4 to 6 servings.

# French Fruit Parfait

2 cups blueberries
2 cups ripe pineapple chunks
2 cups ripe strawberry halves
½ cup crumbled Roquefort cheese
2 tablespoons finely chopped California walnuts

Arrange alternate layers of fruits in each of 6 parfait glasses. Mash Roquefort cheese lightly; add walnuts and mix well. Shape cheese mixture into small balls (about ¾-inch in diameter). Arrange cheese balls on cocktail picks. Serve with fruit. Makes 6 servings.

The Roquefort Association

# Strawberry Soufflé

1 pint fresh strawberries, hulled and crushed
1¼ cups sugar
4 eggs, separated
1 envelope unflavored gelatin
⅛ teaspoon salt
1 cup heavy cream, whipped

Cut strip of waxed paper about 4-inches deep and long enough to extend around sides of 1½ quart soufflé dish; fasten with string. Lightly brush inside surface of collar with oil. Force crushed strawberries through food mill or sieve (there should be about 1¾ cups puree). Stir in ½ cup of the sugar. Remove ¼ cup sweetened puree; sprinkle gelatin over top to soften. Combine egg yolks with ½ cup of the sugar in top of double boiler. Stir over boiling water until thickened. Stir in gelatin mixture until dissolved; cool and blend in remaining strawberry puree. Beat egg whites and salt until soft peaks form. Gradually add remaining ¼ cup sugar and continue beating until stiff peaks form. Fold in whipped cream, then strawberry mixture. Turn into prepared soufflé dish and chill until firm. Remove collar and serve with Brandied Strawberry Sauce. Makes 6 servings.

## Brandied Strawberry Sauce

1 cup sugar
2 tablespoons cornstarch
1 pint fresh strawberries, hulled and crushed
2 tablespoons lemon juice
2 tablespoons cognac or brandy

In saucepan, blend sugar and cornstarch. Stir in lemon juice. Add strawberries. Stir over medium heat until thickened and clear. Cool slightly; stir in cognac. Chill. Makes about 1½ cups.

California Strawberry Advisory Board

# Cherries Jubilee

**1 (1 lb.) can light or dark sweet cherries, pitted**
**⅓ cup jelly (blackberry, currant, loganberry)**
**Vanilla ice cream**
**2 tablespoons syrup, drained from cherries**
**⅓ to ½ cup brandy or cognac**

Drain cherries, reserve syrup. Melt jelly in saucepan or chafing dish over low heat. Stir in cherries and two tablespoons syrup. When ready to serve, heat cherry mixture in chafing dish. Pour all but 1 tablespoon of the brandy over heated cherries. Do not stir. Pass spoon of brandy through flame until ignited and pour over cherries. When flames begin to burn down, stir gently and ladle over vanilla ice cream. Makes 4 to 5 servings.

Wine Institute

# Sherry Toddy Pudding

**1 (14½ oz.) package gingerbread mix**
**¼ cup Sherry**
**¾ cup water**
**1 (3½ oz.) can flaked coconut**

Prepare gingerbread according to package directions using ¼ cup Sherry and ¾ cup water for liquid called for. Add half the coconut to the batter. Turn batter into a 9-inch square pan; sprinkle remaining coconut on top. *Or,* turn batter into a well-greased ring or other fancy mold sprinkled with remaining coconut (batter should fill mold ½ to ⅔ full). Bake in a moderate oven (350°F.) about 30 minutes or until cake-pudding is done. Serve warm with Creamy Sherry Sauce. Makes 8 to 10 servings.

### Creamy Sherry Sauce

Combine 1 cup sugar, ½ cup butter or margarine, ¼ cup light or heavy cream and ⅛ teaspoon salt in a saucepan. Heat slowly to boiling, stirring now and then. Add ¼ cup California Sherry and 1 teaspoon grated lemon rind. Heat slightly to blend flavors. Makes about 1⅓ cups sauce.

Washington State Apple Commission

# Cascade Apple-Meringue Dessert

6 tablespoons butter
3 tablespoons sugar
2 egg yolks
¾ cup plus 2 tablespoons sifted flour
6 tablespoons finely cut blanched almonds
3 teaspoons shredded lemon peel
5 tablespoons sugar
2 tablespoons lemon juice
5 apples, peeled, halved and cored
6 tablespoons raspberry jam
Meringue:
4 egg whites
Dash of salt
½ cup sugar

Cream together butter and sugar. Beat in egg yolks. Add flour, almonds and lemon peel; mix well. Press dough on bottom of 8 x 8 x 2″ cake pan. *Brush with slightly beaten egg white.* (Use a bit of the egg whites from which the meringue will be made.) Bake in a moderate oven (350°F.) 15 minutes, or until crust is golden brown. Cool. Meanwhile, place sugar and lemon juice in large skillet. Add apple halves, cover tightly and cook slowly until apples are just tender. Spread cooled crust with jam, then arrange apple halves in pan. Beat egg whites and salt until stiff. Continue beating, adding 1 tablespoon sugar at a time. Beat until sugar is completely dissolved. Pile lightly over apples, bake in a moderate oven (350°F.) about 15 minutes, or until meringue is lightly browned. A rich dessert that will serve 12 to 16.

# Peanut Butterscotch Squares

1 package butterscotch pudding and pie filling mix
½ cup peanut butter
2 cups milk
¼ cup sugar
3 tablespoons butter
1¼ cups graham cracker crumbs
1 peanut chocolate candy bar, sliced

Combine pie filling mix, ¼ cup peanut butter and milk in saucepan. Cook and stir over medium heat until mixture comes to a full boil. Remove from heat and cover to avoid surface film. Meanwhile, add sugar, remaining ¼ cup peanut butter and butter to crumbs and blend thoroughly. Line an 8 x 8 x 2-inch pan with aluminum foil. Press half the crumb mixture in the bottom of the pan. Stir pudding and pour over crumbs in pan. Sprinkle with remaining crumbs and sliced candy bar. Chill until firm. Lift out with foil and cut into squares. Makes 6 to 8 servings.

The Peanut Growers of Alabama and Georgia

# Strawberry Charlotte

1 package ladyfingers
¾ cup instant nonfat dry milk
¾ cup cold water
¼ cup cold water
2 tablespoons unflavored gelatin
2 packages (10 oz. each) frozen sliced strawberries
¼ cup sugar
¾ cup boiling water
Red food coloring

Line side of a buttered 2-quart bowl with ladyfingers split in half lengthwise. In small-sized electric mixer bowl place dry milk and the ¾ cup water; whip on high speed until stiff, 6 to 8 minutes. Chill in refrigerator. In a pint measure or jar soften gelatin in the ¼ cup water 5 minutes. Meanwhile sprinkle sugar on strawberries; break frozen strawberries into pieces using a fork. Stir boiling water into gelatin and continue stirring until gelatin is dissolved. Combine with strawberries and stir until blended; chill until a small amount dropped from a spoon mounds. Fold in whipped, chilled dry milk. Stir food coloring, a drop at a time, until mixture is of desired shade. Turn into ladyfinger-lined bowl. Chill in refrigerator until set, 2 to 3 hours. Unmold. If desired, garnish with additional whipped and sweetened dry milk and strawberries. Makes 6 to 8 servings.

The Borden Company

California Strawberry Advisory Board

# Whipped Pudding with Strawberries

**1 package (3¼ ounces) vanilla pudding and pie filling mix**
**1 tablespoon (1 envelope) unflavored gelatin**
**⅛ teaspoon nutmeg**
**1⅔ cups (large can) undiluted evaporated milk**
**1 cup water**
**2 tablespoons lemon juice**
**½ teaspoon vanilla**
**1 cup fresh California strawberries, sliced**
**1 cup angel food or other cake squares**

Combine pudding, gelatin, nutmeg, 1 cup undiluted evaporated milk and water in saucepan. Cook and stir over medium heat until mixture comes to a boil. Cover and chill until pudding mounds from spoon. Chill remaining ⅔ cup evaporated milk in refrigerator tray until soft ice crystals form around edges (10 to 15 minutes). Whip until stiff (about 1 minute). Add lemon juice and vanilla; whip very stiff (about 2 minutes). Beat pudding until smooth. Fold in sliced strawberries and whipped milk. Layer pudding and cake in a 1½-quart mold or bowl. Chill until firm about 2 hours. Unmold and garnish with whole strawberries and whipped topping, if desired. Makes 6 to 8 servings.

# Peanut Butter Parfait

**½ cup crunchy peanut butter**
**½ cup butterscotch dessert topping**
**¼ cup milk**
**Whipped cream or topping**
**½ cup red maraschino cherries, (about 20 cherries)**
**1 pint vanilla ice cream**
**½ pint cherry-vanilla ice cream**

Blend together peanut butter, butterscotch topping and milk. Reserve 6 whole cherries; chop remaining cherries and set aside. Place small scoop vanilla ice cream in individual parfait glasses. Add 1 to 1½ tablespoons peanut butter sauce. Top each with scoop cherry vanilla ice cream, additional sauce, vanilla ice cream, chopped cherries, whipped cream and a whole cherry. Makes 6 servings.

Peter Pan Peanut Butter Company

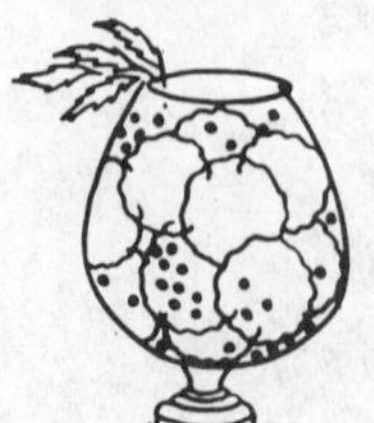

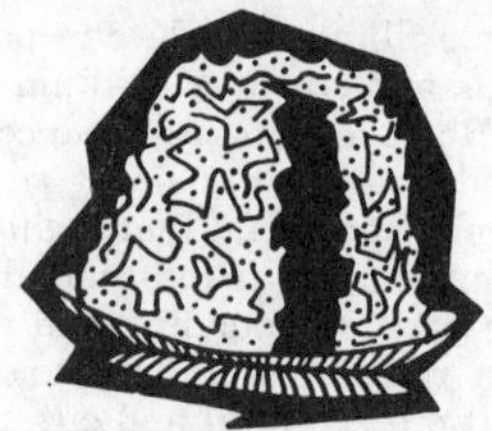

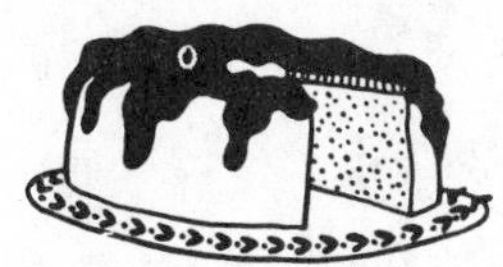

Ralston Purina

# Almond Bavarian Cream

2 eggs, separated
1 cup milk
1 tablespoon (1 envelope) unflavored gelatin
10 tablespoons sugar, divided
¼ teaspoon salt
¼ teaspoon almond extract
1 teaspoon vanilla
1½ cups bite size shredded rice biscuits crushed to ⅓ cup
¼ cup chopped toasted almonds
3 tablespoons *soft* butter or margarine
1 cup heavy cream, whipped

Beat egg yolks and milk together. Add gelatin, ¼ cup sugar and salt. Heat and stir over low heat until thickened and smooth (about 10 minutes). Add almond and vanilla extract. Cool while preparing crumbs. Stir occasionally. Combine cereal crumbs, almonds and 2 tablespoons sugar. Add butter. Mix until uniform. Press one heaping tablespoon crumb mixture into bottom of each of 6 individual molds. Beat egg whites until foamy. Add ¼ cup sugar gradually. Beat until whites hold a stiff peak. Fold into gelatin mixture with whipped cream. Spoon into molds. Sprinkle with remaining crumb mixture. Chill 2-3 hours until firm or overnight. Makes 6 servings.

# Coeur à la Crème

2 teaspoons unflavored gelatin
3 tablespoons cold water
2 cups (1 lb.) cottage cheese
2 packages (3 oz. each) cream cheese
1 cup heavy cream
1 tablespoon confectioners' sugar
3 packages (10 oz. each) frozen strawberry halves

Soften gelatin in cold water. Place over hot water until gelatin is dissolved. Force cottage cheese through a fine sieve. Stir cream cheese until softened. Gradually blend in the cream. Stir in sugar and cottage cheese; then stir in gelatin. Spoon into 1-quart mold or individual molds. Chill until firm. Meanwhile, thaw strawberries as directed on package. Unmold cheese mixture. Top with strawberries. Makes 3¾ cups, enough for 10 servings.

Courtesy of Birds Eye Strawberry Halves

# Nut Pudding with Vanilla Sauce

(See picture between pgs. 160-161.)

¼ lb. margarine
½ cup sugar
Drop of vanilla
Ginger
3 eggs
¼ cup flour
⅛ cup cornstarch
1 oz. cocoa
2½ teaspoons baking powder
About 6 tablespoons milk
3 tablespoons ground nuts
Ladyfingers

Cream butter, add sugar, spices, eggs and beat until fluffy. Sift together flour, cornstarch, cocoa and baking powder. Blend into batter alternately with the milk. Beat batter until smooth, add ground nuts and pour into a greased pudding dish. Place dish in pan of boiling water. Bake one hour in moderate oven (350°). Remove. After a few minutes, invert entire pudding on a serving platter. Garnish with ladyfingers.

¼ lb. powdered sugar
4 tablespoons black coffee

Stir until smooth and thick. Sprinkle ladyfingers with this icing.

1 pt. milk
1 oz. sugar
Few drops vanilla
1 tablespoon cornstarch
1 egg yolk

Combine and stir in a double boiler until thickened. Serve this sauce with pudding.

Florida Citrus Commission

# Florida Orange Soufflé

3 tablespoons flour
1/3 cup sugar
1/2 cup milk
4 egg yolks
4 tablespoons frozen Florida orange juice concentrate, thawed, undiluted
1 tablespoon butter
1/4 teaspoon grated Florida orange rind
5 egg whites
1 teaspoon salt
1 tablespoon sugar

Prepare 2-quart soufflé dish by oiling or buttering entire inside surface and sprinkling evenly with granulated sugar; set aside. Preheat oven to hot (425°F.) Combine flour with 1/3 cup sugar in small saucepan; gradually blend in milk. Cook over low heat, stirring with whisk or wooden spoon until it boils. Continue stirring and boil 30 seconds. Sauce will be very thick. Remove from heat; beat 2 minutes. Beat in butter, yolks one at a time, then orange juice concentrate and rind. Reserve. Beat whites and salt until soft peaks form. Add 1 tablespoon sugar gradually. Beat until stiff peaks form. Fold creamy orange mixture into whites. Pour into prepared soufflé dish. Place in preheated hot oven and turn heat down to moderate oven (375°F.); bake 30 minutes until golden brown. For a darker top, sprinkle with confectioners' sugar after first 20 minutes of baking time. Serve immediately. Makes 6 to 8 servings.

**STEP ONE: After combining flour with sugar in small saucepan, gradually blend in milk. Cook over low heat, stirring with whisk or wooden spoon until it boils.**

**STEP TWO: After beating in butter and egg yolks, add orange juice concentrate.**

**STEP THREE: After beating egg whites and salt into soft peaks, add sugar gradually and beat until stiff peaks form. Fold creamy orange mixture into whites.**

# Coffee Cakes

## Dutch Apple Cake

1 cup milk
¼ cup sugar
2 teaspoons salt
¼ cup shortening
¼ cup warm water
1 package or cake yeast, active dry or compressed
1 egg
½ teaspoon cinnamon
2½ cups sifted flour
6 medium apples
2 tablespoons melted butter or margarine
3 tablespoons sugar
1 teaspoon nutmeg

Scald milk. Stir in sugar, salt and shortening. Cool to lukewarm. Measure water into a large mixing bowl (warm, not hot, water for active dry yeast; lukewarm water for compressed yeast). Sprinkle or crumble in yeast. Stir until dissolved. Stir in lukewarm milk mixture. Beat in egg. Stir in cinnamon and flour to make a soft dough. Turn out on a lightly floured board and knead until smooth and elastic. Place dough in an oiled bowl. Cover and let rise until doubled in bulk. Punch down; knead a few moments and divide dough in half. Pat into 2 oiled 8-inch layer pans. Peel and core apples. Slice in very thin slices. Arrange in rows on top of dough. Brush with butter and sprinkle with combined sugar and nutmeg. Let rise 15 minutes. Bake in a moderate oven (350°F.) 45 minutes to 1 hour. Makes two 8-inch apple cakes.

## Hungarian Coffee Cake

¼ cup milk
½ cup sugar
½ teaspoon salt
¼ cup melted shortening
¼ cup warm water
1 package or cake yeast, active dry or compressed
1 egg
2¼ cups sifted flour
¼ cup butter or margarine, melted
¾ cup sugar
3 teaspoons cinnamon
¼ cup raisins

Scald milk. Stir in sugar, salt and shortening. Cool to lukewarm. Measure water into a large mixing bowl (warm, not hot, water for active dry yeast; lukewarm water for compressed yeast). Sprinkle or crumble in yeast. Stir until dissolved. Stir in lukewarm milk mixture. Beat in egg. Stir in flour. Turn out on a lightly floured board and knead until smooth and elastic. Place dough in an oiled bowl. Cover and let rise until doubled in bulk. Punch down and shape dough into sixteen 1½-inch balls. Roll in butter and combined sugar and cinnamon. Place 8 balls on bottom of an oiled 8-inch tube pan. Arrange remaining balls on top of first layer, so that each ball covers the space between the two below. Sprinkle with raisins. Cover and let rise until double in bulk. Bake in a moderate oven (350°F.) about 40-50 minutes. Makes one 8-inch coffee cake.

## Jingle Bread

1 cup buttermilk or sour milk
2 teaspoons salt
⅓ cup sugar
¼ cup shortening, melted
¼ cup lukewarm water
2 packages or cakes yeast, active dry or compressed
2 eggs
4 cups sifted flour
¼ cup honey
¼ cup sugar
½ cup chopped nuts
1 teaspoon cinnamon
¼ cup grated orange rind
2 tablespoons orange juice

Warm buttermilk but do not scald. Add sugar, salt and shortening and stir until sugar is dissolved. Measure water into a large mixing bowl (warm, not hot, water for active dry yeast; lukewarm water for compressed yeast). Sprinkle or crumble in yeast. Stir until dissolved. Stir in lukewarm milk mixture. Beat in eggs. Stir in flour. Turn out on a lightly floured board and knead until smooth and elastic. Place in an oiled bowl; cover and let rise in a warm place until double in bulk. Punch down. Roll dough into a square 18 inches by 18 inches. Spread with the combined remaining ingredients; roll as for a jelly roll. Cut in 1-inch slices and arrange in layers in a greased 9-inch tube pan. Let rise in a warm place until double in bulk. Bake in a moderate oven (350°F.) 1 hour. Remove from pan and pour over the top any syrup remaining in pan.

# Date Braided Cake

½ cup milk
½ cup sugar
1½ teaspoons salt
¼ cup shortening
½ cup warm water
2 packages or cakes yeast, active dry or compressed
2 eggs, beaten
5 cups sifted flour

Scald milk. Stir in sugar, salt and shortening. Cool to lukewarm. Measure water into a large mixing bowl (warm, not hot, water for active dry yeast; lukewarm water for compressed yeast). Sprinkle or crumble in yeast. Stir until dissolved. Stir in lukewarm milk mixture. Add eggs and 3 cups of the flour. Beat until smooth. Stir in remaining 2 cups of flour. Turn dough out on lightly floured board. Knead until smooth and elastic. Place in greased bowl; brush top with melted shortening. Cover. Let rise in a warm place, free from draft, until doubled in bulk, about 1 hour. Meanwhile, prepare Date Filling. When dough has doubled in bulk, punch it down and turn it out on a lightly floured board. Divide dough in half. Roll out each half into an oblong about 16x8 inches. Spread half the Date Filling down center third of each oblong. Cut 15 slits in dough along each side of filling, making strips about 1 inch wide. Fold strips at an angle across filling, alternating from side to side. Place on greased baking sheet. If desired, form into a ring, placing one end in the other. Seal together firmly. Cover. Let rise in a warm place, free from draft, until doubled in bulk, about 1 hour. Brush cakes with mixture of 1 egg yolk and 2 tablespoons milk. Sprinkle with Crumb Topping and bake in a moderate oven (350°F.) about 35 minutes. Makes 2 Braided Date Cakes.

### DATE FILLING

1 cup chopped, pitted dates
¼ cup brown sugar
⅔ cup water
½ cup chopped nuts
1 tablespoon lemon juice

Combine all ingredients in a saucepan. Bring to a boil over medium heat, stirring constantly, and continue boiling until mixture is thick enough to spread.

### CRUMB TOPPING

2 tablespoons butter or margarine
2 tablespoons sugar
⅓ cup sifted flour
½ teaspoon cinnamon

Blend together all ingredients with a fork.

Cut 15 slits in dough along each side of filling, making each strip of dough about one inch wide.

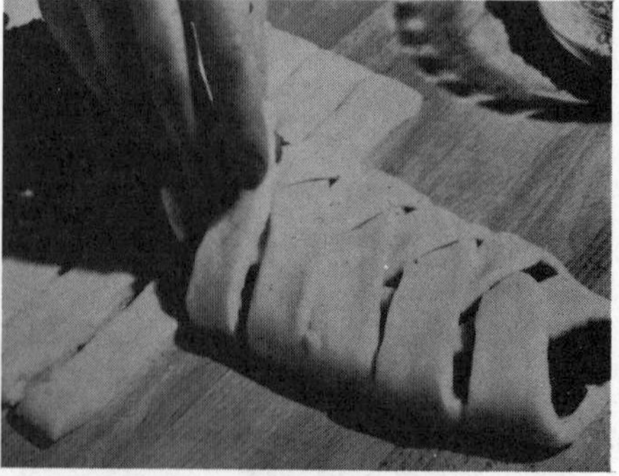

Fold strips at an angle across filling, alternating from side to side; place on a greased baking sheet.

# Baba Au Rhum

½ cup milk
⅓ cup butter or margarine
1 teaspoon salt
¼ cup sugar
1 package or cake yeast, active dry or compressed
¼ cup warm, not hot, water
2 eggs
½ teaspoon grated lemon peel
2¼ cups sifted flour
½ cup water
1 cup sugar
½ cup molasses
½ cup rum

Scald milk; add butter, salt and sugar and stir until melted. Cool to lukewarm. Add yeast to water (warm, not hot, for active dry yeast; lukewarm for compressed) and stir until dissolved. Add to cooled milk mixture and mix well. Beat eggs; add with lemon peel. Add flour and beat until smooth. Cover; let rise about 6 hours. Beat until smooth and elastic. Fill greased muffin pans, baba molds or ring mold ½ full. Let rise, uncovered, about 20 minutes. Bake in a hot oven (425°F.) 20 minutes. Remove at once from pans. Combine water, sugar and molasses and boil 10 minutes. Cool slightly and add rum. Place babas while still piping hot in serving dishes and spoon warm syrup over each. Let stand several hours. Serve with extra sauce and top with whipped cream, if desired. Makes 8 to 12 Babas.

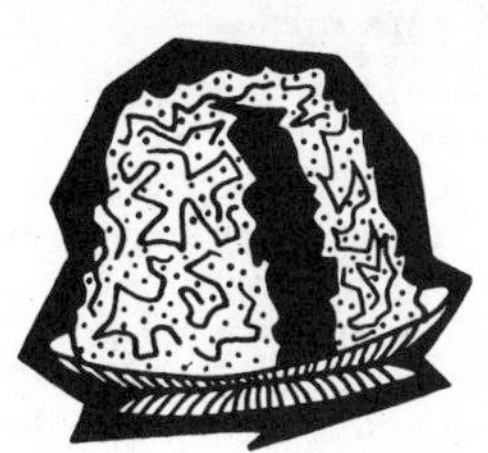

# Strawberry Savarin

½ cup milk, scalded
1 package or cake yeast, active dry or compressed
2 cups sifted flour
½ teaspoon salt
4 eggs
2 tablespoons sugar
⅔ cup butter, softened
½ cup rum
1 cup apricot jam
½ cup sugar
¼ cup water
1½ cups heavy cream
1 pint strawberries, cleaned

Pour milk into a bowl and cool until it is lukewarm. Sprinkle or crumble in yeast and stir until yeast is dissolved. Sift together flour and salt into a large bowl. Beat eggs lightly and stir in yeast mixture. Add to flour all at once, beat until bubbles begin to form. Cover and let stand in a warm place, free from drafts until double in bulk, about 1½ hours. With a wooden spoon punch down dough. Sprinkle sugar over dough and dot with butter. Beat hard for about 4 minutes or until large bubbles form. Turn dough into a buttered 10-inch ring mold and let stand until the dough rises to the top of the mold, about 1 hour. Bake in a hot oven (400°F.) about 35 minutes or until top is quite brown. Loosen edges carefully and turn out on a large platter. Pour rum over the cake and let stand until thoroughly cool. Combine jam, sugar and water in a small saucepan. Heat about 10 minutes, or until mixture becomes thin and runny. Remove from heat and force through a fine sieve. Brush mixture evenly over cooled ring. Chill. Just before serving, whip cream until stiff. Sweeten and flavor to taste. Fill ring with cream and top with berries.

# Croissants

1 cake or package yeast, compressed or active dry
¾ cup milk
2 cups sifted flour
½ teaspoon salt
½ cup sweet butter
1 egg yolk

Dissolve the yeast in lukewarm milk. Sift together flour and salt and add to yeast and milk. Sift until smooth. Turn out on a lightly floured board and knead until smooth and elastic. Place in a greased bowl and grease top of the dough. Let rise in a warm place until double in bulk. Roll dough out on a lightly floured board into a long strip. Dot top of dough with bits of the butter. Fold in thirds. Turn half way around and roll out into a large strip. Fold into thirds; wrap in waxed paper and chill well. Roll out again and fold in thirds. Wrap and chill. Remove from refrigerator and roll out a fourth time. This time roll dough out as thin as possible. Cut into 4-inch triangles. Roll each triangle from wide end to the tip, pressing in the tip to seal the roll. Shape into half moons or crescents. Place on a well buttered cookie sheet, cover and let rise until double in bulk. Brush the tops with beaten egg yolk and bake in a hot oven (425°F.) 20 to 25 minutes. Serve hot. Makes 1½ dozen rolls.

# Brioche

**½ cup milk**
**½ cup butter or margarine**
**⅓ cup sugar**
**½ teaspoon salt**
**¼ cup warm water**
**1 package or cake yeast, active dry or compressed**
**4 eggs**
**3¼ cups sifted enriched flour**
**1 tablespoon sugar**

Scald milk. Cool to lukewarm. Cream butter thoroughly. Gradually cream in sugar and salt. Measure water into a large mixing bowl (warm, not hot, water for active dry yeast; lukewarm water for compressed yeast). Sprinkle or crumble in yeast; stir until dissolved. Stir in lukewarm milk and creamed mixture. Separate one of the eggs, add the yolk to yeast mixture and put white into a small bowl for later use. Add remaining 3 whole eggs and flour. Beat 10 minutes. Cover. Let rise in a warm place, free from draft, about 2 hours or until more than doubled in bulk. Stir down. Beat thoroughly. Cover tightly with waxed paper or aluminum foil. Store in refrigerator overnight. Stir down and turn out soft dough onto a floured board. Divide into 2 pieces, one about ¾ the weight of the dough and the other about ¼ the weight of the dough. Cut large piece into 16 equal pieces. Form into smooth balls. Place in well greased muffin pans 2¾x1¼ inches. Cut smaller piece into 16 equal pieces. Form into smooth balls. Make a deep indentation in center of each large ball; dampen slightly with cold water. Press a small ball of dough into each indentation. Cover. Let rise in a warm place, free from draft, about 1 hour or until more than doubled in bulk. Mix reserved egg white with the 1 tablespoon sugar and brush mixture over rolls. Bake in a moderate oven (375°F.) about 20 minutes. Makes 16 Brioche.

Make a depression in center of the large dough balls. Dampen and press in smaller balls.

After brushing egg white mixture on each roll, bake in moderate oven 20 minutes and serve.

# Palm Leaf Buns

**½ cup milk**
**2 cups sugar, divided**
**1½ teaspoons salt**
**¼ cup shortening**
**½ cup lukewarm water**
**3 packages or cakes yeast, active dry or compressed**
**2 eggs, beaten**
**5 cups sifted flour (about)**
**Melted butter or margarine**
**2 teaspoons cinnamon**
**⅔ cups raisins**

Scald milk. Stir in ½ cup of the sugar, salt and shortening. Cool to lukewarm. Measure water into a large mixing bowl (warm, not hot, for active dry yeast; lukewarm water for compressed yeast). Sprinkle or crumble in yeast. Stir until dissolved. Stir in lukewarm milk mixture. Add eggs and 3 cups of the flour. Beat until smooth. Stir in remaining 2 cups of the flour. Turn dough out on a lightly floured board. Knead until smooth and elastic. Place in greased bowl; brush top with soft shortening.

Cover. Let rise in warm place, free from draft, until doubled in bulk, about 45 minutes. Punch down and turn out on lightly floured board. Divide dough in half. Roll out each half into a square about 12x12 inches. Brush lightly with melted butter. Combine remaining sugar, cinnamon and nuts. Sprinkle each square with one-half the raisin-sugar mixture. Roll up as for a jelly roll. Seal edges firmly. Cut into 8 equal pieces (about 1¼ inches wide). Make 2 cuts through each piece, parallel to cut sides and extending to within ½ inch of other side. Turn each leaf on its side and spread the three leaves apart into a fan shape. Place on a greased baking sheet about 2 inches apart. Cover. Let rise in a warm place, free from draft, until doubled in bulk, about 30 minutes. Bake in a moderate oven (350°F.) about 35 minutes. Makes 16 Palm Leaf Buns.

Sprinkle each square of dough with half of raisin-sugar mixture. Roll into cylinder, seal edges and cut into 8 equal pieces.

Make 2 parallel cuts almost through each piece and spread three sections into a fan. Let rise 30 minutes, then bake.

# Kugelhupf

**½ cup milk**
**½ cup sugar**
**½ teaspoon salt**
**¼ cup butter or margarine**
**¼ cup warm, not hot, water**
**1 package or cake yeast, active dry or compressed**
**2 eggs, beaten**
**2½ cups sifted flour**
**Fine bread crumbs**
**14-16 whole blanched almonds**
**½ cup seedless raisins**
**½ teaspoon grated lemon peel**

Scald milk. Stir in sugar, salt and butter. Cool to lukewarm. Measure water into a large mixing bowl (warm, not hot, for active dry yeast; lukewarm water for compressed yeast). Sprinkle or crumble in yeast. Stir until dissolved. Stir in lukewarm milk mixture. Add eggs and flour. Beat vigorously, about 5 minutes. Cover. Let rise in a warm place, free from draft, until doubled in bulk, about 1 hour and 30 minutes. Sprinkle fine bread crumbs over sides and bottom of well-greased 1½-quart casserole or fancy mold. Arrange almonds on bottom of casserole or mold. Stir batter down. Beat thoroughly. Stir in raisins and lemon peel. Turn into prepared casserole or mold. Let rise in a warm place, free from draft, until doubled in bulk, about 1 hour. Bake in a moderate oven (350°F.) about 50 minutes.

Line mold with bread crumbs and place a few almonds on bottom. Pour in Kugelhupf batter.

# Coffee Kringle

¼ cup milk
¼ cup sugar
½ teaspoon salt
2¼ cups sifted flour
¼ cup shortening
¼ cup warm water
1 package or cake yeast, active dry or compressed
1 egg, beaten

Scald milk. Cool to lukewarm. Mix together sugar, salt and flour. Cut in shortening. Measure water into a large mixing bowl (warm, not hot, water for active dry yeast; lukewarm water for compressed yeast). Sprinkle or crumble in yeast. Stir until dissolved. Stir in lukewarm milk. Add egg and flour mixture. Stir until well blended, about 2 minutes. Place in a greased bowl; brush top with soft shortening. Cover. Let rise in warm place, free from draft, until doubled in bulk, about 1 hour and 30 minutes. Meanwhile, prepare Prune, Date-Nut or Poppy Seed filling. (Recipes follow.) When dough has doubled in bulk, punch down and turn out on lightly floured board. Divide in half. Roll out each half into an oblong about 16 by 12 inches. Place one oblong on a large greased baking sheet. Spread with desired filling. Cover with other oblong of dough. Cover. Let rise in a warm place, free from draft, until doubled in bulk, about 1 hour. Bake in a moderate oven (350°F.) about 20 minutes. Cool.

1 cup sifted confectioners' sugar
1 tablespoon milk
¼ teaspoon vanilla

Combine all ingredients and mix well. Spread over top of Kringle. Cut in squares to serve.

Place one oblong of dough on baking sheet.

Spread with filling and cover with rest of dough.

### PRUNE FILLING

1½ cups chopped stewed pitted prunes
3 tablespoons lemon juice
½ teaspoon grated lemon peel
3 tablespoons sugar

Mix all ingredients well. Use for filling on Coffee Kringle.

### DATE-NUT FILLING

½ cup chopped nuts
½ cup chopped dates
Grated peel of 1 lemon
¼ cup chopped candied fruit
¼ cup sugar
½ teaspoon nutmeg

Mix all ingredients well. Use for filling on Coffee Kringle.

### POPPY SEED FILLING

1 cup ground poppy seeds
1 cup chopped dates
¾ cup chopped walnuts
¼ cup melted semi-sweet chocolate

Mix all ingredients together well. Use for filling on Coffee Kringle.

After baking and cooling Kringle, top with sugar icing.

When ready to serve, cut into squares.

# Jule Kaga

1 cup milk
½ cup sugar
1 teaspoon salt
½ cup shortening
¼ cup warm, not hot, water
2 packages or cakes yeast, active dry or compressed
4½ cups sifted flour
1½ teaspoons ground cardamom
½ cup raisins
¼ cup chopped citron
¼ cup chopped candied cherries
¼ cup chopped almonds

Scald milk. Stir in sugar, salt and shortening. Cool to lukewarm. Measure water into a large mixing bowl (warm, not hot, water for active dry yeast; lukewarm water for compressed yeast). Sprinkle or crumble in yeast. Stir until dissolved. Stir in lukewarm milk mixture. Add 2 cups of the flour. Beat thoroughly. Cover. Let rise in a warm place, free from draft, until doubled in bulk, about 30 minutes. Stir down. Stir in cardamom, raisins, citron, cherries and almonds. Stir in remaining 2½ cups of the flour. Turn dough out on a floured board. Knead until smooth and elastic. Place in a greased bowl; brush with shortening. Cover. Let rise in a warm place, free from draft, until doubled in bulk, about 55 minutes. Punch down. Form into round ball and place on a large greased baking sheet. Cover. Let rise in a warm place, free from draft, until doubled in bulk, about 1 hour. Bake in a hot oven (400°F.) about 10 minutes; reduce heat to moderate (350°F.) and continue baking 40 minutes. Cool.

1 cup sifted confectioners' sugar
1 tablespoon milk
¼ teaspoon vanilla
Whole nuts
Candied fruits

Combine sugar, milk and vanilla. Frost cake with this mixture and decorate with nuts and fruits.

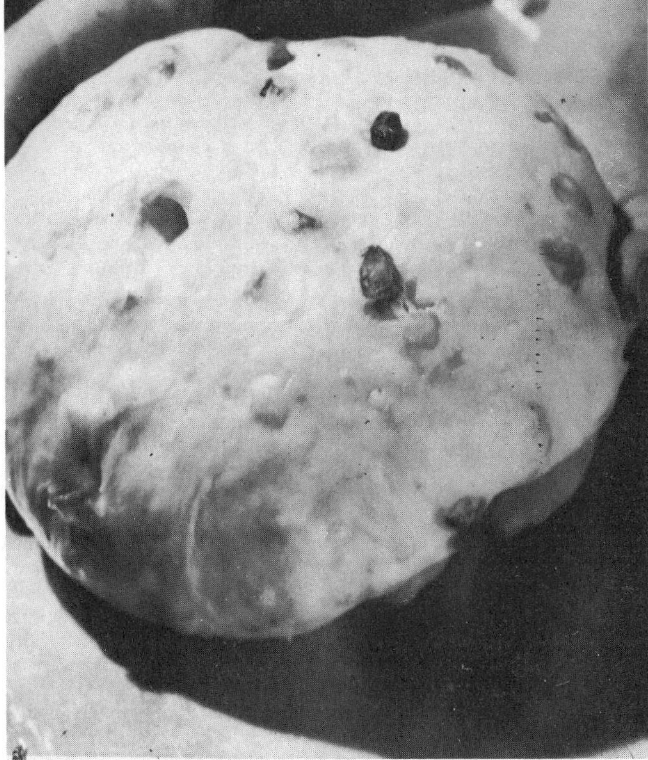

Let dough rise to twice its size. Bake in hot oven 10 minutes.

Reduce heat, bake 40 minutes.

# Hoska

1 cup milk
½ cup shortening
¾ cup sugar
½ teaspoon salt
¼ cup warm water
2 packages or cakes yeast, active dry or compressed
3 eggs
5½ cups sifted enriched flour
¼ cup chopped citron
¼ cup raisins
¼ cup chopped almonds
¼ cup whole blanched almonds
Melted butter or margarine

Scald milk. Stir in shortening, sugar and salt. Cool to lukewarm. Measure water into a large mixing bowl (warm, not hot, water for active dry yeast; lukewarm water for compressed yeast). Sprinkle or crumble in yeast. Stir until dissolved. Stir in lukewarm milk mixture. Beat 2 of the eggs and add to yeast mixture. Add 3 cups of the flour. Beat until smooth. Stir in citron, raisins and chopped almonds. Stir in remaining flour. Turn dough out on a lightly floured board. Knead until smooth and elastic. Place in a greased bowl; brush with melted shortening. Cover. Let rise in a warm place, free from draft, until doubled in bulk, about 1 hour and 15 minutes. Punch dough down and turn it out on a lightly floured board. Divide dough in half. Divide one half into 3 equal pieces. Roll each piece into a strip about 18 inches long. Place 3 strips on greased baking sheet. Form into a braid. Brush top lightly with melted butter or margarine. Divide ⅔ of remaining dough into 3 equal pieces. Form into a second braid about 18 inches long. Place on top of first braid. Brush top lightly with melted butter or margarine. Form remaining dough into a third braid about 18 inches long. Place on top of second braid. If necessary, use toothpicks to hold braids in place. Let rise in a warm place, free from draft, until doubled in bulk, about 1 hour. Mix remaining egg with 1 tablespoon water and brush on loaf. Decorate with whole blanched almonds. Bake in a moderately hot oven (375°F.) about 45 minutes. Makes 1 Hoska.

Place three braids on top of each other and, if necessary, use toothpicks to hold in place.

# French Pastry

## Palmiers Glacés

Press scraps of Puff Paste gently together. Roll out on a lightly floured board into a rectangle. Sprinkle with sugar. Fold into thirds and roll out into a rectangle. Sprinkle heavily with sugar and fold in thirds again. Roll out into a square about ⅛ inch thick. Fold each side of the square over to the center. Then fold in half, making 4 layers of pastry. Slice across into 1-inch slices. Place on a baking sheet covered with brown paper. Bake in a hot oven (425°F.) about 8 minutes. Turn over so that they do not burn on the bottom and bake another 8 minutes.

## Puff Paste

**2 cups sifted flour**
**½ teaspoon salt**
**½ cup ice water**
**1 cup butter**

Mix together the flour and salt in a bowl. Stir in ice water gradually, tossing moistened parts aside gently so that the dough is not overmixed. Stir just until blended. Cover dough with waxed paper and let stand for 20 minutes at room temperature. Roll dough out on a lightly floured board into a rectangle about ¼ inch thick. Cut butter into ¼-inch-thick squares. Arrange on pastry so that squares are equal distance from each other. Fold pastry into thirds crosswise, right and left portions over the center. Let rest about 10 minutes. Roll out to ¼-inch thickness. Fold again in thirds crosswise and reroll to ¼-inch thickness; fold in thirds again. Wrap lightly in waxed paper and chill in the refrigerator about 10 minutes. Reroll and fold two more times, chilling 10 minutes between each rolling. Roll dough into an oblong about 16 inches wide and ¼ inch thick. Cut into desired shapes. Place on a baking sheet lined with brown paper. Bake in a hot oven (425°F.) 20 to 25 minutes until paste is puffed high and delicately browned.

The Borden Company

PUFF PASTE

Sift together 2 cups sifted flour and ½ teaspoon salt. Gradually add ½ cup ice water, tossing moistened parts aside gently so that the dough is not overmixed. Stir until just blended. Cover dough with waxed paper and let stand about 20 minutes at room temperature.

Roll dough out on a lightly floured board into a rectangle about ¼-inch thick. Cut butter into ¼-inch squares. Arrange on pastry so that squares are equal distances from each other. Fold pastry into thirds crosswise, right and left portions over the center. Let rest about 10 minutes.

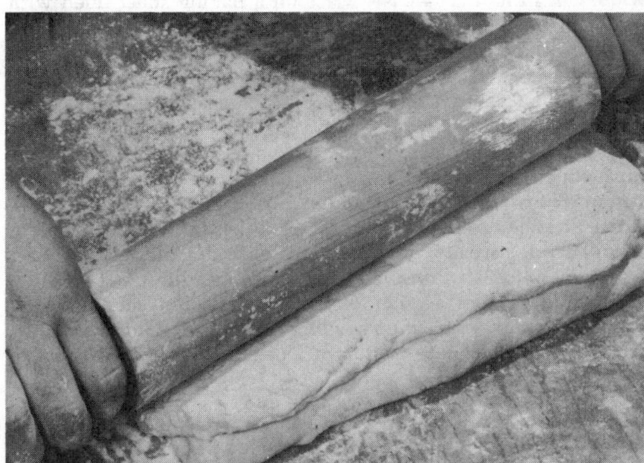

Roll dough out gently into a rectangle about ¼-inch thick. Be sure that none of the butter pops through the dough in rolling. Turn the rectangle and fold dough into thirds crosswise again. Roll dough out to ¼-inch thickness. Fold in thirds again. Wrap lightly in waxed paper and chill in the refrigerator about 10 minutes. Roll dough, turn and fold twice more, chilling between each rolling. Roll dough into an oblong about 16-inches wide and ¼-inch thick. Cut into desired shapes. Place on a baking sheet lined with browned paper. Bake in a hot oven (425° F) 20 to 25 minutes or until dough is puffed high and delicately browned.

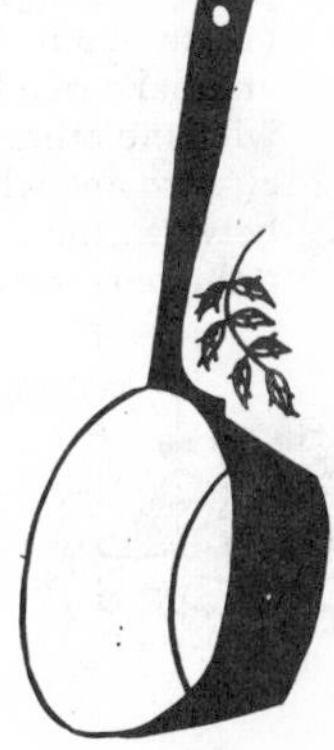

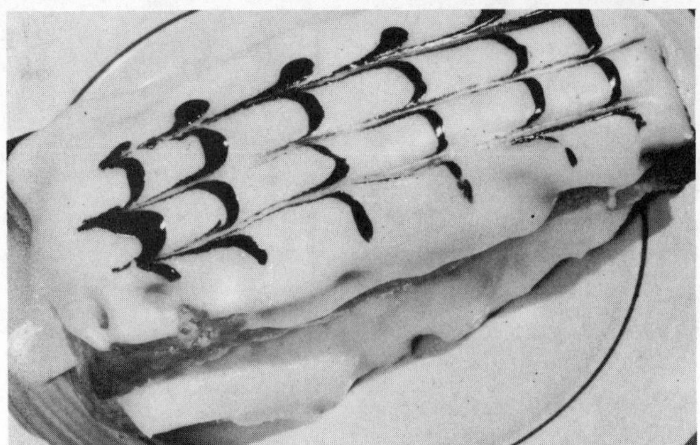
The Borden Company

# Napoleons

1 recipe Puff Paste
⅔ cup sugar
5 tablespoons flour
¼ teaspoon salt
2 cups milk
2 eggs, slightly beaten
1 teaspoon vanilla
¾ cup butter
1 cup sifted confectioners' sugar
1 tablespoon cold milk
Melted unsweetened chocolate

Roll Puff Paste into an oblong piece about 16 inches wide and ¼ inch thick. Cut lengthwise into 2 sections about 8 inches wide. Cut in half crosswise. Place on a baking sheet lined with brown paper. Bake in a hot oven (425°F.) 20 to 25 minutes. Cool. Combine sugar, flour and salt in the top of a double boiler. Add milk slowly, while stirring, to keep mixture smooth. Cook over boiling water, stirring constantly, until thickened. Cover and cook 10 minutes longer. Stir a little of the hot mixture into the slightly beaten eggs. Slowly add to the remaining hot mixture while stirring rapidly. Cook over hot but not boiling water, stirring constantly, for 2 minutes. Cool; stir in vanilla; chill. Cream butter, gradually beat in the thoroughly chilled cream filling. Chill. Spread 2 of the sections with this filling. Cut other 2 sections into 2-inch-wide strips. Place on filling, cut through filling and bottom section of pastry. Combine confectioners' sugar and milk. Stir until smooth. Spread over top of pastry layers. Swirl chocolate on top of frosting. Makes 8 Napoleons.

# Crispy Berry Napoleons

2 cups sifted flour
½ teaspoon salt
⅓ cup butter or margarine
⅓ cup shortening
5 tablespoons ice water
2 cups vanilla custard
1 cup whipped cream
2 cups sweetened berries

Sift together flour and salt. With a pastry blender or two knives cut in the butter and shortening until mixture looks like corn meal. Sprinkle water over mixture and toss gently until dough holds together. Divide dough in quarters. Roll 1 piece of dough out on a lightly floured board into a thin rectangle about 4 by 8 inches. Slide a cookie sheet under dough and bake in a hot oven (425°F.) about 15 minutes. Do the same with the other 3 quarters of the dough. When cool, combine the custard and whipped cream. Fold in berries. Spread this mixture between the 4 layers of pastry. Save enough of the mixture for a thin coating on the top. Makes 8 servings.

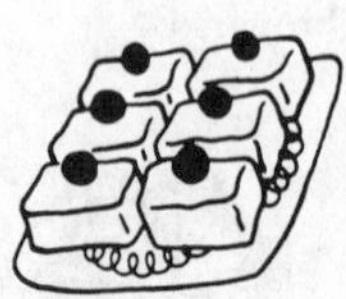

# Almond Cream Cake

1 recipe Puff Paste
½ cup finely ground, blanched almonds
½ cup sugar
¼ cup butter
2 egg yolks
2 tablespoons rum
1 drop almond extract
1 beaten egg
1 tablespoon milk
Confectioners' sugar

Roll out Puff Paste about ⅓ inch thick. Cut into two 8-inch circles. Place one circle on a baking sheet that has been lined with heavy brown paper. Combine almonds, sugar, butter, egg yolks, rum and almond extract. Spread over top of puff paste, leaving a ½-inch border around the edge. Moisten border lightly with water. Place second circle over top and press all around with thumbs to seal tightly. Brush the top with the combined egg and milk. With a sharp pointed knife prick the top all over, making a design if desired. Place the cake in the refrigerator and chill about 30 minutes. Bake in a hot oven (425°F.) 20 to 25 minutes, or until puffed and lightly browned. About 5 minutes before cake is baked sprinkle the top with confectioners' sugar and continue baking until the sugar is carmelized.

# Lady Locks

Press scraps of Puff Paste gently together. Roll out on a lightly floured board into a rectangle about ⅛ inch thick. Cut into strips about 1 inch wide and 10 inches long. Wind each strip around a buttered metal tube called a cream horn case, overlapping the edges slightly. Start at the point of the tube and finish at the wide part. Fasten the end securely. Put tubes on a baking sheet covered with heavy brown paper. Bake in a hot oven (425°F.) about 15 minutes. Slip off the tubes and cool. To serve fill with sweetened whipped cream.

The Borden Company

# Butter Cream Puffs

2 cups milk
¾ cup butter
Dash of salt
2 cups sifted flour
6 large eggs

Place milk and butter in a saucepan. Bring to a fast boil. Add salt and flour, stirring rapidly, until mixture is smooth and forms a ball. Remove from heat at once. Cool. Place mixture in large bowl of electric mixer. Add the eggs, one at a time, beating constantly at slow speed until each egg is thoroughly blended in. Dough should be firm enough to hold its shape when dropped from a spoon. Drop by tablespoonfuls onto well-greased, floured baking sheets. Bake in a moderately hot oven (375°F.) 45 minutes or until puffs are golden brown and crisp. Do not open oven door during first 40 minutes of baking period. Cool. Split puffs only enough to fill with ice cream, flavored whipped cream or custard. Makes 12 large puffs.

# Cream Puff Swans

**½ cup water**
**¼ cup butter or margarine**
**½ cup sifted flour**
**¼ teaspoon salt**
**2 eggs**
**Heavy cream, whipped**

Put water and butter in a saucepan. Bring mixture to a boil. Add flour and salt all at once. Cook over medium heat, stirring constantly, until mixture leaves sides of pan and forms a ball of dough. Remove from heat. Add eggs one at a time and beat well after each addition. Drop 4 very large tablespoonfuls of this mixture on a buttered baking sheet, about 3 inches apart. Press one side of each mound of paste with a spoon, to flatten and elongate it slightly, to make the tail of the swan. Put the remaining paste in a pastry bag with a plain round tube. Press out S-shaped pieces of paste to simulate swans' necks, onto a greased pie plate. Bake puffs and necks in a hot oven (425°F.) 20 to 25 minutes. The necks will be done before the puffs, so remove as soon as they are puffed and browned. Let cool. Cut off ⅓ from the top of each large puff and fill the puff with the whipped cream. Cut the top in halves and press them into the filling on either side to represent the wings. Insert the neck into the filling. Makes 4 cream puff swans.

# Gateau Saint Honore

**1 cup sifted flour**
**¼ cup butter**
**Dash of salt**
**½ tablespoon sugar**
**2 to 3 tablespoons cold water**
**1 double recipe Cream Puff Pastry**
**1 egg yolk**
**½ tablespoon milk**

Sift together flour, salt and sugar. Cut in butter with a pastry blender or 2 knives. Add just enough cold water to make a dough. Form into a ball and roll out on a lightly-floured board into a circle about 9 inches in diameter. Place on a cookie sheet. Place half the cream puff pastry in a pastry bag fitted with a plain tube. Make an edge around the dough about ¾ inch thick. Combine egg yolk and milk and beat. Brush top of cream puff paste with this mixture. Bake in a hot oven (425°F.) about 20 to 25 minutes, or until cream puff edge is puffed and browned. With remaining cream puff pastry make puffs about the size of large walnuts on a baking sheet. Brush with egg yolk and milk. Bake in a hot oven (425°F.) 20 to 25 minutes until puffed and browned.

### CREME PATISSIERE

**4 cups milk**
**1 one-inch stick vanilla bean**
**¾ cup sifted flour**
**1 teaspoon cornstarch**
**1 cup sugar**
**8 egg yolks**

Heat the milk and the vanilla bean to the boiling point. In another saucepan combine the flour, cornstarch, sugar and egg yolks and mix thoroughly. Gradually stir in the hot milk and continue stirring until smooth. Cook over very low heat, stirring constantly, until mixture is thickened. Cool. Take one cup of this mixture and fill the small cream puffs.

**1 cup sugar**
**⅓ cup water**
**¼ teaspoon cream of tartar**

Combine ingredients in a saucepan. Bring to a boil and cook over low heat, without stirring, until the syrup turns light brown. While syrup is still hot, dip small filled cream puffs in the mixture and arrange them around the edge of the cake. They will stay nicely if they are placed on edge while still dripping.

# Crown

**1 recipe Cream Puff Pastry**
**1 egg, beaten**
**½ cup slivered, blanched almonds**
**2 cups whipped, sweetened cream**

Shape the cream puff pastry into a circle about 8 inches in diameter on a greased baking sheet. Brush with the beaten egg and sprinkle with the almonds. Bake in a hot oven (425°F.) 20 to 25 minutes or until ring is puffed and lightly browned. Cool. Split and fill with whipped cream. Dust generously with confectioners' sugar just before serving.

# Creme Saint Honore

**1 unfilled Crown Ring**
**1 envelope unflavored gelatin**
**2 tablespoons cold water**
**3 cups hot Crème Patissiere**
**6 egg whites**
**6 tablespoons sugar**

Soften gelatin in cold water. Stir into the hot Crème Patissiere sauce and stir until the gelatin is dissolved. Cool. Beat the egg whites until stiff but not dry. Gradually beat in sugar and continue beating until mixture stands in stiff peaks. Fold into the cooled custard sauce. Pour into center of cream puff ring. Chill well. Top with whipped cream before serving, if desired.

# Josephines

**2 cups sifted flour**
**1 teaspoon salt**
**⅔ cup shortening**
**¼ cup milk**
**¼ cup butter**

Sift together flour and salt. Cut in ⅓ cup of the shortening until mixture looks like corn meal. Cut in last ⅓ cup of shortening until particles are size of peas. Sprinkle milk over mixture and mix with a fork until all flour is moistened. Press with hands into a smooth ball. Roll out dough ⅛ inch thick on a lightly floured board. Dot with bits of butter. Fold so that the two sides meet in the center and seal by pressing the side edge of pastry with fingers. Fold ends to center and seal. Roll dough out again about ⅛ inch thick into a rectangle. Cut into twenty-four oblongs about 2x3 inches. Place on a cookie sheet. Prick with a fork. Bake in a very hot oven (475°F.) 8 to 10 minutes or until delicately browned.

**½ cup sugar**
**⅓ teaspoon salt**
**2 tablespoons cornstarch**
**¾ tablespoon flour**
**2¼ cups milk**
**2 large egg yolks, beaten**
**¾ teaspoon butter**
**1 teaspoon vanilla**
**1 cup confectioners' sugar**
**2 tablespoons water**
**Chopped walnuts**

Mix together in the top of a double boiler the sugar, salt, cornstarch and flour. Stir in the milk. Cook over moderate heat, stirring constantly, until mixture thickens and boils. Boil 1 minute. Remove from heat. Slowly stir the hot mixture into egg yolks. Return to top of double boiler and cook over boiling water 3 minutes. Remove from heat and add butter and vanilla. Cool, stirring occasionally. Then chill thoroughly. Combine confectioners' sugar and water. Spread over twelve of the oblongs, then sprinkle with chopped nuts. Put oblongs together with the chilled vanilla cream between, using the frosted oblongs for the tops. Makes 12 Josephines.

# Croquembouche

½ package pie crust mix
3 recipes Cream Puff Pastry

Roll out the pie pastry on a lightly-floured board into a circle 9 inches in diameter. Place on a baking sheet and bake in a hot oven (425°F.) about 10 minutes or until lightly browned. Shape the cream puff dough into puffs about the size of walnuts. Bake in a hot oven (425°F.) about 20 to 25 minutes, or until puffed and browned.

### VANILLA BAVARIAN CRÈME

1 envelope unflavored gelatin
2 tablespoons cold water
4 egg yolks
½ cup sugar
1 cup hot milk
1 teaspoon vanilla
1 cup heavy cream, whipped

Combine gelatin and cold water. In a saucepan mix together the egg yolks and sugar. Slowly add the hot milk and stir well. Cook over low heat, stirring constantly, until mixture thickens. Remove from heat and stir in gelatin. Stir until dissolved. Add vanilla. Cool. Fold in whipped cream. Fill tiny cream puffs with this Bavarian Crème mixture. Combine 1 cup sugar, ⅓ cup water and ¼ teaspoon cream of tartar. Bring to a boil and simmer very slowly until light tan in color. Remove from heat, but keep hot. Place the pastry ring on a large serving dish. Dip the bottoms of the filled cream puffs in the hot syrup and place a row of them around the outside edge of the pastry ring. Place a second row of puffs on top of the first row, over the spaces between the puffs. Continue to build up the cream puffs in this manner, slanting it slightly in all the time. Continue to build the pyramid until it is topped off with one last puff. This may be garnished with rosettes of whipped cream as a final flourish.

# Apple Sauce Cream Puffs

½ cup water
¼ cup butter or margarine
½ cup sifted all-purpose flour
2 eggs
¼ teaspoon salt

Bring water to boiling point in saucepan; add butter or margarine; stir until melted. Bring to boiling point; quickly add all of the flour and salt. Cook, stirring constantly, about 2 minutes, or until mixture forms smooth, compact mass. Cool slightly; add eggs one at a time beating after each. Beat 5 minutes, or until mixture is thick and shiny. Using tablespoon or pastry bag, immediately shape 2″ apart on greased baking sheet in mounds 2½″ in diameter. Bake in very hot oven, (450°F.) 10 minutes, reduce to moderate oven, (350°F.), bake 20-25 minutes. Makes 8-9 medium puffs.

### Apple Sauce Filling

¼ lb. marshmallows, diced
2 tablespoons chopped maraschino cherries
2 cups canned apple sauce
½ cup heavy cream

Stir marshmallows and cherries into apple sauce. Beat cream until stiff; fold into apple sauce mixture. Makes enough filling for 8-9 cream puffs.

*To make Apple Sauce Cream Puffs:* Split cream puff shells; spoon in Apple Sauce filling. Place on serving plate; sprinkle tops with confectioners' sugar.

# Lemon Cream Puffs

1 cup water
½ cup butter
¾ cup sifted enriched flour
¼ teaspoon salt
½ cup rolled oats (quick or old fashioned, uncooked)
3 eggs
1 recipe lemon cream pudding
½ pint heavy cream, whipped

Heat water and butter to boiling in a large saucepan. Quickly stir in flour, salt and rolled oats. Beat vigorously over medium heat for about 2 minutes or until mixture leaves sides of pan and forms a ball. Remove from heat. Add eggs, one at a time, beating well after each addition; then beat for a minute more after the last egg has been well combined. Drop by tablespoonfuls (or a medium-sized ice cream scoop) onto greased cooky sheets. Bake in a very hot oven (450°F.) 15 minutes; then reduce temperature to 350°F. and continue baking 20 to 25 minutes. (The puffs should be firm and brown with no beads of perspiration.) Cool. To serve, cut off tops and fill with lemon whipped cream (made by preparing your favorite lemon cream sauce or lemon pudding mix, cooling thoroughly, then folding into the whipped cream.) Top with chocolate sauce. Makes 1½ dozen.

The Quaker Oats Company

# Cherry Eclairs

1 cup hot water
½ cup butter or margarine
1 cup sifted flour
¼ teaspoon salt
4 large eggs
1 No. 2 can pitted red cherries
1½ tablespoons cornstarch
¾ cup sugar
¼ teaspoon cinnamon
2 tablespoons margarine
1 cup heavy cream, whipped

Combine water and butter in a saucepan and bring to a boil. Add salt and flour all at once. Stir vigorously with a wooden spoon until a ball of dough is formed leaving sides of pan clean. Cool about 5 minutes. Add eggs one at a time, beat until mixture is smooth and glossy after each addition. Force dough through a pastry tube onto a lightly greased baking sheet in strips about 1 inch wide and 4 inches long. Bake in a hot oven (425°F.) 20 to 25 minutes. Drain juice from cherries. Combine cornstarch, sugar and cherry juice. Cook, stirring constantly, until thickened and clear. Add cinnamon and margarine. Cool slightly. Fold cherries into whipped cream. Slit cooled eclairs in half, fill with cream mixture. Pour hot sauce over eclairs. Makes 12 large eclairs.

# Strudels

## Strudel Dough

**3 cups sifted flour**
**2 eggs**
**½ teaspoon salt**
**3 tablespoons oil**
**⅔ cup warm water**

Sift flour onto a pastry board. Make a well in center and add eggs, salt and oil. Add water slowly and work mixture into a soft dough. Knead dough until it becomes elastic and leaves the board clean. Or, pick up the dough and throw it on the board about one hundred times. Form dough into a smooth ball. Cover with a warm bowl and let stand about 1 hour. Spread a clean cloth over a large table. Secure cloth with thumbtacks in several spots so that it will be easier to work on. Dust the whole cloth lightly with flour. Place dough in middle of cloth and roll out into a large oblong. Then reach under the dough with palms up and stretch the dough until it is transparent. With kitchen shears cut off the thick edges. Cover about ⅔ of dough with the desired filling. Roll strudel, starting with end covered with filling. The dough will roll easily by simply lifting the cloth high in the air, and pulling gently at the same time. With the last roll deposit the strudel in a greased baking pan. Brush with melted butter. Bake in a moderate oven (350°F.) 35 to 45 minutes or until browned.

With palms up, stretch the dough until it becomes very thin and almost transparent.

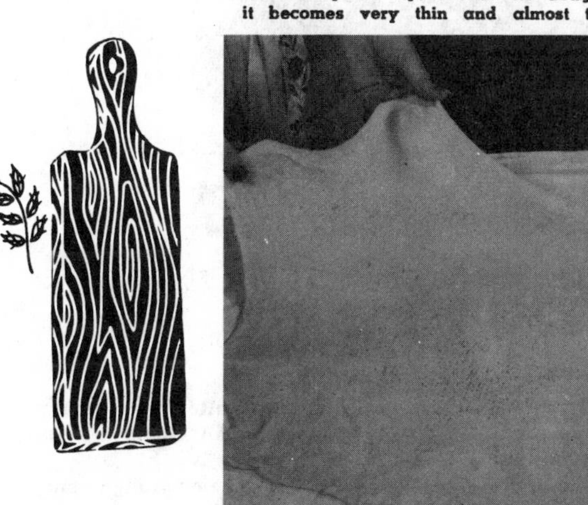

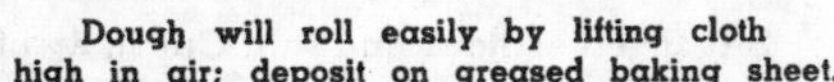

Dough will roll easily by lifting cloth high in air; deposit on greased baking sheet.

## Apple Strudel

**1 recipe strudel dough**
**½ cup melted butter**
**½ cup fine bread crumbs**
**6 tart apples, peeled, cored and thinly sliced**
**1 cup sugar**
**1 teaspoon cinnamon**
**1 cup raisins**
**1 cup chopped walnuts (optional)**
**Confectioners' sugar**

Make and stretch strudel dough according to directions. Brush the surface of dough with some of the melted butter. Sprinkle the bread crumbs over ⅔ of the dough. Sprinkle remaining ingredients over bread crumbs. Roll and place on a buttered baking sheet. Brush top of roll with remaining butter. Bake in a moderate oven (350°F.) about 45 minutes. Sprinkle generously with confectioners' sugar and serve warm with whipped cream, if desired.

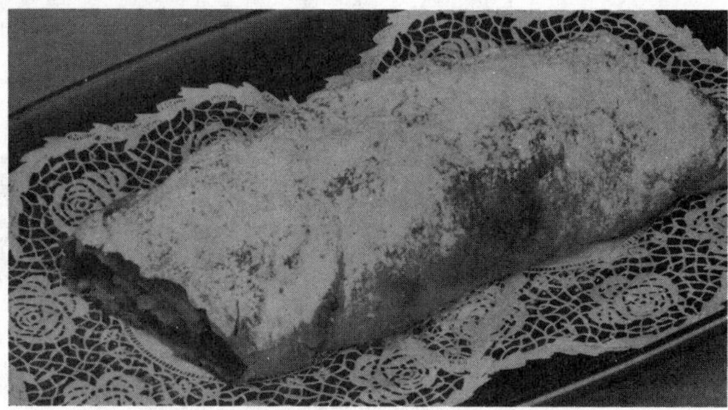

## Poppy Seed Strudel

**1 recipe strudel dough**
**1 cup poppy seeds, ground**
**½ cup sugar**
**Grated rind of ½ lemon**
**½ cup milk**
**⅓ cup raisins**
**2 tablespoons melted butter**

Combine poppy seeds, sugar, lemon rind and milk in the top of a double boiler. Cook over hot water until slightly thickened. Add raisins and cool. Prepare and stretch strudel dough according to directions. Brush with melted butter. Spread poppy seed mixture over ⅔ of the dough. Roll up tightly and place on a baking sheet. Bake in a moderate oven (350°F.) 45 minutes or until browned.

## Cottage Cheese Strudel

**1 recipe strudel dough**
**½ cup butter, divided**
**⅓ cup sugar**
**4 eggs, separated**
**½ cup sour cream**
**1 pound cottage cheese**
**1 teaspoon grated lemon rind**
**¼ cup white raisins**

Make and stretch strudel dough according to directions. Cream ¼ cup of the butter with the sugar. Beat in egg yolks and sour cream. Press the cottage cheese through a fine strainer and add to butter mixture. Add lemon rind. Beat egg whites until stiff and fold into cheese mixture. Sprinkle surface of strudel dough with some of the remaining butter which has been melted. Spread cheese mixture over ½ of the dough. Sprinkle raisins over cheese mixture. Roll and place on a buttered baking sheet. Brush with remaining melted butter. Bake in a moderate oven (350°F.) about 45 minutes or until golden brown Serve warm.

Processed Apples Institute

# Holiday Apple Strudel

- **2 cups canned apple sauce**
- **½ cup light brown sugar**
- **1 teaspoon cinnamon**
- **½ teaspoon nutmeg**
- **½ cup seedless raisins**
- **1 cup chopped walnuts**
- **1½ cups sifted all-purpose flour**
- **¼ teaspoon salt**
- **1 egg, slightly beaten**
- **⅓ cup warm water**
- **¾ cup melted butter**

Combine apple sauce, brown sugar, cinnamon, nutmeg, raisins and walnuts. Mix well. Mix together flour, salt, egg and water. Mix to dough with fork. Knead dough on board stretching and pulling dough to make it elastic. Knead until dough no longer sticks to board. Place ball of dough on floured board and cover with hot bowl. Let stand 40 to 50 minutes. Flour a board or table surface 18" x 24". Roll dough in an oblong piece; spread with ¼ cup melted butter. Carefully stretch dough all around to measure 18" x 24", at this point the dough should be very thin. Cut off torn and rough edges. Spread dough with another ¼ cup melted butter. Spread apple sauce filling over dough. Roll up jelly-roll fashion beginning at the long side. Place on a greased baking sheet, shaping roll into a ring. Brush with remaining ¼ cup butter, several times during baking. Bake in hot oven, 400°F., ½ hour, reduce heat to 350°F., and bake 15 minutes longer, or until brown and crisp. Cool and decorate according to the occasion. Makes 16-18 servings.

# Baklava

- **4 cups sifted flour**
- **2 teaspoons salt**
- **1⅓ cups shortening**
- **½ cup cold water**
- **1 cup cornstarch**
- **½ cup butter or margarine**
- **1 cup finely chopped black walnuts**
- **1 cup sage or orange honey**

Sift together flour and salt. Cut in ½ of the shortening with a pastry blender or two knives until mixture is the consistency of corn meal. Cut in remaining shortening to about the size of peas. Add water by the spoonful, tossing until mixture just sticks together, about like pie crust. Turn into a piece of waxed paper and press dough together. Chill in refrigerator about 5 to 6 hours. Divide dough into 30 equal sized balls. Roll each ball into as thin a rectangular sheet as can be handled. Stack in a baking pan one on top of the other, dusting each sheet lightly with cornstarch to prevent sticking. As you stack every sixth sheet, brush with melted butter and sprinkle with chopped walnuts. Pour ½ cup of the honey on top sheet. Bake in a very slow oven (300°F.) 30 minutes, or until lightly browned. Cut into diamond shaped pieces. Serve individually on plates with a heaping tablespoon of honey. Makes about 10 servings.

# MEAT, FISH & POULTRY

Do you shy away from roasting a turkey because it might not be as good as mother's? Would you like to know how to cook a succulent Ribs of Beef? Are you afraid that you might ruin that lovely sirloin steak if you attempt to cook it?

Here is the cook book that will unlock the secret of low temperature meat cookery. If you follow the times and the temperatures for roasting meat given in the charts, your roasts will be moist, succulent and done to your taste every time. You no longer will have to worry about over-cooking the steak, if you take a quick peek at our broiling chart first.

As for fish, many experienced cooks as well as new cooks, don't like to cook fish because it doesn't seem to taste just right. The real trick is not to over-cook it. Fish has no tough connective tissue, so it doesn't take long to cook and as soon as it flakes easily with a fork, serve it with pride, at once.

Roasting turkey and chicken is easy, if you follow a few simple directions. A quick trick for a perfect thanksgiving turkey is a simple tent of aluminum foil over the top of the turkey, to keep it from drying out and becoming tasteless. And if you want to know what to do with the left over turkey, you will find scores of recipes showing you how to use it up, right down to the last drumstick.

# MEAT

## How to Cook Meat

Basically, there are two methods for cooking meat. They are the dry heat method or moist heat, depending upon whether liquid is used in the cooking process. Dry heat methods are ideal for tender cuts of meat, whereas moist heat creates steam which softens connective tissue and cooks the less tender cuts to juicy goodness.

Oven roasting is used for large tender cuts of meat. The meat is placed, fat side up, in a shallow roasting pan. It is wise to use a meat thermometer, inserted into the thickest part of the muscle, being careful the bulb does not touch bone or rest in fat. Do not add water. Do not cover. Roast in a 325° F. oven and cook to desired degree of doneness as registered on the meat thermometer. Refer to time table on page 8 for approximate cooking time.

Broiling is used for small tender cuts of meat such as steaks, chops and ground meat patties. Steaks and chops should be cut at least 1-inch thick for best flavor results. Broiling is not recommended for fresh pork, which requires longer cooking time, or for veal, which is lacking in fat. Follow your range manufacturers' directions for broiling. Check times for broiling in chart on page 11.

Pan broiling is a variation of broiling in which the meat is cooked by direct contact with the hot metal of the pan instead of by direct heat as in actual broiling. No fat is added. Fat from the meat is poured off as it accumulates in the pan. Pan frying is similar to pan broiling except that a small amount of fat is added to the pan. This method is used for breaded and floured meats, for small frozen cuts and for meats that are very low in fat, such as liver or cubed steaks.

Braising is used for cooking less tender cuts of meat, and for some tender cuts, such as pork and veal chops. After meat is browned, a small amount of liquid is added, and meat is simmered until fork-tender.

Stewing is the method used for small pieces of meat, cut from economical, less tender cuts of beef, veal and lamb. Beef cubes are usually browned in hot fat; liquid is added, with or without vegetables and then covered tightly and simmered until fork tender.

### TIME AND TEMPERATURE CHART
### ROASTING—Use oven temperature of 325°F

| Cut | Weight Range | Internal Meat Temp | Approximate Total Time—(Hours) |
|---|---|---|---|
| **BEEF** | | | |
| Standing Ribs (3) | 8-9 lbs. | 140° F. rare | 2¼-2½ |
| | | 160° F. med. | 2¾-3 |
| | | 170° F. well done | 3½-4 |
| Standing Ribs (2) | 6-6½ lbs. | 140° F. rare | 1¾-2 |
| | | 160° F. med. | 2¼-2½ |
| | | 170° F. well done | 3-3¼ |
| Rolled Rib | 4-5 lbs. | Use times for 3-rib standing rib. | |
| Rolled Rump | 5-7 lbs. | 170° F. well done | 2½-3½ |
| Sirloin Tip | 3-3½ lbs. | 160° F. med. | 2-2½ |
| **VEAL** | | | |
| Leg (Center Cut) | 7-8 lbs. | 170° F. | 3-3½ |
| Loin | 4½-5 lbs. | 170° F. | 2½-3 |
| Boned Rolled Shoulder | 5-6 lbs. | 170° F. | 3½-4 |
| Boned Rolled Shoulder | 3 lbs. | 170° F. | 3 |
| **LAMB** | | | |
| Leg (whole) | 6-7 lbs. | 175-180° F. | 3½-3¾ |
| Leg (half) | 3-4 lbs. | 175-180° F. | 3-3½ |
| Boned Rolled Shoulder | 4-6 lbs. | 175-180° F. | 3-4 |
| Bone-in, Stuffed | 4-5 lbs. | 175-180° F. | 2½-2¾ |
| **FRESH PORK** | | | |
| Fresh Ham | 10-14 lbs. | 185° F. | 6-7 |
| Fresh Ham (half) | 5-6 lbs. | 185° F. | 3½-4 |
| Loin | 4-5 lbs. | 185° F. | 3¼-3½ |
| Loin End | 2½-3 lbs. | 185° F. | 2¼-2½ |
| Shoulder Butt | 4-6 lbs. | 185° F. | 3½-4 |

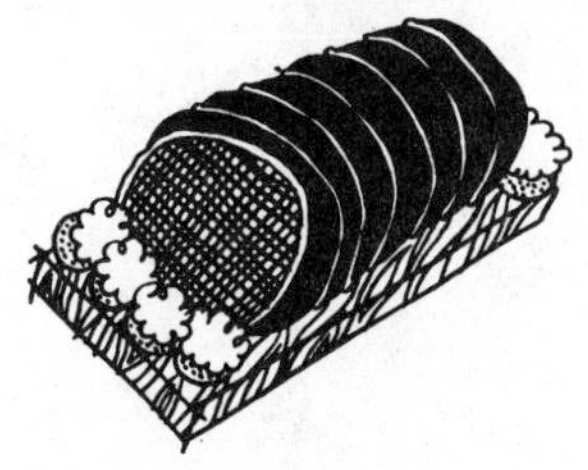

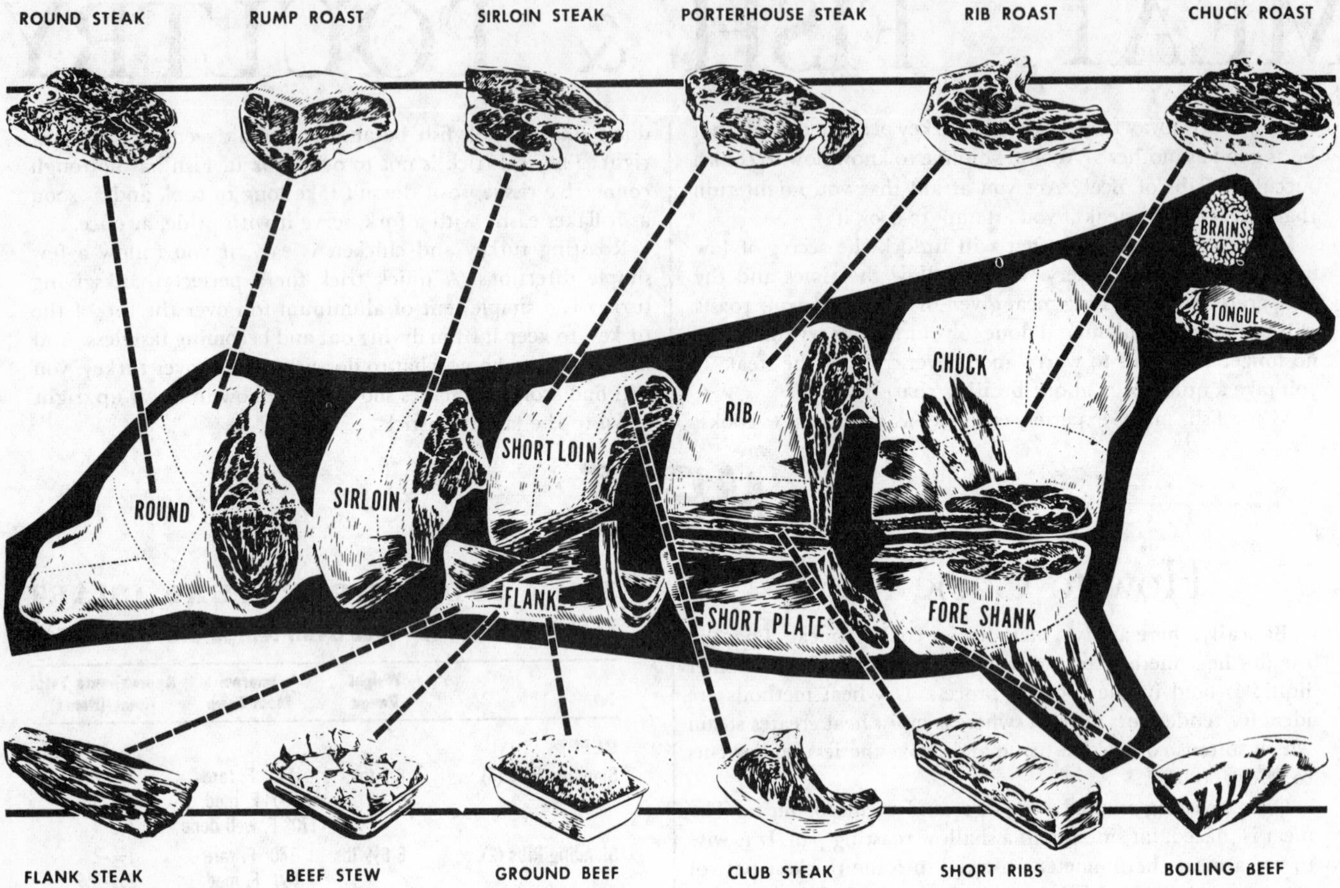

ROUND STEAK
RUMP ROAST
SIRLOIN STEAK
PORTERHOUSE STEAK
RIB ROAST
CHUCK ROAST
BRAINS
TONGUE
CHUCK
RIB
SHORT LOIN
SIRLOIN
ROUND
FLANK
SHORT PLATE
FORE SHANK
FLANK STEAK
BEEF STEW
GROUND BEEF
CLUB STEAK
SHORT RIBS
BOILING BEEF

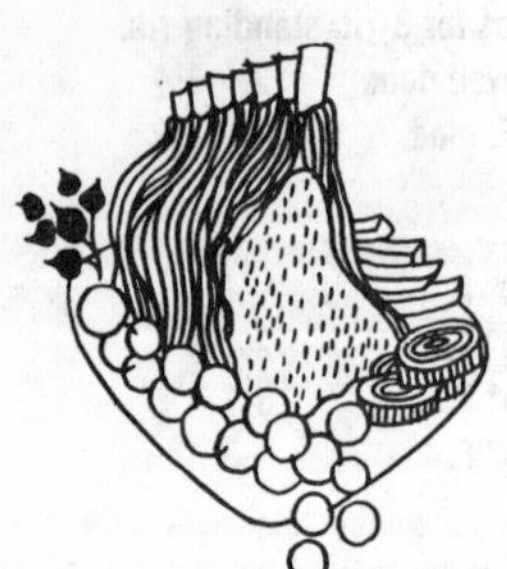

By referring to the following chart, you will be able to tell at a glance, which cuts of meat can be used for the dry heat or moist heat method of cooking.

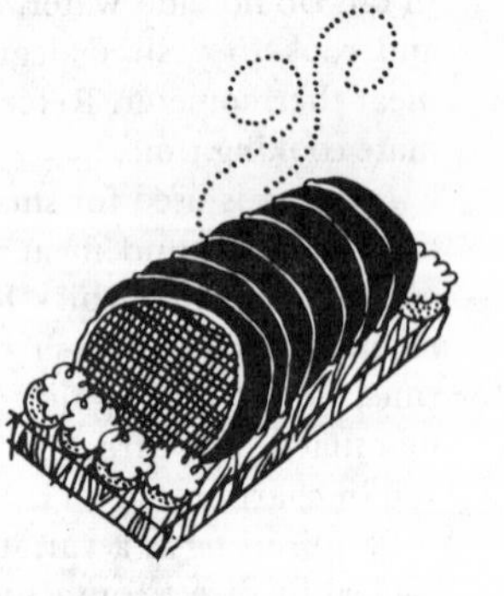

**PICTURED BELOW ARE FAMILIAR BONE SHAPES**

**These Can Help You Identify a Cut of Meat and Predict Tenderness**

TENDER
LESS TENDER
BEEF
VEAL
PORK
LAMB
T-BONE
RIB BONE
WEDGE BONE
ROUND BONE
BLADE BONE

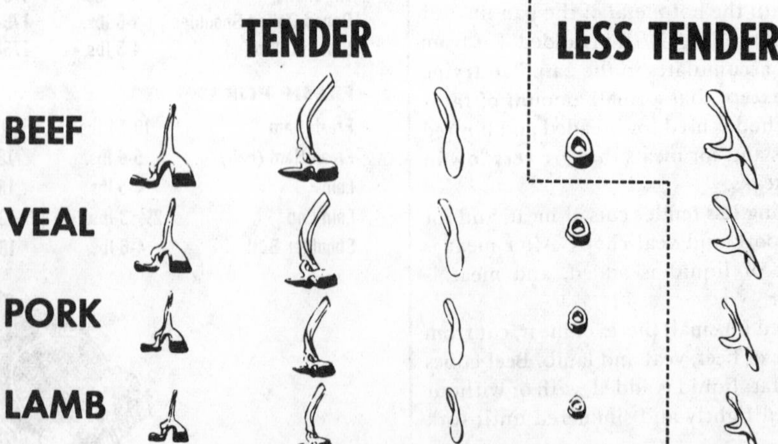

# How to Roast Ribs of Beef

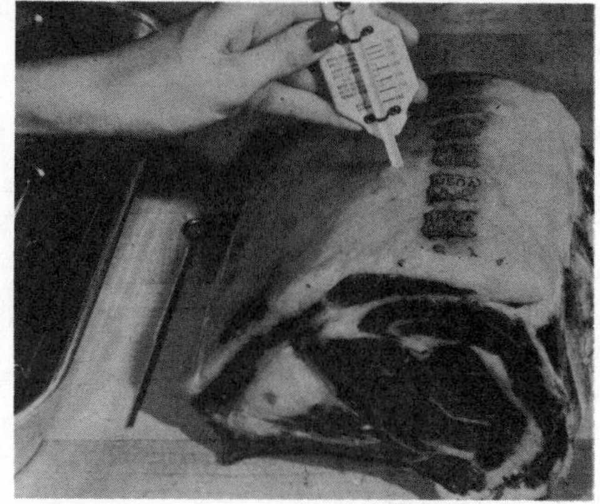

Place roast, fat side up, on a rack in an open, low-sided pan. Do not add water. Do not cover. Insert the point of a meat thermometer into the center of the thickest part of the meat, not touching bone. As the meat roasts, the thermometer indicates the internal temperature of the meat. Roast in a moderately slow oven (325° F). Use the time table in the chart

# How to Carve a Rib Roast of Beef

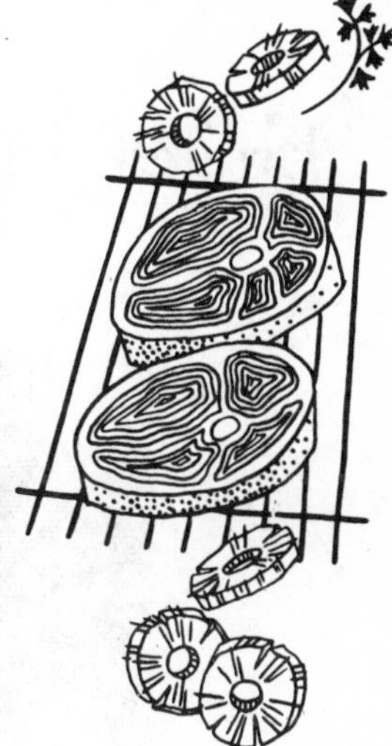

Use a large flat platter. Place the roast with flat side down, ribs to the left of the carver. The ribs' ends should be toward the carver. Insert the carving fork, tines down, between the top and second rib. Slice across the roast from right to left, making a ¼-inch slice.

Swift & Co.

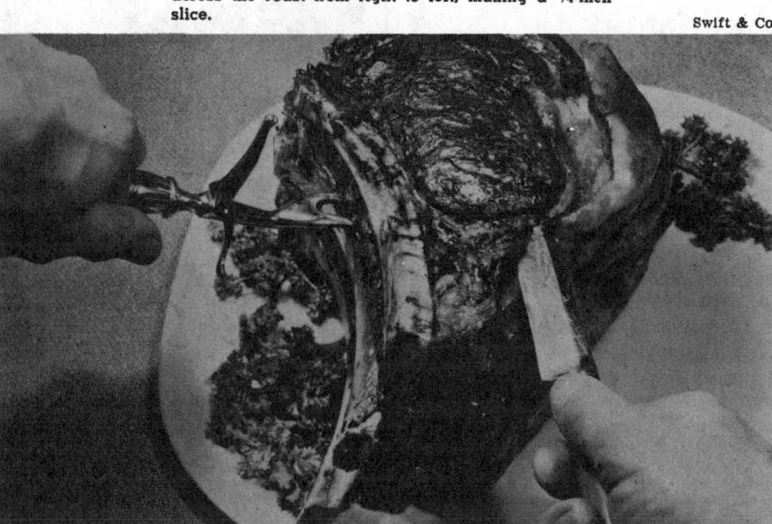

Continue slicing, removing rib bones as each one is cut from the meat. Or you may make a few extra thick slices, leaving a bone attached to the serving of roast beef.

Remove the knife and with the tip, cut along the side of the rib bone to free the slice. With the fork and knife, remove the slice to another heated plate or platter for serving.

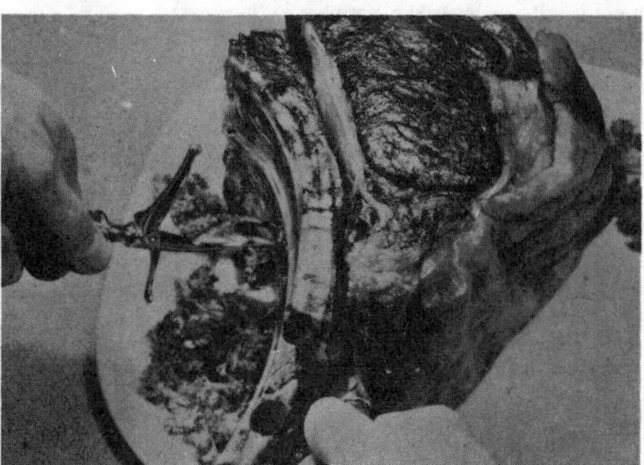

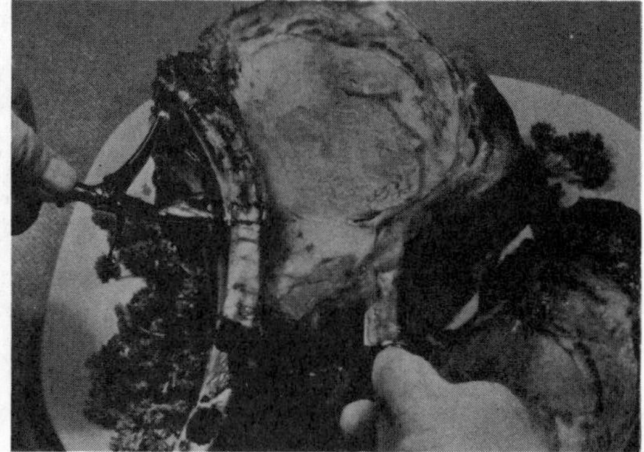

## TIME AND TEMPERATURE CHART

### BROILING

| Cut | Thickness | Weight | Approximate Total Time (Minutes) Rare | Medium | Well Done |
|---|---|---|---|---|---|
| **BEEF** | | | | | |
| Rib Steak | 1 inch | 1½ lbs. | 8-10 | 12-14 | 18-20 |
| Club Steak | 1 inch | 1½ lbs. | 8-10 | 12-14 | 18-20 |
| Porterhouse | 1 inch | 1½-2 lbs. | 10-12 | 14-16 | 20-25 |
| | 1½ inch | 2½-3 lbs. | 14-16 | 18-20 | 25-30 |
| | 2 inch | 3-3½ lbs. | 20-25 | 30-35 | 40-45 |
| Sirloin | 1 inch | 2½-3½ lbs. | 10-12 | 14-16 | 20-25 |
| | 1½ inch | 3½-4½ lbs. | 14-16 | 18-20 | 25-30 |
| | 2 inch | 5-5½ lbs. | 20-25 | 30-35 | 40-45 |
| Ground Beef Patties | ¾ inch | 4 oz. each | 8 | 12 | 15 |
| Tenderloin | 1 inch | —— | 8-10 | 12-14 | 18-20 |
| **LAMB** | | | | | |
| Rib or Loin Chops (1 rib) | ¾ inch | 2-3 oz. each | —— | —— | 14-15 |
| Double Rib | 1½ inch | 4-5 oz. each | —— | —— | 22-25 |
| Lamb Shoulder Chops | ¾ inch | 3-4 oz. each | —— | —— | 14-15 |
| Lamb Patties | ¾ inch | 4 oz. each | —— | —— | 14-15 |

# Broiled Sirloin Steak

Nation Live Stock & Meat Board

A Sirloin steak may be identified by the size of the meat and the shape of the bone. This steak should be broiled, panbroiled or panfried depending on the thickness of the steak.

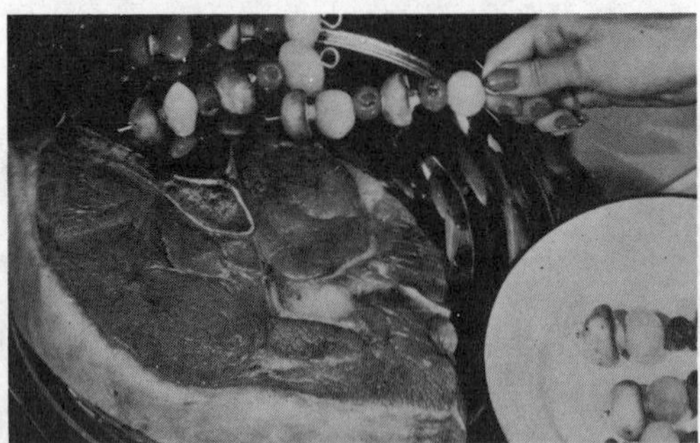

Steaks for broiling should be cut 1 to 2 inches thick. Place meat on broiling rack so that surface of meat is about 3-inches from the source of heat. After one side is browned, season and turn to finish cooking on second side.

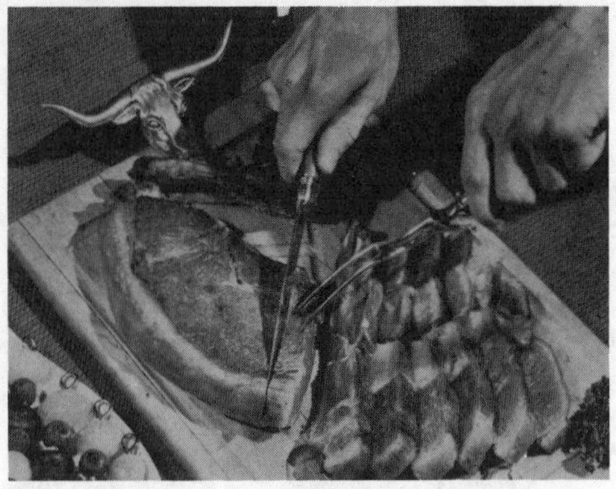

When steak is cooked, place on a cutting board. Cut around the bone, and place on side of board. Cut steak in strips, with the grain, from ½ to 1-inch wide. Serve 2 to 3 strips per serving.

# How to Cook a Beef Stew

Cook 4 slices of bacon in a heavy skillet. Remove bacon. Brown 2 pounds of boneless beef cubes in the drippings. Cook and turn until all sides of the beef cubes are browned.

After beef cubes are browned, return crumbled bacon to skillet. Sprinkle over the meat 2 teaspoons salt, ¼ teaspoon pepper, ½ teaspoon marjoram and 1 minced clove of garlic. Stir in 2 cups water. Cover tightly and cook over low heat for 2 hours.

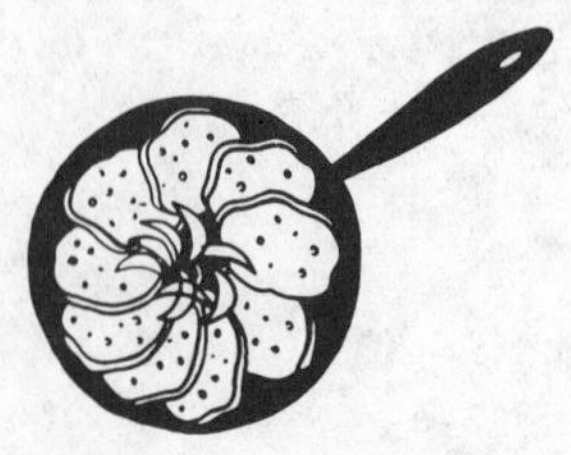

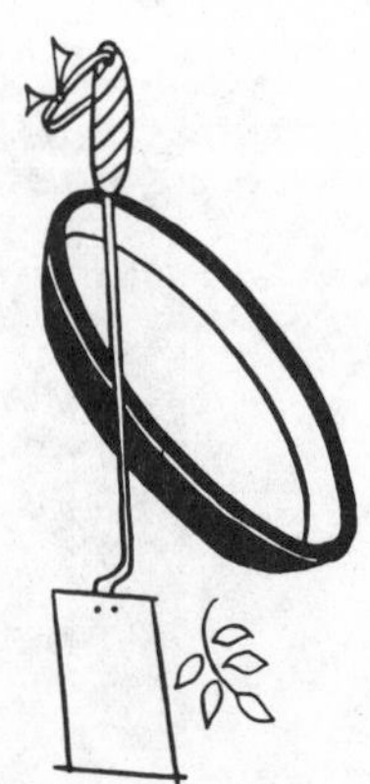

When meat is almost cooked, add 4 medium potatoes, cut in halves or quarters, 6 medium carrots, halved, 6 small onions and 2 turnips cut in quarters. Cover tightly and cook over low heat until the vegetables are done and meat is tender, about 30 minutes.

Remove meat and vegetables and place on serving platter. Measure liquid in pan and add enough water to make 2 cups liquid. Combine 3 tablespoons of flour with a little water to make a smooth paste. Stir into liquid in pan and cook, stirring, until mixture boils and thickens. Season to taste and serve with meat and vegetables.

# Beef

## Swiss Steak

**1 beef round steak, cut 1-inch thick**
**¼ cup flour**
**3 teaspoons salt**
**⅛ teaspoon pepper**
**1 medium onion, sliced**
**1 clove garlic, minced**
**3 tablespoons shortening**
**1 can (2-ounces) mushroom stems and pieces**
**1 teaspoon Worcestershire sauce**
**¼ cup water**
**¼ teaspoon oregano**
**⅛ teaspoon rosemary**
**⅛ teaspoon cayenne pepper**
**1 can (6-ounces) tomato paste**
**¼ cup catsup**
**1 can (8½-ounces) applesauce**

Cut round steak into 5 or 6 pieces. Combine flour, salt and pepper. Pound flour mixture into both sides of the meat with the back of a heavy knife or the edge of a saucer. Brown meat, onion and garlic in hot shortening in a skillet. Pour off drippings. Add mushrooms, Worcestershire sauce, water, oregano, rosemary and cayenne pepper to skillet. Cover tightly and simmer 2 hours. Stir in tomato paste, catsup and applesauce. Continue cooking about 30 minutes, or until fork tender. Makes 5 to 6 servings.

National Live Stock & Meat Board

## Round Steak and Vegetables

**2 pounds round steak, cut ½-inch thick**
**Flour**
**1 teaspoon salt**
**8 carrot strips**
**8 celery strips**
**4 dill pickles, cut in half lengthwise**
**3 tablespoons fat**
**1 cup beef bouillon**
**¼ teaspoon pepper**
**¼ teaspoon onion salt**

Cut round steak in 8 pieces about 3 by 4 inches. Pound in flour with edge of heavy saucer. Sprinkle on salt. Lay 1 strip each of carrot, celery and dill pickle on each piece. Fold meat in half. Fasten with a pick. Brown meat in hot fat in a heavy skillet. Add remaining ingredients. Cover and simmer about 1¼ hours or until tender. Makes 6 to 8 servings.

Swift & Co.

# Sweet Sour Pot Roast

2 tablespoons shortening
5 pounds round-bone pot roast
½ cup sliced onion
1 cup vinegar
¾ cup brown sugar
¼ teaspoon nutmeg
½ teaspoons salt

Melt shortening in a heavy kettle. Brown meat in melted fat. Remove meat. Add onions and cook until transparent. Return meat to kettle. Add remaining ingredients. Cover and simmer over low heat until meat is tender. This will take about 3½ hours. If desired thicken broth, using 1½ tablespoons of flour for every cup of liquid. Makes 8 to 10 servings.

# Veal Cutlets, Oriental

4 Frenched veal cutlets
Flour
3 tablespoons fat
½ cup chopped celery
¼ cup chopped onion
½ cup sliced mushrooms
3 tablespoons soy sauce
1 cup chicken bouillon
1 tablespoon cornstarch
½ cup slivered almonds, toasted
Cooked rice

Dip veal cutlets into flour. Pan-brown veal in hot fat in a heavy skillet. Remove veal. Cook celery, onion and mushrooms until tender. Return veal to pan. Add soy sauce and ½ cup bouillon. Cover and simmer 30 minutes. Combine remaining ½ cup bouillon and cornstarch. Stir into veal mixture. Cook 5 minutes or until thickened. Stir in almonds. Serve over hot rice. Makes 4 servings.

Swift & Co.

# Pot Roast with Kidney Beans

2 tablespoons shortening
5-pound bladebone pot roast
1 tablespoon salt
1 teaspoon chili powder
1 large onion, sliced
2 cups water
1 can (pound) kidney beans

Melt shortening in a heavy kettle. Brown meat in melted fat. Add salt, chili powder, sliced onion and water. Cover and simmer 3 hours or until tender. Pour kidney beans over meat. Cover and simmer until beans are hot. Remove roast from kettle. Serve with beans in gravy. Makes 8 to 10 servings.

# Baked Short Ribs Mount Vernon

4 tablespoons flour
1 teaspoon salt
¼ teaspoon pepper
4 pounds beef short ribs
2 tablespoons butter or margarine
2 medium onions, chopped
2 tablespoons brown sugar
1 tablespoon vinegar
½ teaspoon dry mustard
½ cup catsup
½ cup beer or ale
1 cup beef bouillon
6 whole carrots, scraped and halved

Combine flour, salt and pepper; roll short ribs in mixture. Brown ribs on all sides in hot butter in skillet. Reduce heat; add onion and cook until tender, but not brown. Combine brown sugar, vinegar, dry mustard, catsup, beer and bouillon. Turn into a 2-quart casserole. Bake in a moderate oven (350°F.) 1½ hours. Add carrots; bake 1 hour longer. Makes 6 servings.

U. S. Brewers' Association

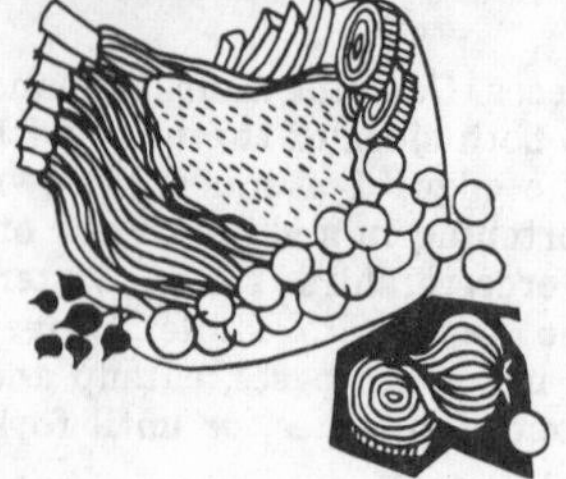

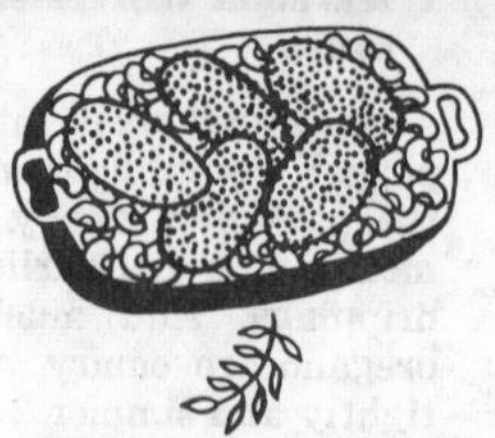

Swift & Co.

# Beef Short Ribs and Cabbage with Herbs

**3 pounds short ribs, cut into servings**
**2 tablespoons fat**
**1 tablespoon salt**
**¼ teaspoon pepper**
**½ cup wine vinegar**
**1 cup water**
**½ teaspoon oregano**
**⅛ teaspoon sage**
**1 tablespoon dry mustard**
**1 bay leaf**
**½ cup sliced onions**
**½ head cabbage cut in 4 wedges**

Brown short ribs in hot fat in a skillet. Sprinkle with salt and pepper. Add remaining ingredients, except cabbage. Cover and simmer 1 to 1½ hours. Add cabbage and cook about 20 minutes, or until cabbage is tender. Makes 4 servings.

# Sauerbraten

**1½ cups vinegar**
**1½ cups water**
**2 bay leaves**
**12 whole cloves**
**¼ teaspoon pepper**
**¼ teaspoon mace**
**1½ teaspoons salt**
**1 tablespoon sugar**
**2 large onions, sliced**
**½ cup salad oil**
**3 to 4 pound beef roast, heel of round**
**½ cup flour, divided**
**3 tablespoons shortening**
**½ cup crumbled ginger snaps**

Heat vinegar, water, spices, salt and sugar to boiling. Pour over sliced onions and allow to stand until cool. Stir in oil. Pour marinade over roast in a deep bowl. Allow to stand in refrigerator 2 to 4 days, turning meat once a day so it will marinate evenly. Remove meat from marinade and pat dry. Dredge with half the flour. Brown on all sides in hot shortening in a dutch oven. Place rack under meat and add 1 cup of strained marinade. Save remaining marinade. Cover meat tightly and simmer 3 to 4 hours or until meat is fork tender. Remove to hot platter. Add enough strained marinade to liquid in dutch oven to make 2 cups liquid. Make a smooth paste with remaining flour and ¼ cup cold marinade. Stir into liquid in kettle. Bring to boil, stirring constantly. Stir in ginger snaps and heat thoroughly. Season to taste. Serve hot gravy with sauerbraten. Makes 6 to 8 servings.

National Live Stock & Meat Board

# Raisin Pot Roast

**3½ pounds pot roast of beef**
**2 tablespoons shortening**
**1 medium onion, chopped**
**1 bay leaf**
**1 teaspoon salt**
**¾ cup water**
**1 tablespoon brown sugar**
**2 tablespoons vinegar**
**3 tablespoons catsup**
**⅓ cup raisins**
**1 cup cold water**
**1 tablespoon cornstarch**

Brown beef in hot shortening in a heavy kettle. Add onion, bay leaf, salt and ¾ cup water. Cover and simmer 1 hour. Mix together brown sugar, vinegar, catsup and raisins. Add to beef in kettle. Cover and continue simmering 1 to 1½ hours, or until meat is fork tender. Remove pot roast to hot platter. Skim excess fat from broth remaining in kettle, leaving about 2 tablespoons fat. Gradually combine 1 cup cold water with cornstarch. Mix until smooth. Add to broth and stir until gravy is clear and thickened. Serve gravy over roast. Makes 6 to 8 servings.

# Pot Roast Supreme

4 to 5 pound blade pot roast, 2-inches thick
1 tablespoon salt
¼ teaspoon black pepper
1 tablespoon shortening
1 cup water
2 teaspoons Worcestershire sauce
1 bay leaf
½ stalk celery, cut in pieces
6 to 8 medium onions
¼ cup catsup
2 tablespoons mustard
8 carrots, pared
½ teaspoon herb seasoning

Wipe surface of roast with damp towel. Sprinkle salt and pepper over entire roast. Heat shortening in large Dutch oven. Brown roast on both sides, 10 to 15 minutes. Slip a low rack under meat to prevent burning during long cooking period. Add water, Worcestershire sauce, bay leaf, celery and 1 of the onions, sliced. Blend together catsup and mustard; spread half on top surface of roast. Cover with tight-fitting lid. Cook slowly over low heat. Water should simmer enough to make steam. Add water, if needed, to keep about an inch of liquid in bottom of kettle. After 1½ hours, turn roast; spread with remaining catsup-mustard mixture. Add whole onions and whole carrots (split in half lengthwise if large). Continue cooking until meat and vegetables are tender. About 1½ hours.

Remove meat and vegetables to hot platter. Keep hot. Strain broth. Pour off excess fat. Add water to make 3 cups liquid. Add herb seasoning. Make into gravy. To thicken, add 3 to 4 tablespoons flour, blended smooth with cold water. Bring to a boil. Simmer 4 to 5 minutes. Serve with potato pancakes. Makes 8 to 10 servings.

National Live Stock & Meat Board

# Mexicana Veal

6 veal cutlets, cut ½-inch thick
1 egg, beaten
⅔ cup fine dry bread crumbs
¼ cup shortening
1 can (1 pound) tomatoes
1½ teaspoons salt
¼ teaspoon oregano
3 medium zucchini squash

Put cutlets into egg and then in bread crumbs. Brown on both sides in hot shortening in heavy skillet. Pour off drippings. Add tomatoes and seasonings. Cover tightly and simmer 30 minutes. Slice zucchini in about ½-inch slices and add to veal. Continue cooking 30 minutes or until meat is fork tender. Makes 6 servings.

# Parisian Oxtails with Vegetables

4 pounds disjointed oxtails
½ cup flour, divided
1 tablespoons salt
¼ teaspoon pepper
¼ cup shortening
2 medium onions, sliced
2 carrots, cut into chunks
½ cup diced celery and leaves
1 bay leaf
1 clove garlic, chopped
¼ teaspoon thyme
1 can (1 pound) tomatoes
2 cups water
4 to 6 peeled potatoes
½ cup water
Chopped parsley

Roll oxtails in ¼ cup flour mixed with salt and pepper. Brown in hot shortening in a heavy kettle. Add onions, carrots, celery, bay leaf, garlic, thyme, tomatoes and 2 cups water. Cover and simmer 3 to 4 hours or until meat is tender. Chill in refrigerator overnight. Skim off all surface fat. A half hour before serving time, pare and quarter potatoes. Cook in simmering salted water until just tender. Heat oxtails to boiling point. Combine remaining ¼ cup flour and ½ cup water and stir into broth. Cook, stirring constantly, until mixture thickens. Reduce heat and simmer 10 minutes. Drain potatoes and stir into meat mixture. Serve topped with chopped parsley. Makes 4 to 6 servings.

# Spicy Brown Beef Stew

2 pounds beef stew meat, cut into 2-inch cubes
⅓ cup flour
3 tablespoons fat
1½ teaspoons salt
½ teaspoon celery salt
¼ teaspoon dry thyme
1 small clove garlic, finely chopped
2 cups water
2 teaspoons Worcestershire sauce
2 tablespoons catsup
6 whole cloves
1 can (1 pound) onions
1 package (10 ounces) frozen peas and carrots
1 can (1 pound) whole potatoes

Coat meat on all sides with flour. Save extra flour. Melt fat in a heavy kettle. Add meat and brown well on all sides. Remove browned meat from kettle. Sprinkle salt, celery salt, thyme, garlic and extra flour into kettle with fat, stirring to make a smooth paste. Gradually add water, stirring constantly, until gravy is smooth and thickened. Stir in Worcestershire sauce and catsup. Return browned meat to kettle. Cover and cook over low heat about 2 hours. Stick whole cloves into onions. Add onions, carrots and potatoes to kettle. Cover and continue cooking about 30 minutes or until meat is fork-tender. Makes 6 servings.

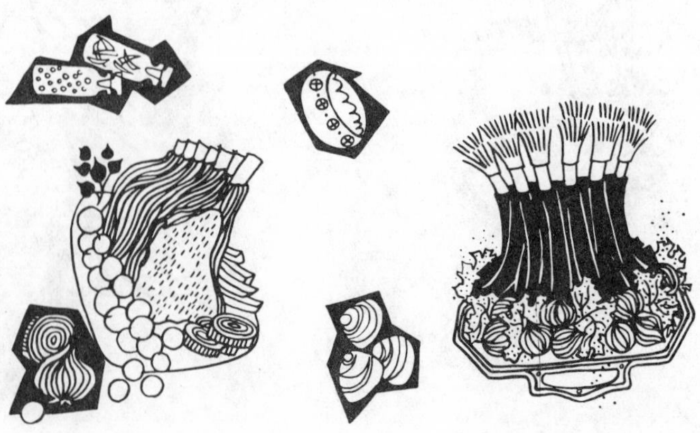

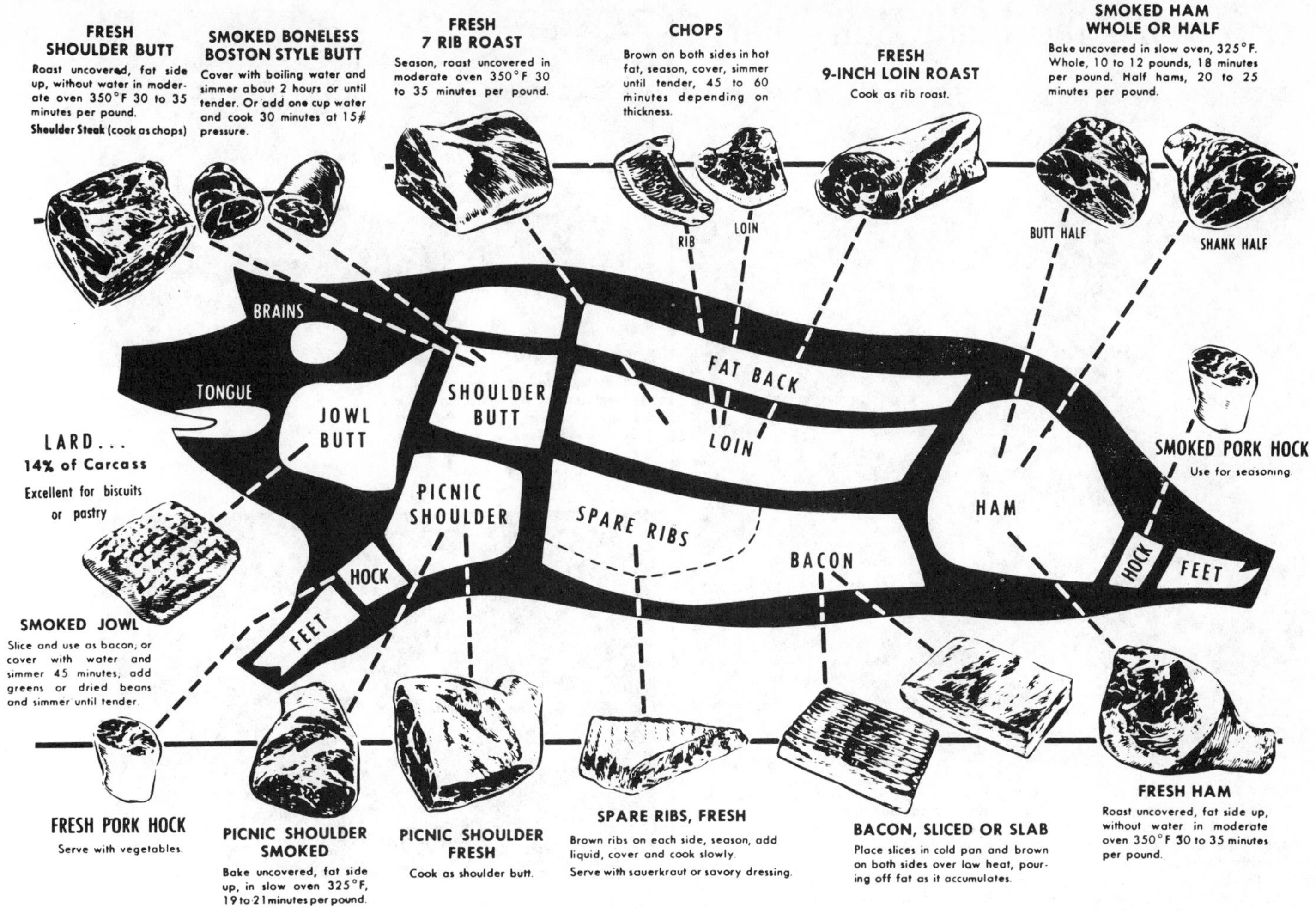

**FRESH SHOULDER BUTT**
Roast uncovered, fat side up, without water in moderate oven 350°F 30 to 35 minutes per pound.
**Shoulder Steak** (cook as chops)

**SMOKED BONELESS BOSTON STYLE BUTT**
Cover with boiling water and simmer about 2 hours or until tender. Or add one cup water and cook 30 minutes at 15# pressure.

**FRESH 7 RIB ROAST**
Season, roast uncovered in moderate oven 350°F 30 to 35 minutes per pound.

**CHOPS**
Brown on both sides in hot fat, season, cover, simmer until tender, 45 to 60 minutes depending on thickness.

RIB

LOIN

**FRESH 9-INCH LOIN ROAST**
Cook as rib roast.

**SMOKED HAM WHOLE OR HALF**
Bake uncovered in slow oven, 325°F. Whole, 10 to 12 pounds, 18 minutes per pound. Half hams, 20 to 25 minutes per pound.

BUTT HALF

SHANK HALF

BRAINS

TONGUE

JOWL BUTT

SHOULDER BUTT

FAT BACK

LOIN

PICNIC SHOULDER

SPARE RIBS

BACON

HAM

HOCK

FEET

HOCK

FEET

**LARD...**
**14% of Carcass**
Excellent for biscuits or pastry

**SMOKED PORK HOCK**
Use for seasoning.

**SMOKED JOWL**
Slice and use as bacon; or cover with water and simmer 45 minutes; add greens or dried beans and simmer until tender.

**FRESH PORK HOCK**
Serve with vegetables.

**PICNIC SHOULDER SMOKED**
Bake uncovered, fat side up, in slow oven 325°F, 19 to 21 minutes per pound.

**PICNIC SHOULDER FRESH**
Cook as shoulder butt.

**SPARE RIBS, FRESH**
Brown ribs on each side, season, add liquid, cover and cook slowly.
Serve with sauerkraut or savory dressing.

**BACON, SLICED OR SLAB**
Place slices in cold pan and brown on both sides over low heat, pouring off fat as it accumulates.

**FRESH HAM**
Roast uncovered, fat side up, without water in moderate oven 350°F 30 to 35 minutes per pound.

# Pork

## How to Select and Cook Ham

There are two kinds of ham sold in most retail stores today. They are either fully-cooked or cook-before-eating hams. Fully cooked hams can be served cold, without further cooking. Or, if you prefer, they may be reheated, as suggested in the following chart. Canned hams are also fully cooked and may be served cold or reheated according to taste.

Cook-before-eating hams require additional cooking time before being served, as shown in the following chart. Another kind of ham, the so called "Country Style" hams, is not readily available in all localities. These hams are heavily cured and usually require soaking and simmering in water before baking.

Hams are available in several styles: bone in; skinless, shankless (only the shank removed and the meat skinned and trimmed of excess fat); semi-boneless; boneless; boneless (shaped into rolls) and canned hams which are also boneless and skinless.

To bake a ham, place the meat, fat side up, on a rack in a shallow roasting pan. Do not add water or cover and do not baste. Insert a meat thermometer into the thickest part of the meat and bake in a moderately slow oven (325°F) oven.

Cook-before-eating hams would be baked to an internal temperature of 160°F. according to cooking time in the chart. Center slices of ham can be cooked by oven-baking, broiling, pan-broiling or frying.

Fully-cooked hams may be reheated to an internal temperature of 130°F. according to cooking time in chart. Center slices can be browned lightly on each side to heat through.

Cooking time for Hams

| Cuts | Minutes per pound |
|---|---|
| Cook-Before-Eating | |
| Whole Ham | 18 to 20 |
| Half Ham | 22 to 25 |
| Boned Ham Roll | 30 |
| Fully-Cooked | |
| Whole Ham | 10 |
| Half Ham | 14 |
| Boned Ham Roll | 12 to 15 |
| Canned, 8 to 13 pounds | 10 to 15 |
| 6 pounds | 15 to 20 |

# Carving the Ham Butt Half

The butt end of the ham is recognized by the small round bone just off center. The flat wedge bone showing on the side opposite the fat covered area also helps to identify the cut.
Place the half ham upright with the cut surface down on a flat platter. The bone end and the wedge-shaped bone should be placed to the left of the carver.

Plunge the fork firmly into the ham. Begin slicing horizontally, using a firm, sawing stroke across the grain of the muscle to the round bone. Cut several slices. Next make a vertical cut close to the bone to free and remove the slices. After four or five half-inch thick slices have been removed, the round bone increases in size. If necessary, cut around the joint to cut the size slices desired.

# Roast Loin of Pork

Place pork roast on a rack in a shallow roasting pan. Rub with 1 teaspoon salt to each pound.

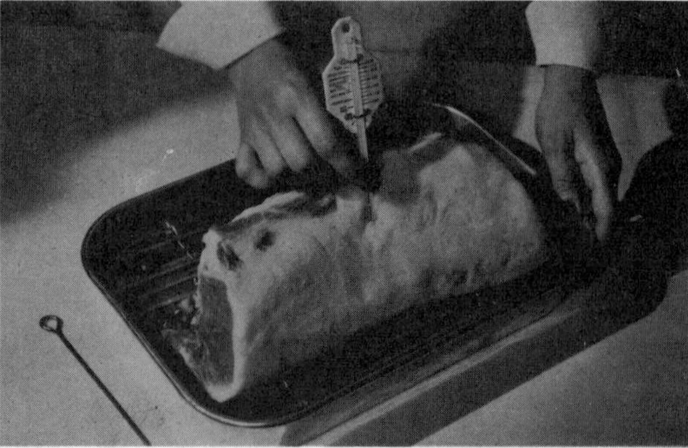

Make a hole in roast with a skewer and insert thermometer to center of meaty part. Be sure thermometer does not touch bone. Let pork roast thoroughly to internal temperature to 185° F.

Roast meat, uncovered, in a moderate oven (350° F). Cook 30 minutes per pound for loin of pork, 35 minutes per pound for pork shoulder.

Perfect finished product is thoroughly and evenly cooked, well browned, juicy and flavorful. Garnish with spicy crabapples, and serve with applesauce if desired.

# Pork Oriental

1 tablespoon shortening
1 pound lean pork, loin or shoulder
1 teaspoon salt
2 teaspoons Worcestershire sauce
2 teaspoons lemon juice
1 tablespoon brown sugar
2 medium onions, sliced
1 can (13½ ounces) pineapple tidbits
1 green pepper, cut into strips
1 envelope curry sauce mix
½ cup cold water

Heat shortening in skillet. Cut pork into ½-inch slices; cut slices into 2½-inch strips. Brown lightly in hot shortening—about 5 minutes. Sprinkle pork with salt. Add Worcestershire sauce, lemon juice, sugar, and onion slices. Drain syrup from can of pineapple into a measuring cup. Add water to make 1¾ cups. Pour over pork. Stir ingredients in pan, bring to a boil. Cover; reduce heat; cook gently 20 minutes. Add green pepper. Continue to cook 2 or 3 minutes. Meanwhile combine contents of envelope of Curry sauce mix with cold water. Push meat to one side of pan, add curry mixture and pineapple, stirring constantly. Mix all together. Bring to boiling point. Serve hot over fluffy cooked rice. Makes 4 servings.

R. T. French Co.

# Miniature Glazed Ham Loaves

¾ pound ground cooked ham
¾ pound ground pork
¾ cup rolled oats, uncooked
2 eggs
½ cup milk
⅔ cup brown sugar, firmly packed
2 tablespoons flour
1 teaspoon dry mustard
⅛ teaspoon ground cloves
⅔ cup apricot nectar
1 tablespoon vinegar
1 tablespoon lemon juice

Combine ham, pork, rolled oats, eggs and milk. Blend well. Shape into 8 small round loaves. Bake in a slow oven (325°F.) 1 hour. Pour excess fat from pan. Blend together brown sugar, flour, mustard and cloves in a small saucepan. Add apricot nectar, vinegar and lemon juice. Stir and cook over low heat until thickened. Pour over ham loaves and continue baking 20 minutes.

# Spicy Ham Loaf

3 cups ground cooked ham
½ cup fine bread crumbs
¼ cup finely chopped onion
2 tablespoons finely chopped green pepper
½ teaspoon dry mustard
⅛ teaspoon allspice
⅛ teaspoon ground cloves
2 eggs, slightly beaten
½ cup milk

Combine ham, bread crumbs, onion, green pepper, mustard, allspice and cloves. Add eggs and milk and mix until combined. Pack into a 1-quart loaf pan. Bake in a moderate oven (350°F) 45 minutes. Unmold and serve hot. Makes 6 servings.

# Ham and Potato Casserole

1 medium onion, chopped fine
3 tablespoons chopped green pepper
¼ cup butter or margarine
3 tablespoons flour
2 cups milk
½ teaspoon salt
⅛ teaspoon pepper
3 cups cubed cooked ham
4 cups cubed or sliced, cooked potatoes
¾ cup shredded, processed American cheese

Cook onion and green pepper in butter about 5 minutes. Stir in flour. Add milk, salt, and pepper. Stir, cooking constantly until mixture is thickened. Add ham and potatoes. Pour into a 2-quart casserole. Sprinkle with cheese. Bake in a moderate oven (350°F.) about 25 to 30 minutes. Makes 6 to 8 servings.

Florida Citrus Commission

# Easter Ham

1 uncooked whole ham (10-12 pounds) (smoked or ready-to-eat)
Whole cloves
⅓ cup unsulphured molasses
⅓ cup prepared mustard

Bake ham in a moderate oven (325°F.). For smoked ham, bake 18 to 20 minutes per pound or until meat thermometer registers 160°F. For ready-to-eat ham, bake 10-12 minutes per pound or until meat thermometer registers 130°F. One hour before ham is done, take from oven. If ham has rind, remove. Score fat surface with tulip cookie cutter; outline tulips with cloves. Carefully place each Orange Tulip inside clove outline. Combine unsulphured molasses and mustard; brush part of mixture over ham. Return to oven and continue baking, brushing with remaining glaze.

### Orange Tulips

4 oranges
1 cup sugar
¾ cup water
2 tablespoons vinegar
1 teaspoon whole cloves
1 2-inch piece stick cinnamon

With tip of paring knife, cut peel of each orange into 4 quarters. Carefully remove peel; reserve. Cut membrane from oranges; section to use in dessert fruit bowl. Cut each quarter of peel with a tulip cookie cutter; discard excess peel. Place "orange tulips" in saucepan; add 3 cups water. Bring to a boil; boil gently 20 minutes. Drain off water, remove peel. Combine sugar, water, vinegar and spices in saucepan; stir over low heat until sugar is dissolved. Bring to a boil; add "orange tulips" and simmer 30 minutes. Remove and cool. Place on ham according to directions.

# Stuffed Ham Steak

2 ham steaks, ¼ inch thick
Whole cloves
½ cup finely chopped onion
¾ cup finely chopped celery
2 tablespoons butter
1½ cups bread cubes
2 tablespoons chopped parsley
1 teaspoon salt
⅛ teaspoon cinnamon
1 egg, slightly beaten

Slash fat around ham steaks; stud with whole cloves; set aside. Sauté onion and celery in butter 10 minutes. Add bread cubes, parsley, salt, cinnamon, egg; toss lightly. Place one ham steak in center of large double-thick square of aluminum foil, cover steak with stuffing mixture. Top with second ham steak; if necessary, hold in place with toothpicks. Bring two sides of foil up over ham; seal together with double fold; fold each end up close to ham. Place on oven rack; bake 25 minutes in hot oven (450°F.). Open foil wrap; bake 10 minutes longer. Place ham on platter to serve. Makes 4-5 servings.

# Pork and Apple Casserole

6 medium-sized apples
⅓ cup water
1 teaspoon salt
2 cups chopped, cooked pork
½ cup brown sugar
¾ cup soft breadcrumbs

Pare, core and slice apples. Add water and salt. Simmer about 10 minutes or until apples are soft. Arrange half the apples in a 1½-quart casserole. Add pork cubes. Add remaining apple slices. Combine sugar and crumbs. Spread mixture over top of casserole. Bake in a moderate oven (350°F.) about 45 minutes. Makes 4 to 5 servings.

# Savory Pork in Sweet Potato Nests

2 cups mashed sweet potatoes
Milk
1 tablespoons melted butter or margarine
1½ cups finely chopped cooked pork
1 cup peas
½ cup pork gravy
½ teaspoon salt
⅛ teaspoon thyme

To the mashed sweet potatoes add enough milk to make mixture smooth and easy to shape. Divide in flour mounds on a baking sheet. Make a well in the center of each mound with the back of a spoon. Brush with melted butter. Combine remaining ingredients in a baking dish. Place pork mixture and sweet potato mounds in a moderate oven (350°F.) 15 to 20 minutes. Spoon pork into sweet potato nest and serve at once. Makes 4 servings.

# Baked Ham En Casserole

1 cooked boneless ham, 3 to 5 lbs.
¼ cup Sherry
¼ cup honey
¼ cup brown sugar
1 teaspoon grated orange rind
1 cup sweet mixed pickles

Place ham in 2½-quart shallow casserole. If ham is canned, scrape off gelatin first to remove excess salt flavor. If ham is not fully-cooked, allow longer cooking time as directed on meat package. Combine Sherry, honey, brown sugar, and orange rind; pour over ham. Bake in slow oven, (325°F.), for 40 to 45 minutes, basting once. Baste again and pour pickles over top. Continue baking for 20 to 30 minutes or until ham is heated thoroughly.

Corning Glass Works

# Ham and Cheese Fondue

10 slices bread
1 cup cubed cooked ham
¼ pound shredded Cheddar cheese
1¼ cups milk
Dash cayenne pepper
2 eggs, beaten slightly
2 tablespoons butter or margarine

Remove crusts from bread and place in a layer in a buttered 2-quart casserole, or shallow baking dish. Sprinkle half of the ham and cheese over bread. Cover with remaining slices of bread, then remaining ham and cheese. Combine milk, pepper and eggs. Pour over bread and ham. Dot with butter and bake in a moderate oven (350°F.) 30 to 35 minutes. Makes 6 servings.

# Ham and Noodle Casserole

2 tablespoons butter or margarine
2 tablespoons flour
1 cup milk
1 cup shredded American cheese
1 teaspoon salt
2 tablespoons catsup
1 tablespoon horse-radish
1 cup cooked peas
2 cups diced cooked ham
1½ cups cooked noodles
¼ cup dry bread crumbs
1 tablespoon butter

Melt 2 tablespoons butter in a saucepan. Blend in flour. Pour in milk and stir. Cook, stirring constantly, until sauce is thick and smooth. Add cheese and cook, stirring until melted. Add salt, catsup, horseradish, peas, ham and noodles. Blend well. Turn mixture into a 1-quart casserole. Top with crumbs and dot with butter. Bake in a moderate oven (350°F.) 30 minutes. Makes 4 servings.

# Scalloped Pork and Potato Casserole

2 cups chopped cooked pork
3 cups thinly sliced potatoes
2 tablespoons finely chopped green pepper
2 tablespoons finely chopped onion
1 can (10½ ounces) cream of celery soup
½ cup milk
1 teaspoon salt
⅛ teaspoon pepper
⅛ teaspoon savory
½ cup shredded cheese

Combine all ingredients, except cheese, and place in a 1-quart casserole. Bake in a moderate oven (350°F.) 30 minutes. Remove from oven and sprinkle cheese on top. Return to oven and continue baking 30 minutes or until potatoes are done. Makes 4 to 5 servings.

# Glazed Baked Ham

Buy a ham the size and type you want and place in the oven, fat side up in an open roasting pan. Follow the time and temperature directions in the Time and Temperature Chart. About 45 minutes before the ham is done, remove from the oven. Remove the skin if necessary and score the fat (cut in criss-cross gashes to form a diamond pattern). In each diamond, place a whole clove. Combine 1 cup brown sugar and 1 cup crushed pineapple. Coat ham with this mixture. Return to oven and finish baking.

*Tip.* In baking half a ham, place cut side down on a rack to keep it from drying out. Half an hour before it is done, score and glaze.

National Live Stock & Meat Board

# Broiled Center Ham Slice

slice of ham 1 to 1½ inches thick
¼ teaspoon cloves
1 can (1 lb.) cling peaches
½ cup brown sugar
1 tablespoon cornstarch
1 tablespoon butter or margarine

Heat broiler and grease broiler rack with a piece of ham fat. Gash the fat in several places to prevent curling during cooking. Place meat on the rack, 2 inches from the source of heat. Broil 20 to 25 minutes on each side. While meat is broiling, drain can of peaches. Combine cloves, sugar and cornstarch. Add to peach juice and cook over low heat, stirring constantly until thickened. When ham slice is turned, arrange drained peaches on broiler. Dot with bits of the tablespoon of butter and broil until slightly brown. Serve on platter around ham slice. Pass the sauce separately. Makes 4 servings. Serve with corn on the cob, buttered asparagus, carrot and raisin salad, lemon sponge pudding.

*Tip.* Any tag ends of leftover ham slice can be scrambled with eggs for another meal.

# Barbecued Pork Tenderloin

**2 whole pork tenderloins**
**2 tablespoons butter or margarine**
**½ cup flour**
**¼ cup vinegar**
**½ teaspoon salt**
**½ teaspoon dry mustard**
**2 teaspoons celery seed**
**1½ teaspoons chili sauce**
**½ cup catsup**
**2 tablespoons sugar**
**2 tablespoons paprika**
**Pepper**

Cut each tenderloin lengthwise and crosswise. This will make 8 pieces. Melt butter in a skillet. Coat meat with flour and brown in hot butter. Combine remaining ingredients and pour over meat. Cover and simmer over very low heat about 2 hours. Makes 8 servings.

Swift & Co.

# Spiced Ham on a Rotisserie

**5 to 6 pound canned ham**
**¼ teaspoon each ground cloves and nutmeg**
**½ cup apricot, peach or pineapple preserves**
**2 teaspoons lemon juice**

Tie ham with string in 2 or 3 places. Insert rotisserie spit lengthwise through the center of the meat and secure with prongs. Sprinkle spices evenly over surface of ham. Insert a roast meat thermometer parallel to spit in the meat. Place spit in position in a rotisserie or over a bed of hot coals. Heat to 130°F. internal temperature, allowing 10 to 15 minutes per pound. Combine preserves and lemon juice. Spoon sweet sauce over ham last 5 minutes of cooking period, or after ham is removed from the spit.

Swift & Co.

# Lamb

## How to Buy and Cook Lamb

Among the most popular oven roasts is the leg of lamb. The full leg includes the sirloin and the leg; it may weigh as much as 8 or 9 pounds. Sometimes the retailer removes the sirloin section and markets it as a fine small oven roast weighing 2 to 2½ pounds. Or he may cut it into sirloin chops as shown here. The sirloin chop, tender enough for charcoal, oven or pan broiling, can be recognized by the wedge-shaped bone.

In addition to the wedge bone, the rib, T-bone and round bone chops are fine for broiling. The rib chops are often cut 1 to 2-inches thick for charcoal and oven broiling. When served in fine restaurants, they are often cut with 2 ribs per chop and are listed as double lamb chops. The rib section also makes a fine small oven roast and is called a rack of lamb.

The T-bone lamb chops are highly prized for broiling because of their meatiness and the fact that the tenderloin muscle, known for its tenderness is included. A T-bone chop cut 1-inch thick weighs from 4 to 6 ounces.

The round bone shoulder chop is a chop of good size weighing 5 to 7 ounces when cut about ¾-inch thick. Because it is a little less tender and less picturesque than the T-bone and rib chop, it is usually priced cheaper in the market. Another big chop, cut from the shoulder section, is identified by the blade bone. It is usually cut ½ to ¾-inch thick and will weigh 7 to 8 ounces. Both of these chops are especially good when braised.

Broiling is a form of dry heat cooking reserved for tender chops and steaks. The meat is cooked by direct heat. Moisture and cover are not needed.

Lamb chops for charcoal and oven-broiling should be cut 1 to 2-inches thick. Thinner chops should be pan-broiled to be served at their juicy best. Tender lamb chops for broiling are the rib, T-bone, wedge bone and round bone cuts.

Slash the edges of the chops in several places to prevent curling. Place the meat on the broiling rack so that the surface of the meat is about 3-inches from the source of the heat. Allow about 5 minutes per side for medium-done chops cut 1-inch thick. Add 1 minute per side for well-done chops. Turn once and season before serving.

Lamb chops especially suitable for braising are the blade bone chops. Some prefer to braise the round bone shoulder chops, also. To braise, the lamb chops may be dipped into seasoned flour, then browned in a small amount of hot fat. Liquid is added before covering to cook slowly on top of the range or in a moderate oven (350° F).

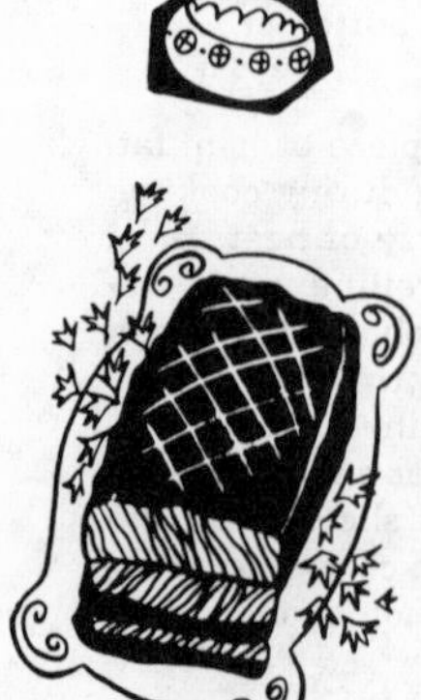

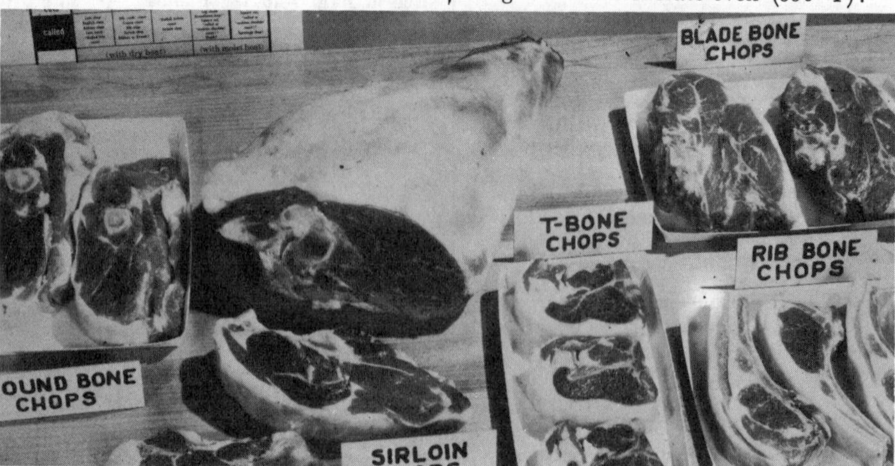


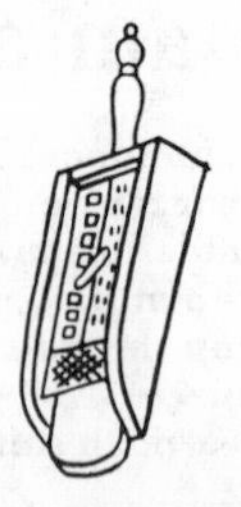

# How to Carve
# Leg of Lamb

Place the roast with the legbone to the right of the carver. The aitchbone, a wedge-shaped bone located at the butt end of the leg of lamb, is slanted toward the meaty horseshoe section of the roast. With the meat held firmly in place with the fork, cut 3 or 4 lengthwise slices from the side opposite the horseshoe section. Turn the roast to rest on the flat just-cut surface.

Beginning at the shank end of the roast, cut down to the bone with firm strokes, slicing the meat about ¼-inch thick. Continue cutting until the aitchbone is reached. Remove the slices by cutting along the legbone. A 6 to 7 pound leg of lamb will yield 15 to 18 slices from this horseshoe cut. Second helpings may be carved from the meat remaining on the legbone.

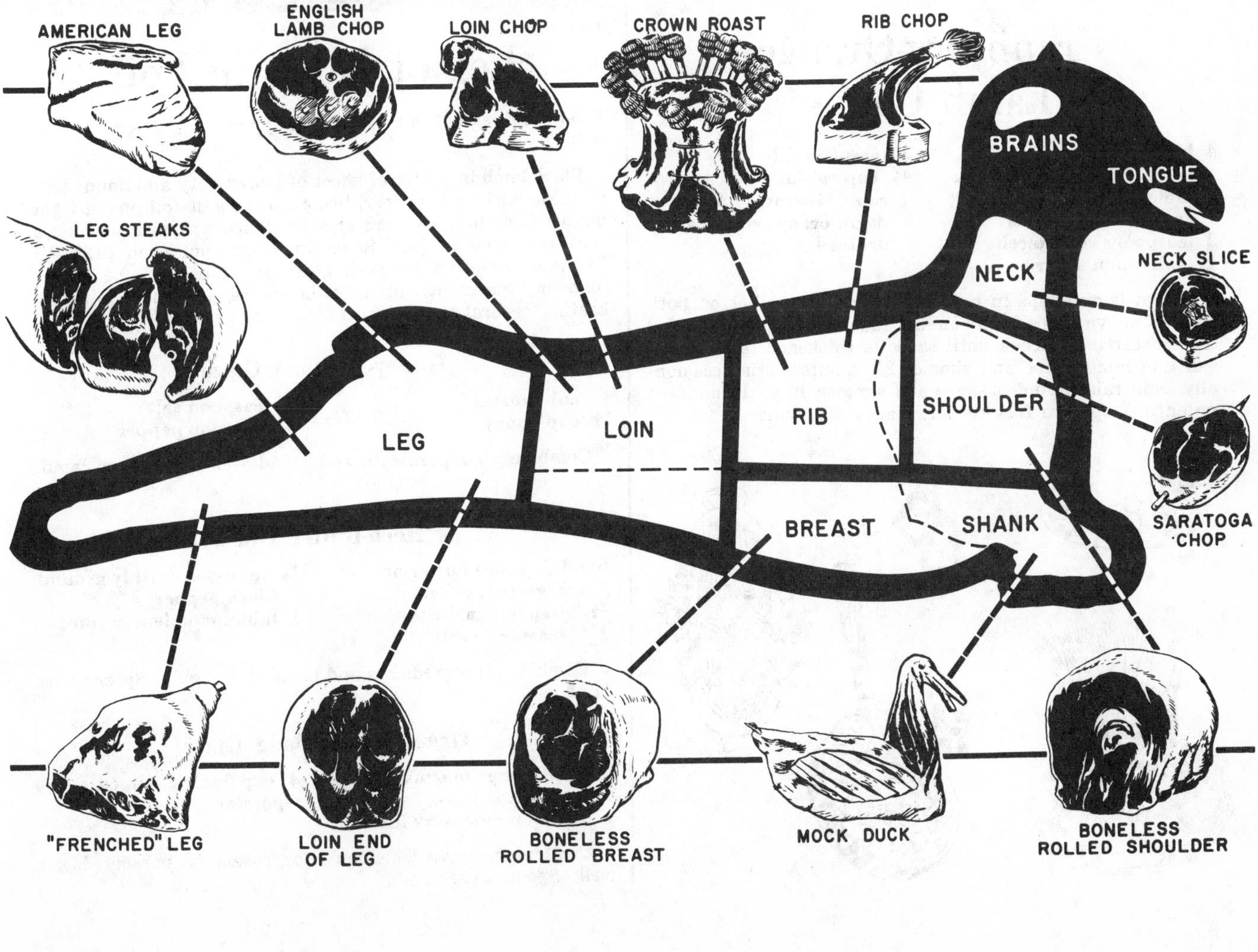

AMERICAN LEG
ENGLISH LAMB CHOP
LOIN CHOP
CROWN ROAST
RIB CHOP
BRAINS
TONGUE
LEG STEAKS
NECK
NECK SLICE
LEG
LOIN
RIB
SHOULDER
SARATOGA CHOP
BREAST
SHANK
"FRENCHED" LEG
LOIN END OF LEG
BONELESS ROLLED BREAST
MOCK DUCK
BONELESS ROLLED SHOULDER

# Minted Rack of Lamb

**5-pound rack of lamb**
**Salt and pepper**
**½ cup mint jelly**
**¼ teaspoon cinnamon**
**¼ teaspoon cloves**
**1 can (1 pound) applesauce**

Place lamb on rack in shallow roasting pan; sprinkle with salt and pepper. Bake in moderate oven (325°F) 1½ hours. Meanwhile, combine jelly, cinnamon and cloves in saucepan; bring to a boil and stir until jelly melts. Stir ¼ cup into applesauce; chill. Drain off lamb drippings; heat remaining mint glaze and brush over lamb. Bake 30 minutes longer or until meat thermometer registers 175°F. to 180°F. (depending upon desired degree of "doneness"). Serve lamb with minted applesauce. Makes 6 servings.

# Touch-of-Dill Lamb Chops

**4 blade or round bone lamb chops, ½-inch thick**
**1 tablespoon shortening**
**1 can (11-ounces) condensed cream of celery soup**
**½ cup water**
**1 teaspoon ground dill seed**

Brown chops on both sides in shortening in a skillet. Add soup, water and dill seed. Blend well and simmer 35 to 40 minutes, stirring occasionally, until chops are fork-tender. Makes 4 servings.

# Cranberry-Orange Lamb Chops

**4 blade or round bone lamb chops, ½-inch thick**
**1 tablespoon shortening**
**1 cup cranberry juice**
**2 teaspoons cornstarch**
**1 tablespoon sugar**
**1 teaspoon salt**
**½ cup raisins**
**1 can (11-ounces) Mandarin orange sections, drained**

Brown lamb chops in hot shortening in a skillet on both sides. Remove chops from pan and add cranberry juice. Blend in cornstarch and cook until sauce is thickened. Add sugar, salt and lamb chops and simmer 25 minutes. Stir occasionally. Add raisins and oranges and simmer 10 to 15 minutes or until chops are fork-tender. Makes 4 servings.

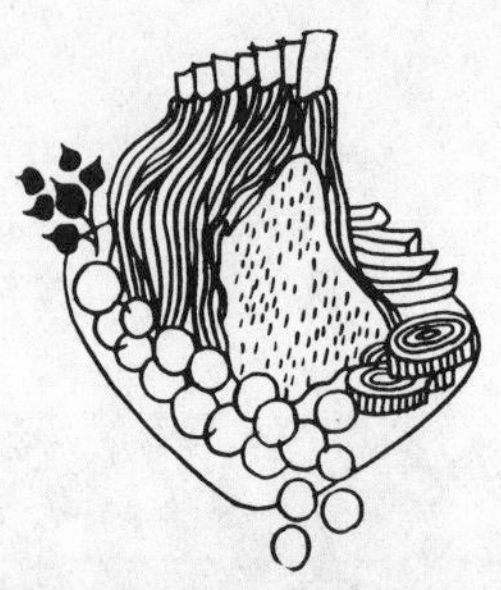

Alcoa Wrap

# Leg of Lamb in Foil

**1 5-pound leg of lamb**
**Salt**
**Pepper**

Place lamb in center of sheet of heavy duty aluminum foil; sprinkle with salt, pepper, bring up sides of foil, using tight double folds over top and at ends. Place wrapped lamb on a rack in a shallow pan. Roast in a very hot oven (425°F.) 2½ hours. Open foil; push away and top with one of the following glazes. Return to oven and bake 30 more minutes, basting several times.

### Honey-Mustard Glaze

**¼ cup mustard**
**¼ cup honey**
**½ teaspoon salt**
**⅛ teaspoon pepper**

Combine all ingredients and blend well. Pour over lamb.

### Herb-Butter Glaze

**6 tablespoons butter or margarine, softened**
**½ teaspoon garlic salt**
**1½ teaspoons salt**
**¼ teaspoon freshly ground black pepper**
**1 tablespoon lemon juice**

Combine all ingredients and blend thoroughly. Spread over lamb.

### Orange-Marmalade Glaze

**½ cup orange marmalade**
**⅓ cup lemon juice**
**1 teaspoon rosemary leaves**
**¼ cup finely chopped parsley**

Combine marmalade, lemon juice, rosemary, parsley; blend well. Spoon over lamb.

# Lemon-Clove Lamb Shoulder Roast

5 pounds boned lamb shoulder, rolled and tied
Salt and pepper
1 lemon, sliced
Whole cloves
2 tablespoons honey

Place lamb on rack in shallow roasting pan; sprinkle with salt and pepper. Bake in moderate oven (325°F.) 2 hours. Place lemon slices on lamb, securing each one with cloves. Drizzle honey over lamb; continue baking 30 to 60 minutes or until meat thermometer registers 175°F. to 180°F. (depending upon desired degree of "doneness." Makes 6 to 8 servings.

# Lamb Paprikash

3 pounds lamb shoulder, cut into 1-inch cubes
3 tablespoons salad oil
1 tablespoons salt
½ teaspoon freshly ground black pepper
3 tablespoons paprika
2 medium onions, thinly sliced
1 cup hot water
2 cups dairy sour cream
1 pound medium egg noodles
1 cup slivered blanched almonds
1 tablespoon poppy seed

Brown lamb well in hot oil; drain off drippings. Sprinkle with salt, pepper and paprika. Add onions and water; cover and simmer 45 minutes or until lamb is tender, stirring occasionally. Gradually stir in sour cream; heat but do not boil.

Meanwhile, cook noodles according to package directions; drain in colander. Toss with almonds and poppy seed; arrange on serving platter; pour lamb with sauce over noodles. Makes 8 servings.

# Peruvian Shoulder Chops and Scallions

3 tablespoons flour
1 teaspoon salt
¼ teaspoon pepper
⅛ teaspoon oregano
4 lamb shoulder chops, about ¾-inch thick
¼ cup salad oil
¼ cup chopped scallions
¼ cup coffee
¼ cup sour cream
¼ cup grated Gruyere cheese (about 1 ounce)

Combine flour, salt and pepper and oregano; mix well. Pound flour mixture into lamb. Heat oil. Add lamb and scallions and cook over medium heat, until lamb is browned on both sides. Arrange lamb and scallions in a greased shallow casserole. Combine coffee and sour cream; mix well. Pour sour cream mixture over lamb. Top with cheese. Bake in a moderate oven (350°F) 30 minutes. Makes 4 servings.

# French Leg of Lamb

1 cup French dressing
2 small onions, sliced
2 cloves garlic, slivered
1 teaspoon ginger
5-pound leg of lamb

Mix together French dressing, onions, garlic and ginger. Pour over leg of lamb. Chill 6 hours or overnight, turning occasionally. Drain lamb, reserving marinade. Place meat on a rack in a shallow roasting pan. Insert meat thermometer into the center of the thickest part of the roast, making sure it does not rest in fat or on bone. Bake in a moderate oven (350°F.) 2½ hours or until meat thermometer registers 175 to 180°F., depending upon desired degree of "doneness." Baste occasionally with marinade during cooking period. Remove to platter and garnish as desired. Makes 6 to 8 servings.

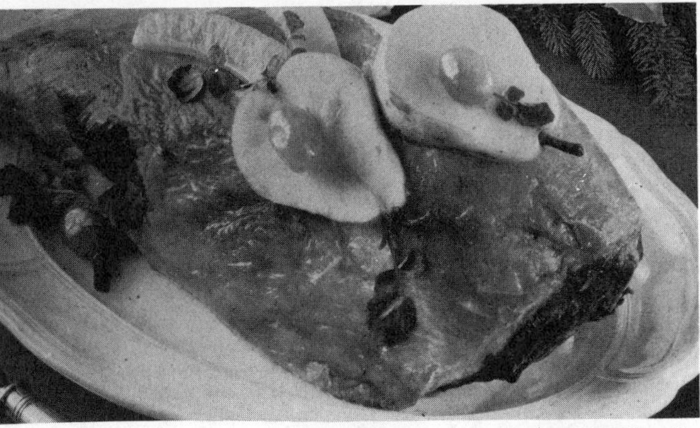

American Lamb Council

American Lamb Council

# Flaming Cherry Rack of Lamb

3-pound rack of lamb*
Seasoned salt
⅓ cup maraschino cherry juice
⅓ cup lemon juice
¼ cup chopped red maraschino cherries (about 10 cherries)
1 teaspoon cornstarch
½ teaspoon mace or nutmeg
4 orange baskets
Grapes and whole red maraschino cherries
3 tablespoons Brandy

Place lamb on rack in shallow roasting pan; sprinkle with seasoned salt. Bake in moderate oven (325°F) 1½ hours. Meanwhile, stir cherry juice, lemon juice and chopped cherries into cornstarch and mace in saucepan; cook, stirring constantly until mixture boils. Drain off lamb drippings; pour ½ the cherry glaze over lamb. Bake 30 minutes; pour remaining cherry glaze over lamb and bake 10 minutes longer or until meat thermometer registers 175° to 180°F. (depending upon desired degree of "doneness"). Place lamb on serving platter and garnish with orange baskets filled with grapes and cherries. Heat brandy and ignite; pour over lamb. Makes 4 servings.

* Have butcher crack bones.

# Glazed Rolled Leg of Lamb

**4½ to 5-pound leg of lamb, boned and rolled**
**Salt and pepper**
**1 cup whole cranberry sauce**
**⅓ cup cherry wine (or substitute 1 cup orange juice)**
**½ teaspoon ginger**
**2 medium oranges**
**1 vegetable bouillon cube**
**½ cup boiling water**
**Orange slices**

Sprinkle lamb roast with salt and pepper. In saucepan, combine cranberry sauce (reserving a few berries for garnish), cherry wine and ginger. Halve oranges crosswise; remove seeds and force oranges through food grinder. Stir orange pulp into sauce mixture and simmer over low heat 5 to 8 minutes. Place lamb on rack in shallow roasting pan; pour ½ of the orange-cranberry sauce over lamb and bake in moderate oven (325°F) 2½ hours, or until meat thermometer registers 175°F. for medium "doneness." Dissolve bouillon cube in water; baste lamb with bouillon after 1 hour of roasting time. Twenty minutes before lamb is done, baste with remainder of orange-cranberry sauce. Garnish with notched orange slices and reserved whole cranberries. Makes 6 to 8 servings.

# Holiday Lamb Cushion-Style Roast

**½ package (8-ounce size) prepared stuffing mix**
**½ cup chopped walnuts**
**1 cup mixed candied fruit**
**1 vegetable bouillon cube**
**1 cup hot water**
**2 tablespoons melted butter or margarine**
**3½ to 4-pounds lamb shoulder, prepared cushion style**
**Salt and pepper**
**2 tablespoons flour**
**½ teaspoon salt**
**1¼-cups cold water**

Combine in mixing bowl the stuffing mix, walnuts and half the candied fruit. Dissolve bouillon cube in hot water and lightly stir half the bouillon and the butter into mixture. Fill lamb pocket with stuffing and sew edges or skewer to hold edges tightly. Sprinkle meat with salt and pepper. Bake in moderate oven (325°F) about 2½ hours or until meat thermometer reads 180°F. Baste occasionally with remaining bouillon and pan drippings. To prepare gravy, blend flour and salt into pan drippings and brown over low heat, stirring constantly. Add cold water; cook and stir until gravy is thickened. Add rest of candied fruit and serve with holiday lamb. Makes 6 servings.

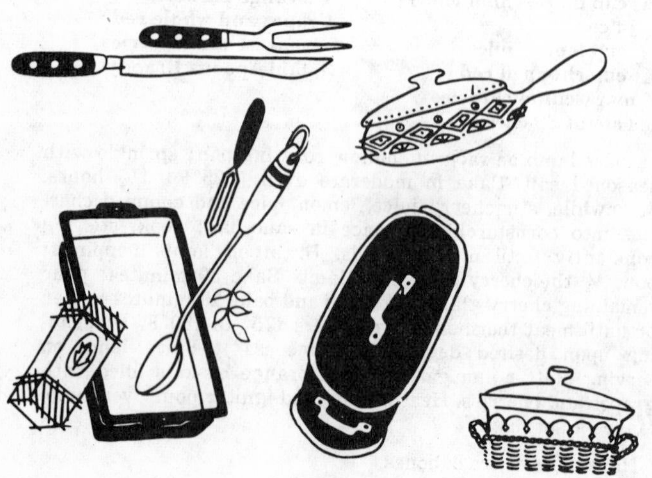

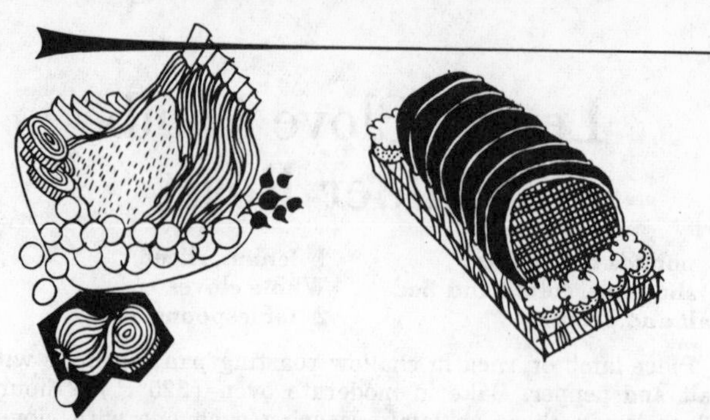

American Lamb Council

# Leg of Lamb Neopolitan

**5-pound leg of lamb**
**2 teaspoons salt**
**1 teaspoon crushed oregano**
**4 medium onions, chopped**
**1 medium green pepper, chopped**
**1 clove garlic, crushed**
**1 can (1 pound, 12 ounces) tomatoes**

Sprinkle lamb with salt and oregano; place on rack in shallow roasting pan. Bake in moderate oven (325°F.) 1½ hours; drain off drippings. Mix together the onions, green pepper, garlic and tomatoes. Baste lamb with some of the tomato mixture and bake, basting occasionally, for 1 hour or until meat thermometer registers 175°F. for medium "doneness." Add water to sauce if needed during latter part of cooking time. Serve roast with sauce. Makes 6 to 8 servings.

# Stuffed Lamb Rib Chops Dijonnais

**6 double rib lamb chops**
**1 can (3 ounces) sliced mushrooms**
**½ teaspoon salt**
**3 tablespoons dry Sherry wine**
**1 egg, beaten**
**½ cup fine dry bread crumbs**
**Salt and pepper**

Using sharp knife, make slit from bone side between rib bones into center of meat on each chop. Drain mushrooms, reserving 2 tablespoons liquid. Mix together reserved mushroom liquid, ½ teaspoon salt, Sherry, egg, mushrooms and bread crumbs; stuff chops with mushroom mixture. Sprinkle lamb with salt and pepper; broil 4 to 5 inches from source of heat 12 minutes on each side or until desired degree of "doneness." **Note:** If desired, have meat man french the chops; before serving place a frill on each chop. Makes 6 servings.

# FISH

## Fried

### Pan Fried Fish Fillets

**1 package frozen fish fillets**
**¼ cup flour**
**½ teaspoon salt**
**¼ teaspoon pepper**
**1 teaspoon paprika**
**¼ cup butter or margarine**

Let fillets thaw on refrigerator shelf. Separate fillets. Mix together flour, salt, pepper and paprika. Turn out mixture onto a piece of waxed paper. Dip each fillet into the flour mixture to coat both sides. Melt butter or margarine in a frying pan. Add fillets, and cook about 5 to 8 minutes or until golden brown and fish flakes easily when tested with a fork.

National Fisheries Institute

### Fish and Rice with Curry Sauce

**1½ pounds fish fillets**
**4 cups corn flakes**
**1 tablespoon salt**
**1 cup milk**
**4 teaspoons cooking oil**
**2 tablespoons butter or margarine**
**2 tablespoons flour**
**¼ cup minced onion**
**2 teaspoons curry powder**
**¾ teaspoon sugar**
**⅛ teaspoon powdered ginger**
**1 cup milk**
**1 teaspoon lemon juice**
**4 cups seasoned cooked rice**
**⅓ cup chopped parsley**

Cut fish into serving pieces. Roll corn flakes into fine crumbs. Dip fish in salted milk, then in crumbs and arrange on a well oiled baking sheet. Sprinkle oil over top of fish. Bake on top shelf of a very hot oven (500°F.) 12 to 15 minutes. Melt butter in a saucepan; add onion and fry until tender but not brown. Stir in flour, curry powder, sugar and ginger. Add milk and cook, stirring constantly, until mixture thickens. Stir in lemon juice just before serving. Combine rice and parsley and pile in center of serving platter. Surround with pieces of fish and serve with sauce on the side. Makes 6 servings.

### Fish Cutlets

**1 pound fish, cooked and flaked**
**1 egg, beaten**
**½ cup milk**
**½ teaspoon salt**
**2 tablespoons pickle relish**
**1 cup fine bread crumbs, divided**
**¼ cup fat**

Blend together fish, egg, milk, salt, relish and ¾ cup of the bread crumbs. Shape into cutlets; dredge with remaining crumbs. Fry in hot fat until golden brown. Serve with desired sauce. Makes 4 to 6 servings.

### Spicy Fillets

**1 package frozen fish fillets**
**¼ cup olive oil**
**¼ cup vinegar**
**⅛ teaspoon thyme**
**¼ teaspoon tarragon**
**1 bay leaf, crumbled**
**1 small onion, minced**
**1 teaspoon salt**
**¼ teaspoon pepper**
**¼ cup flour**
**2 tablespoons butter or margarine**

Thaw fish at room temperature until fillets can be separated. Place olive oil, vinegar and seasonings in a bowl large enough to hold fillets. Add fish and let stand for 1 hour. Drain and dry slightly with a paper towel. Roll in flour. Melt butter in a skillet. Sauté fish 5 minutes on 1 side, turn and sauté 5 minutes more, or until golden brown. Makes 3 to 4 servings.

# Pan Fried Fish

**6 pan-dressed fish**
**1 teaspoon salt**
**⅛ teaspoon pepper**
**1 egg**
**1 tablespoon milk**
**1 cup bread crumbs, cracker crumbs, cornmeal or flour**

Wash fish and be sure that they are well cleaned inside. Sprinkle both sides with salt and pepper. Beat egg slightly, and blend in the milk. Dip fish in egg and roll in crumbs. Place fish in a heavy frying pan which contains about ⅛ inch melted fat, hot but not smoking. Fry at moderate heat. When fish is brown on one side, turn carefully and brown the other side. Cooking time is about 10 minutes depending on thickness of the fish. Drain on absorbent paper. Serve immediately plain or with desired sauce. Makes 6 servings.

# Perch Almondine

**1 package frozen ocean perch fillets**
**Seasoned flour**
**¼ cup fat**
**¼ cup butter or margarine**
**⅓ cup finely shredded blanched almonds**
**2 teaspoons lemon juice**

Thaw fillets just enough to separate. Roll in seasoned flour. Fry in fat in skillet over medium heat 8 to 10 minutes, or until done, turning to brown both sides. Meanwhile, melt butter in another skillet or saucepan. Add almonds and sauté over medium heat until delicately browned. Arrange fish on hot platter. Top with sautéed almonds and sprinkle with lemon juice. Garnish with parsley and lemon juice. Makes 4 servings.

# Deep Fat Fried Fish

**2 pounds fresh or frozen fillets or steaks**
**1 teaspoon salt**
**⅛ teaspoon pepper**
**1 egg**
**1 tablespoon milk**
**1 cup bread crumbs, cracker crumbs, cornmeal or flour**

Cut fish into serving-size portions. Sprinkle both sides with salt and pepper. Beat egg slightly and blend in the milk. Dip fish in the egg and roll in crumbs. Use a deep kettle with a frying basket and enough fat to cover the fish, but do not have the kettle more than half full of fat. Heat the fat to 375°F. Place 1 layer of fish in the frying basket and cook to an even golden brown, about 3 to 5 minutes. Raise basket, remove fish, and drain on absorbent paper. Serve immediately plain or with desired sauce. Makes 6 servings.

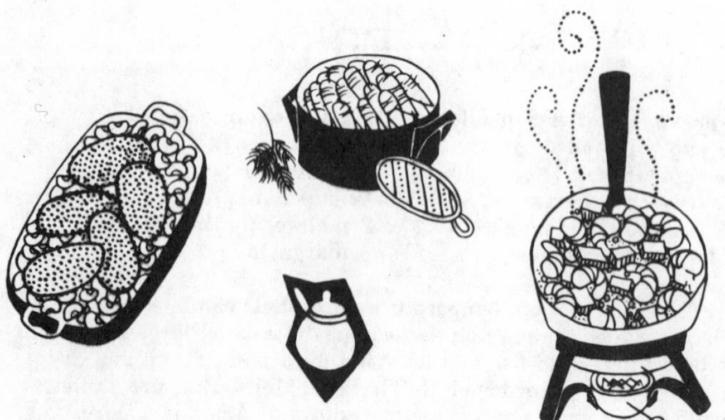

# Italian Festival Fillets

**1 pound fish fillets, fresh or frozen (sole, flounder, cod, haddock or ocean perch)**
**3 tablespoons olive oil**
**3 tablespoons butter or margarine**
**1 can (8-ounce) spaghetti sauce with mushrooms**
**½ cup water**
**½ teaspoon oregano**
**¼ teaspoon dried basil**
**3 tablespoons minced parsley**
**Hot spaghetti or noodles**

Thaw fillets if necessary. Heat olive oil and butter in a large skillet. Add fillets. Cook over low heat about four minutes per side or until golden brown. (Turn fillets gently, using a pancake turner.) Meantime, in a second saucepan, simmer spaghetti sauce with water, oregano, basil and parsley. When fillets are browned, pour sauce over them, and stir in the open areas of skillet to blend sauce with pan drippings. Turn heat low and simmer ten minutes, basting fish with sauce occasionally. This is sufficient to dress 3 cups hot cooked spaghetti or noodles. Makes 4 servings.

National Fisheries Institute

# Brook Trout Supreme

**4 brook trout**
**Lemon juice**
**Salt**
**Pepper**
**1 egg, beaten**
**2 tablespoons milk**
**Fine dry bread crumbs**
**½ cup butter, divided**
**1 can (2-ounces) sliced mushrooms, drained**

Sprinkle cleaned and dressed brook trout inside and out with lemon juice, salt and pepper. Dip in egg combined with milk. Cover with bread crumbs. Melt half of the butter in a skillet. Add fish and sauté until golden brown on both sides, about 3 to 4 minutes, or until fish flakes easily when tested with a fork. Melt remaining butter. Add mushrooms, 1 tablespoon lemon juice and ½ teaspoon salt. Serve brook trout with hot sauce. Makes 4 servings.

# Salmon Croquettes

**4 tablespoons butter or margarine**
**5 tablespoons flour**
**½ teaspoon salt**
**1 cup milk**
**2 cups salmon, flaked**
**1 teaspoon lemon juice**
**½ teaspoon onion juice**
**Dash of pepper**
**1 egg, slightly beaten**
**1 tablespoon water**
**½ cup bread crumbs**
**Shortening**

Melt butter. Add flour and salt and blend. Stir in milk, and cook, stirring constantly, until thickened. Remove from heat. Add salmon, lemon juice, onion juice and pepper. Blend well. Spread mixture in shallow pan and chill until stiff. Shape into cylinders, roll in crumbs, then in combined egg and water and roll again in crumbs. Fry in deep hot shortening (375°F.) until browned. Makes 6 servings.

# Sole Amandine

**¼ cup blanched slivered almonds**
**6 tablespoons butter or margarine, divided**
**4 fillets of sole or flounder**
**4 fresh tomatoes, chopped**
**½ clove garlic, minced**
**½ teaspoon dried tarragon**
**Salt and pepper**

Heat slivered almonds in 1 tablespoon butter, stirring constantly. Salt and set aside. Dust fillets lightly in seasoned flour and brown very quickly on each side in 4 tablespoons of hot butter. In a different pan cook tomatoes, garlic, remaining butter, tarragon and seasonings for about 1 minute. Arrange tomato mixture on serving dish and place fillets on top. Cover with heated almonds. Makes 4 servings.

# Golden Fish Gado Gado

1 package breaded fish portions
2 tablespoons cooking oil
⅓ cup sliced onion (½ medium)
1 clove garlic, minced
¼ teaspoon crushed Italian-style red pepper (if you like hot-tasting food, use ½ teaspoon)
½ teaspoon salt
1 teaspoon brown sugar
1 teaspoon lemon juice
4 tablespoons peanut butter or finely ground peanuts
½ cup water, or vegetable or chicken broth

Heat fish following package directions. Meantime, make sauce: Heat the oil in a medium skillet. Add onion, garlic, and red pepper. Cook, stirring occasionally until onion is soft and lightly browned. Then stir in salt, brown sugar, lemon juice and peanut butter. Stir in water (or broth) bit by bit until sauce looks like gravy. More water or broth may be added, if desired. Serve with hot fish. Makes 4 servings.

National Fisheries Institute

# Steamed and Poached

PLACE fish fillets or steaks in skillet with boiling water that just barely covers. Season water with parsley, celery, onions, wine, salt and pepper or any desired spices. Cut a circle of waxed (or buttered white) paper to fit the skillet. Tear a hole in the center and place over fish. Cover tightly and simmer from 6 to 10 minutes or until fish flakes easily with a fork. Remove from skillet and serve with desired sauce. If desired, fish may be poached in a sauce instead of water.

*For steamed fish,* use a deep saucepan or Dutch oven with a greased rack in the bottom. Fill with 1½ to 2 inches of water. Season water with desired seasonings. Tie large pieces of fish in cheesecloth or place directly on rack or place in a basket in saucepan. Cover tightly and steam: If fish is under 2 inches thick, steam about 1 minute for each ounce of fish. If fish is over 2 inches thick, steam 10 to 12 minutes for each pound, or until fish flakes easily with a fork. Lift fish out to a heated platter and serve with desired sauce. Large pieces of fish are excellent chilled in the refrigerator and served icy cold as a main course with any desired sauce; or flake the fish and use in salads, sandwiches or main dishes. Allow ½ pound whole or ⅓ pound sliced fish per portion; 1 pound steamed fish makes 2 cups flaked fish.

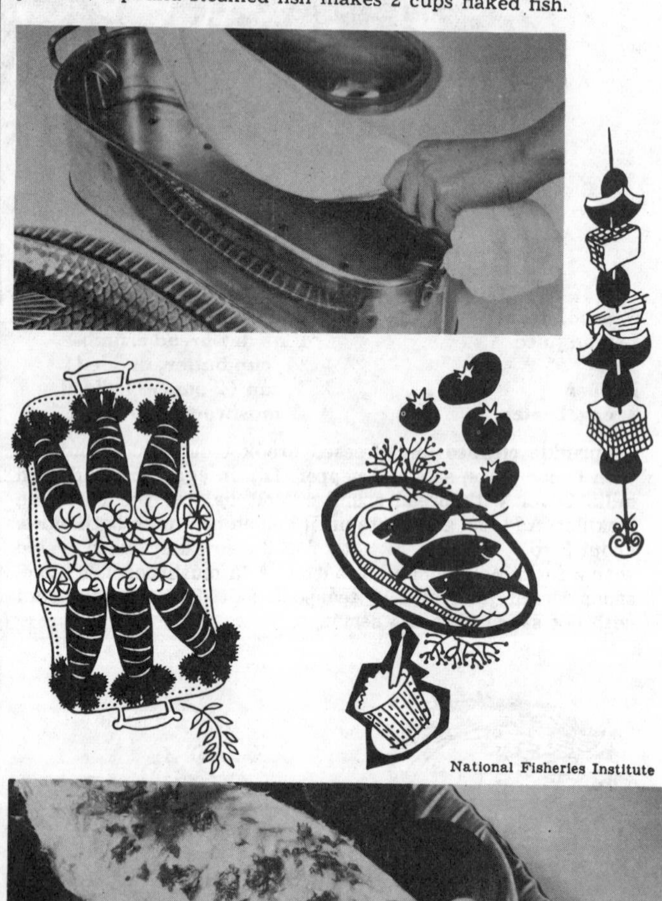

National Fisheries Institute

# Fish Duglere

4 fish fillets
1 teaspoon salt
Dash of pepper
3 tablespoons butter or margarine
1 medium onion, chopped
1 clove garlic
4 ripe tomatoes, peeled and chopped
1 teaspoon chopped parsley
¼ cup dry white wine
½ cup water
1 tablespoon flour
2 tablespoons butter

Season fillets with salt and pepper. Melt butter in a skillet. Add onion and garlic and cook gently until onions are soft. Place fillets in pan. Arrange tomatoes and parsley over fillets. Add wine and water. Cover with a circle of waxed paper with a hole in the center. Cover tightly and simmer about 8 minutes, or until fish flakes easily with a fork. Remove fish to a hot platter. Cook liquid until it is reduced to ⅓ its original quantity. Remove garlic. Mix flour and butter and stir into liquid. Stir over low heat until it is thickened. Pour sauce over fish. Makes 4 servings.

# Fish Fillets Creole

1 package frozen fillets
2 tablespoons butter or margarine
¼ cup chopped onion
1 tablespoon flour
1 No. 2 can tomatoes
¼ teaspoon pepper
½ teaspoon salt
3 whole cloves
1 bay leaf
¼ cup chopped parsley
¼ teaspoon allspice
3 tablespoons lemon juice
4 cups cubed fried potatoes

Thaw fillets. Melt butter in a skillet. Add onions and cook until tender. Add flour and stir over low heat until browned. Stir in tomatoes, seasonings and lemon juice. Cook over moderate heat 10 minutes. Add fillets. Cover with a circle of buttered white paper or waxed paper with a hole in the center. Cover pan tightly and simmer 8 to 10 minutes or until fish flakes easily with a fork. Remove fish to platter, cover with sauce and serve with potatoes. Makes 4 servings.

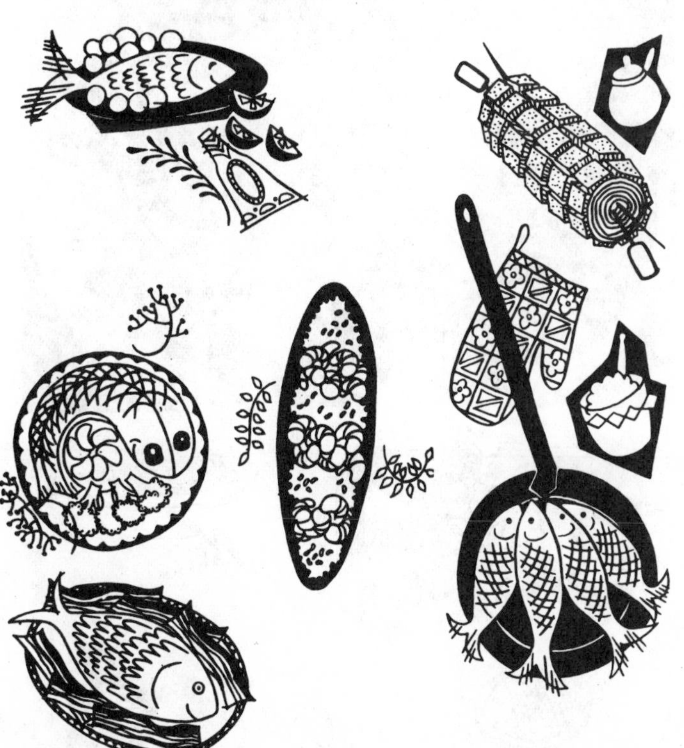

# Poached Fillet of Flounder with Lobster Sauce

1 small cooked lobster
2 pounds cooked shrimp
6 tablespoons butter or margarine
6 tablespoons flour
3 cups milk
3 cups cream
1½ teaspoons paprika
2½ teaspoons salt
Dash of pepper
8 large flounder fillets
½ cup milk
½ cup water
2 teaspoons salt
Dash of pepper

Remove lobster meat from shell and cut in chunks. Shell and clean shrimp. Melt butter in the top of a double boiler. Stir in flour, gradually add milk and cook over hot water stirring frequently until sauce is thickened. Add paprika, salt, pepper, lobster and shrimp and let simmer in top of double boiler while fixing flounder. Split fillets down the center. Begin at the larger end of the fillet and roll it up. Fasten each fillet with a toothpick. Place in a large skillet. Add milk, water, salt and pepper. Cover with a circle of waxed paper with a hole in the center. Cover skillet tightly and simmer fish gently 10 minutes. Remove fish to a hot platter; remove toothpicks and cover with the sauce. Makes 8 servings.

National Fisheries Institute

# Fillet of Sole in Wine Sauce

1 cup white wine
1 cup water
2 pounds frozen fillet of sole, defrosted
1 pint oysters
½ pound cooked shrimp
1 tablespoon butter

*Sauce:*

¼ cup butter or margarine
¼ cup flour
1 cup milk
½ cup light cream
½ cup reserved fish stock
½ teaspoon Worcestershire sauce
½ teaspoon lemon juice
1 teaspoon salt
½ teaspoon monosodium glutamate
¼ teaspoon pepper
⅛ teaspoon basil
¼ teaspoon dry mustard
¼ teaspoon paprika

Combine wine and water in 10½-inch fry pan; bring to a boil. Add sole fillets; cover; simmer gently 3-5 minutes or until fish flakes easily. Reserve ½ cup fish stock for sauce; set fillets aside to keep warm. Heat oysters in sauce pan until edges curl; drain; set aside to keep warm. Sauté cooked shrimp in butter until heated through; set aside to keep warm. Melt butter in sauce pan; stir in flour; add milk, cream, reserved fish stock; blend thoroughly. Cook over low heat, stirring constantly until thickened. Blend in Worcestershire sauce, lemon juice, salt, monosodium glutamate, pepper, basil, dry mustard, paprika. Shape shallow individual fish casseroles from double thick sheets of super-strength aluminum foil.* Arrange sole fillets in casseroles, top with oysters, shrimp; pour sauce over all. Sprinkle with papkrika; place casseroles on baking sheet. Place under broiler about 3-4 inches from source of heat; broil 4-5 minutes or until lightly browned. Makes 6 servings.

**How to make Aluminum Foil Casseroles:* Invert a shallow round or oval bowl of one serving size on your work table. Tear off a sheet of aluminum foil, regular or heavy duty, and place it, shiny side down, over the dish. Cover with another sheet of foil, shiny side up. Crush the foil tightly around the bowl. Shape excess foil at one end into a pointed fish nose; the other into a tail. The rest of the foil is molded into a rim around the edge. Easy, isn't it.

Alcoa Wrap

# Fish Fillets à la Orange

1 package frozen fish fillets
1 orange
3 tablespoons butter or margarine
½ small onion, minced
Juice of 1 lemon
Juice of 1 orange
¼ cup water
1 tablespoon butter or margarine
1 tablespoon flour

Let fillets thaw at room temperature until they can be pulled apart easily. Sprinkle with salt and pepper. Cut peel from 1 orange removing just a very thin layer of orange peel. Slice into thin strips. Cook about 2 minutes in boiling water. Drain. Finish peeling orange and slice, set aside for use as garnish. Melt butter in a frying pan. Add onion and cook until tender. Add lemon juice, orange juice and water. Bring to boil. Add fish fillets. Cover with a circle of buttered white paper or circle of waxed paper with a hole in the center. Cover and simmer about 7 minutes or until fish flakes easily when tested with a fork. Remove fish to heated platter and keep warm. Cook liquid in pan until it is reduced to about ½ cup. Cream together butter and flour. Stir into liquid and cook until thickened. Add orange rind and season to taste if needed. Pour sauce over fish. Garnish with orange slices. Makes 4 servings.

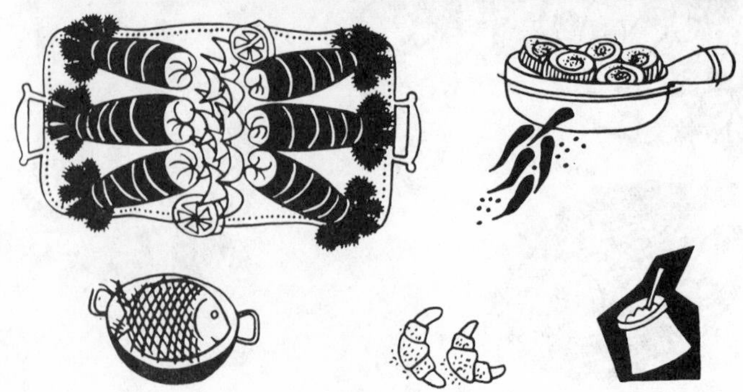

# Broiled

BROILING fish is probably the easiest and quickest way to prepare an excellent fish dinner. As an added inducement try one of the new broiler-to-table platters—easy to use, nice for serving and a breeze to clean. If you use your broiler pan, place aluminum foil under the fish, and after it has cooked throw away the foil. You will have no dirty broiler to worry about.

Any kind or variety of fish can be broiled. If the fish is frozen, thaw before cooking. For 4 servings allow 1 to 1½ pounds fish fillets, 2 pound fish steak or a 3 pound whole or split fish.

Quick cooking makes broiled fish juicy, tender and full of flavor. If fish finds favor with your family at a restaurant but gets a cold reception at home, look to your cooking. Broiled whole, in steaks or fillets, the cardinal rule is—don't overcook!

Use cold salted water if fish needs washing (1 tablespoon salt to 1 quart water). Wipe with clean, damp cloth. Line broiler pan with aluminum foil and turn edges up to prevent drippings from running into pan. Preheat broiler compartment and pan at full heat, 550°F., for 10 minutes. Remove heated pan and grease aluminum foil (or broiler rack). Lay fish on foil and brush with melted fat. Use a pastry brush or waxed paper held with kitchen tongs. Return pan to broiler unit 2 inches from heat. Broil at full heat until fish flakes easily with fork. Brush with fat once or twice during cooking. Do not overcook. Salt and pepper, and serve very hot.

*Whole fish* should be broiled 4-15 minutes on each side. Time depends on thickness of fish.

*Steaks* are cut ready for cooking. Broil ½-inch steaks about 3 minutes on each side; 1-inch steaks about 5 minutes.

*Fillets* are also cut ready for cooking and are available fresh or frozen all year round. If frozen, let thaw before cooking. If skin is left on, place fillets skin side down on broiler. Broil for 5-10 minutes. Do not turn during cooking.

# Broiled Ocean Perch in French Dressing

**4 perch fillets (about 1¼ pounds**

**½ cup bottled French dressing**

Place fillets in shallow pan; pour French dressing over; marinate 1-2 hours in refrigerator. Place marinated fillets in disposable aluminum broiler pan; place 3 inches away from broiler unit. Broil 7-8 minutes or until fish flakes easily when pierced with fork; baste several times with French dressing. Makes 4 servings.

# Broiled Halibut Steaks with Coffee Butter

2 pounds halibut steaks, fresh or frozen
1 tablespoon lemon juice
1 tablespoon instant coffee
¼ cup melted butter
¼ teaspoon onion salt
2 tablespoons chopped parsley

If steaks are frozen, let them thaw on refrigerator shelf or at room temperature. Combine lemon juice with instant coffee powder; add to melted butter with onion salt and parsley. Brush liberally on fish steaks. Broil, 3 inches from heat, 5 minutes. Turn fish; brush with butter mixture. Broil 5 minutes, or until fish flakes easily when tested with a fork. Brush again with butter mixture; sprinkle with more parsley if desired and serve. Makes 6 servings.

Halibut Association of North America

# Broiled Salmon with Herbs

4 salmon steaks ¾ inch thick
1 tablespoon grated onion
Juice of 1 lemon
6 tablespoons melted butter or margarine
1 teaspoon salt
¼ teaspoon pepper
½ teaspoon marjoram
1 tablespoon minced chives
2 tablespoons minced parsley

Place salmon steaks on a broil-and-serve platter. Mix remaining ingredients and pour half of mixture over steaks. Broil 2 inches from source of heat about 4 minutes. Turn steaks, pour remaining mixture over steaks. Broil 6 to 7 minutes or until fish flakes easily with a fork. Makes 4 servings.

# Broiled Shad Roe

1½ pounds shad roe
1 quart boiling water
1 tablespoon vinegar
Melted butter or margarine
Salt and pepper
Lemon juice

Wash shad roe. Place in boiling water and vinegar and simmer about 10 minutes. Drain. Remove membrane. Place shad roe on broil and serve platter or lined broiling pan. Brush with butter, sprinkle with salt and pepper and lemon juice. Broil 2 inches from heat, turn and broil 3 to 4 minutes longer. Makes 6 servings.

# Deviled Fish Steaks

4 fish steaks
2 tablespoons prepared mustard
1 tablespoon oil
2 tablespoons chili sauce
2 tablespoons horse-radish
1 teaspoon salt

Place fish steaks on broil-and-serve platter or broiling pan. Mix together remaining ingredients and spread half of mixture on steaks. Broil 2 inches from heat 4 minutes. Turn, cover with rest of mixture, and broil 7 to 8 minutes, or until fish flakes easily with a fork. Makes 4 servings.

# Salmon Rounds

2 large tomatoes
Salt and pepper
1 pound can salmon
1 tablespoon lemon juice
8 slices American cheese

Slice each tomato into four rounds, season with salt and pepper and place on a baking sheet. Flake salmon and pile on each slice of tomato. Sprinkle with lemon juice and cover each tomato round with a slice of cheese. Broil in a preheated broiling compartment about 6 inches from heat, about 5 minutes or until cheese melts. Makes 4 servings.

# Fillet de Sole Amandine

2 pounds fillet of sole
Melted fat
Salt and pepper
½ cup almonds, blanched and slivered
2 tablespoons butter or margarine

Wipe fillets with damp cloth. Place fillets, skin side down, on preheated broiling pan. Brush with melted fat. Season with salt and pepper. Place pan 2 inches from source of heat. Broil about 8 minutes or until fish flakes easily when tested with a fork. Meanwhile, lightly brown almonds in hot butter. Serve over top of fillets. Makes 4 to 6 servings.

National Fisheries Institute

# Deviled Fish Sticks

¼ cup very soft butter or margarine
¼ teaspoon dry mustard
1½ teaspoons Worcestershire sauce
½ teaspoon lemon juice
Dash Tabasco
2 teaspoons grated onion
¼ cup finely chopped parsley (optional)
2 packages fish sticks

Combine butter, mustard, Worcestershire sauce, lemon juice, Tabasco, onion and parsley. (Mixture will not be completely blended.) Place fish sticks close together in broiler pan; spread with butter mixture. Broil, 4 inches from heat, about 7 to 8 minutes or until golden and done. Or bake in hot oven (450°F) 12 to 15 minutes. Makes 4 to 6 servings.

National Fisheries Institute

# Baked

ANY fish from salt or fresh water, regardless of size or cut is excellent baked. For ease in cooking and serving, use one of the new oven glass platters or special aluminum platters that you also use for broiling. Or else line your baking pan with aluminum foil so that you will have no clean-up problem.

# Baked Whole Fish

Select a fish weighing from 3 to 5 pounds, with or without head and tail as desired. Clean and rub insides with salt. Stuff fish with any of the following stuffings. Fasten with toothpicks or skewers, loop string over row of skewers as you would lace shoes. Place fish, underside down in a greased baking dish or baking dish lined with aluminum foil. Rub outside with salt and brush with melted fat or lay strips of bacon or salt pork over top of fish. Bake in a moderate to hot oven (350-400°F.) 10 to 16 minutes per pound, or until fish flakes easily with a fork. Remove to hot platter and garnish with lemon slices and parsley and serve with any desired sauce. Allow ½ pound fish per serving.

# Bread Stuffing

1½ cups bread cubes
½ teaspoon salt
⅛ teaspoon pepper
¼ teaspoon thyme or marjoram
½ medium onion, minced
3 tablespoons butter, melted

Combine all ingredients thoroughly. Makes enough stuffing for a 3 to 4 pound fish.

# Mushroom Stuffing

3 tablespoons butter or margarine
1 tablespoon onion, chopped
½ cup chopped mushrooms
2 cups fresh bread crumbs
½ cup cream
2 eggs, beaten
1 teaspoon chopped parsley
Salt and pepper

Put butter in a saucepan. Add onion and sauté until onion is golden. Add chopped mushrooms and cook until water from mushrooms cooks away. Add remaining ingredients and stir until well mixed. Cook over low heat until mixture is thickened. Season to taste with salt and pepper. Makes enough stuffing for a 3 to 4 pound fish.

# Clam-Stuffed Fish Fillets

2 packages (1 pound) fish fillets
2 cans (5 ounces) minced clams
½ cup butter or margarine
¼ cup chopped onion
¼ cup chopped celery
4 cups soft bread crumbs
2 tablespoons lemon juice
Salt and pepper

Let fish fillets thaw on refrigerator shelf or at room temperature. Arrange half of fillets, close together, in buttered baking dish. Drain minced clams, reserving liquid. Melt butter or margarine in skillet. Pour off about half of butter and save. To butter in skillet add onion and celery and cook until tender. Stir in bread crumbs until butter is soaked up. Continue tossing crumbs until they brown slightly. Stir in clams, lemon juice, and enough clam liquid to moisten. Season to taste with salt and pepper. Spoon stuffing over fillets. Cover with remaining fillets. Brush with reserved butter. Bake in moderate oven (375°F) 20 minutes, or until fish flakes easily when tested with fork. Serve in baking dish. Makes 6 to 8 servings.

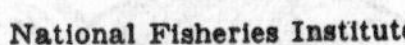
National Fisheries Institute

# Red Snapper with Shrimp Stuffing

- 3 to 4 pound red snapper
- ¼ cup chopped celery
- 2 tablespoons chopped onion
- 2 tablespoons butter
- 3 slices cooked bacon, crumbled
- 1 cup soft bread crumbs
- ½ cup chopped cooked shrimp
- 1 egg
- Salt and pepper
- Melted shortening

Have fish dressed. Clean and rub salt inside and out. Cook celery and onion in butter until soft. Add remaining ingredients and mix well. Stuff fish with mixture. Fasten together with skewers. Brush with melted shortening and place in baking pan. Bake in a moderate oven (350°F) 40 minutes, or until fish flakes easily when tested with a fork. Makes 3 to 4 servings.

National Fisheries Institute

# Fish Rolls

- 2 tablespoons pickle relish
- 1 tablespoon minced onion
- 1 pound frozen cod or halibut fillets, defrosted
- 2 tablespoons butter
- 2 tablespoons flour
- 1 cup milk
- ½ teaspoon salt
- Dash of pepper
- ½ teaspoon Worcestershire sauce
- ½ pound American cheese, shredded

Combine relish and onion. Spread evenly over tops of fish fillets. Roll up jelly roll fashion, secure with toothpicks and place in baking dish. Melt butter in a saucepan. Stir in flour, milk and seasonings. Cook over moderate heat, stirring constantly, until smooth and thickened. Stir in cheese and stir until cheese melts. Spoon sauce over top of rolled fish fillets. Bake in a moderate oven (325°F) 25 to 30 minutes. Serve hot. Makes 4 servings.

The Borden Company

# Stuffed Striped Bass

- 1 cup oysters, chopped
- 3 cups stale bread cubes
- 2 teaspoons salt
- ⅛ teaspoon pepper
- ⅛ teaspoon sage
- 3 tablespoons butter
- 1 onion, minced
- 2 tablespoons minced parsley
- ½ cup minced celery
- 1 striped bass, about 6 pounds, split and boned
- Melted butter
- Salt and pepper

Place oyster in a skillet, cover and simmer 5 minutes. Drain. Combine bread cubes, salt, pepper, sage and oyster. Melt butter in a skillet; add onion, parsley and celery and cook until tender. Add to oyster mixture and blend well. Place half of fish, skin side down, in center of a lightly greased sheet of heavy duty aluminum foil. Spread fish with oyster mixture. Place other half of fish, skin side up, on top of stuffing. Fasten both sides with skewers. Brush with melted butter and sprinkle with salt and pepper. Bring up sides of foil over fish in a tight double fold; fold up ends. Place on baking sheet and bake in a hot oven (400°F) 1 hour. Open foil; push down around fish and brush with melted butter. Return to oven for an additional 15 to 20 minutes or until fish flakes easily with a fork. Makes 6 servings.

Alcoa Wrap

# Soup-Baked Fish Fillets au Gratin

**1 package (14 ounces) equal portions breaded fish fillets**
**2 tablespoons melted butter**
**Black pepper**
**1 can (10½ ounces) condensed tomato soup**
**2 tablespoons chopped parsley**
**½ cup shredded Cheddar cheese**
**Thin cucumber slices**

Arrange fillets in shallow baking dish; spread portions with melted butter. Sprinkle lightly with pepper. Bake in very hot oven (500°F) until fish flakes easily with a fork, about 25 minutes. Spoon soup, combined with parsley, over fillets; sprinkle with cheese. Return to oven 5 to 10 minutes or until cheese melts. Garnish with cucumber slices. Makes 6 servings.

Campbell Soup Company

# Lobster

## Baked

Plan on buying one 2-pound lobster for each person. Have fish dealer split and clean or follow these directions yourself. Place lobster on its back. Cross the large claws and hold firmly with the left hand. Insert the point of a sharp knife into the lobster at the head and cut the shell open from head to tail. Cut through to the back shell. Remove the stomach and the intestinal vein that runs the length of the tail section close to the back. Do not remove juices or the liver. The liver is the grayish looking meat found in the body cavity which turns green when it is cooked. Fill the cavity in the head with the following dressing: Combine 1½ cups cracker crumbs, ½ teaspoon salt, 2 tablespoons Worcestershire sauce and 4 tablespoons melted butter or margarine. This is enough dressing for 4 lobsters. Pour melted butter over lobster and bake in a hot oven (450°F.) 19 minutes. Serve immediately with hot melted butter.

## Boiled

Bring to a full rolling boil, 3 quarts of water and 3 tablespoons of salt. Drop into water a 1 to 1½-pound live lobster. Cover tightly and return to boil. Cook 5 minutes for the first pound and 3 minutes for each additional pound. Remove from boiling water immediately. Split, and prepare according to directions and pictures for baked lobster. Serve with melted butter blended with a squeeze of lemon juice.

National Fisheries Institute

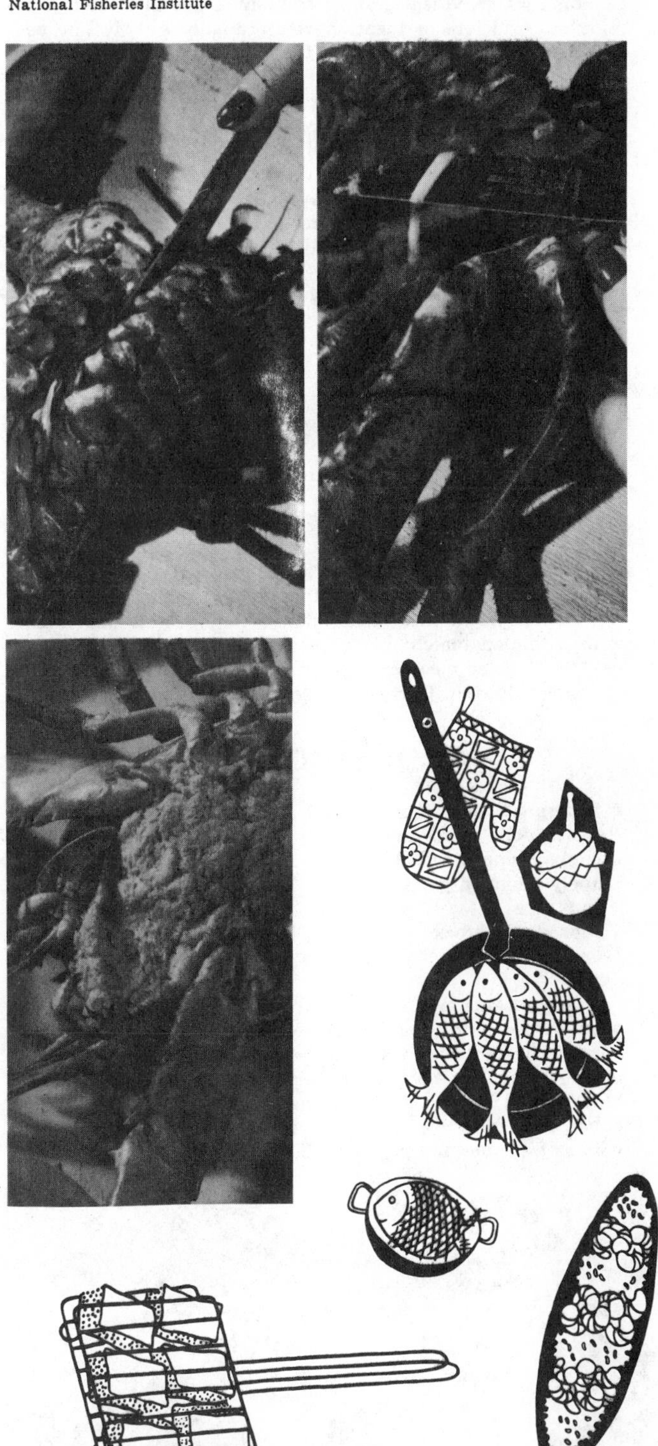

# Lobster Vinaigrette

**2 lobsters**
**¾ cup water**
**6 tablespoons tarragon vinegar**
**2 teaspoons minced onion**
**2 teaspoons minced chives**
**6 egg yolks, beaten**
**½ teaspoon dry mustard**
**1 tablespoon chopped parsley**

Cook lobsters according to directions for boiled lobster. Remove meat from shells; reserve shells. Cut meat into cubes. Combine water, vinegar, onion and chives and simmer about 5 minutes. Add lobster meat; heat thoroughly but do not boil. Arrange shells on a preheated fireproof dish and keep warm. Remove lobster meat from sauce and fill shells. Combine egg yolks and mustard. Pour some of the hot liquid into egg yolks, mix well. Return to pan and cook, stirring constantly, over low heat until sauce is smooth and thickened. Season with salt, add chopped parsley. Pour sauce over lobster meat in shells and serve immediately. This dish may be served over buttered toast instead of in lobster shells. Makes 4 to 6 servings.

# Lobster au Charin

**½ cup butter or margarine**
**4 chopped scallions**
**1 tablespoon curry powder**
**1 cup heavy cream**
**Salt**
**2 cooked lobsters**
**⅓ cup brandy**
**Parsley**

Melt ¼ cup of the butter in a skillet over low heat. Add scallions and cook about 2 minutes. Stir in curry powder and cream; heat thoroughly but do not boil. Season with salt to taste and keep hot over very low heat. Melt remaining butter in another skillet. Remove meat from lobsters and cut in chunks. Add to melted butter and heat thoroughly over low heat. When hot remove from heat; add brandy. Set lobster meat ablaze with a lighted match; blaze ½ minute and extinguish flame. Arrange lobster meat on a preheated platter. Pour hot cream sauce over lobster. Garnish with parsley. Makes 4 servings.

# Lobster Pilaf

**2 tablespoons oil**
**2 tablespoons shortening**
**1 finely chopped onion**
**1 finely chopped garlic clove**
**2 cups rice**
**4 cups strong stock**
**1 bay leaf**
**2 tablespoons grated Parmesan cheese**
**2 lobsters, cooked**
**4 tablespoons sour cream**
**Salt and pepper**
**Paprika**

Heat oil and fat in a pan. Add onion and garlic and cook over low heat until soft. Add rice and cook about 5 minutes, stirring constantly. Cover with the stock, bring to a boil and add bay leaf. Reduce heat, cover tightly and steam until rice is tender. Add grated cheese. Remove lobster meat and cut in cubes. Add to rice with sour cream, mix well. Season to taste with salt, pepper and paprika. Makes 6 servings.

# Rock Lobster Tails

Place rock lobster tails, either thawed or frozen, into a large kettle with boiling salted water (1 teaspoon of salt for each quart of water). When water reboils, lower heat so that water boils gently and begin counting time. Keep kettle tightly covered. Boil tails 1 minute longer than their individual weight in ounces. For instance, boil a 5 ounce tail for 6 minutes. Add 2 minutes to all boiling times when tails are cooked frozen. Drain off water and cover with cold water. With scissors, cut lengthwise through center of membrane covering flesh; insert fingers under meat at open end and pull meat out. *In boiling whole lobster, boil 5 minutes for first pound, 3 more for each additional pound.*

# Lobster Chops

**2 tablespoons butter or margarine**
**3 tablespoons flour**
**1 cup light cream, warm**
**¼ teaspoon salt**
**⅛ teaspoon pepper**
**1 7-ounce can lobster, shredded**
**3 egg yolks, slightly beaten**
**3 cups corn flakes**
**1 egg, well beaten**
**2 tablespoons shortening**

Melt butter in a saucepan; stir in flour and cook until lightly browned. Add cream, salt and pepper; cook, stirring constantly, until thickened. Fold in lobster meat. Stir small amount of hot mixture into egg yolks; add to remaining hot mixture and cook over low heat about 3 minutes, stirring constantly. Spread ½-inch thick in greased shallow pan. Cool; shape into chops. Crush corn flakes into fine crumbs. Dip chops in beaten egg, then roll in corn flake crumbs. Fry in heated shortening until lightly browned. Serve with lemon slices. Makes 6 chops.

# Seafood Coquilles

**1 6-ounce can lobster meat**
**1 4-ounce can mushrooms**
**¼ cup butter or margarine**
**¼ cup flour**
**1⅔ cups milk**
**½ teaspoon salt**
**Dash of pepper**
**2 tablespoons chopped green pepper**
**2 tablespoons dry bread crumbs**

Drain lobster meat; remove hard fiber and flake meat. Drain mushrooms; reserve liquor. Melt butter in a saucepan; stir in flour. Add milk to mushroom liquor; gradually stir into flour mixture. Cook, stirring constantly, until smooth and thickened. Add salt, pepper, green pepper, mushrooms and lobster. Turn into individual casseroles. Top with bread crumbs and bake in a moderate oven (375°F.) 20 minutes. Makes 4 to 5 servings.

# Lobster Bordelaise

**1 2-pound lobster**
**¼ cup butter or margarine**
**2 tablespoons flour**
**¼ teaspoon salt**
**Pinch of cayenne**
**Pinch of nutmeg**
**1 cup milk**
**1 small onion, minced**
**½ small carrot, minced**
**¼ teaspoon oregano**
**¼ cup claret wine**
**4 slices toast**

Cook lobster according to directions for boiled lobster. Remove meat from shell and cut in pieces. Melt butter in top of double boiler over hot water. Stir in flour, salt cayenne and nutmeg. Combine milk, onion, carrot and oregano in a small saucepan. Bring to a boil and simmer 5 minutes. Slowly add hot milk to mixture in double boiler and cook until thick. Add lobster meat and cook 5 minutes. Add wine and heat thoroughly. Serve over hot buttered toast. Makes 4 servings.

# Broiled Live Lobster

To kill the lobster, insert a sharp knife between the body and tail shells; this severs the spinal cord. Place lobster on back and make a deep cut lengthwise from head to end of tail; open and remove stomach, dark vein and liver. Season liver with salt, pepper, grated onion, lemon juice and fine bread crumbs and replace in lobster cavity. Crack large claws and lay lobster as flat as possible, flesh side up, on broiler. Brush meat with melted butter or margarine and sprinkle lightly with salt and pepper. Broil about 4 inches away from source of heat, meat side up, until delicately browned. Allow 12 to 14 minutes for smaller lobster; 16 to 18 minutes for larger lobsters.

# Lobster à la Newburg

**6 tablespoons butter or margarine**
**2 tablespoons flour**
**3 cups cut-up lobster**
**Dash paprika**
**1 teaspoon salt**
**3 tablespoons sherry**
**3 egg yolks**
**2 cups cream**
**Toast**

Melt butter in double-boiler top; stir in flour; add lobster, seasoning and sherry. Place over hot water. Beat egg yolks slightly, stir in cream and mix well. Stir slowly into lobster mixture, cook, stirring, until thickened. Serve over toast. Makes 6 servings.

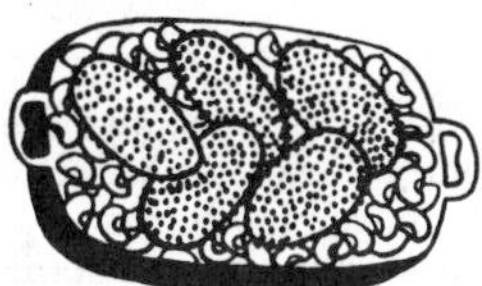
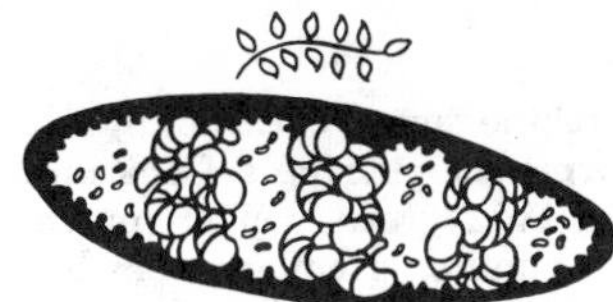

# Scallops

THE scallop is a shell fish, much like the oyster or clam. Its shell is rounded with a wavy scalloped edge and a large muscle holds the 2 shells together as it opens and closes, propelling itself along through the water. This muscle is called the eye and is the only part of the scallop eaten in the United States.

There are 2 kinds of scallops: the sweet tender, small bay scallop taken from inshore waters and the large succulent sea scallop, fished from off shore banks and other deep waters. Besides fresh scallops you will find quick-frozen ones on the market. One pound of scallops will make 4 servings.

# Scallops with Herbs

**1 pound scallops**
**2 cups cracker crumbs**
**1 cup bread crumbs**
**½ teaspoon salt**
**Pinch of cayenne**
**1 tablespoon minced parsley**
**⅛ teaspoon rosemary**
**⅛ teaspoon dill**
**⅛ teaspoon marjoram**
**¼ cup sherry wine**
**¼ cup butter**
**1 cup cream**
**4 tablespoons chopped green olives**

If scallops are large, cut in half across grain; wipe with damp cloth. Combine remaining ingredients, except cream and olives and mix well. Arrange layer of crumb mixture in a casserole, place layer of scallops over crumbs and continue with layers until all is used. Pour cream over top. Bake in a moderate oven (350°F.) 20 minutes. Serve piping hot. Garnish each serving with 1 tablespoon chopped green olives. Makes 4 servings.

# Scallops in White Wine

**1 pound scallops**
**¾ cup dry white wine**
**3 tablespoons butter**
**2 tablespoons flour**
**½ cup cream**
**Salt and pepper**

Wash scallops. Poach in wine until just tender, about 5 minutes. Drain, save wine. Melt butter in a saucepan, add flour and blend well. Add wine and cream and cook, stirring constantly until thick. Add scallops, season to taste and serve hot. Makes 3 to 4 servings.

# Baked Scallops

**1 cup dry white wine**
**1 cup water**
**1 teaspoon salt**
**Herb bouquet (4 sprigs parsley, 1 sprig thyme, ½ bay leaf in cheese cloth)**
**2 pounds scallops, washed**
**2 cans (4-ounce) sliced mushrooms, drained**
**¼ cup minced onions**
**1 tablespoon minced parsley**
**3 tablespoons butter or margarine**
**2 tablespoons water**
**1 teaspoon lemon juice**
**¼ cup butter or margarine**
**¼ cup flour**
**2 egg yolks, slightly beaten**
**¼ cup heavy cream**
**⅓ cup dry bread crumbs**

Combine wine, water, salt, herb bouquet in sauce pan; bring to a boil. Add scallops; cover; simmer 10 minutes or until tender. Remove herb bouquet; drain scallops; reserve liquid. Cut scallops in quarters; set aside. Combine mushrooms, onions, parsley, butter, water, lemon juice; cover pan; simmer 5-10 minutes; add to scallops. Melt ¼ cup butter in sauce pan; stir in flour; add reserved liquid, blending thoroughly. Cook over low heat, stirring constantly until thickened. Blend egg yolks and cream together; gradually blend in white sauce; add scallops. Make eight individual foil casseroles using two aluminum foil squares for each. Pour scallop mixture into foil casseroles; sprinkle top with crumbs. Place foil casseroles on baking sheet; bake in hot oven (450°F), 8-10 minutes or until golden brown. Makes 8 servings.

Alcoa Wrap

Alcoa Wrap

# Scallops Orly

1 pound scallops
Salt and pepper
Few grains nutmeg
Juice of 1 lemon
4 tablespoons olive oil
½ teaspoon finely chopped onion
Fat

Combine scallops, salt and pepper to taste, nutmeg, lemon juice, olive oil and onions in a bowl. Let stand 1 hour, stirring occasionally. Drain. Roll in crumbs or flour and fry in hot fat until golden brown on all sides. Serve with tomato sauce. Makes 3 to 4 servings.

# Broiled Scallops

2 pounds scallops
1 cup milk
Dry bread crumbs
2 tablespoons butter

Dip scallops in milk and roll in bread crumbs. Place one layer deep in a greased shallow pan, dot with butter and broil 2 inches from source of heat 3 minutes, or until browned, turning frequently. Serve with melted butter and lemon wedges. Makes 6 servings.

# Oven Fried Scallops

1 pound scallops
Salt and pepper
1 egg, beaten
2 tablespoons water
¾ cup fine bread crumbs
¼ cup melted shortening

If scallops are large, cut into cubes of about ¾-inch size. Season with salt and pepper. Beat egg and water together. Dip scallops in egg, crumbs and then into melted shortening. Place in a shallow baking dish. Bake in a hot oven (450°F.) 20 to 25 minutes. Makes 4 servings.

# Shrimp

SHRIMP is probably the most popular shellfish in the United States. Only the meat of the tail on the shrimp is eaten; it comes to market either fresh or frozen in sizes tiny, medium and large. One pound of fresh or frozen fish makes 1⅓ to 1½ cups prepared shrimp. As for planning for service, 1 pound will serve 2 to 4, depending on how it is served. Some canned shrimp come de-veined and most cans make about 1 cup prepared shrimp.

# Boiled Shrimp

1 quart water
½ stalk celery
1 carrot, sliced
1 small onion, sliced
Juice of ½ lemon
1 teaspoon salt
½ teaspoon pepper
1 pound shrimp

Put water in saucepan. Add all ingredients except shrimp. Bring to a boil. Add shrimp, let water come to a boil again. Turn heat down so water just simmers. Cover saucepan and let shrimp cook 5 minutes, never longer. Drain shrimp and cool quickly.

Shrimp may be shucked either before or after boiling. To clean shrimp, hold tail end in right hand, slip thumb under shell, between feelers and lift off 2 or 3 segments in one motion. Then still holding firmly to tail, pull out shrimp from remaining shell section and tail. With a knife, cut along outside curvature and lift out black sand vein, if desired. Vein is harmless but some people object to the appearance of the black line.

# Curried Shrimp with Spaghetti

6 tablespoons butter or margarine
3 tablespoons minced onion
2 cloves garlic, finely minced
6 tablespoons flour
3 teaspoons curry powder
½ teaspoon salt
⅛ teaspoon pepper
1 can condensed consomme
3 cups milk
3 tablespoons chutney
⅓ cup lemon juice
2 pounds cooked shrimp or 2 5-ounce cans shrimp
1½ pounds thin spaghetti, cooked

Melt butter, sauté onion and garlic for several minutes. Stir in flour, curry powder, salt and pepper. Add consommé and milk slowly. Cook, stirring constantly, until thickened. Add chutney, lemon juice and shrimp. Heat thoroughly and serve over hot cooked spaghetti. Makes 6 servings.

# Sweet and Pungent Shrimp

¼ cup brown sugar
2 tablespoons cornstarch
½ teaspoon salt
¼ cup vinegar
1 tablespoon soy sauce
1 No. 2 can pineapple chunks
1 green pepper, cut in strips
1 onion, sliced
1 pound cooked, cleaned shrimp
Hot cooked rice

Combine sugar, cornstarch, salt, vinegar, soy sauce and the juice from the pineapple. Cook until slightly thick, stirring constantly. Add green pepper, onion and pineapple chunks and cook 3 minutes. Remove from heat, add shrimp and let stand covered 10 minutes. Just before serving, bring mixture to a boil, stirring constantly. Serve with hot rice. Makes 4 servings.

# Roast Turkey with Glazed Chestnuts

(See picture opposite.)

1 small turkey, about 7 lbs.
½ teaspoon white pepper
1 tablespoon salt
3 or 4 apples
5 tablespoons melted butter
4 to 8 tablespoons dry sherry

Wash and dry turkey carefully. Make bouillon of neck, heart, liver, etc. Rub salt and pepper all over turkey and fill with slices of apple. Sew together at neck and breast openings. Put turkey, breast upward, on a grid on baking tin. Brush with butter and place in warm oven, 350 degrees. Roast at this temperature for about 2½ hours and then turn turkey on side. Brush with butter and after 30 minutes turn on other side; brush with butter and leave in oven for 30 minutes before turning. Roast the rest of time with breast upwards. Brush with butter occasionally and in the end, brush with sherry. When turkey is tender wrap in aluminum foil while making sauce.

3 cups bouillon and turkey gravy
3 tablespoons flour
1 cup cream
Salt, pepper, sherry

Strain the bouillon and gravy from turkey together. Thicken with the flour and add cream. Add pepper and salt to gravy and a little sherry.

8 cups of chestnuts
1 teaspoon salt
3 tablespoons butter
1 cup bouillon

While the turkey is roasting, prepare the chestnuts by cutting a cross in each tip. Boil for 12 minutes. Remove shells. Brown in butter in frying pan and then add bouillon. Cover with lid and simmer for 15 minutes. Makes 8 - 10 servings.

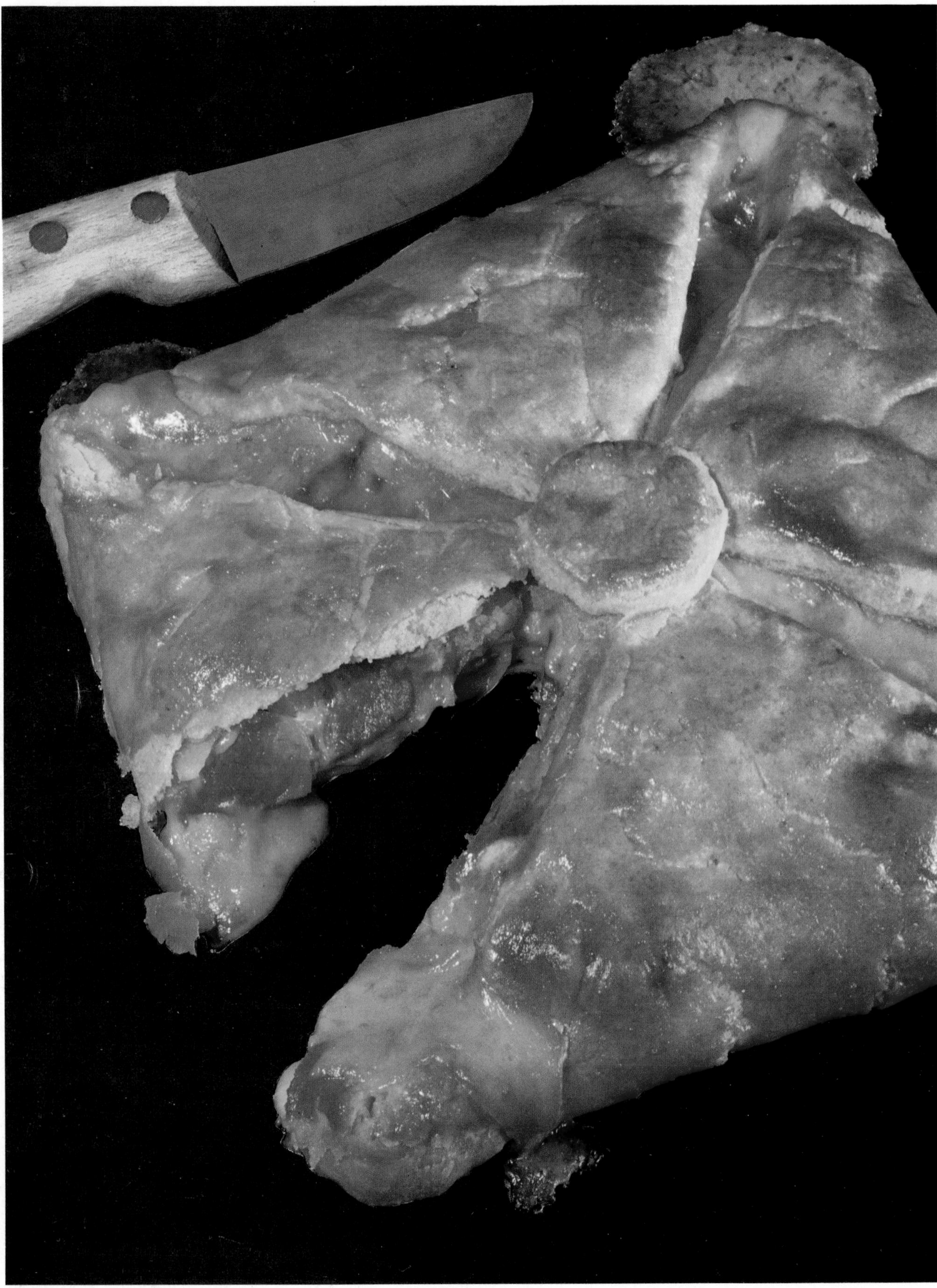

*Swiss Pie, p. 70*

*Pizza a la Reine, p. 125, Bechamel Sauce, p. 125*

# Roast Turkey

(See picture opposite.)

Roast turkey needs about 4 hours cooking in a medium oven for a 10-12 lb. bird, drawn weight. Spread a little butter over the breast of the bird before wrapping in foil and putting in the oven. About ½ hour before the turkey is finished open the foil and allow the breast to brown. Roast potatoes need to be parboiled first then put in a baking tin with fat and placed at top of oven. Turn the heat up to 425° to brown potatoes and turkey for final half hour. Serve with crispy bacon rolls, sausages, potato croquettes, and brussel sprouts.

# Shrimp Diavolo

**2 pounds shrimp, fresh or frozen**
**⅓ cup olive oil**
**1 medium onion, chopped**
**2 cloves garlic, minced**
**2 cans (No. 2) stewed tomatoes**
**⅛ teaspoon cloves**
**⅛ teaspoon mace**
**1 teaspoon salt**
**⅛ teaspoon pepper**
**2 tablespoons cornstarch**
**2 tablespoons water**
**5 cups hot rice**
**¼ cup brandy, if desired**

**Shell and clean shrimp removing sand veins, but do not cook. Heat olive oil. Add onion, garlic and shrimp. Cook and stir over low heat until shrimp are barely pink. Add tomatoes and seasonings. Stir to combine, then cover and simmer ten minutes to blend flavors. Blend cornstarch and water, then stir into bubbling liquid. Cook until thickened. Pack hot rice into 9-inch ring mold, then invert on plate or platter. Or spoon rice to form ring on platter. Stir half the brandy into shrimp mixture. Pour shrimp into center of ring. Warm remaining brandy, ignite rising vapors, pour over shrimp and serve. Makes 6 servings.**

# Deviled Shrimp

**2 tablespoons chopped onion**
**2 tablespoons chopped green pepper**
**½ cup chopped celery**
**2 tablespoons butter or margarine**
**2 tablespoons flour**
**¼ teaspoon dry mustard**
**½ teaspoon salt**
**1 cup milk**
**½ teaspoon Worcestershire sauce**
**¼ cup diced pimiento**
**1 cup cleaned, cooked shrimp**
**¾ cup ripe olives, slivered**
**½ cup buttered bread crumbs**

Cook onion, green pepper and celery slowly in butter until vegetables are tender but not browned. Blend in flour, mustard, salt and milk, cook and stir until thickened. Blend in Worcestershire sauce, pimiento, shrimp and olives. Turn into ramekins or baking shells and top with crumbs. Bake in a hot oven (400°F.) about 15 minutes. Makes 4 servings.

# Shrimp Mull

**3 slices bacon**
**1½ cups diced onion**
**1 green pepper, diced**
**2 stalks celery, chopped**
**1 pound raw, cleaned shrimp**
**Boiling water**
**1 cup catsup**
**Pepper to taste**
**1 teaspoon Worcestershire sauce**
**Salt to taste**
**Dash of Tabasco**

Fry bacon slices until cooked. Add onion and sauté until golden, add pepper and celery; simmer, lid on pan, 5 minutes. Add shrimp, and just enough water to cover; add remaining ingredients and simmer about 30 minutes or until thickened. Makes 4 servings.

# Shrimp Fricassee

**2 tablespoons butter or margarine**
**2 tablespoons flour**
**1½ cups canned tomatoes**
**2 tablespoons finely minced onion**
**2 tablespoons chopped green pepper**
**¼ teaspoon garlic salt**
**⅛ teaspoon thyme**
**½ teaspoon dried parsley**
**1 bay leaf**
**½ teaspoon celery salt**
**⅛ teaspoon pepper**
**Salt to taste**
**1 pound shrimp, cooked and cleaned**
**2 cups cooked rice**

Melt butter in skillet. Add flour and heat, stirring constantly until lightly browned. Add tomatoes, onion, green pepper and seasonings. Simmer 15 minutes. Add shrimp and simmer 5 minutes. Pack cooked rice into greased cups and place in moderate oven (350°F.) about 5 minutes. Unmold on platter and pour shrimp mixture over them. Makes 4 servings.

# Oysters

OYSTERS in the shell are generally sold by the dozen and must be alive when purchased. You will find that many fish dealers will open them for you, for oysters on the half shell. You can buy shucked oysters in ½ pint, 1 pint or quart containers. If your shucked oysters are frozen they should not be thawed until ready to use, once thawed they should never be refrozen. To serve 4 you will need to purchase 2 dozen shell oysters, 1 pint of shucked oysters or one No. 1 can of oysters.

# Oyster Soufflé

**1 pint oysters**
**3 tablespoons butter or margarine**
**3 tablespoons flour**
**1 cup milk**
**1 teaspoon salt**
**⅛ teaspoon pepper**
**Dash nutmeg**
**3 eggs, separated**

Drain and chop oysters. Melt butter, blend in flour, add milk and cook, stirring constantly, until thick. Remove from heat. Add oysters, seasonings and beaten egg yolks. Beat egg whites until stiff but not dry. Fold into oyster mixture. Pour into buttered casserole and bake in moderate oven (350°F.) 30 minutes or until brown. Makes 6 servings.

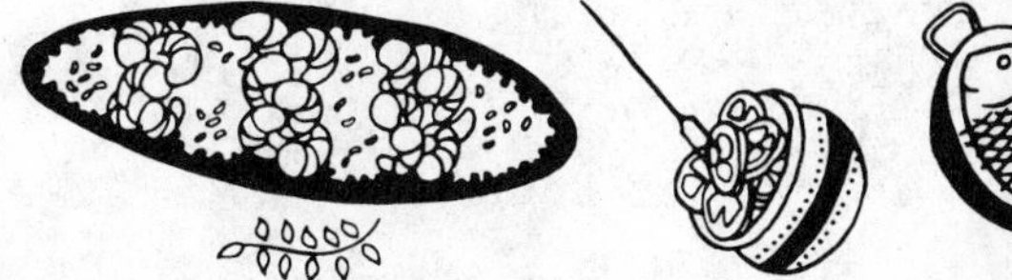

# Oysters Creole

2 dozen oysters, drained (reserve liquor)
6 tablespoons bacon fat, divided
1 small onion, diced
½ green pepper, diced
1 stalk celery, diced
2 cups cooked tomatoes
¾ teaspoon salt
½ teaspoon chili powder
2 teaspoons brown sugar
4 large hard rolls
3 tablespoons butter or margarine
Dill pickles
Lemon wedges

Cook oysters in 3 tablespoons of the drippings for 1 minute. Remove oysters from skillet. Simmer onion, green pepper and celery in 3 tablespoons hot fat 5 minutes. Add oyster liquor, tomatoes and seasonings and continue cooking, stirring occasionally, 20 minutes or until thick. Split rolls in half, remove centers and brush hollows with melted butter. Toast rolls. Drop oysters into hot creole sauce; cook 1 minute; ladle into toasted rolls. Garnish with dill pickle slices and lemon wedges. Makes 4 servings.

# Oysters Casino

3 slices bacon, chopped
4 tablespoons chopped onion
2 tablespoons chopped green pepper
2 tablespoons chopped celery
1 teaspoon lemon juice
½ teaspoon salt
⅛ teaspoon pepper
½ teaspoon Worcestershire sauce
2 drops Tabasco sauce
1 pint oysters

Fry bacon, add onion, green pepper, celery, and cook until tender. Add seasonings and mix well. Arrange drained oysters on buttered baking dish. Spread bacon mixture over oysters. Bake in a moderate oven (350°F.) about 10 minutes or until browned. Makes 4 to 6 servings.

# Oysters Rockefeller

36 shell oysters
2 cups cooked spinach
4 tablespoons chopped onion
2 bay leaves
2 sprigs parsley
½ teaspoon celery salt
½ teaspoon salt
6 drops Tabasco sauce
½ cup bread crumbs
6 tablespoons butter

Shuck and drain oysters; place on deep half of shells. Put spinach, onion, bay leaves and parsley through food grinder. Add seasonings and cook in butter for 5 minutes. Add bread crumbs and mix well. Spread mixture over oysters and bake in a hot oven (400°F.) for about 10 minutes. Makes 6 servings.

National Fisheries Institute

# Crabs

THE edible Atlantic coast crab is called the Blue crab. Crabs have a hard shell except during the molting season in the spring and summer; between the shedding of the old shell and the hardening of the new larger shell, they have a soft shell and at this time are known as soft-shell crabs.

Soft-shell crabs are generally broiled or pan fried and the whole crab, shell and all, is eaten. Hard-shell crabs are cooked like lobster and the meat eaten hot or cold from the shell, or it is taken from the shell and in the market can be found as fresh frozen or canned crab meat. Most of the canned crab on the retail market is from the Pacific coast from a hard-shelled crab known as the Dungeness Crab.

# Crab Cakes

1½ cups chopped raw potatoes
½ cup milk
⅛ teaspoon cayenne
½ teaspoon salt
2 cups cooked or canned crab meat
2 eggs, beaten

Put potatoes and milk in top part of a double boiler and cook over boiling water until tender. Add seasonings. Flake crab meat and add to potato mixture. Beat in eggs. Drop mixture from a tablespoon onto a hot well-greased griddle or heavy frying pan. Brown on both sides and serve hot with plenty of tartar sauce. Makes 6 servings.

# Sea Shell Oven Bake

1½ cups macaroni shells
2 small onions, chopped
1 green pepper, chopped
4 stalks celery, chopped
3 tablespoons butter or margarine
½ cup mayonnaise
1 14-ounce can evaporated milk
1 teaspoon salt
1 teaspoon paprika
1 teaspoon dry mustard
1 teaspoon Worcestershire sauce
6 ripe olives, slivered
1 can crab meat

Cook macaroni until tender in a large saucepan of boiling salted water. Sauté onion, green pepper and celery in butter until tender. Stir in mayonnaise, evaporated milk, salt, paprika, mustard and Worcestershire sauce. Add macaroni and olives; fold in seafood. Spoon mixture into greased 1½-quart casserole or 6 individual casseroles. Bake in a moderate oven (350°F.) 30 minutes. Makes 6 servings.

# Broiled Soft-Shell Crabs

Dust dressed crabs very lightly with flour. Preheat broiling compartment. Place crabs on broiler 6 inches from heat. Broil small and medium-size crabs 4 minutes on the first side, and 4 minutes on the second. Large crabs should be broiled 5 minutes on each side. Do not baste during cooking time. When done, remove crabs, dot with butter and serve immediately. Two large or 3 small soft-shell crabs make 1 serving.

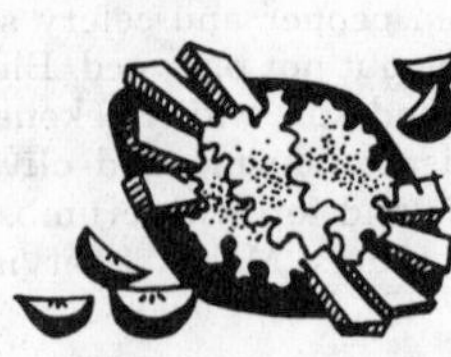

# Spiced Crab

**3 tablespoons butter or margarine**
**3 tablespoons flour**
**2 teaspoons Worcestershire sauce**
**Dash of cayenne**
**½ teaspoon salt**
**¼ teaspoon pepper**
**1 cup milk**
**2½ cups cooked crab**
**¼ cup chopped mushrooms**
**1 tablespoon chopped parsley**
**1 teaspoon minced onion**
**2 cups corn flakes, crushed**
**1 egg yolk, beaten**
**½ teaspoon dry mustard**
**1 teaspoon lemon juice**
**¼ teaspoon salt**
**Butter or margarine**
**Paprika**

Melt butter; add flour and seasonings; add milk and cook, stirring constantly, until thick. Add crab meat, mushrooms, parsley and onion; mix well. Place in buttered shells or ramekins. Top with a mixture of corn flakes, egg yolk, mustard, lemon juice and salt. Dot with butter and sprinkle with paprika. Bake in a hot oven (400°F.) about 10 to 15 minutes or until golden brown. Makes 6 servings.

# Meeting-Street Crab

**4 tablespoons butter or margarine**
**4 tablespoons flour**
**1 cup cream**
**Salt and pepper to taste**
**4 tablespoons sherry**
**1 pound crab meat**
**¾ cup grated Cheddar cheese**

Melt butter; stir in flour; gradually stir in milk and cook, stirring constantly, until thickened. Add salt, pepper and sherry. Remove from heat and add crab meat. Pour mixture into a butter casserole or individual baking dishes. Sprinkle with cheese and bake in a hot oven (400°F.) until cheese melts. Makes 4 servings.

# Clams

ON THE Atlantic coast there are two kinds of clams: hard and soft shell. The hard-shell clams, called Quahaugs, in the largest size are best for chowders and broths. Smaller sizes, known as Little Necks and Cherrystones, are best served raw on the half shell or in cocktails. Soft-shell clams are somewhat oval in shape and are best steamed, fried, in chowders or used for clambakes.

Pacific coast clams range in size from tiny clams to giant ones weighing several pounds. Most common are the Razor or Long clams; these are best for soups and chowders and also used for commercially canned clams.

# Clam Scallop

**2 dozen shucked clams**
**¾ cup cracker crumbs**
**2 tablespoons butter**
**⅛ teaspoon paprika**
**⅛ teaspoon oregano**
**½ teaspoon salt**
**2 stalks celery, chopped**
**2 tablespoons chopped parsley**
**1 cup light cream**
**½ cup sherry**

Drain clams. Place a layer of clams in bottom of a buttered casserole. Combine cracker crumbs, butter, paprika, oregano and salt and spread a layer of mixture over clams, then a layer of celery and parsley. Alternate until all ingredients are used finishing with a layer of crumbs. Combine cream and sherry and pour over top. Bake in a moderate oven (350°F.) about 20 minutes. Makes 4 servings.

# Clam Chowder

**2 dozen clams and liquid or**
**2 cans minced clams**
**½ cup finely diced salt pork**
**¼ cup chopped onion**
**2 cups cubed potatoes**
**2 cups clam juice and water**
**1 cup tomato juice**
**Dash of pepper**
**¼ teaspoon baking soda**
**2 cups scalded milk**
**¼ cup chopped parsley**

Prepare clams and chop. Sauté salt pork until lightly browned; add onion and cook until soft. Add potatoes, clam juice and water. Cover, bring to boil, reduce heat and simmer about 15 minutes or until potatoes are tender. Add tomato juice, clams and pepper. Cook slowly uncovered about 8 minutes; add soda, mix well and add milk. If necessary season with salt. Sprinkle with parsley and serve at once. Makes 7½ cups.

# Clam Pancakes

**¾ cup sifted flour**
**1¼ teaspoons baking powder**
**¼ teaspoon salt**
**⅛ teaspoon pepper**
**1 egg, slightly beaten**
**1 10½-ounce can minced clams**
**1 tablespoon buttter or margarine**
**¼ cup cooking oil**

Sift together flour, baking powder, salt and pepper. Combine egg, undrained clams and butter; add sifted dry ingredients and blend well. Heat cooking oil in a large skillet over medium heat; drop batter by spoonfuls into hot fat and cook about 2 minutes on each side or until lightly browned. Makes 12 pancakes.

# Clams Casino

**12 clams**
**Juice of 1 lemon**
**2 tablespoons minced green pepper**
**2 tablespoons minced onion**
**Salt and pepper**
**2 slices bacon**

Open clams carefully to retain juice. Remove upper shell, leaving clams in deeper half. Sprinkle each with a few drops of lemon juice, green pepper and onion. Season with salt and pepper. Cut bacon into small bits and put a few pieces on top of each clam. Set clams in a pan and bake in a hot oven (450°F.) or under a hot broiler until bacon crisps. Makes 4 servings.

# POULTRY

## Turkey

### Roast Stuffed Turkey

Rinse turkey in cold running water and pat dry with paper towels. Fill with bone or with stuffing. Fasten neck skin to back with skewers. Fill body cavity lightly. Push drumsticks under band of skin at tail, or tie them to the tail. Place turkey, breast side up, on rack in shallow open roasting pan. Insert meat thermometer in thigh muscle or thickest part of breast. Be sure that the thermometer does not touch bone. Place a loose covering or "tent" of aluminum foil over turkey. Roast in a moderately slow oven (325° F) according to time table. Remove foil during last half hour to brown turkey. When turkey is done the meat thermometer should read 185° F.

For serving, plan cooking schedule so that the turkey is out of the oven 20 to 30 minutes before it is to be served. This gives the meat a chance to absorb the juices and it will be easier to carve.

CHART FOR ROASTING WHOLE TURKEY

| Ready-to-cook Weight | Oven Temperature | Total Cooking Hours |
|---|---|---|
| 4 to 8 pounds | 325°F. | 3 to 4 |
| 8 to 12 pounds | 325°F. | 4 to 4½ |
| 12 to 16 pounds | 325°F. | 4½ to 5 |
| 16 to 20 pounds | 325°F. | 5½ to 7 |
| 20 to 24 pounds | 325°F. | 7 to 8½ |

Internal temperature—meat thermometer—185°F.

CHART FOR ROASTING HALF AND QUARTER TURKEY

| Ready-to-cook Weight | Oven Temperature | Total Cooking Hours |
|---|---|---|
| 3½ to 5 pounds | 325°F. | 3 to 3½ |
| 5 to 8 pounds | 325°F. | 3½ to 4 |
| 8 to 12 pounds | 325°F. | 4 to 4½ |

**Since turkeys vary in type and size, roasting periods in this chart are approximate. If the wrapper of the turkey has a printed time-temperature chart, use those directions.**

## How to Carve Turkey

### SIDE STYLE

1. REMOVE THE WING TIP AND FIRST JOINT. Grasp the wing tip firmly with fingers, lift up, and cut between first and second joint. Place the wing tip and first joint portion on the side of the platter. Leave the second joint attached to the turkey.

2. REMOVE THE DRUMSTICK. Grasp the end of the drumstick and lift it up and away from the body, disjointing it from the thigh. The thigh is left attached to the turkey. Place the drumstick on the service plate for slicing the meat. Hold the drumstick upright at a convenient angle and cut down toward the plate, parallel with the bone, turning the drumstick to make uniform slices.

3. SLICING WHITE MEAT. Begin at the front end of the turkey and slice until the wing socket is exposed. Remove the second joint of the wing. Continue slicing white meat until enough slices have been provided, or until the breastbone is reached.

4. REMOVING STUFFING FROM HOLE CUT INTO CAVITY UNDER THIGH. Slit the thin tissue in the thigh region with the tip of the knife and make an opening large enough for a serving-spoon. The stuffing in the breast cavity may be served by laying the skin back onto the platter.

NOTE: *Use this "Side Style" method for carving half and quarter turkeys.*

# STANDARD STYLE

1. TO REMOVE LEG (drumstick and thigh). Hold the drumstick firmly with fingers, pulling gently away from turkey body. At the same time cut through skin between leg and body. Continue as follows:

2. PRESS LEG AWAY FROM BODY WITH FLAT SIDE OF KNIFE. Then cut through joint joining leg to backbone and skin on the back. Hold leg on service plate with drumstick at a convenient angle to plate. Separate drumstick and thigh by cutting down through the joint to the plate.

3. SLICE DRUMSTICK MEAT. Hold drumstick upright at a convenient angle to plate and cut down, turning drumstick to get uniform slices. Drumsticks and thighs from smaller turkeys are usually served without slicing.

4. SLICE THIGH MEAT. Hold thigh firmly on plate with a fork. Cut slices of meat parallel to the bone.

5. CUT INTO WHITE MEAT PARALLEL TO WING. Make a cut deep into the breast to the body frame parallel to and as close to the wing as possible.

6. SLICE WHITE MEAT. Beginning at front, starting halfway up the breast, cut thin slices of white meat down to the cut made parallel to the wing. The slices will fall away from the turkey as they are cut to this line. Continue carving until enough meat has been carved for first servings. Additional turkey may be carved as needed.

*Remove servings of stuffing from an opening cut into side of turkey where leg has been removed. OR: Enlarge opening of body cavity at tail and spoon out stuffing.*

# Barbecued Turkey and Stuffing

**5-pound ready-to-cook broiler-fryer turkey**
**2½ cups barbecue sauce**
**⅓ cup shortening**
**⅓ cup chopped onion**
**2 quarts soft (½-inch) bread cubes**
**1 teaspoon salt**
**½ teaspoon ground sage**
**½ teaspoon ground thyme**
**½ teaspoon rosemary leaves**
**1 egg, beaten**

Have butcher saw turkey in half, lengthwise. Place halves of turkey, skin side up, on a sheet of aluminum foil placed over a rack in a large shallow baking pan. Pour about a cup of barbecue sauce over turkey. Roast, uncovered, in a slow oven (325°F) for about one hour. Turn pieces and baste with more sauce. Roast for another hour. Melt shortening in a skillet. Add onion and sauté until tender. Pour over soft bread cubes, adding salt, sage, thyme, rosemary and beaten egg. Remove turkey from oven and turn the halves on their sides. Divide Stuffing in half and form it into two mounds on the foil. Replace turkey halves over the stuffing and continue roasting until done (allow twenty-five to thirty minutes per pound). Baste occasionally with barbecue sauce during baking period. Makes 10 servings.

# Dressing Bac-Chant

3 cups day-old bread cubes
1 cup white wine
Liver of bird, chopped
¼ cup chopped green onions
2 tablespoons minced parsley
¼ cup chopped pistachio nuts
¼ cup seedless raisins
½ teaspoon sage
¼ teaspoon thyme
⅛ teaspoon allspice
½ teaspoon salt
⅛ teaspoon pepper
3 tablespoons melted butter or margarine

Sprinkle bread crumbs with wine and squeeze dry. Reserve excess wine for basting. Combine bread with remaining ingredients in the order given. Makes about 4 cups of dressing. Especially fine for chicken, duck or game birds.

# Rice and Orange Dressing

1 cup raw rice
1 small onion, minced
2 tablespoons shortening or fat from fowl
1 large orange
2 tablespoons seedless raisins
½ teaspoon salt
⅛ teaspoon pepper
½ teaspoon celery salt

Cook rice in boiling lightly-salted water until barely tender. Drain thoroughly. Sauté onion in shortening until golden. Grate skin of orange; peel and remove membrane and seeds; chop orange meat coarsely. Place peel, chopped orange, rice, onion and raisins in a bowl. Add combined seasonings and mix well. Makes about 4 cups of dressing, enough for a 5- to 6-pound bird. For duck, turkey, chicken or goose.

# Giblet Dressing

Giblets, neck and wing tips
1 quart bread cubes
1 small onion
1 stalk celery
¼ cup butter or margarine
1 teaspoon salt
⅛ teaspoon pepper
¼ teaspoon poultry seasoning
⅓ to ½ cup giblet broth

Simmer giblets (except liver) with neck and wing tips in salted water to cover for 1 to 1½ hours or until gizzard is tender; add liver during last 20 minutes of cooking. Dice giblets and remove meat from neck bones. Toast bread cubes until lightly browned in moderate oven 350°F. Sauté onion and celery in butter until soft but not brown; combine with giblets, neck meat, bread cubes and seasonings. Moisten lightly with broth; too much liquid will make a soggy dressing. Makes about 4 cups, enough for a 4-pound ready-to-cook bird. Triple ingredients for a 12-pound turkey.

# Bread and Butter Dressing

½ cup butter or margarine
½ cup chopped onion
2 tablespoons minced parsley
1 tablespoon minced celery leaves
3 cups day-old bread cubes
1 teaspoon salt
⅛ teaspoon pepper
½ teaspoon poultry seasoning

Heat butter and sauté onion until soft. Combine remaining ingredients and mix well with butter and onions. Makes about 4 cups of dressing.

# Cornbread and Olive Dressing

½ cup chopped onion
½ cup chopped celery
½ cup butter or margarine
1 quart cornbread crumbs
1 pint stale bread crumbs
½ teaspoon salt
½ teaspoon sage
¼ teaspoon black pepper
¼ cup chopped parsley
1 cup ripe olives

Sauté onion and celery in butter until transparent but not browned. Combine cornbread and bread crumbs and sprinkle with seasoning and parsley. Pour onion and celery mixture over crumbs, tossing to blend. Stir in olives cut from pits in large pieces. Sprinkle with ¼ cup hot water if mixture is too dry, tossing to blend. Makes enough stuffing for 8- to 9-pound ready-to-cook turkey. Divide proportions in half for a 5-pound roasting chicken.

# Chestnut Dressing

½ pound chestnuts
2 cups lightly-packed crumbs
3 tablespoons melted butter or margarine
1 teaspoon salt
1 teaspoon dried sage
⅛ teaspoon pepper
1 egg, well beaten
¼ cup cream or top milk

Wash chestnuts and make a gash in each shell. Bake in a very hot oven 500°F. for 15 minutes. Cool and remove shells and skins. Cook in boiling salted water for 20 minutes. Drain and chop fine. Add remaining ingredients and mix well. Makes about 4 cups of dressing.

# Orange Wild Rice Stuffing

2 tablespoons butter
¼ cup chopped onion
½ cup chopped celery
¼ teaspoon Tabasco
1 cup uncooked wild rice
3½ cups toasted bread cubes
1 teaspoon poultry seasoning
½ teaspoon rosemary
2 teaspoons salt
2 teaspoons orange rind
6 oranges

Melt butter in skillet. Add onion and celery; cook until tender but not brown. Stir in Tabasco. Prepare and cook wild rice according to package directions. Combine onion, celery, wild rice, bread cubes, seasoning and rind. To section oranges, cut slice from top and bottom; cut off peel around and round, spiral fashion. Go over fruit again, removing any remaining white membrane. Remove sections; cut each section in half. Add to wild rice mixture. Toss lightly. Makes approximately 7 cups or enough for an 8 to 10-pound turkey.

Florida Citrus Commission

# Turkey in Aspic

- 1 package gelatin (1 tablespoon)
- 2 cups strained, well-seasoned turkey or chicken broth
- 1 tablespoon lemon juice
- 6 hard-cooked eggs
- 2½ cups shredded, cooked or canned turkey
- ¼ cup finely chopped parsley
- 6 large stuffed olives
- Carrot curls for garnish
- Lemon slices for garnish
- Parsley for garnish

Soften gelatin in ¼ cup cold water. Dissolve in hot broth: add lemon juice. Arrange egg slices on bottom of a well-greased loaf pan. Alternate layers of turkey, egg, parsley and sliced olives. Pour hot gelatin mixture over layers in loaf pan. Cover with wax paper. Chill well. Garnish with carrot curls, lemon slices and parsley. Serves 6.

# Cranberry Tom

- 16-pound ready-to-cook tom turkey
- 2 teaspoons Accent
- 1 pound fresh cranberries
- 1 cup sugar
- 4 quarts small bread cubes
- 1 cup melted butter or margarine
- 2 cups raisins
- 1 tablespoon salt
- 1 teaspoon cinnamon
- 2 teaspoons lemon rind
- 1 cup turkey broth

Prepare turkey for roasting as per Modern Method of Roasting Turkey. Dust cavity with Accent. To make cranberry dressing chop cranberries; place in a sauce pan with sugar and bring to a boil. Remove from heat. Moisten bread cubes with melted butter; combine with cranberries, raisins, seasonings, lemon rind and broth; mix well. Stuff and truss turkey. Roast according to chart. Serves 18.

# Raleigh Dressing

- ½ cup sausage meat
- 1 small onion, chopped
- ½ teaspoon paprika
- ½ teaspoon salt
- ¼ cup diced carrots
- ¼ cup chopped celery
- 3 cups soft bread crumbs
- 2 tablespoons parsley
- 2 tablespoons milk

Cook sausage meat and onion, stirring frequently until lightly browned. Combine with remaining ingredients and mix well. Makes 3½ cups dressing.

# Roast Boneless Turkey Roll

Leave rolls in original wrapper and thaw in refrigerator for 1 to 2 days, or under running cold water. Remove wrapper and leave string in place while cooking. Rinse roast with cold water; drain and pat dry. Place on rack in shallow roasting pan. Brush with melted butter. Cover roll with a loose tent of aluminum foil. Bake in a moderate oven (350°F) about 2½ hours for a 4-pound roast, or follow directions printed on label. A meat thermometer inserted in center of roll should register 175°F when roll is done.

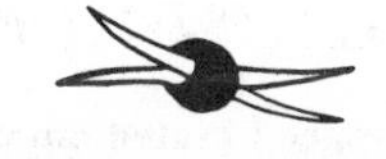

Poultry and Egg National Board

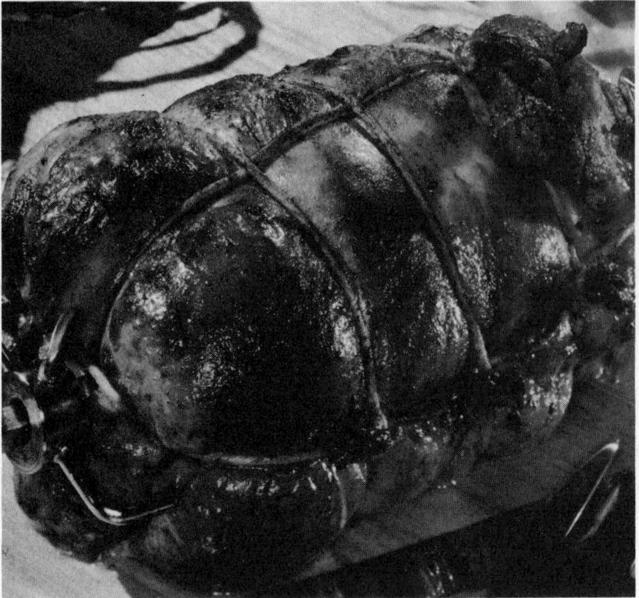

Poultry and Egg National Board

# Rotisseried Turkey

Turkeys of any size may be cooked on a rotisserie. It is wise to check manufacturer's weight suggestions before buying a turkey for rotisserie cooking. For operation of rotisserie, follow manufacturer's directions.

Rub body cavity lightly with salt, if desired. Push drumsticks under band of skin at tail, or tie drumsticks securely to tail. Fasten neck skin to back with skewer. Flatten wings over breast, then tie cord around breast to hold wings securely. Insert spit rod through center of bird from tail end toward front. Insert skewers firmly in place in bird and screw tightly. Test the balance. Bird must balance on spit so it will rotate smoothly throughout the cooking period. Place spit in rotisserie. Brush turkey with melted butter. Follow manufacturer's directions for rotisserie temperature setting and times.

# Texas Turkey Trot

**2 tablespoons vegetable oil**
**1 medium onion, chopped**
**1 green pepper, chopped**
**½ cup catsup**
**⅓ cup pickle relish**
**Juice and grated rind of 1 lemon**
**1 tablespoon prepared mustard**
**8 generous slices or small pieces of cooked turkey**

Heat oil and sauté onion and green pepper for 5 minutes. Add catsup, relish, lemon juice and rind and mustard. Simmer for 5 minutes. Add turkey and heat through. Serves 4.

# Braised Turkey Wings

**4 large turkey wings**
**⅓ cup flour**
**½ teaspoon salt**
**⅛ teaspoon paprika**
**3 tablespoons butter or margarine**
**½ cup tomato juice**
**4 small onions**
**1 bay leaf**
**1 clove**

Toss turkey wings in a bag with flour seasoned with salt and paprika. Brown thoroughly in butter. Add tomato juice, onions, bay leaf and clove. Cover tightly and simmer for 1½ hours or until tender. Add more tomato juice as needed during cooking, and turn wings several times. Serve turkey, onions and pan juices on a bed of cooked noodles. Serves 4.

# Creamed Turkey à la Pasha

**1 small onion, chopped**
**⅓ cup butter or margarine**
**⅓ cup flour**
**3 cups milk**
**4 chicken bouillon cubes**
**½ cup slivered blanched almonds**
**¼ cup seedless raisins**
**1 whole clove**
**1 bay leaf**
**12 slices turkey meat**
**24 buttered toast points (6 slices bread)**

Sauté onion in butter until soft. Blend in flour; add milk and bouillon cubes; stir until thickened. Mix in almonds, raisins, clove and bay leaf. Simmer for 5 minutes; remove clove and bay leaf. Add turkey and heat through. Spoon over toast points. Serves 6.

# Turkey-in-the-Corn Pudding

**1 tablespoon grated onion**
**2 tablespoons melted butter or margarine**
**1 teaspoon salt**
**¼ teaspoon pepper**
**¼ teaspoon paprika**
**3 eggs, well beaten**
**14½-oz. can undiluted evaporated milk**
**1½ cups diced cooked or canned turkey**
**1 cup whole-kernel corn**

Combine onion, butter and seasonings with well beaten eggs; blend thoroughly. Mix in remaining ingredients. Pour into a greased 1½-quart casserole. Set it in a pan of warm water and bake in preheated moderate oven 375°F. for 40 minutes or until a knife inserted in the center comes out clean. Serves 6.

# Turkey-Noodle Cocottes

**6 ounces raw noodles**
**2 tablespoons butter or margarine**
**2½ cups diced cooked turkey**
**10½-oz. can condensed cream of mushroom soup**
**1 cup thin cream**
**2 tablespoons capers**
**½ cup grated Cheddar cheese**
**Paprika for garnish**

Cook noodles according to package directions; drain and toss with butter. Grease 4 individual shirring dishes or casseroles and line with noodles. Combine turkey, mushroom soup, cream and capers; spoon over noodles. Sprinkle with grated cheese and a dash of paprika. Bake in a slow oven 325°F. for about 25 minutes or until golden brown on top. Serves 4.

# Turkey Calvados

**4- to 5-pound turkey breast or hind quarter**
**2 teaspoons salt**
**½ teaspoon pepper**
**1 teaspoon allspice**
**¼ cup butter or margarine**
**2 medium onions, thinly sliced**
**2 carrots, finely diced**
**1 cup apple cider**

Sprinkle turkey quarter with salt, pepper and allspice. Brown in a heavy skillet in moderately hot butter, turning frequently for about 30 minutes. Remove from pan. Arrange a bed of onions and carrots in the skillet with turkey on top. Pour apple cider over. Cover and cook over low heat for about 2½ hours or until fork-tender in the thickest parts. Baste occasionally and add more cider if necessary. Remove turkey to a warm serving dish. Strain pan juices, mashing the vegetables through a sieve to make a rich gravy. Season to taste. Garnish platter with Garlic Croutons and halves of canned fruit filled with seedless raisins. Serves 6.

# Roast Half Turkey

**6- to 7-pound turkey half**
**Salt**
**Pepper**
**⅓ cup melted butter or margarine**
**⅓ cup turkey or chicken broth**
**6 cups your favorite dressing**

Rinse turkey in cold water; pat dry. Rub all over with salt and pepper. Skewer or stitch skin to cut edges to prevent shrinking from heat during roasting. Secure leg to tail; fold wing to back. Place skin side down on a rack in a shallow pan. Brush with butter. Roast in a slow oven 325°F. about 3½ hours or until tender and meat in thickest part is soft; turn when two-thirds done. Baste every 30 minutes with a mixture of butter and broth. Meanwhile, prepare dressing; place in a casserole and bake with turkey for 1¼ hours; cover if moist dressing is desired. Stuffing may be arranged on a sheet of aluminum foil in the roasting pan with turkey atop it, skin side up. Serves 8.

# Turkey Aux Claret

**4- to 5-pound turkey breast or hind quarter, cut in pieces**
**½ cup flour**
**2 teaspoons salt**
**1 teaspoon paprika**
**½ teaspoon pepper**
**½ cup butter or margarine (1 stick)**
**1 clove garlic, minced**
**½ cup diced cooked ham**
**18 small white onions**
**1 tablespoon minced parsley**
**½ teaspoon thyme**
**2 bay leaves**
**½ pound whole mushrooms, cleaned**
**2 tablespoons brandy**
**1 cup claret or other red wine**

Shake turkey pieces in a bag with flour seasoned with salt, paprika and pepper. Heat butter in a heavy skillet or Dutch oven; sauté turkey with garlic, turning frequently for about 30 minutes or until browned evenly all over. Add ham, onions, parsley, thyme, bay leaves, and a sprinkling of salt and pepper. Cover tightly and bake in a slow oven 325°F. for 1½ hours or until the thickest part is fork-tender. Add mushrooms, brandy and wine during last 30 minutes of cooking. Sauce may be thickened with 1 or 2 teaspoons cornstarch mixed to a paste with water if desired. This dish is improved by standing and reheating; it may be cooked in the morning or the day before. Serves 6.

# Baked Curried Turkey and Rice

**1 cup raw rice**
**1 medium onion, chopped**
**⅓ cup butter or margarine**
**2 tablespoons curry powder**
**3 cups diced, cooked turkey meat**
**2½ cups turkey broth**
**Salt**

Sauté rice and onion in butter, stirring often until rice turns pale yellow. Blend in curry powder and cook for 2 minutes. Combine with turkey, broth and salt to taste depending on seasoning in broth. Turn into a 2-quart greased casserole; bake uncovered in a moderate oven 350°F. for 25 minutes or until liquid is absorbed and rice is fluffy. Serves 4.

Poultry and Egg National Board

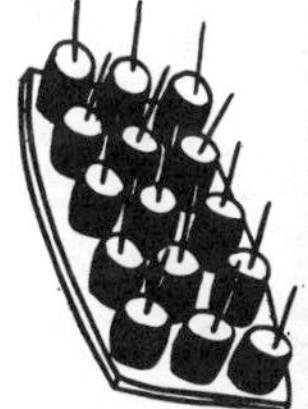

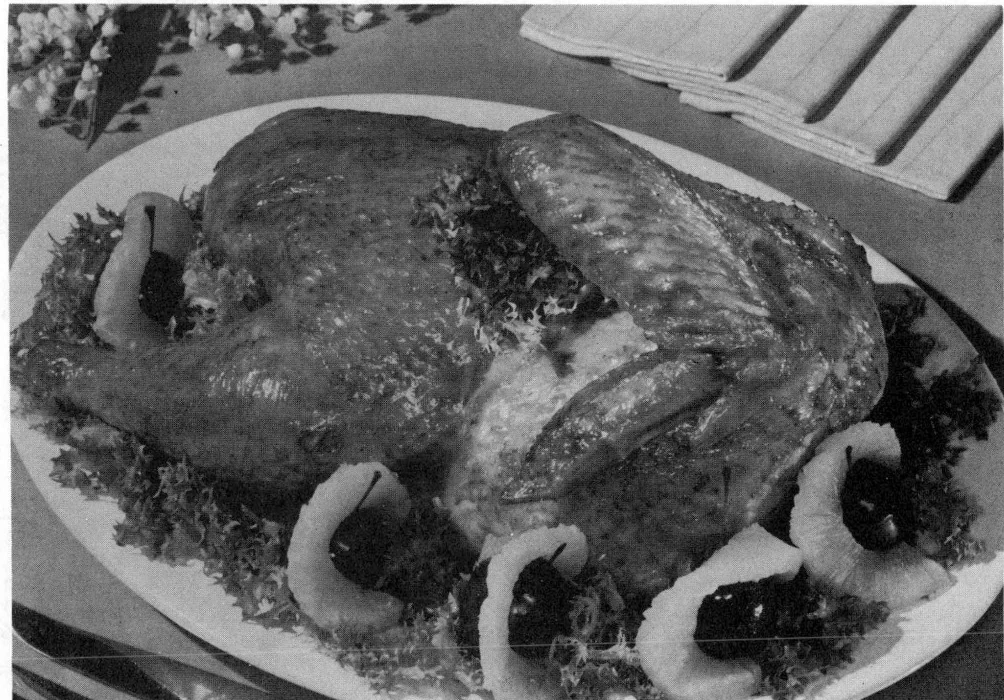

National Broiler Council

# Basic Fried Chicken

½ cup flour
1 teaspoon monosodium glutamate
1 teaspoon salt
1 teaspoon paprika
⅛ teaspoon pepper
1 broiler-fryer chicken, cut in serving pieces

Combine flour and seasonings; roll chicken pieces in seasoned flour. Heat shortening or salad oil ½-inch deep in skillet. Place chicken, skin side down, in skillet. Put in larger meatier pieces first. Cook, uncovered, 15 to 25 minutes on each side, turning only once. Drain well on absorbent paper.

# Broiled Chicken

1 tender young broiler, drawn and split or quartered
3 tablespoons melted butter, margarine or fat
½ teaspoon salt
⅛ teaspoon pepper
½ teaspoon Accent (optional but flavor-wise)

A. Select chickens weighing 2½ pounds or less, allowing ½ bird for each serving; completely defrost frozen birds. Rinse under cold running water and dry. Preheat broiler oven. Place chicken on broiler pan, skin side down. (For added piquancy rub with cut clove garlic.) Brush with melted butter or fat. Season with a mixture of salt, pepper and Accent. Place in broiler 3 to 5 inches from source of heat. Leave oven door ajar.

B. Broil at low temperature for 15 minutes.

C. Turn. Brush again with butter and season second side. Continue to broil for about 15 minutes turning once again and brushing with butter. Remove to a warm serving dish and garnish with parsley.

D. Cold broiled chicken is just as good as cold fried chicken for lunch box purposes and for a child it is more easily digested. For people of all ages it is easy to manage finger-food.

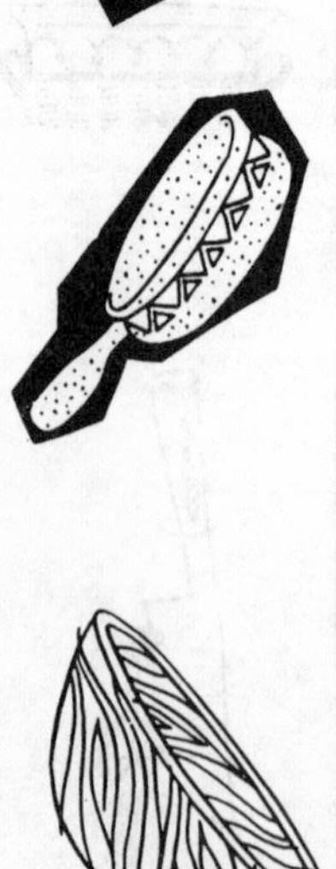

Poultry & Egg National Board

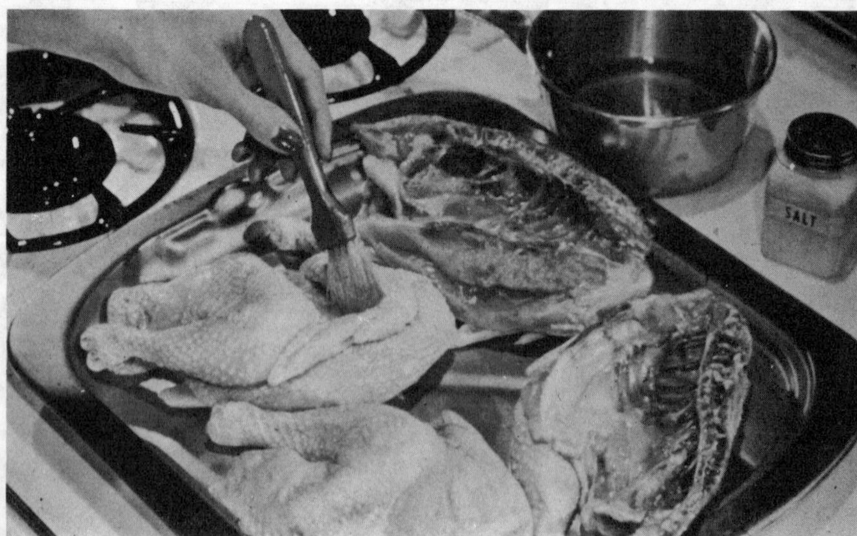


Preheat oven. Place chicken on broiler pan, skin sides down. Brush with butter or fat and season.

Let cook for 15 minutes with oven door ajar. Turn and brush all skin sides again with butter or fat.

# Bird of Paradise

½ cup melted butter
½ cup honey
¼ teaspoon ginger
2 garlic cloves, minced
¼ cup lemon juice
2 broiler-fryer chickens, halved
2 teaspoons monosodium glutamate
Salt
Pepper
2 pineapple slices, quartered
8 kumquats
8 maraschino cherries

Combine melted butter, honey, ginger, garlic and lemon juice. Sprinkle chicken with monosodium glutamate, salt and pepper. Turn oven temperature control to moderate (350°F) and broil 3 to 4 inches from heat; or set control to "broil" and place broiler pan about 7 to 8 inches from the heat. Place chicken skin side down on broiler pan. Brush with sauce. Broil 30 minutes, brushing occasionally. Turn and brush again. Broil 15 to 30 minutes longer, brushing occasionally. Reserve remaining sauce. Thread a pineapple piece, kumquat, and cherry on each skewer. Thread a chicken half lengthwise on each skewer; repeat with remaining fruit. Place under broiler heat 2 minutes, turning once. Serve with Polynesian Sauce and rice. Makes 4 servings.

## Polynesian Sauce

Reserved basting sauce
½ cup kumquat syrup
⅓ cup lightly toasted chopped nuts
½ cup pineapple juice

Combine all ingredients in saucepan. Heat to serving temperature.

# Twin Roast Chickens

2 2½ to 3 pound broiler-fryer chickens
1 package (8-ounces) prepared stuffing mix
2 tablespoons melted butter
8 canned peach halves
Pickle relish

Prepare chickens for roasting. Prepare stuffing according to package directions. Stuff and truss chickens. Place chickens on rack in shallow open roasting pan; brush with melted butter. Roast in a moderate oven (375°F) 30 minutes per pound. Last 20 minutes of roasting, place drained peaches, cut side down around chicken. Place chickens on a heated serving platter; garnish with peach halves. Fill centers with pickle relish. Makes 8 servings.

National Broiler Council

# Golden-Crisped Chicken

**2½ cups packaged corn flake crumbs**
**1 tablespoon salt**
**½ teaspoon pepper**
**Aluminum foil**
**3 broiler-fryer chickens, cut in serving pieces**
**1 cup evaporated milk**

Combine corn flake crumbs with salt and pepper in pie plate or shallow baking dish. Line 2 shallow baking pans with aluminum foil. Dip chicken pieces in evaporated milk then roll immediately in seasoned corn flake crumbs. Place chicken pieces, skin side up, in foil-lined pan; do not crowd. Bake in a moderate oven (350°F) 1½ hours, or until tender. At the end of one hour, exchange place of pans on shelves; continue to bake. No need to cover or turn chicken while cooking. Makes 12 servings.

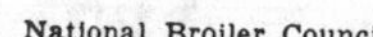
National Broiler Council

# Oven Fried Chicken

**¼ cup butter or margarine**
**⅓ cup flour**
**⅓ cup yellow corn meal**
**½ teaspoon salt**
**1 broiler-fryer chicken, cut in serving pieces**
**⅓ cup evaporated milk**

Melt butter in 7 x 11 x 2-inch baking pan in moderate oven (375°F.). Combine flour, corn meal and salt in shallow dish. Dip chicken pieces in evaporated milk, then roll immediately in flour mixture. Place chicken, skin side down, in butter. Bake 30 minutes. Turn skin side up; bake 30 minutes longer, or until tender. Makes 4 servings.

National Broiler Council

# Spiced Cranberry Chicken

**½ cup flour**
**1 teaspoon salt**
**⅛ teaspoon pepper**
**6 fryer legs and thighs**
**¼ inch salad oil in large fry pan**
**Cranberry Spice Sauce**

In paper bag mix together flour, salt and pepper. Shake chicken pieces in seasoned flour mixture to coat. Brown chicken on all sides in hot oil. Cover tightly. Reduce heat and cook gently 20-30 minutes, turning occasionally, until tender. Drain on paper towels. Serve chicken topped with Cranberry Spice Sauce.

## Cranberry Spice Sauce

**2 tablespoons brown sugar**
**1 tablespoon cornstarch**
**¾ cup cranberry juice cocktail**
**1 lb. can whole cranberry sauce**
**1 teaspoon ground nutmeg**
**1 teaspoon ground marjoram**
**1 tablespoon minced onion**

Mix together brown sugar and cornstarch in saucepan. Slowly stir in cranberry juice cocktail until smooth. Add whole cranberry sauce, spices and minced onion. Cook over medium heat, stirring, until mixture comes to a boil. Spoon over top of fried chicken.

Ocean Spray Cranberries, Inc.

Ocean Spray Cranberries, Inc.

# Rosa's Easy Chicken Cacciatore

2½-pound ready-to-cook chicken, cut in pieces
¼ cup flour
1 teaspoon salt
¼ teaspoon pepper
¼ cup olive or salad oil
No. 1 can small white onions
1 medium-size green pepper, cut in strips
4-oz. can drained mushrooms
1 small clove garlic, minced
10½-oz. can condensed tomato soup
½ cup water
2 tablespoons vinegar or lemon juice
1 tablespoon Worcestershire sauce
½ teaspoon oregano

Rinse chicken pieces and pat dry. Roll in flour seasoned with salt and pepper. Brown chicken in olive oil in a large skillet; remove chicken. Sauté onions, green pepper, mushrooms and garlic in same skillet; blend in remaining ingredients. Add chicken; cover and simmer about 30 minutes or until chicken is done. Stir occasionally. Serve over cooked spaghetti. Serves 4.

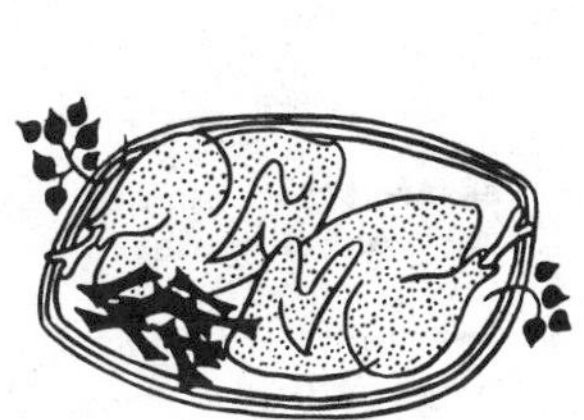

# Patio Chicken

2 pounds chicken breasts and legs
¼ cup melted butter
1 cup bread crumbs
1 teaspoon onion salt
¼ teaspoon garlic salt
½ teaspoon pepper
½ teaspoon monosodium glutamate
1 tablespoon chopped parsley
½ teaspoon curry powder
1 cup mayonnaise

Brush chicken with melted butter. Roll in a mixture of bread crumbs, onion salt, garlic salt, pepper, monosodium glutamate, parsley and curry powder. Arrange crumb coated chicken on foil-lined cookie sheet, skin side up and not overlapping. Place in hot oven (400°F) for 15 minutes to set crumbs. Remove from oven. Brush generously with mayonnaise. Reduce heat to 300°F and bake for 1 hour or until chicken is tender.

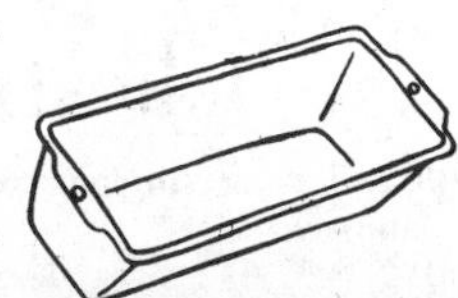

# Skillet Herb-Fried Chicken

⅔ cup evaporated milk
1¼ cups all-purpose flour
1½ teaspoons salt
½ teaspoon paprika
⅛ teaspoon pepper
¼ teaspoon rosemary
¼ teaspoon thyme
2 broiler-fryer chickens, cut in serving pieces
Corn oil for frying

Pour evaporated milk into bowl. Combine flour, salt, paprika, pepper and herbs in shallow dish. Dip chicken pieces in evaporated milk, then roll in flour mixture. Pour corn oil in skillet to a depth of ½ inch; heat. Place chicken, skin side down, in skillet and brown. When chicken is brown on one side, turn and brown second side. For crisp fried chicken, cook uncovered 15 to 25 minutes on each side, turning once. Makes 6 to 8 servings.

National Broiler Council

# Fruit and Nut Stuffed Chicken Breasts

¾ cup butter (1½-sticks) divided
1 cup diced apple
½ cup coarsely chopped nuts
½ cup golden raisins
1 can (1 pound, 4-ounces) crushed pineapple
1 cup soft bread crumbs, toasted
1 teaspoon salt, divided
1 teaspoon cinnamon
½ teaspoon nutmeg
¼ teaspoon ginger
¼ teaspoon ground cloves
6 whole chicken breasts, boned

Melt ½ cup (1 stick) butter in skillet; sauté diced apple and chopped nuts 10 minutes. Remove from heat. Add raisins, ½ cup drained crushed pineapple (reserve remaining pineapple), toasted bread crumbs, ½ teaspoon salt, cinnamon, nutmeg, ginger and cloves. Sprinkle inside of chicken breasts with ½ teaspoon salt. Place 1/3 cup stuffing on inside of each breast; fold the sides over, and fasten with skewers or string. Place remaining ¼ cup butter in 9 x 13 inch baking pan lined with foil; place in moderate oven (375°F) until melted, about 5 minutes. Place breasts top-side down in melted butter; return pan to oven and bake chicken 25 minutes. Turn chicken over and bake 20 minutes more. Serve with Fruit Sauce. Makes 6 servings.

### Fruit Sauce

1 tablespoon sugar
1 tablespoon cornstarch
⅛ teaspoon salt
½ teaspoon cinnamon
¼ teaspoon nutmeg
⅛ teaspoon ginger
1 cup orange juice
Pineapple and syrup reserved from stuffing
¼ cup golden raisins
1 tablespoon butter
Sections and slivered peel from 1 orange

Combine sugar, cornstarch, salt, cinnamon, nutmeg, and ginger. Stir in orange juice; add pineapple and pineapple syrup, raisins, butter, and slivered peel. Cook, stirring constantly, over medium heat until mixture comes to a boil and thickens. Add orange sections and heat.

National Broiler Council

# Creamed Chicken and Eggs on Waffles

¼ cup chopped green pepper
3 tablespoons butter or margarine
3 tablespoons flour
1½ cups milk
1 teaspoon salt or seasoned salt
¼ teaspoon pepper
1 cup diced cooked or canned chicken
4 hard-cooked eggs, quartered
2 cups waffle mix
2 cups milk
⅓ cup melted butter or margarine
2 eggs, slightly beaten
Parsley

Sauté green pepper in butter for 5 minutes and remove from pan. Blend flour into butter remaining in the pan. Gradually add milk; cook, stirring constantly until thickened and smooth. Season with salt and pepper; add green pepper, chicken and hard-cooked eggs (reserve 5 quarters for garnish). Heat through. Meanwhile, combine waffle mix, milk, butter and slightly-beaten eggs. Beat with a rotary beater until fairly smooth. Bake on a hot waffle iron until steaming stops. Keep warm on a heated platter. Pour creamed mixture into a heated serving dish; center remaining egg quarters flower-fashion around a tuft of parsley. Spoon over crisp hot waffles. Serves 6.

# Chicken Fried with Bacon Bits

1-pound package frozen chicken
¼ cup flour
1 teaspoon onion salt
½ teaspoon paprika
⅛ teaspoon pepper
¼ pound bacon, finely chopped

Thaw chicken according to carton directions. Combine flour, onion salt, paprika and pepper in a paper bag. Shake three pieces of chicken at a time until well coated. Spread bacon bits over the bottom of 9-inch cold skillet. Arrange coated chicken on top. Do not cover. Cook very slowly 45 minutes or until tender, turning frequently. As chicken browns, bits of bacon should adhere to chicken. Spoon bacon in bottom of pan over chicken before serving. Serves 2.

# Roast Capon with Chestnut Dressing

6-pound ready-to-cook whole capon
Salt
6 cups Chestnut Dressing, page 92
3 slices of bacon
½ cup hot chicken broth
3 tablespoons butter

Rinse capon, pat dry and rub inside and out with salt. Stuff with Chestnut Dressing (do not pack). Close opening with skewers and truss. Place in baking pan breast up. Lay bacon over breast. Bake uncovered in moderate oven 375°F. for 30 minutes. Reduce heat to 325°F. and continue roasting for 1¾ hours or until the bird's second joints move easily. Baste often during roasting with hot broth mixed with butter. Transfer bird to a warm platter. Serves 6 to 8.

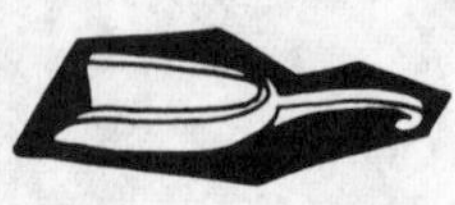

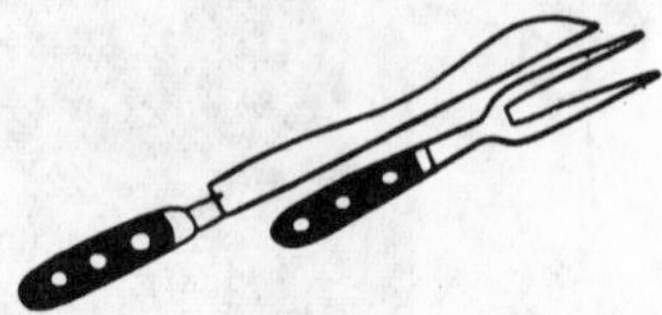

# Baltimore Dinner Belle

3-pound dressed frying chicken, cut in pieces
1 egg
⅓ cup milk
¾ cup fine cracker crumbs
¼ cup flour
1 tablespoon corn meal
½ teaspoon salt
½ teaspoon paprika
¼ cup butter or margarine
¼ cup olive or salad oil

Dip cleaned chicken pieces in egg and milk beaten together, then in a combination of cracker crumbs, flour, corn meal, salt and paprika. Heat butter and salad oil, and brown chicken thoroughly on all sides. Turn heat very low. Flick a little water over chicken with your fingers. Cover and cook until tender, about 30 minutes. Serves 4.

# Danish Chicken Fricassee

3 slices bacon, chopped
5-pound dressed-weight fowl, cut in pieces
1 large onion, chopped
¼ teaspoon powdered cloves
1 teaspoon Accent
¼ teaspoon pepper
1 teaspoon salt
4 cups cooked rice
1 cup heavy cream
1 tablespoon cornstarch
2 egg yolks
2 teaspoons lemon juice

Fry bacon in a large sauce pan or Dutch oven until nearly crisp. Remove and reserve bits. Brown chicken in bacon fat. Add onion during last 5 minutes of browning. Sprinkle with seasonings, bacon bits and ½ cup water. Cover and steam over low heat for 2 hours. Transfer chicken to a warm platter. Surround with fluffy hot rice. Beat cream, cornstarch, egg yolks and lemon juice over low heat until very smooth. Pour over chicken. Serves 6.

# Squab-Chickens Baked in Sherry

6 whole squab-chickens (tiny broilers 1 to 1½ pounds each), cleaned and drawn
½ lemon
Salt
6 green onions
3 bay leaves
6 cloves
¼ cup chopped celery leaves
1 tablespoon chopped parsley
6 thin slices larding pork
4 peppercorns
1 medium onion, chopped
12 medium mushrooms
1 cup sherry or Marsala
1 cup chicken bouillon
2 teaspoons flour (optional)
¼ cup currant jelly

Rub birds inside and out with lemon and salt. Place in each cavity 1 green onion, ½ bay leaf, 1 clove and equal divisions of celery leaves and parsley. Sew or skewer cavities. Cover breasts with larding pork. Arrange birds in an adequate casserole or roasting pan. Add peppercorns, chopped onion, mushrooms, sherry and bouillon. Cover tightly and bake in a preheated moderate oven 350°F. for about 1 hour or until fork-tender. Transfer birds and mushrooms to a warm platter. Remove peppercorns from drippings and, if thick sauce is desired, blend in flour mixed to a paste with a little water; stir in jelly; heat through and serve sauce separately. Serves 6.

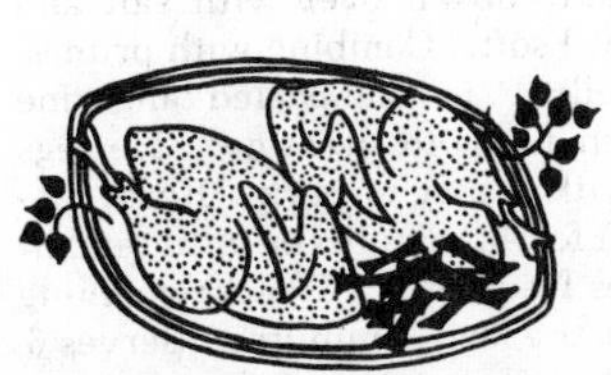

# Jig-Time Chicken Supper

3½-pound dressed frying chicken, cut in serving pieces
⅓ cup corn meal
⅓ cup flour
2 teaspoons salt
½ teaspoon celery salt
¼ teaspoon pepper
3 tablespoons shortening
4 medium-sized sweet potatoes, pared
4 slices pineapple
⅛ teaspoon powdered allspice
½ teaspoon cinnamon
¼ cup brown sugar
2 tablespoons melted butter or margarine
1 tablespoon lemon juice
Parsley

Shake chicken pieces in a paper bag containing a combination of corn meal, flour, 1 teaspoon salt, celery salt and pepper. Heat shortening in pressure cooker over medium heat and fry chicken to an even golden brown. Place sweet potatoes on an 18" square of aluminum foil. Arrange pineapple slices over them. Sprinkle with spices, sugar, remaining teaspoon salt and drizzle with melted butter. Pull edges of aluminum foil up and twist together making a tightly sealed package. Slip rack under chicken, sprinkle with lemon juice and add ½ cup water and foil package. Cover and cook at 15 pounds pressure for 15 minutes. Let pressure reduce gradually. Serves 4.

# Baked-Fried Savory Chicken

3½-pound dressed fryer, cut in pieces
1 teaspoon Accent
½ teaspoon thyme
½ teaspoon marjoram
1 egg, slightly beaten
2 tablespoons milk
¼ cup flour
½ cup fine cracker crumbs
1 teaspoon salt
¼ teaspoon pepper
¼ cup wine vinegar
¼ cup melted butter or margarine

Sprinkle cleaned chicken pieces with Accent, thyme and marjoram and let stand for 1 hour. Dip in egg beaten with milk and then in flour combined with cracker crumbs, salt and pepper. Place in greased baking pan. Do not crowd. Bake uncovered in a moderate oven 350°F. for 1½ hours or until chicken is tender. Turn occasionally; sprinkle twice with wine vinegar and once with melted butter. Serves 4.

# Crusty Baked Delmarva Chicken

2 eggs
2 teaspoons Worcestershire sauce
1 teaspoon onion juice
2 3-pound ready-to-cook broiler-fryers, cut in pieces
2 cups fine bread crumbs
1 teaspoon sage
½ teaspoon paprika
Dash garlic salt
½ teaspoon salt
⅛ teaspoon pepper
¼ cup vegetable oil
4 slices bacon
⅓ cup milk

Beat eggs, Worcestershire sauce and onion juice until thoroughly mixed. Dip chicken pieces in this mixture, then roll in a combination of bread crumbs and seasonings. Pour oil in a flat baking dish. Arrange chicken in dish with bacon slices spread over it. Bake in moderate oven 350°F. for 1 hour. Add milk. Cover with a lid or foil and continue to bake for 15 to 20 minutes. Serves 6.

# Chicken Dillicassee

**4½-pound ready-to-cook stewing fowl, cut in pieces**
**6 cups boiling water**
**2 teaspoons Accent**
**1 onion, quartered**
**2 celery tops**
**3 peppercorns**
**5 tablespoons flour**
**Salt**
**Dash cayenne**
**2 tablespoons minced fresh dill**
**1 egg yolk**
**⅓ cup light cream**
**Baking powder biscuits**

Cover fowl with boiling water; add Accent, onion, celery tops and peppercorns. Cover and simmer for 2½ hours or until fowl is tender; remove to a warm platter. Strain broth and measure 2½ cups; thicken with flour mixed smooth with ⅓ cup water. Season to taste with salt, cayenne and dill. Beat egg yolk with cream and stir in. Pour over chicken pieces; surround with split baking powder biscuits. Serves 6 to 8.

# Chicken Barbecued in a Skillet

**3-pound ready-to-cook chicken, cut for frying**
**¼ cup shortening**
**⅓ cup thinly-sliced onion**
**⅓ cup chopped green pepper**
**1 small clove garlic, minced**
**10½-oz. can condensed tomato soup**
**2 tablespoons brown sugar**
**2 tablespoons Worcestershire sauce**
**2 tablespoons lemon juice or vinegar**
**2 teaspoons prepared mustard**
**Dash Tabasco sauce**

Brown chicken on all sides in hot shortening in a heavy skillet; remove chicken and sauté onion, green pepper and garlic for 5 minutes. Mix in remaining ingredients and simmer until thoroughly blended. Return chicken to the skillet and spoon sauce over. Cover and simmer about 30 minutes or until chicken is done, turning occasionally. Serves 4.

# Creamed Chicken with Pancake-Omelet

**¼ cup butter, margarine or chicken fat**
**¼ cup flour**
**1 cup rich chicken broth**
**1 cup heavy cream**
**½ teaspoon Accent**
**¼ teaspoon salt**
**Dash cayenne**
**2 cups diced cooked or canned chicken**
**2 tablespoons minced parsley**
**1 tablespoon sherry**
**4 egg yolks**
**¾ cup milk**
**3 tablespoons cream**
**1¼ cups pancake mix**
**4 egg whites, beaten stiff**
**1 tablespoon butter**

Heat butter and blend in flour. Stir in cool or lukewarm broth and cream. Cook, stirring constantly, until sauce is smooth and thick. Add Accent, salt to taste, and the cayenne, chicken, and parsley. Keep warm over lowest heat. Just before serving stir in sherry. Meanwhile prepare pancakes by combining egg yolks, milk and cream. Add the liquid mixture all at once to the pancake mix. Fold in egg whites. Heat butter in a 10-inch fry pan over moderate heat. Cook omelet for about 3 minutes or until golden brown on bottom. Place in preheated broiling unit about 3 inches from heat and continue cooking until top has browned lightly. Transfer to a warm serving dish. Crease through center. Fill with about half of the creamed chicken. Fold over and pour remaining creamed chicken over. Serves 6.

# Roast Squabs

**6 squabs, cleaned and trussed for roasting**
**¼ cup butter or margarine**
**1 teaspoon salt**
**¼ teaspoon pepper**
**½ teaspoon rosemary**
**Celery tops**
**½ cup chopped onion**
**½ cup chopped celery**
**1 small clove garlic, minced**
**½ cup sauterne**

Allow 1 squab for each person. Rub with softened butter; dust with a mixture of salt, pepper and rosemary. Stuff with celery tops. Arrange in a shallow baking dish on a bed of onion, celery and garlic. Pour sauterne over. Roast in hot oven 425°F. for 30 minutes or until tender and thoroughly done. Baste every 10 minutes with wine. Serves 6.

# Orange-Mushroom Sauce

**1 small onion, finely chopped**
**2 tablespoons butter or margarine**
**2 cups orange juice**
**1 tablespoon lemon juice**
**1 tablespoon grated orange rind**
**1 teaspoon grated lemon rind**
**1 3-oz. can sliced mushrooms**
**2 tablespoons cornstarch**
**½ teaspoon salt**
**½ teaspoon ginger**

Sauté onion in butter or pan drippings from roast fowl until soft. Combine with citrus juices and rind. Heat to boiling. Blend cornstarch to a paste with mushroom liquid, salt and ginger. Add to sauce; cook and stir until smooth and thickened. Add mushrooms. Makes about 2½ cups. Serve with duck, goose or chicken.

# Duckling with Applekraut

**4-pound ready-to-cook duckling, quartered**
**2 tablespoons rendered duck fat**
**½ cup chopped onion**
**1 pound sauerkraut**
**1 teaspoon caraway seeds**
**3 tart apples, diced**

Cook duck in fat in a heavy skillet over moderate heat until nicely browned on all sides, about 40 minutes. Remove pieces of duck; pour off excess fat leaving 3 or 4 tablespoons drippings. Add onion, cook until soft. Drain off most of liquid from sauerkraut; mix 'kraut with caraway seeds, apples and onions in skillet. Arrange duck, skin side down, on this savory bed. Cover and simmer for 30 minutes. Serve with fluffy mashed potatoes. Serves 4.

# Squabs Mercedes

**6 fat squabs**
**Salt**
**Pepper**
**1 small onion, chopped**
**3 tablespoons butter or margarine**
**½ cup chopped seeded prunes**
**½ cup minced apple**
**1 cup cooked rice**
**1 tablespoon minced parsley**
**1 tangerine**
**6 thin slices salt pork**
**½ cup sherry**

Clean birds inside and out and rub all over with salt and pepper. Sauté onion in butter until soft. Combine with prunes, apple, rice and parsley, mixing well. Place one peeled tangerine section in each squab cavity then fill with dressing. Tie legs together and cover each breast with a slice of pork. Roast uncovered in a moderate oven 325°F. for 45 minutes or until tender, basting with sherry and pan juices frequently. Roast remaining tangerine sections beside birds for the last 15 minutes. Serves 6.

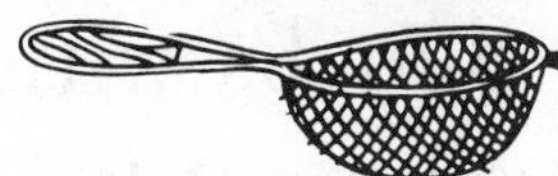

# Roast Goose with Sweet Potato and Apple Dressing

8-pound young goose, cleaned and drawn
Salt
1 cup finely chopped onions
3 cups finely chopped apples
2 tablespoons butter or margarine
2 cups mashed sweet potatoes
¼ teaspoon thyme
¼ teaspoon sage
1 teaspoon salt
½ teaspoon pepper
½ cup cider or orange juice

Rub goose inside and out with salt. Stuff with a dressing made as follows: Sauté onions and apples in butter for 5 minutes. Combine with sweet potatoes and seasoning; stuff into cavity. Close cavities with skewers; fasten neck skin to back with a skewer. Prick skin all over. Place breast down on a rack in a roasting pan. Roast in a slow oven 325°F. for 2 hours. Draw off excess fat; baste goose with cider. Continue to roast for 1½ hours or until tender, basting every 20 minutes. Transfer to a warm platter; garnish with orange slices and currant jelly. Serves 8.

# Rock Cornish Game Hen in Foil

1 Rock Cornish Game Hen (about one pound)
Wild Rice Stuffing
Melted butter
Salt

Clean, wash, dry cornish hen. Stuff hen with Wild Rice Stuffing (3 variations follow). Tie legs to tail. Brush with melted butter; sprinkle with salt. Place in center of a sheet of heavy duty aluminum foil; wrap tightly, using double folds over top and at each end. Place on rack in shallow pan. Roast in hot oven (425°F) 1 hour and 15 minutes; for last 15 minutes, open foil for browning. One cornish hen per serving.

# Wild Rice Stuffing #1

1 cup minced onion
½ cup minced celery
¼ cup butter or margarine
1 cup seedless grapes, cut in fourths
¼ cup Sherry
1 teaspoon salt
2 cups cooked wild rice

Sauté onion and celery in butter until tender (about five minutes). Add grapes, Sherry, salt, wild rice; blend well. Makes about 4 cups stuffing or enough to stuff 4 Rock Cornish Hens.

# Wild Rice Stuffing #2

½ cup minced onion
¼ pound sausage meat
1 tablespoon butter or margarine
1 teaspoon salt
½ teaspoon tarragon
2 cups cooked wild rice

Sauté onion and sausage in butter about 10 minutes. Add salt, tarragon, wild rice; blend well. Makes about 2¾ cups stuffing or enough to stuff 3 Rock Cornish Hens.

# Wild Rice Stuffing #3

¾ cup minced onion
¾ cup minced green pepper
½ cup minced celery
2 tablespoons butter or margarine
1 teaspoon salt
1 teaspoon sweet basil
1 egg, slightly beaten
¼ cup red wine
2 cups cooked wild rice

Sauté onion, green pepper and celery in butter until tender (about five minutes). Add salt, basil, egg, wine, wild rice; blend well. Makes about three cups stuffing or enough to stuff three Rock Cornish Hens.

***To Cook Wild Rice:***

1 cup water
1 teaspoon salt
½ cup wild rice, raw

Bring water to boil; add salt, wild rice; cover. Cook 40-45 minutes over low heat. Makes two cups wild rice.

Alcoa Wrap

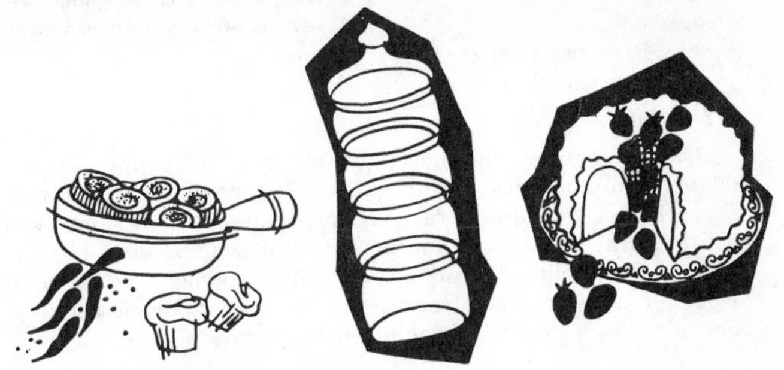

# Roast Guinea Hen Aux Garni

**2 2-pound ready-to-cook guinea hens**
**Salt**
**½ lemon (optional)**
**4 small onions**
**¼ pound salt pork cut in thin strips**
**2 cups Garlic Croutons,**
**12 large mushroom caps, sautéed in butter**
**1 cup cooked peas**
**½ pimiento**

Clean, rinse and dry the hens. Rub inside and out with salt and cut lemon if desired. Insert 2 onions in each hen. Place breast down on rack in uncovered roaster. Place pork strips over back. Roast in moderate oven 325°F. for 1¼ hours or until tender. Halfway through roasting turn bird; re-arrange pork strips over breast. Place birds on a hot platter, garnish around with Garlic Croutons, mushroom caps filled with peas and slivers of pimiento. Serves 4 to 6.

# Suprêmes of Guinea Hen au vin Blanc

**2-pound ready-to-cook guinea hen**
**½ small onion, sliced**
**2 celery tops**
**½ small carrot, sliced**
**3 tablespoons flour**
**½ teaspoon salt**
**¼ teaspoon white pepper**
**2 tablespoons butter or margarine**
**1 cup heavy cream**
**¼ cup white wine**
**4 mushroom caps, sautéed**

Disjoint guinea hen taking care to keep breasts intact. For this dish we use only the breasts which are considered very choice. Reserve legs for future use. Place neck, back and giblets in water, cover with onion, celery tops, and carrot and simmer for 1 hour. Dredge breasts with flour seasoned with salt and pepper. Sauté in butter until golden brown. Add ½ cup rich strained broth. Cover and cook over low heat for 15 minutes. Combine cream and wine. Heat through but do not boil. Pour over breasts; garnish with mushroom caps. Serves 2.

# Roast Ducklings à la Orange

**2 4½-pound ready-to-cook ducklings**
**Salt**
**Pepper**
**8 cups Rice and Orange or Bread and Butter Dressing**
**¼ cup honey**
**1 teaspoon ginger**
**2 teaspoons Kitchen Bouquet**
**2½ cups Orange-Mushroom Sauce**

Clean ducklings; rub thoroughly with salt and pepper. Spoon dressing into cavities; do not pack. Sew or skewer openings. Place breast side up on rack in open pan; roast in slow oven 325°F. for about 1½ to 2 hours or until brown and done to your liking. Baste with a combination of honey, ginger and Kitchen Bouquet several times during the last half hour of cooking. Serve with Orange-Mushroom Sauce. Serves 8.

# Squabs with White Grapes

**4 squabs, cleaned and trussed**
**¼ cup softened butter**
**1 teaspoon salt**
**⅓ cup chicken consommé**
**⅓ cup white wine**
**1½ cups seedless white grapes**

Preheat oven to moderate 375°F. Rub squabs with butter. Sprinkle cavities with salt. Place in a buttered casserole; cover and bake for 10 minutes. Add consommé and wine. Cover again and continue to bake at 325°F. for 45 minutes or until tender. Five minutes before squabs are done add grapes. Serves 4.

# Sherry-Glazed Duckling

**4-pound ready-to-cook duckling**
**1 teaspoon salt**
**1 teaspoon celery salt**
**1 chopped green pepper**
**2 chopped green onions**
**4 sprigs parsley**
**½ cup sherry**
**¼ cup honey**
**1 clove**
**Dash cayenne**
**1 teaspoon cornstarch**
**3-oz. can mushrooms**

Wash duckling and wipe dry. Rub with salt and sprinkle with celery salt inside and out. Insert green pepper, onions and parsley into cavity. Skewer neck skin to back; fold back wings. Place breast side up on a rack in an open roasting pan. Roast in a slow oven 325°F. for 1 hour. Meanwhile, combine sherry, honey, clove and cayenne. Bring to a boil; remove from heat. Siphon excess fat from roasting pan. Continue to roast duck for 45 minutes or until tender basting every 15 minutes with the wine sauce. Remove duck to a warm platter. Thicken sauce in pan with cornstarch. Mix in drained mushrooms; serve sauce in a separate bowl. Serves 4.

# Sweet and Pungent Duckling

**4-pound ready-to-cook duckling**
**2 tablespoons soy sauce**
**2 tablespoons honey**
**2 tablespoons sherry**
**1 clove garlic, minced**
**½ teaspoon ginger**
**2 tablespoons rendered duck fat**
**1 cup pineapple juice**
**1 large green pepper, diced**
**1 cup canned pineapple chunks**
**1 tablespoon lemon juice**
**2 tablespoons cornstarch**

Score duck skin from neck to vent; remove skin with a sharp pointed knife leaving flesh intact. Cut in serving-size pieces. Combine soy sauce, honey, sherry, garlic and ginger; pour over bird. Set aside for 1 hour, turning pieces occasionally. Brown duck on all sides in hot fat in a heavy skillet. Drain off excess fat. Combine pineapple juice with marinade; pour over duck. Cover and simmer for 50 minutes. Add green pepper, pineapple chunks, lemon juice and cornstarch mixed to a paste with ¼ cup cold water. Simmer for 10 minutes. Serve with rice. Serves 4.

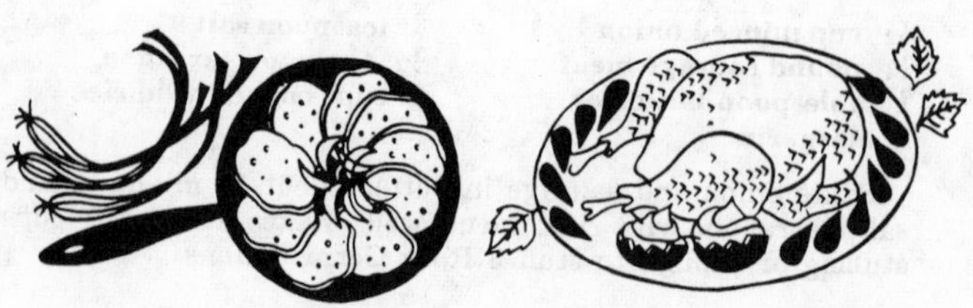

# PIE

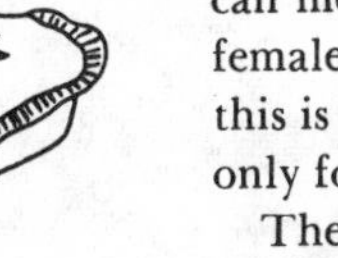

By and large, the favorite dessert of the majority of American men is Apple Pie. Therefore it behooves every American female to know how to bake an apple pie to perfection—and this is the book to show her how. It will unlock the secret, not only for a good apple pie, but many, many other kinds of pie.

The secret of success for any pie is the crust. Step-by-step pictures show how to make a basic flaky pie crust, using shortening. It shows how to make a pie shell, how to make a double crust pie and how to seal and flute the edges. We also have step-by-step photos on an oil pastry, that is as simple as 1-2-3. And of course we have included graham cracker crusts, cookie crusts and how to make a meringue shell.

As for the fillings, they come in all the fruit flavors, either plain or with cream or chiffon base. Try mixing fruits in a pie, or try something new, such as a pear pie. Chiffon pies, that come in all the colors of the rainbow, are usually a favorite with the ladies.

**Pastry should be flaky, tender and delicate; it should not crumble when broken but shatter in layers. Use light touch in mixing and rolling.**

## TENDER PASTRY

**This complete how-to recipe makes one two-crust nine-inch pie or two nine-inch pie shells. To start with, sift 2 cups of flour and 1¼ teaspoons of salt into a bowl. Measure out ⅔ cup of shortening.**

**With a pastry blender, cut in ⅓ cup of the shortening until mixture is consistency of cornmeal. Cut in second ⅓ cup until mixture is size of small peas.**

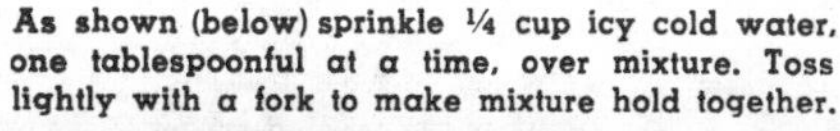

**As shown (below) sprinkle ¼ cup icy cold water, one tablespoonful at a time, over mixture. Toss lightly with a fork to make mixture hold together.**

**Turn mixture out onto a piece of waxed paper, press gently with hands into ball shape, chill for a while.**

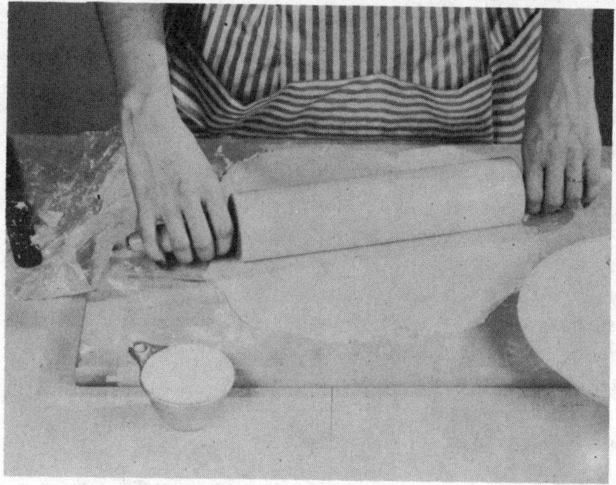

Divide ball of dough in half. On a lightly-floured board, roll dough into a circle about ⅛ inch thick. Roll lightly from center, lift near edges.

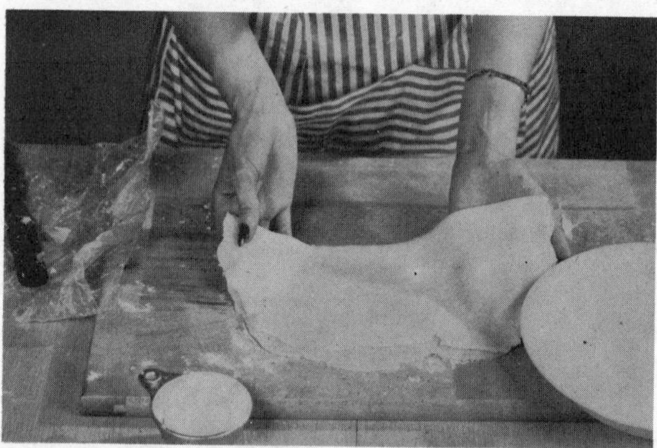

Now fold dough in half (see above), then lift gently and lay fold line across center of pan. Carefully, now, unfold the dough in pan to original circle.

Fit pastry into pan by lifting and patting gently. The thing to remember here is: do not stretch it to make it fit. If you do it will shrink when baked.

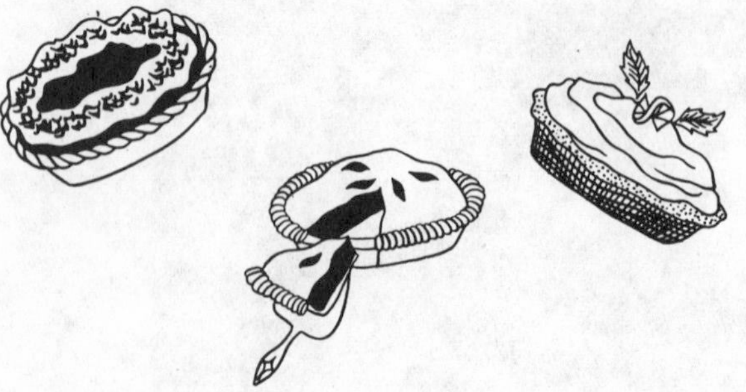

In order to have enough pastry dough to work with when fluting the edges (see next photo) trim edges (above) leaving ½ inch beyond plate.

Fold edges of crust under so that it stands up. Flute edges by pressing index finger of one hand between thumb and index finger of other hand.

Prick pastry all over with a fork to allow steam to escape and bake in a very hot oven (450°) 12 to 15 minutes, or until crust is lightly browned.

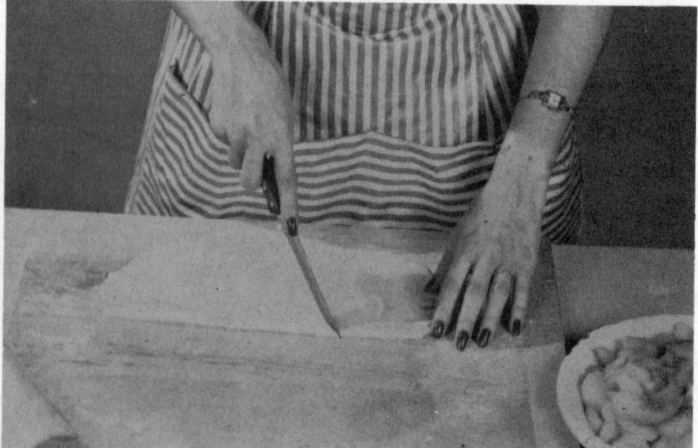

For a two-crust pie, roll half of pastry and fit into pan for a single crust. Fill. Trim even with plate. Remaining half is slashed with pattern.

After cutting slits, moisten lower edges of top pastry with water, place on filling and unfold. Pat edges together, trim ½ inch over, tuck under.

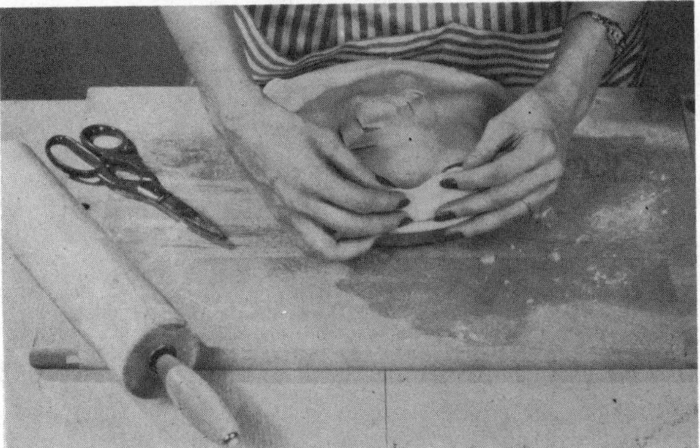

Seal crust (below) by pressing at an angle with thumb and bent index finger. Or, use any other kind of edge desired. Bake according to recipe.

# Flaky Pastry

**2 cups sifted flour**
**1 teaspoon salt**
**⅔ cup shortening**
**⅓ cup milk**

Mix together flour and salt. Cut in shortening with a pastry blender or 2 knives until mixture looks like coarse cornmeal. Remove ¼ cup of this mixture. Mix well with the milk and stir into the flour shortening mixture until a dough is formed. Press into a ball and flatten slightly. Roll half the dough between 2 pieces of waxed paper as shown for Salad Oil Pastry. Proceed according to directions for either pie shells or a double crust pie. Makes two 8 or 9-inch shells or one double crust pie.

## GRAHAM CRACKER PIE CRUST

To make the graham cracker pie crust shown, place twenty graham crackers in a plastic or cellophane bag, roll into fine crumbs. Pour crumbs into a bowl, add one-quarter cup of sugar and one-quarter cup of softened butter. Mix ingredients with blender. Pour crumb mixture into a nine-inch pie plate. Set an eight-inch pie plate on top of crumbs and press them firmly into an even layer against bottom and sides of pan. Bake in moderately hot oven (375°F) for eight minutes. Take out and cool before filling.

# Chocolate Coconut Pie Crust

**2 squares unsweetened chocolate**
**2 tablespoons butter**
**2 tablespoons hot milk or water**
**⅔ cup sifted confectioners' sugar**
**1½ cups shredded coconut**

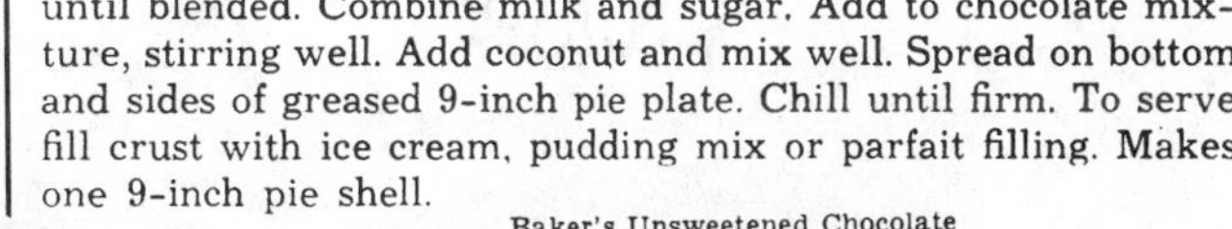

Melt chocolate and butter in top of a double boiler, stirring until blended. Combine milk and sugar. Add to chocolate mixture, stirring well. Add coconut and mix well. Spread on bottom and sides of greased 9-inch pie plate. Chill until firm. To serve fill crust with ice cream, pudding mix or parfait filling. Makes one 9-inch pie shell.

Baker's Unsweetened Chocolate

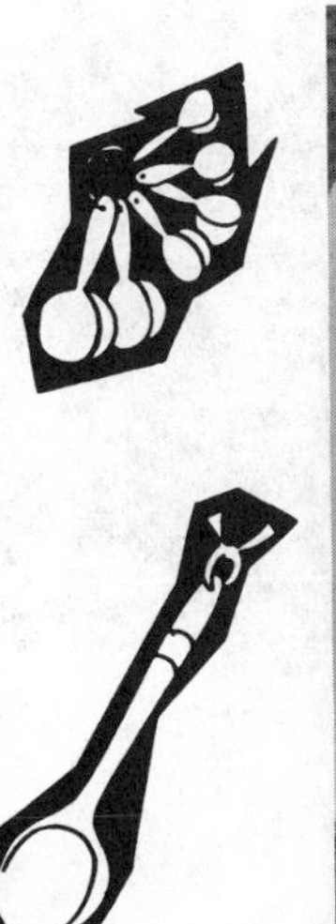

LATTICE-TOP

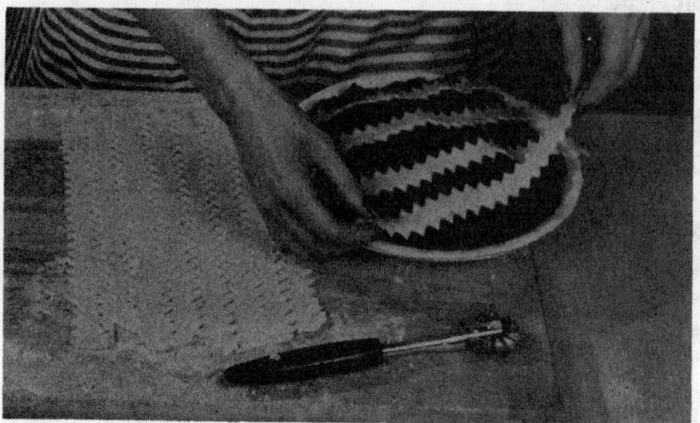

**To make a lattice-top pie crust, use half of the pastry for bottom shell, roll second half into twelve-inch circle, cut into one-half inch strips with a pastry wheel or sharp knife. Lay four or five strips loosely across top of filling as shown in above photograph.**

**Take remaining strips and, in basket-weave fashion, complete lattice-top design. Trim even with plate edge, moisten with water, press down.**

# Quick Oatmeal Pie Crust

**2 cups quick oats**
**⅓ cup melted butter or margarine**
**¼ teaspoon salt**
**2 teaspoons grated lemon rind**
**3 tablespoons light corn syrup**

Combine quick oats and melted butter and stir well. Add salt, lemon rind and corn syrup. With the back of a spoon press mixture lightly into a pie plate. Bake in a moderately hot oven (375° F) 15 to 20 minutes or until lightly browned. Cool before filling. Makes one 8 or 9-inch pie crust.

# Quick Coconut Crust

**2 tablespoons soft butter**
**1 package (1½ cups) shredded coconut**

Spread butter evenly in an 8 or 9-inch pie plate. Sprinkle coconut in pan, pressing gently into butter on bottom and sides. Bake in a slow oven (300° F) 15 to 20 minutes. Cool crust before filling. Makes one 8 or 9-inch shell.

SALAD OIL PASTRY

Sift together into a bowl two cups of flour and one teaspoon of salt, combine one-half cup salad oil and one-quarter cup milk in a measuring cup.

Pour salad oil and milk mixture (all at once) over flour. These and the next five photos comprise Salad Oil how-to picture-recipe set.

Stir and mix lightly with a fork until flour is entirely moistened.

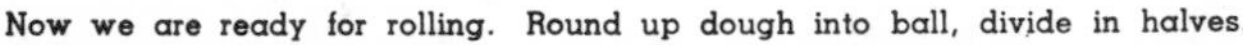

Now we are ready for rolling. Round up dough into ball, divide in halves.

Place half of dough between two squares of waxed paper. Wipe table with a damp cloth to keep paper from slipping while rolling. Roll dough lightly from center until circle reaches edges of waxed paper.

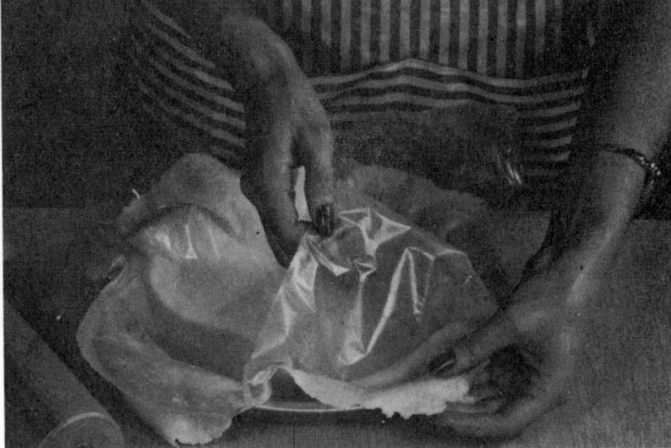

Remove top sheet of waxed paper. Lift paper and pastry by top corners and place paper-side up over pie pan. Peel off paper, ease into pan.

Trim bottom crust even with sides of pan. Fill. Roll out remaining dough and repeat process. Invert over filling and peel off paper.

# Spicy Pastry

**2 cup sifted flour**
**¼ teaspoon baking soda**
**¼ cup sugar**
**1 teaspoon salt**
**½ teaspoon cinnamon**
**¼ teaspoon ginger**
**¼ teaspoon cloves**
**⅔ cup shortening**
**1 tablespoon vinegar**
**3 tablespoons orange juice**

Sift together dry ingredients. Cut in ⅓ cup of the shortening to the consistency of cornmeal. Cut in remaining ⅓ cup of the shortening to the consistency of peas. Mix together vinegar and orange juice. Add slowly to dry ingredients, mixing lightly with a fork. Turn onto a piece of waxed paper and shape into a ball. Chill. Roll out dough on a lightly floured board according to picture directions. Makes one 9-inch 2 crust pie or two 9-inch pie shells.

# Margarine Pie Crust

½ cup margarine
¼ cup boiling water
1½ cups sifted flour
¼ teaspoon salt

Cream margarine until soft and light. Add boiling water and mix thoroughly. Cool. Combine flour and salt and add to margarine mixture, stirring lightly with a fork. Wrap dough in waxed paper and chill. Roll out on a lightly floured board. Fit according to directions . For a baked shell follow directions for baking. Otherwise fill and bake according to directions in recipe. Makes one 9-inch shell.

# Chocolate Cookie Crumb Crust

1¼ cups finely crushed chocolate cookies
½ cup sugar
¼ cup softened butter or margarine

Combine all ingredients and mix thoroughly. Press evenly around bottom and sides of pie plate. Fill with desired filling and chill well before serving. Makes one 9-inch pie crust.

# Bran Pie-Crust Shells

⅓ cup bran
2 cups sifted flour
½ teaspoon salt
⅔ cup shortening
6 tablespoons cold water, about

Crush bran into fine crumbs; mix with flour and salt. Cut in ⅓ cup of the shortening to the consistency of cornmeal. Cut in remaining shortening to the consistency of peas. Sprinkle cold water over top a little at a time, mixing with a fork until dough is just moist enough to hold together. Turn onto a piece of waxed paper and shape into a ball. Roll out according to directions . Makes two 8 or 9-inch pie shells or four 4-inch tart shells.

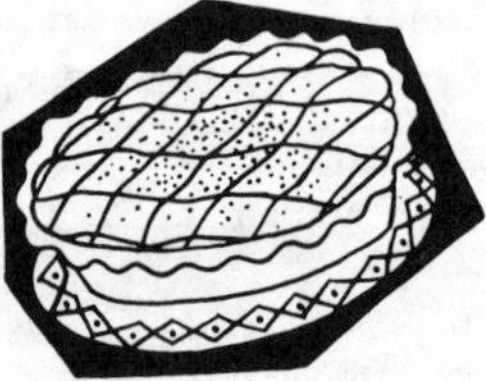

# Brazil Nut Pie Crust

1½ cups ground Brazil nuts (¾ pound unshelled nuts)
3 tablespoons sugar

Mix nuts and sugar in a 10-inch pie plate. Press mixture with the back of a tablespoon against the bottom and sides of pie plate. Crust is ready for filling now or it can be baked before filling. If a toasted flavor is desired, bake in a hot oven (400° F) 8 minutes or until lightly browned. Chill before filling. Makes one 10-inch shell.

# Macaroon Pie Crust

1 egg white
2 tablespoons sugar
1 tablespoon light corn syrup
½ teaspoon vanilla
2 cups coconut, finely chopped

Beat egg whites until foamy. Add sugar and beat until mixture will stand in soft peaks. Add corn syrup and flavoring. Fold in coconut. Using the back of a spoon, press macaroon mixture firmly on bottom and sides of a well-buttered 9-inch pie plate. Bake in a moderate oven (350° F) 15 minutes, or until lightly browned. Cool before using. Makes one 9-inch shell.

# Gingersnap Pie Crust

20 gingersnaps
3 tablespoons sugar
½ teaspoon cinnamon
½ cup softened butter or margarine

Crush gingersnaps with a rolling pin; measure out 1¼ cups. Place in a bowl and add sugar and cinnamon. Blend in softened butter with a fork and mix well. Press crumb mixture with the back of a spoon into a 9-inch pie plate. Bake crust in a moderate oven (350° F) 10 minutes. Cool before filling. Good with pumpkin chiffon mixture. Makes one 9-inch pie shell.

### PASTRY VARIATIONS
### (for single crust pie)

*Lemon Pastry:* Follow recipe for 1-2-3 Pastry, stirring in ½ teaspoon grated lemon rind with flour and salt and substituting lemon juice for water.

*Cheddar Cheese Pastry:* Follow recipe for 1-2-3 Pastry, adding ½ cup finely shredded Cheddar cheese to flour and salt.

*Nut Pastry:* Follow recipe for 1-2-3 Pastry, adding ¼ cup finely chopped nuts to flour and salt.

*Cream Cheese Pastry:* Follow recipe for 1-2-3 Pastry, cutting 3 ounces cream cheese into flour and salt with pastry blender or 2 knives.

*Chocolate Pastry:* Follow recipe for 1-2-3 Pastry sifting ¼ cup cocoa and 1 tablespoon sugar with flour and salt.

# 1-2-3 Pastry

| *Single Crust Pie* | *Double Crust Pie* |
|---|---|
| **1⅓ cups sifted flour** | **2 cups sifted flour** |
| **½ teaspoon salt** | **1 teaspoon salt** |
| **⅓ cup corn oil** | **½ cup corn oil** |
| **2 tablespoons cold water** | **3 tablespoons cold water** |

Combine flour and salt in mixing bowl. Blend in corn oil, mixing thoroughly with fork. Sprinkle all water on top; mix well. Press firmly into ball with hands. (If slightly dry, mix in 1 to 2 tablespoons additional corn oil.)

*Single Crust:* Flatten dough slightly, and immediately roll out to 12 inch circle between 2 pieces of waxed paper. (Wipe table with damp cloth to keep paper from slipping.) Peel off top paper; place pastry circle in 9-inch pie pan, paper side up. Peel off paper; fit pastry loosely into pan. Trim pastry ½ inch beyond rim of pan, if necessary. Flute edge. If shell is to be baked before filling, prick thoroughly and bake in hot oven (450°F.) until golden brown, 12 to 15 minutes. If shell and filling are to be baked together, do not prick shell; bake pie according to filling used.

*Double Crust:* Divide dough almost in half. Flatten larger portion slightly; roll out and place in pie pan as directed above. Fill as desired. Trim pastry, if necessary. Roll out remaining pastry for top crust. Peel off paper, cut slits in pastry to permit steam to escape during baking, and place over filling. Trim ½ inch beyond rim of pan. Fold edges of both crusts under; seal and flute. Bake pie according to filling used.

**Note:** If unsifted flour is used, measure 1 cup plus 2 tablespoons flour for single crust, and 1¾ cups for double crust. To measure, dip dry nested measuring cups and measuring spoons (as needed) into flour; level off with straight edged spatula.

Mix together flour and salt. Pour in corn oil; blend with a fork.

Sprinkle all of water over mixture. Mix well. Press dough firmly into a ball with hands.

Roll dough out between 2 sheets of waxed paper. To keep paper from slipping, wipe table top with a damp cloth.

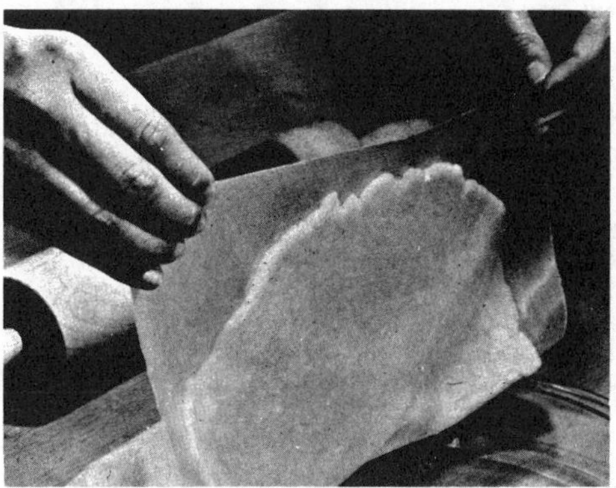

After removing top sheet of waxed paper, use bottom sheet of paper to lift crust, carefully placed rolled pie crust over pie pan.

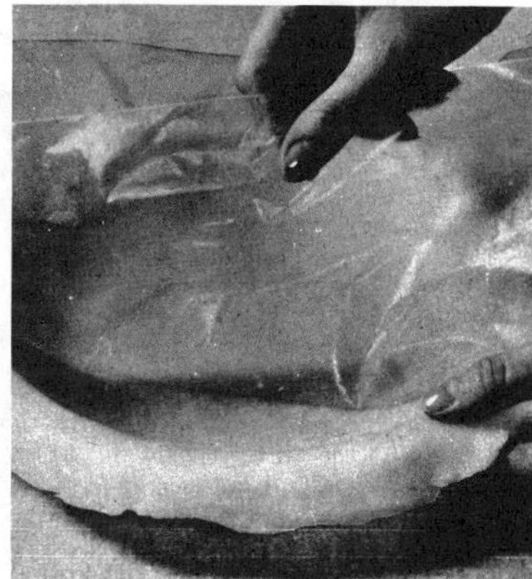

Remove waxed paper and fit pastry carefully into pan.

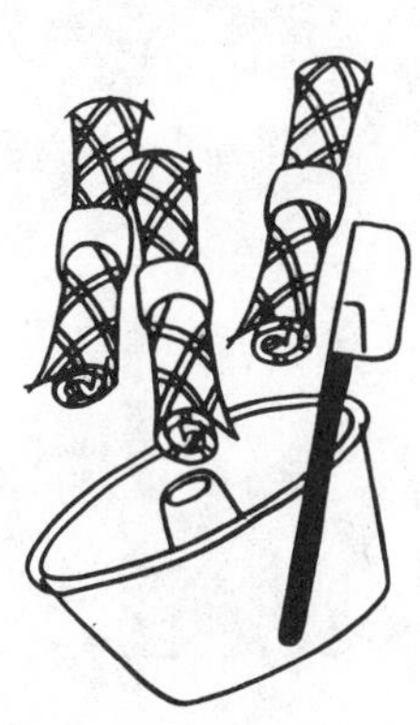

# Coconut Macaroon Crust

**1 egg white**
**2 tablespoons sugar**
**1 tablespoon light corn syrup**
**½ teaspoon vanilla or ¼ teaspoon almond extract**
**2 cups flaked coconut**
**1 quart vanilla or peppermint ice cream**
**Chocolate sauce**

Beat egg white until foamy. Add sugar and beat until mixture will stand in soft peaks. Add corn syrup and flavoring. Fold in coconut. Using the back of a fork, press macaroon mixture firmly on bottom and sides of well-buttered 9-inch pie pan. Bake in moderate oven (350°F.) for 15 minutes, or until lightly browned. Cool. To serve, fill cold crust with ice cream and pass Chocolate Sauce.

### Chocolate Sauce

**1 package (4 ounces) sweet cooking chocolate**
**2 tablespoons water**
**3 tablespoons cream or evaporated milk**

Combine chocolate and water in saucepan. Place over low heat and stir constantly until chocolate is melted—about 3 to 5 minutes. Remove from heat. Add cream and stir until smooth. Serve warm or cold. Makes ¾ cup sauce.

# Spicy Walnut Meringue Shell

**½ cup toasted walnuts**
**3 egg whites**
**¼ teaspoon cream of tartar**
**⅛ teaspoon salt**
**1 cup sugar**
**½ teaspoon cinnamon**

Chop walnuts fine. Beat egg whites with cream of tartar and salt, in a medium sized bowl, to soft peaks. Gradually beat in sugar, about 2 tablespoons at a time, until meringue stands up in stiff glossy peaks. Beat in cinnamon along with the last ¼ cup sugar. Gently fold in walnuts. Pile meringue in a lightly greased 9 or 10-inch pie plate. Spread over bottom and up sides to form crust. Bottom of shell should be about ¼-inch thick, sides about 1-inch thick. Bake in a slow oven (275°F.) 50 to 60 minutes or until a very light tan in color. Turn off oven and leave meringue to cool with door closed. Meringue will crack and fall in center while cooling. Makes 1 large shell.

# Mayonnaise Pie Crust

**1 cup sifted flour**
**¼ teaspoon salt**
**⅓ cup mayonnaise**
**1½ tablespoons water**
**½ teaspoon grated lemon rind**

Mix flour and salt. Stir in mayonnaise with a fork. Add water and rind and mix well. Roll dough out on a lightly floured board to a 12-inch circle. Fit lightly into a 9-inch pie plate. Flute edges. Or divide dough into 6 portions and roll each into a circle. Fit into individual pie plates and flute edges. Makes one 9-inch shell or 6 tart shells.

Baker's Angel Flake Coconut

Start with two or three egg whites, according to the recipe you are using. Be sure whites are at room temperature for greatest volume. Beat until frothy.

Add sugar gradually, one tablespoon at a time (two tablespoons to each egg white), beating well after each addition, until egg whites stand in stiff peaks.

Spoon mounds of meringue around edges of the filling, making sure to touch crust all around, heap the remaining meringue inside as shown. Pull up points of meringue with back of spoon, bake in hot oven (400°F) five to ten minutes until delicately browned. Cool away from drafts.

## Meringue Pie Crust

**2 egg whites**
**¼ teaspoon salt**
**¼ teaspoon cream of tartar**
**½ cup sugar**

Beat egg whites until frothy; add salt and cream of tartar and beat until stiff but not dry. Gradually add sugar and beat until meringue stands in stiff peaks and is smooth and glossy. Spread in bottom and sides of a well greased 9-inch pie plate. Bake in a slow oven (250° F) about 1 hour or until lightly browned. Fill with berries or ice cream just before serving. Makes one 9-inch shell.

# Tarts

Here are tarts that will steal the hearts of your family—and you'll be crowned Queen of the Day!

## Fresh Cherry Tarts

**½ cup sugar**
**¼ cup cornstarch**
**¼ teaspoon salt**
**½ cup light corn syrup**
**3 cups fresh, sour cherries, pitted**
**¼ teaspoon almond extract**
**6 3½-inch baked tart shells**

Combine sugar, cornstarch and salt in top of a double boiler. Add corn syrup and mix well. Add cherries. Place over boiling water and cook, stirring frequently, until mixture thickens. Cover and continue cooking about 20 minutes, stirring occasionally. Remove from heat and add almond extract. Cool. Pour into baked tart shells and chill. Serve with whipped cream, if desired. Makes 6 tarts.

## 1-2-3 Tart Shells

**1⅓ cups sifted flour**
**½ teaspoon salt**
**⅓ cup corn oil**
**2 tablespoon cold water**

Combine flour and salt in a mixing bowl. Blend in corn oil, mixing thoroughly with a fork. Sprinkle all water on top; mix well. Press firmly into ball with hands. (If slightly dry, mix in 1 to 2 tablespoons additional corn oil.) Place ball of dough on a piece of heavy duty aluminum foil about 15 inches long. Flatten ball slightly and cover with waxed paper. Roll out dough to a 12-inch square. Remove waxed paper. Mark off dough into desired shapes with edge of knife. (Makes 4-inch squares or circles, or triangles 4-inches long on each side.) Cut through dough and foil with scissors. Turn up sides of dough and foil, about 1-inch all around. Pinch corners, or flute circles, to hold in place. Prick and place on ungreased baking sheet. Bake in a very hot oven (450°F.) until shells are golden brown, 12 to 15 minutes. Cool. Remove foil. Fill shells as desired. Makes 9 squares or circles, or 15 triangles.

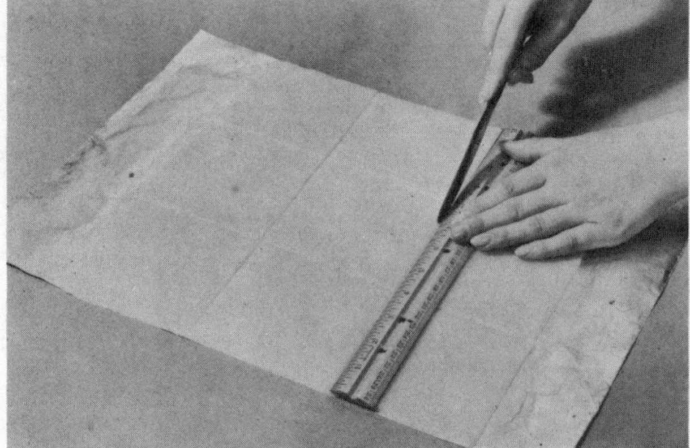

# Lunch Box Turnovers

**1 recipe pastry**
**⅔ cup cooked prunes**
**⅓ cup cooked apricots**
**¼ cup sugar**
**1 tablespoon cornstarch**
**¼ teaspoon salt**
**1 tablespoon lemon juice**

Roll out pastry ⅛-inch thick. Cut into twelve 4-inch squares. Combine remaining ingredients in a saucepan and cook over low heat about 5 minutes. Place 1½ tablespoons of the filling on half of each square; fold pastry over to form a triangle. Seal edges and flute with fingers or a fork. Prick holes in top with a fork. Bake in a hot oven (425° F) about 15 minutes or until lightly browned. Makes 12 turnovers.

Roll out pastry to ⅛-inch thickness and cut into 4-inch squares with a pastry wheel or sharp knife. Next place not more than a tablespoon of mincemeat or other filling in the corner of each square.

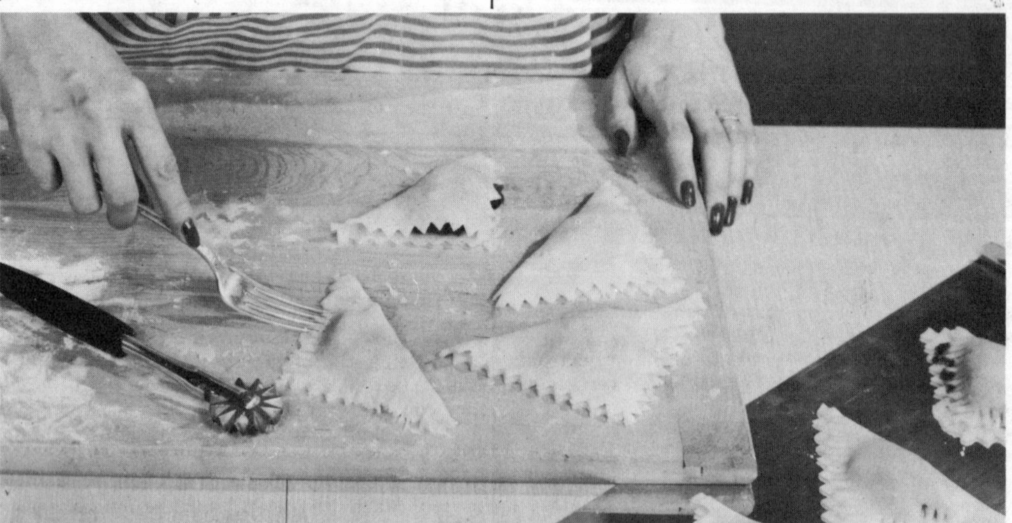

Moisten edges of turnovers with water and fold over dough from one corner to the other. Seal edges of each by pressing with a fork. Prick tops and bake in a very hot oven (450° F) for about 15 minutes.

# Tom Thumb Tarts

### Pastry

1 cup butter or margarine
2 packages (3-ounces) cream cheese
2 cups sifted flour

Soften butter at room temperature. Add cream cheese; beat until smooth and creamy. Add flour ½ cup at a time, blending well after each addition. Work with fingers to a smooth dough. Shape into balls about ½" in diameter. Place each ball in cup of small muffin pans; press with thumb to line bottom and sides easily.

### Filling

2 eggs
1½ cups brown sugar
1 tablespoon instant coffee
Dash of salt
2 tablespoons melted butter or margaine
1 teaspoon vanilla
¾ cup coarsely broken pecans

Beat eggs with fork just enough to blend yolks and whites. Combine sugar, instant coffee and salt; add gradually to eggs, beating well after each addition. Add melted butter and vanilla. Sprinkle pecans in pastry cup; spoon filling over pecans, filling cups not quite to tops. Bake in moderate oven (350°F.), 20 minutes or until set. Makes about two dozen.

Pan American Coffee Bureau

Processed Apples Institute, Inc.

# Individual Apple Sauce-Date Pies

1½ cups sifted all-purpose flour
¼ teaspoon salt
½ cup shortening
½ cup grated American cheese
3 tablespoons cold water
2 cups canned apple sauce
1 cup chopped pitted dates
⅓ cup brown sugar
½ teaspoon nutmeg
1½ teaspoons grated lemon rind

Sift together flour and salt. Cut in shortening with 2 knives or pastry blender. Add cheese; mix well. Add enough water to hold ingredients together. Chill. (Or use your favorite pastry mix and add the grated cheese.) Combine apple sauce, dates, brown sugar, nutmeg and lemon rind; mix well. Line individual pie plates with pastry, reserving enough for tops. Place an equal amount of apple sauce mixture into pie plates. Moisten edges of pastry with cold water. Roll out remaining pastry; cover tops of pies. Press edges with tines of fork; trim pastry to edge of pie plate. Prick tops to allow steam to escape. Bake in hot oven (400°F.) 30 minutes. Makes six 4-inch individual pies, or one 9-inch pie.

# Fruit Turnovers

1 recipe pastry
1 No. 2 can sliced peaches, well drained
½ cup brown sugar
½ teaspoon ginger

Roll out pastry ⅛ inch thick. Cut in 8 rounds 6 inches across. Place 3 peach slices on half of each circle. Sprinkle with sugar and ginger. Moisten edge of pastry with water; fold over and press edges together with a fork. Prick tops with a fork. Bake in a moderately hot oven (400° F) 30 minutes. Makes 8 turnovers.

# ·Quick Lemon Meringue Tarts

**1 package lemon pudding or pie mix**
**½ cup sugar**
**2½ cups water**
**2 eggs, separated**
**6 large or 12 small baked tart shells**
**¼ cup sugar**

Combine lemon pudding, sugar and water in a saucepan. Beat yolks slightly and add to mixture. Cook over medium heat, stirring constantly, until mixture thickens and comes to a boil. Cool slightly. Pour into baked tart shells. Beat egg whites until stiff but not dry; gradually beat in sugar until mixture stands in peaks. Pile lightly on tarts. Bake in a hot oven (425° F) about 5 minutes until lightly browned. Makes 6 large or 12 small tarts.

Corn Products Company

Washington State Apple Commission

# Apple Blossom Tarts

**Pastry for one crust pie**
**½ cup sugar**
**3 tablespoons cinnamon drop candies**
**¾ cup warm water**
**Dash of salt**
**2-3 apples**
**24 tiny marshmallows**
**4 tablespoons broken walnut meats**
**2 tablespoons crushed peppermint stick candy**

Roll out pastry. Cut rounds to fit bottom of custard cups. Invert 4 custard cups on a cookie sheet. Place one round of pastry on the bottom of each cup, then overlap 4 or 5 rounds for "petal" sides, moistening the rounds where they overlap. Prick well with fork, bake in very hot oven (450°F.) for 15 minutes or until browned. Cool.

Combine sugar, cinnamon candies, water and salt in a saucepan. Simmer until candies are completely dissolved. Peel, quarter and core apples; then cut quarters into thick half-slices. Add apples to syrup gradually so that the temperature of the syrup is not reduced sharply. Simmer apples, turning and basting with the syrup, until *barely tender*. Lift apples from syrup and spread out on platter to cool. Boil down syrup until it falls heavily from a spoon. Cool. Toss cinnamon apple chunks, marshmallows, walnuts and peppermint candy together, lightly, adding syrup as desired. Fill pastry cups. Serve, chilled, with a dollop of whipped cream, tinted apple green, if you wish.

# Nut Cookie Tarts

⅓ cup sifted flour
¼ teaspoon salt
¼ teaspoon baking soda
1½ cups quick-cooking oats
3 tablespoons finely chopped nuts
¼ cup margarine
¼ cup granulated sugar
¼ cup brown sugar
1 egg
½ teaspoon vanilla
¼ teaspoon maple flavor
Mixed fruits
Whipped cream

Sift together flour, salt and soda. Stir in oats and nuts. Cream margarine well. Add sugars and blend well. Add egg and flavorings and beat well. Add dry ingredients and blend well. Divide dough into 6 individual greased pie pans and press in dough to the thickness of pie crust. Bake in a moderate oven (350°F.) 20 to 25 minutes. After about 10 minutes of baking time it may be necessary to press down dough in the pans again. Cool. Fill with any desired combination of cooked or fresh fruit. Top with whipped cream. Makes 6 servings.

# French Glaze Cherry Tart

1 cup sifted flour
½ teaspoon salt
⅓ cup shortening
2 tablespoons milk
2 tablespoons butter

Sift together flour and salt. With a pastry blender or 2 knives, cut in the shortening. Sprinkle milk over mixture, tossing with a fork until dough stays together. Round up into a ball and roll out on a lightly floured board to ⅛-inch thickness. Dot with butter. Fold so that the two sides meet in the center and seal by pressing the side edge of pastry with fingers. Fold ends to center and seal. Roll dough out again into a circle 1½ inches larger than 9-inch pie pan. Place in pie pan. Fold edge under and flute to make a stand-up collar. Prick thoroughly with a fork. Bake in a very hot oven (475°F.) 8 to 10 minutes. Cool.

1 3-ounce package cream cheese
4 cups sweet cherries, pitted
1 cup water
⅔ cup sugar
2⅔ tablespoons cornstarch
1 tablespoon lemon juice
Sweetened whipped cream

Mash cream cheese and stir until smooth. Spread over bottom of pie shell. Cover cheese with 2 cups of the cherries. Combine remaining cherries and water and boil 5 minutes. Stir in combined sugar and cornstarch. Boil 1 minute, stirring constantly. Remove from heat. Blend in lemon juice. Cool and pour over cherries in pie shell. Just before serving decorate with whipped cream. Makes one 9-inch pie.

# Chess Pies

½ cup butter or margarine
1 teaspoon vanilla
1 cup sugar
1 egg white
3 egg yolks, beaten
1 cup chopped raisins
1 cup chopped nuts
10 unbaked tart shells in 2¾-inch muffin pans

Cream butter and vanilla. Gradually beat in sugar until light and fluffy. Beat egg white until stiff and fold into beaten egg yolks. Blend well into sugar mixture. Add raisins and nuts. Pour into tart shells. Bake in a hot oven (400° F) 25 minutes. Serve topped with whipped cream, if desired. Makes 10 tarts.

# Meringue Tart Shells

4 egg whites
1 cup sugar

Beat egg whites until foamy. Beat sugar in gradually, 1 tablespoon at a time beating thoroughly after each addition. Continue beating until meringue forms sharp peaks when beater is raised. Shape meringue into nests with a spoon or pastry bag on brown paper on a baking sheet. Bake in a very slow oven (250° F) 1 hour and 20 minutes until shells are dried and the tops are cream colored. Remove from paper as soon as baked. Cool completely before serving. Fill with fruit or ice cream for serving. Makes 12 shells.

# Pumpkin Marmalade Tarts

¾ cup strained cooked or canned pumpkin
⅓ cup firmly packed brown sugar
½ teaspoon cinnamon
¼ teaspoon ginger
¼ teaspoon nutmeg
½ teaspoon salt
2 egg yolks, beaten
¾ cup milk
¼ cup evaporated milk
6 unbaked tart shells
3 tablespoons orange marmalade
2 egg whites
4 tablespoons sugar

Combine pumpkin, brown sugar, spices and salt. Stir in egg yolks, milk and evaporated milk. Pour mixture into unbaked tart shells. Bake in a hot oven (450° F) 15 minutes; reduce temperature to 325° F and continue baking about 20 minutes or until set. Spread tarts with orange marmalade. Beat egg whites until stiff. Gradually beat in sugar and continue beating until well mixed. Spread over top of marmalade. Bake in a hot oven (425° F) about 5 minutes, or until lightly browned. Makes 6 tarts.

Washington State Pears

# Pear Squares

**2 to 3 fresh pears**
**Pie pastry (using 3 cups flour)**
**½ cup sugar**
**1 tablespoon butter**
**1 cup water**
**1½ cups brown sugar**
**1 tablespoon lemon juice**
**1 tablespoon butter**
**1 stick cinnamon, broken**
**Pinch of salt**

Wash, peel and core pears. Save peelings in saucepan. Make pastry using 3 cups of flour. Chill, then roll out into rectangle. Cut into strips, 4 x 8 inches. Slice pears and place on half of each pastry strip. Sprinkle pears with sugar, dot with butter. Fold pastry over and seal edges with tines of fork. Cut slits or pear shape on top of pastry. Bake on baking sheet in hot oven (425°F.) for 20 minutes or until golden brown. Serve warm with Cinnamon Sauce.

*Cinnamon Sauce:* Boil pear peelings with 1 cup water for 5 minutes. Strain and discard peelings. Add brown sugar, lemon juice, butter, cinnamon and salt to water in which pear peelings cooked. Bring to boil and simmer for 5 to 6 minutes. Strain out cinnamon stick pieces. Serve warm.

# Lemon Cheese Tart

1 cup sifted flour
½ teaspoon salt
⅓ cup shortening
3 to 4 tablespoons cold water
1 8-ounce package cream cheese
2 eggs
½ cup sugar
1 teaspoon vanilla
1 teaspoon grated lemon rind
1 tablespoon lemon juice
½ cup heavy cream

Sift together the flour and salt. Cut in shortening until particles are the size of small peas. Sprinkle cold water gradually over mixture, tossing lightly with a fork until dough is moist enough to hold together. Form into a ball. Roll out on a lightly floured board into a circle 1½ inches larger than an 8-inch pie pan. Fit pastry loosely into pie pan. Fold edge to form a standing rim; flute edge. Prick crust with a fork. Bake in a hot oven (425°F.) 8 to 10 minutes. Soften cream cheese and whip until fluffy. Add eggs, one at a time, beating well after each addition. Blend in sugar, vanilla, lemon rind and lemon juice. Mix well. Turn into baked pie shell. Bake in a moderate oven (350°F.) 15 to 20 minutes until slightly firm. Cool. Chill at least 1 hour before serving. Whip cream until stiff. Flavor to taste. Spread over pie before serving. Garnish with grated lemon rind. Makes one 8-inch pie.

# French Strawberry Cream Tart

1½ cups sifted flour
½ teaspoon baking powder
¼ teaspoon salt
½ cup butter
1 egg
½ cup sugar

Sift together flour, baking powder and salt. Cut in butter until it is the consistency of corn meal. Beat egg slightly, add sugar and beat until just blended. Stir into flour mixture and mix well. Place dough in a greased 9-inch pie pan and press it out so that it covers bottom and sides of pan. Bake in a hot oven (425°F.) about 20 minutes. When cool, fill with the following custard mixture.

⅔ cup sugar
4 tablespoons cornstarch
¼ teaspoon salt
2 cups milk
2 eggs
½ teaspoon vanilla
½ teaspoon lemon extract
1 pint strawberries

Combine sugar, cornstarch and salt in top part of a double boiler. Stir in milk. Cook over low heat, stirring constantly, until mixture is thick and smooth. Beat eggs slightly. Pour hot mixture slowly over eggs and beat well. Return mixture to top of double boiler and cook over boiling water 5 minutes, stirring constantly. Cool. Stir in flavorings. Pour into tart shell. Wash, hull and halve berries. Arrange on top of custard just before serving. Makes 6 to 8 servings.

# Streusel Peach Tarts

½ cup sugar
2 tablespoons flour
2 tablespoons butter
¼ teaspoon cinnamon
10 unbaked tart shells
10 well drained canned peach halves

Mix together sugar, flour, butter and cinnamon. Sprinkle half of the crumb mixture in the bottoms of the tart shells. Place a peach half in each tart shell. Sprinkle remaining crumb mixture over peach halves. Bake in a hot oven (425° F) 20 to 30 minutes or until crust is delicately browned. Serve warm. Makes 10 tarts.

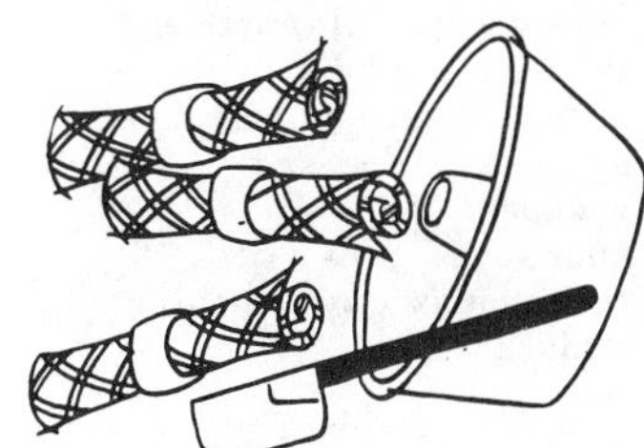

# Coconut Pumpkin Chiffon Tarts

1 envelope unflavored gelatine
½ cup cold water
2 eggs, separated
1 cup evaporated milk
1¼ cups strained cooked or canned pumpkin
¾ cup firmly packed brown sugar
½ teaspoon salt
½ teaspoon nutmeg
½ teaspoon cinnamon
¼ teaspoon ginger
1 cup toasted shredded coconut
8 baked tart shells
⅓ cup heavy cream, whipped

Soften gelatine in cold water. Put egg yolks in top of double boiler, add evaporated milk and beat until blended. Stir in pumpkin, ½ cup of the brown sugar, salt and spices. Cook over boiling water 10 minutes, stirring constantly. Remove from heat. Add gelatine and stir until dissolved. Chill until slightly thickened. Beat egg whites until stiff, but not dry; add remaining brown sugar gradually and continue beating. Fold pumpkin mixture into egg whites with ¾ cup of the toasted coconut. Fill tart shells and chill until firm. To serve, top with whipped cream and remaining coconut. Makes 8 servings.

# Banana Coconut Cream Tarts

¾ cup heavy cream
2 tablespoons sugar
¼ teaspoon vanilla
1 cup moist shredded coconut
6 baked 3½-inch tart shells
3 ripe bananas

Beat cream until stiff. Fold in sugar and vanilla. Sprinkle shredded coconut into tart shells. Peel bananas and slice over coconut. Cover banana slices at once with whipped cream. Garnish tarts with additional coconut and sliced berries if desired. Makes 6 servings.

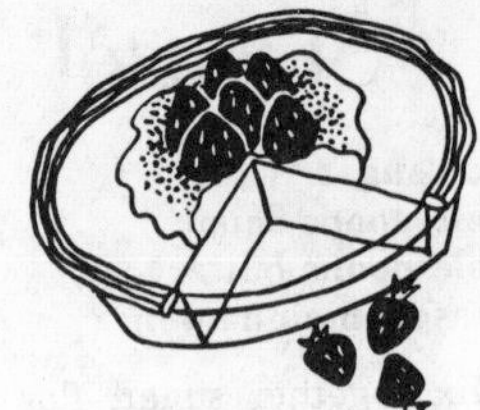

## Cranberry Tarts

**4 cups chopped cranberries**
**1 teaspoon grated orange rind**
**2 oranges, peeled and chopped**
**2 cups sugar**
**3 tablespoons quick-cooking tapioca**
**1 tablespoon butter or margarine, melted**
**½ teaspoon salt**
**1 orange, sectioned**
**6 mayonnaise pie crust tart shells, unbaked**

Combine cranberries, orange rind, oranges, sugar, tapioca. margarine and salt. Pour into tart shells. Arrange orange sections on top of filling. Bake in a very hot oven (450° F) 10 minutes: reduce temperature to moderate 350° F and bake 25 to 30 minutes. Makes 6 tarts.

## Java Cream Tarts

**6 tablespoons flour**
**⅔ cup sugar**
**⅛ teaspoon salt**
**2 cups strong coffee**
**1 cup evaporated milk**
**2 eggs, beaten**
**1 teaspoon vanilla**
**2 tablespoons butter**
**8 baked tart shells**

Combine flour, sugar and salt in top of a double boiler. Add coffee and milk and mix well. Cook over low heat, stirring constantly, until thick. Pour slowly over beaten eggs, mix well and return to double boiler and cook over boiling water 3 minutes. Add vanilla and butter. Cool. Pour into tart shells and chill thoroughly. Makes 8 tarts.

## Fruit Sherbet Tarts

**20 graham crackers, finely crushed**
**¼ cup softened butter or margarine**
**¼ cup sugar**
**1 large banana**
**¼ cup orange juice**
**2 tablespoons lime juice**
**¾ cup sugar**
**1¼ cups milk**
**1 egg white**

Thoroughly blend together graham cracker crumbs, butter and sugar. Divide mixture into 8 fluted paper cups set in muffin pans. Press crumbs firmly against bottom and sides of paper cups with a spoon or a straight sided glass. Place in freezing compartment of refrigerator. Mash banana with a fork, add orange juice, lime juice and sugar. Stir in milk. Freeze 1 hour. Beat mixture with a rotary beater. Beat egg white until stiff but not dry and fold into sherbet mixture. Spoon sherbet into tart shells. Place in freezing compartment of refrigerator and freeze 3 to 4 hours. Remove fluted paper cups before serving. Makes 8 tarts.

## Black and White Tarts

**1 cup shredded coconut**
**1 cup candy-coated rice cereal or puffed wheat**
**¼ cup honey**
**2 tablespoons sugar**
**¼ teaspoon salt**
**1 tablespoon butter**
**1 package vanilla pudding mix**
**1 package chocolate pudding mix**

Spread coconut in a shallow baking pan. Bake in a moderate oven (350° F) 5 to 7 minutes, or until delicately browned. Stir or shake often during browning time. Place toasted coconut and cereal in a greased bowl and set aside. Combine honey, sugar and salt in a small saucepan. Bring to a boil over medium heat, stirring to dissolve sugar. Continue boiling until a small amount of syrup forms a firm ball in cold water or to a temperature of 246° F. Add butter. Pour syrup over coconut and cereal and stir lightly to coat. Press mixture on bottom and sides of well greased custard cups or tart tins. Chill. Fill tarts with chocolate and vanilla pudding. Garnish with shaved chocolate and shredded coconut. Makes 6 tarts.

## Cheese Apricot Turnovers

**3 3-ounce packages cream cheese**
**⅓ cup butter**
**2 cups sifted flour**
**1 teaspoon salt**
**½ pound dried apricots, cooked and puréed**
**½ cup sugar**

Blend together cream cheese and butter. Gradually cut in mixed and sifted dry ingredients; chill. Roll out very thin on a lightly floured board. Cut into 4-inch squares. Combine apricots and sugar. Place 1 tablespoon of the apricot mixture on each square of pastry. Fold squares into triangles and seal edges with a fork. Prick tops with a fork. Place on a cookie sheet. Bake in a moderate oven (375° F) 20 to 25 minutes. Makes 18 to 20 turnovers.

## Open-Face Raspberry Tarts

**2 tablespoons sugar**
**1 tablespoon cornstarch**
**⅛ teaspoon salt**
**¾ cup fruit juice**
**1 teaspoon lemon juice**
**4 to 6 baked tart shells**
**1 pint fresh raspberries**

Blend together in a saucepan sugar, cornstarch and salt. Stir in fruit juice and cook over low heat until thick and clear. Cool. Add lemon juice. Fill tart shells with raspberries. Pour fruit sauce over berries. Chill. Top with whipped cream, if desired. Makes 4 to 6 tarts.

# Peach Patisseries

⅓ cup sugar
3 tablespoons flour
½ teaspoon cornstarch
Few grains salt
1 cup milk
2 egg yolks, slightly beaten
¼ teaspoon vanilla
¼ teaspoon almond extract
6 3-inch baked tart shells
6 peach halves

In the top of a double boiler mix together sugar, flour, cornstarch and salt. Stir in milk. Cook over low heat, stirring constantly, until thick. Pour slowly into beaten egg yolks, return to double boiler and cook over boiling water 3 minutes. Cool. Add flavorings. Pour mixture into tart shells. Place a peach half on each, cut side up. If desired, garnish with whipped cream. Makes 6 tarts.

# Cookie Tart Shells

⅓ cup margarine
½ cup sugar
1 egg
1 tablespoon orange juice
1½ cups sifted flour
1 teaspoon baking powder
¼ teaspoon salt

Cream margarine; add sugar gradually and mix well. Add egg and orange juice; mix well. Sift flour, baking powder and salt together. Add to creamed mixture and blend well. Chill dough. Roll dough on a lightly floured board to ⅛-inch thickness; cut into rounds. Invert muffin tins and grease outside of cups. Place rounds over cups, press down and pinch edges of dough at intervals to fit cups. Prick with a fork. Bake in a moderate oven (375° F) 6 to 8 minutes. Cool 1 minute before removing shells. Fill with berries, pudding or ice cream for serving. Makes 10 or 12 tart shells.

To shape cookie tart shells, invert muffin tins, grease outside of cups. Place rounds over cups, press down and pinch edges of dough at intervals.

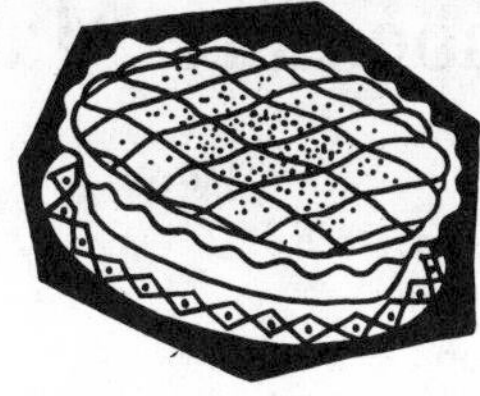

# Fig-Nut Turnovers

½ cup sugar
½ cup figs, finely chopped
1 cup finely chopped peeled apple
1 cup almonds, chopped
1 teaspoon grated orange rind
1 cup liquid (juice of 1 orange plus water)
¼ teaspoon cinnamon
¼ teaspoon mace
1 recipe pastry

Combine sugar, figs, apple, almonds, orange rind, liquid, cinnamon and mace in a saucepan. Simmer until thick and apples are soft, about 5 minutes. Cool. Divide dough in halves. Roll out one-half on a lightly floured board to a 15 by 10-inch rectangle. Cut into 5-inch squares. Place a rounded tablespoon of the fig filling on each. Fold squares in half to form rectangles. Seal edges with a fork. Place on a cookie sheet. Prick tops to allow escape of steam. Bake in a hot oven (425° F) 12 to 15 minutes. Makes 12 turnovers.

# Banbury Turnovers

1 recipe pastry
½ cup sugar
1 tablespoon flour
1 egg, slightly beaten
1 cup seedless raisins
¼ cup chopped nuts
1 tablespoon lemon juice
2 teaspoons grated lemon rind

Roll pastry out ⅛ inch thick. Cut into twelve 4-inch squares. Combine sugar and flour and stir into beaten egg. Add remaining ingredients and mix well. Place 2 tablespoons of the filling on half of each square and fold over pastry to form a triangle. Seal edges and flute with fingers or a fork. Prick tops with a fork and place on a baking sheet. Bake in a hot oven (425° F) about 15 minutes or until lightly browned. Makes 12 turnovers.

# Cranberry Apple Tarts

2½ cups cranberries, coarsely chopped
1½ cups chopped peeled apples
1¼ cups sugar
Grated rind of 1 orange
1 tablespoon flour
3 tablespoons water
6 unbaked tart shells

Combine all ingredients except tart shells. Let stand about 10 minutes. Pour into tart shells. Bake in a hot oven (425° F) 25 to 30 minutes. Makes six 2½-inch tarts.

## Chocolate Macaroon Tarts

**¼ cup cornstarch**
**¾ cup sugar**
**⅛ teaspoon salt**
**2 cups milk, scalded**
**2 eggs, separated**
**1 tablespoon butter**
**3 squares unsweetened chocolate, melted**
**1 teaspoon vanilla**
**1½ cups macaroon cookie crumbs**
**2 egg whites, stiffly beaten**
**8 baked tart shells**
**1 cup heavy cream, whipped**

Mix cornstarch, sugar and salt together in top of a double boiler. Add milk and blend well. Cook over low heat, stirring constantly, until thick. Beat egg yolks. Pour hot mixture slowly over egg yolks and mix well. Return to double boiler. Stir in butter and chocolate. Cook over boiling water 3 minutes. Cool. Add vanilla, macaroon crumbs and egg whites. Fill tart shells. Chill well. Garnish with whipped cream. Makes 8 tarts.

# Fruit Pies

**Whether you bake a Nectar Mince or Apple Crumb your family will chorus, "Yum! Yum! Yum!"**

## Nectar Mince Pie

**1 recipe spicy pastry**
**¼ cup butter or margarine**
**½ cup sugar**
**½ cup molasses**
**½ teaspoon salt**
**2 eggs**
**1 cup prepared mincemeat**
**½ cup seedless raisins**
**½ cup chopped nuts**
**2 tablespoons grated orange rind**

Line a 9-inch pie plate with one-half the pastry. Cream together butter and sugar and blend in molasses and salt. Add eggs one at a time, beating thoroughly after each addition. Add mincemeat, raisins, nuts and orange rind. Pour filling into pastry lined pie plate. Roll out remaining crust and cut into pumpkin shapes. Place on top of filling. Bake in a hot oven (400° F) 30 to 40 minutes. Makes one 9-inch pie.

The Borden Company

Corn Products Company

# Metropolitan Apple Pie

**1 recipe pastry**
**1 cup sugar**
**1⅓ cups pineapple juice**
**½ teaspoon salt**
**6 medium-size apples**
**2 teaspoons cornstarch**
**½ teaspoon vanilla**
**2 tablespoons butter or margarine**

Line a 9-inch pie plate with half the pastry. Combine sugar, pineapple juice and salt and heat to boiling. Peel, core and quarter apples. Simmer in pineapple juice until tender, moving apples just enough to keep them covered with syrup. Lift the apples out carefully and arrange in pastry shell. Blend cornstarch with a little cold water and add to syrup. Cook over low heat until syrup thickens. Add the vanilla and butter and pour over apples. Roll out remaining pastry and cut in a long strip. Starting at center of pie, twist and coil the strip over the apples to form a curled spiral top crust. Bake in a hot oven (450° F) 10 minutes and then reduce the heat to moderate 375° F and bake about 20 minutes. Makes one 9-inch pie.

# Peach Pie

**1 recipe pastry**
**¼ to ½ cup sugar**
**¼ cup flour or 3 tablespoons quick-cooking tapioca**
**½ teaspoon cinnamon**
**Dash of nutmeg**
**6 cups sliced fresh peaches**
**1 tablespoon lemon juice**
**Butter or margarine**

Line a 9-inch pie plate with half the pastry. Combine sugar flour, cinnamon, nutmeg and peaches. Place in pie plate. Sprinkle with lemon juice and dot with butter. Cover with top crust. Bake in a hot oven (450° F) 10 minutes; reduce heat to moderate 375° F and bake 30 to 40 minutes. Makes one 9-inch pie.

# Dutch Peach Pie

**6 fresh peaches**
**1 9-inch unbaked pie shell**
**1 cup sugar**
**¼ teaspoon salt**
**2 tablespoon cornstarch or quick-cooking tapioca**
**1 cup cream**
**1 teaspoon vanilla**

Peel peaches. Remove stones and cut in eighths. Arrange in pie shell. Mix sugar, salt and cornstarch thoroughly. Add cream and vanilla and pour over peaches. Bake in a hot oven (450° F) 15 minutes; reduce temperature to 325° F and bake 30 minutes longer or until peaches are tender. Makes one 9-inch pie.

# Apple Crumb Pie

**6 tart apples, peeled, cored and sliced**
**2 tablespoons butter, melted**
**¾ cup sugar**
**½ teaspoon nutmeg**
**½ teaspoon cinnamon**
**⅛ teaspoon salt**
**1 9-inch unbaked pie shell**
**½ cup brown sugar, firmly packed**
**¼ cup flour**
**¼ cup butter or margarine**
**½ cup chopped nuts**

Mix together apples, butter, sugar, nutmeg, cinnamon and salt. Arrange in the pie shell. Combine brown sugar and flour. Cut in the butter and add nuts. Sprinkle evenly over apples. Bake in a moderate oven (375° F) about 50 minutes, or until apples are tender. Serve warm or cold. Makes one 9-inch pie.

# Lattice Top Cherry Pie

**1 recipe pastry**
**2½ to 3 tablespoons quick-cooking tapioca**
**1 cup sugar**
**⅛ teaspoon salt**
**4 cups (two No. 2 cans) drained, pitted red sour cherries, water packed**
**½ cup cherry juice**
**1 tablespoon butter or margarine**

Line a 9-inch pie pan with half the pastry. Combine tapioca, sugar, salt, cherries and juice. Fill pie shell with cherry mixture and dot with butter. Cover with a lattice crust. Bake in a hot oven (425° F) 45 minutes, or until syrup boils with heavy bubbles that do not burst. Makes one 9-inch pie.

# Cranberry Apple Pie

**1 recipe pastry**
**4 cups peeled, cored and sliced apples**
**¼ cup sugar**
**2 tablespoons flour**
**¼ teaspoon salt**
**1 can whole cranberry sauce**
**2 teaspoons lemon juice**
**1 teaspoon grated lemon rind**

Line a 9-inch pie plate with half the pastry. Arrange apples in pie plate. Combine remaining ingredients and pour over sliced apples. Cover with a lattice crust. Bake in a hot oven (425° F) 10 minutes. Reduce heat to moderate 350° F and bake 35 minutes longer. Makes one 9-inch pie.

# Apple Crunch Pie

**1 recipe pastry**
**5 cups pared, sliced apples**
**¾ cup sugar**
**¼ teaspoon cinnamon**
**¼ teaspoon salt**
**1 tablespoon flour**
**1 tablespoon lemon juice**
**1 tablespoon butter or margarine**
**Topping:**
**1 tablespoon shortening**
**1 tablespoon sugar**
**3 tablespoons flour**
**¼ teaspoon salt**

Line a 9-inch pie plate with one-half the pastry. Combine apples with sugar, cinnamon, salt, flour and lemon juice. Place in pastry lined pie plate. Dot the top with butter. Cover with top crust. Mix topping ingredients of shortening, sugar, flour and salt until crumbly. Sprinkle over top of pie. Bake in a hot oven (425° F) about 10 minutes; reduce temperature to 350° F and continue baking about 25 to 30 minutes or until apples are tender and crust is browned. Makes one 9-inch pie.

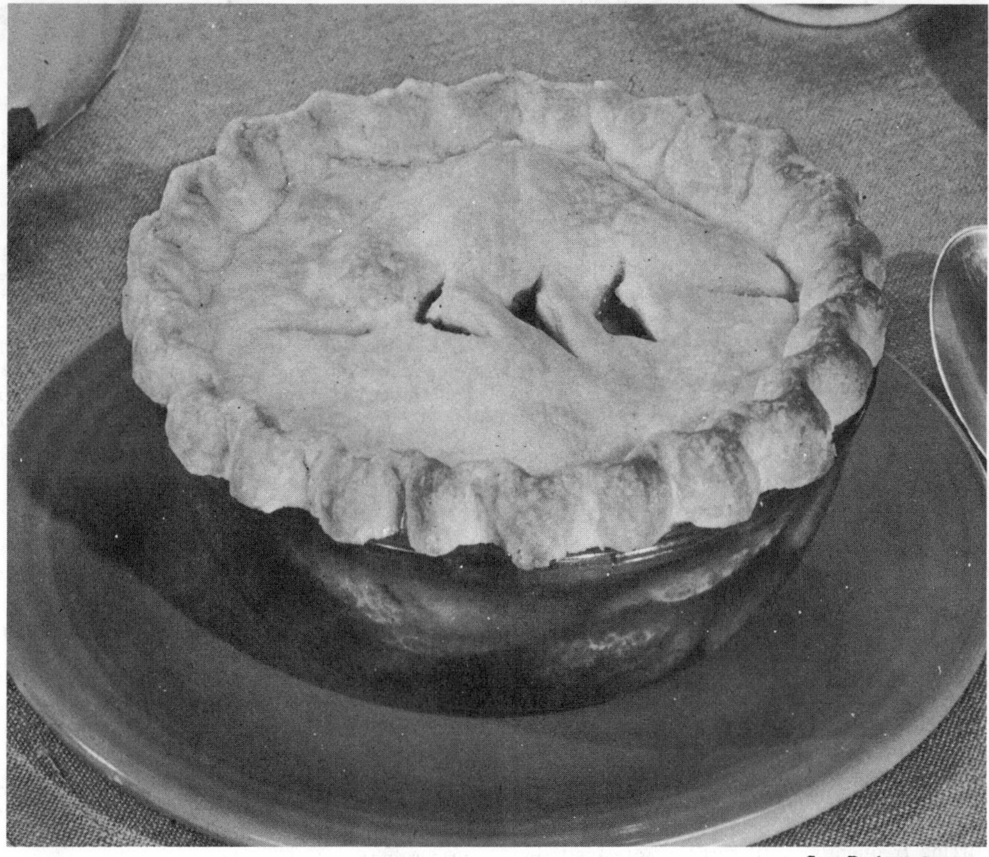

Corn Products Company

# Individual Deep-Dish Apple Pie

**6 to 8 medium apples**
**1 tablespoon cornstarch or quick-cooking tapioca**
**1 teaspoon cinnamon**
**¼ teaspoon salt**
**¼ cup sugar**
**1 teaspoon grated lemon rind**
**1 teaspoon lemon juice**
**3 tablespoons butter or margarine, melted**
**1 cup corn syrup**
**½ recipe pastry**

Peel and core apples. Cut in wedges about ¼ inch thick. Arrange in 4 small casseroles. Combine remaining ingredients, except pastry; stir until blended. Pour mixture evenly over apples. Roll pastry and cut in four small circles to fit casseroles. Cut slashes to allow escape of steam. Place over apples and seal edges. Bake in a hot oven (450° F) for ten minutes, reduce temperature to moderate 350° F and bake for 30 minutes or until apples are tender. Makes 4 individual pies.

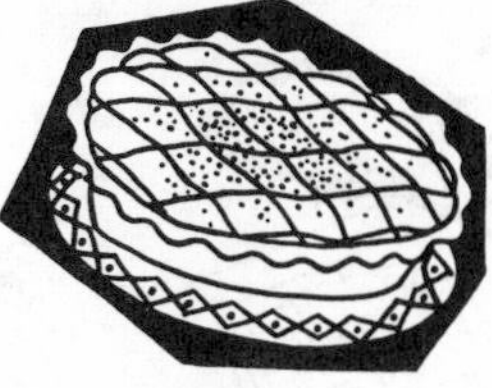

# Apricot Pie

**1 recipe pastry**
**⅔ cup sugar**
**¼ teaspoon salt**
**1 tablespoon cornstarch or quick-cooking tapioca**
**3½ cups drained, cooked or canned apricots**
**½ cup apricot juice**
**2 tablespoons lemon juice**
**1 tablespoon butter**

Line a 9-inch pie plate with half the pastry. Mix sugar, salt and cornstarch. Add apricots, apricot juice and lemon juice. Place in pastry lined pie plate and dot top with butter. Cover with top crust. Bake in a hot oven (425° F) 10 minutes; reduce temperature to 350° F and continue baking about 25 minutes or until crust is browned. Makes one 9-inch pie.

# Cranberry Pineapple Pie

**1 cup sugar**
**3 tablespoons flour**
**¼ teaspoon salt**
**½ cup corn syrup**
**½ cup pineapple syrup**
**4 cups washed cranberries**
**4 slices canned pineapple, cut in pieces**
**1 teaspoon grated lemon rind**
**1 9-inch unbaked pie shell**

Combine sugar, flour, salt, corn syrup and pineapple syrup. Bring to a boil over low heat. Add cranberries and cook gently until skins pop. Remove from heat and add pineapple and lemon rind. Cool slightly without stirring. Pour into pie shell. Bake in a hot oven (425° F) 10 minutes; reduce heat to moderate 350° F and bake 30 minutes longer. Makes one 9-inch pie.

# Prune and Apricot Pie

1 tablespoon flour
6 tablespoons sugar
1 cup prune and apricot juice
2 tablespoons lemon juice
Grated rind of 1 lemon
2 tablespoons butter or margarine
1 cup cooked dried apricots
1 cup cooked dried prunes
1 recipe pastry

Mix flour and sugar thoroughly. Add fruit juices and mix well. Cook over low heat, stirring until thick. Remove from heat and add rind, butter, apricots and prunes. Let cool. Line an 8-inch pie plate with half the pastry. Turn prune mixture into lined pie dish. Cover with lattice top. Bake in a hot oven (450° F) 20 to 25 minutes. Makes one 8-inch pie.

# Caramel Apple Pie

3½ cups canned apple slices
1 9-inch unbaked pie shell
¾ cup sugar
¾ cup graham cracker crumbs
¼ cup flour
Dash of salt
½ cup chopped pecans
½ teaspoon cinnamon
⅓ cup butter or margarine, melted
¼ pound caramels
¼ cup hot water

Place apple slices in pie shell. Combine sugar, crumbs, flour, salt, pecans, cinnamon and butter. Sprinkle mixture over apple slices. Bake in a hot oven (450° F) 10 minutes; reduce temperature to moderate 350° F and continue baking 20 minutes. Combine caramels and hot water in top of a double boiler. Cook over hot water, stirring frequently, until caramels are melted and sauce smooth. Pour mixture over top of crumbs on apple pie. Return to oven and continue baking for 10 minutes. Makes one 9-inch pie.

# French Apple Pie

4 to 5 large apples
¾ cup sugar
½ teaspoon cinnamon
½ teaspoon salt
2 tablespoons flour
1 9-inch unbaked pie shell
½ cup cream

Pare, core and slice apples. Combine sugar, cinnamon, salt and flour. Sprinkle half the mixture in the bottom of pie shell. Place apple slices on dry ingredients. Sprinkle remaining dry mixture on top of apples. Pour cream over apples. Bake in a hot oven (400° F) 15 minutes; reduce temperature to 350° F and continue baking 45 to 60 minutes until apples are tender. Makes one 9-inch pie.

# Strawberry Glaze Pie

1 quart ripe strawberries
¾ cup water
1 cup sugar
3 tablespoons cornstarch
1 teaspoon lemon juice
2 3-ounce packages cream cheese
4 tablespoons cream
1 9-inch baked pie shell

Wash and hull strawberries; drain well. Combine 1 cup of the berries with water and simmer 5 minutes. Reserve remaining berries. Mix sugar and cornstarch together. Stir in cooked berries and cook, stirring constantly, until syrup is clear and thick. Stir in lemon juice and cool slightly. Mix together cheese and cream until light and fluffy. Spread over bottom of baked pie shell. Cover with remaining whole berries. Pour thickened syrup over top of berries. Chill well before serving. Makes one 9-inch pie.

# Deep Dish Rhubarb Pie

2 pounds rhubarb, cut in ½ inch pieces
1¼ cups sugar
¼ cup flour or 3 tablespoons quick cooking tapioca
⅛ teaspoon nutmeg
2 tablespoons shredded orange rind
2 tablespoons butter or margarine
½ recipe pastry

Combine rhubarb with sugar, flour, nutmeg and orange rind and mix lightly. Place in 8-inch square pan and dot with butter. Top with pastry. Bake in a hot oven (425° F) 30 minutes. Makes 4 to 6 servings.

# Paradise Pie

6 large apples
¾ cup sugar
1 tablespoon red cinnamon candies
4 tablespoons orange juice
1 tablespoon lemon juice
1 tablespoon grated lemon rind
1 9-inch baked pie shell
1 cup whipped cream
¼ cup chopped nuts

Wash, pare and core apples. Cut each apple in eight sections. Arrange in a large saucepan, add the sugar, cinnamon candies and enough water to just cover apples. Simmer until tender, turning often. Remove apples and place in a dish. To the remaining syrup in the saucepan add orange juice, lemon juice and lemon rind. Simmer until syrup is thick. Pour over apples and let stand until cool. Arrange apple sections in the baked pie shell. Chill thoroughly. Garnish with whipped cream and nuts before serving. Makes one 9-inch pie.

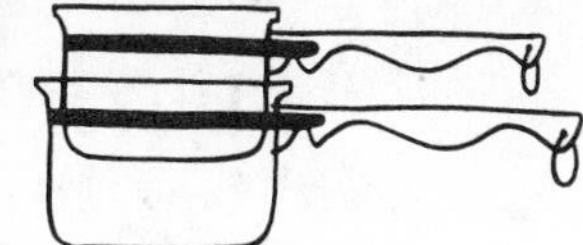

# French Peach Pie

**1½ cups sifted flour**
**½ teaspoon salt**
**½ cup shortening**
**2 to 3 tablespoons cold water**
**4 cups sliced fresh peaches**
**½ cup granulated sugar**
**¾ cup brown sugar, firmly packed, divided**
**1 tablespoon lemon juice**
**3 tablespoons cornstarch**

Sift together flour and salt. Cut in shortening with a pastry blender or two knives. Measure ½ cup of the flour-shortening mixture and set aside. Sprinkle remaining flour mixture with cold water, tossing lightly with a fork until dough forms a ball. Roll out and fit into a 9-inch pie plate. Flute edges. Combine peaches, sugar, ½ cup of brown sugar, lemon juice and cornstarch. Toss lightly. Place in pie shell. Combine reserve flour mixture and remaining ¼ cup brown sugar. Sprinkle over top of peach filling. Bake in a hot oven (425°F.) 45 to 50 minutes. Makes 1 pie.

# Rhubarb Pie

**1 recipe pastry**
**4 cups cut rhubarb**
**1 cup sugar**
**⅓ cup light brown sugar**
**¼ teaspoon salt**
**6 tablespoons flour or 5 tablespoons quick cooking tapioca**
**¼ teaspoon cinnamon**
**2 tablespoons butter or margarine**

Line a 9-inch pie plate with half the pastry. Combine rhubarb, sugars, salt, flour and cinnamon and pour into pie shell. Dot top with butter. Cover with a lattice top. Bake in a hot oven (400° F) 45 minutes. Makes one 9-inch pie.

# Raspberry Glaze Pie with Gingersnap Crust

**⅓ cup melted margarine**
**1¼ cups gingersnap crumbs**
**2 tablespoons confectioners' sugar**
**½ teaspoon cinnamon**
**1 pint raspberries**
**⅓ cup sugar**
**2 teaspoons unflavored gelatine**
**1½ tablespoons cold water**
**2 tablespoons melted margarine**
**½ teaspoon lemon juice**
**1 package prepared vanilla pudding**
**½ teaspoon almond extract**
**1 cup cream, whipped**

Add margarine to gingersnap crumbs; stir in confectioners' sugar and cinnamon and blend well. Spread in a 9-inch pie plate. Pat mixture firmly onto bottom and sides. Bake in a hot oven (400° F) 10 minutes. Cool. Combine raspberries and sugar in a saucepan; heat gently. Strain off juice and set raspberries aside. Soften gelatine in water; dissolve over hot water. Stir into berry juice; add margarine and lemon juice. Cool until slightly thickened. Meanwhile, prepare pudding according to directions on package; add almond extract. Cool and pour into gingersnap shell. Spread raspberries over pudding and cover with gelatine mixture. Chill until set. Before serving, spread with whipped cream and garnish with additional raspberries. Makes one 9-inch pie.

# Crunchy Pear Pie

**¼ cup sugar**
**2 tablespoons cornstarch**
**⅛ teaspoon salt**
**½ teaspoon ginger, divided**
**1½ cups juice drained from pears**
**1 teaspoon grated lemon rind**
**1 tablespoon lemon juice**
**2 cups pear halves, drained**
**1 unbaked 9-inch pie shell**
**1 cup sifted flour**
**½ cup brown sugar, firmly packed**
**½ cup butter or margarine**
**½ cup chopped nuts**

Combine sugar, corn starch, salt and ¼ teaspoon ginger in a saucepan. Blend in pear juice. Cook over medium heat, stirring constantly, until mixture thickens and comes to a boil. Remove from heat. Add lemon rind and lemon juice. Cut pear halves in half lengthwise, arrange in pastry shell. Pour thickened syrup over top of pears. Blend together flour, brown sugar, butter and remaining sugar with a pastry blender until mixture looks like coarse crumbs. Stir in nuts. Sprinkle over top of pears. Bake in a hot oven (425°F.) 20 to 25 minutes. Makes one 9-inch pie.

# Melody Pie

**1 cup chopped, cooked, pitted prunes**
**3½ cups chopped, peeled, cored apples**
**1 tablespoon grated orange rind**
**¼ cup orange juice**
**2 tablespoons flour**
**½ teaspoon salt**
**½ cup sugar**
**¼ cup prune juice**
**¼ cup molasses**
**1 9-inch unbaked pie shell**
**1 cup whipped cream**

Mix prunes, apples, orange rind and juice. Mix together dry ingredients, prune juice and molasses. Add to prune mixture and pour into pastry shell. Bake in a hot oven (450° F) 10 minutes; reduce temperature to 375° F and continue baking 50 minutes. Cool before serving. Garnish with whipped cream. Makes one 9-inch pie.

# Apricot Crumb Pie

**1 9-inch unbaked pie shell**
**4 cups sliced fresh apricots**
**½ cup sugar**
**¼ teaspoon nutmeg**
**¾ cup flour**
**¼ cup firmly packed brown sugar**
**⅓ cup butter**

Fill pie shell with apricots mixed with sugar and nutmeg. Mix flour and brown sugar together. Cut in butter until mixture is crumbly. Sprinkle over top of apricots. Bake in a hot oven (400° F) 45 minutes. Makes one 9-inch pie.

# Mock Mince Pie

½ lemon
1½ cups raisins
2 apples, unpeeled, cored and chopped
½ cup suet
¼ cup sugar
½ cup molasses
½ teaspoon salt
½ teaspoon cinnamon
¼ teaspoon allspice
¼ teaspoon ground cloves
⅓ cup boiling water
1 beef bouillon cube
1 recipe pastry

Put lemon and raisins through food chopper. Add remaining ingredients, except pastry. Heat to boiling and simmer, stirring occasionally, about 30 minutes. Cool slightly. Line a 9-inch pie plate with about two-thirds of the pastry. Pour filling into pie plate. Cover with lattice top. Bake in a hot oven (450° F) 10 minutes; reduce temperature to 350° F and continue baking 30 to 40 minutes. Makes one 9-inch pie.

# Winter Fruit Pie

1 recipe pastry
2 cups raw cranberries
2 cups peeled, chopped apples
½ cup water
½ cup sugar
2 tablespoons flour
½ cup corn syrup
Dash of salt
½ teaspoon grated orange rind

Line a 9-inch pie plate with half the pastry. Cook cranberries and apples in water until cranberries pop, about 5 minutes. Add sugar and blend. Cover and allow to cool. Add flour, corn syrup, salt and orange rind. Mix well and pour into pastry lined pie plate. Cover with lattice top. Bake in a hot oven (425° F) 35 to 45 minutes. Makes one 9-inch pie.

# Apple-Peach Pie

1 recipe pastry
2 cups sliced apples
1 cup sugar
¼ cup flour or 3 tablespoons tapioca
2 teaspoons cinnamon
⅛ teaspoon cloves
¼ teaspoon salt
2 cups sliced peaches

Line a 9-inch pie plate with half the pastry. Arrange apples in bottom of pie plate. Combine sugar, flour, cinnamon, cloves and salt. Sprinkle apples with half of this mixture. Top with sliced peaches and sprinkle with remaining dry ingredients. Cover with top crust. Bake in a hot oven (425° F) 10 minutes; reduce heat to 375° F and continue baking 20 to 30 minutes or until apples are done. Makes one 9-inch pie.

# Fresh Apricot Pie

1 recipe pastry
⅔ cup sugar
1 cup pineapple juice
1½ dozen fresh apricots, pitted and halved
2 teaspoons cornstarch
½ teaspoon salt
2 tablespoons margarine
½ teaspoon vanilla

Line a 9-inch pie plate with half the pastry. Combine sugar and pineapple juice and boil 1 minute. Simmer apricots, a few at a time, until just tender. Lift apricots carefully from juice and arrange in pie shell. Mix cornstarch with a little cold water; add to juice and cook until thickened. Add salt, margarine and vanilla and pour over apricots. Cover with lattice top. Bake in a hot oven (450° F) 10 minutes; reduce heat to 350° F and bake about 20 minutes. Makes one 9-inch pie.

Corn Products Company

# Cherry Almond Pie

1 recipe pastry
4 cups fresh sour cherries
¾ cup sugar
2 tablespoons flour or 1½ tablespoons quick-cooking tapioca
⅛ teaspoon salt
2 tablespoons butter or margarine
¼ cup blanched slivered almonds

Line a 9-inch pie plate with half the pastry. Wash, pit and drain cherries. Combine with sugar, flour and salt. Pour into lined pie plate. Dot top with butter. Cover with a lattice top. Sprinkle almonds over top of pie. Bake in a hot oven (400° F) about 45 minutes. Makes one 9-inch pie.

# Deep Dish Prune and Apricot Pies

1½ cups cooked prunes, drained
1½ cups cooked apricots, drained
1 tablespoon cornstarch or quick-cooking tapioca
¼ teaspoon salt
2 tablespoons lemon juice
1 tablespoon grated lemon rind
1½ tablespoons melted butter or margarine
1 cup corn syrup
1 recipe pastry

Pit and halve prunes. Mix with apricots and place in 6 individual deep pie dishes. Combine remaining ingredients except pastry; stir until blended. Pour mixture equally over fruit. Roll pastry ⅛ inch thick and cut in narrow strips. Arrange in a lattice pattern across top of pies. Make a rim with one long strip. Bake in a hot oven (450° F) 10 minutes; reduce heat to moderate 350° F and bake 35 minutes longer or until crust is brown. Makes 6 deep dish pies.

# Blueberry Pie

3 tablespoons quick-cooking tapioca
¾ to 1 cup sugar*
¼ teaspoon salt
⅛ teaspoon cinnamon
4 cups wild or cultivated fresh blueberries
1 to 2 tablespoons lemon juice
Pastry for two-crust 9-inch pie
1 tablespoon butter

Combine tapioca, sugar, salt, cinnamon, blueberries and lemon juice. Roll half the pastry ⅛ inch thick. Line a 9-inch pie pan and trim pastry at edge of rim. Roll remaining pastry ⅛ inch thick and cut several 2-inch slits or a fancy design near center. Fill pie shell with blueberry mixture. Dot with butter. Moisten edge of bottom crust. To adjust top crust, fold pastry in half or roll loosely on rolling pin; center on filling. Open slits with a knife. (Well-opened slits are important to permit escape of steam during baking.) Trim top crust, allowing it to extend ½ inch over rim. To seal, press top and bottom crusts together on rim. Then fold edge of top crust under bottom crust and flute. Bake in hot oven (425° F) 55 minutes, or until syrup boils with heavy bubbles that do not burst. Makes one 9-inch pie.

*If desired, ½ cup granulated sugar and ½ cup firmly packed brown sugar may be used.

# Eggnog Pear Pie

1 can (1 pound) pear halves
1 envelope unflavored gelatine
1½ cups eggnog
⅓ cup heavy cream
3 tablespoons brandy
8-inch graham cracker crumb shell
Nutmeg

Drain pear halves, reserving syrup. Soften gelatine in 1/3 cup pear syrup. Heat over hot water until dissolved. Stir in eggnog and chill until syrupy. Whip cream. Whip eggnog-gelatine mixture. Fold whipped cream and brandy into gelatine mixture. Slice three pear halves and place in bottom of pie shell. Pour eggnog mixture over sliced pears. Chill until firm. Slice remaining pear halves. Dip edges in nutmeg and use to garnish top of pie. Makes 6 servings.

## Strawberry Pie

**1 quart strawberries**
**½ cup sugar**
**1 tablespoon cornstarch**
**½ cup water**
**1 9-inch baked pie shell**
**1 cup heavy cream, whipped**

Wash and hull berries. Cut all large and perfect berries into 2 or 3 slices. Take remaining berries and mash. Combine sugar and cornstarch in a saucepan. Add water and crushed berries. Cook over low heat until clear and slightly thickened. Cool. Stir in sliced berries. Spread bottom of pie shell with half the whipped cream. Add half of berry mixture. Repeat layers. Chill in refrigerator before serving. Makes one 9-inch pie.

## Blueberry Cheese Pie

**1⅔ cups finely rolled graham cracker crumbs**
**¼ cup soft butter or margarine**
**¼ cup brown sugar, firmly packed**
**½ teaspoon cinnamon**
**1 envelope unflavored gelatine**
**½ cup sugar**
**¼ teaspoon salt**
**3 egg yolks**
**1 cup milk**
**1 package (8-ounces) cream cheese, softened**
**1 teaspoon vanilla**
**1 cup heavy cream**
**½ cup confectioner's sugar**
**½ cup dairy sour cream**
**1 teaspoon vanilla**
**1 cup fresh blueberries**

Combine graham cracker crumbs, butter, brown sugar and cinnamon. Pour into a 9-inch pie plate. Press crumbs firmly against bottom and sides of pie plate. Bake in a moderate oven (375°F.) 8 minutes. Cool. Combine gelatine, sugar and salt in top of a double boiler. Beat yolks. Beat in milk. Stir into dry ingredients in top of double boiler. Cook over boiling water, until mixture begins to thicken, about 15 minutes. Slowly add cream cheese and vanilla. Stir until well blended. Cool. Pour into chilled shell. Chill until firm. Whip cream and confectioners' sugar together until it stands in stiff peaks. Continue beating while gradually adding sour cream and vanilla. Fold in blueberries. Spread over cheese filling. Chill thoroughly. Makes one 9-inch pie.

## Raspberry Pie

**1 pint red raspberries, divided**
**¾ cup water**
**½ cup sugar**
**1 tablespoon cornstarch**
**1½ teaspoons unflavored gelatine**
**2 tablespoons cold water**
**1 tablespoon lemon juice**
**1 9-inch cereal flake pie shell**
**1 cup whipped cream**

Cook one cup of raspberries with water for 5 minutes. Strain. Mix sugar and cornstarch; add hot raspberry juice and cook, stirring constantly, until thickened and clear. Soften gelatine in cold water. Dissolve in hot raspberry mixture. Cool until the consistency of unbeaten egg whites. Fold in remaining raspberries and lemon juice. Turn into pie shell. Chill in refrigerator until pie is firm enough to cut. Garnish with whipped cream before serving. Makes one 9-inch pie.

## Prune Pie

**2 cups cooked prunes**
**1 orange**
**½ cup brown sugar, firmly packed**
**¼ teaspoon salt**
**2 tablespoons cornstarch**
**1 cup liquid from prunes**
**2 tablespoons butter or margarine**
**1 8-inch baked pie shell**
**2 egg whites**
**¼ cup sugar**
**Few drops lemon flavoring**

Pit prunes and cut in half. Peel orange, removing white inner part completely, and dice orange. Combine sugar, salt and cornstarch; add prune liquid and bring to a boil, stirring constantly until thickened. Add prunes, orange and butter and continue cooking for 10 minutes, stirring occasionally. Pour into a baked pie shell. Beat egg whites until stiff but not dry. Add sugar and flavoring gradually, beating until mixture stands in peaks. Pile over pie filling. Bake in a hot oven (425° F) 5 to 10 minutes or until lightly browned. Makes one 8-inch pie.

National Biscuit Company

Corn Products Company

# Apple Raisin Crumb Pie

6 apples
¾ cup raisins
1 cup water
1 tablespoon flour
1 teaspoon cinnamon
½ teaspoon nutmeg
¼ teaspoon salt
1 cup sugar, divided
1 unbaked 9-inch pie shell
½ cup margarine, melted
1 cup quick oats
½ cup flour

Peel, core and slice apples. Add raisins and water and stew about 10 minutes. Mix flour, spices and 2 tablespoons of the sugar. Add to apples, stir until smooth, and bring to boil. Turn into pie shell. Combine remaining ingredients and sprinkle over top of apples. Bake in a hot oven (450° F) 10 minutes. Reduce heat to moderate 350° F and bake 40 to 45 minutes or until crumbs are brown and crisp. Makes one 9-inch pie.

# Cheese-Apple Pie

2½ cups sliced apples
1 cup brown sugar, divided
2 tablespoons flour
1 tablespoon cinnamon
½ teaspoon nutmeg
1 tablespoon lemon juice
⅔ cup flour
⅓ cup butter
⅔ cup grated American cheese

Combine apples, ½ cup sugar, 2 tablespoons flour, cinnamon, nutmeg and lemon juice. Place in deep dish pie pan. Mix remaining ½ cup sugar and 2/3 cup flour; cut in butter with 2 knives or pastry blender. Add cheese, toss lightly; sprinkle mixture over apples. Bake in hot oven (400°F.) for 45-50 minutes. Serve with wedges of cheese on top.

# Strawberry Bavarian Pie

1 cup brown sugar
2 cups rolled oats (quick or old fashioned, uncooked)
⅔ cup butter, melted
2 envelopes unflavored gelatine
½ cup cold water
2 eggs, separated
¼ cup water
¼ cup sugar
Few drops red food coloring
1 tablespoon lemon juice
2 cups crushed fresh strawberries
⅔ cup evaporated milk, chilled
Few Whole Strawberries

Combine brown sugar and oats. Add melted butter. Mix well. Reserve ½ cup of mixture for topping. Press remaining oats mixture onto the bottom and sides of a deep pie plate (9½ x 2 inches). Chill until firm in freezer or refrigerator.

Soften gelatine in ½ cup cold water. Beat together egg yolks, ¼ cup water and sugar. Add a few drops of red food coloring, if desired. Add softened gelatine. Place over low heat (may use double boiler). Stir frequently. Cook until gelatine is dissolved and mixture begins to thicken slightly. Remove from heat; add lemon juice. Cool until thickened; fold in strawberries.

Beat egg whites until stiff. Beat well-chilled evaporated milk until stiff. Fold strawberry mixture into egg whites, then into whipped milk. Pour into crumb-lined pie plate. Sprinkle edge with the ½ cup remaining crumbs. Chill until firm. Garnish with whole strawberries.

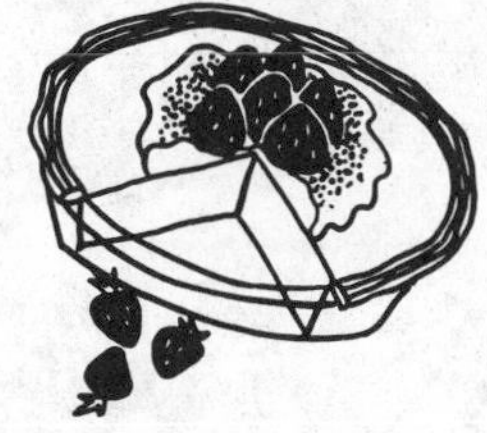

# Coffee Coconut Prune Pie

1 cup hot strong coffee
1 can (3½ ounces) flaked coconut
3 tablespoons soft butter
½ pound plumped, pitted chopped prunes, reserve a few whole prunes for garnish
⅓ cup prune juice
2 tablespoons grated orange rind
3 eggs
½ cup brown sugar, firmly packed
¼ cup granulated sugar
1 envelope unflavored gelatine
½ teaspoon salt
1 package (3-ounces) cream cheese, softened
1 cup dairy sour cream
Whipped cream
Maraschino cherries

Combine coffee and coconut. Let stand 30 minutes. Drain coconut and spread between pieces of paper toweling and pat dry. Spread softened butter on the bottom and sides of a 9-inch pie plate. Turn coconut into pie plate and pat out to cover bottom and sides of plate. Bake in a moderate oven (350°F.) 10 minutes. Cool. In a saucepan combine chopped prunes, prune juice and orange rind. Bring to a boil and remove from heat. Beat together eggs, brown sugar, granulated sugar, gelatine and salt. Mix in cheese and sour cream and beat until smooth. Stir into prune mixture and cook over moderate heat, stirring constantly, until mixture is smooth and thickened. Cool slightly. Pour mixture into prepared pie shell and chill until firm. Garnish with reserved whole prunes, whipped cream and cherries. Makes one 9-inch pie.

Washington Apricots

# Tangy Apricot Pie

1 pastry recipe
4 cups sliced fresh apricots
¼ cup orange juice
2 teaspoons grated orange rind
½ teaspoon nutmeg
1¼ cups sugar
2½ teaspoons quick-cooking tapioca

Line a 9-inch pie plate with half the pastry. Combine remaining ingredients and pour into pie shell. Cover with top crust. Bake in a hot oven (425°F.) 40 minutes. Makes one 9-inch pie.

# Cherry Cheese Pie

1 No. 2 can sour red cherries
1 envelope unflavored gelatine
½ cup sugar
1 teaspoon grated lemon rind
1 3-ounce package cream cheese
1 tablespoon milk
1 9-inch baked pie shell

Drain cherries. To the juice add enough water to make 1½ cups of liquid. Place in a saucepan with the gelatine, sugar and lemon rind. Bring almost to a boil over very low heat. Cool until the consistency of unbeaten egg white. Mix cream cheese and milk together until smooth. Spread on the bottom of the pie shell. Spread cherries over cheese. Pour syrup over cherries. Chill in the refrigerator until firm. Makes one 9-inch pie.

United Fresh Fruit and Vegetable Association

# Marmalade Mince Pie

1 reçipe pastry
2 cups mincemeat
½ cup orange marmalade
2 tablespoons flour
1 tablespoon lemon juice

Line a 9-inch pie plate with half the pastry. Combine mincemeat, marmalade, flour and lemon juice. Turn into pie plate. Cover with top crust. Bake in a hot oven (425° F) 35 to 40 minutes. Makes one 9-inch pie.

# Banana-Apple Pie

2 cups sliced bananas
1 9-inch baked pie shell
1 tablespoon lemon juice
2 cups sweetened applesauce
1 cup heavy cream, whipped and sweetened

Place sliced bananas on bottom of baked pie shell. Sprinkle with lemon juice. Pour applesauce over bananas and top with whipped cream. Chill well. Makes one 9-inch pie.

# Sweet Red Cherry Pie

1 recipe pastry
1½ pounds large sweet cherries
⅔ cup sugar
1 tablespoon lemon juice
1 teaspoon grated lemon rind
⅛ teaspoon allspice
¼ teaspoon salt
3 tablespoons flour or 2½ tablespoons quick-cooking tapioca

Line a 9-inch pie plate with half the pastry. Remove stones from cherries with a sharp knife. Toss cherries with remaining ingredients. Pour into pie plate. Cover with lattice top. Bake in a hot oven (425° F) 30 minutes; reduce temperature to moderate 350° F and continue baking until fruit is tender, about 15 minutes. Makes one 9-inch pie.

# Raisin Nut Pie

1 recipe pastry
¾ cup water
2 cups raisins
1 tablespoon vinegar
1 tablespoon butter or margarine
½ cup chopped nuts
⅔ cup sugar
1 tablespoon flour
¼ teaspoon salt

Line an 8-inch pie plate with one-half the pastry. Combine water and raisins and simmer until about ¼ of the liquid remains. Add vinegar, butter and nuts. Cool slightly. Combine sugar, flour and salt. Stir into raisin nut mixture. Pour into pastry lined pie plate. Cover with top crust. Bake in a very hot oven (450° F) 10 minutes; reduce heat to moderate F and bake for 25 minutes. Serve slightly warm. Makes 8-inch pie.

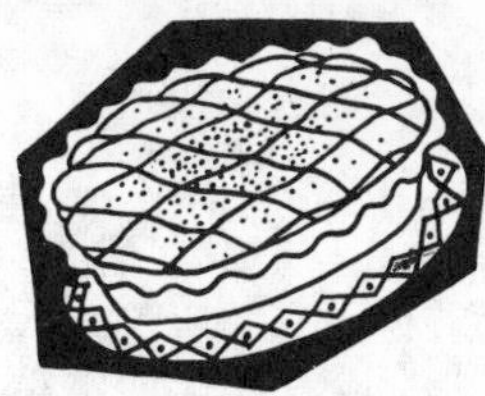

# Citrus Prune Pie

3 cups cooked, pitted prunes
1 cup prune juice
4 tablespoons lemon juice
½ cup corn syrup
2 tablespoons cornstarch
⅛ teaspoon salt
1 tablespoon water
1 8-inch baked pie shell
Orange sections

Combine prunes, juices and corn syrup in saucepan. Stir in cornstarch, salt and water. Cook over low heat until thickened, about 15 minutes, stirring occasionally. Cool. Pour into baked pie shell and garnish with orange sections. Makes one 8-inch pie.

# Apple Sunday Pie

1 cup chocolate wafer crumbs
⅔ cup finely chopped pecans
¼ cup softened (or melted) butter or margarine
1 quart vanilla ice cream
1½ cups shredded fresh, peeled apple
½ cup pecan halves
Unpeeled apple slices for garnish
½ pint heavy cream, whipped

Mix wafer crumbs, pecans and butter or margarine together until crumbly. Press onto bottom and sides of a 9-inch pie plate. Bake in moderate oven (375°F.) about 7 minutes. Chill thoroughly until well set. Soften ice cream and combine with shredded apple. Spread apple-ice cream mixture into pie shell. Sprinkle with pecans. Place in freezer or keep thoroughly chilled until ready to serve; then garnish with thin, unpeeled apple slices. Before serving, top the pie with whipped cream and then garnish with the apple slices if you wish.

Blueberry Institute

## Blueberry Meringue Pie

1½ cups fresh cultivated blueberries
3 cups cornflakes (about 1½ cups crumbs)
2 tablespoons sugar
4 tablespoons butter
4 egg whites
¾ cup sugar
½ teaspoon almond extract
¼ teaspoon salt
½ teaspoon cream of tartar

Rinse fresh cultivated blueberries and spread between layers of absorbent towels to dry thoroughly. Crush cornflakes to make 1½ cups of crumbs. Mix crumbs with 2 tablespoons sugar. Let butter soften to room temperature and mix cornflake crumbs and butter together thoroughly. Use crumb mixture to line a 9-inch pie plate, pressing crumbs with back of spoon to get an even layer on bottom and sides of pie plate. Bake shell in moderate oven (375°F.) for 10 minutes. Let cool. Beat egg whites until stiff. Gradually add sugar in very small amounts, beating continuously after each addition. Alternately add almond extract, salt and cream of tartar, beating until thick and glossy. Carefully fold in dried blueberries, being careful not to break the berries. Pile blueberry meringue into baked crumb crust. With back of wet tablespoon, make swirl designs in meringue. Bake at 300°F. for about 15 minutes or just until top browns slightly. Let cool before cutting. Makes 8 servings.

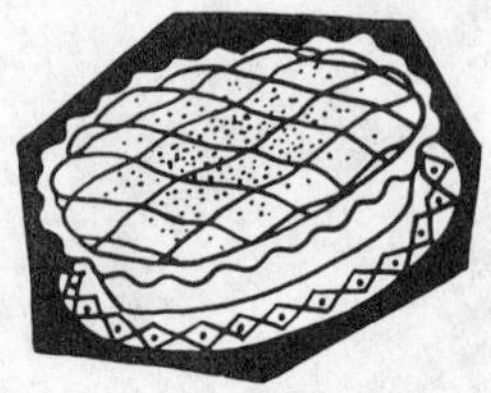

# Chiffon Pies

**From Chocolate Imperial to Strawberry Fluff, you can make 'em and bake 'em 'till you've had enough!**

## Coffee Rum Chiffon Pie

1 9-inch chocolate crumb crust
1 envelope unflavored gelatine
3 tablespoons rum
⅓ cup sugar
¼ teaspoon salt
⅛ teaspoon cinnamon
3 egg yolks, beaten
1 cup strong cold coffee
3 egg whites
½ teaspoon vanilla
⅓ cup sugar

In the top of a double boiler away from the heat, mix the gelatine and rum. Let stand 5 minutes. Add the first ⅓ cup sugar, salt, cinnamon and egg yolks. Gradually add the coffee, a little at a time, beating briskly after each addition. When thoroughly blended, place over hot water and cook, stirring constantly, until the mixture makes a readily visible film on the back of a silver spoon. Remove from heat and chill thoroughly. Beat egg whites until stiff. Add vanilla and the second ⅓ cup sugar, gradually, beating after each addition. Fold egg whites into the coffee mixture. Pour into the crumb shell and chill until firm. Garnish with whipped cream and shaved chocolate.

Knox Gelatine

# Chocolate Imperial Pie

1 envelope unflavored gelatine
¼ cup cold water
3 squares unsweetened chocolate
¼ teaspoon salt
2 egg whites
¼ cup sugar
¾ cup dark corn syrup
½ teaspoon vanilla
1 9-inch baked pie shell

Soften gelatine in cold water. Dissolve over boiling water. Melt chocolate over hot water. Add salt to egg whites and beat until mixture forms soft peaks. Gradually add sugar, beating until smooth and glossy. Continue beating and add corn syrup gradually. Fold in vanilla, cooled gelatine and cooled chocolate. Turn into pie shell. Chill for 3 hours or until firm. If desired, garnish with whipped cream and grated chocolate. Makes one 9-inch pie.

# Strawberry Chiffon Pie

1 envelope unflavored gelatine
2 tablespoons cold water
2 egg yolks
¾ cup white corn syrup
1 cup crushed strawberries
1 tablespoon lemon juice
2 egg whites
⅛ teaspoon salt
2 tablespoons sugar
¾ cup heavy cream, whipped
1 9-inch baked pie shell

Soften gelatine in cold water. Beat egg yolks slightly in top of a double boiler. Add corn syrup. Cook over boiling water about 5 minutes, stirring constantly. Add gelatine and stir until dissolved. Cool slightly. Combine strawberries and lemon juice and add to gelatine mixture. Chill until slightly thickened. Beat egg whites and salt until stiff but not dry; gradually beat in sugar. Fold in strawberry mixture; then fold in whipped cream. Pile into baked pie shell. Chill thoroughly. Makes one 9-inch pie.

# Peppermint Chiffon Pie

1 envelope unflavored gelatine
¼ cup water
3 egg whites
½ cup sugar
¼ teaspoon peppermint flavoring
¼ cup chopped almonds
½ cup crushed peppermint stick candy
1 cup heavy cream, whipped
1 9-inch chocolate cookie crust

Soften gelatine in cold water; then dissolve over hot water. Beat egg whites until stiff. Gradually beat in sugar. Add gelatine, flavoring, almonds and candy. Fold in whipped cream. Pour into cookie crust and chill until firm. Makes one 9-inch pie.

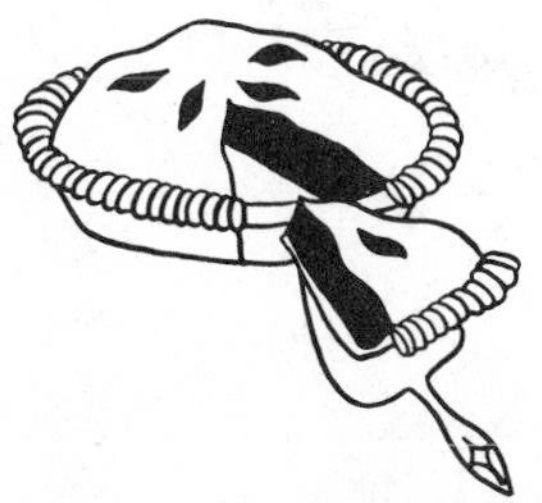

# Sherry Chiffon Pie

1 envelope unflavored gelatine
¼ cup cold water
½ cup boiling water
½ cup sugar
½ cup sherry
½ cup evaporated milk, chilled icy cold
2 tablespoons lemon juice
1 9-inch baked crumb crust

Soften gelatine in cold water. Add boiling water and stir until completely dissolved. Stir in sugar and sherry. Cool until the consistency of unbeaten egg whites. Whip milk until stiff. Fold in lemon juice and gelatine mixture. Pour into crust and chill until firm. Makes one 9-inch pie.

# Florida Chiffon Pie

1 envelope unflavored gelatine
1¼ cups orange juice
⅔ cup sugar
1 tablespoon flour
¼ teaspoon salt
1 tablespoon grated orange rind
2 tablespoons lime juice
1 cup heavy cream, whipped
1 9-inch chocolate cookie crumb crust or
9 baked tart shells

Combine gelatine, orange juice, sugar, flour and salt. Place over medium heat; stir constantly until gelatine is dissolved and mixture is slightly thickened. Remove from heat; add orange rind, and lime juice. Chill until mixture is slightly thicker than the consistency of unbeaten egg white. Fold into whipped cream. Turn into pie crust or tart shells and chill until firm. If desired, garnish with whipped cream, orange sections and shaved chocolate. Makes one 9-inch pie.

# Lime Chiffon Pie

1 package lime-flavored gelatin
⅛ teaspoon salt
2 tablespoons sugar
1 cup hot water
½ cup cold water
2 to 3 tablespoons lime juice
1½ teaspoons grated lime rind
⅓ cup cream, whipped
1 9-inch baked quick coconut pie crust, cooled

Dissolve gelatin, salt and sugar in *hot* water. Add cold water, lime juice and grated lime rind. Chill until slightly thickened. Then place in bowl of ice and water and whip with rotary beater until fluffy and thick like whipped cream. Fold in whipped cream. Turn into pie shell and chill until firm. Garnish with additional whipped cream, if desired. Makes one 9-inch pie.

Best Foods, Inc.

# Chocolate Bavarian Pie

**1 envelope unflavored gelatine**
**¼ cup cold water**
**1 cup fortified chocolate flavored syrup**
**1 pint heavy cream**
**½ teaspoon vanilla**
**1 baked 9-inch pastry shell**

Soften gelatine in cold water. Heat chocolate syrup in a medium saucepan to a full boil. Remove from heat. Add softened gelatine and stir until gelatine is completely dissolved. Chill until mixture is thick and syrupy, stirring once or twice while chilling. Beat cream until stiff and fold into slightly thickened chocolate-gelatine mixture. Fold in vanilla. Pile into baked pastry shell and chill until firm.

**Note:** Rum or rum flavoring may be substituted for the vanilla. Use 1 teaspoon rum extract or 1 to 2 tablespoons rum.

# Lemon Chiffon Pie

**1 envelope unflavored gelatine**
**¼ cup cold water**
**1 cup sugar, divided**
**½ cup lemon juice**
**½ teaspoon salt**
**4 egg yolks, beaten**
**1 teaspoon grated lemon rind**
**4 egg whites**
**1 8-inch baked pie shell**
**½ cup heavy cream, whipped**

Soften gelatine in cold water. Add ½ cup of the sugar, lemon juice and salt to beaten egg yolks in top of double boiler; cook over boiling water until thick. Add lemon rind and softened gelatine. Stir until gelatine is dissolved. Cool. Beat egg whites until stiff. Gradually beat in sugar until mixture is smooth and glossy. Fold egg whites into gelatine mixture. Pour into baked pie shell. Chill until firm. Just before serving garnish with whipped cream. Makes one 8-inch pie.

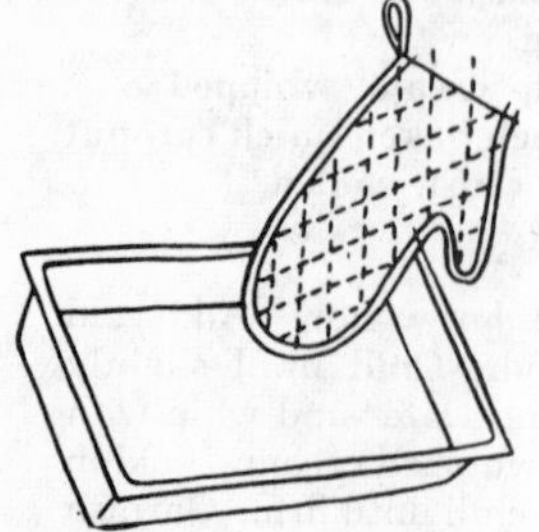

# Fresh Fruit Chiffon Pie

**¼ cup sugar**
**1 tablespoon lemon juice**
**1 pint prepared fresh strawberries, sliced**
**1 envelope unflavored gelatine**
**¼ cup cold water**
**¼ teaspoon salt**
**Water to make ½ cup liquid**
**3 egg whites**
**½ cup light corn syrup**
**1 (9-inch) baked pastry shell**

Sprinkle 2 tablespoons of the sugar and the lemon juice over strawberries; let stand 30 minutes. Soften gelatine in ¼ cup cold water. Mix together the remaining sugar and salt in a saucepan. Drain juice from strawberries and add water to make ½ cup liquid; add to sugar and stir over low heat, add softened gelatine and stir until dissolved. Add strawberries. Chill until the consistency of unbeaten egg white.

*Caution:* Do not let gelatine mixture become too stiff. Beat egg whites until stiff, not dry. Gradually beat in the corn syrup. Fold in chilled gelatine mixture. Chill until thick enough to pile up. Pile lightly into baked pastry shell and swirl gently with a spatula.

# Coconut Pie

**1 envelope unflavored gelatine**
**½ cup sugar**
**¼ teaspoon salt**
**3 eggs, separated**
**1¼ cups milk**
**½ teaspoon almond flavoring**
**¾ cup flaked coconut, divided**
**1 9-inch graham cracker crust**
**¼ cup chopped toasted almonds**

Combine gelatine, sugar and salt in top of a double boiler. Stir in beaten egg yolks and milk. Cook over hot water, stirring constantly, until mixture coats a silver spoon. Chill until mixture is consistency of unbeaten egg whites. Add flavoring and ½ cup of the coconut. Beat egg whites until stiff and fold into gelatine mixture. Pour gelatine mixture into pie crust. Chill until firm. Combine remaining coconut and almonds and sprinkle over pie just before serving. Makes one 9-inch pie.

# Toffee Chiffon Pie

**1 envelope unflavored gelatine**
**⅔ cup sugar, divided**
**⅛ teaspoon salt**
**2 eggs, separated**
**⅓ cup molasses**
**1 cup milk**
**½ cup heavy cream, whipped**
**1 9-inch baked pie shell**

Combine gelatine, ⅓ cup of the sugar and salt in top of double boiler. Add beaten egg yolks and molasses and milk. Cook over hot water until mixture coats a silver spoon. Cool until mixture is the consistency of unbeaten egg whites. Beat egg whites until stiff. Beat in remaining ⅓ cup of sugar. Fold in gelatine mixture. Fold in whipped cream. Pour into pie shell. Chill until firm. Makes one 9-inch pie.

Best Foods, Inc.

Diamond Walnuts

# Cranberry Chiffon Pie

1½ envelopes unflavored gelatine
2 tablespoons water
1 cup sugar, divided
1 cup canned whole cranberry sauce
2 egg whites
¼ teaspoon cream of tartar
⅛ teaspoon salt
1 cup heavy cream
1 baked Spicy Walnut Meringue Shell

Soften gelatine in water. Add 2/3 cup of the sugar and cranberry sauce. Heat mixture to boiling, stirring constantly. Remove and chill until mixture begins to thicken. Beat egg whites to soft peaks with cream of tartar and salt. Beat in remaining 1/3 cup sugar to form meringue. Beat cream stiff. Fold meringue and cream into cranberry filling. Turn into shell. Chill until firm. Garnish with walnut halves and whole cranberries if desired. Makes 6 to 8 servings.

# Strawberry Gelatin Pie

1½ cups strawberries
½ cup sugar, divided
1 package strawberry-flavored gelatin
1 cup hot water
3 eggs, separated
¼ teaspoon salt
1 9-inch baked crumb pie shell
½ cup heavy cream, whipped

Wash and hull berries. Place in a bowl and cut through with a knife several times. Sprinkle ¼ cup of the sugar over berries and let stand 30 minutes. Dissolve gelatin in hot water. Beat egg yolks slightly in top of a double boiler. Drain ¼ cup juice from strawberries and combine with egg yolks. Cook over hot water, stirring constantly, until thickened. Remove from heat and stir in gelatin. Chill until slightly thickened. Fold in strawberries. Beat egg whites until stiff. Gradually beat in salt and ¼ cup of sugar. Fold into gelatin mixture. Pour into graham cracker pie shell. Chill until firm. Garnish with whipped cream before serving. Makes one 9-inch pie.

# Chocolate Nesselrode Pie

3 eggs, separated
1½ cups milk
¼ teaspoon salt
⅔ cup sugar, divided
1 envelope unflavored gelatine
2 tablespoons margarine
2 tablespoons finely chopped citron
3 tablespoons chopped almonds
¼ cup chopped maraschino cherries
1 teaspoon maraschino cherry juice
2 tablespoons rum flavoring
½ cup heavy cream, whipped
1 9-inch baked pie shell
Shaved sweet chocolate

Combine slightly beaten egg yolks, milk, salt, ⅓ cup of the sugar and gelatine in the top of a double boiler. Cook over hot water, stirring constantly, until mixture coats a silver spoon. Remove from heat and stir in margarine. Chill until mixture begins to thicken. Fold in citron, almonds, cherries, cherry juice and rum flavoring. Beat egg whites until stiff; beat in remaining ⅓ cup of the sugar. Fold into custard mixture. Fold in whipped cream. Pour into a baked pie shell. Chill until firm. Before serving sprinkle chocolate over top of pie. Makes one 9-inch pie.

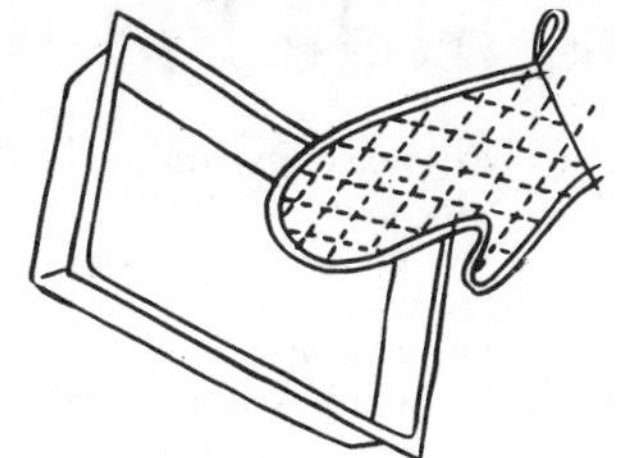

# Butterscotch Fluff Pie

1 cup sifted all-purpose flour
½ teaspoon salt
⅓ cup shortening
½ cup rolled oats (quick or old fashioned, uncooked)
4 to 5 tablespoons cold water
1 envelope unflavored gelatine
¼ cup cold water
½ teaspoon salt
1½ cups milk
2 eggs, separated
1 package (6-ounces) butterscotch pieces
½ cup heavy cream
2 tablespoons sugar
Toasted coconut

Sift together flour and salt into bowl. Cut in shortening until mixture resembles coarse crumbs; stir in oats. Add water, a tablespoon at a time, mixing with a fork until pastry can be formed into a ball. Turn out on lightly floured board or canvas. Roll out to form 13-inch circle. Fit pastry loosely into 9-inch pie plate. Turn edge under and flute. Prick bottom and sides with a fork. Bake in hot oven (425°F.) 12 to 15 minutes. Cool.

Soften gelatine in cold water. Place salt, milk, egg yolks and butterscotch pieces in top of double boiler. Cook over hot water until butterscotch pieces are melted and mixture thickens, stirring frequently. Add softened gelatine and stir until dissolved. Cool until mixture begins to thicken. Beat egg whites until stiff and glossy. Fold cooled gelatine mixture into egg whites. Whip cream until frothy; gradually add sugar, whipping until stiff. Fold into butterscotch mixture. Pour into pie crust; chill until set. Decorate with toasted coconut. Makes one 9-inch pie.

The Quaker Oats Company

# Eggnog Nesselrode Pie

2 envelopes unflavored gelatine
¼ cup sugar
1 quart commercially prepared eggnog
2 teaspoons rum flavoring
1 cup heavy cream, whipped
⅓ cup chopped maraschino cherries
⅓ cup chopped nuts
1 10-inch baked pie shell

Combine gelatine and sugar in saucepan. Stir in 1 cup of the cold eggnog. Place over low heat, stirring constantly until gelatine and sugar are dissolved, about 3-5 minutes. Remove from heat; stir in rum flavoring and remaining eggnog. Chill until slightly thicker than the consistency of unbeaten egg white. Whip gelatine mixture until light and fluffy; fold in whipped cream. Fold in maraschino cherries and nuts. Turn into baked pie shell; chill until firm. If desired, garnish with additional whipped cream, pieces of maraschino cherry and citron "holly" leaves. Makes one 10-inch pie.

Knox Gelatine

# Pumpkin Chiffon Pie

1 envelope unflavored gelatine
¼ cup cold water
1½ cups cooked or canned strained pumpkin
1 tablespoon grated lemon rind
½ cup brown sugar, firmly packed
3 eggs, separated
1 tablespoon cinnamon
½ teaspoon ginger
½ teaspoon mace
¼ teaspoon allspice
½ teaspoon salt
½ cup evaporated milk
2 tablespoons margarine
⅓ cup granulated sugar
1 9-inch baked pie shell

Soften gelatine in cold water. Combine remaining ingredients, except egg whites, granulated sugar and pie shell in top of a double boiler. Cook over boiling water about 10 minutes. Add gelatine and stir until dissolved. Remove from heat and chill until mixture begins to set. Beat egg whites until stiff; beat sugar in gradually. Fold into pumpkin mixture and pour into pie shell. Chill until firm. Just before serving, top with whipped cream. Makes one 9-inch pie.

# Peach Chiffon Pie

1 envelope unflavored gelatine
⅓ cup sugar
⅛ teaspoon salt
1 tablespoon flour
1 No. 2½ can peach slices
3 tablespoons lemon juice
½ teaspoon grated lemon rind
1 cup evaporated milk, chilled
1 10-inch baked pie shell or
1 10-inch chocolate cookie crust

Combine in a small saucepan gelatine, sugar, salt and flour. Drain peaches; add 1½ cups of the peach syrup to sugar mixture. Cook, stirring constantly, until mixture thickens. Remove from heat and add lemon juice and rind. Chill until mixture is consistency of unbeaten egg whites. Beat with a rotary beater until fluffy. Whip chilled evaporated milk until it is the consistency of whipped cream. Fold the gelatine mixture into the whipped milk. Reserve eleven peach slices to garnish top of pie; fold remaining peach slices into gelatine mixture. Pour custard into pie shell. Chill until firm. Garnish top of pie with remaining peach slices. Makes one 10-inch pie.

# Nesselrode Pie

1 envelope unflavored gelatine
1½ cups milk, divided
3 eggs, separated
⅓ cup mixed candied fruit
2 tablespoons ground almonds
1 cup crushed macaroons
⅛ teaspoon salt
2 tablespoons brandy flavoring
1 teaspoon vanilla
⅓ cup sugar
1 9-inch baked pie shell

Soften gelatine in ¼ cup of the milk. Scald remaining milk in top of double boiler. Beat egg yolks slightly. Stir in hot milk, a little at a time; return to double boiler and add gelatine mixture. Cook over hot water, stirring occasionally, until mixture coats a silver spoon. Stir in candied fruit, almonds, macaroons, salt and flavorings. Cool mixture until thickened but not set. Beat egg whites until stiff and gradually beat in sugar until mixture is thick. Fold in gelatine mixture. Pour into pie shell and chill until firm. Makes one 9-inch pie.

# Banana Bavarian Pie

½ cup melted butter or margarine
2 cups crushed chocolate cookie crumbs
1 envelope unflavored gelatine
¼ cup cold water
2 egg whites
1½ cups mashed bananas
3 tablespoons lemon juice
½ cup sugar
⅛ teaspoon salt
¾ cup heavy cream, whipped

Combine butter and cookie crumbs. Reserve ⅓ cup of this mixture. Press remaining cookie mixture into bottom and sides of a 9-inch pie pan. Soften gelatine in cold water; dissolve over hot water. Beat egg whites until stiff; add gelatine slowly, beating until mixture stands in peaks. Combine bananas, lemon juice, sugar and salt. Fold in egg whites and whipped cream. Pour mixture into chocolate cookie crust. Sprinkle reserved crumbs over top of pie. Chill until firm. Makes one 9-inch pie.

# Brazil Nut Black Bottom Pie

1½ cups ground Brazil nuts
3 tablespoons sugar
1 envelope unflavored gelatine
¼ cup cold water
⅔ cup sugar, divided
1 tablespoon cornstarch
4 eggs, separated
2 cups milk, scalded
1 package semi-sweet chocolate pieces
1 teaspoon vanilla
¼ teaspoon salt

Mix together Brazil nuts and 3 tablespoons sugar. Press this mixture with the back of a tablespoon against the bottom and sides of a 10-inch pie plate. Bake in a hot oven (400° F) 8 minutes, or until lightly browned. Cool. Soften gelatine in cold water. Combine ⅓ cup of the sugar and cornstarch. Beat egg yolks slightly; slowly add scalded milk. Stir in sugar mixture. Cook in double boiler, stirring constantly, until mixture is slightly thickened. To 1 cup custard, add semi-sweet chocolate pieces. Stir until chocolate is melted; set aside. To remaining custard, add softened gelatine. Stir until gelatine is dissolved, add vanilla. Cool. Beat egg whites until stiff; gradually beat in salt and remaining ⅓ cup of sugar. Fold in custard-gelatine mixture. Turn chocolate mixture into Brazil nut pie shell. Spoon gelatine mixture over chocolate layer and chill until firm. Garnish with whipped cream, maraschino cherries and Brazil nut slices. Makes one 10-inch pie.

# No-Bake Cheese Pie

1 envelope unflavored gelatine
½ cup sugar
⅛ teaspoon salt
1 cup milk
2 packages (8-ounces each) cream cheese
1 teaspoon lemon rind
1 tablespoon lemon juice
1 cup heavy cream, whipped
1 9-inch graham cracker crumb crust

Mix together gelatine, sugar and salt in saucepan. Stir in milk. Place over low heat, stirring constantly, until gelatine is dissolved, about 3 minutes. Remove from heat. Cool.

Beat cream cheese, lemon rind and lemon juice together on high speed of electric mixer. Gradually beat in gelatine mixture. Chill until mixture mounds, about 15 minutes. Fold in whipped cream. Turn into crumb shell. Chill until firm. If desired, garnish with graham cracker crumbs. Makes one 9-inch pie.

Knox Gelatine

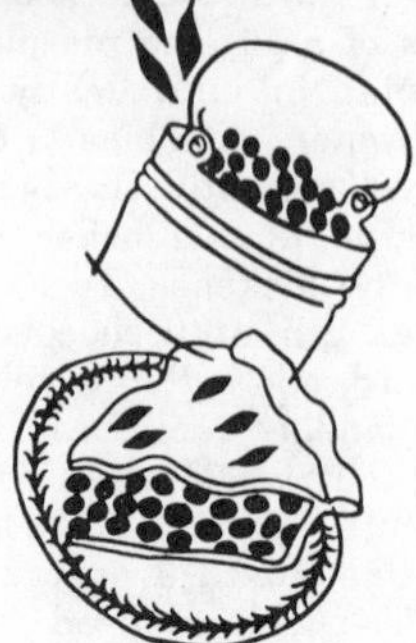

# White Christmas Pie

1 envelope unflavored gelatine
1 cup sugar, divided
¼ cup flour
½ teaspoon salt
1¾ cups milk
¾ teaspoon vanilla
¼ teaspoon almond extract
½ cup heavy cream, whipped
3 egg whites
1 cup moist shredded coconut
1 9-inch baked pie shell

Combine gelatine, ½ cup of the sugar, flour and salt in a saucepan. Stir in milk. Cook over low heat, stirring until it comes to a full boil. Remove from heat. Cool. When partially set, beat with a rotary beater until smooth. Blend in vanilla and almond extract. Fold in cream. Beat egg whites until foamy. Gradually beat in remaining sugar until mixture stands in stiff peaks. Fold into gelatine mixture. Fold in coconut. Pile into pie shell. Chill until set. Makes one 9-inch pie.

# Grape Chiffon Pie

1 envelope unflavored gelatine
¼ cup cold water
1 cup grape juice
¼ cup sugar
1 tablespoon lemon juice
⅛ teaspoon salt
1 cup heavy cream, whipped
1 8-inch graham cracker crust

Soften gelatine in cold water; dissolve over hot water. Combine grape juice, sugar, lemon juice and salt and stir until sugar is dissolved. Add gelatine and stir well. Chill until mixture is the consistency of unbeaten egg whites. Fold in whipped cream. Pour into cracker crust. Chill until firm. Makes one 8-inch pie.

# Cream Pies

**From pie in the sky to pie in your eye, these are the cream of the crop, Pop, you'll eat 'em 'till you drop!**

## Chocolate Polka Dot Pie

**1 envelope unflavored gelatine**
**⅔ cup sugar, divided**
**1 tablespoon cornstarch**
**2¼ cups milk**
**3 eggs, separated**
**1 package semi-sweet chocolate**
**1 teaspoon vanilla**
**¼ teaspoon salt**
**½ cup heavy cream, whipped**
**1 10-inch baked pie shell**

Combine gelatine, ⅓ cup of the sugar and cornstarch in top of double boiler. Stir in milk. Place over boiling water and stir until gelatine and sugar are dissolved. Beat egg yolks slightly; add small amount of hot mixture, return to double boiler and cook, stirring constantly, until thickened. To 1 cup of the gelatine mixture add ¾ package semi-sweet chocolate morsels; stir until chocolate is melted; set aside. To remaining custard add vanilla. Chill until the consistency of unbeaten egg white. Beat egg whites until stiff; gradually beat in salt and remaining ⅓ cup of sugar. Fold into vanilla-gelatine mixture. Fold in whipped cream. Pour chocolate mixture into baked pie shell. Spoon vanilla custard mixture over chocolate layer; chill until firm. Place remaining chocolate morsels upside down over pie to resemble polka dots. Makes one 10-inch pie.

## Peanut Brittle Pie

**2 cups milk, scalded**
**3 tablespoons cornstarch**
**¼ cup sugar**
**¼ teaspoon salt**
**1 egg, slightly beaten**
**⅔ cup finely crushed peanut brittle, divided**
**1 teaspoon vanilla**
**1 9-inch baked graham cracker pie shell**

Stir milk into combined cornstarch, sugar, salt and egg. Add ⅓ cup peanut brittle. Cook over hot water until thick, stirring frequently. Cool and add vanilla. Pour into pie shell. Sprinkle remaining peanut brittle over top of pie and chill well before serving. Makes one 9-inch pie

## Lemon Meringue Pie

**1 package lemon pudding and pie filling mix**
**½ cup sugar**
**2 cups water**
**2 egg yolks**
**1 8- or 9-inch baked pie shell**
**2 egg whites**
**4 tablespoons sugar**

Combine pie filling mix, ½ cup sugar and ¼ cup of the water in saucepan. Add egg yolks and blend well. Then add remaining 1¾ cups water. Cook and stir until mixture comes to a *full* boil and is thickened—about 5 minutes. Remove from heat. Cool only about 5 minutes, stirring once or twice. Pour into pie shell.

Beat egg whites until foamy throughout. Add 4 tablespoons sugar, 2 tablespoons at a time, beating after each addition until sugar is blended. Then continue beating until meringue will stand in peaks. Spread over pie filling. Bake in hot oven (425° F) 5 to 10 minutes, or until meringue is delicately browned. Makes one 8- or 9-inch pie.

Jell-o Pudding and Pie Filling

# Grape Cream Pie

½ cup sugar
6 tablespoons cornstarch
¼ teaspoon salt
1 tablespoon grated lemon rind
½ teaspoon cinnamon
2½ cups grape juice
1 tablespoon lemon juice
1 9-inch baked pie shell
½ cup heavy cream, whipped

Combine sugar, cornstarch, salt, lemon rind and cinnamon in a saucepan. Stir in grape juice and cook, over low heat, stirring constantly until thick. Add lemon juice. Cool and chill until very thick. Spoon mixture into pie shell and chill. Top with whipped cream. Makes one 9-inch pie.

# Peach Cream Pie

1 package vanilla pudding mix
1¾ cups milk
1 egg, separated
1 tablespoon margarine
½ teaspoon almond extract
1 9-inch baked pie shell
8 peach halves
2 tablespoons sugar
Slivered almonds

Combine pudding mix, milk and egg yolk and cook according to directions on package. Stir in margarine and almond extract. Cool 5 minutes, stirring occasionally. Pour into pie shell. Slice 2 peach halves and arrange slices on top of pie. Arrange 6 peach halves on top of filling. Beat egg whites until stiff. Slowly beat in sugar until mixture is smooth and glossy. Fill centers of peach halves with a spoonful of the egg white mixture. Stick almond slivers in the egg white. Bake in a hot oven (425° F) about 5 minutes or until delicately browned. Makes one 9-inch pie.

# Lemon Fluff Pie

4 eggs, separated
1⅓ cups sugar, divided
¼ teaspoon nutmeg
¼ cup lemon juice
2 teaspoons grated lemon rind
1 9-inch baked pie shell
½ cup coconut

Beat egg yolks in top of double boiler until thick and lemon colored. Add ⅔ cup sugar, gradually, beating well after each addition. Cook over hot water until mixture begins to thicken around sides of pan, about 5 to 7 minutes. Blend in nutmeg, lemon juice and lemon rind. Continue cooking until thick, about 10 minutes, stirring constantly. Beat egg whites until foamy. Add remaining ⅔ cup sugar gradually, beating well after each addition. Continue beating until egg whites stand in heavy peaks when beater is raised. Blend ⅓ of this meringue into lemon mixture. Cool. Turn into pie shell. Fold coconut into remaining meringue. Spread on top of filling. Bake in a hot oven (425° F) 5 to 10 minutes, or until lightly browned. Makes one 9-inch pie.

# Coconut Crunch Pie

3 eggs, separated
1¼ cups sugar
1 teaspoon salt
½ cup milk
2 tablespoons soft butter or margarine
½ teaspoon almond extract
¼ teaspoon lemon extract
1 cup shredded coconut
1 9-inch unbaked pie shell

Beat egg yolks well. Add sugar and salt and mix well. Stir in milk, butter, and extracts. Fold in coconut. Beat egg whites until stiff but not dry. Fold into egg yolk mixture. Pour into pie shell. Bake in a moderate oven (350° F) 35 to 40 minutes or until a knife inserted in center comes out clean. Makes one 9-inch pie.

# Caramel Candy Pie

1 envelope unflavored gelatine
¼ cup cold water
½ pound candy caramels
½ cup milk, divided
1 cup heavy cream, whipped
1 9-inch baked pie shell

Soften gelatine in cold water. Combine caramels and ¼ cup of the milk in top of a double boiler. Cook over boiling water until caramels melt. Stir until smooth. Add softened gelatine and stir until dissolved. Remove from heat and stir in ¼ cup of cold milk. Chill until the consistency of unbeaten egg whites. Add caramel mixture to whipped cream and beat with a rotary beater until well blended. Turn into baked pie shell. Chill until firm. Makes one 9-inch pie.

# Mississippi Pecan Pie

3 eggs, slightly beaten
¼ cup sugar
1¼ cups corn syrup
¼ teaspoon salt
1 teaspoon vanilla
⅔ cup whole pecans
1 9-inch unbaked pie shell

Combine all ingredients, except pie shell, in order listed. Blend well and pour into pie shell. Bake in a hot oven (450° F) 10 minutes; reduce temperature to 325° F and bake 30 minutes or until a silver knife, inserted in the center, comes out clean. Makes one 9-inch pie.

# Mocha Chocolate Pie

1 package chocolate pudding mix
4 teaspoons instant coffee
1½ cups milk
½ cup heavy cream, whipped
1 8-inch baked pie shell

Combine pudding mix, instant coffee and milk in a saucepan according to directions on package. Cook and stir over medium heat until mixture comes to a full boil. Remove from heat. Cool about 5 minutes, stirring once or twice. Fold in whipped cream. Pour into pie shell. Chill well before serving. If desired, garnish with a border of whipped cream and chopped nuts. Makes one 8-inch pie.

# Peanut Scotch Pie

½ cup sugar
¾ cup brown sugar, firmly packed
¼ cup sifted flour
½ teaspoon salt
3 eggs, separated
2 cups milk
1 tablespoon butter or margarine
3 tablespoons peanut butter
1 9-inch baked pie shell
6 tablespoons sugar
¼ cup finely chopped peanuts

Combine sugar, brown sugar, flour and salt in top of a double boiler. Stir in egg yolks, milk and butter. Cook over boiling water, stirring occasionally, until thickened. Remove from heat. Add peanut butter and blend well. Cover and cool. Pour into baked pie shell. Beat egg whites until foamy. Gradually beat in 6 tablespoons sugar until mixture stands in stiff peaks. Spread meringue over filling in pie shell. Sprinkle peanuts over top of meringue. Bake in a hot oven (425° F) 5 to 10 minutes, or until golden brown. Makes one 9-inch pie.

# Pennsylvania Cheese Pie

2 teaspoons cornstarch
⅔ cup sugar
1 cup cottage cheese, riced
2 eggs, separated
2 tablespoons milk
⅛ teaspoon salt
1 tablespoon grated lemon rind
1 9-inch unbaked pie shell

Mix cornstarch and sugar; add cottage cheese, egg yolks, milk, salt and lemon rind and blend well. Fold in stiffly beaten egg whites and pour into pie shell. Bake in a hot oven (450° F) 10 minutes. Reduce temperature to 325° F and continue baking 25 to 30 minutes. Makes one 9-inch pie.

# Pineapple Cheese Pie

1 No. 2 can crushed pineapple
2 tablespoons cornstarch
2 teaspoons cold water
½ pound creamy cottage cheese
¼ cup butter or margarine
1 cup sugar
2 eggs, unbeaten
½ cup sifted flour
¾ cup milk
1 teaspoon vanilla
1 9-inch unbaked pie shell

Cook pineapple in a saucepan over low heat 5 minutes. Combine cornstarch and water; stir into pineapple and cook until clear. Cool. Combine cheese and butter; add sugar gradually, beating until light and fluffy. Add eggs singly, beating well after each addition. Add flour alternately with combined milk and vanilla. Pour pineapple mixture into unbaked pie shell. Top with cheese mixture. Bake in a hot oven (450° F) 10 minutes; reduce temperature to 350° F and continue baking 30 minutes. Makes one 9-inch pie.

# Fresh Peach Pie

**1 recipe pastry**
**⅔ cup sugar**
**¾ teaspoon nutmeg**
**¼ teaspoon salt**
**2 teaspoons cornstarch**
**1 egg yolk, slightly beaten**
**3 cups peeled, sliced peaches**
**2½ tablespoons butter or margarine, melted**
**2 tablespoons evaporated milk**
**2 teaspoons lemon juice**

Line an 8-inch pie plate with one-half the pastry. Blend together sugar, nutmeg, salt and cornstarch. Blend in egg yolk. Add remaining ingredients and mix thoroughly. Pour into pastry-lined pie plate. Cover with lattice top. Bake in a hot oven (450° F) 15 minutes; reduce temperature to 350° F and continue baking 35 minutes. Makes one 8-inch pie.

# Mincemeat Custard Pie

**1½ cups prepared mincement**
**1 9-inch unbaked pie shell**
**3 eggs, slightly beaten**
**¼ cup sugar**
**¼ teaspoon salt**
**2 cups milk**
**Nutmeg**

Spread mincemeat in the pie shell. Combine eggs, sugar, salt and milk and mix well. Pour over mincemeat. Sprinkle with nutmeg. Bake in a very hot oven (450° F) 15 minutes; reduce heat to moderate 350° F and bake 30 minutes, or until a knife inserted in the center comes out clean. Serve warm. Makes one 9-inch pie.

The Borden Company

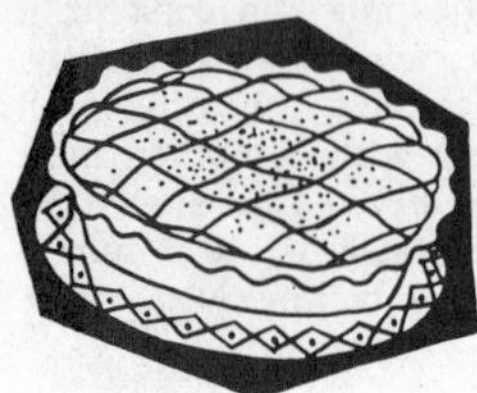 

# Perfect Pie

**4 eggs, separated**
**¼ teaspoon cream of tartar**
**1½ cups sugar, divided**
**3 tablespoons lemon juice**
**1 tablespoon grated lemon rind**
**⅛ teaspoon salt**
**1 pint heavy cream**

Beat egg whites and cream of tartar until stiff. Add 1 cup of the sugar, 1 tablespoon at a time, beating well after each addition. Continue beating until stiff and glossy. Line bottom and sides of a 9-inch pie plate with this mixture. Bake in a low oven (275° F) about 1 hour or until lightly browned. Cool. Beat egg yolks slightly. Stir in remaining sugar, lemon juice, lemon rind and salt. Cook in top of double boiler, over boiling water, until very thick. Remove from heat and cool. Whip 1 cup of the cream until stiff. Fold into cooked egg mixture. Fill meringue shell. Chill in refrigerator 24 hours before serving. Just before serving top with 1 cup cream, whipped. Makes one 9-inch pie.

# Silky Chocolate Pie

**½ cup butter**
**¾ cup sugar**
**1 square unsweetened chocolate, melted and cooled**
**1 teaspoon vanilla**
**2 eggs**
**1 8-inch baked pie shell**

Cream butter. Add sugar gradually and cream well. Blend in chocolate and vanilla. Add eggs, one at a time, and beat 5 minutes with a rotary beater after each addition. Turn into baked pie shell and chill 1 to 2 hours before serving. Top with whipped cream before serving if desired. Makes one 8-inch pie.

# Graham Cracker Butterscotch Pie

**2 cups milk, divided**
**1 cup dark brown sugar, firmly packed**
**2 egg yolks**
**3 tablespoons cornstarch**
**3 tablespoons butter or margarine**
**1 9-inch graham cracker pie crust**
**½ cup whipped cream**

Heat ½ cup of the milk and the brown sugar in the top part of a double boiler until sugar is dissolved. Beat egg yolks well, add cornstarch and remaining 1½ cups of milk. Add mixture to milk and sugar in top of double boiler. Cook over hot water until mixture is thickened, then cook 5 minutes longer, stirring constantly. Remove from heat and stir in butter. Pour into graham cracker lined pie plate and chill in refrigerator. Serve topped with whipped cream. Makes one 9-inch pie.

# Pecan Crumb Pie

½ cup eggs (about 3)
1 cup sugar, divided
2 cups graham cracker crumbs
¼ cup flour
1 teaspoon baking powder
½ cup chopped pecans
2 tablespoons butter or margarine, melted
1 teaspoon vanilla
¼ cup apricot jam
½ cup heavy cream, whipped

Beat eggs until very light with ½ cup of the sugar. Combine remaining sugar with crumbs, flour, baking powder and pecans. Add butter, vanilla and beaten eggs and mix lightly. Pour into a buttered 9-inch pie plate. Bake in a moderate oven (350° F) 30 to 35 minutes. Cool. Serve garnished with apricot jam and cream. Makes one 9-inch pie.

# Apricot Whip Pie

1 cup pureéd cooked dried apricots
¼ teaspoon salt
¾ cup sugar
2 egg whites
¼ teaspoon almond extract
1 tablespoon lemon juice
1 8-inch oatmeal pie crust
Apricot halves, cooked

Place apricots, salt, sugar, unbeaten egg whites, extract and lemon juice in a large bowl. Beat with rotary beater until light and fluffy and stiff enough to stand in peaks. Heap into oatmeal pie crust. Chill. Garnish with apricot halves. Makes one 8-inch pie.

# Deep South Pie

1 cup cooked rice
¼ cup butter or margarine
¾ cup molasses
1 cup sugar
2 eggs, beaten
¼ teaspoon salt
1 teaspoon vanilla
1 9-inch unbaked pie shell
1 cup whole pecans

Cook rice until very soft (at least twice as long as customary). Drain and mash with a fork. Melt butter in a large saucepan. Stir in molasses, sugar, eggs, salt, vanilla and rice and pour into pie shell. Sprinkle pecans evenly over the top. Bake in a moderate oven (375° F) 50 minutes. Cool before serving. Makes one 9-inch pie.

# Creamy Lemon Pie

1 cup sugar
½ teaspoon salt
¼ cup flour
1 cup milk
2 eggs, separated
Rind and juice of 1 lemon
⅓ cup butter or margarine
1 8-inch baked pie shell
4 tablespoons sugar

Combine sugar, salt and flour in the top of a double boiler. Mix well and stir in milk. Cook over very low heat, stirring constantly, until thickened. Beat egg yolks. Pour the hot mixture slowly over egg yolks and mix well. Return mixture to double boiler. Cook over hot water about 3 minutes. Remove from heat. Add lemon juice and rind and butter. Cool, stirring occasionally. Pour into baked pie shell. Beat egg whites until stiff but not dry. Gradually beat in sugar until mixture stands in peaks. Pile on top of lemon filling in pie shell. Bake in a hot oven (425° F) 5 to 10 minutes, or until lightly browned. Makes one 8-inch pie.

# Apple Custard Pie

3 eggs
¼ cup sugar
¼ teaspoon salt
Grated rind of ½ lemon
1 cup grated raw apple
2 cups milk, scalded
1 9-inch unbaked pie shell
Cinnamon

Beat eggs slightly, add sugar, salt, lemon rind and apple. Add milk and strain, forcing the apple through the sieve. Pour into unbaked pie shell. Sprinkle a little cinnamon on the top. Bake in a hot oven (400° F) 10 minutes, reduce the temperature to 300° F and continue baking 30 to 45 minutes or until a silver knife inserted in the center comes out clean. Makes one 9-inch pie.

# Golden Nugget Orange Pie

⅓ cup sugar
4 tablespoons cornstarch
1¼ cups orange juice
1 cup pineapple juice
3 eggs, separated
1½ cups pineapple pieces, drained
1 tablespoon butter or margarine
1 9-inch baked pie shell
6 tablespoons sugar

Combine sugar, cornstarch, orange juice, and pineapple juice in a saucepan. Mix until smooth. Cook over medium heat, stirring constantly, until thick and clear. Stir a little of the hot mixture into the beaten egg yolks and return to saucepan. Cook over very low heat, and cook about 2 minutes, stirring constantly. Remove from heat. Stir in pineapple pieces and butter. Cover and cool. Pour into baked shell. Beat egg whites until foamy. Gradually beat in sugar until stiff. Spread meringue over filling. Bake in a hot oven (425° F) 5 to 10 minutes. Makes one 9-inch pie.

# Sweet Potato Mince Pie

1 cup cooked, mashed sweet potatoes
1 cup evaporated milk
¼ cup brown sugar, packed
1 egg, slightly beaten
½ teaspoon salt
¼ teaspoon cinnamon
¼ teaspoon ginger
1 teaspoon grated lemon rind
1½ tablespoons margarine, melted
1 package mincemeat
1 9-inch unbaked pie shell

Combine sweet potatoes, milk, sugar, egg, seasonings, rind and margarine; cook over low heat 3 minutes, stirring constantly. Prepare mincemeat according to directions on package; spread on bottom of pastry in pie dish; pour potato mixture over mincemeat. Bake in hot oven (450° F) 15 minutes; reduce temperature to 350° F and continue baking 25 to 30 minutes or until a silver knife comes out clean when inserted in the center. Makes one 9-inch pie.

# Chocolate Brownie Pie

2 squares unsweetened chocolate
2 tablespoons butter or margarine
3 eggs
½ cup sugar
¾ cup dark corn syrup
¾ cup pecan halves
1 9-inch unbaked pie shell

Melt chocolate and butter together over hot water. Beat eggs thoroughly. Beat in sugar, chocolate mixture and corn syrup. Stir in pecan halves. Pour mixture into pastry lined pie dish. Bake in a moderate oven (375° F) 40 to 50 minutes, just until pie is set. Makes one 9-inch pie.

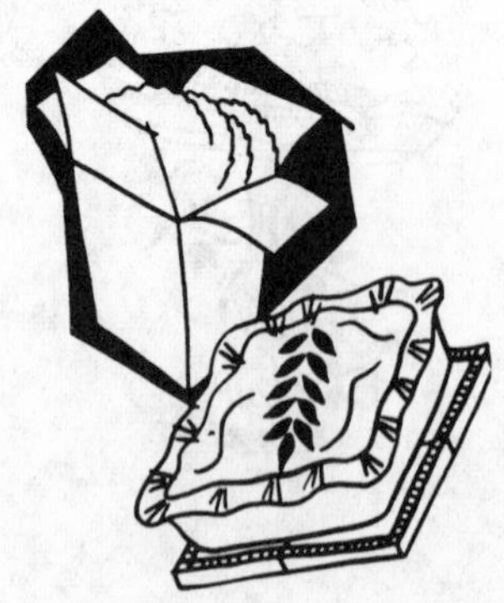

Best Foods, Inc.

# Peanut Butter Pie

1 cup light or dark corn syrup
1 cup sugar
3 eggs, slightly beaten
½ teaspoon vanilla
⅓ cup creamy or chunk style peanut butter
1 unbaked (9-inch) pastry shell

Blend corn syrup, sugar, eggs, vanilla and peanut butter in a bowl. Pour into unbaked pastry shell. Bake in hot oven (400°F.) for 15 minutes. Reduce heat to 350°F. and bake 30 to 35 minutes longer. (Filling should appear slightly less set in center than around edge.)

# Shoo-Fly Pie

1 cup molasses
1 cup boiling water
1 teaspoon baking soda
3 cups sifted flour
1 cup sugar
½ cup butter
1 9-inch unbaked pie shell

Combine molasses, water and baking soda; bring to a boil. Boil 1 minute or until light in color. Sift together flour and sugar. Cut in butter with 2 knives or a pastry blender, to a crumb consistency. Pour molasses mixture into pastry shell; top with crumb mixture. Bake in a hot oven (425° F) 40 minutes. Cool. Makes one 9-inch pie.

# Sour Cream Raisin Pie

2 tablespoons cornstarch
1 cup sugar, divided
¼ teaspoon salt
¼ teaspoon cinnamon
½ teaspoon nutmeg
2 eggs, separated
1 cup sour cream
1 cup raisins
1½ teaspoons lemon juice
1 9-inch baked pie shell

In the top of a double boiler mix together cornstarch, ¾ cup of the sugar, salt, cinnamon and nutmeg. Add egg yolks and mix well. Add sour cream. Cook over hot water until thick, stirring constantly. Stir in raisins and lemon juice. Cool. Pour into baked pie shell. Beat egg whites until stiff. Gradually beat in the remaining ¼ cup of sugar. Spread over filling. Bake in a hot oven (425° F) 5 to 10 minutes, or until delicately browned. Makes one 9-inch pie.

# Chocolate Pie

1 cup sugar
1 teaspoon salt
3½ tablespoons cornstarch
3 cups milk
3 squares unsweetened chocolate
3 eggs, separated
1 tablespoon butter or margarine
1 teaspoon vanilla
1 9-inch baked pie shell
6 tablespoons sugar

Beat the yolks until light and thick. Combine sugar, salt, cornstarch in top of double boiler. Stir in the milk and chocolate. Cook over boiling water, stirring, until thick. Cover and cook for 10 more minutes. Beat egg yolks. Pour hot mixture slowly over egg yolks and mix well. Return to double boiler and cook, stirring constantly, about 2 minutes. Add butter and vanilla. Cool. Pour into baked pie shell. Beat egg whites until stiff but not dry. Add sugar gradually, beating until mixture stands in peaks. Cover top of chocolate with meringue. Bake in a hot oven (425° F) 5 to 10 minutes or until lightly browned. Makes one 9-inch pie.

# Custard Pie with Crispy Crust

**4 eggs, slightly beaten**
**2½ cups milk**
**½ cup sugar**
**1 teaspoon vanilla**
**½ teaspoon salt**
**⅛ teaspoon nutmeg**
**1 9-inch baked pie shell**

Combine eggs, milk, sugar, vanilla, salt and nutmeg and blend well. Strain into an oiled 9-inch pie pan. Place pan in a shallow pan of hot water. Bake in a moderate oven (350° F) about 35 minutes. Cool to room temperature. Loosen custard from sides of pan with a spatula. Shake gently to loosen from pan. Slide custard quickly into baked pie shell. Makes one 9-inch pie.

# Apricot Cottage Cheese Pie

**2 cups mashed, cooked apricots**
**1 teaspoon lemon extract**
**¼ teaspoon almond extract**
**1 cup sugar, divided**
**1 9-inch unbaked pie shell**
**⅛ teaspoon salt**
**2 eggs, beaten**
**1 cup milk**
**1 teaspoon vanilla**
**1 cup cottage cheese**

Combine apricots, lemon extract, almond extract and ½ cup of the sugar. Spread in bottom of pie shell. Bake in a hot oven (425° F) 10 minutes. Combine remaining sugar and salt with eggs and mix well. Add remaining ingredients. Pour mixture over apricots in pie shell. Reduce temperature to low 325° F and continue baking 50 minutes. Serve with whipped cream if desired. Makes one 9-inch pie.

# Baked Chocolate Sponge Pie

**¼ cup butter or margarine**
**1 cup sugar, divided**
**3 tablespoons flour**
**6 tablespoons cocoa**
**3 eggs, separated**
**1 teaspoon vanilla**
**2 cups milk**
**1 9-inch unbaked pie shell**

Cream together butter and ⅔ cup of the sugar. Stir in flour and cocoa. Add egg yolks separately, beating well after each addition. Stir in vanilla and milk. Beat egg whites until stiff. Gradually beat in remaining ⅓ cup of the sugar and continue beating until egg whites stand in peaks. Fold whites into chocolate mixture and turn into unbaked pie shell. Bake in a hot oven (425° F) 15 minutes, then reduce heat to low (325° F) and continue baking 30 minutes or until firm to the touch. Makes one 9-inch pie.

# Fruit in Cream Pie

**1 cup canned, sliced peaches, drained**
**½ cup chopped dates**
**½ cup quartered marshmallows**
**1½ cups sliced bananas**
**3 tablespoons lemon juice**
**3 tablespoons honey**
**½ cup heavy cream, whipped**
**1 9-inch baked pie shell**
**2 tablespoons crushed cheese crackers**

Combine peaches, dates, marshmallows, bananas, lemon juice and honey. Chill thoroughly. Fold fruit mixture carefully into whipped cream. Turn into pie shell. Sprinkle with crushed cheese crackers. Chill until ready to serve. Makes one 9-inch pie.

# Scotch Banana Pie

2 bananas
1 8-inch cornflake pie crust
1 package butterscotch pudding mix
1¾ cups milk
2 tablespoons margarine
⅓ cup chopped pecans

Slice one banana and arrange in bottom of cornflake pie crust. Prepare pudding with the milk according to directions on the package. When mixture comes to a full boil remove from heat and stir in margarine and pecans. Cool about 5 minutes, stirring occasionally. Pour into pie crust. Chill until firm. Just before serving garnish top with sliced banana and chopped nuts. Makes one 8-inch pie.

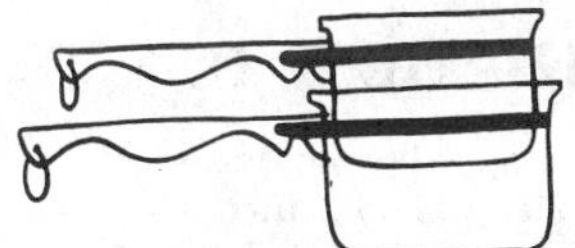

# Coffee Meringue Pie

⅔ cup sugar
5 tablespoons cornstarch
½ teaspoon salt
1 cup milk
1½ cups strong coffee
2 eggs, separated
1 9-inch baked pie shell
⅛ teaspoon salt
4 tablespoons sugar

Mix sugar, cornstarch and salt in top part of double boiler. Add combined milk and coffee. Cook over direct heat, stirring constantly, until smooth and thick. Beat egg yolks slightly. Pour hot mixture slowly over egg yolks and mix well. Return to double boiler and cook over hot water about 5 minutes, stirring occasionally. Cool. Pour into baked pie shell. Beat egg whites with salt until stiff. Gradually beat in sugar and continue beating until mixture stands in peaks. Arrange on top of filling. Bake in a hot oven (425° F) 5 to 10 minutes or until lightly browned. Makes one 9-inch pie.

Sunkist Growers

# Prize-Winning Lemon Meringue Pie

**One 9-inch baked pie shell**
**7 tablespoons cornstarch**
**1⅓ cups sugar**
**¼ teaspoon salt**
**1½ cups hot water**
**3 egg yolks, beaten**
**½ cup lemon juice**
**1 teaspoon grated lemon rind**
**2 tablespoons butter or margarine**

Mix cornstarch, sugar and salt in a saucepan. Stir in hot water gradually and bring to a boil over direct heat. Cook for 8 to 10 minutes over medium heat, stirring constantly until thick and clear. Remove from the heat. Stir several spoonfuls of this hot mixture into the beaten egg yolks. Mix well. Pour egg yolks back into the saucepan. Bring to a boil then reduce heat and cook slowly for 4 to 5 minutes, stirring constantly. Remove from heat and gradually add lemon juice, rind and butter. Cool thoroughly, then pour into the cooled baked pie shell. Top with meringue: put the 3 egg whites (at room temperature) in a deep medium sized bowl. Add 1 tablespoon lemon juice. Beat until whites stand in soft peaks. Add 6 tablespoons sugar gradually, beating well after each addition. Beat until egg whites stand in firm glossy peaks. Spread over cooled filling, starting at the edges and working toward the center of the pie, attaching meringue securely to the edges of the crust. Bake at 350° F. for 15 to 20 minutes. Cool but do not refrigerate before serving.

# Old-South Butterscotch Pie

**1¼ cups dark brown sugar, firmly packed**
**¼ teaspoon salt**
**2 tablespoons water**
**2 cups milk, divided**
**4½ tablespoons cornstarch**
**3 egg yolks, slightly beaten**
**2 tablespoons butter or margarine**
**½ teaspoon vanilla**
**1 9-inch baked pie shell**
**⅓ cup pecans, chopped**
**1 cup heavy cream, whipped**

Combine brown sugar, salt and water in top of a double boiler. Cook over direct heat for 5 minutes. Blend ¼ cup of the milk with the cornstarch. Add the remaining milk and combine with the brown sugar mixture. Place over hot water and cook until thick and smooth, about 20 minutes, stirring occasionally. Stir a small amount of the hot mixture over the beaten egg yolks and mix well; return to double boiler and cook 5 minutes longer. Add butter and vanilla; remove from hot water and cool. Pour into baked shell and chill well. Before serving, sprinkle top with pecans and garnish with whipped cream. Makes one 9-inch pie.

# Heavenly Chocolate Pie

**1 cup sifted flour**
**¾ teaspoon salt, divided**
**⅓ cup shortening**
**3 to 4 tablespoons cold water**
**2 eggs, separated**
**½ teaspoon vinegar**
**¾ cup sugar, divided**
**1 package (6-ounces) semi-sweet chocolate morsels**
**¼ cup water**
**1 cup heavy cream**
**¼ teaspoon cinnamon**

Combine flour and ½ teaspoon salt in mixing bowl. Cut in shortening until consistency of coarse meal. Sprinkle water, over mixture, tossing quickly and lightly with fork until dough is just moist enough to hold together. Roll out pastry and fit into a 9-inch pie plate. Flute edges and prick bottom with a fork. Bake in a very hot oven (450°F.) 12 minutes. Beat together egg whites, vinegar and remaining ¼ teaspoon salt until stiff but not dry. Gradually add ½ cup of the sugar and beat until very stiff. Spread meringue over bottom and up sides of baked shell. Bake in a moderate oven (325°F.) 15 to 18 minutes, or until lightly browned. Cool. Melt chocolate morsels over hot water. Beat together egg yolks and ¼ cup water until smooth. Beat in melted chocolate. Spread 3 tablespoons of chocolate mixture over cooled meringue. Chill remaining chocolate mixture until it begins to thicken. Beat together heavy cream, remaining ¼ cup sugar and cinnamon until thick. Spread ½ of the whipped cream mixture over chocolate layer in pie shell. Fold chilled chocolate mixture into remaining whipped cream. Spread over plain whipped cream in pie shell. Chill pie at least 4 hours before serving. Makes one 9-inch pie.

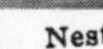
Nestle

# Gingerbread Meringue Pie

**3 tablespoons sugar**
**¼ cup molasses**
**¼ cup corn syrup**
**3 tablespoons shortening**
**1 teaspoon ginger**
**½ teaspoon cinnamon**
**Pinch of salt**
**½ cup boiling water**
**1 teaspoon soda**
**1¼ cups sifted flour**
**1 egg, well beaten**
**1 9-inch unbaked pie shell**
**2 egg whites**
**4 tablespoons sugar**

Combine 3 tablespoons sugar, molasses, corn syrup, shortening, ginger, cinnamon and salt. Combine water and soda and add to molasses mixture. Stir in flour. Beat together with rotary beater. Add egg, and beat again. Pour into shell. Bake in a moderate oven (375° F) until firm, about 40 minutes. Beat egg whites until stiff but not dry. Gradually beat in 4 tablespoons sugar until mixture stands in peaks. Cover pie with meringue and bake in a hot oven (425° F) 5 to 10 minutes or until browned. Makes one 9-inch pie.

National Dairy Council

# Rainbow Ice Cream Pie

½ cup chopped mixed candied fruits
¼ cup chopped pecans
½ cup light corn syrup
¼ cup sugar
¼ cup orange juice
½ teaspoon rum flavoring
⅔ cup brown edge or vanilla wafer fine cookie crumbs
3 tablespoons melted butter
12 whole brown edge or vanilla wafer cookies
1 pint chocolate ice cream
1 pint vanilla ice cream
1 pint strawberry ice cream

Combine candied fruits, pecans, corn syrup, sugar and orange juice in a saucepan. Bring to a boil and simmer 1 minute. Remove from heat and stir in rum flavoring. Chill. Combine cookie crumbs and butter and blend well. Press mixture evenly over bottom of a 9-inch pie plate. Stand whole cookies upright around edge. Chill. Spoon chocolate ice cream into a layer in cookie crust and drizzle ¼ of the sauce over top. Repeat process using vanilla and strawberry ice cream and sauce. Freeze until serving time. Serve with remaining sauce. Makes one 9-inch pie.

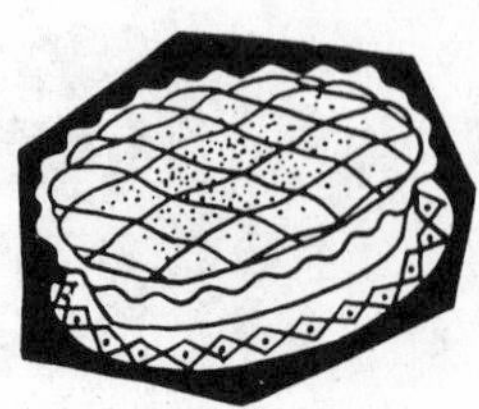

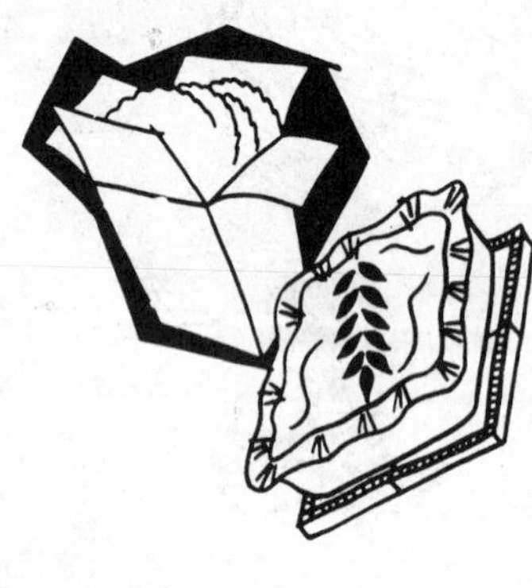

# Raisin Chocolate Pie

1 cup raisins
2¼ cups milk, scalded
½ teaspoon salt
1 cup sugar, divided
¼ cup cocoa
¼ cup cornstarch
2 eggs, separated
2 tablespoons cold water
2 teaspoons vanilla
1 9-inch baked pie shell

Boil raisins 5 minutes in water to cover; drain well and set aside. Scald milk in top of double boiler. Combine salt, ¾ cup sugar, cocoa and cornstarch and blend thoroughly. Add slowly to scalded milk, stirring to prevent lumping. Beat together egg yolks and water. Pour the hot mixture slowly over egg yolks and mix well. Return mixture to double boiler and cook over hot water until thick and clear, stirring occasionally. Remove from heat. Cool and fold in vanilla and raisins. Pour into baked pie shell. Beat egg whites until stiff but not dry. Add sugar gradually, beating until mixture stands in peaks. Pile over pie filling. Bake in a hot oven (425° F) 5 to 10 minutes or until meringue is lightly browned. Makes one 9-inch pie.

# Yambilee Ice Cream Pie

¾ cup ginger snap crumbs (about 12 2-inch cookies)
2 tablespoons melted butter or margarine
1 tablespoon sugar
11 2-inch ginger snaps
1 pint vanilla ice cream, softened
¼ cup chopped pecans
3 cups mashed cooked yams
¼ cup maple-blended syrup
½ cup heavy cream
¼ teaspoon orange extract
1 tablespoon sugar
¼ teaspoon cinnamon
Pecans

Mix crumbs, butter and 1 tablespoon sugar; press into bottom of 9-inch pie plate. Place ginger snaps around edge of pie plate. Combine ice cream, chopped pecans, yams and syrup; blend thoroughly. Pour yam mixture into pie plate; freeze. Combine heavy cream, orange extract, 1 tablespoon sugar and cinnamon; whip until soft peaks form. Garnish frozen pie with whipped cream and pecans.

**Note:** If pie is very firm, let stand at room temperature 15 minutes before serving.

Louisiana Yam Commission

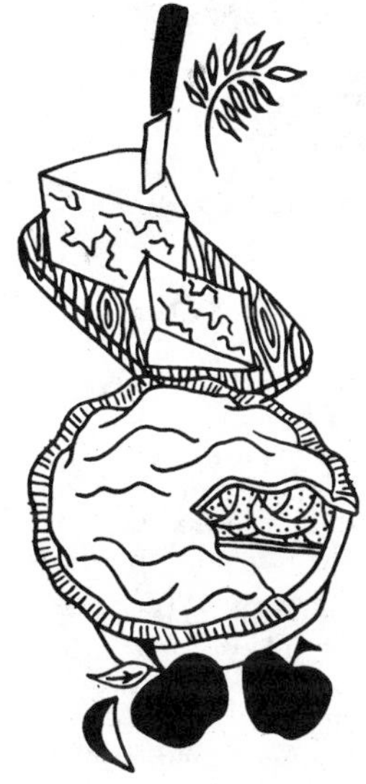

# Never-Fail Lemon Meringue Pie

24 vanilla cookie wafers
1⅓ cups (15-ounce can) sweetened condensed milk
½ cup lemon juice
1 teaspoon grated lemon rind
¼ teaspoon salt
2 eggs, separated
¼ teaspoon cream of tartar
4 tablespoons sugar

Line an 8-inch pie pan with vanilla wafers; crumble several of the wafers to fill spaces between cookies in bottom of pie pan. Pour sweetened condensed milk into mixing bowl; add lemon juice, rind, salt and egg yolks. Beat with a rotary beater until blended. Turn filling into pie shell. Add cream of tartar to egg whites and beat until stiff but not dry. Add sugar gradually, beating until mixture stands in peaks. Spread over lemon filling. Bake in a hot oven (425° F) 5 to 10 minutes or until lightly browned. Cool before serving. Makes one 8-inch pie.

# Currant Pie

3 eggs, separated
1¼ cups brown sugar, firmly packed
½ teaspoon cinnamon
¼ teaspoon cloves
2 teaspoons butter
1 teaspoon vinegar
½ cup dried currants
¾ cup chopped walnuts
1 8-inch unbaked pie shell

Combine egg yolks, brown sugar, cinnamon, cloves and butter and beat until well blended. Stir in vinegar, currants and walnuts. Beat egg whites until stiff but not dry. Fold into fruit mixture. Pour into pie shell. Bake in a very hot oven (450° F) 10 minutes, reduce temperature to 325° F and bake 20 to 25 minutes. Makes one 8-inch pie.

The Borden Company

# Eggnog Coconut Pie

1 package vanilla pudding and pie filling mix
1 tablespoon brandy
2 tablespoons rum extract
1 9-inch baked coconut pie crust

Prepare pudding mix as directed on package. Add brandy and rum extract. Cool about 5 minutes, stirring once or twice. Turn into coconut pie crust. Chill well before serving. Garnish with whipped cream, if desired. Makes one 9-inch pie.

# Peaches and Cream Pie

1 No. 2½ can peach halves, drained
or
5 fresh peaches, peeled and sliced
1 9-inch unbaked pie shell
2 eggs
1 cup sour cream
¼ cup honey
½ cup brown sugar, firmly packed
2 tablespoons flour

Arrange peach halves or slices in pie shell. Beat eggs slightly, add cream and honey and mix well. Pour over peaches. Blend together brown sugar and flour and sprinkle over egg mixture. Bake in a very hot oven (450° F) 15 minutes; reduce temperature to 350° F and bake 25 to 30 minutes. Makes one 9-inch pie.

# Sweet Potato Pie

2 cups hot mashed sweet potatoes
1 cup evaporated milk
2 tablespoons brown sugar
1 cup hot water
¼ cup molasses
1 soda cracker, finely crushed
½ teaspoon ginger
½ teaspoon salt
2 tablespoons raisins
1 9-inch unbaked pie shell

Combine potatoes, milk, sugar, water and molasses. Blend together cracker crumbs, ginger and salt; add to potato mixture. Stir in raisins. Pour into unbaked pastry shell. Bake in a hot oven (450° F) 10 minutes; reduce temperature to 350° F and continue baking 25 minutes or until firm. Makes one 9-inch pie.

# Lemon-Lime Meringue Pie

1¼ cups sugar, divided
1 tablespoon butter or margarine
1¾ cups water, divided
⅛ teaspoon salt
5 tablespoons cornstarch
2 eggs, separated
2½ tablespoons lime juice
2½ tablespoons lemon juice
Grated rind of 1 lemon
Grated rind of 1 lime
1 9-inch baked pie shell

Mix together 1 cup sugar, butter, 1½ cups of the water and salt in top of a double boiler. Cook over low heat until mixture boils. Mix cornstarch with remaining water, add to sugar syrup and cook over hot water 20 minutes. Beat egg yolks. Pour the hot mixture slowly into egg yolks and mix well. Return to double boiler and cook 3 minutes, stirring constantly. Remove from hot water and cool. Add fruit juices and rinds; blend well. When filling is cold, pour into baked pie shell. Beat egg whites until stiff but not dry. Add sugar gradually, beating until mixture stands in peaks. Pile on top of filling. Bake in a hot oven (425° F) 5 to 10 minutes or until lightly browned. Makes one 9-inch pie.

National Dairy Council

# Pumpkin Pie

2 cups cooked or canned mashed pumpkin
½ cup firmly packed brown sugar
1 teaspoon salt
½ teaspoon cinnamon
½ teaspoon nutmeg
½ teaspoon ginger
¼ teaspoon cloves
3 eggs, slightly beaten
2 cups milk
1 9-inch unbaked pie shell

Combine pumpkin, sugar and seasonings. Blend in eggs and milk and mix well. Pour into unbaked pie shell. Bake in a hot oven (450° F) 10 minutes; reduce temperature to 350° F and continue baking 25 to 30 minutes or until knife inserted in center comes out clean. Serve with whipped cream if desired. Makes one 9-inch pie.

# Chocolate Marshmallow Pie

2 squares unsweetened chocolate
2 tablespoons sugar
½ cup milk
12 marshmallows
1½ cups heavy cream, whipped
1 8-inch baked pie shell
½ cup toasted chopped almonds

Put chocolate, sugar, milk and marshmallows in top of a double boiler. Melt over hot water. Cool, stirring frequently. Fold in whipped cream. Pour into baked pie shell. Sprinkle with chopped almonds. Chill well before serving. Makes one 8-inch pie.

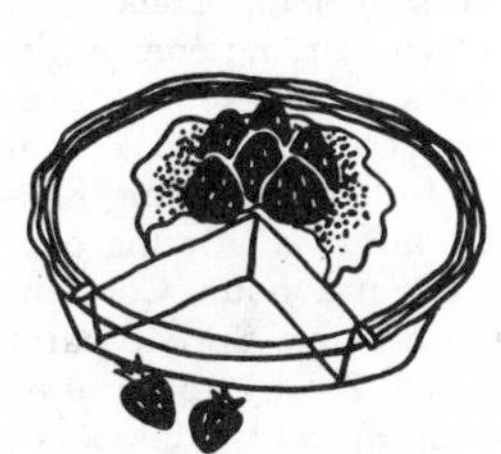

# Baked Ice Cream Pie In Cocoa Crust

⅓ cup shortening
1 cup sifted flour
¼ teaspoon salt
4 teaspoons cocoa
4 teaspoons sugar
¾ teaspoon vanilla
3 tablespoons water
1 quart peppermint or vanilla ice cream
3 egg whites
¼ teaspoon salt
¾ teaspoon cream of tartar
6 tablespoons sugar
1 teaspoon vanilla

Cut shortening into sifted dry ingredients until mixture is consistency of corn meal and small peas. Combine vanilla and water. Gradually sprinkle enough liquid over flour mixture to dampen dough. Blend with fork or pastry blender. Place dough on waxed paper. Knead 3 times. Let stand at room temperature for 15 to 20 minutes. Roll out dough. Fit into pie pan. Flute edge. Prick pastry. Bake in a very hot oven (450°F.) 8 to 10 minutes. Cool. Pack ice cream firmly into thoroughly cooled pie crust. Wrap, mark and place in freezer if pie is not to be served immediately. Just before serving make meringue by beating egg whites with salt until definite peaks will form when beater is lifted. Gradually beat in cream of tartar and sugar until meringue is very stiff. Add vanilla. Pile meringue lightly over ice cream making sure meringue touches pie crust all the way around. Bake in a very hot oven (450°F.) 3 minutes, or until meringue is delicately browned. Serve immediately. Makes 8 inch deep pie or 9 inch shallow pie.

Swift & Co.

National Biscuit Company

# Graham Cracker Cream Pie

1 packet of graham crackers, finely rolled (1⅔ cups crumbs)
¼ cup butter or margarine, softened
¾ cup sugar, divided
3 cups milk
2 packages vanilla pudding and pie filling mix
4 eggs, separated

Thoroughly blend crumbs with softened butter or margarine and ¼ cup sugar. Pour into a 9-inch pie plate and press firmly against bottom and sides of pie plate. (The easy way is to use an 8-inch pie plate.) Bake in a moderate oven (375°F.) for 7 minutes. Cool.

In a saucepan gradually add milk to pudding and pie filling mix. Stir in beaten egg yolks. Cook over medium heat, stirring constantly until pudding thickens. Cool. Pour into baked crust. Beat egg whites until foamy. Gradually add remaining sugar. Continue beating until stiff. Pile meringue over filling sealing to edges of crust. Bake in a hot oven (425°F.) 4 to 5 minutes, or until lightly browned. Chill 3 to 4 hours. Makes 6 to 8 servings.

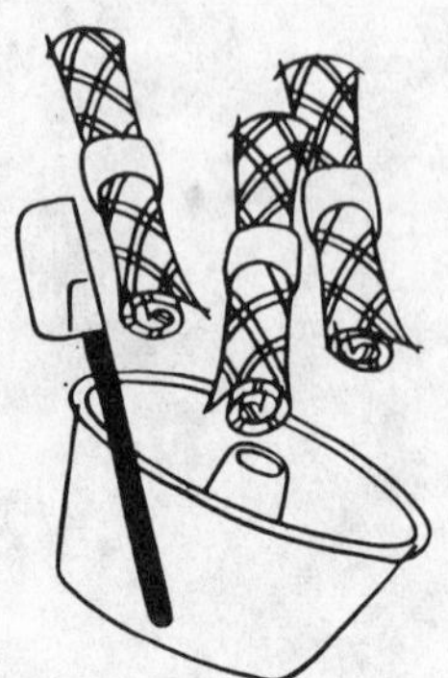

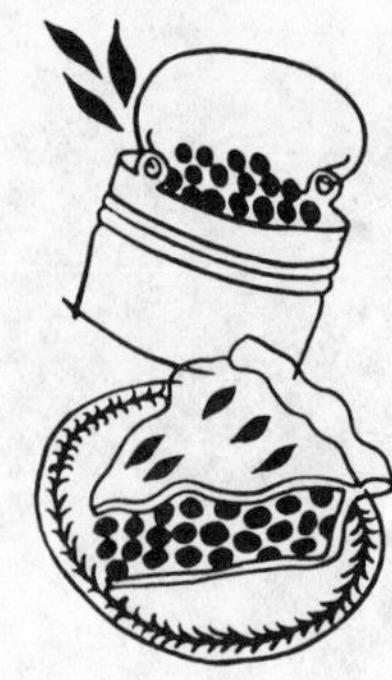

# Lime Meringue Pie

4 tablespoons cornstarch
¾ cup sugar
¼ teaspoon salt
1¼ cups water
3 eggs, separated
1 tablespoon butter
2 teaspoons grated lime rind
5 tablespoons lime juice
1 8-inch baked pie shell
6 tablespoons sugar

Blend cornstarch, sugar and salt in top of a double boiler. Stir in water. Cook over direct heat, stirring constantly, until mixture is very thick and transparent. Beat egg yolks. Pour hot mixture slowly over egg yolks and mix well. Return to double boiler and cook over hot water 3 minutes, stirring constantly. Remove from heat. Stir in butter, lime rind and juice. Turn into baked pie shell. Beat egg whites until stiff but not dry. Add 6 tablespoons of sugar gradually, beating until mixture stands in peaks. Pile over pie filling. Bake in a hot oven (425° F) 5 to 10 minutes. Makes one 8-inch pie.

# Peanut Coconut Pie

3 eggs, well beaten
1 cup light corn syrup
¾ cup sugar
2 tablespoons soft butter or margarine
1 teaspoon vanilla
⅛ teaspoon salt
1 cup peanuts
½ cup flaked coconut
1 9-inch unbaked pie shell

Combine all ingredients except pie shell. Mix well and turn into pie shell. Bake in a moderately hot oven (375° F) 35 to 45 minutes or until a knife inserted in the center comes out clean. Makes one 9-inch pie.

# Quick Coconut Pie

1 cup flaked coconut
2 tablespoons butter
1 package butterscotch pudding mix
1¾ cups milk
1 8-inch baked pie shell
3 tablespoons brown sugar
1½ tablespoons light cream

Combine coconut and butter in a saucepan. Cook over medium heat until coconut is golden brown, stirring constantly. Remove half the coconut from saucepan and reserve. Add pudding mix and milk to coconut in saucepan and cook over medium heat until mixture comes to a full boil, stirring constantly. Remove from heat. Cool about 5 minutes, stirring once or twice. Pour into pie shell and cool about 1 hour. Combine reserved coconut with brown sugar and cream. Spread carefully over cooled pie. Bake in a hot oven (425° F) 15 minutes, or until top is bubbly. Serve either warm or cold. Makes one 8-inch pie.

# Dutch Cottage Cheese Pie

1⅛ cups creamed cottage cheese
3 eggs
1¼ teaspoons salt
3 tablespoons molasses
¼ teaspoon ground cinnamon
½ cup dark brown sugar
1 teaspoon lemon juice
¼ cup heavy cream
4 tablespoons flour
6 well-drained canned peach halves
1 unbaked 9-inch pie shell

Sieve or beat cottage cheese until smooth. Add and thoroughly beat in eggs one at a time. Blend in salt, molasses, cinnamon, sugar, lemon juice and cream. Sprinkle half of the flour over the cut sides of the peach halves. Add remaining flour to cottage cheese mixture and mix until smooth.

Place floured peach halves, cut side down, in bottom of pie shell, allowing a whole half for each pie serving. Pour in cottage cheese filling carefully. Bake pie in a moderate oven (350°F.), about 50 minutes or until a silver knife inserted in the center comes out clean. Cool before serving. Makes 6 servings.

# Squash Pie

1½ cups cooked, strained squash
1 cup brown sugar, firmly packed
½ teaspoon salt
2 teaspoons cinnamon
1 teaspoon ginger
2 tablespoons molasses
3 eggs, slightly beaten
1 cup evaporated milk
1 9-inch unbaked pie shell

Mix squash, sugar, salt, spices and molasses. Add eggs and milk and mix thoroughly. Pour mixture into unbaked pie shell. Bake in a hot oven (425° F) 40 to 45 minutes or until a knife inserted in the center comes out clean. Makes one 9-inch pie.

# Refrigerator Cheese Pie

20 graham crackers
¼ cup sugar
¼ cup softened butter or margarine
1 envelope unflavored gelatine
¼ cup cold water
1 egg, separated
¼ cup milk
½ cup sugar
1 cup cottage cheese
1 3-ounce package cream cheese
Grated rind of ½ lemon
½ teaspoon vanilla
½ cup light cream
Juice of ½ lemon

Place crackers in a bag and crush fine with a rolling pin. Combine with ¼ cup sugar and softened butter and mix well. Put crumbs in a refrigerator ice cube tray. Press firmly against bottom and sides of tray with a cup. Soften gelatine in cold water. Combine slightly beaten egg yolk, milk and ½ cup sugar; cook over low heat for 5 minutes, stirring constantly. Remove from heat; add gelatine and stir until dissolved. Blend cheeses together; add lemon rind and vanilla. Add gelatine mixture and blend well. Chill until mixture begins to thicken. Beat cream until foamy; add lemon juice and whip until thickened. Beat egg white until stiff. Fold cream and egg white into cheese mixture. Pour into crumb lined refrigerator tray. Chill until firm. Cut into pie shaped wedges for serving. Makes 6 servings.

# Apple Butter Pumpkin Pie

1 cup apple butter
1 cup cooked or canned mashed pumpkin
½ cup brown sugar, firmly packed
½ teaspoon salt
¾ teaspoon cinnamon
¾ teaspoon nutmeg
⅛ teaspoon ginger
3 eggs
¾ cup evaporated milk
1 9-inch unbaked pie shell

Combine apple butter, pumpkin, brown sugar, salt, cinnamon, nutmeg and ginger. Beat eggs and stir into mixture. Gradually add evaporated milk and mix thoroughly. Pour into pie shell. Bake in a hot oven (425° F) 40 to 45 minutes or until a knife inserted in pie comes out clean. Makes one 9-inch pie.

Sealtest Consumer Service

# NOTES

# SALAD

A salad is probably the most versatile course in the whole meal and can be made from almost any combination of foods. Try a small piquant salad as a first course, and start your meal with a flourish. Serve a salad with the main course, as a contrast with the main dish. With a bland creamy entree, serve a crisp spicy salad. With a hot spicy main dish, present a bland salad, even one that is slightly sweet.

Salads are, of course, delightful as the main dish in a meal. This should be hearty, using meat, fish or eggs, combined with fruits or vegetables. In the summer time especially, one needs only hot rolls, dessert and a beverage for a complete luncheon or dinner.

And don't forget salads for dessert. Frozen or molded salads, of fruits or cheese, make a light and satisfying finale for any meal.

United Fresh Fruit and Vegetable Association

# Salad Greens

## About Salads

When shopping for fruits and vegetables for salads, choose only those that are fresh and crisp. Salad greens are the soul and basis for the best salads, so special attention should be given to them. Select the best quality available, then clean and refrigerate the greens as quickly as possible.

Wash salad greens well, the sand and dirt are washed away more quickly if you use lukewarm water. Trim wilted leaves from greens and discard. Drain excess water from a head of lettuce on a rack or towel. Drain or toss leafy salad greens in a tea towel, or twirl them in a lettuce basket. For the best salad, greens should be bone dry. Store greens promptly in the refrigerator crisper, or place them in plastic bags in the refrigerator. To make perfect lettuce cups; remove the core from a head of lettuce, run water into the cavity and the force of the water will push the leaves apart, making them easy to separate.

Don't forget, there are many salad greens on the market besides lettuce. At one time or other in the market there are 14 different varieties of lettuce. Look over the accompanying sketches, try a new salad green for dinner this evening and see if it might not open a whole new salad world to your family.

Garlic

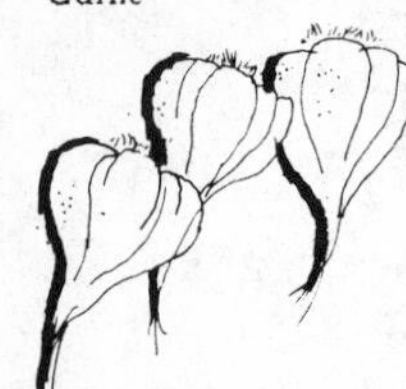

Garlic, a European bulbous herb of the lily family, has pungent bulb which is composed of cloves.

Romaine

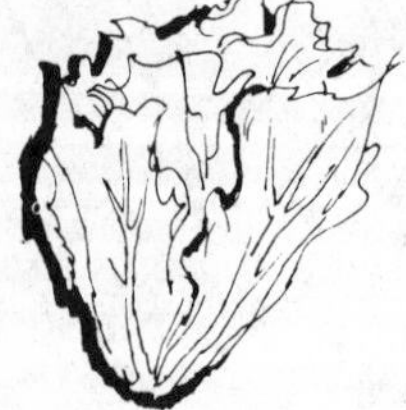

Romaine is dark green with elongated head, has a coarse leaf of medium firmness, is strong-flavored.

Iceberg lettuce, a top favorite, is crisp, solid, slices well, has medium green outside, pale inside.

Parsley is a European aromatic garden herb of the carrot family, used (leaves) to garnish and flavor.

Iceberg Lettuce

Chinese cabbage has characteristics of romaine and cabbage family; it should be crisp, well-blanched.

Boston lettuce is softer and lighter than Iceberg; leaves have waxy texture; it is not crisp or solid.

Parsley

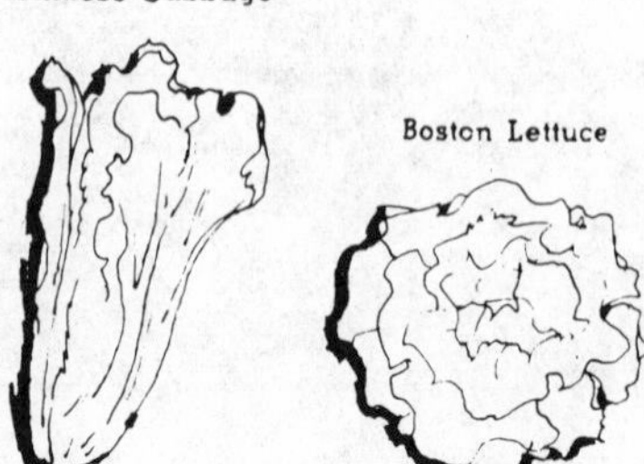


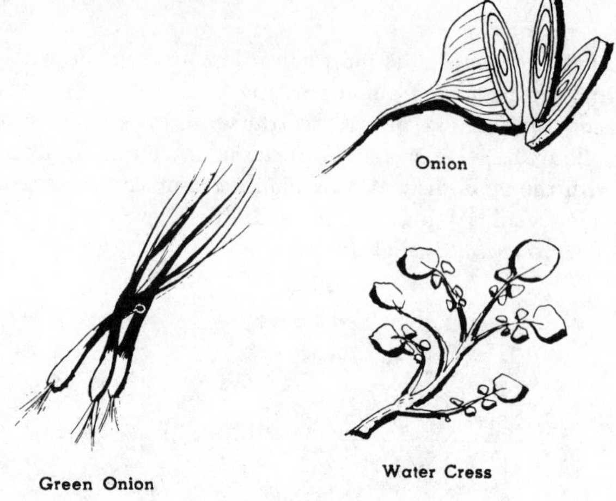


Green onions (also known as scallions or shallots) are mild-flavored and usually eaten in raw state.

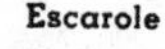


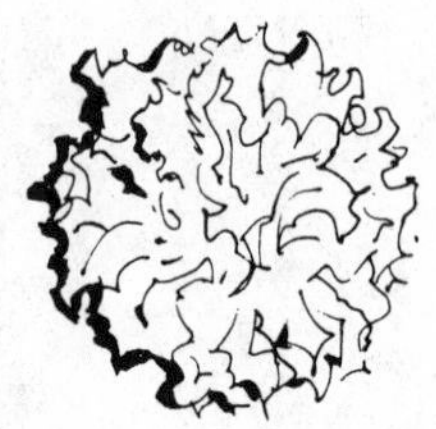

Onions have an Asiatic ancestry, are of the lily family; it's edible bulb is, of course, pungent.

Water cress has moderately pungent leaves, has numerous relatives in the mustard plant family.

Escarole is sometimes called broad leaf endive, has flat, slightly curled leaves, is mild to bitter.

Chicory is often called curly endive, is mild to slightly bitter, has white and dark green leaves.

French Endive

French endive is best served alone with a spicy dressing rather than mixed with other greens.

Chives are perennial plants allied to the onion; its slender leaves are used to flavor many salads.

Celery stems should snap readily and have a good head formation; they should also be thick, meaty.

Celery

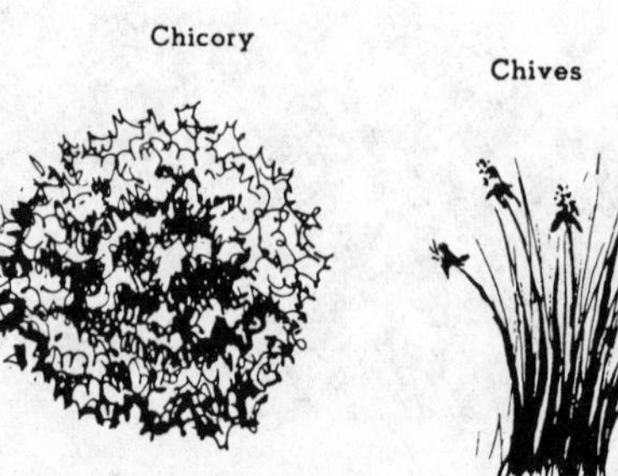

Choose any shape or kind of salad bowl you prefer, just be sure it is large enough for easy tossing.

If you use a wooden salad bowl, be sure it is made of a hardwood and always wash immediately after using.

Lettuce, romaine and other salad greens look fresher and prettier if you tear them into bite size pieces.

Cut other salad ingredients; celery into bias half-moons, pepper into rings and tomatoes into wedges.

When salad is ready, cover with foil and refrigerate. Do not add dressing until ready to toss and serve.

Get in the habit of using your kitchen scissors for mincing parsley and chives and cutting up fruits.

A shredder is a necessity for shredding cabbage, carrots, cheese and other foods in many salads.

Fill a lettuce basket with washed salad greens, a couple of good twirls and ready for the refrigerator.

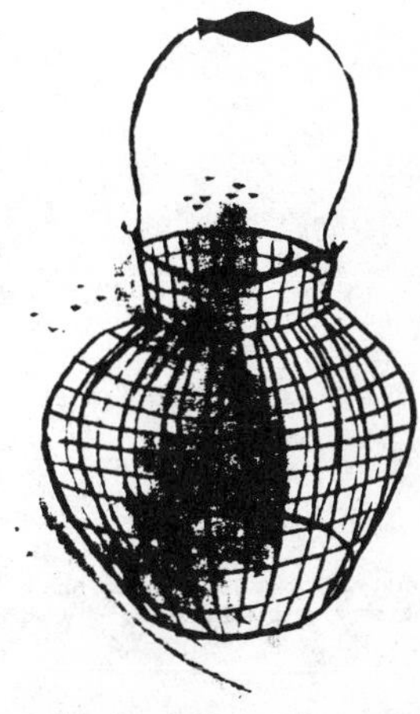

## Herbs for Salads

Learn to use herbs, both fresh and dried, in your salads. Try a bit of chopped fresh basil on fresh tomato slices. Add a pinch of oregano in a green salad. Keep a pot of chives on your window sill and snip off a bit for your next salad. Look at the herb chart in this section and try something different in your next salad.

Basil

Basil comes from the Greek meaning king. Flavor is sweet and warm with a pungent undertone.

Tarragon

Tarragon is a rich, racy herb with a slightly anise flavor. Careful, a pinch goes a long ways.

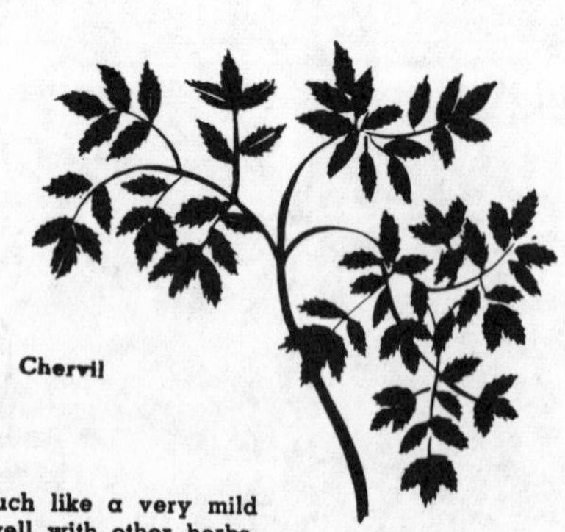

Chervil

Chervil looks and tastes much like a very mild parsley. It combines very well with other herbs.

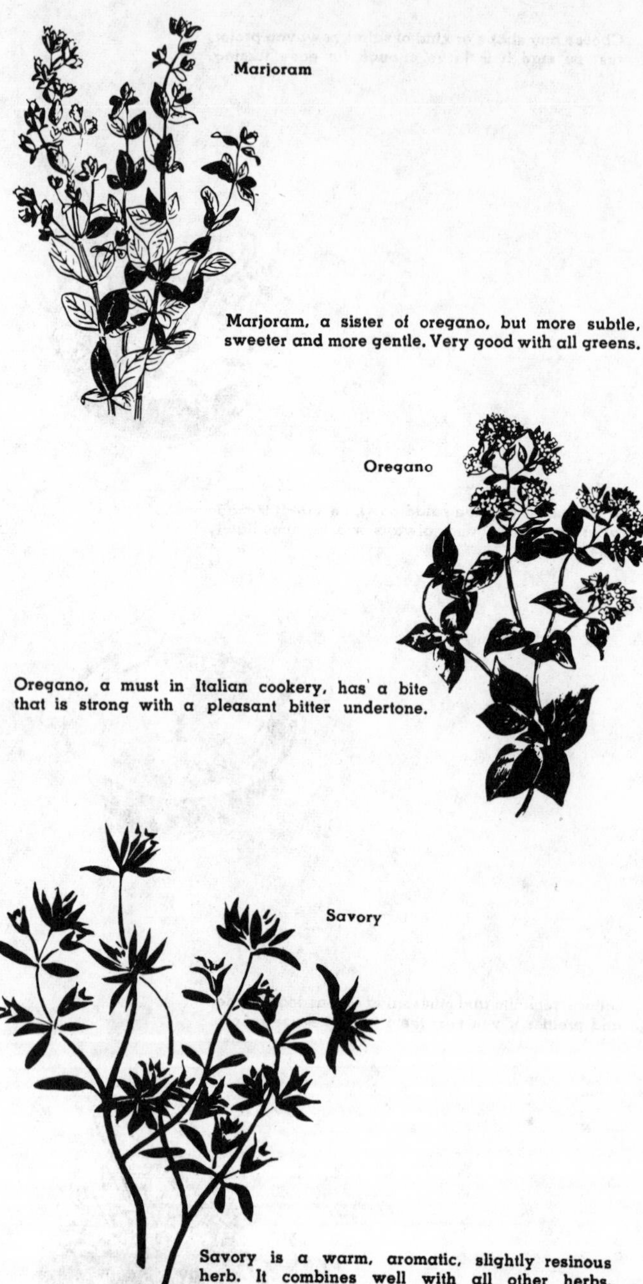

Marjoram

Marjoram, a sister of oregano, but more subtle, sweeter and more gentle. Very good with all greens.

Oregano

Oregano, a must in Italian cookery, has a bite that is strong with a pleasant bitter undertone.

Savory

Savory is a warm, aromatic, slightly resinous herb. It combines well with all other herbs.

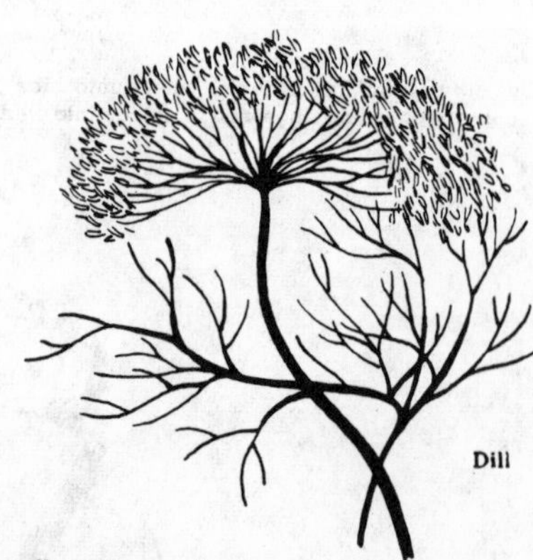

Dill

The tender fresh leaves, as well as the seeds of dill have a crisp flavor with a slight caraway tang.

# Salad Dressing

## Fruit Cream Dressing

¼ cup pineapple juice
½ cup orange juice
3 tablespoons reconstituted lemon juice
2 eggs
Dash of salt
⅓ cup sugar
⅓ cup evaporated milk, whipped*

Combine pineapple, orange and lemon juices in top of double boiler; place boiler top over boiling water. Beat eggs slightly; stir in salt and sugar. Slowly stir a little of the heated fruit juices into beaten egg mixture; gradually return it to remaining hot fruit juices, while stirring constantly. Cook 2 minutes longer over boiling water, stirring constantly. Remove from heat and chill. Just before serving fold in whipped evaporated milk. Makes 2 cups.

*To whip evaporated milk, chill it in refrigerator tray in freezer until crystals form at edges. Put into chilled mixing bowl and whip with chilled rotary beater or electric mixer until stiff.

The Borden Company

## French Dressing

½ cup lemon juice or vinegar
1 ½ cups olive or other salad oil
2 teaspoons salt
¼ teaspoon pepper
1 teaspoon dry mustard
Dash cayenne

Mix all ingredients in a 1-quart glass jar; cover tightly, and shake until thoroughly blended. Store in the refrigerator. Makes 2 cups.

VARIATIONS

**CHIFFONADE DRESSING:** To ¾ cup French Dressing, add 1 chopped hard-cooked egg, 1 teaspoon minced parsley, 1 tablespoon minced pimiento, 1 teaspoon minced green onion, and ⅛ teaspoon paprika. Good on vegetables.

**CHILI MAYONNAISE:** Mix 1 cup mayonnaise, ¼ cup chili sauce, 2 tablespoons chopped green pepper and 2 tablespoons chopped green onion. Makes 1¼ cups. Good on lettuce wedges or mixed greens.

**COTTAGE-CHEESE DRESSING:** To ¾ cup French Dressing, add 2 tablespoons cottage cheese, 1 tablespoon pickle relish, and 2 tablespoons chopped parsley. Good on fruit, greens, and vegetables.

**DE LUXE FRENCH DRESSING:** Use French Dressing recipe, adding several gashed cloves garlic, ⅓ cup chili sauce, 1 tablespoon horseradish, and 1 teaspoon paprika.

**HERB DRESSING:** To ¾ cup French Dressing, add 2 teaspoons chopped fresh dill, marjoram, rosemary, summer savory, or other herbs. Good on greens, seafood, or meat.

**OLIVE DRESSING:** To ¾ cup French Dressing, add ¼ cup chopped stuffed green or ripe olives. Good on fish, fruit, or vegetables.

**VINAIGRETTE DRESSING:** To ¾ cup French Dressing, add 1 chopped hard-cooked egg and 1 teaspoon chopped chives. Good on vegetables or greens.

**WATERMELON-PICKLE DRESSING:** To ¾ cup French Dressing, add 2 tablespoons chopped watermelon pickle. Good on greens, fruit, meat, or vegetable salads.

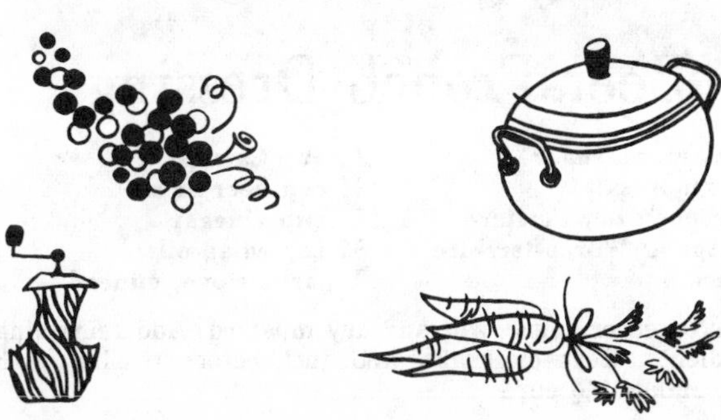

Sealtest Kitchens

# Cottage Cheese Fruit Dressing

**1 cup creamed cottage cheese**
**½ cup sour cream**
**Dash salt**
**½ cup maraschino cherry juice**
**½ teaspoon lemon juice**
**6 tablespoons drained, canned crushed pineapple**

Sieve cottage cheese; fold in sour cream. Add salt and cherry and lemon juices; blend well. Fold in crushed pineapple. Refrigerate. A colorful dressing for fruit salads. Yields 2 cups.

# Cottage Cheese Vegetable Dressing

**1 cup creamed cottage cheese**
**½ cup sour cream**
**¼ teaspoon onion salt**
**¼ teaspoon dry mustard**
**½ cup tomato juice**
**1 teaspoon lemon juice**
**2 tablespoons catsup**
**1 teaspoon soy sauce**

Sieve cottage cheese; fold in sour cream. Sprinkle onion salt and mustard over mixture; gently blend in. Add tomato and lemon juices, catsup and soy sauce; mix well. Refrigerate. A unique dressing for green salads or vegetables. 1¾ cups dressing.

# Mayonnaise Variations

*Curry Mayonnaise*: To 1 cup mayonnaise, add 1 teaspoon curry powder and ½ clove crushed garlic.

*Cream Mayonnaise*: Whip ½ cup heavy cream until stiff and fold in 1 cup mayonnaise.

*Cucumber Mayonnaise*: To 1 cup mayonnaise, add ½ cup chopped cucumber and 2 tablespoons chopped parsley.

*Chiffonade Mayonnaise*: To 1 cup mayonnaise, add 2 tablespoons chopped green pepper, 2 tablespoons chopped pimiento, 1 tablespoon chopped green olives, 1 tablespoon chopped sweet pickle and 1 teaspoon prepared horse-radish.

*Spicy Mayonnaise*: To 1 cup mayonnaise, add 2 teaspoons prepared mustard, 1 teaspoon prepared horse-radish, ½ teaspoon Worcestershire sauce and 1 tablespoon minced onion.

*Russian Dressing*: To 1 cup mayonnaise, add 2 tablespoons chili sauce, 2 tablespoons chopped pimiento, ½ teaspoon vinegar, ½ teaspoon paprika, 1 hard-cooked egg, chopped, and 1 tablespoon chopped chives.

# Mayonnaise

**1 egg yolk**
**½ teaspoon salt**
**½ teaspoon dry mustard**
**¼ teaspoon paprika**
**Dash of cayenne**
**2 tablespoons vinegar or lemon juice**
**1 cup salad oil**

Put egg yolk and seasonings into a small bowl and beat thoroughly; add 1 tablespoon vinegar and beat again. Gradually beat in oil, adding ½ teaspoon oil at a time until ¼ cup is used. Then add 1 to 2 tablespoons at a time. As mixture thickens, add remaining vinegar. If oil is added too rapidly, mayonnaise will curdle. To remedy this, at once beat curdled mixture gradually into a second egg yolk and continue as above. Store mayonnaise in a covered jar in a moderately cold place. Makes about 1¼ cups mayonnaise.

# Beer French Dressing

**1 tablespoon sugar**
**1 teaspoon salt**
**½ teaspoon dry mustard**
**1 teaspoon Worcestershire sauce**
**¼ cup Catsup**
**¼ cup beer or ale**
**¼ cup vinegar**
**¾ cup salad oil**
**1 garlic clove, minced**

Stir together sugar, salt and dry mustard. Add remaining ingredients. Beat or shake well just before tossing with salad. Makes 1½ cups.

# Florida French Dressing

1 cup Florida grapefruit juice, divided
2 teaspoons cornstarch
2 tablespoons salad oil
¾ teaspoon salt
1 teaspoon sugar
½ teaspoon paprika
½ teaspoon dry mustard
¼ teaspoon Tabasco
¼ cup Catsup

Blend ½ cup of the Florida grapefruit juice and cornstarch. Cook over low heat, stirring constantly until thickened and clear. Remove from heat; add remaining ½ cup grapefruit juice. Combine remaining ingredients; add cornstarch mixture and beat with rotary beater until smooth. Cover and store in refrigerator. Shake before using. Makes 1¼ cups.

# Boiled Dressing

¾ cup cider vinegar
¼ cup water
1 tablespoon butter
⅓ cup sugar
2 tablespoons flour
½ teaspoon salt
1 teaspoon dry mustard
1 teaspoon celery seed
1 egg, beaten
Milk

Heat the vinegar, water and butter together in the top of a double boiler. Combine in a bowl, sugar, flour, salt, mustard, celery seed and egg. Add enough milk to make a thin paste. Stir a little of the hot liquid into the mixture in the bowl, return contents to double boiler and cook over hot water, stirring constantly, until the mixture is smooth and thick. Cool slightly and then store in the refrigerator in a covered container. Makes about 2 cups dressing.

# Ruby French Dressing

½ cup sugar
¼ cup lemon juice
½ cup catsup
1 cup olive oil
2 tablespoons vinegar
½ teaspoon salt
1 teaspoon onion juice
2 teaspoons celery seed

Combine sugar and lemon juice and boil for 5 minutes; let cool. Add remaining ingredients and beat well. Good with fruit salads. Makes about 2 cups dressing.

# Salad Dressing Supreme

1½ cups sugar
1 cup water
1 teaspoon salt
1 teaspoon celery salt
1 teaspoon paprika
4 tablespoons vinegar
½ cup lemon juice
2 teaspoons grated onion
2 cups salad oil
½ cup catsup

Cook the sugar and water together until it is about as thick as molasses. Cool slightly and add the remaining ingredients. Beat with a rotary beater until a smooth mixture is formed. Cover and store in a cool place. Makes about 1 quart dressing.

# Green Goddess Dressing

1 egg yolk
½ teaspoon salt
½ teaspoon dry mustard
¼ teaspoon monosodium glutamate
2 tablespoons tarragon vinegar
1 tablespoon anchovy paste
1 cup salad oil
¼ cup cream
1 tablespoon lemon juice
1 teaspoon onion juice
Dash of garlic powder
2 tablespoons chopped parsley

In a deep bowl, mix egg yolk, salt, mustard, monosodium glutamate, vinegar and anchovy paste. Add 2 tablespoons oil; beat with a rotary or electric beater until blended. Beat in remaining oil, 2 tablespoons at a time. Stir in rest of ingredients. Store in tightly covered jar in refrigerator until needed. Makes about 1⅓ cups dressing.

# Hot Salad Dressing

1 teaspoon salt
1 tablespoon sugar
½ teaspoon dry mustard
⅓ cup vinegar
2 tablespoons salad oil
1 hard-cooked egg, minced
2 cucumbers, thinly sliced and pared or
1 head lettuce

Combine salt, sugar and mustard. Add vinegar and oil and heat to boiling point. Stir in egg. Pour over thinly sliced cucumbers or over lettuce broken into bite-sized pieces. Dust with paprika and serve at once. Makes ¾ cups dressing.

# Thousand Island Dressing

1 cup mayonnaise
3 tablespoons chili sauce
1 tablespoon chopped sweet pickle
2 tablespoons chopped stuffed olives
1 hard-cooked egg, chopped
½ teaspoon grated onion
½ cup French dressing

Mix ingredients in the order given and chill thoroughly before serving. Makes about 2 cups dressing.

Best Foods

# Mystery French Dressing

1 cup salad oil
⅓ cup vinegar
1 tablespoon sugar
1½ teaspoons salt
½ teaspoon paprika
½ teaspoon dry mustard
1 clove garlic, minced
1 egg white

Combine all ingredients in a bowl. Beat with a rotary beater until thoroughly blended. Store in the refrigerator in a covered jar. This dressing thickens slightly on standing and does not separate as readily as plain French dressing. Mix thoroughly before serving. Makes about 1½ cups dressing.

## Sour Cream Dressing

**1 cup dairy sour cream**
**3 tablespoons fresh lemon juice**
**½ cup salad oil**
**1½ tablespoons prepared horseradish**
**1½ teaspoons salt**
**1 teaspoon dry mustard**
**1 teaspoon whole dill seed**
**¼ teaspoon ground black pepper**
**¼ cup minced onion**

Combine all ingredients, blending well. Allow to stand in refrigerator for several hours for flavors to blend. Makes 2 cups.

## Peanut Butter Dressing

**2 tablespoons peanut butter**
**2 tablespoons cream**
**2 tablespoons lemon juice**
**¼ teaspoon horse-radish**
**½ teaspoon sugar**
**¼ teaspoon paprika**
**¼ teaspoon salt**

Cream peanut butter until light and fluffy. Add remaining ingredients and beat until very light. Good with salad greens. Makes about ½ cup dressing.

## Stuffed Olive Dressing

**1 teaspoon salt**
**1 teaspoon dry mustard**
**1 teaspoon paprika**
**1 teaspoon sugar**
**¼ teaspoon cayenne**
**2 tablespoons catsup**
**1 cup salad oil**
**¼ cup vinegar**
**½ cup sliced stuffed olives**

Mix all the dry ingredients and the catsup together. Beat well with a rotary or electric beater. Add the oil one tablespoon at a time, beating well after each addition. Add vinegar gradually beating all the while. Add the olives and chill. Makes about 1½ cups dressing.

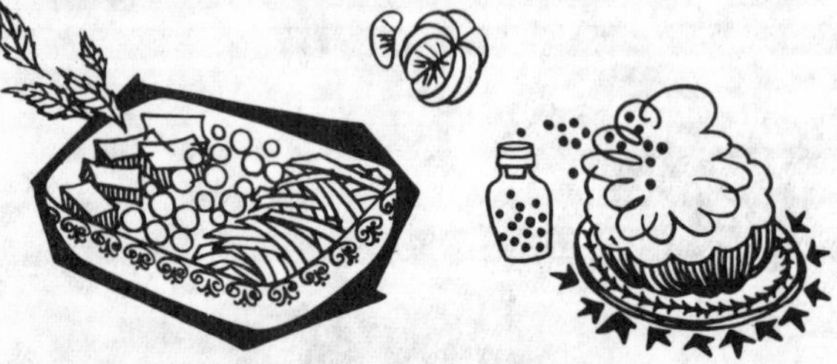

# Fruit Salads

## Fruit Salad Bowl

**2 bananas, cut lengthwise**
**4 crescents of avocado**
**Lemon juice**
**4 slices pineapple**
**4 slices red shined apples**
**4 fingers of cantaloupe**
**8 orange sections**
**Strawberries**

Dip the banana, avocado and apples in lemon juice to prevent them from darkening. Arrange lettuce and water cress in a glass salad bowl. Arrange on the lettuce the bananas and cantaloupe then place the other fruit around, sandwiching each apple slice between 2 sections of orange. Garnish with the strawberries. When serving, be sure each person receives some of each fruit. Pass sweetened fruit French dressing. Makes 4 servings.

Best Foods

## Cranberry-Avocado Salad

**2 medium sized avocados**
**Salt**
**Lemon juice**
**1 cup cubes of cranberry jelly**
**¾ cup halved orange sections**
**French dressing**

Cut the avocados in halves lengthwise, remove the seed and peel avocados. Sprinkle with salt and lemon juice to prevent darkening. Mix the cranberry cubes lightly with the orange sections and pile into the avocado halves. Place on lettuce cups and serve with plenty of French dressing. Makes 4 servings.

## Pineapple-Cranberry Salad

**4 slices canned pineapple**
**4 slices canned jellied cranberry sauce**
**1 3-ounce package cream cheese**
**⅛ teaspoon salt**
**⅛ teaspoon ground ginger**
**Chopped nuts**

Place pineapple and cranberry slices, put together sandwich fashion, on crisp greens. Blend cream cheese, salt and ginger; pat into four balls and roll in chopped nuts. Place one cheese ball on each salad. Serve with mayonnaise thinned with a little pineapple juice. Makes 4 servings.

# Molded Apple Salad

6 apples
3 cups water
1 cup sugar
Red vegetable coloring
½ cup crushed pineapple
¼ cup raisins
¼ cup chopped nuts
1 package lemon-flavored gelatin

Peel and core the apples. Combine water, sugar and a few drops of red vegetable coloring. Drop apples in syrup and cook gently until apples are tender. Do not overcook so apples lose their shape. Remove apples from syrup and place each in a large cup. Combine pineapple, raisins and nuts. Stuff centers of apples with this mixture. Make up gelatin according to directions on package. When cool, pour gelatin over apples. Chill well until set. Unmold on crisp lettuce and serve with mayonnaise. Makes 6 servings.

# Spicy Salad Del Sol

1 head lettuce
2 oranges peeled and thinly sliced
1 Bermuda onion, thinly sliced
1 cup French dressing
1 can (4½-ounces) deviled ham

Break lettuce into large pieces, arrange on plate with orange slices and onion rings. Shake dressing with delived ham. Serve with salad. Makes 4 to 6 servings.

Underwood Kitchens

# Banana Waldorf Salad

2 cups diced banana
½ cup diced celery
½ cup broken nut meats
1 tablespoon lemon juice
Mayonnaise
Salt

Combine banana, celery and nuts. Add lemon juice, enough mayonnaise to moisten and season with salt to taste. Chill thoroughly and serve on lettuce leaves. Makes 4 servings.

# Cinnamon Apple Salad

1 cup sugar
1 cup water
1 cup red cinnamon candies
6 cooking apples
1 cup cottage cheese
½ cup chopped walnuts

Combine sugar; water and cinnamon candies in a saucepan. Cook over low heat until candy is dissolved. Pare and core the apples and place in the syrup; cover and cook very slowly until apples are tender but not broken. Turn apples several times during cooking period so they will take on an even color. Remove apples carefully from syrup, drain and chill thoroughly. Mix the cottage cheese and walnuts. Fill apple centers with cheese mixture; arrange on salad greens and serve with mayonnaise. Makes 6 servings.

# Raw Cranberry Salad

2 cups raw cranberries
1 large orange
1 cup sugar
1 package lemon-flavored gelatin
1 cup boiling water

Pick over and wash cranberries, then put them through the food grinder. Put unpeeled orange through the grinder. Add the sugar to the ground cranberries and orange and mix well. Dissolve gelatin in boiling water and chill. When mixture is slightly thickened. fold in cranberry-orange mixture. Pour into molds and chill until firm. Serve on lettuce cups with mayonnaise. Makes 6 servings.

# Lime-Fruit and Cheese Salad

1 No. 303 can fruit cocktail
1 No. 2 can crushed pineapple
1 package lime-flavored gelatin
2 teaspoons grated lemon rind
2 tablespoons lemon juice
½ cup processed grated American cheese
Crisp greens

Drain syrup from fruit cocktail and pineapple into measuring cup; add water to make 2 cups liquid. Heat in saucepan; add gelatin and stir until dissolved; add lemon rind and juice. Chill mixture until slightly thickened. Fold in drained fruits and cheese. Spoon into individual molds. Chill until firm. Unmold and serve with crisp greens and French or Whipped Cream Mayonnaise. Makes 6 servings.

Florida Citrus Commission

# Grapefruit Salad Mold

1 package (3-ounce) cream cheese
2 envelopes unflavored gelatin
¼ cup sugar
¼ teaspoon salt
3½ cups canned grapefruit juice, divided
3 cups grapefruit sections, divided
¼ cup diced pimiento
Salad greens

Form cream cheese into 8 small balls; chill. Mix together gelatin, sugar and salt in saucepan. Add 1 cup of the grapefruit juice. Place over medium heat, stirring occasionally, until gelatin is thoroughly dissolved. Remove from heat; add remaining 2½ cups grapefruit juice. Chill. Arrange a few of the grapefruit sections, cream cheese balls and pieces of pimiento in a 5-cup ring mold to make attractive design. Spoon in a little of the chilled gelatin and chill until almost firm. Chill remaining gelatin until the consistency of unbeaten egg white. Fold in 1½ cups grapefruit sections and remaining pimiento. Spoon into mold; chill until firm. Unmold and fill center with salad greens, remaining grapefruit sections and cream cheese balls. Makes 8 servings.

**Note:** If desired, a few drops green food coloring may be added to full amount liquid before chilling.

# Bunch of Grapes

4 large canned pear halves
1 3-ounce package cream cheese
2 tablespoons milk
1 large bunch Tokay grapes
French dressing

Place each pear half cut-side down on a bed of lettuce on a salad plate. Combine softened cream cheese and milk and blend until smooth. Cover each pear half with cream cheese. Cut grapes in half and remove seeds. Press the grape halves, cut-side down, into the cheese covering the pear completely so that it resembles a large bunch of grapes. Serve with French dressing. Makes 4 servings.

# Wine-Cranberry Molds

1 envelope unflavored gelatin
¼ cup cold water
1¼ cups strained, sweetened cranberry sauce
1 cup red table wine, divided
1 orange, peeled and sectioned
Pecans

Soften gelatin in cold water. Heat cranberry sauce, add softened gelatin and stir until gelatin is dissolved. Cool. Add ½ cup of the red wine; pour into individual ring molds and chill until firm. Combine remaining ½ cup of red wine and the orange and chill until ready to serve. Unmold salads on crisp salad greens. Fill center of each ring with orange sections and garnish with pecan halves. Serve with mayonnaise or fruit French dressing. Makes 4 servings.

# Molded Grapefruit Salad

2 envelopes unflavored gelatin
½ cup cold water
¼ teaspoon salt
¼ cup sugar
1 No. 2 can grapefruit sections
1 No. 2 can grapefruit juice

Soften gelatin in cold water. Place over hot water and stir until gelatin is dissolved. Add salt and sugar and stir until dissolved. Drain syrup from grapefruit sections, combine with grapefruit juice to make 3 cups. Add dissolved gelatin to the 3 cups of citrus juice; chill until mixture is the consistency of unbeaten egg white. Fold in drained grapefruit sections. Turn into 1¼ quart mold. Chill until firm. Unmold and garnish with fresh or canned fruit. Makes 8 to 10 servings.

The Borden Company

# Autumn Pinwheel Salad

Line a large salad bowl with cups of crisp iceberg lettuce. Arrange several smaller cups on top. Fill alternate lettuce cups with wedges of crisp, thin apple slices with the red skin left on. Heap a mound of seeded grape halves on top of apple slices. Arrange pomegranate seeds in alternate lettuce cups. Serve with a very light fruit French dressing.

# Fresh Pear Salad

**½ cup mayonnaise**
**¼ cup shredded sharp cheese**
**3 large pears**
**Lemon juice**
**2 large blue plums, cut in rings**
**6 whole walnut meats**

Combine mayonnaise and cheese. Peel pears, cut in half lengthwise and core. Sprinkle with lemon juice to keep from darkening. Place a plum ring in the center of each half and then a spoonful of the mayonnaise mixture. Top each salad with a whole nut meat. Arrange on lettuce leaves and serve with additional cheese-mayonnaise. Makes 6 servings.

# Jellied Pineapple Cream Cheese Salad

**1 package (3-ounce) lime gelatin**
**3 cups hot water**
**1 cup drained, canned crushed pineapple (reserve juice)**
**½ cup finely chopped unpeeled cucumber**
**1 package (3-ounce) lemon gelatin**
**1 package (8-ounce) cream cheese, softened**

Dissolve lime gelatin in 2 cups of hot water. Chill until consistency of unbeaten egg whites. Stir in pineapple and cucumber. Rinse 9 x 5 x 2-inch loaf pan with cold water. Pour in gelatin mixture. Chill until almost firm. Dissolve lemon gelatin in remaining hot water. Measure pineapple juice; add cold water to make 1 cup of liquid. Stir into lemon gelatin. Add cream cheese and beat until mixture is smooth. Pour on top of lime layers. Chill until firm, about 3 hours. Unmold. If desired, garnish loaf with cream cheese. Makes 10 servings.

# Frozen Fruit Salad

**2 teaspoons unflavored gelatin**
**6 tablespoons water**
**2 teaspoons powdered sugar**
**4 tablespoons lemon juice**
**2 tablespoons maraschino cherry juice**
**⅔ cup mayonnaise**
**1 cup heavy cream, whipped**
**1 large banana, cut in cubes**
**1½ cups diced pineapple**
**1 cup sliced maraschino cherries**

Soften gelatin in cold water. Dissolve over hot water and add sugar, lemon juice and maraschino juice. Fold mayonnaise into whipped cream. Fold in gelatin mixture and then the prepared fruits. Turn into refrigerator trays and freeze, stirring once before mixture is firm. Freeze from 4 to 5 hours. Slice and serve on salad greens with mayonnaise if desired. Makes 6 servings.

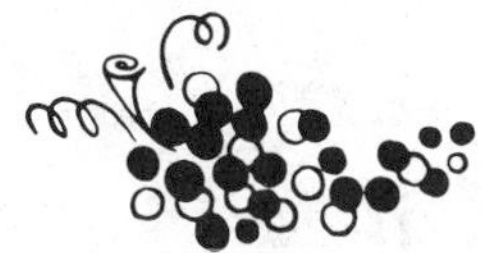

Processed Apples Institute

# Two-For-The-Money Salads

**1 envelope unflavored gelatin**
**¼ cup cold water**
**2 cups canned apple sauce**
**¼ cup sugar**
**¼ cup cider vinegar**
**1 tablespoon prepared horseradish**
**½ teaspoon salt**
**¼ cup chopped raisins**
**½ cup diced celery**
**½ cup finely shredded cabbage**
**Lettuce or chicory**
**Mayonnaise or salad dressing**

Soften gelatin in cold water; heat apple sauce; add gelatin, stir until dissolved. Add sugar, vinegar, prepared horseradish and salt; cool. Add raisins, celery and cabbage; mix well. Pour into individual molds, which have been rinsed in cold water; chill until set. Unmold on lettuce or chicory; serve with mayonnaise or salad dressing. Makes 6 servings. (12 of the little molds)

# Ambrosia Salad

**2 bananas, sliced**
**1 orange, sectioned**
**½ cup seedless grapes**
**¼ cup chopped dates**
**3 tablespoons lemon juice**
**¼ cup grated coconut**

Combine fruits and sprinkle with lemon juice. Chill well. Toss lightly with Whipped Cream Mayonnaise. Serve on crisp lettuce cups and sprinkle with coconut. Makes 4 to 6 servings.

# Valentine Salad

2 3-ounce packages cream cheese
1 cup drained, crushed pineapple
¼ cup pineapple juice
¼ cup walnuts, chopped, divided
6 slices yellow apples, ½ inch thick and unpeeled
6 lettuce cups
6 heart-shaped cranberry jelly slices, ½ inch thick

Soften cream cheese and mix with pineapple, pineapple juice and half the chopped walnuts. Chill in refrigerator. Arrange apple slices in the lettuce cups. Mound cream cheese mixture evenly over each apple slice. Top each with a cranberry heart and sprinkle with remaining walnuts. Serve with mayonnaise. Makes 6 servings.

# Waldorf Salad

3 large, tart, eating apples
1 tablespoon lemon juice
1 cup celery, coarsely chopped
½ cup chopped walnuts
½ cup mayonnaise
2 tablespoons cream
⅛ teaspoon salt

Peel apples, or leave unpeeled if skins are tender and a bright red color. Core apples and cut in ½-inch cubes. Place in a bowl and sprinkle with lemon juice. Add celery and marinate in refrigerator for 10 minutes. Add nuts, mayonnaise combined with cream and salt. Toss lightly and pile in lettuce cups and serve immediately. Makes 5 to 6 servings.

# Blackberry-Pineapple Mold

2 cups fresh blackberries
3 tablespoons sugar
2 packages orange-flavored gelatin
2 cups hot water
2 cups canned pineapple juice and water
2 cups drained pineapple chunks

Combine blackberries and sugar and let stand 10 minutes. Dissolve gelatin in hot water; add fruit juice and water and turn into a 2-quart loaf pan. Add pineapple chunks, distributing the fruit as evenly as possible. Then add blackberries. (Pineapple will sink and the blackberries will float, forming two fruit layers with a clear layer between.) Chill until firm. Unmold and serve with mayonnaise. Makes 8 servings.

# Jellied Waldorf Salad

1 envelope unflavored gelatin
½ cup cold water
1 cup hot water
⅓ cup sugar
½ teaspoon salt
¼ cup lemon juice
½ cup diced celery
2 cups diced, unpeeled tart apples
¼ cup chopped walnuts

Soften gelatin in cold water. Dissolve in hot water. Stir in sugar, salt and lemon juice. Chill until consistency of unbeaten egg white. Fold in celery, apples and nut meats. Turn into individual molds. Chill until firm. Unmold on salad greens and serve with mayonnaise. Makes 6 servings.

# Catalina Luncheon Cooler

Cut chilled cantaloupes into halves crosswise. Remove seeds and peel cantaloupe halves. Place on crisp lettuce cups. Fill the cantaloupe halves with a combination of fresh fruits—peeled and pitted fresh apricots and peaches, ripe banana slices dipped in lemon juice, plump bing cherries—or any other fresh fruits or berries that are in season. Garnish with a bunch of tiny, cool seedless grapes. Tuck in a sprig of fresh mint. For a different dressing use fresh lime juice sweetened to taste with honey.

# Moran's Party Salad

Cut a large ripe watermelon in half lengthwise. Scoop out the pulp in shape of small balls with a melon ball cutter or a teaspoon. Combine watermelon balls with balls of cantaloupe and honeydew. Mix lightly and pile back into watermelon half. Garnish if desired, with fresh unhulled strawberries and serve with Honey French dressing.

Instead of using all melon balls you may use any kind of fruits desired such as pineapple, either fresh or canned, bananas, orange or grapefruit sections, and any fresh berries that are in season.

# Fruit Slaw

3 medium oranges
4 cups shredded cabbage
⅓ cup crushed, drained pineapple
½ cup chopped green pepper
¼ cup mayonnaise
1 tablespoon pineapple juice
½ teaspoon salt

Peel and section oranges. Add cabbage, pineapple, green pepper and toss together. Combine mayonnaise, pineapple juice and salt and mix with the salad. Makes 6 servings.

# Black Cherry Salad

1 No. 2½ can pitted black cherries
2 packages orange-flavored gelatin
⅓ cup lemon juice
1 3-ounce bottle stuffed olives
¾ cup pecans

Drain cherries and add water to cherry syrup to make 3¾ cups liquid. Heat and pour over gelatin and stir until dissolved. Add lemon juice and chill until syrupy. Slice olives and add to gelatin with cherries and pecans. Pour into molds and chill until firm. Makes 12 servings.

# Cheese Stuffed Apricots

8 canned apricot halves
1 No. 2 can grapefruit sections
2 tablespoons milk
Dash of salt
1 3-ounce package cream cheese
¼ cup chopped dates
4 lettuce cups

Drain apricots and grapefruit. Add milk and salt to cream cheese and blend until smooth. Stir in dates. Fill apricot centers with cream cheese mixture. Arrange two apricot halves and three grapefruit sections on each lettuce cup. Serve with French dressing. Makes 4 servings.

# Pink Party Mold

1 cup milk
1 (10½ ounce) package miniature marshmallows
2 envelopes unflavored gelatin
¼ cup cold water
2 - 3 drops red food coloring
¾ cup sugar
½ cup fresh lemon juice
⅓ cup fresh orange juice
1 teaspoon grated lemon peel
1 (14½ ounce) can evaporated milk, chilled
6 maraschino cherries, halved
½ cup crushed pineapple

Heat milk and marshmallows in top of double boiler until marshmallows dissolve. Soak gelatin in cold water 5 minutes; dissolve in marshmallow mixture. Add food coloring, sugar, citrus juices and peel. Chill until mixture begins to set. Whip chilled evaporated milk and fold into gelatin mixture. Fold in halved cherries and crushed pineapple. Pour into a mold and refrigerate until set. Makes 6 servings.

"Courtesy of Sunkist Growers"

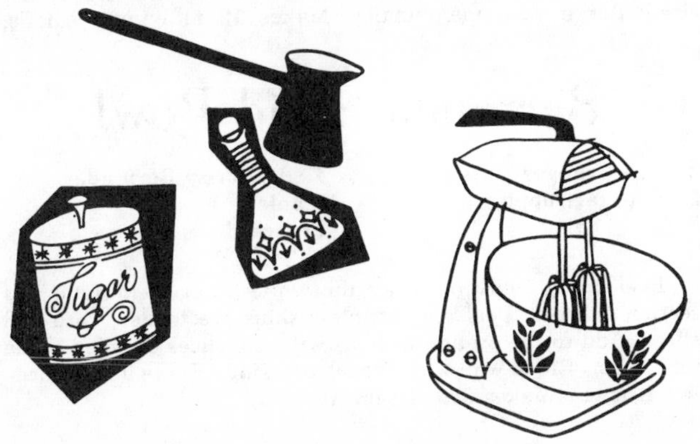


# Molded Pineapple Vegetable Loaf

1¾ cups canned pineapple juice
1 package lemon-flavored gelatin
¼ cup lemon juice
1 cup finely shredded raw cabbage
½ cup grated carrots
1 package cream cheese
2 tablespoons cream
¼ cup chopped nuts
8 slices canned pineapple

Pour 1 cup of the pineapple juice into a saucepan and bring to a boil. Add to lemon-flavored gelatin and stir until dissolved. Add remaining ¾ cup pineapple juice. Stir in lemon juice and cool until mixture is slightly thickened. Add vegetables. Soften cream cheese with cream and blend in nuts. Form into 8 small balls and fit into the center of the pineapple rings. Press firmly in place. Arrange 2 of the filled rings on the bottom of a loaf pan, 2 on each side and 1 on each end. Pour in gelatin mixture and chill in refrigerator until firm. Unmold on a bed of lettuce or other greens. Makes 8 servings.

# Our-Favorite Cranberry Salad

1 package lemon-flavored gelatin
1¼ cups cold water
1 quart cranberries
1 whole orange
¾ cup chopped celery
1 apple, peeled, cored and diced
½ cup chopped nuts
1 cup sugar

Combine gelatin and hot water and stir until gelatin is dissolved. Chill until syrupy. Pick over cranberries and put through food chopper with orange, rind and all. Add celery, apple and nuts to cranberry mixture; cover with sugar and let stand while gelatin cools. Mold fruit into gelatin, pour into mold and chill until firm. Unmold on salad greens. Makes 10 servings.

# Stuffed Pear Salad

4 fresh pears
Lemon juice
½ cup grated carrot
½ cup grated American cheese
¼ cup French dressing

Peel pears, cut in half lengthwise and remove cores. Sprinkle with lemon juice to keep pears from turning dark. Combine remaining ingredients. Fill centers of pears with mixture and serve on lettuce cups with additional French dressing. Makes 4 servings.

# Golden Peach Gels

1 No. 2½ can cling peach halves
2 envelopes unflavored gelatin
6 tablespoons lemon juice
2 teaspoons grated lemon rind
⅔ cup sugar
1 8-ounce package cream-style cottage cheese

Drain peaches thoroughly. Reserve syrup; add water to measure 3 cups. Soften gelatin in 1 cup of the cold liquid; heat remaining liquid. Add softened gelatine, lemon juice, lemon rind and sugar; stir until dissolved. Pour into a 7x12x2-inch glass dish. Chill until consistency of unbeaten egg whites. Place 8 peach halves in gelatin; put a scoop of cottage cheese in the center of each peach half. Chill until firm. To serve, cut gelatin into 8 squares with a filled peach half in center of each. Serve on salad greens. Makes 8 servings.

Florida Citrus Commission

# St. Patrick's Day Salad

**3 or 4 grapefruit (4 cups of sections) grapefruit juice**
**3 envelopes unflavored gelatin**
**½ cup sugar**
**1½ teaspoons salt**
**1½ cups cold water**
**6 tablespoons white vinegar**
**6 tablespoons lime juice**
**Green food coloring**
**1 cup shredded cabbage**
**1 cup finely diced celery**
**½ cup chopped nuts**
**1 package (3 ounces) cream cheese**
**12 pecan halves**

**To section grapefruit, cut slice from top, then cut off peel in strips from top to bottom, cutting deep enough to remove white membrane, then cut slice from bottom. Or cut off peel, round and round spiral fashion. Go over fruit again, removing any remaining white membrane. Cut along side of each dividing membrane from outside to middle of core. Remove section by section, over bowl to retain juice from fruit. Drain sections; add additional grapefruit juice to make 2¼ cups; reserve. Combine gelatin, sugar and salt in saucepan; stir in cold water. Place over low heat and stir until gelatin is dissolved. Add grapefruit juice, vinegar and lime juice. Add green food coloring to desired color. Pour 3 cups of this mixture into shallow pan, about 10 by 15 inches. Chill until firm. Place remaining gelatin mixture in refrigerator and chill to consistency of unbeaten egg white. Fold in grapefruit sections, cabbage, celery and chopped nuts. Pour into 12 muffin tins, 2 inches deep. Chill until firm. Remove flat pan from refrigerator. Cut circles in gelatin mixture about 3 inches round. Remove with spatula and place on individual salad plates to form base of hat. Remove gelatin from muffin tins; place on top of circle to form top of hat. Flute base with softened cream cheese; place pecan half for buckle. Garnish with salad greens and additional grapefruit sections if desired. Serve with mayonnaise. Makes 12 individual salads.**

# Melon Cooler

**1 package lemon-flavored gelatin**
**1 cup hot water**
**1 cup cold water**
**1 tablespoon lemon juice**
**1½ cups melon balls (cantaloupe, honeydew)**

Dissolve gelatin in hot water. Add cold water and lemon juice. Chill until slightly thickened. Then fold in melon balls. Turn into a 1-quart mold. Chill until firm. Unmold. Garnish with additional melon balls and crisp lettuce. Makes 6 servings.

# Peach Ginger Ale Salad

**1 package lemon-flavored gelatin**
**1 cup hot water**
**1 cup ginger ale**
**¼ cup chopped nut meats**
**¼ cup chopped celery**
**1 cup drained, sliced, sweetened fresh peaches**

Dissolve gelatin in hot water. Add ginger ale. Chill until slightly thickened. Then fold in nut meats, celery and peaches. Turn into 8x8x2-inch pan. Chill until firm. Cut in squares. Serve on crisp lettuce with mayonnaise or whipped cream salad dressing. Makes 6 servings.

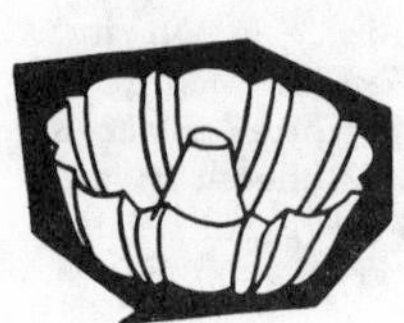

# Bermuda Salad Bowl

**2 large oranges**
**2 crisp, tart apples**
**4 slices crisp Bermuda onion**
**French dressing**

Peel orange, cutting away the white outer membrane and section orange. Peel apples unless skins are tender; core and slice. Add to the orange sections with the slices of onion made into rings. Blend well with French dressing. Serve in a lettuce-lined bowl. Makes 3 to 4 servings.

United Fresh Fruit and Vegetable Association

# Molded Citrus Fruit Salad

2 packages unflavored gelatin
¾ cup fresh lemon juice
¼ cup water
2 cups fresh orange juice
½ teaspoon salt
¾ cup sugar
½ cup sliced bananas
¼ cup fresh tangerine sections
1½ cups fresh grapefruit sections
1 cup fresh orange sections
1 cup sliced unpeeled red apples
¾ cup sliced unpeeled green pears

Soften gelatin in fresh lemon juice and place over hot water to melt. Stir in water, fresh orange juice, salt and sugar. Pour ½-inch layer of clear gelatin into an oiled 6-cup mold. Chill until stiff. Arrange a layer of sliced bananas and tangerine sections as desired over the firm gelatin. Pour in another ½-inch layer of gelatin mixture. Chill until firm. Repeat this process, using layers of grapefruit sections, orange sections, sliced apples and pears. Chill until firm and ready to serve. Unmold onto a serving plate and garnish as desired. Makes 8 servings.

Corn Products Company

# Fresh Fruit Salad

1 honeydew melon
2 oranges
1 fresh pineapple
1 pint strawberries
Boston lettuce
¾ cup mayonnaise
⅓ cup honey
¼ cup orange juice
⅛ teaspoon grated onion

Cut melon in half, remove seeds and scoop out fleshy part with a ball cutter or a teaspoon. Peel and section oranges. Cut pineapple in ¾ inch slices and remove rind and eyes. Cut in cubes, discarding center core of each slice. Hull and wash berries thoroughly. Place greens in a large bowl and arrange fruit attractively in bowl. Combine remaining ingredients and beat with a rotary beater. Serve with honey dressing on the side or toss together to serve. Makes 6 to 8 servings.

# Frozen Pineapple Salad

1 cup shredded pineapple
1 cup shredded cabbage
1 cup chopped celery
½ cup shredded almonds
1 cup heavy cream, whipped
1 cup mayonnaise
Juice of 1 lemon
½ teaspoon salt
½ teaspoon paprika

Combine all ingredients and pack into a large freezing tray of refrigerator and freeze until firm about 2 hours. Cut in squares and serve on lettuce cups. Makes 6 to 8 servings.

# Orange Pyramid Salad

**6 medium-sized oranges**
**3 3-ounce packages cream cheese**
**3 tablespoons onion juice**
**6 lettuce cups**
**Water cress**
**Mayonnaise**

Peel oranges, being careful to remove all white part of rind. Slice crosswise into 3 or 4 slices. Blend together cream cheese and onion juice. Spread mixture between slices of orange. Place oranges in lettuce cups, top with water cress and serve with mayonnaise. Makes 6 servings.

Corn Products Company

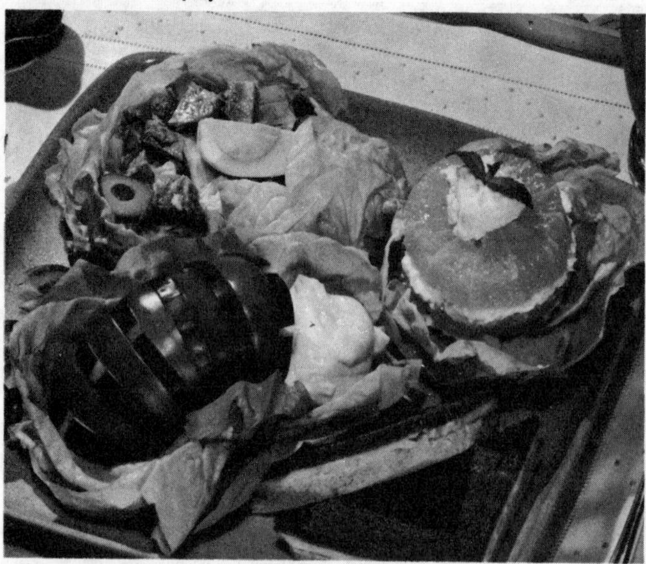

# Salad Patrish

**1 pint strawberries**
**4 oranges**
**1 large cantaloupe**
**3 pears**
**3 bananas**
**Juice of 2 lemons**
**Salad greens**
**1 cup mayonnaise**
**⅓ cup honey**
**1 tablespoon lemon juice**
**2 teaspoons celery seed**

Wash and hull strawberries. Pare and slice oranges. Slice melon in half, scoop out balls with a fruit ball cutter or teaspoon. Remove skins from pears and scoop out core. Slice bananas lengthwise into quarters. Brush pears and bananas with lemon juice. Place a bed of washed, drained chicory or other salad greens on a large salad plate. Arrange fresh fruit on salad greens. Combine mayonnaise, honey, lemon juice and celery seed. Place in a small bowl and serve with the fresh fruit. Makes 6 servings.

# Hawaiian Salad

**2 bunches water cress**
**1 head endive**
**1 papaya**
**1 fresh pineapple**

Wash salad greens and dry thoroughly with a towel or salad drying basket. Line a shallow bowl with the greens. Remove skin and seed of the papaya; cut lengthwise slices. Use a sharp knife for peeling the pineapple. Cut off the base and crown. Stand pineapple on the cutting board. Remove peel by cutting from top to bottom. Cut out bracs. Quarter the pineapple and remove the core; slice lengthwise. Arrange slices of pineapple with papaya on salad greens. Serve Water Cress French dressing. Makes 4 to 6 servings.

Western Growers Association

# Pear Cucumber Aspic

**1 package lime-flavored gelatin**
**1 cup hot water**
**1 cup pear juice and water**
**4 teaspoons vinegar**
**¾ cup diced cucumber**
**½ teaspoon salt**
**¾ cup diced canned pears**

Dissolve gelatin in hot water. Add pear juice and water and vinegar. Chill until slightly thickened. Season cucumber with salt; add pears. Fold into gelatin. Turn into ring mold. Chill until firm. Unmold. Garnish with sliced cucumber and crisp lettuce. Fill center with cottage cheese. Makes 6 servings.

# Fruit in Wine Jelly

3 envelopes unflavored gelatin
3/4 cup cold water
1 cup sugar
1/4 teaspoon salt
1 1/2 cups boiling water
3 tablespoons lemon juice
2 1/4 cups white table wine
2 large navel oranges
1 cup halved and seeded red grapes
2 whole fresh pears

Soften gelatin in cold water. Add sugar, salt and boiling water and stir until gelatin is dissolved. Add lemon juice and wine and chill until the consistency of unbeaten egg whites. Peel oranges, remove all membrane and section. Prepare grapes. Peel and core pears and cut into sections. Fold in fruit and pour into a 1 1/2-quart mold. Chill until firm. Unmold on salad greens. Makes 8 servings.

# Pineapple-Strawberry Salad

1 large fresh pineapple
1 pint fresh strawberries
Sour cream mayonnaise

Cut large ripe pineapple lengthwise into sixths. Remove core and cut meat from peel leaving about 1/2 inch. Cut 5 or 6 gashes crosswise on each piece and insert slices of fresh strawberry. Garnish with pieces of pineapple tops. Serve with Sour Cream Mayonnaise. Makes 6 servings.

Corn Products Company

# Vegetable Salads

## Fresh Raw Spinach Salad

1/2 pound raw spinach
1/4 cup chopped sweet green pepper
1/2 cup onion rings
1 1/2 tablespoons fresh lemon juice
1 tablespoon salad oil
1/2 teaspoon tarragon leaves
1/2 teaspoon salt
1/8 teaspoon ground black pepper
Hard-cooked eggs
Anchovies

Thoroughly wash spinach, drain and wrap in a clean towel to absorb excess water. Tear leaves into bite-size pieces and put into a salad bowl. Add chopped green pepper, onion rings, lemon juice, salad oil, tarragon leaves, salt and black pepper. Toss lightly. Garnish with hard-cooked eggs and anchovies. Makes 6 servings.

United Fresh Fruit and Vegetable Association

# Vegetable Chop Suey

**2 cups bean sprouts, well drained**
**1 cup thinly sliced celery**
**1 cup thinly sliced radishes**
**1 cup thinly sliced unpeeled cucumber**
**1 green pepper, cut in strips**
**1 raw carrot, cut in thin sticks**
**3 green onions, thinly sliced**
**French dressing**
**Soy sauce**

Combine vegetables in a large salad bowl. Moisten with the desired amount of French dressing. Season to taste with soy sauce. Makes 6 servings.

# Laguna Cabbage Salad

**3 cups shredded cabbage**
**½ cup diced celery**
**½ cup shredded carrot**
**1 cup thick sour cream**
**2 tablespoons vinegar**
**1 tablespoon fresh lemon juice**
**1 tablespoon finely minced onion**
**½ teaspoon salt**
**3 tablespoons sugar**
**Pepper**

Toss together the prepared vegetables. Mix together the remaining ingredients and toss with the prepared vegetables. Serve very cold on lettuce cups. Makes 6 servings.

# Caesar Salad

**3 to 4 heads crisp, chilled lettuce and romaine**
**¼ cup garlic-flavored oil**
**½ cup salad oil**
**1 tablespoon Worcestershire sauce**
**½ teaspoon dry mustard**
**Salt and freshly ground black pepper**
**¾ to 1 cup grated parmesan cheese**
**1 raw egg**
**Juice of 3 lemons**
**2 cups crisp croutons**

Tear lettuce into not-too-small pieces in a big salad bowl. Pour garlic-flavored oil and salad oil over greens. Add Worcestershire sauce, mustard, salt, pepper and grated cheese. Break raw egg directly over salad greens. Sprinkle lemon juice over greens and toss and mix very thoroughly until all trace of egg has disappeared. Add crisp croutons, mix thoroughly and serve immediately. Makes 6 to 8 servings.
*Note: Chop or mash 2 or 3 peeled cloves of garlic. Cover with olive oil and let stand at room temperature several hours before using. To make croutons; cut thin slices of bread in small cubes and toast in a slow oven until thoroughly crisp and lightly brown. Cubes may be fried in 2 tablespoons of olive oil also.*

# Valentine Aspics

**2 envelopes unflavored gelatin**
**3½ cups tomato juice, divided**
**¼ teaspoon Tabasco**
**½ teaspoon salt**
**1 teaspoon sugar**
**1 teaspoon Worcestershire sauce**
**¼ cup lemon or lime juice**
**8 bread slices**
**6 stuffed olives**
**1 3-ounce package cream cheese**

Sprinkle gelatin on 1 cup of the tomato juice in saucepan to soften. Place over low heat, stirring constantly, until gelatin is dissolved. Remove from heat; add remaining 2½ cups tomato juice, Tabasco, salt, sugar, Worcestershire sauce and lemon juice. Pour into 8½-cup individual heart shaped molds; chill until firm. To serve, cut bread slices into heart shapes, the same size as molds. Finely chop olives; add to cream cheese and cream well. Spread bread with mixture. Unmold aspice on cream cheese topped bread. Serve with mayonnaise using ¼ teaspoon Tabasco to each ½ cup mayonnaise used. Makes 8 servings.

McIlhenny's Tabasco

# Emerald Macedoine Salad

**1 package lime-flavored gelatin**
**1 teaspoon salt**
**1 cup hot water**
**¾ cup cold water**
**2 tablespoons vinegar**
**¾ cup finely chopped celery**
**½ cup sliced stuffed olives**
**¼ cup diced green pepper**

Dissolve gelatin and salt in hot water. Add cold water and vinegar. Chill until slightly thickened. Then fold in celery, olives and green pepper. Turn into large mold. Chill until firm. Unmold and serve with mayonnaise. Makes 5 servings.

# Stuffed Tomato Salads

Wash medium-sized to large tomatoes. Peel if desired. Remove core and cut tomatoes in quarters almost to the base; spread apart. Salt and chill thoroughly. Just before serving fill with any desired filling or one of the following. Serve on crisp lettuce leaves with either mayonnaise or French dressing.
*Egg Salad*: Chop one hard-cooked egg for each tomato. Add tomato pulp, pickle relish, chopped celery, minced onion, seasonings to taste and moisten with mayonnaise.
*Egg and Olive*: Chop one hard-cooked egg for each tomato. Add sliced stuffed olives, minced onion, mayonnaise and season to taste.
*Fish Salad*: Mix equal amounts of fish such as crab, shrimp, or lobster with chopped celery. Add minced onion to taste, with mayonnaise and season.
*Chicken Salad*: Mix minced chicken with an equal amount of chopped celery. Add mayonnaise and minced onion to taste.
*Cottage Cheese*: Mix cottage cheese with tomato pulp and minced onion. Or mix with chopped chives, chopped parsley or any desired seasonings.

# Old Fashioned Potato Salad

**6 cooked potatoes, cubed**
**¼ cup thinly sliced radishes**
**½ cup diced celery**
**¼ cup minced onion**
**4 hard-cooked eggs, diced**
**1 cup Boiled Dressing**

Combine all ingredients and mix lightly. Chill well. Serve on lettuce cups and garnish with quartered hard-cooked eggs and tomato wedges. Makes 6 servings.

# Bean Salad

**1½ cups cooked dried beans, drained**
**3 hard-cooked eggs, sliced**
**½ cup chopped sweet pickle**
**½ cup mayonnaise**

Combine all ingredients and chill well. Serve on lettuce cups and garnish with parsley. Makes 4 servings.

# Tomato Vegetable Salad

**3½ cups tomato juice**
**1 bay leaf**
**1 tablespoon chopped onion**
**½ teaspoon salt**
**Dash of cayenne**
**2 envelopes unflavored gelatin**
**¼ cup cold water**
**1 teaspoon Worcestershire sauce**
**1 teaspoon lemon juice**
**1 cup diced celery**
**1 cup grated raw carrots**
**1 small green pepper, chopped**

Combine tomato juice, bay leaf, onion, salt and cayenne; cook over low heat 15 minutes. Remove bay leaf. Soften gelatin in cold water. Add to hot tomato juice and stir until dissolved. Add Worcestershire sauce and lemon juice. Chill in refrigerator until slightly thickened. Blend in vegetables. Pour into an 8-inch ring mold. Chill until firm. Unmold and garnish as desired. Makes 8 servings.

United Fresh Fruit and Vegetable Association

# Molded Fresh Beet and Cucumber Salad

**2 packages unflavored gelatin**
**½ cup cold water**
**⅓ cup sugar**
**½ teaspoon salt**
**2 cups boiling water**
**¾ cup fresh lemon juice**
**10 cucumber slices**
**1½ cups (¾ pound) diced fresh beets cooked**
**Cucumber slices for garnish**
**Salad greens for garnish**

Soften gelatin in cold water. Add sugar, salt and boiling water. Stir until dissolved. Add lemon juice. Pour ½ cup of this mixture into bottom of a 5-cup ring mold. Chill until partially set. Chill remaining gelatin mixture in bowl until it is the consistency of unbeaten egg whites. Arrange 10 cucumber slices in ring pattern in bottom layer of partially-set gelatin. Chill until firm. Fold beets into remaining gelatin. Pour into mold over cucumber layer. Chill until firm. Unmold onto serving plate and garnish with cucumber slices and salad greens. Makes 8 servings.

# Beet Salad Ring

**1 No. 2 can diced beets**
**1 package lemon-flavored gelatin**
**⅔ cup orange juice**
**2 teaspoons horse-radish**
**2 teaspoons vinegar**
**1 teaspoon minced onion**
**1 teaspoon salt**
**1 cup finely chopped celery**

Drain juice from beets; measure 1 cup juice into a saucepan and bring to a boil. Dissolve gelatin in hot beet juice. Add remaining ingredients except celery. When mixture is slightly thickened fold in celery and beets. Turn into a ring mold and chill until firm. Unmold on crisp salad greens and fill center with any desired filling. Serve with mayonnaise. Makes 6 servings.

# Christmas Garden Salad

1 small head cauliflower
2 medium onions, thinly sliced
1 large green pepper, slivered
⅔ cup vinegar
⅓ cup salad oil
2 teaspoons sugar
¼ teaspoon marjoram
¼ teaspoon thyme
¼ teaspoon paprika
4 cups fresh spinach, washed
4 pimientos, cut in star shapes

Let cauliflower stand 30 minutes in cold salted water. Drain, rinse, break into flowerets. Mix with onions and green pepper. Pour combined vinegar, oil and seasonings over vegetables and toss together. Chill in refrigerator about 30 minutes. Just before serving break spinach leaves into salad mixture; toss lightly. Garnish with pimiento stars. Makes 6 to 8 servings.

# Frozen Tomato Salad

6 small firm tomatoes
1 cup cottage cheese
½ cup chopped cucumbers
2 tablespoons minced onion
3 tablespoons chopped green pepper
2 tablespoons chopped pimiento
½ teaspoon salt
1 cup cooked dressing
1 cup heavy cream, whipped

Wash and peel tomatoes, remove stem ends and scoop out centers to form cups. Combine cheese, cucumbers, onion, green pepper, pimiento, salt and 3 tablespoons of the cooked dressing. Fill centers of tomatoes with mixture. Place tomatoes cut-side down in freezing tray of refrigerator. Mix remaining salad dressing with whipped cream and pour around tomatoes. Freeze about 2 hours. Cut in squares so that each portion is a stuffed tomato in a square of frozen dressing. Serve on lettuce cups. Makes 6 servings.

# Golden Glow Salad

1 cup grated raw carrots
½ cup chopped salted peanuts
½ teaspoon salt
4 tablespoons mayonnaise
6 slices pineapple
Salad greens
French dressing

Combine carrots, peanuts, salt and mayonnaise. Place pineapple slices on salad greens and top each pineapple slice with a large spoonful of the carrot mixture. Serve with French dressing. Makes 6 servings.

# Tomato and Avocado Salad Bowl

3 medium-sized tomatoes
½ cup French dressing
1 head lettuce
1 small avocado
¼ cup crumbled Roquefort cheese

Wash and stem the tomatoes and cut into eighths. Pour the French dressing over tomatoes and let stand ½ hour in the refrigerator. Meanwhile, wash the lettuce, separate leaves and break into small chunks. Cut avocado in halves, remove seed, peel and then cut into crescent slices. Arrange lettuce in a salad bowl, cover with tomatoes, avocado slices and Roquefort cheese. Pour French dressing from marinated tomatoes over top of salad and toss well before serving. Makes 6 servings.

Best Foods, Inc.

# Avocado Soufflé Salad

**1 cup boiling water**
**1 package (3-ounce) lime-flavored gelatin**
**½ cup cold water**
**2 tablespoons lemon juice**
**½ cup mayonnaise**
**½ teaspoon salt**
**1 medium avocado**
**1 cup diced grapefruit sections**
**½ cup diced celery**
**Iceberg lettuce**

**Pour boiling water over gelatin in bowl; stir until gelatin is completely dissolved. Add cold water, lemon juice, mayonnaise and salt; blend with rotary beater. Pour into freezing tray or metal loaf pan. Chill in freezing unit until firm about 1 inch from edge of pan but still soft in center, about 20 to 25 minutes. Peel and mash avocado. Turn chilled gelatin mixture into bowl and whip with rotary beater until fluffy and thick. Fold avocado, celery and grapefruit into whipped gelatin mixture. Pour into 1-quart mold or individual molds. Chill in refrigerator (not freezing unit) until firm, about 45 to 60 minutes. Unmold. Serve, garnished with Iceberg lettuce and** additional **mayonnaise, if desired. Makes 4 to 6 servings.**

# Bacon and Spinach Salad Bowl

8 slices bacon
1 pound cleaned raw spinach
3 hard-cooked eggs, chopped
French dressing

Fry bacon until crisp. Drain on paper and crumble. Tear spinach into bite-sized pieces in a salad bowl. Add bacon and chopped eggs. Add just enough French dressing to moisten and toss lightly. Makes 6 servings.

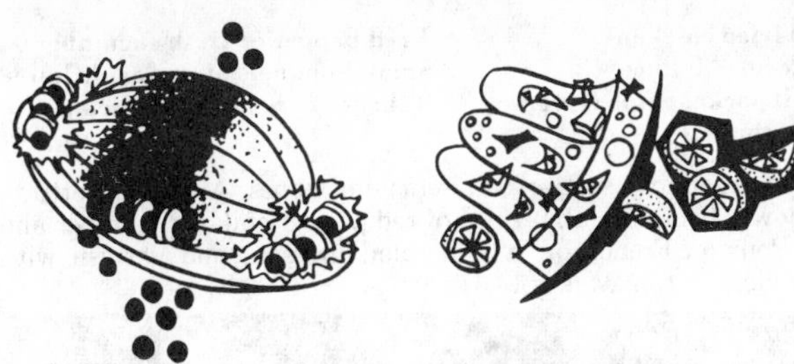

Wine Institute

# Jellied Cranberry-Turkey Salad

1 cup bottled cranberry juice
1 package (3-ounce) raspberry or cherry gelatin
½ cup Port
Tiny sprigs romaine or other lettuce
Turkey Salad (recipe below)

Heat cranberry juice to boiling. Stir in gelatin until dissolved. Remove from heat; add Port and cool. Turn into oversize wine glasses, goblets or individual molds. Chill until firm. When ready to serve, arrange small spears of romaine in each glass. Spoon in turkey salad. If small molds are used, turn out on crisp greens and surround with salad mixture. Makes 4 or 5 servings.

### Turkey Salad

1½ cups bite-size cooked turkey or chicken pieces
¾ cup chopped celery
2 tablespoons chopped green onion
¾ teaspoon seasoned salt
⅛ teaspoon seasoned or plain pepper
3 or 4 tablespoons mayonnaise
½ cup seedless grapes

Combine all ingredients, except mayonnaise and grapes, thoroughly and chill for several hours. Add mayonnaise and grapes just before serving.

Brewers Foundation

# Insalata Mista

## (Mixed Salad)

1 clove garlic
1 small head romaine
1 head chicory or escarole and stalk endive
1 small onion, minced
2 teaspoons chopped parsley
4 hard-cooked eggs, sliced
4 medium cold boiled potatoes, cubed
1 medium tomato, quartered
6 radishes, sliced
6 pitted black olives
1 teaspoon capers
½ teaspoon crushed oregano
Salt to taste

Rub salad bowl with cut clove of garlic. Tear washed, crisped greens into bite-size pieces, dropping them into salad bowl. Add onion and parsley. Place egg slices in row across center of salad. Arrange cubed potatoes, tomato wedges and sliced radishes in groups. Garnish with olives and capers. Chill in refrigerator until ready to serve. Sprinkle with oregano and salt. Serve with Beer French Dressing. Makes 4 generous servings.

# Lima Bean Salad

6 cups hot cooked dried lima beans
1 clove garlic
½ teaspoon salt
¼ teaspoon pepper
2 tablespoons sugar
¼ cup finely minced onion
¼ cup chopped parsley
⅓ cup wine vinegar
⅔ cup bean liquid

Drain hot beans and save the liquid. Crush garlic thoroughly, add salt and remaining ingredients and mix well. Add the beans and toss lightly. Let stand in the refrigerator for several hours before serving. Makes 6 to 8 servings.

# Cauliflower Salad

1 small head cauliflower, raw
¼ cup finely chopped green pepper
½ cup finely chopped celery
2 tablespoons finely chopped pimiento
1 teaspoon salt
1 cup tomato French dressing
Lettuce cups

Slice the cauliflower into paper-thin slices, so that it will fall apart into tiny pieces. Mix with the other ingredients, except lettuce, and let stand in refrigerator several hours. Serve in a salad bowl lined with lettuce cups. Makes 6 servings.

# Tossed Rice Bowl

Large can bean sprouts, drained and rinsed
1 cup thinly sliced unpeeled radishes
1 cup diced unpeeled cucumber
1 cup thinly sliced celery
1 cup chopped water cress
2 small sweet onions, chopped
¼ cup chopped green pepper
1½ cups cold cooked rice
1 teaspoon monosodium glutamate
1 cup mayonnaise
Soy sauce, to taste

Rub a salad bowl with garlic. Have all vegetables and rice chilled and layer them into bowl in order given. Blend monosodium glutamate (MSG) and mayonnaise and pour over top layer of salad. Lift and toss carefully to blend but not crush. Taste and if salt is needed try adding soy sauce for a change. Makes 6 to 8 servings.

# Cranberry Holiday Salad

2 cups raw cranberries
1 orange, thinly sliced
1 cup water
¾ cup sugar
1 envelope unflavored gelatin
¼ cup cold water
½ cup seedless grapes, sliced
1 cup diced celery
¼ cup chopped nuts

Cook cranberries, orange and water in covered saucepan until cranberry skins pop open. Press through fine sieve; add sugar and heat to boiling. Soften gelatin in cold water, add hot cranberries and stir until gelatin is dissolved. Chill until syrupy. Add remaining ingredients and turn into a ring mold. Chill in refrigerator until firm. Unmold and garnish as desired. Makes 6 servings.

# Chicken Salad

(See picture opposite.)

1 cold fried chicken
1 large head lettuce
1 small package fine frozen peas, thawed
1 red pepper or fresh cucumber
Small bouquets of raw cauliflower
8 slices of crisply fried bacon

Cut chicken into small pieces removing bones. Mix with lettuce, cauliflower bouquets, thin rings of red pepper and/or cucumber and peas. Pour on French or Italian salad dressing and garnish with bacon slices on top. Makes 4 - 6 servings.

# Savory Potato Salad

6 medium potatoes, cooked
½ teaspoon savory
¼ teaspoon marjoram
¼ cup salad oil
¼ cup vinegar
2 teaspoons salt
¼ teaspoon pepper
1 tablespoon caraway seeds
1 medium onion, minced
1 small cucumber, diced
½ cup mayonnaise
2 tablespoons mustard
Tomato quarters
Cucumber slices
Lettuce leaves

Slice potatoes into a large bowl. Put seasonings in a jar with the oil and vinegar; shake to blend well. Pour mixture over potatoes and let stand about 1 hour. Add caraway seeds, onion, cucumber, mayonnaise and mustard. Toss gently to combine all ingredients thoroughly. Garnish with tomatoes, cucumber slices and lettuce leaves. Makes 6 servings.

# String Bean and Bacon Salad

1 teaspoon salt
Dash of pepper
½ teaspoon sugar
⅓ cup salad oil
2 tablespoons vinegar
3 tablespoons catsup
2 cups cooked green beans
3 slices cooked bacon
Salad greens

Combine salt, pepper, sugar, oil, vinegar and catsup and mix well. Toss beans in mixture. Crumble bacon and add to beans. Line a bowl with salad greens and top with mixed beans and bacon. Makes 6 servings.

*Toasted Cheese Squares on Long Rolls, p. 453*

*Baked Cheese Tidbits, p. 453*

# Perfection Salad

1 package lemon- or orange-flavored gelatin
1 cup hot water
1 cup cold water
1 teaspoon salt
1 tablespoon vinegar
1 cup shredded cabbage
½ cup chopped celery
½ cup shredded carrot
1 tablespoon finely minced onion

Dissolve gelatin in hot water; add the cold water, salt and vinegar and chill. When mixture is slightly thickened, fold in remaining ingredients. Pour into mold and chill until firm. Unmold on salad greens and top with mayonnaise. Makes 6 to 8 servings.

# Dutch Potato Salad

1 teaspoon flour
2 tablespoons brown sugar
½ cup water
¼ cup vinegar
1 cup mayonnaise
8 hot cooked potatoes
4 strips bacon, fried and diced
3 hard-cooked eggs, sliced
3 tablespoons minced onion
1 cup cooked green beans

Combine flour, brown sugar, water and vinegar in top of double boiler. Add mayonnaise and cook over boiling water until slightly thickened. Dice hot potatoes, add bacon, hard-cooked eggs and onions. Pour hot dressing over mixture and toss lightly. Top with cooked green beans and serve immediately. Makes 6 servings.

Corn Products Company

# Summer Salad

1 envelope unflavored gelatin
½ cup cold water
¾ cup hot water
¼ cup sugar
½ teaspoon salt
1 tablespoon lemon juice
½ cup finely shredded cabbage
1 cup diced celery
2 tablespoons minced green pepper
¼ cup vinegar

Soften gelatin in cold water. Add hot water, sugar and salt and stir until sugar is dissolved. Add vinegar and lemon juice. Chill until mixture is the consistency of unbeaten egg whites. Stir in cabbage, celery and green pepper. Turn into large or individual molds and chill until firm. Unmold on lettuce and serve with mayonnaise. Makes 6 servings.

# August Salad

(See picture opposite.)

One large solid lettuce is the basis for this quick dish. Everything in one bowl, cheese and wine afterwards.

Smoked mackerel is used in this dish but all other kinds of smoked fish can be used.

Rub the salad bowl with a slice of garlic before filling it with fresh crisp lettuce, slices of radishes, and cucumber, strips of paprika, pieces of smoked mackerel, hard-boiled eggs, slices and strips of celery and chopped dill. Use either a French salad dressing or the following sauce.

Mix the juice of ½ lemon with 2 teaspoons mixed mustard, a little salt, white pepper and sugar. Stir thoroughly and add 1½ cups thick cream.

# Frosted Vegetables Salad Loaf

2 envelopes unflavored gelatin
½ cup cold water
2 cups boiling water
2 tablespoons sugar
½ cup vinegar
2 tablespoons lemon juice
1 teaspoon salt
1 scallion, minced
½ cup coarsely grated carrot
½ cup sliced celery
¼ cup diced green pepper
¼ cup sliced radishes
1 teaspoon unflavored gelatin
1 tablespoon cold water
1 cup mayonnaise
Salad greens

Soften gelatin in cold water, add boiling water, sugar, vinegar, lemon juice and salt; stir until gelatin is dissolved. Chill until the consistency of unbeaten egg white. Fold in vegetables and turn into loaf pan; chill till firm. Soak gelatin in 1 tbs. cold water and dissolve over hot water; fold in mayonnaise. Unmold salad loaf on serving platter, frost with mayonnaise mixture and return to refrigerator until firm. Garnish with salad greens before serving. Makes 6 to 8 servings.

# Spring Salad with Roquefort Cream

**1 head lettuce**
**½ head chicory**
**1 small bunch water cress**
**2 tomatoes, cut in wedges**
**1 onion, thinly sliced**
**1 cucumber, sliced**
**1 small can anchovy fillets**
**1 cup French dressing**
**¼ cup mayonnaise**
**¼ cup crumbled Roquefort cheese**

Tear lettuce and chicory into bite-size pieces in a salad bowl. Add tomato wedges, green pepper rings, onion rings, cucumber and anchovies. Combine French dressing and mayonnaise, fold in cheese and blend well. Pour dressing over salad and toss lightly. Serve immediately. Makes 6 servings.

Best Foods

# Hot Beet Salad

**1 No. 2 can diced beets**
**1 8-ounce jar sweet mixed pickles**
**1 tablespoon butter or margarine**
**Salt and pepper to taste**

Place diced beets and liquid in a saucepan. Drain juice from the pickles and add to beets. Add butter. Cover and allow to simmer until the spicy juice has permeated the diced beets. Remove from heat and add ½ cup chopped sweet mixed pickles and salt and pepper to taste. Drain thoroughly and serve immediately with mayonnaise. Makes 4 servings.

# Hearts of Lettuce with Bleu Cheese

**1 medium head lettuce**
**3 tomatoes**
**½ cup mayonnaise**
**1 tablespoon vinegar**
**1 tablespoon cream**
**1 tablespoon crumbled Bleu cheese**

Cut lettuce into 4 wedges. Cut tomatoes in wedges. Blend mayonnaise, vinegar, cream and Bleu cheese together. Place lettuce and tomatoes on serving platter with cheese mixture on the side. Makes 4 servings.

# Cooked Vegetable Salad

**2 cups cooked mixed vegetables**
**¼ cup chopped green pepper**
**½ cup grated raw carrot**
**1 tablespoon minced onion**
**½ cup chopped celery**
**¼ cup French dressing**
**¼ cup crumbled Roquefort cheese**

Combine all ingredients and toss well. Chill several hours in the refrigerator. Serve in crisp lettuce cups. Makes 4 servings.

# Spring Green Salad

**½ cup sliced scallions**
**½ cup shredded carrots**
**⅓ cup sliced radishes**
**3 cups broken salad greens**
**½ cup salad oil**
**¼ cup vinegar**
**2 hard-cooked eggs, chopped**
**½ teaspoon prepared mustard**
**1 teaspoon salt**
**Dash of pepper**
**1 teaspoon sugar**

Combine all ingredients and toss lightly. Chill thoroughly before serving. Makes 6 servings.

# Asparagus Appetizer Salad

**1 cup mayonnaise**
**2 tablespoons French dressing**
**2 tablespoons cider vinegar**
**1 tablespoon chopped parsley**
**1 tablespoon chopped chives**
**1 tablespoon chopped pimiento**
**2 tablespoons pickle relish**
**18 stalks asparagus, cooked**
**3 hard-cooked eggs, sliced**
**Salad greens**

Combine mayonnaise, French dressing, cider vinegar, parsley, chives, pimiento and pickle relish. Mix well and let stand in refrigerator for at least one hour for flavors to blend. Arrange on individual salad plates 3 stalks of asparagus and slices of egg on salad greens. Cover with sauce. Makes 6 servings.

Asparagus Appetizer Salad

# Vegetable and Pineapple Soufflé Salad

**1 package lime-flavored gelatin**
**1 cup hot water**
**½ cup cold water**
**1½ tablespoons vinegar**
**½ cup mayonnaise**
**¼ teaspoon salt**
**Dash of pepper**
**½ cup drained crushed pineapple**
**½ cup drained finely diced cucumber**
**½ cup finely diced celery**
**1 tablespoon finely chopped onion**

Dissolve gelatin in hot water. Add cold water, vinegar, mayonnaise, salt and pepper. Blend well with rotary beater. Pour into refrigerator freezing tray. Quick-chill in freezing unit 15 to 20 minutes, or until firm about 1-inch from edge but soft in center. Turn mixture into bowl and whip with rotary beater until fluffy. Fold in pineapple and vegetables. Pour into individual molds. Chill until firm in refrigerator. Unmold and garnish with salad greens. Serve with additional mayonnaise, if desired. Makes 4 to 6 servings.

The Roquefort Association

# Celery Pinwheels

**1 medium stalk celery**
**1 3-ounce package cream cheese**
**2 tablespoons crumbled Roquefort cheese**
**Mayonnaise**
**Worcestershire sauce**

Clean the celery and separate the branches. Blend together the softened cream cheese with the Roquefort. Add mayonnaise to make it of spreading consistency and season with a dash of Worcestershire sauce. Fill the branches with cheese mixture. Press branches back into the original form of the stalk. Roll in waxed paper and chill overnight in refrigerator. Just before serving slice celery crosswise forming pinwheels. Arrange 3 slices on crisp lettuce cups for each serving.

## Grapefruit Perfection Salad

**2 cans (1 pound each) grapefruit sections**
**Canned grapefruit juice**
**2 envelopes unflavored gelatin**
**½ cup sugar**
**½ teaspoon salt**
**1 pimiento**
**2 cups shredded cabbage**
**½ cup diced celery**

Drain grapefruit sections; add enough canned grapefruit juice to make 3½ cups. Sprinkle gelatin on 1 cup of the liquid in saucepan to soften; place over medium heat, stirring constantly, until gelatin is dissolved. Remove from heat; add sugar and salt; stir until dissolved. Stir in remaining grapefruit juice. Cut pimiento with small star cutter. Arrange pimiento stars with several grapefruit sections in bottom of 6 cup mold. Pour in ½ cup of the gelatin liquid; chill until almost firm. Chill remaining liquid until the consistency of unbeaten egg white. Fold in cabbage, celery and 1 cup of the grapefruit sections. Turn into ring mold; chill until firm. Unmold and garnish with remaining sections and salad greens. Makes 8 to 10 servings.

# Seafood Salads

## Orange and Seafood Salad

**3 cups orange pieces, cut bite-size**
**3 cups cooked seafood (shrimp, lobster crab-meat, tuna or fillet of sole), cut into bite-size pieces**
**3 pints shredded lettuce for salad plate or bowl**
**Sour Cream Dressing**

Combine orange pieces and seafood. Cover with enough Sour Cream Dressing to coat nicely. Serve on bed of shredded lettuce.

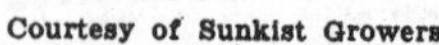
Courtesy of Sunkist Growers

Carnation Evaporated Milk

## Salmon Salad Supreme

**2 envelopes unflavored gelatin**
**¼ cup lemon juice**
**1⅔ cups (large can) undiluted evaporated milk**
**⅓ cup water**
**½ teaspoon paprika**
**⅓ cup chopped celery**
**1 can (1 pound) salmon, drained, boned and flaked**
**¾ cup water**
**1 tablespoon prepared horseradish or to taste**
**1 teaspoon prepared mustard**
**Dash tabasco**
**1 teaspoon salt**
**⅛ teaspoon pepper**
**½ cup pitted ripe olives, halved**
**Additional sliced ripe olives for garnish**

Soften 1 envelope gelatin in lemon juice. Combine gelatin with 2/3 cup evaporated milk, 1/3 cup water and paprika. Cook over boiling water, stirring constantly, until dissolved. Add celery and salmon; turn into 1-quart mold; chill until firm. Soften remaining envelope gelatin in ¾ cup water; stir in remaining 1 cup evaporated milk. Cook over boiling water, stirring constantly until gelatin dissolves. Remove from heat and stir in horseradish, mustard, tabasco, salt and pepper. Chill to consistency of unbeaten egg white. Fold in ½-cup olives and spoon on top of salmon layer. Chill 2-3 hours. Unmold and garnish with additional ripe olive slices. Makes 4 to 6 servings.

Shrimp Association of the Americas

# Shrimp Aspic

**2 chicken bouillon cubes**
**2 envelopes unflavored gelatin**
**¼ cup cold water**
**1 cup boiling water**
**1 cup dry white wine**
**2 cups cooked shrimp**
**½ cup diced cucumber**
**¼ cup diced celery**
**¼ cup diced black olives**

**Soak the bouillon cubes and gelatin in cold water until soft. Add the boiling water and stir till gelatin is dissolved. Then add the wine. Chop shrimp, reserving about 6 whole shrimp. Arrange the whole shrimp in a mold and cover with a layer of the gelatin. Chill until set. Meanwhile, cool remaining gelatin until thick but not set. Stir in cucumber, celery, olives and chopped shrimp. Spoon the mixture into the mold. Chill until set. Unmold on lettuce leaves and serve with a dressing of mayonnaise thinned with a little white wine. Makes 6 servings.**

# Southern Shrimp Salad

**¼ cup salad oil**
**1 tablespoon prepared mustard**
**2 tablespoons lemon juice**
**2 scallions, thinly sliced**
**¼ cup chopped celery**
**½ teaspoon salt**
**¼ teaspoon pepper**
**1 cup whole shrimp**
**Shredded lettuce**

Measure first 7 ingredients into a bowl in order given; blend thoroughly with a fork. Add shrimp and toss well. Cover and set in refrigerator for about 2 hours. Mix again just before serving and heap on plates with shredded lettuce. Makes 3 servings.

# Molded Crab Salad

**1 envelope unflavored gelatin**
**¼ cup cold water**
**1½ teaspoons dry mustard**
**1½ teaspoons salt**
**2 tablespoons sugar**
**2 eggs**
**1 cup sour cream**
**¼ cup vinegar**
**1½ cups flaked, cooked crab meat**

Soften gelatin in cold water. Combine mustard, salt, sugar and eggs in the top of a double boiler. Add the cream and vinegar and cook over hot water, stirring constantly, until mixture coats a silver spoon. Add the gelatin and stir until gelatin is dissolved. Cool slightly. Strain custard over the crab meat. Turn into a mold and chill until firm. Unmold on crisp greens and garnish with tomato wedges. Makes 6 servings.

# Lobster Salad

**2 cans lobster**
**½ cup chopped cucumber**
**1 cup chopped celery**
**¼ cup French dressing**
**2 envelopes unflavored gelatin**
**½ cup cold water**
**3 chicken bouillon cubes**
**3 cups boiling water**
**2 tablespoons chopped pimiento**
**1 teaspoon grated onion**
**1 teaspoon salt**
**Mayonnaise**

Cut lobster in chunks. Combine with cucumber and celery. Pour French dressing over mixture and allow to stand while preparing rest of salad. Soak gelatin in cold water 5 minutes. Dissolve bouillon cubes in boiling water; add to gelatin and stir until gelatin is dissolved. Chill until mixture is the consistency of unbeaten egg whites. Add pimiento, onion, salt and lobster mixture. Pour into a ring mold and chill until firm. Unmold on lettuce leaves. Serve with mayonnaise. Makes 6 to 8 servings.

Corn Products Company

# Filled Avocados

(See picture between pgs. 64-65.)

**4 ripe avocados**
**6 hard boiled eggs**
**1 lb. cooked shelled shrimp**
**Mayonnaise**
**Chopped parsley**

Cut avocados in half, lengthwise and remove stone. Scoop out a little of the center and mix with half of the shrimp, the mayonnaise and the chopped egg whites. Fill the avocados with the shrimp mixture and garnish with remaining shrimp and sieved egg yolks.

# Tuna Fish Salad

**1 7-ounce can tuna fish, drained and flaked**
**1 cup diced celery**
**1 cup diced avocado**
**¼ teaspoon salt**
**Dash of white pepper**
**¼ cup salad dressing**
**1 tablespoon lemon juice**
**Chicory**

Toss together, lightly, tuna fish, celery, diced avocado, salt and pepper. Combine salad dressing and lemon juice. Add to tuna fish mixture and blend carefully. Pile in a bowl and garnish with chicory. Makes 4 servings.

# Tuna Temptation

2 teaspoons unflavored gelatin
3 tablespoons cold water
¼ cup mayonnaise
½ cup chopped celery
2 cans (7 ounce) flaked tuna fish, drained
½ pint sour cream
¼ cup Indian relish
1 tablespoon reconstituted lemon juice

In medium-sized mixing bowl sprinkle gelatin onto cold water and let stand 5 minutes to soften; dissolve over hot water. Cool gelatin slightly; stir in mayonnaise, celery and tuna. Combine sour cream, relish and lemon juice. Stir into tuna mixture. Rinse a 1-quart mold with cold water. Spoon mixture into mold. Chill until firm, about 3 hours. Unmold. Garnish with lemon slices and watercress. Makes 6 servings.

The Borden Company

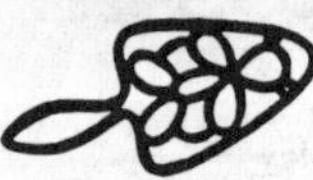

# Salmon Mousse

1 tablespoon unflavored gelatin
2 tablespoons cold water
½ tablespoon flour
1½ tablespoons sugar
1 teaspoon dry mustard
1 teaspoon salt
Few grains cayenne
2 eggs
¾ cup milk
¼ cup vinegar
1½ tablespoons melted butter
1½ cups flaked salmon
½ cup heavy cream, whipped

Soften gelatin in cold water. Mix flour, sugar and seasonings in top part of double boiler. Add eggs and stir until smooth. Add milk, then vinegar slowly and mix well. Cook over hot water until mixture thickens, stirring constantly. Stir in butter and softened gelatin. Stir until gelatin is dissolved. Stir in flaked salmon. Chill, stirring occasionally. When slightly thickened fold in whipped cream and turn into a mold. Chill until firm. Unmold on crisp lettuce and serve with Cucumber Dressing. Makes 6 servings.

# Crab Louie

Lettuce cups
2 to 3 cups crab meat
3 hard-cooked eggs, sliced
Chopped chives
½ cup French dressing
½ cup chili sauce
2 tablespoons mayonnaise
1 teaspoon Worcestershire sauce
Salt and pepper to taste

Arrange lettuce leaves around the inside of a salad bowl, place a bed of shredded lettuce in bottom of bowl. Pick over crab meat and place on top of lettuce. Arrange egg slices around crab meat and sprinkle with chives. Combine remaining ingredients, mix well. Pour over top of crab meat. Makes 4 to 6 servings.

# Crab Meat Apple Salad

2 small cans crab meat
3 stalks celery, minced
Mayonnaise to moisten
Salt and pepper
Lettuce cups
1 large red apple
Juice of 1 lemon

Empty crab meat into a mixing bowl. Pick over crab meat and remove shells and membrane. Add celery, moisten with mayonnaise and season with salt and pepper. Pile crab meat mixture into lettuce cups. Core apple, but do not peel, and slice in wedges. Garnish each salad with slices, sprinkle lemon juice over apple slices. Makes 4 servings.

# Artichoke Seafood Salad

4 large artichokes
Salt
Sharp French dressing
1½ cups cooked shrimp, crab, lobster or tuna
1½ cups sliced celery
⅓ cup sliced ripe olives
⅓ cup mayonnaise
1 tablespoon fresh lemon juice

Wash artichokes. Trim stems and pull off any tough outer leaves. Cut off top half of artichokes and clip off thorny tip of each leaf with scissors. Drop artichokes into boiling salted water. Cover and boil until tender, 20 to 45 minutes, depending on size. Drain artichokes upside down for a few minutes. Pull out center core of tiny leaves and scoop out fuzzy portion with a teaspoon. Gently spread outer leaves apart to form a broad shallow cup. Drizzle French dressing over artichokes and chill. Toss together remaining ingredients and heap into chilled artichokes. Serve on lettuce cups. Makes 4 servings.

# Tuna Stuffed Tomatoes

4 small tomatoes
1 7-ounce can tuna
1 cup chopped celery
2 tablespoons onion, minced
½ green pepper, chopped
4 stuffed olives, chopped
2 tablespoons liquid from olives
Pepper and salt to taste
Mayonnaise to moisten

Cut tomatoes into wedges leaving tomato uncut on bottom. Spread wedges and invert for a while. Drain tuna; flake into a bowl. Add remaining ingredients and toss lightly. Pile into tomato shells and serve with additional mayonnaise. Makes 4 servings.

# Fish and Vegetable Salad

1 can whole tiny beets
1 can whole green beans
7 tablespoons French dressing
1½ pound fish fillets, steamed and flaked
¾ cup mayonnaise
2 tablespoons catsup
2 tablespoons chopped chives
1 teaspoon prepared horse-radish
2 hard-cooked eggs

Drain beets and beans. Place each in a separate bowl. Cover each with 1½ tablespoons French dressing and chill well. Chill fish thoroughly. Combine remaining French dressing, mayonnaise, catsup, chives and horse-radish. Toss the fish flakes with this mixture. Place in lettuce cups on a large platter and top with sliced hard-cooked eggs. Garnish with marinated beets and beans arranged in lettuce cups. Makes 4 servings.

Maine Sardine Council

# Sardine "Coast o' Maine" Salad

**1 envelope unflavored gelatin**
**¼ cup cold water**
**½ cup boiling water**
**¼ cup vinegar**
**1 pint creamy cottage cheese**
**¼ cup crumbled bleu cheese**
**1 cup mayonnaise**
**1 small onion, chopped**
**1 tablespoon minced parsley**
**2 tablespoons horseradish**
**⅛ teaspoon celery seed**
**1 tablespoon grated lemon rind**
**½ cup grated and drained cucumber**
**2 cans (4 ounce) sardines, drained and broken**
**Salt and pepper**

**Soften gelatin in cold water; dissolve in boiling water. Add vinegar and fold in cheeses and mayonnaise. Add remaining ingredients and mix well. Season to taste with salt and pepper. Turn mixture into oiled mold and chill until firm, about 4 hours. Turn out on serving plate. If desired, garnish with onion rings, tomato slices and extra sardines. For a party effect, use molded fish as top garnish. Serve with horseradish, mayonnaise and greens. Makes 6-8 servings.**

# Pineapple Shrimp Salad

2 cups cooked shrimp
¼ cup French dressing
1 cup sliced celery
1 cup pineapple tidbits or pineapple chunks

Marinate cleaned shrimp in French dressing for ½ hour. Combine shrimp with celery and pineapple. Arrange on crisp lettuce and serve with additional French dressing. Makes 6 servings.

# Maine Sardine Summer Salad

**2 cans (4 ounce) sardines**
**1 container (8 ounce) cottage cheese**
**3 tablespoons mayonnaise**
**3 tablespoons sour cream**
**2 tablespoons chili sauce**
**¼ cup minced celery**
**2 hard-cooked eggs, coarsely chopped**
**1 tablespoon grated lemon rind**
**Salt and pepper to taste**
**4 large ripe tomatoes**
**Salad greens**
**2 hard-cooked eggs, sieved**

**Drain sardines. Mash one can, reserving remaining can for garnish. Combine mashed sardines with next 8 ingredients. Cut tomatoes crosswise into 4 thick slices. Spoon sardine filling between slices. Place tomatoes on bed of greens. Spoon Sardine mixture over top and sprinkle with sieved egg. Garnish with remaining can of sardines. Makes 4 servings.**

Maine Sardine Council

Maine Sardine Council

# Jellied Beet and Salmon Salad

1 1-pound can salmon
1½ envelopes unflavored gelatin
1¼ cups cold water, divided
¼ cup lemon juice
¼ cup juice from salmon
2 tablespoons vinegar
¼ cup beet juice
⅓ cup water
2 teaspoons salt
⅛ teaspoon pepper
1 tablespoon sugar
1 cup chopped cooked beets
2 teaspoons minced onion
½ cup diced celery
2 hard-cooked eggs, sliced

Drain salmon and reserve juice. Remove skin and bones and flake fish. Soften gelatin in ¼ cup of the cold water. Heat remaining cup of water to boiling; add to gelatin and stir until dissolved. Add remaining liquids and seasonings. Chill in refrigerator until the consistency of unbeaten egg whites. Stir in salmon and vegetables. Arrange slices of egg in bottom of 9-inch ring mold and cover with gelatine mixture. Chill in refrigerator until firm. Unmold on crisp salad greens. Makes 6 to 8 servings.

# Swedish Aspic

2 quarts water
1½ tablespoons white vinegar
1½ teaspoons salt
8 peppercorns
8 whole allspice
2 bay leaves
1½ teaspoons dill seed
¾ pound shrimp
1 pound salmon
4 envelopes unflavored gelatin
½ cup cold water
2 egg whites
Salt and pepper
3 hard-cooked eggs
¼ cup mayonnaise

Put water in a large saucepan; add vinegar, salt, peppercorns, allspice, bay leaves, and dill seed and bring to a boil. Add shrimp; tie salmon loosely in a piece of cheese cloth and add to boiling liquid. Cover tightly and simmer 5 to 8 minutes. Remove fish and strain stock. Add water, if necessary, to make 1½ quarts. Soak gelatin in ½ cup cold water, add to stock. Add egg whites and bring slowly to a boiling point, stirring constantly. Cover and allow to stand 15 minutes. Strain, add salt and pepper to taste. Pour a thin layer of gelatin stock on bottom of a mold Chill. When set, arrange 2 eggs cut in quarters and cleaned shrimp in a pattern on gelatin. Combine 1½ cups of gelatin mixture with mayonnaise and pour gently over arranged shrimp. Chill. Arrange cooked salmon cut into serving pieces on top of set gelatin, add rest of stock and chill until firm. Unmold on chop plate and garnish with remaining hard cooked egg. Makes 6 to 8 servings.

# Atlantic Banks Salad

**2 cans (4 ounce) sardines**
**2 large heads greens**
**¼ cup grated Parmesan cheese**
**½ cup grated sharp Cheddar cheese**
**1 raw egg**
**¾ cup tart French dressing**
**1 cup potato chips, coarsely broken**

**Drain sardines. Break greens into a big shallow bowl, and sprinkle with grated cheeses. Add raw egg and French dressing. Toss thoroughly. Add sardines and potato chips. Toss again. Makes 4 servings.**

# Vegetable and Salmon Soufflé Salad

1 package lemon-flavored gelatin
1 cup hot water
½ cup cold water
2 tablespoons vinegar
½ cup mayonnaise
¼ teaspoon salt
Dash of pepper
1 cup diced celery
¼ cup chopped pimiento
1 tablespoon finely chopped onion
1 7-ounce can salmon, drained and flaked

Dissolve gelatin in hot water. Add cold water, vinegar, mayonnaise, salt and pepper. Blend well with rotary beater. Pour into refrigerator freezing tray. Quick-chill in freezing unit 15 to 20 minutes, or until firm about 1-inch from edge but soft in center. Turn mixture into a bowl and whip with rotary beater until fluffy. Fold in vegetables and salmon. Pour into 1-quart mold or individual molds. Chill until firm in refrigerator. Unmold and garnish with salad greens. Serve with mayonnaise. Makes 4 to 6 servings.

# Shrimp Tomato Ribbon Loaf

**PART I**

**1 envelope unflavored gelatin**
**½ cup cold tomato juice**
**1½ cups hot tomato juice**
**½ teaspoon salt**
**1 teaspoon horse-radish**
**1 tablespoon lemon juice**

Soften gelatin in cold tomato juice. Add hot tomato juice and stir until gelatin is dissolved. Add salt, horse-radish and lemon juice. Pour ½ of mixture into a 4x8-inch loaf pan or individual molds. Chill until almost firm. Chill remaining tomato mixture to the consistency of unbeaten egg white.

**PART II**

**1 envelope unflavored gelatin**
**1 cup cold milk**
**2 egg yolks**
**¼ teaspoon salt**
**1 teaspoon prepared mustard**
**¼ teaspoon paprika**
**¼ teaspoon Tabasco**
**2 tablespoons vinegar**
**2 5-ounce cans shrimp, drained and chopped**

Soften gelatin in cold milk in top of double boiler. Put over boiling water and stir until gelatin is dissolved. Combine egg yolks; salt, mustard, and paprika and beat slightly. Add small amount of milk to egg yolk mixture and return to double boiler. Cook over hot water, stirring constantly, until slightly thickened. Cool. Stir in Tabasco, vinegar and shrimp. Chill until mixture is the consistency of unbeaten egg white. Turn on top of tomato layer in loaf pan. Chill until almost firm. Add remaining layer of tomato mixture. Chill until firm. Unmold and serve with mayonnaise. Makes 8 servings.

# Florida Salmon Loaf

**1 envelope unflavored gelatin**
**1 cup tomato juice**
**2 egg yolks**
**1¼ teaspoons salt**
**1 teaspoon prepared mustard**
**¼ teaspoon paprika**
**2 tablespoons vinegar**
**2 cups cooked, flaked salmon**
**1 No. 2 can grapefruit sections, drained and diced**

Soften gelatin in tomato juice in top of double boiler. Put over boiling water and stir until gelatin is dissolved. Combine the egg yolks, salt, mustard and paprika and beat slightly. Add small amount of the tomato juice to the egg yolk mixture and return to double boiler. Cook over hot, not boiling water, stirring constantly, until mixture is very slightly thickened. Remove from heat and cool. Stir in vinegar and flaked salmon. Fold in grapefruit. Turn into a loaf pan and chill until firm. Unmold and garnish with additional grapefruit sections. Serve with mayonnaise. Makes 6 servings.

# Supper Salad Ring

**1 package lemon-flavored gelatin**
**1 cup hot water**
**⅛ teaspoon salt**
**1½ cups grapefruit sections, cut in pieces**
**Grapefruit juice**
**1 cup flaked tuna fish**
**½ cup diced celery**
**½ cup cooked peas**
**1 tablespoon chopped pimiento**
**1 tablespoon chopped green pepper**
**½ teaspoon salt**
**Dash of pepper**
**2 teaspoons lemon juice**
**5 tablespoons mayonnaise**

Dissolve gelatin in hot water. Sprinkle salt over grapefruit; drain thoroughly, add water to juice to make 1 cup and add to gelatin. Chill until slightly thickened. Add grapefruit and pour into a ring mold. Chill until firm. Combine remaining ingredients and mix lightly. Chill thoroughly. Unmold gelatin on crisp lettuce and fill center of ring with tuna fish mixture. Serve with additional mayonnaise. Makes 6 servings.

# Crab Stuffed Cucumbers

**3 tender young cucumbers**
**1 small can crab meat**
**3 tablespoons mayonnaise**
**Salt and pepper**

Slice off ends of cucumbers. Remove centers with an apple corer. Pick over crab meat and remove any hard fibers. Mix with mayonnaise and season to taste. Stuff crab meat into hollowed out cucumbers. Score cucumber skins with a fork. Wrap stuffed cucumber in waxed paper or aluminum foil and chill thoroughly. Slice and serve on crisp lettuce with sour cream. Makes 4 to 6 servings.

# Summer Salmon Mold

**1 envelope unflavored gelatin**
**1 cup milk**
**2 egg yolks**
**1 teaspoon salt**
**1 teaspoon mustard**
**¼ teaspoon paprika**
**2 tablespoons lemon juice**
**1 large can salmon, flaked**

Soften gelatin in milk in top of double boiler. Dissolve over hot water. Beat together egg yolks, salt, mustard and paprika. Add small amount of milk to the egg mixture, beat well and stir into milk in double boiler. Cook over hot, not boiling water, stirring constantly, until mixture thickens. Remove from heat and cool. Stir in lemon juice and fish. Turn into fish mold or loaf pan and chill until firm. Unmold and garnish with parsley and crab apples. Makes 6 servings.

# Shrimp Curry Salad

**2½ cups chopped shrimp**
**½ cup cooked cold rice**
**¼ cup chopped celery**
**½ cup mayonnaise**
**½ teaspoon curry powder**
**½ clove garlic, finely minced**
**Salt and pepper**
**1 teaspoon lemon juice**
**1 hard-cooked egg**

Combine shrimp, rice and celery. Blend together mayonnaise, curry powder, garlic, salt and pepper and lemon juice. Add mayonnaise to shrimp mixture and toss lightly, season with additional salt and pepper if necessary. Pile in crisp lettuce cups. Mince hard-cooked egg and sprinkle over top of salad. Makes 4 servings.

Maine Sardine Council

# Sea Bounty Salad

2 cans (4 ounce) sardines
1 container (8 ounce) cottage cheese
¼ cup mayonnaise
2 tablespoons sour cream
2 tablespoons chili sauce
¼ cup minced celery
2 hard-cooked eggs, chopped
Grated rind of ½ lemon
Salt and pepper
4 frozen fillets of flounder, haddock or cod (about 1 lb.)
Crisp salad greens
2 hard-cooked eggs, sieved

Drain sardines. Mash one can, reserving second can. Combine mashed sardines with cottage cheese, mayonnaise, sour cream, chili sauce, celery, chopped eggs and lemon rind. Season to taste with salt and pepper. Cut fish fillets in halves. Poach until tender. Chill. Place 4 fish fillets on bed of crisp greens; spoon prepared filling over fish; repeat layers. Top with sardines and sieved eggs. Makes 4 servings.

# Hawaiian Shrimp Salad

2 medium pineapples
1 cup cleaned cooked shrimp
½ cup diced celery
¼ cup diced cumumber
3 teaspoons lemon juice
½ cup mayonnaise

Wash pineapple and cut in halves lengthwise. Scoop out centers; remove core and dice pulp. To the diced pineapple add shrimp, celery, cucumber and lemon juice. Chill in refrigerator about ½ hour. Toss lightly with mayonnaise and refill pineapple shells. Garnish with additional mayonnaise. Makes 4 servings.

# Hearty Shrimp Bowl

2 hard-cooked eggs, chopped
1 cup cleaned shrimp
2 tomatoes, cut in eighths
1 avocado, cut in lengthwise slices
½ cup chopped celery
6 radishes, sliced
½ small head lettuce
French dressing

Place all ingredients in a salad bowl, including the lettuce which has been broken into bite-sized pieces. Add enough French dressing so that each ingredient is lightly coated. Makes 6 servings.

# Seafood Potpourri

1 7-ounce can tuna fish
1 small can crab meat
1 small can shrimp
2 tablespoons French dressing
1 cup diced celery
½ cup diced cucumber
2 tablespoons chopped radishes
1 tablespoon capers
2 tablespoons lemon juice
½ cup mayonnaise
Salt and pepper, to taste

Flake tuna fish and crab meat. Clean shrimp and mix with tuna fish and crab meat. Add French dressing and chill in refrigerator for 30 minutes. Add remaining ingredients and toss lightly. Serve on crisp salad greens. Makes 6 servings.

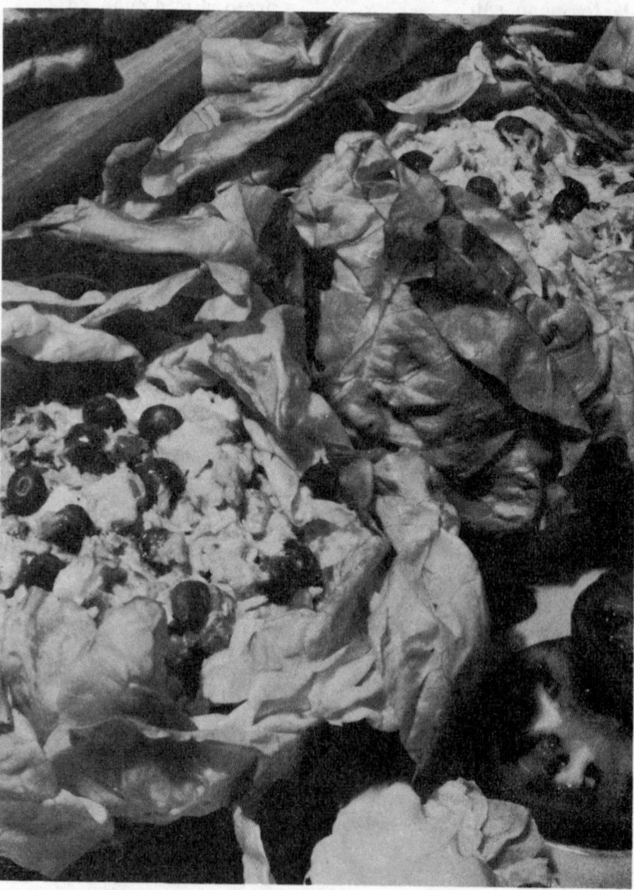

Corn Products Company

# Tuna Stuffed Lettuce Cups

3 medium heads Boston lettuce
2 cups flaked tuna fish
3 hard-cooked eggs, chopped
1 cup cooked green peas
2 tablespoons minced onion
1 cup thinly sliced celery
½ cup mayonnaise
Salt and pepper
Sliced tomatoes

Wash lettuce well, remove turned outer leaves and cut off stems so head will stand up. Pull leaves back carefully and cut out hearts. Turn lettuce heads upside down and drain well. Combine tuna fish, eggs, peas, onion, celery, mayonnaise and seasonings to taste. Fill lettuce heads with mixture. Chill thoroughly. Serve garnished with tomato slices and additional mayonnaise. Makes 6 servings.

Corn Products Co.

# Molded Avocado and Tuna Loaf

**PART I**

**1 envelope unflavored gelatin**
**¼ cup cold water**
**1 cup hot water**
**3 tablespoons lemon juice**
**1 teaspoon salt**
**1 7-ounce can tuna fish, flaked**
**1 cup diced celery**
**⅓ cup chopped pimiento**

Soften gelatin in cold water; add hot water and stir until dissolved. Add lemon juice and salt; chill until the mixture is the consistency of unbeaten egg white. Fold in flaked tuna fish, celery and pimiento. Turn into a 9x5x3-inch loaf pan and chill until almost firm.

**PART II**

**1 envelope unflavored gelatin**
**¼ cup cold water**
**½ cup boiling water**
**1 teaspoon sugar**
**2 tablespoons lemon juice**
**1 cup mashed avocado (1 large)**
**½ cup sour cream**
**½ cup mayonnaise**
**1 teaspoon salt**
**⅛ teaspoon Tabasco**

Soften gelatin in cold water, pour in boiling water and stir until dissolved. Add sugar and 1 tablespoon of the lemon juice. Chill until the consistency of unbeaten egg white. Immediately after mashing avocado, add remaining tablespoon lemon juice, sour cream and seasonings. Mix thoroughly with chilled gelatin mixture. Turn on top of fish layer. Chill until firm. Unmold on crisp salad greens. Makes 8 servings.

# Seafood Mold

**1 envelope unflavored gelatin**
**1 cup milk**
**2 egg yolks**
**½ teaspoon salt**
**1 teaspoon prepared mustard**
**½ teaspoon Tabasco**
**2 tablespoons lemon juice**
**2 cups cooked, flaked fish**

Soften gelatin in cold milk in top of double boiler. Put over boiling water and stir until gelatin is dissolved. Combine egg yolks, salt, mustard and Tabasco and beat slightly. Add small amount of the milk to the egg yolk mixture and return to the double boiler. Cook over hot, not boiling water, stirring constantly until mixture thickens. Remove from heat and cool. Stir in lemon juice and fish. Turn into large mold and chill until firm. Unmold and garnish with water cress and sliced stuffed green olives. Makes 6 to 8 servings.

Corn Products Co.

# Shrimp and Potato Salad

**2 cups cooked shrimp, cleaned and chopped**
**6 small sweet pickles, chopped**
**2 teaspoons salt**
**½ teaspoon pepper**
**½ cup tarragon vinegar**
**2 tablespoons prepared mustard**
**4 tablespoons finely chopped parsley**
**1 cup mayonnaise**
**1 cup diced apples**
**2 cups cooked peas**
**2 cups cooked diced potatoes**

Combine shrimp, pickles, seasonings and vinegar and let stand for 10 minutes. Drain off vinegar and mix with mustard, parsley and mayonnaise. Combine shrimp, mayonnaise mixture and remaining ingredients. Mix well and chill for 1 hour in refrigerator. Mound on crisp salad greens in a salad bowl. Makes 6 to 8 servings.

# Crab Meat Salad with Tomato Aspic

**1½ pounds crab meat**
**6 hard-cooked eggs, chopped**
**1 teaspoon chopped onion**
**2 tablespoons lemon juice**
**Salt and pepper**
**Mayonnaise**

Pick over crab meat and break into pieces. Add eggs, onion, lemon juice, salt and pepper to taste and moisten with mayonnaise. Mix well and chill thoroughly. Arrange salad on greens on a platter. Surround with tomato aspic molds and serve with more mayonnaise. Makes 6 servings.

# Crab Meat Salad Bowl

**1 grapefruit**
**1 avocado**
**1 small can crab meat**
**Salt and pepper**
**1 small head lettuce**
**¼ cup mayonnaise**
**¼ cup chili sauce**

Pare grapefruit, remove membrane and separate into sections. Cut avocado in half, peel and cube. Combine with grapefruit. Flake crab meat coarsely. Break lettuce into bite-sized pieces and combine with grapefruit, avocado and crab meat. Season to taste with salt and pepper. Blend together mayonnaise and chili sauce and toss with crab mixture. Makes 4 servings.

# Shrimp Salad

**1 pound cooked, cleaned shrimp**
**Juice of ½ lemon**
**1 cup chopped celery**
**2 tablespoons capers**
**¼ cup chopped green pepper**
**¼ cup French dressing**
**½ cup mayonnaise**
**Salt and pepper**

Combine shrimp, lemon juice, celery, capers, green pepper, French dressing and mayonnaise. Mix well and season to taste. Serve garnished with lettuce leaves. Makes 3 to 4 servings.

Corn Products Co.

# Seafood Stuffed Avocados

**3 ripe avocados**
**1 tablespoon lemon juice**
**Salt**
**1½ cups tuna fish or other cooked seafood**
**1 cup chopped celery**
**2 teaspoons lemon juice**
**¼ teaspoon salt**
**½ cup sandwich spread**
**¼ cup mayonnaise**
**Salad greens**

Peel avocados, cut in half lengthwise, dip in lemon juice and sprinkle with salt. Chill. Break tuna fish into pieces and toss with celery, lemon juice, salt, sandwich spread and mayonnaise. Fill avocados with fish mixture. Arrange 6 lettuce cups on chop plate and place stuffed avocado on each. Makes 6 servings.

# India Salad

**1 cup cooked flaked fish**
**2 teaspoons lemon juice**
**½ cup boiled dressing**
**¼ teaspoon salt**
**¼ teaspoon curry powder**
**¼ teaspoon prepared mustard**
**1 cup diced celery**
**1 cup diced unpeeled apple**
**6 lettuce cups**

Sprinkle fish with lemon juice. Add combined remaining ingredients except lettuce cups. Chill in refrigerator for about 1 hour. Serve in lettuce cups. Makes 6 servings.

## Herring and Beet Salad

1 cup diced pickled herring
2 apples, peeled and chopped
5 cooked potatoes, diced
6 beets, cooked and diced
2 tablespoons minced onion
Salt and pepper
1 cup sour cream
2 tablespoons mayonnaise
Sugar
Vinegar

Combine herring, apples, potatoes, beets and onion. Sprinkle with salt and pepper. Combine sour cream and mayonnaise with sugar and vinegar to taste. Add to fish and vegetables and mix well. Place in refrigerator for at least 1 hour before serving. Makes 4 to 6 servings.

## Sardine Salad

1 head romaine
½ pound spinach
1 head Boston lettuce
1 can sardines
¼ pound cheese, cut in strips
2 hard-cooked eggs

Wash greens thoroughly. Drain and chill well. Tear greens into a salad bowl. Add sardines, cheese and eggs. Toss with either French dressing or mayonnaise. Makes 4 servings.

Corn Products Company

# Meat Salads

Check the dining room for large appetites on the prowl—

They are best allayed with salads of beef, pork or fowl.

## Bologna-'Tater Salad

5 cups cooked diced potatoes
½ cup mayonnaise
1 teaspoon salt
½ teaspoon celery seed
¼ teaspoon pepper
2 tablespoons minced onion
8½ inch piece of Bologna
Romaine

Mix potatoes, mayonnaise, seasonings and onions thoroughly. Line a 9x5x3-inch loaf pan with waxed paper. Press potato salad against bottom and sides of pan. Place whole piece of skinned bologna in loaf pan. Pack remaining potato salad around bologna. Chill thoroughly. Unmold on romaine and garnish with sliced radishes. Makes 6 servings.

Corn Products Company

Knox Gelatine

# Ruby Ring Mold

2 envelopes unflavored gelatin
1 cup cranberry juice cocktail
2 cans (1 pound) whole cranberry sauce
2 tablespoons lemon juice
2 cups diced cooked chicken
½ cup diced celery
½ cup mayonnaise
½ teaspoon salt
⅛ teaspoon Tabasco
2 teaspoons lemon juice

Sprinkle gelatin on cranberry juice cocktail in saucepan to soften. Place over low heat, stirring constantly, until gelatin is dissolved. Stir in whole cranberry sauce and lemon juice. Turn into a 5-cup ring mold. Chill until firm. Mix together chicken and celery. Add mayonnaise, salt, Tabasco and lemon juice. Toss together lightly. Unmold cranberry ring on serving platter. Fill center of ring with chicken salad. Makes 6 servings.

# Ham and Macaroni Salad

½ pound cooked ham, diced
½ cup diced American cheese
2 cups cooked elbow macaroni
1 cup chopped celery
1 small onion, chopped
½ cup diced dill pickle
½ cup mayonnaise
2 teaspoons prepared mustard

Mix together lightly the ham, cheese, macaroni, celery, onion and dill pickle. Combine the mayonnaise and mustard and mix well. Add to macaroni mixture and toss lightly. Chill well before serving. Serve on lettuce cups, garnished with hard-cooked eggs and tomato wedges. Makes 6 servings.

# Jellied Chicken and Pimiento Loaf

1 envelope unflavored gelatin
¼ cup cold water
1 cup hot chicken stock
2 tablespoons vinegar
½ teaspoon salt
1 cup chopped cooked chicken
½ cup chopped celery
2 teaspoons minced onion
2 tablespoons chopped pimiento

Soften gelatin in cold water. Add chicken stock and stir until gelatin is dissolved. Add vinegar and salt. Chill in refrigerator until mixture is consistency of unbeaten egg whites. Add remaining ingredients. Pour into loaf pan and chill in refrigerator until firm. Unmold on salad greens on large platter. Makes 4 servings.

# Ham Glories

6 large tomatoes
2 cans deviled ham
1 cup chopped celery
1 dozen stuffed olives, sliced
2 hard-cooked eggs, sliced
2 tablespoons mayonnaise

Remove a thin slice from the top of each tomato and scoop out the center pulp. Chop pulp and tomato top very fine and mix with the remaining ingredients. Refill tomatoes, top with a parsley sprig and chill until ready to serve. Makes 6 servings.

# Molded Ham and Potato Salad

**PART I**

1 12-ounce can luncheon meat or
1½ cups ground, cooked ham
2 tablespoons minced onion
½ cup mayonnaise
½ cup chili sauce
1 teaspoon horse-radish
2 teaspoons mustard
¼ teaspoon Tabasco
1 envelope unflavored gelatin
½ cup cold water

Grind or finely chop luncheon meat. Combine with remaining ingredients except gelatin and water. Soften gelatin in cold water; dissolve thoroughly over hot water. Blend into meat mixture. Turn into a 6-cup ring mold and chill until almost firm.

**PART II**

2 cups diced cooked potatoes
1 cup diced celery
1 small onion, minced
2 tablespoons finely chopped green pepper
½ cup mayonnaise
1 tablespoon vinegar
1¼ teaspoons salt
⅛ teaspoon pepper
1 envelope unflavored gelatin
½ cup cold water

Combine potato with celery, onion, green pepper, mayonnaise, vinegar, salt and pepper. Soften gelatin in cold water; dissolve thoroughly over hot water. Blend into potato mixture. Turn over top of meat mixture and chill until firm. Unmold and garnish with salad greens and wedges of tomato. Makes 8 servings.

# Smoked Turkey Salad

1 cup diced smoked turkey
1 cup diced Swiss cheese
2 cooked beets, diced
2 cold boiled potatoes, diced
1 pimiento, chopped
1 cup shredded romaine
1 teaspoon chopped chives
French dressing

Combine all ingredients with enough French dressing to moisten. Season to taste and garnish with water cress and sliced hard-cooked egg. Makes 8 servings.

# Jellied Tongue and Potato Salad

**1½ envelopes unflavored gelatin**
**½ cup cold water**
**1½ cups boiling stock**
**1 cup finely-diced tongue**
**¼ teaspoon Worcestershire sauce**
**¼ teaspoon dry mustard**
**Few grains cayenne**
**2 cups diced cooked potatoes**
**½ cup diced celery**
**¼ cup diced green pepper**
**¼ cup mayonnaise**
**2 tablespoons vinegar**
**½ teaspoon salt**
**⅛ teaspoon pepper**

Soften gelatin in cold water; dissolve in boiling stock; cool gelatin and divide in half. To half the gelatin mixture add the tongue, Worcestershire sauce, mustard and cayenne. Pour into a loaf pan 8x5x3-inch and chill until firm. Combine remaining ingredients with rest of gelatin and pour over tongue layer. Chill in refrigerator until firm. Unmold and garnish as desired. Makes 6 to 8 servings.

# Tongue and Potato Salad

**3 cups diced cooked potatoes**
**⅛ teaspoon savory**
**¼ cup French dressing**
**1 finely chopped onion**
**½ cup mayonnaise**
**2 tablespoons chopped parsley**
**2 cups diced cooked tongue**
**2 hard-cooked eggs, sliced**

Combine potatoes, savory, French dressing and onion in a mixing bowl. Toss lightly and chill well. Add mayonnaise, parsley and tongue and toss well. Garnish with hard-cooked eggs. Makes 4 servings.

# Chop Suey Salad

**2 cups diced chicken**
**1½ cups thinly sliced celery**
**1 cup coarsely chopped walnuts**
**4 sweet pickles, cut in strips**
**2 tablespoons minced onion**
**2 hard-cooked eggs, chopped**
**¾ cup mayonnaise**
**3 tablespoons lemon juice**

Combine chicken, celery, walnuts, pickles, onion and eggs. Mix together mayonnaise and lemon juice and blend until smooth. Add enough of this mixture to chicken mixture to moisten well; season to taste with salt and pepper and chill in refrigerator for 30 minutes. Heap in a lettuce lined salad bowl and garnish with green pepper rings, raw carrot straw and walnut halves. Serve additional dressing separately. Makes 4 to 6 servings.

# Florida Chicken Salad

**1 No. 2 can grapefruit sections**
**2 cups diced cooked chicken**
**1 cup diced celery**
**2 tablespoons lime juice**
**¼ cup mayonnaise**
**¼ teaspoon salt**
**⅛ teaspoon pepper**
**Salad greens**

Drain grapefruit thoroughly. Add sections to chicken and celery in mixing bowl. Mix together lime juice, mayonnaise and seasonings. Add to salad and toss lightly. Serve in a bowl lined with salad greens garnished with more sections of grapefruit. Makes 5 to 6 servings.

# Frankfurter Salad Bowl

**1 No. 2 can kidney beans**
**1½ cups sliced frankfurters**
**¾ cup sliced sour pickles**
**¾ cup French dressing**
**1 head lettuce**
**½ large onion, sliced**

Drain kidney beans. Add the frankfurters, pickles, and ½ cup of the French dressing. Chill. Break lettuce leaves into pieces. Alternate layers of the bean mixture, lettuce and onion in a shallow salad bowl. Pour the remaining French dressing over all and serve. Makes 8 servings.

# Molded Chicken Salad

**1 envelope unflavored gelatin**
**¼ cup cold water**
**1 cup hot chicken broth**
**2 tablespoons chopped green pepper**
**2 cups diced cooked chicken**
**1 tablespoon chopped onion**
**1 cup chopped celery**
**1 cup cooked rice**
**1 teaspoon salt**
**¼ cup French dressing**
**½ cup mayonnaise**

Combine gelatin and cold water, let stand 5 minutes. Add chicken broth and stir until gelatin is dissolved. Place chopped green pepper in bottom of 2-quart mold. Cover with 2 tablespoons of the gelatin and chill until firm. Combine remaining ingredients and stir into remaining gelatin. Pour into mold over firm green pepper and gelatin. Chill until firm. Unmold and serve on salad greens. Makes 6 servings.

# Molded Ham and Cheese Loaf

**1 envelope unflavored gelatin**
**½ cup cold water**
**¾ cup hot water**
**¼ teaspoon salt**
**¼ teaspoon vinegar**
**¼ cup diced celery**
**¼ cup diced sweet pickle**
**1 cup grated American cheese**
**1 cup diced cooked ham**

Soften gelatin in cold water. Add hot water and salt and stir until dissolved. Add vinegar. Chill until the mixture is the consistency of unbeaten egg white. Mix in celery and pickle; divide mixture into 2 parts; to one add the grated cheese, to the other the diced ham. Turn ham mixture into loaf pan and chill until almost firm; add cheese mixture. Chill until firm. Unmold on crisp greens and serve with tomato wedges, parsley potatoes and asparagus. Makes 6 servings.

# Chicken Almond Salad

2 cups diced cooked chicken
1 cup chopped celery
⅓ cup sliced ripe olives
½ cup shredded toasted almonds
½ cup mayonnaise
1 teaspoon salt
2 teaspoons vinegar

Combine all ingredients and toss lightly. Line a bowl with lettuce and place chicken salad on lettuce. Garnish with additional almond slivers. Makes 4 to 6 servings.

# Kraut-Ham-Egg Salad

**4 cups sauerkraut, undrained**
**¼ cup finely chopped onion**
**½ pound boiled ham, cut in strips**
**3 hard-cooked eggs, chopped**
**⅓ cup salad oil**
**2 tablespoons vinegar**
**1 teaspoon dry mustard**
**2 teaspoons sugar**
**Salt and pepper to taste**

Drain kraut; reserve 1/3 cup kraut juice. Combine kraut, onion, ham and eggs; toss lightly and chill. Combine 1/3 cup kraut juice and remaining ingredients; beat or shake until well-blended. Add dressing mixture to kraut mixture; toss lightly, but thoroughly. Garnish with ham strips and egg slices, as desired. Makes 6 servings.

National Kraut Packers Association

Underwood Kitchens

# Double Ring Salad

**2 envelopes unflavored gelatin**
**¼ cup cold water**
**2 cups boiling water**
**2 chicken bouillon cubes**
**4 tablespoons tomato puree**
**2 cans (4½ ounce) deviled ham**
**1 cup heavy cream, whipped**
**½ cup chopped green pepper**

Soften gelatin in cold water. Dissolve in boiling water with bouillon cubes. Add tomato puree and mix well. Chill until slightly thickened, then fold in deviled ham, whipped cream and pepper. Pour into 1-quart ring mold and chill until firm. Unmold onto salad greens. Makes 6 to 8 servings. To make the double ring, double recipe and join rings.

# Tossed Whole-Meal Salad

**1 medium-sized head lettuce**
**½ bunch water cress**
**½ 12-ounce can luncheon meat, cut in strips**
**1 6-ounce can tongue, cut in strips**
**½ cup drained, canned julienne beets**
**½ cup sliced celery**
**3 hard-cooked eggs, cut in eighths**
**1 teaspoon grated onion**
**1 3-ounce package cream cheese, cut in ½-inch cubes**
**½ cup French dressing**

Rub the salad bowl with a cut clove of garlic. Break lettuce in small pieces and place in the bowl. Add all remaining ingredients except cream cheese and dressing. Just before serving add cheese and French dressing. Toss lightly and serve immediately. Makes 6 servings.

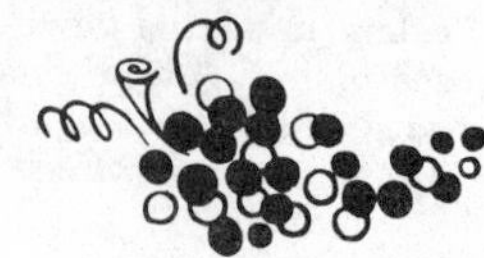

Knox Gelatine

# Molded Corned Beef and Cabbage Layer

1 envelope unflavored gelatin
2 tablespoons sugar
½ teaspoon salt
1¼ cups cold water, divided
2 tablespoon lemon juice
¼ cup vinegar
2 tablespoons chopped green pepper
2 cups finely shredded cabbage

Mix together gelatin, sugar and salt in a saucepan. Add ½ cup of the water. Place over low heat, stirring constantly, until gelatin is dissolved. Remove from heat; stir in remaining ¾ cup water, lemon juice and vinegar. Chill until mixture is the consistency of unbeaten egg white. Mix in green pepper and cabbage. Turn into an 8-inch square pan; chill until almost firm.

### Corned Beef Layer

1 envelope unflavored gelatin
½ cup cold water
¼ teaspoon salt
2 tablespoons lemon juice
¾ cup mayonnaise or salad dressing
¼ cup minced onion
½ cup chopped sweet pickle
½ cup diced celery
1 can (12-ounces) corned beef, finely cut

Sprinkle gelatin on cold water in saucepan to soften. Place over low heat, stirring constantly, until gelatin is dissolved. Remove from heat; add salt and lemon juice; cool. Gradually add to mayonnaise; mix in remaining ingredients. Turn on top of almost firm first layer and chill until firm. Unmold on serving platter. To serve, cut into squares. Makes 9 servings.

# He-Man Special

½ pound American cheese
½ pound salami
2 tomatoes
1 cucumber, sliced
1 Bermuda onion, sliced
Lettuce
French dressing

Cut cheese and salami in finger size strips. Cut tomatoes in eighths. Break onion slices into rings. Arrange cheese, salami, tomatoes, cucumber and onion on broken chunks of lettuce in a salad bowl. Toss with French dressing or serve it on the side. Makes 6 servings.

Corn Products Company

# Ham Salad Ring

2 12-ounce cans luncheon meat
1½ envelopes unflavored gelatin
¼ cup cold water
½ cup minced celery
¼ cup grated horse-radish
2 teaspoons prepared mustard
¾ cup mayonnaise
½ teaspoon salt
Salad greens

Line an oiled 8-inch ring mold with 8 to 10 very thin slices of the meat. Soften gelatin in cold water; dissolve over boiling water. Chill gelatin. Grind remaining meat and combine with remaining ingredients except salad greens and mix thoroughly with the gelatin. Pour into lined ring mold and chill until firm in the refrigerator. Unmold on salad greens and serve with additional mayonnaise. Makes 8 to 10 servings.

## Chicken Olive Salad Mold

2 envelopes unflavored gelatin
¼ cup cold water
1 cup hot water
1½ tablespoons vinegar
1 tablespoon sugar
½ teaspoon salt
1 teaspoon prepared mustard
2 tablespoons salad oil
2 tablespoons catsup
2 eggs, well beaten
2 cups cooked, diced chicken
½ cup minced celery
1 cup sliced ripe olives
⅓ cup chopped pimiento

Combine gelatin and cold water, let stand 5 minutes. Add water and stir until gelatin is dissolved. Add vinegar, sugar, salt, mustard, salad oil and cool. Add beaten eggs, catsup and mayonnaise and beat with a rotary beater. Add chicken, celery olives and pimiento. Pour into a large mold and chill until firm. Unmold on salad greens. Makes 6 to 8 servings.

## Hearty Dixie Salad

2 cups diced cooked sweet potatoes
6 medium oranges, peeled and diced
1½ cups diced cooked ham
1½ cups diced celery
½ teaspoon vinegar
½ cup mayonnaise
6 lettuce cups

Toss together all ingredients, except lettuce cups. Chill in refrigerator about 1 hour. Heap in lettuce cups and garnish as desired. Makes 6 servings.

## Meat Salad Sandwiches

5 cups cooked, diced potatoes
1 tablespoon chopped onion
1 cup diced celery
2 teaspoons salt
1 tablespoon vinegar
3 tablespoons oil
¼ cup mayonnaise
¼ teaspoon Tabasco
2 12-ounce cans luncheon meat

Combine potatoes with onion, celery, salt, vinegar, oil, mayonnaise and Tabasco. Toss lightly with two forks being careful not to break potatoes. Cover and chill. Cut luncheon meat into 18 slices; spoon potato salad on half the slices; top with remaining luncheon meat slices. If desired sandwiches may be served open face and garnished with pimiento, olives and green pepper rings. Makes 9 sandwiches.

## Salmagundi Salad

2 cups diced, cooked ham
1 cup cubed, cooked potatoes
½ cup diced celery
½ cup cooked peas
1 pimiento, chopped
2 sweet pickles, chopped
¾ cup mayonnaise
Salt and pepper

Combine all ingredients and mix well. Season to taste. Serve on crisp lettuce cups. Garnish with slices of hard-cooked eggs and pickled beets. Makes 5 to 6 servings.

Wish-Bone

## Summer Supper Platter

1 package (10 ounce) frozen peas
½ pound carrots, sliced
¼ cup sliced radishes
¼ cup sliced water chestnuts
Cooked asparagus spears
1 bottle Italian dressing
½ cup French dressing
Raw cauliflower flowerettes
Lettuce
¾ pound luncheon meat, sliced
¾ pound sliced boiled ham
Cheddar cheese cut in finger lengths
Hard cooked egg, finely chopped

Cook peas and carrots separately until just tender and crisp. Drain. In each of 3 bowls place the following: peas and radishes, carrots and water chestnuts, and asparagus. To each bowl add ¼ cup Italian dressing. Marinate and refrigerate for three or more hours.

*To serve:* place small bowl of French dressing in center of large round platter. Arrange cauliflower flowerettes around bowl. Drain vegetables; arrange in lettuce cups. Roll luncheon meat and boiled ham around cheese fingers; place between vegetables. Sprinkle asparagus with chopped hard cooked egg. Makes 8 to 10 servings.

## Veal and Green Bean Salad

1½ cups slivered cooked veal
1 cup cooked green beans
⅓ cup French dressing
½ head lettuce
6 stuffed olives, chopped
1 tomato, cut in eighths
1 stalk celery, sliced

Combine veal and beans, add French dressing and let stand in refrigerator for about 1 hour. Tear lettuce into bite-sized pieces. Add to veal and beans with rest of ingredients and toss lightly. Makes 4 servings.

# Chef's Salad Bowl

1 cup broken lettuce
1 cup broken romaine
1 cup escarole pieces
1 bunch water cress
2 tomatoes, cut in wedges
French dressing
4 hard-cooked eggs, cut in wedges
¼ pound American cheese, strips
½ green pepper, cut in rings
½ can luncheon meat, cut in strips

Rub a wooden salad bowl with a cut clove of garlic. Place all ingredients except dressing in bowl. Add about ½ cup of French dressing, toss lightly so that all ingredients are lightly coated. Taste and add seasonings if necessary. Serve immediately. Makes 6 servings.

Western Growers Association

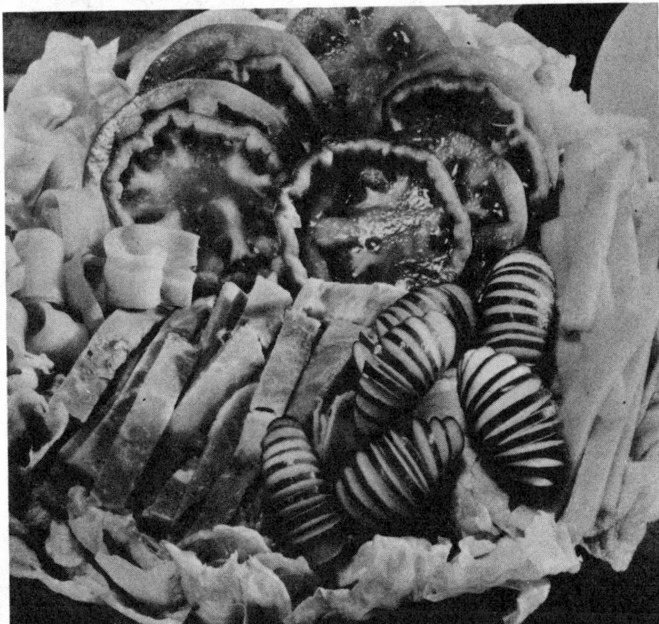

# Beef, Macaroni and Vegetable Salad

2 tablespoons salt
4 to 6 quarts boiling water
1 pound elbow macaroni
2 packages (10 ounce) frozen Brussels sprouts
2 cups cooked corned beef strips
1 large onion, chopped
⅓ cup canned pimientos, sliced
1 cup mayonnaise
1 to 2 tablespoons prepared horseradish
2 tablespoons sugar
⅓ cup vinegar

Add 2 tablespoons salt to rapidly boiling water. Gradually add macaroni so that water continues to boil. Cook uncovered, stirring occasionally, until tender. Drain in colander. Rinse with cold water; drain.

Cook Brussels sprouts according to package directions; drain, if necessary.

Combine macaroni, Brussels sprouts, corned beef, onion and pimientos; toss lightly. Chill. Combine remaining ingredients for dressing and chill. To serve: arrange on bed of crisp lettuce, and top with salad dressing. Makes 8 to 10 servings.

Brussels Sprout Marketing Program

# Antipasto Platter with Ceci Salad

Assortment of salami
Prosciutto
Ham
Assortment of cheeses
Sliced tomatoes
Quartered hard-cooked eggs
Celery hearts
Artichoke hearts
Olives
Anchovies
Eggplant in vinegar
Sweet fried peppers
Ceci salad (recipe below)

## Ceci Salad

1 can (1 pound-4 ounce) chick peas
¼ cup sliced ripe olives
1 tablespoon coarsely chopped pimento
1 small onion, thinly sliced
½ cup Italian dressing
¼ teaspoon salt
⅛ teaspoon black pepper

Drain the chick peas and rinse well under running cold water. Toss with remaining ingredients. Cover and marinate in refrigerator for 6 to 8 hours. Makes 4 to 6 servings.

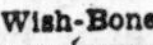
Wish-Bone

Sealtest Consumer Service

# Turkey Mousse

1 envelope unflavored gelatin
1½ cups turkey or chicken stock
1½ cups of leftover ground turkey or chicken
¼ teaspoon curry powder
¼ cup mayonnaise
1 teaspoon celery salt
2 teaspoons grated onion
Salt and pepper
¾ cup heavy cream, whipped
Lettuce and salad dressing

Soften gelatin in ½ cup cold stock. Dissolve over hot water. Combine remaining stock, ground turkey, curry powder, mayonnaise, celery salt and onion. Add dissolved gelatin. Mix well. Season to taste with salt and pepper. Chill until thick and syrupy. Beat until light and foamy. Fold in whipped cream. Pour into a shaped mold or loaf pan of about 1 quart capacity. Chill until firm. Unmold on serving platter. Serve with lettuce and salad dressing. Makes 6 servings. If desired, garnish the mousse with salted whipped cream (put on with a pastry tube). Arrange six slices pineapple around the mousse. Top each pineapple slice with a turkey-shaped cut-out of canned jellied cranberry sauce.

# Liverwurst Salad

¼ pound liverwurst
⅓ cup salad oil
⅓ cup vinegar
⅓ cup chili sauce
1 tablespoon prepared horse-radish
½ teaspoon salt
3 tablespoons finely chopped onion
¼ cup finely chopped green pepper
¾ cup sliced carrots
1 cup diced celery
1 small head lettuce, broken

Cut liverwurst in thin strips. Mix salad oil, vinegar, chili sauce, horse-radish and salt. Chill remaining ingredients. Add the salad dressing to the liverwurst and vegetables and toss just before serving. Makes 6 servings.

# Olive and Tongue Salad

1½ cups diced boiled tongue
½ cup minced ripe olives
1 cup finely cut celery
2 tablespoons minced onion
French dressing

Combine tongue, olives, celery and onion. Chill thoroughly. Add enough French dressing to moisten and season to taste. Serve in lettuce cups with cooked salad dressing. Makes 4 to 5 servings.

# Jellied Deviled Ham Loaf

2 cans (4½ ounce) deviled ham
2 hard-cooked eggs, sliced
1 envelope unflavored gelatin
½ cup cold water
½ cup chopped celery
1 green pepper, chopped
1 tablespoon lemon juice
1 cup cottage cheese
¼ cup mayonnaise
¼ cup halved cocktail onions or ¼ cup chopped scallions
Lettuce

Spread 1 can deviled ham on bottom of loaf pan with sliced egg as garnish. Sprinkle gelatin in cold water to soften for 5 minutes. Then dissolve over boiling water. Mix second can of ham with remaining ingredients except lettuce. Stir in gelatin and turn into 9x5x2 aluminum loaf pan. Refrigerate until firmly set. Unmold on a bed of lettuce and garnish sides with remaining sliced egg. Makes 8 servings.

Underwood Kitchens

# Tropical Chicken Salad

2 cups diced cooked chicken
4 slices pineapple, diced
2 bananas, diced
1 cup chopped celery
½ teaspoon salt
⅓ cup mayonnaise
2 tablespoons lemon juice
Salad greens

Toss together all ingredients except salad greens. Chill in refrigerator about 1 hour. Serve on crisp salad greens. Makes 6 to 8 servings.

# Ham Soufflé Salad

1 package lemon-flavored gelatin
1 cup hot water
½ cup cold water
1 to 2 tablespoons vinegar
½ cup mayonnaise
¼ cup salt
Dash of pepper
1 cup finely diced cooked ham
½ cup diced celery
2 tablespoons chopped sweet pickle

Dissolve gelatin in hot water. Add cold water, vinegar, mayonnaise, salt and pepper. Blend well with rotary beater. Pour into refrigerator freezing tray. Quick-chill in freezer for 15 to 20 minutes, or until firm about 1-inch from edge but soft in center. Turn mixture into bowl and whip with rotary beater until fluffy. Fold in ham, celery and pickle. Pour into a 1-quart mold. Chill until firm in refrigerator. Unmold and garnish with salad greens. Serve with mayonnaise. Makes 4 to 6 servings.

# Toasted Cheese Frankfurter Salad

6 medium potatoes
½ teaspoon celery seed
1 teaspoon salt
Pepper to taste
½ cup chopped green onions
1½ cups thinly sliced celery
½ cup sweet pickle relish
3 hard-cooked eggs, diced
2 teaspoons mustard
2 tablespoons vinegar
½ cup mayonnaise
1 pound frankfurters
1 cup grated American cheese

Boil potatoes until tender. Drain and chill. When cold, peel and dice. Add seasonings, onion, relish, celery and eggs. Blend mustard with vinegar and mayonnaise. Add to potatoes and toss lightly until everything is well coated. Line sides of a loaf pan with frankfurter halves. Pack potato salad in pan and chill thoroughly. Unmold on a cooky sheet or broil and serve platter. Sprinkle with grated cheese and broil until lightly browned and bubbly. Makes 6 to 8 servings.

Corn Products Company

# Chicken Salad California

3 ripe avocados
¼ cup orange juice
2 cups cooked diced chicken
2 oranges, sectioned and diced
1 cup diced celery
½ cup mayonnaise
3 tablespoons chili sauce
⅛ teaspoon paprika
1 teaspoon salt
2 tablespoons chopped pimiento

Peel avocados, cut in half lengthwise and brush with orange juice. Combine chicken, oranges and celery. Combine mayonnaise, chili sauce and seasonings. Add to chicken mixture and blend thoroughly. Fill avocado halves with chicken mixture and top with chopped pimiento. Serve on a bed of salad greens and garnish with additional orange sections. Makes 6 servings.

Best Foods

# Turkey Vegetable Salad

**2 cups diced cooked turkey**
**1 cup cooked peas**
**1 cup diced celery**
**¾ cup chopped walnuts**
**1 teaspoon grated onion**
**½ teaspoon salt**
**Dash pepper**
**½ cup mayonnaise**
**Lettuce**
**Walnut halves for garnish**

**Lightly mix turkey with peas, celery, walnuts, grated onion, salt and pepper. Toss with mayonnaise until evenly coated. Chill. Serve with lettuce. Garnish with walnut halves. Makes 6 servings.**

# Chicken Salad Deluxe

**2 cups cubed cooked chicken**
**1 cup diced celery**
**2 tablespoons lemon juice**
**¾ cup seedless grapes**
**¾ cup toasted, salted almonds**
**1 tablespoon capers**
**Dash of nutmeg**
**Salt and pepper to taste**
**Mayonnaise**

Combine chicken and celery. Add lemon juice and let stand in refrigerator for 1 hour. Combine with grapes, almonds, capers, nutmeg, seasonings and enough mayonnaise to moisten. Pile on lettuce cups and serve with mayonnaise. Makes 6 servings.

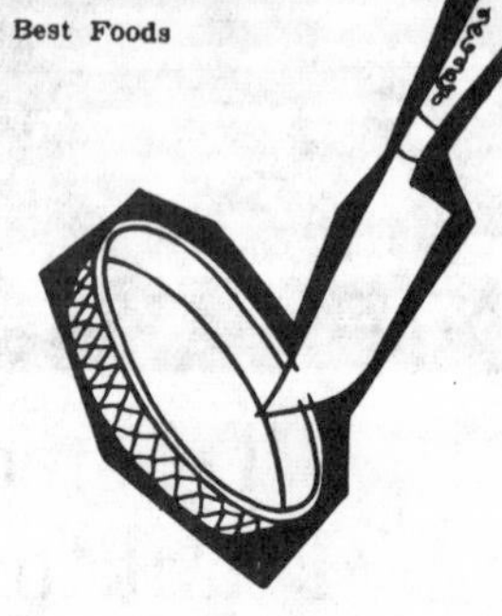

# Chicken and Rice Salad

**½ cup dry rice**
**¼ cup minced onion**
**1 tablespoon vinegar**
**2 tablespoons salad oil**
**¾ teaspoon curry powder**
**2 cups minced cooked chicken**
**1 cup chopped celery**
**¼ cup chopped green pepper**
**¾ cup salad dressing**
**6 medium tomatoes**

Cook rice according to directions on package. Drain well and cool. Add onion, vinegar, oil and curry powder; mix well and refrigerate several hours. Combine marinated rice with chicken, celery, green pepper and salad dressing. Core and peel tomatoes. Cut down in quarters almost to bottom of tomato. Spread apart slightly and pile centers with salad mixture. Makes 6 servings.

## Jellied Chicken Aspic Ring

1 envelope unflavored gelatin
2 tablespoons cold water
2 cups hot tomato juice
1 tablespoon lemon juice
1 teaspoon salt
1 envelope unflavored gelatin
2 tablespoons cold water
1 cup mayonnaise
1½ cups cooked rice
½ cup light cream
1 cup diced cooked chicken
½ cup chopped celery
¼ cup chopped green pepper
½ teaspoon salt
¼ teaspoon paprika
¼ teaspoon dried tarragon

Combine 1 envelope gelatin and 2 tbs. cold water, let stand to soften. Add hot tomato juice and stir until dissolved. Add lemon juice and salt. Pour into 1½-quart ring mold and chill until firm. Soften the remaining gelatin in 2 tbs. cold water. Dissolve over hot water. Add mayonnaise and blend. Add rice, cream, chicken, celery, green pepper, salt, paprika and tarragon. Pour over firm tomato layer in ring mold. Chill until firm. Serve on a bed of salad greens, garnished with mayonnaise. Makes 6 to 8 servings.

## Kidney Bean and Bologna Salad

1 cup cubed bologna
2 cups drained kidney beans
⅓ cup minced onion
1 cup chopped celery
⅓ cup chopped sweet pickle
1 teaspoon salt
Mayonnaise
Lettuce cups

Combine bologna, beans, onion, celery, sweet pickle and salt. Add enough mayonnaise to moisten. Place lettuce cups in a large bowl and pile salad in bowl. Serve with slices of brown bread. Makes 6 servings.

## Hot Weather Salad

1 cucumber
1 pound boiled ham
1 pound American cheese
3 hard-cooked eggs
1 bunch scallions
Salad greens
¾ cup mayonnaise
¼ cup catsup

Score cucumber with a fork and slice in thin slices. Cut ham and cheese in finger strips. Slice eggs. Arrange ham, cheese, eggs, cucumber and scallions on crisp salad greens. Combine mayonnaise and catsup and serve on the side with the salad. Makes 6 servings.

# Egg and Cheese Salads

To earth flew Hermes, so goes the ancient fable,
When he spied a dairy salad on the kitchen table.

## Egg Salad Royale

1 head iceberg lettuce
6 hard-cooked eggs
3 tablespoons chopped chives
½ cup sour cream
¼ teaspoon salt
⅛ teaspoon paprika
¼ cup chopped pimiento
¼ cup chopped cucumber
½ cup mayonnaise

Break lettuce in bite-size pieces and arrange in a salad bowl. Cut eggs in quarters and tuck in among the greens. Sprinkle with chives. Combine remaining ingredients and mix well. Arrange two lettuce cups on top of salad bowl and fill with mayonnaise dressing. Makes 6 servings.

Corn Products Company

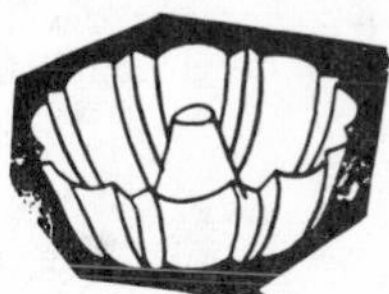

The Roquefort Association

# Roquefort Cheese Dessert Salad

3 envelopes unflavored gelatin
2 cups cold water
1 cup crumbled Roquefort cheese
1 cup cream-style cottage cheese
1 package (3 ounces) cream cheese, softened
1 cup heavy cream, whipped
3 cups orange sections
1 cup strawberry halves
Water cress

Sprinkle gelatin over cold water to soften. Cook over boiling water, stirring constantly, until gelatin is dissolved. Cool. Beat Roquefort, cottage and cream cheeses until smooth. Gradually add gelatin mixture, beating until smooth. Chill until slightly thickened. Fold in whipped cream. Turn into 9-inch ring mold (about 6 cups capacity). Chill until set (about 3 hours). Unmold. Fill with orange sections and strawberries. Garnish with water cress. Makes 8 servings.

# Cottage Cheese Fruit Salad

Mound creamy cottage cheese on slices of canned pineapple, peach halves or pear halves on top of crisp salad greens. Serve with fruit French dressing or with chilled sour cream.

For variety blend ⅓ cup grated carrots, 2 tablespoons chopped chives, 1 pound cottage cheese, ½ teaspoon salt, 3 tablespoons French dressing and 1 tablespoon lemon juice. Mix well and pile on 6 slices of canned or fresh pineapple.

Or try mixing cottage cheese with chopped pecans or walnuts, raisins or bits of candied fruit before piling on pineapple slices or peach halves.

California Prune Advisory Board

# Prune Beauty

2 packages unflavored gelatin
1 cup orange juice
2 cups (1 pound) cottage cheese
½ teaspoon salt
1 cup diced celery
2 tablespoons chopped green pepper
½ cup chopped pitted plumped prunes
18 halved, pitted, plumped prunes
Walnut meats

Soften gelatin on orange juice 5 minutes. Then dissolve gelatin over boiling water. Combine cottage cheese, salt, celery, green pepper and chopped prunes. Add gelatin mixture; mix well. Arrange prune halves, fill with walnut meats, cut side up in bottom of loaf mold. Carefully spoon cottage cheese mixture over prunes. Chill until firm. Makes 8 to 10 servings.

# Cottage Cheese, Fruit Soufflé Salad

1 package lemon-flavored gelatin
1 cup hot water
½ cup cold water
1 tablespoon lemon juice
½ cup mayonnaise
¼ teaspoon salt
Dash of pepper
½ cup diced grapefruit sections
½ cup diced orange sections
¾ cup cottage cheese
½ cup shredded carrots
¼ cup chopped walnuts

Dissolve gelatin in hot water. Add cold water, lemon juice, mayonnaise, salt and pepper. Blend well with rotary beater. Pour into refrigerator freezing tray. Quick-chill in freezing until 15 to 20 minutes, or until firm about 1-inch from edge but soft in center. Turn mixture into bowl and whip with rotary beater until fluffy. Fold in fruit, cheese, carrots and walnuts. Pour into individual molds. Chill until firm in refrigerator. Unmold and garnish with salad greens. Serve with mayonnaise. Makes 4 to 6 servings.

# Rainbow Ring-Around Salad

**1 envelope plain gelatin**
**2 cups milk**
**½ teaspoon salt**
**½ teaspoon grated onion**
**¼ teaspoon Worcestershire sauce**
**6 packages (3 ounces) cream cheese**
**4 ounces Roquefort or Bleu cheese**
**12 cantaloupe slices**
**12 pineapple slices**
**Fresh fruit**

**Soak gelatin in ½ cup milk and dissolve in remaining milk, which has been heated to the boiling point. Add salt, grated onion and Worcestershire sauce; chill until slightly thickened. Blend softened cheeses thoroughly and fold gelatin mixture into cheeses. Mix well and pour into oiled 2-3 ounce paper soufflé cups. Chill until firm. Arrange cantaloupe slices on tray, top each with a pineapple slice; unmold roquefort salad and place in center of fruit slices. Serve a selection of other fresh fruits with the salad. Makes 12 servings.**

Western Growers Association

# Pop's Egg Salad

**Lettuce leaves**
**4 cups shredded cabbage**
**6 medium onions, sliced**
**12 hard-cooked eggs, sliced**
**2 tablespoons vinegar**
**4 tablespoons salad oil**
**1½ teaspoons salt**
**¼ teaspoon pepper**
**Dash of paprika**
**1 teaspoon Worcestershire sauce**
**¼ cup grated sharp cheese**

Line a salad bowl with the lettuce leaves. Fill with layers of shredded cabbage, onion slices and egg slices. Combine vinegar, oil, salt, pepper, paprika and Worcestershire sauce. Mix well and pour over top of salad. Sprinkle with the cheese and garnish with parsley. Makes 6 servings.

# Bacon and Egg Bowl

**8 slices bacon**
**1 clove garlic, cut in half**
**½ head lettuce**
**½ bunch chicory**
**½ cucumber, sliced**
**3 scallions, chopped**
**3 radishes, sliced**
**2 stalks celery, sliced**
**2 tomatoes, quartered**
**4 hard-cooked eggs**
**⅓ cup French dressing**

Fry bacon until crisp and drain on paper. Crumble 6 slices of bacon, reserving 2 for the top garnish. Rub salad bowl with cut side of garlic. Tear lettuce and chicory into bite-sized pieces into salad bowl. Add cucumber, scallions, radishes, celery, tomatoes and 3 of the eggs, quartered. Add French dressing and toss lightly. Garnish top with 2 slices of bacon and the last egg cut in slices. Makes 4 servings.

# Cheese Salad

**1 medium head lettuce**
**1 cup cooked peas**
**1 cup sliced celery**
**½ pound American cheese, cut in ¼-inch cubes**
**½ cup sweet pickle relish**
**¼ cup chopped green onions**
**½ cup mayonnaise**
**2 tablespoons chili sauce**
**¾ teaspoon salt**
**2 tomatoes, quartered**

Trim lettuce and wash. Remove outside leaves for garnish. Break remaining lettuce into bite-sized chunks in a bowl. Add remaining ingredients and toss lightly. Garnish with whole lettuce leaves. Makes 6 servings.

# Frozen Oriental Salad

**1 3-ounce package cream cheese**
**3 tablespoons mayonnaise**
**⅛ teaspoon salt**
**1 cup heavy cream, whipped**
**¼ cup chopped kumquats**
**¼ cup chopped dates**
**¼ cup chopped maraschino cherries**
**¼ cup crushed pineapple**
**1 tablespoon finely chopped preserved ginger**
**½ cup chopped blanched almonds**

Soften cream cheese; stir in mayonnaise and blend until smooth. Add salt. Fold in whipped cream, fruit and ginger. Pour into freezing tray of refrigerator. Sprinkle top with almonds. Freeze in freezing compartment until firm. Cut in squares and serve on crisp lettuce. Makes 8 servings.

# Jellied Deviled Egg Salad

**1 package lemon-flavored gelatin**
**½ teaspoon salt**
**1 cup hot water**
**1 cup cold water**
**1 tablespoon vinegar**
**Dash of hot pepper sauce**
**4 deviled eggs (8 halves)**
**¾ cup coarsely chopped celery**
**⅓ cup coarsely chopped stuffed olives**

Dissolve gelatin and salt in hot water. Add cold water, vinegar and pepper sauce. Pour into a 9x5x3-inch loaf pan to a depth of ¼ inch. Chill this layer until almost firm. Chill remaining gelatin mixture until slightly thickened. Spread tops of deviled egg halves with a small amount of slightly thickened gelatin. Chill until firm. Carefully invert egg halves on chilled gelatin layer. Fold celery and olives into remaining slightly thickened gelatin. Turn into loaf pan over eggs. Chill until firm. Unmold and cut into slices. Serve on salad greens with mayonnaise. Makes 4 servings.

The Borden Company

# Cottage Cheese Apple Salad

1 package lime-flavored gelatin
1 cup hot water
2 cups unsweetened applesauce
1 cup cottage cheese

Combine gelatin and hot water and stir until gelatin is dissolved. Fold in applesauce and cottage cheese. Pour into individual molds and chill until firm. Unmold on lettuce cups and serve with mayonnaise. Makes 6 servings.

# Macaroni and Cheese Salad Ring

2 cups cooked elbow macaroni
¼ cup French dressing
2 cups cottage cheese
¼ cup diced pimiento
¼ cup diced green pepper
2 tablespoons finely chopped onion
2 tablespoons chopped parsley

Combine macaroni and French dressing; mix well and chill for about ½ hour. Add remaining ingredients, mix together gently but thoroughly. Press mixture lightly into a 9-inch ring mold. Chill for several hours. Unmold by loosening sides of salad from mold with a knife. Turn out on a bed of salad greens. Makes 6 to 8 servings.

# Tomato Egg Mold

**PART I**

1 envelope unflavored gelatin
½ cup cold tomato juice
1¼ cups hot tomato juice
½ teaspoon salt
1 tablespoon lemon juice

Soften gelatin in cold tomato juice. Add hot tomato juice and stir until dissolved. Add salt and lemon juice. Pour into loaf pan and chill until almost firm.

**PART II**

1 envelope unflavored gelatin
½ cup cold water
1 teaspoon salt
2 tablespoons lemon juice
¼ teaspoon Worcestershire sauce
Dash of cayenne pepper
¾ cup mayonnaise
1½ teaspoons grated onion
½ cup finely diced celery
¼ cup finely diced green pepper
¼ cup chopped pimiento
4 hard-cooked eggs, chopped

Soften gelatin in cold water. Place over boiling water and stir until dissolved. Add salt, lemon juice, Worcestershire sauce and pepper. Cool. Add mayonnaise and remaining ingredients. Turn on top of tomato layer in loaf pan. Chill until firm. Unmold on crisp salad greens and serve with French dressing. Makes 8 servings.

# Cheese Lime Ring

2 packages lime-flavored gelatin
3¾ cups boiling water
¼ cup lemon juice
2 cups cottage cheese
½ cup slivered blanched almonds

Add gelatin to boiling water and stir until dissolved. Add lemon juice and cool until it is syrupy. Fold in cheese and almonds. Pour into a 1½-quart ring mold. Chill until firm. Unmold on salad greens and serve with mayonnaise. Makes 6 to 8 servings.

Corn Products Company

Knox Gelatin

# Cheese-Tomato Aspic Platter

**1 envelope unflavored gelatin**
**1 cup milk**
**½ teaspoon salt**
**2 teaspoons instant minced onion**
**2 packages (3-ounce) cream cheese**
**¾ cup salad dressing**
**2 tablespoons lemon juice**
**1 teaspoon Worcestershire sauce**
**1 cup sliced, pimiento-stuffed olives**

Sprinkle gelatin over milk in saucepan. Place over low heat; stir constantly until gelatin dissolves, 3 to 4 minutes. Remove from heat; stir in salt and instant minced onion. Soften cream cheese in medium-size bowl. Gradually blend in salad dressing until smooth; stir in lemon juice and Worcestershire sauce. Gradually stir gelatin mixture into salad dressing mixture; beat with rotary beater if necessary until smooth. Chill, stirring occasionally, until mixture mounds slightly when dropped from spoon. Fold in sliced olives and turn into 9 x 5 x 3-inch loaf pan or 2-quart mold. Chill until almost firm.

## Tomato Aspic Layer

**3 envelopes unflavored gelatin**
**2 cups cold water, divided**
**3 cans (8 ounces each) tomato sauce**
**1 tablespoon Worcestershire sauce**
**¼ teaspoon Tabasco**
**1 tablespoon lemon juice**

Sprinkle gelatin over 1½ cups cold water in 2½-quart saucepan. Place over low heat; stir constantly until gelatin dissolves, 2 to 3 minutes. Remove from heat; stir in remaining ½ cup cold water and other remaining ingredients. Cool if necessary to room temperature. Pour over almost-firm cheese layer. Chill until firm. Unmold on serving platter. If desired, serve with cooked shrimp that have been marinated in a well-seasoned French dressing. Garnish top of loaf with sliced stuffed olives and additional shrimp. Serve with salad greens. Makes 8 servings.

# Swiss Salad Platter

**½ pound Swiss cheese**
**12 slices tomato**
**12 slices cucumber**
**12 radish roses**
**Romaine**
**Clove of garlic**
**⅓ cup mayonnaise**
**⅔ cup French dressing**
**1 tablespoon chopped chives**

Cut cheese in match-like sticks and arrange on romaine in center of a platter. Surround with slices of tomato and cucumber and radishes. Rub bowl in which dressing is to be mixed with cut side of clove of garlic. Mix mayonnaise, French dressing and chives in bowl. Serve in a separate bowl with salad. Makes 6 servings.

Corn Products Company

# Cottage Cheese Salad Rings

**2 cups cottage cheese**
**¾ teaspoon salt**
**1 teaspoon sugar**
**1 tablespoon lemon juice**
**½ cup cream**
**1 envelope unflavored gelatin**
**¼ cup cold water**
**Lettuce cups**
**Mixed fruit**

Combine cottage cheese, salt, sugar, lemon juice and cream. Combine gelatin and water and let stand 5 minutes. Place over boiling water and stir until dissolved. Stir gelatin into cheese mixture. Pour into individual ring molds or into one large ring mold. Chill until firm. Unmold on lettuce cups. Fill centers with mixed chilled fruit. Makes 6 servings.

# Frozen Fruit Salad

2 No. 2½ cans fruit cocktail
¼ cup juice from fruit
32 marshmallows
2 3-ounce packages cream cheese
2 cups heavy cream
½ teaspoon salt

Drain fruit cocktail. Place juice and marshmallows in top part of double boiler. Place over hot water and heat until marshmallows are melted. Soften cream cheese in a large mixing bowl with a little of the heavy cream. Beat remaining cream until thick and glossy. Stir salt and melted marshmallows into softened cream cheese. Fold in whipped cream and fruit cocktail. Spoon into four No. 2 cans and cover tops with aluminum foil. Place in freezing compartment of refrigerator and freeze at least 4 hours. To serve, remove bottom of can with can opener, loosen salad around edges with a knife. Push out from bottom. Cut into slices. Serve on crisp lettuce. Makes 16 servings.

# Roquefort Salad Ring

2 teaspoons unflavored gelatin
3 tablespoons cold water
¼ pound Roquefort cheese
2 cups cottage cheese
1 teaspoon Worcestershire sauce
Dash of Tabasco sauce
Salt
½ cup mayonnaise
½ cup heavy cream, whipped

Combine gelatin and cold water, let stand 5 minutes. Dissolve over hot water. Mash Roquefort cheese, stir in cottage cheese and blend thoroughly. Add seasonings and melted gelatin. Fold in mayonnaise and cream. Pour into 6-inch ring mold and chill. Unmold on lettuce cups and garnish with tomatoes and ripe olives. Serve with French dressing. Makes 6 servings.

# Mushroom Stuffed Eggs

6 eggs
¼ teaspoon salt
½ teaspoon prepared mustard
½ teaspoon vinegar
1 tablespoon mayonnaise
Dash pepper
Dash Worcestershire sauce
1 3-oz. can sliced mushrooms

Cook eggs until hard. Peel, halve, and place yolks in a bowl. Mash well until smooth. Add remaining ingredients except mushrooms and blend well. Drain mushrooms, reserving juice for soup or gravy, and save out 12 pieces of mushroom. Chop remaining mushrooms until fairly fine and add to egg mixture. Fill egg whites lightly and use reserved slices of mushroom to garnish.

# Fruit and Cheese Combination

1 package lime-flavored gelatin
1 cup boiling water
⅔ cup orange juice
1 cup orange sections
1 unpeeled apple, cut in strips
2 cups cottage cheese
Salad greens

Dissolve gelatin in boiling water. Add orange juice and chill until thick and syrupy. Gently fold in well drained orange sections and apple strips. Spoon into molds. Press a spoonful of cottage cheese in center of each mold. Chill until firm. Unmold on a circle of salad greens and pile cottage cheese in center of circle. Serve with sour cream or any desired dressing. Makes 6 to 8 servings.

# Cheese Salad Ring

2 envelopes unflavored gelatin
1 cup cold water
2 cups milk
½ cup crumbled Bleu cheese
½ cup mayonnaise
1 teaspoon Worcestershire sauce
1 teaspoon scraped onion
⅛ teaspoon paprika
¾ teaspoon salt
Dash of pepper
2 cups cottage cheese

Soften gelatin in cold water; then dissolve over hot water. Gradually stir in milk and chill until thick. Mash Bleu cheese and blend in mayonnaise. Add Worcestershire sauce, onion, paprika, salt and pepper. When well mixed stir in cottage cheese. Beat chilled gelatin until foamy and then fold in cheese mixture. Pour into a ring mold and chill until firm. Unmold on salad greens and fill center with favorite vegetable salad. Makes 10 to 12 servings.

Corn Products Company

# Fruit Salad Cheese Chest

1 cup mayonnaise
2 3-ounce packages cream cheese
2 envelopes unflavored gelatin
4 tablespoons cold water
1 pint heavy cream
2 large cans fruit cocktail

Combine mayonnaise and softened cream cheese, mix until smooth. Soak gelatin in cold water for 5 minutes; dissolve over hot water. Blend into cheese mixture. Whip heavy cream until stiff and fold into cheese mixture. Chill until gelatin begins to set, about 15 minutes. Rinse a loaf pan 8½x4½x2½-inch with cold water. Line the sides of the pan about ½-inch thick with gelatin mixture. Fill inside with fruit cocktail, packing firmly. Spread remainder of cheese mixture on top and chill 3 or 4 hours. Unmold on a platter. Garnish with orange sections and salad greens. Makes 8 servings.

# Sour Cream Ring

1 envelope unflavored gelatin
¼ cup cold water
½ cup boiling water
2 cups sour cream
1 teaspoon salt
⅛ teaspoon cayenne
1 teaspoon Worcestershire sauce

Soften gelatin in cold water. Add boiling water and stir until gelatin is dissolved. Gradually add sour cream and blend until smooth. Add seasonings and mix well. Pour into a 1-quart ring mold and chill until firm. Unmold on salad greens and fill center with thinly sliced cucumbers and radishes which have been marinated in French dressing. Makes 4 to 6 servings.

# Tomato Soup Mold

2 envelopes unflavored gelatin
½ cup cold water
1 can condensed tomato soup
3 3-ounce packages cream cheese
1 cup mayonnaise
1½ cups chopped celery
2 tablespoons chopped green pepper
2 tablespoons chopped green onion
¼ cup chopped green or ripe olives
½ cup chopped nuts

Soften gelatin in cold water. Heat tomato soup to boiling, remove from heat, add the softened gelatin and stir until it is dissolved. Soften cream cheese and add to the soup. Stir until smooth and well blended. Cool slightly. Fold in mayonnaise, vegetables and nuts. Turn into large mold; chill till firm. Turn out on lettuce cups and serve with mayonnaise or French dressing. Makes 6 servings.

# NOTES

# SANDWICH and PARTY SNACK

Are you having a party or are you going on a picnic? Are you planning lunch for the children or afternoon tea for the ladies? Maybe it is going to be a cocktail party or a midnight supper for the couples club. In any case food will be a "must" on the agenda and, whatever your problem, you will more than likely find the answer to many of your questions in this book.

You will find easy to make dips and dunks, fun to serve and easy to eat. For a picnic, lunch box or late night snack we have many hearty sandwiches for your selection. Many of the hot, hearty sandwiches will also make an excellent luncheon, with dessert and coffee, for the bridge club.

Fancy sandwiches can sometimes be a lot of work, but ours look so pretty, and will be eaten with so much enjoyment, that you will be amply rewarded for your extra time and effort. So, what ever your sandwich problem, big or small, this book will provide the answer.

## Dips and Dunks

FEW GUESTS CAN RESIST the lure of a big platter of crisp vegetables, potato chips or shrimp and a big bowl of savory sauce into which they can dip or dunk their selection. What can you dunk? In addition to potato chips, you can dunk crackers, toast, nuts, pretzels, and even corn flakes. In the vegetable field you can dunk carrots, celery, radishes, cucumber, raw mushrooms, cauliflowerets, tiny tomatoes, fenuchi with the delicate anise flavor, endive, asparagus, green onions and olives. You can also dunk shrimp, lobster chunks, frankfurters, cheese cubes, and others. You can dip and dunk in as simple a sauce as Pink Mayonnaise made with chili sauce, mayonnaise and onion juice, or in one of the more elaborate ones whose recipes are given here. Place your dunks in the prettiest bowls you have, or you can hollow out fruits and vegetables like cabbage, apples and lemons to hold them.

Sealtest Kitchens

# Five-In-One Cream Cheese Dip

**1 package (8 ounce) cream cheese**
**1½ tablespoons lemon juice**
**1½ teaspoons grated onion**
**2 cups (1 pint) sour cream**

Let cream cheese stand at room temperature to soften. Cream until smooth. Add lemon juice and onion; blend well. Gradually blend in sour cream. Chill. Serve with potato chips, crisp crackers or crisp fresh vegetables. Makes 2½ cups.

Vary the above basic dip with *one* of these flavors:

Caper: Fold in ½ cup drained capers. Makes 3 cups.

Anchovy: Fold in a 2-oz. can anchovies, drained and mashed. Makes 2¾ cups.

Curry-Clam: Fold in 2 cans (7½-oz. each or 2 cups) drained minced clams; add ½ teaspoon curry powder. Makes 3½ cups.

Mushroom: Fold in 1 cup finely chopped, lightly sauteed mushrooms. Makes 3½ cups.

The Borden Company

# Barbecue Cheese Dip

**¾ cup sour cream**
**¾ cup cottage cheese**
**⅛ teaspoon each, onion and celery salt**
**2 tablespoons catsup**
**1 tablespoon bottled barbecue sauce**

Place all ingredients in the glass container of a blender, and run about 1 minute or until sauce is smooth. If you have no blender, beat well with a wooden spoon.

# Spicy Dunking Sauce

**1 cup chili sauce**
**2 tablespoons lemon juice**
**½ teaspoon salt**
**¼ teaspoon Tabasco**
**1 tablespoon horse-radish**
**3 tablespoons finely minced celery**

Combine all ingredients and let stand to blend flavors.

# Chicken Liver and Mushroom Dip

**½ pound chicken livers**
**4 tablespoons butter**
**1 can (3-oz.) mushroom slices**
**2 tablespoons chopped onion**
**¼ cup chopped parsley**
**½ cup mayonnaise**
**Salt and pepper to taste**

Sauté livers in butter until brown. Place in chopping bowl, add mushrooms and chop. Add remaining ingredients and blend well adding more mayonnaise if necessary to make of dipping consistency.

# Dunk 'Em Sauce

**1 cup mayonnaise**
**¼ cup catsup**
**2 tablespoons mustard-with-horse-radish**
**1 teaspoon powdered onion**
**Dash of Tabasco sauce**
**Red apples**

Combine first five ingredients. Cut a slice from the tops of apples. Scoop out most of insides. Fill with sauce and stick picks with foods to be dunked into apples.

# Guacamole

**1 small avocado, peeled**
**2 tablespoons lemon juice**
**1 teaspoon onion juice**
**Dash salt, pepper, cayenne pepper**
**1 clove garlic, mashed**
**2 teaspoons Worcestershire sauce**

Mash the avocado and stir in lemon juice immediately to prevent discoloration. Add remaining ingredients. Mix well. A little cooked crumbled bacon may be added or a fresh, diced tomato. Unless you're going to serve this immediately, cover with a thin layer of mayonnaise to prevent discoloration.

# Avocado-Cream Cheese Dip

**2 3-oz. packages cream cheese**
**1 tablespoon lemon juice**
**1 medium avocado, peeled and cut**
**¼ teaspoon onion juice**
**Dash salt and pepper**
**2 tablespoons milk**

Soften cream cheese at room temperature. Sprinkle lemon juice over cut pieces of avocado and mash finely. Beat cream cheese until smooth and fluffy. Stir in onion juice, salt and pepper. Gradually beat in avocado, blending well. Add enough milk to give good dipping consistency. Serve with crisp raw vegetables or potato chips.

# Egg-Parsley Dip

**4 hard-cooked eggs, chopped**
**1 tablespoon minced parsley**
**2 tablespoons lemon juice**
**1 teaspoon onion juice**
**Dash each, salt and pepper**
**Pinch of mixed dried herbs**
**½ cup mayonnaise**

Combine ingredients and serve garnished with parsley.

# Tomato-Sour Cream Dip

**1 8-oz. can tomato sauce**
**1 cup thick sour cream**
**Dash salt, pepper, paprika**
**2 teaspoons onion juice**
**⅓ cup horse-radish**

Combine all ingredients and chill before serving.

# Deviled Crab Dip

**1 6½-oz. can crab meat**
**2 hard-cooked eggs, chopped**
**½ teaspoon prepared mustard**
**Dash salt and pepper**
**1 tablespoon lemon juice**
**½ cup mayonnaise**
**Parsley**

Drain, bone and flake crab meat. Combine with remaining ingredients. Mix well. Garnish with parsley.

# Cheese Sputnik

(See picture between pgs. 64-65.)

**Cheese cubes**
**Pineapple cubes**
**Green and purple grapes**
**Banana slices**
**Halves of nuts**
**Mandarin oranges**
**Maraschino cherries**

. . . and so on. Just use your imagination! Stick the toothpicks into an orange levelled at the bottom. And you have a special treat.

# Smoky Pea Dip

**1 envelope Swiss recipe smoky green pea soup mix**
**1 pint dairy sour cream**

Combine soup mix and sour cream. Chill 2 hours for crunchy dip and 4 hours for softer dip. Makes 2 cups. Serve with cheese doodles.

Best Foods

# Leek Dip

**1 envelope Swiss recipe cream of leek soup mix**
**1 pint dairy sour cream**

Combine soup mix and sour cream. Let stand in refrigerator at least 2 hours before serving. Makes 2 cups. Serve with dipsy doodles.

# Spring Vegetable Dip

**1 envelope Swiss recipe spring vegetable soup mix**
**1 pint dairy sour cream**

Combine soup mix and sour cream. Let stand in refrigerator at least 2 hours before serving. Makes 2 cups. Serve with corn doodles.

## Ginger Cream Dip

**1½ cups sour cream**
**½ cup chilled mayonnaise**
**¼ cup minced parsley**
**¼ cup finely chopped water-chestnuts**
**2 to 4 tablespoons finely chopped onion**
**2 tablespoons finely chopped crystallized ginger**
**1 tablespoon soy sauce**
**Dash salt**

Combine sour cream and mayonnaise. Blend in remaining ingredients. Chill until ready to use. Serve as a dip for crisp vegetables and crackers. Makes 2½ cups.

## Chiffonade Dip

**¼ cup minced pimiento**
**¼ cup minced parsley**
**3 tablespoons minced onion**
**¼ cup finely diced green pepper**
**Dash salt, garlic salt, Tabasco**
**2 hard-cooked eggs, chopped**
**¼ cup mayonnaise**

Combine all ingredients and chill until ready to serve.

## Blue Cheese Dip

**¼ pound blue cheese, crumbled**
**½ cup chili sauce**
**2 tablespoons mayonnaise**
**2 tablespoons chopped onion**
**¼ cup chopped parsley**
**Salt and pepper to taste**

Combine all ingredients. Blend well and chill before serving.

## Chili Dip

**1 can baked beans, sieved**
**2 tablespoons minced onion**
**¼ cup chopped dill pickle**
**1 tablespoon chili sauce**
**1 teaspoon chili powder**
**2 hard-cooked eggs, chopped**
**Salt and pepper to taste**

Combine all ingredients and chill until serving time.

Western Growers Association

## Cocktail Curry Sauce

**¼ cup butter**
**1 green onion, minced**
**1 teaspoon minced ginger root or 3 tablespoons chopped crystallized ginger**
**2 tablespoons flour**
**½ cup chopped apple**
**1-2 teaspoons curry powder**
**1 teaspoon salt**
**1 teaspoon sugar**
**4 whole cloves**
**Dash of Cayenne pepper**
**2 cups milk**
**½ cup moist shredded coconut**
**¼ cup lemon juice**
**Thin cream**

Set out chafing dish and melt butter in the chafing dish blazer. Cook onion until transparent, stirring occasionally. Blend in flour until mixture bubbles. Add ginger, apple, curry powder, salt, sugar, cloves and pepper.

Remove from heat and gradually add milk. Stir constantly until sauce thickens. Place over pan of simmering water and cook 30 minutes covered. Remove whole cloves.

Stir in coconut. Gradually add lemon juice. Thin cream may be added if consistency is too thick. Makes 3 cups of sauce. Suggestions: An electric skillet can be used to cook the sauce and a casserole with candle warmer substituted for a chafing dish. Serve a side dish of fruit chutney.

## A Basic Dunk

**1 cup mayonnaise**
**½ cup chili sauce**
**1 teaspoon onion juice or powder**
**1 tablespoon horse-radish**
**¼ teaspoon each, salt, paprika**
**Dash of freshly ground pepper**

Combine all ingredients and chill before serving.

Western Growers Association

# Cream Cheese Olive Dip

2 3-oz. packages cream cheese
½ cup chopped ripe olives
1 tablespoon chopped onion
About 3 tablespoons milk
Salt and pepper to taste

Combine cream cheese with remaining ingredients. Add a little more milk if necessary to make a good dip consistency.

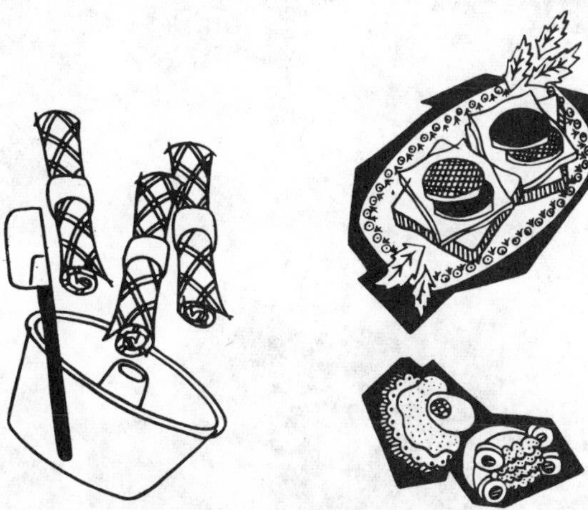

# Creamy Egg-Chive Dip

6 oz. chive cheese
2 tablespoons mayonnaise
1 teaspoon prepared mustard
½ teaspoon Worcestershire sauce
Dash each, salt and pepper
2 hard cooked eggs, finely chopped
About 3 tablespoons milk

Soften cream cheese at room temperature. Beat until smooth and fluffy. Add next four ingredients and mix well. Add eggs, then enough milk to make dip consistency.

# Roquefort Cottage Cheese Dip

2 sections (1¼-oz.) Roquefort cheese
1 container (8-oz.) cottage cheese
½ teaspoon onion juice
About 6 tablespoons sour cream

Crumble Roquefort cheese into cottage cheese. Mix well. Add onion juice and enough sour cream to bring to dip consistency. Serve with chips, crackers or vegetables.

# Sour Cream Dip

**1 cup sour cream**
**½ tablespoon prepared mustard**
**2 tablespoons chili sauce**
**¼ teaspoon celery seed**
**Dash each, salt and pepper**

Combine ingredients. Chill and serve with sliced cucumbers, celery and green onions.

National Dairy Council

# Roquefort Cheese Holiday Dip

**2 cups sour cream**
**1 envelope (1⅞ ounces) dehydrated cream of leek soup**
**¾ cup crumbled Roquefort cheese**
**1 package (10 ounces) pie crust mix**
**Sesame seeds or paprika**

Combine sour cream, soup mix, and Roquefort cheese; mix well. Chill 2 hours.

Meanwhile, prepare pie crust as directed on package for mixing. Divide pastry in half; shape each half into ball. Roll each out on lightly floured surface to 9-inch square. Cut each square into strips (approximately ½" x 4"). Place strips on ungreased baking sheet. Twist each strip. Sprinkle end of each strip with sesame seeds or paprika. Bake in hot oven (425° F.) about 8 minutes or until lightly browned. Serve pastry strips with dip. (Makes about 6 dozen pastry twists and about 3 cups dip.)

The Roquefort Association

Underwood Kitchens

# "Devilicious" Dunking-Bowl

**1 package hot roll mix**
**1 cup cottage cheese**
**1 cup sour cream**
**½ package onion soup mix**
**1 4½-ounce can deviled ham**

Prepare hot roll mix according to package directions. After the first rising, shape dough into a round loaf and place in a lightly greased 8-inch cake pan. Let rise again. Bake in a moderate oven (375° F.) for 35-45 minutes. Remove from pan and let cool on cake rack. Blend cottage cheese and sour cream; add onion soup mix and deviled ham. Mix well and chill. When bread cools, cut an 8 pointed star, about 6 inches in diameter and 2½ inches deep, from the center of round loaf. Cut the center bread chunk into 24-30 cubes for dunking; toast lightly. Just before serving time, place deviled ham mixture in hollow center of bread. Serve with toasted bread cubes, or allow guests to cut "dunking bowl" in chunks to spread with mixture. Makes about 2½ cups mixture.

# Remoulade Dunk

**2 cups salad dressing**
**1 tablespoon finely chopped onion**
**1 tablespoon chopped sweet pickle**
**3 tablespoons chopped parsley**
**1 tablespoon anchovy paste**
**1 tablespoon prepared mustard**
**Dash of salt, pepper**

Combine all ingredients well and serve from a scooped out head of cabbage. Delicious with shrimp.

# Artichoke Antipasto

**Prepare 3 artichokes as directed***
**1½ cups sour cream**
**2 jars (5 ounces each) processed Bleu cheese spread**
**Cherry tomatoes**
**Cocktail frankfurters**
**Fresh pineapple spears**
**Pimiento-stuffed olives**
**Carrot curls**
**Scallions**
**Celery fans**
**Cheddar cheese, cut into wedges**
**Sliced mushrooms**

Chill artichokes. Meanwhile, combine sour cream, and Bleu cheese spread; blend well. Chill. Fill artichokes with Bleu cheese dip and arrange in center of large serving platter. Arrange remaining ingredients as desired around artichokes. Makes about 12 servings.

**To prepare artichokes:* wash artichokes. Turn them upside down and press firmly. Remove chokes (thistle portion) using sharp knife and metal spoon. Stand them upright in deep saucepan large enough to hold snugly. Add 1-inch boiling water and ¼ teaspoon salt for each artichoke. Cover and boil gently 20 to 45 minutes or until stems can be pierced easily with a fork (add a little more boiling water if needed). Turn artichokes upside down to drain. Cut off stems.

Artichoke Advisory Board

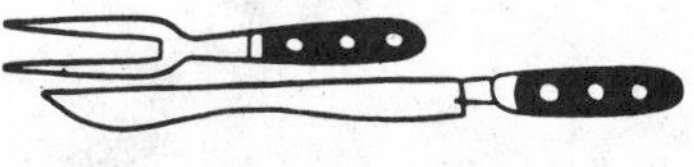

# Spreads

BY FAR THE MOST practical party fare is a bowl of some flavorful spread and an assortment of breads and crackers on which to smear it. This has the advantage of taking much less time to prepare than fancy sandwiches or decorative canapés. Also with spreads, a delay in serving will not cause the bread or crackers to become soggy and limp, and the guests can custom-make their own open sandwiches with exactly the amount of spread they like on them. An added advantage is that any leftovers can be used for days after in sandwiches. You can make spreads out of any of the food categories, and if you own a blender, you can use it to whip them to a velvet-smooth consistency that makes spreading easy. Many of the spreads, particularly those with wine or brandy, can be kept for weeks, and in fact, taste better when the flavors have had a chance to mellow and blend. To keep spreads for any length of time, place them in an earthenware crock or a covered glass container and refrigerate. Warm them to room temperature before serving for easy spreading.

## Cheese Ball

**2 3-oz. packages cream cheese**
**1 5-oz. jar sharp Cheddar cheese spread**
**1 5-oz. jar Roquefort cheese spread**
**1 5-oz. jar Smoky cheese spread**
**½ teaspoon grated onion or onion juice**
**½ teaspoon Worcestershire sauce**
**¼ cup undiluted evaporated milk**
**½ cup finely chopped walnuts**

Let the four cheeses stand at room temperature for an hour or so. Put them in a mixing bowl with the onion and Worcestershire. Mix with a fork until smooth and well blended. Stir in milk, a little at a time, and then cover and chill until firm. This will take about 4 hours or overnight. Shape the cheeses into a ball. Roll in the chopped nuts. Chill until ready to serve. Serve on a large platter with a parsley or water cress garnish and crisp crackers or wafers.

## Tuna Pâté

**1 7-oz. can tuna fish**
**6 slices crisp, brown bacon**
**6 tablespoons mayonnaise**
**2 teaspoons lemon juice**
**¼ teaspoon salt**
**Few drops Tabasco**

Grind or mash the tuna and bacon very well together. Blend in mayonnaise, lemon juice, salt and Tabasco. Rub a pretty mold very lightly with mayonnaise and pack tuna mixture into it. Chill thoroughly. Unmold to serve and garnish with lemon wedges. Makes 1½ cups.

## Chicken-Almond Spread

**¾ cup cooked chicken, cut in pieces**
**2 tablespoons canned diced, roasted almonds**
**1 stalk celery, minced**
**Dash each salt, cayenne pepper**
**1 teaspoon lemon juice**
**2 tablespoons mayonnaise**

Have the chicken in small pieces. Add the almonds, celery, seasonings, lemon juice and mayonnaise. Toss until well combined. Serve in a bowl surrounded by crackers and garnished with more almonds and parsley. Makes 1 cup.

Corn Products Company

ONE OF THE MOST universally liked spreads at any party is the highly seasoned ground beef concoction known as Steak Tartare. This can be served on a platter surrounded by parsley sprigs and accompanied by thin slices of rye or pumpernickel breads and thin slices of onion.

## Steak Tartare

**2 pounds top round, ground**
**12 anchovies**
**1 onion, very finely minced**
**Worcestershire sauce, salt, fresh pepper to taste**
**3 raw yolks**

Grind the meat three times with the anchovies. Season highly to taste with onion, Worcestershire, salt and freshly ground pepper. Mix in egg yolks. Make into a mound and serve with onion rings and anchovies.

## Curried Tuna Spread

**1 7-oz. can tuna fish**
**¼ teaspoon salt**
**½ teaspoon curry powder**
**2½ tablespoons mayonnaise**
**2 teaspoons lemon juice**
**2 teaspoons onion powder**

Drain the tuna and break into small pieces. Add the remaining ingredients and toss together lightly with a fork until well-mixed. Garnish with strips of pimiento and parsley. Makes 1 cup.

## Roquefort-Camembert Mousse

**1 tablespoon (1 envelope) unflavored gelatine**
**¼ cup cold water**
**2 small triangles Camembert cheese**
**¼ pound Roquefort cheese**
**1 teaspoon Worcestershire sauce**
**1 egg, separated**
**½ cup heavy cream**

Place gelatine in the cold water and let stand for five minutes Then place the gelatine over hot water and dissolve it. Blend the two cheeses together until the mixture is smooth. Beat in the Worcestershire and egg yolk. Add gelatine. Beat egg white until stiff. Whip cream. Fold egg white and whipped cream into cheese mixture. Pour into a one pint mold. Chill until firm. Unmold onto a platter and serve with crackers or slices of salty rye bread.

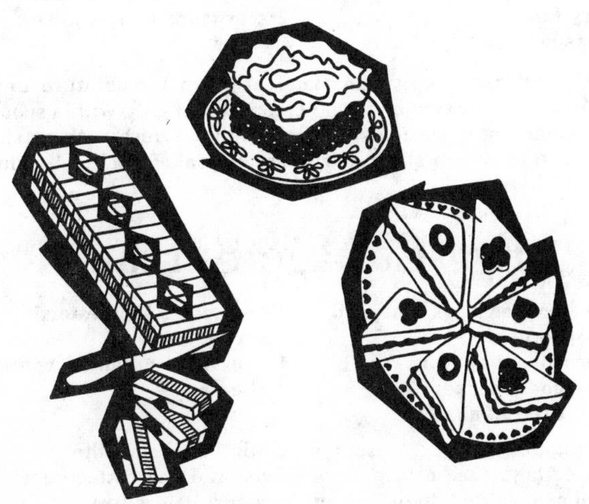

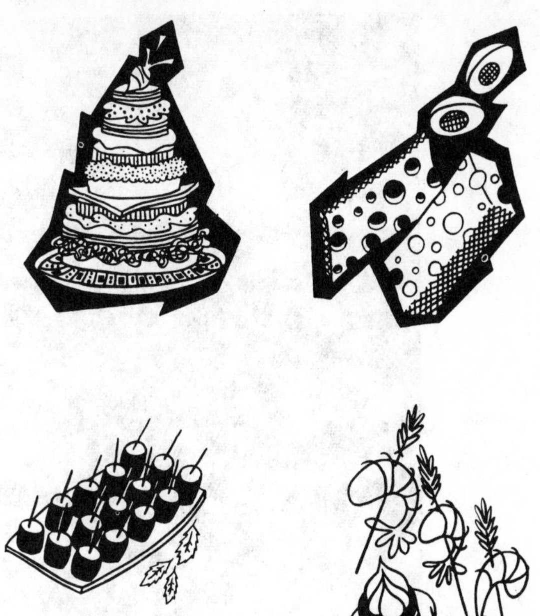

## Hungarian Cheese Spread

**½ pound cottage cheese**
**1 3-oz. package cream cheese**
**1 tablespoon butter**
**½ teaspoon paprika**
**½ teaspoon caraway seeds**
**½ teaspoon prepared mustard**
**1 teaspoon chopped capers**
**½ teaspoon onion juice**

Cream the cheeses and butter together until well blended. Add the seasonings and chill for several hours to let the flavors blend. Serve on thinly sliced rye or pumpernickel bread.

## Garlic Lamb Spread

**1 3½-oz. can chopped lamb**
**1 cup cottage cheese**
**2 tablespoons catsup**
**½ small onion, finely minced**
**Dash each, salt, pepper, garlic powder**

Combine all ingredients and blend well. Cover and chill before serving. Makes 1¼ cups.

## Sardine Appeteaser

**1 3½-oz. can sardines**
**2 hard-cooked eggs**
**2 tablespoons lemon juice**
**2 tablespoons mayonnaise**
**1 teaspoon onion juice**
**1 tablespoon finely chopped parsley**
**¾ teaspoon salt**
**Dash cayenne pepper**
**½ teaspoon monosodium glutamate**
**3 tablespoons nonfat dry milk solids**
**1 teaspoon anchovy paste**

Mash sardines well with a fork. Mince the egg whites and set aside the yolks to use as a garnish. Combine all ingredients except the egg yolks and mix very well. Place in a bowl and top with sieved egg yolks. Makes 1 cup.

R. T. French Co.

## Cheese-Pecan Spread

**1 envelope cheese sauce mix**
**¾ cup milk**
**8 ounces cream cheese**
**4 ounces Bleu cheese**
**¾ cup pecans, finely chopped**
**2 tablespoons finely chopped parsley**
**1 teaspoon Worcestershire Sauce**
**Stuffed olives for garnish**

Combine cheese sauce and milk in a small saucepan. Heat just to boiling, stirring constantly. Cool to lukewarm. Add cream cheese and crumbled Bleu cheese; mix until smoothly blended. Mix in all but 2 or 3 tablespoons of pecans, the parsley, and the Worcestershire Sauce. Chill. With spoon and spatula, mold into a mound. Garnish top with a gay Christmas tree fashioned with slices of stuffed olives. Or mound the spread into a small bowl. Garnish top with nuts and olives. A help-yourself-spread good on toast rounds and a variety of crisp crackers. About 2½ cups.

## Layered Spread

*Cheese Layer:* Cream together 2 3-oz. packages cream cheese and 1 1½-oz. package blue cheese. Season to taste with Worcestershire sauce and chopped parsley. Mix in enough milk or cream to make into spreading consistency. Spread evenly on bottom of an 8-inch pie plate.

*Ham Layer:* Combine 1 can (4½ oz.) deviled ham with a little mayonnaise and spread over cheese layer.

*Egg Layer:* Hard-cook and chop 4 eggs. Season to taste with salt, pepper, pimiento and mayonnaise. Spread on top of ham layer. Cover and chill several hours or overnight. Cut in thin wedges to serve.

## Shrimp Paste

**2 tablespoons chili sauce**
**2 tablespoons mayonnaise**
**1 tablespoon lemon juice**
**⅛ teaspoon dill powder**
**1 5-oz. can shrimp, drained**

Place ingredients in order listed in the container of an electric blender. Cover and turn on blender about 30 seconds, stopping to stir down the paste once or twice. Place in a bowl and garnish with sprays of water cress. Makes ¾ cup.

## Viking Spread

**1 bar (½ cup) butter or margarine**
**4 hard-cooked eggs, chopped very fine**
**⅛ teaspoon salt**
**¼ cup ripe olives, cut in pieces**
**¼ cup mashed sardines**
**2 teaspoons lemon juice**

Let butter or margarine stand at room temperature until soft. Place in a mixing bowl and cream thoroughly with a spoon. Add remaining ingredients and mix well. Garnish with parsley and serve with thin slices of rye bread. Makes about 1½ cups.

## Egg-Cottage Spread

**8 hard-cooked eggs, chopped**
**1 teaspoon salt**
**¼ teaspoon dry mustard**
**¼ teaspoon pepper**
**4 to 6 drops Tabasco**
**½ teaspoon Worcestershire sauce**
**1 container creamed cottage cheese**

Combine eggs and seasonings. Chill. For a smoother spread, press cottage cheese through a sieve. Add the cottage cheese, sieved or unsieved, to the egg mixture just before serving. Serve with crisp wafers or bread. Makes 2 cups.

## Brandied Cheese Spread

2 3-oz. packages cream cheese
¼ pound Roquefort cheese
2 tablespoons olive oil
1 teaspoon dry mustard
3 tablespoons brandy

Let cream cheese soften at room temperature. Beat until fluffy. Crumble Roquefort cheese into cream cheese. Add olive oil and beat until well blended. Stir in mustard and brandy. Chill for ½ hour. Serve with crackers. This may be kept in the refrigerator for several weeks.

## Favorite Egg Spread

12 hard-cooked eggs, riced or sieved
2 tablespoons softened butter
4 teaspoons lemon juice
1½ teaspoons prepared mustard
2 teaspoons Worcestershire sauce
1 teaspoon salt
¼ teaspoon pepper
About ¾ cup salad dressing
Paprika, chives or parsley

Combine all ingredients. Beat until smooth, adding more seasonings if desired. Refrigerate until ready to serve. Garnish with paprika, parsley or chives. Makes 4 cups.

## Almond Piquant Spread

¼ cup chopped blanched, roasted almonds
1 3-oz. package cream cheese
¼ cup sweet pickle relish
½ teaspoon prepared horse-radish
Salt to taste
Few drops Tabasco
Mayonnaise

Combine the first 6 ingredients with enough mayonnaise to make into spreading consistency. Blend thoroughly, then place in a bowl and sprinkle with paprika. Makes about ¾ cup of spread.

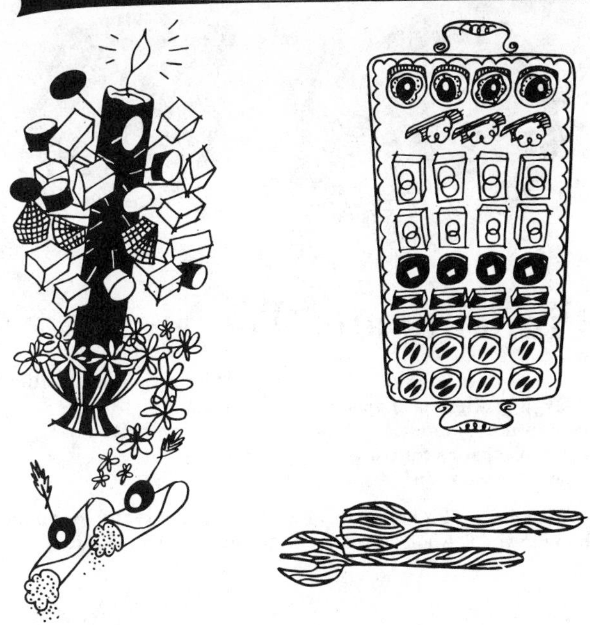

## Curried Olive Spread

1 3-oz. package cream cheese
2 tablespoons milk
⅛ teaspoon curry powder
¼ teaspoon onion powder
½ cup chopped ripe olives
Dash each, pepper, paprika

Combine cream cheese and milk until smooth and of spreading consistency. Add remaining ingredients and blend. Serve with crisp crackers. Makes about ¾ cup spread.

## Cheese Pineapple

This interesting looking spread can make an attractive edible decoration for the table.

2 3-oz. packages cream cheese
1 small jar stuffed olives
Pointed leaves

Mash the cheese until soft and smooth. Add a very small amount of milk if necessary. Slice half the olives and chop the rest. Add the chopped olives to the cream cheese and stuff into a large jelly glass. Invert and place on a serving plate. Smooth around with a spatula and mark the surface with diagonal lines centering each square with an olive slice. Place the leaves on top to complete the effect of a pineapple. Serve with crackers.

## Cream Cheese-Anchovy Spread

2 3-oz. packages cream cheese
Anchovy paste to taste
1 tablespoon onion juice
1 tablespoon finely minced chives
1 small jar stuffed olives, minced

Mash the cream cheese with milk or cream until smooth and soft. Add anchovy paste to taste and then add remaining ingredients. Mix well and store in a cool place until ready to serve. Makes enough spread for about 6 dozen crackers.

# Pimiento and Tongue Spread

1 cup ground tongue
1 large pimiento, chopped
⅓ cup mayonnaise
1½ tablespoons mustard with horse-radish
1 tablespoon finely minced onion
1 teaspoon salt

Combine all ingredients and mix well. Let blend for about an hour in the refrigerator before serving. Makes 1½ cups.

# Pungent Liver Pâté

½ cup ground, cooked chicken livers
2 teaspoons minced onion
2 teaspoons chopped sweet pickle
1 tablespoon pickle juice
¼ cup mayonnaise
1 chopped hard-cooked egg
Salt and pepper to taste

Combine all ingredients and mix well. Mash finely for a smooth paste or leave coarse if desired. Makes 1 cup.

Small cans of strained and chopped baby foods make a wonderful and quick base for many different spreads. They can be speedily combined with seasonings, cheese or cream to make a great variety of flavorful spreads in a matter of minutes.

# Chicken Pâté

2 tablespoons consommé
⅓ cup blanched almonds
½ teaspoon powdered ginger
¼ cup mayonnaise
1 cup cooked chicken, cut in pieces

Place consommé and almonds in container of a blender. Cover and turn on blender until contents are smoothly blended. Add ginger, mayonnaise and chicken. Cover and blend until smooth. Place in a covered container and chill until ready to serve. Makes 1 cup.

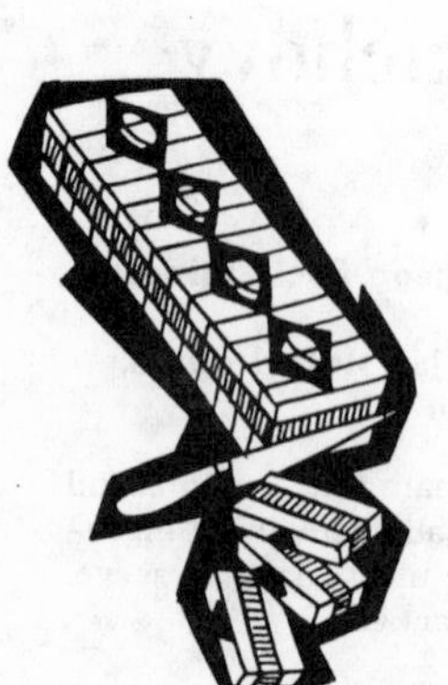

Tuna Research Foundation

# Christmas Tuna Pâté

1 package (8 ounces) cream cheese
2 tablespoons chili sauce
2 tablespoons minced parsley
¼ cup minced onion
1 tablespoon Worcestershire Sauce
½ teaspoon tabasco sauce
3 cans (6½ or 7 ounces each) tuna
3 to 4 tablespoons mayonnaise
Pimiento
Capers
Parsley sprigs

With an electric beater, beat together the cream cheese, chili sauce, parsley, onion, Worcestershire and tabasco. Turn tuna into a colander or strainer to drain; gradually add drained tuna to cream cheese mixture, beating until thoroughly blended. Chill 8 hours or overnight in tightly covered container. To shape tuna paté into Christmas tree shape, mold tuna mixture on serving plate into a pyramid. Cover with the mayonnaise, using a small spatula. Make garlands around tree by alternating pimiento strips and capers in two rows around tree. Cut star out of pimiento with miniature star cutter and secure with toothpick on top of tree. Arrange parsley sprigs around bottom or tree. Makes 4 cups tuna paté.

**Note:** If you want to chill the tuna mixture speedily, spread it in a shallow pan and place it in the freezer, but do not freeze.

Diamond Walnuts

## California Walnut Cheese Logs

**1 pound soft Cheddar cheese**
**2 (3-ounce) packages cream cheese**
**¼ pound Bleu cheese**
**¼ pound smoked cheese**
**1 tablespoon prepared mustard**
**1 teaspoon grated onion**
**3 tablespoons Port wine**
**Cream**
**1 cup chopped walnuts**

Grate cheddar cheese; combine with one package of the cream cheese, the Bleu cheese, and smoked cheese. Mix in mustard, grated onion and port, using electric mixer or your hands. Shape into logs about an inch in diameter. Blend remaining package of cream cheese with enough cream until of spreading consistency and spread over the logs. Roll in walnuts. Wrap in aluminum foil and chill in refrigerator. Slice and serve on assorted crackers. Makes 24 servings.

## Snappy Deviled Spread

**1 2¼-oz. can deviled ham**
**½ Snappy cheese roll**
**1 teaspoon prepared mustard**

Mash ham and cheese together, then blend in the mustard. Makes ¾ cup.

## Creamy Beef Spread

**1 3½-oz. can chopped beef**
**1 cup sour cream**
**¼ teaspoon salt**
**Dash each, garlic salt, pepper**
**Few drops Tabasco**

Blend all ingredients together well. Cover and chill. Makes 1¼ cups.

## Curried Egg Spread

**4 hard-cooked egg yolks**
**2 3-oz. packages cream cheese**
**¼ cup mayonnaise**
**½ cup chopped stuffed olives**
**1 teaspoon curry powder**
**Dash each, salt and Worcestershire**

Mash egg yolks until smooth. Add cream cheese and blend well. Add remaining ingredients and stir until well combined. Cover and chill until serving time. Makes about 1¾ cups.

## Chopped Liver Spread

**1 3½-oz. can chopped liver**
**1 3-oz. package cream cheese, softened**
**1 small onion, browned in butter**
**Salt and pepper to taste**

Combine all ingredients and blend well. Cover and chill well before serving. Makes 1¼ cups.

# Biscuits, Breads and Batters

**Here's one of the book's most essential chapters—practically all hors d'oeuvres use bread as a base.**

MOST HORS D'OEUVRES are served on or with some kind of bread. This can be as simple as a cracker from a box or as complicated as French puff paste. If you decide on packaged crackers as your bread base, you can dress them up with little effort. Use any *crisp cracker;* brush with butter and dust lightly with grated hard cheese, caraway seeds, or any of the savory salts. Heat for a short time in a moderate (350°F.) oven. *Soda crackers* can be puffed up to make an attractive base by soaking them in ice cold water for 6 to 7 minutes, then draining on paper towels. Then place them on a cookie sheet and brush lightly with butter. Dust lightly with any of the flavorful herbs or spices and bake in a hot (400°F.) oven for about half an hour.

Unless the hors d'oeuvres are to be served as soon as they are prepared or very shortly thereafter, *bread* used as a base should be toasted. Cut rounds or any fancy shapes desired from slices of bread and either brown in melted butter or margarine in a skillet or brush lightly with melted butter and place under the broiler until brown. The bread can also be cut into finger strips and treated the same way or you can make *bread sticks* tasty enough to be served on their own. Brush the bread fingers with melted butter and sprinkle with poppy or caraway, dill or celery seeds and toast for about 15 minutes in a moderate (350°F.) oven.

The commercially prepared *melba toasts* are so excellent that few people take the trouble to make their own any more. However, if you have some stale bread you want to make into melba toast, slice it thinly and bake it in a slow oven (275° to 300°F.) for about 30 minutes or until it is brown and dry.

## Plain Pastry

**¾ cup shortening**
**¼ cup boiling water**
**1 tablespoon milk**
**2 cups flour, sifted before measuring**
**1 teaspoon salt**

Place shortening in a mixing bowl and pour boiling water and milk over it. Tilt the bowl and break up shortening with a fork. Whip with rapid, cross-the-bowl strokes until all liquid is absorbed and mixture is thick and smooth as whipped cream. It should hold soft peaks when the fork is lifted. Combine flour and salt in a sifter and sift onto the whipped shortening. With vigorous round-the-bowl strokes, stir the ingredients together into a dough that clings together and leaves the bowl clean. Roll between two squares of waxed paper from the center out. Makes enough for a nine-inch, two-crust pie.

## Mayonnaise Pastry

**2 cups flour, sifted before measuring**
**½ teaspoon salt**
**⅔ cup mayonnaise**
**2 tablespoons water**

Mix together flour and salt. Blend mayonnaise and water. Combine with dry ingredients, tossing lightly with a fork. Turn out on a floured surface, press together and divide into 2 or more balls for rolling.

Best Foods

**Add cold water to the mayonnaise and blend the two together well.**

**Finally, roll out on floured wax paper.**

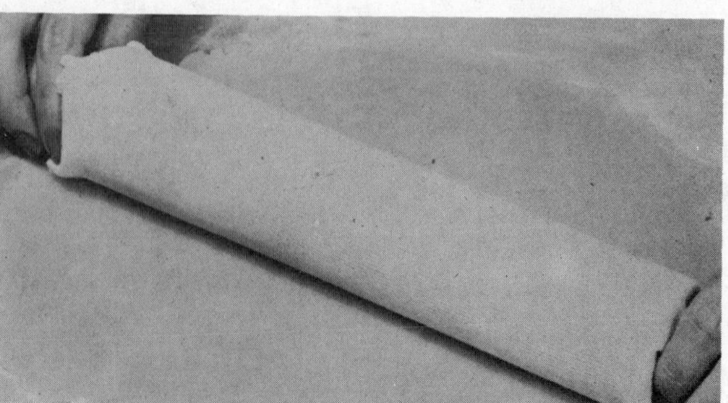

**Pour the thinned mayonnaise into the flour and stir mixture quickly.**

# Basic Biscuits

**2 cups flour, sifted before measuring**
**3 teaspoons double acting baking powder**
**1 teaspoon salt**
**1/4 cup shortening**
**About 3/4 cup milk**

Heat oven to hot (450°F.). Sift the dry ingredients together. With a pastry blender or two knives, cut in the shortening. The mixture should look like a coarse "meal." Then add almost all the milk tossing dough with a fork to wet it evenly. Add the remaining milk a little at a time until the dough is neither dry nor sticky. Round up into a ball and knead five or six times. Handle very lightly or the dough will toughen. Roll out 1/4 inch thick for the thin, crisp Southern type of biscuits; 1/2 inch thick for the thicker, softer Northern biscuits. Cut in rounds with a tiny biscuit cutter or to eliminate rerolling, cut in small squares or diamonds with a knife. Place on an ungreased baking pan, close together for high, soft-sided biscuits; an inch apart for biscuits with crusty sides. Bake in the middle of the oven until golden brown. Makes about 36 small biscuits.

*Herb Biscuits:* Make up the biscuit dough from a mix or the above recipe and to the dry ingredients add 1/4 teaspoon nutmeg, 1/4 teaspoon dry mustard, 1/2 teaspoon crumbled dry sage and 1 1/4 teaspoons caraway seeds.

*Curry Biscuits:* Make up the biscuit dough and to the dry ingredients add 1/2 teaspoon curry powder. This would be delicious with a shrimp mixture or cold sliced turkey or chicken.

*Bacon Biscuits:* Cook five strips of bacon until crisp. Drain well, then crumble. Add bacon bits to dry ingredients, and proceed as above.

*Cheese Biscuits:* Decrease shortening to 3 tablespoons and add 1 cup grated processed American cheese to the dry ingredients. Proceed as above.

*Chive Biscuits:* Make up the biscuit dough and to the dry ingredients add 1/4 cup minced chives.

*Drop Biscuits:* Follow the directions for the Basic Biscuits but increase the milk to 1 cup. Grease the baking sheet and take tablespoons of the dough and drop them onto it. Bake as above.

*Blushing Biscuits:* Make up the biscuit dough using tomato juice instead of milk. Proceed as above.

# Simple Puff Paste

For the tiny flaky patty shells which the French call Bouchées, it is necessary to make a puff paste. This type of pastry is richer and flakier than the ordinary but it also is more difficult and time-consuming to make. Here is a simplified version of this delicacy which will give you the desired effect with a minimum of effort.

Make the recipe for plain pastry and roll out 1/8 inch thick. Measure out 1/3 cup of firm but not hard butter. Butter that is either too soft or too hard will not work successfully. Put bits of the butter over the dough and roll it up. With your rolling pin roll it out to a rectangle and fold it so that the first two sides meet in the center, and then the other two sides meet in the center. Wrap in foil or waxed paper and chill. To make the bouchées, roll the dough 1/4 inch thick and cut 1/3 of it into rounds with a biscuit cutter. Cut remaining 2/3 into rings with a doughnut cutter. Use the centers for canapé bases, and place 2 rings on top of each round sticking them together with water. Bake in a hot oven (425°F.) for 20 to 30 minutes. If they start to get too brown, cover them with pieces of brown paper.

# Little Cream Puffs

**1/2 cup water**
**1/4 cup butter or margarine**
**1/2 cup flour, sifted before measuring**
**2 eggs**

Heat oven to hot (450°F.). Lightly grease a baking sheet. Heat water to boiling in a saucepan. Add butter or margarine and stir until melted. Add flour all at once and stir constantly and vigorously until mixture leaves the sides of the pan and forms a ball. This should take about 1 minute. Remove from heat and allow to cool slightly. Add eggs, one at a time, beating until mixture is smooth and velvety. Drop from the tip of a teaspoon onto the baking sheet keeping the balls two inches apart. They should be the size of small walnuts. Bake 20 to 25 minutes in all, using the hot oven for the first 10 minutes, a moderate oven (350°F.) for the remaining time. After they are baked, allow them to cool slowly away from drafts. When cool, cut off the tops with a sharp knife and scoop out any stray pieces of soft dough. Fill the puffs with any desired mixture. Makes 18 puffs.

# Speedy Waffles

2 cups pancake mix
2 cups milk
⅓ cup melted shortening
2 eggs

Heat waffle iron. Place all ingredients in a mixing bowl. Beat with a rotary beater until fairly smooth, but do not overbeat. Bake waffles until iron stops steaming. Cut into small squares, triangles, diamonds or rounds as desired and top with any of the following:

*Bacon-Cress topping:* Combine 2 3-oz. packages cream cheese and three tablespoons milk. Cream until fluffy. Add 8 strips of cooked crumbled bacon, ¼ cup finely chopped water cress and ¼ teaspoon onion powder. Spread on waffle bases.

*Ham and Pickle topping:* Combine ½ pound cooked ham, ground, with ¼ cup sweet pickle relish, 2 tablespoons prepared mustard and ¼ cup mayonnaise. Spread on waffle bases.

*Tuna-Cheese topping:* Mash 1 package cream cheese well. Add 1 can tuna, well drained and blend together. Add ¼ cup chopped ripe olives and season to taste with salt, pepper and onion powder. Spread on waffles.

*Ready-Spread toppings:* Spread the waffles with any of the prepared cheese spreads and garnish with stuffed olive slices, ripe olive slices or parsley.

# Speedy Salt Sticks

2 cups flour, sifted before measuring
1 teaspoon baking soda
½ teaspoon salt
⅓ cup shortening
¼ cup vinegar
½ cup milk
1 cup crisp rice cereal, crushed
1 teaspoon salt
1½ teaspoons caraway or poppy seeds

Heat oven to hot (450°F.). Grease a baking sheet. Sift dry ingredients together. With a pastry blender or two knives, cut in the shortening until the mixture resembles a coarse corn meal. Add vinegar and milk all at once, stirring only enough to combine them. Turn out on a lightly floured board and knead gently 5 or 6 times. Divide dough into 16 equal parts. Roll each part on the board with the palms of the hands until it becomes a cylinder about 6 inches long. Brush with milk. Combine cereal, salt and seeds. Roll each stick in this mixture. Place on baking sheets and bake about 15 minutes.

The Quaker Oats Company

# Little Eclairs

Prepare the cream puff dough and using a spatula or a pastry tube, shape it into finger width strips about 1½ inches long, leaving plenty of room between each. Bake as above and fill with:

# Crab Meat Filling

¼ cup butter or margarine
¼ cup flour
1 cup top milk or light cream
½ cup white table wine
1 chicken bouillon cube
½ teaspoon each, onion powder, lemon rind, Worcestershire sauce
Salt and pepper to taste
2 cups cooked or canned crab meat
½ cup finely chopped celery
1 tablespoon minced parsley

Melt butter and stir in flour. Add milk, wine and bouillon cube. Cook, stirring constantly, until mixture boils and thickens and bouillon cube is dissolved. Add remaining ingredients and serve hot in little eclairs.

Arnold Bakers, Inc.

# Miniature Patty Shells

**1 1-pound loaf white bread (18 slices)**
**5 tablespoons butter, melted**

Cut 5 rounds, the size of a fifty-cent piece, out of each slice of bread with a 1¼" cookie cutter, making 90 rounds. Make rings out of 45 of these rounds by removing center with a ¾" cutter, the size of a dime.

Brush the rounds on one side with melted butter and place on baking sheet, buttered side up. Dip rings in melted butter and place on each round. Toast in hot oven (425° F.) for approximately 6 minutes, until golden brown. Cool.

## Egg Filling

**2 eggs**
**2 packages (3 ounces each) cream cheese**
**4 teaspoons prepared mustard**
**2 teaspoons chopped chives**
**2 tablespoons capers (well-drained)**
**2 tablespoons chopped parsley**
**Parsley or pimiento for decoration**

Hard-boil the eggs and separate the yolks from the whites while still hot. Blend the hot yolks with the cream cheese and mustard. Chop the egg whites and the capers coarsely and combine all ingredients.

Fill Patty Shells and decorate with either parsley or pimiento. Makes filling for 45 patty shells.

# Golden Cheese Straws

Make recipe for cheese pastry (p. 38) and roll out a small amount at a time to ⅛-inch thickness. Cut with a pastry wheel into strips 5 inches long and ½ inch wide. With a third of the strips, bring ends together to form rings. When baked slip two straws through each ring. Bake on a greased cookie sheet in a hot oven (400°F.) about 8 minutes. Makes about 4 dozen strips.

Tiny bite-sized biscuits make an ideal base for slivers of Virginia style ham, anchovies, smoked turkey or any of the pâtés. With herbs or cheese added, they can be served as cocktail snacks just as they are. You will find the biscuit mixes on the market very satisfactory and handy to keep around for emergencies. In the event that you have the time and prefer to make your own, here is a fool-proof recipe for biscuits.

# Basic Waffle Recipe

**2 cups sifted flour**
**3 teaspoons double-acting baking powder**
**2 tablespoons sugar**
**1¼ teaspoons salt**
**2 eggs, separated**
**2 cups minus 2 tablespoons milk**
**⅓ cup melted shortening**

Heat the waffle iron until it is smoking hot. Sift together the flour, baking powder, sugar and salt. Combine the yolks, milk and shortening. Add liquid ingredients to dry ingredients all at once and mix until blended. Beat egg whites until stiff, and fold gently into the batter. Bake until steaming stops and waffle is golden. Makes 6 large waffles which can then be cut into smaller pieces for serving.

# Tuna Cheese Tarts

**½ recipe for Cheese Pastry**
**1 tablespoon fat**
**¼ cup (2-oz.) canned mushrooms**
**1 tablespoon finely chopped onion**
**1 tablespoon flour**
**¼ teaspoon salt, dash pepper**
**1 cup milk**
**2 tablespoons finely chopped pimiento**
**1 can (7-oz.) tuna**

Roll out pastry ⅛ inch thick and cut into 4- or 5-inch rounds. Place lightly in tart pans or into the bottoms of ungreased muffin cups. Bake in hot oven (425°F.) for 8 to 10 minutes. This will make 6 large shells or 1 dozen small party size ones. While the shells are baking, melt the fat and in it brown the mushrooms and onions lightly. Blend in flour, salt and pepper, then gradually stir in the milk. Cook over low heat until thickened, stirring constantly. Add pimiento and tuna, broken in large pieces. Heat together then serve in small tart shells.

The Quaker Oats Company

# Shrimp-Filled Pannequets

Prepare the pancakes as for Beef-Filled Pancakes.

## Filling:

**2 tablespoons fat**
**1 onion, finely chopped**
**½ pound shrimp, cooked and shelled**
**1 teaspoon salt**
**¼ teaspoon pepper**
**6 eggs**
**2 tablespoons parsley, finely minced**

Heat fat and brown onion in it. Chop the shrimp and add to onion. Cook, stirring, for five minutes. Add seasonings, eggs and parsley. Cook slowly, stirring until eggs are thickened but still moist. Place a heaping tablespoon of filling at the edge of each pancake. Roll up jelly roll fashion. Serve on a warm platter or in a chafing dish. Makes 12 filled pannequets.

# Cheese Pastry

**2 cups flour, sifted before measuring**
**1 teaspoon salt**
**⅔ cup shortening**
**1 cup grated processed American cheese**
**6 to 7 tablespoons cold water**

Place flour and salt in a mixing bowl. With a pastry blender or two knives, cut in the shortening and cheese until the particles are the size of small peas. Add the water gradually, tossing and stirring until the dough is just moist enough to hold together. Form into 2 balls. Roll each to ⅛-inch thickness and make into cups, turnovers and straws.

*Cheese Cups:* Cut pastry into rounds with a 3-inch scalloped cutter. Fit into small ungreased muffin pans and prick with a fork. Bake in a hot oven (425°F.) for 10 to 12 minutes. Fill with chicken or tuna salad and garnish with olive slices.

*Tiny Turnovers:* Cut pastry into 3-inch squares. Place a teaspoon of some savory spread or filling on each square. Fold over to form triangles. Seal edges and prick or gash the top. Bake as above. Serve hot.

# Cheese Balls

**1 cup biscuit mix**
**½ cup grated sharp cheddar cheese**
**2 tablespoons mayonnaise**
**⅓ cup milk, approximately**
**½ cup minced parsley**
**1 tablespoon grated onion**

Heat oven to hot (450°F.). Grease a cookie sheet. Combine first four ingredients adding only enough of the milk to moisten the dough. Shape into small balls. Combine parsley and grated onion and roll balls in this mixture. Place on the cookie sheet and bake 8 to 10 minutes. Makes about 30 balls.

Little cream puffs with their hollow insides are excellent carriers for moist fillings like chicken and lobster salads. They are not difficult to make and can be prepared days ahead of time.

# Cheese Custard Pie

1 recipe plain pastry
12 strips lean bacon
¼ pound Swiss cheese, grated
4 eggs
2 cups top milk or light cream
Dash each, salt, sugar, nutmeg, cayenne, black pepper

Prepare plain pastry (p. 30); divide in two. Roll out one half and fit into a nine-inch pie plate. Heat oven to hot (450°F.). Cook bacon in a skillet until brown and crisp. Drain and then crumble into unbaked pie shell. Place grated cheese over the bacon. Combine eggs, milk and seasonings and pour over cheese-bacon mixture. Place in the hot oven for 10 minutes, then reduce the heat to slow (300°F.) and bake for 25 to 30 minutes longer or until the custard is set. If the pie is not brown enough after this baking period, pop it under the broiler for a few seconds to brown up the top. You can use browned onions in place of the cheese and have an onion and bacon pie.

# Corn Meal Wafers

**1½ cups flour, sifted before measuring**
**½ cup corn meal**
**½ teaspoon each salt, celery seed**
**2 teaspoons mustard-with-horse-radish**
**⅔ cup mayonnaise**
**3 tablespoons cold water**

Heat oven to hot (425°F.). Combine dry ingredients and seasonings. Blend mustard with mayonnaise. Add water to mustard-mayonnaise mixture. Stir quickly into flour with a fork. Shape into a ball and roll out on a pastry cloth or wax paper. Cut in any desired shapes with a pastry wheel or cookie cutters. Place on an ungreased cookie sheet and bake 8 to 10 minutes. Makes 5 to 6 dozen wafers.

# Cheese Puffs

**½ cup water**
**¼ teaspoon salt**
**1½ tablespoons butter**
**¼ pound Swiss cheese, grated**
**⅔ cup flour**
**3 eggs**

Heat water, salt and butter in a saucepan until butter is melted. Add the cheese gradually, keeping the temperature even and low and stir until the cheese is melted and the mixture is creamy. Add the flour and stir vigorously until dough forms a ball. Add eggs and proceed as for regular cream puffs. These are delicious filled or they can be served plain with cheese and fruit.

# Mayonnaise Pastry Canapés

Divide dough into 2 balls (p. 31); roll to ¼-inch thickness. Cut one part into rounds or diamond shapes. Bake 6 to 8 minutes in a (425°F.) oven. Spread and garnish as desired.

*Meat Strips:* Roll pastry into a rectangle. On one half of the pastry spread a spicy meat mixture. Fold over the other half and lightly press together. With a pastry cutter or a sharp knife cut the meat-filled pastry into ½- by 2-inch strips. Bake as above.

*Pastry Cases:* Roll the pastry into a rectangle. Cut into 1½-inch squares with a pastry cutter or a sharp knife. Pinch together each of the corners to form a little case. Bake upside down on a baking sheet using the same time and temperature as above.

*Turnovers:* Roll the pastry into a rectangle and cut it into large squares. Put a spoonful of any tasty filling on the square and fold in half horizontally or diagonally. Seal edges with a fork and prick the top. Bake as above.

The Quaker Oats Company

# Beef-Filled Pancakes

**3 eggs, beaten**
**½ cup milk**
**½ cup pancake mix**

Combine beaten eggs and milk. Add pancake mix and stir until smooth. For each pancake, place ½ teaspoon butter in a six or seven-inch skillet. Heat until bubbly. Pour in two tablespoons of batter and roll pan until bottom is coated. Cook until underside is brown. Turn and brown. Keep hot on a baking sheet in a warm oven while making filling.

## Filling:

**1 tablespoon fat**
**1 onion, chopped**
**1 clove garlic**
**1 pound beef, ground**
**½ teaspoon paprika**
**1 teaspoon salt**
**1 tablespoon flour**
**½ cup milk**
**1 tablespoon parsley**

Melt fat and in it brown onion, garlic and meat. Add paprika and salt and blend. Add flour and mix well. Add milk gradually and stir until thick. Cover and simmer 10 minutes, stirring occasionally. Add parsley just before rolling. Place two tablespoons of filling at the edge of each pancake and roll up jelly roll fashion. Serve in a chafing dish or on a hot platter with or without mushroom sauce. Makes twelve filled pancakes.

# Cocktail Crêpes

**½ cup sifted flour**
**½ teaspoon salt**
**2 eggs**
**1 cup milk**

Place all ingredients in a bowl and beat with a rotary beater until velvety smooth. Butter a six or seven-inch skillet lightly. Pour in just enough batter to coat the bottom. Cook until brown, then turn and brown the other side. Makes about 1½ dozen crêpes.

## Fill With:

**Minced chicken and chopped olives moistened and heated with heavy cream**

**Chopped mushrooms and onions moistened and heated with sour cream**

**Minced chicken, pimiento and green pepper heated with heavy cream sauce**

**Minced tongue and chopped raisins heated with Port or Madeira**

**Minced duck, mushrooms and ginger (fresh if you can get it) heated with soy sauce, pineapple juice and a little cornstarch**

Or spread the crêpes with any of the savory butters, roll them up and serve.

# Hot Hors d'Oeuvres

There is such an endless variety of hot hors d'oeuvres that a whole book could be written about them alone. A selection has been made for this chapter from among those built around meat, fish, cheese, poultry and vegetables. You can start with these ideas and vary them according to your own tastes.

# Shrimp Roundelays

Shred ½ pound sharp Cheddar cheese and combine with ¼ pound soft butter. Add 5 tablespoons grated onion, 1 teaspoon Worcestershire, ¼ cup lemon juice, ½ teaspoon dry mustard and ½ teaspoon paprika. Stir in 2 cups finely chopped or ground cooked or canned shrimp. Spread on crackers, toast rounds or split finger rolls. On each canapé place a tiny whole cooked shrimp (if desired). Broil 3 inches from heat until cheese is brown and bubbling.

The Shrimp Association of the Americas

# Cheese Wafers

**1 package snappy cheese**
**¼ cup butter**
**½ cup sifted flour**
**¼ teaspoon salt**
**1 cup sugar-coated rice cereal**

Heat oven to hot (450°F.). Combine cheese, butter, flour, salt and cereal. Blend well. Shape into small balls. Place on an ungreased baking sheet and flatten with the back of a spoon. Bake in a hot oven 7 to 10 minutes. Serve with cocktails or salads Makes about 3 dozen wafers.

Ralston-Purina

# Ry-Buildups

**8 seasoned rye crackers**
**8 thin slices tomato, peeled**
**¼ cup diced green pepper**
**¼ cup finely chopped onion**
**⅔ cup (5-ounce jar) sharp cheese spread**
**¼ cup chopped bacon, cooked**
**Cayenne pepper**
**Paprika (optional)**

Heat oven to hot (425° F.) Place rye crackers on unbuttered cookie sheet. Put tomato slice on each cracker. Mix green pepper and onion with cheese spread. Place heaping tablespoon of cheese mixture on each sandwich. Spread evenly over tomato and cracker. Top with bacon, dash of cayenne pepper and paprika. Bake 8-9 minutes or until cheese melts and is slightly brown. Makes 4 servings, 2 sandwiches/serving.

# Peanut Butter Cheese Dip

**½ cup chopped onion**
**1 cup chopped green pepper**
**1 clove garlic, chopped**
**2 tablespoons peanut oil**
**2 tomatoes, peeled, chopped**
**¾ cup tomato juice**
**¼ teaspoon thyme**
**¼ teaspoon oregano**
**½ bay leaf**
**½ teaspoon salt**
**⅛ teaspoon pepper**
**½ pound American Cheddar Cheese, grated**
**¾ cup peanut butter (smooth or crunchy)**

Cook onion, green pepper and garlic in peanut oil until tender, but not browned. Add tomatoes and tomato juice with seasonings, cover and cook over low heat 10 minutes. Stir once or twice. Put in top of double boiler and add cheese and peanut butter. Cook and stir over boiling water until cheese is melted and mixture blended. Serve in chafing dish with Fritos or potato chips. Makes 1 quart dip.

Peanut Growers of Alabama and Georgia

# Peanut Butter Ham Squares

**½ cup peanut butter (smooth or crunchy)**
**2 teaspoons grated onion—or ½ teaspoon instant minced onion**
**6 thin slices boiled ham**
**1 egg, beaten**
**2 tablespoons water**
**½ cup fine, dry bread crumbs**
**1 cup peanut oil**

Mix peanut butter and onion. Spread mixture on half the ham slices. Top with remaining ham slices. Wrap in waxed paper and chill in refrigerator for about an hour. Cut into 1-inch squares.

Mix beaten egg with water. Dip squares in egg and then in bread crumbs. Fry in hot peanut oil about 2 minutes or until golden brown. Serve at once on toothpicks. Makes 5 dozen canapés.

# Deviled Peanut Spread

**½ cup peanut butter (smooth or crunchy)**
**1 2¼-ounce can deviled ham**
**½ teaspoon celery salt**

Mix all ingredients lightly. Makes ⅔ cup. Serve on crackers.

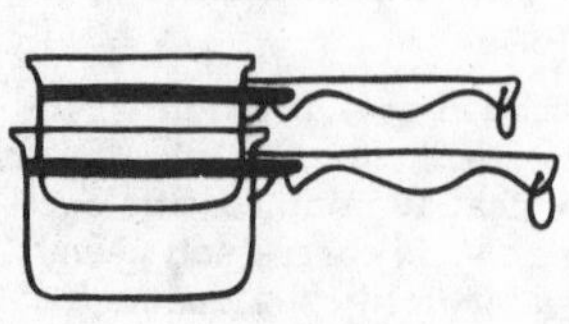

# Peanut Butter Biscuits

**2 cups sifted flour**
**¾ teaspoons salt**
**2½ teaspoons baking powder**
**2 tablespoons shortening**
**¼ cup smooth peanut butter**
**About ¾ cup milk**

Sift dry ingredients together. Cut in shortening and peanut butter until mixture is like coarse cornmeal. Add the milk and stir until a soft dough is formed.

Roll or pat on floured board to ½ inch thickness. Cut with 1-inch round biscuit cutter and place on ungreased baking sheet. Bake in hot (450° F.) oven 10-12 minutes. Makes about 40 biscuits.

Split and serve with thin sliced baked ham.

# Peanut Butter-Bacon Spread

**4 slices bacon**
**½ cup peanut butter (smooth or crunchy)**
**½ cup finely chopped dill pickle**
**2 tablespoons dill pickle juice**
**¼ teaspoon salt**
**Dash Tabasco Sauce**

Cook bacon until crisp. Drain on paper towels. Crumble into small pieces. Mix with peanut butter, dill pickles, juice and seasoning. Makes about 1 cup. Serve on crackers.

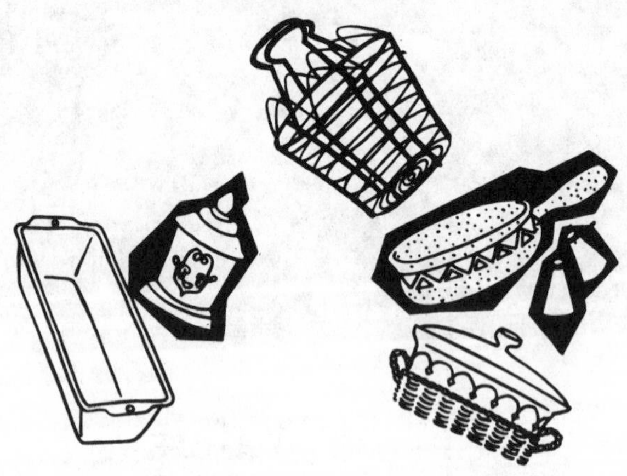

# Olive-Ham Turnovers

## Spicy Pastry:

**2 cups flour measured after sifting**
**½ teaspoon salt**
**⅔ cup mayonnaise**
**2 teaspoons prepared mustard**
**2 tablespoons water**

## Filling:

**⅔ cup ground cooked ham**
**⅔ cup chopped ripe olives**
**3 to 4 tablespoons mayonnaise**

Pastry: Heat oven to hot (425°F.). Sift flour with salt. Add mayonnaise, mustard and water. Mix well together. Turn onto a lightly floured board and roll thin. Cut into 2½-inch squares. Put a generous half teaspoon of filling on each square, moisten edges with a little water. Then fold over into triangles and pinch the edges to seal. Bake about 12 to 15 minutes or until pastry is nicely browned. Makes 2½ dozen turnovers.

Filling: Combine ham, olives and mayonnaise and mix well.

# Clam Puffs

2 5-oz. jars Relish cheese spread
1 egg yolk
½ teaspoon baking powder
Dash of freshly ground pepper
¼ teaspoon Worcestershire sauce
Dash of cayenne pepper
½ teaspoon salt
1 can (7-oz.) minced clams, drained
Pastry
20 aluminum foil circles, about 2½ inches each

Blend together cheese, egg yolk, baking powder and seasonings. Add the drained clams and mix well. Heat oven to very hot (450°F.). Roll the pastry to ⅛-inch thickness and cut into rounds with a 1¾-inch cutter. Cover each round generously with the relish mixture. Place each round in the center of an aluminum foil circle. Sprinkle cheese mixture with paprika if desired and bring up the edges of the aluminum foil around the pastry rounds. Place in the oven for about 15 minutes or until the pastry is done and the cheese mixture is puffed and brown. Remove the foil and serve hot.

# Gem Beef Tidbits

¼ pound ground beef
½ teaspoon salad oil
2 tablespoons finely chopped onion
2 tablespoons chili sauce
½ teaspoon salt
¼ teaspoon chili powder
¼ teaspoon Tabasco sauce
1 (8 ounce) can gem flake rolls
Grated American cheese

In a small skillet brown the meat in oil. Stir in onion, chili sauce, salt, chili powder, and Tabasco sauce. Cook until onion is tender but not browned. Remove from heat. With fingers, separate each roll in half. Use the palm of hand or the bottom of a glass to flatten each half-roll into a round or clam shape until it is twice its original size. Place two rounded teaspoonfuls meat mixture in center of half of the flattened roll halves. With a sharp knife, cut a cross in center of remaining roll halves. Pull back cut corners to open center of each. Place one cut half atop each meat filled half. Seal edges by pressing together with tines of a fork. Sprinkle tops with cheese. Place each on ungreased cookie sheet. Bake in moderate oven (at 375°) for 12 to 14 minutes, or until lightly browned. Serve piping hot. Makes 12 servings.

The Borden Company

The Shrimp Association of the Americas

# French Fried Shrimp

1 pound shrimp, fresh or frozen
¼ cup flour
1 egg
¼ cup milk
2 tablespoons salad oil
½ cup fine dry bread crumbs
½ teaspoon salt
Dash of pepper

Peel and clean the shrimp. Spread the flour on waxed paper. Beat the egg in a small bowl. To it add the milk and salad oil. Mix together the bread crumbs, salt and pepper. Spread these on another sheet of waxed paper. Coat each shrimp with flour, shaking off the excess. Dip into egg mixture. Drain slightly, then coat with bread crumbs. Fry in deep fat heated to 350°F. for about three minutes or until golden brown. Drain on paper towels.

# Hot Cheese Whirls

**1 (8 ounce) can gem flake rolls**
**1 (8 ounce) package sharp Cheddar cheese bar**
**Worcestershire Sauce**
**12 stuffed green olive halves**

Open gem rolls according to package directions. Use fingers to flatten and shape dough into a circle 3½-inches in diameter. Depress center of each with bottom of roll can or a floured small glass to form a rim around edges. Place on ungreased cookie sheet. Cut cheddar cheese bar into 12 equal (¼-inch thick) slices. Place a slice of cheese on the middle of each roll. Place a drop of Worcestershire sauce and half an olive on top of cheese. Bake in a moderate oven (375° F.) for 12 to 14 minutes. Serve piping hot. Makes 12 appetizers.

# Gem Sticks

**1 (8 ounce) can gem flake rolls**
**1 (2 ounce) can grated American cheese**

With fingers, separate each of the 12 rolls in half. Roll each half of the roll between palms of hands until the thickness of a pencil and about 4 inches long. Place the contents of grated American Cheese canister on a sheet of waxed paper. Roll the prepared dough sticks in the cheese, until the stick is completely covered. Place on ungreased baking sheet. Bake in moderate oven (375° F.) for 8 to 10 minutes, or until browned. Serve hot or cold.

### Variations

Any one of the following seasonings may be used in place of Grated American Cheese. Follow above directions for preparation.

1. A mixture of equal amounts of onion salt, oregano, and paprika.
2. Sesame seeds.
3. Garlic salt (roll only one side of stick in this seasoning).
4. Onion salt (roll only one side of stick in this seasoning).
5. Celery salt (roll only one side of stick in this seasoning).
6. Grated Parmesan and Romano Cheese. (brush stick with melted butter before rolling it in this cheese).
7. Caraway seeds.
8. Poppy seeds.
9. Coarse salt.

# Fish Sticks

**1 (8 ounce) package frozen fish sticks (about 10 sticks)**

Open gem rolls as directed on package. Use fingers to separate into half, each of the 12 rolls. Stretch each half roll into a triangular shape about twice its original size.

Place one-half fish stick at widest part of dough. Start at wide end and roll dough tightly around the fish sticks. Press the small end of dough tightly against the side to seal. Place on ungreased baking sheet with the sealed side down. Bake in a moderate oven at 375° for about 12 minutes, or until golden brown. Serve hot.

### Cocktail Frankfurters

**1 (6 ounce) jar cockail style frankfurters (about 24 frankfurters)**

Place one frank on the widest part of dough and follow above directions.

# Saucy Mushrooms In Cheese-Pastry Shells

**2 sticks (one 9-ounce package) pie crust mix**
**¾ cup (3 ounce) finely shredded Cheddar cheese**
**3 tablespoons boiling water**
**1½ cups (two 7-ounce cans) of mushrooms**

Crumble pie crust mix into small bowl. Add shredded cheese and boiling water. Stir with a fork until dough loses stickiness, forms a ball and completely cleans side of bowl. Line tart shell pans by lightly pressing, with fingers, a small amount of dough in each shell. Spoon 1 tablespoon mushroom mixture into each shell. Bake in a hot oven (425° F.) for 10 to 12 minutes. Remove from shell pans. If desired, garnish with a dab of sour cream and top with pimiento and green pepper cutouts or small cutouts of baked pastry. A small cooky cutter does nicely for this purpose. Serve hot. Makes about 20 shells, 2½-inch diameter.

### Variations

Mix pastry as above. Roll out dough on lightly floured board. Cut into desired shapes using a two-inch cooky cutter. Cut two identical pieces for each case. Place a teaspoonful of mushroom mixture in center of pastry shape. Cover with identical shape. Press edges of pastry together with tines of fork. Place on ungreased cooky sheet. Bake in a hot oven (425° F.) until pastry is golden brown, 10 to 12 minutes. Remove from cooky sheet and cool on rack. Makes about 40 pastry cases, 2-inch size.

The Borden Company

# Pizza Appetizers

## Pastry Base:

**½ cup corn meal**
**1½ cups flour, measured after sifting**
**1 teaspoon salt**
**½ teaspoon baking powder**
**⅓ cup shortening**
**⅓ cup water**

Sift together the dry ingredients into a medium sized bowl. With a pastry blender or two knives cut in the shortening until the mixture resembles a coarse meal. Add water a little at a time until the pastry will just hold together. Divide the pastry in two parts. On a lightly floured board, knead each part gently for a few seconds. Let rest and heat the oven to hot (425°F.). Roll out each part to about ¼-inch thickness. Cut with a small round cutter and prick each round with a fork. Place on an ungreased baking sheet and turn the outside edge up slightly to flute. Bake for 10 to 12 minutes. Cool.

## Filling:

**3 tablespoons olive oil**
**⅓ cup Parmesan cheese**
**1 small can tomato sauce**
**Dash of salt**
**¼ pound cooked pork sausage**
**¼ pound processed American cheese, grated**
**½ teaspoon oregano**

Brush each cooled pastry round with a little olive oil. Top each with about ¼ teaspoon Parmesan cheese and add a thin layer of tomato sauce. Sprinkle with salt and add a bit of cooked sausage to each. Add more Parmesan cheese and top with some American cheese. Brush with remaining olive oil and sprinkle lightly with the oregano. Pop under the broiler and heat for a minute or two or until the cheese melts.

# Cheese and Rice Balls

**1 cup processed sharp cheese**
**1 tablespoon prepared mustard**
**Horse-radish to taste**
**Salt**
**2 cups cooked rice**
**Fat for deep frying**

Heat fat to hot (375°F.) Work the cheese into small balls, not over ½ inch in diameter. Spread each ball lightly with mustard and horse-radish. Salt the cooked rice and roll the balls in this until the rice completely covers the cheese balls. Press in to make a compact ball. Fry in the hot deep fat until golden brown. These can be fried ahead of time and reheated in a hot oven.

# Cheese Tempters

These may look like cookies but actually they are delicious little wafers with a wonderful cheese flavor.

**1 bar (¼-lb.) butter or margarine**
**½ pound grated sharp cheese**
**¼ teaspoon salt**
**Dash of cayenne pepper**
**1 cup, plus 2 tablespoons flour, sifted before measuring**
**Pecan halves**

Let butter or margarine soften slightly in the mixing bowl. Add cheese, salt and cayenne and mix until well blended. Add flour and mix well. Shape dough into 3 rolls, about 1½ inches in diameter. Wrap in waxed paper and chill overnight in the refrigerator. When ready to serve, heat the oven to moderately hot (375°F.). Cut the chilled rolls into ⅛-inch slices and place on ungreased cookie sheets. Place a pecan half on each slice and bake 11 to 13 minutes or until lightly brown around the edges.

# Suy Gow

## Pastry:

**1 cup boiling water**
**2 cups sifted flour**
**1 egg, slightly beaten**
**6 cups broth**

Pour the water into a one-quart bowl. Add the flour all at once, stirring rapidly. Grease a board with salad oil and place dough on it. Knead until smooth. Allow to cool. Divide in quarters. Divide each quarter into four pieces. Shape each piece into a ball and flatten with greased hands. Put on the greased board and roll until paper thin, about 3 inches in diameter. Place one rounded teaspoon of filling on each circle. Brush the edge of the circle with the egg and fold in half diagonally, pressing the edges together with the fingers. Bring the broth to a boil. Drop Suy Gow in and allow the broth to come to a boil again. Boil for 8 minutes or until the dumplings float to the surface.

## Shrimp Filling:

**2 tablespoon oil**
**½ teaspoon salt**
**Dash pepper**
**1 teaspoon ginger**
**1 tablespoon soy sauce**
**¾ pound raw shrimp, cleaned and minced**
**½ white turnip, finely minced**
**½ green pepper, finely minced**
**2 tablespoons minced scallions**

Heat oil in a skillet. Add salt, pepper and soy sauce. Add shrimp, turnip and green pepper. Cook over medium heat, stirring constantly for about 3 minutes. Cool, then remove from pan with a slotted spoon. Add the scallions and use as filling.

# Tamale Boats

## Boats:

1½ cups flour, measured after sifting
½ cup corn meal
1 teaspoon salt
1 teaspoon chili powder
⅓ cup shortening
⅓ cup water

Sift together the dry ingredients. With a pastry blender or two knives, cut in the shortening until the mixture resembles coarse crumbs. Add water, mixing lightly only until dampened. Roll out on a lightly floured board to form a rectangle about 12x18. Cut in half lengthwise. Place a rectangle of dough over the inside of a corn stick pan shaping each section to form a boat. Cut almost through the dough between each corn stick mold. Bake in a hot oven (425°F.) 10 to 12 minutes or until pastry is lightly browned. Separate the boats by cutting the rest of the way through the pastry between each corn stick mold. Arrange the boats on a platter and fill with meat mixture.

## Filling:

1 medium onion, chopped
1 pound ground beef
1 tablespoon shortening
1 tablespoon chili powder
1½ teaspoons salt
½ teaspoon pepper
1 can tomato paste
1 cup water

Lightly brown onion and beef in shortening. Add remaining ingredients and simmer, stirring occasionally for 20 to 25 minutes. Makes 14 boats.

The Quaker Oats Co.

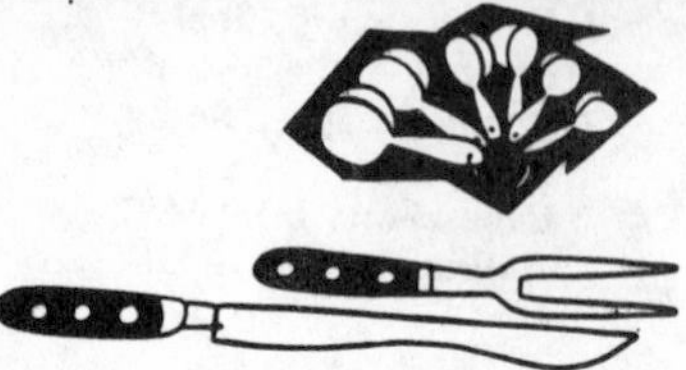

South African Lobster Association

# Rock Lobster Quiche

6 (4 ounce) South African rock lobster tails
2 cups milk
3 eggs
2 egg yolks
1 tablespoon flour
½ teaspoon salt
½ teaspoon dry mustard
1 tablespoon butter
1 recipe pie pastry for a double-crust pie

Parboil South African rock lobster tails by dropping in boiling salted water and cooking for 1 minute after water reboils. Drain immediately and drench with cold water. Remove meat from shells and grind or finely shred meat. Make the pastry and roll out a scant ⅛-inch thick. With glass or cookie cutter, cut out shapes to fit tart pans and line slightly oiled 2-bite tartlet pans with dough. Trim edges and brush lightly with unbeaten egg yolk. Combine milk, eggs, egg yolks, flour and seasonings. Beat together until well mixed. Heat the butter until golden brown and stir in. Add the ground or shredded rock lobster meat. Spoon mixture into the pastry-lined tart pans and bake 25 minutes in moderate (375° F.) oven. Remove from tart pans and keep warm on hot tray so guests can help themselves. Makes about 50 3-inch tarts.

**Note:** Rock Lobster Quiche can also be made as one large or several small "pies" and cut in serving pieces when done.

# Cocktail Fish Balls

1 can codfish cakes
1 egg, well beaten
1 tablespoon butter, melted
Dash of pepper
Fine dry bread crumbs

Place codfish cakes in a bowl. Add eggs, butter and pepper. Mix well. Form into little balls. Roll in fine crumbs and fry in hot deep fat (385°F.) until brown. Drain on paper towels and serve with picks.

# Clams Casino

Open clams carefully to retain the juice. Remove the upper shell, leaving the clams in the deeper half. Sprinkle each with a few drops of lemon juice and a pinch of finely minced green pepper and chopped onion. Season each with a dash of salt and pepper and put 3 small bits of bacon on each. Set in a pan; broil until bacon is crisp. You can also use canned clams to make Clams Casino. Buy the whole clams, drain them well and either place in a shallow baking pan or else place a serving or two or three into bought clam shells. Proceed as above.

# Anchovy Puffs

**1 cup flour, measured after sifting**
**1½ teaspoons baking powder**
**¼ teaspoon salt**
**1 teaspoon lemon rind**
**½ teaspoon onion salt**
**3 tablespoons mayonnaise**
**3 tablespoons milk**
**12 rolled anchovies**

Grease small muffin pans. Heat oven to hot (400°F.). Sift together the flour, baking powder and salt. Add the lemon rind and onion salt. Blend together the mayonnaise and milk and add all at once to the flour, mixing quickly and lightly with a fork. Fill muffin pans ⅔ full and press a rolled anchovy into the top of each muffin. Bake 12 to 15 minutes.

# Bambinos

**1 jar (5 ounces) olive and pimiento cheese spread**
**½ clove garlic, minced very fine**
**4 cans (4 ounces each) Maine sardines**
**8 to 10 medium radishes**
**5 to 6 scallions**
**1 can (4 ounces) pimientos**
**18 finger rolls (hard, or soft poppy seed)**

Blend cheese spread with garlic and let stand, refrigerated until ready to use. Drain sardines. Trim and wash radishes and slice very thin. Peel and wash scallions and cut into four or six pieces lengthwise, then one-inch pieces crosswise. Cut drained pimientos into thin slivers. Slice finger rolls almost in two, leaving a hinge. Spread with cheese mixture. Over this place a layer of radishes. Next, the whole sardine, one to a roll. Top with scallions and pimientos. Close rolls. For hors d'oeuvres service, cut in half crosswise with sharp knife, but arrange with halves remaining together. Wrap in transparent plastic wrap and chill until ready to use. If desired, skewer each portion with food pick. Makes eighteen Bambinos or thirty-six hors d'oeuvres.

# Little Rice and Cheese Puffs

**3 tablespoons butter**
**3 tablespoons flour**
**1 cup milk**
**1 teaspoon salt**
**Dash of pepper**
**Dash of cayenne pepper**
**1½ cups grated sharp cheese**
**½ teaspoon dry mustard**
**¼ teaspoon Worcestershire sauce**
**1 teaspoon grated onion or onion powder**
**3 cups cooked rice**
**2 tablespoons milk**
**2 eggs, well beaten**
**Fine dry bread crumbs**

Melt butter in a sauce pan. Add flour and stir until blended. Add milk gradually, stirring constantly. Add salt, pepper and cayenne, and cook, stirring, over low heat until thick and smooth. Add cheese, mustard, Worcestershire and onion. Mix well then add rice and mix thoroughly. Chill. Shape chilled mixture into 1-inch balls using about 1½ teaspoons of the mixture for each ball. Add milk to eggs, and blend. Dip each ball in egg-milk mixture, then roll in bread crumbs. Fry in shallow hot fat until golden brown. Drain on absorbent paper. Serve piping hot. Makes about 85 puffs.

National Fisheries Institute

# Swedish Meat Balls

**1 pound finely ground beef**
**½ cup dry bread crumbs**
**1 egg**
**⅔ cup milk**
**½ small onion, grated**
**1 teaspoon salt**
**Dash each, pepper, nutmeg**

Mix together lightly and form into about 3 dozen 1½-inch balls. Brown well in hot fat or bacon drippings using a heavy skillet over low heat. Add ¼ cup hot water, bouillon or wine (more may be added as needed). Cover tightly and simmer about 20 minutes. To serve, stick each meat ball with a pick.

# Deviled Meat Balls

**¼ pound Roquefort cheese**
**¼ cup mayonnaise**
**2 tablespoons Worcestershire sauce**
**1 teaspoon prepared mustard**
**2 cups corn flakes**
**½ cup milk**
**1 egg, slightly beaten**
**1 pound ground beef**
**1½ teaspoons salt**
**⅛ teaspoon pepper**

Crumble cheese with a fork and blend in mayonnaise, Worcestershire and mustard. Crush corn flakes slightly. Add remaining ingredients and Roquefort mixture and mix well. Form into small balls about 1 inch in diameter. Broil or pan fry until browned. Serve hot on toothpicks. Makes about 3½ dozen balls.

# Baked Filled Rolls

**1 small onion**
**½ medium green pepper**
**6 slices well cooked bacon**
**½ pound processed American cheese**
**½ cup condensed tomato soup**
**½ teaspoon salt**
**Dash of cayenne pepper**
**Dash of Worcestershire**
**Small French rolls**

Cut the onion into quarters and the green pepper into strips. Together with the bacon strips put the onion and green pepper through the food chopper. Cut the cheese into quarter sticks lengthwise. Put the cheese sticks through the food chopper. To the chopped mixture, add the soup, salt, pepper and Worcestershire. Split the French rolls and spread the bottom with one tablespoon of the filling. Cover with the top of the roll. Heat oven to moderately hot (400°F.). Bake for a short while until the filling is melted.

National Biscuit Company

# Oyster-Turkey Balls

**¼ cup oysters**
**½ cup cooked turkey**
**½ teaspoon ground mace**
**¼ teaspoon pepper**
**¼ teaspoon celery salt**
**1 tablespoon oyster liquid**
**2 tablespoons heavy cream**
**2 egg yolks, slightly beaten**
**¼ cup blanched almonds, chopped fine**
**¼ cup dry bread crumbs**

Heat oysters for a few minutes in a small quantity of water. Remove, and set aside one tablespoon of the liquid. Grind oysters and turkey in the food chopper. Add next six ingredients and stir until well blended. Pack into a jar or covered bowl and chill for 24 hours. Form into small balls. Combine almonds and bread crumbs and roll balls in this mixture until well coated. Fry in deep fat until golden brown. Serve hot on picks. Makes about 3 dozen.

# Scallipops

1 package (7 ounces) frozen breaded scallops
¼ cup fine bread crumbs
3 teaspoons paprika, about
¼ cup minced parsley
¼ cup grated Swiss cheese
½ cup mayonnaise
10 to 20 wooden skewers from your butcher (or sucker sticks or food picks)

Following package directions, begin preheating oven for scallops. Bake as package directs. During last five minutes, sprinkle bread crumbs in flat pan and place in oven to brown lightly. Stir once during baking. When browned, add two teaspoons of the paprika to crumbs. Place parsley, Swiss cheese and mayonnaise in separate dishes. To make "Red Scallipops" roll one-third of the scallops in mayonnaise (use a knife to even the coating) then in bread-crumb paprika mixture. Last dust tops lightly with plain paprika. Insert point or skewer. To make "Green Scallipops," roll one-third of the scallops in mayonnaise, then in parsley. Skewer these, too. To make "Yellow Scallipops," roll one-third of the scallops in mayonnaise and Swiss cheese. Serve as hot as possible (although Scallipops are good cold, too). Makes ten to twenty, or hors d'oeuvres for six.

Note: For party service, use a small head of lettuce or cabbage or a turnip cut in flower shape as a holder for scallipops. Before starting recipe, use one skewer to make the holes to receive the skewer sticks.

# Top Hatters

12 squares of cornbread
12 tomato slices
3 egg whites
3 egg yolks
1 cup grated sharp cheese
¼ cup crumbled cooked bacon

Cut 6 square pieces of cornbread in half crosswise to make 12 thin squares. Brush with melted butter or margarine and place in the broiler for three minutes or until the cornbread is delicately browned. Top each square with a tomato slice and set aside for a moment. Beat egg whites until stiff but not dry. Beat egg yolks until thick and lemon colored. Fold egg yolks into egg whites, then fold in cheese and bacon into egg mixture. Place a spoonful of this soufflé mixture on each tomato slice. Return to the broiler for a few minutes or until the soufflé topping is puffed and brown. This hors d'oeuvre should be served immediately since it won't wait.

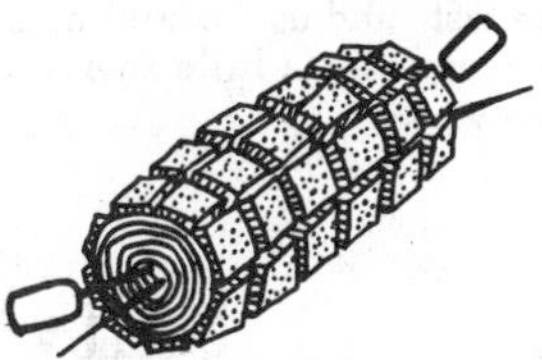

# Peanut Butter Meat Balls

½ cup peanut butter (smooth or crunchy)
½ pound ground beef
¼ cup finely chopped onion OR 2 teaspoons instant minced onion
2 tablespoons chili sauce
1 teaspoon salt
⅛ teaspoon pepper
1 egg, beaten
2 tablespoons peanut oil

Mix peanut butter lightly with beef, onion, chili sauce, salt, pepper and egg. Form into 3 dozen small meat balls. Fry in hot peanut oil, turning to brown on all sides.

# Potato Puff Cheese d'Oeuvres

1 head cabbage
1 small can of canned heat
1 package (8 ounces) frozen potato puffs
Grated sharp Cheddar Cheese
Catsup

In top center of cabbage, cut a "well" large enough to insert canned heat so top rim of can is level with top of cabbage. Heat potato puffs as directed on package; arrange some around base of cabbage and secure remaining puffs to cabbage with wooden picks. Serve with grated cheese and catsup (seasoned, if desired) as dips. Just before serving, light canned heat. Reheat potato puffs over flame; then dip in cheese and/or catsup. Makes 3 to 3½ dozen.

Courtesy of Birds Eye Potato Puffs

# Cold Hors d'Oeuvres

## Fried Mozzarella

**6 ¼-inch slices Mozzarella**
**2 eggs, slightly beaten**
**1 cup fine cracker crumbs**
**2 tablespoons olive oil**

Dip the cheese slices into the egg and then into the cracker crumbs. Heat the oil in a skillet and fry the breaded cheese until crisp and brown. Cut into small pieces to serve and stick each with a pick.

Cocktail franks, meatballs and French fried shrimp are probably the most frequently served of the hot hors d'oeuvres. To fix the shrimp for frying, shell them and bread them with egg and crumbs. You can bread them hours before you are going to fry them or even the day before. The rest period in the refrigerator helps to set the coating so that the crust will fry crisp and unbroken. Since they fry in less than five minutes, do not plan to start cooking until the last possible moment. You can use packaged bread crumbs, but for really fine French fried shrimp carefully prepared homemade crumbs are better. To make them, cut the crusts from eight slices of white bread. Leave the bread out overnight, uncovered. Then crush the bread into fine crumbs using a rolling pin, a food grinder or an electric blender. Sift the crumbs through a medium fine sieve.

## Cheese Croustades

Remove crusts from a day-old unsliced sandwich loaf. Cut into 12 slices of about 1½ inches thick. Cut each slice into four squares. With a sharp pointed scissors, hollow out the center of each square. Brush the little box that is formed with melted butter on all sides. Heat oven to hot (400°F.). Place bread boxes on a baking sheet and toast in the oven until delicately browned. Prepare the following filling:

**1 pound processed American cheese**
**¼ cup sherry wine**
**1 teaspoon Worcestershire sauce**
**½ teaspoon dry mustard**

Cut cheese in pieces and place in top of a double boiler over boiling water. Heat until melted. Add wine and seasonings. Let cool slightly, then place some of this mixture in the hollows of the bread boxes. Before serving, place back in the oven for a short time until heated through. Makes 4 dozen croustades.

## Mushroom-Nut Canapés

**1 3-oz. can chopped mushrooms**
**1 cup shelled Brazil nuts, about 4 oz.**
**1 3-oz. package cream cheese**
**1 tablespoon grated or finely minced onion**
**Dash salt and pepper**
**Few drops Tabasco**

Drain mushrooms, reserving broth for other use. Put drained mushrooms and nuts through a food chopper. Soften cream cheese at room temperature. Add onion, salt and pepper, and Tabasco. Blend well. Add ground mushrooms and nuts. Mix lightly but thoroughly. Spread on small circles and rectangles of bread. Makes about 48 canapés.

## Melon Balls and Prosciutto

Take a ripe cantaloupe or honeydew melon and make it into balls with a French melon baller. Take paper thin slices of prosciutto (Italian Ham) and cut into thin strips. Wrap one strip around each melon ball. Spear with a pick to serve.

## Raw Stuffed Mushrooms

Buy tiny white mushrooms. Remove the stems, reserving them for soups and gravies. Soften cream cheese at room temperature or by adding a little milk. Combine with curry powder to taste and use to stuff mushroom crowns. Or soften the cream cheese with a little sherry wine and use to stuff the mushroom crowns.

## Salty Radishes

Wash radishes and trim away large green leaves, leaving a few of the more tender green leaves on. Wrap a flat filet of anchovy around each one and fasten with half a pick. Serve cold.

Brewers Foundation

# Make-Your-Own Assortments

As with the spreads and smears, and dips and dunks, many people prefer to make their own hors d'oeuvres. Some just find this fun and others have very strong preferences and like to fix their hors d'oeuvres in the way that suits them best. The responsibility of the hostess is to provide an attractive and tasty combination of meats and/or cheese and breads on which to put them. The meats used in a make-your-own assortment can be as simple or as unusual as you wish to make them. You can have any of the luncheon meats and these can be handsomely arranged if some thought is given to shapes and colors in their selection. Or you can use delicacies like smoked turkey, paper-thin slivers of Virginia style ham, or slices of a goose-liver pâté.

# Pickled Mushrooms

**2 6-oz. cans whole mushrooms**
**½ cup vinegar**
**1 cup brown sugar**
**2 teaspoons mixed pickling spices**

Drain mushrooms, reserving broth. Cut the mushrooms in quarters. Combine ½ cup mushroom broth with vinegar, sugar and mixed pickling spices in a small saucepan. Bring to a boil and pour over quartered mushrooms. Cover tightly and place in the refrigerator for at least 24 hours. Spear with toothpicks to serve.

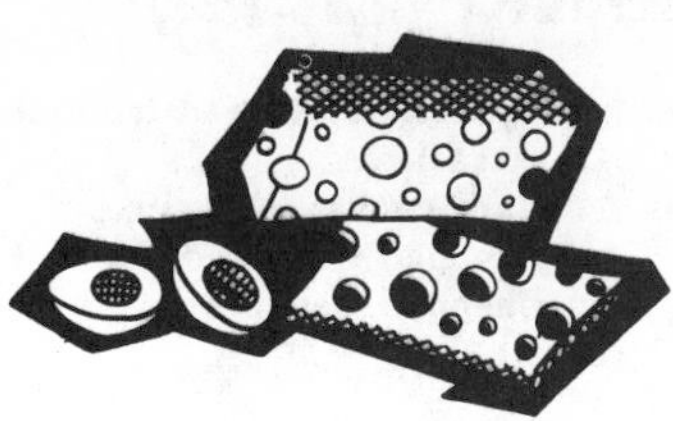

# Hors d'Oeuvre Pie

**1 round rye loaf of bread (7 to 9 inches)**
**Butter or margarine**

## Egg Filling

**6 hard-cooked eggs, chopped**
**3 tablespoons mayonnaise**
**1 tablespoon lemon juice**
**½ teaspoon instant minced onion or 1 teaspoon snipped chives**
**¼ teaspoon salt**
**Dash pepper**

## Bologna Filling

**1 cup chopped bologna**
**¼ cup minced celery**
**2 tablespoons sweet pickle relish, drained**
**2 tablespoons mayonnaise**
**1 to 2 teaspoons prepared mustard**

Cut a slice of bread from center of loaf, about ½ inch thick. Spread with butter or margarine. In two bowls, combine ingredients for egg and bologna fillings. Spread egg mixture in circle around edge of slice of bread, about 2 inches wide. Spread bologna mixture to fill in center of round. Garnish with cucumber slices and/or slices of stuffed olives, if desired. Cut in wedges to serve. Makes about 8 servings.

Campbell Soup Company

# Curried Turkey Canapés

1 cup finely chopped turkey
¼ cup mayonnaise
1 tablespoon finely chopped chutney
1 tablespoon chutney juice
1 teaspoon curry powder
Square, round and triangle crackers
Hard-cooked egg slices
Chopped shredded coconut
Chopped peanuts

Blend turkey, mayonnaise, chutney and juice, and curry powder well. Spread on different kinds of crackers. Top some with egg slices, some with shredded coconut and some with chopped peanuts. Makes about 3 dozen. This would be very good with leftover chicken or lamb as well as with turkey.

# Dark and Light Rye Rounds

Combine potted meat spread with a dash of garlic and celery salt. Spread on slices of small salty rye bread. Spread other slices of salty rye with a bacon-cheese spread. Arrange the two spreads alternately on a tray.

# Burning Bush

Sliced dried beef
½ pound cream cheese
1 tablespoon minced chives

Chop the dried beef very finely. Divide the cream cheese into 32 cubes, then roll each cube into a ball using butter paddles. Toss each ball into the chopped dried beef and roll around until entirely coated. Spear each ball with a toothpick and serve stuck into a grapefruit or a large apple.

# Celery Swirls

2 3-oz. packages cream cheese
Few tablespoons milk
3 tablespoons sweet pickle relish, drained
Celery stalks from one medium bunch

Combine cheese and milk until soft and fluffy. Add relish. Dry the celery stalks thoroughly. Fill 5 to 6 inside stalks with cheese mixture and fit back together to resemble the original bunch. Fill 4 to 5 outer stalks with cheese mixture and fit back together. Wrap each bunch in waxed paper and tie with a string. Chill overnight. Just before serving, slice with a sharp knife to ¼ to ½ inch thickness and arrange on a platter.

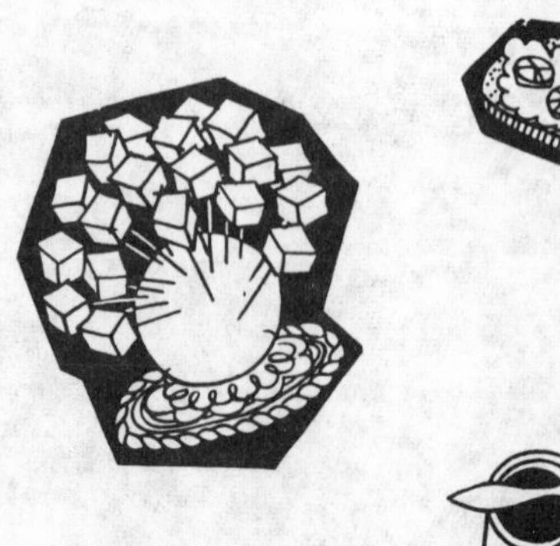

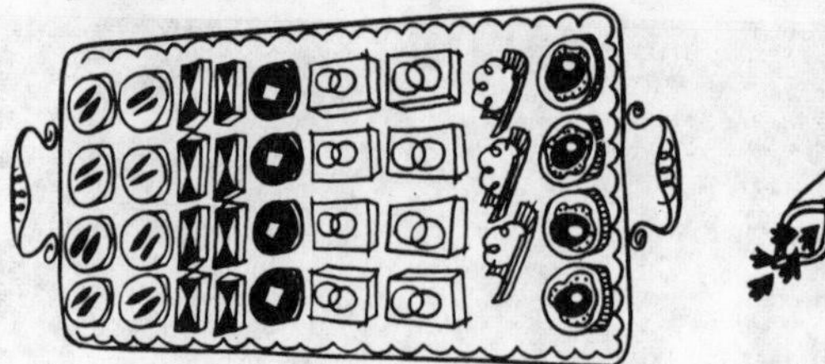

# Devil Fingers

Combine deviled ham with chive cheese and spread on thin slices of white bread from which the crusts have been removed. Cut into fingers by cutting bread slices in half and then cutting each half in three pieces; garnish with slices of stuffed olive.

# Garlic Olives

Place one peeled clove of garlic in a bowl. Add 1 tablespoon of olive oil and the olives, either ripe or green. Toss together and chill for several hours before serving. If you like a strong garlic flavor, cut the garlic clove in quarters or else put it through a press.

# Stuffed Mushroom Crowns

**2 6-oz. cans mushroom crowns**
**1 3-oz. package cream cheese**
**2 tablespoons diced toasted almonds**
**⅔ cup leftover duck or chicken**
**½ teaspoon onion juice**
**2 teaspoons lemon juice**
**⅛ teaspoon salt**
**Dash pepper and paprika**

Drain mushrooms, reserving the broth for other use. Remove stems with a sharp knife. Chop the stems finely. Soften the cream cheese at room temperature. Add the mushroom stems and all remaining ingredients. Combine well and heap the mixture in the hollow center of each mushroom crown. Dust lightly with paprika. Makes about 50 crowns.

# Cheese Canapé Roll

**½ pound package of processed American cheese**
**3 tablespoons milk**
**½ teaspoon Worcestershire sauce**
**2 tablespoons minced stuffed olives**

Melt cheese and milk in top of a double boiler over hot water, stirring until blended. Add Worcestershire sauce and olives. Cool until cheese thickens and is easy to handle. Form into a 1-inch roll on waxed paper. Wrap up and chill thoroughly. To serve slice thinly and place each slice on a round cracker. If you have an egg slicer, it will be a great help in producing even slices.

Underwood Kitchens

# Chilled Canapé "Pie"

**Pastry for 2-crust pie**
**6 egg yolks**
**3 tablespoons soft butter**
**2 cups sour cream**
**3 tablespoons flour**
**½ teaspoon salt**
**¼ teaspoon garlic salt**
**1½ cups grated Swiss cheese**
**2 4½-ounce cans deviled ham**

Roll crust to fit a 12" round shallow pizza pie pan. Bake at 425° F. about 10 minutes or until lightly browned. Cool. Blend eggs, butter and sour cream in top of double boiler, then stir in flour and seasonings. Cook over boiling water until quite thick, add Swiss cheese, blend well and cook just until cheese is melted. Cool thoroughly. Spread deviled ham on baked pie shell, then spread cheese mixture evenly over the top. Cover with protective film and refrigerate for at least two hours (this can be chilled overnight). Just before serving cut into 24 wedges and garnish with watercress, radishes, olives, cherry tomatoes, pickle fans or cucumbers. Serves 24 or more depending on size of wedges.

# Liver Chips

Soften liver sausage or canned pâté with a little cream or mayonnaise. Add catsup to taste, and drop by spoonfuls onto crisp potato chips.

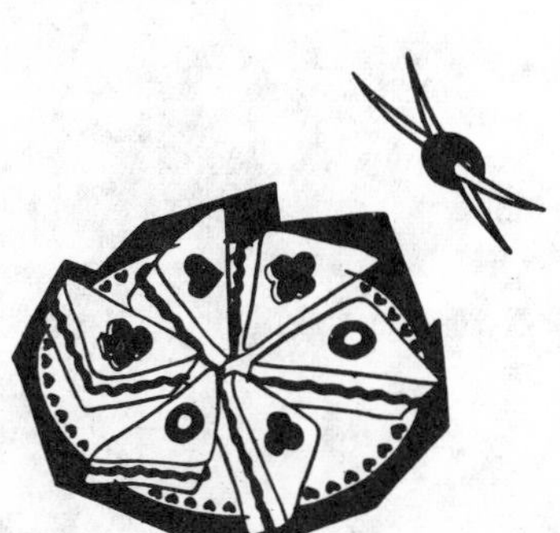

# Cucumber Pâté Canapés

Run the tines of a fork down the sides of a cucumber to make grooves. Slice into ¼-inch slices. Brown chicken livers and onions in a little butter, then mash well, and season with a small amount of salt and freshly ground pepper. Place a mound of chicken liver pâté on each slice of cucumber and serve.

# Cottage Cheese-Cucumber Mixture

**½ cup finely chopped cucumber**
**½ cup cottage cheese**
**Dash of salt**
**Dash of freshly ground pepper**

Blend all ingredients and spread on bread. Garnish with minced chives.

# Celery-Cucumber Mixture

**½ cup finely chopped cucumber**
**½ cup finely chopped celery**
**Dash of salt and onion salt**

Blend all ingredients. Chill. Place a spoonful on circles of bread. Garnish with water cress.

# Cucumber-Onion Filling

**1 cup finely chopped cucumber**
**2 tablespoons minced onion**
**Dash of salt**

Blend ingredients. Serve on bread and garnish with fresh dill.

Tip Top Bakers

# Low Calorie Hors d'Oeuvres

There comes a time in every person's life when for one reason or another, watching calories becomes important. There is no need to cut out hors d'oeuvres at this point but it is advisable to choose among the many hors d'oeuvres available, those with the fewest calories. The best appetizer a dieter can eat is raw vegetables in a cottage cheese, lemon juice and herb dunk. This will not only be very low in calories but will make a positive contribution to the nutritional content of the day's food intake. There is no need to eliminate bread on a reducing diet but choosing a protein bread with fewer than 50 calories a slice makes very good sense. Here are some highly flavorful, low calorie spreads to put on the protein bread.

# Smoked Salmon Cornucopia

Cut thin slices of smoked salmon into 2-inch squares. Select tender sprigs of water cress and roll salmon around water cress, starting at one corner to form a cornucopia. Or spread the smoked salmon with a thin layer of softened chive cheese and either roll or form into a cornucopia. Or spread crescent shaped pieces of bread with softened butter or cream cheese and top with crescents of smoked salmon. Garnish with a caper.

# Ham and Cheese Roll-Ups

Spread thinly sliced boiled ham with relish cheese spread. Roll up tightly and chill well to make the cheese firm. Cut into ¾-inch slices and spear with toothpicks. You can use any cheese or spicy spread as filling before rolling.

# Crispy Balls

Prepare cream cheese and chives as for Burning Bush. Just before serving, melt 2 teaspoons butter in a skillet and sauté ½ cup slightly crushed corn flakes in it for about 3 or 4 minutes. Roll cheese balls in the toasted corn flakes.

# Bologna Wedges

Spread 4 slices of about ⅛-inch thick bologna with chive cheese. Place together layer cake fashion. Chill and then slice into wedges to serve. Or else spread cheese over the top and around the sides. Place thin slices of stuffed olives in a circle close to the top edge. Cut into wedges so that an olive slice appears on each wedge. You can use cervelat, salami or ham and Swiss cheese to make wedges.

# Shrimp Cooked in Court Bouillon

**1 quart water**
**½ stalk celery**
**1 carrot, sliced**
**1 small onion, sliced**
**Juice of ½ lemon**
**1 teaspoon salt**
**½ teaspoon pepper**
**1 pound shrimp**

Put water and all ingredients except shrimp into a sauce pan. Bring to a boil. Add shrimp, and, if necessary, enough water to cover. Let water come to a boil, then reduce heat to simmer. Cover saucepan and let shrimp cook 3 to 5 minutes and no longer. Drain and cool quickly.

# Pickle Pretties

Cut a slice from each end of medium or large-sized dill pickles. Remove the centers with an apple corer. Drain on paper towels. Fill the hollows with your favorite jarred cheese spread or with grated sharp cheddar cheese, packing it in firmly. Wrap the pickles in waxed paper and chill. Just before serving, slice with a sharp knife. Arrange on a tray and serve with crackers or pretzels.

National Biscuit Company

# Liverwurst Log

Blend ½ pound ground liverwurst, ½ cup shredded cheddar cheese, ¼ cup chopped black olives, ½ medium onion chopped; ½ teaspoon salt, and ⅛ teaspoon ground black pepper. Form into a log about 1½ inches in diameter. Wrap in wax paper and chill for 2 to 3 hours to allow flavors to blend. Before serving garnish with pimiento and chopped hard-cooked egg yolk. Serve with assorted snack crackers. Makes about 1½ cups.

# Vegetable Dip

**1 cup finely chopped celery**
**1 tablespoon chopped chives**
**3 tomatoes, finely chopped**
**1 carrot, shredded**
**½ small cucumber, finely chopped**
**1 teaspoon garlic vinegar**
**½ teaspoon salt**
**⅛ teaspoon ground black pepper**
**Dash Worcestershire Sauce**

Combine first five ingredients. Blend remaining ingredients. Combine the vegetables and vinegar mixture. Chill 2 to 3 hours. Serve with assorted Snack Crackers. Makes about 2 cups.

## Glazed Spicy Shrimp

**1 pound cooked shrimp**
**1 envelope (1 tablespoon) unflavored gelatine**
**⅔ cup catsup**
**3 tablespoons chili sauce**
**2 tablespoons horse-radish**
**3 tablespoons lemon juice**
**⅛ teaspoon onion powder**
**2 teaspoons Worcestershire sauce**
**Dash cayenne pepper**

Peel and devein shrimp, and chill. Soften gelatine in ¼ cup cold water, then dissolve over boiling water. Combine remaining ingredients, then add gelatine. Chill until syrupy. Spear each shrimp with a toothpick and dip into spicy sauce. Stick into a grapefruit or cabbage. If desired, you can dip them twice to build up the amount of spicy coating. Chill until ready to serve.

## Cheese Teasers

Take pieces of sharp, medium or mild cheddar and cut into cubes. Top some with small stuffed olives and some with small pickled onions. Spear both together with a toothpick and arrange on a platter.

Armour and Co.

## Cold Egg Hors d'Oeuvres

Stuffed eggs are probably the most popular hors d'oeuvre served. This popularity is well merited since stuffed eggs are enjoyed by almost everybody, they are easy to prepare and lend themselves to an infinite variety. To make them, hard-cook your eggs in water just below boiling. If you boil the eggs, the whites will be tough and the yolks will develop a green ring on the outside. Cold eggs plunged into hot water will crack. If your eggs are chilled, start them in cold or lukewarm water. Cook for about 15 minutes. Chill in cold water before peeling to make the peeling easier. Cut in half, lengthwise, and scoop out the yolks into a bowl. Mash with anchovy paste, red or black caviar, cheese, deviled ham or any other spicy meat, fish or seasoning. Refill the whites and garnish with olive slices, pimiento, parsley, paprika or chives.

## Cream Cheese and Anchovy Toast

Cut toast into 2-inch squares. Spread thinly with anchovy paste. Soften cream cheese with a little milk and using a pastry tube, make a border of cream cheese all around the square.

## Shell Appetizers

Buy the large macaroni shells and cook as directed on the package or as you would any macaroni. Cool and dry them. Then fill with shrimp paste, anchovy and chopped egg paste, black or red caviar.

## Lincoln Cheese Log

**½ pound cream cheese**
**¼ cup grated Swiss cheese**
**2 teaspoons prepared horse-radish**
**Cream, if necessary**
**¼ cup coarsely chopped dried beef**

Blend together cream cheese, Swiss cheese and horse-radish, adding a few drops of cream if the mixture seems too stiff. Form into one long roll about 1½ inches in diameter. Spread the dried beef on waxed paper and roll the cheese around in it until the outside of the roll is coated. Chill overnight to blend the flavors. To serve, cut in slices and place on crackers.

# Cheese Treats

**1 jar (1 pound) cheese spread**
**1 package salty rye bread, sliced**
**Small stuffed olives**
**Small pickled onions**

Spread cheese spread on slices of rye bread. On half the slices place a small olive with a cocktail toothpick stuck through it. On the remaining slices, place small pickled onions on toothpicks.

# Vegetable Hors d'Oeuvres

Many raw vegetables like celery, radishes, carrots, green onions, sliced mushrooms, peeled broccoli stems, cauliflowerets, fenuchi, to name a few, are delicious nibbles just served in a bowl of shaved ice. They can be served just salted or with any one of the dunking sauces given in chapter on dunks. They can also be combined with fish, meat and cheeses and used as carriers of these foods in many appetizing ways.

The Borden Company

# Hearty Sandwiches

## SAVORY FRENCH TOAST SANDWICHES

Lightly spread 12 slices enriched or whole wheat bread with softened butter or margarine. Fit on thin-sliced cooked ham, meat loaf, tongue, luncheon meat, chicken, turkey, Swiss or American cheese, or spread with deviled ham or chunk-style peanut butter. Put the slices together in pairs. Cut in half if you like. Dip quickly in and out of egg wash; fry 4 minutes or until golden brown on both sides in 3 tablespoons butter or margarine. Garnish of vegetable nibblers; or currant jelly, or a spiced peach or crabapple in a lettuce leaf. Makes 6 whole sandwiches.

**Egg Wash:** Beat 3 eggs until frothy with ¾ cup milk. Add ¼ teaspoon salt, and a choice of ⅛ teaspoon ground cinnamon, clove or nutmeg.

R. T. French Co.

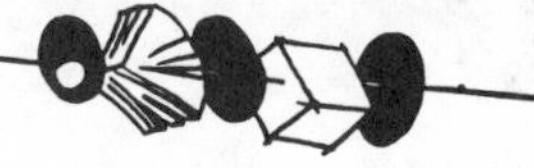

American Institute of Baking

**Salad Sandwiches**

THESE may be glamorous or simple. Use rolls of your choice, or enriched, specialty white, whole wheat, wheat germ, cracked wheat, or Roman meal bread. Spread with softened butter or margarine, or a harmonizing or contrasting flavored butter. If they are to be eaten at once, put together with crisp lettuce or romaine; or with thin-sliced tomato or cucumber. But if they are to be packed for a carried lunch, pack the greens and fresh vegetables separately in a polyethelene bag or paraffin-covered paper container, and add them at eating time.

### The Salad Dressing

For sandwich making use mayonnaise or Russian dressing, or any special commercial thick salad dressing. Most commercial mayonnaise is so bland that the flavor is improved by stirring in additional seasonings as follows:

**"Pepped-Up" Mayonnaise:** To 1 quart commercial mayonnaise add 1 teaspoon Worcestershire, ¼ teaspoon Tabasco, ½ teaspoon garlic salt, ¼ teaspoon Ac'cent and 1 tablespoon vinegar.

**Russian Dressing:** To ¾ cup "pepped-up" mayonnaise add ¼ cup chili sauce and 1 tablespoon each minced celery, pimiento and green pepper.

If the day is hot, or if salad sandwiches are to stand for hours in a warm place, do not use a dressing made with eggs. Instead whip up the following:

**White Mayonnaise:** In a deep pint bowl combine ½ teaspoon salt, ¼ teaspoon each pepper and sugar, and ⅓ teaspoon mustard. Stir in 3 tablespoons undiluted evaporated milk. Gradually beat in ½ cup salad oil with a rotary or electric beater. Then gradually beat in 2 tablespoons vinegar. Use as you would any mayonnaise.

# Tasty Frankfurter Sandwich Filling

**¾ cup (¼ pound) grated processed American cheese**
**3 tablespoons milk**
**3 frankfurters, chopped**
**1 tablespoon prepared mustard**

Combine cheese and milk in top of a double boiler; when cheese has melted, add chopped frankfurters and mustard; mix well. Makes approximately 1 cup, or filling for 5 sandwiches

American Institute of Baking

# Denver or Western Sandwich

*Single Serving*

**1 teaspoon butter or margarine**
**1 egg**
**1 tablespoon each fine-chopped onion and green pepper**
**2 tablespoons milk**
**⅛ teaspoon salt**
**2 tablespoons chopped cooked ham or crisp bacon**
**⅛ teaspoon Ac'cent**
**Speck pepper**
**2 slices buttered rounds bread or toast**

In a small skillet heat the butter until moderately hot. Meantime, beat the egg, and add the onion, green pepper, milk, ham, or bacon, salt and pepper. Pour into the skillet. Cook, stirring and lifting the mixture to cook evenly. At the same time draw the mixture toward the center to keep it round and make a "cake" to fit the bread. Brown slightly on the bottom. Turn to cook other side. Place between bread or toast slices. Serve hot.

# Bologna Salad Sandwich Filling

**½ cup (3 ounces) ground bologna sausage**
**1 hard-cooked egg, chopped**
**2 tablespoons chopped sweet pickles**
**1 tablespoon chopped onion**
**2 tablespoons mayonnaise or salad dressing**
**¼ teaspoon salt**

Combine bologna sausage, chopped egg, sweet pickle, onion, mayonnaise and salt. Makes ¾ cup, or filling for 4 sandwiches.

# Cream Cheese-Raisin Sandwich Filling

**½ cup seedless raisins**
**½ cup water**
**1 (3 ounce) package cream cheese**
**4 teaspoons milk**

Soak raisins in water for thirty minutes. Pour liquid off. Combine cream cheese and milk until soft. Add raisins and mix well. Makes ⅞ cup, or filling for 4 sandwiches.

Best Foods

# Seafood Toastwiches

**2 tablespoons enriched margarine**
**2 tablespoons minced onion**
**1 (5 ounce) can lobster**
**1 (4½ ounce) can shrimp**
**½ cup real mayonnaise**
**¼ cup milk**
**2 tablespoons dry white wine**
**12 slices toasted white or cheese bread**

Melt the margarine; sauté the onion in it 3 minutes. Dice and add the seafood. Slow-heat 5 minutes. Blend the mayonnaise and milk in the top of a double boiler; heat 5 minutes over hot but not boiling water. Stir in the seafood and wine. Spoon half over the toast; top with a second piece of toast and spoon over the remaining filling.

# Toasted Cheese Squares on Long Rolls

(See picture between pgs. 381-385.)

Cut squares of processed cheese into four and place long ways overlapping down the center of halves of soft rolls. Pop under the grill and toast until cheese bubbles. Serve with green pea soup.

# Baked Cheese Tidbits

(See picture between pgs. 381-385.)

**6 slices of toast**
**2 ozs. butter**
**¼ lb. cheddar cheese, grated**
**1 egg yolk**
**Mustard**
**Salt**
**Paprika**
**Radish**
**Stuffed olives**

Stir butter until soft, add cheese, yolk and seasonings. Spread on 6 slices of toast. Grill to a golden brown. Cut slices into triangles and garnish with radishes and olives. Serve hot.

# Egg and Bacon Muffin Puffs

**1 cup real mayonnaise**
**1 egg white, stiff-beaten**
**8 split toasted halved English muffins**
**8 sliced hard-cooked eggs**
**Crisp bacon slices**
**Crisp pickle slices**

Fold the mayonnaise into the egg white. Spread lightly on toasted muffin halves and put together. Place sliced egg on top. Pile mayonnaise mixture over. Brown 1 minute under a broiler. Top with crisp bacon slices. Serve at once. Garnish with pickle slices.

# Toast-Quick Waffled Sandwiches

Their streamlined preparation is made possible by three home-making electrical time-savers: The waffle iron, the food freezer and the toaster. Waffle "toast-quicks" are made in advance, cooled, wrapped in moisture-vapor-proof covering and stored in the freezer, ready to toast and serve at a moment's notice.

**To Prepare:** Sandwich together enriched or whole wheat bread with the spread of your choice. Spread butter or margarine on the *outside*. Place in the waffle-baker; toast until light brown. Serve piping hot.

American Institute of Baking

# Egg Sandwich Mexicana

**4 coarse-chopped hard-cooked eggs**
**2 tablespoons each chopped green pepper, pimiento, stuffed olives and scallions**
**½ cup grated sharp American cheese**
**¼ cup chili sauce**
**⅓ teaspoon salt**
**¼ teaspoon Ac'cent**
**¼ teaspoon chili powder**
**¼ teaspoon pepper**
**4 large rolls**
**¼ cup butter or margarine**

Combine all ingredients except the butter or margarine and rolls. Split the rolls. Hollow out the soft interior; brush with the melted butter or margarine. Heap in the egg mixture. Place on a baking sheet. Bake about 20 minutes in a hot oven, 400°F, or until the cheese starts to melt and the edges are delicately browned.

### French Omelet Sandwiches

*New and Satisfying Whether Hot or Cold*

It's amazing what can be done with French omelets in sandwiches and how good they taste! Cut in sections, and use to fill sandwiches made with enriched cheese, wheat germ, cracked wheat, whole wheat, Roman meal or onion bread or toast, spread lightly with softened butter or margarine.

Broiler Council

# The Original Club Sandwich

*Single Serving*

**3 slices toast**
**Butter or margarine**
**Lettuce**
**Mayonnaise**
**2 slices cooked white chicken meat**
**2 crisp cooked bacon slices**
**2 slices tomato**

Toast the bread and spread with butter or margarine. Cover one slice with chicken; spread with mayonnaise and top with a lettuce leaf. Cover with a slice of toast and spread with mayonnaise. Place bacon and tomato slices on top. Cover with the remaining toast slice. Fasten securely with 4 wooden toothpicks. Cut the sandwich diagonally into 4 triangles. Stand them upright on a plate. Garnish with pickles, olives, or halved slices tomato.

### Turkey, Duck or Goose Club Sandwiches

Follow the preceding recipe using sliced turkey, duck or goose instead of chicken dusted with Ac'cent.

### Tongue Club Sandwiches

Follow the recipe for the original club sandwich using cooked ham instead of chicken, and Thousand Island dressing instead of mayonnaise.

### Roast Pork Club Sandwich

Follow the recipe for the original club sandwich using sliced roast pork instead of chicken, and "pepped-up" mayonnaise.

### Lobster Club Sandwich

Follow the original club sandwich using fresh, canned or thawed frozen lobster meat instead of chicken and tartar sauce in place of mayonnaise.

### Salmon Club Sandwich

Make as the original club sandwich recipe using thin-sliced fresh cooked salmon, or flaked, well-drained canned salmon. Season with black pepper. Add chopped scallions.

### Flounder Club Sandwich

Follow the original recipe for club sandwich substituting for chicken thin slices butter-broiled fillets of flounder. Add chopped scallions and radishes and tartar sauce.

### Cheese Club Sandwich

Make as the original recipe but use sliced Swiss cheese, or American or provolone cheese instead of chicken.

### Boston Club Sandwich

Follow the original recipe but use hot Boston baked beans instead of chicken and add plenty of chopped green peppers.

### Mushroom Club Sandwich

Make according to directions for the original club sandwich; but use, instead of chicken, a layer of coarse-chopped butter-fried fresh mushrooms. Add a little chopped scallion or minced chives, and use "pepped-up" mayonnaise.

### Oyster Club Sandwich

For each sandwich allow 4 shucked oysters. Roll in ½ cup flour mixed with ¼ teaspoon each salt and Ac'cent, and ⅛ teaspoon pepper. Sauté in butter until golden brown. Place on a slice of enriched bread toast. Put together with lettuce, bacon, sliced tomato, and tartar sauce; top with toast. Serve as described in recipe for Original Club Sandwich.

# Vealburgers

**1 pound twice-ground raw veal**
**¼ cup twice-ground ham, cooked or raw**
**½ cup milk**
**½ cup enriched bread crumbs**
**¼ cup minced parsley**
**1 tablespoon lemon juice**
**1 tablespoon tomato ketchup**
**1 teaspoon salt**
**1 teaspoon Ac'cent**
**¼ teaspoon pepper**

Combine the ingredients in the order given. Mix until very smooth. Make into 8 flat round patties ½ inch thick. Dust with flour. Pan-fry in butter or margarine 10 to 12 minutes or until lightly browned.

# Peanut-Cheese Crunch Stack Sandwich

**1 cup chopped peanuts**
**¼ cup pickle relish**
**⅓ cup salad dressing**
**⅛ teaspoon Worcestershire**
**¼ teaspoon salt**
**⅛ teaspoon pepper**
**¼ teaspoon Ac'cent**
**6 slices pasteurized processed cheese spread**
**6 stuffed olives**

Blend the peanuts, pickle relish, salad dressing, Worcestershire and seasonings. Spread 6 of the toast rounds with this mixture. Top each with a slice of cheese spread. Place in a moderate oven, 350°F for 10 minutes or until the cheese melts. Cover with the remaining toast rounds. Garnish with olives.

# Shrimp Salad Rolls

**1 pound cooked shrimp, fresh or frozen**
**1½ cups shredded lettuce**
**3 tablespoons chopped parsley or cress**
**½ cup chopped celery**
**½ cup chopped cucumber**
**1 teaspoon chopped onion**
**4 tablespoons mayonnaise**
**⅛ teaspoon Ac'cent**
**¼ teaspoon Tabasco**
**Salt and pepper**
**Long rolls**

Reserve a few whole shrimp for garnishing; chop the remainder. Toss with the lettuce, parsley, celery, cucumber, and onion. Moisten with the mayonnaise; add Ac'cent and Tabasco. Season to taste with salt and pepper. Chill. Split the rolls, but do not cut all the way through. Spread with softened butter or margarine; fill with the shrimp salad.

The Shrimp Association of the Americas

# Sliced Cheese Mustard Sandwiches

Spread slices of enriched or rye bread or pumpernickel with mustard sauce. Top half the slices with sliced American or Swiss cheese. Cover with the remaining bread. Sliced cooked or canned ham or tongue, sliced cooked pork butt, liverwurst and other sausages may be used instead of cheese, or make it half and half!

### Mustard Sandwich Sauce

Beat 1 egg in a saucepan. Add 2 tablespoons sugar, 2 tablespoons flour, and 2 tablespoons dry mustard; blend well. Stir in 1 cup vinegar a little at a time: Boil until it thickens. Add 2 tablespoons butter.

### Scallion Mustard Sauce

Add ⅓ cup fine-chopped scallions to cooled mustard sauce; use at once.

# Cheese-Vegetable Sandwiches

Combine 1 cup minced celery, 1 cup grated raw carrot, ½ cup thin radish slices ¼ cup minced green pepper and ¼ cup "pepped-up" mayonnaise. Spread on 4 well-buttered or margarined slices whole wheat or enriched bread. Top each with shredded American cheese, or use a thin slice; top with another slice of bread.

**Menu:** Tapioca cream, salted peanuts and cocoa complete this lunch.

American Institute of Baking

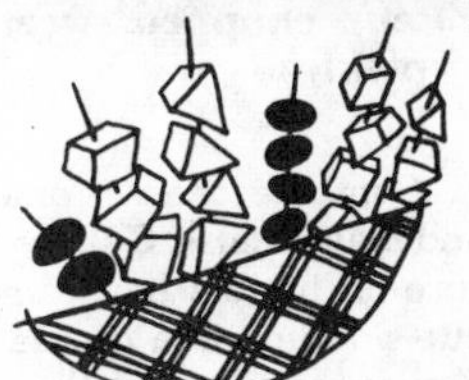

# Bologna Salad Stack Sandwich

**½ cup (3 ounces) ground bologna sausage**
**1 chopped hard-cooked egg**
**2 tablespoons pickle relish**
**1 tablespoon chopped onion**
**2 tablespoons mayonnaise or salad dressing**
**¼ teaspoon salt**
**12 slices whole wheat or enriched bread**
**¼ cup soft butter or margarine**
**4 slices American cheese**

Combine the bologna, egg, pickle relish, onion, mayonnaise and salt; blend into the butter. Cover 4 slices of bread with the bologna salad filling. Top with a second slice of bread; then with 1 slice cheese and a third slice of bread.

# Beanburgers

**1 medium-sized onion sliced**
**1 tablespoon butter or margarine**
**1 can (1¾ cups) pork and beans**
**1 can (1¼ cups) spaghetti sauce-with-meat**
**6 slices processed cheese**
**6 hamburger buns, split and toasted**

Brown the onion lightly in butter or margarine. Stir in beans and spaghetti sauce; heat. Place the cheese slices on the toasted buns; spoon over the sauce. Serves 6.

American Institute of Baking

# Cheeseburgers

**1½ cups (½ pound) grated processed or American cheese**
**2 tablespoons fine-chopped onion**
**⅓ cup chopped sweet pickles**
**2 hard-cooked eggs, chopped**
**½ teaspoon Worcestershire**
**¼ teaspoon salt**
**½ cup mayonnaise or salad dressing**
**6 hamburger buns**

Combine cheese, onion, pickles, eggs, Worcestershire, salt, and mayonnaise. Cut the buns in half; spread ¼ cup cheese mixture on bottom half of each bun. Place all halves of the buns, cut-side up, on a cookie sheet; toast under a preheated broiler 5 minutes, or until the tops are toasted and the cheese melts. Makes 6.

# Tuna Towers

**¼ cup mayonnaise or salad dressing**
**1 teaspoon Worcestershire sauce**
**¼ teaspoon celery salt**
**2 cans (6½ or 7 ounces) tuna in vegetable oil**
**4 hamburger buns, toasted**
**4 slices tomato**
**4 slices onion**
**4 slices cucumber**
**2 hard-cooked eggs, halved crosswise**
**4 pimiento-stuffed olives**

Blend together mayonnaise, Worcestershire sauce and celery salt. Add tuna, toss until well mixed. Pile tuna mixture on bottom halves of hamburger buns. Top each with a tomato slice, onion slice, cucumber slice, hard-cooked egg half and olive. Use 7-inch knitting needles as skewers, spearing all the ingredients in the "towers" from the top to secure them. Tape pennant with "Tuna Tower" or any desired legend on end of each needle. To eat, pull out knitting needles, remove cucumber slices, eggs and olives; eat separately; cover remaining towers with top halves of buns. Makes 4 servings.

Tuna Research Foundation

# Deviled Scrambled Egg

**2 tablespoons butter or margarine**
**1 green pepper chopped**
**1 medium-sized onion chopped**
**4 eggs**
**1 (4 inch) piece celery diced**
**1 family-size can deviled ham**
**6 soft round buns**

Melt the butter or margarine in a skillet; add the green pepper, onion, and celery, and sauté. Beat and add the eggs and the deviled ham. Scramble as usual. Serve sandwich-style between toasted, split round buns.

### Scrambled Egg-Ham

Follow the directions for scrambled egg-onion spread, using ¼ cup minced cooked ham, and 1 tablespoon tomato ketchup instead of 1 tablespoon milk.

### Scrambled Egg-Tongue

Follow the directions for scrambled egg-onion spread; add 1 (3¼ ounce) can tongue spread.

### Scrambled Egg-Cheese

Plain scramble 3 eggs with ¼ cup grated American cheese.

### Scrambled Egg-Bacon-Cheese

Plain scramble 3 eggs with the contents 1 (3¼ ounce) can commercial bacon spread and ⅓ cup fine-grated sharp American cheese.

### Scrambled Egg-Ham-Bologna

Grind enough ham-bologna to make ¼ cup. Add to 1 recipe scrambled eggs; cook and blend.

# Little Olive-Ham Pizzas

Use halved English muffins as a base. Spread with tomato sauce. Cover with small thin squares of ham and sliced stuffed olives. Dribble ½ teaspoon olive oil over each. Cover with a half inch topping of cottage cheese, and dust with Parmesan cheese. Place on a pan lined with aluminum foil. Bake 10 to 12 minutes in a hot oven, 450°F.

# California Cream Cheese Sandwich

Combine and blend 1 (3 ounce) package cream cheese, 2 tablespoons butter or margarine, 2 tablespoons mayonnaise and ½ teaspoon lemon juice until light and fluffy. Spread on whole wheat, nut, raisin or cracked wheat bread. Garnish with peeled orange sections.

American Institute of Baking

# Grilled Cheese-Peanut Butter Sandwich

**16 slices enriched bread**
**4 tablespoons soft butter or margarine**
**½ cup peanut butter**
**½ cup (4 ounces) pimiento cream cheese**
**4 slices American cheese**

Spread all the bread with butter or margarine. Then spread 4 slices with pimiento cream cheese, using 2 tablespoons on each slice; cover with the second slice of bread. Spread this slice with peanut butter using 2 tablespoons on each; cover with a third slice of bread. Place 1 slice American cheese on this layer, and top with the fourth slice of bread. Cut the sandwiches into thirds. Insert a toothpick into each cut section; place cut-side down, on a cookie sheet. Toast under a preheated broiler 5 minutes on each side. Serve with fruit salad.

# "Stack" Bunwiches

**8 large round soft buns**
**½ cup prepared mustard**
**1 cup pickle relish**
**2 pounds assorted sliced ready-to-serve meats (bologna, liver sausage, spiced ham, tongue, ham, salami, etc.)**

Split buns crosswise; spread bottom slices lightly with mustard. Pile alternate slices of 3 or 4 different kinds of ready-to-serve meats on the bottom slice of each bun, then spread the slices with relish and mustard. Place bun tops on sandwiches. Makes 8. (Instead of buns, sliced white, rye, pumpernickel, etc., bread slices may be used.)

R. T. French Co.

# Grilled Deep-Sea Sandwiches

**1 package (12 ounces) frozen haddock or cod fillets, partly thawed**
**½ cup water**
**½ teaspoon salt**
**¼ cup light cream**
**¼ cup catsup**
**2 tablespoons chopped sweet pickle**
**1 tablespoon grated onion**
**2 teaspoons prepared horse-radish**
**½ teaspoon salt**
**Dash of pepper**
**8 slices bread or 4 hot dog or hamburger rolls, split**
**Softened butter**
**Cheese Sauce**

Cut fish into 1-inch pieces. Place fish, water, and ½ teaspoon salt in a saucepan. Cover, bring to a boil, and simmer until fish is easily flaked with a fork, about 5 minutes. Drain and flake the fish.

Combine the cream, catsup, pickle, onion, horse-radish, salt, and pepper. Add the flaked fish and mix well. Spread on bread, making 4 sandwiches. Spread outside of sandwiches with softened butter. Brown in sandwich grill or sauté in a skillet. Serve with Cheese Sauce or top with a slice of cheese. Makes 4 servings.

### Cheese Sauce

**1 tablespoon butter**
**1 tablespoon flour**
**¼ teaspoon salt**
**Dash of pepper**
**¾ cup light cream or milk**
**¾ cup grated sharp Cheddar cheese or 1 cup mild Cheddar or process cheese**

Melt butter in saucepan. Add flour, salt, and pepper and stir until blended. Then add cream gradually, stirring constantly. Cook and stir over medium heat until smooth and thickened. Then add cheese and stir until melted. Makes about 1 cup sauce, or 4 servings.

# Beefburgers (Hamburgers)

**1½ pounds twice-ground chopped beef**
**1 teaspoon salt**
**¼ teaspoon pepper**
**½ teaspoon Ac'cent**
**2 tablespoons raw oatmeal**
**2 tablespoons milk**
**1 tablespoon scraped onion (optional)**

Combine the ingredients and work together until smooth. Shape into 8 flat round patties ½ inch thick. Slowly pan-fry 8 minutes in butter or margarine. Turn once.

### Wine Beefburgers

Follow the recipe for beefburgers using 2 tablespoons any dry wine instead of milk.

### Venisonburgers

Use twice-ground venison steak instead of beef. Follow the method for making beefburgers.

Courtesy of Birds Eye Fish Fillets

# Beefburgers With Cheese Sauce

Split and toast round buns. Spread the bottom half of each with salad dressing; cover with a slice of onion, then a hot broiled beef or vealburger. Top each with 1 tablespoon of commercial cheese spread. Cover with the tops of the buns.

# Savory Meat Stack Bunwiches

**1½ cups any ground, cooked meat**
**¼ teaspoon Ac'cent**
**1 teaspoon Worcestershire**
**¼ cup minced green pepper**
**1½ tablespoons pickle relish**
**½ tablespoon onion salt**
**Few grains cayenne**
**2 tablespoons chili sauce**
**3 tablespoons mayonnaise**

Combine all ingredients. Cool, and spread between 6 split buttered buns. Top with a slice of tomato and crisp lettuce. Makes 6. Serve at once, or wrap in Saran or waxed paper; chill and pack in the lunch box.

# Zesty Dill Beef Rolls

**1 pound ground beef**
**¼ cup chopped dill pickle**
**½ teaspoon salt**
**1 tablespoon grated onion**
**1 tablespoon table mustard**
**1 tablespoon ketchup**
**6 frankfurter rolls**

Combine and mix the beef, pickles, salt, grated onion, mustard and ketchup. Split the rolls lengthwise, but do not cut through the bottom. Divide the beef-pickle mixture into 6 equal parts. Fill meat into the frankfurter rolls. Place on broiler rack and broil 4 inches from source of heat, about 8 minutes, or until meat is done.

# Cheese-Frankfurter Sandwich Filling

Combine 1 cup grated American cheese and 3 tablespoons milk in the top of a double boiler; when the cheese melts, mix in 4 chopped skinless frankfurters and 1½ tablespoons table mustard and 1 tablespoon mayonnaise.

### Salad Sandwich and Soup Luncheon

A brimming bowl of hot vegetable soup gives a lift to any meal. With it enjoy a big ham-egg, veal-nut or salmon-cucumber salad roll.

# Tomboy Sandwich

**4 individual loaves Italian bread**
**Enriched margarine**
**12 slices salami (skin removed)**
**1 can baked beans with tomato sauce**
**2 tablespoons mustard-with-horse-radish**
**Chilled crisp pickle slices**

Slice the loaves in half lengthwise; spread the cut sides with softened enriched margarine. Place 3 slices salami on the bottom slice of each loaf. Blend the baked beans and mustard-with-horse-radish. Spoon over the salami. Cover with the top slices of bread. Heat in a moderate oven 5 minutes. Makes 4.

# "Devilicious" Patio Platter

**1 4½-ounce can deviled ham**
**2 tablespoons chili sauce**
**½ cup chopped peanuts**
**1 jar American cheese spread**
**1 loaf French bread**
**1 tomato**
**Radish roses**
**Cucumber slices**
**Green pepper rings**
**Parsley**

Combine deviled ham, chili sauce and nuts. Slice bread and spread every two slices with deviled ham mixture and cheese spread. Make sandwiches and reshape loaf. Serve on a wooden board—garnish ends with tomato halves—center with parsley and serve fresh vegetables on board. When ready to serve, separate unspread slices for individual sandwiches. Makes about 12 double sandwiches.

Underwood Kitchens

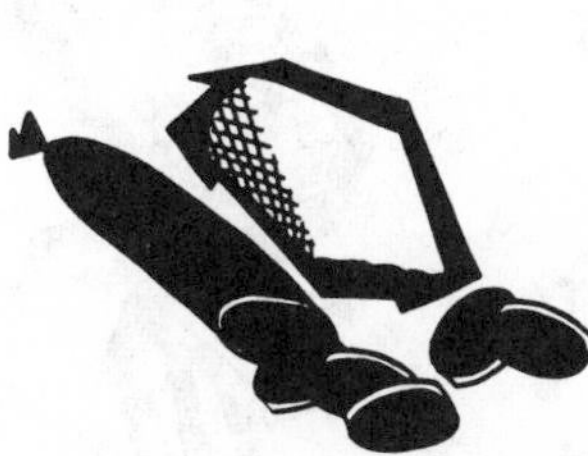

International Tuna Fish Association

# Tuna Heroes

**4 individual hero rolls, split**
**Romaine**
**1 can (6½ to 7 ounces) tuna, drained**
**2 tablespoons sweet pickle relish**
**American cheese, cut in strips**
**Sliced pimiento-stuffed olives**
**¼ cup mayonnaise**
**2 tablespoons catsup**

Cover bottom halves of hero rolls with romaine. Break tuna into pieces, toss with pickle relish and spread over romaine. Top with strips of cheese and olive slices. Mix together mayonnaise and catsup; spoon over all. Cover with top halves of hero rolls. Makes 4 servings.

South African Lobster Association

# South African Rock Lobster Rolls

**2 (6 to 8 ounce) South African rock lobster tails *or* 2 cans South African rock lobster**
**2 tablespoons butter or margarine**
**3 tablespoons flour**
**½ teaspoon salt**
**½ teaspoon paprika**
**1 cup milk**
**2 tablespoons mayonnaise**
**2 tablespoons minced parsley**
**6 to 8 frankfurter rolls**

Boil South African rock lobster tails according to directions. Remove meat and dice. Melt butter or margairne and stir in flour and seasonings. Add milk and stir over low heat until sauce thickens and boils. Beat in mayonnaise and parsley. Split rolls almost through. Toast lightly and fill with hot rock lobster mixture. Brush top of rolls with butter and serve. Makes 6-8 servings.

*Directions for Boiling:* Place South African rock lobster tails, either thawed or frozen, into large kettle boiling salted water (1 teaspoon salt for each quart water). When water reboils, lower heat so water boils gently and begin counting time. Keep covered. Boil tails 1 minute longer than their individual weight in ounces. For instance boil a 6-ounce tail 7 minutes. Add 2 minutes to all boiling times when tails are cooked frozen. To remove meat easily from shell, drain off hot water, drench with cold water. Using scissors, cut lengthwise through center of membrane covering flesh and insert fingers under meat at open end and pull meat out.

# Egg and Green Pepper Family Club Sandwich

Remove the crusts from a day-old loaf of unsliced enriched or a specialty white bread. Cut in 3 lengthwise slices. Toast lightly under the broiler. Spread with mayonnaise. Place on a tray or platter. Arrange sliced green pepper on 1 slice. Cover with another slice of bread, then with a layer of hard-cooked egg. Cover this with the remaining slice of bread. Top with seasoned sliced tomatoes. And here's a tip—pass hot mayonnaise sauce.

### Hot Mayonnaise Sauce

Combine ⅓ cup real mayonnaise, 1 (3 ounce) package cream cheese and ¾ cup milk. Beat with a rotary beater until smooth. Add ⅓ cup each sliced olives and diced pimientos; heat thoroughly in the top of a double boiler; stir occasionally.

Corn Products Company

# Chickenburgers

**1 pound twice-ground raw chicken meat**
**1 teaspoon salt**
**½ teaspoon Ac'cent**
**⅛ teaspoon pepper**
**1 egg**
**¼ cup enriched bread crumbs**
**2 tablespoons milk**
**1 tablespoon minced parsley**

Combine the ingredients in the order given. Mix thoroughly until smooth. Form into 8 round flat cakes a scant ½ inch thick. Slow-fry 12 minutes in butter or margarine.

National Kraut Packers Association

# Kraut Round Dogs on Horseradish Buttered Rolls

**3 cups drained sauerkraut**
**½ cup chili sauce**
**2 tablespoons drained capers**
**¼ cup butter or margarine**
**1 tablespoon prepared horse-radish**
**⅛ teaspoon dry mustard**
**6 frankfurters (about ½ pound)**
**6 hard poppy seed rolls**

Combine kraut, chili sauce and capers. Cream together butter, horseradish and mustard. Cut 10 deep slits in each frankfurter without cutting all the way through. Place in boiling water; cover and remove from heat. Let stand 8 minutes. Meanwhile, cut slice off top of roll; scoop out centers* to form cups. Toast rolls lightly in broiler; spread with horseradish butter. Top with round dog. Fill with kraut mixture. Serve with potato chips and assorted relishes. Makes 6 servings.

*Save centers to make bread crumbs.

# Salmon Salad Loaf

### Ingredients

1 (20 ounce) loaf day-old enriched bread, unsliced
4 chopped hard-cooked eggs
1 (No. 2) can red salmon, flaked
1 tablespoon grated lemon rind
1 tablespoon lemon juice
¾ cup fine-chopped parsley
1 teaspoon salt
⅔ cup mayonnaise or salad dressing
1 tablespoon chopped green pepper
2 tablespoons sliced green olives

### Topping for Loaf

1 envelope unflavored gelatine
1 tablespoon mild vinegar
1 cup mayonnaise or salad dressing
¼ teaspoon Tabasco
½ teaspoon Worcestershire
1 sliced hard-cooked egg
Strips of green pepper

Mix gelatine with vinegar; dissolve over hot water. Slowly stir into mayonnaise; add seasonings.

**Step 1.** With a sharp knife, remove the crusts from a loaf of bread to make an even, box-shaped loaf. Cut a lengthwise slice from the top.

**Step 2.** Hollow out the center of the loaf, leaving side walls and bottom at least ½ inch thick. Place on a cookie sheet. (Save the center of the loaf for bread crumbs or stuffing.)

In a bowl combine and mix the chopped eggs, flaked salmon, lemon rind, lemon juice, celery, salt, mayonnaise, green pepper and green olives. With this fill the hollowed loaf. Cover with a top slice of bread.

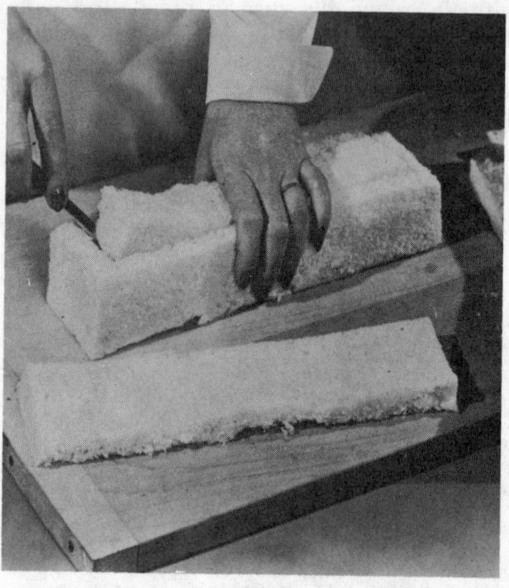

**Step 3.** Spread top and sides of the loaf with the topping mixture. Garnish with the sliced egg and green pepper strips. Cover the finished loaf with heavy waxed paper to prevent discoloration of mayonnaise. Refrigerate twelve hours before serving. Do not freeze because a zero temperature causes mayonnaise to separate.

## Chicken or Turkey Salad Loaf

Follow the recipe for salmon salad loaf, using 2½ cups minced cooked oddments of chicken or turkey instead of salmon, and adding ¼ cup fine-chopped pecan meats and ¼ teaspoon Ac'cent.

## Ham Salad Loaf

Follow the recipe for salmon salad loaf; using 2½ cups minced cooked or canned smoked ham, and adding 1 teaspoon table mustard.

# Beef-Vegetable-Burgers

**1 pound chopped beef**
**2 peeled medium-sized potatoes**
**2 peeled small carrots**
**½ cup cut celery**
**1 peeled medium-sized onion**
**3 sprigs parsley**
**1 egg**
**¼ teaspoon thyme**
**½ teaspoon salt**
**⅛ teaspoon pepper**
**½ teaspoon Ac'cent**

Put the beef and vegetables through the food chopper twice. Beat and add the egg; add the seasonings. Form into flattened balls containing 1 tablespoon each. Dust with flour. Slow-brown on both sides in 2 tablespoons fat. Then add ¼ cup hot water and ½ teaspoon beef extract. Cover and simmer 30 minutes. Turn once.

# Pork and Vealburgers

**¾ pound fresh lean pork**
**¾ pound lean veal**
**1½ teaspoons salt**
**1 teaspoon Ac'cent**
**¼ cup fine-chopped sweet green pepper or canned pimientoes**
**¼ teaspoon pepper**
**½ cup soft enriched bread crumbs**
**¼ cup water**
**1 tablespoon grated onion**
**½ teaspoon poultry seasoning**

Order the meats ground together twice. Combine with the remaining ingredients in the order given. Mix thoroughly until smooth. Shape into 8 round patties ½ inch thick. Dust with flour; slow-fry 25 minutes in butter or margarine. Add 2 tablespoons hot water after browning; finish covered to avoid drying out the meat.

### Lambburgers

Follow the preceding recipe, using 1½ pounds twice-ground lean lamb instead of veal and pork.

# Big Salad Rolls for Every Day

Put together with crisp lettuce and a choice of the following fillings:

### Ham-Egg

To 1¼ cups small-diced ready-to-eat or cooked smoked ham, add 2 chopped hard-cooked eggs, ¼ cup fine-chopped celery, 2 tablespoons pickle relish, ½ teaspoon table mustard, enough mayonnaise or salad dressing for spreadability, ⅛ teaspoon Ac'cent, and salt and pepper to taste.

### Veal-Nut

Dice oddments of roast veal to make 1¼ cups. Add ¼ cup each minced celery and fine-chopped walnut meats. Stir in ⅛ teaspoon Ac'cent and enough mayonnaise or salad dressing for spreadability. Add salt and pepper to taste.

### Salmon-Cucumber

Drain the contents of 1 (7½ ounce) can salmon. Flake fine. Add 2 chopped hard-cooked eggs, ¼ cup fine-chopped firm portion cucumber, 2 tablespoons minced dill pickle, enough salad dressing or bought tartar sauce for spreadability, ⅛ teaspoon Ac'cent, and salt and pepper to taste.

# California Tuna Salad Rolls

Combine the contents of 1 (7 ounce) can solid-pack tuna, ½ cup grated Swiss cheese, 1 tablespoon chopped parsley, 2 teaspoons lemon juice, and ⅓ cup mayonnaise. Mix with a fork. Use with lettuce as a filling on split crusty rolls spread with softened butter or margarine.

# Grilled Tomato-Burgers

**1½ pounds ground beef**
**1 teaspoon salt**
**⅛ teaspoon pepper**
**4 firm, ripe tomatoes**
**1 sweet onion, sliced into rings**
**6 large mushroom caps, cooked or canned, marinated in Italian style low-calorie salad dressing**

Lightly mix meat with salt and pepper; shape into 6 burgers. Cook over glowing charcoal on outdoor grill or cook in skillet or broil as desired. Cut each tomato into 3 slices, crosswise. Lightly brown with hamburgers for a few minutes, being sure tomatoes remain firm; place hamburgers on 6 tomato slices; top with remaining slices. Arrange a few onion rings on top and put a mushroom cap in center. Garnish serving platter with additional onion rings if desired. Makes 6 servings.

Campbell Soup Company

# Party Sandwiches

**For more substantial snacks, the ever-popular sandwich is usually seen; here are dozens of recipes and methods of serving these hors d'oeuvres.**

BREAD IS THE background for your sandwiches, and you can achieve much greater interest by varying your breads. Try rye, whole wheat, raisin, date, nut or brown bread, and for more colorful sandwiches, combine two different kinds. Close, fine-textured breads are the easiest to work with. Use 24-hour-old bread for open and closed sandwiches. It is easier to slice and easier to spread. Use very fresh bread for pinwheel and rolled sandwiches. For very thin sandwiches, buy an unsliced loaf and cut it into slices of the desired thickness with a very sharp knife. If you are planning to cut the sandwiches into fancy shapes with a cookie cutter, you will get more out of the loaf if you cut it lengthwise instead of the usual cross-section slices. Select *fillings* that have eye appeal and taste interest. Save your cream cheese or other white fillings for the dark breads. Use the more colorful fillings for the white breads. Soften the butter or margarine before using so as not to tear the bread when spreading. Do this by creaming it, but don't melt it. Spread a thin layer of the soft butter or margarine over the entire area of the bread getting it into all corners, and covering both slices. This prevents the filling from soaking into the bread. Keep the fillings moist but not wet by using a small amount of salad dressing. If you are going to add tomato, lettuce, cucumber or bacon, do so just before serving. If you can possibly arrange it that way, serve sandwiches with moist fillings soon after they are made. If you have to hold them for an hour or so, wrap the sandwiches in waxed paper, then in a damp cloth and store in a cool place. If a quantity of sandwiches is to be stored, use a large shallow pan. Place a damp tea towel in the bottom of the pan, next a layer of waxed paper. Stack the sandwiches in layers with waxed paper between and on top. Then fold the towel snugly over the paper and sandwiches.

If you have a freezer you can make up large quantities of sandwiches any time you have a chance. With proper wrapping, they will keep for months and always be on hand when you need them. Wrap the sandwiches separately in moisture-vapor-proof material. If ycu pack many different varieties, label them so you know what you have. If you are freezing only a few, place the wrapped sandwiches in an ice-cube tray. A larger number can be placed in freezer boxes or any suitable box, in layers. Wrap the entire outside of the box with a moisture-vapor-proof material. and freeze Place open-faced sandwiches on cardboard for support before wrapping. Leave rolled, ribbon and loaf sandwiches uncut.

In case you're in a quandary about quantities, here are some figures you will want to know. Plan on having at least three fancy sandwiches for each guest. Allow a slice of bread for each three to five small sandwiches. Use two tablespoons of filling for each slice of bread and figure that one cup of filling will cover six slices.

To make 100 open-faced sandwiches you will need the following:

**1⅓ regular 28-slice loaves of bread**
**1 pound butter or margarine**
**3 8-ounce glasses jelly**
**1 quart jam or preserves**
**2 pounds American or Swiss cheese, sliced very thin**
**½-pint jar mayonnaise if the fillings require mayonnaise**

# Individual Sandwich Loaves

**2 tablespoons mayonnaise**
**1 tablespoon minced parsley**
**1 hard-cooked egg, chopped fine**
**8 slices bread**
**1 can (2¼ oz.) deviled ham**
**2 3-oz. packages cream cheese**
**1 tablespoon milk or cream**

Combine mayonnaise, parsley and egg to make a fairly smooth mixture. Spread on four of the slices of bread. Spread remaining four slices with deviled ham. Make two stacks of four slices each, alternating the fillings. Remove crusts and cut each stack in half to make 2 small loaves. Beat cream cheese and milk until soft and light. Frost the four individual loaves and garnish with sliced stuffed olives.

American Institute of Baking

# tips for making SANDWICHES

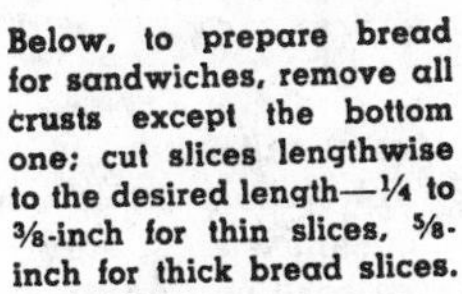

Below, to prepare bread for sandwiches, remove all crusts except the bottom one; cut slices lengthwise to the desired length—¼ to ⅜-inch for thin slices, ⅝-inch for thick bread slices.

American Institute of Baking

For pinwheel sandwiches, spread the lengthwise slices of fresh bread with soft butter or margarine and top with filling; cut each slice in half crosswise and roll. Wrap in waxed paper, twisting the ends, then place on flat surface on last turn of bread. Store in refrigerator until ready to serve; slice thinly when ready to use them.

Ribbon sandwiches look best with light and dark breads; ready-sliced bread may be used. Spread each slice with butter and selected filling. Trim crusts, wrap and chill; when served, cut into fours.

# "Christmas Tree" Sandwiches

## (2 Variations)

***20 slices white bread**
**1 4½-ounce can deviled ham**
**1 3-ounce package cream cheese, softened**
**2 tablespoons orange marmalade**
**1 8-ounce package cream cheese, softened**
**1 cup cottage cheese**
**1 tablespoon milk**
**Green vegetable coloring**
**Wide strip of orange peel**

****20 slices dark bread**
**2 4½-ounce cans deviled ham**
**4 tablespoons chopped raisins**
**4 tablespoons chopped nuts**
**1 8-ounce package cream cheese, softened**
**1 cup cottage cheese**
**1 tablespoon milk**
**Wide strip of orange peel**

*Variation 1: To cut out "tree" shape (triangle) start at top center of bread slice, cut down to right corner of slice, then down to left corner. Trim remaining crust; repeat to make 20 "trees". Combine deviled ham, cream cheese and marmalade. Spread half the slices with deviled ham mixture, top with remaining slices. To form loaf, stand sandwiches upright on a platter. Chill. Combine cream cheese, cottage cheese, milk and 4 drops coloring. Cut out 10 stars from orange peel. Frost loaf with cheese mixture. Place "stars" on center top of each sandwich. At serving time, cut between stars to separate sandwiches. Serves 10.

**Variation 2: Proceed as above, use dark bread instead of white. Combine deviled ham, raisins and nuts for filling; and omit green coloring from the cheese frosting.

The Underwood Kitchen

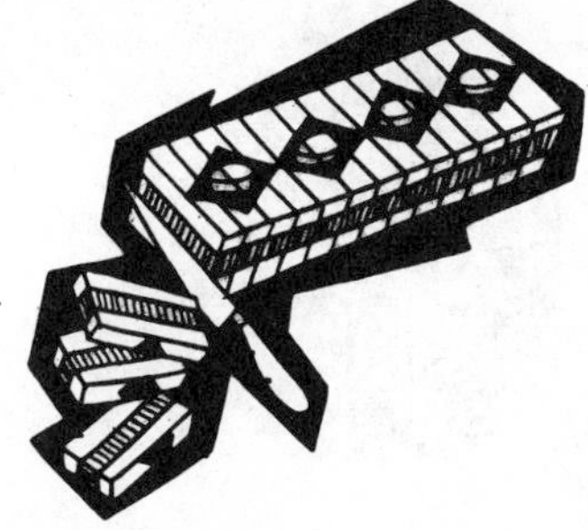

Ward Foods

# Sliced Bread Sandwich Loaf

**1 tablespoon unflavored gelatine**
**¼ cup cold water**
**1½ cups mayonnaise**
**1 #1 can salmon, drained and flaked**
**1 tablespoon chopped parsley**
**1 pimiento, chopped**
**⅛ teaspoon pepper**
**¼ teaspoon lemon juice**
**18 slices enriched white bread**
**1 tube anchovy paste**

Soften gelatine in cold water. Set over hot water until thoroughly dissolved. Stir in 1 cup of the mayonnaise. Allow mayonnaise mixture to thicken while loaf is being prepared. Mix together salmon, the remaining ½ cup mayonnaise, parsley, pimiento, pepper and lemon juice. Make 6 three-decker sandwiches with salmon spread, using 3 slices of bread for each sandwich. Arrange these six sandwiches close together on a tray. Ice with the mayonnaise mixture to form one loaf and place in the refrigerator until mayonnaise icing is set. Garnish with anchovy paste marking the individual sandwich portions. Makes 6 servings.

# Frosted Sandwich Loaf

**1 small can tuna**
**3 tablespoons tartar sauce or sandwich spread**
**Dash each salt and pepper**
**1 cup grated processed American cheese**
**2 tablespoons chopped pimiento**
**2 tablespoons mayonnaise**
**Dash each salt and pepper**
**2 hard-cooked eggs, finely chopped**
**6 ripe olives, finely chopped**
**1 teaspoon prepared mustard**
**2 tablespoons mayonnaise**
**Dash each salt and pepper**
**4 3-oz. packages cream cheese**
**About ⅓ cup top milk or light cream**
**1 day-old loaf unsliced bread**

Drain oil from tuna and turn into a mixing bowl. Add tartar sauce. Blend and season to taste. Set aside. Put cheese, pimiento and mayonnaise in a bowl and blend. Season to taste. Set aside. Put eggs, olives, mustard and mayonnaise in another bowl and mix. Season to taste and set aside. Soften cream cheese with milk. Set aside. With a very sharp knife trim top, bottom and sides of bread. Slice lengthwise into four even slices. Spread the lowest slice with tuna spread. Cover with second slice. Spread with cheese and pimiento spread. Cover with third slice. Spread with egg salad and top with last slice. Frost sides and top with softened cream cheese, leaving a little cheese to tint for decoration if desired.

R. T. French Co.

# Holiday Sandwich "Package"

**1 2-pound loaf unsliced white bread**
**2 4½ ounce cans deviled ham**
**2 tablespoons mayonnaise**
**½ cup chopped sweet pickle relish**
**2 tablespoons catsup**
**Radish roses**

Cut out center of loaf leaving ½ inch shell around ends and sides. Slice bread thinly and spread with a mixture of deviled ham, relish, mayonnaise and catsup. Place sandwiches in bread shell and garnish with radishes. "Tie" loaf with holiday ribbon. Makes 24 small sandwiches.

# Sandwedge Swirl

**Round loaf white bread (about 1½ pounds)**
**¼ pound soft-butter**
**Mustard-Mayonnaise Mix**
**1 package (8 ounces) sliced process American Cheese**
**2 firm ripe tomatoes, thinly sliced**
**Crisp garden lettuce**
**6 or 8 thin slices summer sausage**
**Ham Salad Filling**
**Egg Salad Filling**
**4 radishes**
**4 sweet gherkin pickles**

Round loaves of bread vary some in height but all will yield 2 thick slices from bottom of loaf. (Save crusty top slice remaining to use as you wish.) For ease in eating finished sandwich with a fork, remove a portion of the thick brown bottom crust, leave just enough for a firm sandwich base. Cut two round slices about 1½-inches thick from bottom of loaf. Spread bottom slice with butter. Then using just enough mustard-mayonnaise between layers of filling to hold them together, top with slices of cheese, tomato, frills of garden lettuce and summer sausage. Spread second round of bread with butter. Place buttered side down over fillings. Spread top of sandwich with butter. Place a large round cookie cutter or turn a small custard cup up-side down in the center. Spread a thick layer of ham filling in a ring around custard cup. Remove cup; fill with egg salad filling. Garnish center with radish slices; garnish ham border with pickle halves. Cut into thick wedges to serve. Makes 8 servings.

R. T. French Co.

### Egg Salad Filling

**4 hard-cooked eggs, chopped**
**¼ cup Mustard-Mayonnaise***
**½ teaspoon seasoning salt**
**¼ cup finely diced celery**

Combine all ingredients. Keep refrigerated until ready to use.

### Ham Salad Filling

**1½ cups ground cooked ham**
**1 tablespoon pickle relish**
**⅓ cup Mustard-Mayonnaise***

Combine all ingredients, using additional mustard-mayonnaise, if needed, to make a moist mixture.

*Mustard-Mayonnaise: Blend together ¾ cup mayonnaise with 6 tablespoons prepared mustard.

Brewers Association

# Danish Smorrebrod

### (Open Faced Sandwiches)

For Danish sandwiches, use dark rye, pumpernickel or whole grain wheat bread. If bread is unsliced, cut very thin. Spread bread slices lightly with butter. (For authentic Danish sandwiches, bread should be spread with sweet butter.) For meat sandwiches, blend small amount of prepared mustard with butter. A variety of sandwiches should be served at one time.

### Sandwich Toppings

Smoked salmon with hard cooked egg slices.
Lobster salad and asparagus spears.
Chopped egg and herring salad garnished with lemon slices.
Stuffed eggs with liver paste.
Bleu cheese with radishes and sliced egg yolk.
Sliced smoked meat and potato salad.
Liver paste and dill pickle slices garnished with sieved egg yolk.
Sliced tomatoes with finely chopped raw onion.
Sardines, hard cooked egg slices and twisted lemon slices.

Pan American Coffee Bureau

# Combination Fillings for a Sandwich Loaf

### Filling 1:

**1 small can crab meat**
**1 stalk of celery, finely chopped**
**2 tablespoons chopped sweet pickle**
**2 tablespoons mayonnaise**
**½ teaspoon salt**
**1 teaspoon lemon juice**

Drain and shred the crab meat. Add remaining ingredients and mix well. Set aside.

### Filling 2:

**2 hard-cooked eggs, chopped**
**⅓ cup chopped pickled beets**
**1 tablespoon mayonnaise**
**Salt and pepper to taste**

Mix all ingredients together and set aside.

### Filling 3:

**1 3-oz. package cream cheese**
**5 large stuffed olives, chopped**
**¼ green pepper, finely chopped**

Mix ingredients well together and set aside.

Prepare bread; spread with fillings and frost with softened cream cheese.

# Egg Salad Filling

**6 hard-cooked eggs, finely chopped**
**3 tablespoons pickle relish**
**⅓ cup finely diced green pepper**
**3 tablespoons chopped parsley**
**3 tablespoons salad dressing**
**Salt, pepper, dry mustard to taste**

Combine eggs, pickle relish, green pepper, parsley and salad dressing. Season to taste.

# Chicken Filling

**1½ cups finely chopped cooked chicken**
**½ cucumber, very finely chopped**
**½ cup salad dressing**
**Salt, pepper and dill powder to taste**

Combine all ingredients and blend well.

# Jelly Cube Sandwiches

Cut an unsliced loaf of bread into one-inch cubes. With kitchen tweezers pull out part of the center of each cube. Combine one 3-oz. package of cream cheese with 1 tablespoon of milk and spread over the rim on top of each cube. Fill the little hollow with any tart red jelly or jam.

Armour & Co.

# Rolled Sandwiches

Remove the crusts from thin slices of fresh bread. Spread with soft butter or margarine, and then any tasty sandwich spread. Roll up each slice and fasten with a wooden toothpick. Wrap two or three rolls in waxed paper and cover with a damp towel. Chill well. Just before serving remove the toothpick and tuck sprigs of water cress into each end.

Any of the prepared cheese spreads make excellent fillings for rolled sandwiches. The bread can also be rolled around a cooked vegetable like asparagus or carrot and in this case use a savory butter as the spread. Other delicious spreads for this type of sandwich would be Deviled Ham and Chopped Fresh Dill, Chopped Pimiento with Crushed Pineapple and Cream Cheese, and Chive Cheese and Minced Clams. Water cress and parsley are the best greens to tuck into the ends, although bits of chicory and celery tops are good, too.

# Peanut Butter Cheese Stuffies

2 thin loaves French bread
½ cup peanut butter
¾ cup cottage cheese
2 tablespoons chopped black olives
½ cup finely diced celery
1 tablespoon finely chopped onion
2 tablespoons chili sauce
1 tablespoon milk
½ teaspoon salt
½ teaspoon A-1 sauce

Cut bread almost through lengthwise; carefully open loaves and pull out inside of each loaf being careful not to split the back. Combine remaining ingredients and mix until well blended; pack into loaves and press them together; chill. At serving time slice each roll thinly. Makes about 20 stuffies.

Campbell Soup Company

# Avocado-Pineapple Tea Sandwiches

1 medium avocado, mashed
2 teaspoons lemon juice
¼ cup drained, crushed pineapple
2 tablespoons mayonnaise
16 slices of whole-wheat bread
16 small pieces of green pepper

Combine mashed avocado with lemon juice, pineapple and mayonnaise. Make a leaf-shaped pattern out of cardboard and cut two leaves from each slice of bread. Spread each leaf with the avocado mixture and mark the veins of the leaf with a blunt toothpick. Insert the small piece of green pepper for the stem.

# Checkerboard Sandwiches

These are a little more difficult to make but they are so attractive on a platter that they are worth the effort. First make a ribbon loaf using two slices of white and two of whole-wheat bread. Cut this in six lengthwise slices about ⅓ inch thick. Spread the strips lengthwise with cheese butter (see below for the recipe) and put together in such a way that a white block is over every dark one forming a checkerboard at the ends. Wrap the loaf in waxed paper and chill. Slice thinly in cross section to serve.

# Ham and Cucumber Filling

Mix 3 cups ground cooked ham with 1 cup diced cucumber, ½ teaspoon salt, a dash of pepper and about ½ cup mayonnaise.

# Sardine Filling

Mix and moisten with mayonnaise, 3 cup sardines and 4 tablespoons prepared horse-radish. Add a dash of salt and pepper.

# Chicken Salad Filling

Mix 3 cups finely minced cooked chicken with 2 stalks celery, diced, 4 tablespoons chopped olives and ½ teaspoon salt. Add enough mayonnaise to moisten, about ½ cup.

# Cheese Butter

Grind ¼ pound processed American cheese. Cream ½ pound of butter and blend the two together to make a smooth spread. This makes enough for three ribbon loaves.

# Chicken and Nut Filling

Combine 2½ cups finely minced cooked chicken with ⅔ cup chopped walnuts, ½ cup mayonnaise, ⅓ cup sour cream, 2 tablespoons lemon juice and salt and pepper to taste.

# Fancy Open Sandwiches

You will get many more of these sandwiches out of a loaf if you slice the bread lengthwise, then cut the long slices into hearts, stars, shamrocks, crescents, diamonds or whatever shapes your fancy and the occasion call for. Decorate with softened cream cheese put through a cookie press or pastry tube, with bits of pimiento, parsley, ripe olive or any other colorful touch.

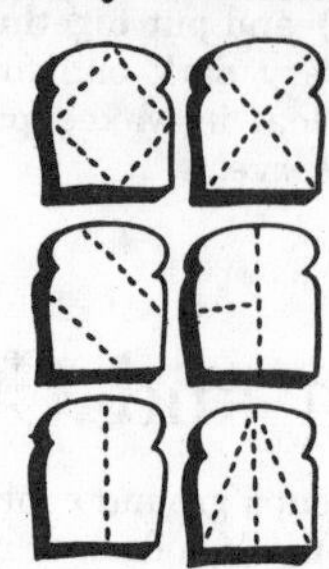

American Institute of Baking

# Fancy Covered Sandwiches

These are best made on the day on which they are to be served, but the spreads for them can be made in advance and kept covered, in the refrigerator, for several days. Interesting varieties can be produced through the use of different kinds of breads, different assortments of fillings and varied shapes of cookie cutters. If you can't find a cookie cutter for a particular shape you want to make, you can trace it on cardboard, cut out the cardboard and use that for your model. Lay it on the slice of bread and cut around it with a sharp knife.

To fill covered sandwiches use a combination of cream cheese and chopped ripe olives, minced cucumber, onion and water cress, chopped egg and anchovies, or shrimp and celery mixed with curried mayonnaise. Or you can try one of these fillings.

# Ribbon Sandwiches

These can be made from one kind of bread but are more effective in their design if white and dark breads are both used. Trim the crusts from two unsliced loaves, one white and one whole wheat. Cut two long slices 1/3 inch thick from each. Put the four slices together with the desired filling, alternating the white with the dark. Wrap, chill, and slice to the desired thickness. Two loaves of bread make three ribbon loaves. Here are some fillings that go very well with ribbon-style sandwiches.

## Chicken Ribbon Filling

**1¼ cups finely minced cooked chicken**
**2 stalks finely diced celery**
**1 teaspoon lemon juice**
**¼ teaspoon ground nutmeg**
**½ teaspoon salt**
**2 tablespoons mayonnaise**

Combine all ingredients and spread between layers of bread.

## Olive-Cheese Filling

**1 3-oz. package cream cheese**
**¼ cup prepared olive butter or 12 olives very finely minced**
**2 tablespoons soft butter or margarine**
**20 medium-sized stuffed olives**
**2 lengthwise slices bread**

Combine cream cheese and olives or olive butter. Spread each slice of bread with butter or margarine and then with the cream cheese-olive mixture. Cut each slice in half. Place a row of five olives across the width of each half slice of bread, pressing the olives firmly together end to end. Roll each half slice of bread. Wrap, chill and cut as above.

## Cottage Cheese-Cucumber Filling

**1 small cucumber very finely, chopped**
**½ cup cottage cheese**
**2 teaspoons fresh dill, if obtainable**
**Salt and freshly ground pepper to taste**

Blend all ingredients and spread between layers of bread.

Wheat Flour Institute

# Lincoln "Log Cabin" Sandwiches

**1 4½-ounce can deviled ham**
**1 3-ounce package cream cheese**
**2 tablespoons chopped olives**
**1 6-ounce can boned chicken**
**2 tablespoons mayonnaise**
**2 tablespoons chopped celery**
**16 slices bread, dark or light**

Blend deviled ham, cream cheese and olives. Spread on 4 slices of bread. Top with 4 more slices. Blend chicken, mayonnaise and celery. Repeat with remaining bread. Cut each sandwich into 4 strips or "logs". Build log cabin with sandwich strips of both light and dark bread. Make a roof from folded piece of cardboard or bread. Top with a tiny American flag. Serve on individual plates, surrounded by "grass" made of parsley or chicory. Makes 4 log cabins.

# Happy Hooligans

Spread one slice bread generously with deviled ham, place cheese cutout on top and garnish.

PUMPKIN: Cut bread with 3-inch round cutter. Spread with deviled ham. Cut cheese with same cutter. Cut out eyes, nose, mouth with knife or tiny cutter. Place cheese on bread. Garnish with parsley hair, raisin eyes, and bow tie made from green pepper under pimiento.

GHOST: Using cardboard for pattern, cut ghost shape out of cheese. Place on bread spread with deviled ham. Garnish with black olive eyes, nose and pimiento mouth.

CAT: Use cheese square to fit bread. Cut 1⅓" circle from center of cheese. Cut ears with knife. Garnish with black olive pieces for eyes and nose, pimiento tongue, and gherkin strips for whiskers.

The Underwood Kitchen

# NOTES

# INDEX